Official
BASEBALL GUIDE

1982 EDITION

Editors / Baseball Guide

LARRY WIGGE
CARL CLARK
DAVE SLOAN
CRAIG CARTER
BARRY SIEGEL

President-Chief Executive Officer
RICHARD WATERS

Editor
DICK KAEGEL

Director of Books and Periodicals
RON SMITH

Published by

The Sporting News

1212 North Lindbergh Boulevard
P.O. Box 56 — St. Louis, Mo. 63166

Copyright © 1982
The Sporting News Publishing Company
a Times Mirror company

TABLE OF CONTENTS

REVIEW OF 1981—A Recap of the Strike-Torn Season, MVP Tables, Cy Young Tables **3**

NATIONAL LEAGUE—Team Reviews of '81 Season, Day-by-Day Scores, Official Batting, Fielding and Pitching Averages **31**

AMERICAN LEAGUE—Team Reviews of '81 Season, Day-by-Day Scores, Official Batting, Fielding and Pitching Averages **93**

DIVISION PLAYOFFS—National and American League Playoff Reviews, Box Scores **165**

CHAMPIONSHIP SERIES—National and American League Series Reviews, Box Scores, Composite Box Scores **177**

WORLD SERIES—Dodgers-Yankees Series Review, Official Box Scores, Play-by-Play, Rosters of Eligible Players **189**

ALL-STAR GAME—Review, Official Box Score, Play-by-Play, Results of Previous Games **205**

BATTING AND PITCHING FEATURES—Len Barker's Perfect Game and Other No-Hitters, Low-Hit Games, Top Strikeout Performances, Top Firemen, Pitchers Winning 1-0 Games, Grand Slam Hitters, Multi-Homer Games, One-Game Hitting Feats, Top Pinch-Hitters, Homers by Parks, Award Winners, Hall of Fame Electees **213**

1981 REENTRY DRAFT, MINOR LEAGUE DRAFT, MAJOR LEAGUE TRANSACTIONS, NECROLOGY **243**

INFORMATION ON LEAGUES AND CLUBS—Major League and Minor League Directories, National League Directory, National League Club Directories, American League Directory, American League Club Directories, Minor League Presidents, Major League Farm Systems **259**

OFFICIAL 1981 MINOR LEAGUE AVERAGES **295**

1982 NATIONAL LEAGUE SCHEDULE **450**

1982 AMERICAN LEAGUE SCHEDULE **452**

For Index to Contents See Page 455

(Index to Minor League Cities on Page 456)

ON THE COVER: Cincinnati's Tom Seaver compiled a 14-2 record in 1981, finishing with the best winning percentage in the National League (.875). Seaver, who had a 2.55 earned-run average, finished second in the Cy Young voting to Fernando Valenzuela.

—Photo by Malcolm Emmons

Baseball Takes Lumps, Survives Stormy, Strike-Plagued Season

By CLIFFORD KACHLINE

If there ever was A Year to Forget in baseball, 1981 would probably be it. Or, more properly, The Year That Baseball Management and Fans Alike Would Prefer to Forget, certainly at the major league level.

What began as a season of tremendous promise—and an apparent all-time high in fan interest—developed into the most acrimonious, strife-riddled campaign in the sport's history.

For the first two months of the season, the stage seemed to be set for A Year to Remember. Spectacular accomplishments by rookies Fernando Valenzuela and Tim Raines, together with stirring bids by veterans Pete Rose, Carl Yastrzemski and Gaylord Perry to reach several of baseball's most coveted plateaus, had the turnstiles humming at a record-smashing clip.

Behind the scenes, however, a smoldering issue that carried over from the 1980 labor-management dispute was bringing new confrontation. It culminated in June with the first midseason player strike in the annals of professional sports in the U.S. and Canada. The walkout forced a complete shutdown of major league baseball for almost two months, wiping out one-third of the schedule, and for a time threatened to cancel the remainder of the season.

Even events such as Len Barker's perfect game, Nolan Ryan's record fifth no-hitter, and the departure of two of baseball's oldest family ownerships (via the sale of the Chicago Cubs and Philadelphia Phillies) paled in significance when weighed against the blow dealt to the game's image by the strike.

The shocking turn of events left baseball personnel and fans alike in a catatonic state of boredom for much of the summer. Worse yet, the strike generated bad feelings between management and the players, between hard-line and moderate club owners, and among the fans who were deprived of their summer pastime. A large segment of the public was embittered to the point where many observers expressed concern that the adverse effects of the 50-day strike might be felt for years.

One hit away from a National League career record, Pete Rose had to pack his bags and wait for the players and owners to reach agreement.

Although the walkout involved only approximately 650 players—a relatively small group of workers in a strike—the prolonged absence of baseball attracted as much attention as work stoppages in industries like coal mining, mail delivery and air travel. The terms "negotiations", "law suits" and "courtrooms" were used frequently in the sports pages and on the electronic media.

With the average major league player

salary in 1981 being $193,000, the shut-down cost the athletes around $28 million. Individual losses ranged from Dave Winfield's estimated $7,770 per day, or $388,500 for the 50-day layoff, to about $180 per day, or a total of $9,000, for those players earning the minimum of $32,500.

Based on average ticket prices and concessions sales, the 712 cancelled games cost the clubs approximately $116 million. A $50 million strike insurance policy—known as "business interruption insurance"—helped to reduce the owners' red ink.

Losses at the club level varied greatly. According to estimates compiled by Jane Gross of the New York Times, the 26 teams dropped anywhere from $7.6 million to $1.6 million before insurance payments. She calculated that the Los Angeles Dodgers, turnstile leaders and one of five clubs to play in a privately-owned stadium, lost approximately $345,000 in ticket revenues and concessions for each of 22 home dates, for a total of $7.6 million. The New York Yankees, whose lease on city-owned Yankee Stadium cost them around $7,000 per game in rental, dropped about $285,000 for each of 25 cancelled games—or $7.1 million. By contrast, the Minnesota Twins, last in attendance, lost only about $1.6 million and may have even collected more than that in insurance.

The strike-interrupted season had a devastating economic impact that extended far beyond the players and clubs. It seriously affected virtually every major league city through the loss of stadium rentals, concessions, parking, and hotel and restaurant business. The airlines and radio and television likewise were hard hit.

In New York City, comptroller Harrison J. Goldin said a conservative estimate indicated the strike cost the city at least $8.4 million in lost business and wages. Mayor David Mann of Cincinnati figured that for each Reds' game that was not played, the community lost $900,000. At one point he sought to force the Reds to pay rental on Riverfront Stadium for the cancelled games. Philadelphia civic officials estimated the stoppage cost the city $100,000 per game in rent, parking receipts and various taxes, plus lost wage taxes of laidoff employees.

The New York Times said a study done by Dun & Bradstreet showed 58 percent of business establishments within walking distance of parks were hurt by the baseball shutdown. Two restaurants in the vicinity of Chicago's Comiskey Park were forced to close; and a restaurant near Yankee Stadium reported an 80 percent drop in trade.

Besides being the major leagues' first midseason player walkout, the strike was responsible for several other "firsts." They included the only indefinite postponement—and subsequent rescheduling—of an All-Star Game and the first split-season pennant races in this century. The latter move stirred controversy and, ironically, resulted in keeping the team with the best won-lost record in 1981 (Cincinnati) from a place in the playoffs. And the inclusion of another round of playoffs led to the latest start and latest finish in World Series history.

From a historical perspective, the strike represented another chapter in the baseball revolution that started in 1975. That year two veteran pitchers, Andy Messersmith and Dave McNally, challenged the game's nearly century-old reserve system and were declared free agents by arbiter Peter Seitz. The following summer the Major League Baseball Players Association negotiated a new Basic Agreement with management. It provided that any player with at least six seasons of major league service became a free agent at the expiration of his contract.

The 1981 walkout had its origins in the last-minute compromise the players and owners reached on May 23, 1980. Free-agent compensation was the main issue. Under the system in effect since free agency and the re-entry draft began in 1976, the only compensation a team losing a player to free agency received from the signing team was a choice in the June draft of high school and college talent. Management was insistent that compensation instead take the form of a professional player from the signing team. The players balked at the idea, contending such an arrangement would severely reduce the bargaining power and mobility of free agents.

Terms of the 1980 Memorandum of Agreement called for creation of a four-member joint study committee that would seek to negotiate a settlement of the compensation question. In the event that failed, the agreement stipulated that (1) management had the right to announce during the period February 16-19, 1981 that it would put its compensation proposal into effect, and (2) the Players Association, if still dissatisfied, could serve notice by March 1 that it planned to strike, with the walkout to begin no later than June 1 of the '81 season.

The study group of general managers Frank Cashen (New York Mets) and Harry Dalton (Milwaukee), representing management, and players Bob Boone (Philadelphia) and Sal Bando (Milwaukee), met a number of times, but reported in January that they could not reach an agreement. Negotiations then were resumed by each side's chief negotiators—Ray Grebey, director of the owners' Players Relations Committee, and Marvin Miller, executive director of the Players Association.

Following two weeks of fruitless sessions, Grebey announced on February 19 that, in keeping with the 1980 accord, management was invoking its right to implement its compensation proposal. Six days later, the 29-member executive board of the Players Association met in Tampa, Fla., and voted unanimously for a strike beginning on Friday, May 29, if the dispute was not resolved by that date.

"Today's action was a procedural step to keep our options open," commented Doug DeCinces, American League player representative. "We're trying to avoid a strike. Hopefully we will have some legitimate negotiations."

Under the plan the owners sought to implement, compensation to a team losing a free agent who was a "ranking player" would be an unprotected player from the signing club's major league roster plus the usual amateur draft choice. To be considered a "ranking player," the free agent would have to meet two criteria: (1) During the previous season, he had to rate among the top 50 percent of the league's players at his position in number of plate appearances or pitching appearances, and (2) He would have to be selected by at least eight teams in the re-entry draft. The signing club would protect only 15 players on its roster if the free agent ranked in the top 33 percent, and protect 18 in the case of any other "ranking player."

With the talks obviously deadlocked, the two chief negotiators invited Kenneth E. Moffett, acting head of the Federal Mediation and Conciliation Service, to join the sessions beginning April 20. Moffett had been instrumental in helping avert a strike in 1980.

The squabble produced an unusual sidelight on May 5 when it was revealed that Harry Dalton had been fined $50,000 under the owners' "gag rule," also known in the media as the "Grebey discipline code." It was believed to be the stiffest levy ever imposed on a baseball executive other than a club owner.

A story by Thomas Boswell in the March 6 edition of the Washington Post was the cause of Dalton's difficulties. Boswell had quoted the Milwaukee executive as saying: "I hope management is really looking for a compromise and not a victory, but I'm not certain that's the case. The Players Association is genuinely looking for a compromise if we'll just give them something they can accept without losing too much face." Those familiar with the circumstances behind the story claimed Dalton believed he was having a confidential conversation with Boswell and that his comments had not been meant for publication. (The "gag rule," calling for fines of up to $500,000, reportedly was set up at the suggestion of Grebey to prevent management representatives from making public statements considered detrimental to their negotiating cause.) The fine was later rescinded.

The labor dispute took a new turn on May 7. Charging the Player Relations Committee with failing to bargain, Miller announced the Players Association was filing a charge of unfair labor practice with the National Labor Relations Board. The petition asked that the owners be required to turn over financial data to help the players determine the validity of claims that the free-agent sweepstakes were bankrupting any clubs. Grebey responded by denying that management ever had claimed at the bargaining table that free agency was causing financial hardship.

In the meantime, there were reports that a growing number of owners were expressing dissatisfaction with the lack of progress in the ongoing negotiations. The fear of fines, however, kept them from speaking out publicly. And despite minor modifications in their positions, the two sides remained far apart. The basic stumbling block was the source and quality of compensation.

Less than 36 hours before the strike deadline, the possibility of a delay arose. William A. Lubbers, general counsel for the NLRB, disclosed on May 27 that his agency would seek a temporary restraining order to postpone the strike. The next day, after spending some seven hours in conference with Miller and Grebey, NLRB regional director Daniel Silverman announced the two parties had agreed to extend the strike deadline while the NLRB sought the injunction. The petition, which put the entire situation on hold, sought to postpone the compensation issue to the same dates in 1982. Late that same afternoon, the principals appeared before Judge Henry R. Werker in U.S. District Court in Manhattan, and he agreed to hear the NLRB petition the following week.

Baseball's tangled labor situation next moved to Rochester, N.Y. Because another judge was ill, Judge Werker was assigned to the Western District court in Rochester for two weeks to hear criminal cases, but arranged to squeeze in the baseball hearing.

Only three witnesses—Grebey, Miller and Commissioner Bowie Kuhn—were heard during the day-long session on June 3. Kuhn was called to testify because of his gloom-and-doom State of Baseball message at the annual meetings in Dallas the previous December. In that talk, the commissioner predicted considerable financial difficulty for the sport because of rising salaries. However, Grebey emphasized during his appearance that Kuhn wasn't speaking for the owners and added, "At no time in my dealings with the owners have any expressed the inability to pay salaries." The hearing concluded the following day with a 90-minute session.

While awaiting Judge Werker's decision, the MLBPA offered a new compensation proposal on June 6. It called for a pool of professional players from which teams losing players to free agency could choose. Grebey rejected the plan.

The pool concept was a change in theory from direct compensation sought by the owners. Each team would be able to protect an as yet determined number of players and all remaining talent would be placed in the pool. When a Type A player was signed by another club, instead of the signing club paying direct compensation, the compensation would be selected from the pool.

Four days later, Judge Werker issued his ruling. It denied the NLRB request for an injunction to postpone the walkout. In his 23-page decision, Judge Werker noted: "The evidence adduced at the hearing is insufficient to support a finding that the replacement player compensation proposal . . . presents economic issues. I am bound by the law. The possibility of a strike, although a fact of life in labor relations, offers no occasion for this court to distort the principles of law and equity."

Upon learning of the ruling, Miller immediately distributed a strike memorandum. It stated: "As directed by the executive board's unanimous decision, no games will be played on Friday, June 12, or thereafter until a settlement is reached and approved by the players."

Nevertheless, Moffett summoned the negotiators to the bargaining table on June 11. During the day-long sessions, the PRC proposed several new ideas and the players offered a modification of their player-pool concept. But at 12:30 a.m., when the talks ended, Miller announced the strike was definitely on. He also said he was removing himself physically from the bargaining sessions because the owners considered him a roadblock to a settlement. He said that the elected officers of the Players Association, along with attorneys Donald Fehr and Peter Rose, would handle future negotiations.

A last-ditch attempt to forestall the walkout took place on Friday morning, June 12. Ten players from the Mets, Astros, Reds, Phillies and Braves joined the talks, but the meeting in New York's Doral Inn broke off after two hours with no progress—and the work stoppage began.

So the strike that neither management nor the players claimed to want was a reality. The confusion was greatest among the 13 teams playing on the road. Two had opened in new cities on Thursday night, and the others were due to switch sites on Friday. Although several teams had flown to their next destination, most were waiting for chartered airlines to take off in the morning if a settlement came. Players stood around hotel lobbies awaiting definitive word. With the walkout underway, they had to pay their own way home.

The first game actually affected by the strike was the San Diego-Chicago contest set for 1:35 CDT on Friday at Wrigley Field. Twelve more games were wiped out that night and another 27, including one doubleheader, on Saturday and Sunday as the gates of all 26 major league stadiums were padlocked.

Prior to the interruption, the turnstiles had boomed. The 26 teams had drawn 1,140,645 more fans than at a corresponding point in 1980, and it appeared almost certain they would break the all-time attendance record of 43,550,398 set in 1979. Fernando Fever—named after Fernando Valenzuela—had helped the Dodgers average 46,238 at home, which projected to a potential season record of around 3,800,000.

Commissioner Kuhn, in a statement issued shortly after the strike began, said "fan compensation" was the real issue. "We have heard over and over again that

Houston pitcher Don Sutton (left) and teammate Joe Niekro answered questions June 12 after the Major League Baseball Players Association, led by Executive Director Marvin Miller (right), had voted to go out on strike.

the single issue at hand is player compensation," his statement read. "In reality it is fan compensation. For several years I have strongly espoused compensation for free agents lost. I feel the free agent system adopted in 1976 and recognized as experimental was not fair to the fans of a club which lost a ranking free agent and got nothing in exchange but an unproven amateur player. What the clubs' plan means is that the club and its fans would receive a player who has the potential to step into their lineup."

Faced with their first summer vacations, many players did what other Americans normally do—take their families on picnics, to the beach or watch TV reruns. Managers and coaches found themselves in a different situation. They

remained on the club payroll, and after a few days off, many were assigned to farm teams to look over and assist minor league prospects.

The owners had geared themselves for potential losses in a shutdown. Besides $50 million in strike insurance, they had tucked away $10-$15 million in a mutual assistance fund. The bulk of the fund was created by assessing each club two percent of gate receipts since the start of the 1979 season.

Most of the insurance was placed through Lloyds of London, but it was spread among more than 100 carriers throughout the world. The total premium for the policies, which had expiration dates of December 31, 1981, was said to be around $2.2 million and was paid in three installments. The final one was authorized on February 27—two days after the players filed notification of a strike. At the time, Grebey was quoted by The Associated Press as saying: "We have taken the same prudent steps any industry would take. We have a combination of insurance and an industry-wide fund to cover the contingencies." By contrast, the Players Association had no strike insurance, according to Miller, who passed up his salary—estimated at $160,000 or more—during the strike.

The absence of games also created a big vacuum for newspapers and the electronic media. Three days after the walkout began, two Philadelphia newspapers startled their readers with stories about Pete Rose "breaking Stan Musial's National League record for hits as the Phillies down the Braves." Each was accompanied by an explanatory note emphasizing the story was a "mythical account." Subsequently, other papers took similar trips into the world of fictional baseball or reprinted stories written about great games of past years. The radio and television outlets that normally carried major league games began repeating broadcasts and telecasts of famous games, and later several stations sent their announcers to minor league cities to air games played by farm teams.

During the first 48 days of the strike, 17 negotiating sessions were held. True to his word, Miller skipped the initial meetings. In his absence, players Bob Boone of Philadelphia, Steve Rogers of Montreal and Mark Belanger of Baltimore became the union's principal negotiators. Grebey, league presidents Lee MacPhail and Chub Feeney, and attorneys Barry Rona, James Garner and Louis Hoynes continued to represent the PRC. After missing seven meetings, Miller returned to the bargaining table on July 1. A few days later, while other U.S. citizens were celebrating the country's birthday on July 4, the negotiators met for five hours, only to have the talks blow up. "There's a philosophical difference," Moffett explained afterward. "There's the pool arrangement versus direct compensation. Until there's a resolution to that issue, in my opinion the strike will continue."

Meanwhile, there were developments on other fronts. Four players, three of them Dodgers, were charged with playing in an exhibition series in violation of their contracts; the Major League Umpires Association sought to block payment of strike insurance to the clubs; the Players Association filed default notices on behalf of players who claimed they should be paid; several minor league teams shifted games to major league parks; the NLRB began its hearings into the players' unfair labor charges against the owners, and the owners called a meeting of their own.

At the request of Richie Phillips, counsel for the Umpires Association, Judge Stanley M. Greenberg of Philadelphia's Common Pleas Court issued a temporary injunction on June 24 to block Lloyds of London from paying out strike insurance. The class-action suit contended the insurance provided management with an incentive not to bargain. Two days later, however, Judge Donald W. Van Artsdalen of the U.S. District Court in Philadelphia dissolved the temporary restraining order.

On July 1 it was disclosed the players' union had filed salary claims for players who contended they had guaranteed contracts with no exceptions, were on the disabled list, or had too much taken from their last paycheck on June 15. Those who claimed to have guaranteed contracts included Steve Carlton, Steve Garvey, Larry Hisle, Bill Madlock, John Montefusco and Gene Garber. Joel Youngblood, Tommy John, Rudy May, Bruce Robinson, Dave Palmer, Bake McBride and John Candelaria were among the disabled-list group. The clubs paid under protest and, at the same time, filed grievances.

Four minor league teams played games in the vacant big league stadiums. Redwood and Reno, farm clubs of the California Angels and San Diego Padres, respectively, attracted a crowd of 9,556 for a California League game played at Anaheim Stadium on July 3. The following night the same two teams drew 37,665 at San Diego's Jack Murphy Stadium. A Midwest League game at Milwaukee County Stadium between Burlington, a Brewers farm club, and Wausau, a Mariners farm team, on July 15 lured fewer than 2,000 fans. An earlier effort by Cleveland's Gabe Paul to have the Indians' Charleston farm play an International League game at Cleveland Stadium fell through when the Charleston and Tidewater players nixed the idea.

The NLRB hearing, originally scheduled for June 15 but postponed three times, began on July 6 in New York City before Melvin Welles, the agency's chief administrative law judge. It lasted four days. During his appearance, Grebey testified that his early conversations with team officials "reflected resentment and

STEINBERG

Detroit's Richie Hebner spent his strike time digging graves under the guidance of his father in Boston while Tigers relief ace Kevin Saucier called different kinds of strikes for youngsters in Pensacola, Fla.

concern" over rising salaries for players. But he insisted management never claimed inability or incapacity to pay during negotiations. "Free agents are here to stay," he said. "They are a benefit to baseball. I know some people in management don't share my opinion, but there is no intention or desire to attack the system." After the hearings, Judge Welles gave both sides two weeks to submit briefs.

Even while the NLRB hearing was going on, owners of the 26 clubs were being summoned to New York City for a July 9 meeting—their first since the strike began. The meeting was called by the PRC's board of directors after the owners of eight teams sent telegrams to Kuhn requesting the session. The owners had been scheduled to meet in Kansas City on June 24—originally to discuss the major league broadcasting agreement and then the labor situation—but that meeting was cancelled.

"Baseball is in its biggest crisis since the Black Sox scandal (1919), and it is no time to sit around and do nothing," declared Edward Bennett Williams, the outspoken Baltimore owner, in commenting on the call for the meeting. Another alleged dissident, John McMullen of Houston, said: "Those of us not directly involved in negotiations have a difficult time finding out what's going on. We have to see what our future strategy will be."

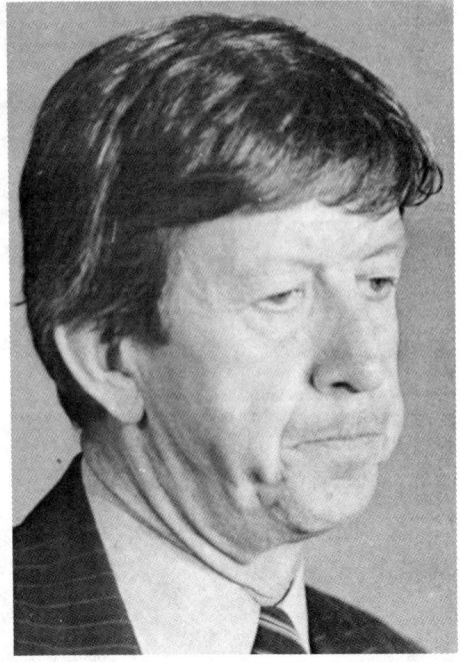

The comments and the timing of the meeting prompted reports of disagreements among the owners. However, following a session of more than three hours, the owners and their representatives announced they were united in their support of Grebey and the bargaining team.

The somber faces of Kenneth Moffett (above) and owners' negotiator Ray Grebey tell the story during the latter stages of the 1981 baseball strike.

The longer the strike continued, the more numerous and complex became the problems. The matter of service credit for players became an explosive issue because it affects eligibility for free agency, salary arbitration, pension benefits and the right to demand or reject a trade. If denied credit for days lost during the stoppage, a number of players would lose the right to free agency at the close of the 1981 season. Other problems involved umpires' salaries, what to do about the All-Star Game and the money the players' pension fund received from it, and how to handle the remainder of the schedule—if and when the season resumed.

The thirty-fourth day of the strike, July 15, saw U.S. Labor Secretary Ray-

mond J. Donovan enter the picture. He accompanied Moffett from Washington to New York and, in a 45-minute appearance before the negotiators, advised them of the concern that President Ronald Reagan's administration had about the prolonged stoppage.

At Donovan's urging, the talks were moved to Washington starting on Monday, July 20, and a news blackout was imposed. Two days later, the Players Association negotiators and the PRC's executive board met secretly in their only face-to-face session. The six-member PRC board consisted of Ed Fitzgerald, Milwaukee, chairman; Joe Burke, Kansas City; Clark Griffith, Minnesota; Bob Howsam, Cincinnati; John McHale, Montreal, and Dan Galbreath, Pittsburgh. Although the two sides met four consecutive days for the first time, the talks broke down again. As the principals departed Washington, there was growing concern that the season was over.

"I don't think there's going to be any baseball for a long while, perhaps into next season," declared Miller on his return to New York following the session. He immediately arranged a meeting of the Players Association executive board for July 27 in Chicago and set up a series of other meetings to brief the players. Subsequently, the owners were notified to be in New York on July 29 for a meeting of their own.

Despite the gloomy outlook, Moffett called for yet another negotiating session at 2 p.m. on Thursday, July 30, at New York's Doral Inn, site of most of the negotiatons. Early the next morning, exactly seven weeks after it started, baseball's longest strike came to a halt.

Ironically, Moffett never got to participate in the final round of discussions. While he and mediation service counsel Nancy Broff waited at the Doral Inn, two-man committees of Miller and Fehr for the players and Grebey and MacPhail for the PRC met secretly in National League headquarters. After breaking at 5 p.m. to caucus with other members of their negotiating teams, the four men resumed talks around 6:30. As midnight approached the full committees were called in, and by 1:30 a.m. they had reached agreement on all the primary points. Finally, at 5 o'clock Friday morning, July 31, all details were resolved. Shortly after 6 a.m., the negotiators arrived at the Doral Inn for a news conference to announce the agreement that ended the 20-month dispute.

Except for several minor points, the proposal that became the strike-terminating agreement actually was suggested by Miller to MacPhail on July 27, Murray Chass of the New York Times reported. MacPhail, who played an increasingly more significant role in the days leading up to the settlement, acknowledged that Miller's ideas were proposed because they "were not far off what we (management) had in mind."

Besides player compensation, the most difficult issue to resolve was service credit for players for time lost during the strike. The owners said they wouldn't give that time, but the players insisted on it.

"When I called the meeting," Moffett said, "I was the only one who wanted it." Asked by a reporter what finally ended the strike, Moffett responded "fear," referring to the fear of both sides that the season might otherwise be over.

The basic terms of the 22-page Memorandum of Agreement were as follows:

—A player pool to compensate teams losing free agents was established. A maximum of five teams can choose to be an "excluded club" and bypass the re-entry procedure for a three-year period, meaning they will not select or sign a Type A free agent and will not participate in the player pool during that time. Of the teams remaining, each club signing a Type A free agent can protect 24 players in its entire organization and the other teams can protect 26. All other players go into the pool.

—No team can lose more than one player from the pool each year. Once a team loses a player, it will be eliminated from the pool (a) for two years or (b) until it signs a Type A free agent, with the following exceptions: A team signing two Type A players in a year is eligible to lose one player per year for two years, while a team signing three or more Type A players in a year is eligible to lose one player per year for a maximum of three years.

—A team losing a player from the pool will receive $150,000 from an industry fund created by equal contributions from all 26 teams. A team will be compensated only for the loss of one player per year. Should that same team lose players from the pool in the following two years, it will not receive any payment, but thereafter the team will again be eligible for payment under the same arrangement.

—Selections from the pool are to be made the first week in January (or when all of the Type A players have signed) and clubs will select in the reverse order of the preceding season's standings. An "excluded club" losing a Type A free agent is eligible for compensation from the pool.

—Two classes of "ranking" free agents were created. Type A free agents—those ranking in the top 20 percent of all players at their respective positions over the last two years, as determined by a statistical formula—shall entitle the teams losing them to professional compensation from the pool as well as an amateur draft choice. Compensation for Type B free agents—those in the 21-30 percent category—will be two amateur draft choices. A team losing an unranked player to free agency will continue to receive an amateur draft choice unless the player is selected by fewer than four teams.

—The statistical formula for batters includes plate appearances, batting average, on-base percentage, home runs and RBIs. It also includes fielding percentage and assists for catchers and fielding percentage and total chances for second basemen, third basemen and shortstops. For starting pitchers, the formula consists of games started (plus half a game for each relief appearance), innings pitched, victories, winning percentage, earned-run average and strikeouts. For relief pitchers, the formula includes number of relief appearances (plus credit for two appearances for each start), innings pitched, combined total of victories and saves, games finished, ERA and strikeouts.

—Players who have completed the repeat rights cycle (those who went through the re-entry draft previously) and players with 12 or more seasons of credited major league service shall not be "ranking" players. Free-agent players signed after being taken in the re-entry draft do not have to be protected, but any player with a no-trade or trade-by-consent clause in his contract must be included on the protected list.

—There is no limit on the number of teams which can select a free agent in the re-entry draft. (Previously only 12 teams —plus the last team for which he played— could select a player.) If fewer than four teams take a ranking free agent, he will be eligible to negotiate will all teams.

—The maximum number of Type A free agents requiring professional compensation in 1981 was set at seven if only 21 to 23 teams participate or eight if 24 or more participate, with the maximum rising to nine in 1982 and 1983 if all teams participate. In the event there are more Type A free agents than the maximum requiring professional compensation,

teams losing such players beyond the maximum will receive an additional amateur draft choice.

In addition to the thorny compensation issue, the agreement embraced the following points:

—Play would resume on Sunday, August 9, with the All-Star Game in Cleveland, and the championship season would resume on Monday, August 10. No games cancelled because of the strike would be rescheduled.

—Players' salaries would resume on Saturday, August 1, except for players reporting thereafter, unless for unavoidable causes.

—No deductions of credited major league service would be made for the period of the strike.

—Incentive bonus clauses that some players had for home runs and other performance statistics in 1981 would be prorated both as to performance and bonus unless the original incentive level was reached.

—The contribution of $2,139,000 from the All-Star Game to the players' benefit plan would be made within two weeks of the game even if the game were not played.

—The players would withdraw their complaint before Judge Welles of the NLRB.

—The Basic Agreement was extended one year to December 31, 1984, assuring an additional year of labor peace and the pension plan was also extended one year to March 31, 1985.

—The minimum player salary for 1984 was set at $40,000.

—The owners were given the right to decide how to finish the season, i.e., whether to continue the standings from the point of the strike or to play a split-season. This applied to 1981 only.

—In the event of a split-season, each player on the eight teams in the divisional playoffs would receive five days' additional pay. In addition, 60 percent of the gate receipts from the divisional playoffs would go into a pool to be shared equally by players on the eight teams.

Like most strikes, this one left animosity between the parties and mixed feelings about the settlement. Lee MacPhail admitted some of the owners didn't like the agreement. As for the athletes, player representative Doug DeCinces said: "I very seriously doubt that the owners will try to challenge the players again." His boss, Baltimore General Manager Hank Peters, also had a word of caution. "If we ever let it (a strike) happen again, kiss baseball goodbye."

The clubs moved quickly to piece together the shreds of the season. All 26 teams began workouts on August 1 and started lining up exhibitions for late the following week. Because Olympic Stadium in Montreal was booked for football and soccer, the Expos ordered their players to report to the club's spring training camp at West Palm Beach, Fla. The Cincinnati Reds, faced with a similar situation, trained at the University of Michigan at Ann Arbor. Two other clubs—Oakland and Seattle—also found their home stadiums occupied and worked out on nearby college fields.

The most interesting issue involved with the settlement was the question of whether to pick up the standings of June 12 (when the strike began) or declare a split season and have all clubs start another, shorter, season. "We're 18 games behind," declared Calvin Griffith, the Minnesota owner, "and if we don't split the season we might as well not open our gates." Baseball purists, of course, cringed at the thought of a split season, but some fans and owners of teams far off the pace thought it was a good idea. The majors' only previous split-season race occurred during the 1892 National League season.

Formal ratification of the agreement as well as a decision on how to handle the remainder of the season came quickly. The players voted 627-37 in favor of the pact, while at a joint meeting of the two leagues in Chicago on August 6, the owners approved it by a 21-2 margin with three teams abstaining. Only Cincinnati and St. Louis voted in the negative, according to Joseph Durso of the New York Times.

In separate meetings that same day, the two leagues okayed a split-season format. American League clubs favored the idea by a 12-0 margin with the Orioles and White Sox abstaining. In the National League, the vote was 9-3 with Cincinnati, Philadelphia and St. Louis voting no. In explaining his vote, president Dick Wagner of the Reds said: "Circumstances could lead a team that won the first half, in effect, to help pick its opponent in the second half."

The decision to divide the season meant that teams on top when the strike started became first-half champions. In the American League, the Yankees were in front in the East by two games over Baltimore at the time of the stoppage, while Oakland led the West by a game and a half over Texas. In the National League,

Philadelphia was a game and a half ahead of St. Louis in the East, and Los Angeles held a half-game edge over Cincinnati in the West. The second-half leader would automatically qualify for the divisional series, unless that champion was also the first-half leader. In that case, the second playoff team would be the club with the best overall record.

The loophole to which Wagner referred soon became evident. Responding to a hypothetical question, the White Sox' 36-year-old lawyer-manager, Tony LaRussa, pointed out it was possible his team could gain a playoff spot by deliberately losing some late-season games with Oakland, making the A's champions in both halves and giving his White Sox the best overall record in the A.L. West. His comment started a storm. One newspaper headline read: "Sox Players Would Throw Games." Whitey Herzog, St. Louis' manager, also hinted he might forfeit a late-season game if that would help his team gain a playoff spot. To avoid any possible question of integrity, Commissioner Kuhn and league presidents subsequently revamped the playoff structure. The revised setup provided that if the same team won both halves, it would meet the second-half runnerup—rather than the team with the next best overall record—in the Division playoff, and play four of the five games at home as an incentive for a team to win both halves.

While creating a new tier of playoffs, the split-season format also forced the leagues to negotiate new terms with the umpires. The league presidents proposed using four-man umpire crews for the mini-playoffs and offered to pay each arbiter $4,000. The umpires' union insisted on six umpires—the same as in the league Championship Series and World Series—and demanded $6,500 each. In addition, their attorney, Richie Phillips, wanted the umpires to be paid for the entire 50 days of the strike instead of for 30 days as provided in their 1979 agreement. The dispute almost led to a boycott by the arbiters chosen for the All-Star Game, but the leagues eventually agreed to assign six umpires to the divisional playoffs and pay them $5,150 apiece. When their offer to pay the umps for 45 days of the strike was rejected, both sides agreed to submit that issue to arbitration.

A walkout of the nation's air traffic controllers on August 3 added to baseball's problems. During the latter stages of the baseball talks, Kenneth Moffett also was mediating in the air traffic controllers' dispute. Fortunately, that walk-out resulted in only minor travel disruptions for the All-Star Game and for the games played afterward.

The second season got underway officially on Monday afternoon, August 10, at Chicago's Wrigley Field. Only 7,551 fans turned out. The game, which saw the Mets edge the Cubs in 13 innings, 7-5, was televised in both cities, but all other "second openers" that night were blacked out locally because of ABC's national Monday night baseball telecast.

Only two of the August 10 reopeners attracted capacity or near-capacity crowds. The largest was at Philadelphia where 60,561 showed up to cheer on Pete Rose. The Phillies veteran rewarded them by singling off Bruce Sutter, the Cardinal relief ace, in the eighth inning for hit No. 3,631, breaking Musial's National League record.

At San Diego that same evening, Ray Kroc, the Padres owner, threw the gates open to the public, and a crowd of 52,608 jammed Jack Murphy Stadium. Several other clubs sought to win back their fans during the remaining weeks with special inducements such as reduced ticket prices.

Attendance was off during the second half. "Baseball is in for its worst financial year," commented the Phillies' Bill Giles on August 20. "We're going to have to sweat it out. I think hard times are pretty much the pattern."

Because the original schedule was followed, the second season found teams slated for an unequal number of games and contained many other built-in imbalances. For instance, Baltimore enjoyed a 31-20 break in home-away games while Milwaukee had a 22-31 home-away disadvantage. Other clubs faced similar situations. In addition, some important head-to-head series between contenders were erased by the shutdown.

Despite these drawbacks, the second half produced its share of excitement. Besides Rose, Nolan Ryan achieved a historic milestone. The Houston fire-baller hurled his fifth no-hitter—a record —in beating Los Angeles, 5-0, at the Astrodome on September 26. It was the year's third pitching gem. Charlie Lea of Montreal held San Francisco hitless in a 4-0 conquest at Olympic Stadium on May 10. And Len Barker of Cleveland did even better, pitching the eleventh perfect game in major league history when he stopped Toronto, 3-0, at Cleveland's Municipal Stadium on May 15.

After winning his first eight decisions,

five via shutouts, Fernando Valenzuela ran into some difficulties but remained a prime attraction. The Dodgers' phenomenal 20-year-old Mexican southpaw finished the abbreviated campaign with 13 victories, including eight shutouts, to tie the rookie record. Montreal's Tim Raines, who posed a threat to Lou Brock's record by stealing 50 bases in 55 games before the strike, continued his base-swiping heroics until he broke a bone in his right hand while sliding on September 13. The injury relegated him to pinch-running the remainder of the way, but his 71 steals in 88 games led the majors and set a rookie record.

All four second-half races proved to be thrillers. Of the first-half leaders, Oakland came closest to repeating. Playing four more games than the A's, Kansas City edged Billy Martin's team by one game for the A.L. West title. In fact, the Royals had to win a makeup contest at Cleveland on October 5, the day after the regular season closed, to clinch first place. Otherwise the Royals would have had to play four of the possible five divisional playoff games in Oakland.

Milwaukee captured the A.L. East crown by one and one-half games over Boston and Detroit.

In the National League, Montreal assured Canada of its first representation in the playoffs by finishing half a game in front of St. Louis in the East, and Houston nosed out Cincinnati by one and one-half games in the West.

To emphasize that 1981 was the game's strangest season ever, Cincinnati wound up with the year's best overall record at 66-42, and St. Louis (59-43) had the best record in the N.L. East, yet neither the Reds nor the Cardinals gained a spot in the playoffs. By contrast, one playoff team—Kansas City—had a 50-53 record for the season.

Three of the Divisional Series went the five-game distance. The exception saw Oakland oust Kansas City in three straight. In the others, the Yankees defeated Milwaukee, Los Angeles beat Houston and Montreal knocked off Philadelphia. The Dodgers, who eventually captured the World Series, had to win three successive games at home to take the series after losing the first two games in the Astrodome.

The Yankees followed their division series win by crushing Oakland in three games to capture the American League pennant. And the Dodgers, after being down two games to one, rebounded again to gain the N.L. flag when Valenzuela

Chuck Kasprisin finally got to peddle his wares when the All-Star Game opened the second season August 9 in Cleveland's Municipal Stadium.

The National and American League ERA titles went to Houston's Nolan Ryan (above) and Oakland's Steve McCatty (below).

stopped Montreal, 2-1, in the fifth game.

The Dodgers further demonstrated their resiliency in the World Series. Beaten in the first two games at Yankee Stadium, they rallied to win the next four and claim the world championship.

Despite losing one-third of the season to the strike, the two leagues drew 26,544,376 fans for the regular season, led by the American League with 14,065,986. Seven A.L. teams and six in the National exceeded the million mark. The Dodgers were the only club to surpass two million with 2,381,292, while the Yankees topped the A.L. with 1,614,353. Even though limited to 51 home games, the A's set an all-time Oakland attendance record of 1,304,052. A record 11 straight victories to open the season, together with "Billy Ball" and new ownership, helped stimulate interest in the A's.

Two third basemen—Bill Madlock of Pittsburgh and Carney Lansford of Boston—won the batting championships. With the Pirates playing only 103 games, tying for the lowest total in either league, Madlock just managed to qualify with 320 plate appearances—one over the minimum—in gaining his third National League title with a .341 average. Rose was runnerup at .325. Lansford, an off-season acquisition, hit .336 for the Red Sox to edge his nearest rival, Tom Paciorek of Seatttle, by ten points.

Another third baseman, Mike Schmidt of Philadelphia, led the National League for the second successive year in home runs (31), runs batted in (91), total bases (228) and slugging percentage (.644). Four players—Tony Armas of Oakland, Bobby Grich of California, Eddie Murray of Baltimore and Dwight Evans of Boston—shared American League home run honors with 22. Murray led in RBIs with 78, Evans in total bases with 215 and Grich in slugging at .543.

Nolan Ryan achieved his first ERA title when he paced the National League with 1.69. Houston teammate Bob Knepper was next at 2.18. In the American League, a special ruling gave Oakland's Steve McCatty the earned-run leadership over Sammy Stewart of Baltimore. On the basis of his 112⅓ innings pitched, Stewart finished with a 2.32 ERA compared to 2.33 for McCatty, who worked 185⅔ innings. However, baseball rules require that the innings of both had to be rounded off, leaving McCatty the ERA winner by an identical 2.32 to 2.33 margin. (Late in the year, the Scoring Rules Committee recommended changing the rule so that, starting in 1983, the round-

Fernando Valenzuela became one of the game's top personalities in '81.

ing off of fractional innings would be eliminated for all pitchers.)

McCatty also shared American League laurels for most victories (14) with Dennis Martinez of Baltimore, Jack Morris of Detroit and Pete Vuckovich of Milwaukee. Vuckovich had the best winning percentage with his 14-4 record. In the National League, Tom Seaver of Cincinnati led in victories as well as winning percentage with a 14-2 ledger. Valenzuela's eight shutouts for the Dodgers paced the senior circuit and were double the highest total by any American League pitcher. Rollie Fingers of Milwaukee paced A.L. relievers in saves with 28 while notching six victories, and St. Louis' Bruce Sutter topped National League firemen with 25 saves to go with three victories.

Even without a strike, 1981 would have been a historic season. For the first time, two black managers were in charge of big league teams—Maury Wills with Seattle and Frank Robinson with San Francisco. Robinson, who piloted Cleveland in the mid-1970s, was one of five new appointees. The others were Ralph Houk, Boston; Don Zimmer, Texas; Gene Michael, New York Yankees, and Frank Howard, San Diego.

Wills, who took the Seattle helm on August 4, 1980, failed to last one full season. With the Mariners off to the worst start in their five-year history and sporting a dismal 6-18 record, Wills was dismissed on May 6. Rene Lachemann was brought up from the club's Spokane farm team to replace him.

John Goryl of Minnesota became the second skipper to feel the axe. Like Wills, he had held the job less than a year. Goryl was ousted on May 22 following an eight-game losing streak that left the Twins at 12-25. Billy Gardner, the team's third base coach, succeeded Goryl.

Jim Fregosi of California was next to go. On May 28 the Angels released him, and Gene Mauch took the reins. Mauch, who resigned as Minnesota manager the previous summer, had joined the Angels early in the year as director of player personnel.

Less than a year after guiding Kansas City into the World Series, Jim Frey was handed his walking papers by the Royals on August 31. The club's poor showing and dissatisfaction among the players sped his departure. Dick Howser, who had been fired by the Yankees the previous fall, but who was still under contract to them as a scout, was given a three-year contract to succeed Frey.

Ironically, shortly before Howser's appointment to the Kansas City job, some members of the New York press speculated that owner George Steinbrenner might bring Howser back to manage the Yankees. Gene Michael, in the first season of a three-year contract as Yankee skipper, and his boss had had several disagreements. Late in May, Steinbrenner summoned Michael to Tampa, Fla., for a meeting that led to Stan Williams being replaced as Yankee pitching coach by Clyde King. Continued interference and second guessing by the owner finally aroused Michael's ire, and on August 28 he informed the media that Steinbrenner had called him again that morning and threatened dismissal. Michael said he challenged his boss by saying: "George, if you're going to fire me, then do it. Don't keep threatening me."

After a period of uncharacteristic silence, Steinbrenner responded on the morning of September 6. He announced that Michael was through and that Bob Lemon, who managed the club less than a year in 1978-79, was taking over the helm immediately. Lemon thus became the eighth manager, counting himself and Billy Martin twice each, in Steinbrenner's nine years as Yankee owner.

In another surprise move, the Montreal Expos fired Dick Williams on September 8 in the majors' third managerial change in nine days. To replace him, president John McHale reached into the club's front office and tapped Jim Fanning, former major league catcher and the Expos' director of player development, for the job.

Six other managerial positions changed hands following the season. Joe Torre was dismissed by the New York Mets on the final day of the campaign, and on October 20 the club hired George Bamberger as his successor. Two more jobs were vacated on October 7 when Bobby Cox disclosed that he had been fired by Atlanta and 65-year-old Bobby Mattick announced he was giving up the Toronto post in favor of a newly-created role as executive coordinator of baseball operations for the Blue Jays. Eight days later, Toronto appointed Cox as manager, and on October 23 Torre was named to the Atlanta helm.

After watching San Diego finish last in his rookie season as manager, Frank Howard was fired on October 13 with a year remaining on his contract. President Ballard Smith said Howard's refusal to communicate with the front office was a key factor in the decision. The

Padres filled the vacancy by signing Dick Williams to a three-year pact on November 18.

Ownership changes involving the Phillies and Cubs led to the year's last two shifts in pilots. Shortly after the season ended, Dallas Green resigned as Philadelphia skipper and on October 15 took over officially as executive vice-president and general manager of the Cubs. A week later he named Lee Elia, one of his former Phillies coaches, as manager of the Cubs, succeeding Joe Amalfitano. On November 4 the Phillies appointed Pat Corrales as Green's replacement.

The managerial musical chairs scenario of the Yankees took an odd twist late in the year. On December 8, during the winter meetings in Hollywood, Fla., the club called a press conference to announce that Lemon would return as manager in 1982. The club's collapse in the World Series had prompted speculation that Steinbrenner might not bring him back for the final year of his five-year contract. One day after the Lemon announcement, the Yankees revealed that Gene Michael would be back as manager in 1983. At the same time, vice-president Bill Bergesch disclosed that Steinbrenner had extended Michael's contract through 1985.

Four clubs, including both Chicago teams, underwent major changes in ownership in 1981. The two others were the Seattle Mariners and Philadelphia Phillies.

The sales of the White Sox and Mariners both were consummated early in the year. On January 8, a group headed by Jerry Reinsdorf, a real estate tycoon, and television executive Eddie Einhorn purchased the White Sox and Comiskey Park from Bill Veeck and company for $20 million. Reinsdorf, 44, assumed the title of chairman and handled the baseball end of operations. Einhorn, 45, former executive producer of CBS' "Sports Spectacular," became president and ran the non-baseball operations.

Six days later, George Argyros bought controlling interest in the Seattle club for a reported $13 million. Four of the Mariners' original owners—Stanley Golub, Danny Kaye, Lester Smith and Walter Schoenfield—remained as limited partners, while Warren Finley, Argyros' personal attorney, also became a limited partner. Argyros, 43, headed up real estate and financial interests on the West Coast.

Barely four months after seeing the Phillies win their first world champion-

Dallas Green left the Phillies dugout to take over as general manager of the lowly Chicago Cubs.

ship, president Ruly Carpenter sent shock waves through the baseball world by announcing on March 6 that the Philadelphia club was for sale. Carpenter, whose family bought the club in 1943, said he was fed up with escalating player salaries, bizarre free-agent signings and the actions of some maverick owners.

"It was one of the most difficult decisions the family ever had to make," Carpenter said. "It has become apparent to me that some deeply-ingrained philosophical differences exist between the Carpenter family and some of the other owners as to how the baseball business should be conducted." He added that the frantic bidding for free agents following the 1980 re-entry draft was "the final nail in the coffin."

Bill Giles, the Phillies' executive vice-president whose father was National League president for 18 years, immediately began to put together a group to purchase the club. But the subsequent players' strike and other complications delayed any transaction.

In the meantime, another family's 65-year association with baseball came to an end. On June 16, William Wrigley sold the Cubs to the Tribune Company, parent firm of two newspapers (The Chicago Tribune and New York Daily News) and several other media operations. The purchase price for Wrigley's 81 percent holdings and all remaining 1,900 shares was $20.5 million. Wrigley Field itself was not included in the deal. The Tribune Company was expected to buy the park in a later transaction. The Tribune Company's radio and television outlets in Chicago, WGN and WGN-TV, had long aired the Cubs' games.

Wrigley cited estate tax problems resulting from the death of his parents, and attempts to find a solution to the Cubs' long-term financial needs, as factors in the sale. His grandfather, William Wrigley, Jr., first acquired an interest in the team in 1916 and became majority stockholder in 1921. After he died in 1932, his son, Philip K. Wrigley, was the chief owner until his death in 1977. The Cubs, the only publicly-owned major league club, with 600 stockholders, lost $1.7 million in 1980.

The Tribune's acquisition of the Cubs led to speculation that lights might be installed at Wrigley Field, the major league's lone bastion of all day games. Early in September, however, the team announced that they had no plans for lights.

An agreement on the sale of the Phillies finally was announced on October 29. A group of six investors brought together by Giles paid a record $30,175,000 for the franchise. The Carpenter family purchased the club 38 years earlier for less than a million dollars. Although no real estate was included in the latest transaction, the total price exceeded by almost 50 percent the previous high of $21.1 million paid for the Mets in 1980.

The new owners established a limited partnership, with Giles as the general partner. The five limited partners were: Taft Broadcasting Co. of Cincinnati, which acknowledged putting up $15 million, for slightly less than 50 percent ownership, and thus was the biggest investor; J.D.B. Associates, a partnership involving John Drew Betz and Robert D. Hedbert; Tri-Play Associates, a partnership of brothers Alexander, James and William Buck; Fitz Eugene Dixon, former owner of the Philadelphia 76ers basketball team, and Rochelle Levy, wife of Robert P. Levy, chief executive officer of DRT Industries.

In buying into the Phillies, Taft Broadcasting was forced to divest itself of a five-percent holding in the Cincinnati Reds. Taft owned seven television and 12 radio stations, including WTAF-TV in Philadelphia. As part of the deal, WTAF-TV will take over the Phillies' telecasts for nine years starting in 1984, after the club's current contract with WPHL-TV ends. The new Taft connection with the Phillies provided a touch of irony. Back in 1909, Charles P. Taft of Cincinnati, brother of President William Howard Taft, put up the money that enabled another syndicate to purchase the Philadelphia club. Charles Taft also was the money man behind the Cubs during that same period. Giles' Cincinnati ties went back to the days when his father headed the Reds as general manager and later president.

Under the new setup, Giles assumed the title of president of the Phillies. David Montgomery, director of sales, moved up to executive vice-president. Paul Owens agreed to remain on for five years as vice-president and general manager.

Two other National League teams, the Pittsburgh Pirates and St. Louis Cardinals, claimed heavy losses and were the subjects of possible relocation or ownership change during the year.

Unable to negotiate new terms with the city, the Pirates filed suit to nullify their lease on Three Rivers Stadium, which still had 30 years to run. Club officials contended the team had experienced a deficit of $2,165,000 in 1980, and losses of more than $6.5 million since moving into the facility in 1970. Stadium maintenance costs contributed heavily to the problem. A dispute over who would pay for an estimated $2-$3 million in stadium repairs, and charges that the city failed to improve highway access, were other factors leading to the suit.

Fuel was added to the situation when Cliff N. Wallace, general manager of the Superdome in New Orleans, met with Pirates president Dan Galbreath on April 26 to explore a possible move to the Louisiana city. The following day, the City of Pittsburgh filed suit in Federal court to keep Superdome officials from attempting to lure away the Pirates. As the year drew to a close, the dispute between the club and the city remained unresolved, prompting Galbreath to comment: "We're now at the crossroads. Baseball cannot exist in Pittsburgh under this lease."

A bid by Anheuser-Busch Companies, owner of the Cardinals, to buy Busch Memorial Stadium touched off a furor in St. Louis. When the stadium was built in the early 1960s, the Cardinals agreed to give up concessions and parking rights to help Civic Center Redevelopment Corporation, which headed up the project. Club officials in 1981 claimed the concessions and parking revenues were needed to offset high player salaries.

On April 13, Anheuser-Busch, already owner of a 24.6 percent interest in CCRC, offered $33.5 million for the remaining common stock of Civic Center, which owned not only the stadium but four nearby parking garages and the city's largest hotel, Stouffer's Riverfront Towers. Several months later, when an increased bid of $41 million was rejected, Anheuser-Busch officials revealed the Cardinals had a pre-tax loss of $2.9 million in 1980. They added that they would be forced to sell the team if efforts to buy the stadium failed. Subsequently, the team reportedly was offered to Apex Oil Co., of suburban Clayton, for $23.5 million. (Apex also was bidding for the CCRC properties.) Everything was resolved in late August when Anheuser-Busch acquired all Civic Center stock for $53 million.

While the Pirates and Cardinals were battling stadium problems, the Minnesota Twins waited as their new home neared completion. After playing 21 seasons at Metropolitan Stadium in Bloomington, the Twins were scheduled to open the 1982 season in the $55-million Hubert H. Humphrey Metrodome in Minneapolis. The domed stadium, boasting an inflatable Teflon-coated fabric roof, also will become the home of the Minnesota Vikings football team, and will seat 55,200 for baseball and 63,000 for football.

The four clubs which changed ownership weren't the only ones to experience major shifts at the executive level. The Cubs changed general managers twice. Bob Kennedy resigned as executive vice-president-G.M. on May 22 and was succeeded by Herman Franks. Franks remained in charge until Dallas Green took over in October. Green proceeded to revamp much of the Cubs front office.

San Francisco also had a midseason change in general managers. Spec Richardson was replaced on July 7 as vice-president of baseball operations by Tom Haller, who had been coordinator of player personnel for the Giants.

Joe Burke was elevated to the Kansas City Royals' presidency on October 8. John Schuerholz moved up to Burke's former role as executive vice-president and general manager.

In a surprise move, Peter Bavasi resigned as president and chief operating officer of the Toronto Blue Jays on November 24. Bavasi said he would become a private sports consultant. Most of his baseball duties were turned over to General Manager Pat Gillick.

Other changes in executive personnel included: Harry Gibbs, a 24-year veteran of the U.S. Secret Service, was appointed director of security by Commissioner Kuhn in January to succeed Henry Fitzgibbon, who retired; Paul Richards was named assistant to Eddie Robinson, executive vice-president of the Texas Rangers; Lou Saban, longtime football coach, was appointed president of the Yankees on March 1; Kip Horsburgh resigned as executive director of the Seattle Mariners in June; Harry Renaud resigned as Montreal vice-president in August; Jim Weigel was dismissed as San Diego farm director in October and replaced by Bob Cluck, who had worked in Houston's minor league department; Bobby Winkles was promoted from coach to director of player development by the White Sox in October; Gordon Goldsberry became the Cubs' scouting and minor league director; Bing Devine, former longtime major league executive, resigned after three years as vice-president of the St. Louis football Cardinals to join the Montreal Expos in November as vice-president in charge of player development, and Branch Rickey III was promoted to the position of farm director of the Pittsburgh Pirates.

Two developments at the coaching level emphasized the new stature being attained by field assistants. Charlie Lau, widely considered the game's premier batting coach, left the Yankees to sign a six-year contract as batting instructor with the White Sox. He reportedly will be paid a total of $500,000 or more. Around the same time another Yankees coach, Jeff Torborg, was given a seven-year contract by Owner George Steinbrenner to remain with the club as a coach and future front-office executive. Prior to the 1981 season, Torborg had announced he was leaving the Yankees at year's end to become baseball coach at Princeton University, but the new long-term pact changed his mind.

Free agents fared better than ever in 1981. And a new twist was added to free agency at year's start. On January 5, it was disclosed that two Boston players—outfielder Fred Lynn and catcher Carlton Fisk—had filed for free agency. Both claimed the contracts sent them by the Red Sox arrived in envelopes postmarked December 22—two days after the deadline stipulated in the Major League Rules.

While grievances were pending in the two cases, the Red Sox negotiated a five-player deal that sent Lynn and pitcher Steve Renko to California for outfielder Joe Rudi and pitchers Frank Tanana and Jim Dorsey. The swap was announced January 23 after Lynn agreed to a four-year contract with the Angels. The contract was estimated to be worth between $4.1 and $5.25 million.

In an attempt to avoid losing Fisk, the Red Sox made him a new offer of a four-year pact which, with incentive clauses, would have paid him around $425,000 per season. However, he rejected it and, following an arbitration hearing, was declared a free agent on February 12 by baseball's permanent arbitrator, Raymond Goetz. Five weeks later, Fisk signed a five-year, $2.9 million contract with the White Sox.

Approximately 70 players were eligible to become free agents at season's end, but nearly half of them signed new contracts before the re-entry draft. At least ten were rewarded with long-term contracts worth $500,000 or more per season to pass up free agency. Dave Concepcion of Cincinnati and Bill Madlock of Pittsburgh headed the list. The Reds gave their star shortstop a five-year pact for a reported $4,630,000, an average of $926,000 per season. Madlock signed for six years and $5.1 million, an average of $850,000, but can pick up another $125,000 each year if he maintains his weight at no more than 206 pounds.

Others who skipped the draft for big contracts were: Bobby Grich, California, who signed for four years and around $4 million, including a reported $700,000 signing bonus; Greg Luzinski, White Sox, three years for $2.25 million; Phil Garner, Houston, three years for $2.05 million; Jerry Mumphrey, Yankees, six years for nearly $4 million; Amos Otis, Kansas City, two years for $1,275,000; Ray Burris, Montreal, three years for $1.8 million; Vern Ruhle, Houston, three years for $1.5 million, and Ken Griffey, signed by the Yankees for five years for around $5 million after being obtained in a trade with Cincinnati.

Seven clubs—two above the maximum—filed for status as "excluded clubs" for three years under the new rules. In a drawing conducted on November 3, the five teams chosen were Boston, California, Los Angeles, Minnesota and Seattle. The two others were not identified.

By the time the sixth re-entry draft took place in New York City on November 13, the number of free agents had dwindled to 41. Ron Guidry was chosen by the largest number of clubs (18) while John Denny was picked by 14 and Joaquin Andujar by 12. Eleven players were passed up by all clubs. They and nine others who were selected by fewer than four teams thus became free to negotiate with any club. Three teams—Detroit, Minnesota and San Diego—made no selections.

The complete list of 41 players included in the re-entry process, with the number of teams selecting them shown in parentheses, follows:

AMERICAN LEAGUE

Baltimore—Mark Belanger (3); **Boston**—Bill Campbell (6), Jerry Remy (6), Joe Rudi (5), Frank Tanana (6); **California**—Bert Campaneris (0), Jesse Jefferson (0), Ed Ott (5); **Chicago**—Ed Farmer (5), Lamar Johnson (2), Jerry Turner (4); **Cleveland**—John Denny (14), Sid Monge (10), Rick Waits (9); **Detroit**—Ron Jackson (0); **Kansas City**—Dave Chalk (1), Cesar Geronimo (0); **Milwaukee**—None; **Minnesota**—Glenn Adams (0), Pete Mackanin (2); **New York**—Ron Guidry (18), Reggie Jackson (0), Dave LaRoche (5), Bobby Murcer (0); **Oakland**—None; **Seattle**—Glenn Abbott (5), Jeff Burroughs (0); **Texas**—Ferguson Jenkins (2), Tom Poquette (0); **Toronto**—Buck Martinez (5).

NATIONAL LEAGUE

Atlanta—John Montefusco (0); **Chicago**—Tim Blackwell (7), Hector Cruz (0), Dick Tidrow (2); **Cincinnati**—Dave Collins (10), Mike Vail (3); **Houston**—Tony Scott (5); **Los Angeles**—Rick Monday (3), Reggie Smith (0); **Montreal**—Chris Speier (0); **New York**—None; **Philadelphia**—Larry Christenson (9), Ron Reed (6); **Pittsburgh**—None; **St. Louis**—Joaquin Andujar (12); **San Diego**—None; **San Francisco**—None.

The new "ranking" statistics used to determine Type A and Type B free agents produced interesting comparisons for management and fans alike. There was speculation the statistics would also find their way into salary arbitration hearings. Using the statistical formula spelled out in the new compensation agreement, the Elias Sports Bureau produced a document rating all players at their posi-

Carlton Fisk won his free agency and played the '81 season with the White Sox.

tions within their leagues. Of the 695 players involved, Steve Carlton of the Phillies achieved the highest ranking— 1.667. The top-rated non-pitcher was first baseman Cecil Cooper of Milwaukee at 2.100.

The document showed the top three players at each position, based on combined 1980-1981 statistics, as follows:

AMERICAN LEAGUE

Starting pitchers—Mike Norris, Oakland, 6.750; Dennis Leonard, Kansas City, 6.833; Scott McGregor, Baltimore, 8.167; **Relief pitchers**—Doug Corbett, Minnesota, 3.917; Rollie Fingers, Milwaukee, 4.286; Goose Gossage, New York, 8.917; **Catchers**—Jim Sundberg, Texas, 4.286; Lance Parrish, Detroit, 5.429; Carlton Fisk, Chicago, 6.143; **First basemen**—Cecil Cooper, Milwaukee, 2.100; Eddie Murray, Baltimore, 3.200; Willie Aikens, Kansas City, 5.100; **Second basemen**—Bobby Grich, California, 3.000; Rich Dauer, Baltimore, 6.000; Bump Wills, Texas, 7.286; **Third basemen**—Buddy Bell, Texas, 2.429; George Brett, Kansas City, 3.857; Toby Harrah,

Cleveland, 5.071; **Shortstops**—Rick Burleson, California, and Alan Trammell, Detroit, both 3.000; Robin Yount, Milwaukee, 3.571; **Outfielders**—Ken Singleton, Baltimore, 8.000; Al Oliver, Texas, 9.800; Steve Kemp, Detroit, 10.800; **Designated hitters**—Richie Zisk, Seattle, 2.800; Hal McRae, Kansas City, 5.400; Champ Summers, Detroit, 5.600.

NATIONAL LEAGUE

Starting pitchers—Steve Carlton, Philadelphia, 1.667; Steve Rogers, Montreal, 7.917; Nolan Ryan, Houston, 9.500; **Relief pitchers**—Tom Hume, Cincinnati, 9.333; Bruce Sutter, St. Louis, 9.750; Rick Camp, Atlanta, 10.333; **Catchers**—Gary Carter, Montreal, 5.286; Milt May, San Francisco, 6.429; Johnny Bench, Cincinnati, 7.571; **First basemen**—Keith Hernandez, St. Louis, 2.400; Bill Buckner, Chicago, and Steve Garvey, Los Angeles, both 4.900; **Second Basemen**—Manny Trillo, Philadelphia, 3.000; Joe Morgan, San Francisco, 4.429; Phil Garner, Houston and Glenn Hubbard, Atlanta, both 7.000; **Third baseman**—Mike Schmidt, Philadelphia, 3.286; Ron Cey, Los Angeles, 5.714; Darrell Evans, San Francisco, 6.429; **Shortstops**—Dave Concepcion, Cincinnati, 3.714; Garry Templeton, St. Louis, 4.571; Larry Bowa, Philadelphia, 5.286; **Outfielders**—Andre Dawson, Montreal, 6.800; George Foster, Cincinnati, 8.000; Dusty Baker, Los Angeles, 9.700.

The scramble for free agents following the 1981 re-entry draft was considerably less spirited than in previous years. Fewer than half of the 41 players had been signed by year's end. The top contracts were those achieved by Guidry, Collins and Remy. Guidry agreed to a reported five-year, $5 million package to remain with the Yankees. The Yankees also landed Collins with a three-year, $2.3 million contract, while Remy accepted a five-year deal worth more than $2.8 million to stay with the Red Sox.

Numerous other players received lucrative new pacts. On December 21, the Phillies disclosed they had signed Mike Schmidt to a new six-year agreement estimated at $1.2 million per season. His old six-year, $560,000-a-year pact was due to expire at the end of 1982.

Shortly before the 1981 spring training ended, the Phillies tore up Carlton's contract, which would have earned him around $400,000 per season through 1983. They gave him a new one which, with incentive bonuses, could pay him approximately $1 million per season through 1984. Early in the season, Kansas City pitching ace Dennis Leonard, on the last season of a five-year pact, signed a five-year extension involving a $3.4 million package. Atlanta gave Chris Chambliss a five-year pact through 1986 worth an estimated $3.5-$4 million.

A record number of 98 players filed for salary arbitration in January 1981, but most of them signed before the hearings. Several wound up with million-dollar contracts, including John Mayberry of Toronto, who signed for four years and $3.2 million; Gorman Thomas of Milwaukee, five years and $3 million, and Roy Smalley of Minnesota, four years and $2.6 million. Earlier, the Twins had broken with tradition by signing Butch Wynegar to a five-year, $2.3 million contract.

Only 21 salary disputes actually went to arbitration. The hearings were conducted by Monroe Berkowitz, economics professor at Rutgers University. He ruled in favor of the player in 11 instances and for the club in the 10 others. Three players tried the arbitration route for the second consecutive year. Steve Kemp won again, while Dave Collins of Cincinnati

and Ron Jackson of Minnesota fared the opposite of their previous attempt (Collins lost and Jackson won the second time around). The salary figures which follow were obtained by Murray Chass and published in the New York Times and THE SPORTING NEWS.

The 11 players who gained the salaries they sought, with the club's offer in parentheses, were: Kemp, $600,000 ($360,000); Ed Farmer, White Sox, $495,000 ($300,000); Rick Cerone, Yankees, $440,000 ($350,000); Jason Thompson, Angels, $395,000 ($250,000); Tony Scott, Cardinals, $225,000 ($180,000); John Castino, Twins, $210,000 ($150,000); Ron Jackson, Twins, $200,000 ($130,525); Rick Honeycutt, Rangers, $167,000 ($110,000); Johnnie LeMaster, Giants, $155,000 ($135,000); Dave Frost, Angels, $112,500 ($95,000), and Dave Rajsich, Rangers, $65,000 ($35,000).

The 10 who had to settle for the club's offer, with the figure the player sought in parentheses, were: Dave Skaggs, Angels, $60,000 ($75,000); Rick Sutcliffe, Dodgers, $85,000 ($110,000); Paul Moskau, Reds, $90,000 ($125,000); Julio Cruz, Mariners, $106,000 ($160,000); Wayne Nordhagen, White Sox, $160,000 ($255,379); Mike Vail, Reds, $175,000 ($225,000); Greg Minton, Giants, $180,000 ($265,000); Tony Armas, A's, $210,000 ($500,000); Dave Collins, Reds, $267,500 ($360,000), and Mike Norris, A's, $325,000 ($450,000).

Commissioner Bowie Kuhn experienced another busy and trying year. Several owners and many fans were critical of the low profile he maintained during the player strike. They felt he should have been more actively involved in efforts to end it. A splinter group of owners was especially outspoken, but as two court hearings during the shutdown demonstrated, the owners' Player Relations Committee alone was empowered to act in the dispute.

"The commissioner's role is a difficult one and not perhaps that well understood by the public," Kuhn told Joseph Durso of the New York Times in an interview during the third week of the strike. "The commissioner's powers are mostly restraining. I don't make labor policy or labor decisions."

Early in the year, Kuhn issued two decisions that directly affected several players. In one decision he ruled against Aqua Velva's awarding of a prize for the season's longest hitting streak. The company wanted to put up a cup and $1,000 for each game in the hitting streak, but the commissioner decided money should not be offered "for a specific performance as opposed to general excellence" because of possible adverse influence on the outcome of a game.

The other ruling nullified part of a three-team player deal. On April 1, Pittsburgh sent catcher Ed Ott and pitcher Mickey Mahler to California for first baseman Jason Thompson. The Pirates immediately traded Thompson to the Yankees for first baseman Jim Spencer, minor league pitchers Greg Cochran and Fred Toliver, and cash. According to Jane Gross of the New York Times, the Pirates were to receive $850,000, of which $450,000 was earmarked to pay Spencer's salary for the next several years. Because the cash involved exceeded the $400,000 guideline he set in 1977, Kuhn vetoed the Yankee-Pirate portion of the swap.

The commissioner was in the spotlight again in December during the annual major-minor league winter meetings at Hollywood, Fla. In his annual state-of-baseball address, he painted another gloomy financial picture—but added that he was optimistic about the future. "It appears that only nine major league clubs earned a profit in 1980 as compared to 11 teams in 1979," he reported. "The combined losses of the 17 other clubs reached approximately $40 million. These figures translate into a net loss in 1980 for baseball of about $25 million.

"It appears that we are well on our way toward the very considerable losses over the five-year period 1980-1984 that I predicted last year," he continued. "It is clear that our industry continues to operate in a precarious financial condition."

During the meetings it was disclosed that an attempt to oust Kuhn had been sidetracked. According to Murray Chass of the New York Times, the owners of nine clubs signed a letter aimed at inducing Kuhn to resign or at least not to run again when his term expires in August, 1983. Later, the letter was torn up when other owners expressed outrage at the handling of the matter. Chass reported those who signed the letter were August Busch, Jr., St. Louis; William Williams, Cincinnati; John McMullen, Houston; Ballard Smith, San Diego; Nelson Doubleday, New York Mets; George Steinbrenner, Yankees; Edward Bennett Williams, Baltimore; Eddie Chiles, Texas, and George Argyros, Seattle.

These same owners nevertheless won some points during the winter meetings. Two were elected to positions in the game's high councils. Edward Bennett Williams was named to a four-year term on the Executive Council, replacing John Fetzer of Detroit, and Chiles was elected to a similar term on the Player Relations Committee, succeeding Clark Griffith of Minnesota. Bud Selig of Milwaukee and Ballard Smith of San Diego also were named to the Executive Council, replacing Ed Fitzgerald of Milwaukee and Peter Bavasi of Toronto, while Selig succeeded Fitzgerald on the Player Relations Committee. The two leagues also voted to create a 12-member committee to study the game's organizational structure and policies.

In other action at the winter meetings, American League owners announced that they favored a three-division concept, starting possibly in 1983, but National League owners were opposed to the idea. The proposal would put four teams, including a "wild card", in each league's playoffs. The owners also voted to limit player rosters after August 31 to 28 players—instead of 40—and, prompted by Ron Cey's beaning in the World Series, decided to require all players to wear double ear-flap helmets in the future, pending approval by the Players Association.

While everyone conceded the Cey beaning was accidental, violence both on the playing field and in the stands was a growing concern. Several players were injured when struck by objects thrown by fans, and the commissioner called on clubs to "vigorously prosecute" fans who attack players.

Two managers were subjects of disciplinary action for attacks on umpires. They were Billy Martin of Oakland and Dallas Green of Philadelphia. Martin drew a $1,000 fine and one-week suspension for bumping umpire Terry Cooney and then throwing dirt on him during a dispute in a game at Toronto on May 29. It was the stiffest penalty ever imposed on a manager by A.L. president Lee MacPhail. After missing three days, Martin filed an appeal and returned to uniform. He later dropped the appeal and sat out the remainder of the suspension starting September 6. In the meantime, Cooney filed criminal charges against the manager, but that action was dropped when Martin apologized.

Two weeks after the Martin-Cooney clash there were other developments. MacPhail sent telegrams to the three umpire crews working on the West Coast ordering them to remain in the same cities—rather than rotating—following their June 8-10 series. The change in schedule was ordered so Cooney would not have to work in Oakland. When the three crews disregarded the order and switched cities, MacPhail fined the 12 umpires each a day's pay plus travel expenses. The arbiters then threatened a walkout, but the player strike began the next day and the issue was subsequently resolved.

Green was fined $1,000 and banned for five games following an incident in a game with Atlanta at Philadelphia on August 24. A rhubarb developed when umpire Steve Fields ruled shortstop Larry Bowa failed to touch second base on a routine double-play attempt. In the ensuing argument Green jostled Fields, knocked his cap off and then kicked it. Bowa was docked $500 for his part in the dispute. Further repercussions occurred after the game. While departing the field, umpires Nick Colosi and Frank Pulli became embroiled in a quarrel with a TV commentator, and Colosi allegedly grabbed the TV crewman's camera and threw it to the ground, causing $18,000 damage. League president Chub Feeney fined Colosi $500 and Pulli $300 for the incident.

Players also were involved in especially stormy scenes. Garry Templeton, the St. Louis shortstop, was fined $5,000 and suspended indefinitely by Manager-General Manager Whitey Herzog after making obscene gestures toward a Busch Stadium crowd on August 26. Following psychiatric evaluation and an apology to the fans, Templeton returned to action on September 16. Cesar Cedeno of Houston was tagged with a $5,000 fine by Feeney for going into the stands in Atlanta on September 8 and scuffling with a fan, while Reggie Smith of Los Angeles was fined $5,000 and suspended five days by Feeney for going into the stands in San Francisco on September 24 and engaging in fisticuffs with a heckler.

A decision to switch sports brought one player into the courts. Danny Ainge, a 22-year-old infielder, signed a three-year contract with Toronto in 1980 for a reported $75,000 annually, plus a $300,000 payment for agreeing not to play pro basketball. Following another disappointing season in which he batted only .187 for the Blue Jays, Ainge sought permission to play basketball with the Boston Celtics. The Celtics had selected the former Brigham Young All-America in the second round of the NBA draft in June. On October 2, after a three-day trial, a six-preson jury in Federal District Court in Manhattan ruled his Toronto contract was binding and precluded his joining the Celtics. However, late in November, the Celtics and Toronto worked out an arrangement allowing Ainge to play basketball.

Several aspects of baseball again came under review by the Federal government. On May 4 the U.S. Supreme Court, in response to an appeal by the defunct Boise (Idaho) minor league club of a lower court ruling, refused without comment to reconsider its long-held position that anti-trust laws do not apply to major league baseball. Late in May a House Judiciary Subcommittee held hearings on a bill directed at cable television, which many observers contended was threatening local TV, including free sports telecasts. Commissioner Kuhn was among those to testify. And in July another House Judiciary Subcommittee conducted hearings into the effects of antitrust law and policy on professional sports. Ted Turner, owner of the Atlanta Braves, told the panel that he felt there was no reason for baseball to be exempt from the antitrust laws.

The Kansas City Royals almost became the first American team to lose a series in Japan. The 17-game tour, sponsored by the Yomiuri Shimbun Corp., extended from October 31 through November 23 and featured games against the Yomiuri Giants, winners of the Japanese World Series, as well as other teams. Rusty from a three-week layoff, the Royals began poorly, but then won six of their last seven games to finish with nine victories against seven losses and one tie. In games with the Yomiuri Giants, the Royals were 6-2, including three shutouts.

Mike Schmidt, Rollie Fingers and Fernando Valenzuela dominated the year-end individual awards. The Philadelphia third baseman again was an overwhelming choice in the Baseball Writers' poll as the National League's Most Valuable Player. He became only the third N.L. player to win MVP honors two successive years. Fingers, veteran relief ace with Milwaukee, captured both the MVP and Cy Young Awards in the American League. Valenzuela became the first player in major league history to win Cy Young and Rookie of the Year honors in the same year.

A breakdown of the Most Valuable Player voting in the two leagues, based on 14 points for first place, nine for second, eight for third and on down to one point for 10th place, follows:

American League

Player—Club	1	2	3	4	5	6	7	8	9	10	Pts.
Fingers, Milwaukee	15	9	2	1	—	1	—	—	—	—	319
Henderson, Oakland	12	13	2	1	—	—	—	—	—	—	308
Evans, Boston	—	1	5	7	3	2	—	4	—	2	140
Armas, Oakland	1	1	3	2	7	2	3	4	1	—	139
Murray, Baltimore	—	—	5	6	2	6	1	1	3	—	137
Lansford, Boston	—	1	4	2	3	2	3	3	2	1	109
Winfield, New York	—	—	3	2	3	3	4	3	1	—	98
Cooper, Milwaukee	—	1	1	2	3	3	6	—	3	2	96
Gossage, New York	—	1	1	1	1	2	1	3	3	3	62
Paciorek, Seattle	—	—	—	2	2	—	1	1	3	7	46
Murphy, Oakland	—	1	1	1	—	—	4	—	2	1	45
Gibson, Detroit	—	—	—	1	3	—	—	2	3	3	40
McCatty, Oakland	—	—	—	—	1	2	—	1	1	1	22
Grich, California	—	—	—	—	—	—	4	—	1	1	19
Morris, Detroit	—	—	—	—	—	2	1	1	—	—	17
Oliver, Texas	—	—	1	—	—	—	—	—	—	—	8
Yount, Milwaukee	—	—	—	—	—	1	—	—	1	—	7
Bell, Texas	—	—	—	—	—	—	—	1	2	—	7
Almon, Chicago	—	—	—	—	—	1	—	—	—	1	6
Mumphrey, New York	—	—	—	—	—	1	—	—	—	—	5
Hargrove, Cleveland	—	—	—	—	—	—	—	—	1	2	4
Trammell, Detroit	—	—	—	—	—	—	—	1	—	1	4
Singleton, Baltimore	—	—	—	—	—	—	—	1	—	—	3
Kemp, Detroit	—	—	—	—	—	—	—	1	—	—	3
D. Martinez, Baltimore	—	—	—	—	—	—	—	1	—	—	3
Luzinski, Chicago	—	—	—	—	—	—	—	—	1	1	3
Stieb, Toronto	—	—	—	—	—	—	—	—	—	1	1
G. Brett, Kansas City	—	—	—	—	—	—	—	—	—	1	1

National League

Player—Club	1	2	3	4	5	6	7	8	9	10	Pts.
Schmidt, Philadelphia	21	3	—	—	—	—	—	—	—	—	321
Dawson, Montreal	2	16	4	—	1	1	—	—	—	—	215
Foster, Cincinnati	—	3	6	4	2	4	1	2	—	1	146
Concepcion, Cincinnati	—	1	7	2	—	3	3	—	—	2	108
Valenzuela, L. A.	1	—	—	7	2	2	—	1	1	—	90
Carter, Montreal	—	1	1	—	3	2	2	6	2	2	77
Baker, Los Angeles	—	—	—	1	4	5	2	—	—	1	65
Sutter, St. Louis	—	—	2	3	2	—	—	1	3	1	59
Carlton, Philadelphia	—	—	1	—	3	1	—	2	2	—	41
Seaver, Cincinnati	—	—	1	—	1	1	3	1	—	1	35
Rose, Philadelphia	—	—	1	—	—	1	2	3	1	3	35
Buckner, Chicago	—	—	—	—	1	1	2	2	3	4	35
Matthews, Philadelphia	—	—	—	3	1	—	—	—	2	—	31
Cruz, Houston	—	—	—	1	1	—	2	1	—	1	25
Hendrick, St. Louis	—	—	—	1	1	1	—	—	3	1	25
Ryan, Houston	—	—	—	2	—	—	—	2	1	1	23
Madlock, Pittsburgh	—	—	—	—	—	1	3	—	1	1	20
Howe, Houston	—	—	1	—	1	—	—	—	1	—	16
Raines, Montreal	—	—	—	—	1	—	1	—	2	1	15
Camp, Atlanta	—	—	—	—	—	1	—	—	2	—	9
Hernandez, St. Louis	—	—	—	—	—	—	1	1	—	2	9
Herr, St. Louis	—	—	—	—	—	—	—	1	1	—	7
Minton, San Francisco	—	—	—	—	—	—	1	—	—	—	4
Cromartie, Montreal	—	—	—	—	—	—	—	1	—	—	3
Garvey, Los Angeles	—	—	—	—	—	—	—	—	—	1	1
May, San Francisco	—	—	—	—	—	—	—	—	—	1	1

Fingers was a runaway choice by the Baseball Writers' committee for the Cy Young prize in the American League, drawing 22 of 28 first-place votes. In winning in the senior circuit, Valenzuela became the first rookie ever to gain Cy Young honors. He barely edged Tom Seaver of Cincinnati, a three-time winner. A breakdown of the Cy Young poll in each league, based on a 5-3-1 vote system, follows:

American League

Pitcher-Club	1	2	3	Pts.
Fingers, Milw	22	5	1	126
McCatty, Oakland	6	17½	2	84½
Morris, Detroit	−	3½	10½	21
Vuckovich, Milw	−	1	5½	8½
D. Martinez, Balt	−	−	3½	3½
Gossage, N. York	−	1	−	3
Guidry, New York	−	−	2½	2½
Burns, Chicago	−	−	2	2
Gura, Kansas City	−	−	1	1

National League

Pitcher-Club	1	2	3	Pts.
Valenzuela, Los Angeles	8	8	6	60
Seaver, Cincinnati	8	7	6	67
Carlton, Philadelphia	5	6	7	50
Ryan, Houston	3	3	4	28
Sutter, St. Louis	−	−	1	1

Valenzuela edged Montreal's Tim Raines for National League Rookie of the Year laurels, 107 points to 85, in the BBWAA poll. The duo accounted for all 24 first-place votes, with 17 writers naming Valenzuela, six picking Raines and the other listing both in the No. 1 slot. In the American League another lefthanded pitcher, Dave Righetti of the Yankees, was an overwhelming choice for Rookie of the Year. Twenty-three of the 28 writers who participated favored Righetti, and he piled up 127 points compared to 64 for runner-up Rich Gedman of Boston.

Valenzuela also dominated THE SPORTING NEWS awards, being named major league Player of the Year as well as the National League's No. 1 pitcher and top rookie pitcher. Other Man of the Year designations went to Billy Martin, Oakland manager, and John McHale, Montreal president. Winners of TSN No. 1 Man awards in the minors were: Player of the Year—Mike Marshall, first baseman of Albuquerque (Pacific Coast); Manager of the Year—Del Crandall of Albuquerque, and Executives of the Year—Pat McKernan of Albuquerque in Class AAA, Allie Prescott of Memphis (Southern) in Class AA and Dan Overstreet of Hagerstown (Carolina) in Class A. Other award winners named by THE

SPORTING NEWS included: A.L. Player and Pitcher of the Year—Tony Armas of Oakland and Jack Morris of Detroit, respectively; and N.L. Player and Pitcher of the Year—Andre Dawson of Montreal and Valenzuela, respectively. Named A.L. Rookie Player and Pitcher of the Year were Gedman and Righetti, respectively; and the N.L. Rookie Player and Pitcher honors went to Raines and Valenzuela, respectively. Fingers was named the A.L. Fireman of the Year and Bruce Sutter of St. Louis received the N.L. honor. Comeback Player of the Year awards were given to Richie Zisk of Seattle in the A.L. and Bob Knepper of Houston in the N.L.

The players themselves again voted for THE SPORTING NEWS All-Star Teams and selected the following:

American League: 1B—Cecil Cooper, Milwaukee; 2B—Bobby Grich, California; 3B—Buddy Bell, Texas; SS—Rick Burleson, California; LF—Rickey Henderson, Oakland; CF—Dwayne Murphy, Oakland; RF—Tony Armas, Oakland; C—Jim Sundberg, Texas; RHP—Jack Morris, Detroit; LHP—Ron Guidry, New York; DH—Richie Zisk, Seattle.

National League: 1B—Pete Rose, Philadelphia; 2B—Manny Trillo, Philadelphia; 3B—Mike Schmidt, Philadelphia; SS—Dave Concepcion, Cincinnati; LF—George Foster, Cincinnati; CF—Andre Dawson, Montreal; RF—Pedro Guerrero, Los Angeles; C—Gary Carter, Montreal; RHP—Tom Seaver, Cincinnati; LHP—Fernando Valenzuela, Los Angeles.

Gold Glove winners for fielding excellence, as chosen by each league's managers and coaches, were: 1B—Mike Squires, Chicago White Sox, in the American League and Keith Hernandez, St. Louis, in the National; 2B—Frank White, Kansas City, and Manny Trillo, Philadelphia; 3B—Buddy Bell, Texas, and Mike Schmidt, Philadelphia; SS—Alan Trammell, Detroit, and Ozzie Smith, San Diego; OF—Dwayne Murphy, Oakland; Dwight Evans, Boston, and Rickey Henderson, Oakland, in the American and Andre Dawson, Montreal; Garry Maddox, Philadelphia, and Dusty Baker, Los Angeles, in the National; C—Jim Sundberg, Texas, and Gary Carter, Montreal; P—Mike Norris, Oakland, and Steve Carlton, Philadelphia.

Silver Glove winners for fielding supremacy in the minors were: 1B—Gregory Guin, Erie (New York-Pennsylvania); 2B—Bill Crone, Lynn (Eastern); 3B—Jerome Lorenz, Utica (NY-P); SS—Jim Smith, Portland (Pacific Coast); OF—Rusty Torres, Portland (PC); Jim Len-

Montreal's Andre Dawson was TSN's National League Player of the Year.

Milwaukee's Cecil Cooper repeated as a TSN Silver Slugger.

tine, Charleston (International), and Wayne Harer, Columbus (Int.); C—Robert Melvin, Macon (Southern), and P—Randall Town, Waterbury (Eastern).

The Hillerich & Bradsby Silver Slugger winners for hitting prowess were: 1B—Cecil Cooper, Milwaukee, in the American and Pete Rose, Philadelphia, in the National; 2B—Bobby Grich, California, and Manny Trillo, Philadelphia; 3B—Carney Lansford, Boston, and Mike Schmidt, Philadelphia; SS—Rick Burleson, California, and Dave Concepcion, Cincinnati; OF—Rickey Henderson, Oakland; Dwight Evans, Boston, and Dave Winfield, New York Yankees, in the American League, and Andre Dawson, Montreal; Dusty Baker, Los Angeles, and George Foster, Cincinnati, in the National; C—Carlton Fisk, Chicago White Sox, and Gary Carter, Montreal; P—Fernando Valenzuela, Los Angeles, and DH—Al Oliver, Texas.

The minor leagues were the scene of many significant events in 1981, including several record-making achievements. The International League produced the longest game in professional baseball history when Rochester and Pawtucket battled 32 innings at Pawtucket the night of April 18-19 before play was halted at 4:07 Easter Sunday morning with the score 2-2. The game was completed on June 23 with Pawtucket winning in the bottom of the thirty-third inning, 3-2. Elapsed playing time of the marathon was eight hours and 25 minutes.

Denver established an all-time minor league attendance record when a post-game fireworks display helped attract a crowd of 59,691 to Mile High Stadium on July 2 for an American Association game with Omaha.

Working her fifth season in pro ball, Pamela Postema became the first woman umpire to advance to Class AA as she worked in the Texas League.

And Jeff Stone, a 20-year-old outfielder with Spartanburg, set what was believed to be a minor league record by stealing 123 bases in 134 games in the South Atlantic League.

NATIONAL LEAGUE

Including

Team Reviews of 1981 Season

Team Day-by-Day Scores

1981 Standings, Home-Away Records

1981 Official N.L. Batting Averages

1981 Official N.L. Fielding Averages

1981 Official N.L. Pitching Averages

1981 Pitching Against Each Club

1981 was a high-five season for Fernando Valenzuela, Ron Cey and L.A. fans.

The Dodgers' Dream Came True

By GORDON VERRELL

The Los Angeles Dodgers' regular season started with rookie Fernando Valenzuela, the sensational 21-year-old left-hander, hurling a shutout and it ended with the same Valenzuela hurling them into the World Series.

It was the Mexican-born Valenzuela who was baseball's brightest star the first half of the strike-interrupted season, winning his first eight starts, five by shutout, and drawing capacity crowds to Dodger Stadium 11 times (the one game he didn't fill the stadium, the crowd was 45,817).

The Dodgers, with Valenzuela leading the way, were never out of first place in the National League West in the first half, although their lead over Cincinnati at the time of the strike was only one-half game.

Still, that was enough to get the Dodgers into the divisional series, where they rebounded from a 0-2 deficit to overcome Houston, the second half winner. And they came back again, from 1-2, in the NL Championship Series to defeat Montreal, the East Division champion.

Overall, the Dodgers' regular-season record of 63-47 was the third best in baseball (only Cincinnati, with 66, and Oakland, with 64, won more games).

And the Dodgers, despite the strike that cost them 25 home dates, still played to 2,381,292 fans, an average of 42,523, and sold out Dodger Stadium 27 of their 57 home dates.

But it was Valenzuela who was by far the biggest attraction. And he responded by leading the National League in complete games (11), shutouts (8), innings pitched (192 1-3) and strikeouts (180).

He was the first rookie to lead a league in strikeouts since Herb Score fanned 245 for Cleveland in 1957, and his eight shutouts set an NL record and tied a major league record. Those statistics resulted in a Cy Young award and earned Valenzuela honors as THE SPORTING NEWS National League Pitcher of the Year.

Valenzuela, who did not allow an earned run in 18 innings in 1980, began the '81 season with five shutouts in seven games. He allowed only one run in each of the other two starts. And he finished the N.L. season by defeating the Expos, 2-1, in the final game of the Championship Series.

He started the season with 36 straight

Burt Hooton. . .Consistent.

scoreless innings, the streak finally ending in Montreal om May 3. Valenzuela's revenge came in the Championship Series when he defeated the Expos, 2-1, to lift the Dodgers to the NL pennant.

The 1981 season was not the private domain of the rookie pitcher, however. It marked the eighth season the infield of Steve Garvey, Dave Lopes, Bill Russell and Ron Cey played as a unit.

And Garvey extended his playing streak to 945 consecutive games, the fifth longest on record.

Combined with Valenzuela, who ended the season 13-7, veterans Burt Hooton (11-6, 2.28) and Jerry Reuss (10-4, 2.29) gave the Dodgers a solid 1-2-3 punch in their starting pitching.

It became especially evident in the post-season, prior to the World Series, when the three combined for a 6-2 record and 1.27 ERA in the playoffs against Houston and Montreal.

"I said all season we had excellent starting pitching, and you saw it," bubbled Manager Tom Lasorda, who won his third NL pennant in five years.

Dusty Baker was the most consistent Dodger, his .320 average good enough for third in the NL batting race. He led the club in hits with 128 and he had the Dodgers' longest hitting streak of the year, 15 games.

Baker also earned an All-Star berth for the first time in his career, as did Hooton. Other Dodger All-Stars were Garvey, for the eighth year in a row, Lopes, Valenzuela and Pedro Guerrero.

It was Guerrero who made one of the Dodgers' biggest contributions, taking over in right field at the start of the season when it was clear Reggie Smith, who had undergone a shoulder operation, would not be able to start. Guerrero hit .325 the first half, finishing the season at .300.

The Dodgers made a key acquisition in the spring, adding center fielder Ken Landreaux in a trade with Minnesota.

Rick Monday, who knocked in the winning run in the deciding game of the playoff with Houston and then homered to win the pennant clincher against Montreal, slugged 11 home runs in only 130 at bats. Cey was the club's home run leader with 13.

The Dodgers' bullpen—playpen, actually—had its moments. Lefthander Steve Howe, in his second year, led with eight saves, and rookie Dave Stewart, who became the righthanded short man, saved six games and won four. Two other rookies, Tom Niedenfuer and Alejandro Pena, combined with veteran Terry Forster to fill out the bullpen.

SCORES FOR LOS ANGELES DODGERS' 1981 GAMES

APRIL			Winner	Loser
9 — Houston	W	2-0	Valenzuela	Niekro
11 — Houston	W	7-4	Hooton	Sutton
12 — Houston	W	3-2	Sutcliffe	Ruhle
13 — At S. Fran.	W	4-3	Stewart	Ripley
14 — At S. Fran.	W	7-1	Valenzuela	Blue
15 — At S. Fran.	W	4-2	Hooton	Whitson
17 — At S. Diego	L	2-3*	Lollar	Howe
18 — At S. Diego	W	2-0	Valenzuela	Wise
19 — At S. Diego	W	6-1	Welch	Curtis
20 — At Hous.	W	5-2	Hooton	Andujar
21 — At Hous.	L	0-1	Knepper	Reuss
22 — At Hous.	W	1-0	Valenzuela	Sutton
23 — San Diego	W	3-1	Sutcliffe	Wise
24 — San Diego	L	5-6	Lucas	Castillo
25 — San Diego	W	2-1†	Howe	Littlefield
26 — San Diego	W	3-2	Reuss	Lucas
27 — San Fran.	W	5-0	Valenzuela	Griffin
28 — San Fran.	L	1-6	Ripley	Sutcliffe
29 — San Fran.	L	2-3	Blue	Welch
Won 14, Lost 5				

MAY				
1 — At Mon.	L	8-9§	Lee	Castillo
2 — At Mon.	W	4-0	Reuss	Sanderson
3 — At Mon.	W	6-1*	Valenzuela	Gullickson
4 — At Mon.	L	3-4	Rogers	Sutcliffe
5 — At Phila.	L	7-8	Lyle	Castillo
6 — At Phila.	W	2-1	Hooton	Espinosa
7 — At Phila.	W	2-1	Reuss	Bystrom
8 — At N. York	W	1-0	Valenzuela	Scott
9 — At N. York	L	4-7	Allen	Castillo
10 — At N. York	W	5-3	Welch	Jones
12 — Montreal	W	5-0	Hooton	Burris
13 — Montreal	W	8-6	Howe	Fryman
14 — Montreal	W	3-2	Valenzuela	Ratzer
15 — New York	W	6-5	Howe	Allen
16 — New York	W	9-0	Hooton	Roberts
17 — New York	W	6-1	Reuss	Zachry
18 — Phila.	L	0-4	Bystrom	Valenzuela
19 — Phila.	L	2-3	Ruthven	Welch
20 — Phila.	W	3-2*	Howe	McGraw
22 — At Cinn.	W	4-2‡	Stewart	Bair
23 — At Cinn.	W	9-6*	Stewart	Moskau
24 — At Cinn.	L	2-3	Moskau	Welch
24 — At Cinn.	W	10-3	Castillo	Berenyi
25 — At Atlanta	W	7-1	Hooton	Walk
27 — At Atlanta	L	2-3	Camp	Howe
28 — At Atlanta	L	4-9	Perry	Valenzuela
29 — Cincinnati	W	5-2	Welch	LaCoss
30 — Cincinnati	L	1-9	Pastore	Hooton
31 — Cincinnati	W	16-4	Goltz	Soto
Won 19, Lost 10				

JUNE				
1 — Atlanta	W	5-2	Valenzuela	Boggs
2 — Atlanta	L	1-3*	Perry	Stewart
3 — Atlanta	L	2-4	Niekro	Hooton
5 — At Chicago	L	3-4	Reuschel	Reuss
6 — At Chicago	L	5-11	McGlothen	Valenzuela
7 — At Chicago	W	7-0	Welch	Martz
9 — At St. L.	L	1-6	Forsch	Hooton
10 — At St. L.	W	4-1	Reuss	Sorensen
11 — At St. L.	L	1-2	Martinez	Valenzuela
Won 3, Lost 6				

AUGUST			Winner	Loser
10 — Cincinnati	W	4-0	Reuss	Pastore
11 — Cincinnati	L	6-7	Brown	Forster
12 — Cincinnati	W	8-5	Stewart	Seaver
13 — Atlanta	L	0-9	Boggs	Hooton
14 — Atlanta	W	5-0	Goltz	Montefusco
15 — Atlanta	L	4-6	Bedrosian	Reuss
16 — Atlanta	W	6-5	Niedenfuer	Bedrosian
17 — At Chicago	L	1-3	Bird	Welch
18 — At Chicago	W	5-0	Hooton	Griffin
19 — At Chicago	L	3-4	Krukow	Goltz
21 — At St. L.	W	4-0	Reuss	Andujar
22 — At St. L.	W	3-2	Valenzuela	Forsch
23 — At St. L.	L	7-11	Shirley	Welch
24 — At Pitts.	W	3-0	Hooton	Jones
25 — At Pitts.	W	9-7†	Pena	Tekulve
26 — At Pitts.	W	16-6	Reuss	Rhoden
27 — Chicago	W	6-0	Valenzuela	Martz
28 — Chicago	W	6-1	Welch	Krukow
29 — Chicago	L	1-3	Griffin	Hooton
30 — Chicago	L	1-2	Bird	Goltz
31 — Pittsburgh	L	4-5*	Jones	Stewart
Won 12, Lost 9				

SEPTEMBER				
1 — Pittsburgh	W	3-2x	Niedenfuer	Jones
2 — Pittsburgh	W	6-2	Welch	Long
3 — St. Louis	L	3-5	Littell	Howe
4 — St. Louis	L	2-7	Martin	Goltz
5 — St. Louis	W	4-3†	Niedenfuer	Kaat
6 — St. Louis	W	5-0	Valenzuela	Forsch
7 — San Fran.	W	5-1	Welch	Whitson
8 — San Fran.	W	4-0	Hooton	Alexander
9 — San Fran.	L	3-6†	Holland	Niedenfuer
11 — At Cinn.	L	2-3*	Price	Pena
12 — At Cinn.	L	5-6†	LaCoss	Power
13 — At Cinn.	W	4-2	Castillo	Pastore
14 — At S. Diego	W	10-5	Power	Show
15 — At S. Diego	L	2-8	Eichelberger	Goltz
16 — Atlanta	W	3-2	Reuss	Perry
17 — Atlanta	W	2-0	Valenzuela	Mahler
18 — Cincinnati	L	4-5	Price	Stewart
19 — Cincinnati	L	3-7	Edelen	Hooton
20 — Cincinnati	L	1-5	Soto	Power
22 — At S. Fran.	L	2-5	Whitson	Valenzuela
23 — At S. Fran.	L	4-8	Lavelle	Goltz
24 — At S. Fran.	W	7-3	Welch	Griffin
25 — At Hous.	W	3-0	Hooton	Ruhle
26 — At Hous.	L	0-5	Ryan	Power
27 — At Hous.	L	1-4	Sutton	Valenzuela
28 — At Atlanta	L	1-2	Mahler	Reuss
29 — At Atlanta	W	5-3	Howe	Garber
30 — San Diego	L	0-2	Boone	Goltz
Won 13, Lost 15				

OCTOBER				
1 — San Diego	L	0-1	Kuhaulua	Valenzuela
2 — Houston	W	6-1	Reuss	Sutton
3 — Houston	W	7-2	Welch	Niekro
4 — Houston	L	3-5	Smith	Goltz
Won 2, Lost 2				

*10 innings.   †11 innings.   ‡12 innings.   §13 innings.   x14 inn

Anemic Batting Hurt Astros

By HARRY SHATTUCK

The Houston Astros and their supporters could evaluate the 1981 season with either of two approaches. The negative-minded could say that the Astros regressed. In 1980, they took the Philadelphia Phillies to the final game of the National League Championship Series before losing in 10 innings to the eventual world champions. This season, they were eliminated by Los Angeles in a five-game series trying to defend their Western Division title.

But a more positive sort would point out that the Astros compiled the best second-half record in the major leagues; that in the divisional series, they came within a whisker of eliminating the Dodgers (who went on to win the World Series); that after a horrible start. Houston played as well as any team in baseball.

"When you start spring training, your goal for the year is to get yourself in a position that you have a chance to go to the World Series," Astros Manager Bill Virdon said. "We gave ourselves that chance, so I think the season was a success."

"Any time you reach the playoffs, you've achieved some success," pitcher Joe Niekro said. "But I don't feel we took the game to (Los Angeles) in the playoffs the way we did last year."

Indeed, 1981 probably will be remembered as a disappointment for the Astros, if only because more was expected of this team than any other in Houston's 20-year big-league history. In several pre-season forecasts, the Astros were picked to gain their first World Series berth.

But a 4-12 start ruined any hopes of a first-half championship. By the June 12 strike, Houston's record had improved to only 28-29, good for third place behind Los Angeles and Cincinnati in the Western Division.

The split-season format provided renewed hope and the Astros went 5-2 on their first trip. They maintained the pace and clinched the second-half title on the next-to-last day of the regular season.

As expected, pitching was the strong point. The team earned run average the first half was 2.71, and remarkably the figure was even better (2.62) after the strike. The full-season ERA of 2.66 was easily the best in the league and an Astro record.

Nolan Ryan won his first career ERA championship, compiling a 1.69 ERA in 21 starts. Teammate Bob Knepper was second in the league with 2.18. Ryan provided the individual pitching highlight of the season on September 26 with his record fifth career no-hitter, against the Dodgers, 5-0. The next day, Don Sutton two-hit Los Angeles, pinning a record on the Dodgers for the fewest hits produced against one team in consecutive games.

Sutton, Niekro and Vern Ruhle became almost lost amid the attention accorded Ryan and Knepper, but they, too, enjoyed excellent seasons. Sutton's ERA was 2.60. Niekro's 2.82 and Ruhle's 2.91 to complete a starting rotation having not one pitcher with an ERA above 3.00. Ryan and Sutton led in victories with 11, and Sutton prevailed in six of seven second-half decisions before suffering a broken kneecap October 2 when hit by a Jerry Reuss fastball in Los Angeles.

Joe Sambito and Dave Smith were leaders out of the bullpen with 10 and eight saves, respectively.

Offensively, the first half was miserable. The team batting average was only .250. "We couldn't hit with runners in scoring position. We couldn't take advantage of our opportunities," Virdon said.

After the strike, the bats perked up. The Astros hit .264 in the second half and reached a peak near the end of the regular season. They were winning games by scores of 9-1 and 9-2, almost unheard of for Houston clubs. Nineteen straight Astro games were decided by more than one run.

But the bats went silent at the most inappropriate time. Against L.A. in the divisional series, Houston scored only six runs in five games. The pitching of Ryan and Niekro was enough to salvage two victories, but two were not enough.

Third baseman Art Howe was the first-half standout, leading the league with a .344 batting average. But Howe, bothered by an Achilles tendon injury, hit only .244 with nine RBIs the second half. Jose Cruz hit .278 the first half but only .251 after the strike. Cesar Cedeno fell from .305 to .230 and Terry Puhl dropped from .269 to .255.

So from where did the offensive improvement come? Primarily from center fielder Tony Scott and catcher Alan Ashby. Scott, acquired in June in a trade with St. Louis, hit .293 as an Astro. Ashby hit .276 in the second half.

Reserves also contributed toward the end of the season. Dickie Thon came off the bench to hit .409 the second half. Fellow infielder Kiko Garcia hit .317.

Nobody expected the Astros to set any records for power—and they didn't. Houston players totaled only 45 home runs, but that was five more than Astro pitching allowed the opposition. Cruz led with 13, but nobody else homered more than five times.

The biggest individual disappointments were Puhl, who experienced his first bad season offensively (but he did

not make an error all year in the outfield) and Dave Roberts, who signed a $1.1, five-year contract as a free agent last year.

Two trades helped the Astros in the second half. One was Scott's accquisiton. The other was General Manager Al Rosen's August 31 deal with Pittsburgh to get second baseman Phil Garner.

The season also included the continuing comeback efforts of pitcher James Rodney Richard, who suffered a near-fatal stroke in July 1980. Richard worked out with the club all year and was reactivated September 1, but he did not pitch in a game.

SCORES FOR HOUSTON ASTROS' 1981 GAMES

APRIL			Winner	Loser		AUGUST			Winner	Loser
9 – At L.A.	L	0-2	Valenzuela	Niekro		10 – At S. Fran.	W	6-5	Sambito	Breining
11 – At L.A.	L	4-7	Hooton	Sutton		11 – At S. Fran.	L	2-3	Griffin	Niekro
12 – At L.A.	L	2-3	Sutcliffe	Ruhle		12 – At S. Fran.	W	5-4	Sambito	Holland
13 – Atlanta	L	1-2*	Camp	Sambito		13 – At S. Diego	L	1-9	Welsh	Knepper
14 – Atlanta	W	8-2	Niekro	Walk		14 – At S. Diego	W	5-1	Ryan	Lollar
15 – Atlanta	W	2-0	Ryan	Boggs		15 – At S. Diego	W	5-0	Sutton	Eichelberger
17 – Pittsburgh	L	3-4	Rhoden	Sutton		16 – At S. Diego	W	3-0	Niekro	Mura
18 – Pittsburgh	L	3-6†	Jackson	D. Smith		17 – Montreal	L	2-6	Burris	Ruhle
19 – Pittsburgh	L	0-2	Scurry	Niekro		18 – Montreal	W	4-2	Knepper	Rogers
20 – Los Ang.	L	2-5	Hooton	Andujar		19 – Montreal	W	9-1	Ryan	Sanderson
21 – Los Ang.	W	1-0	Knepper	Reuss		21 – At Phila.	L	4-5	Lyle	Ruhle
22 – Los Ang.	L	0-1	Valenzuela	Sutton		22 – At Phila.	L	4-8	Ruthven	Niekro
23 – Cincinnati	L	4-5*	Price	D. Smith		23 – At Phila.	L	0-6	Carlton	Knepper
24 – Cincinnati	L	0-3	Pastore	Niekro		25 – At N. York	L	1-2	Marshall	Sambito
25 – Cincinnati	L	1-2	Berenyi	Ryan		26 – At N. York	W	9-3	Sutton	Zachry
26 – Cincinnati	W	1-0	Knepper	Soto		27 – At N. York	L	2-3*	Marshall	Sambito
28 – At Atlanta	W	2-1	Sutton	Montefusco		28 – Phila.	W	3-2*	D. Smith	Lyle
29 – At Atlanta	W	5-4	LaCorte	Camp		29 – Phila.	W	6-1	Ruhle	Davis
30 – At Atlanta	W	5-1	Niekro	Boggs		29 – Phila.	W	2-1	L. Smith	Noles
						30 – Phila.	W	5-4*	D. Smith	Lyle
Won 7, Lost 12						31 – New York	W	6-1	Sutton	Zachry
MAY						**Won 13, Lost 6**				
1 – At Pitts.	W	5-3	Sambito	Solomon						
2 – At Pitts.	L	4-5‡	Solomon	D. Smith		**SEPTEMBER**				
3 – At Pitts.	W	3-1	Sutton	Bibby		1 – New York	W	3-2	Sambito	Marshall
4 – At Chicago	W	5-4	Andujar	Krukow		2 – New York	W	8-0	Knepper	Scott
5 – At Chicago	W	4-3	D. Smith	Smith		3 – At Mon.	W	2-1	Ruhle	Sanderson
6 – At Chicago	L	1-2†	Smith	LaCorte		4 – At Mon.	W	5-0	Ryan	Gullickson
7 – At Chicago	W	6-0	Knepper	Martz		5 – At Mon.	L	2-5	Burris	Sutton
8 – At Cinn.	L	0-4	Seaver	Sutton		6 – At Mon.	W	4-3‡	LaCorte	Sosa
9 – At Cinn.	L	5-9	Berenyi	Andujar		7 – At Atlanta	W	3-2	D. Smith	Camp
10 – At Cinn.	W	7-5	Niekro	Pastore		8 – At Atlanta	L	2-3	Camp	B. Smith
11 – At Cinn.	W	5-0	Ryan	LaCoss		9 – At Atlanta	L	0-9	Niekro	Ryan
12 – St. Louis	L	2-3*	Sutter	Sambito		11 – San Fran.	W	6-0	Sutton	Blue
13 – St. Louis	W	3-0	Sutton	Shirley		12 – San Fran.	W	5-2	Niekro	Whitson
14 – St. Louis	L	6-7	Otten	Sambito		13 – San Fran.	W	3-0	Knepper	Alexander
15 – Chicago	W	5-0	Niekro	Caudill		14 – Cincinnati	L	2-4	Berenyi	Ruhle
16 – Chicago	W	6-1	Ryan	Martz		15 – Cincinnati	L	0-4	Leibrandt	Ryan
17 – Chicago	W	6-1	Knepper	Krukow		16 – At S. Diego	W	5-2	Sutton	Lollar
19 – At St. L.	L	12-15	Kaat	Sprowl		17 – At S. Diego	W	9-0	Niekro	Mura
20 – At St. L.	W	4-3†	Niekro	Sutter		18 – At S. Fran.	L	2-5	Alexander	Knepper
21 – At St. L.	L	1-3	Martin	Ryan		19 – At S. Fran.	W	8-1	Ruhle	Griffin
22 – San Fran.	L	3-6x	Minton	Andujar		20 – At S. Fran.	W	7-3	Ryan	Lavelle
23 – San Fran.	W	5-3	LaCorte	Whitson		22 – Atlanta	W	3-0	Sutton	Perry
24 – San Fran.	L	1-2	Blue	Sutton		23 – Atlanta	L	1-3	Mahler	Niekro
25 – San Diego	W	6-3	Niekro	Mura		24 – Atlanta	W	5-3	Knepper	McWilliams
26 – San Diego	W	1-0	Ryan	Eichelberger		25 – Los Ang.	L	0-3	Hooton	Ruhle
27 – San Diego	W	1-0	Knepper	Welsh		26 – Los Ang.	W	5-0	Ryan	Power
29 – At S. Fran.	L	1-3	Blue	Sutton		27 – Los Ang.	W	4-1	Sutton	Valenzuela
30 – At S. Fran.	W	9-8§	Andujar	Breining		28 – San Diego	W	2-1	Sambito	Eichelberger
31 – At S. Fran.	L	1-6	Griffin	Ryan		29 – San Diego	L	1-2	Wise	Knepper
						30 – At Cinn.	L	2-5	Soto	Ruhle
Won 17, Lost 12						**Won 18, Lost 10**				
JUNE										
2 – At S. Diego	W	2-1	LaCorte	Welsh		**OCTOBER**				
3 – At S. Diego	W	6-1	Sutton	Wise		1 – At Cinn.	W	8-1	Ryan	Berenyi
4 – At S. Diego	L	5-7	Mura	Niekro		2 – At L.A.	L	1-6	Reuss	Sutton
5 – New York	W	3-0	Ryan	Jones		3 – At L.A.	L	2-7	Welch	Niekro
6 – New York	W	6-2	Ruhle	Zachry		4 – At L.A.	W	5-3	D. Smith	Goltz
7 – New York	L	1-3	Scott	Knepper		**Won 2, Lost 2**				
8 – At Phila.	L	3-4	Ruthven	Sutton						
9 – At Phila.	L	3-10	Bystrom	Niekro						
10 – At Phila.	L	4-5	Carlton	LaCorte						
Won 4, Lost 5										

*10 innings.   †11 innings.   ‡12 innings.   §14 innings.   x15 innings.

Nolan Ryan's record-setting fifth no-hitter touched off a celebration.

The big bat of George Foster powered the Reds in '81.

Reds' Season Went Unrewarded

By EARL LAWSON

The 1981 season will go into the record books as one of the most memorable in Cincinnati Reds history, but not the most rewarding.

Because of the strike that began June 12 and ended July 31, major league baseball instituted a split-season format for the first time in the game's history. And, because of this format, the Reds wound up watching post-season play on their television sets—even though they had completed the season with the best overall record of any club in the majors (66-42).

Naturally, cries of "We wuz robbed" came from players, management and the club's loyal fans. But, as Reds Manager John McNamara is so fond of saying, "There's no sense in becoming upset about matters over which you have no control."

McNamara preferred talking about the more pleasant aspects of the 1981 season. And there were more than a few. At age 35, Tom Seaver, the Reds' three-time Cy Young winner, finished the 1981 season with a 14-2 record, the best winning percentage by a National League pitcher since Roy Face in 1959. There were those ready to write off Seaver after the veteran right-hander, sidelined for the first time by shoulder problems, finished the 1980 season with a 10-8 record, the lowest victory total of his illustrious career. In 1981 Seaver also became one of four active pitchers to pass the 3,000 strikeout milestone. Gaylord Perry, Nolan Ryan and Steve Carlton are the others.

No one in the Reds' organization ever doubted that pitcher Bruce Berenyi had the natural ability to make it big. Ever since he was signed as the club's No. 1 choice in the secondary phase of the June 1976 free agent draft, it was just a matter of his conquering control problems. The 27-year-old, 6-3, 215-pound Berenyi took a giant step toward realizing his potential during the 1981 season. He became a regular in the starting rotation, finishing the season with a 9-6 record and three shutouts. And one of those shutouts was a one-hitter against the Montreal Expos.

Mario Soto, a 25-year-old Dominican righthander who compiled a 10-8 record and performed the dual role of starter and reliever in 1980, proved that was no fluke when he finished the 1981 season

Mario Soto. . .No fluke.

with a 12-9 record. Unfortunately, his teammates didn't support his sparkling pitching with timely hits on many occasions. The last of his 12 victories came on the final day of the season, when he blanked the Atlanta Braves on one hit.

The biggest disappointment of the Reds pitching staff was Frank Pastore, the club's top winner in 1980 with 13 victories, who dipped to a 4-9 record in 1981.

However, Pastore's disappointing season was offset by Joe Price, who, after being coverted from a starter to a reliever, finished the season with a 6-1 record, a 2.50 earned run average and four saves. And Tom Hume again proved he rates as one of the league's premier relief pitchers when he registered a 9-4 record with 13 saves.

Even though George Foster's outfield

play can be poor at times, he proved again in 1981 that he's one of baseball's most prolific run producers. He pounded out 22 homers and drove home 90, second only to the league-leading total of the Phils' Mike Schmidt.

The year 1981 also will be remembered as the season Johnny Bench relinquished his role as a full-time catcher. His catching days ended permanently after he suffered a broken ankle in late May sliding into second base. After returning to action, he played first base when physically able. His timely hitting played a prominent role in one of the club's most successful trips ever during a mid-September tour of the Western Division. The Reds finished with an 11-2 record that kept them in the race for the second-half title until the last five days of the season.

Perhaps the most memorable aspect of the 1981 season was the fact that the Reds broke their long-standing policy of refusing to guarantee contracts. They signed shortstop Dave Concepcion, who had been eligible for free agency, to a five-year, $5 million pact.

Still, despite the brighter aspects of 1981, Reds President Dick Wagner admitted that if the team were to regain the Western Division title, which has eluded them since 1979, they must improve their overall team speed, bolster their catching and improve their left-handed pitching.

SCORES FOR CINCINNATI REDS' 1981 GAMES

APRIL

Date	W/L	Score	Winner	Loser
8 — Phila.	W	3-2	Hume	Lyle
10 — At Atlanta	L	3-5	Garber	Soto
11 — At Atlanta	W	3-2	Bair	Garber
12 — At Atlanta	L	2-3	Bradford	Hume
13 — At S. Diego	W	7-1	Seaver	Wise
14 — At S. Diego	W	4-0	Berenyi	Curtis
15 — At S. Diego	W	10-1	Soto	Mura
17 — St. Louis	L	5-9	Sorensen	LaCoss
18 — St. Louis	L	4-10	Shirley	Seaver
21 — Atlanta	L	1-10	Boggs	Soto
22 — Atlanta	L	3-7	Perry	LaCoss
23 — At Hous.	W	5-4*	Price	D. Smith
24 — At Hous.	W	3-0	Pastore	Niekro
25 — At Hous.	W	2-1	Berenyi	Ryan
26 — At Hous.	L	0-1	Knepper	Soto
28 — San Diego	W	11-2	Seaver	Lollar
29 — San Diego	W	8-5	Moskau	Littlefield
30 — San Diego	W	4-3	LaCoss	Mura

Won 11, Lost 7

MAY

Date	W/L	Score	Winner	Loser
1 — At St. L.	L	6-7	Forsch	Soto
2 — At St. L.	L	3-7	Shirley	Berenyi
3 — At St. L.	L	4-5†	Edelen	Hume
6 — Pittsburgh	W	9-8	Hume	Jackson
7 — Pittsburgh	L	1-3	Rhoden	Soto
7 — Pittsburgh	L	1-7	Solomon	LaCoss
8 — Houston	W	4-0	Seaver	Sutton
9 — Houston	W	9-5	Berenyi	Andujar
10 — Houston	L	5-7	Niekro	Pastore
11 — Houston	L	0-5	Ryan	LaCoss
12 — Chicago	W	2-1	Soto	Tidrow
13 — Chicago	W	8-3	Seaver	Krukow
14 — Chicago	W	6-1	Berenyi	Reuschel
15 — At Pitts.	W	4-1	Price	Romo
16 — At Pitts.	W	4-0	LaCoss	Scurry
17 — At Pitts.	W	4-3	Soto	Solomon
19 — At Chicago	W	5-0	Seaver	Reuschel
20 — At Chicago	W	10-7	Price	Smith
21 — At Chicago	L	1-5	Martz	Pastore
22 — Los Ang.	L	2-4‡	Stewart	Bair
23 — Los Ang.	L	6-9*	Stewart	Moskau
24 — Los Ang.	W	3-2	Moskau	Welch
24 — Los Ang.	L	3-10	Castillo	Berenyi
25 — San Fran.	W	6-3	Combe	Holland
27 — San Fran.	W	3-2	Soto	Alexander
28 — San Fran.	W	7-4	Price	Lavelle
29 — At L.A.	L	2-5	Welch	LaCoss
30 — At L.A.	W	9-1	Pastore	Hooton
31 — At L.A.	L	4-16	Goltz	Soto

Won 16, Lost 13

JUNE

Date	W/L	Score	Winner	Loser
1 — At S. Fran.	W	8-5	Hume	Minton
2 — At S. Fran.	L	7-15	Whitson	LaCoss
3 — At S. Fran.	W	6-2	Pastore	Blue
5 — Montreal	W	6-3	Soto	Rogers
6 — Montreal	W	9-3	Seaver	Lea
7 — Montreal	W	2-0	Berenyi	Burris
9 — At N. York	W	8-4	Hume	Falcone
10 — At N. York	W	2-0	Soto	Jones
11 — At N. York	W	5-2	Seaver	Zachry

Won 8, Lost 1

AUGUST

Date	W/L	Score	Winner	Loser
10 — At L.A.	L	0-4	Reuss	Pastore
11 — At L.A.	W	7-6	Brown	Forster
12 — At L.A.	L	5-8	Stewart	Seaver
14 — San Fran.	L	0-4	Whitson	Berenyi
14 — San Fran.	W	7-6*	Hume	Holland
15 — San Fran.	L	2-5	Alexander	Pastore
16 — San Fran.	W	2-1	Soto	Griffin
18 — Phila.	W	3-1	Seaver	Carlton
19 — Phila.	W	6-3	Hume	Lyle
21 — New York	W	2-0	Soto	Zachry
22 — New York	L	4-7	Boitano	Pastore
23 — New York	L	2-3*	Allen	Hume
24 — New York	W	2-0	Berenyi	Scott
25 — At Mon.	L	1-9	Sanderson	LaCoss
26 — At Mon.	L	0-6	Gullickson	Soto
27 — At Mon.	L	0-12	Burris	Pastore
28 — At N. York	W	5-2	Seaver	Allen
29 — At N. York	L	2-3	Scott	Berenyi
30 — At N. York	W	6-3	LaCoss	Harris
31 — Montreal	W	9-8	Bair	Lee

Won 10, Lost 10

SEPTEMBER

Date	W/L	Score	Winner	Loser
1 — Montreal	L	3-4	Lea	Price
2 — Montreal	W	7-0	Seaver	Bahnsen
3 — At Phila.	W	9-3	Berenyi	Davis
4 — At Phila.	L	6-7	Lyle	Bair
5 — At Phila.	L	4-5	R. Reed	Soto
6 — At Phila.	W	5-4	Hume	Lyle
7 — San Diego	W	8-7	Seaver	Show
8 — San Diego	L	1-6	Eichelberger	Berenyi
9 — San Diego	W	5-4	Hume	Urrea
11 — Los Ang.	W	3-2*	Price	Pena
12 — Los Ang.	W	6-5†	LaCoss	Power
13 — Los Ang.	L	2-4	Castillo	Pastore
14 — At Hous.	W	4-2	Berenyi	Ruhle
15 — At Hous.	W	4-0	Leibrandt	Ryan
16 — At S. Fran.	L	7-12	Breining	Soto
17 — At S. Fran.	W	1-0*	Seaver	Holland
18 — At L.A.	W	5-4	Price	Stewart
19 — At L.A.	W	7-3	Edelen	Hooton
20 — At L.A.	W	5-1	Soto	Power
21 — At S. Diego	L	0-6	Welsh	Leibrandt
22 — At S. Diego	W	3-2	Seaver	Eichelberger
23 — At S. Diego	W	5-1	Pastore	Wise
25 — At Atlanta	W	10-2	Soto	Boggs
26 — At Atlanta	W	2-0	Berenyi	Niekro
27 — At Atlanta	W	4-2	Seaver	Perry
28 — San Diego	L	0-4	Hargesh'mer	Pastore
29 — San Fran.	W	4-3	Hume	Minton
30 — Houston	W	5-2	Soto	Ruhle

Won 20, Lost 8

OCTOBER

Date	W/L	Score	Winner	Loser
1 — Houston	L	1-8	Ryan	Berenyi
2 — Atlanta	L	5-11	Perry	Pastore
3 — Atlanta	L	3-4	Mahler	Hume
4 — Atlanta	W	3-0	Soto	Boggs

Won 1, Lost 3

*10 innings.   †11 innings.   ‡12 innings.

Giant Success Came Slowly

By NICK PETERS

The Giants' 1981 season was a schizophrenic's delight.

For much of the strike-interrupted campaign, the club gave rookie Manager Frank Robinson a "splitting" headache. But a fast finish established an aura of optimism.

Robinson contributed by establishing firm leadership and added stability to the organization by signing a two-year contract extension through 1984.

New direction also was provided by Tom Haller, who was appointed vice-president of baseball operations during the strike, a layoff that proved more advantageous to the Giants than to most clubs.

After the stunning dismissal of Manager Dave Bristol by Owner Bob Lurie during the winter baseball meetings, Robinson was named the National League's first black skipper January 15 and immediately promised to change the attitude of the club.

Spec Richardson, general manager at the time, contributed by altering the roster with winter swaps. Pitchers John Montefusco and Bob Knepper, both unhappy losers with the Giants, were traded. Troubled Mike Ivie was traded to the Astros in mid-April.

By spring training, Robinson already was beginning to see results. Free-agent second baseman Joe Morgan brought much-needed leadership and a reliable glove that helped tighten the infield.

Rookie outfielder Chili Davis, who started the season with the club before being shipped to Phoenix for regular duty, showed promise.

But the Giants, who finished 11 games under .500 in 1980, were not going to achieve success overnight.

The Giants dropped five of their first seven, including a three-game sweep by the Dodgers at Candlestick Park. A five-game losing streak against San Diego and Atlanta left the club in fifth place with a 5-11 record on April 25, already 7½ games behind.

Were it not for the quick starts of newcomers Doyle Alexander and Enos Cabell and the robust hitting of Larry Herndon, who edged Jerry Martin for the left-field job in the spring, it might have been worse.

After the five-game losing streak, the club won eight of its next nine series, including an 8-6 trip to Los Angeles, Philadelphia, New York and Montreal, punctuated by a no-hit loss to the Expos' Charlie Lea.

The Giants hovered around .500 until the second week in June, when a pair of losses in Pittsburgh and a three-game sweep by the Cubs at Wrigley dropped them to 27-32 at the time of the strike.

"Maybe the strike will help us," Robinson remarked sarcastically as his club languished 10 games behind the Dodgers during the seven-week layoff. "We haven't been doing too many things right, so it can't hurt.

"This ballclub has got to make a move. We cannot continue with some of these same players if we are to become a winner. The only way we can be a good ballclub with our present roster is to play smart baseball."

Robinson was especially perturbed by the fielding of Cabell and center fielder Billy North and baserunning blunders that ran the club out of potential victories.

On the bright side, both Herndon and catcher Milt May were .300 hitters in the first half. Johnnie LeMaster blossomed as a solid shortstop and batted .252. And the pitching staff had such standouts as Alexander (2.69 ERA), Vida Blue (2.22), Greg Minton (nine saves) and rookie Fred Breining (2-1, 1.75 in relief).

But those performances were overshadowed by a 5-9 record in one-run decisions, a puny .241 team batting average and slumps by sluggers Jack Clark and Darrell Evans, batting .224 and .223, respectively, at the time of the strike.

As Robinson declared, something had to be done, and Owner Bob Lurie didn't take long to send shock waves through the organization. He started at the top, replacing Richardson with Haller. Before play resumed, veterans North, Mike Sadek and Randy Moffitt were released.

North's departure made Martin a regular and it also elevated Morgan to the leadoff spot. A more subtle change was the promotion of outfielder Jeff Leonard from Phoenix. Leonard, acquired along with Dave Bergman in the Ivie deal, was batting .401 with the PCL club.

The strike was beneficial in other ways. A tired pitching staff was rejuvenated. The split-season format gave the pitchers a second chance and they made the most of it by remaining in mathematical contention for the playoffs until the final week.

The club didn't start the second half quickly, splitting its first 16 games and continuing the trend of blowing the close ones. Finally, after a mistake-marred victory over the Pirates August 27, Robinson lashed out at his troops in a closed-door meeting.

Clark, who took exception with Robinson and said so publicly, suddenly began to hit with authority and assumed a leadership role. The Giants enjoyed an 8-2 home stand, leaving them 1½ games behind Houston and with a 16-10 record on Labor Day.

But the bottom fell out swiftly. In a one-week swing to Los Angeles and Houston, the Giants kissed their pennant hopes goodbye by going 1-5 and returning home 17-15 on September 14.

They held their own the rest of the way and finished the second half at 29-23. A victory on the final day of the season made them 56-55, a "winner" for the first time since 1978.

Clark powered the second-half comeback with a .315 average, 11 homers and 28 RBIs, but he had lots of help. Morgan

SCORES OF SAN FRANCISCO GIANTS' 1981 GAMES

APRIL			Winner	Loser
9 – San Diego	L	1-4‡	Lucas	Holland
10 – San Diego	L	2-4	Urrea	Lavelle
11 – San Diego	W	2-0	Alexander	Eichelberger
12 – San Diego	W	7-6x	Breining	Lucas
13 – Los Ang.	L	3-4	Stewart	Ripley
14 – Los Ang.	L	1-7	Valenzuela	Blue
15 – Los Ang.	L	2-4	Hooton	Whitson
17 – At Atlanta	W	6-2	Alexander	Perry
18 – At Atlanta	W	4-1	Griffin	Montefusco
19 – At Atlanta	L	3-4	Camp	Minton
20 – At S. Diego	W	9-0	Blue	Mura
21 – At S. Diego	L	1-3	Welsh	Alexander
22 – At S. Diego	L	0-4	Eichelberger	Whitson
23 – Atlanta	L	3-7	Montefusco	Griffin
24 – Atlanta	L	1-7	Walk	Ripley
25 – Atlanta	L	0-4	Niekro	Blue
26 – Atlanta	W	3-1	Alexander	Perry
26 – Atlanta	W	8-5	Holland	Boggs
27 – At L.A.	L	0-5	Valenzuela	Griffin
28 – At L.A.	W	6-1	Ripley	Sutcliffe
29 – At L.A.	W	3-2	Blue	Welch
		Won 9, Lost 12		
MAY				
2 – At Phila.	W	6-2	Alexander	Espinosa
2 – At Phila.	L	1-3	Bystrom	Whitson
3 – At Phila.	L	5-7	Ruthven	Lavelle
4 – At Phila.	L	4-6	Carlton	Ripley
5 – At N. York	W	9-7	Griffin	Jones
6 – At N. York	W	6-4	Minton	Zachry
7 – At N. York	L	2-3	Lynch	Alexander
8 – At Mon.	W	4-3	Ripley	Gullickson
9 – At Mon.	W	8-2	Blue	Rogers
10 – At Mon.	W	5-1	Griffin	Lee
10 – At Mon.	L	0-4	Lea	Whitson
12 – Phila.	W	4-0	Alexander	Espinosa
13 – Phila.	W	5-2	Ripley	Bystrom
14 – Phila.	L	1-3	Ruthven	Blue
15 – Montreal	W	4-2	Whitson	Rogers
16 – Montreal	L	0-5	Lea	Griffin
17 – Montreal	W	5-4‡	Holland	Lee
18 – New York	W	3-1	Ripley	Lynch
19 – New York	W	4-1	Holland	Scott
20 – New York	L	3-4*	Reardon	Minton
22 – At Hous.	W	6-3y	Minton	Andujar
23 – At Hous.	L	3-5	LaCorte	Whitson
24 – At Hous.	W	2-1	Blue	Sutton
25 – At Cinn.	L	3-6	Combe	Holland
27 – At Cinn.	L	2-3	Soto	Alexander
28 – At Cinn.	L	4-7	Price	Lavelle
29 – Houston	W	3-1	Blue	Sutton
30 – Houston	L	8-9x	Andujar	Breining
31 – Houston	W	6-1	Griffin	Ryan
		Won 16, Lost 13		
JUNE				
1 – Cincinnati	L	5-8	Hume	Minton
2 – Cincinnati	W	15-7	Whitson	LaCoss
3 – Cincinnati	L	2-6	Pastore	Blue
5 – At Pitts.	W	5-3	Breining	Romo
6 – At Pitts.	L	6-7	Scurry	Griffin
7 – At Pitts.	L	2-3	Solomon	Blue
9 – At Chicago	L	1-2z	Krukow	Ripley
10 – At Chicago	L	4-7	Reuschel	Alexander
11 – At Chicago	L	1-6	Martz	Griffin
		Won 2, Lost 7		

AUGUST			Winner	Loser
10 – Houston	L	5-6	Sambito	Breining
11 – Houston	W	3-2	Griffin	Niekro
12 – Houston	L	4-5	Sambito	Holland
14 – At Cinn.	W	4-0	Whitson	Berenyi
15 – At Cinn.	L	6-7*	Hume	Holland
15 – At Cinn.	W	5-2	Alexander	Pastore
16 – At Cinn.	L	1-2	Soto	Griffin
17 – At Pitts.	W	5-1†	Minton	Scurry
18 – At Pitts.	W	4-2	Whitson	Tiant
19 – At Pitts.	L	3-7	Jones	Alexander
21 – At Chicago	W	4-3	Breining	Tidrow
22 – At Chicago	W	2-1	Blue	Bird
23 – At Chicago	L	5-6	Capilla	Lavelle
24 – At St. L.	L	1-2*	Kaat	Minton
25 – At St. L.	W	4-2	Griffin	Martin
26 – At St. L.	L	4-9	Andujar	Lavelle
27 – Pittsburgh	W	5-4§	Holland	D. Robinson
28 – Pittsburgh	W	5-1	Whitson	Scurry
29 – Pittsburgh	W	8-3	Alexander	Tiant
30 – Pittsburgh	W	5-0	Griffin	Perez
		Won 12, Lost 8		
SEPTEMBER				
1 – St. Louis	W	4-2	Blue	Forsch
2 – St. Louis	L	2-5	Sorensen	Whitson
3 – Chicago	W	12-0	Alexander	Bird
4 – Chicago	W	3-2*	Holland	Tidrow
5 – Chicago	L	2-8	Krukow	Hargesh'mer
6 – Chicago	W	3-0	Blue	Griffin
7 – At L.A.	L	1-5	Welch	Whitson
8 – At L.A.	L	0-4	Hooton	Alexander
9 – At L.A.	W	6-3†	Holland	Niedenfuer
11 – At Hous.	L	0-6	Sutton	Blue
12 – At Hous.	L	2-5	Niekro	Whitson
13 – At Hous.	L	0-3	Knepper	Alexander
14 – Atlanta	W	4-2	Griffin	Boggs
15 – Atlanta	W	6-5	Minton	Garber
16 – Cincinnati	W	12-7	Breining	Soto
17 – Cincinnati	L	0-1*	Seaver	Holland
18 – Houston	W	5-2	Alexander	Knepper
19 – Houston	L	1-8	Ruhle	Griffin
20 – Houston	L	3-7	Ryan	Lavelle
22 – Los Ang.	W	5-2	Whitson	Valenzuela
23 – Los Ang.	W	8-4	Lavelle	Goltz
24 – Los Ang.	L	3-7	Welch	Griffin
25 – At S. Diego	W	3-0	Holland	Fireovid
26 – At S. Diego	W	6-5	Lavelle	Armstrong
27 – At S. Diego	W	7-3	Alexander	Welsh
28 – At Cinn.	W	4-0	Hargesh'mer	Pastore
29 – At Cinn.	L	3-4	Hume	Minton
30 – At Atlanta	L	2-9	McWilliams	Whitson
		Won 15, Lost 13		
OCTOBER				
1 – At Atlanta	W	6-2	Alexander	Niekro
3 – San Diego	L	3-4§	Lucas	Rowland
3 – San Diego	L	2-7	Lollar	Hargesh'mer
4 – San Diego	W	4-3	Breining	Show
		Won 2, Lost 2		

*10 innings. †11 innings. ‡12 innings. §13 innings. x14 innings. y15 innings. zSuspended game, completed June 10.

Jack Clark's bat and Greg Minton's arm kept the Giants respectable.

constantly was getting on base, Evans hit .300, LeMaster continued to sparkle afield, May batted .312 and Leonard batted .307.

For the season, May batted .310, the highest average ever for a San Francisco Giants catcher. Clark topped the club with 17 homers, 53 RBIs and 11 game-winning RBIs. LeMaster batted .253 and improved defensively with Morgan a stabilizing influence at second base.

But pitching remained the strong suit and Robinson handled the staff deftly. He knew the club was thin in starters and utlized his bullpen frequently and efficiently.

Minton, despite the shortened schedule, earned a club-record 21 saves and extended his homerless innings string to 255. The bullpen registered 33 saves, tying St. Louis for the league lead, and the staff ERA of 3.28 was bettered only by the Astros, Yankees and Dodgers in all of major league baseball.

Atlanta's Dale Murphy suffered a power outage in '81.

Poor Offense Doomed Braves

By TIM TUCKER

The Atlanta Braves' 1981 season began with Manager Bobby Cox declaring, "For the first time, I really believe we can win the pennant."

And it ended, one fourth-place and one fifth-place finish later, with Owner Ted Turner firing Cox and making a declaration of his own. "We went backward this year," he said, "and you should continue to improve."

Unquestionably, the Braves did go backward. A team that had seemed on the verge of contention when it finished 81-80 in 1980 regressed to six games below .500. It finished the first half of the strike-interrupted season in fourth place, 9½ games behind Los Angeles. It finished the second half in fifth place, 7½ behind Houston. In the inconsequential overall standings, it finished 50-56, 15 games behind Cincinnati.

Turner responded by firing Cox and hiring Joe Torre to a three-year contract as manager. Turner admitted he acted only because "sometimes in baseball you're supposed to make a change, just for the sake of making a change." He did not pretend to believe that Cox was the club's biggest problem in 1981.

The problem was lack of hitting. Once again failing to live up to their heavy-hitting reputation, the Braves finished next to last in the National League with a team batting average of .243, better only than the Cubs. They did not have a .300 hitter and had no one with more than 51 RBIs, 15 home runs, 23 stolen bases or 44 runs scored. The offense obviously needed a thorough reevaluation.

Much of the problem was that the heart of the order did not produce. Bob Horner fell from 35 homers in 1980 to 15. Dale Murphy fell from 33 to 13, and his batting average dropped to .247. Chris Chambliss fell from 18 homers to eight.

Claudell Washington did not hit as many home runs (5) or steal as many bases (12) as the Braves had expected, but hit a solid .291 and played superbly in right field. He and late-season arrival Brett Butler (.256 in 40 games as the left fielder) solidified the top of the order.

Defensively, the club was solid at every position except shortstop, where young Rafael Ramirez committed 30 errors in 95 games and lost the job in late September. Catcher Bruce Benedict played so well in the first half that he was named to

Claudell Washington . . . Solid.

the All-Star team and, although he did not play as well in the second half, firmly entrenched himself at the position. Glenn Hubbard played as well defensively as any second baseman in the league, keeping himself in the lineup despite a .235 batting average. Butler, Murphy and Washington formed the best defensive outfield the club had fielded since moving to Atlanta.

But just as it was the lack of hitting that doomed the Braves, it was the pitching that kept them from total collapse.

The staff's earned-run average of 3.45 was fifth best in the league, the Braves' best since 1974. For the second half, the Braves' staff ERA was 2.81.

Rookie Rick Mahler was the most significant find on the pitching staff, coming from nowhere to post an 8-6 record and 2.81 earned-run average to qualify himself as a full-fledged member of the starting rotation. The only starter to equal Mahler in wins was Gaylord Perry, released after the season despite an 8-9 record.

Phil Niekro showed no signs of aging, pitching some of the best baseball of his career in the second half to finish 7-7 with a 3.11 ERA. Tommy Boggs did not meet his 12-win form of the year before,

but he pitched better than his 3-13 record. The rotation spent most of the season in dire need of a lefthander. Larry McWilliams pitched well after joining the club in September.

The bullpen was perhaps the club's biggest strength. Rick Camp had his second straight marvelous season, going 9-3 with a 1.78 earned run average and 17 saves. Veterans Al Hrabosky (1-1, 1.06) and Gene Garber (4-6, 2.59) made strong comebacks from disappointing 1980 seasons.

Obviously, it was not the year the Braves had expected. The preseason promotional campaign was "This Could Be the Year." And with a little hitting— and a good shortstop—it just might have been.

SCORES OF ATLANTA BRAVES' 1981 GAMES

APRIL

Date		Score	Winner	Loser
10—Cincinnati	W	5-3	Garber	Soto
11—Cincinnati	L	2-3	Bair	Garber
12—Cincinnati	W	3-2	Bradford	Hume
13—At Hous.	W	2-1*	Camp	Sambito
14—At Hous.	L	2-8	Niekro	Walk
15—At Hous.	L	0-2	Ryan	Boggs
17—San Fran.	L	2-6	Alexander	Perry
18—San Fran.	L	1-4	Griffin	Montefusco
19—San Fran.	W	4-3	Camp	Minton
21—At Cinn.	W	10-1	Boggs	Soto
22—At Cinn.	W	7-3	Perry	LaCoss
23—At S. Fran.	W	7-3	Montefusco	Griffin
24—At S. Fran.	W	7-1	Walk	Ripley
25—At S. Fran.	W	4-0	Niekro	Blue
26—At S. Fran.	L	1-3	Alexander	Perry
26—At S. Fran.	L	5-8	Holland	Boggs
28—Houston	L	1-2	Sutton	Montefusco
29—Houston	L	4-5	LaCorte	Camp
30—Houston	L	1-5	Niekro	Boggs

Won 9, Lost 10

MAY

Date		Score	Winner	Loser
1—At Chicago	W	2-1	Perry	Caudill
2—At Chicago	L	2-5	Martz	Niekro
3—At Chicago	W	9-7	Hanna	Kravec
4—At St. L.	W	9-6	Bradford	Sutter
5—At St. L.	L	1-4	Sorensen	Boggs
6—At St. L.	W	10-2	Perry	Forsch
7—At St. L.	W	4-3	Camp	Martinez
8—Chicago	W	4-3†	Mahler	Tidrow
9—Chicago	L	3-7	Reuschel	Walk
10—Chicago	T	5-5x	....	....
11—Pittsburgh	W	3-2*	Mahler	Tekulve
12—Pittsburgh	W	2-0	Niekro	Solomon
13—Pittsburgh	L	5-7§	Cruz	Boggs
15—St. Louis	W	11-3	Hanna	Sorensen
16—St. Louis	L	2-6	Martinez	Boggs
17—St. Louis	L	3-4	Forsch	Perry
19—At Pitts.	L	0-5	Bibby	Niekro
20—At Pitts.	L	1-6	Rhoden	Walk
22—San Diego	L	2-5	Eichelberger	Boggs
23—San Diego	W	7-6†	Camp	Lucas
24—San Diego	L	5-7	Curtis	Niekro
25—Los Ang.	L	1-7	Hooton	Walk
27—Los Ang.	W	3-2	Camp	Howe
28—Los Ang.	W	9-4	Perry	Valenzuela
29—At S. Diego	W	7-1	Niekro	Wise
30—At S. Diego	L	1-11	Mura	Hanna
31—At S. Diego	L	1-5	Eichelberger	Mahler

Won 13, Lost 13, Tied 1

JUNE

Date		Score	Winner	Loser
1—At L.A.	L	2-5	Valenzuela	Boggs
2—At L.A.	W	3-1*	Perry	Stewart
3—At L.A.	W	4-2	Niekro	Hooton
5—Phila.	W	4-1	Mahler	Carlton
6—Phila.	L	0-3	Christenson	Boggs
7—Phila.	L	5-7	Lyle	Perry
9—At Mon.	L	1-12	Sanderson	Niekro
10—At Mon.	L	2-11	Gullickson	Mahler
11—At Mon.	L	0-7	Rogers	Boggs

Won 3, Lost 6

AUGUST

Date		Score	Winner	Loser
10—At S.D.	W	3-2	Garber	Urrea
11—At S.D.	W	5-1	Perry	Mura
12—At S.D.	W	4-3†	Camp	Curtis
13—At L.A.	W	9-0	Boggs	Hooton
14—At L.A.	L	0-5	Goltz	Montefusco
15—At L.A.	W	6-4	Bedrosian	Reuss
16—At L.A.	L	5-6	Niedenfuer	Bedrosian
18—New York	L	0-4	Lynch	Mahler
19—New York	W	5-2	Boggs	Scott
20—New York	W	6-4	Niekro	Harris
21—Montreal	L	1-4†	Fryman	Garber
22—Montreal	L	4-5	Bahnsen	Bedrosian
22—Montreal	W	9-1	Montefusco	Lea
23—Montreal	W	2-1	Mahler	Rogers
24—At Phila.	L	5-7§	McGraw	Hrabosky
25—At Phila.	W	12-2	Niekro	Davis
26—At Phila.	W	5-3*	Camp	R. Reed
28—At Mon.	L	0-3	Rogers	Mahler
29—At Mon.	L	3-4	Reardon	Garber
30—At Mon.	W	5-4†	Garber	Lee
31—Phila.	L	8-11	Ruthven	Perry

Won 12, Lost 9

SEPTEMBER

Date		Score	Winner	Loser
1—Phila.	L	0-3	Carlton	Mahler
2—Phila.	W	3-2	Garber	Brusstar
4—At N. York	L	1-4	Harris	Niekro
5—At N. York	L	2-4	Zachry	Perry
6—At N. York	W	5-2	Mahler	Jones
7—Houston	L	2-3	D. Smith	Camp
8—Houston	W	3-2	Camp	B. Smith
9—Houston	W	9-0	Niekro	Ryan
11—San Diego	W	4-1	Perry	Mura
12—San Diego	W	5-4†	Camp	Armstrong
13—San Diego	L	4-6*	Lucas	Camp
14—At S. Fran.	L	2-4	Griffin	Boggs
15—At S. Fran.	L	5-6	Minton	Garber
16—At L.A.	L	2-3	Reuss	Perry
17—At L.A.	L	0-2	Valenzuela	Mahler
18—At S. Diego	W	3-0	McWilliams	Wise
19—At S. Diego	L	3-6	Show	Garber
20—At S. Diego	W	3-1†	Hrabosky	Mura
22—At Hous.	L	0-3	Sutton	Perry
23—At Hous.	W	3-1	Mahler	Niekro
24—At Hous.	L	3-5	Knepper	McWilliams
25—Cincinnati	L	2-10	Soto	Boggs
26—Cincinnati	L	0-2	Berenyi	Niekro
27—Cincinnati	L	2-4	Seaver	Perry
28—Los Ang.	W	2-1	Mahler	Reuss
29—Los Ang.	L	3-5	Howe	Garber
30—San Fran.	W	9-2	McWilliams	Whitson

Won 11, Lost 16

OCTOBER

Date		Score	Winner	Loser
1—San Fran.	L	2-6	Alexander	Niekro
2—At Cinn.	W	11-5	Perry	Pastore
3—At Cinn.	W	4-3	Mahler	Hume
4—At Cinn.	L	0-3	Soto	Boggs

Won 2, Lost 2

*10 innings.   †11 innings.   ‡12 innings.   §13 innings.   x14 innings.

Youthful Padres Paid the Price

By PHIL COLLIER

The San Diego Padres' 13th National League season may long be remembered as their most disappointing.

Jack McKeon, beginning his first full year as general manager, began a rebuilding program. But by season's end, the youthful San Diego team had shown so little progress that rookie Manager Frank Howard became the fifth field leader to be fired in five years.

The Padres, 22-33 before the June 12 work stoppage and 18-36 after resuming play, finished 41-69—their lowest winning percentage (.373) since 1974.

It was in August 1980 that McKeon, formerly a manager at Kansas City and Oakland, began weeding out the old players on one of major league baseball's oldest rosters. His wheeling and dealing continued during the winter when he exchanged established, high-salaried players such as Rollie Fingers, Gene Tenace and Randy Jones for youngsters such as Terry Kennedy and John Urrea.

The Padres were still in a state of flux March 30 when McKeon made his last major changes. He acquired an exciting young second baseman, Juan Bonilla, from Cleveland, and then picked up two outfielders, Ruppert Jones and Joe Lefebvre, and two young lefthanders, Chris Welsh and Tim Lollar, in a trade that sent centerfielder Jerry Mumphrey to the Yankees.

The Padres, who had allowed All-Star right fielder Dave Winfield to defect to the Yankees in the reentry draft, went into their 13th season much as they had their first—with some of the youngest players in the majors.

They opened the season with such newcomers as catchers Kennedy and Steve Swisher, Bonilla at second, Jones in center, and Lefebvre and Dave Edwards in right. Welsh, Lollar, Dan Boone, John Littlefield and Urrea started on the mound.

The Padres were handicapped by having to play 21 of their first 30 games on the road. They lost 20 of the 30, largely because Jones, Lefebvre, shortstop Ozzie Smith, third baseman Luis Salazar, left fielder Gene Richards and first baseman Randy Bass all got off to miserable starts at the plate.

In spring training, Howard had talked of a .500 season and predicted the Padres would score 100 more runs than they had

Ozzie Smith . . . Golden glove.

the previous year. It soon became evident, however, how much the Padres would miss Winfield, their perennial leader in home runs and runs batted in; Mumphrey, who had batted .298 and stolen 52 bases in 1980, and Fingers, who had recorded 23 of the team's 39 saves.

Losing Winfield, Tenace and Mumphrey took away 41 of the 67 homers the Padres had hit in 1980. In 1981, the Padres were last in the majors in homers with 32 in 110 games. Lefebvre, an eighth-place hitter in San Diego's batting order much of the season, led the team with eight.

In 1980, when they finished with a 73-89 record, the Padres led the majors in stolen bases with 239. Mumphrey (52), Richards (61) and Smith (57) became the first three National League teammates ever to steal 50 or more bases in one season.

In 1981, however, the San Diego running game deteriorated to such an extent that the Padres finished eighth in the National League. They dropped off from

239 to 83 and were caught stealing 62 times. Smith declined from 57 to 22 and Richards from 61 to 20.

Ironically, the Padres set an all-time team record with their .256 batting average, ranking seventh in the league. And they were ninth in the N.L. in pitching with an earned run average of 3.72. Thanks largely to Smith and Bonilla, they led the league in double plays (117), but their 102 errors were exceeded by only two teams—Chicago (113) and New York (130).

Sophomore lefthander Gary Lucas took up some of the slack caused by Fingers' departure. He had a 7-7 record, a 2.00 ERA and 13 of the Padres' 23 saves.

However, the Padres lacked a comparable righthander for short relief.

"We could certainly use a righthanded power hitter and I think we need to make better use of our speed," Dick Williams said after becoming manager in November.

Williams, who guided Oakland to World Series titles in 1972 and '73 and led the Expos into contention in the past couple of years before being fired by Montreal in September, compared the Padres' young talent to that of Montreal's when he took over that club in 1976.

"The Padres are set up to do the same thing we did in Montreal; they're going to build from within," said Williams.

SCORES OF SAN DIEGO PADRES' 1981 GAMES

ARPIL

			Winner	Loser
9—At S. Fran.	W	4-1‡	Lucas	Holland
10—At S. Fran.	W	4-2	Urrea	Lavelle
11—At S. Fran.	L	0-2	Alexander	Eichelberger
12—At S. Fran.	L	6-7x	Breining	Lucas
13—Cincinnati	L	1-7	Seaver	Wise
14—Cincinnati	L	0-4	Berenyi	Curtis
15—Cincinnati	L	1-10	Soto	Mura
17—Los Ang.	W	3-2*	Lollar	Howe
18—Los Ang.	L	0-2	Valenzuela	Wise
19—Los Ang.	L	1-6	Welch	Curtis
20—San Fran.	L	0-9	Blue	Mura
21—San Fran.	W	3-1	Welsh	Alexander
22—San Fran.	W	4-0	Eichelberger	Whitson
23—At L.A.	L	1-3	Sutcliffe	Wise
24—At L.A.	W	6-5	Lucas	Castillo
25—At L.A.	L	1-2†	Howe	Littlefield
26—At L.A.	L	2-3	Reuss	Lucas
28—At Cinn.	L	2-11	Seaver	Lollar
29—At Cinn.	L	5-8	Moskau	Littlefield
30—At Cinn.	L	3-4	LaCoss	Mura

Won 6, Lost 14

MAY

1—At N. York	W	4-2	Urrea	Zachry
2—At N. York	L	2-6	Falcone	Welsh
3—At N. York	W	4-1	Wise	Roberts
3—At N. York	L	4-7	Scott	Lollar
5—At Mon.	L	3-4	Fryman	Mura
6—At Mon.	W	13-5	Eichelberger	Burris
7—At Mon.	L	1-2	Sanderson	Welsh
8—At Phila.	L	7-11	Lyle	Lucas
9—At Phila.	L	6-9	Carlton	Lollar
10—At Phila.	W	8-4	Mura	Christenson
12—New York	W	3-0	Eichelberger	Zachry
13—New York	W	5-0	Welsh	Lynch
14—New York	W	10-6	Lucas	Falcone
15—Phila.	L	1-2	Carlton	Mura
16—Phila.	W	2-1	Littlefield	McGraw
17—Phila.	L	3-6	Espinosa	Eichelberger
18—Montreal	L	2-3*	Fryman	Lucas
19—Montreal	W	3-1	Wise	Gullickson
20—Montreal	L	2-6	Rogers	Mura
22—At Atlanta	W	5-2	Eichelberger	Boggs
23—At Atlanta	L	6-7†	Camp	Lucas
24—At Atlanta	W	7-5	Curtis	Niekro
25—At Hous.	L	3-6	Niekro	Mura
26—At Hous.	L	0-1	Ryan	Eichelberger
27—At Hous.	L	0-1	Knepper	Welsh
29—Atlanta	L	1-7	Niekro	Wise
30—Atlanta	W	11-1	Mura	Hanna
31—Atlanta	W	5-1	Eichelberger	Mahler

Won 13, Lost 15

JUNE

2—Houston	L	1-2	LaCorte	Welsh
3—Houston	L	1-6	Sutton	Wise
4—Houston	W	7-5	Mura	Niekro
5—At St. L.	L	1-2§	Kaat	Curtis
6—At St. L.	L	1-11	Martin	Lollar
7—At St. L.	W	5-1	Welsh	Shirley
9—At Pitts.	W	7-4	Mura	Rhoden
10—At Pitts.	W	3-2	Eichelberger	Perez

Won 4, Lost 4

AUGUST

			Winner	Loser
10—Atlanta	L	2-3	Garber	Urrea
11—Atlanta	L	1-5	Perry	Mura
12—Atlanta	L	3-4†	Camp	Curtis
13—Houston	W	9-1	Welsh	Knepper
14—Houston	L	1-5	Ryan	Lollar
15—Houston	L	0-5	Sutton	Eichelberger
16—Houston	L	0-3	Niekro	Mura
17—At St. L.	L	1-2§	Kaat	Lucas
18—At St. L.	W	4-3	Welsh	Martinez
19—At St. L.	L	6-7	Sutter	Littlefield
21—At Pitts.	L	2-4	Rhoden	Mura
21—At Pitts.	L	2-3	Bibby	Lollar
22—At Pitts.	W	7-6	Curtis	Tekulve
23—At Pitts.	L	2-5	Scurry	Welsh
24—At Chicago	L	8-9†	Smith	Lucas
25—At Chicago	L	3-4	Kravec	Lollar
26—At Chicago	L	7-9	Smith	Curtis
27—St. Louis	L	2-3§	Kaat	Curtis
29—St. Louis	L	1-6	Sorensen	Welsh
29—St. Louis	L	5-6	Sykes	Eichelberger
30—St. Louis	W	9-6	Lucas	Littell
31—Chicago	W	4-1	Mura	Kravec

Won 5, Lost 17

SEPTEMBER

1—Chicago	W	3-2	Wise	Krukow
2—Chicago	W	5-4*	Lucas	Tidrow
3—Pittsburgh	L	3-7	Tiant	Eichelberger
4—Pittsburgh	W	5-4	Littlefield	D. Robinson
5—Pittsburgh	L	1-2	Rhoden	Mura
6—Pittsburgh	L	5-9	Solomon	Wise
7—At Cinn.	L	7-8	Seaver	Show
8—At Cinn.	W	6-1	Eichelberger	Berenyi
9—At Cinn.	L	4-5	Hume	Urrea
11—At Atlanta	L	1-4	Perry	Mura
12—At Atlanta	L	4-5†	Camp	Armstrong
13—At Atlanta	W	6-4*	Lucas	Camp
14—Los Ang.	L	5-10	Power	Show
15—Los Ang.	W	8-2	Eichelberger	Goltz
16—Houston	L	2-5	Sutton	Lollar
17—Houston	L	0-9	Niekro	Mura
18—Atlanta	L	0-3	McWilliams	Wise
19—Atlanta	W	6-3	Show	Garber
20—Atlanta	L	1-3†	Hrabosky	Mura
21—Cincinnati	W	6-0	Welsh	Leibrandt
22—Cincinnati	L	2-3	Seaver	Eichelberger
23—Cincinnati	L	1-5	Pastore	Wise
25—San Fran.	L	0-3	Holland	Fireovid
26—San Fran.	L	5-6	Lavelle	Armstrong
27—San Fran.	L	3-7	Alexander	Welsh
28—At Hous.	L	1-2	Sambito	Eichelberger
29—At Hous.	W	2-1	Wise	Knepper
30—At L.A.	W	2-0	Boone	Goltz

Won 10, Lost 18

OCTOBER

1—At L.A.	W	1-0	Kuhaulua	Valenzuela
3—At S. Fran.	W	4-3§	Lucas	Rowland
3—At S. Fran.	W	7-2	Lollar	Hargesh'mer
4—At S. Fran.	L	3-4	Breining	Show

Won 3, Lost 1

*10 innings. †11 innings. ‡12 innings. §13 innings. x14 innings.

When Gene Richards' average dropped, so did his stolen bases.

Expos catcher Gary Carter often was the center of attention in '81.

Expos Enjoyed Best Season

By IAN MacDONALD

The Montreal Expos were National League Eastern Division champions and finally had something more than "ifs" and "might-have-beens" on which to reflect.

Wins and losses, of course, are what count and the Expos have done well in that department. Their overall record for the past three years is the best in the National League. But a successful winning percentage was not enough to lift them into the playoffs until 1981.

Once they made it, they performed well. After surving the Philadelphia Phillies in the division mini-series brought about by the split schedule following the 50-day players' strike, the Expos took the Los Angeles Dodgers into the ninth inning of the fifth game of the best-of-five N.L. Championship Series before falling when Rick Monday hit a dramatic two-run homer.

The Expos reached their greatest heights despite finding it necessary to switch managers down the stretch. President and General Manager John McHale fired Manager Dick Williams on September 8 and asked his executive aide, Jim Fanning, to guide the ship through the final weeks.

Under Fanning, the Expos went 17-10 through the balance of the schedule and earned their first post-season appearance.

Excellent pitching and better-than-adequate defense carried the Expos. Offensively, they were inconsistent, despite the early-season heroics of speedster Tim Raines and the powerful bats of Gary Carter and THE SPORTING NEWS' N.L. Player of the Year Andre Dawson.

The Expos were second in the N.L. to the Dodgers in home runs with 81 and they led the majors with 138 steals. But their team batting average of .246 was 10th.

The Expos remained consistent through both halves of the split season. They were 30-25 in the first half, finishing four games behind the Phillies, and 30-23 in the second, earning their playoff berth when the Cardinals stumbled down the stretch.

As has become their custom since moving into Olympic Stadium, the Expos were tough at home. After leading the league with 56-25 and 51-29 marks for the previous two years, the Expos were

Steve Rogers . . . Staff leader.

38-18 this year.

The pitching staff was led by starters Steve Rogers, Ray Burris, Scott Sanderson and hard-luck Bill Gullickson. Charlie Lea contributed one of the outstanding individual efforts when he no-hit the Giants at Montreal on April 10, but the righthander came up with a tender elbow after the strike and was unable to contribute.

After being acquired from the New York Mets in exchange for outfielder Ellis Valentine, Jeff Reardon proved an excellent righthanded complement to veteran lefty Woodie Fryman in the bullpen.

In late August, Gullickson, Burris and Rogers pitched consecutive shutouts.

Then, during the third week in September, the staff pitched 36⅔ consecutive shutout innings. Gullickson started that streak when he whiffed 13 Cubs during a September 20 victory.

It took this kind of pitching to offset frequent lapses on offense. The only consistency through the season was provided by Dawson and the rookie Raines. Raines, however, was injured September 13 and was used only as a pinch-runner down the stretch. Dawson went into his only slump of the season at about that time.

Dawson finished the season with 24 home runs, second in the majors only to Mike Schmidt, and his .553 slugging percentage was second in the league. Dawson also won his second consecutive Gold Glove as a center fielder.

Raines stole 71 bases in 82 attempts, breaking the rookie record of 56 set by Gene Richards. Had he not missed 78 games because of the strike and hand injury, Raines might have taken aim at Lou Brock's single-season record of 118 steals.

Carter carried the team for several stretches with his powerful bat and added to his growing reputation as the best defensive catcher in the game.

The Gold Glover caught 42 straight games at the end of the season and led the league in games caught for a fifth straight year, equaling a record set by Del Crandall. Carter threw out 42 would-be stealers while the opposition was successful 50 times.

Warren Cromartie tied Raines for the team lead with a .304 average. He had an interesting spurt at the end when he was inserted into the leadoff position. Over that 15-game stretch, Cromartie was 22 for 53 (.415) and had 13 walks for an on-base average of .530.

Third baseman Larry Parrish, hampered by a wrist injury suffered when he was hit by a pitch on May 30, 1980, rallied for a strong September when he hit .316, drove in 24 runs and was named N.L. Player of the Month.

SCORES FOR MONTREAL EXPOS' 1981 GAMES

APRIL

Date		Score	Winner	Loser
9 – At Pitts.	W	6-5	Fryman	Tekulve
12 – At Pitts.	L	2-3	Rhoden	Burris
15 – Chicago	W	5-4	Bahnsen	Tidrow
16 – Chicago	W	7-0	Sanderson	McGlothen
18 – At N. York	W	5-3	Gullickson	Jones
19 – At N. York	W	4-3	Burris	Swan
19 – At N. York	L	2-7	Zachry	Lea
20 – Phila.	W	9-8	Rogers	McGraw
21 – Phila.	W	10-3	Sanderson	Ruthven
22 – Phila.	W	4-3†	Sosa	McGraw
25 – New York	W	4-2	Rogers	Jones
26 – New York	W	8-4	Burris	Zachry
26 – New York	W	7-6	Sanderson	Swan
27 – At Phila.	L	1-3	Ruthven	Gullickson
28 – At Phila.	W	6-3	Ratzer	Christenson
29 – At Phila.	L	2-6	Carlton	Rogers

Won 12, Lost 4

MAY

Date		Score	Winner	Loser
1 – Los Ang.	W	9-8§	Lee	Castillo
2 – Los Ang.	L	0-4	Reuss	Sanderson
3 – Los Ang.	L	1-6*	Valenzuela	Gullickson
4 – Los Ang.	W	4-3	Rogers	Sutcliffe
5 – San Diego	W	4-3	Fryman	Mura
6 – San Diego	L	5-13	Eichelberger	Burris
7 – San Diego	W	2-1	Sanderson	Welch
8 – San Fran.	L	3-4	Ripley	Gullickson
9 – San Fran.	L	2-8	Blue	Rogers
10 – San Fran.	L	1-5	Griffin	Lee
10 – San Fran.	W	4-0	Lea	Whitson
12 – At L.A.	L	0-5	Hooton	Burris
13 – At L.A.	L	6-8	Howe	Fryman
14 – At L.A.	L	2-3	Valenzuela	Ratzer
15 – At S. Fran.	L	2-4	Whitson	Rogers
16 – At S. Fran.	W	5-0	Lea	Griffin
17 – At S. Fran.	L	4-5‡	Holland	Lee
18 – At S. Diego	W	3-2*	Fryman	Lucas
19 – At S. Diego	L	1-3	Wise	Gullickson
20 – At S. Diego	W	6-2	Rogers	Mura
22 – At Chicago	W	6-3	Lea	Krukow
23 – At Chicago	L	4-6	Reuschel	Burris
24 – At Chicago	L	2-6	Caudill	Sanderson
25 – St. Louis	W	5-3	Gullickson	Sorensen
26 – St. Louis	W	4-3	Rogers	Kaat
27 – St. Louis	W	4-1	Lea	Martin
29 – Pittsburgh	W	3-2	Sanderson	Bibby
30 – Pittsburgh	L	2-3	Rhoden	Gullickson
31 – Pittsburgh	W	5-1	Rogers	Perez

Won 14, Lost 15

JUNE

Date		Score	Winner	Loser
1 – At St. L.	L	2-4	Martin	Lea
2 – At St. L.	W	8-1	Burris	Shirley
3 – At St. L.	L	2-3†	Sutter	Sosa
4 – At St. L.	L	1-4	Sorensen	Gullickson
5 – At Cinn.	L	3-6	Soto	Rogers
6 – At Cinn.	L	3-9	Seaver	Lea
7 – At Cinn.	L	0-2	Berenyi	Burris
9 – Atlanta	W	12-1	Sanderson	Niekro
10 – Atlanta	W	11-2	Gullickson	Mahler
11 – Atlanta	W	7-0	Rogers	Boggs

Won 4, Lost 6

AUGUST

Date		Score	Winner	Loser
10 – Pittsburgh	W	3-1	Lee	Perez
11 – Pittsburgh	L	3-6	Tekulve	Fryman
12 – At Pitts.	W	3-2	Burris	Solomon
13 – At Pitts.	W	7-2	Rogers	Tiant
14 – St. Louis	L	1-3	Andujar	Sanderson
17 – At Hous.	W	6-2	Burris	Ruhle
18 – At Hous.	L	2-4	Knepper	Rogers
19 – At Hous.	L	1-9	Ryan	Sanderson
21 – At Atlanta	W	4-1†	Fryman	Garber
22 – At Atlanta	W	5-4	Bahnsen	Bedrosian
22 – At Atlanta	L	1-9	Montefusco	Lea
23 – At Atlanta	L	1-2	Mahler	Rogers
25 – Cincinnati	W	9-1	Sanderson	LaCoss
26 – Cincinnati	W	6-0	Gullickson	Soto
27 – Cincinnati	W	12-0	Burris	Pastore
28 – Atlanta	W	3-0	Rogers	Mahler
29 – Atlanta	W	4-3	Reardon	Garber
30 – Atlanta	L	4-5‡	Garber	Lee
31 – At Cinn.	L	8-9	Bair	Lee

Won 11, Lost 8

SEPTEMBER

Date		Score	Winner	Loser
1 – At Cinn.	W	4-3	Lea	Price
2 – At Cinn.	L	0-7	Seaver	Bahnsen
3 – Houston	L	1-2	Ruhle	Sanderson
4 – Houston	L	0-5	Ryan	Gullickson
5 – Houston	W	5-2	Burris	Sutton
6 – Houston	L	3-4‡	LaCorte	Sosa
7 – At Phila.	W	5-4	Fryman	Proly
8 – At Phila.	L	5-10	Larson	Sanderson
9 – At Phila.	L	8-11	R. Reed	Fryman
11 – At Chicago	L	5-6	Griffin	Burris
12 – At Chicago	W	2-0	Rogers	Bird
13 – At Chicago	W	10-6	Sanderson	Krukow
15 – St. Louis	L	2-3	Martin	Gullickson
15 – St. Louis	W	4-3	Lee	Littell
16 – St. Louis	L	1-7	Forsch	Burris
16 – St. Louis	W	4-3†	Reardon	Kaat
17 – St. Louis	L	4-7	Andujar	Rogers
18 – Chicago	W	11-0	Sanderson	Bird
19 – Chicago	L	1-2	Krukow	Lee
20 – Chicago	W	4-0	Gullickson	Griffin
21 – Phila.	W	1-0x	Smith	J. Reed
22 – Phila.	W	6-2	Rogers	Ruthven
23 – Pittsburgh	W	3-2	Jackson	Rhoden
24 – Pittsburgh	W	7-1	Lee	Jones
25 – New York	W	6-3	Gullickson	Zachry
26 – New York	W	4-2	Burris	Harris
27 – New York	L	1-2	Scott	Rogers
28 – At St. L.	L	2-6	Martin	Sanderson
29 – At St. L.	L	4-8	Andujar	Lee
30 – At Pitts.	W	3-2	Gullickson	Solomon

Won 16, Lost 14

OCTOBER

Date		Score	Winner	Loser
1 – At Pitts.	W	5-2	Burris	Tiant
2 – At N. York	W	3-0	Rogers	Zachry
3 – At N. York	W	5-4	Lee	Allen
4 – At N. York	L	1-2	Falcone	Gullickson

Won 3, Lost 1

*10 innings.   †11 innings.   ‡12 innings.   §13 innings.   x17 innings.

Phils' Express Came Up Empty

By HAL BODLEY

After winning their first world championship in 1980, the Philadelphia Phillies' express came to a screeching halt in the late stages of 1981.

The Phillies won the first half of the strike-torn season with a 34-21 record, 1½ games better than the St. Louis Cardinals, but the Phils were never a threat during the second half, ending with a 25-27 mark.

And in the National League East Division playoffs against the Expos, the Phils were beaten in the deciding fifth game. They lost the first two games in cold, damp Olympic Stadium in Montreal and returned to Veterans Stadium to take two in a row before losing the clincher, 3-0, to Steve Rogers. Rogers was outstanding in the Series, out-pitching Steve Carlton twice within a week.

Dallas Green, in what was supposed to be his second full season as manager, insisted the 50-day players' strike cost the Phillies.

"We had a good carry-over from 1980 and were rolling when the strike was called," said Green, who resigned from the Phils after the season to become vice-president and general manager of the Chicago Cubs. "We never got it going in the second half and I blame the strike for that."

The Phils, who drew the major leagues' second-best attendance—1,638,932 (30,351 average)—had a 36-19 record at the Vet, second only to the Expos' 38-18 home record. They led the National League in team batting with a .273 average and in runs scored with 491.

The Phils were the only major league team with five base stealers in double figures. Lonnie Smith led the way with 21 and was followed by Larry Bowa (16), Gary Matthews (15), Mike Schmidt (12) and Manny Trillo (10).

Schmidt led the major leagues in homers for the fifth time in his nine-year career with 31. His .316 average was a personal high and fourth-best in the league. He was the league leader in homers, slugging percentage (.644), runs (78), walks (73), RBIs (91) and on-base percentage.

Schmidt homered off New York's Mike Scott on August 14 at New York to become the 44th player to hit 300 or more home runs. When he homered off Pittsburgh's Kent Tekulve on September 20

Steve Carlton . . . Silent but deadly.

for his 310th, he set an all-time record for Philadelphia baseball. Jimmie Foxx, who played for both the Phillies and Philadelphia Athletics, hit 309.

The season also was memorable for 40-year-old Pete Rose. On August 10, he singled off St. Louis' Mark Littell in the eighth inning at Veterans Stadium to break Stan Musial's all-time National League hits record of 3,631. He ended the year with 3,697 career hits, trailing only Hank Aaron (3,771) and Ty Cobb (4,190). On the all-time National League lists, Rose ranks first in at-bats, singles and hits, fourth in games played, runs and total bases.

Rose, who had 140 hits in 107 games, led the N.L. in hits for the seventh time, breaking Musial's record of six. Cobb led the American League eight times.

Rose also ended the season with a .325 average, second only to Bill Madlock of

Pittsburgh, who won the batting title with a .341 mark. Rose has played in 464 consecutive games (the last 28 with the 1978 Cincinnati Reds and every game since signing with the Phillies). The Dodgers' Steve Garvey held the longest active streak at 945 following the '81 season.

Carlton finished with a 13-4 record, second only to Tom Seaver's 14-2 in National League winning percentage. He had a 2.42 ERA.

On April 29, Carlton fanned Montreal's Tim Wallach to become the sixth (first lefthander) pitcher to reach 3,000 strikeouts. On September 21, he fanned Montreal's Andre Dawson in the third inning

for 3,118 strikeouts, an all-time National League record.

Gary Matthews, who came to the Phils from Atlanta during spring training, hit .301, 13 points above his lifetime average, and finished second behind Schmidt (10-9) in game-winning RBIs.

Second-year outfielder Lonnie Smith, who was dealt to the St. Louis Cardinals during the off-season, wound up with a 23-game hitting streak to tie Houston's Art Howe for the longest in 1981. Smith hit .415 in those 23 games to boost his average from .250 to a season-ending .324.

Larry Bowa's .283 average was the third highest of his career.

SCORES OF PHILADELPHIA PHILLIES' 1981 GAMES

APRIL			Winner	Loser
8 – At Cinn.	L	2-3	Hume	Lyle
11 – At St. L.	W	5-2	Ruthven	Forsch
12 – At St. L.	L	3-7	Sorensen	Christenson
13 – Pittsburgh	W	5-1	Carlton	Candelaria
15 – Pittsburgh	W	4-3†	McGraw	Romo
16 – Pittsburgh	W	5-3	Ruthven	D. Robinson
17 – Chicago	W	6-2	Christenson	Kravec
18 – Chicago	W	4-3*	Carlton	Smith
19 – Chicago	W	7-3	Espinosa	Reuschel
20 – At Mon.	L	8-9	Rogers	McGraw
21 – At Mon.	L	3-10	Sanderson	Ruthven
22 – At Mon.	L	3-4†	Sosa	McGraw
24 – At Chicago	W	6-4	Carlton	Reuschel
25 – At Chicago	W	7-5	Lyle	Tidrow
26 – At Chicago	W	6-2	Bystrom	Caudill
27 – Montreal	W	3-1	Ruthven	Gullickson
28 – Montreal	L	3-6	Ratzer	Christenson
29 – Montreal	W	6-2	Carlton	Rogers

Won 12, Lost 6

MAY				
2 – San Fran.	L	2-6	Alexander	Espinosa
2 – San Fran.	W	3-1	Bystrom	Whitson
3 – San Fran.	W	7-5	Ruthven	Lavelle
4 – San Fran.	W	6-4	Carlton	Ripley
5 – Los Ang.	W	8-7	Lyle	Castillo
6 – Los Ang.	L	1-2	Hooton	Espinosa
7 – Los Ang.	L	1-2	Reuss	Bystrom
8 – San Diego	W	11-7	Lyle	Lucas
9 – San Diego	W	9-6	Carlton	Lollar
10 – San Diego	L	4-8	Mura	Christenson
12 – At S. Fran.	L	0-4	Alexander	Espinosa
13 – At S. Fran.	L	2-5	Ripley	Bystrom
14 – At S. Fran.	W	3-1	Ruthven	Blue
15 – At S. Diego	W	2-1	Carlton	Mura
16 – At S. Diego	L	1-2	Littlefield	McGraw
17 – At S. Diego	W	6-3	Espinosa	Eichelberger
18 – At L.A.	W	4-0	Bystrom	Valenzuela
19 – At L.A.	W	3-2	Ruthven	Welch
20 – At L.A.	L	2-3*	Howe	McGraw
22 – At Pitts.	L	1-3	Perez	Christenson
23 – At Pitts.	W	6-4	Proly	Tekulve
24 – At Pitts.	L	1-7	Bibby	Bystrom
25 – At N. York	L	3-13	Harris	Ruthven
26 – At N. York	W	7-5	R. Reed	Allen
27 – At N. York	L	1-3	Zachry	Christenson
29 – St. Louis	L	4-11	Forsch	Espinosa
30 – St. Louis	W	10-2	Ruthven	Sorensen
31 – St. Louis	W	6-1	Carlton	Martinez

Won 15, Lost 13

JUNE				
1 – New York	W	5-4	Lyle	Allen
2 – New York	W	9-7	Proly	Lynch
3 – New York	L	2-6	Harris	Ruthven
5 – At Atlanta	L	1-4	Mahler	Carlton
6 – At Atlanta	W	3-0	Christenson	Boggs
7 – At Atlanta	W	7-5	Lyle	Perry
8 – Houston	W	4-3	Ruthven	Sutton
9 – Houston	W	10-3	Bystrom	Niekro
10 – Houston	W	5-4	Carlton	LaCorte

Won 7, Lost 2

AUGUST			Winner	Loser
10 – St. Louis	L	3-7	Forsch	Christenson
11 – St. Louis	W	6-5*	R. Reed	Kaat
12 – St. Louis	L	3-11	Sykes	Ruthven
13 – St. Louis	L	2-5	Martin	Carlton
14 – At N. York	W	8-4	Christenson	Scott
15 – At N. York	L	1-3	Falcone	Espinosa
16 – At N. York	L	2-5	Zachry	Ruthven
18 – At Cinn.	L	1-3	Seaver	Carlton
19 – At Cinn.	L	3-6	Hume	Lyle
21 – Houston	W	5-4	Lyle	Ruhle
22 – Houston	W	8-4	Ruthven	Niekro
23 – Houston	W	6-0	Carlton	Knepper
24 – Atlanta	W	7-5‡	McGraw	Hrabosky
25 – Atlanta	L	2-12	Niekro	Davis
26 – Atlanta	L	3-5*	Camp	R. Reed
28 – At Hous.	L	2-3*	D. Smith	Lyle
29 – At Hous.	L	1-6	Ruhle	Davis
29 – At Hous.	L	1-2	B. Smith	Noles
30 – At Hous.	L	4-5*	D. Smith	Lyle
31 – At Atlanta	W	11-8	Ruthven	Perry

Won 7, Lost 13

SEPTEMBER				
1 – At Atlanta	W	3-0	Carlton	Mahler
2 – At Atlanta	L	2-3	Garber	Brusstar
3 – Cincinnati	L	3-9	Berenyi	Davis
4 – Cincinnati	W	7-6	Lyle	Bair
5 – Cincinnati	W	5-4	R. Reed	Soto
6 – Cincinnati	L	4-5	Hume	Lyle
7 – Montreal	L	4-5	Fryman	Proly
8 – Montreal	W	10-5	Larson	Sanderson
9 – Montreal	W	11-8	R. Reed	Fryman
11 – At Pitts.	W	8-0	Carlton	Rhoden
12 – At Pitts.	L	2-6	Solomon	Noles
13 – At Pitts.	L	2-3	Jones	R. Reed
16 – At N. York	W	3-1	Ruthven	Zachry
16 – At N. York	L	4-5	Marshall	Carlton
17 – At N. York	W	3-2	Noles	Scott
18 – Pittsburgh	L	6-7	Scurry	R. Reed
19 – Pittsburgh	W	8-2	Larson	Jones
20 – Pittsburgh	W	5-4	Lyle	Solomon
21 – At Mon.	L	0-1§	Smith	J. Reed
22 – At Mon.	L	2-6	Rogers	Ruthven
23 – At St. L.	W	9-4	Noles	Martin
24 – At St. L.	W	14-6	Davis	Sorensen
25 – At Chicago	W	9-2	Larson	Kravec
27 – At Chicago	W	5-2	Carlton	Bird
27 – At Chicago	L	0-14	Krukow	Ruthven
28 – New York	W	12-4	Christenson	Lynch
29 – New York	L	0-7	Falcone	Davis
30 – St. Louis	W	8-5	Lyle	DeLeon

Won 16, Lost 12

OCTOBER				
1 – St. Louis	L	2-3*	Bair	Christenson
2 – Chicago	W	9-7	R. Reed	Tidrow
3 – Chicago	L	4-8	Howell	Lyle
4 – Chicago	W	2-1	Ruthven	Smith

Won 2, Lost 2

*10 innings.   †11 innings.   ‡13 innings.   §17 innings.

Mike Schmidt ran away with his second straight MVP Award.

Keith Hernandez' glove matches his productive bat.

Cards Finished Second Twice

By RICK HUMMEL

"We finished first," insisted Whitey Herzog. Well, yes and no.

The Cardinals' general manager-manager was referring to his club's best overall record of 59-43 in the National League East Division. That was two games better than the Montreal Expos and 2½ games better than the Philadelphia Phillies. But there was no payoff for best overall record in the baseball season that wasn't.

Finishing 1½ games behind the Phillies in the first half and ½ game behind Montreal in the second half got the Cardinals nothing except an early ticket home.

But that the Cardinals were that close to winning the division at all was remarkable considering the injuries and assorted misfortunes that befell them.

"If you had told me that I would lose Andy Rincon and Darrell Porter for 3½ months and that Tempy (Garry Templeton) would play like he played before he became part of the team, I wouldn't have given us a chance of finishing higher than fifth. Maybe fifth. But the guys really picked it up," said Herzog, after completing his first full year as a dual executive.

Rincon, who won three of his first four decisions and had a 1.75 earned-run average, suffered a broken right forearm when hit by a line drive May 9 and never returned to pitch in the major leagues. Herzog optioned him to Springfield (American Association) before the players' strike June 12 in hopes that he would be ready when play resumed, but Rincon was beset by back and arm injuries in the minors.

Silvio Martinez, bothered by arm injuries for the second season in succession, won only two games. In 1979, he posted an impressive 15-8 mark. John Fulgham, a 10-game winner over the final three months of '79, underwent surgery for a torn rotator cuff and didn't pitch at all.

Porter, Herzog's former catcher at Kansas City, had signed a five-year contract for $3.5 million, but suffered a torn rotator cuff in his right shoulder and was unable to play from early May until late August. Though he hit four home runs in the last 2½ weeks as the Cardinals desperately tried to hang on in the race, the season was a .224 disappointment.

Templeton, who had been the center of previous St. Louis storms, was fined

George Hendrick . . . Power man.

$5,000 and suspended August 26 for making a series of obscene gestures at St. Louis fans during a game with San Francisco. The suspension was lifted when Templeton checked into a hospital for treatment of depression and the shortstop returned the last three weeks to hit .367 and regain the respect of teammates who had been shocked by his actions and dismayed by his attitude.

"He showed me something," said Gene Tenace, who had been harshly critical of Templeton. "Some of us said things that we now regret because we didn't know what really was wrong."

The Cardinals improved 15 games from their 74-88 disaster of 1980 and they passed the 1,000,000 attendance mark for the 19th straight year, a streak that ranks only behind that of the Los Angeles Dodgers in the National League.

Second baseman Tom Herr was the catalyst in the Redbirds' success. A part-time player the year before, Herr inherited a regular job when third baseman Ken Reitz was traded to Chicago and former second baseman Ken Oberkfell shifted to third. Herr started all 103 Cardinals games and hit .268. He drove in 46 runs, which ranked him third on the team, only two RBIs behind Keith Hernandez. He also made only five errors.

Hernandez, who hit .306, was the Cardinals' top everyday batter for the third year in succession. George Hendrick easily won the team home run and RBI honors. His 18 home runs were 10 more than anyone else and he had 61 RBIs.

Outfielder Dane Iorg, playing more than at any time in his career, batted .327 in 217 at-bats. Templeton finished at .288 and Oberkfell at .293.

But outfielder Sixto Lezcano, acquired in the big Milwaukee trade of the off-season, was a disappointment. He batted just .266, drove in only 28 runs and missed much of the last month with an elbow injury.

Reliever Bruce Sutter won his second National League Fireman of the Year award with 25 saves and three victories. Sutter, however, faltered down the stretch, turning in five sub-par outings in three weeks.

The staff leader was Bob Forsch, who missed by one victory his fourth straight 11-triumph season. Forsch had a 10-5 record and 3.19 ERA.

Joaquin Andujar, obtained from Houston June 7, provided a lift by winning six of seven decisions as a Cardinal, including three straight over Montreal, running his career mark against the Expos to 10-0.

Lefthander John Martin was the team's top rookie, winning eight of 13 decisions and leading the staff in complete games with four. The Cardinals had only 11 complete games.

The Cardinals had one of the league's best road marks, 27-22, and their strong bullpen did not lose any game in which the team entered the ninth inning with a lead.

"But," said Herzog, "nobody remembers who finished second."

SCORES OF ST. LOUIS CARDINALS' 1981 GAMES

APRIL			Winner	Loser
11 – Phila.	L	2-5	Ruthven	Forsch
12 – Phila.	W	7-3	Sorensen	Christenson
15 – At N. York	L	3-5	Zachry	Martinez
16 – At N. York	W	5-1	Rincon	Scott
17 – At Cinn.	W	9-5	Sorensen	LaCoss
18 – At Cinn.	W	10-4	Shirley	Seaver
20 – Chicago	W	6-1	Forsch	McGlothen
21 – Chicago	W	8-0	Rincon	Kravec
22 – Chicago	W	3-0	Sorensen	Krukow
25 – At Pitts.	W	5-1	Shirley	Candelaria
26 – At Pitts.	W	3-2	Kaat	Jackson
29 – At Chicago	L	1-6	Krukow	Rincon
29 – At Chicago	T	2-2†	....	....

Won 9, Lost 3, Tied 1

MAY				
1 – Cincinnati	W	7-6	Forsch	Soto
2 – Cincinnati	W	7-3	Shirley	Berenyi
3 – Cincinnati	W	5-4†	Edelen	Hume
4 – Atlanta	L	6-9	Bradford	Sutter
5 – Atlanta	W	4-1	Sorensen	Boggs
6 – Atlanta	L	2-10	Perry	Forsch
7 – Atlanta	L	3-4	Camp	Martinez
8 – Pittsburgh	W	5-4	Shirley	Bibby
9 – Pittsburgh	W	13-0	Rincon	Scurry
10 – Pittsburgh	L	2-8	Candelaria	Sorensen
12 – At Hous.	W	3-2*	Sutter	Sambito
13 – At Hous.	L	0-3	Sutton	Shirley
14 – At Hous.	W	7-6	Otten	Sambito
15 – At Atlanta	L	3-11	Hanna	Sorensen
16 – At Atlanta	W	6-2	Martinez	Boggs
17 – At Atlanta	W	4-3	Forsch	Perry
19 – Houston	W	15-12	Kaat	Sprowl
20 – Houston	L	3-4†	Niekro	Sutter
21 – Houston	W	3-1	Martin	Ryan
22 – New York	L	3-9	Zachry	Martinez
23 – New York	W	8-2	Forsch	Falcone
24 – New York	L	1-3*	Allen	Sutter
25 – At Mon.	L	3-5	Gullickson	Sorensen
26 – At Mon.	L	3-4	Rogers	Kaat
27 – At Mon.	L	1-4	Lea	Martin
29 – At Phila.	W	11-4	Forsch	Espinosa
30 – At Phila.	L	2-10	Ruthven	Sorensen
31 – At Phila.	L	1-6	Carlton	Martinez

Won 14, Lost 14

JUNE				
1 – Montreal	W	4-2	Martin	Lea
2 – Montreal	L	1-8	Burris	Shirley
3 – Montreal	W	3-2†	Sutter	Sosa
4 – Montreal	W	4-1	Sorensen	Gullickson
5 – San Diego	W	2-1§	Kaat	Curtis
6 – San Diego	W	11-1	Martin	Lollar
7 – San Diego	L	1-5	Welsh	Shirley
9 – Los Ang.	W	6-1	Forsch	Hooton
10 – Los Ang.	L	1-4	Reuss	Sorensen
11 – Los Ang.	W	2-1	Martinez	Valenzuela

Won 7, Lost 3

AUGUST			Winner	Loser
10 – At Phila.	W	7-3	Forsch	Christenson
11 – At Phila.	L	5-6*	R. Reed	Kaat
12 – At Phila.	W	11-3	Sykes	Ruthven
13 – At Phila.	W	5-2	Martin	Carlton
14 – At Mon.	W	3-1	Andujar	Sanderson
17 – San Diego	W	2-1§	Kaat	Lucas
18 – San Diego	L	3-4	Welsh	Martinez
19 – San Diego	W	7-6	Sutter	Littlefield
21 – Los Ang.	L	0-4	Reuss	Andujar
22 – Los Ang.	L	2-3	Valenzuela	Forsch
23 – Los Ang.	W	11-7	Shirley	Welch
24 – San Fran.	W	2-1*	Kaat	Minton
25 – San Fran.	L	2-4	Griffin	Martin
26 – San Fran.	W	9-4	Andujar	Lavelle
27 – At S. Diego	W	3-2§	Kaat	Curtis
28 – At S. Diego	W	6-1	Sorensen	Welsh
29 – At S. Diego	W	6-5	Sykes	Eichelberger
30 – At S. Diego	L	6-9	Lucas	Littell

Won 12, Lost 6

SEPTEMBER				
1 – At S.F.	L	2-4	Blue	Forsch
2 – At S.F.	W	5-2	Sorensen	Whitson
3 – At L.A.	W	5-3	Littell	Howe
4 – At L.A.	W	7-2	Martin	Goltz
5 – At L.A.	L	3-4†	Niedenfuer	Kaat
6 – At L.A.	L	0-5	Valenzuela	Forsch
7 – Chicago	L	0-10	Bird	Sorensen
8 – Chicago	L	3-4‡	Geisel	Kaat
9 – Chicago	L	3-7	Krukow	Martin
11 – New York	W	4-2	Forsch	Zachry
12 – New York	W	4-2§	Bair	Marshall
13 – New York	W	4-2	Andujar	Leach
15 – At Mon.	W	3-2	Martin	Gullickson
15 – At Mon.	L	3-4	Lee	Littell
16 – At Mon.	W	7-1	Forsch	Burris
16 – At Mon.	L	3-4†	Reardon	Kaat
17 – At Mon.	W	7-4	Andujar	Rogers
18 – At N. York	L	1-8	Lynch	Shirley
19 – At N. York	L	2-6	Falcone	Martin
20 – At N. York	L	6-7	Allen	Sutter
21 – At Chicago	W	2-0	Andujar	Kravec
22 – At Chicago	L	3-4	Martz	Littell
23 – Phila.	L	4-9	Noles	Martin
24 – Phila.	L	6-14	Davis	Sorensen
25 – Pittsburgh	L	4-5	Solomon	Kaat
26 – Pittsburgh	W	5-3	Forsch	Lee
27 – Pittsburgh	W	7-5	LaPoint	Perez
28 – Montreal	W	6-2	Martin	Sanderson
29 – Montreal	W	8-4	Andujar	Lee
30 – At Phila.	L	5-8	Lyle	DeLeon

Won 14, Lost 16

OCTOBER				
1 – At Phila.	W	3-2*	Bair	Christenson
2 – At Pitts.	L	7-8	Tekulve	Sutter
3 – At Pitts.	W	8-3	Martin	Camacho
4 – At Pitts.	W	4-0	Shirley	Jones

Won 3, Lost 1

*10 innings. †11 innings. ‡12 innings. §13 innings.

Crippled Bucs Slumped Badly

By CHARLEY FEENEY

The Pittsburgh Pirates, a contending club since division play began in 1969, had the bottom drop out during the 1981 season. Overall, they were a fourth-place club. They finished Part 1 of the strike-interrupted season in fourth place and finished last in Part 2.

Age played a part in the decline of the Bucs. Willie Stargell, the grand old pro who will be 41 years old in March, tried to play on two gimpy knees. Stargell, who has a career home run total of 472, didn't hit one out of the park in 60 at-bats in 38 games. Dave Parker, who is only 30, often played like a man 10 years older; and the two-time batting champion (1977-78) finished with a .258 average. There was a suspicion that Parker's batting average may have been only a few points higher than his weight. And that weight did nothing to help Parker's chronic sore knees.

The Pirates acquired Jason Thompson from California just before the season opened and he drew mixed reviews. He batted .170 in the first season and over .300 in the second half, hitting 15 homers, driving in 42 runs and leading the club with 59 walks.

The season opened with Phil Garner at second base, but in September he was traded to the Astros for rookie second baseman Johnny Ray. Veteran pinch-hitter John Milner in August was sent to Montreal for Willie Montanez. In September, veteran Pirate reliever Grant Jackson became Milner's teammate with the Expos.

Like most clubs, the Pirates had injuries. The winners survive the bad breaks. The losers do not. Pitcher John Candelaria strained his left bicep pitching on a cold, rainy day in St. Louis in May and was through for the season. Jim Bibby hurt his shoulder in August and rarely pitched the rest of the season. Bibby finished with a 6-3 record.

Rick Rhoden, who was 9-4, led the staff and Eddie Solomon was 8-6. Kent Tekulve was ineffective in relief in April, but found his winning form in May. Tekulve had a good year, but his value lessened because the Pirates often were too far behind in the late innings.

Don Robinson spent parts of the season on the disabled list with various aches and pains. Rod Scurry was a starter early and ended the season working short re-

Jim Bibby . . . Injury problems.

lief. Victor Cruz, acquired from Cleveland in the Bert Blyleven swap, opened the season with the Bucs' Portland farm club. He joined the club in May and had only fair success as a reliever. The same went for Enrique Romo, who was inconsistent despite leading the club with nine saves. Romo had a 1-3 record.

"We just couldn't keep our pitchers healthy," Manager Chuck Tanner said. "I don't want to blame injuries because they're part of the game, but it's a fact."

There also were other factors in the fall of the Pirates. Bill Robinson, who was supposed to platoon at first base, underwent surgery on his heel in April. When he returned in August, he was only about 80 percent healthy. Shortstop Tim Foli was in and out of the lineup because of chronic leg injuries. Mike Easler and Lee Lacy platooned in left field with fair success and both became starters when Parker couldn't play right field.

By August, Tanner had new faces on the mound. People like 40-year-old Luis Tiant, who had won 13 games at Portland, and Odell Jones, who was leading the Pacific Coast League in strikeouts when he was brought up in August.

There were some Bucs who had positive statistics. Third baseman Bill Madlock led the league in hitting with a .342 average. It was Madlock's third batting title, the others coming in 1975 and 1976 when he was with the Chicago Cubs. But he barely qualified for the batting cham-

pionship because of a hand injury in September.

Center fielder Omar Moreno hiked his batting average 27 points over his 1980 mark of .249. Moreno's defense in center was always above average and often spectacular.

Rookie catcher Tony Pena emerged as the star of the future. He and Steve Nicosia caught the games in early April, but it wasn't long before Pena, who batted .300 in 66 games, became the regular. Late in the season, Tanner gave Nicosia more playing time and when the season ended, Nicosia had a .231 average. The Pirates rarely played like a team that was capable of contending. The once-mighty Pirates of the 1970s were no longer there.

SCORES OF PITTSBURGH PIRATES' 1981 GAMES

APRIL			Winner	Loser
9 — Montreal	L	5-6	Fryman	Tekulve
12 — Montreal	W	3-2	Rhoden	Burris
13 — At Phila.	L	1-5	Carlton	Candelaria
15 — At Phila.	L	3-4‡	McGraw	Romo
16 — At Phila.	L	3-5	Ruthven	D. Robinson
17 — At Hous.	W	4-3	Rhoden	Sutton
18 — At Hous.	W	6-3‡	Jackson	D. Smith
19 — At Hous.	W	2-0	Scurry	Niekro
22 — New York	T	2-2*	......	......
25 — St. Louis	L	1-5	Shirley	Candelaria
26 — St. Louis	L	2-3	Kaat	Jackson
28 — At N. York	W	8-0	Rhoden	Scott
29 — At N. York	W	10-0	Bibby	Roberts
30 — At N. York	W	7-4	Candelaria	Jones

Won 7, Lost 6, Tied 1

MAY				
1 — Houston	L	3-5	Sambito	Solomon
2 — Houston	W	5-4§	Solomon	D. Smith
3 — Houston	L	1-3	Sutton	Bibby
6 — At Cinn.	L	8-9	Hume	Jackson
7 — At Cinn.	W	3-1	Rhoden	Soto
7 — At Cinn.	W	7-1	Solomon	LaCoss
8 — At St. L.	L	4-5	Shirley	Bibby
9 — At St. L.	L	0-13	Rincon	Scurry
10 — At St. L.	W	8-2	Candelaria	Sorensen
11 — At Atlanta	L	2-3†	Mahler	Tekulve
12 — At Atlanta	L	0-2	Niekro	Solomon
13 — At Atlanta	W	7-5x	Cruz	Boggs
15 — Cincinnati	L	1-4	Price	Romo
16 — Cincinnati	L	0-4	LaCoss	Scurry
17 — Cincinnati	L	3-4	Soto	Solomon
19 — Atlanta	W	5-0	Bibby	Niekro
20 — Atlanta	W	6-1	Rhoden	Walk
22 — Phila.	W	3-3	Perez	Christenson
23 — Phila.	L	4-6	Proly	Tekulve
24 — Phila.	W	7-1	Bibby	Bystrom
25 — At Chicago	L	9-10‡	Tidrow	Cruz
26 — At Chicago	W	6-4	Tekulve	Krukow
27 — At Chicago	W	3-2	Perez	Reuschel
28 — At Chicago	W	9-4	Solomon	Caudill
29 — At Mon.	L	2-3	Sanderson	Bibby
30 — At Mon.	W	3-2	Rhoden	Gullickson
31 — At Mon.	L	1-5	Rogers	Perez

Won 13, Lost 14

JUNE				
2 — Chicago	W	16-3	Solomon	Caudill
3 — Chicago	W	3-2	Bibby	Martz
4 — Chicago	W	5-4†	Tekulve	McGlothen
5 — San Fran.	L	3-5	Breining	Romo
6 — San Fran.	W	7-6	Scurry	Griffin
7 — San Fran.	W	3-2	Solomon	Blue
9 — San Diego	L	4-7	Mura	Rhoden
10 — San Diego	L	2-3	Eichelberger	Perez

Won 5, Lost 3

AUGUST			Winner	Loser
10 — At Mon.	L	1-3	Lee	Perez
11 — At Mon.	W	6-3	Tekulve	Fryman
12 — Montreal	L	2-3	Burris	Solomon
13 — Montreal	L	2-7	Rogers	Tiant
15 — At Chicago	L	3-4z	Martz	Scurry
16 — At Chicago	W	4-3‡	Tekulve	Smith
16 — At Chicago	L	4-6	Howell	Perez
17 — San Fran.	L	1-5‡	Minton	Scurry
18 — San Fran.	L	2-4	Whitson	Tiant
19 — San Fran.	W	7-3	Jones	Alexander
21 — San Diego	W	4-2	Rhoden	Mura
21 — San Diego	W	3-2	Bibby	Lollar
22 — San Diego	L	6-7	Curtis	Tekulve
23 — San Diego	W	5-2	Scurry	Welsh
24 — Los Ang.	L	0-3	Hooton	Jones
25 — Los Ang.	L	7-9‡	Pena	Tekulve
26 — Los Ang.	L	6-16	Reuss	Rhoden
27 — At S. Fran.	L	4-5x	Holland	D. Robinson
28 — At S. Fran.	L	1-5	Whitson	Scurry
29 — At S. Fran.	L	3-8	Alexander	Tiant
30 — At S. Fran.	L	0-5	Griffin	Perez
31 — At L.A.	W	5-4†	Jones	Stewart

Won 7, Lost 15

SEPTEMBER				
1 — At L.A.	L	2-3y	Niedenfuer	Jones
2 — At L.A.	L	2-6	Welch	Long
3 — At S. Diego	W	7-3	Tiant	Eichelberger
4 — At S. Diego	L	4-5	Littlefield	D. Robinson
5 — At S. Diego	W	2-1	Rhoden	Mura
6 — At S. Diego	W	9-5	Solomon	Wise
7 — New York	W	2-1	Jones	Allen
7 — New York	W	5-4	Long	Boitano
8 — New York	L	1-3	Lynch	Tiant
9 — New York	L	3-5	Leach	Perez
11 — Phila.	L	0-8	Carlton	Rhoden
12 — Phila.	W	6-2	Solomon	Noles
13 — Phila.	W	3-2	Jones	R. Reed
15 — At Chicago	W	8-2	Tiant	Griffin
18 — At Phila.	W	7-6	Scurry	R. Reed
19 — At Phila.	L	2-8	Larson	Jones
20 — At Phila.	L	4-5	Lyle	Solomon
21 — At N. York	L	3-4x	Boitano	Lee
22 — At N. York	W	5-3	Bibby	Scott
23 — At Mon.	L	2-3	Jackson	Rhoden
24 — At Mon.	L	1-7	Lee	Jones
25 — At St. L.	W	5-4	Solomon	Kaat
26 — At St. L.	L	3-5	Forsch	Lee
27 — At St. L.	L	5-7	LaPoint	Perez
28 — Chicago	W	4-0	Rhoden	Griffin
28 — Chicago	L	1-3	Geisel	Long
29 — Chicago	W	10-6	Romo	Tidrow
30 — Montreal	L	2-3	Gullickson	Solomon

Won 13, Lost 15

OCTOBER				
1 — Montreal	L	2-5	Burris	Tiant
2 — St. Louis	W	8-7	Tekulve	Sutter
3 — St. Louis	L	3-8	Martin	Camacho
4 — St. Louis	L	0-4	Shirley	Jones

Won 1, Lost 3

*8½ innings. †10 innings. ‡11 innings. §12 innings. x13 innings. y14 innings. z15 innings.

Dave Parker suffered through an un-Parkerlike season.

Homecoming celebrations are a big part of Dave Kingman's baseball life.

Mets' Improvement Not Enough

By JACK LANG

Their relationship from the start was strained, so it was inevitable that Frank Cashen would eventually dump Joe Torre as manager of the Mets. He wanted to do it earlier—the strike actually saved Torre's job—and when the general manager finally did do it on the final Sunday of the season, the move caught everyone by surprise.

During the first-half season, Torre's Mets were a stumbling aggregation that lost two games for every victory. But there was improvement when play resumed in August after the players' strike. The Mets actually contended for the second-half title. That they did finish with a 24-28 record the second time around was due mainly to Torre's player moves and juggling of the pitching staff.

Nevertheless, on October 4, Torre and his entire coaching staff were fired, even though the manager had a year to go on his contract. Two weeks later, Cashen hired his old buddy from Baltimore, George Bamberger, to run the club in 1982. Torre had lasted 4½ years, the secon longest reign of any Mets manager.

Cashen had inherited Torre when he became the general manager. He was pressured into signing him to a two-year contract when Torre brought the team home fifth in 1980. But Cashen and Torre had many philosophical differences and they never worked well together despite outward appearances.

Problems developed in the spring when Torre and his coaching buddy, Bob Gibson, urged Cashen to elevate rookie Tim Leary to the varsity roster. Leary's spring performances were sensational but Cashen wanted the pitcher to have at least a half season in Triple-A. Torre and Gibson won, but also lost. On the third day of the season, Leary left a game in Chicago after only two innings. He complained of an elbow problem he had concealed earlier. Leary never threw another pitch all season.

Torre counted on Leary as a regular starter because Craig Swan was slow recovering from a slight tear of the rotator cuff in his right shoulder. When Swan did pitch for the first time, on the third week of the season, he showed little. One week later, he was the victim of a freak accident when catcher Ron Hodges hit him in the ribs and fractured one of them while attempting a throw to second.

Neil Allen . . . Saving grace.

Swan made two relief appearances in June, but after the strike he had the same old shoulder problems and was disabled for the balance of the year.

The Mets also lost John Stearns the day before the season opened when the catcher stepped on a ball while running in the outfield and sprained his left ankle. Stearns had accepted the challenge to play third base after Joel Youngblood rejected the opportunity in spring training.

As a result of the Stearns injury, Hubie Brooks was handed the job and the rookie turned out to be one of the few bright spots of the season.

Brooks fielded well and was one of the team's leading hitters with a .307 average.

The Mets started the season with an outfield of Dave Kingman in left, Lee Mazzilli in center and Mookie Wilson in right. It was weak defensively and Mazzilli also endured the worst slump of his career while playing with multiple injuries. Wilson, normally a center fielder, had trouble adjusting to his new position.

It wasn't until Torre shifted Mazzilli to left, Kingman to first, Wilson to center and installed Joel Youngblood in right that the Mets began to play better. Wilson began hitting and stealing bases and

Youngblood, happy at last in the outfield, battered the ball at a .350 clip and was selected to the All-Star team.

Nevertheless, Youngblood griped and was continually at odds with Torre. When second-half play started, Youngblood injured his left knee and spent the balance of the season on the bench.

A big disappointment was Randy Jones, the veteran lefthander obtained from San Diego. Jones never did master his control and won only one game all season. He was not even used during the final month.

The Mets also suffered at shortstop where the moody Frank Taveras was hot and cold. He would make a brilliant play and then botch up the routine grounder. When the second half began, the Mets made a decision that was to benefit them and keep them interesting throughout September. They decided to go with young pitchers as starters, get five or six innings out of them, and let Neil Allen or Mike Marshall try to save them.

The veteran Pat Zachry continued to start, but people like Mike Scott, Ed Lynch, Pete Falcone, Terry Leach, Greg Harris and Dan Boitano helped keep the Mets in contention.

Allen had a sensational season in the bullpen, winning seven and saving 18.

Kingman led the Mets in home runs with 22 but suffered long slumps and batted only .221. Ellis Valentine, obtained from Montreal in May, suffered through a .208 season. Mazzilli never did get started and batted .228 for the year.

SCORES OF NEW YORK METS' 1981 GAMES

APRIL			Winner	Loser
9—At Chicago	W	2-0	Zachry	Reuschel
11—At Chicago	L	1-3	Tidrow	Hausman
12—At Chicago	W	2-1	Allen	Eastwick
15—St. Louis	W	5-3	Zachry	Martinez
16—St. Louis	L	1-5	Rincon	Scott
18—Montreal	L	3-5	Gullickson	Jones
19—Montreal	L	3-4	Burris	Swan
19—Montreal	W	7-2	Zachry	Lea
22—At Pitts.	T	2-2*	....	....
25—At Mon.	L	2-4	Rogers	Jones
26—At Mon.	L	4-8	Burris	Zachry
26—At Mon.	L	6-7	Sanderson	Swan
28—Pittsburgh	L	0-8	Rhoden	Scott
29—Pittsburgh	L	0-10	Bibby	Roberts
30—Pittsburgh	L	4-7	Candelaria	Jones
Won 4, Lost 10, Tied 1				
MAY				
1—San Diego	L	2-4	Urrea	Zachry
2—San Diego	W	6-2	Falcone	Welsh
3—San Diego	L	1-4	Wise	Roberts
3—San Diego	W	7-4	Scott	Lollar
5—San Fran.	L	7-9	Griffin	Jones
6—San Fran.	L	4-6	Minton	Zachry
7—San Fran.	W	3-2	Lynch	Alexander
8—Los Ang.	L	0-1	Valenzuela	Scott
9—Los Ang.	W	7-4	Allen	Castillo
10—Los Ang.	L	3-5	Welch	Jones
12—At S. Diego	L	0-3	Eichelberger	Zachry
13—At S. Diego	L	0-5	Welsh	Lynch
14—At S. Diego	L	6-10	Lucas	Falcone
15—At L.A.	L	5-6	Howe	Allen
16—At L.A.	L	0-9	Hooton	Roberts
17—At L.A.	L	1-6	Reuss	Zachry
18—At S. Fran.	L	1-3	Ripley	Lynch
19—At S. Fran.	L	1-4	Holland	Scott
20—At S. Fran.	W	4-3†	Reardon	Minton
22—At St. L.	W	9-3	Zachry	Martinez
23—At St. L.	L	2-8	Forsch	Falcone
24—At St. L.	W	3-1†	Allen	Sutter
25—Phila.	W	13-3	Harris	Ruthven
26—Phila.	L	5-7	R. Reed	Allen
27—Phila.	W	3-1	Zachry	Christenson
29—Chicago	W	6-1	Scott	Martz
30—Chicago	L	3-10	Krukow	Harris
31—Chicago	W	3-2	Jones	Reuschel
Won 11, Lost 17				
JUNE				
1—At Phila.	L	4-5	Lyle	Allen
2—At Phila.	L	7-9	Proly	Lynch
3—At Phila.	W	6-2	Harris	Ruthven
5—At Hous.	L	0-3	Ryan	Jones
6—At Hous.	L	2-6	Ruhle	Zachry
7—At Hous.	W	3-1	Scott	Knepper
9—Cincinnati	L	4-8	Hume	Falcone
10—Cincinnati	L	0-2	Soto	Jones
11—Cincinnati	L	2-5	Seaver	Zachry
Won 2, Lost 7				

AUGUST			Winner	Loser
10—At Chicago	W	7-5‡	Miller	McGlothen
11—At Chicago	W	4-2	Searage	Smith
12—At Chicago	W	7-4†	Allen	Tidrow
13—At Chicago	L	1-6	Bird	Harris
14—Phila.	L	4-8	Christenson	Scott
15—Phila.	W	3-1	Falcone	Espinosa
16—Phila.	W	5-2	Zachry	Ruthven
18—At Atlanta	W	4-0	Lynch	Mahler
19—At Atlanta	L	2-5	Boggs	Scott
20—At Atlanta	L	4-6	Niekro	Harris
21—At Cinn.	L	0-2	Soto	Zachry
22—At Cinn.	W	7-4	Boitano	Pastore
23—At Cinn.	W	3-2†	Allen	Hume
24—At Cinn.	L	0-2	Berenyi	Scott
25—Houston	W	2-1	Marshall	Sambito
26—Houston	L	3-9	Sutton	Zachry
27—Houston	W	3-2	Marshall	Sambito
28—Cincinnati	L	2-5	Seaver	Allen
29—Cincinnati	W	3-2	Scott	Berenyi
30—Cincinnati	L	3-6	LaCoss	Harris
31—At Hous.	L	1-6	Sutton	Zachry
Won 11, Lost 10				
SEPTEMBER				
1—At Hous.	L	2-3	Sambito	Marshall
2—At Hous.	L	0-8	Knepper	Scott
4—Atlanta	W	4-1	Harris	Niekro
5—Atlanta	W	4-2	Zachry	Perry
6—Atlanta	L	2-5	Mahler	Jones
7—At Pitts.	L	1-2	Jones	Allen
7—At Pitts.	L	4-5	Long	Boitano
8—At Pitts.	W	3-1	Lynch	Tiant
9—At Pitts.	W	5-3	Leach	Perez
11—At St. L.	L	2-4	Forsch	Zachry
12—At St. L.	L	2-4‡	Bair	Marshall
13—At St. L.	L	2-4	Andujar	Leach
16—Phila.	L	1-3	Ruthven	Zachry
16—Phila.	W	5-4	Marshall	Carlton
17—Phila.	L	2-3	Noles	Scott
18—St. Louis	W	8-1	Lynch	Shirley
19—St. Louis	W	6-2	Falcone	Martin
20—St. Louis	W	7-6	Allen	Sutter
21—Pittsburgh	W	4-3‡	Boitano	Lee
22—Pittsburgh	L	3-5	Bibby	Scott
23—At Chi.	L	1-2	Krukow	Lynch
24—At Chi.	L	9-10	Tidrow	Orosco
25—At Mon.	L	3-6	Gullickson	Zachry
26—At Mon.	L	2-4	Burris	Harris
27—At Mon.	W	2-1	Scott	Rogers
28—At Phila.	L	4-12	Christenson	Lynch
29—At Phila.	W	7-0	Falcone	Davis
30—Chicago	W	2-1	Allen	Martz
Won 12, Lost 16				
OCTOBER				
1—Chicago	T	2-2*	....	....
2—Montreal	L	0-3	Rogers	Zachry
3—Montreal	L	4-5	Lee	Allen
4—Montreal	W	2-1	Falcone	Gullickson
Won 1, Lost 2, Tied 1				

*8½ innings. †10 innings. ‡13 innings.

Another Bad Year for the Cubs

By JOE GODDARD

The beginning was depressing but the end encouraging for the Chicago Cubs in 1981.

The depression started with the trading of Dave Kingman to the Mets the first day of spring training. It continued with the firing in June of General Manager Bob Kennedy by principal owner William Wrigley, who replaced him with Kennedy's former manager, Herman Franks.

The picture remained bleak right up to the strike. The team had the worst record in the major leagues (15-37) and ace pitcher Rick Reuschel was traded to the Yankees.

But during the strike, Wrigley sold his majority interest in the league's oldest continuing franchise to the Tribune Co., and immediately hope sprung anew. The team made a run for the second-half Eastern Division championship and a new management team, headed by Phillies Manager Dallas Green, took over.

Green, who signed a five-year contract for an estimated $1 million, saw problems everywhere, including a lack of speed and pitching throughout the organization. "I can't tell if it was lack of funds or total incompetence," he said. He named Phillies coach Lee Elia to replace Joey Amalfitano as manager for 1982. And he hired long-time friend Gordon Goldsberry to oversee both the farm and scouting departments.

The players quietly heralded the change of ownership, expressing hope that new management—and more money —would make them competitive. This year, with the benefit of the split-season format, they were competitive right up to the end of the second half, falling by the wayside with only five days remaining. They won 22 games in the second half, 15 in the first.

"First we reached respect for ourselves, then we earned it from the people we played against, then from our own fans," said Mike Krukow, the only pitcher who was close to double figures in victories (9-9 record).

The pitching, bolstered by former Yankee Doug Bird in the starting rotation and rookie Randy Martz in the bullpen, improved dramatically in the second half. The staff earned-run average went from 4.34 at the strike to 4.01 at the end of the season. Bird won four games in his

Bill Buckner . . . Another good year.

brief stretch and kept the team close in the five he lost. Mike Griffin, also picked up in the Reuschel-Bird swap, had a few encouraging starts. Martz saved six games in the second half.

Still, the staff missed Reuschel and Bruce Sutter, who was traded to the Cardinals during the winter meetings. The Cubs only had two shutouts. Dick Tidrow, playing out his option, and Lee Smith did not live up to expectations. Tidrow saved nine games, but had a 3-10 record and 5.04 ERA. Smith, troubled with an arm injury, was 3-6 with just one save.

The hitting was last in the league (.236) despite a big season from Bill Buckner, who had won the batting championship the previous year. Disappointed when Kennedy would not reward his batting title with a renegotiated contract, Buckner not only hit .311, but drove in 75 runs, third best in the league. He had 11 game-winning RBIs, fifth best and two more than Ron Cey, the leading game-winner for the world champion Dodgers.

One of Green's first announcements as chief executive was to assure fans the popular Buckner would not be traded.

Another certain to stay was Leon

(Bull) Durham, the principal acquisition in the Sutter deal. He was hurt when the season opened and was batting under .200 going into May, but zoomed toward .300 while stealing every base in sight. He had a 12-for-12 stretch in one week and finished with 25 thefts. Although Durham tailed off to .290, he was among the league batting leaders late in September.

Fellow outfielders Steve Henderson (.293) and Jerry Morales (.286), both former Mets, also had good years. There were dropoffs among the others, however, most notably Ivan DeJesus. Although he continued to field well at shortstop, DeJesus never got above .200 at the plate.

Tim Blackwell lost his catching job to rookie Jody Davis, drafted from the Cardinals' system in one of Kennedy's better deals in five years.

Second base remained a problem and third base became a new one. Joe Strain, Steve Dillard and Mike Tyson took turns at second until Pat Tabler was acquired from the Yankees. Tabler, though, hit only .188. And at third, Ken Reitz, acquired from the Cardinals, never got untracked. He eventually lost out to still another Redbird in the Sutter deal, Ty Waller.

A total housecleaning by Green, including a cleaning of Wrigley Field, was indicated after the season.

SCORES OF CHICAGO CUBS' 1981 GAMES

APRIL			Winner	Loser
9 — New York	L	0-2	Zachry	Reuschel
11 — New York	W	3-1	Tidrow	Hausman
12 — New York	L	1-2	Allen	Eastwick
15 — At Mon.	L	4-5	Bahnsen	Tidrow
16 — At Mon.	L	0-7	Sanderson	McGlothen
17 — At Phila.	L	2-6	Christenson	Kravec
18 — At Phila.	L	3-4†	Carlton	Smith
19 — At Phila.	L	3-7	Espinosa	Reuschel
20 — At St. L.	L	1-6	Forsch	McGlothen
21 — At St. L.	L	0-8	Rincon	Kravec
22 — At St. L.	L	0-3	Sorensen	Krukow
24 — Phila.	L	4-6	Carlton	Reuschel
25 — Phila.	L	5-7	Lyle	Tidrow
26 — Phila.	L	2-6	Bystrom	Caudill
29 — St. Louis	W	6-1	Krukow	Rincon
29 — St. Louis	T	2-2‡	....	....
Won 2, Lost 13, Tied 1				

MAY				
1 — Atlanta	L	1-2	Perry	Caudill
2 — Atlanta	W	5-2	Martz	Niekro
3 — Atlanta	L	7-9	Hanna	Kravec
4 — Houston	L	4-5	Andujar	Krukow
5 — Houston	L	3-4	D. Smith	Smith
6 — Houston	W	2-1‡	Smith	LaCorte
7 — Houston	L	0-6	Knepper	Martz
8 — At Atlanta	L	3-4‡	Mahler	Tidrow
9 — At Atlanta	W	7-3	Reuschel	Walk
10 — At Atlanta	T	5-5y	....	....
12 — At Cinn.	L	1-2	Soto	Tidrow
13 — At Cinn.	L	3-8	Seaver	Krukow
14 — At Cinn.	L	1-6	Berenyi	Reuschel
15 — At Hous.	L	0-5	Niekro	Caudill
16 — At Hous.	L	1-6	Ryan	Martz
17 — At Hous.	L	1-6	Knepper	Krukow
19 — Cincinnati	L	0-5	Seaver	Reuschel
20 — Cincinnati	L	7-10	Price	Smith
21 — Cincinnati	W	5-1	Martz	Pastore
22 — Montreal	L	3-6	Lea	Krukow
23 — Montreal	W	6-4	Reuschel	Burris
24 — Montreal	W	6-2	Caudill	Sanderson
25 — Pittsburgh	W	10-9‡	Tidrow	Cruz
26 — Pittsburgh	L	4-6	Tekulve	Krukow
27 — Pittsburgh	L	2-3	Perez	Reuschel
28 — Pittsburgh	L	4-9	Solomon	Caudill
29 — At N. York	L	1-6	Scott	Martz
30 — At N. York	W	10-3	Krukow	Harris
31 — At N. York	L	2-3	Jones	Reuschel
Won 8, Lost 20, Tied 1				

JUNE				
2 — At Pitts.	L	3-16	Solomon	Caudill
3 — At Pitts.	L	2-3	Bibby	Martz
4 — At Pitts.	L	4-5†	Tekulve	McGlothen
5 — Los Ang.	W	4-3	Reuschel	Reuss
6 — Los Ang.	W	11-5	McGlothen	Valenzuela
7 — Los Ang.	L	0-7	Welch	Martz
9 — San Fran.	W	2-1a	Krukow	Ripley
10 — San Fran.	W	7-4	Reuschel	Alexander
11 — San Fran.	W	6-1	Martz	Griffin
Won 5, Lost 4				

AUGUST			Winner	Loser
10 — New York	L	5-7x	Miller	McGlothen
11 — New York	L	2-4	Searage	Smith
12 — New York	L	4-7†	Allen	Tidrow
13 — New York	W	6-1	Bird	Harris
15 — Pittsburgh	W	4-3z	Martz	Scurry
16 — Pittsburgh	L	3-4‡	Tekulve	Smith
16 — Pittsburgh	W	6-4	Howell	Perez
17 — Los Ang.	W	3-1	Bird	Welch
18 — Los Ang.	L	0-5	Hooton	Griffin
19 — Los Ang.	W	4-3	Krukow	Goltz
21 — San Fran.	L	3-4	Breining	Tidrow
22 — San Fran.	L	1-2	Blue	Bird
23 — San Fran.	W	6-5	Capilla	Lavelle
24 — San Diego	W	9-8‡	Smith	Lucas
25 — San Diego	W	4-3	Kravec	Lollar
26 — San Diego	W	9-7	Smith	Curtis
27 — At L.A.	L	0-6	Valenzuela	Martz
28 — At L.A.	L	1-6	Welch	Krukow
29 — At L.A.	W	3-1	Griffin	Hooton
30 — At L.A.	W	2-1	Bird	Goltz
31 — At S. Diego	L	1-4	Mura	Kravec
Won 11, Lost 10				

SEPTEMBER				
1 — At S. Diego	L	2-3	Wise	Krukow
2 — At S. Diego	L	4-5†	Lucas	Tidrow
3 — At S. Fran.	L	0-12	Alexander	Bird
4 — At S. Fran.	L	2-3†	Holland	Tidrow
5 — At S. Fran.	W	8-2	Krukow	Hargesh'mer
6 — At S. Fran.	L	0-3	Blue	Griffin
7 — At St. L.	W	10-0	Bird	Sorensen
8 — At St. L.	W	4-3§	Geisel	Kaat
9 — At St. L.	W	7-3	Krukow	Martin
11 — Montreal	W	6-5	Griffin	Burris
12 — Montreal	L	0-2	Rogers	Bird
13 — Montreal	L	6-10	Sanderson	Krukow
15 — Pittsburgh	L	2-8	Tiant	Griffin
18 — At Mon.	L	0-11	Sanderson	Bird
19 — At Mon.	W	2-1	Krukow	Lee
20 — At Mon.	L	0-4	Gullickson	Griffin
21 — St. Louis	L	0-2	Andujar	Kravec
22 — St. Louis	W	4-3	Martz	Littell
23 — New York	W	2-1	Krukow	Lynch
24 — New York	W	10-9	Tidrow	Orosco
25 — Phila.	L	2-9	Larsen	Kravec
27 — Phila.	L	2-5	Carlton	Bird
27 — Phila.	W	14-0	Krukow	Ruthven
28 — At Pitts.	L	0-4	Rhoden	Griffin
28 — At Pitts.	W	3-1	Geisel	Long
29 — At Pitts.	L	6-10	Romo	Tidrow
30 — At N. York	L	1-2	Allen	Martz
Won 11, Lost 16				

OCTOBER				
1 — At N. York	T	2-2*	....	....
2 — At Phila.	L	7-9	R. Reed	Tidrow
3 — At Phila.	W	8-4	Howell	Lyle
4 — At Phila.	L	1-2	Ruthven	Smith
Won 1, Lost 2, Tied 1				

*8½ innings. †10 innings. ‡11 innings. §12 innings. x13 innings. y14 innings. z15 innings. aSuspended game, completed June 10.

Cubs catcher Jody Davis was a bright spot in a dismal season.

National League Averages for 1981

CHAMPIONSHIP WINNERS IN PREVIOUS YEARS

Year			Year			Year		
1876	Chicago	.788	1911	New York	.647	1946	St. Louis°	.628
1877	Boston	.646	1912	New York	.682	1947	Brooklyn	.610
1878	Boston	.683	1913	New York	.664	1948	Boston	.595
1879	Providence	.705	1914	Boston	.614	1949	Brooklyn	.630
1880	Chicago	.798	1915	Philadelphia	.592	1950	Philadelphia	.591
1881	Chicago	.667	1916	Brooklyn	.610	1951	New York†	.624
1882	Chicago	.655	1917	New York	.636	1952	Brooklyn	.627
1883	Boston	.643	1918	Chicago	.651	1953	Brooklyn	.682
1884	Providence	.750	1919	Cincinnati	.686	1954	New York	.630
1885	Chicago	.777	1920	Brooklyn	.604	1955	Brooklyn	.641
1886	Chicago	.726	1921	New York	.614	1956	Brooklyn	.604
1887	Detroit	.637	1922	New York	.604	1957	Milwaukee	.617
1888	New York	.641	1923	New York	.621	1958	Milwaukee	.597
1889	New York	.659	1924	New York	.608	1959	Los Angeles‡	.564
1890	Brooklyn	.667	1925	Pittsburgh	.621	1960	Pittsburgh	.617
1891	Boston	.630	1926	St. Louis	.578	1961	Cincinnati	.604
1892	Boston	.680	1927	Pittsburgh	.610	1962	San Francisco§	.624
1893	Boston	.662	1928	St. Louis	.617	1963	Los Angeles	.611
1894	Baltimore	.695	1929	Chicago	.645	1964	St. Louis	.574
1895	Baltimore	.669	1930	St. Louis	.597	1965	Los Angeles	.599
1896	Baltimore	.698	1931	St. Louis	.656	1966	Los Angeles	.586
1897	Boston	.705	1932	Chicago	.584	1967	St. Louis	.627
1898	Boston	.685	1933	New York	.599	1968	St. Louis	.599
1899	Brooklyn	.677	1934	St. Louis	.621	1969	New York (East)a	.617
1900	Brooklyn	.603	1935	Chicago	.649	1970	Cincinnati (West)b	.630
1901	Pittsburgh	.647	1936	New York	.597	1971	Pittsburgh (East)c	.599
1902	Pittsburgh	.741	1937	New York	.625	1972	Cincinnati (West)b	.617
1903	Pittsburgh	.650	1938	Chicago	.586	1973	New York (East)d	.509
1904	New York	.693	1939	Cincinnati	.630	1974	Los Angeles (West)b	.630
1905	New York	.686	1940	Cincinnati	.654	1975	Cincinnati (West)b	.667
1906	Chicago	.763	1941	Brooklyn	.649	1976	Cincinnati (West)e	.630
1907	Chicago	.704	1942	St. Louis	.688	1977	Los Angeles (West)e	.605
1908	Chicago	.643	1943	St. Louis	.682	1978	Los Angeles (West)e	.586
1909	Pittsburgh	.724	1944	St. Louis	.682	1979	Pittsburgh (East)d	.605
1910	Chicago	.675	1945	Chicago	.636	1980	Philadelphia (East)f	.562

°Defeated Brooklyn, two games to none, in playoff for pennant. †Defeated Brooklyn, two games to one, in playoff for pennant. ‡Defeated Milwaukee, two games to none, in playoff for pennant. §Defeated Los Angeles, two games to one, in playoff for pennant. aDefeated Atlanta (West) in Championship Series. bDefeated Pittsburgh (East) in Championship Series. cDefeated San Francisco (West) in Championship Series. dDefeated Cincinnati (West) in Championship Series. eDefeated Philadelphia (East) in Championship Series. fDefeated Houston (West) in Championship Series.

COMPOSITE STANDING OF CLUBS AT CLOSE OF SEASON

EAST DIVISION

Club	St.L.	Mon.	Phil.	Pitt.	N.Y.	Chi.	Cin.	L.A.	Hou.	S.F.	Atl.	S.D.	W.	L.	Pct.	G.B.
St. Louis	..	9	6	8	5	4	5	5	4	3	3	7	59	43	.578	.....
Montreal	6	..	7	10	9	7	4	2	2	2	7	4	60	48	.556	2
Philadelphia	7	4	..	7	7	10	2	3	6	4	5	4	59	48	.551	2½
Pittsburgh	3	3	5	..	6	10	2	1	4	3	3	6	46	56	.451	13
New York	6	3	7	3	..	8	3	1	3	2	3	2	41	62	.398	18½
Chicago	5	4	2	4	5	..	1	6	1	5	2	3	38	65	.369	21½

WEST DIVISION

Club	Cin.	L.A.	Hou.	S.F.	Atl.	S.D.	St.L.	Mon.	Phil.	Pitt.	N.Y.	Chi.	W.	L.	Pct.	G.B.
Cincinnati	..	8	8	9	5	10	0	5	5	4	7	5	66	42	.611	.....
Los Angeles	8	..	8	7	7	6	5	5	3	5	5	4	63	47	.573	4
Houston	4	4	..	9	8	11	2	5	4	2	6	6	61	49	.555	6
San Francisco	5	5	6	..	7	7	2	5	3	7	4	5	56	55	.505	11½
Atlanta	6	7	4	5	..	9	4	3	4	2	3	3	50	56	.472	15
San Diego	2	5	3	6	6	..	3	2	2	4	5	3	41	69	.373	26

Tie Games: New York at Pittsburgh, St. Louis at Chicago, Chicago at Atlanta and Chicago at New York.

Cancelled Games: Here are the teams and their total number of games that originally were scheduled to be played from June 12 through August 9, 1981, but were cancelled due to the players' strike: Atlanta (54), Chicago (55), Cincinnati (53), Houston (52), Los Angeles (51), Montreal (52), New York (56), Philadelphia (55), Pittsburgh (57), St. Louis (56), San Diego (52), San Francisco (51). Total of 322 games.

The following games were scheduled to be made up during the players' strike but were not: St. Louis at Cincinnati, Chicago at Montreal, St. Louis at New York, Montreal at Pittsburgh, New York at Pittsburgh, Chicago at Atlanta, St. Louis at Pittsburgh, Los Angeles at Atlanta, St. Louis at Chicago suspended game of April 29 and rescheduled for July 3, but later cancelled. Total of 9 games.

The total games cancelled for each team during the players' strike. Atlanta (56), Chicago (58), Cincinnati (54), Houston (52), Los Angeles (52), Montreal (54), New York (58), Philadelphia (55), Pittsburgh (60), St. Louis (60), San Diego (52), San Francisco (51). Total of 329 games.

Division Series:Montreal defeated Philadelphia, three games to two,
          Los Angeles defeated Houston, three games to two.
Championship Series: Los Angeles defeated Montreal, three games to two.

RECORD AT HOME

EAST DIVISION

Club	Mon.	Phil.	St.L.	Chi.	N.Y.	Pitt.	Hou.	Cin.	L.A.	S.F.	Atl.	S.D.	W.	L.	Pct.
Montreal	.....	5-0	5-4	4-1	5-1	5-2	1-3	3-0	2-2	1-3	5-1	2-1	38	18	.679
Philadelphia.....	4-2	.....	4-5	5-1	3-2	5-1	6-0	2-2	1-2	3-1	1-2	2-1	36	19	.655
St. Louis..........	5-1	1-3	.....	3-3	4-2	4-2	2-1	3-0	3-3	2-1	1-3	4-2	32	21	.604
Chicago	3-3	1-5	2-1	.....	4-5	3-5	1-3	1-2	4-2	4-2	1-2	3-0	27	30	.474
New York	2-4	5-4	4-1	3-1	.....	1-4	2-1	1-5	1-2	1-2	2-1	2-2	24	27	.471
Pittsburgh........	1-5	4-2	1-4	5-1	2-2	.....	1-2	0-3	0-3	3-3	2-0	3-3	22	28	.440

WEST DIVISION

Club	Hou.	Cin.	L.A.	S.F.	Atl.	S.D.	Mon.	Phil.	St.L.	Chi.	N.Y.	Pitt.	W.	L.	Pct.
Houston..........	.....	1-5	3-3	4-2	4-2	4-1	2-1	4-0	1-2	3-0	5-1	0-3	31	20	.608
Cincinnati	3-3	.....	3-4	6-3	1-4	5-1	5-1	3-0	0-2	3-0	2-2	1-2	32	22	.593
Los Angeles	5-1	4-5	.....	3-3	5-4	3-3	3-0	1-2	2-2	2-2	3-0	2-1	33	23	.589
San Francisco..	4-5	2-3	2-4	.....	4-3	3-4	2-1	2-1	1-1	3-1	2-1	4-0	29	24	.547
Atlanta............	2-4	2-4	3-2	2-3	.....	3-3	2-2	2-4	1-2	1-1	2-1	2-1	22	27	.449
San Diego........	2-7	1-5	2-3	2-4	3-6	.....	1-2	1-2	1-3	3-0	3-0	1-3	20	35	.364

RECORD ABROAD

EAST DIVISION

Club	St.L.	Pitt.	Phil.	Mon.	N.Y.	Chi.	Cin.	L.A.	Hou.	Atl.	S.F.	S.D.	W.	L.	Pct.
St. Louis..........	.....	4-1	5-4	4-5	1-4	1-2	2-0	2-2	2-1	2-1	1-1	3-1	27	22	.551
Pittsburgh........	2-4	.....	1-5	2-5	4-1	5-3	2-1	1-2	3-0	1-2	0-4	3-1	24	28	.462
Philadelphia.....	3-1	2-4	.....	0-5	4-5	5-1	0-3	2-1	0-4	4-2	1-2	2-1	23	29	.442
Montreal	1-5	5-1	2-4	.....	4-2	3-3	1-5	0-3	1-2	2-2	1-2	2-1	22	30	.423
New York	2-4	2-2	2-3	1-5	.....	5-4	2-2	0-3	1-5	1-2	1-2	0-3	17	35	.327
Chicago	3-3	1-5	1-5	1-4	1-3	.....	0-3	2-2	0-3	1-1	1-3	0-3	11	35	.239

WEST DIVISION

Club	Cin.	L.A.	Hou.	Atl.	S.F.	S.D.	St.L.	Pitt.	Phil.	Mon.	N.Y.	Chi.	W.	L.	Pct.
Cincinnati	.....	5-4	5-1	4-2	3-2	5-1	0-3	2-2	0-3	5-1	2-1	2-1	34	20	.630
Los Angeles	4-3	.....	3-3	2-3	4-2	3-2	3-3	3-0	2-1	2-2	2-1	2-4	30	24	.556
Houston..........	3-3	1-5	.....	4-2	5-4	7-2	1-2	2-1	0-6	3-1	1-2	3-1	30	29	.508
Atlanta............	4-1	4-5	2-4	.....	3-4	6-3	3-1	0-2	2-1	1-5	1-2	2-1	28	29	.491
San Francisco..	3-6	3-3	2-4	3-2	.....	4-2	1-2	2-3	1-3	3-1	2-1	2-4	27	31	.466
San Diego........	1-5	3-3	1-4	3-3	4-3	.....	2-4	3-3	1-2	1-2	2-2	0-3	21	34	.382

SHUTOUT GAMES

Club	L.A.	Mon.	Hou.	Cin.	Phil.	St.L.	S.F.	Pitt.	S.D.	Atl.	N.Y.	Chi.	W.	L.	Pct.
Los Angeles	..	2	3	1	0	2	2	1	1	2	2	3	19	5	.792
Montreal	0	..	0	2	1	0	2	0	0	2	1	4	12	5	.706
Houston..........	2	1	..	2	0	1	2	0	5	2	2	2	19	9	.679
Cincinnati	0	2	3	..	0	0	1	1	1	2	3	1	14	8	.636
Philadelphia.....	1	0	1	0	..	0	0	1	0	2	0	0	5	4	.556
St. Louis..........	0	0	0	0	0	..	0	2	0	0	0	3	5	4	.556
San Francisco..	0	0	0	2	1	0	..	1	3	0	0	2	9	9	.500
Pittsburgh........	0	0	1	0	0	0	0	..	0	1	2	1	5	7	.417
San Diego........	2	0	0	1	0	0	1	0	..	0	2	0	6	11	.353
Atlanta............	0	0	1	0	0	0	1	1	1	..	0	0	4	12	.250
New York	0	0	0	0	1	0	0	0	0	1	..	1	3	12	.200
Chicago	0	0	0	0	1	1	0	0	0	0	0	..	2	17	.105

OFFICIAL NATIONAL LEAGUE BATTING AVERAGES

Compiled by Elias Sports Bureau, New York, N.Y.

CLUB BATTING

Club	Pct.	G.	AB.	R.	OR.	H.	TB.	2B.	3B.	HR.	RBI.	SH.	SF.	SB.	CS.	LOB.
Phila.	.273	107	3665	491	472	1002	1424	165	25	69	453	44	37	103	46	793
Cinc'ati	.267	108	3637	464	440	972	1402	190	24	64	429	53	40	58	37	789
St. Louis....	.265	103	3537	464	417	936	1334	158	45	50	431	46	35	88	45	747
Los Ang.....	.262	110	3751	450	356	984	1403	133	20	82	427	62	27	73	46	776
Pittsb'gh....	.257	103	3576	407	425	920	1321	176	30	55	384	54	36	122	52	717
Houston.....	.257	110	3693	394	331	948	1313	160	35	45	369	79	35	81	43	795
S. Diego	.256	110	3757	382	455	963	1299	170	35	32	350	72	30	83	62	769
S. Fran.....	.250	111	3766	427	414	941	1343	161	26	63	399	65	27	89	50	797
N. York	.248	105	3493	348	432	868	1245	136	35	57	325	41	34	103	42	726
Montreal ...	.246	108	3591	443	394	883	1328	146	28	81	407	63	30	138	40	722
Atlanta.....	.243	107	3642	395	416	886	1270	148	22	64	366	56	18	98	39	731
Chicago	.236	106	3546	370	483	838	1205	138	29	57	348	53	30	72	41	721
Totals	.255	644	43654	5035	5035	11141	15887	1881	354	719	4688	688	379	1108	543	9083

INDIVIDUAL BATTING
(Top Fifteen Qualifiers for Batting Championship)

°Bats lefthanded. †Switch-hitter.

Player and Club	Pct.	G.	AB.	R.	H.	TB.	2B.	3B.	HR.	RBI.	GW.	SH.	SF.	SB.	CS.
Madlock, Bill, Pitt.	.341	82	279	35	95	138	23	1	6	45	5	0	4	18	6
Rose, Peter, Phila.†	.325	107	431	73	140	168	18	5	0	33	5	1	3	4	4
Baker, Johnnie, L.A.	.320	103	400	48	128	178	17	3	9	49	8	3	5	10	7
Schmidt, Michael, Phila.	.316	102	354	78	112	228	19	2	31	91	10	0	3	12	4
Buckner, William, Chi.°	.311	106	421	45	131	202	35	3	10	75	11	0	5	5	2
Griffey, G. Kenneth, Cin.°	.311	101	396	65	123	162	21	6	2	34	3	2	4	12	4
May, Milton, S.F.°	.310	97	316	20	98	121	17	0	2	33	8	3	1	1	4
Brooks, Hubert, N.Y.	.307	98	358	34	110	147	21	2	4	38	2	1	6	9	5
Concepcion, David, Cin.	.306	106	421	57	129	172	28	0	5	67	14	2	7	4	5
Hernandez, Keith, St. L.°	.306	103	376	65	115	174	27	4	8	48	10	0	5	12	5
Cromartie, Warren, Mtl.°	.304	99	358	41	109	150	19	2	6	42	8	0	3	2	3
Raines, Timothy, Mtl.†	.304	88	313	61	95	137	13	7	5	37	3	0	3	71	11
Salazar, Luis, S.D.	.303	109	400	37	121	161	19	6	3	38	3	5	2	11	8
Dawson, Andre, Mtl.	.302	103	394	71	119	218	21	3	24	64	9	0	5	26	4
Kennedy, Terrence, S.D.°	.301	101	382	32	115	147	24	1	2	41	6	4	2	0	2

DEPARTMENTAL LEADERS: G—Garvey, O. Smith, 110; AB—O. Smith, 450; R—Schmidt, 78; H—Rose, 140; TB—Schmidt, 228; 2B—Buckner, 35; 3B—Reynolds, Richards, 12; HR—Schmidt, 31; RBI—Schmidt, 91; GW—Concepcion, 14; SH—Reynolds, 18; SF—Maddox, 8; SB—Raines, 71; CS—O. Moreno, 14.

(All Players—Listed Alphabetically)

Player and Club	Pct.	G.	AB.	R.	H.	TB.	2B.	3B.	HR.	RBI.	GW.	SH.	SF.	SB.	CS.
Aguayo, Luis, Phila.	.214	45	84	11	18	25	4	0	1	7	1	2	0	1	0
Alexander, Doyle, S.F.	.176	24	51	5	9	13	4	0	0	6	0	4	1	0	0
Alexander, Gary, Pitt.	.213	21	47	6	10	19	4	1	1	6	1	0	1	0	0
Alexander, Matthew, Pitt.†	.364	15	11	5	4	4	0	0	0	0	0	0	0	3	2
Allen, Neil, N.Y.	.200	43	5	0	1	3	0	1	0	0	0	2	0	0	0
Alvarez, Jose, Atl.	.000	1	0	0	0	0	0	0	0	0	0	0	0	0	0
Andujar, Joaquin, Hou-StL†	.000	21	23	0	0	0	0	0	0	0	0	2	0	0	0
Armstrong, Michael, S.D.	.000	10	0	0	0	0	0	0	0	0	0	0	0	0	0
Ashby, Alan, Hou.†	.271	83	255	20	69	94	13	0	4	33	4	3	2	0	2
Asselstine, Brian, Atl.°	.256	56	86	8	22	33	5	0	2	10	3	0	1	0	0
Aviles, Ramon, Phila.	.214	38	28	2	6	7	1	0	0	3	0	3	0	0	0
Backman, Walter, N.Y.†	.278	26	36	5	10	12	2	0	0	0	0	2	0	1	0
Bahnsen, Stanley, Mtl	.111	25	9	0	1	1	0	0	0	0	0	0	0	0	0
Bailor, Robert, N.Y.	.284	51	81	11	23	28	3	1	0	8	2	4	1	2	0
Bair, C. Douglas, Cin.-St.L.	.167	35	6	1	1	4	0	0	1	3	0	0	0	0	0
Baker, Johnnie, L.A.	.320	103	400	48	128	178	17	3	9	49	8	3	5	10	7
Barranca, German, Cin.°	.333	9	6	2	2	2	0	0	0	1	0	0	0	0	0
Bass, Randy, S.D.°	.210	69	176	13	37	55	4	1	4	20	2	3	1	0	1
Bedrosian, Stephen, Atl.	.000	15	2	0	0	0	0	0	0	0	0	0	0	0	0
Bench, Johnny, Cin.	.309	52	178	14	55	87	8	0	8	25	6	1	0	0	2
Benedict, Bruce, Atl.	.264	90	295	26	78	107	12	1	5	35	4	5	3	1	1
Berenyi, Bruce, Cin.	.190	21	42	4	8	11	3	0	0	1	0	3	1	0	0
Bergman, David, Hou.-S.F.°	.252	69	151	17	38	59	9	0	4	14	1	2	1	2	0
Berra, Dale, Pitt.	.241	81	232	21	56	74	12	0	2	27	2	2	0	11	1
Bevacqua, Kurt, Pitt.	.259	29	27	2	7	11	1	0	1	4	0	1	2	0	0
Bibby, James, Pitt.	.143	14	28	4	4	9	2	0	1	3	1	4	0	0	0
Biittner, Larry, Cin.°	.213	42	61	1	13	17	4	0	0	8	0	0	1	0	0
Bird, J. Douglas, Chi.	.100	12	20	0	2	2	0	0	0	0	0	2	0	0	0
Blackwell, Timothy, Chi.†	.234	58	158	21	37	54	10	2	1	11	1	1	0	2	1
Blue, Vida, S.F.°	.200	18	35	4	7	9	2	0	0	1	0	5	0	0	0
Boggs, Thomas, Atl.	.152	25	46	2	7	8	1	0	0	3	0	1	0	0	0
Boitano, Danny, N.Y.	.000	16	0	0	0	0	0	0	0	0	0	0	0	0	0
Bonds, Bobby, Chi.	.215	45	163	26	35	62	7	1	6	19	1	1	0	5	6
Bonilla, Juan, S.D.	.290	99	369	30	107	127	13	2	1	25	3	9	2	4	9
Boone, Daniel, S.D.°	.500	37	4	0	2	2	0	0	0	0	0	1	0	0	0
Boone, Robert, Phila.	.211	76	227	19	48	67	7	0	4	24	2	2	2	2	2
Bowa, Lawrence, Phila.†	.283	103	360	34	102	122	14	3	0	31	4	4	1	16	7
Boyland, Dorian, Pitt.°	.000	11	8	0	0	0	0	0	0	0	0	0	0	0	0
Bradford, Larry, Atl.	1.000	25	1	1	1	1	0	0	0	0	0	0	0	0	0
Bradley, Mark, N.Y.	.167	9	6	2	1	2	1	0	0	0	0	0	0	0	0
Braun, Stephen, St.L.°	.196	44	46	9	9	13	2	1	0	2	0	1	0	1	0
Breining, Fred, S.F.	.000	45	11	0	0	0	0	0	0	0	0	1	0	0	0
Brenly, Robert, S.F.	.333	19	45	5	15	22	2	1	1	4	0	0	0	0	1
Briggs, Dan, Mtl.°	.091	9	11	0	1	1	0	0	0	0	0	0	0	0	1
Brooks, Hubert, N.Y.	.307	98	358	34	110	147	21	2	4	38	2	1	6	9	5
Brown, Scott, Cin.	.000	10	1	0	0	0	0	0	0	0	0	0	0	0	0
Brummer, Glenn, St.L.	.200	21	30	2	6	7	1	0	0	2	1	1	1	0	0
Brusstar, Warren, Phila.	.000	14	0	0	0	0	0	0	0	0	0	0	0	0	0
Buckner, William, Chi.°	.311	106	421	45	131	202	35	3	10	75	11	0	5	5	2
Burris, B. Ray, Mtl.	.189	22	37	4	7	7	0	0	0	2	1	7	1	0	0
Butler, Brett, Atl.°	.254	40	126	17	32	40	2	3	0	4	1	0	0	9	1
Bystrom, Martin, Phila.	.118	9	17	0	2	2	0	0	0	0	0	1	0	0	1
Cabell, Enos, S.F.	.255	96	396	41	101	129	20	1	2	36	9	4	2	6	7
Camacho, Ernie, Pitt.	.000	7	4	0	0	0	0	0	0	0	0	1	0	0	0

Player and Club	Pct.	G.	AB.	R.	H.	TB.	2B.	3B.	HR.	RBI.	GW.	SH.	SF.	SB.	CS.
Camp, Rick, Atl.	.000	48	12	1	0	0	0	0	0	0	0	1	0	0	0
Candelaria, John, Pitt.°	.231	6	13	0	3	3	0	0	0	3	0	2	1	0	0
Capilla, Douglas, Chi.°	.000	42	3	0	0	0	0	0	0	0	0	0	0	0	0
Carlton, Steven, Phila.°	.134	24	67	5	9	15	2	2	0	4	1	2	0	0	0
Carter, Gary, Mtl.	.251	100	374	48	94	166	20	2	16	68	7	3	6	1	5
Castillo, Robert, L.A.	.444	34	9	1	4	6	2	0	0	1	0	0	0	0	0
Caudill, William, Chi.	.143	30	14	0	2	2	0	0	0	1	0	1	0	0	0
Cedeno, Cesar, Hou.	.271	82	306	42	83	117	19	0	5	34	5	2	5	12	7
Cey, Ronald, L.A.	.288	85	312	42	90	148	15	2	13	50	9	1	3	0	2
Chambliss, C. Chris., Atl.°	.272	107	404	44	110	163	25	2	8	51	9	2	3	4	1
Christenson, Larry, Phila.	.100	20	30	2	3	3	0	0	0	1	1	3	1	0	0
Clark, Jack, S.F.	.268	99	385	60	103	177	19	2	17	53	11	0	6	1	1
Collins, David, Cin.†	.272	95	360	63	98	137	18	6	3	23	2	3	2	26	10
Combe, Geoffrey, Cin.	.000	14	0	0	0	0	0	0	0	0	0	0	0	0	0
Concepcion, David, Cin.	.306	106	421	57	129	172	28	0	5	67	14	2	7	4	5
Cromartie, Warren, Mtl.°	.304	99	358	41	109	150	19	2	6	42	8	0	3	2	3
Cruz, Hector, Chi.	.229	53	109	15	25	51	5	0	7	15	1	0	1	2	2
Cruz, Jose, Hou.°	.267	107	409	53	109	174	16	5	13	55	12	0	7	5	7
Cruz, Victor, Pitt.	.000	22	4	0	0	0	0	0	0	0	0	0	1	0	0
Cubbage, Michael, N.Y.°	.213	67	80	9	17	26	2	2	1	4	1	0	1	0	0
Curtis, John, S.D.°	.077	28	13	1	1	1	0	0	0	2	0	1	2	0	0
Davis, Charles, S.F.†	.133	8	15	1	2	2	0	0	0	0	0	0	0	2	0
Davis, Jody, Chi.	.256	56	180	14	46	65	5	1	4	21	2	3	2	0	1
Davis, Mark, Phila.°	.091	9	11	2	1	1	0	0	0	1	0	1	0	0	0
Davis, Richard, Phila.	.333	45	96	12	32	46	6	1	2	19	1	0	1	1	2
Dawson, Andre, Mtl.	.302	103	394	71	119	218	21	3	24	64	9	0	5	26	4
DeJesus, Ivan, Chi.	.194	106	403	49	78	94	8	4	0	13	1	10	1	21	9
DeLeon, Luis, St.L.	.000	10	1	0	0	0	0	0	0	0	0	0	0	0	0
Dernier, Robert, Phila.	.750	10	4	0	3	3	0	0	0	0	0	0	0	2	1
Dillard, Stephen, Chi.	.218	53	119	18	26	41	7	1	2	11	2	0	0	0	0
Driessen, Daniel, Cin.°	.236	82	233	35	55	90	14	0	7	33	5	2	3	2	4
Durham, Leon, Chi.°	.290	87	328	42	95	151	14	6	10	35	2	0	0	25	11
Easler, Michael, Pitt.°	.286	95	339	43	97	146	18	5	7	42	6	0	6	4	7
Eastwick, Rawlins, Chi.	.000	30	2	0	0	0	0	0	0	0	0	0	0	0	0
Edelen, B. Joe, St.L.-Cin.	.200	18	5	0	1	1	0	0	0	0	0	0	0	0	0
Edwards, David, S.D.	.214	58	112	13	24	36	4	1	2	13	2	1	1	3	1
Eichelberger, Juan, S.D.	.087	25	46	1	4	4	0	0	0	0	0	6	0	0	0
Engle, Richard, Mtl.°	.000	1	0	0	0	0	0	0	0	0	0	0	0	0	0
Espinosa, Arnulfo, Phila.	.200	14	20	0	4	4	0	0	0	2	0	3	0	0	0
Evans, Barry, S.D.	.323	54	93	11	30	35	5	0	0	7	1	1	3	2	2
Evans, Darrell, S.F.°	.258	102	357	51	92	149	13	4	12	48	4	3	3	2	3
Falcone, Peter, N.Y.°	.182	35	22	1	4	7	0	0	1	5	1	0	0	0	0
Ferguson, Joseph, L.A.	.143	17	14	2	2	3	1	0	0	1	1	0	0	0	0
Fiala, Neil, St.L.-Cin.°	.200	5	5	1	1	1	0	0	0	1	0	0	0	0	0
Fireovid, Stephen, S.D.†	.143	5	7	0	1	1	0	0	0	0	0	0	0	0	0
Flannery, Timothy, S.D.°	.254	37	67	4	17	23	4	1	0	6	2	1	2	1	0
Fletcher, Scott, Chi.	.217	19	46	6	10	14	4	0	0	1	0	0	0	0	0
Flynn, R. Douglas, N.Y.	.222	105	325	24	72	95	12	4	1	20	2	7	0	1	2
Foli, Timothy, Pitt.	.247	86	316	32	78	94	12	2	0	20	1	14	3	7	7
Foote, Barry, Chi.	.000	9	22	0	0	0	0	0	0	0	1	0	0	1	0
Forsch, Robert, St.L.	.122	20	41	0	5	6	1	0	0	3	1	6	0	0	0
Forster, Terry, L.A.°	.000	21	2	0	0	0	0	0	0	0	0	0	0	0	0
Foster, George, Cin.	.295	108	414	64	122	215	23	2	22	90	13	0	4	4	0
Francona, Terry, Mtl.°	.274	34	95	11	26	31	0	1	1	8	0	3	0	1	0
Frias, Jesus, L.A.	.250	25	36	6	9	10	1	0	0	3	0	0	1	0	0
Fryman, Woodrow, Mtl.	.667	35	3	0	2	2	0	0	0	0	0	0	0	0	0
Garber, H. Eugene, Atl.	.000	35	5	0	0	0	0	0	0	0	0	0	0	0	0
Garcia, Alfonso, Hou.	.272	48	136	9	37	45	6	1	0	15	0	2	1	2	2
Gardenhire, Ronald, N.Y.	.271	27	48	2	13	14	1	0	0	3	0	0	0	2	2
Garner, Philip, Pitt.-Hou.	.248	87	294	35	73	91	9	3	1	26	4	6	4	10	8
Garvey, Steven, L.A.	.283	110	431	63	122	177	23	1	10	64	6	1	3	3	5
Gates, Michael, Mtl.°	.500	1	2	1	1	3	0	1	0	1	0	0	0	0	0
Geisel, J. David, Chi.°	.000	11	3	0	0	0	0	0	0	0	0	0	0	0	0
Giles, Brian, N.Y.	.000	9	7	0	0	0	0	0	0	0	0	0	1	0	0
Goltz, David, L.A.	.059	26	17	0	1	1	0	0	0	0	0	2	0	0	0
Gomez, Luis, Atl.	.200	35	35	4	7	7	0	0	0	1	0	0	0	0	1
Gonzalez, Julio, St.L.	.318	20	22	2	7	11	1	0	1	3	1	1	0	0	0
Gorman, Thomas, Mtl.°	.000	9	0	0	0	0	0	0	0	0	0	0	0	0	0
Green, David, St.L.	.147	21	34	6	5	6	1	0	0	2	0	0	0	0	1
Griffey, G. Kenneth, Cin.°	.311	101	396	65	123	162	21	6	2	34	3	2	4	12	4
Griffin, Michael, Chi.	.154	16	13	0	2	2	0	0	0	0	0	2	0	0	0
Griffin, Thomas, S.F.	.195	22	41	1	8	12	1	0	1	5	1	6	1	0	0
Gross, Gregory, Phila.°	.225	83	102	14	23	31	6	1	0	7	0	0	2	2	2
Grote, Gerald, L.A.	.000	2	2	0	0	0	0	0	0	0	0	0	0	0	0
Guerrero, Pedro, L.A.	.300	98	347	46	104	161	17	2	12	48	4	3	1	5	9
Gullickson, William, Mtl.	.152	22	46	1	7	8	1	0	0	1	0	4	0	0	0
Gwosdz, Douglas, S.D.	.167	16	24	1	4	6	2	0	0	3	0	1	2	0	0
Hall, Albert, Atl.†	.000	6	2	1	0	0	0	0	0	0	0	0	0	0	0
Hall, Melvin, Chi.°	.091	10	11	1	1	4	0	0	1	2	0	0	0	0	0
Hanna, Preston, Atl.	.250	20	4	0	1	1	0	0	0	0	0	0	0	0	0

Player and Club	Pct.	G.	AB.	R.	H.	TB.	2B.	3B.	HR.	RBI.	GW.	SH.	SF.	SB.	CS.
Hargesheimer, Alan, S.F.	.200	6	5	0	1	1	0	0	0	1	0	1	0	0	0
Harper, Terry, Atl.	.260	40	73	9	19	26	1	0	2	8	1	0	1	5	1
Harris, Greg, N.Y.†	.182	17	22	1	4	5	1	0	0	0	0	0	0	0	0
Hausman, Thomas, N.Y.	.000	20	2	0	0	0	0	0	0	0	0	0	0	0	0
Hayes, William, Chi.	.000	1	0	0	0	0	0	0	0	0	0	0	0	0	0
Heep, Daniel, Hou.°	.250	33	96	6	24	27	3	0	0	11	2	0	0	0	0
Henderson, Stephen, Chi.	.293	82	287	32	84	118	9	5	5	35	3	2	4	5	7
Hendrick, George, St.L.	.284	101	394	67	112	191	19	3	18	61	10	0	2	4	2
Hernandez, Guillermo, Chi.°	.000	13	0	0	0	0	0	0	0	0	0	0	0	0	0
Hernandez, Keith, St.L.°	.306	103	376	65	115	174	27	4	8	48	10	0	5	12	5
Herndon, Larry, S.F.	.288	96	364	48	105	151	15	8	5	41	4	3	3	15	6
Herr, Thomas, St.L.†	.268	103	411	50	110	142	14	9	0	46	4	6	5	23	7
Hodges, Ronald, N.Y.°	.302	35	43	5	13	18	2	0	1	6	0	0	1	0	0
Holland, Alfred, S.F.	.063	47	16	1	1	1	0	0	0	1	0	5	0	1	0
Hooton, Burt, L.A.	.190	23	42	3	8	11	3	0	0	3	0	7	0	0	0
Horner, J. Robert, Atl.	.277	79	300	42	83	138	10	0	15	42	6	0	3	2	3
Hostetler, David, Mtl	.500	5	6	1	3	6	0	0	1	1	0	0	0	0	0
Householder, Paul, Cin†	.275	23	69	12	19	29	4	0	2	9	1	0	0	3	1
Howard, Michael, N.Y.†	.167	14	24	4	4	5	1	0	0	3	1	0	1	2	0
Howe, Arthur, Hou.	.296	103	361	43	107	146	22	4	3	36	3	1	3	1	3
Howe, Steve, L.A.°	.000	41	1	0	0	0	0	0	0	0	0	0	0	0	0
Howell, Jay, Chi	.000	10	2	0	0	0	0	0	0	0	0	2	0	0	0
Hrabosky, Alan, Atl	.000	24	1	0	0	0	0	0	0	0	0	0	0	0	0
Hubbard, Glenn, Atl.	.235	99	361	39	85	126	13	5	6	33	3	3	1	4	2
Hume, Thomas, Cin	.000	51	4	0	0	0	0	0	0	0	0	0	0	0	0
Hutton, Thomas, Mtl°	.103	31	29	1	3	3	0	0	0	2	0	0	0	0	0
Iorg, Dane, St.L.°	.327	75	217	23	71	92	11	2	2	39	5	0	3	2	0
Ivie, Michael, S.F.-Hou.	.254	26	59	3	15	20	5	0	0	9	2	0	2	0	1
Jackson, Grant, Pitt.-Mtl†	.000	45	2	0	0	0	0	0	0	0	0	0	0	0	0
Jacoby, Brook, Atl.	.200	11	10	0	2	2	0	0	0	1	0	0	0	0	0
Johnson, Anthony, Mtl	.000	2	1	0	0	0	0	0	0	0	0	0	0	0	0
Johnson, Wallace, Mtl†	.222	11	9	1	2	4	0	1	0	3	1	0	0	1	1
Johnstone, John, L.A.°	.205	61	83	8	17	29	3	0	3	6	1	0	0	0	1
Jones, Odell, Pitt	.200	13	10	0	2	2	0	0	0	0	0	3	0	0	0
Jones, Randall, N.Y.	.118	13	17	0	2	2	0	0	0	0	0	1	0	0	0
Jones, Ruppert, S.D.°	.249	105	397	53	99	147	34	1	4	39	5	4	7	7	9
Jorgensen, Michael, N.Y.°	.205	86	122	8	25	43	5	2	3	15	1	2	3	4	0
Kaat, James, St.L.°	.375	41	8	2	3	4	1	0	0	2	0	0	0	0	0
Kennedy, Junior, Cin	.250	27	44	5	11	12	1	0	0	5	0	2	0	0	0
Kennedy, Terrence, S.D.°	.301	101	382	32	115	147	24	1	2	41	6	4	2	0	2
Kingman, David, N.Y.	.221	100	353	40	78	161	11	3	22	59	6	1	2	6	0
Knepper, Robert, Hou°	.149	22	47	3	7	12	2	0	1	3	0	5	0	0	0
Knicely, Alan, Hou.	.571	3	7	2	4	10	0	0	2	2	0	0	0	0	0
Knight, C. Ray, Cin	.259	106	386	43	100	143	23	1	6	34	7	3	3	2	4
Kravec, Kenneth, Chi°	.000	25	15	1	0	0	0	0	0	0	0	4	0	0	0
Krug, Gary, Chi°	.400	7	5	0	2	2	0	0	0	0	0	0	0	0	0
Krukow, Michael, Chi.	.180	25	50	5	9	11	2	0	0	3	0	6	0	0	0
Kuhaulua, Fred, S.D.°	.111	5	9	0	1	1	0	0	0	1	0	1	0	0	0
LaCorte, Frank, Hou	.333	37	3	0	1	1	0	0	0	0	0	0	0	0	0
LaCoss, Michael, Cin	.000	20	19	0	0	0	0	0	0	0	0	7	0	0	0
Lacy, Leondaus, Pitt.	.268	78	213	31	57	82	11	4	2	10	2	1	0	24	3
Landestoy, Rafael, Hou-Cin†	.153	47	85	8	13	16	1	1	0	5	1	4	0	5	1
Landreaux, Kenneth, L.A.°	.251	99	390	48	98	143	16	4	7	41	4	3	1	18	4
Landrum, Terry, St.L.	.261	81	119	13	31	44	5	4	0	10	1	5	2	4	2
LaPoint, David, St.L.°	.000	3	5	0	0	0	0	0	0	0	0	0	0	0	0
Larson, Daniel, Phila	.111	5	9	2	1	1	0	0	0	0	0	1	0	0	0
Lavelle, Gary, S.F.°	.273	34	11	1	3	4	1	0	0	1	0	2	0	0	1
Law, Vance, Pitt	.134	30	67	1	9	11	0	1	0	3	1	1	1	1	1
Lea, Charles, Mtl	.133	16	15	1	2	2	0	0	0	0	0	4	0	0	0
Leach, Terry, N.Y.	.000	21	1	1	0	0	0	0	0	0	0	0	0	0	0
Leary, Timothy, N.Y.	.000	1	1	0	0	0	0	0	0	0	0	0	0	0	0
Lee, Mark, Pitt	.500	12	2	0	1	1	0	0	0	0	0	0	0	0	0
Lee, William, Mtl°	.364	31	22	1	8	11	0	0	1	2	0	0	0	0	0
Lefebvre, Joseph, S.D.°	.256	86	246	31	63	108	13	4	8	31	0	2	1	6	4
Leibrandt, Charles, Cin	.000	7	8	0	0	0	0	0	0	0	0	0	0	0	0
LeMaster, Johnnie, S.F.	.253	104	324	27	82	93	9	1	0	28	2	4	1	3	7
Leonard, Jeffrey, Hou-S.F.	.290	44	145	21	42	74	12	4	4	29	1	1	1	5	2
Lezcano, Carlos, Chi	.071	7	14	1	1	1	0	0	0	2	0	0	0	0	0
Lezcano, Sixto, St.L.	.266	72	214	26	57	84	8	2	5	28	3	0	4	0	1
Linares, Rufino, Atl	.265	78	253	27	67	95	9	2	5	25	3	2	1	8	4
Littell, Mark, St.L.°	.250	28	8	0	2	2	0	0	0	2	0	0	0	0	0
Littlefield, John, S.D.	.000	42	1	0	0	0	0	0	0	0	0	1	0	0	0
Lollar, W. Timothy, S.D.°	.167	24	18	2	3	6	0	0	1	1	0	0	0	0	0
Long, Robert, Pitt	.000	5	4	1	0	0	0	0	0	0	0	1	0	0	0
Lopes, David, L.A.°	.206	58	214	35	44	61	2	0	5	17	2	4	0	20	2
Loucks, Scott, Hou	.571	10	7	2	4	4	0	0	0	0	0	0	0	1	0
Lucas, Gary, S.D.°	.100	57	10	1	1	1	0	0	0	1	0	2	0	0	0
Lum, Michael, Atl-Chi°	.217	51	69	6	15	22	1	0	2	7	0	0	1	0	0
Lyle, Albert, Phila°	.400	48	5	2	2	2	0	0	0	0	0	1	0	1	0
Lynch, Edward, N.Y.	.143	17	21	0	3	4	1	0	0	1	0	2	1	0	0

Player and Club	Pct.	G.	AB.	R.	H.	TB.	2B.	3B.	HR.	RBI.	GW.	SH.	SF.	SB.	CS.
Maddox, Garry, Phila	.263	94	323	37	85	109	7	1	5	40	5	1	8	9	4
Madlock, Bill, Pitt	.341	82	279	35	95	138	23	1	6	45	5	0	4	18	6
Mahler, Richard, Atl	.148	34	27	0	4	5	1	0	0	2	0	2	0	0	1
Maldonado, Candido, L.A.	.083	11	12	0	1	1	0	0	0	0	0	0	0	0	0
Manuel, Jerry, Mtl	.200	27	55	10	11	25	5	0	3	10	1	0	2	0	0
Marshall, Michael A., L.A.	.200	14	25	2	5	8	3	0	0	1	0	0	0	0	0
Marshall, Michael G., N.Y.	.000	20	0	0	0	0	0	0	0	0	0	0	0	0	0
Martin, Jerry, S.F.	.241	72	241	23	58	81	5	3	4	25	3	1	1	6	2
Martin, John, St.L.†	.212	18	33	2	7	11	2	1	0	8	1	7	0	0	0
Martinez, Silvio, St.L	.200	18	35	1	7	9	2	0	0	2	0	1	0	0	0
Martz, Randy, Chi°	.214	34	28	0	6	6	0	0	0	2	1	2	0	0	0
Matthews, Gary, Phila	.301	101	359	62	108	162	21	3	9	67	9	1	6	15	2
Matula, Richard, Atl	.000	5	1	0	0	0	0	0	0	0	0	0	0	0	0
Matuszek, Leonard, Phila°	.273	13	11	1	3	4	1	0	0	1	0	0	0	0	1
May, Milton, S.F.°	.310	97	316	20	98	121	17	0	2	33	8	3	1	1	4
Mazzilli, Lee, N.Y.†	.228	95	324	36	74	116	14	5	6	34	4	0	4	17	7
McBride, Arnold, Phila°	.271	58	221	26	60	85	17	1	2	21	2	1	2	5	0
McCormick, Donald, Phila	.250	3	4	0	1	1	0	0	0	0	0	0	0	0	0
McGlothen, Lynn, Chi°	.083	20	12	1	1	2	1	0	0	0	0	0	0	0	0
McGraw, Frank, Phila	.000	34	1	0	0	0	0	0	0	0	0	1	0	0	0
McWilliams, Larry, Atl°	.100	6	10	0	1	1	0	0	0	0	0	1	0	0	0
Mejias, Samuel, Cin	.286	66	49	6	14	16	2	0	0	7	2	3	2	1	0
Miller, Dyar, N.Y.	.333	23	3	0	1	1	0	0	0	0	0	0	0	0	0
Miller, Edward, Atl†	.231	50	134	29	31	36	3	1	0	7	2	2	0	23	5
Mills, J. Bradley, Mtl°	.238	17	21	3	5	6	1	0	0	1	0	0	0	0	0
Milner, Eddie, Cin°	.200	8	5	0	1	2	1	0	0	1	0	0	0	0	0
Milner, John, Pitt-Mtl°	.237	65	135	12	32	53	6	0	5	18	2	1	1	0	1
Minton, Gregory, S.F.†	.000	55	12	1	0	0	0	0	0	0	0	1	0	0	0
Mitchell, Robert, L.A.°	.125	10	8	0	1	1	0	0	0	0	0	0	0	0	0
Moffitt, Randall, S.F.	.000	10	0	0	0	0	0	0	0	0	0	0	0	0	0
Monday, Robert, L.A.°	.315	66	130	24	41	79	1	2	11	25	6	0	1	1	2
Montanez, Glrmo., Mtl-Pitt°	.210	55	100	8	21	26	0	1	1	6	4	0	0	0	0
Montefusco, John, Atl	.067	26	15	1	1	2	1	0	0	0	0	0	0	0	0
Morales, Julio, Chi	.286	84	245	27	70	83	6	2	1	25	3	1	3	1	1
Moreland, B. Keith, Phila	.255	61	196	16	50	75	7	0	6	37	6	0	3	1	2
Moreno, Jose, S.D.†	.229	34	48	5	11	13	2	0	0	6	0	1	0	4	1
Moreno, Omar, Pitt°	.276	103	434	62	120	157	18	8	1	35	6	1	4	39	14
Morgan, Joe, S.F.°	.240	90	308	47	74	116	16	1	8	31	3	1	3	14	5
Moskau, Paul, Cin	.000	27	6	0	0	0	0	0	0	0	0	2	0	0	0
Mura, Stephen, S.D.	.136	24	44	2	6	7	1	0	0	4	0	2	0	0	0
Murphy, Dale, Atl	.247	104	369	43	91	144	12	1	13	50	3	1	2	14	5
Nahorodny, William, Atl	.231	14	13	0	3	4	1	0	0	2	1	0	0	0	0
Nicosia, Steven, Pitt	.231	54	169	21	39	57	10	1	2	18	2	2	0	3	1
Niedenfuer, Thomas, L.A.	.000	17	0	0	0	0	0	0	0	0	0	0	0	0	0
Niekro, Joseph, Hou	.176	24	51	1	9	10	1	0	0	6	0	11	0	0	0
Niekro, Philip, Atl°	.077	22	52	1	4	4	0	0	0	1	0	3	0	0	0
Nolan, Joseph, Cin°	.309	81	236	25	73	96	18	1	1	26	4	0	3	1	2
Noles, Dickie, Phila	.105	13	19	1	2	2	0	0	0	1	0	2	0	0	0
North, William, S.F.†	.221	46	131	22	29	39	7	0	1	12	2	3	0	26	8
O'Berry, P. Michael, Cin	.180	55	111	6	20	28	3	1	1	5	0	3	0	0	0
Oberkfell, Kenneth, St.L.°	.293	102	376	43	110	140	12	6	2	45	4	3	4	13	5
Oester, Ronald, Cin†	.271	105	354	45	96	141	16	7	5	42	4	5	7	2	5
Office, Rowland, Mtl°	.175	26	40	4	7	7	0	0	0	0	0	0	0	0	0
Orosco, Jesse, N.Y.	.000	8	2	0	0	0	0	0	0	0	0	0	0	0	0
Otten, James, St.L	.000	24	2	0	0	0	0	0	0	0	0	1	0	0	0
Owen, Lawrence, Atl	.000	13	16	0	0	0	0	0	0	0	0	0	0	0	0
Parker, David, Pitt°	.258	67	240	29	62	109	14	3	9	48	3	0	3	6	2
Parrish, Larry, Mtl	.244	97	349	41	85	134	19	3	8	44	4	5	3	0	0
Pastore, Frank, Cin	.114	22	44	1	5	6	1	0	0	1	0	6	0	0	0
Pate, Robert, Mtl	.333	8	6	0	2	2	0	0	0	0	0	0	0	0	0
Pena, Adalberto, Hou	.500	4	2	0	1	1	0	0	0	0	0	1	0	0	0
Pena, Alejandro, L.A.	.000	14	6	0	0	0	0	0	0	0	0	0	0	0	0
Pena, Antonio, Pitt	.300	66	210	16	63	80	9	1	2	17	4	2	2	1	2
Perconte, John, L.A.°	.222	8	9	2	2	4	0	1	0	1	1	0	0	1	1
Perez, Pascual, Pitt	.136	18	22	3	3	5	0	1	0	0	0	2	0	0	0
Perkins, Broderick, S.D.°	.280	92	254	27	71	101	18	3	2	40	5	4	3	0	4
Perry, Gaylord, Atl	.250	24	48	5	12	17	2	0	1	7	0	5	0	0	0
Pettini, Joseph, S.F.	.069	35	29	3	2	3	1	0	0	2	0	1	0	1	0
Phillips, Michael, S.D.-Mtl°	.214	48	84	6	18	22	2	1	0	4	0	1	1	1	1
Pittman, Joseph, Hou	.281	52	135	11	38	46	4	2	0	7	2	2	1	4	4
Pladson, Gordon, Hou	.000	2	0	0	0	0	0	0	0	0	0	0	0	0	0
Pocoroba, Biff, Atl°	.180	57	122	4	22	26	4	0	0	8	2	4	0	0	0
Porter, Darrell, St.L.°	.224	61	174	22	39	71	10	2	6	31	4	0	3	1	2
Porter, Robert, Atl°	.286	17	14	2	4	5	1	0	0	4	0	0	0	0	0
Power, Ted, L.A.	.000	5	3	0	0	0	0	0	0	0	0	0	0	0	0
Price, Joseph, Cin	.000	41	3	0	0	0	0	0	0	0	0	0	0	0	0
Proly, Michael, Phila	.000	35	7	0	0	0	0	0	0	0	0	0	0	0	0
Puhl, Terry, Hou°	.251	96	350	43	88	124	19	4	3	28	8	4	5	22	4
Pujols, Luis, Hou	.239	40	117	5	28	36	3	1	1	14	2	0	1	1	0

Player and Club	Pct.	G.	AB.	R.	H.	TB.	2B.	3B.	HR.	RBI.	GW.	SH.	SF.	SB.	CS.
Puleo, Charles, N.Y.	.000	4	2	0	0	0	0	0	0	0	0	0	0	0	0
Raines, Timothy, Mtl†	.304	88	313	61	95	137	13	7	5	37	3	0	3	71	11
Ramirez, Mario, S.D.	.077	13	13	1	1	1	0	0	0	1	0	0	0	0	0
Ramirez, Rafael, Atl	.218	95	307	30	67	93	16	2	2	20	1	9	1	7	3
Ramos, Roberto, Mtl	.195	26	41	4	8	12	1	0	1	3	1	0	0	0	0
Ramsey, Michael, St.L.†	.258	47	124	19	32	35	3	0	0	9	4	1	0	4	0
Ransom, Jeffrey, S.F.	.267	5	15	2	4	5	1	0	0	0	0	0	0	0	0
Ratzer, Steven, Mtl.	.000	12	2	0	0	0	0	0	0	0	0	0	0	0	0
Ray, John, Pitt. †	.245	31	102	10	25	36	11	0	0	6	0	0	1	0	0
Reardon, Jeffrey, N.Y.-Mtl.	.000	43	5	0	0	0	0	0	0	0	0	0	2	0	0
Reed, Jerry, Phil.	.000	4	0	0	0	0	0	0	0	0	0	0	0	0	0
Reed, Ronald, Phil.	.500	39	6	1	3	4	1	0	0	1	0	0	0	0	0
Reitz, Kenneth, Chi.	.215	82	260	10	56	73	9	1	2	28	4	2	6	0	0
Reuschel, Ricky, Chi.	.080	16	25	1	2	2	0	0	0	1	0	4	0	0	0
Reuss, Jerry, L.A.°	.196	22	51	3	10	10	0	0	0	3	0	7	0	0	0
Reynolds, G. Craig, Hou.°	.260	87	323	43	84	130	10	12	4	31	4	18	1	3	3
Rhoden, Richard, Pitt.	.188	21	48	4	9	11	2	0	0	0	0	3	0	0	0
Richards, Eugene, S.D.°	.288	104	393	47	113	160	14	12	3	42	4	5	1	20	8
Rincon, Andrew, St.L.	.231	5	13	1	3	4	1	0	0	5	0	2	0	0	0
Ripley, Allen, S.F.	.133	19	30	0	4	4	0	0	0	2	0	2	0	0	0
Roberts, David, N.Y.°	.250	7	4	1	1	1	0	0	0	0	0	0	0	0	0
Roberts, David, Hou.	.241	27	54	4	13	19	3	0	1	5	0	0	2	1	0
Robinson, Don, Pitt.	.250	17	12	1	3	3	0	0	0	1	0	0	0	0	0
Robinson, William, Pitt.	.216	39	88	8	19	28	3	0	2	8	0	1	0	1	0
Roenicke, Ronald, L.A.†	.234	22	47	6	11	11	0	0	0	0	0	1	0	1	1
Rogers, Stephen, Mtl.	.145	23	55	5	8	9	1	0	0	3	1	4	0	0	0
Romo, Enrique, Pitt.	.000	33	4	0	0	0	0	0	0	0	0	2	0	0	0
Roof, Eugene, St.L.†	.300	23	60	11	18	24	6	0	0	3	0	0	1	5	1
Rooney, Patrick, Mtl.	.000	4	5	0	0	0	0	0	0	0	0	0	0	0	0
Rose, Peter, Phil.†	.325	107	431	73	140	168	18	5	0	33	5	1	3	4	4
Rowland, Michael, S.F.	1.000	9	1	0	1	1	0	0	0	1	0	0	0	0	0
Royster, Jeron, Atl.	.204	64	93	13	19	25	4	1	0	9	1	4	1	7	5
Ruhle, Vernon, Hou.	.250	20	24	1	6	7	1	0	0	3	1	4	0	0	0
Runge, Paul, Atl.	.259	10	27	2	7	8	1	0	0	2	0	0	0	0	0
Russell, William, L.A.	.233	82	262	20	61	74	9	2	0	22	3	5	3	2	1
Ruthven, Richard, Phil.	.140	23	50	2	7	10	3	0	0	5	1	5	0	0	0
Ryan, L. Nolan, Hou.	.216	21	51	3	11	12	1	0	0	1	0	4	0	0	0
Sadek, Michael, S.F.	.167	19	36	5	6	9	3	0	0	3	1	2	0	0	0
Salazar, Luis, S.D.	.303	109	400	37	121	161	19	6	3	38	3	5	2	11	8
Sambito, Joseph, Hou.°	.000	49	5	0	0	0	0	0	0	0	0	0	0	0	0
Sanchez, Orlando, St.L.°	.286	27	49	5	14	18	2	1	0	6	2	0	1	1	0
Sandberg, Ryne, Phil.	.167	13	6	2	1	1	0	0	0	0	0	0	0	0	0
Sanderson, Scott, Mtl.	.114	22	35	2	4	6	2	0	0	6	2	5	0	0	0
Sax, Stephen, L.A.	.277	31	119	15	33	41	2	0	2	9	1	1	0	5	7
Schmidt, Michael, Phil.	.316	102	354	78	112	228	19	2	31	91	10	0	3	12	4
Scioscia, Michael, L.A.°	.276	93	290	27	80	96	10	0	2	29	5	4	4	0	2
Scott, Michael, N.Y.	.073	23	41	4	3	3	0	0	0	1	0	1	0	0	0
Scott, Rodney, Mtl.†	.205	95	336	43	69	84	9	3	0	26	3	13	2	30	7
Scott, Tony, St.L.-Hou.†	.264	100	401	49	106	144	18	4	4	39	3	5	0	18	10
Scurry, Rodney, Pitt.°	.158	27	19	1	3	3	0	0	0	0	0	0	0	0	0
Searage, Raymond, N.Y.°	1.000	26	1	0	1	1	0	0	0	0	0	0	0	0	0
Seaver, G. Thomas, Cin.	.200	23	55	3	11	15	1	0	1	6	0	4	1	0	0
Shirley, Robert, St.L.	.136	28	22	0	3	3	0	0	0	1	0	1	0	0	0
Show, Eric, S.D.	.000	15	0	0	0	0	0	0	0	0	0	0	0	0	0
Sinatro, Matthew, Atl.	.281	12	32	4	9	12	1	1	0	4	2	0	0	1	0
Smith, Billy, Hou.	.000	10	2	0	0	0	0	0	0	0	0	0	0	0	0
Smith, Billy, S.F.†	.180	36	61	6	11	14	0	0	1	5	0	0	1	0	0
Smith, Bryn, Mtl.	.000	7	1	0	0	0	0	0	0	0	0	2	0	0	0
Smith, C. Reginald, L.A.†	.200	41	35	5	7	11	1	0	1	8	3	0	2	0	0
Smith, Christopher, Mtl.†	.000	7	7	0	0	0	0	0	0	0	0	0	0	0	0
Smith, David, Hou.	.250	42	8	0	2	2	0	0	0	0	0	0	0	0	0
Smith, Kenneth, Atl.°	.333	5	3	0	1	2	1	0	0	0	0	0	0	0	0
Smith, Lee, Chi.	.000	40	9	0	0	0	0	0	0	0	0	1	0	0	0
Smith, Lonnie, Phil.	.324	62	176	40	57	83	14	3	2	11	3	3	0	21	10
Smith, Osborne, S.D.†	.222	110	450	53	100	115	11	2	0	21	4	10	1	22	12
Solomon, Eddie, Pitt.	.163	25	43	3	7	7	0	0	0	3	2	5	0	0	0
Sorensen, Lary, St.L.	.065	23	46	1	3	4	1	0	0	0	0	5	0	0	0
Sosa, Elias, Mtl.	1.000	32	2	0	2	2	0	0	0	1	0	0	0	0	0
Soto, Mario, Cin.	.068	25	59	4	4	4	0	0	0	0	0	6	0	0	0
Speier, Chris, Mtl.	.225	96	307	33	69	89	10	2	2	25	4	6	0	1	2
Spilman, W. Harry, Cn-Ho°	.241	51	58	9	14	15	1	0	0	4	0	1	0	0	1
Sprowl, Robert, Hou.°	.167	15	6	0	1	1	0	0	0	1	0	0	0	0	0
Stargell, Wilver, Pitt.°	.283	38	60	2	17	21	4	0	0	9	0	0	1	0	0
Staub, Daniel, N.Y.°	.317	70	161	9	51	75	9	0	5	21	4	0	2	1	0
Stearns, John, N.Y.	.271	80	273	25	74	91	12	1	1	24	4	7	1	12	2
Stennett, Renaldo, S.F.	.230	38	87	8	20	23	0	0	1	7	0	1	0	2	1
Stewart, David, L.A.°	.400	32	5	2	2	4	0	1	0	1	0	0	0	0	0
Stimac, Craig, S.D.	.111	9	9	0	1	1	0	0	0	0	0	0	0	0	0
Strain, Joseph, Chi.	.189	25	74	7	14	15	1	0	0	1	0	0	0	0	0
Sularz, Guy, S.F.	.200	10	20	0	4	4	0	0	0	2	0	0	1	0	1

Player and Club	Pct.	G.	AB.	R.	H.	TB.	2B.	3B.	HR.	RBI.	GW.	SH.	SF.	SB.	CS.
Sutcliffe, Richard, L.A.°	.182	14	11	2	2	2	0	0	0	2	1	0	0	0	0
Sutter, H. Bruce, St.L.	.000	48	9	0	0	0	0	0	0	1	0	0	0	0	0
Sutton, Donald, Hou.	.137	23	51	1	7	7	0	0	0	3	0	5	0	0	0
Swan, Craig, N.Y.	.000	5	3	0	0	0	0	0	0	0	0	0	0	0	0
Swisher, Steven, S.D.	.143	16	28	2	4	4	0	0	0	0	0	0	0	0	0
Sykes, Robert, St.L.†	.000	22	2	0	0	0	0	0	0	0	0	0	0	0	0
Tabler, Patrick, Chi.	.188	35	101	11	19	27	3	1	1	5	1	3	0	0	1
Taveras, Franklin, N.Y.	.230	84	283	30	65	82	11	3	0	11	0	5	3	16	4
Tekulve, Kenton, Pitt.	.000	45	2	0	0	0	0	0	0	0	0	0	0	0	0
Templeton, Garry, St. L.†	.288	80	333	47	96	131	16	8	1	33	1	1	2	8	12
Tenace, F. Gene, St.L.	.233	58	129	26	30	52	7	0	5	22	2	1	2	0	0
Thomas, Derrel, L.A.†	.248	80	218	25	54	70	4	0	4	24	2	7	2	7	2
Thompson, Jason, Pitt.°	.242	86	223	36	54	112	13	0	15	42	6	0	3	0	0
Thompson, V. Scot, Chi.°	.165	57	115	8	19	24	5	0	0	8	1	2	3	2	0
Thon, Richard, Hou.	.274	49	95	13	26	32	6	0	0	3	0	1	0	6	1
Tiant, Luis, Pitt.	.188	9	16	0	3	5	2	0	0	4	0	2	0	0	0
Tidrow, Richard, Chi.	.000	51	5	0	0	0	0	0	0	0	0	1	0	0	0
Tolman, Timothy, Hou.	.125	4	8	0	1	1	0	0	0	0	0	0	0	0	0
Tracy, James, Chi.°	.238	45	63	6	15	19	2	1	0	5	0	0	1	1	0
Trevino, Alejandro, N.Y.	.262	56	149	17	39	41	2	0	0	10	2	1	1	3	0
Trillo, J. Manuel, Phil.	.287	94	349	37	100	138	14	3	6	36	4	5	4	10	4
Tufts, Robert, S.F.°	.000	11	1	0	0	0	0	0	0	0	0	0	0	0	0
Turner, John, S.D.°	.226	33	31	5	7	13	0	0	2	6	0	1	0	0	1
Tyson, Michael, Chi.†	.185	50	92	6	17	25	2	0	2	8	2	2	1	1	0
Unser, Delbert, Phila.°	.153	62	59	5	9	12	3	0	0	6	0	0	1	0	0
Urrea, John, S.D.	.250	38	4	0	1	1	0	0	0	0	0	0	0	0	0
Vail, Michael, Cin.	.161	31	31	1	5	5	0	0	0	3	0	0	0	0	0
Valentine, Ellis, Mtl.-N.Y.	.208	70	245	23	51	88	11	1	8	36	6	0	5	0	4
Valenzuela, Fernando, L.A.°	.250	25	64	3	16	18	0	1	0	7	2	6	0	0	0
Venable, W. McKinley, S.F.°	.188	18	32	2	6	10	0	2	0	1	0	0	0	3	1
Virgil, Osvaldo, Phila.	.000	6	6	0	0	0	0	0	0	0	0	0	0	0	0
Vukovich, George, Phila.°	.385	20	26	5	10	13	0	0	1	4	1	0	0	1	0
Vukovich, John, Phila.	.000	11	1	0	0	0	0	0	0	0	0	1	0	0	0
Walk, Robert, Atl.	.143	12	7	1	1	1	0	0	0	0	0	3	0	0	0
Wallach, Timothy, Mtl.	.236	71	212	19	50	73	9	1	4	13	1	0	0	0	1
Waller, E. Tyrone, Chi.	.268	30	71	10	19	32	2	1	3	13	0	1	1	2	0
Walling, Dennis, Hou.°	.234	65	158	23	37	58	6	0	5	23	4	1	2	2	1
Washington, Claudell, Atl.°	.291	85	320	37	93	136	22	3	5	37	3	8	2	12	6
Weiss, Gary, L.A.†	.105	14	19	2	2	2	0	0	0	1	1	0	1	0	0
Welch, Robert, L.A.	.222	23	45	3	10	12	0	1	0	2	0	7	0	0	0
Welsh, Christopher, S.D.°	.146	22	41	4	6	7	1	0	0	1	0	3	0	0	0
Whisenton, Larry, Atl.°	.200	9	5	1	1	1	0	0	0	0	0	0	0	0	0
White, Jerome, Mtl.†	.218	59	119	11	26	42	5	1	3	11	3	2	1	5	2
Whitson, Eddie, S.F.	.091	22	33	2	3	3	0	0	0	1	0	9	0	0	0
Wieghaus, Thomas, Mtl.	.000	1	1	0	0	0	0	0	0	0	0	0	0	0	0
Wiggins, Alan, S.D.†	.357	15	14	4	5	5	0	0	0	0	0	0	0	2	0
Wilson, William, N.Y.†	.271	92	328	49	89	122	8	8	3	14	2	0	0	24	12
Wise, Richard, S.D.	.040	18	25	1	1	2	1	0	0	1	0	3	0	0	0
Wohlford, James, S.F.	.162	50	68	4	11	17	3	0	1	7	2	0	1	0	0
Woods, Gary, Hou.	.209	54	110	10	23	29	4	1	0	12	2	3	2	2	1
Yeager, Stephen, L.A.	.209	42	86	5	18	29	2	0	3	7	0	0	0	0	0
Youngblood, Joel, N.Y.	.350	43	143	16	50	76	10	2	4	25	2	0	4	2	5
Zachry, Patrick, N.Y.	.158	24	38	1	6	6	0	0	0	2	0	4	1	0	0

AWARDED FIRST BASE ON INTERFERENCE: Berra, Pitts. 3 (May 2, Stearns); Rose, Phila. 2 (Carter Tenace); Ashby, Hous. (Kennedy); Chambliss, Atl. (Kennedy); Herr, St.L. (Kennedy); Howard, N.Y. (Porter); Landreaux, L.A. (Kennedy); Phillips, S.D. (Scioscia).

PLAYERS WITH TWO OR MORE CLUBS
(Alphabetically Arranged With Player's First Club on Top)

Player and Club	Pct.	G.	AB.	R.	H.	TB.	2B.	3B.	HR.	RBI.	GW.	SH.	SF.	Tot. BB.	Int. BB.	HP.	SO.	SB.	CS.	GI. DP.
Andujar, Hou.	.000	9	4	0	0	0	0	0	0	0	0	1	0	1	0	0	3	0	0	0
Andujar, St.L.	.000	12	19	0	0	0	0	0	0	0	0	1	0	0	0	0	9	0	0	0
Bair, Cin.	.333	24	3	1	1	4	0	0	1	3	0	0	0	0	0	0	1	0	0	0
Bair, Cin.	.000	11	3	0	0	0	0	0	0	0	0	0	0	0	0	0	3	0	0	0
Bergmàn, Hou.	.167	6	6	1	1	4	0	0	1	1	0	0	0	0	0	0	0	0	0	0
Bergman, S.F.	.255	63	145	16	37	55	9	0	3	13	1	2	1	19	3	0	18	2	0	4
Edelen, St.L.	.333	13	3	0	1	1	0	0	0	0	0	0	0	0	0	0	1	0	0	0
Edelen, Cin.	.000	5	2	0	0	0	0	0	0	0	0	0	0	0	0	0	1	0	0	0
Fiala, St.L.	.000	3	3	0	0	0	0	0	0	0	0	0	0	0	0	0	1	0	0	0
Fiala, Cin.	.500	2	2	1	1	1	0	0	0	1	0	0	0	0	0	0	1	0	0	0
Garner, Pitt.	.254	56	181	22	46	59	6	2	1	20	2	2	3	21	1	0	21	4	6	3
Garner, Hou.	.239	31	113	13	27	32	3	1	0	6	2	4	1	15	1	0	11	6	2	1
Ivie, S.F.	.294	7	17	1	5	7	2	0	0	3	1	0	1	0	0	0	1	0	0	0
Ivie, Hou.	.238	19	42	2	10	13	3	0	0	6	1	0	1	2	0	0	11	0	1	0
Jackson, Pitt.	.000	35	2	0	0	0	0	0	0	0	0	0	0	0	0	0	1	0	0	0
Jackson, Mtl.	.000	10	0	0	0	0	0	0	0	0	0	0	0	0	0	0	0	0	0	0

Player and Club	Pct.	G.	AB.	R.	H.	TB.	2B.	3B.	HR.	RBI.	GW.	SH.	SF.	Tot. BB.	Int. BB.	HP.	SO.	SB.	CS.	GI. DP.
Landestoy, Hou.	.149	35	74	6	11	14	1	1	0	4	1	4	0	16	4	0	9	4	1	4
Landestoy, Cin.	.182	12	11	2	2	2	0	0	0	1	0	0	0	1	0	0	0	1	0	2
Leonard, Hou.	.167	7	18	1	3	6	1	1	0	3	0	0	1	0	0	0	4	1	0	0
Leonard, S.F.	.307	37	127	20	39	68	11	3	4	26	1	1	0	12	3	1	21	4	2	5
Lum, Atl.	.091	10	11	1	1	1	0	0	0	0	0	0	0	2	1	0	2	0	0	0
Lum, Chi.	.241	41	58	5	14	21	1	0	2	7	0	0	1	5	2	1	5	0	0	1
Milner, Pitt.	.237	34	59	6	14	21	1	0	2	9	1	1	1	5	0	0	3	0	0	2
Milner, Mtl.	.237	31	76	6	18	32	5	0	3	9	1	0	0	12	2	0	6	0	1	1
Montanez, Mtl.	.177	26	62	6	11	13	0	1	0	5	3	0	0	4	0	0	9	0	0	5
Montanez, Pitt.	.263	29	38	2	10	13	0	0	1	1	1	0	0	1	0	0	2	0	0	1
Phillips, S.D.	.207	14	29	1	6	8	0	1	0	0	0	0	0	0	0	0	3	1	0	3
Phillips, Mtl.	.218	34	55	5	12	14	2	0	0	4	0	1	1	5	0	0	15	0	1	2
Reardon, N.Y.	.000	18	1	0	0	0	0	0	0	0	0	0	0	0	0	0	0	0	0	0
Reardon, Mtl.	.000	25	4	0	0	0	0	0	0	0	0	0	2	0	0	0	2	0	0	0
Scott, St.L.	.227	45	176	21	40	55	5	2	2	17	0	2	0	5	0	1	22	10	7	3
Scott, Hou.	.293	55	225	28	66	89	13	2	2	22	3	3	0	15	1	0	32	8	3	1
Spilman, Cin.	.167	23	24	4	4	5	1	0	0	3	0	1	0	3	0	0	7	0	0	1
Spilman, Hou.	.294	28	34	5	10	10	0	0	0	1	0	0	0	2	0	0	3	0	1	0
Valentine, Mtl.	.211	22	76	8	16	28	3	0	3	15	3	0	3	6	0	0	11	0	1	2
Valentine, N.Y.	.207	48	169	15	35	60	8	1	5	21	3	0	2	5	0	0	38	0	3	2

OFFICIAL MISCELLANEOUS NATIONAL LEAGUE BATTING RECORDS

CLUB MISCELLANEOUS BATTING RECORDS

Club	Slg. Pct.	G.	Tot. BB.	Int. BB.	HP.	SO.	GIDP.	ShO.
Philadelphia	.389	107	372	42	23	432	79	4
Cincinnati	.385	108	375	38	18	553	98	8
St. Louis	.377	103	379	41	16	495	82	4
Los Angeles	.374	110	331	38	17	550	83	5
Pittsburgh	.369	103	278	37	15	494	60	7
Houston	.356	110	340	49	8	488	69	9
San Diego	.346	110	311	39	14	525	87	11
San Francisco	.357	111	386	49	14	543	91	9
New York	.356	105	304	35	13	603	78	12
Montreal	.370	108	368	55	16	498	74	5
Atlanta	.349	107	321	38	18	540	83	12
Chicago	.340	106	342	44	13	611	78	17
Totals	.364	644	4107	505	185	6332	962	103

INDIVIDUAL MISCELLANEOUS BATTING RECORDS
(Top Fifteen Qualifiers for Slugging Championship)

Player—Club	Slg. Pct.	Tot. BB.	Int. BB.	HP.	SO.	GI DP.
Schmidt, Phila.	.644	73	18	4	71	9
Dawson, Mtl.	.553	35	14	7	50	6
Foster, Cin.	.519	51	5	3	75	12
Madlock, Pitt.	.495	34	7	3	17	5
Hendrick, St.L.	.485	41	7	4	44	10
Buckner, Chi.	.480	26	9	1	16	17
Cey, L.A.	.474	40	3	3	55	7
Guerrero, L.A.	.464	34	3	2	57	12
Hernandez, St.L.	.463	61	6	2	45	9
Durham, Chi.	.460	27	6	0	53	6
Horner, Atl.	.460	32	3	1	39	6
Clark, S.F.	.460	45	6	1	45	12
Kingman, N.Y.	.456	55	7	1	105	9
Matthews, Phila.	.451	59	2	3	42	8
Baker, L.A.	.445	29	1	1	43	9

DEPARTMENTAL LEADERS: Tot. BB—Schmidt, 73; Int. BB—Schmidt, 18; HP—Dawson, 7; SO—Kingman, 105; GIDP—Knight, 18.

(All Players—Listed Alphabetically)

Player—Club	Slg. Pct.	Tot. BB.	Int. BB.	HP.	SO.	GI DP.
Aguayo, Phila.	.298	6	0	2	15	0
Alexander, S.F.	.255	2	0	0	12	2
G. Alexander, Pitt.	.404	3	0	0	12	1
M. Alexander, Pitt.	.364	0	0	0	1	0
Allen, N.Y.	.600	0	0	0	4	0
Alvarez, Atl.	.000	0	0	0	0	0
Andujar, Hou.-St.L.	.000	1	0	0	12	0
Armstrong, S.D.	.000	0	0	0	0	0
Ashby, Hou.	.369	35	6	0	33	6
Asselstine, Atl.	.384	5	0	0	7	4
Aviles, Phila.	.250	3	0	0	5	0
Backman, N.Y.	.333	4	0	0	7	0
Bahnsen, Mtl.	.111	0	0	0	4	0
Bailor, N.Y.	.346	8	0	1	11	3
Bair, Cin.-St.L.	.667	0	0	0	4	0
Baker, L.A.	.445	29	1	1	43	9
Barranca, Cin.	.333	0	0	0	0	0
Bass, S.D.	.313	20	1	1	28	7
Bedrosian, Atl.	.000	0	0	0	1	0
Bench, Cin.	.489	17	3	0	21	4
Benedict, Atl.	.363	33	4	3	21	8
Berenyi, Cin.	.262	2	0	0	18	1
Bergman, Hou.-S.F.	.391	19	3	0	18	4
Berra, Pitt.	.319	17	4	3	34	3
Bevacqua, Pitt.	.407	4	0	0	6	1
Bibby, Pitt.	.321	1	0	1	11	0
Biittner, Cin.	.279	4	1	0	4	3
Bird, Chi.	.100	1	0	0	11	0
Blackwell, Chi.	.342	23	4	0	23	2
Blue, S.F.	.257	3	0	0	10	1
Boggs, Atl.	.174	0	0	0	6	1
Boitano, N.Y.	.000	0	0	0	0	0
Bonds, Chi.	.380	24	5	2	44	4

Player—Club	Slg. Pct.	Tot. BB.	Int. BB.	HP.	SO.	GI DP.
Bonilla, S.D.	.344	25	5	2	23	7
Boone, S.D.	.500	0	0	0	0	0
Boone, Phila.	.295	22	2	0	16	6
Bowa, Phila.	.339	26	2	0	17	8
Boyland, Pitt.	.000	1	0	0	3	0
Bradford, Atl.	1.000	0	0	0	0	0
Bradley, L.A.	.333	0	0	0	1	0
Braun, St.L.	.283	15	0	0	7	1
Breining, S.F.	.000	1	0	0	7	0
Brenly, S.F.	.489	6	0	1	4	1
Briggs, Mtl.	.091	0	0	0	3	0
Brooks, N.Y.	.411	23	2	1	65	9
Brown, Cin.	.000	0	0	0	1	0
Brummer, St.L.	.233	1	0	0	2	1
Brusstar, Phila.	.000	0	0	0	0	0
Buckner, Chi.	.480	26	9	1	16	17
Burris, Mtl.	.189	4	0	0	12	0
Butler, Atl.	.317	19	0	0	17	0
Bystrom, Phila.	.118	0	0	0	10	0
Cabell, S.F.	.326	10	0	1	47	6
Camacho, Pitt.	.000	0	0	0	1	0
Camp, Atl.	.000	0	0	0	6	0
Candelaria, Pitt.	.231	0	0	0	1	0
Capilla, Chi.	.000	0	0	0	1	0
Carlton, Phila.	.224	2	0	0	16	2
Carter, Mtl.	.444	35	4	1	35	6
Castillo, L.A.	.667	0	0	0	2	0
Caudill, Chi.	.143	2	0	0	6	0
Cedeno, Hou.	.382	24	2	1	31	6
Cey, L.A.	.474	40	3	3	55	7
Chambliss, Atl.	.403	44	10	1	41	11
Christenson, Phila.	.100	1	0	0	16	0
Clark, S.F.	.460	45	6	1	45	12
Collins, Cin.	.381	41	1	6	41	6
Combe, Cin.	.000	0	0	0	0	0
Concepcion, Cin.	.409	37	1	1	61	13
Cromartie, Mtl.°	.419	39	12	0	27	8
Cruz, Chi.	.468	17	0	0	24	3
Cruz, Hou.	.425	35	4	0	49	7
Cruz, Pitt.	.000	0	0	0	3	0
Cubbage, N.Y.	.325	9	1	0	15	2
Curtis, S.D.	.077	0	0	0	6	1
Davis, S.F.	.133	1	0	0	2	1
Davis, Chi.	.361	21	3	1	28	6
M. Davis, Phila.	.091	2	0	0	2	0
R. Davis, Phila.	.479	8	0	1	13	1
Dawson, Mtl.	.553	35	14	7	50	6
DeJesus, Chi.	.233	46	2	0	61	2
DeLeon, St.L.	.000	0	0	0	0	0
Dernier, Phila.	.750	0	0	0	0	0
Dillard, Chi.	.345	8	0	0	20	1
Driessen, Cin.	.386	40	3	2	31	5
Durham, Chi.	.460	27	6	0	53	6
Easler, Pitt.	.431	24	7	0	45	10
Eastwick, Chi.	.000	0	0	0	2	0
Edelen, St.L.-Cin.	.200	0	0	0	2	0
Edwards, S.D.	.321	11	0	0	24	3
Eichelberger, S.D.	.087	0	0	0	21	1
Engle, Mtl.	.000	0	0	0	0	0
Espinosa, Phila.	.200	0	0	0	8	0
Evans, S.D.	.376	9	2	0	9	4
Evans, S.F.	.417	54	8	2	33	4
Falcone, N.Y.	.318	0	0	0	4	1
Ferguson, L.A.	.214	2	0	0	5	0
Fiala, St.L.-Cin.	.200	0	0	0	2	0
Fireovid, S.D.	.143	0	0	0	4	0
Flannery, S.D.	.343	2	1	0	4	1
Fletcher, Chi.	.304	2	0	0	4	0
Flynn, N.Y.	.292	11	8	0	19	12
Foli, Pitt.	.297	17	0	1	10	2
Foote, Chi.	.000	3	0	0	7	1
Forsch, St.L.	.146	1	0	0	10	2
Forster, L.A.	.000	0	0	0	0	0
Foster, Cin.	.519	51	5	3	75	12
Francona, Mtl.	.326	5	1	1	6	0
Frias, L.A.	.278	1	1	1	3	0
Fryman, Mtl.	.667	0	0	0	0	0
Garber, Atl.	.000	0	0	0	1	0
Garcia, Hou.	.331	10	3	1	16	2
Gardenhire, N.Y.	.292	5	2	0	9	0
Garner, Pitt.-Hou.	.310	36	2	0	32	4
Garvey, L.A.	.411	25	6	1	49	8
Gates, Mtl.	1.500	0	0	0	1	0
Geisel, Chi.	.000	1	0	0	2	0
Giles, N.Y.	.000	0	0	0	3	0
Goltz, L.A.	.059	1	0	1	9	0
Gomez, Atl.	.200	6	0	0	4	0
Gonzalez, St.L.	.500	1	0	0	3	2
Gorman, Mtl.	.000	0	0	0	0	0
Green, St.L.	.176	6	1	0	5	0
Griffey, Cin.	.409	39	6	1	42	9
Griffin, Chi.	.154	0	0	0	8	0
Griffin, S.F.	.293	2	0	0	12	1
Gross, Phila.	.304	15	4	0	5	4
Grote, L.A.	.000	0	0	0	1	1
Guerrero, L.A.	.464	34	3	2	57	12
Gullickson, Mtl.	.174	3	0	0	13	1
Gwosdz, S.D.	.250	3	2	0	6	0
Hall, Atl.	.000	1	0	0	1	0
Hall, Chi.	.364	1	0	0	4	0
Hanna, Atl.	.250	1	0	0	0	0
Hargesheimer, S.F.	.200	0	0	0	2	0
Harper, Atl.	.356	11	0	0	17	2
Harris, N.Y.	.227	0	0	0	13	0
Hausman, N.Y.	.000	1	0	0	1	0
Hayes, Chi.	.000	0	0	0	0	0
Heep, Hou.	.281	10	2	0	11	3
Henderson, Chi.	.411	42	7	2	61	7
Hendrick, St.L.	.485	41	7	4	44	10
Hernandez, Chi.	.000	0	0	0	0	0
Hernandez, St.L.	.463	61	6	2	45	9
Herndon, S.F.	.415	20	2	1	55	12
Herr, St.L.	.345	39	3	1	30	9
Hodges, N.Y.	.419	5	2	0	8	0
Holland, S.F.	.063	1	0	0	8	0
Hooton, L.A.	.262	4	0	0	13	0
Horner, Atl.	.460	32	3	1	39	6
Hostetler, Mtl	1.000	0	0	0	2	0
Householder, Cin	.420	10	0	0	16	2
Howard, N.Y.	.208	4	0	0	6	0
Howe, Hou.	.404	41	7	0	23	8
Howe, L.A.	.000	1	0	0	1	0
Howell, Chi	.000	1	0	0	1	0
Hrabosky, Atl	.000	0	0	0	1	0
Hubbard, Atl	.349	33	2	2	59	7
Hume, Cin	.000	0	0	0	2	0
Hutton, Mtl	.103	2	0	0	1	0
Iorg, St.L	.424	7	0	0	9	7
Ivie, S.F.-Hou	.339	2	0	0	12	0
Jackson, Pitt-Mtl	.000	0	0	0	1	0
Jacoby, Atl	.200	0	0	0	3	1
A. Johnson, Mtl	.000	0	0	0	0	0
W. Johnson, Mtl	.444	1	1	0	1	1
Johnstone, L.A.	.349	7	0	0	13	3
Jones, Pitt	.200	0	0	0	3	0
Jones, N.Y.	.118	0	0	0	9	0
Jones, S.D.	.370	43	2	0	66	7
Jorgensen, N.Y.	.352	12	1	0	24	2
Kaat, St.L	.500	1	0	0	0	0
Kennedy, Cin	.273	1	0	0	5	0
Kennedy, S.D.	.385	22	6	2	53	7
Kingman, N.Y.	.456	55	7	1	105	9
Knepper, Hou	.255	0	0	1	15	0
Knicely, Hou	1.429	0	0	0	1	0
Knight, Cin	.370	33	3	4	51	18
Kravec, Chi	.000	2	0	0	8	0
Krug, Chi	.400	1	0	0	1	0
Krukow, Chi	.220	0	0	0	13	2
Kuhaulua, S.D.	.111	0	0	0	5	0
LaCorte, Hou	.333	0	0	0	0	0
LaCoss, Cin	.000	0	0	0	8	0
Lacy, Pitt	.385	11	2	1	29	1
Landestoy, Hou-Cin	.188	17	4	0	9	6
Landreaux, L.A.	.367	25	3	0	42	6
Landrum, St.L.	.370	6	0	1	14	2
LaPoint, St.L	.000	0	0	0	3	0

Player—Club	Slg. Pct.	Tot. BB.	Int. BB.	HP.	SO.	GI DP.
Larson, Phila	.111	2	0	0	0	0
Lavelle, S.F.	.364	1	0	0	3	1
Law, Pitt	.164	2	0	0	15	2
Lea, Mtl	.133	1	0	0	7	0
Leach, N.Y.	.000	2	0	0	0	0
Leary, N.Y.	.000	0	0	0	0	0
Lee, Pitt	.500	0	0	0	1	0
Lee, Mtl	.500	0	0	0	4	0
Lefebvre, S.D.	.439	35	7	2	33	12
Leibrandt, Cin	.000	2	0	0	4	0
LeMaster, S.F.	.287	24	7	1	46	9
Leonard, Hou-S.F.	.510	12	3	1	25	5
Lezcano, Chi	.071	0	0	0	4	0
Lezcano, St.L.	.393	40	2	0	40	8
Linares, Atl	.375	9	2	0	28	12
Littell, St.L.	.250	0	0	0	2	0
Littlefield, S.D.	.000	0	0	0	0	0
Lollar, S.D.	.333	2	0	0	5	0
Long, Pitt	.000	1	0	0	2	0
Lopes, L.A.	.285	22	1	3	35	7
Loucks, Hou	.571	1	0	0	3	0
Lucas, S.D.	.100	0	0	0	2	0
Lum, Atl-Chi	.319	7	3	1	7	1
Lyle, Phila	.400	1	0	0	1	0
Lynch, N.Y.	.190	4	0	0	10	0
Maddox, Phila	.337	17	1	1	42	6
Madlock, Pitt	.495	34	7	3	17	5
Mahler, Atl	.185	0	0	0	4	0
Maldonado, L.A.	.083	0	0	0	5	0
Manuel, Mtl	.455	6	1	0	11	1
Marshall, N.Y.	.000	1	0	0	0	0
Marshall, L.A.	.320	1	0	1	4	1
Martin, S.F.	.336	21	2	3	52	9
Martin, St.L.	.333	2	0	0	14	0
Martinez, St.L.	.257	1	0	0	12	0
Martz, Chi	.214	3	0	0	13	1
Matthews, Phila	.451	59	2	3	42	8
Matula, Atl	.000	0	0	0	0	0
Matuszek, Phila	.364	3	1	0	1	0
May, S.F.	.383	34	10	0	29	7
Mazzilli, N.Y.	.358	46	3	2	53	5
McBride, Phila	.385	11	1	0	25	6
McCormick, Phila	.250	0	0	0	1	1
McGlothen, Chi	.167	0	0	0	3	0
McGraw, Phila	.000	0	0	0	0	0
McWilliams, Atl	.100	1	0	0	7	0
Mejias, Cin	.327	2	1	0	9	1
Miller, N.Y.	.333	0	0	0	0	0
Miller, Atl	.269	7	1	3	29	1
Mills, Mtl	.286	2	1	0	1	1
Milner, Cin	.400	1	0	0	1	0
Milner, Pitt-Mtl	.393	17	2	0	9	3
Minton, S.F.	.000	0	0	0	2	1
Mitchell, L.A.	.125	1	0	0	4	0
Moffitt, S.F.	.000	0	0	0	0	0
Monday, L.A.	.608	24	3	1	42	0
Montanez, Mtl-Pitt	.260	5	0	0	11	6
Montefusco, Atl	.133	0	0	0	9	0
Morales, Chi	.339	22	0	1	29	6
Moreland, Phila	.383	15	1	1	13	10
Moreno, S.D.	.271	1	1	0	8	2
Moreno, Pitt	.362	26	4	3	76	1
Morgan, S.F.	.377	66	7	0	37	3
Moskau, Cin	.000	1	0	0	3	0
Mura, S.D.	.159	2	0	0	7	1
Murphy, Atl	.390	44	8	0	72	10
Nahorodny, Atl	.308	1	1	0	3	0
Nicosia, Pitt	.337	13	2	0	10	7
Niedenfuer, L.A.	.000	0	0	0	0	0
Niekro, Hou	.196	2	0	0	10	0
Niekro, Atl	.077	0	0	0	11	0
Nolan, Cin	.407	24	6	1	19	7
Noles, Phila	.105	0	0	0	7	1
North, S.F.	.298	26	0	1	28	1
O'Berry, Cin	.252	14	0	0	19	3
Oberkfell, St.L	.372	37	6	0	28	11
Oester, Cin	.398	42	8	0	49	8
Office, Mtl	.175	4	0	0	6	2
Orosco, N.Y.	.000	0	0	0	2	0
Otten, St.L.	.000	0	0	0	0	0
Owen, Atl	.000	1	0	0	4	0
Parker, Pitt	.454	9	3	2	25	5
Parrish, Mtl	.384	28	2	0	73	10
Pastore, Cin	.136	1	0	0	13	0
Pate, Mtl	.333	1	0	0	0	0
Pena, Hou	.500	0	0	0	0	0
Pena, L.A.	.000	0	0	0	6	0
Pena, Pitt	.381	8	2	1	23	4
Perconte, L.A.	.444	2	0	0	2	0
Perez, Pitt	.227	0	0	0	10	0
Perkins, S.D.	.398	14	4	0	16	6
Perry, Atl	.354	0	0	1	10	3
Pettini, S.F.	.103	4	0	0	5	0
Phillips, S.D.-Mtl	.262	5	0	0	18	5
Pittman, Hou	.341	11	3	0	16	3
Pladson, Hou	.000	0	0	0	0	0
Pocoroba, Atl	.213	12	1	2	15	5
Porter, St.L	.408	39	7	1	32	3
Porter, Atl	.357	2	0	0	1	0
Power, L.A.	.000	0	0	0	3	0
Price, Cin	.000	0	0	0	1	0
Proly, Phila	.000	0	0	0	1	1
Puhl, Hou	.354	31	5	4	49	3
Pujols, Hou	.308	10	3	0	17	4
Puleo, Hou	.000	0	0	0	2	0
Raines, Mtl	.438	45	5	2	31	7
Ramirez, S.D.	.077	2	1	0	5	0
Ramirez, Atl	.303	24	3	1	47	3
Ramos, Mtl	.293	3	0	0	5	2
Ramsey, St.L	.282	8	1	0	16	6
Ransom, S.F.	.333	1	1	0	1	1
Ratzer, Mtl	.000	0	0	0	0	0
Ray, Pitt	.353	6	2	0	9	3
Reardon, N.Y.-Mtl	.000	0	0	0	2	0
J. Reed, Phila	.000	0	0	0	0	0
R. Reed, Phila	.667	0	0	0	1	0
Reitz, Chi	.281	15	3	3	56	9
Reuschel, Chi	.080	1	0	0	7	1
Reuss, L.A.	.196	0	0	0	18	0
Reynolds, Hou	.402	12	2	0	31	6
Rhoden, Pitt	.229	1	0	0	7	1
Richards, S.D.	.407	53	3	1	44	6
Rincon, St.L.	.308	1	0	0	6	0
Ripley, S.F.	.133	0	0	0	5	1
Roberts, N.Y.	.250	0	0	0	2	0
Roberts, Hou	.352	3	0	0	6	1
D. Robinson, Pitt.	.250	1	0	0	4	0
W. Robinson, Pitt.	.318	5	1	0	18	2
Roenicke, L.A.	.234	6	0	0	8	0
Rogers, Mtl	.164	2	0	0	21	0
Romo, Pitt	.000	0	0	0	4	0
Roof, St.L	.400	12	2	0	16	1
Rooney, Mtl	.000	0	0	0	3	0
Rose, Phila	.390	46	5	3	26	8
Rowland, S.F.	1.000	0	0	0	0	0
Royster, Atl	.269	7	0	0	14	2
Ruhle, Hou	.292	6	0	0	11	0
Runge, Atl	.296	4	0	0	4	1
Russell, L.A.	.282	19	3	1	20	13
Ruthven, Phila	.200	2	0	0	14	0
Ryan, Hou	.235	5	0	0	18	1
Sadek, S.F.	.250	8	0	0	7	0
Salazar, S.D.	.403	16	2	1	72	7
Sambito, Hou	.000	0	0	0	3	0
Sanchez, St.L.	.367	2	1	0	6	2
Sandberg, Phila.	.167	0	0	0	1	0
Sanderson, Mtl	.171	9	0	0	18	0
Sax, L.A.	.345	7	1	0	14	0
Schmidt, Phila.	.644	73	18	4	71	9
Scioscia, L.A.	.331	36	8	1	18	8
Scott, N.Y.	.073	3	0	0	18	2
Scott, Mtl	.250	50	0	1	35	7
Scott, S.L.-Hou.	.359	20	1	1	54	4
Scurry, Pitt.	.158	2	0	0	10	0
Searage, N.Y.	1.000	0	0	0	0	0
Seaver, Cin.	.273	8	0	0	16	2

Player—Club	Slg. Pct.	Tot. BB.	Int. BB.	HP.	SO.	GI DP.
Shirley, St.L.	.136	0	0	0	7	0
Show, S.D.	.000	0	0	0	0	0
Sinatro, Atl.	.375	5	1	0	4	0
B. Smith, Hou.	.000	0	0	0	2	0
Smith, S.F.	.230	9	0	0	16	1
B. Smith, Mtl.	.000	0	0	0	0	0
Smith, L.A.	.314	7	3	0	8	4
C. Smith, Mtl.	.000	0	0	0	2	0
D. Smith, Hou.	.250	0	0	0	4	0
Smith, Atl.	.667	0	0	0	1	0
Smith, Chi.	.000	0	0	0	7	0
Smith, Phila.	.472	18	1	5	14	1
Smith, S.D.	.256	41	1	5	37	8
Solomon, Pitt.	.163	0	0	0	15	0
Sorensen, St.L.	.087	0	0	1	21	0
Sosa, Mtl.	1.000	0	0	0	0	0
Soto, Cin.	.068	1	0	0	24	0
Speier, Mtl.	.290	38	10	0	29	9
Spilman, Cin-Hou.	.259	5	0	0	10	1
Sprowl, Hou.	.167	0	0	0	2	0
Stargell, Pitt.	.350	5	1	0	9	0
Staub, N.Y.	.466	22	3	1	12	6
Stearns, N.Y.	.333	24	2	0	17	10
Stennett, S.F.	.264	3	0	1	6	3
Stewart, L.A.	.800	1	0	0	0	0
Stimac, S.D.	.111	0	0	0	3	0
Strain, Chi.	.203	5	0	1	7	1
Sularz, S.F.	.200	2	0	1	4	0
Sutcliffe, L.A.	.182	2	0	0	3	0
Sutter, St.L.	.000	0	0	1	4	0
Sutton, Hou.	.137	5	0	1	12	2
Swan, N.Y.	.000	0	0	0	1	0
Swisher, S.D.	.143	2	0	0	11	1
Sykes, St.L.	.000	1	0	0	2	0
Tabler, Chi.	.267	13	0	0	26	4
Taveras, N.Y.	.290	12	0	2	36	3
Tekulve, Pitt.	.000	0	0	0	1	0
Templeton, St.L.	.393	14	3	0	55	4
Tenace, St.L.	.403	38	2	4	26	1
Thomas, L.A.	.321	25	2	0	23	2
Thompson, Pitt.	.502	59	1	0	49	6
Thompson, Chi.	.209	7	1	0	8	2
Thon, Hou.	.337	9	1	0	13	3
Tiant, Pitt.	.313	1	0	0	3	0
Tidrow, Chi.	.000	0	0	0	2	0
Tolman, Hou.	.125	0	0	0	0	0
Tracy, Chi.	.302	12	0	0	14	2
Trevino, N.Y.	.275	13	0	1	19	4
Trillo, Phil.	.395	26	3	3	37	6
Tufts, S.F.	.000	0	0	0	0	0
Turner, S.D.	.419	4	1	0	3	1
Tyson, Chi.	.272	7	1	1	15	0
Unser, Phila.	.203	13	1	0	9	1
Urrea, S.D.	.250	0	0	0	1	0
Vail, Cin.	.161	0	0	0	9	1
Valentine, Mtl.-N.Y.	.359	11	0	0	49	4
Valenzuela, L.A.	.281	1	0	0	9	0
Venable, S.F.	.313	4	0	0	3	0
Virgil, Phila.	.000	0	0	0	2	0
G. Vukovich, Phila.	.500	1	0	0	0	0
J. Vukovich, Phila.	.000	0	0	0	1	0
Walk, Atl.	.143	0	0	0	3	0
Wallach, Mtl.	.344	15	2	4	37	3
Waller, Chi.	.451	4	1	0	18	0
Walling, Hou.	.367	28	1	0	17	4
Washington, Atl.	.425	15	1	4	47	6
Weiss, L.A.	.105	1	0	0	4	0
Welch, L.A.	.267	1	0	0	16	0
Welsh, S.D.	.171	2	0	0	15	0
Whisenton, Atl.	.200	2	0	0	1	0
White, Mtl.	.353	13	0	0	17	0
Whitson, S.F.	.091	3	0	0	13	0
Wieghaus, Mtl.	.000	0	0	0	0	0
Wiggins, S.D.	.357	1	0	0	0	0
Wilson, N.Y.	.372	20	3	2	59	3
Wise, S.D.	.080	1	0	0	11	2
Wohlford, S.F.	.250	4	0	0	9	5
Woods, Hou.	.264	11	4	0	22	4
Yeager, L.A.	.337	6	0	0	14	2
Youngblood, N.Y.	.531	12	1	2	19	4
Zachry, N.Y.	.158	3	0	0	12	1

OFFICIAL NATIONAL LEAGUE FIELDING AVERAGES

CLUB FIELDING

Club	Pct.	G.	PO.	A.	E.	TC.	DP.	TP.	PB.
St. Louis	.981	103	2829	1347	82	4258	108	1	5
Cincinnati	.981	108	2897	1132	80	4109	99	0	3
Montreal	.980	108	2925	1123	81	4129	88	0	5
Los Angeles	.980	110	2991	1244	87	4322	101	0	13
Philadelphia	.980	107	2881	1285	86	4252	90	0	2
Houston	.980	110	2970	1206	87	4263	81	0	8
Pittsburgh	.979	103	2826	1171	86	4083	106	0	7
San Diego	.977	110	3006	1375	102	4483	117	0	5
San Francisco	.977	111	3028	1313	102	4443	102	0	7
Atlanta	.976	107	2904	1284	102	4290	93	0	10
Chicago	.974	106	2870	1284	113	4267	103	0	6
New York	.968	105	2779	1195	130	4104	89	0	5
Totals	.978	644	34906	14959	1138	51003	1177	1	76

INDIVIDUAL FIELDING

°Throws lefthanded.

FIRST BASEMEN

Leader—Club	Pct.	G.	PO.	A.	E.	DP.
GARVEY, L.A.	.999	110	1019	55	1	84

(Listed Alphabetically)

Player—Club	Pct.	G.	PO.	A.	E.	DP.
G. Alexander, Pitt.	.964	9	52	2	2	4
Bass, S.D.	.993	50	390	35	3	38
Bench, Cin.	.983	38	334	23	6	35
Bergman, Hou.-S.F.°	.992	34	235	25	2	21
Biittner, Cin.°	1.000	8	53	3	0	2
Briggs, Mtl°	1.000	3	13	2	0	1
Buckner, Chi.°	.984	105	996	81	17	92
Cabell, S.F.	.987	69	620	63	9	56
Carter, Mtl.	1.000	1	6	0	0	1
Cedeno, Hou.	.991	45	428	27	4	27
Chambliss, Atl.	.997	107	1046	94	4	83
Cromartie, Mtl.°	.992	62	488	32	4	38
Driessen, Cin.	.995	74	558	30	3	54
Durham, Chi.°	1.000	3	16	0	0	1
Evans, S.D.	.987	10	75	2	1	7
Evans, S.F.	.992	12	114	15	1	12
Francona, Mtl.°	1.000	1	1	0	0	0
Garvey, L.A.	.999	110	1019	55	1	84
Guerrero, L.A.	1.000	1	6	0	0	0
Heep, Hou.°	.990	22	198	9	2	12
Hernandez, St.L.°	.997	98	1054	86	3	99
Hostetler, Mtl.	1.000	2	4	0	0	2
Howe, Hou.	1.000	2	15	0	0	3
Hutton, Mtl.°	1.000	9	22	2	0	2
Iorg, St.L.	1.000	8	47	5	0	1
Ivie, S.F.-Hou.	.992	15	113	15	1	7
Johnstone, L.A.	1.000	2	14	1	0	2
Jorgensen, N.Y.°	.991	40	108	8	1	8
Kingman, N.Y.	.974	56	462	31	13	39
Leonard, Hou.-S.F.	.986	7	70	3	1	5
Lum, Chi.°	1.000	1	1	0	0	0
Marshall, L.A.	1.000	3	9	0	0	2
Matuszek, Phila.	1.000	1	2	0	0	1
Milner, Pitt.-Mtl.°	.979	29	213	17	5	16

Player—Club	Pct.	G.	PO.	A.	E.	DP.
Montanez, Mtl.-Pitt.°	.995	27	173	13	1	12
Moreland, Phila.	1.000	2	4	1	0	1
Murphy, Atl.	1.000	3	10	0	0	1
Nahorodny, Atl.	1.000	1	1	0	0	0
Perkins, S.D.°	.997	80	598	38	2	56
Roberts, Hou.	.958	10	83	8	4	6
W. Robinson, Pitt.	1.000	23	131	10	0	9
Rose, Phila.	.996	107	929	91	4	69
Smith, L.A.	1.000	2	15	1	0	1
Smith, Atl.	1.000	4	6	1	0	0
Spilman, Cin.-Hou.	.984	15	58	3	1	3
Stargell, Pitt.°	1.000	9	70	0	0	10
Staub, N.Y.	.989	41	339	20	4	26
Stearns, N.Y.	1.000	9	58	8	0	4
Tenace, St.L.	1.000	7	39	4	0	3
Thompson, Pitt.°	.989	78	590	46	7	65
Thompson, Chi.°	.875	3	7	0	1	0
Unser, Phila.°	1.000	18	44	5	0	4
J. Vukovich, Phila.	1.000	1	3	0	0	0
Wallach, Mtl.	1.000	16	140	5	0	7
Walling, Hou.	.990	27	188	8	2	17

TRIPLE PLAY: Hernandez, St. Louis.

FIRST BASEMEN WITH TWO OR MORE CLUBS

Player—Club	Pct.	G.	PO.	A.	E.	DP.
Bergman, Hou.°	1.000	1	3	1	0	0
Bergman, S.F.°	.992	33	232	24	2	21
Ivie, S.F.	1.000	5	37	4	0	2
Ivie, Hou.	.989	10	76	11	1	5
Leonard, Hou.	1.000	2	23	1	0	0
Leonard, S.F.	.980	5	47	2	1	5
Milner, Pitt.°	.980	8	48	1	1	2
Milner, Mtl.°	.978	21	165	16	4	14
Montanez, Mtl.°	.992	16	117	12	1	8
Montanez, Pitt.°	1.000	11	56	1	0	4
Spilman, Cin.	.929	2	12	1	1	0
Spilman, Hou.	1.000	13	46	2	0	3

SECOND BASEMEN

Leader—Club	Pct.	G.	PO.	A.	E.	DP.
HERR, St.L.	.992	103	211	374	5	74

(Listed Alphabetically)

Player—Club	Pct.	G.	PO.	A.	E.	DP.
Aguayo, Phila.	.938	21	27	33	4	8
Aviles, Phila.	1.000	20	14	19	0	3
Backman, N.Y.	.946	11	14	21	2	2
Bailor, N.Y.	.963	13	12	14	1	3
Berra, Pitt.	1.000	18	26	43	0	9
Bevacqua, Pitt.	.941	4	7	9	1	3
Bonilla, S.D.	.976	97	229	290	13	72
Dillard, Chi.	.974	32	54	96	4	21
Evans, S.D.	1.000	6	13	9	0	2
Flannery, S.D.	.950	7	7	12	1	1

Player—Club	Pct.	G.	PO.	A.	E.	DP.
Fletcher, Chi.	.972	13	31	39	2	10
Flynn, N.Y.	.987	100	220	301	7	58
Frias, L.A.	.875	6	4	3	1	1
Garcia, Hou.	.977	9	16	26	1	2
Gardenhire, N.Y.	1.000	6	7	7	0	0
Garner, Pitt.-Hou.	.973	81	183	250	12	48
Gates, Mtl.	1.000	1	0	1	0	0
Giles, N.Y.	1.000	2	1	2	0	1
Gomez, Atl.	1.000	3	5	3	0	0
Gonzalez, St.L.	.889	4	3	5	1	0
Herr, St.L.	.992	103	211	374	5	74
Hubbard, Atl.	.991	98	188	344	5	50
W. Johnson, Mtl.	1.000	1	1	2	0	1
Kennedy, Cin.	.980	16	21	27	1	8

Player—Club	Pct.	G.	PO.	A.	E.	DP.
Landestoy, Hou.-Cin.	.967	34	55	64	4	11
Law, Pitt.	1.000	19	40	45	0	9
Lopes, L.A.	.993	55	129	161	2	30
Manuel, Mtl.	.987	23	37	40	1	10
Mills, Mtl.	1.000	2	1	1	0	1
Moreno, S.D.	1.000	1	2	1	0	1
Morgan, S.F.	.991	87	177	258	4	61
Oester, Cin.	.980	103	202	328	11	61
Perconte, L.A.	1.000	2	4	13	0	3
Pettini, S.F.	.920	12	7	16	2	1
Phillips, S.D.-Mtl.	.982	15	26	30	1	7
Pittman, Hou.	.980	35	56	89	3	14
Raines, Mtl.	1.000	1	2	2	0	0
Ramsey, St.L.	1.000	1	2	2	0	0
Ray, Pitt.	.987	31	52	96	2	22
Roberts, Hou.	1.000	3	1	0	0	0
Royster, Atl.	.960	13	20	28	2	7
Sandberg, Phila.	1.000	1	1	2	0	1
Sax, L.A.	.975	29	64	93	4	22
Scott, Mtl.	.983	93	187	278	8	41
Smith, S.F.	1.000	5	3	8	0	1
C. Smith, Mtl.	1.000	1	0	1	0	0

Player—Club	Pct.	G.	PO.	A.	E.	DP.
Stennett, S.F.	1.000	19	48	46	0	9
Strain, Chi.	.975	20	38	81	3	10
Sularz, S.F.	1.000	6	9	18	0	3
Tabler, Chi.	.982	35	70	93	3	17
Thomas, L.A.	.986	30	73	71	2	16
Thon, Hou.	.950	28	37	39	4	10
Trevino, N.Y.	1.000	4	1	3	0	0
Trillo, Phila.	.987	94	245	286	7	61
Tyson, Chi.	.940	36	50	76	8	14
J. Vukovich, Phila.	1.000	1	1	0	0	0
Waller, Chi.	1.000	3	5	2	0	0

TRIPLE PLAY: Herr, St. Louis.

SECOND BASEMEN WITH TWO OR MORE CLUBS

Player—Club	Pct.	G.	PO.	A.	E.	DP.
Garner, Pitt.	.968	50	121	148	9	31
Garner, Hou.	.982	31	62	102	3	17
Landestoy, Hou.	.966	31	52	63	4	11
Landestoy, Cin.	1.000	3	3	1	0	0
Phillips, S.D.	.979	9	23	23	1	6
Phillips, Mtl.	1.000	6	3	7	0	1

THIRD BASEMEN

Leader—Club	Pct.	G.	PO.	A.	E.	DP.
REITZ, CHI.	.977	81	57	157	5	11

(Listed Alphabetically)

Player—Club	Pct.	G.	PO.	A.	E.	DP.
Aguayo, Phila.	1.000	3	0	2	0	1
Aviles, Phila.	.909	13	2	8	1	1
Backman, N.Y.	.000	1	0	0	0	0
Bailor, N.Y.	.000	1	0	0	0	0
Berra, Pitt.	.976	42	21	62	2	6
Bevacqua, Pitt.	1.000	2	0	1	0	0
Braun, St.L.	.000	1	0	0	0	0
Brenly, S.F.	.714	3	2	3	2	0
Brooks, N.Y.	.924	93	65	192	21	14
Cabell, S.F.	.854	22	14	27	7	2
Cey, L.A.	.941	84	71	184	16	15
Cruz, Chi.	.925	18	12	25	3	0
Cubbage, N.Y.	.963	12	5	21	1	0
Dillard, Chi	.600	7	3	0	2	0
Evans, S.D.	.969	24	10	21	1	1
Evans, S.F.	.953	87	74	187	13	10
Flannery, S.D.	.967	15	9	20	1	4
Fletcher, Chi.	1.000	1	1	1	0	0
Frias, L.A.	.000	1	0	0	0	0
Garcia, Hou.	.840	13	4	17	4	1
Gardenhire, N.Y.	1.000	1	1	1	0	0
Gomez, Atl.	1.000	9	3	3	0	0
Gonzalez, St.L.	1.000	2	1	1	0	0
Guerrero, L.A.	.903	21	14	51	7	5
Horner, Atl.	.938	79	51	129	12	6
Howe, Hou.	.966	98	52	206	9	16
Iorg, St.L.	1.000	2	0	2	0	0
Jacoby, Atl.	1.000	3	3	4	0	1
Kennedy, Cin.	1.000	5	1	5	0	0

Player—Club	Pct.	G.	PO.	A.	E.	DP.
Knight, Cin.	.957	105	69	176	11	18
Lacy, Pitt.	1.000	1	0	1	0	0
Law, Pitt.	1.000	2	2	0	0	0
Madlock, Pitt.	.956	78	50	147	9	17
Marshall, L.A.	1.000	3	2	2	0	0
Matuszek, Phila.	1.000	1	3	4	0	0
Mills, Mtl.	1.000	7	5	5	0	0
Moreland, Phila.	.810	7	7	10	4	1
Oberkfell, St.L.	.956	102	77	246	15	23
Parrish, Mtl.	.935	95	91	141	16	7
Pettini, S.F.	.875	9	0	7	1	0
Pittman, Hou.	1.000	4	3	3	0	0
Pocoroba, Atl.	.938	21	15	30	3	4
Ramirez, S.D.	1.000	2	3	5	0	1
Ramsey, St.L.	1.000	5	2	6	0	1
Reitz, Chi.	.977	81	57	157	5	11
Roberts, Hou.	.923	7	4	8	1	1
W. Robinson, Pitt.	.500	1	1	0	1	0
Royster, Atl.	.950	24	15	23	2	2
Salazar, S.D.	.955	94	63	189	12	16
Schmidt, Phila.	.956	101	74	249	15	20
Smith, S.F.	1.000	3	2	3	0	1
Spilman, Cin.	1.000	3	4	2	0	0
Stearns, N.Y.	.857	4	0	6	1	0
Sularz, S.F.	1.000	1	0	6	0	0
Thomas, L.A.	.923	10	3	9	1	0
Thon, Hou.	1.000	5	4	7	0	1
Trevino, N.Y.	.000	1	0	0	0	0
J. Vukovich, Phila.	.800	9	0	4	1	0
Wallach, Mtl.	.972	15	12	23	1	1
Waller, Chi.	.978	22	11	33	1	2

TRIPLE PLAY: Oberkfell, St.L.

SHORTSTOPS

Leader—Club	Pct.	G.	PO.	A.	E.	DP.
SMITH, S.D.	.976	110	220	422	16	72

(Listed Alphabetically)

Player—Club	Pct.	G.	PO.	A.	E.	DP.
Aguayo, Phila.	.976	21	12	28	1	6
Aviles, Phila.	1.000	5	0	3	0	0
Bailor, N.Y.	.955	22	18	46	3	6
Berra, Pitt.	.945	30	42	62	6	12
Bowa, Phila.	.975	102	117	309	11	50
Brooks, N.Y.	1.000	1	0	1	0	0
Concepcion, Cin.	.960	106	208	322	22	71
DeJesus, Chi.	.959	106	221	343	24	81
Dillard, Chi.	1.000	2	2	0	0	1
Evans, S.D.	1.000	2	0	1	0	0
Fletcher, Chi.	.857	4	2	4	1	0
Flynn, N.Y.	1.000	5	9	18	0	3

Player—Club	Pct.	G.	PO.	A.	E.	DP.
Foli, Pitt.	.965	81	140	247	14	52
Frias, L.A.	.906	15	11	18	3	2
Garcia, Hou.	.950	28	38	76	6	11
Gardenhire, N.Y.	.969	18	20	42	2	7
Giles, N.Y.	1.000	2	4	6	0	1
Gomez, Atl.	.895	21	15	19	4	2
Gonzalez, St.L.	1.000	5	3	7	0	1
Law, Pitt.	1.000	7	8	13	0	1
LeMaster, S.F.	.964	103	166	294	17	57
Manuel, Mtl.	1.000	2	0	1	0	0
Oberkfell, St.L.	1.000	1	0	1	0	0
Oester, Cin.	1.000	9	11	13	0	3
Pena, Hou.	1.000	3	1	1	0	1
Pettini, S.F.	.870	12	6	14	3	3
Phillips, S.D.-Mtl.	.974	27	31	44	2	9
Ramirez, S.D.	1.000	2	2	6	0	0

SHORTSTOPS—Continued

Player—Club	Pct.	G.	PO.	A.	E.	DP.
Ramirez, Atl.	.942	95	181	306	30	55
Ramsey, St.L.	.966	35	52	118	6	20
Reynolds, Hou.	.973	85	139	261	11	36
Runge Atl.	.911	10	14	27	4	5
Russell, L.A.	.965	80	128	261	14	49
Sandberg, Phila.	1.000	5	6	5	0	0
Smith, S.F.	.971	21	27	39	2	9
Smith, S.D.	.976	110	220	422	16	72
Speier, Mtl.	.964	96	175	280	17	57
Taveras, N.Y.	.931	79	120	202	24	44
Templeton, St.L.	.960	76	160	272	18	54

Player—Club	Pct.	G.	PO.	A.	E.	DP.
Thomas, L.A.	.921	26	42	63	9	13
Thon, Hou.	.935	13	12	17	2	2
Tyson, Chi.	.000	1	0	0	0	0
Weiss, L.A.	.920	13	12	11	2	8

TRIPLE PLAY: Templeton, St.L.

SHORTSTOPS WITH TWO OR MORE CLUBS

Player—Club	Pct.	G.	PO.	A.	E.	DP.
Phillips, S.D.	1.000	1	0	1	0	1
Phillips, Mtl.	.974	26	31	43	2	8

OUTFIELDERS

Leaders—Club	Pct.	G.	PO.	A.	E.	DP.
LANDREAUX, L.A.	1.000	95	210	4	0	0
PUHL, Hou	1.000	88	185	5	0	1

(Listed Alphabetically)

Player—Club	Pct.	G.	PO.	A.	E.	DP.
G. Alexander, Pitt	.941	8	12	4	1	0
M. Alexander, Pitt	1.000	6	8	0	0	0
Asselstine, Atl	.958	16	22	1	1	1
Bailor, N.Y.	1.000	13	13	0	0	0
Baker, L.A.	.990	101	181	8	2	1
Bergman, S.F.*	.952	15	20	0	1	0
Biittner, Cin*	1.000	3	4	2	0	1
Bonds, Chi	.982	45	108	2	2	0
Bradley, L.A.	1.000	6	3	1	0	0
Braun, St.L	1.000	12	15	2	0	1
Brenly, S.F.	.000	1	0	0	0	0
Briggs, Mtl*	1.000	3	3	0	0	0
Brooks, N.Y.	1.000	3	2	0	0	0
Butler, Atl*	.987	37	76	2	1	0
Cedeno, Hou	.988	34	82	1	1	0
Clark, S.F.	.981	98	193	14	4	4
Collins, Cin*	.977	93	167	4	4	2
Cromartie, Mtl*	1.000	38	82	1	0	0
Cruz, Chi.	1.000	16	21	1	0	0
Cruz, Hou*	.984	104	237	5	4	2
Davis, S.F.	1.000	6	7	0	0	0
R. Davis, Phila	.974	32	37	1	1	0
Dawson, Mtl	.980	103	327	10	7	1
Dernier, Phila.	1.000	5	2	0	0	0
Durham, Chi*	.970	83	159	4	5	1
Easler, Pitt	.980	90	188	13	4	2
Edwards, S.D.	.970	49	59	6	2	2
Ferguson, L.A.	.000	1	0	0	0	0
Foster, Cin	.991	108	224	8	2	1
Francona, Mtl*	1.000	26	40	5	0	0
Green, St.L	.970	18	31	1	1	0
Griffey, Cin*	.989	99	268	8	3	1
Gross, Phila*	.982	55	48	7	1	2
Guerrero, L.A.	.974	75	145	4	4	0
Hall, Atl.	.000	2	0	0	0	0
Hall, Chi*	.000	3	0	0	0	0
Harper, Atl	.976	27	38	2	1	1
Heep, Hou*	.000	1	0	0	0	0
Henderson, Chi.	.951	77	152	4	8	2
Hendrick, St.L	.983	101	227	6	4	0
Hernandez, St.L*	1.000	3	2	0	0	0
Herndon, S.F.	.977	93	207	8	5	1
Householder, Cin	1.000	19	32	1	0	0
Howard, N.Y.	.952	14	18	2	1	0
Hutton, Mtl*	1.000	2	1	0	0	0
Iorg, St.L	.963	57	78	0	3	0
A. Johnson, Mtl	.000	1	0	0	0	0
Johnstone, L.A.	.957	16	19	3	1	0
Jones, S.D.*	.993	104	295	9	2	3
Jorgensen, N.Y.*	1.000	19	35	1	0	0
Kingman, N.Y.	.927	48	86	3	7	0
Knicely, Hou	.000	1	0	0	0	0
Lacy, Pitt	.977	63	121	7	3	1
Landreaux, L.A.	1.000	95	210	4	0	0
Landrum, St.L.	1.000	67	72	6	0	1
Lefebvre, S.D.	.994	84	167	6	1	2
Leonard, Hou-S.F.	1.000	30	82	2	0	0

Player—Club	Pct.	G.	PO.	A.	E.	DP.
Lezcano, Chi	1.000	5	7	0	0	0
Lezcano, St.L.	.973	65	103	5	3	1
Linares, Atl	.963	60	124	6	5	1
Loucks, Hou	1.000	5	5	0	0	0
Lum, Atl-Chi*	.938	15	15	0	1	0
Maddox, Phila	.977	93	249	8	6	4
Maldonado, L.A.	1.000	9	8	0	0	0
Marshall, L.A.	1.000	2	3	0	0	0
Martin, S.F.	.993	64	138	4	1	1
Matthews, Phila	.963	100	170	11	7	1
Mazzilli, N.Y.	.970	89	192	5	6	1
McBride, Phila	.987	56	76	2	1	1
Mejias, Cin	.972	58	34	1	1	0
Miller, Atl	.985	36	65	2	1	0
Milner, Cin*	1.000	4	2	0	0	0
Milner, Pitt*	1.000	8	12	0	0	0
Mitchell, L.A.*	1.000	7	6	0	0	0
Monday, L.A.*	.962	41	50	1	2	0
Morales, Chi	.986	72	142	2	2	1
Moreland, Phila	.000	2	0	0	0	0
Moreno, S.D.	1.000	9	13	1	0	0
Moreno, Pitt*	.997	103	302	6	1	1
Murphy, Atl	.981	103	254	11	5	4
North, S.F.	.966	37	84	1	3	0
Office, Mtl*	.938	15	15	0	1	0
Parker, Pitt	.941	60	110	1	7	0
Pate, Mtl	1.000	5	3	0	0	0
Perkins, S.D.*	.800	3	4	0	1	0
Puhl, Hou	1.000	88	185	5	0	1
Raines, Mtl	.976	81	160	6	4	0
Ramsey, St.L	.000	1	0	0	0	0
Richards, S.D.*	.975	101	178	14	5	1
W. Robinson, Pitt	.941	7	16	0	1	0
Roenicke, L.A.*	1.000	20	38	1	0	1
Roof, St.L	.950	20	38	0	2	0
Rooney, Mtl	1.000	2	1	0	0	0
Salazar, Hou	.959	23	45	2	2	1
Scott, St.L-Hou	.992	99	247	7	2	0
Smith, Phila	.971	51	91	10	3	2
Thomas, L.A.	.889	18	15	1	2	1
Thompson, Chi*	.980	30	49	1	1	0
Tolman, Hou*	1.000	3	2	0	0	0
Tracy, Chi	1.000	11	16	0	0	0
Trevino, N.Y.	1.000	2	3	0	0	0
Turner, S.D.*	.883	4	5	0	1	0
Unser, Phila*	1.000	16	19	0	0	0
Vail, Cin	1.000	3	3	0	0	0
Valentine, Mtl-N.Y.	.969	68	115	8	4	0
Venable, S.F.	1.000	5	12	0	0	0
G. Vukovich, Phila	1.000	9	10	0	0	0
Wallach, Mtl	1.000	35	55	3	0	1
Waller, Chi.	1.000	3	2	0	0	0
Walling, Hou	1.000	27	38	1	0	1
Washington, Atl*	.993	79	145	5	1	0
Whisenton, Atl*	.000	2	0	0	1	0
White, Mtl	.952	39	58	2	3	1
Wiggins, S.D.	.750	4	6	0	2	0
Wilson, N.Y.	.983	80	226	3	4	2
Wohlford, S.F.	1.000	10	3	1	0	0
Woods, Hou	.984	40	61	1	1	0
Youngblood, N.Y.	.962	41	70	6	3	0

OUTFIELDERS WITH TWO OR MORE CLUBS

Player—Club	Pct.	G.	PO.	A.	E.	DP.	Player—Club	Pct.	G.	PO.	A.	E.	DP.
Leonard, Hou	1.000	2	3	0	0	0	Scott, St.L.	1.000	44	120	2	0	0
Leonard, S.F.	1.000	28	79	2	0	0	Scott, Hou	.985	55	127	5	2	0
Lum, Atl°	1.000	1	3	0	0	0	Valentine, Mtl	1.000	21	32	2	0	0
Lum, Chi°	.923	14	12	0	1	0	Valentine, N.Y.	.957	47	83	6	4	0

CATCHERS

Leader—Club	Pct.	G.	PO.	A.	E.	DP.	PB.
NOLAN, Cin	.995	81	393	18	2	2	2

(Listed Alphabetically)

Player—Club	Pct.	G.	PO.	A.	E.	DP.	PB.	Player—Club	Pct.	G.	PO.	A.	E.	DP.	PB.
Ashby, Hou	.982	81	434	58	9	6	3	Nicosia, Pitt	.982	52	257	23	5	2	2
Bench, Cin	.979	7	41	5	1	0	1	Nolan, Cin	.995	81	393	18	2	2	2
Benedict, Atl.	.986	90	404	73	7	7	9	O'Berry, Cin	.983	55	208	22	4	2	0
Blackwell, Chi	.993	56	268	28	2	1	2	Owen, Atl	.964	10	23	4	1	2	0
Boone, Phila	.985	75	365	32	6	1	1	Pena, Pitt	.985	64	286	41	5	10	5
Brenly, S.F.	.964	14	50	3	2	2	2	Pocoroba, Atl.	1.000	9	28	4	0	2	0
Brummer, St.L.	1.000	19	43	3	0	1	0	Porter, St.L.	.979	52	206	31	5	2	2
Carter, Mtl	.993	100	509	58	4	11	4	Pujols, Hou	.995	39	192	14	1	1	5
Davis, Chi	.972	56	274	44	9	4	3	Ramos, Mtl	.974	23	70	5	2	2	1
Foote, Chi	1.000	8	30	3	0	2	1	Ransom, S.F.	1.000	5	28	5	0	0	0
Grote, L.A.	1.000	1	2	0	0	0	0	Roberts, Hou	.000	1	0	0	0	0	0
Gwosdz, S.D.	1.000	13	40	5	0	3	0	Sadek, S.F.	.979	19	79	15	2	2	1
Hayes, Chi	.000	1	0	0	0	0	0	Sanchez, St.L.	.926	18	50	0	4	1	1
Hodges, N.Y.	1.000	7	23	1	0	0	0	Scioscia, L.A.	.987	91	493	48	7	4	11
Kennedy, S.D.	.964	100	465	63	20	12	4	Sinatro, Atl	1.000	12	56	10	0	1	1
Knicely, Hou	1.000	2	11	2	0	0	0	Stearns, N.Y.	.983	66	302	38	6	7	2
May, S.F.	.989	93	468	48	6	4	4	Swisher, S.D.	.971	10	33	1	1	0	1
McCormack, Phila	1.000	3	4	2	0	0	0	Tenace, St.L	.980	38	126	18	3	1	2
Moreland, Phila	.982	50	256	20	5	2	1	Trevino, N.Y.	.963	45	211	22	9	1	3
Nahorodny, Atl	1.000	3	6	0	0	0	0	Virgil, Phila	1.000	1	2	0	0	0	0
								Wieghaus, Mtl	1.000	1	5	0	0	0	0
								Yeager, L.A.	.994	40	142	13	1	1	2

TRIPLE PLAY: Porter, St.L.

PITCHERS

Leader—Club	Pct.	G.	PO.	A.	E.	DP.
LEE, Mtl.°	1.000	31	12	27	0	1

(Listed Alphabetically)

Player—Club	Pct.	G.	PO.	A.	E.	DP.	Player—Club	Pct.	G.	PO.	A.	E.	DP.
Alexander, S.F.	1.000	24	9	16	0	1	Engle, Mtl.°	.000	1	0	0	0	0
Allen, N.Y.	1.000	43	4	13	0	1	Espinosa, Phila.	1.000	14	6	8	0	0
Alvarez, Atl.	.000	1	0	0	0	0	Falcone, N.Y.°	.917	35	2	9	1	0
Andujar, Hou.-St.L.	.895	20	5	12	2	0	Fireovid, S.D.	1.000	5	0	5	0	0
Armstrong, S.D.	.000	10	0	0	0	0	Forsch, St.L.	1.000	20	14	20	0	1
Bahnsen, Mtl.	.800	25	2	2	1	0	Forster, L.A.°	1.000	21	0	11	0	0
Bair, Cin.-St.L.	.889	35	2	6	1	0	Fryman, Mtl.°	1.000	35	2	8	0	1
Bedrosian, Atl.	1.000	15	1	2	0	1	Garber, Atl.	.962	35	8	17	1	1
Berenyi, Cin.	1.000	21	7	12	0	2	Geisel, Chi.°	1.000	11	2	1	0	0
Bibby, Pitt.	.929	14	2	11	1	3	Goltz, L.A.	1.000	26	6	14	0	1
Bird, Chi.	1.000	12	7	7	0	1	Gomez, Atl.	.000	1	0	0	0	0
Blue, S.F.°	.976	18	11	29	1	1	Gorman, Mtl.°	1.000	9	0	6	0	0
Boggs, Atl.	.868	25	13	20	5	0	Griffin, Chi.	1.000	16	1	11	0	0
Boitano, N.Y.	1.000	15	0	3	0	0	Griffin, S.F.	.927	22	9	29	3	0
Boone, S.D.°	.955	37	7	14	1	1	Gullickson, Mtl.	.966	22	12	16	1	2
Bradford, Atl.°	1.000	25	1	6	0	0	Hanna, Atl.	1.000	20	3	12	0	2
Breining, S.F.	1.000	45	3	12	0	0	Hargesheimer, S.F.	1.000	6	2	5	0	0
Brown, Cin.	1.000	10	0	2	0	0	Harris, N.Y.	.909	16	3	7	1	2
Brusstar, Phila.	1.000	14	2	1	0	0	Hausman, N.Y.	1.000	20	2	6	0	0
Burris, Mtl.	.893	22	8	17	3	2	Hernandez, Chi.°	1.000	12	0	3	0	0
Bystrom, Phila.	.889	9	3	13	2	0	Holland, S.F.°	.818	47	7	11	4	0
Camacho, Pitt.	1.000	7	0	3	0	1	Hooton, L.A.	1.000	23	4	18	0	2
Camp, Atl.	1.000	48	11	9	0	1	Howe, L.A.°	1.000	41	1	5	0	0
Candelaria, Pitt.°	1.000	6	1	7	0	1	Howell, Chi.	1.000	10	2	9	0	1
Capilla, Chi.°	.909	42	0	10	1	0	Hrabosky, Atl.°	1.000	24	1	1	0	0
Carlton, Phila.°	1.000	24	3	22	0	0	Hume, Cin.	1.000	51	2	12	0	0
Castillo, L.A.	1.000	34	3	4	0	1	Jackson, Pitt.-Mtl.°	.875	45	4	3	1	0
Caudill, Chi.	.923	30	4	8	1	0	Jones, Pitt.	1.000	13	3	10	0	0
Christenson, Phila.	.913	20	8	13	2	0	Jones, N.Y.°	1.000	13	2	19	0	0
Combe, Cin.	1.000	14	0	2	0	0	Kaat, St.L.°	.895	41	4	13	2	1
Cruz, Pitt.	1.000	22	1	5	0	1	Knepper, Hou.°	.914	22	6	26	3	1
Curtis, S.D.°	.923	28	0	12	1	1	Kravec, Chi.°	.950	24	3	16	1	0
M. Davis, Phila.°	1.000	9	0	6	0	0	Krukow, Chi.	.944	25	13	21	2	2
DeLeon, St.L.	1.000	10	0	2	0	0	Kuhaulua, S.D.°	1.000	5	0	1	0	0
Eastwick, Chi.	.923	30	4	8	1	0	LaCorte, Hou.	1.000	37	2	4	0	0
Edelen, St.L.-Cin.	1.000	18	1	2	0	0	LaCoss, Cin.	.952	20	6	14	1	0
Eichelberger, S.D.	.844	25	10	28	7	4	LaPoint, St.L.°	1.000	3	1	2	0	0
							Larson, Phila.	1.000	5	6	2	0	0
							Lavelle, S.F.°	.950	34	3	16	1	3
							Lea, Mtl.	1.000	16	5	8	0	2
							Leach, N.Y.	1.000	21	4	7	0	0

PITCHERS—Continued

Player—Club	Pct.	G.	PO.	A.	E.	DP.
Leary, N.Y.	.000	1	0	0	0	0
Lee, Pitt.	.929	12	6	7	1	0
Lee, Mtl.°	1.000	31	12	27	0	1
Leibrandt, Cin.°	1.000	7	0	7	0	0
Littell, St.L.	.818	28	5	4	2	0
Littlefield, S.D.	.938	42	6	9	1	1
Lollar, S.D.°	.963	24	4	22	1	1
Long, Pitt.	1.000	5	1	1	0	0
Lucas, S.D.°	1.000	57	5	15	0	0
Lyle, Phila.°	1.000	48	6	17	0	0
Lynch, N.Y.	.941	17	7	9	1	0
Mahler, Atl.	.943	34	14	19	2	0
Marshall, N.Y.	.889	20	3	5	1	0
Martin, St.L.°	1.000	17	3	20	0	0
Martinez, St.L.	.950	18	6	13	1	0
Martz, Chi.	1.000	33	7	18	0	2
Matula, Atl.	1.000	5	1	1	0	0
McGlothen, Chi.	1.000	20	3	12	0	0
McGraw, Phila.°	1.000	34	3	4	0	0
McWilliams, Atl.°	1.000	6	4	9	0	2
Miller, N.Y.	.800	23	2	2	1	1
Minton, S.F.	1.000	55	11	25	0	1
Moffitt, S.F.	.000	10	0	0	1	0
Montefusco, Atl.	.947	26	6	12	1	1
Moskau, Cin.	.941	27	4	12	1	0
Mura, S.D.	.976	23	14	26	1	0
Niedenfuer, L.A.	1.000	17	4	2	0	0
Niekro, Hou.	1.000	24	11	23	0	1
Niekro, Atl.	1.000	22	10	22	0	2
Noles, Phila.	.750	13	1	5	2	0
Orosco, N.Y.°	1.000	8	1	2	0	0
Otten, St.L.	.750	24	0	3	1	0
Pastore, Cin.	1.000	22	5	13	0	0
Pena, L.A.	.857	14	1	5	1	0
Perez, Pitt.	.952	17	7	13	1	0
Perry, Atl.	.909	23	11	19	3	0
Pladson, Hou.	.000	2	0	0	0	0
Power, L.A.	.500	5	1	0	1	0
Price, Cin.°	.875	41	1	13	2	0
Proly, Phila.	.958	35	9	14	0	0
Puleo, N.Y.	1.000	4	1	2	0	0
Ratzer, Mtl.	1.000	12	1	6	0	0
Reardon, N.Y.-Mtl.	1.000	43	1	4	0	0
J. Reed, Phila.	1.000	4	3	0	0	0
R. Reed, Phila.	1.000	39	0	8	0	0
Reuschel, Chi.	.926	13	4	21	2	2
Reuss, L.A.°	.980	22	10	38	1	4
Rhoden, Pitt.	1.000	21	8	25	0	4
Rincon, St.L.	1.000	5	2	5	0	0
Ripley, S.F.	.960	19	6	18	1	1
Roberts, N.Y.°	.800	7	0	4	1	0
D. Robinson, Pitt.	1.000	16	7	8	0	1
Rogers, Mtl.	1.000	22	10	20	0	1
Romo, Pitt.	1.000	33	5	3	0	1
Rowland, S.F.	1.000	9	1	2	0	0
Ruhle, Hou.	1.000	20	4	9	0	2
Ruthven, Phila.	.969	23	11	20	1	0
Ryan, Hou.	.955	21	5	16	1	3
Sambito, Hou.°	1.000	49	5	12	0	2
Sanderson, Mtl.	1.000	22	6	14	0	0
Scott, N.Y.	.980	23	14	35	1	2
Scurry, Pitt.°	1.000	27	0	8	0	1
Searage, N.Y.°	1.000	26	2	5	0	0
Seaver, Cin.	.968	23	8	22	1	1
Shirley, St.L.°	1.000	28	1	10	0	0
Show, S.D.	.800	15	0	4	1	0
B. Smith, Hou.	1.000	10	2	3	0	1
B. Smith, Mtl.	.500	7	0	1	1	0
D. Smith, Hou.	.933	42	3	11	1	0
Smith, Chi.	1.000	40	3	9	0	0
Solomon, Pitt.	.962	22	6	19	1	1
Sorensen, St.L.	.947	23	15	21	2	3
Sosa, Mtl.	1.000	32	3	8	0	0
Soto, Cin.	.935	25	10	19	2	1
Sprowl, Hou.°	1.000	15	2	3	0	0
Stewart, L.A.	1.000	32	4	7	0	0
Sutcliffe, L.A.	1.000	14	6	8	0	0
Sutter, St.L.	1.000	48	7	8	0	0
Sutton, Hou.	.946	23	11	24	2	3
Swan, N.Y.	1.000	5	0	2	0	0
Sykes, St.L.°	1.000	22	4	8	0	1
Tekulve, Pitt.	1.000	45	4	16	0	2
Tiant, Pitt.	1.000	9	3	5	0	0
Tidrow, Chi.	.909	51	0	10	1	0
Tufts, S.F.°	1.000	11	3	4	0	0
Urrea, S.D.	.857	38	0	6	1	0
Valenzuela, L.A.°	.938	25	12	33	3	2
Walk, Atl.	1.000	12	3	4	0	0
Welch, L.A.	1.000	23	4	18	0	1
Welsh, S.D.°	1.000	22	3	30	0	0
Whitson, S.F.	.875	22	10	11	3	1
Wise, S.D.	1.000	18	3	21	0	0
Zachry, N.Y.	.909	24	4	26	3	4

PITCHERS WITH TWO OR MORE CLUBS

Player—Club	Pct.	G.	PO.	A.	E.	DP.
Andujar, Hou.	.667	9	1	1	1	0
Andujar, St.L.	.938	11	4	11	1	0
Bair, Cin.	.857	24	2	4	1	0
Bair, St.L.	1.000	11	0	2	0	0
Edelen, St.L.	1.000	13	1	2	0	0
Edelen, Cin.	.000	5	0	0	0	0
Jackson, Pitt.°	.800	35	3	1	1	0
Jackson, Mtl.°	1.000	10	1	2	0	0
Reardon, N.Y.	1.000	18	0	2	0	0
Reardon, Mtl.	1.000	25	1	2	0	0

OFFICIAL NATIONAL LEAGUE PITCHING AVERAGES

CLUB PITCHING

	ERA.	G.	CG.	Sv.	ShO.	IP.	H.	BFP.	R.	ER.	HR.	SH.	SF.	Tot. BB.	Int. BB.	HB.	SO.	WP.	Bk.
Houston	2.66	110	23	25	19	990	842	4034	331	293	40	50	28	300	24	11	610	36	4
Los Angeles	3.01	110	26	24	19	997	904	4099	356	333	54	55	31	302	38	14	603	19	1
San Francisco	3.28	111	8	33	9	1009⅓	970	4302	414	368	57	65	28	393	56	24	561	36	13
Montreal	3.30	108	20	23	12	975	902	4008	394	357	58	44	26	268	21	18	520	28	2
Atlanta	3.45	107	11	24	4	968	936	4078	416	371	62	64	34	330	31	11	471	25	6
New York	3.55	105	7	24	3	926⅓	906	3951	432	365	74	67	35	336	35	13	490	26	10
Pittsburgh	3.56	103	11	29	5	942	953	4029	425	373	60	59	28	346	51	15	492	32	11
St. Louis	3.63	103	11	33	5	943	902	3910	417	380	52	45	22	290	45	15	388	32	11
San Diego	3.72	110	9	23	6	1002	1013	4297	455	414	64	66	26	414	59	17	492	30	19
Cincinnati	3.73	108	25	20	14	965⅔	863	4065	440	400	67	45	38	393	40	12	593	27	7
Chicago	4.01	106	6	20	2	956⅔	983	4165	483	426	59	75	38	388	60	21	532	42	8
Philadelphia	4.05	107	19	23	5	960⅓	967	4086	472	432	72	53	45	347	45	14	580	32	16
Totals	3.49	644	176	301	103	11635⅓	11141	49024	5035	4512	719	688	379	4107	505	185	6332	355	108

NOTE: Total earned runs for two clubs do not agree with composite total of respective club's pitchers due to provisions of Scoring Rule 10.18 (i). The following differences are to be noted: Chicago pitchers add to 427 and San Diego pitchers add to 415. (BFP total includes 11 batsmen awarded first base because of interference.)

PITCHERS' RECORD
(Top Fifteen Qualifiers for Earned-Run Leadership)

Pitcher and Club	ERA.	W.	L.	Pct.	G.	GS.	CG.	GF.	Sv.	ShO.	IP.	H.	R.	ER.	HR.	SH.	SF.	Tot. BB.	Int. BB.	HB.	SO.	WP.	Bk.
Ryan, L. Nolan, Houston	1.69	11	5	.688	21	21	5	0	0	5	149	99	34	28	2	5	3	68	1	1	140	16	2
Knepper, Robert, Houston°	2.18	9	5	.643	22	22	6	0	0	4	157	128	41	38	5	6	8	38	1	4	75	3	0
Hooton, Burt, Los Angeles	2.28	11	6	.647	23	23	5	0	0	5	142	124	42	36	6	5	8	35	2	2	74	3	0
Reuss, Jerry, Los Angeles°	2.29	10	4	.714	22	22	8	0	0	2	153	138	44	39	9	9	0	27	3	4	51	1	0
Carlton, Steven, Philadelphia°	2.42	13	4	.765	24	24	10	0	0	1	190	152	59	51	7	12	4	62	3	3	179	9	4
Blue, Vida, San Francisco°	2.45	8	6	.571	18	18	1	0	0	0	125	97	40	34	7	9	3	54	3	1	63	7	0
Valenzuela, Fernando, Los Angeles°	2.48	13	7	.650	25	25	11	0	0	8	192	140	55	53	11	9	3	61	4	3	180	5	0
Seaver, G. Thomas, Cincinnati	2.55	14	2	.875	23	23	6	0	0	0	166	120	51	47	10	9	8	66	8	3	87	3	1
Sutton, Donald, Houston	2.60	11	9	.550	23	23	6	0	0	3	159	132	52	46	6	9	5	29	3	1	104	4	0
Gullickson, William, Montreal	2.81	7	9	.438	22	22	3	0	0	2	157	142	54	49	6	13	2	34	4	1	115	4	1
Mahler, Richard, Atlanta	2.81	8	6	.571	34	14	3	10	2	0	112	109	41	35	3	5	3	43	4	5	54	7	1
Niekro, Joseph, Houston	2.82	9	9	.500	24	24	5	0	0	2	166	150	60	52	8	8	6	47	5	0	77	7	1
Alexander, Doyle, San Francisco	2.90	11	7	.611	24	24	4	0	0	1	152	156	51	49	11	5	6	44	4	7	77	4	1
Sanderson, Scott, Montreal	2.96	9	7	.563	22	22	4	0	0	0	137	122	50	45	10	7	4	31	2	1	77	4	0
Burris, B. Ray, Montreal	3.04	9	7	.563	22	21	4	0	0	0	136	117	56	46	9	6	6	41	3	3	52	6	1

° Throws lefthanded.

DEPARTMENTAL LEADERS: W—Seaver, 14; L—Mura, Zachry, 14; Pct.—Seaver, .875; G—Lucas, 57; CG—Valenzuela, 11; GF—Minton, 44; Sv—Sutter, 25; ShO—Valenzuela, 8; IP—Valenzuela, 192; H—Perry, 182; BFP—Carlton, 763; R—Ruthven, 84; ER—Ruthven, 94; HR—Soto, Zachry, 13; SH—Mura, 14; SF—Zachry, 9; Tot. BB—Lucas, Tidrow, 15; HB—T. Griffin, 7; SO—Valenzuela, 180; WP—Ryan, 16; Bk—D. Boone, Eichelberger, Sorensen, 5. Int. BB—Berenyi, 77.

(All Pitchers—Listed Alphabetically)

Pitcher and Club	ERA.	W.	L.	Pct.	G.	GS.	CG.	GF.	Sv.	ShO.	IP.	H.	R.	ER.	HR.	SH.	SF.	Tot. BB.	Int. BB.	HB.	SO.	WP.	Bk.
Alexander, Doyle, San Francisco	2.90	11	7	.611	24	24	4	1	0	1	152	156	51	49	11	5	2	44	8	2	77	4	0
Allen, Neil, New York	2.96	7	6	.538	43	0	0	35	18	0	67	64	26	22	4	10	3	26	0	0	50	3	0

Pitcher and Club	ERA.	W.	L.	Pct.	G.	GS.	CG.	GF.	Sv.	ShO.	IP.	H.	BFP.	R.	ER.	HR.	SH.	SF.	Tot. BB.	Int. BB.	HB.	SO.	WP.	Bk.
Alvarez, Jose, Atlanta	0.00	0	0	.000	1	0	0	1	0	0	1	1	6	0	0	0	0	0	0	0	0	2	0	0
Andujar, Joaquin, Hou.-St.L.	4.10	8	4	.667	20	11	1	0	0	0	79	85	336	41	36	6	2	2	23	1	0	37	0	1
Armstrong, Michael, San Diego	6.00	0	2	.000	10	3	0	3	0	0	12	14	58	9	8	1	0	0	11	3	1	9	0	0
Bahnsen, Stanley, Montreal	4.96	4	2	.667	25	0	0	20	1	0	49	45	208	27	27	7	2	0	24	0	0	28	1	0
Bair, C. Douglas, Cin.-St.L.	5.07	2	2	.500	35	0	0	5	0	0	55	55	234	34	31	5	2	0	19	1	1	30	3	0
Bedrosian, Stephen, Atlanta	4.50	1	2	.333	15	1	0	0	0	0	24	15	106	14	12	2	0	0	15	2	0	9	0	2
Berenyi, Bruce, Cincinnati	3.50	9	6	.600	21	20	5	0	0	3	126	97	544	55	49	4	3	4	77	0	0	106	7	0
Bibby, James, Pittsburgh	2.49	6	3	.667	14	14	2	0	0	1	94	79	385	30	26	5	2	4	16	1	2	48	1	2
Bird, J. Douglas, Chicago	3.60	4	5	.444	12	0	0	1	0	0	75	72	305	34	30	7	1	4	54	3	1	34	2	0
Blue, Vida, San Francisco°	2.45	8	6	.571	18	18	5	0	0	1	125	97	513	40	34	11	9	3	54	3	1	63	4	0
Boggs, Thomas, Atlanta	4.09	3	13	.188	25	24	0	0	0	0	143	140	606	72	65	2	13	7	54	7	3	81	0	0
Boitano, Danny, New York	5.63	2	1	.667	15	0	0	4	0	0	16	21	76	10	10	2	2	0	5	0	1	8	0	0
Boone, Daniel, San Diego°	2.86	2	0	1.000	37	0	0	8	2	0	63	63	262	23	20	1	2	2	21	7	0	43	6	5
Bradford, Larry, Atlanta°	3.67	2	2	.500	25	1	0	11	1	0	27	26	113	13	11	4	2	2	12	0	2	14	0	0
Breining, Fred, San Francisco	2.54	5	2	.714	45	0	0	15	1	0	78	66	326	28	22	0	9	5	38	0	1	37	3	3
Brown, Scott, Cincinnati	2.77	1	0	1.000	10	0	0	3	0	0	13	16	53	4	4	0	0	1	1	0	0	7	0	0
Brusstar, Warren, Philadelphia	4.50	0	1	.000	14	0	0	1	0	0	16	12	60	6	4	0	2	1	10	4	1	8	0	0
Burris, B. Ray, Montreal°	3.04	9	7	.563	22	21	4	0	0	0	136	117	554	56	46	9	9	4	41	3	4	52	6	1
Bystrom, Martin, Philadelphia	3.33	4	3	.571	9	9	1	0	0	1	54	55	227	21	20	3	6	6	16	1	3	24	1	1
Camacho, Ernie, Pittsburgh	4.91	0	1	.000	7	0	0	2	0	0	22	23	96	13	12	0	1	1	15	0	1	11	0	3
Camp, Rick, Atlanta	1.78	9	3	.750	48	0	0	33	17	0	76	68	304	17	15	5	5	3	12	0	0	47	0	0
Candelaria, John, Pittsburgh°	3.51	2	2	.500	6	6	0	0	0	0	41	42	168	17	16	3	1	1	11	4	1	14	2	0
Capilla, Douglas, Chicago°	3.18	2	2	.500	42	0	0	16	0	0	51	52	225	20	18	5	1	3	34	2	0	28	3	4
Carlton, Steven, Philadelphia°	2.42	13	4	.765	24	24	10	0	0	5	190	152	763	59	51	9	12	4	62	2	2	179	6	0
Castillo, Robert, Los Angeles	5.29	2	4	.333	34	1	0	15	0	0	51	50	220	31	30	5	5	2	24	2	1	35	0	2
Caudill, William, Chicago	5.83	1	5	.167	30	0	0	10	5	0	71	87	331	50	46	5	2	0	31	3	0	45	3	0
Christenson, Larry, Philadelphia	3.53	4	7	.364	20	15	0	0	0	0	107	108	446	48	42	8	8	8	30	2	0	70	3	2
Combe, Geoffrey, Cincinnati	7.50	7	0	1.000	14	0	0	3	0	0	18	27	85	15	15	4	2	1	10	1	1	9	1	0
Cruz, Victor, Pittsburgh	2.65	1	1	.500	22	0	0	6	0	0	34	33	144	15	10	3	1	0	15	0	1	28	0	0
Curtis, John, San Diego°	5.10	2	6	.250	28	8	0	4	0	0	67	70	293	41	38	6	4	3	30	3	0	31	1	0
Davis, Mark, Philadelphia°	7.74	2	2	.500	9	0	0	8	0	0	43	49	194	37	37	11	1	4	24	2	2	29	3	1
DeLeon, Luis, St. Louis	2.40	0	2	.000	10	0	0	2	0	0	15	11	59	4	4	1	1	0	3	0	0	8	0	0
Eastwick, Rawlins, Chicago	2.30	0	2	.000	30	0	0	9	0	0	43	43	183	16	11	2	4	2	15	2	1	24	1	1
Edelen, B. Joe, St.L.-Cin.	5.70	2	2	.500	18	0	0	6	0	0	30	34	125	19	19	3	0	4	3	0	1	15	1	1
Eichelberger, Juan, San Diego	3.51	8	8	.500	25	24	3	0	0	1	141	136	615	60	55	5	8	4	74	3	3	81	5	5
Engle, Richard, San Diego°	18.00	0	0	.000	1	0	0	1	0	0	2	6	13	4	4	0	0	0	1	0	0	2	0	0
Espinosa, Arnulfo, Philadelphia°	6.08	0	5	.000	14	14	2	0	0	1	74	98	327	52	50	11	7	2	24	2	0	22	2	1
Falcone, Peter, New York°	2.56	5	3	.625	35	14	3	0	0	1	95	84	397	32	27	3	7	6	36	3	4	56	2	0
Fireovid, Stephen, San Diego	2.77	0	1	.000	5	4	0	0	0	0	26	30	110	8	8	2	0	0	7	0	0	11	3	1
Forsch, Robert, St. Louis	3.19	10	5	.667	20	20	0	0	0	0	124	106	501	47	44	7	7	4	29	3	4	41	3	0
Forster, Terry, Los Angeles°	4.06	1	0	1.000	21	0	0	6	0	0	31	37	137	14	14	1	1	0	15	4	1	17	0	1
Fryman, Woodrow, Montreal°	1.88	5	3	.625	35	2	0	16	6	0	43	38	172	16	9	1	2	3	14	1	1	25	1	0
Garber, H. Eugene, Atlanta	2.59	2	3	.400	35	0	0	17	7	0	59	49	251	23	17	2	1	2	20	9	0	34	3	1
Geisel, J. David, Atlanta°	0.56	2	0	1.000	11	0	0	4	2	0	16	11	66	3	1	0	0	0	10	2	0	7	0	0
Goltz, David, Los Angeles	4.09	2	7	.222	26	11	0	3	0	1	77	83	319	35	35	4	1	2	25	2	3	48	1	1
Gomez, Luis, Atlanta	27.00	0	0	.000	1	0	0	1	0	0	1	3	8	3	3	0	0	0	0	0	0	0	0	0
Gorman, Thomas, Montreal°	4.20	0	0	.000	9	0	0	4	0	0	15	12	63	7	7	0	1	1	6	0	1	13	0	2
Griffin, Michael, Chicago	4.50	2	5	.286	16	9	0	0	0	0	52	64	228	27	26	4	5	2	9	2	0	20	2	2
Griffin, Thomas, San Francisco	3.77	8	8	.500	22	22	3	0	0	1	129	121	557	54	54	8	5	2	57	8	7	83	5	5
Gullickson, William, Montreal	2.81	7	9	.438	22	22	3	0	0	2	157	142	640	54	49	3	5	2	34	4	4	115	4	0

Pitcher and Club	ERA.	W.	L.	Pct.	G.	GS.	CG.	GF.	Sv.	ShO.	IP.	H.	BFP.	R.	ER.	HR.	SH.	SF.	Tot. BB.	Int. BB.	HB.	SO.	WP.	Bk.
Hanna, Preston, Atlanta	6.43	2	1	.667	20	3	0	1	0	0	35	45	164	27	25	2	4	5	23	2	2	22	6	0
Hargesheimer, Alan, San Francisco	4.26	2	4	.333	6	1	0	2	0	0	19	20	80	9	9	1	2	1	8	2	1	6	0	0
Harris, Greg, New York	4.43	3	5	.375	16	14	0	2	1	0	69	65	300	36	34	8	1	1	28	2	2	54	3	2
Hausman, Thomas, New York	2.18	0	1	.000	20	0	0	5	2	0	33	28	130	8	8	2	2	2	7	1	0	13	3	1
Hernandez, Guillermo, Chicago°	3.86	0	1	.000	12	0	0	3	0	0	14	14	62	7	6	0	2	1	8	11	2	13	1	0
Holland, Alfred, San Francisco°	2.41	7	5	.583	47	3	0	23	7	0	101	87	431	31	27	4	7	5	44	0	2	78	3	0
Hooton, Burt, Los Angeles	2.28	11	6	.647	23	23	5	0	0	0	142	124	571	42	36	3	3	4	33	3	2	74	3	0
Howe, Steve, Los Angeles°	2.50	5	3	.625	41	0	0	25	8	0	54	51	227	17	15	2	4	4	18	7	0	32	0	0
Howell, Jay, Chicago	4.91	2	0	1.000	10	2	0	9	0	0	22	23	97	13	12	3	2	2	10	2	0	10	0	0
Hrabosky, Alan, Atlanta°	1.06	1	1	.500	24	0	0	9	1	0	34	24	131	5	4	1	4	1	10	9	1	13	3	0
Hume, Thomas, Cincinnati	3.44	9	4	.692	51	0	0	40	13	0	68	63	281	27	26	7	5	2	31	5	0	27	0	1
Jackson, Grant, Pitt.-Mtl.°	3.77	1	4	.200	45	0	0	20	4	0	43	44	189	19	18	3	5	1	19	6	0	30	1	1
Jones, Odell, Pittsburgh	3.33	2	2	.500	13	8	0	0	0	0	54	51	232	20	20	8	4	1	23	8	1	14	2	0
Jones, Randall, New York°	4.88	1	8	.111	13	12	0	16	0	0	59	65	284	48	32	2	5	3	38	1	0	8	1	1
Kaat, James, St. Louis°	3.40	6	6	.500	22	1	0	16	0	0	53	60	229	25	20	2	6	3	17	8	1	8	2	0
Knepper, Robert, Houston°	2.18	9	5	.643	24	22	6	0	0	0	157	128	617	41	38	5	6	3	38	6	4	75	2	0
Kravec, Kenneth, Chicago°	5.08	1	6	.143	25	12	2	2	0	0	78	80	356	48	44	5	10	5	39	6	4	50	0	1
Krukow, Michael, Chicago	3.69	9	9	.500	25	25	2	0	0	0	144	146	622	68	59	11	7	6	55	6	2	101	8	0
Kuhaulua, Fred, San Diego°	2.48	1	0	1.000	5	0	0	2	0	0	29	28	119	10	8	2	1	3	9	1	0	16	1	1
LaCorte, Frank, Houston	3.64	4	2	.667	37	0	0	22	5	0	42	41	184	18	17	1	1	0	21	3	1	40	0	0
LaCoss, Michael, Cincinnati	6.12	4	7	.364	13	13	0	0	0	0	78	102	354	55	53	4	1	5	30	0	0	22	6	0
LaPoint, David, St. Louis°	4.09	1	0	1.000	3	2	0	0	0	0	11	12	45	5	5	1	1	1	2	0	1	4	2	0
Larson, Daniel, Philadelphia	4.18	3	0	1.000	5	4	1	0	0	0	28	27	122	13	13	4	1	1	15	1	0	15	1	1
Lavelle, Gary, San Francisco°	3.82	2	6	.250	34	1	0	10	4	0	66	58	269	28	28	3	6	3	23	4	0	45	3	2
Lea, Charles, Montreal	4.64	5	4	.556	16	11	2	2	0	0	64	63	267	34	33	3	4	0	26	3	0	31	1	0
Leach, Terry, New York	2.57	1	1	.500	21	1	0	3	0	0	35	26	139	11	10	0	3	1	12	2	0	16	4	0
Leary, Timothy, New York	0.00	0	0	.000	1	1	0	0	0	0	2	0	7	0	0	0	0	0	0	0	0	5	1	0
Lee, Mark, Pittsburgh	2.70	0	2	.000	12	0	0	6	2	0	20	17	83	6	6	1	5	1	5	2	0	5	1	0
Lee, William, Montreal°	2.93	5	6	.455	31	7	1	0	0	0	89	90	365	33	29	6	4	3	14	2	2	34	1	1
Leibrandt, Charles, Cincinnati°	3.60	1	1	.500	7	7	0	0	0	0	30	28	128	12	12	0	1	0	15	1	2	9	1	0
Littell, Mark, St. Louis	3.66	2	3	.400	28	3	0	13	2	0	41	36	186	21	20	2	2	0	31	5	2	22	3	0
Littlefield, John, San Diego	6.08	2	3	.400	42	0	0	13	0	0	64	53	262	28	26	5	3	2	28	5	1	21	2	0
Lollar, W. Timothy, San Diego°	5.85	2	8	.200	24	5	0	0	0	0	77	87	361	56	52	8	4	2	51	1	3	38	7	0
Long, Robert, Pittsburgh	2.00	1	2	.333	5	0	0	13	0	0	20	23	90	14	13	1	8	0	10	0	1	8	0	4
Lucas, Gary, San Diego°	4.44	7	7	.500	57	0	0	40	13	0	90	78	369	26	20	4	9	5	36	15	3	53	1	0
Lyle, Albert, Philadelphia°	2.93	9	6	.600	48	0	0	19	9	0	75	85	332	40	37	6	2	4	33	9	1	29	3	1
Lynch, Edward, New York	2.81	4	5	.444	17	13	1	10	0	0	80	79	336	32	26	5	2	1	21	2	1	27	3	2
Mahler, Richard, Atlanta	2.61	8	6	.571	34	14	1	10	0	0	112	109	478	41	35	5	11	5	43	5	2	54	1	1
Marshall, Michael G., New York	3.41	3	2	.600	20	0	0	9	0	0	31	26	127	10	10	0	2	2	8	3	2	8	2	0
Martin, John, St. Louis°	3.99	8	5	.615	17	15	4	0	0	0	103	85	407	43	39	10	8	5	26	3	0	36	3	0
Martinez, Silvio, St. Louis°	3.67	2	5	.286	18	16	1	0	0	0	97	95	413	48	43	4	7	2	39	3	1	34	2	0
Martz, Randy, Chicago	6.43	5	7	.417	33	14	1	4	0	0	108	103	464	49	44	6	2	1	49	3	0	32	3	0
Matula, Richard, Atlanta	4.75	0	4	.000	20	0	0	10	0	0	7	8	30	5	5	1	1	0	2	0	1	0	1	0
McGlothen, Lynn, Chicago	2.66	1	4	.200	20	6	0	5	0	0	55	71	259	32	29	5	6	2	28	4	0	26	2	0
McGraw, Frank, Philadelphia°	3.08	2	4	.333	34	0	0	31	10	0	44	35	178	13	13	3	2	2	14	3	0	26	1	0
McWilliams, Larry, Atlanta°	3.32	2	2	.500	6	5	2	0	0	0	38	31	147	13	13	0	2	1	8	0	0	23	3	0
Miller, Dyar, New York	2.89	2	1	.667	23	0	0	8	2	0	38	49	174	20	14	2	6	2	15	8	0	22	3	0
Minton, Gregory, San Francisco	8.18	4	5	.444	55	0	0	44	21	0	84	84	359	28	27	0	9	3	36	8	0	29	2	1
Moffitt, Randall, San Francisco°	3.51	0	0	1.000	10	0	0	4	0	0	11	15	51	10	10	2	5	1	2	1	0	11	1	2
Montefusco, John, Atlanta	3.51	2	3	.400	26	9	0	4	1	0	77	75	323	32	30	2	5	3	27	2	0	34	2	1

Pitcher and Club	ERA.	W.	L.	Pct.	G.	GS.	CG.	GF.	Sv.	ShO.	IP.	H.	BFP.	R.	ER.	HR.	SH.	SF.	Tot. BB.	Int. BB.	HB.	SO.	WP.	Bk.
Moskau, Paul, Cincinnati	4.91	5	2	.667	27	1	0	14	2	0	55	54	246	31	30	4	1	3	32	5	1	32	2	0
Mura, Stephen, San Diego	4.27	5	14	.263	23	22	2			2	139	156	610	72	66	10	14	1	50	2	2	70	0	0
Niedenfuer, Thomas, Los Angeles	3.81	3	1	.750	17			8	2	0	26	25	107	11	11	1	4	1	7	1	0	12	7	0
Niekro, Joseph, Houston	2.82	9	9	.500	24	24	5			2	166	150	676	60	52	8	6	6	47	4	0	77	2	0
Niekro, Philip, Atlanta	3.11	7	7	.500	22	22	3			1	139	120	578	56	48	6	5	6	56	2	3	62	2	3
Noles, Dickie, Philadelphia	4.19	2	2	.500	13	8	0	1	0	0	58	57	249	30	27	2	2	2	23	2	0	34	4	1
Orosco, Jesse, New York°	1.59	1	0	1.000	8			4	1	0	17	13	69	4	3	2	1	0	6	3	0	18	3	0
Otten, James, St. Louis	5.25	1	9	.308	24	2	2			0	36	44	160	23	21	3	7	5	20	3	1	20	4	2
Pastore, Frank, Cincinnati	4.02	4	9	.500	14	22		10	0	0	132	125	556	73	59	11	0	0	35	7	1	81	5	0
Pena, Alejandro, Los Angeles	2.88	1	7	.222	14			7	1	0	25	18	104	9	8	2	1	0	11	1	3	14	1	1
Perez, Pascual, Pittsburgh	3.98	8	2	.471	17	13	2	1	0	0	86	92	380	50	38	5	7	6	34	5	0	46	5	1
Perry, Gaylord, Atlanta	3.93	8	9	.000	23	23	3			0	151	182	644	70	66	9	12	6	24	0	4	60	0	1
Pladson, Gordon, Houston	9.00	0	3	.250	5	0		1	0	0	4	9	24	6	4	0	0	0	3	0	0	0	0	0
Power, Ted, Los Angeles	3.21	1	3	.857	5			13	4	0	14	16	66	6	5	3	6	3	7	0	0	7	2	0
Price, Joseph, Cincinnati°	2.50	6	1	.667	41	2	0	9	0	0	54	42	216	19	15	3	9	0	18	5	0	41	1	1
Proly, Michael, Philadelphia	3.86	2	1	.000	35	2	0	2	2	0	63	66	262	29	27	6	5	3	19	2	1	19	5	0
Puleo, Charles, New York	0.00	0	1	.500	4					0	13	8	53	1	0	0	0	1	8	2	0	8	1	1
Ratzer, Steven, Montreal	6.35	0	1	1.000	12			7	0	0	17	23	82	14	12	2	0	0	7	0	0	4	1	0
Reardon, Jeffrey, N.Y.-Mtl.	2.19	3	0	1.000	43		0	33	8	0	70	48	279	17	17	5	2	2	21	4	1	49	5	1
Reed, Jerry, Philadelphia	7.20	0	1	.625	4			2	0	0	5	7	27	4	4	0	0	0	6	1	0	5	1	0
Reed, Ronald, Philadelphia	3.10	5	3	.364	39		0	22	8	0	61	54	251	26	21	6	5	3	17	8	3	40	0	0
Reuschel, Ricky, Chicago	3.45	4	7	.714	13	13	1			0	86	87	358	44	33	4	5	7	23	4	2	53	5	0
Reuss, Jerry, Los Angeles°	2.29	10	4	.692	22	22	8			2	153	138	608	40	39	9	9	0	27	4	2	51	9	1
Rhoden, Richard, Pittsburgh	3.90	9	4	.750	21	21	4			0	136	147	588	66	59	6	7	5	53	4	2	76	6	1
Rincon, Andrew, St. Louis	1.75	3	1	.750	5	5	1			0	36	27	133	8	7	0	0	0	7	2	0	13	3	1
Ripley, Allen, San Francisco	4.05	4	4	.500	19	14	0	4	0	0	91	103	396	45	41	11	7	7	27	3	0	47	1	0
Roberts, David, New York°	9.60	0	3	.000	7	4	0			0	15	26	76	18	16	5	3	2	5	1	0	10	3	0
Robinson, Don, Pittsburgh	5.92	12	8	.600	16	2	0	4	3	0	38	47	180	27	25	5	4	4	23	4	1	17	4	0
Rogers, Stephen, Montreal	3.41	1	2	.250	22	22	7			3	161	149	652	64	61	7	7	4	41	7	0	87	1	1
Romo, Enrique, Pittsburgh	4.50	0	3	.000	33			14	5	0	42	47	186	27	21	5	0	7	18	7	2	23	0	0
Rowland, Michael, San Francisco	3.38	1	0	.400	9		0	3	0	0	16	13	66	7	6	1	1	0	20	1	1	8	0	0
Ruhle, Vernon, Houston	2.91	4	6	.632	20	15	1			1	102	97	412	36	33	3	5	7	20	5	1	39	6	0
Ruthven, Richard, Philadelphia	5.14	12	7	.688	23	22	5			0	147	162	648	94	84	10	7	4	54	5	3	80	16	2
Ryan, L. Nolan, Houston	1.69	11	5	.500	21	21	5			3	149	99	605	34	28	8	3	6	68	5	2	140	9	0
Sambito, Joseph, Houston°	2.96	9	7	.563	49		0	32	10	0	64	43	255	17	13	4	1	1	22	4	1	41	2	1
Sanderson, Scott, Montreal	3.90	5	10	.333	22	22	4			1	137	122	560	50	45	11	7	5	31	2	0	77	4	2
Scott, Michael, New York	3.77	1	5	.444	23	23	1			0	136	130	551	65	59	11	7	2	34	2	1	54	4	1
Scurry, Rodney, Pittsburgh°	3.65	14	2	1.000	27			10	1	0	74	74	331	33	31	6	1	1	40	3	3	65	3	2
Searage, Raymond, New York°	2.55	6	4	.875	26			7	0	0	37	34	156	16	15	10	0	8	17	0	3	16	5	2
Seaver, G. Thomas, Cincinnati	4.10	1	4	.600	23	23	6			1	166	120	671	51	47	6	9	2	66	8	3	87	1	1
Shirley, Robert, St. Louis	3.13	1	3	.250	28	11	0	5	1	1	79	78	342	42	36	8	9	5	34	3	2	36	3	0
Show, Eric, San Diego	3.00	1	0	1.000	15	1	0	4	0	0	23	17	92	9	8	2	3	0	9	4	1	22	0	0
Smith, Billy, Houston	1.00	1	0		10			4	1	0	13	20	81	7	7	1	2	0	3	0	0	0	0	0
Smith, Bryn, Montreal	2.77	5	3	.625	7			1	0	0	21	14	53	7	4	2	0	4	9	0	0	9	4	0
Smith, David, Houston	2.76	3	6	.333	42			22	8	0	75	54	305	26	23	2	6	2	23	4	0	52	7	0
Smith, Lee, Chicago	3.49	8	6	.571	40	1	0	12	1	0	67	57	281	31	26	10	2	0	31	2	0	50	3	1
Solomon, Eddie, Pittsburgh	3.12	7	5	.500	22	17	2	5	0	1	127	133	521	49	44	3	8	2	27	2	1	38	3	3
Sorensen, Lary, St. Louis	3.28	7	7	.333	23	23	3			0	140	149	579	59	51	13	11	0	26	3	1	52	1	5
Sosa, Elias, Montreal	3.69	1	2	.571	32		0	17	3	0	39	46	170	16	16	3	3	3	8	0	1	18	1	3
Soto, Mario, Cincinnati	3.29	12	9		25	25	10	0	0	3	175	142	717	69	64	13	3	4	61	3	3	151	4	3

Pitcher and Club	ERA.	W.	L.	Pct.	G.	GS.	CG.	GF.	Sv.	ShO.	IP.	H.	BFP.	R.	ER.	HR.	SH.	SF.	Tot. BB.	Int. BB.	HB.	SO.	WP.	Bk.
Sprowl, Robert, Houston°	5.90	0	3	.000	15	1	0	4	0	0	29	40	138	20	19	1	2	2	14	1	0	18	3	0
Stewart, David, Los Angeles	2.51	4	3	.571	32	0	0	14	6	0	43	40	184	13	12	3	7	1	14	5	0	29	4	0
Sutcliffe, Richard, Los Angeles	4.02	2	2	.500	14	6	0	5	0	0	47	41	197	24	21	5	1	2	20	2	2	16	0	1
Sutter, H. Bruce, St. Louis	2.63	3	5	.375	48	0	0	36	25	0	82	64	328	24	24	5	7	6	24	8	1	57	0	0
Sutton, Donald, Houston	2.60	11	9	.550	23	23	6	0	0	3	159	132	624	51	46	6	13	0	29	3	1	104	0	1
Swan, Craig, New York	3.21	0	2	.000	5	3	0	0	0	0	14	10	50	6	5	0	1	0	1	0	1	9	0	0
Sykes, Robert, St. Louis°	4.62	2	2	.500	22	1	0	7	3	0	37	37	160	20	19	1	2	4	18	5	1	14	3	0
Tekulve, Kenton, Pittsburgh	2.49	5	5	.500	45	0	0	27	3	0	65	61	268	19	18	1	4	2	17	5	1	34	1	0
Tiant, Luis, Pittsburgh	3.95	2	5	.286	9	9	1	0	0	0	57	54	242	31	25	3	1	1	19	2	0	32	0	0
Tidrow, Richard, Chicago	5.04	3	10	.231	51	0	0	30	9	0	75	73	328	45	42	6	11	0	30	15	1	39	2	0
Tufts, Robert, San Francisco°	3.60	0	0	.000	11	0	0	4	0	0	15	20	74	9	6	0	1	1	6	0	0	12	1	0
Urrea, John, San Diego	2.39	2	7	.500	38	0	0	16	2	0	49	43	215	14	13	1	1	3	28	4	0	19	4	0
Valenzuela, Fernando, Los Angeles°	2.48	13	7	.650	25	25	11	0	0	8	192	140	758	55	53	11	9	0	61	3	3	180	1	1
Walk, Robert, Atlanta	4.60	1	4	.200	12	8	0	1	0	0	43	41	189	25	22	6	2	2	23	0	0	16	1	0
Welch, Robert, Los Angeles	3.45	9	5	.643	23	23	2	0	0	1	141	141	601	56	54	11	9	4	41	4	3	88	2	2
Welsh, Christopher, San Diego°	3.77	6	7	.462	22	19	4	2	0	2	124	122	512	55	52	9	5	3	41	1	0	51	1	2
Whitson, Eddie, San Francisco	4.02	6	9	.400	22	22	2	0	0	0	123	130	534	61	55	10	6	2	47	5	2	65	3	2
Wise, Richard, San Diego	3.77	4	8	.333	28	18	0	1	0	0	98	116	419	44	41	13	6	2	19	4	2	27	2	1
Zachry, Patrick, New York	4.14	7	14	.333	24	24	3	0	0	0	139	151	616	78	64	11	11	9	56	1	4	76	1	1

NOTE—Following pitchers combined to pitch shutout games: Cincinnati (4)—Berenyi and Hume, Seaver and Moskau, Seaver and Price, Seaver and Price and Hume; Houston (6)—Ryan and Sambito 2, Knepper and LaCorte, Niekro and D. Smith, Ryan and LaCorte, Sutton and Sambito; Los Angeles (4)—Goltz and Pena, Hooton, Castillo and Howe, Hooton, Pena and Stewart, Reuss and Howe; Montreal (4)—Burris and Reardon, Burris, Reardon, Fryman, Bahnsen and B. Smith, Rogers, Fryman and Reardon, Sanderson, Lea and Sosa; New York (2)—Lynch and Allen, Zachry, Hausman and Allen; Philadelphia (4)—Carlton and McGraw, Carlton and J. Reed, Christenson and Proly, Bystrom and R. Reed; Pittsburgh (1)—Scurry and Solomon; St. Louis (3)—Andujar and Sutter, Rincon and Sykes, Shirley, Martinez and Sykes; San Diego (3)—Eichelberger and Lucas, Fireovid, Boone and Lucas, Kuhaulua and Show; San Francisco (6)—Alexander and Minton 2, Blue and Lavelle, Blue and Minton, Hargesheimer and Minton, Holland and Minton.

PITCHERS WITH TWO OR MORE CLUBS
(Alphabetically Arranged With Pitcher's First Club on Top)

Pitcher and Club	ERA.	W.	L.	Pct.	G.	GS.	CG.	GF.	Sv.	ShO.	IP.	H.	BFP.	R.	ER.	HR.	SH.	SF.	Tot. BB.	Int. BB.	HB.	SO.	WP.	Bk.
Andujar, Houston	4.88	2	3	.400	9	3	0	0	0	0	23⅔	29	113	17	13	4	2	1	12	0	0	18	0	2
Andujar, St. Louis	3.76	6	1	.857	11	8	1	0	0	0	55⅓	56	223	24	23	4	1	0	11	1	0	19	2	1
Bair, Cincinnati	5.77	2	2	.500	24	0	0	12	1	0	39	42	174	28	25	5	2	0	17	4	0	16	3	0
Bair, St. Louis	3.38	2	0	1.000	11	0	0	8	1	0	15⅔	13	60	6	6	0	0	0	2	0	0	14	0	0
Edelen, St. Louis	9.53	1	0	1.000	13	0	0	4	0	0	17⅓	29	85	18	18	1	1	1	10	1	0	10	1	0
Edelen, Cincinnati	0.69	1	0	1.000	5	0	0	2	0	0	12⅔	5	40	1	1	1	2	0	3	0	0	5	0	0
Jackson, Pittsburgh	2.53	1	2	.333	35	0	0	18	4	0	32⅓	30	135	10	9	1	2	2	10	3	0	17	3	1
Jackson, Montreal	7.36	1	0	1.000	10	0	0	2	0	0	10⅔	14	54	9	9	2	3	0	9	2	0	4	1	0
Reardon, New York	3.41	1	1	1.000	18	0	0	14	2	0	28⅔	27	124	11	11	2	0	2	12	4	0	28	0	0
Reardon, Montreal	1.29	1	2	1.000	25	0	0	19	6	0	41⅓	21	155	6	6	3	3	0	9	1	1	21	1	0

1981 N.L. Pitching Against Each Club

ATLANTA—50-56

Pitcher	Chi. W—L	Cin. W—L	Hou. W—L	L.A. W—L	Mtl. W—L	N.Y. W—L	Phil. W—L	Pitt. W—L	St.L. W—L	S.D. W—L	S.F. W—L	Totals W—L
Bedrosian	0—0	0—0	0—0	1—1	0—1	0—0	0—0	0—0	0—0	0—0	0—0	1— 2
Boggs	0—0	1—2	0—2	1—1	0—1	1—0	0—1	0—1	0—2	0—1	0—2	3—13
Bradford	0—0	1—0	0—0	0—0	0—0	0—0	0—0	0—0	1—0	0—0	0—0	2— 0
Camp	0—0	0—0	2—2	1—0	0—0	0—0	1—0	0—0	1—0	3—1	1—0	9— 3
Garber	0—0	1—1	0—0	0—1	1—2	0—0	1—0	0—0	0—0	1—1	0—1	4— 6
Hanna	1—0	0—0	0—0	0—0	0—0	0—0	0—0	0—0	1—0	0—1	0—0	2— 1
Hrabosky	0—0	0—0	0—0	0—0	0—0	0—0	0—1	0—0	0—0	1—0	0—0	1— 1
Mahler	1—0	1—0	1—0	1—1	1—2	1—1	1—1	1—0	0—0	0—1	0—0	8— 6
McWilliams	0—0	0—0	0—1	0—0	0—0	0—0	0—0	0—0	0—0	1—0	1—0	2— 1
Montefusco	0—0	0—0	0—1	0—1	1—0	0—0	0—0	0—0	0—0	0—0	1—1	2— 3
Niekro	0—1	0—1	1—0	1—0	0—1	1—1	1—0	1—1	0—0	1—1	1—1	7— 7
Perry	1—0	2—1	0—1	2—1	0—0	0—1	0—2	0—0	1—1	2—0	0—2	8— 9
Walk	0—1	0—0	0—1	0—1	0—0	0—0	0—0	0—0	0—1	0—0	1—0	1— 4
Totals	3—2	6—5	4—8	7—7	3—7	3—3	4—5	2—3	4—3	9—6	5—7	50—56

No Decisions—Alvarez, Gomez, Matula.

CHICAGO—38-65

Pitcher	Atl. W—L	Cin. W—L	Hou. W—L	L.A. W—L	Mtl. W—L	N.Y. W—L	Phil. W—L	Pitt. W—L	St.L. W—L	S.D. W—L	S.F. W—L	Totals W—L
Bird	0—0	0—0	0—0	2—0	0—2	1—0	0—1	0—0	1—0	0—0	0—2	4— 5
Capilla	0—0	0—0	0—0	0—0	0—0	0—0	0—0	0—0	0—0	1—0	0—0	1— 0
Caudill	0—1	0—0	0—1	0—0	1—0	0—0	0—1	0—2	0—0	0—0	0—0	1— 5
Eastwick	0—0	0—0	0—0	0—0	0—0	0—1	0—0	0—0	0—0	0—0	0—0	0— 1
Geisel	0—0	0—0	0—0	0—0	0—0	0—0	0—0	1—0	1—0	0—0	0—0	2— 0
Griffin	0—0	0—0	0—0	1—1	1—1	0—0	0—0	0—2	0—0	0—0	0—1	2— 5
Howell	0—0	0—0	0—0	0—0	0—0	0—0	1—0	1—0	0—0	0—0	0—0	2— 0
Kravec	0—1	0—0	0—0	0—0	0—0	0—0	0—2	0—0	0—2	1—1	0—0	1— 6
Krukow	0—0	0—1	0—2	1—1	1—2	2—0	1—0	0—1	2—1	0—1	2—0	9— 9
Martz	1—0	1—0	0—2	0—2	0—0	0—2	0—0	1—1	1—0	0—0	1—0	5— 7
McGlothen	0—0	0—0	0—0	0—0	0—1	0—1	0—0	0—1	0—1	0—0	0—0	1— 4
Reuschel	1—0	0—2	0—0	1—0	1—0	0—2	0—2	0—1	0—0	0—0	1—0	4— 7
Smith	0—0	0—1	1—1	0—0	0—0	0—1	0—2	0—1	0—0	2—0	0—0	3— 6
Tidrow	0—1	0—1	0—0	0—0	0—1	2—1	0—2	1—1	0—0	0—1	0—2	3—10
Totals	2—3	1—5	1—6	6—4	4—7	5—8	2—10	4—10	5—4	3—3	5—5	38—65

No Decisions—Hernandez.

CINCINNATI—66-42

Pitcher	Atl. W—L	Chi. W—L	Hou. W—L	L.A. W—L	Mtl. W—L	N.Y. W—L	Phil. W—L	Pitt. W—L	St.L. W—L	S.D. W—L	S.F W—L	Totals W—L
Bair	1—0	0—0	0—0	0—1	1—0	0—0	0—1	0—0	0—0	0—0	0—0	2— 2
Berenyi	1—0	1—0	3—1	0—1	1—0	1—1	0—0	0—0	0—1	1—1	0—1	9— 6
Brown	0—0	0—0	0—0	1—0	0—0	0—0	0—0	0—0	0—0	0—0	0—0	1— 0
Combe	0—0	0—0	0—0	0—0	0—0	0—0	0—0	0—0	0—0	1—0	0—0	1— 0
Edelen	0—0	0—0	0—0	1—0	0—0	0—0	0—0	0—0	0—0	0—0	0—0	1— 0
Hume	0—2	0—0	0—0	0—0	0—0	1—1	3—0	1—0	0—1	1—0	3—0	9— 4
LaCoss	0—1	0—0	0—1	1—1	0—1	1—0	0—0	1—1	0—1	1—0	0—1	4— 7
Leibrandt	0—0	0—0	1—0	0—0	0—0	0—0	0—0	0—0	0—1	0—0	0—0	1— 1
Moskau	0—0	0—0	0—0	1—1	0—0	0—0	0—0	0—0	0—0	1—0	0—0	2— 1
Pastore	0—1	0—1	1—1	0—0	1—0	0—1	0—0	0—0	0—0	1—0	1—2	4— 9
Price	0—0	1—0	1—0	2—0	0—1	0—0	0—0	1—0	0—0	0—0	1—0	6— 1
Seaver	1—0	2—0	1—0	0—1	2—0	2—0	1—0	0—0	0—1	4—0	1—0	14— 2
Soto	2—2	1—0	1—1	1—1	1—1	2—0	1—0	0—1	1—1	0—0	2—1	12— 9
Totals	5—6	5—1	8—4	8—8	5—4	7—3	5—2	4—2	0—5	10—2	9—5	66—42

No Decisions—None.

HOUSTON—61-49

Pitcher	Atl. W—L	Chi. W—L	Cin. W—L	L.A. W—L	Mtl. W—L	N.Y. W—L	Phil. W—L	Pitt. W—L	St.L. W—L	S.D. W—L	S.F. W—L	Totals W—L
Andujar	0—0	1—0	0—1	0—1	0—0	0—0	0—0	0—0	0—0	0—0	1—1	2— 3
Knepper	1—0	2—0	1—0	1—0	1—0	1—1	0—1	0—0	0—0	1—2	1—1	9— 5
LaCorte	1—0	0—1	0—0	0—0	1—0	0—0	0—1	0—0	0—0	1—0	1—0	4— 2
Niekro	2—1	1—0	1—1	0—2	0—0	0—0	0—2	0—1	1—0	3—1	1—1	9— 9
Ruhle	0—0	0—0	0—2	0—2	1—1	1—0	1—1	0—0	0—0	0—0	1—0	4— 6
Ryan	1—1	1—0	2—2	1—0	2—0	1—0	0—0	0—0	0—1	2—0	1—1	11— 5
Sambito	0—1	0—0	0—0	0—0	0—0	0—1	2—0	1—0	0—2	1—0	2—0	5— 5
B. Smith	0—1	0—0	0—0	0—0	0—0	0—0	0—0	1—0	0—0	0—0	0—0	1— 1
D. Smith	1—0	1—0	0—1	1—0	0—0	0—0	2—0	0—2	0—0	0—0	0—0	5— 3
Sprowl	0—0	0—0	0—0	0—0	0—0	0—0	0—0	0—0	0—1	0—0	0—0	0— 1
Sutton	2—0	0—0	0—1	1—3	0—1	2—0	0—1	1—1	1—1	3—0	1—2	11— 9
Totals	8—4	6—1	4—8	4—8	5—2	6—3	4—6	2—4	2—4	11—3	9—6	61—49

No Decisions—Pladson.

LOS ANGELES—63-47

Pitcher	Atl. W–L	Chi. W–L	Cin. W–L	Hou. W–L	Mtl. W–L	N.Y. W–L	Phil. W–L	Pitt. W–L	St.L. W–L	S.D. W–L	S.F. W–L	Totals W–L
Castillo	0–0	0–0	2–0	0–0	0–1	0–1	0–1	0–0	0–0	0–1	0–0	2– 4
Forster	0–0	0–0	0–1	0–0	0–0	0–0	0–0	0–0	0–0	0–0	0–0	0– 1
Goltz	1–0	0–2	1–0	0–1	0–0	0–0	0–0	0–0	0–1	0–2	0–1	2– 7
Hooton	1–2	1–1	0–2	3–0	1–0	1–0	1–0	1–0	0–1	0–0	2–0	11– 6
Howe	1–1	0–0	0–0	0–0	1–0	1–0	1–0	0–0	0–1	1–1	0–0	5– 3
Niedenfuer	1–0	0–0	0–0	0–0	0–0	0–0	0–0	1–0	1–0	0–0	0–0	3– 1
Pena	0–0	0–0	0–1	0–0	0–0	0–0	0–0	1–0	0–0	0–0	0–0	1– 1
Power	0–0	0–0	0–2	0–1	0–0	0–0	0–0	0–0	0–0	1–0	0–0	1– 3
Reuss	1–2	0–1	1–0	1–1	1–0	1–0	1–0	1–0	2–0	1–0	0–0	10– 4
Stewart	0–1	0–0	3–1	0–0	0–0	0–0	0–0	0–1	0–0	0–0	1–0	4– 3
Sutcliffe	0–0	0–0	0–0	1–0	0–1	0–0	0–0	0–0	0–0	1–0	0–1	2– 2
Valenzuela	2–1	1–1	0–0	2–1	2–0	1–0	0–1	0–0	2–1	1–1	2–1	13– 7
Welch	0–0	2–1	1–1	1–0	0–0	1–0	0–1	1–0	0–1	1–0	2–1	9– 5
Totals	7–7	4–6	8–8	8–4	5–2	5–1	3–3	5–1	5–5	6–5	7–5	63–47

No Decisions—None.

MONTREAL—60-48

Pitcher	Atl. W–L	Chi. W–L	Cin. W–L	Hou. W–L	L.A. W–L	N.Y. W–L	Phil. W–L	Pitt. W–L	St.L. W–L	S.D. W–L	S.F. W–L	Totals W–L
Bahnsen	1–0	1–0	0–1	0–0	0–0	0–0	0–0	0–0	0–0	0–0	0–0	2– 1
Burris	0–0	0–2	1–1	2–0	0–1	3–0	0–0	2–1	1–1	0–1	0–0	9– 7
Fryman	1–0	0–0	0–0	0–0	0–1	0–0	1–1	1–1	0–0	2–0	0–0	5– 3
Gullickson	1–0	1–0	1–0	0–1	0–1	2–1	0–1	1–1	1–2	0–1	0–1	7– 9
Jackson	0–0	0–0	0–0	0–0	0–0	0–0	0–0	1–0	0–0	0–0	0–0	1– 0
Lea	0–1	1–0	1–1	0–0	0–0	0–1	0–0	0–0	1–1	1–0	2–0	5– 4
Lee	0–1	0–1	0–1	0–0	1–0	1–0	0–0	2–0	1–1	0–0	0–2	5– 6
Ratzer	0–0	0–0	0–0	0–0	0–1	0–0	1–0	0–0	0–0	0–0	0–0	1– 1
Reardon	1–0	0–0	0–0	0–0	0–0	0–0	0–0	0–0	1–0	0–0	0–0	2– 0
Rogers	2–1	1–0	0–1	0–1	1–0	2–1	2–1	2–0	1–1	1–0	0–2	12– 8
Sanderson	1–0	3–1	1–0	0–2	0–1	1–0	1–1	1–0	0–2	1–0	0–0	9– 7
B. Smith	0–0	0–0	0–0	0–0	0–0	0–0	1–0	0–0	0–0	0–0	0–0	1– 0
Sosa	0–0	0–0	0–0	0–1	0–0	0–0	1–0	0–0	0–1	0–0	0–0	1– 2
Totals	7–3	7–4	4–5	2–5	2–5	9–3	7–4	10–3	6–9	4–2	2–5	60–48

No Decisions—Engle, Gorman.

NEW YORK—41-62

Pitcher	Atl. W–L	Chi. W–L	Cin. W–L	Hou. W–L	L.A. W–L	Mtl. W–L	Phil. W–L	Pitt. W–L	St.L. W–L	S.D. W–L	S.F. W–L	Totals W–L
Allen	0–0	3–0	1–1	0–0	1–1	0–1	0–2	0–1	2–0	0–0	0–0	7– 6
Boitano	0–0	0–0	1–0	0–0	0–0	0–0	0–0	1–1	0–0	0–0	0–0	2– 1
Falcone	0–0	0–0	0–1	0–0	0–0	1–0	2–0	0–0	1–1	1–1	0–0	5– 3
Harris	1–1	0–2	0–1	0–0	0–0	0–1	2–0	0–0	0–0	0–0	0–0	3– 5
Hausman	0–0	0–1	0–0	0–0	0–0	0–0	0–0	0–0	0–0	0–0	0–0	0– 1
Jones	0–1	1–0	0–1	0–1	0–1	0–2	0–0	0–1	0–0	0–0	0–1	1– 8
Leach	0–0	0–0	0–0	0–0	0–0	0–0	0–0	1–0	0–1	0–0	0–0	1– 1
Lynch	1–0	0–1	0–0	0–0	0–0	0–0	0–2	1–0	1–0	0–1	1–1	4– 5
Marshall	0–0	0–0	0–0	2–1	0–0	0–0	1–0	0–0	0–1	0–0	0–0	3– 2
Miller	0–0	1–0	0–0	0–0	0–0	0–0	0–0	0–0	0–0	0–0	0–0	1– 0
Orosco	0–0	0–1	0–0	0–0	0–0	0–0	0–0	0–0	0–0	0–0	0–0	0– 1
Reardon	0–0	0–0	0–0	0–0	0–0	0–0	0–0	0–0	0–0	0–0	1–0	1– 0
Roberts	0–0	0–0	0–0	0–0	0–1	0–0	0–0	0–1	0–0	0–1	0–0	0– 3
Scott	0–1	1–0	1–1	1–1	0–1	1–0	0–2	0–2	0–1	1–0	0–1	5–10
Searage	0–0	1–0	0–0	0–0	0–0	0–0	0–0	0–0	0–0	0–0	0–0	1– 0
Swan	0–0	0–0	0–0	0–0	0–0	0–0	0–2	0–0	0–0	0–0	0–0	0– 2
Zachry	1–0	1–0	0–2	0–3	0–1	1–3	2–1	0–0	2–1	0–2	0–1	7–14
Totals	3–3	8–5	3–7	3–6	1–5	3–9	7–7	3–6	6–5	2–5	2–4	41–62

No Decisions—Leary, Puleo.

PHILADELPHIA—59-48

Pitcher	Atl. W–L	Chi. W–L	Cin. W–L	Hou. W–L	L.A. W–L	Mtl. W–L	N.Y. W–L	Pitt. W–L	St.L. W–L	S.D. W–L	S.F. W–L	Totals W–L
Brusstar	0–1	0–0	0–0	0–0	0–0	0–0	0–0	0–0	0–0	0–0	0–0	0– 1
Bystrom	0–0	1–0	0–0	1–0	1–1	0–0	0–0	0–1	0–0	0–0	1–1	4– 3
Carlton	1–1	3–0	0–1	2–0	0–0	1–0	0–1	2–0	1–1	2–0	1–0	13– 4
Christenson	1–0	1–0	0–0	0–0	0–0	0–1	2–1	0–1	0–3	0–1	0–0	4– 7
M. Davis	0–1	0–0	0–1	0–1	0–0	0–0	0–1	0–0	1–0	0–0	0–0	1– 4
Espinosa	0–0	1–0	0–0	0–0	0–1	0–0	0–1	0–0	0–1	1–0	0–2	2– 5
Larson	0–0	1–0	0–0	0–0	0–0	1–0	0–0	1–0	0–0	0–0	0–0	3– 0
Lyle	1–0	1–1	1–3	1–2	1–0	0–0	1–0	1–0	1–0	1–0	0–0	9– 6
McGraw	1–0	0–0	0–0	0–0	0–1	0–2	0–0	1–0	0–0	0–1	0–0	2– 4
Noles	0–0	0–0	0–0	0–1	0–0	0–0	1–0	0–1	1–0	0–0	0–0	2– 2
Proly	0–0	0–0	0–0	0–0	0–0	0–1	1–0	1–0	0–0	0–0	0–0	2– 1
J. Reed	0–0	0–0	0–0	0–0	0–0	0–1	0–0	0–0	0–0	0–0	0–0	0– 1
R. Reed	0–1	1–0	1–0	0–0	0–0	1–0	1–0	0–2	1–0	0–0	0–0	5– 3
Ruthven	1–0	1–1	0–0	2–0	1–0	1–2	1–3	1–0	2–1	0–0	2–0	12– 7
Totals	5–4	10–2	2–5	6–4	3–3	4–7	7–7	7–5	7–6	4–2	4–3	59–48

No Decisions—None.

PITTSBURGH—46-56

Pitcher	Atl. W—L	Chi. W—L	Cin. W—L	Hou. W—L	L.A. W—L	Mtl. W—L	N.Y. W—L	Phil. W—L	St.L. W—L	S.D. W—L	S.F. W—L	Totals W—L
Bibby	1—0	1—0	0—0	0—1	0—0	0—1	2—0	1—0	0—1	1—0	0—0	6— 3
Camacho	0—0	0—0	0—0	0—0	0—0	0—0	0—0	0—0	0—1	0—0	0—0	0— 1
Candelaria	0—0	0—0	0—0	0—0	0—0	0—0	1—0	0—1	1—1	0—0	0—0	2— 2
Cruz	1—0	0—1	0—0	0—0	0—0	0—0	0—0	0—0	0—0	0—0	0—0	1— 1
Jackson	0—0	0—0	0—1	1—0	0—0	0—0	0—0	0—0	0—1	0—0	0—0	1— 2
Jones	0—0	0—0	0—0	0—0	1—2	0—1	1—0	1—1	0—1	0—0	1—0	4— 5
Lee	0—0	0—0	0—0	0—0	0—0	0—0	0—1	0—0	0—1	0—0	0—0	0— 2
Long	0—0	0—1	0—0	0—0	0—1	0—0	1—0	0—0	0—0	0—0	0—0	1— 2
Perez	0—0	1—1	0—0	0—0	0—0	0—2	0—1	1—0	0—1	0—1	0—1	2— 7
Rhoden	1—0	1—0	1—0	1—0	0—1	2—1	1—0	0—1	0—0	2—1	0—0	9— 4
D. Robinson	0—0	0—0	0—0	0—0	0—0	0—0	0—0	0—1	0—0	0—1	0—1	0— 3
Romo	0—0	1—0	0—1	0—0	0—0	0—0	0—0	0—1	0—0	0—0	0—1	1— 3
Scurry	0—0	0—1	0—1	1—0	0—0	0—0	0—0	1—0	0—1	1—0	1—2	4— 5
Solomon	0—1	2—0	1—1	1—1	0—0	0—2	0—0	1—1	1—0	1—0	1—0	8— 6
Tekulve	0—1	3—0	0—0	0—0	0—1	1—1	0—0	0—1	1—0	0—1	0—0	5— 5
Tiant	0—0	1—0	0—0	0—0	0—0	0—2	0—1	0—0	0—0	1—0	0—2	2— 5
Totals	3—2	10—4	2—4	4—2	1—5	3—10	6—3	5—7	3—8	6—4	3—7	46—56

No Decisions—None.

ST. LOUIS—59-43

Pitcher	Atl. W—L	Chi. W—L	Cin. W—L	Hou. W—L	L.A. W—L	Mtl. W—L	N.Y. W—L	Phil W—L	Pitt. W—L	S.D. W—L	S.F. W—L	Totals W—L
Andujar	0—0	1—0	0—0	0—0	0—1	3—0	1—0	0—0	0—0	0—0	1—0	6— 1
Bair	0—0	0—0	0—0	0—0	0—0	0—0	1—0	1—0	0—0	0—0	0—0	2— 0
DeLeon	0—0	0—0	0—0	0—0	0—0	0—0	0—0	0—1	0—0	0—0	0—0	0— 1
Edelen	0—0	0—0	1—0	0—0	0—0	0—0	0—0	0—0	0—0	0—0	0—0	1— 0
Forsch	1—1	1—0	1—0	0—0	1—2	1—0	2—0	2—1	1—0	0—0	0—1	10— 5
Kaat	0—0	0—1	0—0	1—0	0—1	0—2	0—0	0—1	1—1	3—0	1—0	6— 6
LaPoint	0—0	0—0	0—0	0—0	0—0	0—0	0—0	0—0	1—0	0—0	0—0	1— 0
Littell	0—0	0—1	0—0	0—0	0—0	0—1	0—0	0—0	0—0	0—1	0—0	1— 3
Martin	0—0	0—1	0—0	1—0	1—0	3—1	0—1	1—1	1—0	1—0	0—1	8— 5
Martinez	1—1	0—0	0—0	0—0	1—0	0—0	0—2	0—1	0—0	0—1	0—0	2— 5
Otten	0—0	0—0	1—0	0—0	0—0	0—0	0—0	0—0	0—0	0—0	0—0	1— 0
Rincon	0—0	1—1	0—0	0—0	0—0	0—0	1—0	0—0	1—0	0—0	0—0	3— 1
Shirley	0—0	0—0	2—0	0—1	1—0	0—1	0—1	0—0	3—0	0—1	0—0	6— 4
Sorensen	1—1	1—1	1—0	0—0	0—1	1—1	0—0	1—2	0—1	1—0	1—0	7— 7
Sutter	0—1	0—0	0—0	1—1	0—0	1—0	0—2	0—0	0—1	1—0	0—0	3— 5
Sykes	0—0	0—0	0—0	0—0	0—0	0—0	0—0	1—0	0—0	1—0	0—0	2— 0
Totals	3—4	4—5	5—0	4—2	5—5	9—6	5—6	6—7	8—3	7—3	3—2	59—43

No Decisions—None.

SAN DIEGO—41-69

Pitcher	Atl. W—L	Chi. W—L	Cin. W—L	Hou. W—L	L.A. W—L	Mtl. W—L	N.Y. W—L	Phil. W—L	Pitt. W—L	St.L. W—L	S.F. W—L	Totals W—L
Armstrong	0—1	0—0	0—0	0—0	0—0	0—0	0—0	0—0	0—0	0—0	0—1	0— 2
Boone	0—0	0—0	0—0	0—0	1—0	0—0	0—0	0—0	0—0	0—0	0—0	1— 0
Curtis	1—1	0—1	0—1	0—0	0—1	0—1	0—0	0—0	1—0	0—2	0—0	2— 6
Eichelberger	2—0	0—0	0—1	0—3	1—0	1—0	1—0	0—1	1—1	0—1	1—1	8— 8
Fireovid	0—0	0—0	0—0	0—0	0—0	0—0	0—0	0—0	0—0	0—0	0—1	0— 1
Kuhaulua	0—0	0—0	0—0	0—0	1—0	0—0	0—0	0—0	0—0	0—0	0—0	1— 0
Littlefield	0—0	0—0	0—1	0—0	0—1	0—0	0—0	1—0	1—0	0—1	0—0	2— 3
Lollar	0—0	0—1	0—1	0—2	1—0	0—0	0—1	0—1	0—1	0—1	1—0	2— 8
Lucas	1—1	1—1	0—0	0—0	1—1	0—1	1—0	0—1	0—0	1—1	2—1	7— 7
Mura	1—3	1—0	0—2	1—3	0—0	0—2	0—0	1—1	1—2	0—0	0—1	5—14
Show	1—0	0—0	0—1	0—0	0—1	0—0	0—0	0—0	0—0	0—0	0—1	1— 3
Urrea	0—1	0—0	0—0	0—0	0—0	0—0	1—0	0—0	0—0	0—0	1—0	2— 2
Welsh	0—0	0—0	1—0	1—2	0—0	0—1	1—1	0—0	0—1	2—1	1—1	6— 7
Wise	0—2	1—0	0—2	1—1	0—2	1—0	1—0	0—0	0—1	0—0	0—0	4— 8
Totals	6—9	3—3	2—10	3—11	5—6	2—4	5—2	2—4	4—6	3—7	6—7	41—69

No Decisions—None.

SAN FRANCISCO—56-55

Pitcher	Atl. W—L	Chi. W—L	Cin. W—L	Hou. W—L	L.A. W—L	Mtl. W—L	N.Y. W—L	Phil. W—L	Pitt. W—L	St.L. W—L	S.D. W—L	Totals W—L
Alexander	3—0	1—1	1—1	1—1	0—1	0—0	0—1	2—0	1—1	0—0	2—1	11— 7
Blue	0—1	2—0	0—1	2—1	1—1	1—0	0—0	0—1	0—1	1—0	1—0	8— 6
Breining	0—0	1—0	1—0	0—2	0—0	0—0	0—0	0—0	1—0	0—0	2—0	5— 2
Griffin	2—1	0—1	0—1	2—1	0—2	1—1	1—0	0—0	1—1	1—0	0—0	8— 8
Hargesheimer	0—0	0—1	1—0	0—0	0—0	0—0	0—0	0—0	0—0	0—0	0—1	1— 2
Holland	1—0	1—0	0—3	0—1	1—0	1—0	1—0	0—0	1—0	0—0	1—1	7— 5
Lavelle	0—0	0—1	0—1	0—1	1—0	0—0	0—0	0—1	0—0	0—1	1—1	2— 6
Minton	1—1	0—0	0—2	1—0	0—0	0—0	0—1	1—1	0—0	1—0	0—1	4— 5
Ripley	0—1	0—1	0—0	0—0	1—1	1—0	1—0	1—1	0—0	0—0	0—0	4— 4
Rowland	0—0	0—0	0—0	0—0	0—0	0—0	0—0	0—0	0—0	0—0	0—1	0— 1
Whitson	0—1	0—0	2—0	0—2	1—2	1—1	1—0	0—0	0—1	2—0	0—1	6— 9
Totals	7—5	5—5	5—9	6—9	5—7	5—2	4—2	3—4	7—3	2—3	7—6	56—55

No Decisions—Moffitt, Tufts.

AMERICAN LEAGUE

Including

Team Reviews of 1981 Season

Team Day-by-Day Scores

1981 Standings, Home-Away Records

1981 Official A.L. Batting Averages

1981 Official A.L. Fielding Averages

1981 Official A.L. Pitching Averages

1981 Pitching Against Each Club

Dave Winfield added lots of punch to the Yankee lineup.

Yanks 'Apologize' for Losing

By PHIL PEPE

Around the Yankees, you learn to accept the basic truism that the only permanence is change and George Steinbrenner. The two are interchangeable. There is no such thing as standing still, win or lose, as long as Steinbrenner is around.

It started in 1981 when new super star free-agent Dave Winfield came into the picture for an estimated $21 million over 10 years. Then came a new center fielder, Jerry Mumphrey, and a new righthanded starting pitcher, Rick Reuschel.

Of course, it wouldn't be the Yankees—Steinbrenner's Yankees—if there wasn't a new manager, Gene Michael; and another new manager, who turned out to be an old manager, Bob Lemon, the ninth manager to hold that job in Steinbrenner's nine years as owner. Others included Ralph Houk, who was there when Steinbrenner bought the club, Billy Martin and Lemon, who served two hitches, and Dick Williams, who was hired, but never served.

Michael's sin was revealing publicly Steinbrenner's constant threats to his job. This was a no-no to George, who does not believe in airing family linen for all to see. Steinbrenner had expected an apology. When none was forthcoming, goodbye, Gene Michael; hello, Bob Lemon.

"I'm not here to do anything different," Lemon said. "They've been very successful. I just don't want to screw it up."

The change came on September 6. At the time, the Yankees had won 48 and lost 34, including seven victories in their last nine games. More importantly, they had qualified for post-season play by finishing with a rush just before the strike. Michael had led them to the playoffs, but he would not be around to see it through.

Once before, in 1978, Lemon had come into a bad situation and taken the Yankees to a world championship. Steinbrenner was hoping to catch lightning in the same bottle.

But there were too many problems, many of them caused by the seven-week strike and layoff and the split season. Aside from pitchers, only three Yankee regulars played up to their potential.

Winfield was their best player, proving his worth with a .294 average, 13 homers, 68 RBIs, 11 stolen bases and excellent de-

Dave Righetti . . . Heat wave.

fense in 105 games. But he was a bust in post-season play.

Mumphrey led the team with a .307 average and had six homers, 32 RBIs and 13 stolen bases in 80 games, but missed most of the last month with a foot injury and was not at his best for the playoffs and World Series.

Graig Nettles, coming back from hepatitis at age 37, retained his former brilliance in the field and batted .244 with 15 homers and 46 RBIs in 103 games.

But Rick Cerone, out for the first month with a hand injury, slipped from .277, 14 homers and 85 RBIs to .244, two and 21; Bucky Dent missed the entire final month, and the post-season, with a hand injury; Oscar Gamble went from .278, 14 homers, 50 RBIs to .238, 10 and 27; Willie Randolph from .294 to .232 and Bob Watson, playing most of the season with a pulled adductor muscle, dropped from .307, 13 homers and 68 RBIs to .212, 6 and 12.

And then there was Reggie Jackson, struggling through the most frustrating year of his career. Eligible to become a free agent after the season, Jackson battled a horrendous first-half slump, fretted over not signing a new contract, and suffered the humiliation of being ordered to take a thorough physical exam in midseason. His numbers dropped from .300, 41 homers and 111 RBIs to .237, 15 and 54.

The strike naturally reduced all cumulative statistics, but Yankee offense was generally down and it was the defense and pitching that carried them to their 33rd American League pennant, their fourth in the last six years.

Rich Gossage was "miraculous," according to Steinbrenner, with 20 saves and an 0.77 ERA in only 32 games, his season curtailed by a pulled groin muscle in September. Ron Davis won four games, saved six and struck out 83 batters in 73 innings, including a record-tying 10 straight in one stretch. Ron Guidry won seven straight games in one stretch and finished 11-5. And rookie Dave Righetti was 8-4 after being recalled from Columbus (where he was 5-0)

and finished up with a 3-0 mark in the post-season.

The Yankees were sluggish in the second season, finishing fifth. Although their overall record was a respectable 59-48, third best in the A.L. East, they were accused of just going through the motions. Steinbrenner warned them: "You can't just turn it on and off like a faucet."

They came alive to win the division playoffs and the American League pennant, but fell short of Steinbrenner's goal of a 23rd world championship, which prompted the owner to issue a public apology to the people of New York "and Yankee fans everywhere."

SCORES OF NEW YORK YANKEES' 1981 GAMES

APRIL

Date			Winner	Loser
9 — Texas	W	10-3	John	Matlack
11 — Texas	W	5-1	May	Darwin
12 — Texas	L	4-6	Jenkins	Guidry
13 — At Toronto	L	1-5	Clancy	John
15 — At Toronto	W	6-3	May	Todd
17 — At Texas	W	2-1	Guidry	Darwin
18 — At Texas	L	4-6	Comer	Castro
19 — At Texas	L	0-4	Matlack	Underwood
20 — Detroit	W	6-2	May	Rozema
21 — Detroit	W	2-0	Bird	Wilcox
22 — Detroit	W	7-2	LaRoche	Bailey
24 — Toronto	W	4-2	John	Bombback
25 — Toronto	L	2-7	Todd	May
26 — Toronto	L	1-2	Stieb	Underwood
27 — At Detroit	W	3-1	Guidry	Bailey
28 — At Detroit	W	4-1	John	Schatzeder
29 — At Detroit	W	3-2	May	Morris
		Won 11, Lost 6		

MAY

Date			Winner	Loser
1 — At Oak.	L	6-8	Langford	Underwood
2 — At Oak.	L	3-6	Keough	Guidry
3 — At Oak.	W	3-2†	Davis	McCatty
3 — At Oak.	W	2-0	John	Kingman
4 — At Calif.	W	4-2	Nelson	Zahn
5 — At Calif.	L	2-6	Jefferson	Underwood
6 — At Calif.	W	5-2	Guidry	Witt
7 — At Calif.	L	1-2	Forsch	John
8 — At Seattle	L	2-3	Clark	May
9 — At Seattle	L	5-6	Drago	Davis
10 — At Seattle	W	5-2	Underwood	Gleaton
12 — Oakland	W	4-1	Guidry	Langford
13 — Oakland	L	4-5	Keough	John
14 — Oakland	W	9-5	Gossage	Jones
16 — Seattle	W	7-5	Bird	Gleaton
17 — Seattle	L	0-1	Bannister	Davis
18 — Kan. City	W	2-1	John	Splittorff
19 — Kan. City	W	6-5	Bird	Martin
20 — Kan. City	W	5-4‡	Castro	Quisenberry
22 — Cleveland	L	3-7	Blyleven	John
23 — Cleveland	W	3-2	Righetti	Waits
24 — Cleveland	L	5-12	Denny	May
25 — At Balt.	L	1-10	Palmer	Guidry
26 — At Balt.	L	4-6	Stewart	Nelson
27 — At Balt.	L	5-6	T. Martinez	Gossage
29 — At Cleve.	W	5-2	Righetti	Waits
30 — At Cleve.	W	1-0	Nelson	Spillner
31 — At Cleve.	L	2-7	Barker	May
		Won 14, Lost 14		

JUNE

Date			Winner	Loser
1 — At Cleve.	W	5-3	Bird	Garland
2 — Baltimore	W	5-3‡	Gossage	Stewart
3 — Baltimore	W	2-0‡	Davis	T. Martinez
4 — Baltimore	W	12-3	Nelson	Ford
5 — Chicago	W	6-5§	LaRoche	Hickey
6 — Chicago	W	2-0	Bird	Trout
7 — Chicago	W	3-1	Guidry	Baumgarten
8 — At Kan. C.	W	8-3	Righetti	Gale
9 — At Kan. C.	W	8-5	LaRoche	Martin
10 — At Chicago	L	5-6	Burns	May
11 — At Chicago	L	2-3	Trout	Bird
		Won 9, Lost 2		

AUGUST

Date			Winner	Loser
10 — Texas	W	2-0	John	Darwin
11 — Texas	L	0-1	Honeycutt	Righetti
12 — Texas	W	5-4	LaRoche	Jenkins
13 — At Detroit	W	3-0	Guidry	Petry
14 — At Detroit	L	0-1	Wilcox	May
15 — At Detroit	L	5-8	Schatzeder	LaRoche
16 — At Detroit	L	4-5	Lopez	Davis
17 — Chicago	L	1-4	Burns	Reuschel
18 — Chicago	W	4-0	Guidry	Trout
19 — Chicago	L	5-6	Lamp	May
21 — Kan. City	L	0-4	Gura	Righetti
22 — Kan. City	W	5-0	Reuschel	Splittorff
23 — Kan. City	W	8-0	Guidry	Gale
24 — Minnesota	L	2-3§	O'Connor	Frazier
25 — Minnesota	L	0-3	Jackson	May
26 — Minnesota	W	3-2	Gossage	Williams
27 — At Chicago	L	1-3*	Hoyt	Davis
28 — At Chicago	W	6-1	Guidry	Trout
29 — At Chicago	W	12-2	John	Dotson
30 — At Chicago	W	5-1	May	Lamp
31 — At Minn.	W	7-0	Righetti	Williams
		Won 11, Lost 10		

SEPTEMBER

Date			Winner	Loser
1 — At Minn.	W	11-6	Reuschel	Redfern
2 — At Minn.	L	3-4	Cooper	Gossage
3 — At Kan. C.	L	2-3	Jones	John
4 — At Kan. C.	W	4-0	May	Leonard
5 — At Kan. C.	W	2-1	Righetti	Gura
6 — At Kan. C.	W	6-1	Reuschel	Hammaker
7 — Milwaukee	W	4-2	Guidry	Lerch
9 — Milwaukee	W	5-2	John	Vuckovich
9 — Milwaukee	L	3-5	Caldwell	May
11 — Boston	W	4-1	Righetti	Eckersley
12 — Boston	L	1-2	Ojeda	Reuschel
13 — Boston	W	10-6	Guidry	Tanana
14 — At Milw.	W	10-2	John	Caldwell
15 — At Milw.	L	1-2	Haas	May
16 — At Milw.	L	2-3	Lerch	Righetti
18 — At Boston	W	6-4	Davis	Stanley
19 — At Boston	L	5-8	Tudor	Davis
20 — At Boston	L	1-4	Hurst	John
21 — Cleveland	L	0-5	Waits	May
22 — Cleveland	L	4-6	Barker	Righetti
23 — Cleveland	W	6-1	Reuschel	Denny
24 — Baltimore	L	1-5	Palmer	Guidry
25 — Baltimore	L	0-1	McGregor	John
26 — Baltimore	W	6-4	Davis	Stone
27 — Baltimore	W	5-2	Righetti	D. Martinez
28 — At Cleve.	L	2-6	Brennan	Reuschel
29 — At Cleve.	L	2-3	Denny	Guidry
		Won 13, Lost 14		

OCTOBER

Date			Winner	Loser
2 — At Balt.	W	9-0	Righetti	Stewart
3 — At Balt.	L	0-3	McGregor	John
4 — At Balt.	L	2-5	Flanagan	Reuschel
		Won 1, Lost 2		

*8 innings. †10 innings. ‡11 innings. §12 innings.

Brewers Rolled Behind Rollie

By TOM FLAHERTY

It was fitting that Rollie Fingers was the winning pitcher when the Brewers clinched the East Division's second-half title on the next-to-last day of the season.

Without Fingers, the fourth relief pitcher ever to win the Cy Young Award, where would the Brewers have been? "Probably three games behind Toronto," said Manager Buck Rodgers.

The Brewer manager may have been stretching it a bit, but there isn't much doubt that they wouldn't have won their first title ever without the THE SPORTING NEWS' American League Fireman of the Year.

The Brewers had been a relief pitcher short of being a legitimate pennant contender for three seasons, and the addition of the tall man with the famous mustache proved to be even better than anybody had expected. Fingers led the major leagues with 28 saves and had a 6-3 record. He had an earned-run average of 1.04 in 78 innings.

He was phenomenal in the second half with a 5-1 record, 16 saves and a 0.72 ERA. The Brewers won 31 games to clinch the second-half title, and Fingers figured in 21 of the victories.

But while Fingers had General Manager Harry Dalton and Rodgers breathing a sigh of relief, the other two players obtained in last winter's big trade with the St. Louis Cardinals provided more than their share of help. Pete Vuckovich was one of the leading pitchers in the American League with a 14-4 record, tying Mike Caldwell's team record with eight straight victories after dropping his first two decisions.

And while Ted Simmons' .216 batting average was about 70 points lower than he was used to hitting in the National League, he hit 14 home runs and drove in 61 runs. He had 12 game-winning RBIs and was swinging a hot bat in the stretch.

The hottest bat on the team, however, belonged to Cecil Cooper. The Brewer first baseman hit .368 the second half to finish at .320, third best in the league.

Still, the Brewers were supposed to be a team of sluggers, and they never really hit the way they were expected to.

They spent most of the season threatening to play the way they were supposed to, then sliding into lethargy for three or four games. When the hits counted most in September, however, the hitters came

Pete Vuckovich . . . Brewer Stopper.

through. Robin Yount hit a home run in September that certainly made a lot of noise in Detroit and Milwaukee.

With the Brewers trailing the Tigers, 6-5, in an important game at Tiger Stadium, Yount hit a three-run home run off Jack Morris in the ninth inning to win the game. Yount's home run was the team's biggest hit of the season. That blow turned everything around, and the Brewers charged down the stretch.

Gorman Thomas, who was the most consistent hitter all season, had one of the best years of his career with a .259 average while finishing among the league's home run leaders with 21. He also drove in 65 runs. Ben Oglivie drove in 72 runs, but batted just .243 with 14 homers. Yount hit .273 and Paul Molitor, missing a lot of the season with injuries, dropped to .267.

Molitor missed too much time for anybody to really decide if his move to the outfield had been a success, but there was no doubt about the man who replaced him at second base. Jim Gantner, playing his first full season as a regular, hit .267, but that wasn't his main contribution. He stopped almost everything hit toward the right side of the infield while helping the Brewers lead the league with 135 double plays. "He's the adhesive that holds us together," Rodgers said about Gantner.

The pitching kept the Brewers in the race the first half of the season, and Mike

Caldwell and Moose Haas both won 11 games. Caldwell struggled a bit in the pennant drive, but Haas came up with two of his best games of the season in a pair of showdown series with the Tigers. Randy Lerch, obtained in spring training from the Phillies, had an up-and-down season and finished with a 7-9 record, but the tall lefthander did some of his best pitching in September.

The Brewers' biggest season ever only earned a fourth of a pennant, but they stirred a lot of excitement at the end.

"We got a taste of it," Cooper said. He was looking forward to more than a taste in 1982.

SCORES OF MILWAUKEE BREWERS' 1981 GAMES

APRIL

			Winner	Loser
11 — At Cleve.	W	5-3	Caldwell	Blyleven
12 — At Cleve.	W	6-1	Slaton	Denny
14 — At Chicago	L	3-9	Baumgarten	Vuckovich
15 — At Chicago	L	4-5	Hoyt	Fingers
16 — Cleveland	L	0-1	Garland	Caldwell
18 — Cleveland	L	0-5	Blyleven	Slaton
20 — At Toronto	W	5-4†	Lerch	Willis
21 — At Toronto	W	6-2	Haas	Stieb
22 — At Toronto	W	8-1	Caldwell	Leal
24 — Kan. City	W	6-1	Slaton	Gale
25 — Kan. City	L	2-4	Gura	Vuckovich
26 — Kan. City	W	11-1	Lerch	Leonard
27 — Toronto	W	4-3†	Cleveland	Garvin
28 — Toronto	L	2-6	Bomback	Caldwell
29 — Toronto	L	0-5x	Leal	Easterly
30 — At Calif.	W	12-1	Augustine	Jefferson

Won 9, Lost 7

MAY

1 — At Calif.	L	4-8	Witt	Lerch
2 — At Calif.	W	8-5	Haas	Forsch
3 — At Calif.	W	4-3	Caldwell	Renko
4 — At Seattle	W	9-5	Easterly	Allard
5 — At Seattle	W	4-1	Vuckovich	Gleaton
6 — At Seattle	L	1-12	Parrott	Lerch
7 — At Seattle	L	1-4	Bannister	Haas
8 — At Oak.	L	0-2	McCatty	Caldwell
9 — At Oak.	L	5-6†	Owchinko	Lerch
10 — At Oak.	W	13-5	Vuckovich	Norris
12 — California	L	0-4	Forsch	Haas
13 — California	L	3-6	Renko	Caldwell
14 — California	L	1-9	Zahn	Slaton
15 — Oakland	W	3-0	Vuckovich	McCatty
16 — Oakland	W	6-5	Cleveland	Owchinko
17 — Oakland	W	6-2	Haas	Langford
19 — Minnesota	W	4-3	Caldwell	Arroyo
20 — Minnesota	W	6-1	Slaton	Williams
21 — Minnesota	W	8-2	Vuckovich	Redfern
22 — Boston	L	3-7	Tudor	Haas
23 — Boston	L	1-8	Torrez	Lerch
24 — Boston	W	2-1x	Easterly	Stanley
24 — Boston	W	10-7	Haas	Stanley
25 — Detroit	L	3-12	Morris	Augustine
26 — Detroit	W	7-3	Vuckovich	Wilcox
27 — Detroit	W	5-1	Lerch	Bailey
28 — Detroit	W	7-1	Caldwell	Petry
29 — At Boston	W	5-4	Fingers	Burgmeier
30 — At Boston	L	6-7*	Clear	Fingers
31 — At Boston	W	5-2	Vuckovich	Crawford

Won 18, Lost 12

JUNE

1 — At Detroit	L	3-4†	Rozema	Cleveland
2 — At Detroit	W	5-2	Caldwell	Petry
3 — At Detroit	L	1-4	Schatzeder	Slaton
5 — At Kan. C.	W	6-2	Haas	Gura
6 — At Kan. C.	W	4-2	Vuckovich	Leonard
7 — At Kan. C.	L	1-7	Splittorff	Lerch
8 — At Minn.	L	0-1	Erickson	Caldwell
9 — At Minn.	L	1-3	Arroyo	Slaton
10 — Texas	L	5-12	Medich	Haas
11 — Texas	W	6-3	Vuckovich	Jenkins

Won 4, Lost 6

AUGUST

			Winner	Loser
10 — At Cleve.	W	5-2§	Keeton	Stanton
11 — At Cleve.	W	6-5	Caldwell	Denny
11 — At Cleve.	W	6-1	Slaton	Waits
12 — At Cleve.	L	4-9	Barker	Lerch
13 — At Cleve.	W	8-5	Haas	Garland
14 — At Toronto	L	4-5	Garvin	Easterly
15 — At Toronto	L	3-4	Bomback	Cleveland
16 — At Toronto	W	6-2	Caldwell	Stieb
16 — At Toronto	W	2-0	Lerch	Todd
18 — At Texas	W	3-1	Haas	Matlack
18 — At Texas	L	6-8	Comer	Vuckovich
19 — At Texas	L	1-4	Medich	Slaton
21 — Minnesota	L	6-7	Williams	Caldwell
22 — Minnesota	W	4-3*	Fingers	Cooper
23 — Minnesota	W	8-5	Augustine	Arroyo
24 — Chicago	W	5-4	Vuckovich	Dotson
25 — Chicago	L	1-5	Lamp	Slaton
27 — Texas	L	1-5	Darwin	Caldwell
28 — Texas	W	6-3	Haas	Honeycutt
29 — Texas	L	5-8	Matlack	Lerch
30 — Texas	W	6-2	Vuckovich	Medich
31 — At Kan. C.	W	5-1	Caldwell	Leonard

Won 13, Lost 9

SEPTEMBER

1 — At Kan. C.	L	1-3	Gura	Haas
2 — At Kan. C.	L	4-5	Quisenberry	Fingers
3 — At Minn.	W	4-3	Vuckovich	Havens
4 — At Minn.	W	16-5	Caldwell	Arroyo
5 — At Minn.	W	5-3	Slaton	Williams
6 — At Minn.	W	8-7*	Fingers	Corbett
7 — At N. York	L	2-4	Guidry	Lerch
9 — At N. York	L	2-5	John	Vuckovich
9 — At N. York	W	5-3	Caldwell	May
10 — Chicago	L	6-12	Hoyt	Cleveland
11 — Baltimore	L	1-2	D. Martinez	Haas
12 — Baltimore	W	6-3	Lerch	Palmer
13 — Baltimore	W	5-0	Vuckovich	Stone
14 — New York	L	2-10	John	Caldwell
15 — New York	W	2-1	Haas	May
16 — New York	W	3-2	Lerch	Righetti
18 — At Balt.	W	5-1	Vuckovich	Flanagan
19 — At Balt.	W	11-8	Fingers	T. Martinez
20 — At Balt.	L	2-8	Palmer	Caldwell
21 — At Boston	L	3-9	Eckersley	Haas
22 — At Boston	W	10-8	Fingers	Clear
23 — At Boston	L	5-11	Aponte	Easterly
25 — At Detroit	W	8-6	Easterly	Morris
26 — At Detroit	W	4-3	Haas	Wilcox
27 — At Detroit	L	1-2	Petry	Lerch
28 — Boston	W	1-0	Vuckovich	Tanana
29 — Boston	L	2-7	Torrez	Slaton
30 — Boston	W	10-5	Lerch	Stanley

Won 16, Lost 12

OCTOBER

2 — Detroit	W	8-2	Haas	Petry
3 — Detroit	W	2-1	Fingers	Morris
4 — Detroit	L	2-3	Wilcox	Augustine

Won 2, Lost 1

*10 innings. †12 innings. §13 innings. x14 innings.

Gorman Thomas (right) was his usual powerful self in '81.

Orioles first baseman Eddie Murray had another big season in Baltimore.

Orioles Were Too Inconsistent

By KEN NIGRO

To Earl Weaver, it was a very good year.

"How can anybody say we had a bad year?" asked the Orioles' manager, who maintains he will retire after the 1982 season.

"How can you have a bad year when you have one less loss than any other team in your division. They just came up with a formula we couldn't handle. It's just like last year, when we won 100 games but didn't win (the division). There's nothing we can do about it except go home and get ready for next year."

The formula the Orioles couldn't handle, of course, was the split season. Baltimore wound up in second place the first half, fourth in the second half and second overall (59-46). There was a strong feeling among Weaver and his players that the Orioles were not a team built for a pair of 50-game schedules.

"We're not a sprint club personality," said pitching coach Ray Miller. "We're a grind it out club that needs a 162-game schedule. That's the way this team is designed. When we get to September in normal years, the pitching settles down."

But, realistically, Weaver, General Manager Hank Peters and everyone else in the organization knew the split season wasn't the main reason the Orioles did not play like the champions of 1979 and the strong runners-up of '80. Too many players experienced off-years and the club rarely played consistent baseball after the first six weeks. And not only was the hitting lacking; so was the usually strong pitching.

Dennis Martinez and Scott McGregor were the only consistent starters, and Sammy Stewart and Tippy Martinez were the lone steady relievers. Rarely before have the Oriole starters been shelled so often so early. In two important games near the end of the season, for instance, McGregor and Jim Palmer failed to get past the first inning against Detroit on successive days.

Injuries to Palmer, Mike Flanagan and Steve Stone at different times during the season affected the club's performance. But injuries alone hardly account for an eighth-place standing in the overall earned-run average department. Baltimore had never finished lower than sixth since entering the American League in

Dennis Martinez . . . Strong season.

1954.

With the pitching not up to normal standards, the Orioles needed big years from their two powerful switch-hitters—Eddie Murray and Ken Singleton. They got it out of Murray (.294, 22 homers, 78 runs batted in), who would have had a good shot at the Most Valuable Player prize had the Orioles won. But Singleton went into one of the worst slumps of his career down the stretch, going 33 straight games without an extra-base hit. His average dropped almost 60 points in that span, and he finished at .278.

"I don't know what it was," Singleton said. "All I know is I felt very strong the first half because I had been working on the nautilus every day. But during the strike, I didn't go in every day and I didn't stay strong."

Other players, like Dan Graham and Gary Roenicke, also fell off in the power department, and the team's home run total dwindled to 88 in 105 games. Since the Orioles do not possess the greatest speed in baseball, Weaver sat back and waited for the long ball. This year, it didn't come quite so often.

Defense, another strong point in past years, also slipped. The decline was especially noticeable in center field, as opposing baserunners took great liberties on Al Bumbry's arm.

The Orioles also seemed to lack their usual enthusiasm. "I can't explain it, but it was like we had no enthusiasm the final month," catcher Rick Dempsey said. "There was no spark and only a couple of guys seemed to be playing with enthusiasm. If you can't get up any en-

thusiasm, you need a change in people."

But the Orioles aren't likely to change many faces. They still have a young club and Peters and Weaver feel the nucleus is there.

"I don't think we'll have any wholesale changes," Weaver said. "I still believe in the personnel and I've got to be satisfied with most every position, save one or two. I think we have the type of people who can come back."

"I certainly don't want to destroy this ballclub," Peters said. "We're basically a very young club and there's a lot of talent here. It's only a disappointing year if you base judgment on whether you won it all, but I don't look at it that way. It was not a disaster."

SCORES OF BALTIMORE ORIOLES' 1981 GAMES

APRIL

			Winner	Loser
10 – Kan. City	W	5-3	Stone	Gura
12 – Kan. City	L	2-4	Leonard	Flanagan
13 – At Boston	W	5-1	Stoddard	Crawford
15 – At Boston	L	2-7	Stanley	D. Martinez
17 – At Kan. C.	W	3-2	T. Martinez	Leonard
19 – At Kan. C.	L	2-3	Gale	Flanagan
21 – At Chicago	L	1-2	Burns	Stewart
23 – At Chicago	L	5-18	Dotson	McGregor
23 – At Chicago	L	3-5	Barrios	Stone
25 – Boston	W	7-2	Flanagan	Tanana
26 – Boston	L	5-7	Eckersley	Stoddard
27 – Chicago	W	5-2	McGregor	Barrios
28 – Chicago	L	6-8	Dotson	Stone
29 – Chicago	W	3-0	D. Martinez	Trout
30 – Toronto	W	4-0	Flanagan	Todd

Won 7, Lost 8

MAY

			Winner	Loser
2 – Toronto	W	4-3	Palmer	Willis
2 – Toronto	W	8-3	McGregor	Leal
3 – Toronto	L	2-4	Bomback	Stone
4 – Minnesota	W	4-3*	D. Martinez	Koosman
5 – Minnesota	W	3-2	Flanagan	Erickson
6 – Minnesota	W	5-4	Stewart	O'Connor
9 – At Texas	W	7-3	D. Martinez	Jenkins
9 – At Texas	W	4-2	Stone	Schmidt
10 – At Texas	L	3-7	Darwin	Flanagan
12 – At Toronto	L	2-5	Stieb	Palmer
13 – At Toronto	W	4-0	McGregor	Bomback
14 – At Toronto	W	10-0	Flanagan	Clancy
15 – At Minn.	W	9-4	D. Martinez	Redfern
16 – At Minn.	W	7-0	Ford	Koosman
17 – At Minn.	W	6-3	Palmer	Erickson
18 – Oakland	W	5-1	McGregor	Keough
19 – Oakland	W	6-5	Flanagan	Norris
20 – California	W	5-3	D. Martinez	Witt
21 – California	L	0-2	Rau	Palmer
22 – At Detroit	W	4-2	McGregor	Wilcox
23 – At Detroit	W	9-2	Flanagan	Rozema
24 – At Detroit	L	2-8	Petry	D. Martinez
24 – At Detroit	L	3-5	Tobik	T. Martinez
25 – New York	W	10-1	Palmer	Guidry
26 – New York	W	6-4	Stewart	Nelson
27 – New York	W	6-5	T. Martinez	Gossage
29 – Detroit	W	6-5	D. Martinez	Schatzeder
30 – Detroit	L	1-4	Morris	Palmer
31 – Detroit	L	4-5	Lopez	McGregor

Won 21, Lost 8

JUNE

			Winner	Loser
2 – At N. York	L	3-5†	Gossage	Stewart
3 – At N. York	L	0-2†	Davis	T. Martinez
4 – At N. York	L	3-12	Nelson	Ford
5 – At Calif.	W	6-4	McGregor	Witt
6 – At Calif.	L	0-10	Forsch	Flanagan
7 – At Calif.	W	4-1	D. Martinez	Frost
9 – At Oak.	L	2-4	McCatty	Palmer
9 – At Oak.	L	2-3	Jones	Stewart
10 – At Oak.	W	3-1	Flanagan	Langford
11 – At Seattle	L	2-8	Parrott	D. Martinez

Won 3, Lost 7

AUGUST

			Winner	Loser
10 – Kan. City	W	3-2‡	T. Martinez	Martin
12 – Kan. City	L	0-10	Gura	Palmer
12 – Kan. City	W	4-3	McGregor	Wright
13 – Kan. City	W	2-1	Flanagan	Gale
14 – Chicago	L	3-5	Dotson	Stewart
15 – Chicago	W	4-0	D. Martinez	Hoyt
16 – Chicago	L	7-8*	Farmer	Ford
18 – At Calif.	W	6-5	McGregor	Frost
19 – At Calif.	L	3-6	Renko	Flanagan
20 – At Calif.	L	2-6	Zahn	D. Martinez
21 – At Oak.	W	4-2	Palmer	Kingman
22 – At Oak.	L	0-2	Langford	McGregor
23 – At Oak.	W	7-4	Stewart	Norris
24 – At Seattle	W	12-8	D. Martinez	Gleaton
25 – At Seattle	W	6-5‡	Stoddard	Drago
27 – California	W	5-2	McGregor	Forsch
28 – California	L	2-9	Witt	Stone
29 – California	W	4-3	D. Martinez	Zahn
30 – California	L	1-7	Hassler	Palmer
31 – Seattle	L	3-4	Andersen	Stewart

Won 11, Lost 9

SEPTEMBER

			Winner	Loser
1 – Seattle	W	1-0	Stone	Abbott
2 – Seattle	W	3-2†	Stoddard	Rawley
3 – Oakland	L	0-10	McCatty	Palmer
4 – Oakland	L	4-5†	Underwood	Stoddard
5 – Oakland	W	5-3	Stone	Langford
6 – Oakland	W	8-4	D. Martinez	Owchinko
7 – Cleveland	W	9-2	Palmer	Waits
8 – Cleveland	W	14-5	McGregor	Barker
9 – Cleveland	L	5-8	Blyleven	Stone
10 – Cleveland	L	1-4	Denny	Stewart
11 – At Milw.	W	2-1	D. Martinez	Haas
12 – At Milw.	L	3-6	Lerch	Palmer
13 – At Milw.	L	0-5	Vuckovich	Stone
15 – At Cleve.	W	7-6	D. Martinez	Stanton
17 – At Cleve.	W	6-2	McGregor	Barker
18 – Milwaukee	L	1-5	Vuckovich	Flanagan
19 – Milwaukee	L	8-11	Fingers	T. Martinez
20 – Milwaukee	W	8-2	Palmer	Caldwell
21 – Detroit	L	1-5	Wilcox	McGregor
22 – Detroit	L	3-6	Cappuzzello	Stewart
23 – Detroit	W	1-0	D. Martinez	Petry
24 – At N. York	W	5-1	Palmer	Guidry
25 – At N. York	W	1-0	McGregor	John
26 – At N. York	L	4-6	Davis	Stone
27 – At N. York	L	2-5	Righetti	D. Martinez
28 – At Detroit	W	7-3	Stewart	Cappuzzello
29 – At Detroit	L	0-14	Morris	McGregor

Won 14, Lost 13

OCTOBER

			Winner	Loser
1 – At Detroit	W	5-4*	Stoddard	Saucier
2 – New York	L	0-9	Righetti	Stewart
3 – New York	W	3-0	McGregor	John
4 – New York	W	5-2	Flanagan	Reuschel

Won 3, Lost 1

*10 innings.　†11 innings.　‡12 innings.

Gibson Keyed Tiger Success

By TOM GAGE

For half the year, he looked awkward, out of place and practically hopeless. He struck out eight times in his last 10 at-bats before the strike, 13 in his last 20. The Detroit Tigers would be patient, but could not wait forever.

And they wouldn't have to. Almost as if the strike erased the clumsiness and uncertainty, Kirk Gibson returned in August a new player. He cut down on his strikeouts, shortened his swing and became the force the Tigers had envisioned.

Gibson hit .234 before the strike and .375 afterward to finish the year at .328. He bunted for hits and also dented the roof of Tiger Stadium. He gave Manager Sparky Anderson, General Manager Jim Campbell and the Tiger front office much more reason to anticipate the 1982 season.

But, the 1981 Tigers almost snagged part of the 1981 pennant for themselves. They were a good ball club all season, but better the second half. They went into Milwaukee for the last series of the year with a chance at the second-half American League East title.

It was called the most important series in nine years for Detroit. Not since 1972, when Billy Martin directed the remnants of the 1968 World Championship team, had the Tigers entertained a shot at any portion of a pennant.

This year was a chance for the Tigers to earn a share of the long, lost spotlight again, but they couldn't pull it off. Losing the first two games of the series, Detroit lost the division title to the Brewers and settled for a second-place tie with the Boston Red Sox. In the overall standings, they finished with a 60-49 record, just percentage points behind the New York Yankees.

"Either way, win or lose, we were going to learn from the experience," said shortstop Alan Trammell. "It was impossible not to. Most of us had never been in a pennant race before, so we didn't know what it felt like. We didn't know how much pressure to expect.

"There was a certain tension to the final weeks, but nobody wanted to be the first to show it. I think we handled it pretty well."

Anderson thought so, too. He and pitching coach Roger Craig worked with mirrors to keep a team with only three

Jack Morris . . . Tigers ace.

dependable starters in the chase.

"I said all along we weren't going to cry about it," Sparky said. "What good would that do? These guys found out what it's like and they'll be ready next year. I'm already looking forward to spring training."

Gibson was the major reason that Anderson's anticipation of 1982 ran so high. Before the season was over, the former Michigan State football star had replaced Steve Kemp as the No. 3 hitter in the lineup, moving up a notch in the final weeks. The Tiger manager also moved Gibson from right field to center and declared the move permanent. "If I kept him in the corners, either left or right field, he'd injure himself. He'd charge into the wall and get hurt. In center, he has much more room to roam."

If Gibson could be called the find of the year, Kevin Saucier wasn't far behind. Regarded as a minor acquisition when the Tigers sent backup shortstop Mark Wagner to the Texas Rangers, Saucier responded with a 4-2 season, 13 saves and a 1.65 earned-run average. His wild dances off the mound following the final out of a game became a new attraction at Tiger Stadium, and it wasn't long before he acquired the nickname of "Hot Sauce."

The Tigers' pitching improved substantially overall, with the three starters providing consistency. Jack Morris, the All-Star Game starter for the American

League, was 14-7 with a 3.05 ERA; Milt Wilcox was 12-9, 3.04, and Dan Petry 10-9, 3.00. Beyond those three, however, there was little help and the Tigers went into the off-season seeking a fourth starter.

"A fifth starter wouldn't hurt, either," said Wilcox. "They can't expect us to hold up through 162 games without more depth. That's asking too much."

Gibson led the Tigers with his .328 average and received some consideration for Most Valuable Player in the American League. But he was about the only standout on offense.

"I knew we had to improve our pitch-ing from the year before," said Anderson, "but you need runs to win. We led the world in runs scored in 1980. I never thought it would be the problem it turned out to be."

Lou Whitaker was consistent all year and finished at .263. Steve Kemp had nine home runs and 49 runs batted in while his average dipped to .277. Lance Parrish ended up with 10 home runs, 46 RBIs and .244.

Along with another starter, the Tigers needed more power from the right side.

"I never saw a good team get better by standing still," said Anderson. "I think we'll look a little different by next year."

SCORES OF DETROIT TIGERS' 1981 GAMES

APRIL			Winner	Loser
9 – Toronto	W	6-2	Morris	McLaughlin
11 – Toronto	W	6-2	Wilcox	Stieb
12 – Toronto	L	2-6	Leal	Bailey
14 – At Kan. C.	W	6-5	Lopez	Quisenberry
15 – At Kan. C.	W	4-0	Rozema	Gura
16 – At Toronto	W	2-0	Wilcox	Stieb
17 – At Toronto	W	8-5	Bailey	Leal
18 – At Toronto	W	4-3	Schatzeder	Clancy
19 – At Toronto	L	1-9	Bomback	Morris
20 – At N. York	L	2-6	May	Rozema
21 – At N. York	L	0-2	Bird	Wilcox
22 – At N. York	L	2-7	LaRoche	Bailey
24 – Chicago	L	2-3*	Hoyt	Morris
25 – Chicago	L	0-4	Baumgarten	Rozema
26 – Chicago	L	4-5	Burns	Wilcox
27 – New York	L	1-3	Guidry	Bailey
28 – New York	L	1-4	John	Schatzeder
29 – New York	L	2-3	May	Morris
30 – At Seattle	W	2-0	Rozema	Gleaton

Won 8, Lost 11

MAY				
1 – At Seattle	W	7-3	Wilcox	Parrott
2 – At Seattle	L	1-3	Bannister	Petry
3 – At Seattle	W	8-5	Morris	Andersen
5 – At Oak.	L	2-6	Norris	Rozema
6 – At Oak.	W	3-2	Wilcox	Langford
7 – At Oak.	L	3-5	Jones	Petry
8 – At Calif.	W	6-1	Morris	Renko
9 – At Calif.	L	1-15	Zahn	Schatzeder
10 – At Calif.	L	3-4	Hassler	Lopez
12 – Seattle	W	6-2	Wilcox	Bannister
13 – Seattle	W	1-0	Petry	Drago
15 – California	W	5-1	Morris	Witt
16 – California	W	7-5	Tobik	Rau
17 – California	L	1-7	Forsch	Wilcox
18 – Texas	L	5-13	Matlack	Petry
19 – Texas	W	14-1	Schatzeder	Medich
20 – Texas	W	8-4	Morris	Jenkins
22 – Baltimore	L	2-4	McGregor	Wilcox
23 – Baltimore	L	2-9	Flanagan	Rozema
24 – Baltimore	W	8-2	Petry	D. Martinez
24 – Baltimore	W	5-3	Tobik	T. Martinez
25 – At Milw.	W	12-3	Morris	Augustine
26 – At Milw.	L	3-7	Vuckovich	Wilcox
27 – At Milw.	L	1-5	Lerch	Bailey
28 – At Milw.	L	1-7	Caldwell	Petry
29 – At Balt.	L	5-6	D. Martinez	Schatzeder
30 – At Balt.	W	4-1	Morris	Palmer
31 – At Balt.	W	5-4	Lopez	McGregor

Won 15, Lost 13

JUNE				
1 – Milwaukee	W	4-3‡	Rozema	Cleveland
2 – Milwaukee	L	2-5	Caldwell	Petry
3 – Milwaukee	W	4-1	Schatzeder	Slaton
5 – Minnesota	W	2-0	Morris	Havens
6 – Minnesota	W	5-1	Petry	Redfern
7 – Minnesota	W	3-0	Wilcox	Koosman
8 – At Texas	L	1-8	Honeycutt	Schatzeder
9 – At Texas	W	5-0	Lopez	Matlack
10 – At Minn.	W	4-2	Morris	Havens
11 – At Minn.	W	7-2	Petry	Redfern

Won 8, Lost 2

AUGUST			Winner	Loser
10 – Toronto	W	4-3	Saucier	McLaughlin
11 – Toronto	L	4-6	Berenguer	Schatzeder
12 – Toronto	L	3-4	Stieb	Morris
13 – New York	L	0-3	Guidry	Petry
14 – New York	W	1-0	Wilcox	May
15 – New York	W	8-5	Schatzeder	LaRoche
16 – New York	W	5-4	Lopez	Davis
17 – Minnesota	W	12-2	Petry	Koosman
18 – Minnesota	W	3-0	Wilcox	Erickson
19 – Minnesota	W	4-0	Schatzeder	Jackson
21 – Texas	W	7-4	Lopez	Darwin
22 – Texas	W	2-0	Petry	Honeycutt
23 – Texas	W	5-4	Rozema	Kern
24 – Kan. City	L	2-4	Brett	Schatzeder
25 – Kan. City	W	4-3*	Saucier	Quisenberry
26 – Kan. City	L	1-6	Gura	Lopez
27 – At Minn.	L	3-4	Redfern	Saucier
28 – At Minn.	L	0-6	Arroyo	Rozema
29 – At Minn.	L	1-7	Havens	Schatzeder
30 – At Minn.	W	6-1	Morris	Cooper
31 – At Chicago	W	3-1	Wilcox	Baumgarten

Won 13, Lost 8

SEPTEMBER				
1 – At Chicago	W	2-1	Petry	Koosman
2 – At Chicago	W	5-4*	Saucier	Koosman
3 – At Texas	W	8-5	Morris	Matlack
4 – At Texas	L	2-3	Medich	Wilcox
5 – At Texas	W	1-0	Petry	Jenkins
6 – At Texas	W	4-3	Saucier	Mercer
7 – Boston	W	3-1	Morris	Ojeda
8 – Boston	L	3-5	Torrez	Wilcox
9 – Boston	L	5-6†	Stanley	Tobik
11 – Cleveland	W	6-3	Schatzeder	Waits
12 – Cleveland	W	11-9‡	Rozema	Monge
13 – Cleveland	W	8-6	Wilcox	Spillner
14 – At Boston	L	2-5	Stanley	Petry
16 – At Boston	L	1-2*	Eckersley	Morris
16 – At Boston	L	4-5	Burgmeier	Tobik
17 – At Boston	L	1-6	Ojeda	Wilcox
18 – At Cleve.	L	4-8	Denny	Schatzeder
19 – At Cleve.	W	4-3	Petry	Blyleven
20 – At Cleve.	W	5-1	Morris	Brennan
21 – At Balt.	W	5-1	Wilcox	McGregor
22 – At Balt.	W	6-3	Cappuzzello	Stewart
23 – At Balt.	L	0-1	D. Martinez	Petry
25 – Milwaukee	L	6-8	Easterly	Morris
26 – Milwaukee	L	3-4	Haas	Wilcox
27 – Milwaukee	W	2-1	Petry	Lerch
28 – Baltimore	L	3-7	Stewart	Cappuzzello
29 – Baltimore	W	14-0	Morris	McGregor

Won 15, Lost 12

OCTOBER				
1 – Baltimore	L	4-5*	Stoddard	Saucier
2 – At Milw.	L	2-8	Haas	Petry
3 – At Milw.	L	1-2	Fingers	Morris
4 – At Milw.	W	3-2	Wilcox	Augustine

Won 1, Lost 3

*10 innings.   †11 innings.   ‡12 innings.

Kirk Gibson used speed and power to spark enthusiasm in Detroit.

Carney Lansford (right) won a batting title and the hearts of Boston fans.

The Red Sox Were Exciting

By JOE GIULIOTTI

A new manager, a new attitude and a new style of play highlighted the 1981 Red Sox. Yet the result was the same.

Even though the Red Sox didn't win the East Division, they played exciting baseball and went until the third to last game of the season before being eliminated in the second-half race.

With Fred Lynn, Carlton Fisk, Butch Hobson and Rick Burleson gone, the Red Sox were no longer a home run hitting team. The fans did not sit and wait for a big inning and then hope the pitching would be good enough to hold down the opposition.

Ralph Houk replaced the fired Don Zimmer and instilled a new attitude—one that was evident from the first day of spring training. There were no super stars and no complainers. It was a 25-man squad that played hard and made the season exciting. The Red Sox won 16 games on their last time at bat and were beaten by the opposition on their last at bat 14 times.

One of Houk's first statements in spring training raised some eyebrows. He promised the Red Sox would not finish 19 games behind as they had in 1980. Impossible, thought some, especially with the loss of the four players.

But their replacements, Carney Lansford, Rick Miller, Rich Gedman and Mark Clear, had outstanding seasons. So did right fielder Dwight Evans, who had the best season of his 10-year-career.

Lansford won the American League batting title with a .336 mark. Miller played excellent center field and hit .291. Gedman posted a .288 average and was named THE SPORTING NEWS' A.L. Rookie Player of the Year. Clear, the iron man of the bullpen, was 8-3 with nine saves. And Evans led the American League in walks (85), total bases (215) and tied for the lead in home runs with 22.

For the first time in 25 years, the Red Sox failed to hit 100 home runs. But offensively, the team had one of its best seasons. It led the majors in hitting with a .275 mark, was the only team in the majors to score 500 runs (519) and led both leagues with 1,052 hits, 1,524 total bases and a slugging percentage of .399.

The Achilles heel of the team was, as usual, starting pitching. Mike Torrez turned his 9-16 season of 1980 into a 10-3 year in '81, but he was the only consistent

Dwight Evans . . . Productive bat.

Mark Clear . . . Bullpen stopper

starter. Dennis Eckersley was 9-8 while rookie Steve Crawford, counted on to be a big winner, started 10 straight games, didn't win any and ended in the bullpen with an 0-5 record.

What kept the Red Sox in contention all season was the bullpen. But in the end, it was the bullpen that did the damage as well. The Red Sox lost five of six to Cleveland and Milwaukee after pulling into a first-place tie on September 25. Clear, Bob Stanley (10-8 with no saves) and Bill Campbell (1-1 with seven saves) had their problems the final week. The Sox ended up third in the second half and fifth overall (59-49), but only 3½ games behind.

Stanley and Torrez tied for the lead in victories with 10. But Stanley, despite spending the entire season (he made only

one start) in the bullpen, didn't have a save. He was the most inconsistent pitcher on the staff.

The 1981 season was also the 21st for 42-year-old Carl Yastrzemski, who ended with a .246 average, the worst of his career. He was hitting well over .300 after the strike until a hamstring injury put him out of action for a week. He never regained his touch at the plate and ended with 11 hits in his last 69 at-bats. But despite his low average, he had seven home runs, each of which either tied a game or put the Red Sox ahead. Five days after the season ended, Yastrzemski signed his contract for 1982.

SCORES OF BOSTON RED SOX' 1981 GAMES

APRIL			Winner	Loser
10 – Chicago	L	3-5	Hoyt	Stanley
12 – Chicago	W	5-4	Clear	Farmer
13 – Baltimore	L	1-5	Stoddard	Crawford
15 – Baltimore	W	7-2	Stanley	D. Martinez
17 – At Chicago	W	8-5	Eckersley	Dotson
18 – At Chicago	L	1-2	Trout	Tanana
19 – At Chicago	W	9-4	Stanley	Baumgarten
20 – Texas	W	4-2	Torrez	Medich
21 – Texas	W	10-4	Tudor	Jenkins
22 – Texas	L	8-16	Darwin	Eckersley
25 – At Balt.	L	2-7	Flanagan	Tanana
26 – At Balt.	W	7-5	Eckersley	Stoddard
27 – At Texas	L	0-10	Medich	Torrez
28 – At Texas	L	0-9	Comer	Crawford
29 – At Texas	L	0-5	Darwin	Tudor
30 – Minnesota	L	4-6	Erickson	Tanana
Won 7, Lost 9				
MAY				
1 – Minnesota	L	1-6	Arroyo	Eckersley
2 – Minnesota	L	2-11	Williams	Torrez
3 – Minnesota	L	1-3	Redfern	Crawford
4 – At Kan. C.	W	8-7‡	Burgmeier	Quisenberry
5 – At Kan. C.	L	1-2	Gura	Tanana
6 – At Kan. C.	W	3-1	Eckersley	Leonard
8 – At Toronto	W	4-2	Torrez	Bomback
9 – At Toronto	W	10-3	Stanley	Clancy
10 – At Toronto	W	9-5*	Burgmeier	Jackson
11 – At Toronto	W	7-6	Clear	Willis
12 – At Minn.	L	3-4†	Corbett	Burgmeier
13 – At Minn.	W	5-2	Torrez	Arroyo
14 – At Minn.	W	9-7†	Campbell	Cooper
15 – Kan. City	W	4-3	Clear	Martin
16 – Kan. City	L	6-7	Gura	Eckersley
17 – Kan. City	L	4-5	Leonard	Burgmeier
18 – Seattle	W	8-5	Clear	Drago
19 – Seattle	W	4-0	Tanana	Parrott
20 – Oakland	W	5-3	Stanley	McCatty
21 – Oakland	W	3-0	Eckersley	Kingman
22 – At Milw.	W	7-3	Tudor	Haas
23 – At Milw.	W	8-1	Torrez	Lerch
24 – At Milw.	L	1-2§	Easterly	Stanley
24 – At Milw.	L	7-10	Haas	Stanley
25 – Cleveland	W	8-7	Clear	Monge
26 – Cleveland	L	2-5	Garland	Eckersley
27 – Cleveland	W	10-5	Clear	Blyleven
29 – Milwaukee	L	4-5	Fingers	Burgmeier
30 – Milwaukee	W	7-6*	Clear	Fingers
31 – Milwaukee	L	2-5	Vuckovich	Crawford
Won 18, Lost 12				
JUNE				
2 – At Cleve.	W	4-0	Eckersley	Blyleven
3 – At Cleve.	L	1-4	Waits	Tudor
4 – At Cleve.	W	6-5	Torrez	Spillner
5 – At Oak.	W	4-1	Tanana	Keough
6 – At Oak.	L	2-6	Norris	Crawford
7 – At Oak.	L	3-4†	Heaverlo	Clear
8 – At Seattle	L	0-2	Bannister	Tudor
9 – At Seattle	W	10-1	Torrez	Clark
10 – At Seattle	W	4-2	Tanana	Allard
11 – At Calif.	L	2-7	Forsch	Rainey
Won 5, Lost 5				

AUGUST			Winner	Loser
10 – Chicago	L	1-7	Lamp	Eckersley
11 – Chicago	L	2-4	Trout	Stanley
12 – Chicago	W	8-1	Ojeda	Hoyt
13 – Chicago	W	9-6	Clear	Patterson
14 – At Texas	L	2-3	Kern	Burgmeier
15 – At Texas	W	5-3	Stanley	Kern
16 – At Texas	L	0-3	Honeycutt	Ojeda
18 – At Oak.	L	2-3x	Owchinko	Campbell
19 – At Oak.	L	2-4	Keough	Tanana
20 – At Oak.	W	6-4	Eckersley	McCatty
21 – At Seattle	W	7-4	Stanley	Stein
22 – At Seattle	W	5-3	Ojeda	Beattie
23 – At Seattle	W	7-5	Burgmeier	Clark
24 – At Calif.	L	6-8	Jefferson	Tanana
25 – At Calif.	L	7-8*	Aase	Burgmeier
27 – Oakland	W	6-5	Stanley	Underwood
28 – Oakland	W	12-5	Ojeda	Norris
29 – Oakland	W	7-6	Torrez	Keough
30 – Oakland	L	3-5	McCatty	Tanana
31 – California	W	4-1	Eckersley	Frost
Won 11, Lost 9				
SEPTEMBER				
1 – California	L	2-3	Forsch	Stanley
2 – California	W	3-1	Ojeda	Witt
3 – Seattle	L	7-8y	Galasso	Stanley
4 – Seattle	L	2-5	Stoddard	Tanana
5 – Seattle	W	12-5	Tudor	Clay
6 – Seattle	W	6-1	Hurst	Abbott
7 – At Detroit	L	1-3	Morris	Ojeda
8 – At Detroit	W	5-3	Torrez	Wilcox
9 – At Detroit	W	6-5†	Stanley	Tobik
11 – At N. York	L	1-4	Righetti	Eckersley
12 – At N. York	W	2-1	Ojeda	Reuschel
13 – At N. York	L	6-10	Guidry	Tanana
14 – Detroit	W	5-2	Stanley	Petry
16 – Detroit	W	2-1*	Eckersley	Morris
16 – Detroit	W	5-4	Burgmeier	Tobik
17 – Detroit	W	6-1	Ojeda	Wilcox
18 – New York	L	4-6	Davis	Stanley
19 – New York	W	8-5	Tudor	Davis
20 – New York	W	4-1	Hurst	John
21 – Milwaukee	W	9-3	Eckersley	Haas
22 – Milwaukee	L	8-10	Fingers	Clear
23 – Milwaukee	W	11-5	Aponte	Easterly
24 – Cleveland	L	2-5	Spillner	Torrez
25 – Cleveland	W	5-4	Stanley	Garland
26 – Cleveland	L	5-7	Waits	Eckersley
27 – Cleveland	L	7-8†	Monge	Clear
28 – At Milw.	L	0-1	Vuckovich	Tanana
29 – At Milw.	W	7-2	Torrez	Slaton
30 – At Milw.	L	5-10	Lerch	Stanley
Won 16, Lost 13				
OCTOBER				
2 – At Cleve.	L	4-11	Spillner	Eckersley
3 – At Cleve.	W	4-0	Tanana	Brennan
4 – At Cleve.	W	6-2	Torrez	Denny
Won 2, Lost 1				

*10 innings. †11 innings. ‡12 innings. §14 innings. x15 innings. y20 innings.

The Same Old Story for Indians

By TERRY PLUTO

There are a few ways to look at the Cleveland Indians' 1981 season.

If the baseball strike had started May 29th, as scheduled, the Indians would have been in the American League East Division playoffs. They were in first place on that date. But the players postponed their strike until June 12, by which time the Indians had dropped to sixth.

The second half was not much better. Cleveland lost seven of its first nine and ended up in fifth place, just one percentage point ahead of the sixth-place New York Yankees. The Yankees, of course, went on to lose to Los Angeles in the World Series.

Overall, the Indians were 52-51, good for sixth in the East. Despite all the optimism and talk of a "new look," it was the same old story for Indians fans.

For the Tribe, there has been no place but sixth since 1978.

In 1981, some thought it might be different. Indians President Gabe Paul and General Manager Phil Seghi pulled off a big trade when they shipped Victor Cruz, Bob Owchinko, Gary Alexander and Rafael Vasquez to Pittsburgh for Bert Blyleven. Until he was struck with elbow ailments in the middle of September, Blyleven was the anchor of the pitching staff. He went 11-7 with a 2.89 ERA. In 13 of his 20 starts, he yielded three runs or less.

The Indians also received fine pitching from John Denny (10-6, 3.14), who was on the verge of free agency. In the first half, Len Barker and Rick Waits were solid. They combined for a 10-7 record and a 2.54 ERA. After the strike, they were 6-10 with a 6.88 ERA.

Buoyed by strong starting pitching, Cleveland spent 22 days on top of the pack in May. But the Indians' arms faltered and the team's lack of relief and power became evident.

The Indians bullpen had only 13 saves, seven going to Dan Spillner. Sid Monge had his second straight miserable year in the bullpen. He was 3-5 with a 4.34 ERA and only four saves. He was shelled for nine homers in 58 innings.

Joe Charboneau, THE SPORTING NEWS' 1980 A.L. Rookie Player of the Year, was a major flop. He slumped to .210 with four homers and 18 RBIs. He even spent

Toby Harrah . . . Mr. Consistency.

Bert Blyleven . . . Elbow problems.

part of the season in the minors, where he slept on an army cot in the Charleston Charlies clubhouse.

Along with Super Joe, Andre Thornton was supposed to supply the team's punch. Thornton suffered a broken hand when hit by a pitch in the first spring training exhibition game. Later in the season, he went on the disabled list (for the sixth time in the last six years) when he received a badly sprained thumb while pulling Don Baylor off Waits during an August 23 brawl in Anaheim.

Toby Harrah, Bo Diaz, Mike Hargrove, Duane Kuiper, Rick Manning and Miguel Dilone all had fine seasons.

Harrah batted .291, scored 64 runs to lead the team and his 44 RBIs were sec-ond only to Hargrove. He also stole 12 bases in 13 tries. Hargrove led the club with 49 RBIs and batted .317.

Diaz was named to the All-Star team. Platooning with Ron Hassey, he hit .313 with seven homers and 38 RBIs. Kuiper, rebounding from a knee injury some said would end his career, hit .257 and played a solid second base. Dilone clashed with Manager Dave Garcia and demanded to be traded, but still batted .290 and led the team with 29 stolen bases. Manning was excellent defensively in center field, but hit only .244.

The Indians' 39 homers were last in the A.L., but they paced the league with 119 stolen bases. They were caught only 37 times.

SCORES FOR CLEVELAND INDIANS' 1981 GAMES

APRIL

11 – Milwaukee	L	3-5	Caldwell	Blyleven
12 – Milwaukee	L	1-6	Slaton	Denny
14 – At Texas	W	7-1	Waits	Matlack
15 – At Texas	L	0-8	Medich	Barker
16 – At Milw.	W	1-0	Garland	Caldwell
18 – At Milw.	W	5-0	Blyleven	Slaton
20 – At Kan. C.	W	4-2	Denny	Splittorff
21 – At Kan. C.	W	4-1	Waits	Berenguer
22 – At Kan. C.	W	4-0	Barker	Leonard
25 – Texas	L	4-8	Honeycutt	Garland
26 – Texas	W	4-3	Blyleven	Johnson
30 – Chicago	W	3-2	Waits	Baumgarten

Won 8, Lost 4

MAY

1 – Chicago	W	10-2	Denny	Burns
2 – Chicago	W	3-1	Barker	Barrios
3 – Chicago	L	0-6	Dotson	Garland
6 – At Toronto	W	4-1	Blyleven	Todd
7 – At Toronto	L	2-6	Stieb	Waits
8 – At Minn.	L	7-8	O'Connor	Monge
9 – At Minn.	W	2-1†	Monge	Redfern
10 – At Minn.	W	5-1	Garland	Koosman
11 – At Chicago	W	3-1	Blyleven	Baumgarten
12 – At Chicago	L	4-7	Trout	Waits
13 – At Chicago	W	4-3z	Stanton	Lamp
15 – Toronto	W	3-0	Barker	Leal
16 – Toronto	L	1-4	Todd	Garland
17 – Toronto	W	1-0	Waits	Stieb
17 – Toronto	W	2-1†	Blyleven	Jackson
18 – California	L	2-7	Renko	Denny
19 – California	W	7-3	Spillner	Zahn
20 – Seattle	L	1-3	Allard	Barker
21 – Seattle	L	3-6	Abbott	Garland
22 – At N. York	W	7-3	Blyleven	John
23 – At N. York	L	2-3	Righetti	Waits
24 – At N. York	W	12-5	Denny	May
25 – At Boston	L	7-8	Clear	Monge
26 – At Boston	W	5-2	Garland	Eckersley
27 – At Boston	L	5-10	Clear	Blyleven
29 – New York	L	2-5	Righetti	Waits
30 – New York	L	0-1	Nelson	Spillner
31 – New York	W	7-2	Barker	May

Won 15, Lost 13

JUNE

1 – New York	L	3-5	Bird	Garland
2 – Boston	L	0-4	Eckersley	Blyleven
3 – Boston	W	4-1	Waits	Tudor
4 – Boston	L	5-6	Torrez	Spillner
5 – At Seattle	W	8-1	Barker	Parrott
6 – At Seattle	W	5-3	Blyleven	Rawley
7 – At Seattle	L	4-5‡	Drago	Stanton
8 – At Calif.	L	2-10	Zahn	Spillner
9 – At Calif.	L	2-4	Hassler	Barker
10 – At Calif.	L	3-4	Renko	Blyleven

Won 3, Lost 7

AUGUST

10 – Milwaukee	L	2-5x	Keeton	Stanton
11 – Milwaukee	L	5-6	Caldwell	Denny
11 – Milwaukee	L	1-6	Slaton	Waits
12 – Milwaukee	W	9-4	Barker	Lerch
13 – Milwaukee	L	5-8	Haas	Garland
14 – Kan. City	L	1-4	Jones	Blyleven
15 – Kan. City	L	3-5	Leonard	Denny
16 – Kan. City	L	2-6	Gura	Waits
16 – Kan. City	W	8-6	Stanton	Martin
18 – At Seattle	W	5-2	Blyleven	Clark
19 – At Seattle	L	3-4†	Rawley	Monge
20 – At Seattle	W	6-5y	Stanton	Drago
21 – At Calif.	L	2-12	Forsch	Barker
22 – At Calif.	L	2-3†	Aase	Monge
23 – At Calif.	W	6-3	Denny	Frost
24 – At Oak.	L	4-16	Keough	Waits
25 – At Oak.	W	2-0	Barker	McCatty
27 – Seattle	W	12-2	Blyleven	Parrott
28 – Seattle	W	1-0	Denny	Rawley
29 – Seattle	W	7-3	Waits	Bannister
30 – Seattle	W	17-11	Monge	Rawley
31 – Oakland	L	3-5	Langford	Blyleven

Won 10, Lost 12

SEPTEMBER

2 – Oakland	W	2-0	Denny	Norris
2 – Oakland	W	10-4	Spillner	Keough
4 – California	L	1-3*	Zahn	Barker
5 – California	W	4-2	Blyleven	Renko
5 – California	W	4-2	Brennan	Frost
6 – California	W	2-0	Denny	Forsch
7 – At Balt.	L	2-9	Palmer	Waits
8 – At Balt.	L	5-14	McGregor	Barker
9 – At Balt.	W	8-5	Blyleven	Stone
10 – At Balt.	W	4-1	Denny	Stewart
11 – At Detroit	L	3-6	Schatzeder	Waits
12 – At Detroit	W	9-11§	Rozema	Monge
13 – At Detroit	L	6-8	Wilcox	Spillner
15 – Baltimore	L	6-7	D. Martinez	Stanton
17 – Baltimore	L	2-6	McGregor	Barker
18 – Detroit	W	8-4	Denny	Schatzeder
19 – Detroit	L	3-4	Petry	Blyleven
20 – Detroit	L	1-5	Morris	Brennan
21 – At N. York	W	5-0	Waits	May
22 – At N. York	W	6-4	Barker	Righetti
23 – At N. York	L	1-6	Reuschel	Denny
24 – At Boston	W	5-2	Spillner	Torrez
25 – At Boston	L	4-5	Stanley	Garland
26 – At Boston	W	7-5	Waits	Eckersley
27 – At Boston	W	8-7‡	Monge	Clear
28 – New York	W	6-2	Brennan	Reuschel
29 – New York	W	3-2	Denny	Guidry

Won 15, Lost 12

OCTOBER

2 – Boston	W	11-4	Spillner	Eckersley
3 – Boston	L	0-4	Tanana	Brennan
4 – Boston	L	2-6	Torrez	Denny
5 – Kan. City	L	0-9	Splittorff	Waits

Won 1, Lost 3

*5½ innings. †10 innings. ‡11 innings. §12 innings. x13 innings. y14 innings. z16 innings.

Mike Hargrove turned in his third straight .300-plus season in Cleveland.

The right arm of Dave Stieb was one of the few bright spots for Toronto.

The Jays Were Bad—Again

By NEIL MacCARL

Optimism marked the beginning of year No. 5 for the Toronto Blue Jays, but it ended like all the rest—in frustration.

It was fitting that the Jays should be blanked 2-0 in the season finale, because that was the story of their season—a lack of hitting. It marked the 20th time in 106 1981 games that the Jays were blanked, almost one out of every five games they played.

At the time of the strike interruption in early June, the Jays' team batting average was a pathetic .218, and they had won only 16 of 58 games. In the second half, the Jays redeemed themselves by playing .500 ball until the final two weeks of the season. But then they lost nine of their last 11 games.

The key to the improvement in the second half was pitching. The Jays finished the season with a 3.82 earned-run average, lowest in team history.

After the acquisition of righthander Juan Berenguer from the Kansas City Royals, pitching coach Al Widmar and Manager Bobby Mattick decided to go with a four-man starting rotation consisting of Dave Stieb, Jim Clancy, Luis Leal and Berenguer.

Stieb won five of his last six decisions to finish 11-10, the first time a Jays starter had finished with a winning record. His 3.18 ERA also was a team record for a starter. Berenguer won his first two decisions for the Jays, then was a shutout victim in three of his next four starts. He finished the season on a nine-game losing streak.

The bullpen was much improved in the second season. Roy Lee Jackson picked up saves in three successive games in the first week after the strike. But the big hero was Joey McLaughlin, who set a team record with 10 saves. He had a string of 11 consecutive appearances covering 17 innings in which he didn't allow a run, and he picked up five saves. After giving up 16 home runs in 136 innings in 1980, he surrendered only two in 60 innings, and his ERA dropped to 2.85 (from 4.51).

Late in the season, the Jays purchased Dale Murray from their Syracuse farm team to bolster the bullpen. He had a 1-0 record and a 1.20 ERA in 11 appearances.

Offensively, the Jays were inconsistent. Alfredo Griffin, the switch-hitting short-

John Mayberry . . . Jays' slugger.

stop, hit .379 in spring training and was swinging more aggressively than ever before. But when the season started, he had nothing but trouble and finished with a .209 average, his worst in three seasons. He also committed 31 errors, leading American League shortstops for the third successive season.

Former Brigham Young basketball star Danny Ainge missed all but the final week of spring training because of the NCAA playoffs. But when he arrived, he was given the third base job. Ainge quickly demonstrated he could do the job defensively, but he just couldn't hit. He batted only .187 with eight extra-base hits and did not have a single game-winning run batted in.

After the Boston Celtics picked him in the NBA draft last June, Ainge decided to quit baseball for basketball.

First baseman John Mayberry, whose average dipped close to .200 in late August, hit seven home runs in the final five weeks to finish with a team-leading 17. He was the Jays' only consistent long-ball threat.

Alvis Woods, who hit 15 home runs and batted .300 in 1980, slipped to .247 with one homer. Barry Bonnell, who did not play the final six weeks because of a knee injury, dropped from .268 to .220.

But there were some bright spots. Second baseman Damaso Garcia was the

Jays' hottest hitter after the strike, until he was hit by a pitch that broke a bone in his right hand. But he quickly recovered and hit at a .375 clip in the second half to boost his average to a team-leading .252. He also led the team in stolen bases with 13 in 16 attempts.

Outfielder Lloyd Moseby, in his first full season, shared the club RBI lead (43) with Mayberry and had six game-winning RBIs. In successive games in August, he drove in six runs against Kansas City and delivered a game-winning, two-out homer against Chicago in the bottom of the ninth.

A pleasant surprise in September was rookie outfielder Jesse Barfield. A native of the Chicago area, he made his debut in Comiskey Park and drove in six runs in his first four games.

After two seasons as manager, Bobby Mattick was given the choice of continuing for another year or moving into the front office as executive assistant to General Manager Pat Gillick. Mattick, who turned 66 in December, didn't make up his mind until the end of the season. When the Jays lost nine of their final 11 games, Mattick decided to step down. Bobby Cox, fired earlier as manager of the Atlanta Braves, was picked as his successor.

SCORES OF TORONTO BLUE JAYS' 1981 GAMES

APRIL

Date		Score	Winner	Loser
9—At Detroit	L	2-6	Morris	McLaughlin
11—At Detroit	L	2-6	Wilcox	Stieb
12—At Detroit	W	6-2	Leal	Bailey
13—New York	W	5-1	Clancy	John
15—New York	L	3-6	May	Todd
16—Detroit	L	0-2	Wilcox	Stieb
17—Detroit	L	5-8	Bailey	Leal
18—Detroit	L	3-4	Schatzeder	Clancy
19—Detroit	W	9-1	Bomback	Morris
20—Milwaukee	L	4-5†	Lerch	Willis
21—Milwaukee	L	2-6	Haas	Stieb
22—Milwaukee	L	1-8	Caldwell	Leal
24—At N. York	L	2-4	John	Bomback
25—At N. York	W	7-2	Todd	May
26—At N. York	W	2-1	Stieb	Underwood
27—At Milw.	L	3-4†	Cleveland	Garvin
28—At Milw.	W	6-2	Bomback	Caldwell
29—At Milw.	W	5-0§	Leal	Easterly
30—At Balt.	L	0-4	Flanagan	Todd

Won 7, Lost 12

MAY

Date		Score	Winner	Loser
2—At Balt.	L	3-4	Palmer	Willis
2—At Balt.	L	3-8	McGregor	Leal
3—At Balt.	W	4-2	Bomback	Stone
6—Cleveland	L	1-4	Blyleven	Todd
7—Cleveland	W	6-2	Stieb	Waits
8—Boston	L	2-4	Torrez	Bomback
9—Boston	L	3-10	Stanley	Clancy
10—Boston	L	5-9*	Burgmeier	Jackson
11—Boston	L	6-7	Clear	Willis
12—Baltimore	W	5-2	Stieb	Palmer
13—Baltimore	L	0-4	McGregor	Bomback
14—Baltimore	L	0-10	Flanagan	Clancy
15—At Cleve.	L	0-3	Barker	Leal
16—At Cleve.	W	4-1	Todd	Garland
17—At Cleve.	L	0-1	Waits	Stieb
17—At Cleve.	L	1-2*	Blyleven	Jackson
18—Chicago	L	2-7	Trout	Bomback
19—Chicago	W	8-5	Clancy	Hoyt
20—Chicago	L	5-6	Farmer	McLaughlin
22—At Oak.	L	2-6	Langford	Stieb
23—At Oak.	L	2-3x	Jones	Leal
24—At Oak.	L	5-6†	Owchinko	McLaughlin
24—At Oak.	L	0-5	Norris	Garvin
25—At Calif.	L	1-2	Witt	Todd
26—At Calif.	W	8-4	Jackson	Rau
27—At Calif.	W	3-1	Stieb	Forsch
29—Oakland	W	6-3	Clancy	Keough
30—Oakland	W	6-5	Leal	Norris
31—Oakland	L	5-6	Owchinko	McLaughlin

Won 9, Lost 20

JUNE

Date		Score	Winner	Loser
1—California	L	0-3	Forsch	Stieb
2—California	L	0-3	Frost	Leal
3—California	L	6-17	Zahn	Clancy
5—At Texas	L	4-5†	Comer	Leal
6—At Texas	L	1-4	Jenkins	Stieb
7—At Texas	L	0-9	Darwin	Todd
8—At Chicago	L	2-6	Lamp	Clancy
9—At Chicago	L	0-3	Dotson	Leal
10—Kan. City	L	4-7	Leonard	Bomback
11—Kan. City	L	5-10	Martin	Willis

Won 0, Lost 10

AUGUST

Date		Score	Winner	Loser
10—At Detroit	L	3-4	Saucier	McLaughlin
11—At Detroit	W	6-4	Berenguer	Schatzeder
12—At Detroit	W	4-3	Stieb	Morris
14—Milwaukee	W	5-4	Garvin	Easterly
15—Milwaukee	W	4-3	Bomback	Cleveland
16—Milwaukee	L	2-6	Caldwell	Stieb
16—Milwaukee	L	0-2	Lerch	Todd
17—At Kan. C.	L	3-5	Gale	Clancy
18—At Kan. C.	W	5-3	Leal	Jones
19—At Kan. C.	W	9-4	Berenguer	Leonard
21—Chicago	W	5-4	Stieb	Farmer
22—Chicago	L	0-8	Burns	Clancy
23—Chicago	L	2-13	Medich	Leal
24—Texas	L	0-3	Medich	Berenguer
25—Texas	L	5-1	Jenkins	Stieb
27—Kan. City	L	5-11	Martin	Clancy
28—Kan. City	W	4-3	McLaughlin	Brett
29—Kan. City	L	0-2	Jones	Berenguer
31—At Texas	W	3-0	Stieb	Jenkins

Won 9, Lost 10

SEPTEMBER

Date		Score	Winner	Loser
1—At Texas	W	9-3	Clancy	Darwin
2—At Texas	L	1-4	Honeycutt	Leal
3—At Chicago	L	3-4	Hoyt	Berenguer
4—At Chicago	W	6-2	Stieb	Lamp
5—At Chicago	W	3-1	Clancy	Baumgarten
6—At Chicago	W	3-2	Leal	Burns
7—At Minn.	L	0-4	Jackson	Berenguer
8—At Minn.	L	0-1	Havens	Stieb
9—At Minn.	L	1-3	Arroyo	Clancy
10—Seattle	W	2-0	Leal	Clay
11—Seattle	L	1-8	Abbott	Berenguer
12—Seattle	W	3-0	Stieb	Beattie
14—Minnesota	L	3-6	Havens	Clancy
15—Minnesota	W	4-2	Leal	Arroyo
16—Minnesota	L	2-5	Williams	Berenguer
18—California	W	5-1	Murray	Witt
19—California	W	6-4	Clancy	Frost
20—California	W	6-3	Bomback	Zahn
22—Oakland	L	2-3‡	Beard	Leal
22—Oakland	L	2-4	McCatty	Berenguer
23—Oakland	L	0-6	Langford	Clancy
25—At Calif.	L	5-11	Zahn	Leal
26—At Calif.	L	3-6	Renko	Berenguer
27—At Calif.	W	4-3	Stieb	Moreno
29—At Oak.	L	1-5	Underwood	Clancy
30—At Oak.	L	0-3	Norris	Leal

Won 11, Lost 15

OCTOBER

Date		Score	Winner	Loser
2—At Seattle	L	3-8	Clay	Berenguer
3—At Seattle	W	4-3	Stieb	Abbott
4—At Seattle	L	0-2	Bannister	Todd

Won 1, Lost 2

*10 innings. †12 innings. ‡13 innings. §14 innings. x15 innings.

These A's Were Truly Amazin'

By KIT STIER

In just two seasons, baseball's doormat has become one of the game's red carpets.

No longer do opposing teams lick their chops and pound the Oakland A's into oblivion. The gang that became known as the Triple-A's is once again Amazin'.

In 1979, the A's were the worst team in baseball (54-108) and a disgrace at the box office. In one year, Manager Billy Martin turned a bunch of greenhorn kids into a group that believed enough in itself to finish second in the American League West.

The march toward success continued in 1981 when the A's, under new management, finished the regular season with the best overall record in the American League (64-45). They swept Kansas City in the divisional playoffs and then were swept out the door in three games against the New York Yankees in the Championship Series.

Oakland jumped out of the starting gate hungry. Very hungry. The A's set a major league record by winning their first 11 games, including eight on the road, and kept on winning to forge an 18-3 record by the end of April and a 4½-game lead in the West.

While the A's were sprinting their way to an early lead, their fans were coming to the Oakland Coliseum in record numbers. The club surpassed its all-time Oakland attendance record on Labor Day and finished the season with a figure of 1,304,054—despite losing 23 dates to the strike.

By May 24, the A's were six games ahead of the pack with a record of 24-7. But up ahead lurked a 10-game trip to New York, Milwaukee, Baltimore and Boston—all teams that give the A's trouble.

And as they had done in recent years, the A's folded up and died in those Eastern hot spots. They returned home with a record of 25-16 and their cushion had dwindled to 2½ games.

But the club held on. When the strike hit, the A's held a 1½-game lead over Texas and would, as it turned out, be headed for the playoffs for the first time since 1975.

In the second half, the A's didn't piece together any long hot streaks, but managed to play well enough to finish Baseball 1981, Part II, just one game behind Kansas City.

Along the way, the starting outfield of Rickey Henderson in left, Dwayne Murphy in center and Tony Armas in right proved that the fantastic play they provided the previous season was no fluke. Time and again the trio stole runs from the opposition with fine defense while also leading the club with their bats. Henderson led the league with 327 putouts and Murphy was second with 326. They formed two-thirds of THE SPORTING NEWS' 1981 Gold Glove outfield.

Armas finished the season tied for the league lead with 22 home runs and was second with 76 runs batted in.

Henderson, who set a league record in 1980 with 100 stolen bases, once again took top honors in the theft department with 56. The Oakland native also led the league with 89 runs, 135 hits and finished in a tie for second with seven triples.

Murphy decided during spring training that he would not bunt as much in 1981, and with his new power boost hit 15 home runs and led the league with 15 game-winning RBIs.

On the mound, the A's staff once again consisted mainly of four starters who got little relief. The club, which had 94 complete games in 1980, had a league-leading 60 in 1981.

Martin began the season with a five-man rotation consisting of Mike Norris, Rick Langford, Matt Keough, Steve McCatty and Brian Kingman. For a while he used a six-man rotation when lefthander Tom Underwood joined the team from the Yankees, but dropped to four starters in the second half. Underwood made some spot starts in the second season, and Kingman, who lost 20 games in 1980 and finished 1981 with a 3-6 mark, was banished to the bullpen.

It was McCatty who emerged as the star of the A's staff in 1981. The hard-throwing righthander wrapped up the season with a 14-7 record and won the league earned-run average title with 2.32.

McCatty, who had never thrown a shutout at any level of baseball until 1980, tossed four and shared top honors with three others in that department.

Langford, with 18, and McCatty, with 16, were 1-2 in the league in complete games.

The bullpen provided just 10 saves in 109 games, but hope for the future came when righthander Dave Beard was called up from the Triple-A level late in the season. In the last four of his eight outings, Beard had three saves and a victory.

The team that bunted and stole its way to semi-fame in 1980 powered its way to the top in 1981. The A's led the league with 104 home runs. In the second season they went only two games without an extra-base hit.

Shortly after the season ended, the A's ran large ads in all of the Bay Area newspapers. The copy, which accompanied a large baseball with "Billy Ball" written on it, read:

"Magic is the only word for it—the voices, the music, the summer nights, the season.

"Thanks, to the greatest fans in all of baseball, for a year we'll never forget. Spring training begins February 15th and, frankly, we can hardly wait."

Baseball fever had finally invaded Oakland.

SCORES OF OAKLAND ATHLETICS' 1981 GAMES

APRIL

			Winner	Loser
9 – At Minn.	W	5-1	Norris	Koosman
10 – At Minn.	W	6-3	Langford	Erickson
11 – At Minn.	W	3-0	Keough	Williams
12 – At Minn.	W	1-0	McCatty	Redfern
13 – At Calif.	W	3-2	Jones	Sanchez
14 – At Calif.	W	5-2	Norris	Zahn
15 – At Calif.	W	5-3	Langford	Hassler
16 – At Calif.	W	5-1	Keough	Witt
17 – Seattle	W	16-1	McCatty	Bannister
18 – Seattle	W	8-0	Kingman	Clay
19 – Seattle	W	6-1	Norris	Abbott
19 – Seattle	L	2-3	Clark	Langford
20 – Minnesota	W	3-0	Keough	Koosman
21 – Minnesota	W	4-3*	McCatty	Corbett
22 – Minnesota	W	2-1	Kingman	Williams
24 – At Seattle	W	6-2	Norris	Abbott
25 – At Seattle	W	7-4	Langford	Gleaton
26 – At Seattle	W	9-4	Keough	Parrott
27 – California	L	2-3	Forsch	McCatty
28 – California	L	1-3	Renko	Kingman
29 – California	W	6-4	Norris	Zahn

Won 18, Lost 3

MAY

1 – New York	W	8-6	Langford	Underwood
2 – New York	W	6-3	Keough	Guidry
3 – New York	L	2-3*	Davis	McCatty
3 – New York	L	0-2	John	Kingman
5 – Detroit	W	6-2	Norris	Rozema
6 – Detroit	L	2-3	Wilcox	Langford
7 – Detroit	W	5-3	Jones	Petry
8 – Milwaukee	W	2-0	McCatty	Caldwell
9 – Milwaukee	W	6-5‡	Owchinko	Lerch
10 – Milwaukee	L	5-13	Vuckovich	Norris
12 – At N. York	L	1-4	Guidry	Langford
13 – At N. York	W	5-4	Keough	John
14 – At N. York	L	5-9	Gossage	Jones
15 – At Milw.	L	0-3	Vuckovich	McCatty
16 – At Milw.	L	5-6	Cleveland	Owchinko
17 – At Milw.	L	2-6	Haas	Langford
18 – At Balt.	L	1-5	McGregor	Keough
19 – At Balt.	L	5-6	Flanagan	Norris
20 – At Boston	L	3-5	Stanley	McCatty
21 – At Boston	L	0-3	Eckersley	Kingman
22 – Toronto	W	6-2	Langford	Stieb
23 – Toronto	W	3-2x	Jones	Leal
24 – Toronto	W	6-5‡	Owchinko	McLaughlin
24 – Toronto	W	5-0	Norris	Garvin
25 – Chicago	W	5-2	McCatty	Dotson
26 – Chicago	L	1-4	Burns	Kingman
27 – Chicago	L	0-3	Baumgarten	Langford
29 – At Toronto	L	3-6	Clancy	Keough
30 – At Toronto	L	5-6	Leal	Norris
31 – At Toronto	W	6-5	Owchinko	McLaughlin

Won 13, Lost 17

JUNE

2 – At Chicago	W	6-2	McCatty	Baumgarten
3 – At Chicago	W	8-3	Kingman	Barrios
4 – At Chicago	L	2-4	Dotson	Langford
5 – Boston	L	1-4	Tanana	Keough
6 – Boston	W	6-2	Norris	Crawford
7 – Boston	W	4-3†	Heaverlo	Clear
9 – Baltimore	W	4-2	McCatty	Palmer
9 – Baltimore	W	3-2	Jones	Stewart
10 – Baltimore	L	1-3	Flanagan	Langford

Won 6, Lost 3

AUGUST

			Winner	Loser
10 – At Minn.	L	2-6	Erickson	Langford
11 – At Minn.	W	6-5	Norris	Williams
12 – At Minn.	L	3-4	Jackson	Owchinko
14 – California	W	4-2*	McCatty	Aase
15 – California	W	8-7§	Underwood	Witt
16 – California	W	7-6	Langford	Forsch
18 – Boston	W	3-2x	Owchinko	Campbell
19 – Boston	W	4-2	Keough	Tanana
20 – Boston	L	4-6	Eckersley	McCatty
21 – Baltimore	L	2-4	Palmer	Kingman
22 – Baltimore	W	2-0	Langford	McGregor
23 – Baltimore	L	4-7	Stewart	Norris
24 – Cleveland	W	16-4	Keough	Waits
25 – Cleveland	L	0-2	Barker	McCatty
27 – At Boston	L	5-6	Stanley	Underwood
28 – At Boston	L	5-12	Ojeda	Norris
29 – At Boston	L	6-7	Torrez	Keough
30 – At Boston	W	5-3	McCatty	Tanana
31 – At Cleve.	W	5-3	Langford	Blyleven

Won 10, Lost 9

SEPTEMBER

2 – At Cleve.	L	0-2	Denny	Norris
2 – At Cleve.	L	4-10	Spillner	Keough
3 – At Balt.	W	10-0	McCatty	Palmer
4 – At Balt.	W	5-4†	Underwood	Stoddard
5 – At Balt.	L	3-5	Stone	Langford
6 – At Balt.	L	4-8	D. Martinez	Owchinko
7 – Texas	W	2-1	Norris	Honeycutt
8 – Texas	W	3-0	McCatty	Hough
9 – Texas	L	4-9	Comer	Underwood
11 – Kan. City	W	6-1	Keough	Hammaker
12 – Kan. City	L	0-4	Leonard	Norris
13 – Kan. City	L	5-6‡	Splittorff	Beard
14 – At Texas	W	5-2	Langford	Medich
15 – At Texas	L	2-12	Hough	Kingman
16 – At Texas	W	2-1	Norris	Darwin
18 – At Chicago	W	10-5	McCatty	Trout
19 – At Chicago	W	2-1	Langford	Lamp
20 – At Chicago	L	3-11	Dotson	Norris
22 – At Toronto	W	3-2§	Beard	Leal
22 – At Toronto	W	4-2	McCatty	Berenguer
23 – At Toronto	W	6-0	Langford	Clancy
25 – Chicago	L	2-6	Farmer	Norris
26 – Chicago	W	5-1	McCatty	Burns
27 – Chicago	L	5-9	Hoyt	Langford
27 – Chicago	L	3-10	Koosman	Keough
29 – Toronto	W	5-1	Underwood	Clancy
30 – Toronto	W	3-0	Norris	Leal

Won 15, Lost 12

OCTOBER

2 – At Kan. C.	L	0-3	Leonard	McCatty
3 – At Kan. C.	W	8-4	Langford	Jones
4 – At Kan. C.	W	4-3	Keough	Gura

Won 2, Lost 1

*10 innings. †11 innings. ‡12 innings. §13 innings. x15 innings.

Rickey Henderson ignited the surprising A's offense.

It was that kind of a season for George Brett, but he still hit .314.

The Royals' Year to Forget

By MIKE McKENZIE

The Royals began 1981 where they left off in '80—bottomed out.

George Brett left spring training to have surgery for hemorrhoids, which had cost him playing time in the '80 World Series against the Philadelphia Phillies. That was the first in a sequence of off-the-field headlines that plagued what in many regards became the worst summer of Brett's young baseball life, despite a .314 batting average.

And, for the Royals, 1981—50-53 (.485) —became the worst summer since 1974 when they stood fifth, 77-85 (.475), and 13 games out of first place.

Thanks to the strike, the split season and a sudden change in style that coincided with a sudden change in managers, the Royals salvaged some measure of pride. With a strong September under Manager Dick Howser, they won the West Division in what became known as the second season.

Then, they crash-landed again. The Oakland A's swept three straight games from the Royals in the division playoffs, leaving them to lick their wounds after a 50-53 season that translated into an 11-game deficit behind Oakland in the overall standings.

The Royals were much like the fabled little girl with the curl right in the middle of her forehead.

When they were good, they were exceptional—with Brett hitting consistently, Willie Aikens clearing fences, Willie Wilson burning basepaths, Frank White and Amos Otis anchoring the defense, Larry Gura and Dennis Leonard unflappable on the mound and Dan Quisenberry whip-slinging his 78-MPH sinkerball out of the bullpen.

But, when they were bad, they were awful.

"It was the kind of year," said Brett, "that you'd like to forget."

Brett, especially. He began by hitting feebly. His average picked up to .323 by the time the strike came June 12. However, Brett didn't hit a home run until the day before the strike, and he had just 13 RBIs in 43 games.

His frustrations surfaced off the field. Three times he garnered national attention with an outburst of temper: once striking a photographer with a crutch, next breaking property in a restroom behind a dugout, and finally pushing a female sportswriter in a hotel lobby. By the time the playoffs became the final albatross around the Royals' necks, Brett sighed, "It's time to go see my horses."

During the strike, he had sought refuge from the zany season by riding roundup on a ranch in the Texas panhandle owned by Mike Battle, former defensive back with the New York Jets and a lifelong friend of the Brett family.

Meanwhile, Club President Joe Burke (his title advanced during the playoffs when John Schuerholz was elevated to general manager) began to ride roundup on the Royals.

He fired Jim Frey on August 31, calling for "a more aggressive approach."

The Royals, who had stood pat on their lineup and pitching rotation from 1980, stood flat in the A.L. West. By the strike, they were 20-30, in fourth place and 12 games behind Oakland. When Howser took command, they stood 30-40. Where they had run away and hidden from the rest of the West the previous year, they now were running away and hiding from embarrassment.

In '80, the Royals compiled the best team batting average (.286) in the A.L. since the 1950 Boston Red Sox (.302), built a 20-game lead and swept the Yankees three straight in the playoffs.

As the Royals entered June and the strike loomed, their batting average was .252, run production was down 40 percent, one pitcher had a winning record (Rich Gale, 4-3, and he was out of the rotation along with Paul Splittorff soon after the strike ended), one had an ERA under 4.00, the bullpen was 2-9, Brett had no home runs and nine RBIs, and Wilson had four stolen bases in 10 attempts.

And these were 80 percent the same Royals who won the league championship in '80. "That," said designated hitter Hal McRae, "probably was the problem."

After the strike, Frey began to juggle the lineup. Uncertainty seemed to compound the problems. Burke finally reached a breaking point when the Royals played dreadfully in a 9-4 loss to Toronto at home August 19. Burke went shopping for Howser, who had been fired by the Yankees after they lost to the Royals in the '80 playoffs.

Burke obtained Howser on a three-year deal and announced a return to "the Royals' style—running."

Under Frey, only Wilson and Otis had the green light for stealing. Howser gave it to five others—U.L. Washington, White, Brett, John Wathan and McRae.

Before the strike, the Royals—one of the top five base-stealing clubs in the major leagues since 1976—stole just 37 in 62 tries. After the strike, they stole 63 in 91 tries.

Looking back on the Royals' season, however, the negatives outweighed the positives.

Highlights came sporadically.

Quisenberry followed his Fireman of the Year act with a miserable start—0-2, 5.56 ERA after eight appearances. However, he announced in May, "I've found a delivery in my flaw," and proceeded to finish the season with 18 saves in 40

games, a scoreless string of 20⅓ innings and a 1.74 ERA (0.79 after the strike).

Leonard, 13-11 and 2.99, was among the league leaders for the fifth straight year in victories, starts, innings pitched and strikeouts. Gura won five straight after the strike, had a 1.09 ERA in September as co-Pitcher of the Month in the A.L., and his final tally was 11-8, 2.72.

Jones, a 22-year-old tall, husky left-hander they call "The Plumber," entered the rotation in late August and went 6-3 with a 3.20 ERA. The staff ERA was 4.25 before the strike, 2.97 after.

Wilson finished the year with 19 straight stolen bases, giving him 34 for 42, and he hit .369 in September (co-Player of the Month) to wind up .303— .305 righthanded and .299 lefthanded.

SCORES OF KANSAS CITY ROYALS' 1981 GAMES

APRIL			Winner	Loser
10 – At Balt.	L	3-5	Stone	Gura
12 – At Balt.	W	4-2	Leonard	Flanagan
14 – Detroit	L	5-6	Lopez	Quisenberry
15 – Detroit	L	0-4	Rozema	Gura
17 – Baltimore	L	2-3	T. Martinez	Leonard
19 – Baltimore	W	3-2	Gale	Flanagan
20 – Cleveland	L	2-4	Denny	Splittorff
21 – Cleveland	L	1-4	Waits	Berenguer
22 – Cleveland	L	0-4	Barker	Leonard
24 – At Milw.	L	1-6	Slaton	Gale
25 – At Milw.	W	4-2	Gura	Vuckovich
26 – At Milw.	L	1-11	Lerch	Leonard
30 – At Texas	L	0-7	Honeycutt	Gale
Won 3, Lost 10				

MAY				
1 – At Texas	W	4-0	Gura	Comer
2 – At Texas	W	7-2	Leonard	Medich
3 – At Texas	L	8-9*	Johnson	Berenguer
4 – Boston	L	7-8‡	Burgmeier	Quisenberry
5 – Boston	W	2-1	Gura	Tanana
6 – Boston	L	1-3	Eckersley	Leonard
8 – At Chicago	L	5-9	Lamp	Splittorff
9 – At Chicago	L	0-3	Dotson	Gale
11 – Texas	L	1-9	Honeycutt	Gura
12 – Texas	W	3-2	Leonard	Matlack
14 – Texas	L	2-3	Medich	Splittorff
15 – At Boston	L	3-4	Clear	Martin
16 – At Boston	W	7-6	Gura	Eckersley
17 – At Boston	W	5-4	Leonard	Burgmeier
18 – At N. York	L	1-2	John	Splittorff
19 – At N. York	L	5-6	Bird	Martin
20 – At N. York	L	4-5†	Castro	Quisenberry
22 – Minnesota	L	0-7	Koosman	Leonard
23 – Minnesota	W	1-0§	Martin	Cooper
24 – Minnesota	W	6-4	Gale	O'Connor
25 – At Seattle	L	1-7	Allard	Gura
25 – At Seattle	L	2-5	Gleaton	Berenguer
26 – At Seattle	W	5-4	Leonard	Rawley
27 – At Seattle	W	8-5	Splittorff	Bannister
29 – At Minn.	W	3-1	Gale	Arroyo
30 – At Minn.	W	6-5	Wright	Corbett
31 – At Minn.	L	4-5	O'Connor	Leonard
Won 12, Lost 15				

JUNE				
1 – Seattle	W	3-2	Splittorff	Andersen
2 – Seattle	L	3-4	Bannister	Berenguer
3 – Seattle	W	12-9	Gale	Clark
5 – Milwaukee	L	2-6	Haas	Gura
6 – Milwaukee	L	2-4	Vuckovich	Leonard
7 – Milwaukee	W	7-1	Splittorff	Lerch
8 – New York	L	3-8	Righetti	Gale
9 – New York	L	5-8	LaRoche	Martin
10 – At Toronto	W	7-4	Leonard	Bomback
11 – At Toronto	W	10-5	Martin	Willis
Won 5, Lost 5				

AUGUST			Winner	Loser
10 – At Balt.	L	2-3‡	T. Martinez	Martin
12 – At Balt.	W	10-0	Gura	Palmer
12 – At Balt.	L	3-4	McGregor	Wright
13 – At Balt.	L	1-2	Flanagan	Gale
14 – At Cleve.	W	4-1	Jones	Blyleven
15 – At Cleve.	W	5-3	Leonard	Denny
16 – At Cleve.	W	6-2	Gura	Waits
16 – At Cleve.	L	6-8	Stanton	Martin
17 – Toronto	W	5-3	Gale	Clancy
18 – Toronto	L	3-5	Leal	Jones
19 – Toronto	L	4-9	Berenguer	Leonard
21 – At N. York	W	4-0	Gura	Righetti
22 – At N. York	L	0-5	Reuschel	Splittorff
23 – At N. York	L	0-8	Guidry	Gale
24 – At Detroit	W	4-2	Brett	Schatzeder
25 – At Detroit	L	3-4*	Saucier	Quisenberry
26 – At Detroit	W	6-1	Gura	Lopez
27 – At Toronto	W	11-5	Martin	Clancy
28 – At Toronto	L	3-4	McLaughlin	Brett
29 – At Toronto	W	2-0	Jones	Berenguer
31 – Milwaukee	L	3-5	Caldwell	Leonard
Won 10, Lost 11				

SEPTEMBER				
1 – Milwaukee	W	3-1	Gura	Haas
2 – Milwaukee	W	5-4	Quisenberry	Fingers
3 – New York	W	3-2	Jones	John
4 – New York	L	0-6	May	Leonard
5 – New York	L	1-2	Righetti	Gura
6 – New York	L	1-6	Reuschel	Hammaker
7 – California	W	7-1	Jones	Witt
8 – California	W	5-3	Leonard	Zahn
9 – California	W	7-3	Martin	Frost
11 – At Oak.	L	1-6	Keough	Hammaker
12 – At Oak.	W	4-0	Leonard	Norris
13 – At Oak.	W	6-5‡	Splittorff	Beard
14 – At Calif.	W	4-3	Gale	Hassler
15 – At Calif.	W	3-2	Hammaker	Moreno
16 – At Calif.	W	3-1	Leonard	Zahn
18 – At Seattle	W	8-3	Jones	Abbott
19 – At Seattle	L	1-4	Beattie	Wright
20 – At Seattle	L	2-3	Bannister	Leonard
21 – Minnesota	L	2-7	Williams	Hammaker
22 – Minnesota	W	2-1	Gura	Arroyo
23 – Minnesota	L	2-6	Redfern	Jones
24 – Minnesota	W	9-2	Leonard	Havens
25 – Seattle	L	3-8	Bannister	Wright
26 – Seattle	L	2-4	Rawley	Gura
27 – Seattle	W	15-3	Jones	Clay
28 – At Minn.	W	6-1	Leonard	Havens
29 – At Minn.	W	4-2	Wright	Williams
30 – At Minn.	W	5-2	Gura	Arroyo
Won 18, Lost 10				

OCTOBER				
2 – Oakland	W	3-0	Leonard	McCatty
3 – Oakland	L	4-8	Langford	Jones
4 – Oakland	L	3-4	Keough	Gura
5 – At Cleve.	W	9-0	Splittorff	Waits
Won 2, Lost 2				

*10 innings. †11 innings. ‡12 innings. §15 innings.

Were Rangers Jekyll or Hyde?

By RANDY GALLOWAY

Which were the real Texas Rangers? Was it the team that rolled through the first half of the 1981 season like a genuine pennant contender, or the stumbling, bumbling second-half edition that folded up early?

"The day the strike hit, I thought we were the best team in our division. If not the best, we were at least playing the best," said Manager Don Zimmer.

The Rangers' record through June 11 was 33-22, and they were within a shade of edging out Oakland for the first-half championship. In fact, in the final game before the strike, Fergie Jenkins held a 3-1 lead over Milwaukee in the sixth inning. But the Brewers turned on the power and the Rangers ended up losing. Had they won that game, they would have moved into first place by percentage points ahead of Oakland in the A.L. West.

"We were one of those teams the strike hurt most because there was no reward for having a good first half," said Zimmer. "But that made it imperative for us to perform well when play resumed. But we just never got it together again, particularly the hitters."

The bats failed the Rangers in the second half, particularly the top of the order, where Mickey Rivers and Bump Wills became liabilities. And without them on base, the RBI production of Al Oliver and Buddy Bell fell off. Before the strike, the Rangers had led the majors in team batting average and runs scored.

"We obviously weren't a power club, so for us to score runs it took a team effort up and down the batting order," Zimmer said. "It wasn't the kind of club one or two guys could carry. We needed a consistent effort out of five or six people."

By the end of the season, there was speculation the Rangers would undergo a big housecleaning, with the main emphasis on finding new bats.

As expected, Bell and Oliver were the offensive leaders. For the fourth consecutive season as a Ranger, Oliver cleared the .300 mark, hitting .309. But after .324, .323 and .319 seasons, he hit his lowest point. His 55 RBIs were second on the team to Bell, who had 64. Bell ended up with a .294 batting average, but his offense was hampered as he played the last five weeks of the season with a back injury and pulled groin muscle.

Doc Medich . . . Staff leader.

And the Rangers did not get the RBI production they'd hoped for from Pat Putnam and John Grubb.

For consistency over the first and second halves of the season, the Ranger pitching, a question mark coming in, was outstanding. The highlight of the year came in early May when there was a club-record four straight shutouts, three of them against the Boston Red Sox. Boston had fired Zimmer as manager after the 1980 season.

Lefthander Rick Honeycutt, obtained from Seattle after the 1980 season, led the staff with an 11-6 record. He was only 5-5 in the second half, but four of those losses were by scores of 2-1 (twice), 1-0 and 2-0.

Doc Medich, Texas' most consistent pitcher over the last three seasons, had a 10-6 record with a 3.08 ERA. But Danny Darwin didn't produce as expected and ended up 9-9 with a 3.64 ERA.

In early September, Zimmer removed Jenkins from the starting rotation and gave his spot to knuckleballer Charlie Hough. He was impressive in five starts, posting a 4-1 record, striking out 37 in 39 innings and allowing only 21 hits and seven earned runs.

Jon Matlack was also bumped from the rotation and rookie John Butcher took his spot. The righthander looked good. His record was only 1-2 but his ERA in three starts and two relief appearances was 1.61.

Jim Kern was considered the key to the bullpen, but he was bothered by injuries and inconsistency. Instead, Steve Comer

came out of nowhere to become the bullpen ace, posting an 8-2 record with six saves. Comer was sidelined most of the '80 season with a sore shoulder and had not been expected to make the team in spring training. But when he was healthy in the exhibition season, Comer immediately became a Zimmer favorite.

Overall, the Rangers finished with a 57-48 record for 1981, which was still a drastic improvement over the year before, when the team was six games under .500.

"The good thing," said Zimmer, "is that we had a 15-game swing in the win column from the year before. If we can build on that in '82, we'll be in business."

SCORES OF TEXAS RANGERS' 1981 GAMES

APRIL

Date			Score	Winner	Loser
9—At N. York	L		3-10	John	Matlack
11—At N. York	L		1-5	May	Darwin
12—At N. York	W		6-4	Jenkins	Guidry
14—Cleveland	L		1-7	Waits	Matlack
15—Cleveland	W		8-0	Medich	Barker
17—New York	L		1-2	Guidry	Darwin
18—New York	W		6-4	Comer	Castro
19—New York	W		4-0	Matlack	Underwood
20—At Boston	L		2-4	Torrez	Medich
21—At Boston	L		4-10	Tudor	Jenkins
22—At Boston	W		16-8	Darwin	Eckersley
25—At Cleve.	W		8-4	Honeycutt	Garland
26—At Cleve.	L		3-4	Blyleven	Johnson
27—Bc.on	W		10-0	Medich	Torrez
28—Loston	W		9-0	Comer	Crawford
29—Boston	W		5-0	Darwin	Tudor
30—Kan. City	W		7-0	Honeycutt	Gale

Won 10, Lost 7

MAY

Date			Score	Winner	Loser
1—Kan. City	L		0-4	Gura	Comer
2—Kan. City	L		2-7	Leonard	Medich
3—Kan. City	W		9-8*	Johnson	Berenguer
5—Chicago	W		6-1	Darwin	Baumgarten
6—Chicago	W		4-2	Johnson	Burns
7—Chicago	W		9-4	Babcock	Farmer
9—Baltimore	L		3-7	D. Martinez	Jenkins
9—Baltimore	L		2-4	Stone	Schmidt
10—Baltimore	W		7-3	Darwin	Flanagan
11—At Kan. C.	W		9-1	Honeycutt	Gura
12—At Kan. C.	L		2-3	Leonard	Matlack
14—At Kan. C.	W		3-2	Medich	Splittorff
15—At Chicago	W		2-1	Jenkins	Dotson
16—At Chicago	L		1-9	Burns	Darwin
17—At Chicago	L		0-9	Baumgarten	Honeycutt
18—At Detroit	W		13-5	Matlack	Petry
19—At Detroit	L		1-14	Schatzeder	Medich
20—At Detroit	L		4-8	Morris	Jenkins
22—At Seattle	W		6-2	Darwin	Bannister
23—At Seattle	W		6-4‡	Comer	Rawley
24—At Seattle	W		5-3	Matlack	Clay
25—Minnesota	W		4-3	Johnson	Jackson
26—Minnesota	W		2-1	Jenkins	Redfern
27—Minnesota	L		1-2	Koosman	Darwin
28—Minnesota	W		6-2	Honeycutt	Erickson
29—Seattle	L		4-5‡	Drago	Babcock
30—Seattle	W		6-0	Medich	Parrott
31—Seattle	L		3-5	Allard	Jenkins

Won 16, Lost 12

JUNE

Date			Score	Winner	Loser
2—At Minn.	W		5-3	Darwin	Koosman
3—At Minn.	W		6-3	Honeycutt	Erickson
4—At Minn.	L		3-7	Arroyo	Matlack
5—Toronto	W		5-4‡	Comer	Leal
6—Toronto	W		4-1	Jenkins	Stieb
7—Toronto	W		9-0	Darwin	Todd
8—Detroit	W		8-1	Honeycutt	Schatzeder
9—Detroit	L		0-5	Lopez	Matlack
10—At Milw.	W		12-5	Medich	Haas
11—At Milw.	L		3-6	Vuckovich	Jenkins

Won 7, Lost 3

AUGUST

Date			Score	Winner	Loser
10—At N. York	L		0-2	John	Darwin
11—At N. York	W		1-0	Honeycutt	Righetti
12—At N. York	L		4-5	LaRoche	Jenkins
14—Boston	W		3-2	Kern	Burgmeier
15—Boston	L		3-5*	Stanley	Kern
16—Boston	W		3-0	Honeycutt	Ojeda
18—Milwaukee	L		1-3	Haas	Matlack
18—Milwaukee	W		8-6	Comer	Vuckovich
19—Milwaukee	W		4-1	Medich	Slaton
21—At Detroit	L		4-7	Lopez	Darwin
22—At Detroit	L		0-2	Petry	Honeycutt
23—At Detroit	L		4-5	Rozema	Kern
24—At Toronto	W		3-0	Medich	Berenguer
25—At Toronto	W		6-1	Jenkins	Stieb
27—At Milw.	W		5-1	Darwin	Caldwell
28—At Milw.	L		3-6	Haas	Honeycutt
29—At Milw.	W		8-5	Matlack	Lerch
30—At Milw.	L		2-6	Vuckovich	Medich
31—Toronto	L		0-3	Stieb	Jenkins

Won 9, Lost 10

SEPTEMBER

Date			Score	Winner	Loser
1—Toronto	L		3-9	Clancy	Darwin
2—Toronto	W		4-1	Honeycutt	Leal
3—Detroit	L		5-8	Morris	Matlack
4—Detroit	W		3-2	Medich	Wilcox
5—Detroit	L		0-1	Petry	Jenkins
6—Detroit	L		3-4	Saucier	Mercer
7—At Oak.	L		1-2	Norris	Honeycutt
8—At Oak.	L		0-3	McCatty	Hough
9—At Oak.	W		9-4	Comer	Underwood
11—At Calif.	W		11-6	Comer	Aase
12—At Calif.	W		3-2	Honeycutt	Zahn
13—At Calif.	L		7-8‡	Renko	Comer
14—Oakland	L		2-5	Langford	Medich
15—Oakland	W		12-2	Hough	Kingman
16—Oakland	L		1-2	Norris	Darwin
18—Minnesota	L		3-6	Redfern	Honeycutt
19—Minnesota	W		6-0	Medich	Jackson
20—Minnesota	W		4-3	Hough	Corbett
21—Seattle	W		4-1	Darwin	Stoddard
22—Seattle	L		2-3	Clay	Butcher
23—Seattle	L		1-2	Abbott	Honeycutt
24—Seattle	L		1-2†	Rawley	Medich
25—At Minn.	W		5-2	Hough	Williams
26—At Minn.	L		3-7	Arroyo	Darwin
27—At Minn.	L		2-5	Redfern	Butcher
28—At Seattle	W		6-5	Honeycutt	Abbott
29—At Seattle	W		6-2	Medich	Clark
30—At Seattle	W		3-1	Hough	Bannister

Won 13, Lost 15

OCTOBER

Date			Score	Winner	Loser
2—California	W		8-6*	Comer	Hassler
3—California	W		1-0	Butcher	Moreno
4—California	L		2-9	Witt	Whitehouse

Won 2, Lost 1

*10 innings. †11 innings. ‡12 innings.

Buddy Bell's bat and glove kept the Rangers close in the first half.

Greg Luzinski gave the White Sox some needed home run punch.

White Sox Hurt by Poor Finish

By BOB MARKUS

It should have been a season of rejoicing on the South Side of Chicago.

The White Sox (54-52) finished over .500 for the first time since 1977. A team that had been last in the league in runs scored the year before tied for third in 1981. The team batting average was up—from .259 to .272, second in the league—and the pitching staff's earned-run average was down from 3.92 to 3.47.

So why the funeral look around Comiskey Park as the days dwindled down to season's end? In a hyphenated word: split-season.

In the first half of the season everything was new and upbeat for the White Sox. Under the new ownership of Jerry Reinsdorf, a local real estate investor, and Eddie Einhorn, a dynamic television executive from New York, the White Sox had pulled a coup by signing free-agent catcher Carlton Fisk after he defected from the Red Sox. Then they traded for slugger Greg Luzinski from the Phillies.

Fisk was expected to provide leadership for the young pitching staff and an injection of power into a lineup that had finished next to last in home runs the season before.

Luzinski came to Chicago unawed by the dimensions of Comiskey Park, which had been trimmed down by a new fence that cut the distance to center field from 445 feet to 402, and with expectations of hitting 30 home runs. Although he was to find new respect for the venerable ball park, only the 56 games lost by the strike kept him from fulfilling his goal.

Fisk was no disappointment behind the plate. But after a jet-quick getaway—four homers in the first week of the season, including a dramatic game-winner on opening day in Boston—his bat lost its snap. He was to hit only three more all year, two of them coming in successive at-bats on the next to last Sunday of the season.

As they had done the year before, the White Sox jumped off to a fast start, winning 11 of their first 15 games. When play was halted by the strike on June 12, the White Sox had won four in a row. They were nine games over .500, just 2½ games behind the Oakland A's, and tied with Texas for fewest losses in the division.

When the strike ended, 12 A.L. clubs voted for the split-season and two (the White Sox and Orioles) abstained. The team played its first 16 post-strike games on the road and the ownership feared it could be out of contention before it ever had a chance to play at home.

It was during that extended trip that a reporter pointed out to many of the White Sox players that, because a team that won both halves would not draw a bye but would play the team with the next best overall record, it might work to their advantage to lose a four-game series to the Athletics in late September. And after a majority said that if that were the case they'd throw the games, a new split-season format was devised, one that called for teams winning both halves to play the team with the next best second-half record.

But no format, as it turned out, could do the White Sox any good. They finished the trip with a 10-6 record, but then slumped unexpectedly to 3-11 at home.

The team continued to play poorly throughout the rest of the season. The only highlight was the four-game series in Oakland, the one they once thought they might have to lose. The White Sox took three out of four. They also won their last two games of the season at home, taking the finale with a four-run, ninth-inning rally after two were out, to finish above .500.

In the overall standings, the White Sox were in third place, 8½ out, and the owners pronounced themselves satisfied that third was about where they should have finished.

Taken as a whole, the season produced more plusses than minuses. Probably the biggest surprise was the play of the double play combination of Bill Almon and Tony Bernazard. Almon, who made the team in spring training after being released by the Mets, hit .301 and was outstanding at shortstop except for a brief period in the second half. Bernazard hit .276 and made only seven errors all season.

Another pleasant surprise was pitcher Dennis Lamp, who came from the Cubs in a trade for Ken Kravec. Originally used in long relief, Lamp was starting by midseason and needed to pitch a shutout in his last start to win the league ERA title. He didn't, but he did have a one-hitter earlier in Milwaukee, not yielding a hit to the Brewers until the ninth inning.

Britt Burns, THE SPORTING NEWS' A.L. Rookie Pitcher of the Year in 1980, had a strong 10-6 season with a 2.64 ERA. His best work came in the second half while commuting from his Birmingham, Ala., home on game days. The rest of his time was spent at the bedside of his critically injured father, who would die late in the season from injuries suffered when he was hit by a car.

Lamarr Hoyt, who had been a starter in his rookie year, duplicated his 9-3 record, but this time as a short man in the bullpen. He also had 10 saves.

Harold Baines improved on his rookie year with a .286 average and became an exceptional defensive outfielder. Center fielder Chet Lemon hit .302, but a sore right shoulder hampered his throwing most of the year. Luzinski ended up leading the club with 21 homers and 62 runs batted in. He was given a lucrative three-year contract a week after the season ended.

Among the disappointments were Ron LeFlore and Ed Farmer. LeFlore, signed to a long-term contract as a free agent, was better than advertised on defense and stole 36 bases, but his .246 average was the worst of his career. Farmer, who had won a $495,000 salary in arbitration, was 3-3 with 10 saves but his ERA went up to 4.58.

Richard Dotson's four shutouts shared the league lead, but they all came in the first half of the season and he finished 9-8 with a 3.77 ERA.

SCORES OF CHICAGO WHITE SOX' 1981 GAMES

APRIL			Winner	Loser
10 – At Boston	W	5-3	Hoyt	Stanley
12 – At Boston	L	4-5	Clear	Farmer
14 – Milwaukee	W	9-3	Baumgarten	Vuckovich
15 – Milwaukee	W	5-4	Hoyt	Fingers
17 – Boston	L	5-8	Eckersley	Dotson
18 – Boston	W	2-1	Trout	Tanana
19 – Boston	L	4-9	Stanley	Baumgarten
21 – Baltimore	W	2-1	Burns	Stewart
23 – Baltimore	W	18-5	Dotson	McGregor
23 – Baltimore	W	5-3	Barrios	Stone
24 – At Detroit	W	3-2†	Hoyt	Morris
25 – At Detroit	W	4-0	Baumgarten	Rozema
26 – At Detroit	W	5-4	Burns	Wilcox
27 – At Balt.	L	2-5	McGregor	Barrios
28 – At Balt.	W	8-6	Dotson	Stone
29 – At Balt.	L	0-3	D. Martinez	Trout
30 – At Cleve.	L	2-3	Waits	Baumgarten
Won 11, Lost 6				
MAY				
1 – At Cleve.	L	2-10	Denny	Burns
2 – At Cleve.	L	1-3	Barker	Barrios
3 – At Cleve.	W	6-0	Dotson	Garland
5 – At Texas	L	1-6	Darwin	Baumgarten
6 – At Texas	L	2-4	Johnson	Burns
7 – At Texas	L	4-9	Babcock	Farmer
8 – Kan. City	W	9-5	Lamp	Splittorff
9 – Kan. City	W	3-0	Dotson	Gale
11 – Cleveland	L	1-3	Blyleven	Baumgarten
12 – Cleveland	W	7-4	Trout	Waits
13 – Cleveland	L	3-4§	Stanton	Lamp
15 – Texas	L	1-2	Jenkins	Dotson
16 – Texas	W	9-1	Burns	Darwin
17 – Texas	W	9-0	Baumgarten	Honeycutt
18 – At Toronto	W	7-2	Trout	Bomback
19 – At Toronto	L	5-8	Clancy	Hoyt
20 – At Toronto	W	6-5	Farmer	McLaughlin
22 – At Calif.	W	9-5	Burns	Forsch
23 – At Calif.	W	15-4	Baumgarten	Renko
24 – At Calif.	W	10-2	Trout	Zahn
25 – At Oak.	L	2-5	McCatty	Dotson
26 – At Oak.	W	4-1	Burns	Kingman
27 – At Oak.	W	3-0	Baumgarten	Langford
30 – California	W	9-0	Dotson	Zahn
31 – California	L	4-7	Witt	Trout
31 – California	W	2-1†	Hoyt	Aase
Won 15, Lost 11				
JUNE				
2 – Oakland	L	2-6	McCatty	Baumgarten
3 – Oakland	L	3-8	Kingman	Barrios
4 – Oakland	W	4-2	Dotson	Langford
5 – At N. York	L	5-6‡	LaRoche	Hickey
6 – At N. York	L	0-2	Bird	Trout
7 – At N. York	L	1-3	Guidry	Baumgarten
8 – Toronto	W	6-2	Lamp	Clancy
9 – Toronto	W	3-0	Dotson	Leal
10 – New York	W	6-5	Burns	May
11 – New York	W	3-2	Trout	Bird
Won 5, Lost 5				

AUGUST			Winner	Loser
10 – At Boston	W	7-1	Lamp	Eckersley
11 – At Boston	W	4-2	Trout	Stanley
12 – At Boston	L	1-8	Ojeda	Hoyt
13 – At Boston	L	6-9	Clear	Patterson
14 – At Balt.	W	5-3	Dotson	Stewart
15 – At Balt.	L	0-4	D. Martinez	Hoyt
16 – At Balt.	W	8-7†	Farmer	Ford
17 – At N. York	W	4-1	Burns	Reuschel
18 – At N. York	L	0-4	Guidry	Trout
19 – At N. York	W	6-5	Lamp	May
21 – At Toronto	L	4-5	Stieb	Farmer
22 – At Toronto	W	8-0	Burns	Clancy
23 – At Toronto	W	13-2	Trout	Leal
24 – At Milw.	L	4-5	Vuckovich	Dotson
25 – At Milw.	W	5-1	Lamp	Slaton
27 – New York	W	3-1*'	Hoyt	Davis
28 – New York	L	1-6	Guidry	Trout
29 – New York	L	2-12	John	Dotson
30 – New York	L	1-5	May	Lamp
31 – Detroit	L	1-3	Wilcox	Baumgarten
Won 10, Lost 10				
SEPTEMBER				
1 – Detroit	L	1-2	Petry	Koosman
2 – Detroit	L	4-5†	Saucier	Koosman
3 – Toronto	W	4-3	Hoyt	Berenguer
4 – Toronto	L	2-6	Stieb	Lamp
5 – Toronto	L	1-3	Clancy	Baumgarten
6 – Toronto	L	2-3	Leal	Burns
7 – Seattle	L	5-9	Beattie	Dotson
8 – Seattle	W	5-3	Trout	Bannister
9 – Seattle	L	1-3	Stoddard	Lamp
10 – At Milw.	W	12-6	Hoyt	Cleveland
11 – At Minn.	L	3-4	Williams	Burns
12 – At Minn.	L	1-3	Redfern	Dotson
13 – At Minn.	L	6-7	Veselic	Hickey
14 – At Seattle	W	5-2	Lamp	Bannister
15 – At Seattle	L	4-8	Andersen	Koosman
16 – At Seattle	W	3-1	Burns	Drago
18 – Oakland	L	5-10	McCatty	Trout
19 – Oakland	L	1-2	Langford	Lamp
20 – Oakland	W	11-3	Dotson	Norris
21 – At Calif.	L	3-6	Renko	Burns
22 – At Calif.	L	0-1	Moreno	Baumgarten
23 – At Calif.	L	3-7	Witt	Trout
24 – At Calif.	W	4-1	Lamp	Kison
25 – At Oak.	W	6-2	Farmer	Norris
26 – At Oak.	L	1-5	McCatty	Burns
27 – At Oak.	W	9-5	Hoyt	Langford
27 – At Oak.	W	10-3	Koosman	Keough
28 – California	L	0-6	Witt	Lamp
29 – California	L	1-5	Kison	Dotson
30 – California	W	10-3	Burns	Frost
Won 11, Lost 19				
OCTOBER				
2 – Minnesota	L	2-3	Redfern	Koosman
3 – Minnesota	W	5-4	Hoyt	Veselic
4 – Minnesota	W	13-12	Robinson	Corbett
Won 2, Lost 1				

*8 innings.   †10 innings.   ‡12 innings.   §16 innings.

Trades Didn't Help the Angels

By JOHN STREGE

The year wasn't a total loss. Not everything the California Angels did was wrong.

When Jim Fregosi was fired as manager on May 28, the players said it was not his fault their record was 22-25. They were right, of course. Under new Manager Gene Mauch, the Angels were 29-34, 20-30 in the second half. At least they didn't play favorites.

The team is repetitious though. In 1980, the Angels had their worst season, winning 65, losing 95, and finishing in sixth place in the American League West, 31 games behind Kansas City.

The 1981 season, either half, wasn't any better. In the first half they finished 31-29 and six games behind Oakland. In the second half, they finished in last place, 8½ games behind Kansas City.

The deals the club made following last season didn't help, either. The Angels signed four free-agent pitchers, apparently seeking quantity instead of quality. For about $4 million, they added Bill Travers, Geoff Zahn, John D'Acquisto and Jesse Jefferson. Travers pitched just 9⅔ innings and D'Acquisto spent most of the season at Salt Lake City. Zahn was mediocre with a 10-11 record and a 4.42 earned-run average. Jefferson was used in mop-up situations.

At the winter meetings in Dallas last year, the Angels dealt third baseman Carney Lansford, center fielder Rick Miller and pitcher Mark Clear to the Boston Red Sox for shortstop Rick Burleson and third baseman Butch Hobson.

Advantage Red Sox. Lansford led the league in batting and was strong defensively. Burleson, voted by his teammates the Angels' most valuable player, batted .293.

But Miller and Clear had strong seasons, and Hobson had half a season. He played well the first half and poorly the second. He batted just .235.

In January, the Angels obtained center fielder Fred Lynn from Boston in exchange for Frank Tanana, Joe Rudi and Jim Dorsey. Lynn was signed to a four-year, $5.25 million contract, only to be hampered by injuries. He batted just .219.

At the end of spring training, the Angels began trading again. First they dealt infielder Dickie Thon to Houston

Rick Burleson . . . Smooth.

for pitcher Ken Forsch. Then they dealt first baseman Jason Thompson to Pittsburgh for catcher Ed Ott. Forsch became the star of the staff; Ott was a disappointment behind the plate.

Entering the season, the Angels had as formidable a lineup as there was in baseball. They were confident they could repeat their performance of 1979, when they won the A.L. West, and avoid a repeat of their disastrous 1980 season.

They were confident, but Owner Gene Autry was cautious. He had hired Mauch as director of player personnel, but most felt Mauch was hired as heir-apparent to the managerial job. Autry had indirectly made it known that a slow start would not be tolerated, that changes would be made.

The Angels, in turn, stalled at the starting gate. In late May, after a 1-5 homestand in which they lost three to Chicago and two to the Toronto Blue Jays, Fregosi was fired and Mauch hired.

At first the move appeared successful. Under Mauch, the Angels won nine and lost four and stood two games above .500 (31-29) when the strike began on June 12. And the layoff looked like a blessing in disguise. Lynn, who had injured his knee in May, rehabilitated it during the 50-day strike and was nearly 100 percent when the season resumed with the All-Star Game August 9. When baseball's hierarchy voted on a split season, the Angels, then 6½ games out of first, were given a fresh start and a healthy center fielder.

But that all changed. Lynn reinjured his knee in the All-Star Game, and though he was in the Angels' re-opening day lineup, he never resembled the Lynn who had played in Boston.

Of their first six games in the second half, the Angels lost five and the outlook again was bleak. A strong homestand, the Angels winning six of eight, rekindled optimism.

Then they embarked on a 14-game, four-city trip. Eight games into the trip, they were 4-4. They did not win again on the trip, finishing 4-10. They lost eight straight games and 14 of 15, and the Crash of '80 was repeated in '81.

The defense was partly responsible—it finished with the second most errors of any A.L. team. The hitting was partly responsible—never consistent, the Angels batted far below expectations.

But the pitching exceeded expectations. The staff earned-run average was 3.71.

SCORES OF CALIFORNIA ANGELS' 1981 GAMES

APRIL			Winner	Loser
9 – At Seattle	W	6-2	Zahn	Abbott
10 – At Seattle	L	2-10	Gleaton	Jefferson
11 – At Seattle	W	7-4	Aase	Bannister
12 – At Seattle	W	8-6	Hassler	Andersen
13 – Oakland	L	2-3	Jones	Sanchez
14 – Oakland	L	2-5	Norris	Zahn
15 – Oakland	L	3-5	Langford	Hassler
16 – Oakland	L	1-5	Keough	Witt
17 – Minnesota	W	4-0	Forsch	Williams
18 – Minnesota	L	4-6	Redfern	Travers
20 – Seattle	W	6-1	Zahn	Gleaton
21 – Seattle	L	0-3	Bannister	Jefferson
22 – Seattle	W	7-3	Forsch	Clay
24 – At Minn.	L	5-7	Corbett	Sanchez
25 – At Minn.	W	6-4	Zahn	Koosman
26 – At Minn.	W	7-1	Witt	Erickson
26 – At Minn.	L	2-5	Arroyo	Jefferson
27 – At Oak.	W	3-2	Forsch	McCatty
28 – At Oak.	W	3-1	Renko	Kingman
29 – At Oak.	L	4-6	Norris	Zahn
30 – Milwaukee	L	1-12	Augustine	Jefferson
		Won 10, Lost 11		

MAY				
1 – Milwaukee	W	8-4	Witt	Lerch
2 – Milwaukee	L	5-8	Haas	Forsch
3 – Milwaukee	L	3-4	Caldwell	Renko
4 – New York	L	2-4	Nelson	Zahn
5 – New York	W	6-2	Jefferson	Underwood
6 – New York	L	2-5	Guidry	Witt
7 – New York	W	2-1	Forsch	John
8 – Detroit	L	1-6	Morris	Renko
9 – Detroit	W	15-1	Zahn	Schatzeder
10 – Detroit	W	4-3	Hassler	Lopez
12 – At Milw.	W	4-0	Forsch	Haas
13 – At Milw.	W	6-3	Renko	Caldwell
14 – At Milw.	W	9-1	Zahn	Slaton
15 – At Detroit	L	1-5	Morris	Witt
16 – At Detroit	L	5-7	Tobik	Rau
17 – At Detroit	W	7-1	Forsch	Wilcox
18 – At Cleve.	W	7-2	Renko	Denny
19 – At Cleve.	L	3-7	Spillner	Zahn
20 – At Balt.	L	3-5	D. Martinez	Witt
21 – At Balt.	W	2-0	Rau	Palmer
22 – Chicago	L	5-9	Burns	Forsch
23 – Chicago	L	4-15	Baumgarten	Renko
24 – Chicago	L	2-10	Trout	Zahn
25 – Toronto	W	2-1	Witt	Todd
26 – Toronto	L	4-8	Jackson	Rau
27 – Toronto	L	1-3	Stieb	Forsch
30 – At Chicago	L	0-9	Dotson	Zahn
31 – At Chicago	W	7-4	Witt	Trout
31 – At Chicago	L	1-2†	Hoyt	Aase
		Won 13, Lost 16		

JUNE				
1 – At Toronto	W	3-0	Forsch	Stieb
2 – At Toronto	W	3-0	Frost	Leal
3 – At Toronto	W	17-6	Zahn	Clancy
5 – Baltimore	L	4-6	McGregor	Witt
6 – Baltimore	W	10-0	Forsch	Flanagan
7 – Baltimore	L	1-4	D. Martinez	Frost
8 – Cleveland	W	10-2	Zahn	Spillner
9 – Cleveland	W	4-2	Hassler	Barker
10 – Cleveland	W	4-3	Renko	Blyleven
11 – Boston	W	7-2	Forsch	Rainey
		Won 8, Lost 2		

AUGUST			Winner	Loser
10 – At Seattle	L	4-5	Drago	Aase
11 – At Seattle	L	1-4	Beattie	Forsch
12 – At Seattle	W	4-1‡	Aase	Drago
14 – At Oak.	L	2-4†	McCatty	Aase
15 – At Oak.	L	7-8x	Underwood	Witt
16 – At Oak.	L	6-7	Langford	Forsch
18 – Baltimore	L	5-6	McGregor	Frost
19 – Baltimore	W	6-3	Renko	Flanagan
20 – Baltimore	W	6-2	Zahn	D. Martinez
21 – Cleveland	W	12-2	Forsch	Barker
22 – Cleveland	W	3-2†	Aase	Monge
23 – Cleveland	L	3-6	Denny	Frost
24 – Boston	W	8-6	Jefferson	Tanana
25 – Boston	W	8-7†	Aase	Burgmeier
27 – At Balt.	L	2-6	McGregor	Forsch
28 – At Balt.	W	9-2	Witt	Stone
29 – At Balt.	L	3-4	D. Martinez	Zahn
30 – At Balt.	W	7-1	Hassler	Palmer
31 – At Boston	L	1-4	Eckersley	Frost
		Won 9, Lost 10		

SEPTEMBER				
1 – At Boston	W	3-2	Forsch	Stanley
2 – At Boston	L	1-3	Ojeda	Witt
4 – At Cleve.	W	3-1*	Zahn	Barker
5 – At Cleve.	L	2-4	Blyleven	Renko
5 – At Cleve.	L	2-4	Brennan	Frost
6 – At Cleve.	L	0-2	Denny	Forsch
7 – At Kan. C.	L	1-7	Jones	Witt
8 – At Kan. C.	L	3-5	Leonard	Zahn
9 – At Kan. C.	L	3-7	Martin	Frost
11 – Texas	L	6-11	Comer	Aase
12 – Texas	L	2-3	Honeycutt	Zahn
13 – Texas	W	8-7§	Renko	Comer
14 – Kan. City	L	3-4	Gale	Hassler
15 – Kan. City	L	2-3	Hammaker	Moreno
16 – Kan. City	L	1-3	Leonard	Zahn
18 – At Toronto	L	1-5	Murray	Witt
19 – At Toronto	L	4-6	Clancy	Frost
20 – At Toronto	L	3-6	Bomback	Zahn
21 – Chicago	W	6-3	Renko	Burns
22 – Chicago	W	1-0	Moreno	Baumgarten
23 – Chicago	W	7-3	Witt	Trout
24 – Chicago	L	1-4	Lamp	Kison
25 – Toronto	W	11-5	Zahn	Leal
26 – Toronto	W	6-3	Renko	Berenguer
27 – Toronto	L	3-4	Stieb	Moreno
28 – At Chicago	W	6-0	Witt	Lamp
29 – At Chicago	W	5-1	Kison	Dotson
30 – At Chicago	L	3-10	Burns	Frost
		Won 10, Lost 18		

OCTOBER				
2 – At Texas	L	6-8†	Comer	Hassler
3 – At Texas	L	0-1	Butcher	Moreno
4 – At Texas	W	9-2	Witt	Whitehouse
		Won 1, Lost 2		

*5½ innings. †10 innings. ‡11 innings. §12 innings. x13 innings.

Fred Lynn suffered through a dismal, injury-plagued season.

Seattle's Tom Paciorek was second in the A.L. with 13 game-winning RBIs.

The Mariners Improved, But . . .

By TRACY RINGOLSBY

The Seattle Mariners went into spring training with Manager Maury Wills promising a .500 or better season. By the end of the first month, that hope had vanished.

Despite playing the easiest part of their schedule, the Mariners were a miserable 6-18. Wills already had fallen out of favor with fans, players and club officials, so the inevitable decision was made. Wills, the former Los Angeles Dodger base stealing star, was given his walking papers and the Mariners looked to their farm system to finally begin reaping the products of their own cultivation.

Out stepped Rene Lachemann, who had managed the M's Class AAA team since it had been established in 1978. And while he didn't get the M's to play .500 baseball, he did get them to play the best baseball that Seattle fans have seen in the club's five-year history. The M's won their first four games under Lachemann, finished the pre-strike portion of the season with a 15-18 record under his direction, and then put a little excitement into the life of their new owner, George Argyros, in the "second season."

They found themselves involved in a pennant race for the first time in their existence, not being eliminated from the race for the A.L. West's second-half playoff berth until September 29, the day the club printed playoff tickets for the first time in its history.

They finished the second half with a 23-29 record. That gave Lachemann a 38-47 record in his first fling at managing, and it gave the M's a fifth-place finish in the second part of the split-season format. It was the first time the Mariners managed to finish higher than sixth place.

And it was reason for Argyros, the Southern California businessman who had purchased the club from its committee of owners in January, to reward Lachemann with a contract to return in 1982.

"Rene is going to be one of the fine managers in the game," said Argyros. "All we have to do is get him the players."

That could be a tough task. With their farm system only just now beginning to show some positive signs, the Mariners have had to rely on castoff veterans for the most part.

It's not the best way to survive in the big leagues, but it's not all bad, either, as 34-year-old Tom Paciorek showed in 1981.

Given a chance to play every day for the first time in more than nine years in the big leagues, Paciorek put together a big season. He finished among the American League leaders in seven offensive categories, including second-place finishes in the batting race (.326 average) and game-winning RBIs (13).

His two biggest game-winners came on back-to-back nights in the Kingdome May 8 and 9. Both nights he hit home runs in the bottom of the ninth inning to beat the New York Yankees, the second one coming before a crowd of 51,903, the fourth largest in Mariner history.

He even showed some speed on the basepaths, picking up 13 stolen bases, seven more than he had ever stolen before. And despite the strike-shortened campaign, Paciorek drove in 66 runs, seven more than the career-best he put together in 1980.

The fact that Paciorek hit third and winter-acquisition Richie Zisk fourth virtually all season helped Paciorek, too. For most of the season they were the hottest hitting combination in baseball, running one-two in the batting race for a good portion of the final month before Zisk went on a cold streak that saw his average drop from .354 to .311.

And hitting right behind Zisk was Jeff Burroughs. He didn't live up to expectations, hitting only 10 home runs. But he became the only player in the major leagues to hit three home runs in one game in 1981 when he belted three against the Twins at Minnesota August 15.

The other big offensive boost came from Gary Gray, a journeyman minor leaguer who finally got a shot to play regularly with Seattle. He responded in the first half of the season by hitting 13 home runs in 133 at-bats. He didn't hit another homer the remainder of the season.

Still, the combination of Zisk (16 homers), Paciorek (14), Gray and Burroughs helped the Mariners roll up 89 home runs, 13 more than their opponents, the first time in the club's history that it outhomered the opposition.

The M's showed some speed on the bases, too, finishing second in the league in steals with 100. The leader of the ring was Julio Cruz, who, after finishing 1980 with four straight thefts, began 1981 with 28 more, tying the A.L. record set in 1980 by Kansas City's Willie Wilson. Cruz equaled Wilson's mark of 32 straight on June 10, in the last game before the strike. The streak ended August 10, the first game back.

Even the pitching staff showed some promise, setting a club record with a 4.23 earned-run average.

Floyd Bannister, bothered by injuries three different times, managed to split his 18 decisions, giving him a .500 record for the first time in his big-league career.

He also pitched five of the Mariners' 10 complete games and tied the club low-hit record with two-hitters against California and Boston.

Jim Beattie, coming off a 5-15 season in 1980 and sent to Spokane early in 1981, came back when the strike was settled to be one of the best starters in the A.L. during the final months, compiling a 2.02 ERA in the second half. And Bob Stoddard, the first pitcher signed and developed by the M's to start a big-league game, made five starts in the final month, winning two of three decisions and allowing only 10 earned runs in 34⅔ innings.

SCORES OF SEATTLE MARINERS' 1981 GAMES

APRIL			Winner	Loser	AUGUST			Winner	Loser
9 — California	L	2-6	Zahn	Abbott	10 — California	W	5-4	Drago	Aase
10 — California	W	10-2	Gleaton	Jefferson	11 — California	W	4-1	Beattie	Forsch
11 — California	L	4-7	Aase	Bannister	12 — California	L	1-4‡	Aase	Drago
12 — California	L	6-8	Hassler	Andersen	13 — At Minn.	W	11-1	Parrott	Arroyo
14 — Minnesota	L	4-5	Koosman	Abbott	14 — At Minn.	L	1-6	Williams	Galasso
15 — Minnesota	W	6-5	Gleaton	Arroyo	14 — At Minn.	W	13-3	Gleaton	Erickson
17 — At Oak.	L	1-16	McCatty	Bannister	15 — At Minn.	W	6-0	Abbott	Havens
18 — At Oak.	L	0-8	Kingman	Clay	16 — At Minn.	W	7-4	Rawley	Corbett
19 — At Oak.	L	1-6	Norris	Abbott	18 — Cleveland	L	2-5	Blyleven	Clark
19 — At Oak.	W	3-2	Clark	Langford	19 — Cleveland	W	4-3†	Rawley	Monge
20 — At Calif.	L	1-6	Zahn	Gleaton	20 — Cleveland	L	5-6x	Stanton	Drago
21 — At Calif.	W	3-0	Bannister	Jefferson	21 — Boston	L	4-7	Stanley	Stein
22 — At Calif.	L	3-7	Forsch	Clay	22 — Boston	L	3-5	Ojeda	Beattie
24 — Oakland	L	2-6	Norris	Abbott	23 — Boston	L	5-7	Burgmeier	Clark
25 — Oakland	L	4-7	Langford	Gleaton	24 — Baltimore	L	8-12	D. Martinez	Gleaton
26 — Oakland	L	4-9	Keough	Parrott	25 — Baltimore	L	5-6§	Stoddard	Drago
27 — At Minn.	W	8-3†	Andersen	Cooper	27 — At Cleve.	L	2-12	Blyleven	Parrott
28 — At Minn.	L	1-4	Redfern	Clay	28 — At Cleve.	L	0-1	Denny	Rawley
29 — At Minn.	T	7-7*	....	....	29 — At Cleve.	L	3-7	Waits	Bannister
30 — Detroit	L	0-2	Rozema	Gleaton	30 — At Cleve.	L	11-17	Monge	Rawley
					31 — At Balt.	W	4-3	Andersen	Stewart
Won 5, Lost 14, Tied 1					**Won 8, Lost 13**				
MAY									
1 — Detroit	L	3-7	Wilcox	Parrott	SEPTEMBER				
2 — Detroit	W	3-1	Bannister	Petry	1 — At Balt.	L	0-1	Stone	Abbott
3 — Detroit	L	5-8	Morris	Andersen	2 — At Balt.	L	2-3‡	Stoddard	Rawley
4 — Milwaukee	L	5-9	Easterly	Allard	3 — At Boston	W	8-7y	Galasso	Stanley
5 — Milwaukee	L	1-4	Vuckovich	Gleaton	4 — At Boston	W	5-2	Stoddard	Tanana
6 — Milwaukee	W	12-1	Parrott	Lerch	5 — At Boston	L	5-12	Tudor	Clay
7 — Milwaukee	W	4-1	Bannister	Haas	6 — At Boston	L	1-6	Hurst	Abbott
8 — New York	W	3-2	Clark	May	7 — At Chicago	W	9-5	Beattie	Dotson
9 — New York	W	6-5	Drago	Davis	8 — At Chicago	L	3-5	Trout	Bannister
10 — New York	L	2-5	Underwood	Gleaton	9 — At Chicago	W	3-1	Stoddard	Lamp
12 — At Detroit	L	2-6	Wilcox	Bannister	10 — At Toronto	L	0-2	Leal	Clay
13 — At Detroit	L	0-1	Petry	Drago	11 — At Toronto	W	8-1	Abbott	Berenguer
16 — At N. York	L	5-7	Bird	Gleaton	12 — At Toronto	L	0-3	Stieb	Beattie
17 — At N. York	W	1-0	Bannister	Davis	14 — Chicago	L	2-5	Lamp	Bannister
18 — At Boston	L	5-8	Clear	Drago	15 — Chicago	W	8-4	Andersen	Koosman
19 — At Boston	L	0-4	Tanana	Parrott	16 — Chicago	L	1-3	Burns	Drago
20 — At Cleve.	W	3-1	Allard	Barker	18 — Kan. City	L	3-8	Jones	Abbott
21 — At Cleve.	W	6-3	Abbott	Garland	19 — Kan. City	W	4-1	Beattie	Wright
22 — Texas	L	2-6	Darwin	Bannister	20 — Kan. City	W	3-2	Bannister	Leonard
23 — Texas	L	4-6§	Comer	Rawley	21 — At Texas	L	1-4	Darwin	Stoddard
24 — Texas	L	3-5	Matlack	Clay	22 — At Texas	W	3-2	Clay	Butcher
25 — Kan. City	W	7-1	Allard	Gura	23 — At Texas	W	2-1	Abbott	Honeycutt
25 — Kan. City	W	5-2	Gleaton	Berenguer	24 — At Texas	W	2-1‡	Rawley	Medich
26 — Kan. City	L	4-5	Leonard	Rawley	25 — At Kan. C.	W	8-3	Bannister	Wright
27 — Kan. City	L	5-8	Splittorff	Bannister	26 — At Kan. C.	W	4-2	Rawley	Gura
29 — At Texas	W	5-4§	Drago	Babcock	27 — At Kan. C.	L	3-15	Jones	Clay
30 — At Texas	L	0-6	Medich	Parrott	28 — Texas	L	5-6	Honeycutt	Abbott
31 — At Texas	W	5-3	Allard	Jenkins	29 — Texas	L	2-6	Medich	Clark
					30 — Texas	L	1-3	Hough	Bannister
Won 12, Lost 16					**Won 13, Lost 15**				
JUNE									
1 — At Kan. C.	L	2-3	Splittorff	Andersen					
2 — At Kan. C.	W	4-3	Bannister	Berenguer					
3 — At Kan. C.	L	9-12	Gale	Clark	OCTOBER				
5 — Cleveland	L	1-8	Barker	Parrott	2 — Toronto	W	8-3	Clay	Burgmeier
6 — Cleveland	L	3-5	Blyleven	Rawley	3 — Toronto	L	3-4	Stieb	Abbott
7 — Cleveland	W	5-4‡	Drago	Stanton	4 — Toronto	W	2-0	Bannister	Todd
8 — Boston	W	2-0	Bannister	Tudor	**Won 2, Lost 1**				
9 — Boston	L	1-10	Torrez	Clark					
10 — Boston	L	2-4	Tanana	Allard					
11 — Baltimore	W	8-2	Parrott	D. Martinez					
Won 4, Lost 6									

*8 innings.   †10 innings.   ‡11 innings.   §12 innings.   x14 innings.   y20 innings.

Can Youth Save Twins?

By PATRICK REUSSE

In 21 seasons at Metropolitan Stadium in Bloomington, there were more good times than bad for the Minnesota Twins. There were 13 seasons of .500 or better and 12 years in which attendance exceeded 1 million, including the first 10 seasons.

The Twins peaked as a team in 1965 with 102 victories and a spot in the World Series against the Los Angeles Dodgers. There were also two West Division championships, followed by league championship series losses against the Baltimore Orioles in 1969 and 1970.

The Twins peaked at the gate in 1967, when a hectic American League pennant race attracted 1,483,000 fans. But the Twins bottomed out—both on the field and at the gate—in their final season at the Met in 1981. Overall, during the strike-interrupted season, the Twins compiled a record of 41-68, the worst in the American League West.

The attendance total of 469,090 was the worst in the major leagues for the second consecutive year and the average of 7,951 for 59 dates was worse than in 1974 when the Twins reached a low of 662,401 for the full schedule. But the gloom was not total because of some promising developments with the younger players during the final weeks of the season. The Twins had the worst record in the American League, 17-39, before the strike stopped play on June 12. That abysmal performance cost Manager Johnny Goryl his job. He was replaced by third base coach Billy Gardner, who became the Twins' third manager in 10 months and ninth in their history.

But Gardner was unable to turn the Twins around. Calvin Griffith, the Twins' president, had signed two potential free agents, shortstop Roy Smalley and catcher Butch Wynegar, to long-term contracts after the 1980 season. But Wynegar injured his elbow in spring training and started the season on the disabled list, and it was discovered Smalley was suffering from a congenital back injury. Also, the Twins had traded another offensive star, Ken Landreaux, to the Los Angeles Dodgers during spring training, getting Mickey Hatcher in return.

First Goryl and then Gardner found themselves as managers without weapons. For the season, Smalley played in

Doug Corbett . . . 17 saves.

only 56 games and batted .263 with seven home runs and 22 RBIs. Wynegar played in 47 games and batted .247, with no home runs and 10 RBIs.

When the season resumed and their play remained poor, the Twins went through a roster shuffle. Three times they recalled minor league players with statistics as home run hitters, and three times those players responded with home runs in their first games. Kent Hrbek, a first baseman and the Most Valuable Player in the California League, debuted in Yankee Stadium August 24 and homered off New York's George Frazier in the 12th inning to give the Twins a 3-2 victory. Hrbek grew up in Bloomington, within a few blocks of Metropolitan Stadium.

Another Minnesotan, catcher Tim Laudner, debuted with the Twins August 28. Laudner, the MVP in the Southern League and a record-setting home run hitter with 42, homered in his third major league at-bat off Detroit's Dave Rozema. Laudner also homered in his next game, joining New York's Joe Lefebvre as the only players in American League history to homer in their first two games.

Then, on September 16, another slugger from Orlando in the Southern League, third baseman Gary Gaetti, homered in his first major league at-bat off Texas' Charlie Hough.

With the influx of new players, and

with rookie Dave Engle going on a 15-game hitting tear, the Twins managed to push their way into the second-season pennant race for several days in late September. They won seven in a row during part of Engle's streak, and were not officially eliminated until three days before the end of the season. The Twins wound up the second half with a 24-29 record.

While the Twins were concluding the season in Chicago, third baseman John Castino—the team's most valuable player in 1980 and a leading contender for that award again in 1981—underwent a spinal fusion. Castino had complained of back pain periodically for a couple of years,

but continued to play. But the surgery left in doubt Castino's status for 1982.

The Twins traded their most experienced pitcher, Jerry Koosman, to the Chicago White Sox on August 30 for minor leaguers Ivan Mesa, Randy Johnson and Ron Perry.

Pete Redfern became the team's leading winner by winning his last five starts for a 9-8 record. Star reliever Doug Corbett saved all five of those victories for Redfern and finished with 17 for the season, with a 2-6 record and 2.56 ERA. Among the starters, rookie Brad Havens had the lowest ERA, 3.58, while compiling a 3-6 record.

SCORES OF MINNESOTA TWINS' 1981 GAMES

APRIL			Winner	Loser
9—Oakland	L	1-5	Norris	Koosman
10—Oakland	L	3-6	Langford	Erickson
11—Oakland	L	0-3	Keough	Williams
12—Oakland	L	0-1	McCatty	Redfern
14—At Seattle	W	5-4	Koosman	Abbott
15—At Seattle	L	5-6	Gleaton	Arroyo
17—At Calif.	L	0-4	Forsch	Williams
18—At Calif.	W	6-4	Redfern	Travers
20—At Oak.	L	0-3	Keough	Koosman
21—At Oak.	L	3-4†	McCatty	Corbett
22—At Oak.	L	1-2	Kingman	Williams
24—California	W	7-5	Corbett	Sanchez
25—California	L	4-6	Zahn	Koosman
26—California	L	1-7	Witt	Erickson
26—California	W	5-2	Arroyo	Jefferson
27—Seattle	L	3-8†	Andersen	Cooper
28—Seattle	W	4-1	Redfern	Clay
29—Seattle	T	7-7*	....	....
30—At Boston	W	8-4	Erickson	Tanana
			Won 6, Lost 12, Tied 1	
MAY				
1—At Boston	W	6-1	Arroyo	Eckersley
2—At Boston	W	11-2	Williams	Torrez
3—At Boston	W	3-1	Redfern	Crawford
4—At Balt.	L	3-4†	D. Martinez	Koosman
5—At Balt.	L	2-3	Flanagan	Erickson
6—At Balt.	L	4-5	Stewart	O'Connor
8—Cleveland	W	8-7	O'Connor	Monge
9—Cleveland	L	1-2†	Monge	Redfern
10—Cleveland	L	1-5	Garland	Koosman
12—Boston	W	4-3†	Corbett	Burgmeier
13—Boston	L	2-5	Torrez	Arroyo
14—Boston	L	7-9‡	Campbell	Cooper
15—Baltimore	L	4-9	D. Martinez	Redfern
16—Baltimore	L	0-7	Ford	Koosman
17—Baltimore	L	3-6	Palmer	Erickson
19—At Milw.	L	3-4	Caldwell	Arroyo
20—At Milw.	L	1-6	Slaton	Williams
21—At Milw.	L	2-8	Vuckovich	Redfern
22—At Kan. C.	W	7-0	Koosman	Leonard
23—At Kan. C.	L	0-1x	Martin	Cooper
24—At Kan. C.	L	4-6	Gale	O'Connor
25—At Texas	L	3-4	Johnson	Jackson
26—At Texas	L	1-2	Jenkins	Redfern
27—At Texas	W	2-1	Koosman	Darwin
28—At Texas	L	2-6	Honeycutt	Erickson
29—Kan. City	L	1-3	Gale	Arroyo
30—Kan. City	L	5-6	Wright	Corbett
31—Kan. City	W	5-4	O'Connor	Leonard
			Won 8, Lost 20	
JUNE				
2—Texas	L	3-5	Darwin	Koosman
3—Texas	L	3-6	Honeycutt	Erickson
4—Texas	W	7-3	Arroyo	Matlack
5—At Detroit	L	0-2	Morris	Havens
6—At Detroit	L	1-5	Petry	Redfern
7—At Detroit	L	0-3	Wilcox	Koosman
8—Milwaukee	W	1-0	Erickson	Caldwell
9—Milwaukee	W	3-1	Arroyo	Slaton
10—Detroit	L	2-4	Morris	Havens
11—Detroit	L	2-7	Petry	Redfern
			Won 3, Lost 7	

AUGUST			Winner	Loser
10—Oakland	W	6-2	Erickson	Langford
11—Oakland	L	5-6	Norris	Williams
12—Oakland	W	4-3	Jackson	Owchinko
13—Seattle	L	1-11	Parrott	Arroyo
14—Seattle	W	6-1	Williams	Galasso
14—Seattle	L	3-13	Gleaton	Erickson
15—Seattle	L	0-6	Abbott	Havens
16—Seattle	L	4-7	Rawley	Corbett
17—At Detroit	L	2-12	Petry	Koosman
18—At Detroit	L	0-3	Wilcox	Erickson
19—At Detroit	L	0-4	Schatzeder	Jackson
21—At Milw.	W	7-6	Williams	Caldwell
22—At Milw.	L	3-4†	Fingers	Cooper
23—At Milw.	L	5-8	Augustine	Arroyo
24—At N. York	W	3-2§	O'Connor	Frazier
25—At N. York	W	3-0	Jackson	May
26—At N. York	L	2-3	Gossage	Williams
27—Detroit	W	4-3	Redfern	Saucier
28—Detroit	W	6-0	Arroyo	Rozema
29—Detroit	W	7-1	Havens	Schatzeder
30—Detroit	L	1-6	Morris	Cooper
31—New York	L	0-7	Righetti	Williams
			Won 9, Lost 13	
SEPTEMBER				
1—New York	L	6-11	Reuschel	Redfern
2—New York	W	4-3	Cooper	Gossage
3—Milwaukee	L	3-4	Vuckovich	Havens
4—Milwaukee	L	5-16	Caldwell	Arroyo
5—Milwaukee	L	3-5	Slaton	Williams
6—Milwaukee	L	7-8†	Fingers	Corbett
7—Toronto	W	4-0	Jackson	Berenguer
8—Toronto	W	1-0	Havens	Stieb
9—Toronto	W	3-1	Arroyo	Clancy
11—Chicago	W	4-3	Williams	Burns
12—Chicago	W	3-1	Redfern	Dotson
13—Chicago	W	7-6	Veselic	Hickey
14—At Toronto	W	6-3	Havens	Clancy
15—At Toronto	L	2-4	Leal	Arroyo
16—At Toronto	W	5-2	Williams	Berenguer
18—At Texas	W	4-6	Redfern	Honeycutt
19—At Texas	L	0-6	Medich	Jackson
20—At Texas	L	3-4	Hough	Corbett
21—At Kan. C.	W	7-2	Williams	Hammaker
22—At Kan. C.	L	1-2	Gura	Arroyo
23—At Kan. C.	W	6-2	Redfern	Jones
24—At Kan. C.	L	2-9	Leonard	Havens
25—Texas	L	2-5	Hough	Williams
26—Texas	W	7-3	Arroyo	Darwin
27—Texas	W	5-2	Redfern	Butcher
28—Kan. City	L	1-6	Leonard	Havens
29—Kan. City	L	2-4	Wright	Williams
30—Kan. City	L	2-5	Gura	Arroyo
			Won 14, Lost 14	
OCTOBER				
2—At Chicago	W	3-2	Redfern	Koosman
3—At Chicago	L	4-5	Hoyt	Veselic
4—At Chicago	L	12-13	Robinson	Corbett
			Won 1, Lost 2	

*8 innings. †10 innings. ‡11 innings. §12 innings. x15 innings.

John Castino was Minnesota's steadiest performer, both at bat and afield.

American League Averages for 1981

CHAMPIONSHIP WINNERS IN PREVIOUS YEARS

1900—Chicago° .... .607	1927—New York................... .714	1954—Cleveland .... .721
1901—Chicago .... .610	1928—New York................... .656	1955—New York................... .623
1902—Philadelphia.............. .610	1929—Philadelphia.............. .693	1956—New York................... .630
1903—Boston...................... .659	1930—Philadelphia.............. .662	1957—New York................... .636
1904—Boston...................... .617	1931—Philadelphia.............. .704	1958—New York................... .597
1905—Philadelphia.............. .622	1932—New York................... .695	1959—Chicago .... .610
1906—Chicago .... .616	1933—Washington............... .651	1960—New York................... .630
1907—Detroit...................... .613	1934—Detroit...................... .656	1961—New York................... .673
1908—Detroit...................... .588	1935—Detroit...................... .616	1962—New York................... .593
1909—Detroit...................... .645	1936—New York................... .667	1963—New York................... .646
1910—Philadelphia.............. .680	1937—New York................... .662	1964—New York................... .611
1911—Philadelphia.............. .669	1938—New York................... .651	1965—Minnesota.................. .630
1912—Boston...................... .691	1939—New York................... .702	1966—Baltimore.................. .606
1913—Philadelphia.............. .627	1940—Detroit...................... .584	1967—Boston...................... .568
1914—Philadelphia.............. .651	1941—New York................... .656	1968—Detroit...................... .636
1915—Boston...................... .669	1942—New York................... .669	1969—Baltimore (East)‡...... .673
1916—Boston...................... .591	1943—New York................... .636	1970—Baltimore (East)‡...... .667
1917—Chicago .... .649	1944—St. Louis................... .578	1971—Baltimore (East)§...... .639
1918—Boston...................... .595	1945—Detroit...................... .575	1972—Oakland (West)a .... .600
1919—Chicago .... .629	1946—Boston...................... .675	1973—Oakland (West)b .... .580
1920—Cleveland.................. .636	1947—New York................... .630	1974—Oakland (West)b .... .556
1921—New York.................. .641	1948—Cleveland†.............. .626	1975—Boston (East)c.......... .594
1922—New York.................. .610	1949—New York................... .630	1976—New York (East)d...... .610
1923—New York.................. .645	1950—New York................... .636	1977—New York (East)d...... .617
1924—Washington............... .597	1951—New York................... .636	1978—New York (East)d...... .613
1925—Washington............... .636	1952—New York................... .617	1979—Baltimore (East)e...... .642
1926—New York.................. .591	1953—New York................... .656	1980—Kansas City (West)f.... .599

°Not recognized as major league in 1900. †Defeated Boston in one-game playoff for pennant. ‡Defeated Minnesota (West) in Championship Series. §Defeated Oakland (West) in Championship Series. aDefeated Detroit (East) in Championship Series. bDefeated Baltimore (East) in Championship Series. cDefeated Oakland (West) in Championship Series. dDefeated Kansas City (West) in Championship Series. eDefeated California (West) in Championship Series. fDefeated New York (East) in Championship Series.

STANDING OF CLUBS AT CLOSE OF SEASON

EAST DIVISION

Club	Mil.	Balt.	N.Y.	Det.	Bos.	Clev.	Tor.	Oak.	Tex.	Chi.	K.C.	Cal.	Sea.	Min.	W.	L.	Pct.	G.B.
Milwaukee	..	4	3	8	7	6	6	4	4	1	5	3	2	9	62	47	.569	....
Baltimore	2	..	7	6	2	4	5	7	2	3	5	6	4	6	59	46	.562	1
New York	3	6	..	7	3	5	2	4	5	7	10	2	2	3	59	48	.551	2
Detroit	5	7	3	..	1	5	6	1	9	3	3	3	5	9	60	49	.550	2
Boston	6	2	3	6	..	7	4	7	3	5	3	2	9	2	59	49	.546	2½
Cleveland	3	2	7	1	6	..	4	3	2	5	4	5	8	2	52	51	.505	7
Toronto	4	2	3	4	0	2	..	2	2	5	3	6	3	1	37	69	.349	23½

WEST DIVISION

Club	Oak.	Tex.	Chi.	K.C.	Cal.	Sea.	Min.	Mil.	Balt.	N.Y.	Det.	Bos.	Clev.	Tor.	W.	L.	Pct.	G.B.
Oakland.................	..	4	6	3	8	6	8	2	5	3	2	5	2	10	64	45	.587	....
Texas....................	2	..	4	4	4	8	8	5	1	4	3	6	2	6	57	48	.543	5
Chicago.................	7	2	..	2	7	3	2	4	6	5	3	4	2	7	54	52	.509	8½
Kansas City............	3	3	0	..	6	6	9	4	3	2	2	3	4	5	50	53	.485	11
California	2	2	6	0	..	6	3	4	6	2	3	4	7	6	51	59	.464	13½
Seattle	1	5	3	7	4	..	6	2	2	3	1	3	4	3	44	65	.404	20
Minnesota..............	2	5	4	4	3	3	..	3	0	3	3	5	1	5	41	68	.376	23

Tie Game: Seattle at Minnesota.

Cancelled Games: Here are the teams and their total number of games that originally were scheduled to be played from June 12 through August 9, 1981, but were cancelled due to the players' strike: Baltimore (55), Boston (53), California (51), Chicago (55), Cleveland (54), Detroit (52), Kansas City (54), Milwaukee (52), Minnesota (52), New York (52), Oakland (53), Seattle (51), Texas (55), Toronto (53). Total of 371 games.

The following games were scheduled to be made up during the players' strike but were not: Toronto at New York, Texas at Cleveland, Cleveland at Toronto, Kansas City at Chicago, Texas at Kansas City, Seattle at New York, Seattle at Detroit, Cleveland at Milwaukee, Minnesota at California, Baltimore at Kansas City. Total of 10 games.

The following games were scheduled to be played after the players' strike but were not: Kansas City at Toronto, New York at Cleveland, Kansas City at Cleveland (second game). Total of 3 games.

The total games cancelled for each team during and after the players' strike: Baltimore (56), Boston (53), California (52), Chicago (56), Cleveland (59), Detroit (53), Kansas City (59), Milwaukee (53), Minnesota (53), New York (55), Oakland (53), Seattle (53), Texas (57), Toronto (56). Total of 384 games.

Division Series: New York defeated Milwaukee, three games to two,
        Oakland defeated Kansas City, three games to none.
Championship Series: New York defeated Oakland, three games to none.

RECORD AT HOME

EAST DIVISION

Club	N.Y.	Balt.	Det.	Mil.	Bos.	Clev.	Tor.	Oak.	Tex.	Chi.	Cal.	K.C.	Min.	Sea.	W.	L.	Pct.
New York	....	5-2	3-0	2-1	2-1	2-4	1-2	2-1	4-2	4-2	0-0	5-1	1-2	1-1	32	19	.627
Baltimore	5-1	....	2-4	1-2	1-1	2-2	3-1	4-2	0-0	3-3	3-3	4-2	3-0	2-1	33	22	.600
Detroit	3-4	3-4	....	3-3	1-2	3-0	3-3	0-0	5-1	0-3	2-1	1-2	6-0	2-0	32	23	.582
Milwaukee	2-1	2-1	5-2	....	4-3	0-2	1-2	3-0	3-3	1-2	0-3	2-1	5-1	0-0	28	21	.571
Boston	2-1	1-1	4-0	3-3	....	3-4	0-0	5-1	2-1	3-3	2-1	1-2	0-4	4-2	30	23	.566
Cleveland	3-3	0-2	1-2	1-6	2-4	....	3-1	2-1	1-1	3-1	4-2	1-4	0-0	4-2	25	29	.463
Toronto	1-1	1-2	1-3	2-5	0-4	1-1	....	2-4	0-2	2-4	3-3	1-4	1-2	2-1	17	36	.321

WEST DIVISION

Club	Oak.	Tex.	Chi.	Cal.	K.C.	Min.	Sea.	N.Y.	Balt.	Det.	Mil.	Bos.	Clev.	Tor.	W.	L.	Pct.
Oakland	....	2-1	2-5	4-2	1-2	3-0	3-1	2-2	3-3	2-1	2-1	4-2	1-1	6-0	35	21	.625
Texas	1-2	....	3-0	2-1	2-2	5-2	2-5	2-1	1-2	2-4	2-1	5-1	1-1	4-2	32	24	.571
Chicago	2-4	2-1	....	3-3	2-0	2-1	1-2	3-3	3-0	0-3	2-0	1-2	1-2	3-3	25	24	.510
California	0-4	1-2	3-4	....	0-3	1-1	2-1	2-2	3-3	2-1	1-3	3-0	5-1	3-3	26	28	.481
Kansas City	1-2	1-2	0-0	3-0	....	4-3	3-3	1-5	1-1	0-2	3-3	1-2	0-3	1-2	19	28	.404
Minnesota	2-5	3-3	3-0	2-2	1-5	....	2-5	1-2	0-3	3-3	2-4	1-2	1-2	3-0	24	36	.400
Seattle	0-3	0-6	1-2	3-4	4-3	1-1	....	2-1	1-2	1-3	2-2	1-5	2-4	2-1	20	37	.351

RECORD ABROAD

EAST DIVISION

Club	Mil.	Clev.	Bos.	Balt.	Det.	N.Y.	Tor.	K.C.	Oak.	Tex.	Chi.	Sea.	Cal.	Min.	W.	L.	Pct.
Milwaukee	....	6-1	3-3	2-1	3-3	1-2	5-2	3-3	1-2	1-2	0-2	2-2	3-1	4-2	34	26	.567
Cleveland	2-0	....	4-3	2-2	0-3	4-2	1-1	3-0	1-1	1-1	2-1	4-2	1-5	2-1	27	22	.551
Boston	3-4	4-2	....	1-1	2-1	1-2	4-0	2-1	2-4	1-5	2-1	5-1	0-3	2-1	29	26	.527
Baltimore	1-2	2-0	1-1	....	4-3	2-5	2-1	1-1	3-3	2-1	0-3	2-1	3-3	3-0	26	24	.520
Detroit	2-5	2-1	0-4	4-2	....	0-3	3-1	2-0	1-2	4-2	3-0	3-1	1-2	3-3	28	26	.519
New York	1-2	3-3	1-2	1-5	4-3	....	1-1	5-1	2-2	1-2	3-3	1-2	2-2	2-1	27	29	.482
Toronto	2-1	1-3	0-0	1-3	3-3	2-1	....	2-1	0-6	2-4	3-3	1-2	3-3	0-3	20	33	.377

WEST DIVISION

Club	K.C.	Oak.	Tex.	Chi.	Sea.	Cal.	Min.	Mil.	Clev.	Bos.	Balt.	Det.	N.Y.	Tor.	W.	L.	Pct.
Kansas City	....	2-1	2-2	0-2	3-4	3-0	5-1	1-2	4-1	2-1	2-4	2-1	1-5	4-1	31	25	.554
Oakland	2-1	....	2-1	4-2	3-0	4-0	5-2	0-3	1-2	1-5	2-4	0-0	1-2	4-2	29	24	.547
Texas	2-1	1-2	....	1-2	6-0	2-1	3-3	3-3	1-1	1-2	0-0	1-5	2-4	2-0	25	24	.510
Chicago	0-0	5-2	0-3	....	2-1	4-3	0-3	2-1	1-3	3-3	3-3	3-0	2-4	4-2	29	28	.509
Seattle	3-3	1-3	5-2	2-1	....	1-2	5-2	0-0	2-4	2-4	1-2	0-2	1-1	1-2	24	28	.462
California	0-3	2-4	1-2	3-3	4-3	....	2-2	3-0	2-4	1-2	3-3	1-2	0-0	3-3	25	31	.446
Minnesota	3-4	0-3	2-5	1-2	1-1	1-1	....	1-5	0-0	4-0	0-3	0-6	2-1	2-1	17	32	.347

SHUTOUT GAMES

Club	Det.	Cal.	Clev.	Tex.	N.Y.	Oak.	Chi.	Balt.	K.C.	Bos.	Mil.	Sea.	Min.	Tor.	W.	L.	Pct.
Detroit	..	0	0	3	1	0	0	1	1	0	0	2	4	1	13	26	.722
California	0	..	0	0	0	0	2	2	0	0	1	0	1	2	8	4	.667
Cleveland	0	1	..	0	1	2	0	0	1	0	2	1	0	2	10	6	.625
Texas	0	1	1	..	2	0	0	0	1	4	0	1	1	2	13	8	.619
New York	2	0	1	1	..	1	2	2	3	0	0	0	1	0	13	9	.591
Oakland	0	0	0	1	0	..	0	2	0	0	1	1	3	3	11	8	.579
Chicago	1	1	1	1	0	1	..	0	1	0	0	0	2	8	6	.571
Baltimore	1	0	0	0	2	0	2	..	0	0	0	1	1	3	10	9	.526
Kansas City	0	0	1	1	1	2	0	1	..	0	0	0	1	1	8	8	.500
Boston	0	0	2	0	0	1	0	0	0	..	0	1	0	0	4	6	.400
Milwaukee	0	0	0	0	0	1	0	1	0	1	..	0	0	1	4	6	.400
Seattle	0	1	0	0	1	0	0	0	0	1	0	..	1	1	5	9	.357
Minnesota	1	0	0	0	1	0	0	0	1	0	1	0	..	2	6	13	.316
Toronto	0	0	0	1	0	0	0	0	0	0	1	2	0	..	4	20	.167

OFFICIAL AMERICAN LEAGUE BATTING AVERAGES

Compiled by Sports Information Center, No. Quincy, Mass.

CLUB BATTING

Club	Pct.	G.	AB.	R.	OR.	H.	TB.	2B.	3B.	HR.	RBI.	SH.	SF.	SB.	CS.	LOB.
Boston	.275	108	3820	519	481	1052	1524	168	17	90	492	37	33	32	31	814
Chicago	.272	106	3615	476	423	982	1399	135	27	76	438	48	36	86	44	755
Texas	.270	105	3581	452	389	968	1323	178	15	49	418	36	39	46	41	720
Kan. C........	.267	103	3560	397	405	952	1362	169	29	61	381	28	35	100	53	757
Cleve........	.263	103	3507	431	442	922	1231	150	21	39	397	46	43	119	37	742
Milw..........	.257	109	3743	493	459	961	1462	173	20	96	475	35	45	39	36	709
Detroit	.256	109	3600	427	404	922	1323	148	29	65	403	50	37	61	37	790
Calif..........	.256	110	3688	476	453	944	1401	134	16	97	439	51	30	44	33	785
N. York	.252	107	3529	421	343	889	1381	148	22	100	403	40	27	47	30	738
Seattle	.251	110	3780	426	521	950	1391	148	13	89	406	41	24	100	50	759
Balt..........	.251	105	3516	429	437	883	1334	165	11	88	408	26	24	41	34	760
Oakland.....	.247	109	3677	458	403	910	1393	119	26	104	430	46	32	98	47	698
Minn.	.240	110	3676	378	486	884	1244	147	36	47	359	36	27	34	27	692
Toronto	.226	106	3521	329	466	797	1163	137	23	61	314	44	18	66	57	658
Totals	.256	750	50813	6112	6112	13016	18931	2119	305	1062	5763	564	450	913	557	10377

INDIVIDUAL BATTING
(Top Fifteen Qualifiers for Batting Championship)

° Bats lefthanded. †Switch-hitter.

Player and Club	Pct.	G.	AB.	R.	H.	TB.	2B.	3B.	HR.	RBI.	GW.	SH.	SF.	SB.	CS.
Lansford, Carney, Bos.	.336	102	399	61	134	175	23	3	4	52	7	1	2	15	10
Paciorek, Thomas, Sea.	.326	104	405	50	132	206	28	2	14	66	13	1	7	13	10
Cooper, Cecil, Milw.°	.320	106	416	70	133	206	35	1	12	60	11	1	5	5	4
Henderson, Rickey, Oak.	.319	108	423	89	135	185	18	7	6	35	7	0	4	56	22
Hargrove, D. Michael, Clev.°	.317	94	322	43	102	129	21	0	2	49	4	4	7	5	4
Brett, George, K.C.°	.314	89	347	42	109	168	27	7	6	43	6	0	4	14	6
Zisk, Richard, Sea.	.311	94	357	42	111	173	12	1	16	43	4	0	0	0	2
Oliver, Albert, Tex.°	.309	102	421	53	130	173	29	1	4	55	8	0	1	3	0
Remy, Gerald, Bos.°	.307	88	358	55	110	121	9	1	0	31	4	13	3	9	2
Mumphrey, Jerry, N.Y.†	.307	80	319	44	98	137	11	5	6	32	5	5	2	13	9
Carew, Rodney, Cal.°	.305	93	364	57	111	136	17	1	2	21	1	10	2	16	9
Grich, Robert, Cal.	.304	100	352	56	107	191	14	2	22	61	8	5	3	2	4
Wilson, Willie, K.C.†	.303	102	439	54	133	160	10	7	1	32	7	3	1	34	8
Lemon, Chester, Chi.....................	.302	94	328	50	99	161	23	6	9	50	4	5	4	5	8
Almon, William, Chi....................	.301	103	349	46	105	131	10	2	4	41	2	2	3	16	6

DEPARTMENTAL LEADERS: G—Armas, Burleson, Whitaker, 109; AB—Rice, 451; R—R. Henderson, 89; H—R. Henderson, 135; TB—Evans, 215; 2B—Cooper, 35; 3B—Castino, 9; HR—Armas, Evans, Grich, Murray, 22; RBI—Murray, 78; GW—Murphy, 15; SH—Trammell, 16; SF—D. Bell, 10; SB—R. Henderson, 56; CS—R. Henderson, 22.

(All Players—Listed Alphabetically)

Player and Club	Pct.	G.	AB.	R.	H.	TB.	2B.	3B.	HR.	RBI.	GW.	SH.	SF.	SB.	CS.
Adams, Glenn, Minn.°	.209	72	220	13	46	62	10	0	2	24	3	0	2	0	1
Aikens, Willie, K.C.°	.266	101	349	45	93	160	16	0	17	53	6	0	5	0	0
Ainge, Daniel, Tor.	.187	86	246	20	46	56	6	2	0	14	0	4	1	8	5
Allen, Kim, Sea.	.000	19	3	1	0	0	0	0	0	0	0	0	0	2	1
Allenson, Gary, Bos.	.223	47	139	23	31	54	8	0	5	25	4	0	1	0	0
Almon, William, Chi.	.301	103	349	46	105	131	10	2	4	41	2	2	3	16	6
Anderson, James, Sea..................	.204	70	162	12	33	46	7	0	2	19	1	1	0	3	5
Armas, Antonio, Oak..................	.261	109	440	51	115	211	24	3	22	76	11	0	1	5	1
Ashford, Thomas, N.Y.................	.000	3	0	0	0	0	0	0	0	0	0	0	0	0	0
Auerbach, Frederick, Sea.............	.155	38	84	12	13	19	3	0	1	6	0	6	1	1	1
Ayala, Benigno, Balt..................	.279	44	86	12	24	35	2	0	3	13	2	1	1	0	1
Babitt, Mack, Oak....................	.256	54	156	10	40	47	1	3	0	14	0	2	0	5	4
Baines, Harold, Chi.°	.286	82	280	42	80	135	11	7	10	41	4	0	2	6	2
Baker, Charles, Minn.................	.182	40	66	6	12	18	0	3	0	6	0	3	0	0	0
Balboni, Stephen, N.Y.	.286	4	7	2	2	5	1	1	0	2	2	0	0	0	0
Bando, Christopher, Clev.†	.213	21	47	3	10	13	3	0	0	6	1	1	1	0	0
Bando, Salvatore, Milw.	.200	32	65	10	13	23	4	0	2	9	0	2	0	1	1
Bannister, Alan, Clev.	.263	68	232	36	61	77	11	1	1	17	2	1	1	16	2
Barfield, Jesse, Tor.	.232	25	95	7	22	35	3	2	2	9	0	0	0	4	3
Baylor, Donald, Cal.	.239	103	377	52	90	161	18	1	17	66	11	0	6	3	3
Beamon, Charles, Tor.°	.200	8	15	1	3	4	1	0	0	0	0	0	0	0	0
Belanger, Mark, Balt..................	.165	64	139	9	23	33	3	2	1	10	1	5	0	2	1
Bell, David, Tex......................	.294	97	360	44	106	154	16	1	10	64	9	0	10	3	3
Bell, Jorge, Tor......................	.233	60	163	19	38	57	2	1	5	12	1	0	0	3	2
Beniquez, Juan, Cal..................	.181	58	166	18	30	44	5	0	3	13	3	4	1	2	1
Bernazard, Antonio, Chi.†	.276	106	384	53	106	146	14	4	6	34	7	9	1	4	4
Bochte, Bruce, Sea.°	.260	99	335	39	87	121	16	0	6	30	3	1	0	1	3
Bonnell, R. Barry, Tor.	.220	66	227	21	50	77	7	4	4	28	4	3	0	4	3
Bonner, Robert, Balt..................	.296	10	27	6	8	10	2	0	0	2	0	0	1	1	0
Bosetti, Richard, Tor.-Oak...........	.197	34	66	9	13	15	2	0	0	5	0	1	0	0	2
Bosley, Thaddis, Milw.°	.229	42	105	11	24	26	2	0	0	3	0	1	0	2	1
Brett, George, K.C.°	.314	89	347	42	109	168	27	7	6	43	6	0	4	14	6

Player and Club	Pct.	G.	AB.	R.	H.	TB.	2B.	3B.	HR.	RBI.	GW.	SH.	SF.	SB.	CS.
Brookens, Thomas, Det.	.243	71	239	19	58	82	10	1	4	25	5	4	6	5	3
Brouhard, Mark, Milw.	.274	60	186	19	51	69	6	3	2	20	2	2	2	1	1
Brown, Darrell, Det.†	.250	16	4	4	1	1	0	0	0	0	0	0	0	1	0
Brown, Rogers, N.Y.†	.226	31	62	5	14	15	1	0	0	6	0	1	1	4	2
Brunansky, Thomas, Cal.	.152	11	33	7	5	14	0	0	3	6	0	0	0	1	0
Budaska, Mark, Oak.†	.156	9	32	3	5	6	1	0	0	2	0	0	0	0	1
Bulling, Terry, Sea.	.247	62	154	15	38	47	3	0	2	15	4	4	0	0	0
Bumbry, Alonza, Balt.°	.273	101	392	61	107	132	18	2	1	27	2	4	2	22	15
Burleson, Richard, Cal.	.293	109	430	53	126	160	17	1	5	33	3	11	4	4	6
Burroughs, Jeffrey, Sea.	.254	89	319	32	81	126	13	1	10	41	5	0	0	0	1
Butera, Salvatore, Minn.	.240	62	167	13	40	49	7	1	0	18	2	3	2	0	0
Campaneris, Dagoberto, Cal.	.256	55	82	11	21	28	2	1	1	10	2	3	1	5	2
Carew, Rodney, Cal.°	.305	93	364	57	111	136	17	1	2	21	1	10	2	16	9
Castillo, Martin, Det.	.125	6	8	1	1	1	0	0	0	0	0	0	0	0	0
Castino, John, Minn.	.268	101	381	41	102	151	13	9	6	36	8	7	2	4	5
Cerone, Richard, N.Y.	.244	71	234	23	57	80	13	2	2	21	2	4	4	0	2
Chalk, David, K.C.	.224	27	49	2	11	14	3	0	0	5	1	3	0	0	1
Charboneau, Joseph, Clev.	.210	48	138	14	29	50	7	1	4	18	1	1	1	1	0
Clark, Robert, Cal.	.250	34	88	12	22	38	2	1	4	19	2	0	0	0	0
Concepcion, Onix, K.C.	.000	2	0	0	0	0	0	0	0	0	0	0	0	0	0
Cooper, Cecil, Milw.°	.320	106	416	70	133	206	35	1	12	60	11	1	5	5	4
Corcoran, Timothy, Minn.°	.176	22	51	4	9	12	3	0	0	4	0	0	1	0	0
Corey, Mark, Balt.	.000	10	8	2	0	0	0	0	0	0	0	0	0	0	0
Cowens, Alfred, Det.	.261	85	253	27	66	88	11	4	1	18	2	5	3	3	3
Cox, Jeffrey, Oak.	.000	2	0	0	0	0	0	0	0	0	0	0	0	0	0
Cox, Larry, Tex.	.231	5	13	0	3	4	1	0	0	0	0	0	0	0	0
Cox, W. Ted, Tor.	.300	16	50	6	15	25	4	0	2	9	1	0	0	0	1
Crowley, Terrence, Balt.°	.246	68	134	12	33	51	6	0	4	25	5	1	2	0	0
Cruz, Julio, Sea.†	.256	94	352	57	90	114	12	3	2	24	1	4	3	43	8
Dauer, Richard, Balt.	.263	96	369	41	97	136	27	0	4	38	4	3	2	0	0
Davis, Michael, Oak.°	.050	17	20	0	1	2	1	0	0	0	0	0	0	0	0
Davis, Robert, Cal.	.000	1	2	0	0	0	0	0	0	0	0	0	0	0	0
DeCinces, Douglas, Balt.	.263	100	346	49	91	157	23	2	13	55	8	1	2	0	3
Dempsey, J. Rikard, Balt.	.215	92	251	24	54	84	10	1	6	15	3	3	0	0	1
Dent, Russell, N.Y.	.238	73	227	20	54	86	11	0	7	27	3	8	2	0	1
Diaz, Baudilio, Clev.	.313	63	182	25	57	97	19	0	7	38	9	1	2	2	2
Dilone, Miguel, Clev.†	.290	72	269	33	78	93	5	5	0	19	2	2	0	29	10
Downing, Brian, Cal.	.249	93	317	47	79	120	14	0	9	41	2	3	0	1	1
Doyle, Brian, Oak.°	.125	17	40	2	5	5	0	0	0	3	0	2	0	0	1
Drumright, Keith, Oak.°	.291	31	86	8	25	28	1	1	0	11	5	1	1	0	0
Duran, Daniel, Tex.°	.250	13	16	1	4	4	0	0	0	0	0	0	0	0	0
Dwyer, James, Balt.°	.224	68	134	16	30	41	0	1	3	10	2	0	3	0	2
Dybzinski, Jerome, Clev.	.298	48	57	10	17	17	0	0	0	6	1	5	0	7	1
Dyer, Don, Det.	.000	2	0	0	0	0	0	0	0	0	0	0	0	0	0
Edler, David, Sea.	.141	29	78	7	11	14	3	0	0	5	0	2	2	3	3
Edwards, Marshall, Milw.°	.241	40	58	10	14	17	1	1	0	4	0	0	0	6	2
Ellis, John, Tex.	.138	23	58	2	8	14	3	0	1	7	0	0	0	0	1
Engle, R. David, Minn.	.258	82	248	29	64	101	14	4	5	32	4	1	2	0	1
Essian, James, Chi.	.308	27	52	6	16	19	3	0	0	5	0	1	0	0	1
Evans, Dwight, Bos.	.296	108	412	84	122	215	19	4	22	71	6	3	3	3	2
Faedo, Leonardo, Minn.	.195	12	41	3	8	10	0	1	0	6	0	0	1	0	0
Fahey, William, Det.°	.254	27	67	5	17	22	2	0	1	9	1	2	1	0	1
Ferguson, Joseph, Cal.	.233	12	30	5	7	11	1	0	1	5	1	1	1	0	0
Firova, Daniel, Sea.	.000	13	2	0	0	0	0	0	0	0	0	0	0	0	0
Fischlin, Michael, Clev.	.233	22	43	3	10	11	1	0	0	5	1	1	1	3	2
Fisk, Carlton, Chi.	.263	96	338	44	89	122	12	0	7	45	5	1	5	3	2
Foote, Barry, N.Y.	.208	40	125	12	26	48	4	0	6	10	0	4	0	0	0
Ford, Darnell, Cal.	.277	97	375	53	104	165	14	1	15	48	4	5	1	2	2
Funderburk, Mark, Minn.	.200	8	15	2	3	4	1	0	0	2	0	0	1	0	0
Gaetti, Gary, Minn.	.192	9	26	4	5	11	0	0	2	3	0	0	0	0	0
Gamble, Oscar, N.Y.°	.238	80	189	24	45	83	8	0	10	27	3	0	2	0	2
Gantner, James, Milw.°	.267	107	352	35	94	116	14	1	2	33	3	9	4	3	6
Garcia, Damaso, Tor.	.252	64	250	24	63	76	8	1	1	13	1	3	1	13	3
Garcia, Daniel, K.C.°	.143	12	14	4	2	2	0	0	0	0	0	0	0	0	0
Gedman, Richard, Bos.°	.288	62	205	22	59	89	15	0	5	26	2	1	3	0	0
Geronimo, Cesar, K.C.°	.246	59	118	14	29	39	0	2	2	13	1	2	2	6	1
Gibson, Kirk, Det.°	.328	83	290	41	95	139	11	3	9	40	5	1	2	17	5
Goodwin, Danny, Minn.°	.225	59	151	18	34	48	6	1	2	17	1	1	1	3	1
Graham, Daniel, Balt.°	.176	55	142	7	25	34	3	0	2	11	1	0	1	0	0
Gray, Gary, Sea.	.245	69	208	27	51	99	7	1	13	31	3	0	2	2	0
Grich, Robert, Cal.	.304	100	352	56	107	191	14	2	22	61	8	5	3	2	4
Griffin, Alfredo, Tor.†	.209	101	388	30	81	112	19	6	0	21	3	6	2	8	12
Gross, Wayne, Oak.°	.206	82	243	29	50	89	7	1	10	31	3	4	4	2	1
Grote, Gerald, K.C.	.304	22	56	4	17	25	3	1	1	9	1	1	1	1	0
Grubb, John, Tex.°	.231	67	199	26	46	66	9	1	3	26	3	1	1	0	3
Gulden, Bradley, Sea.°	.188	8	16	0	3	5	2	0	0	1	0	0	0	0	0
Hairston, Jerry, Chi.†	.280	9	25	5	7	11	1	0	1	6	1	0	1	0	0
Hancock, R. Garry, Bos.°	.156	26	45	4	7	10	3	0	0	3	0	0	0	0	0
Hargrove, D. Michael, Clev.°	.317	94	322	43	102	129	21	0	2	49	4	4	7	5	4

Player and Club	Pct.	G	AB	R	H	TB	2B	3B	HR	RBI	GW	SH	SF	SB	CS
Harlow, Larry, Cal.°	.207	43	82	13	17	18	1	0	0	4	0	2	0	1	1
Harper, Brian, Cal.	.273	4	11	1	3	3	0	0	0	1	0	0	1	1	0
Harrah, Colbert, Clev.	.291	103	361	64	105	140	12	4	5	44	9	0	8	12	1
Harris, John, Cal.°	.247	36	77	5	19	31	3	0	3	9	1	0	0	0	0
Hassey, Ronald, Clev.°	.232	61	190	8	44	51	4	0	1	25	1	3	3	0	1
Hatcher, Michael, Minn.	.255	99	377	36	96	132	23	2	3	37	3	5	3	3	1
Hayes, Von, Clev.°	.257	43	109	21	28	43	8	2	1	17	1	4	2	8	1
Heath, Michael, Oak.	.236	84	301	26	71	104	7	1	8	30	2	5	1	3	3
Hebner, Richard, Det.°	.226	78	226	19	51	78	8	2	5	28	2	1	2	1	2
Henderson, David, Sea.	.167	59	126	17	21	42	3	0	6	13	1	1	1	2	1
Henderson, Rickey, Oak.	.319	108	423	89	135	185	18	7	6	35	7	0	4	56	22
Hill, Marc, Chi.	.000	16	6	0	0	0	0	0	0	0	0	0	0	0	0
Hisle, Larry, Milw.	.230	27	87	11	20	36	4	0	4	11	2	0	2	0	0
Hobson, Clell, Cal.	.235	85	268	27	63	90	7	4	4	36	2	2	4	1	1
Hoffman, Glenn, Bos.	.231	78	242	28	56	69	10	0	1	20	1	6	0	0	1
Hosley, Timothy, Oak.	.095	18	21	2	2	5	0	0	1	5	0	0	0	0	0
Howell, Roy, Milw.°	.238	76	244	37	58	91	13	1	6	33	6	2	2	0	0
Hrbek, Kent, Minn.°	.239	24	67	5	16	24	5	0	1	7	2	0	0	0	0
Hurdle, Clinton, K.C.°	.329	28	76	12	25	42	3	1	4	15	3	0	0	0	0
Iorg, Garth, Tor.	.242	70	215	17	52	63	11	0	0	10	1	2	0	2	3
Ireland, Timothy, K.C.†	.000	4	0	1	0	0	0	0	0	0	0	0	0	0	1
Jackson, Reginald, N.Y.°	.237	94	334	33	79	143	17	1	15	54	7	0	1	0	3
Jackson, Ronnie, Minn.-Det.	.270	85	270	29	73	107	17	1	5	40	5	4	2	6	3
Johnson, Bobby, Tex.	.278	6	18	2	5	11	0	0	2	4	2	0	0	0	0
Johnson, Clifford, Oak.	.260	84	273	40	71	130	8	0	17	59	3	0	6	5	3
Johnson, Lamar, Chi.	.276	41	134	10	37	47	7	0	1	15	1	1	2	0	2
Johnston, Gregory, Minn.°	.125	7	16	2	2	2	0	0	0	0	0	0	0	0	0
Jones, Robert, Tex.°	.265	10	34	4	9	19	1	0	3	7	0	0	0	0	1
Jones, Lynn, Det.	.259	71	174	19	45	56	5	0	2	19	2	2	2	1	2
Kearney, Robert, Oak.	.000	1	0	0	0	0	0	0	0	0	0	0	0	0	0
Keatley, Gregory, K.C.	.000	2	0	0	0	0	0	0	0	0	0	0	0	0	0
Kelleher, Michael, Det.	.221	61	77	10	17	21	4	0	0	6	0	8	1	0	0
Kelly, H. Patrick, Clev.°	.213	48	75	8	16	23	4	0	1	16	1	0	1	2	4
Kemp, Steven, Det.°	.277	105	372	52	103	156	18	4	9	49	10	0	4	9	3
Klutts, Gene, Oak.	.370	15	46	9	17	32	0	0	5	11	2	0	0	0	0
Krenchicki, Wayne, Balt.°	.214	33	56	7	12	16	4	0	0	6	0	0	0	0	0
Kuiper, Duane, Clev.°	.257	72	206	15	53	59	6	0	0	14	1	4	1	1	1
Kuntz, Russell, Chi.	.255	67	55	15	14	16	2	0	0	4	0	1	0	1	0
Lansford, Carney, Bos.	.336	102	399	61	134	175	23	3	4	52	7	1	2	15	10
Laudner, Timothy, Minn.	.163	14	43	4	7	15	2	0	2	5	0	0	0	0	0
LeFlore, Ronald, Chi.	.246	82	337	46	83	101	10	4	0	24	3	1	2	36	11
Leach, Richard, Det.°	.193	54	83	9	16	24	3	1	1	11	2	1	1	0	1
Lemon, Chester, Chi.	.302	94	328	50	99	161	23	6	9	50	4	5	4	5	8
Lickert, John, Bos.	.000	1	0	0	0	0	0	0	0	0	0	0	0	0	0
Lisi, Riccardo, Tex.	.313	9	16	6	5	5	0	0	0	1	0	0	0	0	1
Littleton, Larry, Clev.	.000	26	23	2	0	0	0	0	0	0	0	0	1	0	0
Loviglio, John, Chi.	.267	14	15	5	4	4	0	0	0	2	1	0	0	2	2
Lowenstein, John, Balt.°	.249	83	189	19	47	72	7	0	6	20	4	0	1	7	6
Lubratich, Steven, Cal.	.143	7	21	2	3	4	1	0	0	1	0	0	1	0	0
Luzinski, Gregory, Chi.	.265	104	378	55	100	180	15	1	21	62	11	0	2	0	0
Lynn, Fredric, Cal.°	.219	76	256	28	56	81	8	1	5	31	5	1	4	1	2
Macha, Kenneth, Tor.	.200	37	85	4	17	19	2	0	0	6	0	0	1	1	1
Mackanin, Peter, Minn.	.231	77	225	21	52	73	7	1	4	18	2	3	1	1	2
Maler, James, Sea.	.348	12	23	1	8	9	1	0	0	2	0	0	0	1	0
Manning, Richard, Clev.°	.244	103	360	47	88	121	15	3	4	33	3	2	2	25	3
Manrique, Fred, Tor.	.143	14	28	1	4	4	0	0	0	1	0	0	0	0	1
Martinez, John, Tor.	.227	45	128	13	29	51	8	1	4	21	3	3	3	1	0
May, Lee, K.C.	.291	26	55	3	16	19	3	0	0	8	2	0	0	0	1
Mayberry, John, Tor.°	.248	94	290	34	72	131	6	1	17	43	4	0	2	1	1
McHenry, Vance, Sea.	.222	15	18	3	4	4	0	0	0	2	0	2	0	0	0
McKay, David, Oak.†	.263	79	224	25	59	84	11	1	4	21	4	3	4	4	1
McRae, Harold, K.C.	.272	101	389	38	106	154	23	2	7	36	4	3	5	3	4
Mendoza, Mario, Tex.	.231	88	229	18	53	61	6	1	0	22	0	14	3	2	1
Meyer, Daniel, Sea.°	.262	83	252	26	66	87	10	1	3	22	1	1	2	4	3
Milbourne, Lawrence, N.Y.†	.313	61	163	24	51	65	7	2	1	12	2	3	1	2	0
Miller, Richard, Bos.°	.291	97	316	38	92	119	17	2	2	33	4	4	2	3	5
Molinaro, Robert, Chi.°	.262	47	42	7	11	17	1	1	1	9	2	0	2	1	0
Molitor, Paul, Milw.	.267	64	251	45	67	84	11	0	2	19	1	5	0	10	6
Money, Donald, Milw.	.216	60	185	17	40	53	7	0	2	14	1	3	3	0	0
Moore, Charles, Milw.	.301	48	156	16	47	64	8	3	1	9	1	3	0	1	4
Moore, Kelvin, Oak.	.255	14	47	5	12	17	0	1	1	3	0	0	0	1	0
Morales, Jose, Balt.	.244	38	86	6	21	30	3	0	2	14	3	0	0	0	0
Morrison, James, Chi.	.234	90	290	27	68	108	8	1	10	34	6	9	4	3	2
Moseby, Lloyd, Tor.°	.233	100	378	36	88	135	16	2	9	43	6	5	4	11	8
Motley, Darryl, K.C.	.232	42	125	15	29	39	4	0	2	8	1	1	1	3	3
Mulliniks, S. Rance, K.C.°	.227	24	44	6	10	13	3	0	0	5	2	0	0	0	1
Mumphrey, Jerry, N.Y.†	.307	80	319	44	98	137	11	5	6	32	5	5	2	14	9
Murcer, Bobby, N.Y.°	.265	50	117	14	31	55	6	0	6	24	5	0	1	0	0
Murphy, Dwayne, Oak.°	.251	107	390	58	98	159	10	3	15	60	15	8	4	10	4

Player and Club	Pct.	G.	AB.	R.	H.	TB.	2B.	3B.	HR.	RBI.	GW.	SH.	SF.	SB.	CS.
Murray, Eddie, Balt.†	.294	99	378	57	111	202	21	2	22	78	10	0	3	2	3
Narron, Jerry, Sea.°	.222	76	203	13	45	59	5	0	3	17	1	3	0	0	0
Nettles, Graig, N.Y.°	.244	103	349	46	85	139	7	1	15	46	7	2	3	0	2
Nettles, James, Oak.°	.000	1	0	0	0	0	0	0	0	0	0	1	0	0	0
Newman, Jeffrey, Oak.	.231	68	216	17	50	71	12	0	3	15	1	2	2	0	2
Nichols, T. Reid, Bos.	.188	39	48	13	9	11	0	1	0	3	0	4	1	0	1
Nordhagen, Wayne, Chi.	.308	65	208	19	64	92	8	1	6	33	3	0	3	0	1
Norman, Nelson, Tex.†	.231	7	13	1	3	4	1	0	0	2	0	0	1	0	0
Oates, Johnny, N.Y.°	.192	10	26	4	5	6	1	0	0	0	0	0	0	0	0
Oglivie, Benjamin, Milw.°	.243	107	400	53	97	158	15	2	14	72	11	1	8	2	2
Oliver, Albert, Tex.°	.309	102	421	53	130	173	29	1	4	55	8	0	1	3	0
Orta, Jorge, Clev.°	.272	88	338	50	92	127	14	3	5	34	5	5	5	4	3
Otis, Amos, K.C.	.269	99	372	49	100	155	22	3	9	57	4	3	9	16	7
Ott, N. Edward, Cal.°	.217	75	258	20	56	72	8	1	2	22	1	4	2	2	1
Paciorek, Thomas, Sea.	.326	104	405	50	132	206	28	2	14	66	13	1	7	13	10
Page, Mitchell, Oak.°	.141	34	92	9	13	26	1	0	4	13	0	1	1	2	1
Pagel, Karl, Clev.°	.267	14	15	3	4	11	0	2	1	4	0	0	0	0	0
Papi, Stanley, Det.	.204	40	93	8	19	32	2	1	3	12	1	1	2	1	0
Parrish, Lance, Det.	.244	96	348	39	85	137	18	2	10	46	7	1	1	2	3
Parsons, Casey, Sea.°	.227	36	22	6	5	9	1	0	1	5	1	2	1	0	0
Patek, Fred, Cal.	.234	27	47	3	11	14	1	1	0	5	0	0	0	1	0
Patterson, Michael, Oak.-NY	.313	16	32	6	10	17	1	3	0	1	0	0	0	0	1
Perez, Atanasio, Bos.	.252	84	306	35	77	121	11	3	9	39	2	0	3	0	0
Peters, Richard, Clev.†	.256	63	207	26	53	66	7	3	0	15	4	5	1	1	6
Phelps, Kenneth, K.C.°	.136	21	22	1	3	5	0	1	0	1	0	0	0	0	0
Picciolo, Robert, Oak.	.268	82	179	23	48	71	5	3	4	13	3	9	1	0	1
Piniella, Louis, N.Y.	.277	60	159	16	44	68	9	0	5	18	2	2	0	0	1
Poquette, Thomas, Bos-Tex°	.152	33	66	2	10	11	1	0	0	7	1	0	1	0	1
Powell, Hosken, Minn.°	.239	80	264	30	63	86	11	3	2	25	1	1	1	7	4
Pruitt, Ronald, Clev.	.000	5	9	0	0	0	0	0	0	0	0	0	0	0	0
Pryor, Gregory, Chi.	.224	47	76	4	17	18	1	0	0	6	1	4	0	0	0
Putnam, Patrick, Tex.°	.266	95	297	33	79	124	17	2	8	35	5	1	2	4	2
Quirk, James, K.C.°	.250	46	100	8	25	32	7	0	0	10	1	0	0	0	2
Randle, Leonard, Sea.†	.231	82	273	22	63	86	9	1	4	25	1	6	3	11	6
Randolph, William, N.Y.	.232	93	357	59	83	109	14	3	2	24	2	5	3	14	5
Remy, Gerald, Bos.°	.307	88	358	55	110	121	9	1	0	31	4	13	3	9	2
Revering, David, Oak.-NY°	.233	76	206	20	48	69	5	2	4	17	3	0	1	0	2
Rice, James, Bos.	.284	108	451	51	128	199	18	1	17	62	6	0	7	2	2
Ripken, Calvin Jr., Balt.	.128	23	39	1	5	5	0	0	0	0	0	0	0	0	0
Rivers, John, Tex.°	.286	99	399	62	114	148	21	2	3	26	3	3	1	9	5
Roberts, Leon, Tex.	.279	72	233	26	65	98	17	2	4	31	3	2	5	3	4
Robertson, Andre, N.Y.	.263	10	19	1	5	6	1	0	0	0	0	0	0	1	1
Rodriguez, Aurelio, N.Y.	.346	27	52	4	18	26	2	0	2	8	3	1	0	0	0
Roenicke, Gary, Balt.	.269	85	219	31	59	84	16	0	3	20	2	5	3	1	2
Romero, Edgardo, Milw.	.198	44	91	6	18	24	3	0	1	10	1	1	2	0	2
Rosello, David, Clev.	.238	43	84	11	20	27	4	0	1	7	0	5	0	0	1
Royster, Willie, Balt.	.000	4	4	0	0	0	0	0	0	0	0	0	0	0	0
Rudi, Joseph, Bos.	.180	49	122	14	22	43	3	0	6	24	1	1	2	0	0
Sakata, Lenn, Balt.	.227	61	150	19	34	53	4	0	5	15	2	1	1	4	0
Sample, William, Tex.	.283	66	230	36	65	90	16	0	3	25	4	3	3	4	1
Schmidt, David F., Bos.	.238	15	42	6	10	17	1	0	2	3	1	0	0	0	0
Sconiers, Daryl, Cal.°	.269	15	52	6	14	20	1	1	1	7	0	0	0	0	0
Serna, Paul, Sea.	.255	30	94	11	24	38	2	0	4	9	2	1	0	2	3
Sexton, Jimmy, Oak.	.000	7	3	3	0	0	0	0	0	0	0	0	0	0	0
Shelby, John, Balt.†	.000	7	2	2	0	0	0	0	0	0	0	0	0	2	0
Sheridan, Patrick, K.C.°	.000	3	1	0	0	0	0	0	0	0	0	0	0	0	0
Simmons, Ted, Milw.†	.216	100	380	45	82	143	13	3	14	61	12	1	6	0	1
Simpson, Joe, Sea.°	.222	91	288	32	64	87	11	3	2	30	1	6	2	12	3
Singleton, Kenneth, Balt.†	.278	103	363	48	101	158	16	1	13	49	7	2	2	0	0
Smalley, Roy, Minn.†	.263	56	167	24	44	74	7	1	7	22	6	0	2	0	0
Smith, Raymond, Minn.	.200	15	40	4	8	12	1	0	1	1	0	0	0	0	0
Sofield, Richard, Minn.°	.176	41	102	9	18	20	2	0	0	5	0	1	1	3	2
Spencer, James, N.Y.-Oak.°	.188	79	234	20	44	64	8	0	4	13	3	0	2	1	0
Squires, Michael, Chi.°	.265	92	294	35	78	87	9	0	0	25	1	13	5	7	2
Stanley, Frederick, Oak.	.193	66	145	15	28	32	4	0	0	7	0	8	0	2	0
Stapleton, David, Bos.	.285	93	355	45	101	150	17	1	10	42	7	3	2	0	4
Stein, William, Tex.	.330	53	115	21	38	50	6	0	2	22	5	1	3	1	2
Summers, John, Det.°	.255	64	165	16	42	59	8	0	3	21	5	0	2	1	1
Sundberg, James, Tex.	.277	102	339	42	94	124	17	2	3	28	3	3	3	2	5
Sutherland, Leonardo, Chi.°	.167	11	12	6	2	3	2	0	0	0	0	1	0	2	1
Thomas, J. Gorman, Milw.	.259	103	363	54	94	179	22	0	21	65	4	0	5	4	5
Thornton, Andre, Clev.	.239	69	226	22	54	84	12	0	6	30	4	2	5	3	1
Tolleson, J. Wayne, Tex.†	.167	14	24	6	4	4	0	0	0	1	0	0	0	2	0
Trammell, Alan, Det.	.258	105	392	52	101	128	15	3	2	31	5	16	3	10	3
Turner, John, Chi.°	.167	10	12	1	2	2	0	0	0	2	1	0	0	0	0
Upshaw, Willie, Tor.°	.171	61	111	15	19	36	3	1	4	10	1	0	0	2	1
Valdez, Julio, Bos.†	.217	17	23	1	5	5	0	0	0	3	0	1	1	0	1
Velez, Otoniel, Tor.	.213	80	240	32	51	97	9	2	11	28	3	2	2	0	3
Veryzer, Thomas, Clev.	.244	75	221	13	54	58	4	0	0	14	1	5	2	1	0

Player and Club	Pct.	G.	AB.	R.	H.	TB.	2B.	3B.	HR.	RBI.	GW.	SH.	SF.	SB.	CS.
Wagner, Mark, Tex.	.259	50	85	15	22	31	4	1	1	14	3	2	0	1	1
Walker, Cleotha, Bos.†	.353	6	17	3	6	6	0	0	0	2	0	0	0	0	2
Walton, Reginald, Sea.	.000	12	6	1	0	0	0	0	0	0	0	0	0	0	0
Ward, Gary, Minn.	.264	85	295	42	78	106	7	6	3	29	1	0	3	5	2
Washington, Ronald, Minn.	.226	28	84	8	19	24	3	1	0	5	0	1	0	4	1
Washington, U.L., K.C.†	.227	98	339	40	77	104	19	1	2	29	2	3	1	10	10
Wathan, John, K.C.	.252	89	301	24	76	94	9	3	1	19	1	5	3	11	6
Watson, Robert, N.Y.	.212	59	156	15	33	60	3	3	6	12	2	0	0	0	0
Wells, Gregory, Tor.	.247	32	73	7	18	23	5	0	0	5	0	0	0	0	2
Werner, Donald, Tex.	.250	2	8	1	2	2	0	0	0	0	0	0	0	0	1
Werth, Dennis, N.Y.	.109	34	55	7	6	7	1	0	0	1	0	4	0	1	0
Whitaker, Louis, Det.°	.263	109	335	48	88	125	14	4	5	36	2	3	3	5	3
White, Frank, K.C.	.250	94	364	35	91	137	17	1	9	38	6	4	3	4	2
Whitmer, Daniel, Tor.	.111	7	9	0	1	2	1	0	0	0	0	0	0	0	0
Whitt, L. Ernest, Tor.°	.236	74	195	16	46	58	9	0	1	16	4	7	0	5	2
Wilfong, Robert, Minn.°	.246	93	305	32	75	101	11	3	3	19	3	5	0	2	4
Williams, Dallas, Balt.°	.500	2	2	0	1	1	0	0	0	0	0	0	0	0	0
Wills, Elliott, Tex.°	.251	102	410	51	103	126	13	2	2	41	4	6	5	12	9
Wilson, Willie, K.C.†	.303	102	439	54	133	160	10	7	1	32	7	3	1	34	8
Winfield, David, N.Y.	.294	105	388	52	114	180	25	1	13	68	9	1	7	11	1
Wockenfuss, Johnny, Det.	.215	70	172	20	37	68	4	0	9	25	4	0	2	0	0
Woods, Alvis, Tor.°	.247	85	288	20	71	89	15	0	1	21	4	8	2	3	4
Wynegar, Harold, Minn.†	.247	47	150	11	37	42	5	0	0	10	0	1	3	0	1
Yastrzemski, Carl, Bos.°	.246	91	338	36	83	120	14	1	7	53	10	0	3	0	1
Yost, Edgar, Milw.	.222	18	27	4	6	15	0	0	3	3	0	0	0	0	0
Yount, Robin, Milw.	.273	96	377	50	103	158	15	5	10	49	6	4	6	4	1
Zisk, Richard, Sea.	.311	94	357	42	111	173	12	1	16	43	4	0	0	0	2

The following pitchers had no plate appearances, primarily because of use of designated hitters; they are listed alphabetically by club with number of games, including pinch-running appearances, in parentheses:

BALTIMORE—Boddicker, Michael (2); Flanagan, Michael (20); Ford, David (15); Luebber, Stephen (7); Martinez, Felix (37); Martinez, J. Dennis (25); McGregor, Scott (24); Palmer, James (22); Schneider, Jeffery (11); Stewart, Samuel (29); Stoddard, Timothy (31); Stone, Steven (15).

BOSTON—Aponte, Luis (7); Burgmeier, Thomas (32); Campbell, William (30); Clear, Mark (34); Crawford, Steve (14); Eckersley, Dennis (23); Hurst, Bruce (5); Ojeda, Robert (10); Rainey, Charles (11); Stanley, Robert (35); Tanana, Frank (24); Torrez, Michael (22); Tudor, John (18).

CALIFORNIA—Aase, Donald (39); D'Acquisto, John (6); Forsch, Kenneth (20); Frost, David (12); Hassler, Andrew (42); Jefferson, Jesse (26); Kison, Bruce (11); Mahler, Michael (6); Martinez, Alfredo (2); Moreno, Angel (8); Rau, Douglas (3); Renko, Steven (22); Sanchez, Luis (17); Travers, William (4); Witt, Michael (22); Zahn, Geoffrey (25).

CHICAGO—Agosto, Juan (2); Barrios, Francisco (8); Baumgarten, Ross (21); Burns, R. Britt (24); Dotson, Richard (27); Farmer, Edward (42); Hickey, Kevin (41); Hoyt, D. Lamarr (43); Koosman, Jerry (27—includes 19 with Minnesota); Lamp, Dennis (27); McGlothen, Lynn (11); Patterson, Reginald (6); Robinson, Dewey (4); Trout, Steven (20).

CLEVELAND—Barker, Leonard (22); Blyleven, Rikalbert (20); Brennan, Thomas (7); Denny, John (19); Garland, M. Wayne (12); Glynn, Edward (4); Lewallyn, Dennis (7); Monge, Isidro (31); Spillner, Daniel (32); Stanton, Michael (24); Waits, M. Richard (22).

DETROIT—Bailey, Howard (9); Cappuzzello, George (18); Kinney, Dennis (6); Lopez, Aurelio (29); Morris, John (25); Petry, Daniel (23); Rothschild, Lawrence (5); Rozema, David (28); Rucker, David (2); Saucier, Kevin (38); Schatzeder, Daniel (17); Tobik, David (27); Ujdur, Gerald (4); Wilcox, Milton (24).

KANSAS CITY—Brett, Kenneth (22); Gale, Richard (19); Gura, Lawrence (23); Hammaker, C. Atlee (10); Jones, Michael (12); Leonard, Dennis (26); Martin, D. Renie (29); Paschall, William (2); Quisenberry, Daniel (40); Schattinger, Jeffery (1); Splittorff, Paul (21); Wright, James (17).

MILWAUKEE—Augustine, Gerald (27); Bernard, Dwight (6); Caldwell, R. Michael (24); Cleveland, Reginald (35); DiPino, Frank (2); Easterly, James (44); Fingers, Roland (47); Haas, Bryan (24); Keeton, Rickey (17); Lerch, Randy (23); McClure, Robert (4); Moore, Donnie (3); Mueller, Willard (1); Porter, Charles (3); Slaton, James (24); Vuckovich, Peter (24).

MINNESOTA—Arroyo, Fernando (23); Cooper, Donald (27); Corbett, Douglas (54); Erickson, Roger (14); Felton, Terry (1); Havens, Bradley (14); Hobbs, John (4); Jackson, Darrell (14); O'Connor, Jack (28); Redfern, Peter (24); Verhoeven, John (25); Veselic, Robert (5); Williams, Alberto (23).

NEW YORK—Bird, J. Douglas (17); Castro, William (11); Davis, Ronald (43); Frazier, George (16); Gossage, Richard (32); Griffin, Michael (2); Guidry, Ronald (23); John, Thomas (20); LaRoche, David (26); May, Rudolph (27); McGaffigan, Andrew (2); Nelson, W. Eugene (8); Reuschel, Ricky (12); Righetti, David (15); Wehrmeister, David (5).

OAKLAND—Beard, David (8); Bordi, Richard (2); Figueroa, Eduardo (2); Heaverlo, David (6); Jones, Jeffrey (33); Keough, Matthew (19); Kingman, Brian (18); Langford, J. Rick (24); McCatty, Steven (22); McLaughlin, Michael (11); Minetto, Craig (8); Norris, Michael (23); Owchinko, Robert (29); Underwood, Thomas (25—9 with New York).

SEATTLE—Abbott, W. Glenn (22); Allard, Brian (7); Andersen, Larry (41); Bannister, Floyd (21); Beattie, James (13); Black, Harry (2); Clark, Bryan (30); Clay, Kenneth (22); Drago, Richard (39); Galasso, Robert (13); Gleaton, Jerry (20); Parrott, Michael (24); Rawley, Shane (46); Stein, W. Randolph (5); Stoddard, Robert (5).

TEXAS—Babcock, Robert (16); Butcher, John (5); Comer, Steven (36); Darwin, Danny (22); Honeycutt, Frederick (20); Hough, Charles (21); Jenkins, Ferguson (19); Johnson, John (24); Kern, James (23); Lacey, Robert (15—14 with Cleveland); Matlack, Jonathan (17); Medich, George (20); Mercer, Mark (7); Schmidt, David J. (14); Whitehouse, Leonard (2).

TORONTO—Barlow, Michael (12); Berenguer, Juan (20—8 with Kansas City); Bomback, Mark (21); Clancy, James (22); Espinosa, Arnulfo (21); Garvin, T. Jared (35); Jackson, Roy (39); Leal, Luis (29); McLaughlin, Joey (40); Mirabella, Paul (8); Murray, Dale (11); Steib, David (29); Todd, Jackson (21); Willis, Michael (20).

AWARDED FIRST BASE ON INTERFERENCE—Adams, Minn. (Narron).

PLAYERS WITH TWO OR MORE CLUBS
(Alphabetically Arranged With Players's First Club on Top)

Player and Club	Pct.	G.	AB.	R.	H.	TB.	2B.	3B.	HR.	RBI.	GW.	SH.	SF.	Tot. BB.	Int. BB.	HP.	SO.	SB.	CS.	GI. DP.
Bosetti, Tor.	.234	25	47	5	11	13	2	0	0	4	0	1	0	2	0	0	6	0	2	2
Bosetti, Oak.	.105	9	19	4	2	2	0	0	0	1	0	0	0	3	0	0	3	0	0	0
Jackson, Minn.	.263	54	175	17	46	67	9	0	4	28	3	4	1	10	0	1	15	2	2	3
Jackson, Det.	.284	31	95	12	27	40	8	1	1	12	2	0	1	8	0	0	11	4	1	0
Patterson, Oak.	.348	12	23	4	8	11	1	1	0	1	0	0	0	2	1	0	5	0	1	0
Patterson, N.Y.	.222	4	9	2	2	6	0	2	0	0	0	0	0	0	0	0	0	0	0	0
Poquette, Bos.	.000	3	2	0	0	0	0	0	0	0	0	0	0	0	0	0	0	0	0	0
Poquette, Tex.	.156	30	64	2	10	11	1	0	0	7	1	0	1	5	0	1	1	0	1	3
Revering, Oak.	.230	31	87	12	20	29	1	1	2	10	2	0	1	11	2	1	12	0	1	2
Revering, N.Y.	.235	45	119	8	28	40	4	1	2	7	1	0	0	11	5	0	20	0	1	2
Spencer, N.Y.	.143	25	63	6	9	17	2	0	2	4	2	0	0	9	2	0	7	0	0	3
Spencer, Oak.	.205	54	171	14	35	47	6	0	2	9	1	0	2	10	1	0	20	1	0	5

OFFICIAL MISCELLANEOUS AMERICAN LEAGUE BATTING RECORDS

CLUB MISCELLANEOUS BATTING RECORDS

Club	Slg. Pct.	G.	Tot. BB.	Int. BB.	HP.	SO.	GIDP.	ShO.
Boston	.399	108	378	18	13	520	98	6
New York	.391	107	391	30	7	434	99	9
Milwaukee	.391	109	300	35	29	461	83	6
Chicago	.387	106	322	16	43	518	90	6
Kansas City	.383	103	301	34	17	419	84	8
California	.380	110	393	23	29	571	97	4
Baltimore	.379	105	404	29	15	454	110	9
Oakland	.379	109	342	26	16	647	75	8
Texas	.369	105	295	40	21	396	84	8
Seattle	.368	110	329	24	27	553	70	9
Detroit	.368	109	404	33	18	500	98	5
Cleveland	.351	103	343	31	13	379	91	6
Minnesota	.338	110	275	28	11	497	95	13
Toronto	.330	106	284	23	20	556	72	20
Totals	.373	750	4761	390	279	6905	1246	117

INDIVIDUAL MISCELLANEOUS BATTING RECORDS
(Top Fifteen Qualifiers for Slugging Championship)

Player—Club	Slg. Pct.	Tot. BB.	Int. BB.	HP.	SO.	GI DP.
Grich, Cal.	.543	40	4	4	71	5
Murray, Balt.	.534	40	10	1	43	10
Evans, Bos.	.522	85	1	1	85	8
Paciorek, Sea.	.509	35	3	4	50	10
Cooper, Milw.	.495	28	2	3	30	16
Thomas, Milw.	.493	50	8	2	85	6
Lemon, Chi.	.491	33	0	13	48	10
Zisk, Sea.	.485	28	3	3	63	8
G. Brett, K.C.	.484	27	7	1	23	7
Armas, Oak.	.480	19	6	2	115	6
Luzinski, Chi.	.476	58	1	3	80	10
Winfield, N.Y.	.464	43	3	1	41	13
Aikens, K.C.	.458	62	12	3	47	11
DeCinces, Balt.	.454	41	2	1	32	12
Mayberry, Tor.	.452	44	4	8	45	7

DEPARTMENTAL LEADERS: Tot. BB—Evans, 85; Int. BB—Aikens, 12; HP—Lemon, 13; SO—Armas, 115; GIDP—Singleton, 21.

(All Players—Listed Alphabetically)

Player—Club	Slg. Pct.	Tot. BB.	Int. BB.	HP.	SO.	GI DP.
Adams, Minn.	.282	20	4	0	26	10
Aikens, K.C.	.458	62	12	3	47	11
Ainge, Tor.	.228	23	1	1	41	5
Allen, Sea.	.000	0	0	0	2	0
Allenson, Bos.	.388	23	0	1	33	6
Almon, Chi.	.375	21	0	2	60	4
Anderson, Sea.	.284	17	0	1	29	4
Armas, Oak.	.480	19	6	2	115	6
Ashford, N.Y.	.000	0	0	0	0	0

Player—Club	Slg. Pct.	Tot. BB.	Int. BB.	HP.	SO.	GI DP.
Auerbach, Sea.	.226	4	0	1	15	1
Ayala, Balt.	.407	11	0	1	9	2
Babitt, Oak.	.301	13	1	0	13	6
Baines, Chi.	.482	12	4	2	41	6
Baker, Minn.	.273	1	0	0	8	3
Balboni, N.Y.	.714	1	0	0	4	0
Bando, Clev.	.277	2	0	0	2	1
Bando, Clev.	.354	6	1	0	3	1
Bannister, Clev.	.332	16	2	0	19	0
Barfield, Tor.	.368	4	0	1	19	4
Baylor, Cal.	.427	42	1	7	51	13
Beamon, Tor.	.267	2	0	0	2	0
Belanger, Balt.	.237	12	0	2	25	4
Bell, Tex.	.428	42	10	3	30	6
Bell, Tor.	.350	5	1	0	27	1
Beniquez, Cal.	.265	15	0	1	16	6
Bernazard, Chi.	.380	54	6	2	66	7
Bochte, Sea.	.361	47	5	2	53	5
Bonnell, Tor.	.339	12	0	1	25	8
Bonner, Balt.	.370	1	0	0	4	0
Bosetti, Tor.-Oak.	.227	5	0	0	9	2
Bosley, Milw.	.248	6	0	0	13	4
G. Brett, K.C.	.484	27	7	1	23	7
Brookens, Det.	.343	14	0	2	43	5
Brouhard, Milw.	.371	7	1	2	41	7
Brown, Det.	.250	0	0	0	1	0
Brown, N.Y.	.242	5	0	0	15	1
Brunansky, Cal.	.424	8	0	0	10	0
Budaska, Oak.	.188	4	0	0	10	0
Bulling, Sea.	.305	21	0	1	20	2
Bumbry, Balt.	.337	51	2	2	51	6
Burleson, Cal.	.372	42	2	3	38	8
Burroughs, Sea.	.395	41	3	0	64	7
Butera, Minn.	.293	22	0	0	14	8

Player—Club	Slg. Pct.	Tot. BB.	Int. BB.	HP.	SO.	GI DP.	Player—Club	Slg. Pct.	Tot. BB.	Int. BB.	HP.	SO.	GI DP.
Campaneris, Cal.	.341	5	0	0	10	0	Henderson, Oak.	.437	64	4	2	68	7
Carew, Cal.	.374	45	7	0	45	8	Hill, Chi.	.000	0	0	0	1	0
Castillo, Det.	.125	0	0	0	2	0	Hisle, Milw.	.414	6	0	2	17	1
Castino, Minn.	.396	18	3	1	52	3	Hobson, Cal.	.336	35	0	1	60	4
Cerone, N.Y.	.342	12	0	0	24	10	Hoffman, Bos.	.285	12	0	1	25	7
Chalk, K.C.	.286	4	0	0	2	1	Hosley, Oak.	.238	2	0	0	5	0
Charboneau, Clev.	.362	7	0	0	22	5	Howell, Milw.	.373	23	4	2	39	6
Clark, Cal.	.432	7	0	0	18	2	Hrbek, Minn.	.358	5	1	1	9	0
Concepcion, K.C.	.000	0	0	0	0	0	Hurdle, K.C.	.553	13	3	0	10	2
Cooper, Milw.	.495	28	2	3	30	16	Iorg, Tor.	.293	7	1	1	31	3
Corcoran, Minn.	.235	6	0	0	7	3	Ireland, K.C.	.000	0	0	0	0	0
Corey, Balt.	.000	2	0	0	2	0	Jackson, N.Y.	.428	46	2	1	82	8
Cowens, Det.	.348	22	3	1	36	3	Jackson, Minn.-Det.	.396	18	0	1	26	3
Cox, Oak.	.000	0	0	0	0	0	B. Johnson, Tex.	.611	1	0	0	3	1
Cox, Tex.	.308	0	0	0	4	0	Johnson, Oak.	.476	28	2	3	60	3
Cox, Tor.	.500	5	0	0	10	0	Johnson, Chi.	.351	5	1	0	14	5
Crowley, Balt.	.381	29	5	0	12	3	Johnston, Minn.	.125	2	0	0	5	0
Cruz, Sea.	.324	39	0	3	40	4	Jones, Tex.	.559	1	0	0	7	0
Dauer, Balt.	.369	27	0	3	18	6	Jones, Det.	.322	18	1	1	10	6
Davis, Oak.	.100	2	0	0	4	1	Kearney, Oak.	.000	0	0	0	0	0
Davis, Cal.	.000	0	0	0	0	0	Keatley, K.C.	.000	0	0	0	0	0
DeCinces, Balt.	.454	41	2	1	32	12	Kelleher, Det.	.273	7	0	0	10	5
Dempsey, Balt.	.335	32	1	1	36	5	Kelly, Clev.	.307	14	2	0	9	4
Dent, N.Y.	.379	19	0	2	17	1	Kemp, Det.	.419	70	5	1	48	13
Diaz, Clev.	.533	13	2	1	23	7	Klutts, Oak.	.696	2	1	0	9	0
Dilone, Clev.	.346	18	1	0	28	6	Krenchicki, Balt.	.286	4	0	0	9	1
Downing, Cal.	.379	46	1	4	35	11	Kuiper, Clev.	.286	8	2	0	13	1
Doyle, Oak.	.125	1	0	0	2	1	Kuntz, Chi.	.291	6	0	1	8	1
Drumright, Oak.	.326	4	0	0	4	3	Lansford, Bos.	.439	34	3	2	28	6
Duran, Tex.	.250	1	0	0	1	1	Laudner, Minn.	.349	3	1	1	17	0
Dwyer, Balt.	.306	20	0	0	19	2	Leach, Det.	.289	16	1	0	15	5
Dybzinski, Clev.	.298	5	0	0	8	0	LeFlore, Chi.	.300	28	0	1	70	9
Dyer, Det.	.000	0	0	0	0	0	Lemon, Chi.	.491	33	0	13	48	10
Edler, Sea.	.179	11	0	1	13	1	Lickert, Bos.	.000	0	0	0	0	0
Edwards, Milw.	.293	0	0	0	2	1	Lisi, Tex.	.313	4	0	0	0	0
Ellis, Tex.	.241	5	1	1	10	3	Littleton, Clev.	.000	3	0	0	6	2
Engle, Minn.	.407	13	1	1	37	9	Loviglio, Chi.	.267	1	0	0	1	2
Essian, Chi.	.365	4	0	0	5	2	Lowenstein, Balt.	.381	22	1	1	32	8
Evans, Bos.	.522	85	1	1	85	8	Lubratich, Cal.	.190	0	0	0	2	1
Faedo, Minn.	.244	1	0	0	5	0	Luzinski, Chi.	.476	58	1	3	80	10
Fahey, Det.	.328	2	0	0	4	1	Lynn, Cal.	.316	38	4	3	42	7
Ferguson, Cal.	.367	9	0	0	8	1	Macha, Tor.	.224	8	0	0	15	2
Firova, Sea.	.000	0	0	0	1	0	Mackanin, Minn.	.324	7	2	1	40	4
Fischlin, Clev.	.256	3	0	0	6	0	Maler, Sea.	.391	2	0	1	1	0
Fisk, Chi.	.361	38	3	12	37	9	Manning, Clev.	.336	40	2	0	57	4
Foote, N.Y.	.384	8	0	0	21	7	Manrique, Tor.	.143	0	0	1	12	0
Ford, Cal.	.440	23	3	5	71	16	Martinez, Tor.	.398	11	0	1	16	6
Funderburk, Minn.	.267	2	0	0	1	0	May, K.C.	.345	3	0	0	14	2
Gaetti, Minn.	.423	0	0	0	6	1	Mayberry, Tor.	.452	44	4	8	45	7
Gamble, N.Y.	.439	35	2	1	23	4	McHenry, Sea.	.222	1	0	0	1	1
Gantner, Milw.	.330	29	5	3	29	6	McKay, Oak.	.375	16	0	2	43	4
Garcia, Tor.	.304	9	1	0	32	6	McRae, K.C.	.396	34	3	2	33	11
Garcia, K.C.	.143	0	0	0	2	0	Mendoza, Tex.	.266	7	0	1	25	9
Gedman, Bos.	.434	9	1	1	31	9	Meyer, Sea.	.345	10	1	1	16	6
Geronimo, K.C.	.331	11	2	0	16	3	Milbourne, N.Y.	.399	9	2	1	14	3
Gibson, Det.	.479	18	1	2	64	9	Miller, Bos.	.377	28	1	1	36	7
Goodwin, Minn.	.318	16	2	0	32	3	Molinaro, Chi.	.405	8	1	1	1	1
Graham, Balt.	.239	13	1	0	32	3	Molitor, Milw.	.335	25	1	3	29	3
Gray, Sea.	.476	4	1	0	44	9	Money, Milw.	.286	19	0	1	27	1
Grich, Cal.	.543	40	4	4	71	5	Moore, Milw.	.410	12	0	0	13	4
Griffin, Tor.	.289	17	1	1	38	6	Moore, Oak.	.362	5	0	0	15	1
Gross, Oak.	.366	34	0	2	28	7	Morales, Balt.	.349	3	0	0	13	6
Grote, K.C.	.446	3	0	1	2	1	Morrison, Chi.	.372	10	0	2	29	9
Grubb, Tex.	.332	23	0	2	25	6	Moseby, Tor.	.357	24	3	1	86	4
Gulden, Sea.	.313	0	0	0	2	0	Motley, K.C.	.312	7	0	1	15	2
Hairston, Chi.	.440	2	0	1	4	0	Mulliniks, K.C.	.295	2	0	0	7	2
Hancock, Bos.	.222	2	1	0	4	2	Mumphrey, N.Y.	.429	24	1	0	27	7
Hargrove, Clev.	.401	60	5	5	16	14	Murcer, N.Y.	.470	12	1	0	15	3
Harlow, Cal.	.220	16	0	0	25	3	Murphy, Oak.	.408	73	6	2	91	6
Harper, Cal.	.273	0	0	0	0	0	Murray, Balt.	.534	40	10	1	43	10
Harrah, Clev.	.388	57	8	1	44	5	Narron, Sea.	.291	16	3	2	35	3
Harris, Cal.	.403	3	0	0	11	4	Nettles, N.Y.	.398	47	4	1	49	5
Hassey, Clev.	.268	17	0	2	11	5	Nettles, Oak.	.000	0	0	0	0	0
Hatcher, Minn.	.350	15	2	2	29	10	Newman, Oak.	.329	9	1	0	28	7
Hayes, Clev.	.394	14	1	2	10	2	Nichols, Bos.	.229	2	0	0	6	0
Heath, Oak.	.346	13	1	1	36	9	Nordhagen, Chi.	.442	10	0	1	25	8
Hebner, Det.	.345	27	5	2	28	5	Norman, Tex.	.308	1	0	0	2	0
Henderson, Sea.	.333	16	1	1	24	4	Oates, N.Y.	.231	2	0	0	0	0

Player—Club	Slg. Pct.	Tot. BB.	Int. BB.	HP.	SO.	GI DP.
Oglivie, Milw.	.395	37	10	6	49	9
Oliver, Tex.	.411	24	10	2	28	17
Orta, Clev.	.376	21	3	1	43	11
Otis, K.C.	.417	31	1	2	59	7
Ott, Cal.	.279	17	1	1	42	7
Paciorek, Sea.	.509	35	3	4	50	10
Page, Oak.	.283	7	0	0	29	1
Pagel, Clev.	.733	4	1	0	1	0
Papi, Det.	.344	3	0	0	18	2
Parrish, Det.	.394	34	6	0	52	16
Parsons, Sea.	.409	1	0	2	4	0
Patek, Cal.	.298	1	0	0	6	1
Patterson, Oak-NY	.531	2	1	0	5	0
Perez, Bos.	.395	27	0	0	66	9
Peters, Det.	.319	29	2	2	28	8
Phelps, K.C.	.227	1	0	0	13	0
Picciolo, Oak.	.397	5	0	1	22	6
Piniella, N.Y.	.428	13	4	0	9	7
Poquette, Bos.-Tex.	.167	5	0	1	1	3
Powell, Minn.	.326	17	0	1	31	6
Pruitt, Clev.	.000	1	0	0	2	1
Pryor, Chi.	.237	6	0	2	8	2
Putnam, Tex.	.418	17	3	0	38	4
Quirk, K.C.	.320	6	1	1	17	5
Randle, Sea.	.315	17	4	1	22	2
Randolph, N.Y.	.305	57	0	0	24	10
Remy, Bos.	.338	36	2	0	30	6
Revering, Oak.-N.Y.	.335	22	7	1	32	4
Rice, Bos.	.441	34	3	3	76	14
Ripken, Balt.	.128	1	0	0	8	4
Rivers, Tex.	.371	24	2	1	31	3
Roberts, Tex.	.421	25	2	1	38	8
Robertson, N.Y.	.316	0	0	0	3	0
Rodriguez, N.Y.	.500	2	0	0	10	1
Roenicke, Balt.	.384	23	1	2	29	12
Romero, Milw.	.264	4	0	0	9	4
Rosello, Clev.	.321	7	0	0	12	2
Royster, Balt.	.000	0	0	0	2	0
Rudi, Bos.	.352	8	1	2	29	2
Sakata, Balt.	.353	11	0	1	18	5
Sample, Tex.	.391	17	1	7	21	3
Schmidt, Bos.	.405	7	0	0	17	1
Sconiers, Cal.	.385	1	0	0	10	0
Serna, Sea.	.404	3	0	2	11	0
Sexton, Oak.	.000	0	0	0	2	0
Shelby, Balt.	.000	0	0	0	1	0
Sheridan, K.C.	.000	0	0	0	1	0
Simmons, Milw.	.376	23	2	3	32	10
Simpson, Sea.	.302	15	0	1	41	3
Singleton, Balt.	.435	61	6	0	59	21
Smalley, Minn.	.443	31	5	0	24	8
Smith, Minn.	.300	10	0	0	3	0
Sofield, Minn.	.196	8	0	0	22	5
Spencer, N.Y.-Oak.	.274	19	3	0	27	8
Squires, Chi.	.296	22	0	0	17	5
Stanley, Oak.	.221	15	0	0	23	0
Stapleton, Bos.	.423	21	1	1	22	11
Stein, Tex.	.435	7	3	0	15	5
Summers, Det.	.358	19	3	3	35	5
Sundberg, Tex.	.366	50	6	1	48	5
Sutherland, Chi.	.167	3	0	0	1	0
Thomas, Milw.	.493	50	8	2	85	6
Thornton, Clev.	.372	23	1	0	37	15
Tolleson, Tex.	.167	1	0	0	5	0
Trammell, Det.	.327	49	2	3	31	10
Turner, Chi.	.167	1	0	0	2	0
Upshaw, Tor.	.324	11	0	1	16	1
Valdez, Bos.	.217	0	0	0	2	0
Velez, Tor.	.404	55	3	3	60	5
Veryzer, Clev.	.262	10	1	1	10	6
Wagner, Tex.	.365	8	0	0	13	2
Walker, Bos.	.353	1	0	0	2	0
Walton, Sea.	.000	1	0	0	2	0
Ward, Minn.	.359	28	4	0	48	10
Washington, Minn.	.286	4	0	1	14	1
Washington, K.C.	.307	41	1	0	43	6
Wathan, K.C.	.312	19	1	2	23	9
Watson, N.Y.	.385	24	2	0	17	10
Wells, Tor.	.315	5	0	0	12	2
Werner, Tex.	.250	0	0	0	2	0
Werth, N.Y.	.127	12	2	0	12	4
Whitaker, Det.	.373	40	3	1	42	5
White, K.C.	.376	19	0	0	50	10
Whitmer, Tor.	.222	1	0	0	2	1
Whitt, Tor.	.297	20	3	0	30	2
Wilfong, Minn.	.331	29	1	0	43	1
Williams, Balt.	.500	0	0	0	0	0
Wills, Tex.	.307	32	2	1	49	8
Wilson, K.C.	.364	18	3	4	42	5
Winfield, N.Y.	.464	43	1	1	41	13
Wockenfuss, Det.	.395	28	1	0	22	5
Woods, Tor.	.309	19	5	0	31	7
Wynegar, Minn.	.280	17	2	1	9	7
Yastrzemski, Bos.	.355	49	4	0	28	10
Yost, Milw.	.556	3	0	0	6	0
Yount, Milw.	.419	22	1	2	37	4
Zisk, Sea.	.485	28	3	3	63	8

OFFICIAL AMERICAN LEAGUE DESIGNATED HITTING

CLUB DESIGNATED HITTING

Club	Pct.	AB.	R.	H.	TB.	2B.	3B.	HR.	RBI.	SH.	SF.	BB.	HP.	SO.	SB.	CS.	GI DP.
Texas	.305	433	56	132	175	29	1	4	54	0	1	26	3	33	4	1	17
Seattle	.292	435	52	127	203	17	1	19	49	0	1	33	3	85	1	2	9
Kansas City	.264	401	37	106	151	23	2	6	36	3	4	33	2	40	3	4	10
Chicago	.262	397	61	104	187	15	1	22	65	0	2	57	4	81	0	0	10
Cleveland	.253	387	46	98	137	19	1	6	51	7	6	51	0	52	10	7	15
Baltimore	.252	381	40	96	144	15	0	11	57	4	2	52	1	51	0	1	13
Milwaukee	.247	425	53	105	156	20	2	9	44	4	6	26	6	58	4	4	13
Detroit	.238	378	47	90	141	13	1	12	41	2	3	72	4	66	5	4	8
California	.233	407	55	95	170	17	2	18	72	0	6	47	7	52	4	3	12
Boston	.232	431	56	100	156	13	2	13	62	1	4	46	3	62	1	2	10
New York	.227	384	38	87	141	18	0	12	49	1	4	64	0	75	1	2	8
Oakland	.217	419	51	91	154	10	1	17	72	1	6	41	2	103	8	5	5
Toronto	.212	363	45	77	134	14	2	13	36	3	2	64	4	75	3	6	5
Minnesota	.208	413	33	86	115	14	0	5	37	2	3	35	0	56	2	1	15
Totals	.247	5655	671	1395	2165	237	16	167	725	28	50	647	39	889	46	42	150

INDIVIDUAL DESIGNATED HITTING
(Listed Alphabetically)

Player and Club	Pct.	G.	AB.	R.	H.	TB.	2B.	3B.	HR.	RBI.	SH.	SF.	BB.	HP.	SO.	SB.	CS.	GI DP.
Adams, Minn.	.193	62	212	13	41	55	8	0	2	20	0	2	18	0	26	0	1	10
Ainge, Tor.	.000	1	1	0	0	0	0	0	0	0	0	0	1	0	0	1	1	0
Allen, Sea.	.000	2	1	0	0	0	0	0	0	0	0	0	0	0	1	0	0	0

Player and Club	Pct.	G.	AB.	R.	H.	TB.	2B.	3B.	HR.	RBI.	SH.	SF.	BB.	HP.	SO.	SB.	CS.	GIDP.
Ayala, Balt.	.265	27	68	9	18	25	1	0	2	8	1	1	7	1	7	0	1	2
Baines, Chi.	.000	1	1	0	0	0	0	0	0	0	0	0	0	0	1	0	0	0
Baker, Minn.	.000	1	3	0	0	0	0	0	0	0	0	0	0	0	1	0	0	0
Balboni, N.Y.	.000	1	2	0	0	0	0	0	0	0	0	0	0	0	2	0	0	0
Bando, Clev.	.200	2	5	0	1	2	1	0	0	0	0	0	0	0	0	0	0	0
Bando, Milw.	.000	2	4	0	0	0	0	0	0	0	0	0	1	0	0	0	0	0
Baumgarten, Chi.	.000	1	0	0	0	0	0	0	0	0	0	0	0	0	0	0	0	0
Baylor, Cal.	.233	97	356	51	83	153	17	1	17	64	0	6	41	7	48	3	3	11
Beamon, Tor.	.300	4	10	0	3	4	1	0	0	0	0	0	1	0	1	0	0	0
Bell, Tor.	.150	8	20	3	3	3	0	0	0	2	0	0	0	0	1	0	1	0
Beniquez, Cal.	.000	1	3	0	0	0	0	0	0	0	0	0	0	0	0	0	0	0
Bochte, Sea.	.000	1	1	0	0	0	0	0	0	0	0	0	1	0	1	0	0	0
Bosetti, Tor.-Oak.	.000	3	7	2	0	0	0	0	0	0	0	0	0	0	0	0	0	0
Bosley, Milw.	.500	1	2	1	1	1	0	0	0	0	0	0	0	0	0	0	0	0
Brouhard, Milw.	.222	7	27	3	6	11	3	1	0	5	0	1	0	1	7	0	0	2
Brown, Det.	.000	4	1	1	0	0	0	0	0	4	0	0	0	0	1	0	0	0
Brown, N.Y.	.000	2	0	0	0	0	0	0	0	0	0	0	0	0	0	1	0	0
Budaska, Oak.	.156	9	32	3	5	6	1	0	0	2	0	0	4	0	10	0	1	0
Burroughs, Sea.	.000	1	3	0	0	0	0	0	0	0	0	0	1	0	1	0	0	0
Butera, Minn.	.750	1	4	1	3	3	0	0	0	1	0	0	0	0	0	0	0	0
Carew, Cal.	.250	2	4	1	1	1	0	0	0	0	0	0	1	0	0	1	0	0
Charboneau, Clev.	.242	14	33	3	8	8	0	0	0	4	1	0	5	0	4	0	0	1
Cooper, Milw.	.273	5	22	1	6	7	1	0	0	2	0	0	0	0	0	0	0	2
Corcoran, Minn.	.429	3	7	1	3	4	1	0	0	0	0	0	1	0	1	0	0	0
Cox, Tor.	.000	1	0	1	0	0	0	0	0	0	0	0	1	0	0	0	0	0
Crowley, Balt.	.257	42	109	12	28	46	6	0	4	20	1	1	23	0	8	0	0	3
Davis, Oak.	.000	3	8	0	0	0	0	0	0	0	0	0	1	0	3	0	0	0
Dempsey, Balt.	.000	1	1	0	0	0	0	0	0	0	0	0	0	0	0	0	0	0
Diaz, Clev.	.000	3	3	0	0	0	0	0	0	0	0	0	1	0	1	0	0	0
Dilone, Clev.	.242	11	33	5	8	8	0	0	0	3	0	0	4	0	7	1	2	2
Downing, Cal.	.222	5	18	1	4	4	0	0	0	2	0	0	3	0	0	0	0	1
Drumright, Oak.	.286	5	21	2	6	8	0	1	0	4	0	0	0	0	1	0	0	1
Dwyer, Balt.	.000	1	0	0	0	0	0	0	0	0	0	0	1	0	0	0	0	0
Dybzinski, Clev.	.000	1	0	0	0	0	0	0	0	0	1	0	0	0	0	0	0	0
Edwards, Milw.	.000	1	0	0	0	0	0	0	0	0	0	0	0	0	0	0	0	0
Ellis, Tex.	.000	1	2	1	0	0	0	0	0	0	0	0	2	0	2	0	0	0
Engle, Minn.	.000	1	1	0	0	0	0	0	0	0	0	0	0	0	0	0	0	0
Foote, N.Y.	.214	4	14	0	3	4	1	0	0	0	0	0	0	0	5	0	0	0
Funderburk, Minn.	.000	1	1	0	0	0	0	0	0	0	0	0	0	0	0	0	0	0
Gaetti, Minn.	.000	1	2	0	0	0	0	0	0	0	0	0	0	0	1	0	0	0
Gamble, N.Y.	.191	33	68	9	13	22	3	0	2	9	0	1	18	0	15	0	1	0
Garcia, Tor.	.000	1	3	0	0	0	0	0	0	0	0	0	0	0	2	0	0	0
Gibson, Det.	.259	9	27	2	7	9	2	0	0	3	0	0	1	0	7	1	0	3
Goodwin, Minn.	.125	5	16	2	2	5	0	0	1	3	1	0	0	0	2	1	0	0
Graham, Balt.	.095	6	21	1	2	2	0	0	0	2	0	0	2	0	5	0	0	0
Gray, Sea.	.213	15	61	8	13	25	3	0	3	6	0	1	1	0	18	1	0	1
Gross, Oak.	.000	1	1	0	0	0	0	0	0	0	0	0	0	0	1	0	0	0
Hancock, Bos.	.091	4	11	1	1	1	0	0	0	0	0	0	1	0	1	0	0	0
Hargrove, Clev.	.556	4	9	1	5	7	2	0	0	2	0	0	5	0	1	0	1	1
Harper, Cal.	.000	1	3	0	0	0	0	0	0	0	0	0	0	0	0	0	0	0
Harrah, Clev.	.333	1	6	1	2	3	1	0	0	0	0	0	1	0	0	0	0	0
Harris, Cal.	.000	1	3	0	0	0	0	0	0	0	0	0	0	0	0	0	0	0
Hassey, Clev.	.000	1	1	0	0	0	0	0	0	0	0	1	0	0	0	0	0	0
Hatcher, Minn.	1.000	1	1	1	1	1	0	0	0	0	0	0	0	0	0	0	0	0
Hayes, Clev.	.246	21	61	10	15	19	2	1	0	6	2	0	6	0	7	4	1	2
Hebner, Det.	.125	11	24	1	3	3	0	0	0	2	0	0	8	1	3	0	0	1
Hisle, Milw.	.238	24	84	11	20	36	4	0	4	11	0	2	6	2	16	0	0	1
Hobson, Cal.	.143	2	7	0	1	1	0	0	0	1	0	0	2	0	1	0	0	0
Hosley, Oak.	.125	4	8	0	1	1	0	0	0	1	0	0	0	0	0	0	0	0
Howell, Milw.	.240	13	50	9	12	17	2	0	1	5	1	0	3	0	5	0	0	2
Hrbek, Minn.	.160	8	25	1	4	5	1	0	0	0	0	0	2	0	3	0	0	0
Iorg, Tor.	1.000	1	1	0	1	2	1	0	0	2	0	0	0	0	0	0	0	0
Jackson, N.Y.	.171	33	105	7	18	29	5	0	2	9	0	1	25	0	28	0	1	3
R. Jackson, Minn.	.421	6	19	2	8	11	0	0	1	7	0	0	1	0	3	0	0	1
Johnson, Oak.	.273	68	245	35	67	117	8	0	14	53	0	5	24	2	57	5	3	3
Johnson, Chi.	.250	2	8	1	2	2	0	0	0	1	0	0	0	0	0	0	0	0
Jones, Det.	.000	4	6	0	0	0	0	0	0	0	0	0	2	0	0	1	0	0
Kelly, Clev.	.245	18	49	6	12	18	3	0	1	10	0	1	8	0	1	2	2	2
Kemp, Det.	.389	12	36	8	14	19	2	0	1	5	0	0	9	0	6	1	0	0
Krenchicki, Balt	.000	1	0	1	0	0	0	0	0	0	0	0	0	0	0	0	0	0
Kuntz, Chi.	.000	5	2	1	0	0	0	0	0	0	0	0	0	0	0	0	0	0
Lansford, Bos.	.316	16	57	9	18	28	4	0	2	8	0	0	3	1	9	1	0	2
Laudner, Minn.	.000	2	6	0	0	0	0	0	0	0	0	0	1	0	4	0	0	0
Leach, Det.	.000	2	1	1	0	0	0	0	0	0	0	0	2	0	0	0	0	0
Loviglio, Chi.	.000	2	1	1	0	0	0	0	0	0	0	0	0	0	0	0	0	0
Lowenstein, Balt	.400	5	0	2	2	2	0	0	0	1	0	0	0	0	0	0	0	0
Luzinski, Chi.	.265	103	378	55	100	180	15	1	21	62	0	2	57	3	80	0	0	10
Macha, Tor.	.200	2	5	0	1	1	0	0	0	0	0	0	1	0	1	0	0	0

Player and Club	Pct.	G.	AB.	R.	H.	TB.	2B.	3B.	HR.	RBI.	SH.	SF.	BB.	HP.	SO.	SB.	CS.	GI DP.
Mackanin, Minn	.059	6	17	0	1	1	0	0	0	0	0	0	1	0	3	0	0	0
Maler, Sea............	.400	2	5	2	2	3	1	0	0	0	0	0	1	0	0	0	0	0
Manrique, Tor.......	1.000	1	1	0	1	1	0	0	0	0	0	0	0	0	0	0	0	0
May, K.C.	.111	4	18	1	2	2	0	0	0	1	0	0	0	0	6	0	0	0
Mayberry, Tor.......	.250	10	32	5	8	13	2	0	1	3	0	0	4	1	7	0	0	0
McHenry, Sea	.000	1	1	0	0	0	0	0	0	0	0	0	0	0	0	0	0	0
McRae, K.C........	.270	97	374	35	101	146	23	2	6	33	3	4	33	2	31	3	4	10
Meyer, Sea	.143	3	7	1	1	2	1	0	0	0	0	0	1	0	2	0	0	0
Milbourne, N.Y.	.200	3	5	1	1	1	0	0	0	0	0	0	0	0	1	0	0	0
Molinaro, Chi	.333	4	6	2	2	5	0	0	1	2	0	0	1	1	0	0	0	0
Molitor, Milw	.350	16	60	9	21	27	3	0	1	5	2	0	6	1	8	4	2	0
Money, Milw	.143	2	7	0	1	2	1	0	0	0	0	0	1	0	2	0	0	0
Moore, Milw	.263	6	19	3	5	5	0	0	0	0	1	0	2	0	4	0	2	0
Morales, Balt........	.221	22	68	5	15	22	1	0	2	11	0	0	2	0	8	0	0	4
Morrison, Chi	.000	1	1	1	0	0	0	0	0	0	0	0	0	0	0	0	0	0
Murcer, N.Y.	.284	33	102	13	29	50	6	0	5	20	0	1	10	0	12	0	0	3
Murphy, Oak	.000	1	2	1	0	0	0	0	0	0	0	0	3	0	0	0	0	0
Nettles, N.Y.........	.333	4	15	1	5	5	0	0	0	3	0	1	0	0	3	0	0	0
Nichols, Bos..........	.000	7	0	1	0	0	0	0	0	0	0	0	0	0	0	0	1	0
Oglivie, Milw	.261	6	23	4	6	8	2	0	0	3	0	0	1	0	1	0	0	0
Oliver, Tex	.307	101	420	53	129	172	29	1	4	54	0	1	24	2	28	3	0	17
Otis, K.C..............	1.000	1	1	0	1	1	0	0	0	1	0	0	0	0	0	0	0	0
Page, Oak...........	.136	29	88	8	12	22	1	0	3	12	1	1	7	0	29	2	1	1
Pagel, Clev...........	.000	1	1	0	0	0	0	0	0	0	0	0	0	0	0	0	0	0
Papi, Det............	.300	3	10	3	3	9	0	0	2	4	0	0	0	0	3	0	0	0
Parrish, Det..........	.250	5	12	3	3	5	0	1	0	0	0	1	0	0	7	0	1	0
Patterson, Oak......	.000	2	6	0	0	0	0	0	0	0	0	0	1	0	2	0	0	0
Perez, Bos	.220	23	82	10	18	26	1	2	1	7	0	2	9	0	17	0	0	2
Peters, Det	.242	19	62	9	15	17	2	0	0	5	1	1	16	0	10	0	2	3
Phelps, K.C..........	.250	4	8	1	2	2	0	0	0	1	0	0	0	0	3	0	0	0
Piniella, N.Y.	.265	19	49	6	13	25	3	0	3	6	0	0	6	0	5	0	0	1
Powell, Minn	.214	8	28	2	6	7	1	0	0	2	0	0	2	0	5	1	0	2
Pruitt, Clev	.000	1	1	0	0	0	0	0	0	0	0	0	0	0	0	0	0	0
Revering, Oak	.000	2	0	0	0	0	0	0	0	0	0	0	1	0	0	0	0	0
Rodriguez, N.Y.......	.333	2	6	0	2	2	0	0	0	1	0	0	0	0	1	0	0	0
Rosello, Clev	.333	4	3	0	1	1	0	0	0	0	1	0	1	0	0	0	0	0
Rudi, Bos	.185	21	81	10	15	29	2	0	4	13	1	1	5	2	20	0	0	2
Sconiers, Cal.........	.462	3	13	2	6	11	0	1	1	5	0	0	0	0	3	0	0	0
Sexton, Oak	.000	1	1	1	0	0	0	0	0	0	0	0	0	0	0	1	0	0
Simmons, Milw	.231	22	91	10	21	35	3	1	3	12	0	3	4	2	7	0	0	6
Singleton, Balt.......	.284	30	109	12	31	47	7	0	3	15	2	0	17	0	23	0	0	4
Smalley, Minn	.211	15	38	7	8	12	1	0	1	3	0	1	5	0	5	0	0	2
Stapleton, Bos	.462	3	13	4	6	9	0	1	2	2	0	0	0	0	0	0	0	0
Stieb, Tor	.000	1	0	0	0	0	0	0	0	0	0	0	0	0	0	0	0	0
Summers, Det	.241	37	112	10	27	40	7	0	2	9	0	1	10	3	28	1	1	0
Thomas, Milw	.217	6	23	2	5	6	1	0	0	1	0	0	1	0	6	0	0	0
Thornton, Clev.......	.253	53	182	20	46	71	10	0	5	25	2	5	20	0	31	3	1	7
Upshaw, Tor	.152	15	46	5	7	13	0	0	2	3	0	0	3	0	5	2	1	0
Velez, Tor	.206	74	233	30	48	91	9	2	10	25	2	2	53	3	57	0	3	5
Walton, Sea..........	.000	1	0	1	0	0	0	0	0	0	0	0	0	0	0	0	0	0
Ward, Minn	.200	2	5	2	1	2	1	0	0	0	0	0	1	0	1	0	0	0
Watson, N.Y.	.222	6	9	0	2	2	0	0	0	1	0	0	3	0	1	0	0	1
Wells, Tor	.500	3	8	0	4	5	1	0	0	0	0	0	0	0	1	0	0	0
Werner, Tex..........	.250	2	8	1	2	2	0	0	0	0	0	0	0	0	2	0	1	0
Werth, N.Y.	.125	4	8	1	1	1	0	0	0	0	1	0	2	0	2	0	0	0
Wills, Tex.............	.333	1	3	1	1	1	0	0	0	0	0	0	0	1	1	1	0	0
Winfield, N.Y.	.000	1	1	0	0	0	0	0	0	0	0	0	0	0	0	0	0	0
Wockenfuss, Det ...	.216	39	88	10	19	40	0	0	7	13	0	1	17	0	7	0	0	1
Woods, Tor	.333	2	3	0	1	1	0	0	0	1	1	0	0	0	0	0	0	0
Wynegar, Minn......	.286	9	28	1	8	9	1	0	0	1	1	0	3	0	1	0	0	0
Yastrzemski, Bos ...	.225	48	187	21	42	63	6	0	5	32	0	1	28	0	15	0	1	4
Yount, Milw	.077	3	13	0	1	1	0	0	0	0	0	0	1	0	2	0	0	0
Zisk, Sea	.312	93	356	42	111	173	12	1	16	43	0	0	28	3	62	0	2	8

Note—The following players made no plate appearances as designated hitters and are listed in the designated hitting statistics only because they pinch-ran for the DH: Baumgarten, Brown (N.Y.), Edwards, Krenchicki, Nichols, Stieb and Walton.

Game-winning RBIs by designated hitters, listed alphabetically by club, follow: Baltimore (7)—Ayala 1, Crowley 3, Lowenstein 1, Morales 1, Singleton 1. Boston (4)—Yastrzemski 4. California (10)—Baylor 10. Chicago (11)—Luzinski 11. Cleveland (6)—Hayes 1, Kelly 1, Thornton 4. Detroit (6)—Kemp 1, Summers 3, Wockenfuss 2. Kansas City (4)—McRae 4. Milwaukee (4)—Hisle 2, Howell 1, Simmons 1. Minnesota (4)—Adams 1, Butera 1, R. Jackson 1, Smalley 1. New York (9)—Gamble 1, Jackson 3, Murcer 3, Piniella 1, Rodriguez 1. Oakland (5)—Drumright 2, Johnson 3. Seattle (5)—Gray 1, Zisk 4. Texas (8)—Oliver 8. Toronto (3)—Velez 3.

OFFICIAL AMERICAN LEAGUE FIELDING AVERAGES

CLUB FIELDING

Club	Pct.	G.	PO.	A.	E.	TC.	DP.	TP.	PB.
Detroit	.984	109	2908	1263	67	4238	109	0	8
Texas	.984	105	2821	1340	69	4230	102	0	10
Baltimore	.983	105	2820	1212	68	4100	114	0	11
New York	.982	107	2844	1157	72	4073	100	0	5
Milwaukee	.982	109	2958	1358	79	4395	135	0	9
Kansas City	.982	103	2767	1100	72	3939	94	0	7
Oakland	.980	109	2979	1080	81	4140	74	1	2
Seattle	.979	110	2992	1285	91	4368	122	1	9
Chicago	.979	106	2822	1218	87	4127	113	1	2
Boston	.979	108	2962	1245	91	4298	108	0	9
Cleveland	.978	103	2793	1156	87	4036	91	1	8
Minnesota	.978	110	2939	1268	96	4303	103	0	3
California	.977	110	2914	1286	101	4301	120	0	6
Toronto	.975	106	2860	1164	105	4129	102	0	4
Totals	.980	750	40379	17132	1166	58677	1487	4	93

INDIVIDUAL FIELDING

FIRST BASEMEN

°Throws lefthanded.

Leader—Club	Pct.	G.	PO.	A.	E.	DP.
MURRAY, Balt.	.999	99	899	91	1	98

(Listed Alphabetically)

Player—Club	Pct.	G.	PO.	A.	E.	DP.
Aikens, K.C.	.992	99	844	56	7	79
Bochte, Sea.°	.995	82	745	49	4	70
Carew, Cal.	.995	90	877	60	5	90
Cooper, Milw.°	.992	101	987	72	9	111
Corcoran, Minn.°	1.000	16	108	9	0	10
Ellis, Tex.	.993	18	140	8	1	16
Goodwin, Minn.	.992	40	341	20	3	27
Gray, Sea.	.993	34	275	16	2	34
Hargrove, Clev.°	.989	88	766	76	9	67
Harris, Calif.°	.976	11	78	5	2	9
Hebner, Det.	.995	61	531	29	3	36
Hrbek, Minn.	1.000	13	124	4	0	14
R. Jackson, Minn.-Det.	.993	65	527	41	4	46
Johnson, Chi.	.989	36	264	15	3	31
Leach, Det.°	1.000	32	133	14	0	15
Macha, Tor.	.990	16	94	8	1	8
Mackanin, Minn.	.964	10	74	6	3	13
Mayberry, Tor.°	.993	80	647	36	5	65
Moore, Oak.°	1.000	13	99	7	0	9
Murray, Balt.	.999	99	899	91	1	98
Newman, Oak.	.995	30	185	13	1	12
Perez, Bos.	.993	56	519	37	4	63
Putnam, Tex.	.993	94	769	64	6	65
Revering, Oak.-N.Y.	.994	73	464	43	3	36
Sconiers, Cal.°	1.000	12	95	8	0	11
Spencer, N.Y.-Oak.°	.998	73	516	53	1	47
Squires, Chi.°	.992	88	729	58	6	68
Stapleton, Bos.	.992	12	126	4	1	10
Stein, Tex.	1.000	20	146	10	0	9
Thornton, Clev.	.986	11	67	5	1	7
Upshaw, Tor.°	1.000	14	58	5	0	7
Watson, N.Y.	.997	50	367	25	1	42
Wells, Tor.	.994	22	146	10	1	10
Werth, N.Y.	1.000	19	82	9	0	7
Wockenfuss, Det.	.984	25	179	5	3	27
Yastrzemski, Bos.	.992	39	353	34	3	26

TRIPLE PLAYS: Bochte, Hargrove, Revering (Oakland), Squires.

(Fewer Than Ten Games)

Player—Club	Pct.	G.	PO.	A.	E.	DP.
Balboni, N.Y.	1.000	3	14	1	0	2
Bando, Milw.	1.000	9	58	3	0	6

Player—Club	Pct.	G.	PO.	A.	E.	DP.
Bannister, Clev.	.833	2	5	0	1	0
Baylor, Cal.	1.000	4	32	3	0	2
Beamon, Tor.°	1.000	1	6	0	0	0
Butera, Minn.	1.000	1	2	0	0	0
Cox, Tor.	1.000	1	10	0	0	1
Crowley, Balt.°	1.000	4	30	2	0	2
Davis, Oak.°	.000	1	0	0	0	0
DeCinces, Balt.	1.000	1	4	0	0	0
Duran, Tex.°	1.000	1	1	0	0	0
Dwyer, Balt.°	1.000	3	13	0	0	2
Fisk, Chi.	.900	1	7	2	1	4
Foote, N.Y.	1.000	1	4	0	0	1
Garcia, K.C.°	1.000	2	1	0	0	0
Gross, Oak.	.750	2	3	0	1	0
Hassey, Clev.	1.000	5	31	6	0	1
Hatcher, Minn.	.984	7	56	7	1	5
Hill, Chi.	.000	1	0	0	0	0
Hosley, Oak.	.750	1	3	0	1	0
Howell, Milw.	1.000	3	20	2	0	1
Iorg, Tor.	1.000	1	4	0	0	1
Ireland, K.C.	1.000	4	3	0	0	0
Johnson, Oak.	1.000	9	42	1	0	2
B. Johnson, Tex.	1.000	1	9	0	0	0
Maler, Sea.	1.000	5	36	2	0	5
May, K.C.	1.000	8	63	2	0	8
Meyer, Sea.	1.000	3	17	0	0	3
Money, Milw.	1.000	1	6	0	0	1
Morales, Balt.	1.000	3	13	0	0	1
Oliver, Tex.	1.000	1	2	0	0	0
Pagel, Cal.°	1.000	6	28	6	0	5
Papi, Det.	1.000	1	1	0	0	0
Parsons, Sea.	1.000	1	2	0	0	0
Phelps, K.C.°	1.000	2	4	1	0	0
Rodriguez, N.Y.	1.000	1	8	1	0	2
Rudi, Bos.	1.000	5	47	1	0	2
Simmons, Milw.	.974	4	33	4	1	4
Smalley, Minn.	1.000	1	10	0	0	0
Velez, Tor.	1.000	1	9	0	0	0
Wathan, K.C.	1.000	1	1	0	0	0

FIRST BASEMEN WITH TWO OR MORE CLUBS

Player—Club	Pct.	G.	PO.	A.	E.	DP.
R. Jackson, Minn.	.988	36	309	26	4	26
R. Jackson, Det.	1.000	29	218	15	0	20
Revering, Oak.	.995	29	188	13	1	12
Revering, N.Y.	.994	44	276	30	2	24
Spencer, N.Y.	1.000	25	172	17	0	17
Spencer, Oak.	.997	48	344	36	1	30

SECOND BASEMEN

Leader—Club	Pct.	G.	PO.	A.	E.	DP.
DAUER, Balt.	.989	95	201	253	5	71

(Listed Alphabetically)

Player—Club	Pct.	G.	PO.	A.	E.	DP.
Babitt, Oak.	.972	52	84	125	6	12
Bannister, Clev.	.992	30	51	74	1	14
Bernazard, Chi.	.987	104	228	320	7	66
Chalk, K.C.	1.000	10	10	19	0	2
Cruz, Sea.	.982	92	239	294	10	72
Dauer, Balt.	.989	94	201	253	5	71
Doyle, Oak.	1.000	17	29	39	0	6
Drumright, Oak.	.989	19	38	50	1	7
Gantner, Milw.	.984	107	251	352	10	95
Garcia, Tor.	.972	62	132	181	9	32
Grich, Cal.	.983	100	230	349	10	85
Iorg, Tor.	.963	46	82	152	9	29
Kelleher, Det.	.962	11	9	16	1	5
Kuiper, Clev.	.983	72	118	174	5	24
Mackanin, Minn.	.980	31	62	87	3	15
McKay, Oak.	.970	38	83	108	6	23
Milbourne, N.Y.	.970	14	35	29	2	10
Mulliniks, K.C.	.900	10	14	13	3	4
Patek, Cal.	.983	16	27	31	1	8
Randle, Sea.	.982	21	40	72	2	14
Randolph, N.Y.	.977	93	205	268	11	74
Remy, Bos.	.984	87	162	272	7	58
Romero, Milw.	.985	18	24	43	1	13
Rosello, Clev.	.979	26	46	49	2	13
Sakata, Balt.	.986	20	30	42	1	10
Stapleton, Bos.	.967	23	61	58	4	19

Player—Club	Pct.	G.	PO.	A.	E.	DP.
Whitaker, Det.	.985	108	227	354	9	77
White, K.C.	.988	93	226	263	6	70
Wilfong, Minn.	.980	93	183	268	9	52
Wills, Tex.	.983	101	268	326	10	70

TRIPLE PLAYS: Bannister, Bernazard, Randle.

(Fewer Than Ten Games)

Player—Club	Pct.	G.	PO.	A.	E.	DP.
Ainge, Tor.	1.000	2	1	5	0	0
Allen, Sea.	.000	2	0	0	0	0
Ashford, N.Y.	.000	2	0	0	0	0
Baker, Minn.	1.000	3	3	10	0	2
Campaneris, Cal.	1.000	2	0	2	0	0
Castino, Minn.	.957	4	10	12	1	5
Cox, Oak.	1.000	1	0	1	0	0
Dybzinski, Clev.	.800	3	0	4	1	0
Fischlin, Clev.	.889	1	4	4	1	1
Griffin, Tor.	1.000	1	1	1	0	1
Krenchicki, Balt.	1.000	7	5	14	0	5
Loviglio, Chi.	1.000	3	5	3	0	0
Morrison, Chi.	1.000	1	0	1	0	1
Papi, Det.	1.000	1	1	1	0	0
Pryor, Chi.	1.000	5	8	9	0	5
Quirk, K.C.	1.000	1	0	1	0	0
Robertson, N.Y.	1.000	3	2	7	0	1
Rodriguez, N.Y.	1.000	3	1	5	0	1
Serna, Sea.	.968	7	13	17	1	5
Stanley, Oak.	1.000	6	2	2	0	0
Stein, Tex.	1.000	3	2	3	0	1
Wagner, Tex.	.966	4	13	15	1	5
Walker, Bos.	1.000	5	4	10	0	1

THIRD BASEMEN

Leader—Club	Pct.	G.	PO.	A.	E.	DP.
CASTINO, Minn.	.975	98	86	224	8	24

(Listed Alphabetically)

Player—Club	Pct.	G.	PO.	A.	E.	DP.
Ainge, Tor.	.949	77	73	133	11	19
Bando, Milw.	.967	15	7	22	1	3
Bell, Tex.	.961	96	66	281	14	18
G. Brett, K.C.	.946	88	74	170	14	7
Brookens, Det.	.952	71	58	139	10	13
Campaneris, Cal.	.900	45	10	44	6	5
Castino, Minn.	.975	98	86	224	8	24
Chalk, K.C.	.955	14	9	12	1	3
Cox, Tor.	.897	14	7	19	3	1
DeCinces, Balt.	.942	100	86	191	17	31
Edler, Sea.	.884	26	18	43	8	4
Gross, Oak.	.946	73	65	127	11	7
Harrah, Clev.	.949	101	63	179	13	12
Hobson, Cal.	.929	83	85	139	17	13
Howell, Milw.	.958	53	38	98	6	9
Iorg, Tor.	.927	17	12	26	3	3
Kelleher, Det.	.930	39	12	28	3	2
Klutts, Oak.	.957	14	7	15	1	1
Lansford, Bos.	.951	86	70	180	13	17
Macha, Tor.	.892	19	5	28	4	2
McKay, Oak.	.926	43	29	59	7	3
Meyer, Sea.	.961	49	36	87	5	12
Money, Milw.	.977	56	27	100	3	8
Morrison, Chi.	.956	87	64	199	12	14
Nettles, N.Y.	.972	97	63	214	8	14
Papi, Det.	.941	32	14	50	4	3
Pryor, Chi.	.931	27	12	42	4	1
Randle, Sea.	.986	59	38	105	2	8
Rodriguez, N.Y.	.951	20	11	28	2	1
Stapleton, Bos.	.946	25	21	49	4	3

TRIPLE PLAY: Harrah.

(Fewer Then Ten Games)

Player—Club	Pct.	G.	PO.	A.	E.	DP.
Anderson, Sea.	1.000	2	0	3	0	1
Baker, Minn.	.500	1	0	1	1	1
Castillo, Det.	1.000	4	3	8	0	3
Dauer, Balt.	1.000	4	0	3	0	0
Dybzinski, Clev.	.800	3	2	2	1	1
Engle, Minn.	.000	1	0	0	0	0
Essian, Chi.	.000	2	0	0	1	0
Fisk, Chi.	1.000	1	1	0	0	0
Gaetti, Minn.	1.000	8	5	17	0	1
Graham, Balt.	.875	4	3	4	1	1
Griffin, Tor.	1.000	4	4	3	0	0
Hatcher, Minn.	1.000	2	1	1	0	0
Hayes, Clev.	.750	5	1	2	1	0
Hill, Chi.	.000	1	0	0	0	0
Hoffman, Bos.	1.000	1	1	1	0	0
R. Jackson, Minn.	.833	3	2	3	1	0
Krenchicki, Balt.	.875	6	2	5	1	0
Loviglio, Chi.	.786	4	4	7	3	2
Lubratich, Cal.	1.000	6	2	17	0	2
Mackanin, Minn.	1.000	4	1	3	0	1
Manrique, Tor.	.000	2	0	0	1	0
Milbourne, N.Y.	1.000	3	2	1	0	1
Mulliniks, K.C.	.900	5	4	5	1	1
Nichols, Bos.	1.000	1	0	1	0	0
Patek, Cal.	.875	7	0	7	1	0
Quirk, K.C.	.857	8	5	13	3	1
Ripken, Balt.	.889	6	2	6	1	1
Romero, Milw.	1.000	3	0	2	0	0
Rosello, Clev.	1.000	8	4	10	0	1
Sexton, Oak.	1.000	1	0	3	0	0
Stein, Tex.	.941	7	4	12	1	0
Tolleson, Tex.	1.000	6	5	8	0	0
Wagner, Tex.	1.000	2	2	4	0	0

SHORTSTOPS

Leader—Club	Pct.	G.	PO.	A.	E.	DP.
YOUNT, Milw.	.985	93	161	370	8	83

(Listed Alphabetically)

Player—Club	Pct.	G.	PO.	A.	E.	DP.
Almon, Chi.	.969	103	190	340	17	78
Anderson, Sea.	.947	68	88	181	15	44

Player—Club	Pct.	G.	PO.	A.	E.	DP.
Auerbach, Sea.	.979	38	44	99	3	26
Baker, Minn.	.969	31	32	61	3	10
Belanger, Balt.	.973	63	86	162	7	21
Burleson, Cal.	.979	109	208	394	13	88
Dent, N.Y.	.970	73	104	217	10	49
Dybzinski, Clev.	.970	34	33	64	3	10

SHORTSTOPS—Continued

Player—Club	Pct.	G.	PO.	A.	E.	DP.
Faedo, Minn.	.971	12	24	42	2	10
Fischlin, Clev.	.955	19	29	35	3	7
Griffin, Tor.	.937	97	186	275	31	64
Hoffman, Bos.	.960	78	131	233	15	52
Krenchicki, Balt.	.964	16	16	37	2	7
Mackanin, Minn.	.935	28	34	53	6	11
Manrique, Tor.	.949	11	10	27	2	7
McHenry, Sea.	.893	13	7	18	3	6
Mendoza, Tex.	.970	88	114	270	12	47
Milbourne, N.Y.	.955	39	37	91	6	15
Picciolo, Oak.	.981	82	99	157	5	30
Pryor, Chi.	.913	13	7	14	2	2
Ripken, Balt.	.946	12	11	24	2	5
Romero, Milw.	.949	22	37	57	5	16
Sakata, Balt.	.963	42	52	106	6	23
Serna, Sea.	.954	23	29	75	5	7
Smalley, Minn.	.946	37	52	89	8	14
Stanley, Oak.	.986	62	94	118	3	25
Stapleton, Bos.	.948	33	52	93	8	18
Trammell, Det.	.983	105	181	347	9	65
Valdez, Bos.	.955	17	12	30	2	3
Veryzer, Clev.	.970	75	121	207	10	48
Wagner, Tex.	.964	43	39	68	4	13
Washington, K.C.	.973	98	135	297	12	58
Washington, Minn.	.951	26	58	79	7	19
Yount, Milw.	.985	93	161	370	8	83

TRIPLE PLAYS: Auerbach, Picciolo.

(Fewer Than Ten Games)

Player—Club	Pct.	G.	PO.	A.	E.	DP.
Ainge, Tor.	.933	6	6	8	1	1
Bannister, Clev.	1.000	1	3	0	0	0
Bell, Tex.	1.000	1	1	3	0	1
Bernazard, Chi.	1.000	1	0	1	0	0
Bonner, Balt.	.976	9	15	26	1	8
Campaneris, Cal.	1.000	3	0	3	0	2
Chalk, K.C.	.000	1	0	0	0	0
Concepcion, K.C.	.000	1	0	0	0	0
Cruz, Sea.	.800	1	1	3	1	0
Edler, Sea.	.000	1	0	0	0	0
Harrah, Clev.	1.000	3	1	1	0	0
Iorg, Tor.	1.000	2	1	4	0	0
Kelleher, Det.	1.000	9	9	31	0	5
McKay, Oak.	1.000	7	6	5	0	0
Mulliniks, K.C.	.966	7	7	21	1	4
Norman, Tex.	.963	5	5	21	1	5
Patek, Cal.	1.000	3	0	4	0	0
Randle, Sea.	.667	3	1	1	1	1
Robertson, N.Y.	1.000	8	7	17	0	2
Rosello, Clev.	.900	4	5	4	1	1
Stein, Tex.	1.000	1	1	0	0	0
Tolleson, Tex.	.000	2	0	0	0	0

OUTFIELDERS

Leader—Club	Pct.	G.	PO.	A.	E.	DP.
SINGLETON, Balt.	1.000	72	125	2	0	2

(Listed Alphabetically)

Player—Club	Pct.	G.	PO.	A.	E.	DP.
Armas, Oak.	.993	109	259	8	2	2
Baines, Chi.°	.985	80	120	10	2	1
Bannister, Clev.	.986	35	70	2	1	0
Barfield, Tor.	1.000	25	71	2	0	1
Bell, Tor.	.969	44	92	3	3	2
Beniquez, Cal.	.959	55	117	0	5	0
Bochte, Sea.°	1.000	14	21	0	0	0
Bonnell, Tor.	.975	66	148	5	4	1
Bosetti, Tor.-Oak.	1.000	24	52	0	0	0
Bosley, Milw.	.966	37	55	1	2	0
Brouhard, Milw.	.990	54	92	7	1	2
Brown, N.Y.	.949	29	54	2	3	0
Brunansky, Cal.	.938	11	27	3	2	1
Bumbry, Balt.	.992	100	255	6	2	2
Burroughs, Sea.	.985	87	127	4	2	1
Charboneau, Clev.	.963	27	51	1	2	0
Clark, Cal.	1.000	34	66	5	0	0
Cowens, Det.	.994	83	166	3	1	0
Dilone, Clev.	.971	56	126	7	4	1
Downing, Cal.	.990	56	97	1	1	0
Dwyer, Balt.°	.977	59	84	2	2	0
Edwards, Milw.°	.979	36	46	1	1	0
Engle, Minn.	.980	76	144	4	3	0
Evans, Bos.	.993	108	259	9	2	1
Ford, Cal.	.960	97	188	3	8	0
Gamble, N.Y.	1.000	43	77	0	0	0
Geronimo, K.C.°	.980	57	96	1	2	0
Gibson, Det.°	.973	67	142	1	4	0
Grubb, Tex.	.990	58	95	2	1	0
Harlow, Cal.°	.981	39	52	1	1	0
Harris, Cal.°	1.000	10	7	0	0	0
Hatcher, Minn.	.992	91	239	3	2	0
Hayes, Clev.	.939	13	29	2	2	1
Henderson, Sea.	1.000	58	105	4	0	1
Henderson, Oak.°	.979	107	327	7	7	0
Hurdle, K.C.	1.000	28	59	1	0	0
Jackson, N.Y.°	.974	61	111	3	3	0
Jones, Det.	.989	60	85	5	1	2
Jones, Tex.°	1.000	10	20	4	0	0
Kemp, Det.°	.986	92	207	4	3	0
Kuntz, Chi.	1.000	51	54	0	0	0
LeFlore, Chi.	.960	82	162	6	7	2
Leach, Det.°	1.000	15	16	0	0	0

Player—Club	Pct.	G.	PO.	A.	E.	DP.
Lemon, Chi.	.984	93	240	2	4	1
Littleton, Clev.	1.000	24	11	0	0	0
Lowenstein, Balt.	.990	73	100	3	1	0
Lynn, Cal.°	.978	69	176	4	4	1
Manning, Clev.	.987	103	305	6	4	3
Meyer, Sea.	.931	14	26	1	2	0
Miller, Bos.°	.987	95	219	5	3	0
Molitor, Milw.	.976	46	119	4	3	1
Moseby, Tor.	.989	100	259	4	3	0
Motley, K.C.	.968	39	88	3	3	1
Mumphrey, N.Y.	.966	79	219	5	8	0
Murphy, Oak.	.985	106	326	6	5	0
Nichols, Bos.	1.000	27	35	3	0	1
Nordhagen, Chi.	.947	60	85	4	5	1
Oglivie, Milw.°	.982	101	211	3	4	1
Orta, Clev.	.994	86	150	11	1	2
Otis, K.C.	.993	97	294	6	2	1
Paciorek, Sea.	.974	103	253	10	7	1
Parsons, Sea.	1.000	24	20	2	0	1
Peters, Det.	.991	38	103	3	1	1
Piniella, N.Y.	.986	36	69	2	1	1
Poquette, Bos.-Tex.	.963	20	26	0	1	0
Powell, Minn.°	.970	64	122	6	4	1
Rice, Bos.	.988	108	237	9	3	0
Rivers, Tex.°	.996	97	225	12	1	3
Roberts, Tex.	.992	71	130	2	1	0
Roenicke, Balt.	.983	83	175	2	3	1
Sample, Tex.	.993	64	132	4	1	1
Simpson, Sea.°	.978	88	219	5	5	1
Singleton, Balt.	1.000	72	125	2	0	2
Sofield, Minn.	.983	34	54	5	1	0
Summers, Det.	.964	18	26	1	1	0
Thomas, Milw.	.979	97	221	8	5	3
Upshaw, Tor.°	1.000	14	14	1	0	1
Ward, Minn.	.975	80	185	8	5	4
Wathan, K.C.	1.000	16	15	2	0	0
Wilson, K.C.	.987	101	299	14	4	3
Winfield, N.Y.	.985	102	196	1	3	0
Woods, Tor.°	.973	77	179	4	5	0

TRIPLE PLAY: Baines.

(Fewer Than Ten Games)

Player—Club	Pct.	G.	PO.	A.	E.	DP.
Ainge, Tor.	1.000	4	8	0	0	0
Allen, Sea.	1.000	2	1	0	0	0
Ayala, Balt.	1.000	4	3	2	0	0
Baylor, Cal.	1.000	1	6	0	0	0

OUTFIELDERS—Continued

Player—Club	Pct.	G.	PO.	A.	E.	DP.
Brown, Det.	1.000	6	2	0	0	0
Castillo, Det.	1.000	1	1	0	0	0
Corey, Balt.	1.000	9	6	1	0	0
Davis, Oak.°	1.000	2	3	0	0	0
DeCinces, Balt.	1.000	1	1	0	0	0
Duran, Tex.°	1.000	7	6	1	0	0
Ferguson, Cal.	1.000	4	6	0	0	0
Fisk, Chi.	1.000	1	1	0	0	0
Funderburk, Minn.	1.000	6	4	1	0	0
Garcia, K.C.°	1.000	6	6	0	0	0
Goodwin, Minn.	1.000	1	1	0	0	0
Gray, Sea.	1.000	4	6	0	0	0
Hairston, Chi.	.933	7	14	0	1	0
Hancock, Bos.°	1.000	8	11	2	0	0
Harper, Cal.	.833	2	5	0	1	0
Heath, Oak.	1.000	6	8	0	0	0
Howell, Milw.	.000	1	0	0	0	0
R. Jackson, Minn.	1.000	7	18	1	0	0
Johnston, Minn.°	1.000	6	11	1	0	1
Kelly, Clev.°	1.000	8	6	0	0	0
Lisi, Tex.	1.000	8	9	0	0	0
McRae, K.C.	.909	4	10	0	1	0
Molinaro, Chi.	1.000	2	3	0	0	0
Moore, Milw.	1.000	8	13	1	0	0
Nettles, Oak.°	.000	1	0	0	0	0
Papi, Det.	.000	1	0	0	0	0
Patterson, Oak.-N.Y.	1.000	9	13	0	0	0

Player—Club	Pct.	G.	PO.	A.	E.	DP.
Pruitt, Clev.	1.000	3	3	0	0	0
Putnam, Tex.	.667	3	2	0	1	0
Quirk, K.C.	.000	1	0	0	0	0
Randle, Sea.	1.000	5	10	0	0	0
Rudi, Bos.	.000	1	0	0	0	0
Shelby, Balt.	1.000	4	1	0	0	0
Sheridan, K.C.	1.000	3	2	0	0	0
Squires, Chi.°	.000	1	0	0	0	0
Stein, Tex.	.933	8	13	1	1	0
Sundberg, Tex.	1.000	2	1	0	0	0
Sutherland, Chi.°	1.000	7	6	0	0	0
Turner, Chi.°	1.000	1	2	0	0	0
Walton, Sea.	.000	4	0	0	0	0
Washington, Minn.	.875	2	6	1	1	0
Werth, N.Y.	1.000	8	7	1	0	0
Williams, Balt.°	1.000	1	1	0	0	0
Wockenfuss, Det.	1.000	1	3	0	0	0

OUTFIELDERS WITH TWO OR MORE CLUBS

Player—Club	Pct.	G.	PO.	A.	E.	DP.
Bosetti, Tor.	1.000	19	40	0	0	0
Bosetti, Oak.	1.000	5	12	0	0	0
Patterson, Oak.	1.000	5	7	0	0	0
Patterson, N.Y.	1.000	4	6	0	0	0
Poquette, Bos.	.000	2	0	0	0	0
Poquette, Tex.	.963	18	26	0	1	0

CATCHERS

Leader—Club	Pct.	G.	PO.	A.	E.	DP.	PB.
DEMPSEY, Balt.	.998	90	384	35	1	6	4

(Listed Alphabetically)

Player—Club	Pct.	G.	PO.	A.	E.	DP.	PB.
Allenson, Bos.	.969	47	235	18	8	3	4
Bando, Clev.	.967	15	53	5	2	0	0
Bulling, Sea.	.977	62	239	21	6	2	4
Butera, Minn.	.970	59	254	41	9	0	1
Cerone, N.Y.	.992	69	353	26	3	1	3
Dempsey, Balt.	.998	90	384	35	1	6	4
Diaz, Clev.	.975	51	247	27	7	0	3
Downing, Cal.	.994	37	140	17	1	2	1
Essian, Chi.	.990	25	92	9	1	0	0
Fahey, Det.	.981	27	96	9	2	3	1
Firova, Sea.	1.000	13	8	0	0	0	1
Fisk, Chi.	.990	95	470	44	5	10	2
Foote, N.Y.	.996	34	227	14	1	3	1
Gedman, Bos.	.990	59	275	30	3	1	3
Graham, Balt.	.975	40	138	20	4	1	7
Grote, K.C.	1.000	22	87	6	0	0	0
Gulden, Sea.	1.000	6	24	3	0	0	0
Hassey, Clev.	.991	56	296	38	3	6	5
Heath, Oak.	.978	78	391	45	10	6	1
Hill, Chi.	1.000	14	11	1	0	0	0
Laudner, Minn.	1.000	12	49	5	0	0	1
Martinez, Tor.	.991	45	192	22	2	3	1
Moore, Milw.	.970	34	147	16	5	0	3
Narron, Sea.	.996	65	248	11	1	3	4
Newman, Oak.	.995	37	182	15	1	2	1
Oates, N.Y.	.963	10	49	3	2	0	0

Player—Club	Pct.	G.	PO.	A.	E.	DP.	PB.
Ott, Cal.	.979	72	287	36	7	1	4
Parrish, Det.	.993	90	407	40	3	6	7
Quirk, K.C.	.985	22	58	9	1	1	5
Schmidt, Bos.	1.000	15	53	4	0	0	2
Simmons, Milw.	.980	75	300	37	7	3	4
Smith, Minn.	1.000	15	65	3	0	0	1
Sundberg, Tex.	.996	98	464	52	2	9	8
Wathan, K.C.	.979	73	300	26	7	1	2
Whitt, Tor.	.991	72	297	46	3	5	3
Wynegar, Minn.	.995	37	162	24	1	4	0
Yost, Milw.	.956	16	37	6	2	2	2

(Fewer Than Ten Games)

Player—Club	Pct.	G.	PO.	A.	E.	DP.	PB.
Castillo, Det.	1.000	1	1	0	0	0	0
Cox, Tex.	1.000	5	33	2	0	0	2
Davis, Cal.	1.000	1	2	0	0	0	0
Dyer, Det.	.000	2	0	0	0	0	0
Ferguson, Cal.	.976	8	35	5	1	1	1
Johnson, Tex.	1.000	5	22	0	0	0	0
Kearney, Oak.	.000	1	0	0	0	0	0
Keatley, K.C.	1.000	2	1	0	0	0	0
Lickert, Bos.	1.000	1	1	0	0	0	0
Macha, Tor.	.000	1	0	0	0	0	0
Pruitt, Clev.	1.000	1	0	0	0	0	0
Royster, Balt.	1.000	4	5	0	0	0	0
Werth, N.Y.	1.000	3	15	1	0	0	1
Whitmer, Tor.	1.000	7	12	3	0	2	0
Wockenfuss, Det.	1.000	5	15	1	0	0	0

PITCHERS

Leaders—Club	Pct.	G.	PO.	A.	E.	DP.
LEONARD, K.C.	1.000	26	13	31	0	3
MORRIS, Detroit	1.000	25	16	28	0	2

(Listed Alphabetically)

Player—Club	Pct.	G.	PO.	A.	E.	DP.
Aase, Calif.	.923	39	2	10	1	1
Abbott, Sea.	.970	22	11	21	1	1
Andersen, Sea.	1.000	41	5	9	0	1
Arroyo, Minn.	1.000	23	7	23	0	1
Augustine, Milw.°	.923	27	1	11	1	2
Babcock, Tex.	1.000	16	2	4	0	0
Bannister, Sea.°	1.000	21	6	15	0	1

Player—Club	Pct.	G.	PO.	A.	E.	DP.
Barker, Clev.	.938	22	9	21	2	1
Barlow, Tor.	1.000	12	0	5	0	0
Baumgarten, Chi.°	1.000	19	7	16	0	1
Beattie, Sea.	.950	13	8	11	1	0
Berenguer, K.C.-Tor.	1.000	20	1	9	0	0
Bird, N.Y.	1.000	17	6	7	0	1
Blyleven, Clev.	.962	20	9	16	1	2
Bomback, Tor.	1.000	20	6	16	0	0
K. Brett, K.C.°	1.000	22	5	6	0	1
Burgmeier, Bos.°	1.000	32	7	13	0	3
Burns, Chi.°	.889	24	0	8	1	0
Caldwell, Milw.°	1.000	24	5	26	0	0
Campbell, Bos.	.917	30	4	7	1	0

PITCHERS—Continued

Player—Club	Pct.	G.	PO.	A.	E.	DP.
Cappuzzello, Det.°	1.000	18	0	5	0	1
Castro, N.Y.	1.000	11	0	3	0	0
Clancy, Tor.	1.000	22	2	10	0	0
Clark, Sea.°	.957	29	0	22	1	0
Clay, Sea.	.941	22	6	10	1	1
Clear, Bos.	1.000	34	5	4	0	0
Cleveland, Milw.	.889	35	3	5	1	1
Comer, Tex.	.958	36	5	18	1	2
Cooper, Minn.	1.000	27	1	6	0	0
Corbett, Minn.	.935	54	7	22	2	0
Crawford, Bos.	1.000	14	8	8	0	1
Darwin, Tex.	.923	22	8	16	2	3
Davis, N.Y.	1.000	43	4	5	0	0
Denny, Clev.	.947	19	14	40	3	7
Dotson, Chi.	1.000	24	7	20	0	4
Drago, Sea.	1.000	39	1	11	0	1
Easterly, Milw.°	1.000	44	7	10	0	0
Eckersley, Bos.	.969	23	12	19	1	1
Erickson, Minn.	.913	14	8	13	2	1
Farmer, Chi.	.933	42	5	9	1	1
Fingers, Milw.	.938	47	2	13	1	1
Flanagan, Balt.°	.966	20	4	24	1	1
Ford, Balt.	1.000	15	2	5	0	0
Forsch, Calif.	.955	20	18	24	2	2
Frazier, N.Y.	.833	16	1	4	1	0
Frost, Calif.	1.000	12	1	9	0	0
Galasso, Sea.	1.000	13	3	4	0	0
Gale, K.C.	.933	19	6	8	1	1
Garland, Clev.	1.000	12	4	11	0	0
Garvin, Tor.°	1.000	35	1	9	0	2
Gleaton, Sea.°	.944	20	5	12	1	0
Gossage, N.Y.	.900	32	2	7	1	1
Guidry, N.Y.°	1.000	23	13	17	0	1
Gura, K.C.°	1.000	23	9	30	0	4
Haas, Milw.	.969	24	16	15	1	1
Hammaker, K.C.°	1.000	10	1	4	0	1
Hassler, Calif.°	1.000	42	4	14	0	1
Havens, Minn.°	1.000	14	1	11	0	1
Hickey, Chi.°	1.000	41	3	11	0	0
Honeycutt, Tex.°	.917	20	3	30	3	1
Hough, Tex.	1.000	21	2	8	0	1
Hoyt, Chi.	1.000	43	6	8	0	1
Jackson, Tor.	.938	39	5	10	1	0
D. Jackson, Minn.°	1.000	14	0	2	0	0
Jefferson, Calif.	.850	26	11	6	3	2
Jenkins, Tex.	1.000	19	10	22	0	3
John, N.Y.°	1.000	20	11	27	0	2
J. Johnson, Tex.°	1.000	24	1	7	0	1
Jones, Oak.	1.000	33	2	6	0	0
Jones, K.C.°	1.000	12	3	14	0	0
Keeton, Milw.	1.000	17	2	6	0	2
Keough, Oak.	.920	19	10	13	2	2
Kern, Tex.	.857	23	3	3	1	0
Kingman, Oak.	.867	18	4	9	2	0
Kison, Calif.	1.000	11	3	9	0	1
Koosman, Minn.-Chi.°	.960	27	7	17	1	0
LaRoche, N.Y.°	1.000	26	5	4	0	0
Lacey, Clev.-Tex.°	1.000	15	2	3	0	0
Lamp, Chi.	.966	27	5	23	1	4
Langford, Oak.	.929	24	16	23	3	3
Leal, Tor.	1.000	29	4	19	0	0
Leonard, K.C.	1.000	26	13	31	0	3
Lerch, Milw.°	.962	23	4	21	1	1
Lopez, Det.	1.000	29	5	10	0	1
Martin, K.C.	.900	29	3	15	2	1
F. Martinez, Balt.°	.842	37	3	13	3	0
J. D. Martinez, Balt.	.970	25	20	44	2	4
Matlack, Tex.°	.917	17	2	20	2	0
May, N.Y.°	.975	27	11	28	1	0
McCatty, Oak.	.974	22	11	26	1	2
McGlothen, Chi.	1.000	11	3	1	0	0
McGregor, Balt.°	1.000	24	8	29	0	2
McLaughlin, Tor.	1.000	40	7	6	0	0
McLaughlin, Oak.	1.000	11	2	1	0	0
Medich, Tex.	.976	20	15	26	1	1
Monge, Clev.°	1.000	31	5	4	0	0
Morris, Det.	1.000	25	16	28	0	2
Murray, Tor.	.889	11	2	6	1	0

Player—Club	Pct.	G.	PO.	A.	E.	DP.
Norris, Oak.	.976	23	16	25	1	0
O'Connor, Minn.°	.833	28	2	8	2	3
Ojeda, Bos.°	.929	10	3	10	1	1
Owchinko, Oak.°	.857	29	0	6	1	1
Palmer, Balt.	1.000	22	12	26	0	2
Parrott, Sea.	1.000	24	6	15	0	0
Petry, Det.	.976	23	14	26	1	6
Quisenberry, K.C.	.969	40	8	23	1	1
Rainey, Bos.	.875	11	5	9	2	0
Rawley, Sea.°	1.000	46	1	14	0	1
Redfern, Minn.	1.000	24	6	18	0	0
Renko, Calif.	1.000	22	2	10	0	0
Reuschel, N.Y.	1.000	12	6	14	0	0
Righetti, N.Y.°	.938	15	6	9	1	0
Rozema, Det.	.952	28	5	15	1	0
Sanchez, Calif.	.778	17	1	6	2	0
Saucier, Det.°	.867	38	3	10	2	1
Schatzeder, Det.°	.857	17	6	12	3	0
Schmidt, Tex.	1.000	14	1	6	0	0
Schneider, Balt.°	.667	11	2	2	2	0
Slaton, Milw.	1.000	24	14	14	0	3
Spillner, Clev.	.957	32	6	16	1	1
Splittorff, K.C.°	1.000	21	2	22	0	2
Stanley, Bos.	.951	35	10	29	2	6
Stanton, Clev.	1.000	24	3	3	0	0
Stewart, Balt.	.963	29	12	14	1	3
Stieb, Tor.	.980	25	11	38	1	3
Stoddard, Balt.	1.000	31	4	3	0	1
Stone, Balt.	1.000	15	3	10	0	0
Tanana, Bos.°	.971	24	9	25	1	2
Tobik, Det.	1.000	27	2	3	0	0
Todd, Tor.	.969	21	11	20	1	0
Torrez, Bos.	.893	22	12	13	3	2
Trout, Chi.°	.929	20	3	23	2	5
Tudor, Bos.°	1.000	18	2	17	0	1
Underwood, N.Y.-Oak.°	.882	25	2	13	2	1
Verhoeven, Minn.	1.000	25	0	11	0	1
Vuckovich, Milw.	1.000	24	11	27	0	1
Waits, Clev.°	1.000	22	12	28	0	2
Wilcox, Det.	.950	24	5	33	2	1
Williams, Minn.	.880	23	9	13	3	2
Willis, Tor.°	1.000	20	3	5	0	1
Witt, Calif.	.885	22	7	16	3	0
Wright, K.C.	1.000	17	2	6	0	0
Zahn, Calif.°	.927	25	7	31	3	2

(Fewer Than Ten Games)

Player—Club	Pct.	G.	PO.	A.	E.	DP.
Agosto, Chi.°	1.000	2	0	1	0	0
Allard, Sea.	.909	7	4	6	1	1
Aponte, Bos.	1.000	7	1	6	0	0
Bailey, Det.°	1.000	9	2	11	0	0
Barrios, Chi.	.875	8	1	6	1	0
Beard, Oak.	1.000	8	2	1	0	0
Bernard, Milw.	.000	6	0	0	0	0
Black, Sea.°	1.000	2	0	1	0	0
Boddicker, Balt.	.500	2	1	0	1	0
Bordi, Oak.	.000	2	0	0	0	0
Brennan, Clev.	.944	7	5	12	1	2
Butcher, Tex.	1.000	5	3	5	0	0
D'Acquisto, Calif.	1.000	6	1	1	0	0
DiPino, Milw.°	.000	2	0	0	0	0
Espinosa, Tor.	.000	1	0	0	0	0
Felton, Minn.	.000	1	0	0	0	0
Figueroa, Oak.	1.000	2	1	1	0	0
Glynn, Clev.°	.000	4	0	0	0	0
Griffin, N.Y.	1.000	2	0	2	0	0
Heaverlo, Oak.	.000	6	0	0	0	0
Hobbs, Minn.°	1.000	4	1	0	0	0
Hurst, Bos.°	1.000	5	0	2	0	0
Kinney, Det.°	1.000	6	1	0	0	0
Lewallyn, Clev.	1.000	7	0	1	0	0
Luebber, Minn.	1.000	7	3	3	0	0
Mahler, Calif.°	1.000	6	0	1	0	0
Martinez, Calif.	1.000	2	0	2	0	0
McClure, Milw.°	1.000	4	1	0	0	0
McGaffigan, N.Y.	.000	2	0	2	0	0
Mercer, Tex.°	1.000	7	0	2	0	0

PITCHERS—Continued

Player—Club	Pct.	G.	PO.	A.	E.	DP.
Minetto, Oak.°	.000	8	0	0	0	0
Mirabella, Tor.°	1.000	8	1	0	0	0
Moore, Milw.	1.000	3	1	1	0	0
Moreno, Calif.°	.833	8	0	5	1	0
Mueller, Milw.	1.000	1	1	0	0	0
Nelson, N.Y.	.900	8	3	6	1	0
Paschall, K.C.	.000	2	0	0	0	0
Patterson, Chi.	1.000	6	0	3	0	0
Porter, Milw.	.000	3	0	0	0	0
Rau, Calif.°	1.000	3	1	0	0	0
Robinson, Chi.	1.000	4	1	0	0	0
Rothschild, Det.	1.000	5	1	3	0	0
Rucker, Det.°	1.000	2	1	0	0	0
Schattinger, K.C.	.000	1	0	0	0	0
Stein, Sea.	1.000	5	0	2	0	1
Stoddard, Sea.	1.000	5	0	6	0	0
Travers, Calif.°	1.000	4	1	1	0	0
Ujdur, Det.	1.000	4	1	3	0	0
Veselic, Minn.	1.000	5	1	1	0	0
Wehrmeister, N.Y.	1.000	5	1	2	0	0
Whitehouse, Tex.°	.000	2	0	0	0	0

PITCHERS WITH TWO OR MORE CLUBS

Player—Club	Pct.	G.	PO.	A.	E.	DP.
Berenguer, K.C.	.000	8	0	0	0	0
Berenguer, Tor.	1.000	12	1	9	0	0
Koosman, Minn.	.952	19	5	15	1	0
Koosman, Chi.	1.000	8	2	2	0	0
Lacey, Clev.	1.000	14	1	3	0	0
Lacey, Tex.	1.000	1	1	0	0	0
Underwood, N.Y.	.857	9	2	4	1	0
Underwood, Oak.	.900	16	0	9	1	1

Royals second baseman Frank White has won five straight Gold Gloves.

OFFICIAL AMERICAN LEAGUE PITCHING AVERAGES

CLUB PITCHING

Club	ERA.	G.	CG.	Sv.	ShO.	IP.	H.	BFP.	R.	ER.	HR.	SH.	SF.	Tot. BB.	Int. BB.	HB.	SO.	WP.	Bk.
New York	2.90	107	16	30	13	948	827	3872	343	305	64	32	30	287	17	10	606	25	5
Oakland	3.30	109	60	10	11	993	883	4166	403	364	80	50	32	370	17	28	505	30	11
Texas	3.40	105	23	18	13	940⅓	851	3909	389	355	67	50	23	322	34	17	488	18	2
Chicago	3.47	106	20	23	8	940⅔	891	3964	423	363	73	39	23	336	17	24	529	24	6
Detroit	3.53	109	33	22	13	969⅓	840	4030	404	380	83	36	34	373	41	27	476	24	5
Kansas City	3.56	103	24	24	8	922⅓	909	3878	405	365	75	41	44	273	36	20	404	13	4
Baltimore	3.70	105	25	23	10	940	923	3970	437	386	83	32	27	347	22	14	489	29	5
California	3.70	110	27	19	8	971⅓	958	4089	453	399	81	36	34	323	24	21	426	18	5
Boston	3.81	108	19	24	8	987⅓	983	4213	481	418	90	49	29	354	28	28	536	18	1
Toronto	3.82	106	20	18	4	953⅓	908	4089	466	404	72	33	36	377	27	14	451	41	4
Cleveland	3.88	103	33	13	10	931	989	4003	442	401	67	47	37	311	15	10	569	30	2
Milwaukee	3.91	109	11	35	4	986	994	4181	459	428	72	34	34	352	33	11	448	31	2
Minnesota	3.98	110	13	22	6	979⅔	1021	4230	486	433	79	45	35	376	53	17	500	19	14
Seattle	4.23	110	10	23	5	997⅓	1039	4274	521	469	76	36	32	360	26	16	478	40	7
Totals	3.66	750	334	304	117	13459⅔	13016	56868	6112	5470	1062	564	450	4761	390	279	6905	359	73

(BFP total includes one batsman awarded first base because of interference.)

NOTE—Totals for earned runs for several clubs do not agree with the composite totals for all pitchers of each respective club due to instances in which provisions of Section 10.18 (i) of the Scoring Rules were applied. The following differences are to be noted: Boston pitchers add to 420; California, 400; Chicago, 366; Detroit, 381; Seattle, 470.

PITCHERS' RECORDS
(Top Fifteen Qualifiers for Earned-Run Leadership)

Pitcher and Club	ERA.	W.	L.	Pct.	G.	GS.	CG.	GF.	Sv.	ShO.	IP.	H.	R.	ER.	BFP.	HR.	SH.	SF.	Tot. BB.	Int. BB.	HB.	SO.	WP.	Bk.
McCatty, Steven, Oakland	2.32	14	7	.667	22	22	16	0	0	4	186	140	50	48	741	12	8	6	61	1	2	91	0	0
Stewart, Samuel, Baltimore	2.33	4	8	.333	29	3	0	18	4	0	112	89	33	29	463	8	4	3	57	3	1	57	1	2
Lamp, Dennis, Chicago	2.41	7	6	.538	27	10	3	5	0	0	127	103	41	34	514	4	5	0	43	1	1	71	4	1
John, Thomas, New York°	2.64	9	8	.529	20	20	7	0	0	1	140	135	50	41	580	10	8	2	39	2	1	50	0	2
Burns, R. Britt, Chicago°	2.64	10	6	.625	24	23	5	0	0	2	157	139	52	46	651	14	5	6	49	1	6	108	6	1
Gura, Lawrence, Kansas City°	2.72	11	8	.579	23	23	12	0	1	2	172	139	61	52	680	11	9	4	35	0	1	61	3	0
Guidry, Ronald, New York°	2.76	11	5	.688	23	21	3	0	0	2	127	100	41	39	497	12	1	9	27	4	1	104	0	0
Forsch, Kenneth, California	2.88	11	7	.611	20	20	10	0	0	4	153	143	54	49	616	7	8	5	27	2	4	55	0	1
Blyleven, Rikalbert, Cleveland	2.89	11	7	.611	20	20	9	0	0	1	159	145	52	51	644	9	3	6	40	1	5	107	3	1
Leonard, Dennis, Kansas City	2.99	13	11	.542	26	26	9	0	0	2	202	202	79	67	837	15	5	8	41	5	3	107	5	0
Langford, J. Rick, Oakland	3.00	12	10	.545	24	24	18	0	0	0	195	190	81	65	823	14	8	8	58	2	3	84	1	1
Petry, Daniel, Detroit	3.00	10	9	.526	23	22	7	1	0	2	141	115	53	47	583	10	9	8	57	4	1	79	3	0
Wilcox, Milton, Detroit	3.04	12	9	.571	24	24	8	0	0	0	166	152	61	56	686	15	8	5	52	1	6	79	4	0
Morris, John, Detroit	3.05	14	7	.667	25	25	15	0	0	1	198	153	69	67	798	14	8	9	78	11	2	97	2	2
Medich, George, Texas	3.08	10	6	.625	20	20	0	4	0	4	143	136	51	49	585	8	8	2	33	5	2	65	1	0

°Throws lefthanded.

DEPARTMENTAL LEADERS: W—J. Dennis Martinez, McCatty, Morris, Vuckovich, 14; L—Berenguer, Koosman, Leal, 13; Pct.—Vuckovich, .778; G—Corbett, 54; GS—Leonard, 26; CG—Langford, 18; GF—Corbett, 45; Sv—Fingers, 28; ShO—Dotson, Forsch, McCatty, Medich, 4; IP—Leonard, 202; H—Leonard, 837; R—Zahn, 93; ER—Zahn, 79; HR—Caldwell, Zahn, 18; SH—Splittorff, 11; SF—Gura, Morris, 9; Tot. BB—Morris, 78; Int. BB—Corbett, 13; HB—Stieb, Witt, 11; SO—Barker, 127; WP—Norris, 14; Bk—Erickson, Norris, 5.

(All Pitchers—Listed Alphabetically)

Pitcher and Club	ERA.	W.	L.	Pct.	G.	GS.	CG.	GF.	Sv.	ShO.	IP.	H.	BFP.	R.	ER.	HR.	SH.	SF.	Tot. BB.	Int. BB.	HB.	SO.	WP.	Bk.
Aase, Donald, California	2.35	4	4	.500	39	0	0	32	11	0	65	56	265	17	17	4	1	1	24	2	1	38	2	0
Abbott, W. Glenn, Seattle	3.95	4	9	.308	22	20	1	1	0	0	130	127	530	64	57	14	6	4	28	1	0	35	1	0
Agosto, Juan, Chicago°	4.50	0	2	.000	2	0	0	1	0	0	6	5	22	3	3	0	1	0	5	0	1	3	0	0
Allard, Brian, Seattle	3.75	3	2	.600	7	7	1	0	0	0	48	48	191	22	20	4	5	0	18	0	1	20	0	0
Andersen, Larry, Seattle	2.65	3	3	.500	41	0	0	23	5	0	68	57	273	27	20	0	2	3	3	2	0	40	0	0
Aponte, Luis, Boston	0.56	1	0	1.000	7	0	0	3	0	0	16	11	57	1	1	1	0	0	3	0	1	11	3	0
Arroyo, Fernando, Minnesota	3.94	7	10	.412	23	19	2	1	0	0	128	144	542	66	56	11	1	2	34	3	1	39	3	0
Augustine, Gerald, Milwaukee°	4.28	2	2	.500	27	2	0	9	1	0	61	75	272	30	29	7	5	1	18	3	1	26	1	0
Babcock, Robert, Texas	2.17	1	1	.500	16	0	0	7	0	0	29	21	117	7	7	2	2	0	16	1	1	18	1	0
Bailey, Howard, Detroit°	7.30	1	4	.200	9	5	0	2	0	0	37	45	165	31	30	4	3	2	13	3	1	17	7	1
Bannister, Floyd, Seattle	4.46	9	9	.500	21	20	5	0	0	2	121	128	522	62	60	14	6	4	39	0	3	85	5	0
Barker, Leonard, Cleveland	3.92	8	7	.533	22	22	5	0	0	3	154	150	660	72	67	7	7	2	46	1	1	127	1	0
Barlow, Michael, Toronto	4.20	0	0	.000	12	0	0	7	2	0	15	22	78	11	7	1	6	4	6	1	4	5	1	0
Barrios, Francisco, Chicago	4.00	1	3	.250	8	7	1	0	0	0	36	45	170	23	16	3	1	2	14	1	1	12	4	2
Baumgarten, Ross, Chicago°	4.06	5	9	.357	19	19	2	0	0	0	102	101	435	56	46	9	4	2	40	1	1	52	2	1
Beard, David, Oakland	2.77	3	3	.500	8	0	0	7	3	0	13	9	53	5	4	1	0	1	4	0	2	15	2	0
Beattie, James, Seattle	2.96	3	2	.600	13	13	1	0	0	1	67	59	275	24	22	2	3	0	18	1	0	36	3	0
Berenguer, Juan, K.C.-Tor.	5.24	2	13	.133	20	14	0	3	0	0	91	84	405	62	53	11	3	7	51	1	5	49	6	1
Bernard, Dwight, Milwaukee	3.60	0	1	.000	6	0	0	4	1	0	5	5	27	3	2	0	1	2	6	3	0	1	0	0
Bird, J. Douglas, New York	2.72	5	1	.833	17	4	0	3	0	0	53	58	229	19	16	5	1	6	16	0	3	28	1	1
Black, Harry, Seattle°	0.00	0	0	.000	2	0	0	0	0	0	1	2	7	0	0	0	0	0	3	0	0	0	3	0
Blyleven, Rikalbert, Cleveland	2.89	11	7	.611	20	20	9	0	0	1	159	145	644	52	51	9	3	5	40	1	5	107	2	1
Boddicker, Michael, Baltimore	4.50	0	0	.000	2	2	0	0	0	0	6	6	25	4	3	1	0	0	2	0	0	2	6	0
Bomback, Mark, Toronto	3.90	5	5	.500	20	11	1	3	0	0	90	84	377	42	39	6	5	3	35	2	1	33	0	1
Bordi, Richard, Oakland	0.00	0	0	.000	7	0	0	0	0	0	2	1	8	0	0	0	0	0	1	0	0	0	0	0
Brennan, Thomas, Cleveland	3.19	2	2	.500	22	7	0	7	0	0	48	49	205	20	17	5	5	2	14	4	4	15	0	0
Brett, Kenneth, Kansas City°	4.22	1	1	.500	32	6	1	14	0	0	32	35	144	16	15	5	2	0	14	4	4	7	1	0
Burgmeier, Thomas, Boston°	2.85	4	5	.444	24	0	0	21	6	0	60	61	255	23	19	5	6	2	17	4	1	35	1	0
Burns, R. Britt, Chicago°	2.64	10	6	.625	24	23	5	0	0	1	157	139	651	52	46	14	5	6	49	1	0	108	3	0
Butcher, John, Texas	1.61	1	2	.333	5	5	3	0	0	1	28	18	106	6	5	0	10	0	8	4	0	19	1	0
Caldwell, R. Michael, Milwaukee°	3.94	11	9	.550	24	23	3	0	7	0	144	151	609	70	63	18	3	2	38	4	0	41	3	1
Campbell, William, Boston	3.19	1	1	.500	30	0	0	23	7	0	48	45	208	23	17	5	2	2	20	2	0	37	4	0
Cappuzzello, George, Detroit°	3.44	1	1	.500	18	3	0	5	0	0	34	28	146	14	13	2	2	0	18	2	0	19	2	0
Castro, William, New York	3.79	1	1	.500	11	0	0	6	1	0	19	26	86	13	8	2	1	0	5	1	0	4	0	0
Clancy, James, Toronto	4.90	6	12	.333	22	22	2	0	0	0	125	126	556	77	68	12	2	4	64	2	5	56	12	0
Clark, Bryan, Seattle°	4.35	2	5	.286	29	14	0	5	2	0	93	92	421	54	45	7	2	3	55	3	2	52	7	0
Clay, Kenneth, Seattle	4.63	2	7	.222	34	0	0	20	0	0	101	116	445	62	52	10	4	2	42	3	1	32	5	0
Clear, Mark, Boston	4.09	8	3	.727	35	0	0	22	9	0	77	69	346	36	35	11	4	0	51	2	3	82	8	0
Cleveland, Reginald, Milwaukee	5.12	2	3	.400	36	1	0	11	2	0	65	57	274	41	37	1	4	4	30	8	1	18	2	3
Comer, Steven, Texas	2.57	8	2	.800	27	22	3	0	0	1	77	70	330	25	22	5	3	2	31	1	1	22	2	0
Cooper, Donald, Minnesota	4.27	1	5	.167	36	0	0	11	0	0	59	61	262	33	28	5	3	5	32	2	1	33	1	0
Corbett, Douglas, Minnesota	2.56	2	6	.250	54	0	0	45	17	0	88	80	377	29	25	10	5	4	34	13	0	60	2	0
Crawford, Steve, Boston	4.97	0	5	.000	14	11	0	0	0	0	58	69	257	38	32	12	3	4	18	3	3	29	1	0
D'Acquisto, John, California	10.89	0	0	.000	6	0	0	2	0	0	19	26	95	24	23	2	4	3	12	1	0	8	4	0
Darwin, Danny, Texas	3.64	9	9	.500	22	22	6	0	0	0	146	115	601	67	59	6	4	3	57	3	6	98	1	1
Davis, Ronald, New York	2.71	4	5	.444	43	0	0	22	6	0	73	47	285	22	22	6	2	5	25	5	3	83	1	1
Denny, John, Cleveland	3.14	10	6	.625	19	19	6	0	0	3	146	139	623	62	51	9	2	5	66	3	3	94	10	0
DiPino, Frank, Milwaukee°	0.00	0	0	.000	2	0	0	2	0	0	2	0	10	5	0	0	0	0	3	0	0	3	0	0

Pitcher and Club	ERA.	W.	L.	Pct.	G.	GS.	CG.	GF.	Sv.	ShO.	IP.	H.	BFP.	R.	ER.	HR.	SH.	SF.	Tot. BB.	Int. BB.	HB.	SO.	WP.	Bk.
Dotson, Richard, Chicago	3.77	9	8	.529	24	24	5	0	0	4	141	145	599	67	59	13	4	5	49	0	4	73	2	2
Drago, Richard, Seattle	5.50	4	6	.400	39	0	0	24	5	0	54	71	240	33	33	4	2	4	15	5	5	27	2	0
Easterly, James, Milwaukee°	3.19	3	3	.500	44	0	0	16	4	0	62	46	253	23	22	0	4	5	34	8	0	31	1	0
Eckersley, Dennis, Boston	4.27	9	8	.529	23	23	8	0	0	2	154	160	649	82	73	9	6	5	35	2	3	79	2	5
Erickson, Roger, Minnesota	3.86	3	8	.273	14	14	1	0	0	0	91	93	399	48	39	7	7	6	31	4	0	44	2	0
Espinosa, Arnulfo, Toronto	9.00	0	0	.000	1	0	0	0	0	0	1	4	6	3	1	0	0	0	0	0	1	0	0	0
Farmer, Edward, Chicago	4.58	3	3	.500	42	0	0	25	10	0	53	53	243	33	27	5	0	6	34	1	1	42	3	0
Felton, Terry, Minnesota	54.00	0	0	.000	1	0	0	0	0	0	1	8	10	6	6	1	4	0	2	0	0	1	0	0
Figueroa, Eduardo, Oakland	5.63	0	3	.000	2	1	0	0	0	0	8	8	37	5	5	1	0	0	6	0	1	1	1	0
Fingers, Roland, Milwaukee	1.04	6	3	.667	47	0	0	41	28	0	78	55	297	9	9	3	4	2	13	5	2	61	6	0
Flanagan, Michael, Baltimore°	4.19	9	6	.600	20	20	5	0	0	2	116	108	482	55	54	11	3	5	37	1	4	72	0	0
Ford, David, Baltimore	6.53	1	2	.333	15	2	0	4	0	0	40	61	185	33	29	7	0	0	10	3	0	12	0	0
Forsch, Kenneth, California	2.88	11	7	.611	20	20	10	0	0	4	153	143	616	54	49	7	8	5	27	2	4	55	1	0
Frazier, George, New York	1.61	0	3	.000	16	0	0	9	3	0	28	26	117	7	5	3	0	0	11	2	0	17	1	0
Frost, David, California	5.55	1	8	.111	16	9	0	1	0	0	47	44	200	30	29	3	2	1	19	0	2	16	0	0
Galasso, Robert, Seattle	4.78	1	1	.500	13	1	0	4	1	1	32	32	136	19	17	2	1	2	13	1	0	14	0	0
Gale, Richard, Kansas City	5.38	6	6	.500	19	15	2	0	0	0	102	107	440	63	61	14	1	0	38	0	2	47	3	0
Garland, M. Wayne, Cleveland	5.79	3	7	.300	12	10	2	0	0	0	56	89	264	40	36	8	6	2	14	2	0	15	0	2
Garvin, T. Jared, Toronto°	3.40	3	6	.333	35	4	0	11	0	0	53	46	221	20	20	4	4	4	23	2	2	25	3	0
Gleaton, Jerry, Seattle°	4.76	4	7	.364	20	13	0	3	0	0	85	88	369	50	45	10	3	3	38	2	0	31	3	0
Glynn, Edward, Cleveland	1.13	0	2	.000	4	0	0	3	0	0	8	5	30	1	1	0	0	1	4	0	1	4	0	0
Gossage, Richard, New York	0.77	3	2	.600	32	0	0	30	20	0	47	22	173	6	4	1	1	0	14	1	0	48	1	0
Griffin, Michael, New York	2.25	0	2	.000	4	0	0	1	0	0	4	5	18	1	1	0	0	0	2	0	1	4	0	0
Guidry, Ronald, New York°	2.76	11	5	.688	23	21	12	1	0	2	127	100	497	41	39	12	9	6	26	4	0	104	6	0
Gura, Lawrence, Kansas City°	2.72	11	8	.579	24	23	12	0	0	2	172	139	680	61	52	11	5	6	35	4	0	61	3	0
Haas, Bryan, Milwaukee	4.47	11	7	.611	24	22	6	0	0	0	137	146	583	69	68	8	5	1	40	8	0	64	3	1
Hammaker, C. Atlee, Kansas City°	5.54	1	3	.250	10	6	0	2	0	0	39	44	169	24	24	2	1	2	12	1	0	11	0	0
Hassler, Andrew, California°	3.20	4	3	.571	42	12	0	21	5	1	76	72	315	29	27	8	5	3	33	8	0	44	3	1
Havens, Bradley, Minnesota°	3.58	3	6	.333	14	12	0	0	0	0	76	76	323	33	31	6	8	4	24	4	1	43	3	2
Heaverlo, David, Oakland	1.50	1	0	1.000	6	0	0	3	0	0	6	7	27	1	1	0	0	0	3	1	1	2	0	0
Hickey, Kevin, Chicago°	3.68	0	2	.000	41	0	0	14	1	0	44	38	188	22	18	3	3	1	18	5	1	17	1	0
Hobbs, John, Minnesota°	3.00	0	2	.000	4	0	0	1	0	0	6	7	29	2	2	0	0	0	6	1	1	1	1	0
Honeycutt, Frederick, Texas°	3.30	11	6	.647	20	20	5	0	0	2	128	120	509	49	47	12	5	2	17	1	3	40	4	0
Hough, Charles, Texas	2.96	4	1	.800	21	5	0	9	2	0	82	61	330	30	27	4	5	4	31	1	3	69	3	2
Hoyt, D. Lamarr, Chicago	3.56	9	3	.750	43	11	7	0	0	3	91	80	371	40	36	10	0	2	28	3	1	60	2	0
Hurst, Bruce, Boston°	4.30	2	2	.500	5	5	1	0	0	0	23	23	104	11	11	1	1	0	12	2	1	11	1	0
Jackson, Darrell, Minnesota°	4.36	4	8	.333	14	5	0	3	0	0	33	35	145	16	16	1	3	1	19	1	1	26	5	0
Jackson, Roy, Toronto	2.61	1	2	.333	39	0	0	21	7	0	62	65	266	23	18	5	4	5	25	7	1	27	4	0
Jefferson, Jesse, California	3.62	9	8	.529	26	16	0	5	0	0	77	80	333	39	31	14	5	6	24	4	0	63	2	2
Jenkins, Ferguson, Texas	4.50	5	8	.385	19	19	0	0	0	0	106	122	467	55	53	10	8	4	40	4	3	50	6	0
John, Thomas, New York°	2.64	9	8	.529	20	20	0	0	0	0	140	135	580	50	41	7	8	5	39	2	3	8	1	0
Johnson, John, Texas°	2.63	4	1	.800	24	0	0	15	7	0	61	51	273	27	23	7	8	3	40	4	3	43	3	2
Jones, Jeffrey, Oakland	3.39	6	3	.667	12	10	4	0	0	1	61	51	158	27	23	7	3	3	11	0	7	29	1	3
Jones, Michael, Kansas City°	3.20	3	1	.750	17	11	0	8	0	0	76	74	323	30	27	7	8	2	28	7	0	9	1	0
Keough, Matthew, Oakland	5.14	10	6	.625	19	19	10	0	0	1	140	125	579	56	53	11	4	1	45	0	0	60	1	2
Keeton, Rickey, Milwaukee	3.41	1	2	.333	14	0	0	15	6	0	35	47	131	21	20	0	6	1	22	3	1	20	5	0
Kern, James, Texas	2.70	3	6	.333	23	0	0	3	6	1	30	21	135	10	9	0	4	2	32	2	4	52	3	0
Kingman, Brian, Oakland	3.96	3	6	.333	18	15	3	0	0	1	100	112	435	48	44	10	0	1	32	1	0	52	0	0
Kinney, Dennis, Detroit°	9.00	0	0	.000	6	0	0	1	0	0	4	5	20	4	4	0	0	2	4	1	0	3	0	0

Pitcher and Club	ERA	W	L	Pct.	G	GS	CG	GF	Sv.	ShO	IP	H	BFP	R	ER	HR	SH	SF	Tot. BB	Int. BB	HB	SO	WP	Bk.
Kison, Bruce, California	3.48	1	1	.500	11	4	0	4			44	40	180	18	17	8	0	0	14	1	0	19	1	0
Koosman, Jerry, Minn.-Chicago	4.02	4	13	.235	27	16	3	3		1	121	125	517	59	54	10	7	5	41	1	7	76	2	1
LaRoche, David, New York°	2.49	4	1	.800	26	1	0	14	5		47	38	192	16	13	3	5	3	16	1	0	24	1	0
Lacey, Robert, Cleveland-Texas°	7.77	0	1	.000	15	1	0	8			22	37	107	21	19	6	0	3	9	0	1	11	1	1
Lamp, Dennis, Chicago	2.41	7	6	.538	27	24	3	0		1	127	103	514	41	34	4	4	8	43	1	1	71	4	1
Langford, J. Rick, Oakland	3.00	12	10	.545	24	24	18	0		2	195	190	823	81	65	14	8	6	58	8	5	84	1	0
Leal, Luis, Toronto	3.67	7	13	.350	24	19	3	4	1		130	127	562	63	53	8	7	6	44	5	5	71	8	1
Leonard, Dennis, Kansas City	2.99	13	11	.542	29	26	9	1			202	202	837	79	67	15	5	5	41	2	3	107	5	1
Lerch, Randy, Milwaukee°	4.30	7	9	.438	26	18	1	4			111	134	495	63	53	8	5	1	43	5	0	53	6	0
Lewallyn, Dennis, Cleveland	5.54	0	2	.000	23	0	0	19			13	16	57	8	8	1	1	4	2	0	0	11	0	0
Lopez, Aurelio, Detroit	3.62	5	2	.714	7	3	0	0	3		82	70	338	34	33	3	0	4	31	2	0	53	1	1
Luebber, Stephen, Baltimore°	7.41	0	0	.000	29	0	0	7			17	26	77	14	14	0	2	0	4	0	0	12	0	0
Mahler, Michael, California°	0.00	0	0	.000	6	0	0	12	4		6	1	20	0	0	0	2	0	2	0	2	5	2	0
Martin, D. Renie, Kansas City	2.76	4	5	.444	29	0	0	24	11	2	62	55	264	25	19	10	3	7	29	7	0	25	6	1
Martinez, Alfredo, California	3.00	0	5	.000	29	9	0	1	0		57	48	248	21	19	4	8	3	32	2	2	50	3	0
Martinez, Felix, Baltimore°	2.90	3	3	.500	11	0	0	1	0		6	5	25	2	2	1	0	0	3	0	0	4	0	0
Martinez, J. Dennis, Baltimore	3.32	14	5	.737	25	24	9	0	0	2	179	173	753	84	66	19	8	6	62	5	0	88	6	0
Matlack, Jonathon, Texas°	4.15	4	7	.364	16	16	4	0	0	0	104	101	447	59	48	8	6	6	41	0	1	43	0	1
May, Rudolph, New York°	4.14	6	11	.353	27	22	0	1	0	0	148	137	610	71	68	8	8	2	61	2	2	79	3	0
McCatty, Steven, Oakland	2.32	14	7	.667	22	22	16	0	0	4	186	140	741	50	48	12	6	9	61	2	0	91	1	1
McClure, Robert, Milwaukee°	3.38	0	0	.000	24	0	0	2	2	0	22	8	34	3	3	1	3	1	7	0	0	6	2	0
McGaffigan, Andrew, New York	2.57	0	0	.000	7	0	0	4	0	0	22	14	83	10	10	0	7	3	7	0	3	12	1	0
McGlothen, Lynn, Chicago	4.09	13	5	.722	24	22	8	2	0	3	160	167	664	63	58	13	5	6	40	5	0	82	3	0
McGregor, Scott, Baltimore°	3.26	1	5	.167	40	0	0	26	10	0	60	55	249	24	19	3	2	1	21	1	2	38	1	0
McLaughlin, Joey, Toronto	2.85	10	6	.625	11	0	0	4	0	0	12	17	61	15	15	1	8	0	9	0	0	65	0	0
McLaughlin, Michael, Oakland	11.25	0	1	.000	20	20	4	0	2	0	143	136	585	51	49	8	8	2	33	5	2	8	5	0
Medich, George, Texas	3.08	0	0	.000	7	0	0	0	0	0	8	7	36	4	4	0	5	0	7	0	0	4	0	0
Mercer, Mark, Texas°	4.50	0	1	.000	8	0	0	2	2	0	7	7	31	2	2	0	0	1	4	1	0	9	0	0
Minetto, Craig, Oakland°	2.57	3	5	.375	8	1	0	2	0	0	15	20	73	16	12	2	0	1	21	1	1	41	2	0
Mirabella, Paul, Toronto°	7.20	0	0	.000	31	0	0	20	0	0	58	58	244	31	28	9	1	3	7	2	0	12	1	2
Monge, Isidro, Cleveland°	4.34	3	5	.375	8	4	1	2	0	0	31	4	19	10	10	0	0	2	14	0	0	12	2	0
Moore, Donnie, Milwaukee°	6.75	4	3	.000	8	0	0	8	0	0	15	27	131	10	10	2	3	1	3	0	2	97	2	0
Moreno, Angel, California°	2.90	14	7	.000	25	4	0	2	0	0	39	153	798	69	67	14	11	7	78	11	0	12	0	0
Morris, John, Detroit	3.05	0	8	.667	25	25	15	2	0	0	198	153	10	1	1	0	0	0	4	0	0	16	11	0
Mueller, Willard, Milwaukee	4.50	1	0	1.000	11	0	0	7	0	0	35	12	62	11	11	0	9	2	5	0	0	12	0	0
Murray, Dale, Toronto	1.20	12	3	.750	8	8	0	0	2	0	39	40	179	24	21	5	6	3	23	6	0	16	2	0
Nelson, W. Eugene, New York	4.85	3	9	.571	23	23	12	0	0	2	173	145	721	77	72	17	4	2	63	0	10	78	14	5
Norris, Michael, Oakland	3.75	12	9	.571	28	28	12	0	0	0	173	145	721	77	72	17	4	4	63	0	2	78	14	0
O'Connor, Jack, Minnesota°	5.91	3	2	.600	28	10	0	11	0	0	66	50	267	27	23	3	3	6	30	6	1	16	6	0
Ojeda, Robert, Boston°	3.14	6	3	.750	10	10	2	0	0	2	66	50	267	25	23	6	4	0	25	3	1	28	2	1
Owchinko, Robert, Oakland°	3.23	4	3	.571	29	0	0	12	2	0	39	34	164	15	14	2	2	2	19	1	1	26	1	0
Palmer, James, Baltimore	3.76	7	8	.467	22	22	5	0	0	1	127	117	532	60	53	14	4	4	46	1	0	35	3	1
Parrott, Michael, Seattle	5.08	3	6	.333	24	12	0	6	0	0	85	102	378	51	48	3	3	6	28	1	0	43	3	1
Paschall, William, Kansas City	4.50	0	0	.000	2	0	0	2	0	0	2	2	7	1	1	0	0	0	0	0	0	1	0	0
Patterson, Reginald, Chicago	14.14	0	1	.000	6	1	0	1	0	0	7	14	40	11	11	0	7	2	6	1	0	1	0	0
Petry, Daniel, Detroit	3.00	10	9	.526	23	22	7	0	0	1	141	115	583	53	47	10	9	4	57	0	0	79	3	1
Porter, Charles, Milwaukee	4.50	0	0	.000	3	0	0	0	0	0	4	6	20	2	2	3	5	2	1	0	1	1	1	0
Quisenberry, Daniel, Kansas City	1.74	1	4	.200	40	0	0	35	18	0	62	59	254	16	12	1	4	4	15	0	8	20	0	0
Rainey, Charles, Boston	2.70	0	1	.000	11	2	0	3	0	0	40	39	171	21	12	2	2	2	13	0	0	20	1	0

Pitcher and Club	ERA.	W.	L.	Pct.	G.	GS.	CG.	GF.	Sv.	ShO.	IP.	H.	BFP	R.	ER.	HR.	SH.	SF.	BB.	Tot. BB.	Int. BB.	HB	SO.	WP.	Bk.
Rau, Douglas, California °	9.00	1	2	.333	3	3	0	0	0	0	10	14	45	10	10	2	2	0	3		1		3	0	0
Rawley, Shane, Seattle °	3.97	4	6	.400	46	3	0	28	8	0	68	64	295	31	30	1	4	4	38	6	1		35	8	0
Redfern, Peter, Minnesota	4.06	9	8	.529	24	23	3	0	0	0	142	140	601	70	64	12	4	4	52	1	1		77	2	1
Renko, Steven, California	3.44	4	8	.667	22	15	3	0	0	0	102	93	424	40	39	7	6	2	42	2	1		50	2	0
Reuschel, Ricky, New York °	2.66	4	4	.500	12	11	2	0	0	0	71	75	282	24	21	4	1	2	10	1	0		22	0	0
Righetti, David, New York °	2.06	8	4	.667	15	15	2	0	0	0	105	75	422	25	24	1	3	2	38	0	1		89	1	1
Robinson, Dewey, Chicago	4.50	0	0	1.000	4	0	0	1	0	0	4	5	18	2	2	0	0	2	1	0	1		2	0	0
Rothschild, Lawrence, Detroit	1.50	0	0	.000	5	0	0	5	0	0	6	4	27	1	1	0	2	0	2	1	0		1	2	0
Rozema, David, Detroit °	3.63	5	5	.500	28	9	2	1	0	2	104	99	419	42	42	12	4	2	25	8	1		46	0	0
Rucker, David, Detroit	6.75	0	0	.000	2	0	0	0	0	0	4	3	18	4	3	0	1	0	1	0	0		2	1	0
Sanchez, Luis, California	2.91	0	4	.000	17	0	0	12	3	0	34	26	150	16	11	4	4	0	11	3	0		13	2	0
Saucier, Kevin, Detroit °	1.65	4	2	.667	38	0	0	23	13	0	49	39	189	11	9	1	1	0	21	3	2		23	0	0
Schattinger, Jeffery, Kansas City	0.00	0	0	.000	1	0	0	0	0	0	3	2	14	0	0	0	0	0	1	0	0		1	3	0
Schmidt, Daniel, Detroit °	6.08	6	8	.429	17	14	1	1	0	0	71	74	318	49	48	13	4	0	29	3	1		20	3	1
Schmidt, David J., Texas	3.09	0	1	.000	14	0	0	8	1	0	32	31	132	11	11	4	3	1	11	1	1		13	5	0
Schneider, Jeffery, Baltimore °	4.88	0	0	.000	11	1	0	7	0	0	24	27	109	15	13	4	1	0	12	3	0		17	5	0
Slaton, James, Milwaukee	4.38	5	7	.417	24	21	1	0	0	0	117	120	500	60	57	10	3	6	50	3	0		47	3	1
Spillner, Daniel, Cleveland	3.15	4	4	.500	32	5	1	21	7	0	97	86	410	41	34	3	5	7	23	0	2		59	0	2
Splittorff, Paul, Kansas City °	4.36	5	5	.500	21	15	1	1	0	0	99	111	419	48	48	12	11	7	23	4	0		48	1	1
Stanley, Robert, Boston	3.82	6	8	.556	35	0	0	14	0	0	99	110	430	46	42	4	8	2	38	4	0		28	1	2
Stanton, Michael, Cleveland	4.40	3	3	.500	24	0	0	15	4	0	43	43	185	21	21	4	8	1	18	6	0		34	3	0
Stein, W. Randolph, Seattle	11.00	0	1	.000	5	3	0	1	0	0	9	18	51	12	11	1	0	1	8	0	0		6	0	0
Stewart, Samuel, Baltimore	2.33	11	8	.333	29	3	0	18	8	0	112	89	463	33	29	8	4	3	57	4	3		57	1	0
Stieb, David, Toronto	3.18	2	10	.524	25	25	11	0	0	2	184	148	748	70	65	10	5	7	61	0	11		89	1	0
Stoddard, Robert, Seattle	2.57	1	2	.667	5	5	1	0	0	0	35	35	141	16	10	1	3	0	9	0	0		22	1	0
Stoddard, Timothy, Baltimore	3.89	4	1	.667	31	0	0	20	7	0	37	38	162	16	16	6	4	0	18	2	1		32	2	0
Stone, Steven, Baltimore °	4.57	4	7	.364	15	12	5	0	0	2	63	63	270	39	32	7	7	4	27	0	2		30	2	0
Tanana, Frank, Boston °	4.02	4	10	.286	24	23	5	0	0	0	141	142	596	70	63	17	9	2	43	3	4		78	2	0
Tobik, David, Detroit	2.70	2	0	.500	27	0	0	9	0	0	60	47	258	19	18	7	6	4	33	3	0		32	1	0
Todd, Jackson, Toronto	3.95	2	7	.222	21	13	3	3	0	0	98	94	415	51	43	10	3	3	31	2	0		41	3	0
Torrez, Michael, Boston	3.69	10	3	.769	22	22	2	0	0	0	127	130	542	61	52	10	4	2	51	2	0		54	1	0
Travers, William, California °	8.10	0	1	.000	4	0	0	0	0	0	10	14	46	11	9	1	4	0	7	0	0		5	0	1
Trout, Steven, Chicago °	3.46	8	7	.533	20	18	3	0	1	0	125	122	517	53	48	8	2	4	38	4	0		54	2	1
Tudor, John, Boston °	4.56	4	3	.571	18	11	1	3	0	0	79	74	331	44	40	11	6	2	28	0	3		44	1	4
Ujdur, Gerald, Detroit	6.43	0	0	.000	4	4	1	0	0	0	14	19	65	12	10	2	6	0	5	1	0		5	1	0
Underwood, Thomas, N.Y.-Oak. °	3.64	4	6	.400	25	11	2	6	0	1	84	69	351	38	34	6	5	4	38	2	2		75	2	0
Verhoeven, John, Minnesota	3.98	3	4	.429	25	0	0	15	0	0	52	57	223	27	23	8	1	2	14	0	4		16	1	0
Veselic, Robert, Minnesota	3.13	1	1	.500	5	0	0	3	0	0	23	22	102	8	8	1	7	1	12	2	0		13	2	0
Vuckovich, Peter, Milwaukee	3.54	14	4	.778	24	23	8	0	0	0	150	137	620	61	59	9	5	5	57	1	1		84	1	0
Waits, M. Richard, Cleveland °	4.93	8	10	.444	22	21	4	0	1	0	126	173	578	74	69	9	7	5	44	2	0		51	5	0
Wehrmeister, David, New York °	5.14	0	0	.000	5	0	0	2	0	0	7	8	33	4	4	4	0	2	7	0	0		7	1	0
Whitehouse, Leonard, Texas °	18.00	0	1	.000	2	0	0	0	0	0	3	7	20	7	6	0	1	0	2	0	0		2	0	0
Wilcox, Milton, Detroit	3.04	12	9	.571	24	24	8	0	0	1	166	152	686	61	56	10	8	5	52	3	6		79	4	3
Williams, Alberto, Minnesota	4.08	6	10	.375	23	22	2	1	0	0	150	160	640	72	68	11	3	5	52	4	1		76	2	0
Willis, Michael, Toronto °	5.91	8	8	.500	20	20	1	0	0	0	35	43	168	25	23	9	2	3	20	1	0		16	2	0
Witt, Michael, California	3.28	8	9	.471	22	21	7	0	1	1	129	123	555	60	47	6	4	4	47	4	7		75	2	0
Wright, James, Kansas City	3.46	2	3	.400	17	4	0	7	0	0	52	57	230	21	20	5	0	2	21	7	2		27	0	0
Zahn, Geoffrey, California °	4.42	10	11	.476	25	25	9	0	0	0	161	181	689	93	79	18	8	2	43	2	0		52	2	2

NOTE—Following pitchers combined to pitch shutout games: Baltimore (3)—J. Dennis Martinez and F. Martinez, Stone and Ford; California (3)—Rau and Aase, Frost and Hassler, Moreno and Aase; Chicago (2)—Baumgarten and Hoyt 2; Cleveland (1)—Waits and Monge; Detroit (7)—Wilcox and Saucier 2, Wilcox, Saucier and Lopez, Lopez and Saucier, Schatzeder and Tobik, Petry, Rozema and Saucier, Morris and Rozema; Kansas City (4)—Splittorff and Martin, Gura and Martin, Jones and Quisenberry, Splittorff, Wright and Hammaker; Milwaukee (3)—Vuckovich, Easterly and Fingers, Lerch and Fingers, Vuckovich, Easterly and McClure; Minnesota (4)—Erickson and Corbett, D. Jackson and Koosman, Arroyo and Koosman, D. Jackson and Corbett; New York (13)—Righetti and Gossage 2, Bird, Castro and Gossage, John and Gossage, Nelson, Davis and Gossage, Righetti and Davis, Bird, Davis and Gossage, John, Davis and May, Guidry, Frazier, Wehrmeister and Davis, Guidry and Frazier, Reuschel, May and Frazier, Guidry, Davis and Gossage, May and Davis; Seattle (3)—Bannister, Drago and Rawley, Abbott and Clark, Bannister and Rawley; Texas (3)—Medich and J. Johnson, Jenkins, Comer and Babcock, Honeycutt, Kern, J. Johnson and Schmidt; Toronto (2)—Garvin, Barlow, Willis, Leal and McLaughlin, Leal and McLaughlin.

PITCHERS WITH TWO OR MORE CLUBS
(Alphabetically Arranged With Pitcher's First Club on Top)

Pitcher and Club	ERA.	W.	L.	Pct.	G.	GS.	CG.	GF.	Sv.	ShO.	IP.	H.	BFP.	R.	ER.	HR.	SH.	SF.	Tot. BB.	Int. BB.	HB.	SO.	WP.	Bk.
Berenguer, Kansas City	8.55	0	4	.000	8	3	0	4	0	0	20	22	97	21	19	4	2	3	16	0	2	20	1	0
Berenguer, Toronto	4.31	2	9	.182	12	11	1	0	0	0	71	62	308	41	34	7	2	4	35	1	3	29	1	0
Koosman, Minnesota	4.21	3	9	.250	19	13	2	5	1	1	94	98	404	49	44	8	5	5	34	7	0	55	1	1
Koosman, Chicago	3.33	1	4	.200	8	3	1	4	5	0	27	27	113	10	10	2	2	0	7	0	0	21	1	0
Lacey, Cleveland	7.71	0	0	.000	14	0	0	7	0	0	21	36	103	20	18	5	0	3	3	0	0	11	0	0
Lacey, Texas	9.00	0	0	.000	1	0	0	1	0	0	1	1	4	1	1	1	0	0	0	0	0	0	1	0
Underwood, New York	4.36	1	4	.200	9	6	0	1	1	0	33	32	138	17	16	2	3	3	13	1	0	29	1	0
Underwood, Oakland	3.18	3	2	.600	16	5	1	5	1	0	51	37	213	21	18	4	3	0	25	1	2	46	2	4

1981 A.L. Pitching Against Each Club

BALTIMORE—59-46

Pitcher	Bos. W-L	Cal. W-L	Chi. W-L	Clev. W-L	Det. W-L	K.C. W-L	Mil. W-L	Min. W-L	N.Y. W-L	Oak. W-L	Sea. W-L	Tex. W-L	Tor. W-L	Totals W-L
Flanagan...	1-0	0-2	0-0	0-0	1-0	1-2	0-1	1-0	1-0	2-0	0-0	0-1	2-0	9- 6
Ford..........	0-0	0-0	0-1	0-0	0-0	0-0	0-0	1-0	0-1	0-0	0-0	0-0	0-0	1- 2
D. Martinez	0-1	3-1	2-0	1-0	2-1	0-0	1-0	2-0	0-1	1-0	1-1	1-0	0-0	14- 5
T. Martinez	0-0	0-0	0-0	0-0	0-1	2-0	0-1	0-0	1-1	0-0	0-0	0-0	0-0	3- 3
McGregor ..	0-0	3-0	1-1	2-0	1-3	1-0	0-0	0-0	2-0	1-1	0-0	0-0	2-0	13- 5
Palmer	0-0	0-2	0-0	1-0	0-1	0-1	1-1	1-0	2-0	1-2	0-0	0-0	1-1	7- 8
Stewart	0-0	0-0	0-2	0-1	1-1	0-0	0-0	1-0	1-2	1-1	0-1	0-0	0-0	4- 8
Stoddard ...	1-1	0-0	0-0	0-0	1-0	0-0	0-0	0-0	0-0	0-1	2-0	0-0	0-0	4- 2
Stone	0-0	0-1	0-2	0-1	0-0	1-0	0-1	0-0	0-1	1-0	1-0	1-0	0-1	4- 7
Totals	2-2	6-6	3-6	4-2	6-7	5-3	2-4	6-0	7-6	7-5	4-2	2-1	5-2	59-46

No Decisions: Boddicker, Luebber, Schneider.

BOSTON—59-49

Pitcher	Balt. W-L	Cal. W-L	Chi. W-L	Clev. W-L	Det. W-L	K.C. W-L	Mil. W-L	Min. W-L	N.Y. W-L	Oak. W-L	Sea. W-L	Tex. W-L	Tor. W-L	Totals W-L
Aponte	0-0	0-0	0-0	0-0	0-0	0-0	1-0	0-0	0-0	0-0	0-0	0-0	0-0	1- 0
Burgmeier..	0-0	0-1	0-0	0-0	1-0	1-1	0-1	0-1	0-0	0-0	1-0	0-1	1-0	4- 5
Campbell ...	0-0	0-0	0-0	0-0	0-0	0-0	0-0	1-0	0-0	0-1	0-0	0-0	0-0	1- 1
Clear..........	0-0	0-0	2-0	2-1	0-0	1-0	1-1	0-0	0-0	0-1	1-0	0-0	1-0	8- 3
Crawford	0-1	0-0	0-0	0-0	0-0	0-0	0-1	0-1	0-0	0-1	0-0	0-1	0-0	0- 5
Eckersley...	1-0	1-0	1-1	1-3	1-0	1-1	1-0	0-1	0-1	2-0	0-0	0-1	0-0	9- 8
Hurst.........	0-0	0-0	0-0	0-0	0-0	0-0	0-0	0-0	1-0	0-0	1-0	0-0	0-0	2- 0
Ojeda........	0-0	1-0	1-0	0-0	1-1	0-0	0-0	0-0	1-0	1-0	1-0	0-0	0-0	6- 2
Rainey.......	0-0	0-1	0-0	0-0	0-0	0-0	0-0	0-0	0-0	0-0	0-0	0-0	0-0	0- 1
Stanley......	1-0	0-1	1-2	1-0	2-0	0-0	0-3	0-0	0-1	2-0	1-1	1-0	1-0	10- 8
Tanana......	0-1	0-1	0-1	1-0	0-0	0-1	0-1	0-1	0-1	1-2	2-1	0-0	0-0	4-10
Torrez.......	0-0	0-0	0-0	2-1	1-0	0-0	2-0	1-1	0-0	1-0	1-0	1-1	1-0	10- 3
Tudor	0-0	0-0	0-0	0-1	0-0	0-0	1-0	0-0	1-0	0-0	1-1	1-1	0-0	4- 3
Totals	2-2	2-4	5-4	7-6	6-1	3-3	6-7	2-5	3-3	7-5	9-3	3-6	4-0	59-49

No Decisions: None.

CALIFORNIA—51-59

Pitcher	Balt. W-L	Bos. W-L	Chi. W-L	Clev. W-L	Det. W-L	K.C. W-L	Mil. W-L	Min. W-L	N.Y. W-L	Oak. W-L	Sea. W-L	Tex. W-L	Tor. W-L	Totals W-L
Aase..........	0-0	1-0	0-1	1-0	0-0	0-0	0-0	0-0	0-0	0-1	2-1	0-1	0-0	4- 4
Forsch.......	1-1	2-0	0-1	1-1	1-0	0-0	1-1	1-0	1-0	1-1	1-1	0-0	1-1	11- 7
Frost.........	0-2	0-1	0-1	0-2	0-1	0-0	0-1	0-0	0-0	0-0	0-0	0-0	1-1	1- 8
Hassler......	1-0	0-0	0-0	1-0	1-0	0-1	0-0	0-0	0-0	0-1	1-0	0-1	0-0	4- 3
Jefferson ...	0-0	1-0	0-0	0-0	0-0	0-0	0-1	0-1	1-0	0-0	0-2	0-0	0-0	2- 4
Kison.........	0-0	0-0	1-1	0-0	0-0	0-0	0-0	0-0	0-0	0-0	0-0	0-0	0-0	1- 1
Moreno	0-0	0-0	1-0	0-0	0-0	0-1	0-0	0-0	0-0	0-0	0-0	0-1	0-1	1- 3
Rau...........	1-0	0-0	0-0	0-0	0-1	0-0	0-0	0-0	0-0	0-0	0-0	0-0	0-1	1- 2
Renko	1-0	0-0	1-1	2-1	0-1	0-0	1-1	0-0	0-0	1-0	0-0	1-0	1-0	8- 4
Sanchez....	0-0	0-0	0-0	0-0	0-0	0-0	0-0	0-1	0-0	0-1	0-0	0-0	0-0	0- 2
Travers......	0-0	0-0	0-0	0-0	0-0	0-0	0-0	0-1	0-0	0-0	0-0	0-0	0-0	0- 1
Witt	1-2	0-1	3-0	0-0	0-1	0-1	1-0	1-0	0-1	0-2	0-0	1-0	1-1	8- 9
Zahn	1-1	0-0	0-2	2-1	1-0	0-2	1-0	1-0	0-1	0-2	2-0	0-1	2-1	10-11
Totals	6-6	4-2	6-7	7-5	3-3	0-6	4-3	3-3	2-2	2-8	6-4	2-4	6-6	51-59

No Decisions: D'Acquisto, Mahler, Martinez.

CHICAGO—54-52

Pitcher	Balt. W-L	Bos. W-L	Cal. W-L	Clev. W-L	Det. W-L	K.C. W-L	Mil. W-L	Min. W-L	N.Y. W-L	Oak. W-L	Sea. W-L	Tex. W-L	Tor. W-L	Totals W-L
Barrios......	1-1	0-0	0-0	0-1	0-0	0-0	0-0	0-0	0-0	0-1	0-0	0-0	0-0	1- 3
B'garten....	0-0	0-1	1-1	0-2	1-1	0-0	1-0	0-0	0-1	1-1	0-0	1-1	0-1	5- 9
Burns........	1-0	0-0	2-1	0-1	1-0	0-0	0-1	2-0	1-1	1-0	1-1	1-1	1-0	10- 6
Dotson	3-0	0-1	1-1	1-0	0-0	1-0	0-1	0-1	0-1	2-1	0-1	0-1	1-0	9- 8
Farmer......	1-0	0-1	0-0	0-0	0-0	0-0	0-0	0-0	0-0	1-0	0-0	0-1	1-1	3- 3
Hickey.......	0-0	0-0	0-0	0-0	0-0	0-0	0-0	0-1	0-1	0-0	0-0	0-0	0-0	0- 2
Hoyt..........	0-1	1-1	1-0	0-0	1-0	0-0	2-0	1-0	1-0	1-0	0-0	0-0	1-1	9- 3
Koosman ...	0-0	0-0	0-0	0-0	0-2	0-0	0-0	0-1	0-0	1-0	0-1	0-0	0-0	1- 4
Lamp.........	0-0	1-0	1-1	0-1	0-0	1-0	1-0	0-0	1-1	0-1	1-1	0-0	1-1	7- 6
Patterson ..	0-0	0-1	0-0	0-0	0-0	0-0	0-0	0-0	0-0	0-0	0-0	0-0	0-0	0- 1
Robinson ...	0-0	0-0	0-0	0-0	0-0	0-0	0-0	1-0	0-0	0-0	0-0	0-0	0-0	1- 0
Trout.........	0-1	2-0	1-2	1-0	0-0	0-0	0-0	0-0	1-3	0-1	1-0	0-0	2-0	8- 7
Totals	6-3	4-5	7-6	2-5	3-3	2-0	4-1	2-4	5-7	7-6	3-3	2-4	7-5	54-52

No Decisions: Agosto, McGlothen.

CLEVELAND—52-51

Pitcher	Balt. W-L	Bos. W-L	Cal. W-L	Chi. W-L	Det. W-L	K.C. W-L	Mil. W-L	Min. W-L	N.Y. W-L	Oak. W-L	Sea. W-L	Tex. W-L	Tor. W-L	Totals W-L
Barker	0-2	0-0	0-3	1-0	0-0	1-0	1-0	1-0	2-0	1-0	1-1	0-1	1-0	8- 7
Blyleven	1-0	0-2	1-1	1-0	0-1	0-1	1-1	0-0	1-0	0-1	3-0	1-0	2-0	11- 7
Brennan	0-0	0-1	1-0	0-0	0-1	0-0	0-0	0-0	1-0	0-0	0-0	0-0	0-0	2- 2
Denny	1-0	0-1	2-1	1-0	1-0	1-1	0-2	0-0	2-1	1-0	1-0	0-0	0-0	10- 6
Garland	0-0	1-1	0-0	0-1	0-0	0-0	1-1	1-0	0-1	0-0	0-1	0-1	0-1	3- 7
Monge	0-0	1-1	0-1	0-0	0-1	0-0	0-0	1-1	0-0	0-0	1-1	0-0	0-0	3- 5
Spillner	0-0	2-1	1-1	0-0	0-1	0-0	0-0	0-0	0-1	1-0	0-0	0-0	0-0	4- 4
Stanton	0-1	0-0	0-0	1-0	0-0	1-0	0-1	0-0	0-0	0-0	1-1	0-0	0-0	3- 3
Waits	0-1	2-0	0-0	1-1	0-1	1-2	0-1	0-0	1-2	0-1	1-0	1-0	1-1	8-10
Totals	2-4	6-7	5-7	5-2	1-5	4-4	3-6	2-1	7-5	3-2	8-4	2-2	4-2	52-51

No Decisions: Glynn, Lacey, Lewallyn.

DETROIT—60-49

Pitcher	Balt. W-L	Bos. W-L	Cal. W-L	Chi. W-L	Clev. W-L	K.C. W-L	Mil. W-L	Min. W-L	N.Y. W-L	Oak. W-L	Sea. W-L	Tex. W-L	Tor. W-L	Totals W-L
Bailey	0-0	0-0	0-0	0-0	0-0	0-0	0-1	0-0	0-2	0-0	0-0	0-0	1-1	1- 4
Cappuzzello	1-1	0-0	0-0	0-0	0-0	0-0	0-0	0-0	0-0	0-0	0-0	0-0	0-0	1- 1
Lopez	1-0	0-0	0-1	0-0	0-0	1-1	0-0	0-0	1-0	0-0	0-0	2-0	0-0	5- 2
Morris	2-0	1-1	2-0	0-1	1-0	0-0	1-2	3-0	0-1	0-0	1-0	2-0	1-2	14- 7
Petry	1-1	0-1	0-0	1-0	1-0	0-0	1-3	3-0	0-1	0-1	1-1	2-1	0-0	10- 9
Rozema	0-1	0-0	0-0	0-1	1-0	1-0	1-0	0-1	0-1	0-1	1-0	1-0	0-0	5- 5
Saucier	0-1	0-0	0-1	0-0	1-0	1-0	0-0	0-1	0-0	0-0	0-0	1-0	1-0	4- 2
Schatzeder	0-1	0-0	0-1	0-0	1-1	0-1	1-0	1-1	1-1	0-0	0-0	1-1	1-1	6- 8
Tobik	1-0	0-2	1-0	0-0	0-0	0-0	0-0	0-0	0-0	0-0	0-0	0-0	0-0	2- 2
Wilcox	1-1	0-2	0-1	1-1	1-0	0-0	1-2	2-0	1-1	1-0	2-0	0-1	2-0	12- 9
Totals	7-6	1-6	3-3	3-3	5-1	3-2	5-8	9-3	3-7	1-2	5-1	9-3	6-4	60-49

No Decisions: Kinney, Rothschild, Rucker, Ujdur.

KANSAS CITY—50-53

Pitcher	Balt. W-L	Bos. W-L	Cal. W-L	Chi. W-L	Clev. W-L	Det. W-L	Mil. W-L	Min. W-L	N.Y. W-L	Oak. W-L	Sea. W-L	Tex. W-L	Tor. W-L	Totals W-L
Berenguer	0-0	0-0	0-0	0-0	0-1	0-0	0-0	0-0	0-0	0-0	0-2	0-1	0-0	0- 4
K. Brett	0-0	0-0	0-0	0-0	0-0	1-0	0-0	0-0	0-0	0-0	0-0	0-0	0-1	1- 1
Gale	1-1	0-0	1-0	0-1	0-0	0-0	0-1	2-0	0-2	0-0	1-0	0-1	1-0	6- 6
Gura	1-1	2-0	0-0	0-0	1-0	1-1	2-1	2-0	1-1	0-1	0-2	1-1	0-0	11- 8
Hammaker	0-0	0-0	1-0	0-0	0-0	0-0	0-0	0-1	0-1	0-1	0-0	0-0	0-0	1- 3
Jones	0-0	0-0	1-0	0-0	1-0	0-0	0-0	0-1	1-0	0-1	2-0	0-0	1-1	6- 3
Leonard	1-1	1-1	2-0	0-0	1-1	0-0	0-3	2-2	0-1	2-0	1-1	2-0	1-1	13-11
Martin	0-1	0-1	1-0	0-0	0-1	0-0	0-0	1-0	0-2	0-0	0-0	0-0	2-0	4- 5
Quisenberry	0-0	0-1	0-0	0-0	0-0	0-2	1-0	0-0	0-1	0-0	0-0	0-0	0-0	1- 4
Splittorff	0-0	0-0	0-0	0-1	1-1	0-0	1-0	0-0	0-2	1-0	2-0	0-1	0-0	5- 5
Wright	0-1	0-0	0-0	0-0	0-0	0-0	0-0	2-0	0-0	0-0	0-2	0-0	0-0	2- 3
Totals	3-5	3-3	6-0	0-2	4-4	2-3	4-5	9-4	2-10	3-3	6-7	3-4	5-3	50-53

No Decisions: Paschall, Schattinger.

MILWAUKEE—62-47

Pitcher	Balt. W-L	Bos. W-L	Cal. W-L	Chi. W-L	Clev. W-L	Det. W-L	K.C. W-L	Min. W-L	N.Y. W-L	Oak. W-L	Sea. W-L	Tex. W-L	Tor. W-L	Totals W-L
Augustine	0-0	0-0	1-0	0-0	0-0	0-2	0-0	1-0	0-0	0-0	0-0	0-0	0-0	2- 2
Caldwell	0-1	0-0	1-1	0-0	2-1	2-0	1-0	2-2	1-1	0-1	0-0	0-1	2-1	11- 9
Cleveland	0-0	0-0	0-0	0-1	0-0	0-1	0-0	0-0	0-0	1-0	0-0	0-0	1-1	2- 3
Easterly	0-0	0-1	1-0	0-0	0-0	1-0	0-0	0-0	0-0	0-0	1-0	0-0	0-2	3- 3
Fingers	1-0	2-1	0-0	0-1	0-0	1-0	0-1	2-0	0-0	0-0	0-0	0-0	0-0	6- 3
Haas	0-1	1-2	1-1	0-0	1-0	2-0	1-1	0-0	1-0	1-0	0-1	2-1	1-0	11- 7
Keeton	0-0	0-0	0-0	0-0	1-0	0-0	0-0	0-0	0-0	0-0	0-0	0-0	0-0	1- 0
Lerch	1-0	1-1	0-1	0-0	0-1	1-1	1-1	0-0	1-1	0-1	0-1	0-1	2-0	7- 9
Slaton	0-0	0-1	0-1	0-1	2-1	0-1	1-0	2-1	0-0	0-0	0-0	0-1	0-0	5- 7
Vuckovich	2-0	2-0	0-0	1-1	0-0	1-0	1-1	2-0	0-1	2-0	1-0	2-1	0-0	14- 4
Totals	4-2	7-6	3-4	1-4	6-3	8-5	5-4	9-3	3-3	4-2	2-2	4-5	6-4	62-47

No Decisions: Bernard, DiPino, McClure, D. Moore, Mueller, Porter.

MINNESOTA—41-68

Pitcher	Balt. W-L	Bos. W-L	Cal. W-L	Chi. W-L	Clev. W-L	Det. W-L	K.C. W-L	Mil. W-L	N.Y. W-L	Oak. W-L	Sea. W-L	Tex. W-L	Tor. W-L	Totals W-L
Arroyo	0-0	1-1	1-0	0-0	0-0	1-0	0-3	1-3	0-0	0-0	0-2	2-0	1-1	7-10
Cooper	0-0	0-1	0-0	0-0	0-0	0-1	0-1	0-1	1-0	0-0	0-1	0-0	0-0	1- 5
Corbett	0-0	1-0	1-0	0-1	0-0	0-0	0-1	0-1	0-0	0-1	0-1	0-1	0-0	2- 6
Erickson	0-2	1-0	0-1	0-0	0-0	0-1	0-0	1-0	0-0	1-1	0-1	0-2	0-0	3- 8
Havens	0-0	0-0	0-0	0-0	0-0	1-2	0-2	0-1	0-0	0-0	0-1	0-0	2-0	3- 6
D. Jackson	0-0	0-0	0-0	0-0	0-0	0-1	0-0	0-0	1-0	1-0	0-0	0-2	1-0	3- 3
Koosman	0-2	0-0	0-1	0-0	0-1	0-2	1-0	0-0	0-0	0-2	1-0	1-1	0-0	3- 9
O'Connor	0-1	0-0	0-0	0-0	1-0	0-0	1-1	0-0	1-0	0-0	0-0	0-0	0-0	3- 2
Redfern	0-1	1-0	1-0	2-0	0-1	1-2	1-0	0-1	0-1	0-1	1-0	2-1	0-0	9- 8
Veselic	0-0	0-0	0-0	1-1	0-0	0-0	0-0	0-0	0-0	0-0	0-0	0-0	0-0	1- 1
Williams	0-0	1-0	0-1	1-0	0-0	0-0	1-1	1-2	0-2	0-3	1-0	0-1	1-0	6-10
Totals	0-6	5-2	3-3	4-2	1-2	3-9	4-9	3-9	3-3	2-8	3-6	5-8	5-1	41-68

No Decisions: Felton, Hobbs, Verhoeven.

NEW YORK—59-48

Pitcher	Balt. W-L	Bos. W-L	Cal. W-L	Chi. W-L	Clev. W-L	Det. W-L	K.C. W-L	Mil. W-L	Min. W-L	Oak. W-L	Sea. W-L	Tex. W-L	Tor. W-L	Totals W-L
Bird	0-0	0-0	0-0	1-1	1-0	1-0	1-0	0-0	0-0	0-0	1-0	0-0	0-0	5- 1
Castro	0-0	0-0	0-0	0-0	0-0	0-0	1-0	0-0	0-0	0-0	0-0	0-1	0-0	1- 1
Davis	2-0	1-1	0-0	0-1	0-0	0-1	0-0	0-0	0-0	1-0	0-2	0-0	0-0	4- 5
Frazier	0-0	0-0	0-0	0-0	0-0	0-0	0-0	0-0	0-1	0-0	0-0	0-0	0-0	0- 1
Gossage	1-1	0-0	0-0	0-0	0-0	0-0	0-0	0-0	1-1	1-0	0-0	0-0	0-0	3- 2
Guidry	0-2	1-0	1-0	3-0	0-1	2-0	1-0	1-0	0-0	1-1	0-0	1-1	0-0	11- 5
John	0-2	0-1	0-1	1-0	0-1	1-0	1-1	2-0	0-0	1-1	0-0	2-0	1-1	9- 8
LaRoche	0-0	0-0	0-0	1-0	0-0	1-1	1-0	0-0	0-0	0-0	0-0	1-0	0-0	4- 1
May	0-0	0-0	0-0	1-2	0-3	2-1	1-0	0-2	0-1	0-0	0-1	1-0	1-1	6-11
Nelson	1-1	0-0	1-0	0-0	1-0	0-0	0-0	0-0	0-0	0-0	0-0	0-0	0-0	3- 1
Reuschel	0-1	0-0	0-0	0-1	1-1	0-0	2-0	0-0	1-0	0-0	0-0	0-0	0-0	4- 4
Righetti	2-0	1-0	0-0	0-0	2-1	0-0	2-1	0-1	1-0	0-0	0-0	0-1	0-0	8- 4
Underwood	0-0	0-0	0-1	0-0	0-0	0-0	0-0	0-0	0-0	0-1	1-0	0-1	0-1	1- 4
Totals	6-7	3-3	2-2	7-5	5-7	7-3	10-2	3-3	3-3	4-3	2-3	5-4	2-3	59-48

No Decisions: Griffin, McGaffigan, Wehrmeister.

OAKLAND—64-45

Pitcher	Balt. W-L	Bos. W-L	Cal. W-L	Chi. W-L	Clev. W-L	Det. W-L	K.C. W-L	Mil. W-L	Min. W-L	N.Y. W-L	Sea. W-L	Tex. W-L	Tor. W-L	Totals W-L
Beard	0-0	0-0	0-0	0-0	0-0	0-0	0-1	0-0	0-0	0-0	0-0	0-0	1-0	1- 1
Heaverlo	0-0	1-0	0-0	0-0	0-0	0-0	0-0	0-0	0-0	0-0	0-0	0-0	0-0	1- 0
Jones	1-0	0-0	1-0	0-0	0-0	1-0	0-0	0-0	0-0	0-1	0-0	0-0	1-0	4- 1
Keough	0-1	1-2	1-0	0-1	1-1	0-0	2-0	0-0	2-0	2-0	1-0	0-0	0-1	10- 6
Kingman	0-1	0-1	0-1	1-1	0-0	0-0	0-0	0-0	1-0	0-1	1-0	0-1	0-0	3- 6
Langford	1-2	0-0	2-0	1-3	1-0	0-1	1-0	0-1	1-1	1-1	1-1	1-0	2-0	12-10
McCatty	2-0	1-2	1-1	4-0	0-1	0-0	0-1	1-1	2-0	0-0	1-0	1-0	1-0	14- 7
Norris	0-2	1-1	2-0	0-2	0-1	1-0	0-1	0-1	2-0	0-0	2-0	2-0	2-1	12- 9
Owchinko	0-1	1-0	0-0	0-0	0-0	0-0	0-0	1-1	0-1	0-0	0-0	0-0	2-0	4- 3
Underwood	1-0	0-1	1-0	0-0	0-0	0-0	0-0	0-0	0-0	0-0	0-0	0-1	1-0	3- 2
Totals	5-7	5-7	8-2	6-7	2-3	2-1	3-3	2-4	8-2	3-4	6-1	4-2	10-2	64-45

No Decisions: Bordi, Figueroa, McLaughlin, Minetto.

SEATTLE—44-65

Pitcher	Balt. W-L	Bos. W-L	Cal. W-L	Chi. W-L	Clev. W-L	Det. W-L	K.C. W-L	Mil. W-L	Min. W-L	N.Y. W-L	Oak. W-L	Tex. W-L	Tor. W-L	Totals W-L
Abbott	0-1	0-1	0-1	0-0	1-0	0-0	0-1	0-0	1-1	0-0	0-2	1-1	1-1	4- 9
Allard	0-0	0-1	0-0	0-0	1-0	0-0	1-0	0-1	0-0	0-0	0-0	1-0	0-0	3- 2
Andersen	1-0	0-0	0-1	1-0	0-0	0-1	0-1	0-0	1-0	0-0	0-0	0-0	0-0	3- 3
Bannister	0-0	1-0	1-1	0-2	0-1	1-1	3-1	1-0	0-0	1-0	0-1	0-2	1-0	9- 9
Beattie	0-0	0-1	1-0	1-0	0-0	0-0	1-0	0-0	0-0	0-0	0-0	0-1	0-0	3- 2
Clark	0-0	0-2	0-0	0-0	0-1	0-0	0-1	0-0	0-0	1-0	1-0	0-1	0-0	2- 5
Clay	0-0	0-1	0-1	0-0	0-0	0-0	0-1	0-0	0-1	0-0	0-1	1-1	1-1	2- 7
Drago	0-1	0-1	1-1	0-1	1-1	0-1	0-0	0-0	0-0	1-0	0-0	1-0	0-0	4- 6
Galasso	0-0	1-0	0-0	0-0	0-0	0-0	0-0	0-0	0-1	0-0	0-0	0-0	0-0	1- 1
Gleaton	0-1	0-0	1-1	0-0	0-0	0-1	1-0	0-1	2-0	0-2	0-1	0-0	0-0	4- 7
Parrott	1-0	0-1	0-0	0-0	0-2	0-1	0-0	1-0	1-0	0-0	0-1	0-1	0-0	3- 6
Rawley	0-1	0-0	0-0	0-0	1-3	0-0	1-1	0-0	1-0	0-0	0-0	1-1	0-0	4- 6
Stein	0-0	0-1	0-0	0-0	0-0	0-0	0-0	0-0	0-0	0-0	0-0	0-0	0-0	0- 1
Stoddard	0-0	1-0	0-0	1-0	0-0	0-0	0-0	0-0	0-0	0-0	0-0	0-1	0-0	2- 1
Totals	2-4	3-9	4-6	3-3	4-8	1-5	7-6	2-2	6-3	3-2	1-6	5-8	3-3	44-65

No Decisions: Black.

TEXAS—57-48

Pitcher	Balt. W-L	Bos. W-L	Cal. W-L	Chi. W-L	Clev. W-L	Det. W-L	K.C. W-L	Mil. W-L	Min. W-L	N.Y. W-L	Oak. W-L	Sea. W-L	Tor. W-L	Totals W-L
Babcock....	0-0	0-0	0-0	1-0	0-0	0-0	0-0	0-0	0-0	0-0	0-0	0-1	0-0	1- 1
Butcher.....	0-0	0-0	1-0	0-0	0-0	0-0	0-0	0-0	0-1	0-0	0-0	0-1	0-0	1- 2
Comer	0-0	1-0	2-1	0-0	0-0	0-0	0-1	1-0	0-0	1-0	1-0	1-0	1-0	8- 2
Darwin	1-0	2-0	0-0	1-1	0-0	0-1	0-0	1-0	1-2	0-3	0-1	2-0	1-1	9- 9
Honeycutt..	0-0	1-0	1-0	0-1	1-0	1-1	2-0	0-1	2-1	1-0	0-1	1-1	1-0	11- 6
Hough	0-0	0-0	0-0	0-0	0-0	0-0	0-0	0-0	2-0	0-0	1-1	1-0	0-0	4- 1
Jenkins......	0-1	0-1	1-0	1-0	0-0	0-2	0-0	0-1	1-0	1-1	0-0	0-1	2-1	5- 8
Johnson.....	0-0	0-0	0-0	1-0	0-1	0-0	1-0	0-0	1-0	0-0	0-0	0-0	0-0	3- 1
Kern..........	0-0	1-1	0-0	0-0	0-0	0-1	0-0	0-0	0-0	0-0	0-0	0-0	0-0	1- 2
Matlack.....	0-0	0-0	0-0	0-0	0-1	1-2	0-1	1-1	0-1	1-1	0-0	1-0	0-0	4- 7
Medich......	0-0	1-1	0-0	0-0	1-0	1-1	1-1	2-1	1-0	0-0	0-1	2-1	1-0	10- 6
Mercer	0-0	0-0	0-0	0-0	0-0	0-1	0-0	0-0	0-0	0-0	0-0	0-0	0-0	0- 1
Schmidt.....	0-1	0-0	0-0	0-0	0-0	0-0	0-0	0-0	0-0	0-0	0-0	0-0	0-0	0- 1
Whitehouse	0-0	0-0	0-1	0-0	0-0	0-0	0-0	0-0	0-0	0-0	0-0	0-0	0-0	0- 1
Totals	1-2	6-3	4-2	4-2	2-2	3-9	4-3	5-4	8-5	4-5	2-4	8-5	6-2	57-48

No Decisions: Lacey.

TORONTO—37-69

Pitcher	Balt. W-L	Bos. W-L	Cal. W-L	Chi. W-L	Clev. W-L	Det. W-L	K.C. W-L	Mil. W-L	Min. W-L	N.Y. W-L	Oak. W-L	Sea. W-L	Tex. W-L	Totals W-L
Berenguer..	0-0	0-0	0-1	0-1	0-0	1-0	1-1	0-0	0-2	0-0	0-1	0-2	0-1	2- 9
Bomback ...	1-1	0-1	1-0	0-1	0-0	1-0	0-1	2-0	0-0	0-1	0-0	0-0	0-0	5- 5
Clancy	0-1	0-1	1-1	2-2	0-0	0-1	0-2	0-0	0-2	1-0	1-2	0-0	1-0	6-12
Garvin	0-0	0-0	0-0	0-0	0-0	0-0	0-0	1-1	0-0	0-0	0-1	0-0	0-0	1- 2
Jackson.....	0-0	0-1	1-0	0-0	0-1	0-0	0-0	0-0	0-0	0-0	0-0	0-0	0-0	1- 2
Leal	0-1	0-0	0-2	1-2	0-1	1-1	1-0	1-1	1-0	0-0	1-3	1-0	0-2	7-13
McLaughlin	0-0	0-0	0-0	0-1	0-0	0-2	1-0	0-0	0-0	0-0	0-2	0-0	0-0	1- 5
Murray	0-0	0-0	1-0	0-0	0-0	0-0	0-0	0-0	0-0	0-0	0-0	0-0	0-0	1- 0
Stieb	1-0	0-0	2-1	2-0	1-1	1-2	0-0	0-2	0-1	1-0	0-1	2-0	1-2	11-10
Todd	0-1	0-0	0-1	0-0	1-1	0-0	0-0	0-1	0-0	1-1	0-0	0-1	0-1	2- 7
Willis	0-1	0-1	0-0	0-0	0-0	0-0	0-1	0-1	0-0	0-0	0-0	0-0	0-0	0- 4
Totals	2-5	0-4	6-6	5-7	2-4	4-6	3-5	4-6	1-5	3-2	2-10	3-3	2-6	37-69

No Decisions: Barlow, Espinosa, Mirabella.

Hard-throwing rookie Dave Righetti was 8-4 with the Yankees after coming up from the minors.

You can always tell the winners from the losers. Gary Carter (left) jumps for joy after Montreal had clinched its division series against Philadelphia. Milwaukee's Rollie Fingers (right) can't believe what the Yankees are doing to him.

1981 DIVISION PLAYOFFS

Including

Review of National League West Series

National League West Box Scores

Review of National League East Series

National League East Box Scores

Review of American League East Series

American League East Box Scores

Review of American League West Series

American League West Box Scores

Jerry Reuss gets a big hug from a Dodger fan after pitching the Dodgers past Houston in the N.L. West playoffs.

NATIONAL LEAGUE WEST

Dodgers Use Comeback Magic

By LARRY WIGGE

Dusty Baker turned philosophical and club comedian Jay Johnstone kept his teammates loose with a little humor.

The Los Angeles Dodgers were on the precipice. They needed a little humor. They trailed the Houston Astros two games to none in the best-of-five National League West Division Series. The Dodgers' only hope was that their 11-2 home record against the Astros in recent games would hold true.

When Johnstone emerged from the Dodgers' dugout October 8, the day before Game 3, he shouted joyously: "Look at the sun! The sun! We've missed the sun. That's all we need, a little vitamin C."

Dr. Johnstone's prescription looked pretty good when the Dodgers erupted for three first-inning runs the next afternoon.

Baker, who had been 1-for-7 in the series, doubled home the first run of the inning and Steve Garvey homered for two more. The Dodgers went on to post a 6-1 victory behind a Burt Hooton-Steve Howe-Bob Welch three-hitter.

There was still life left in the patient.

"I believe in something called the last breath," said Baker. "You haven't beaten people until you've taken away their last breath. We're still breathing, even after we lost those first two games."

Game 4 turned out to be a pitcher's battle. Neither the Dodgers nor the Astros put a runner on base in the first four innings as Fernando Valenzuela and Vern Ruhle were in complete command. Both pitchers begrudgingly permitted four hits in the game, but Pedro Guerrero belted a solo homer in the fifth and Bill Russell added an RBI single in the seventh, giving the Dodgers a 2-1 victory to even the series at two games apiece.

Another pitching struggle ensued in Game 5. It was Nolan Ryan for the Astros—he had no-hit the Dodgers September 26 and then had limited them to two hits for a series-opening victory—against Jerry Reuss. Reuss had allowed the Astros only two runs in 26 innings.

It wasn't until the sixth that the Dodgers got to Ryan. Baker walked and Garvey followed with a single, only the second L.A. hit in the game. Rick Monday singled to score one run.

Mike Scioscia singled home another and a third came in on a throwing error. Reuss breezed to a 4-0 victory, yielding just five hits.

Behind Ryan's pitching and Alan Ashby's two-run homer in the ninth inning, the Astros had won Game 1, 3-1. They took a 2-0 lead in games with a 1-0 triumph in Game 2 when Denny Walling stroked a pinch-single with the bases filled and two out in the 11th inning.

The series will long be remembered for superlative pitching. The Astros as a team batted only .179, while the Dodgers were slightly better at .198.

The Astros, who had beaten the Dodgers in a playoff for the 1980 N.L. West Division title, were okay under the glass in Houston, but they had once again been ambushed on the West Coast —under the sun.

Game of Tuesday, October 6, at Houston (N)

Los Angeles	AB	R.	H.	RBI.	Houston	AB.	R.	H.	RBI.
Lopes, 2b	4	0	0	0	Puhl, rf	4	1	2	0
Landreaux, cf	4	0	1	0	Garner, 2b	3	0	0	0
Baker, lf	3	0	0	0	Scott, cf	4	0	1	1
Garvey, 1b	3	1	1	1	Cruz, lf	4	0	0	0
Monday, rf	2	0	0	0	Cedeno, 1b	4	0	2	0
Guerrero, 3b	3	0	0	0	Howe, 3b	4	0	1	0
Scioscia, c	3	0	0	0	Garcia, ss	3	0	0	0
Russell, ss	3	0	0	0	Reynolds, ph	1	1	1	0
Valenzuela, p	2	0	0	0	Ashby, c	3	1	1	2
Johnstone, ph	1	0	0	0	Ryan, p	3	0	0	0
Stewart, p	0	0	0	0					
Totals	28	1	2	1	Totals	33	3	8	3

Los Angeles .... 0 0 0   0 0 0   1 0 0—1
Houston .... 0 0 0   0 0 1   0 0 2—3
Two out when winning run scored.

Los Angeles	IP.	H.	R.	ER.	BB.	SO.
Valenzuela	8	6	1	1	2	6
Stewart (Loser)	⅔	2	2	2	0	1

Houston	IP.	H.	R.	ER.	BB.	SO.
Ryan (Winner)	9	2	1	1	1	7

Game-winning RBI—Ashby.
Errors—None. Double play—Los Angeles 1. Left on base —Los Angeles 1, Houston 6. Two-base hit—Cedeno. Home runs—Garvey, Ashby. Stolen bases—Cedeno 2. Time—2:22. Attendance—44,836.

Game of Wednesday, October 7, at Houston

Los Angeles	AB.	R.	H.	RBI.	Houston	AB.	R.	H.	RBI.
Lopes, 2b	5	0	2	0	Puhl, rf	5	0	1	0
Marshall, ph	1	0	0	0	Garner, 2b	5	1	2	0
Stewart, p	0	0	0	0	Scott, cf	5	0	1	0
Forster, p	0	0	0	0	Cruz, lf	5	0	2	0
Niedenfuer, p	0	0	0	0	Cedeno, 1b	3	0	0	0
Landreaux, cf	4	0	1	0	A. Howe, 3b	4	0	0	0
Baker, lf	4	0	1	0	Thon, ss	4	0	2	0
Garvey, 1b	5	0	1	0	Walling, ph	1	0	1	1
Monday, rf	4	0	1	0	Pujols, c	3	0	0	0
Thomas, rf	1	0	0	0	Niekro, p	2	0	0	0
Guerrero, 3b	5	0	1	0	Woods, ph	1	0	0	0
Scioscia, c	4	0	1	0	D. Smith, p	0	0	0	0
Yeager, ph-c	1	0	1	0	Pittman, ph	1	0	0	0
Russell, ss	2	0	0	0	Sambito, p	0	0	0	0
Reuss, p	4	0	0	0					
S. Howe, p	0	0	0	0					
R. Smith, ph	1	0	0	0					
Sax, 2b	0	0	0	0					
Totals	41	0	9	0	Totals	39	1	9	1

Los Angeles .... 0 0 0   0 0 0   0 0 0 0—0
Houston .... 0 0 0   0 0 0   0 0 0 1—1
Two out when winning run scored.

Houston catcher Alan Ashby gets a big reception after hitting a game-winning, ninth-inning homer to beat the Dodgers in Game 1.

Los Angeles	IP.	H.	R.	ER.	BB.	SO.
Reuss	9	5	0	0	2	3
S. Howe	1	1	0	0	0	0
Stewart (Loser)	0*	2	1	1	0	0
Forster	1/3	0	0	0	0	0
Niedenfuer	1/3	1	0	0	1	1

Houston	IP.	H.	R.	ER.	BB.	SO.
Niekro	8	7	0	0	3	4
D. Smith	2	1	0	0	0	3
Sambito (Winner)	1	1	0	0	1	2

*Pitched to two batters in eleventh.

Game-winning RBI—Walling.
Error—Russell. Left on base—Los Angeles 13, Houston 10. Two-base hits—Lopes, Yeager. Stolen base—Cruz. Sacrifice hits—Landreaux, Pujols. Time—3:39. Attendance—42,398.

Game of Friday, October 9, at Los Angeles

Houston	AB.	R.	H.	RBI.	Los Ang.	AB.	R.	H.	RBI.
Puhl, rf	4	0	0	0	Lopes, 2b	3	1	1	0
Garner, 2b	2	0	0	0	L'dreaux, cf	4	0	1	1
Scott, cf	4	0	0	0	Baker, lf	5	1	2	1
Cruz, lf	4	0	2	0	Garvey, 1b	4	1	2	2
Cedeno, 1b	4	0	0	0	Guerrero, 3b	3	0	1	0
Ashby, c	2	0	0	0	Monday, rf	3	0	1	0
A. Howe, 3b	2	1	1	1	Th'as, ph-rf	1	1	0	0
Reynolds, ss	2	0	0	0	Yeager, c	4	1	1	0
Thon, ph-ss	1	0	0	0	Russell, ss	4	1	1	1
Knepper, p	1	0	0	0	Hooton, p	3	0	0	0
Spilman, ph	1	0	0	0	S. Howe, p	0	0	0	0
LaCorte, p	0	0	0	0	R. Smith, ph	0	0	0	1
Woods, ph	1	0	0	0	Welch, p	0	0	0	0
Sambito, p	0	0	0	0					
B. Smith, p	0	0	0	0					
Totals	28	1	3	1	Totals	34	6	10	6

Houston .... 0 0 1   0 0 0   0 0 0—1
Los Angeles .... 3 0 0   0 0 0   0 3 x—6

Houston	IP.	H.	R.	ER.	BB.	SO.
Knepper (Loser)	5	6	3	3	2	4
LaCorte	2	0	0	0	0	2
Sambito	2/3	4	3	3	1	0
B. Smith	1/3	0	0	0	0	0

Los Angeles	IP.	H.	R.	ER.	BB.	SO.
Hooton (Winner)	7*	3	1	1	3	2
Howe	1	0	0	0	0	2
Welch	1	0	0	0	1	1

*Pitched to one batter in eighth.

Game-winning RBI—Baker.
Errors—Cruz, Cedeno. Double plays—Los Angeles 2. Left on base—Houston 4, Los Angeles 9. Two-base hits—Cruz, Baker, Guerrero. Home runs—Garvey, A. Howe. Sacrifice hit—Landreaux. Sacrifice fly—R. Smith. Wild pitch—Knepper. Time—2:35. Attendance—46,820.

Game of Saturday, October 10, at Los Angeles (N)

Houston	AB.	R.	H.	RBI.	Los Ang.	AB.	R.	H.	RBI.
Puhl, rf	4	1	1	0	Lopes, 2b	3	0	0	0
Garner, 2b	4	0	0	0	L'dreaux, cf	4	0	0	0
Scott, cf	4	0	1	1	Baker, lf	3	0	0	0
Cruz, lf	4	0	0	0	Garvey, 1b	3	1	1	0
Cedeno, 1b	2	0	1	0	Monday, rf	2	0	0	0
Walling, 1b	1	0	0	0	Thomas, rf	1	0	0	0
Howe, 3b	3	0	1	0	Guerrero, 3b	3	1	1	1
Thon, ss	2	0	0	0	Scioscia, c	2	0	0	0
Pujols, c	3	0	0	0	Russell, ss	3	0	2	1
Ruhle, p	1	0	0	0	Val'zuela, p	2	0	0	0
Garcia, ph	1	0	0	0					
Totals	29	1	4	1	Totals	25	2	4	2

Houston .... 0 0 0   0 0 0   0 0 1—1
Los Angeles .... 0 0 0   0 1 0   1 0 x—2

Houston	IP.	H.	R.	ER.	BB.	SO.
Ruhle (Loser)	8	4	2	2	2	1

Los Angeles	IP.	H.	R.	ER.	BB.	SO.
Valenzuela (Winner)	9	4	1	1	1	4

Game-winning RBI—Guerrero.
Errors—None. Left on base—Houston 3, Los Angeles 3. Two-base hit—Puhl. Home run—Guerrero. Sacrifice hits—Ruhle, Valenzuela, Monday. Time—2:00. Attendance—55,983.

Game of Sunday, October 11, at Los Angeles

Houston	AB.	R.	H.	RBI.	Los Ang.	AB.	R.	H.	RBI.
Puhl, rf	4	0	0	0	Lopes, 2b	5	0	1	0
Garner, 2b	4	0	0	0	L'dreaux, cf	4	1	1	0
Scott, cf	3	0	0	0	Baker, lf	3	1	0	0
Howe, 3b	4	0	1	0	Garvey, 1b	4	0	1	1
Cruz, lf	3	0	2	0	Monday, rf	3	1	1	1
Walling, 1b	4	0	1	0	Th'as, pr-rf	0	0	0	0
Thon, ss	4	0	0	0	Guerrero, 3b	3	0	0	0
Ashby, c	4	0	0	0	Scioscia, c	4	0	1	1
Ryan, p	1	0	1	0	Russell, ss	4	0	1	0
Pittman, ph	1	0	0	0	Reuss, p	4	0	0	0
D. Smith, p	0	0	0	0					
LaCorte, p	0	0	0	0					
Roberts, ph	1	0	0	0					
Totals	33	0	5	0	Totals	34	4	7	3

Houston .... 0 0 0   0 0 0   0 0 0—0
Los Angeles .... 0 0 0   0 0 3   1 0 x—4

Houston	IP.	H.	R.	ER.	BB.	SO.
Ryan (Loser)	6	4	3	2	2	7
D. Smith	1/3	1	1	1	0	1
LaCorte	1 2/3	2	0	0	1	3

Los Angeles	IP.	H.	R.	ER.	BB.	SO.
Reuss (Winner)	9	5	0	0	3	4

Game-winning RBI—Monday.
Errors—Garner, Russell, Thon, Walling, Guerrero. Left on base—Houston 9, Los Angeles 9. Two-base hits—Landreaux, Russell. Three-base hit—Garvey. Stolen bases—Puhl, Guerrero, Lopes. Time—2:52. Attendance—55,979.

NATIONAL LEAGUE EAST

Hungry Expos Shake Jinx

By LARRY WIGGE

Beating Steve Carlton is an accomplishment. Beating Carlton in a playoff game is a feat. Beating Carlton twice in five days, both times in playoff games, is something of a milestone.

The "milestone" belonged to Montreal righthander Steve Rogers, who on October 11 turned back Carlton and the Philadelphia Phillies, 3-0, in the deciding game of the best-of-five National League East Division Series.

Rogers, who had combined with reliever Jeff Reardon for a 3-1 victory in Game 1 of the series, fired a six-hitter at the defending world champions and contributed a two-run single as the Expos advanced into the N.L. Championship Series for the first time in their history after several near misses.

Though the victory came in Philadelphia and was his fourth shutout in his last 12 outings, Rogers knew he would have to face the inevitable question. Sure enough, a reporter asked the 31-year-old to comment on his failures in "big games" of the past.

"Next question, please," Rogers snapped.

It was a long time coming for the Expos. They had been eliminated from the N.L. East race by the Pittsburgh Pirates on the final day of the 1979 season. The Pirates went on to win the World Series. The Expos had been eliminated by the Phillies on the next-to-last day of the 1980 season. The Phillies won the World Series. Now the Expos felt it was their turn to win all the marbles.

"It's sweet, I'll tell you!" shouted Montreal Manager Jim Fanning. "We've been waiting for this for so very long."

The Expos touched Carlton for seven hits and three runs in six innings of Game 1 at Montreal. Rookie Tim Wallach and veteran shortstop Chris Speier stroked doubles in the bottom of the second to give Montreal a 2-1 lead. Warren Cromartie added an insurance run in the fourth to back the combined effort by Rogers and Reardon.

Speier provided his second straight game-winning RBI in Game 2, slamming a run-scoring single in the second inning. Gary Carter hit a two-run homer and Tim Gullickson and Reardon combined on a six-hitter for a second 3-1 Expo vic-

The Phils' George Vukovich arrives home (center) after his game-winning, 10th-inning homer in Game 2.

tory.

When the scene shifted to Philadelphia on October 9, the Phillies pounded out 13 hits and were aided by four Montreal errors in gaining a 6-2 win.

The Phils evened the series at two games apiece on the strength of George Vukovich's 10th-inning pinch homer. It was Vukovich's third pinch-hit of the series and it gave Philadelphia a 6-5 verdict. The Phillies had blown 4-0 and 5-4 leads earlier in the game before Vukovich sent Reardon's 2-0 pitch over the right field fence.

The second Rogers-Carlton confrontation, in Game 5, was scoreless until the fifth inning. With the bases loaded and Rogers at the plate, the Philadelphia lefthander served up a two-run single. Parrish's RBI double in the sixth completed the scoring.

But Rogers was in total control. The Phils' only threat came in the sixth when they put runners on first and third with one out, but Rogers induced Mike Schmidt to bounce into an inning-ending double play.

Phillies Manager Dallas Green said, "We wanted Lefty (Carlton) to pitch like Rogers and our team to play like their team. It just didn't happen."

Game of Wednesday, October 7, at Montreal

Phila'phia	AB.	R.	H.	RBI.	Montreal	AB.	R.	H.	RBI.
Smith, cf	4	0	2	0	Crom'tie, 1b	5	0	2	1
Rose, 1b	4	0	2	0	White, lf-rf	4	1	1	0
Matthews, lf	4	0	1	0	Dawson, cf	4	0	2	0
Schmidt, 3b	3	0	0	0	Carter, c	3	0	1	1
McBride, rf	4	0	0	0	Parrish, 3b	3	0	0	0
Moreland, c	4	1	3	1	Wallach, rf	2	1	1	0
Aguayo, pr	0	0	0	0	Francona, lf	0	0	0	0
Bowa, ss	3	0	0	0	Manuel, 2b	4	0	0	0
G. Vu'ich, ph	1	0	1	0	Speier, ss	1	1	1	1
Trillo, 2b	3	0	0	0	Rogers, p	2	0	0	0
Carlton, p	2	0	1	0	Reardon, p	0	0	0	0
Gross, ph	1	0	0	0					
R. Reed, p	0	0	0	0					
Totals	33	1	10	1	Totals	28	3	8	3

Philadelphia.....................................0 1 0 0 0 0 0 0 0—1
Montreal..1 1 0 1 0 0 0 0 x—3

Philadelphia	IP.	H.	R.	ER.	BB.	SO.
Carlton (Loser)	6	7	3	3	5	6
R. Reed	2	1	0	0	2	3
Montreal	IP.	H.	R.	ER.	BB.	SO.
Rogers (Winner)	8⅔	10	1	1	2	3
Reardon (Save)	⅓	0	0	0	0	0

Game-winning RBI—Speier.

Error—Moreland. Double play—Montreal 2. Left on base—Philadelphia 7, Montreal 10. Two-base hits—Carter, Wallach, Speier, Rose, Cromartie. Three-base hits—Matthews, Dawson. Home Run—Moreland. Stolen bases—White 2, Dawson, Francona. Sacrifice hits—Rogers 2. Wild pitches—Carlton, Reed. Time—2:30. Attendance—34,327.

Game of Thursday, October 8, at Montreal (N)

Phila'phia	AB.	R.	H.	RBI.	Montreal	AB.	R.	H.	RBI.
Smith, cf	4	1	2	0	Crom'tie, 1b	4	1	2	0
Rose, 1b	4	0	1	1	White, rf	3	0	0	0
McBride, rf	4	0	2	0	Dawson, cf	4	0	1	0
Schmidt, 3b	3	0	0	0	Carter, c	4	1	1	2
Matthews, lf	4	0	1	0	Parrish, 3b	4	1	0	0
McGraw, p	0	0	0	0	Francona, lf	3	0	2	0
Moreland, c	3	0	0	0	Speier, ss	2	0	1	1
Bowa, ss	4	0	0	0	Manuel, 2b	3	0	0	0
Trillo, 2b	4	0	0	0	Gul'kson, p	3	0	0	0
Ruthven, p	1	0	0	0	Reardon, p	0	0	0	0
Gross, ph	1	0	0	0					
Brusstar, p	0	0	0	0					
Lyle, p	0	0	0	0					
G. V'h, ph-lf	1	0	0	0					
Totals	33	1	6	1	Totals	30	3	7	3

Philadelphia.....................................0 0 0 0 0 0 0 1 0—1
Montreal..0 1 2 0 0 0 0 0 x—3

Philadelphia	IP.	H.	R.	ER.	BB.	SO.
Ruthven (Loser)	4	3	3	2	1	0
Brusstar	2	2	0	0	1	2
Lyle	1	1	0	0	1	0
McGraw	1	1	0	0	0	0
Montreal	IP.	H.	R.	ER.	BB.	SO.
Gullickson (Winner)	7⅔	6	1	1	1	3
Reardon (Save)	1⅔	0	0	0	1	1

Game-winning RBI—Speier.

Errors—Schmidt, Bowa. Left on base—Philadelphia 7, Montreal 6. Two-base hits—Cromartie, Smith, McBride. Home run—Carter. Stolen bases—White, Francona. Time—2:31. Attendance—45,896.

Game of Friday, October 9, at Philadelphia

Montreal	AB.	R.	H.	RBI.	Phila'phia	AB.	R.	H.	RBI.
Cromartie, 1b	4	0	1	0	Smith, cf	4	0	0	0
White, rf	4	1	1	0	Boone, c	1	0	0	0
Dawson, cf	3	0	1	0	Rose, 1b	4	0	1	1
Carter, c	3	1	2	1	McBride, rf	4	0	0	0
Parrish, 3b	4	0	0	0	Lyle, p	0	0	0	0
Francona, lf	4	0	1	0	Gross, lf	1	0	0	0
Speier, ss	4	0	2	1	Schmidt, 3b	3	1	2	0
Manuel, 2b	3	0	0	0	Matthews, lf	4	2	3	0
W. J'nson, ph	1	0	0	0	R. Reed, p	0	0	0	0
Burris, p	2	0	0	0	Moreland, c	3	1	2	0
Lee, p	0	0	0	0	Aguayo, pr	0	1	0	0
Wallach, ph	0	0	0	0	Maddox, cf	1	0	0	0
Sosa, p	0	0	0	0	Bowa, ss	3	0	2	1
Milner, ph	1	0	0	0	Trillo, 2b	2	1	1	1
					Christ'son, p	2	0	0	0
					G. V'h, ph-rf	2	0	2	1
Totals	33	2	8	2	Totals	34	6	13	4

Montreal..0 1 0 0 0 0 0 1 0—2
Philadelphia.....................................0 2 0 0 0 2 2 0 x—6

Montreal	IP.	H.	R.	ER.	BB.	SO.
Burris (Loser)	5⅓	7	4	3	4	4
Lee	⅔	2	0	0	0	1
Sosa	2	4	2	1	0	0
Philadelphia	IP.	H.	R.	ER.	BB.	SO.
Christenson (Winner)	6	4	1	1	1	8
Lyle	1	2	0	0	1	0
R. Reed	2	2	1	1	0	0

Game-winning RBI—None.

Errors—Dawson, Cromartie, Manuel, Sosa. Double plays—Montreal 2, Philadelphia 1. Left on base—Montreal 7, Philadelphia 9. Two-base hits—Carter, Bowa, Schmidt, White. Sacrifice hit—Bowa. Sacrifice fly—Carter. Time—2:45. Attendance—36,835.

Game of Saturday, October 10, at Philadelphia

Montreal	AB.	R.	H.	RBI.	Phila'phia	AB.	R.	H.	RBI.
Cromartie, 1b	5	0	0	0	Smith, cf	3	0	0	0
White, rf-lf	3	1	0	1	Maddox, cf	2	0	1	0
Dawson, cf	5	0	1	0	Rose, 1b	5	1	1	0
Carter, c	5	1	3	2	McBride, rf	3	1	1	0
Parrish, 3b	5	1	1	0	R. Reed, p	0	0	0	0
Francona, lf	4	0	0	0	Aviles, ph	0	0	0	0
Reardon, p	1	0	0	0	McGraw, p	0	0	0	0
Speier, ss	4	2	2	0	G. V'ich, ph	1	1	1	1
Manuel, 2b	1	0	1	0	Schmidt, 3b	3	2	1	2
Milner, ph	1	0	1	1	Matthews, lf	4	1	2	1
Phillips, pr-2b	1	0	0	0	Moreland, c	3	0	1	2
Sanderson, p	1	0	0	0	Boone, c	1	0	0	0
Bahnsen, p	0	0	0	0	Bowa, ss	4	0	1	0
Mills, ph	0	0	0	0	Trillo, 2b	3	0	0	0
Sosa, p	0	0	0	0	Noles, p	0	0	0	0
W. J'nson, ph	1	0	1	1	Brusstar, p	0	0	0	0
Fryman, p	0	0	0	0	Lyle, p	0	0	0	0
Wallach, rf	1	0	0	0	D. D's, ph-rf	2	0	0	0
Totals	38	5	10	5	Totals	34	6	9	6

Montreal..0 0 0 1 1 2 1 0 0 0—5
Philadelphia.....................................2 0 2 0 0 1 0 0 0 1—6

None out when winning run scored.

Montreal	IP.	H.	R.	ER.	BB.	SO.
Sanderson	2⅔	4	4	2	2	2
Bahnsen	1⅓	1	0	0	1	1
Sosa	1	0	0	0	0	1
Fryman	1⅓	3	1	1	1	0
Reardon (Loser)	2⅔†	1	1	1	0	1
Philadelphia	IP.	H.	R.	ER.	BB.	SO.
Noles	4*	4	2	2	2	5
Brusstar	1⅔	3	2	2	0	1
Lyle	⅓	1	0	0	0	1
R. Reed	1	1	1	1	1	0
McGraw (Winner)	3	1	0	0	0	2

*Pitched to three batters in fifth.
†Pitched to one batter in tenth.

Game-winning RBI—G. Vukovich.

Error—Manuel. Double play—Philadelphia 1. Left on base—Montreal 7, Philadelphia 6. Two-base hits—Speier, Carter, Maddox. Home runs—Carter, Schmidt, Matthews, G. Vukovich. Stolen base—Dawson. Sacrifice hit—Noles. Sacrifice fly—White. Time—2:48. Attendance—38,818.

Game of Sunday, October 11, at Philadelphia

Montreal	AB.	R.	H.	RBI.	Phila'phia	AB.	R.	H.	RBI.
Cromartie, 1b	4	0	0	0	Smith, cf	4	0	1	0
White, lf-rf	4	0	1	0	Rose, 1b	3	0	1	0
Dawson, cf	4	1	1	0	G. Vuk'ch, rf	4	0	0	0
Carter, c	4	0	1	0	R. Reed, p	0	0	0	0
Parrish, 3b	4	1	2	1	Schmidt, 3b	4	0	1	0
Wallach, rf	1	0	0	0	Matthews, lf	4	0	1	0
Francona, lf	1	0	1	0	Trillo, 2b	4	0	2	0
Speier, ss	4	1	0	0	Bowa, ss	3	0	0	0
Manuel, 2b	3	0	0	0	Boone, c	3	0	0	0
Rogers, p	3	0	2	2	Carlton, p	2	0	0	0
					Gross, ph-rf	1	0	0	0
Totals	32	3	8	3	Totals	32	0	6	0

Montreal..0 0 0 0 2 1 0 0 0—3
Philadelphia.....................................0 0 0 0 0 0 0 0 0—0

Montreal	IP.	H.	R.	ER.	BB.	SO.
Rogers (Winner)	9	6	0	0	1	2
Philadelphia	IP.	H.	R.	ER.	BB.	SO.
Carlton (Loser)	8	7	3	3	3	7
R. Reed	1	1	0	0	0	1

Game-winning RBI—Rogers.

Error—Manuel. Double play—Montreal 1. Left on base—Montreal 5, Philadelphia 6. Two-base hit—Parrish. Time—2:15. Attendance—47,384.

Montreal ace Steve Rogers reacts after shutting out the Phillies in the deciding game of the East Division playoffs.

Yankee catcher Rick Cerone went from goat to hero and won the hearts of New York fans in the Yankees' fifth-game victory over Milwaukee.

AMERICAN LEAGUE EAST
Yanks Survive Owner, Brewers

By LARRY WIGGE

New York Yankees Owner George Steinbrenner had plenty of words (most of them unprintable) for everyone after the Milwaukee Brewers had captured their second straight decision at Yankee Stadium to even the best-of-five American League East Division Series October 10.

Some 24 hours later, the fiery criticisms aimed chiefly at Rick Cerone and Reggie Jackson had turned into rosy compliments.

"That home run of Rick's broke their backs," Steinbrenner said. "What can you say about the way Rick played?

"Reggie rose to the occasion. He must have looked at the calendar," he added, referring to the man known as Mr. October.

"It seems that every time George jumps on the club, it responds," New York coach Jeff Torborg said after the Yankees' 7-3 victory over the Brewers October 11.

Steinbrenner cited mental mistakes and shoddy baserunning for the 2-1 loss in Game 4. Without mentioning names, he singled out Cerone's blunder in the seventh inning when the slow-footed catcher rounded first base too far after a single to left field. The series of events that followed resulted in Larry Milbourne straying off third base and being put out.

"----you, George. You don't know what you're talking about," responded Cerone. "You don't know baseball."

"It's over. You're gone next year," reportedly was Steinbrenner's response to Cerone.

Steinbrenner turned to Jackson and said: "I thought you were better than this."

Reggie turned peacemaker the next morning, setting his employer straight and carrying a note from Steinbrenner to Cerone saying that he (Steinbrenner) knew Cerone's words had come out in frustration.

The teams played the series much like the regular season, when Milwaukee's Rollie Fingers and New York's Ron Davis and Rich Gossage ruled the final innings.

The Brewers surrendered a 2-0 lead in Game 1 when the Yankees scored four

Relief ace Goose Gossage slams the door on the Brewers.

times in the fourth inning on a two-run homer by Oscar Gamble and a two-run double by Cerone. Starter Ron Guidry yielded another run in the fifth before Davis and Gossage combined for one-hit relief over the final 4⅔ innings of New York's 5-3 triumph.

Dave Righetti, Davis and Gossage were in complete control in Game 2, striking out 14 Milwaukee batters for a 3-0 victory. Lou Piniella connected for a home run in the fourth inning and Jackson added a two-run homer in the ninth.

When the scene shifted to New York October 9, the Brewers gave the Yanks all the fight they wanted . . . and more, winning Game 3 by a 5-3 score.

Ted Simmons' two-run homer and Sal Bando's RBI single in the seventh inning gave Milwaukee a 3-1 lead and brought Fingers into the game. However, the moustachioed righthander couldn't hold the lead as Cerone and Willie Randolph stroked run-scoring singles.

The Brewers bounced right back with a solo homer by Paul Molitor and an RBI double by Simmons.

A sacrifice fly by Cooper and an RBI double by Ben Oglivie provided the two fourth-inning runs that led the Brewers to their 2-1 victory in the now infamous Game 4.

Trailing 2-0 in Game 5, the Yanks erupted for four runs in the fourth inning with Jackson lofting a two-run homer and Gamble following with another homer off Moose Haas.

Cerone's homer came in the seventh and the Yankees wrapped up the scoring with two runs in the eighth on a run-scoring double by Piniella and Graig Nettles' sacrifice fly.

Game of Wednesday, October 7, At Milwaukee (N)

New York	AB.	R.	H.	RBI.	Milwaukee	AB.	R.	H.	RBI.
Randolph, 2b	5	0	0	0	Molitor, rf	4	0	0	0
Mumphrey, cf	5	1	2	0	Yount, ss	2	1	1	1
Winfield, lf	5	0	1	0	Cooper, 1b	3	0	1	0
Jackson, rf	4	1	1	0	Simmons, c	4	0	1	1
Nettles, 3b	5	0	0	0	Thomas, cf	4	0	0	0
Gamble, dh	4	1	3	2	Oglivie, lf	4	0	0	0
Watson, 1b	4	1	3	0	Bando, 3b	4	1	1	0
Milbourne, ss	4	1	1	0	Moore, dh	2	0	2	1
Cerone, c	4	0	2	2	How'l, ph-dh	2	0	1	0
					Gantner, 2b	4	1	1	0
Totals	40	5	13	4	Totals	33	3	8	3

New York ....0 0 0 4 0 0 0 0 1—5
Milwaukee ....0 1 1 0 1 0 0 0 0—3

New York	IP.	H.	R.	ER.	BB.	SO.
Guidry	4⅓	7	3	3	2	5
Davis (Winner)	2⅔	0	0	0	0	4
Gossage (Save)	2	1	0	0	0	3
Milwaukee	**IP.**	**H.**	**R.**	**ER.**	**BB.**	**SO.**
Haas (Loser)	3⅓	8	4	4	1	1
Bernard	⅔	0	0	0	0	0
McClure	1⅓	3	0	0	0	0
Slaton	2⅓	1	0	0	0	1
Fingers	1⅓	1	1	0	0	1

Game-winning RBI—Cerone.

Errors—Cerone, Yount, Simmons, Gantner. Double play—Milwaukee 1. Left on base—New York 9, Milwaukee 7. Two-base hits—Cerone 2, Gamble, Bando, Gantner. Home run—Gamble. Stolen bases—Yount, Mumphrey. Sacrifice hit—Molitor. Sacrifice fly—Yount. Time—2:57. Attendance—35,064.

Game of Thursday, October 8, at Milwaukee

New York	AB.	R.	H.	RBI.	Milwaukee	AB.	R.	H.	RBI.
Randolph, 2b	4	0	2	0	Molitor, rf	4	0	1	0
Mumphrey, cf	4	0	0	0	Yount, ss	5	0	0	0
Winfield, lf	4	1	3	0	Cooper, 1b	4	0	1	0
Jackson, rf	4	1	1	2	Simmons, c	3	0	1	0
Piniella, dh	4	1	1	1	Thomas, cf	3	0	0	0
Nettles, 3b	4	0	0	0	Oglivie, lf	4	0	0	0
Watson, 1b	3	0	0	0	Bando, 3b	4	0	3	0
Milbourne, ss	3	0	0	0	Moore, dh	2	0	0	0
Cerone, c	3	0	0	0	How'l, ph-dh	0	0	0	0
					B'sley, pr-dh	0	0	0	0
					M'ey, ph-dh	1	0	0	0
					Gantner, 2b	4	0	1	0
Totals	33	3	7	3	Totals	34	0	7	0

New York ....0 0 0 1 0 0 0 0 2—3
Milwaukee ....0 0 0 0 0 0 0 0 0—0

New York	IP.	H.	R.	ER.	BB.	SO.
Righetti (Winner)	6	4	0	0	2	10
Davis	⅓	1	0	0	2	0
Gossage (Save)	2⅔	2	0	0	0	4
Milwaukee	**IP.**	**H.**	**R.**	**ER.**	**BB.**	**SO.**
Caldwell (Loser)	8⅓	7	3	3	0	4
Slaton	⅔	0	0	0	0	0

Game-winning RBI—Piniella.

Errors—None. Double play—Milwaukee 1. Left on base—New York 3, Milwaukee 11. Two-base hits—Winfield, Bando 2. Home runs—Piniella, Jackson. Wild pitch—Davis. Time—2:35. Attendance—26,395.

Game of Friday, October 9, at New York (N)

Milwaukee	AB.	R.	H.	RBI.	New York	AB.	R.	H.	RBI.
Molitor, cf	4	1	3	1	Rand'ph, 2b	5	0	1	1
Yount, ss	4	1	1	0	M'ph'y, cf	4	0	0	0
Cooper, 1b	4	1	1	0	Winfield, lf	3	1	2	0
Simmons, c	3	1	2	3	Jackson, rf	4	0	0	0
Thomas, dh	4	1	1	0	Piniella, dh	3	0	0	0
Oglivie, lf	3	0	0	0	Ga'le, ph-dh	1	0	1	0
Bando, 3b	4	0	1	1	Nettles, 3b	2	0	0	0
Moore, rf	2	0	0	0	Watson, 1b	2	1	2	1
Ed'ws, pr-rf	1	0	0	0	Murcer, ph	1	0	0	0
Gantner, 2b	3	0	0	0	Revering, 1b	0	0	0	0
					Milb'rne, ss	4	1	1	0
					Cerone, c	4	0	1	1
Totals	32	5	9	5	Totals	33	3	8	3

Milwaukee ....0 0 0 0 0 0 3 2 0—5
New York ....0 0 0 1 0 0 2 0 0—3

Milwaukee	IP.	H.	R.	ER.	BB.	SO.
Lerch	6	3	1	1	4	3
Fingers (Winner)	3	5	2	2	0	3
New York	**IP.**	**H.**	**R.**	**ER.**	**BB.**	**SO.**
John (Loser)	7*	8	5	5	2	0
May	2	1	0	0	0	1

*Pitched to two batters in eighth.

Game-winning RBI—Molitor.

Errors—Watson, May. Double plays—Milwaukee 1, New York 1. Left on base—Milwaukee 3, New York 7. Two-base hits—Winfield, Simmons. Home runs—Simmons, Molitor. Sacrifice hit—Oglivie. Wild pitch—May. Time—2:39. Attendance—54,171.

Game of Saturday, October 10, at New York

Milwaukee	AB.	R.	H.	RBI.	New York	AB.	R.	H.	RBI.
Molitor, rf	4	1	1	0	Rand'ph, 2b	3	0	0	0
Yount, ss	3	1	1	0	Mumph'y, cf	4	1	0	0
Cooper, 1b	3	0	0	1	Winfield, lf	4	0	1	0
Simmons, c	4	0	0	0	Jackson, rf	4	0	1	0
Oglivie, lf	3	0	1	1	Gamble, dh	1	0	0	0
Thomas, cf	3	0	0	0	Pin'la, ph-dh	2	0	0	1
Edwards, cf	0	0	0	0	Nettles, 3b	3	0	0	0
Howell, dh	3	0	1	0	Watson, 1b	3	0	1	0
Bando, 3b	3	0	0	0	Brown, pr	0	0	0	0
Gantner, 2b	3	0	0	0	Revering, 1b	0	0	0	0
					Foote, ph	0	0	0	0
					Murcer, ph	0	0	0	0
					Milb'rne, ss	4	0	1	0
					Cerone, c	4	0	1	0
Totals	29	2	4	2	Totals	32	1	5	1

Milwaukee ....0 0 0 2 0 0 0 0 0—2
New York ....0 0 0 0 0 1 0 0 0—1

Milwaukee	IP.	H.	R.	ER.	BB.	SO.
Vuckovich (Winner)	5*	2	1	0	3	4
Easterly	1	0	0	0	0	1
Slaton	1⅔	2	0	0	0	1
McClure	1	0	0	0	0	1
Fingers (Save)	⅓	1	0	0	1	1
New York	**IP.**	**H.**	**R.**	**ER.**	**BB.**	**SO.**
Reuschel (Loser)	6	4	2	2	1	3
Davis	3	0	0	0	0	2

*Pitched to two batters in sixth.

Game-winning RBI—Cooper.

Errors—Cooper, Gantner. Left on base—Milwaukee 2, New York 8. Two-base hits—Oglivie, Winfield. Sacrifice fly—Cooper. Wild pitch—Vuckovich. Time—2:34. Attendance—52,077.

Game of Sunday, October 11, at New York (N)

Milwaukee	AB.	R.	H.	RBI.	New York	AB.	R.	H.	RBI.
Molitor, cf	4	0	0	0	Mumph'y, cf	4	0	0	0
Yount, ss	5	1	3	0	Milb'rne, ss	4	2	3	0
Cooper, 1b	4	0	1	2	Winfield, lf	4	0	0	0
Simmons, c	4	0	0	0	Jackson, rf	4	2	3	2
Thomas, dh	4	1	1	1	Gamble, dh	3	1	1	1
Oglivie, lf	4	0	2	0	Pin'la, ph-dh	1	0	1	1
Bando, 3b	2	0	0	0	Nettles, 3b	3	1	1	1
Moore, rf	3	0	0	0	Watson, 1b	4	0	1	0
Howell, ph	0	0	0	0	Cer'e, c	3	1	2	2
Edw'ds, pr-rf	0	0	0	0	R'dolph, 2b	3	0	1	0
Romero, 2b	2	1	1	0					
M'ey, ph-2b	2	0	0	0					
Totals	34	3	8	3	Totals	33	7	13	7

Milwaukee ....0 1 1 0 0 0 1 0 0—3
New York ....0 0 0 4 0 0 1 2 x—7

Milwaukee	IP.	H.	R.	ER.	BB.	SO.
Haas (Loser)	3⅓	5	3	3	0	0
Caldwell	0*	2	1	1	0	0
Bernard	1⅔	0	0	0	0	0
McClure	1	1	0	0	0	1
Slaton	1⅓	3	2	2	0	0
Easterly	⅓	2	1	1	0	0
Vuckovich	⅓	0	0	0	0	0
New York	**IP.**	**H.**	**R.**	**ER.**	**BB.**	**SO.**
Guidry	4	4	2	2	1	3
Righetti (Winner)	3	4	1	1	1	3
Gossage (Save)	2	0	0	0	2	1

*Pitched to two batters in fourth.

Game-winning RBI—Gamble.

Errors—None. Double plays—Milwaukee 3. Left on base—Milwaukee 9, New York 3. Two-base hits—Milbourne, Piniella. Three-base hit—Yount. Home runs—Thomas, Jackson, Gamble, Cerone. Sacrifice flies—Cooper, Nettles. Time—2:47. Attendance—47,505.

AMERICAN LEAGUE WEST

A's Make Short Work of Royals

By LARRY WIGGE

Maybe George Brett should have choked up on his bat when he came to the plate with the bases loaded and his team trailing 4-1 in the third game of the best-of-five American League West Division Series. It worked for the kid in the 7-Up commercial.

Maybe Clint Hurdle should have been more careful before he was picked off second base in the same inning of Game 3 when the Kansas City Royals had four hits, but failed to score against the Oakland A's.

And maybe the A's and Billy Ball were for real.

When the Royals failed in bases-loaded none out and bases-loaded one out situations in the early going of Game 1, the pattern was established. They lost, 4-0, and collected only four hits, two of them bunt singles. Still, Kansas City second baseman Frank White insisted Oakland pitcher Mike Norris beat them with "slop."

Oakland starter Steve McCatty stymied the Royals on six hits for a 2-1 triumph in Game 2, but the Royals were still unimpressed with the A's pitching. John Wathan said: "The way some of us have been swinging the bat, I think my wife can get us out."

McCatty offered another point of view. After all, these same Royals had lashed out 18 hits against Cleveland October 5 in a makeup game that decided the second-season champion in the A.L. West. Surely, the Royals had not lost all of their hitting magic in 48 hours.

"Maybe we're making good pitches," said McCatty. "What makes a slump? Good pitching makes a slump, doesn't it?"

For the series, the A's frustrated the heart of the Royals lineup: Amos Otis went 0-for-12, Brett 2-for-12, Hal McRae 1-for-10 and White 2-for-11. Willie Wilson, Kansas City's catalyst, was 4-for-13, but had no walks and failed to steal a base.

The A's who had finished at the bottom of the A.L. standings in 1979, were built around excellent starting pitching. Norris, McCatty and Rick Langford provided the firepower that resulted in a quick exit for the defending American League champion Royals.

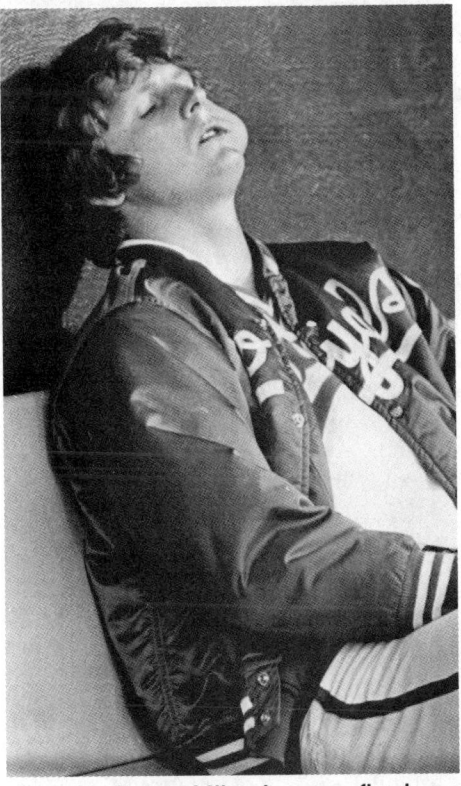

Royals pitcher Mike Jones reflects on his tough luck after a 2-1 Game 2 loss.

Wayne Gross, a .206 hitter in 1981, provided the key blow to support Norris' pitching in Game 1. Gross belted a three-run homer off Dennis Leonard, who had the only two shutouts pitched against the A's in '81. Dwayne Murphy also homered.

Tony Armas took charge of Game 2. After driving in the game's first run with a double in the opening inning, Armas broke a 1-1 deadlock with another RBI double in the eighth as the A's captured their second straight victory on Kansas City turf, 2-1.

Armas again produced the A's first run en route to their series-clinching third victory October 9 with an infield single. Three Kansas City errors opened the gates for Oakland's second run in the third and Dave McKay belted a home run and Murphy added an RBI double in the

A's ace Steve McCatty gets some deserved pats on the back after pitching the A's to a 2-1 win over the Royals in Game 2.

fourth inning. Langford, Tom Underwood and Dave Beard combined on the 4-1 victory.

A's pitchers held the Royals to two runs and just one extra-base hit—an infield double off Langford's leg—in 27 innings.

The Royals problems were typified by a threat they frittered away in the fifth inning of Game 3 when Hurdle and Wathan opened the inning with singles. U.L. Washington was trying to bunt the runners along and Hurdle kept taking longer and longer leads off second base. Suddenly, shortstop Fred Stanley slipped behind Hurdle and catcher Mike Heath rifled a throw to Stanley to nail a red-faced Hurdle. After Washington popped up, Wilson and White singled to load the bases. But Brett, who capitalized on almost every opportunity in 1980 when he chased the .400 mark, weakly popped up.

Game of Wednesday, October 7, at Kansas City

Oakland	AB.	R.	H.	RBI.	Kan. City	AB.	R.	H.	RBI.
Henderson, lf	5	0	0	0	Wilson, lf	5	0	1	1
Murphy, cf	4	2	2	0	White, 2b	4	0	0	0
Johnson, dh	3	0	1	0	G. Brett, 3b	4	0	1	0
Armas, rf	4	0	4	2	Aikens, 1b	1	0	0	0
Bosetti, pr-rf	0	0	0	0	G'nimo, pr	0	0	0	0
Klutts, 3b	3	0	1	0	May, 1b	0	0	0	0
Moore, 1b	4	0	0	0	Otis, cf	4	0	0	0
McKay, 2b	4	0	1	0	McRae, dh	3	0	0	0
Newman, c	3	0	0	0	Hurdle, rf	4	0	1	0
Picciolo, ss	3	0	1	0	Wathan, c	4	1	2	0
Gross, ph	1	0	0	0	Wash'ton, ss	3	0	1	0
Stanley, ss	0	0	0	0					
Totals	34	2	10	2	Totals	32	1	6	1

Oakland.....................1 0 0   0 0 0   0 1 0—2
Kansas City ....0 0 0   0 1 0   0 0 0—1

Oakland	IP.	H.	R.	ER.	BB.	SO.
McCatty (Winner)......	9	6	1	1	4	3

Kansas City	IP.	H.	R.	ER.	BB.	SO.
Jones (Loser).............	8	9	2	2	2	2
Quisenberry	1	1	0	0	0	0

Game-winning RBI—Armas.
Error—Armas. Left on base—Oakland 8, Kansas City 9. Two-base hits—Johnson, Armas 2. Stolen base—Henderson. Sacrifice hits—Klutts, Washington, Johnson, Newman. Time—2:50. Attendance—40,274.

Game of Friday, October 9, at Oakland (N)

Kan. City	AB.	R.	H.	RBI.	Oakland	AB.	R.	H.	RBI.
Wilson, lf	4	0	2	0	Hend'son, lf	2	3	2	0
White, 2b	4	1	2	0	Murphy, cf	4	0	2	1
G. Brett, 3b	4	0	1	0	Johnson, dh	4	0	1	0
Aikens, 1b	4	0	2	0	Armas, rf	3	0	1	1
Otis, cf	4	0	0	1	Klutts, 3b	4	0	0	0
McRae, dh	4	0	1	0	Moore, 1b	4	0	0	0
Hurdle, rf	4	0	1	0	Heath, c	4	0	0	0
Wathan, c	4	0	1	0	McKay, 2b	3	1	1	1
Wash'ton, ss	3	0	0	0	Stanley, ss	2	0	0	0
Totals	35	1	10	1	Totals	30	4	7	3

Kansas City ....0 0 0   1 0 0   0 0 0—1
Oakland ....1 0 1   2 0 0   0 x—4

Kansas City	IP.	H.	R.	ER.	BB.	SO.
Gura (Loser)	3⅔	7	4	3	3	3
Martin	4⅓	0	0	0	2	1

Oakland	IP.	H.	R.	ER.	BB.	SO.
Langford (Winner)	7⅓	10	1	1	0	3
Underwood.................	⅓	0	0	0	0	1
Beard (Save)	1⅓	0	0	0	0	2

Game-winning RBI—Armas.
Errors—Washington, White, Wathan. Double play—Oakland 1. Left on base—Kansas City 7, Oakland 7. Two-base hits—McRae, Murphy. Home run—McKay. Stolen base—Henderson. Time—2:59. Attendance—40,002.

Game of Tuesday, October 6, at Kansas City

Oakland	AB.	R.	H.	RBI.	Kan. City	AB.	R.	H.	RBI.
Henderson, lf	4	0	0	0	Wilson, lf	4	0	1	0
Murphy, cf	3	2	2	1	White, 2b	3	0	0	0
D'right, dh	4	0	1	0	G. Brett, 3b	4	0	0	0
Armas, rf	4	1	1	0	Aikens, 1b	4	0	1	0
Gross, 3b	4	1	2	3	Otis, cf	4	0	0	0
Spencer, 1b	4	0	1	0	McRae, dh	4	0	0	0
Heath, c	4	0	0	0	Hurdle, rf	3	0	1	0
McKay, 2b	4	0	1	0	Wathan, c	2	0	0	0
Stanley, ss	4	0	0	0	Wash'ton, ss	3	0	1	0
Totals	35	4	8	4	Totals	31	0	4	0

Oakland..........................0 0 0   3 0 0   0 1 0—4
Kansas City ....0 0 0   0 0 0   0 0 0—0

Oakland	IP.	H.	R.	ER.	BB.	SO.
Norris (Winner)	9	4	0	0	3	2

Kansas City	IP.	H.	R.	ER.	BB.	SO.
Leonard (Loser).........	8	7	4	1	1	3
Martin........................	1	1	0	0	0	0

Game-winning RBI—Gross.
Errors—Norris, G. Brett, McKay. Double play—Oakland 2, Kansas City 1. Left on base—Oakland 5, Kansas City 7. Two-base hit—Spencer. Home runs—Gross, Murphy. Time—2:35. Attendance—40,592.

1981 CHAMPIONSHIP SERIES

Including

National League Review

National League Box Scores

National League Composite Box Scores

American League Review

American League Box Scores

American League Composite Box Scores

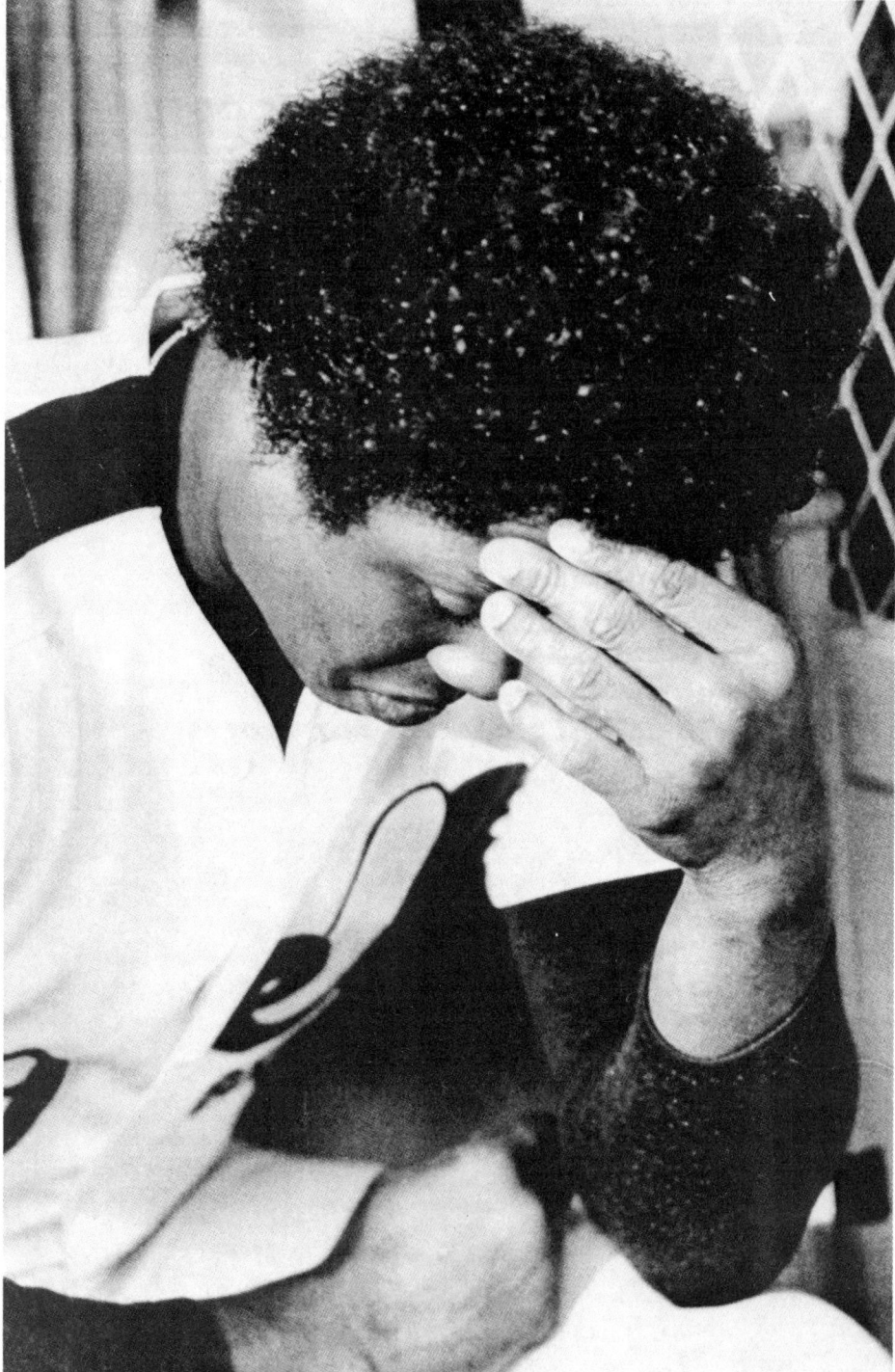

Expos first baseman Warren Cromartie shows the frustration of another near-miss by the Expos.

Dodgers Find Life After Death

By LARRY WIGGE

"I don't know what to think. I'm just numb. I didn't make the pitch where I wanted. Mechanically, I made a mistake. I was called on to do the job and I came up one pitch short."

Montreal ace righthander Steve Rogers was being a little hard on himself October 19 after Rick Monday's two-out, ninth-inning home run had given the Los Angeles Dodgers a 2-1 victory over the Expos and a fifth-game triumph in the National League Championship Series.

"This wasn't supposed to be the last chapter of a book written for a sixth grader," Rogers said. "One pitch different and I could have written a fairy tale ending. Only this was reality."

There was a chill in the air. The rain that had postponed Game 5 one day earlier also had delayed the start of this game by some 26 minutes. Snow was even in the Montreal forecast.

But by mid-afternoon the sun had broken through and Montreal's Ray Burris and rookie sensation Fernando Valenzuela of the Dodgers had dueled on even terms for eight innings.

When Montreal Manager Jim Fanning summoned Rogers from his bullpen, he was calling on his late-season ace. Rogers had won four straight games and had permitted just two runs in 42 innings. But those statistics were compiled in starting roles.

The relief appearance was only the third in Rogers' nine-year major league career and the first since July 3, 1978. His fairy tale did not have a happy ending.

Lightning struck in the form of Monday. Monday's Monday Punch conjured visions of Bobby Thomson vs. Ralph Branca in 1951 and Chris Chambliss vs. Mark Littell in 1976.

"I knew I hit the ball well, but I couldn't see it because of the glare," Monday said. "I saw Andre Dawson racing to the wall in center field, so I thought he was going to catch it. When he didn't catch it, I knew it had cleared the fence. I couldn't control myself."

The 35-year-old Monday was finishing off the final year of a five-year contract with the Dodgers. The only questions he had been answering in recent weeks pertained to what he was going to do in the future—outside of baseball.

Monday batted .315 during the season, including a great month of September

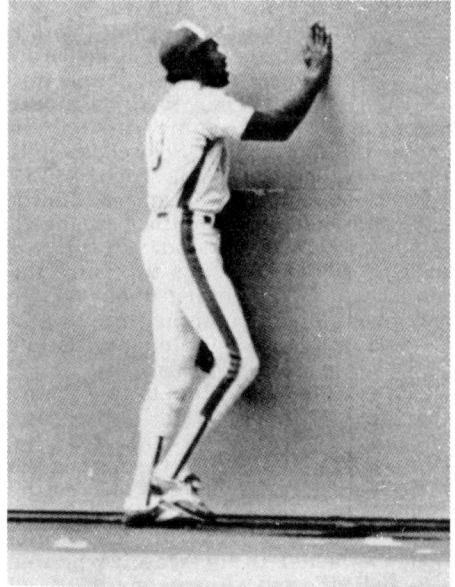

A helpless Andre Dawson taps the wall over which Rick Monday's game-winning homer flew.

when he belted six home runs. He was on the bench when the Championship Series began. Though he started Game 4 in place of a slumping Ken Landreaux, Monday was 1-for-5 in the series. He had struck out four times—hardly the stats of a hero. But. . . .

After the Expos took a 1-0 lead in Game 5, it was Monday who started the Dodgers' fifth inning with a single and eventually came home on Valenzuela's groundout. Then, Monday's clout in the ninth turned the 40-degree chill into a warm wonderful day for Lasorda's Dodger Blue.

The victory kept the Dodgers' record in Championship Series play perfect—they've won all four N.L. series they've played, defeating Pittsburgh in 1974, Philadelphia in '77 and '78 and now the Expos. They had to do it the hard way, too, rebounding from a 2-1 deficit by winning two straight games on the road.

The series opened in warm, sunny Los Angeles, where the Dodgers had beaten the Expos in 18 of their previous 19 meetings. Game 1 of the Championship Series was no different.

The Dodgers were aided by the return

of third baseman Ron Cey, while the Expos were boosted by the return of fleet left fielder Tim Raines, who broke a bone in his hand September 12 and was relegated to pinch-running activity.

Cey, who had missed 28 games with a broken bone in his left forearm, celebrated his return to action with a double into the right-field corner to drive home Steve Garvey for the game's first run in the second inning. Mike Scioscia's single moved Cey to third and he scored on Bill Russell's perfectly placed squeeze bunt.

With two out in the eighth, Cey singled and Pedro Guerrero and Scioscia hit back-to-back home runs to insure the verdict. The Dodgers turned four double plays behind the combined hurling of Burt Hooton, Bob Welch and Steve Howe.

Game 2 pitted Valenzuela for the Dodgers against Burris. Advantage Dodgers?

Burris proved differently, stopping the Dodgers, 3-0, on five singles to even the series at one game apiece. Burris, who said he tried to throw the ball by the Dodgers earlier in the season when he was shelled for six runs in one start and two in another, kept them off balance all night and was never in serious trouble.

With one out in the second inning, Larry Parrish and Jerry White reached Valenzuela for singles. Warren Cromartie followed with a double that scored Parrish. After Chris Speier walked to fill the bases and Burris struck out, Raines singled to left. Singles by Dawson and Gary Carter and Dusty Baker's throwing error provided the Expos with their third run in the sixth inning.

"From Burris to B-R-R-R!!!" read one headline as the series shifted to chilly Montreal for Game 3.

Rogers went the route on a seven-hitter, yielding only one run when the Dodgers put together singles by Baker and Garvey and a run-scoring groundout by Cey. The Dodgers' Jerry Reuss held a 1-0 lead going into the bottom of the sixth.

Dawson touched him for a seemingly harmless two-out single and the tall, blond lefthander walked Carter. Parrish tied the game with an RBI single and White turned from anonymous outfielder (.218 with three homers in '81) into a Canadian national hero when he sent one of Reuss' fastballs over the left-field wall for a 4-1 victory.

The script for Game 4 was similar. With the score knotted at 1-1 going into the eighth inning, it was Dodgers first

baseman Garvey who stepped into the spotlight.

Baker opened the eighth with a single off Bill Gullickson and Garvey followed with a two-run homer. The Dodgers sent 10 men to the plate and added four runs in the ninth, coasting home with a 7-1 triumph.

GAME OF TUESDAY, OCTOBER 13
AT LOS ANGELES

Montreal	AB.	R.	H.	RBI.	PO.	A.
Raines, lf	4	0	1	0	5	0
Scott, 2b	3	0	2	0	1	1
Dawson, cf	4	0	0	0	1	0
Carter, c	3	1	2	0	7	1
Parrish, 3b	4	0	1	1	0	0
Cromartie, 1b	4	0	1	0	8	0
White, rf	4	0	2	0	0	0
Speier, ss	4	0	0	0	2	2
Gullickson, p	1	0	0	0	0	1
Francona, ph	1	0	0	0	0	0
Reardon, p	0	0	0	0	0	0
Totals	32	1	9	1	24	5

Los Angeles	AB.	R.	H.	RBI.	PO.	A.
Lopes, 2b	3	0	1	0	6	4
Landreaux, cf	4	0	1	0	0	0
Baker, lf	3	0	0	0	3	0
Garvey, 1b	4	1	1	0	9	0
Cey, 3b	4	1	2	1	2	2
Thomas, pr-3b	0	1	0	0	0	0
Guerrero, rf	4	1	1	2	2	1
Scioscia, c	3	1	2	1	4	1
Russell, ss	3	0	0	1	1	3
Hooton, p	3	0	0	0	0	0
Welch, p	0	0	0	0	0	0
Howe, p	0	0	0	0	0	0
Totals	31	5	8	5	27	11

Montreal .... 0 0 0   0 0 0   0 0 1—1
Los Angeles .... 0 2 0   0 0 0   0 3 x—5

Montreal	IP.	H.	R.	ER.	BB.	SO.
Gullickson (Loser)	7	5	2	2	2	6
Reardon	1	3	3	3	0	0

Los Angeles	IP.	H.	R.	ER.	BB.	SO.
Hooton (Winner)	7⅓	6	0	0	3	2
Welch	⅔*	2	1	1	0	1
Howe	1	1	0	0	0	0

*Pitched to two batters in the ninth.

Game-winning RBI—Cey.

Errors—None. Double plays—Los Angeles 4. Left on base—Montreal 7, Los Angeles 6. Two-base hits—Carter, White, Cey, Landreaux, Parrish. Home runs—Guerrero, Scioscia. Stolen bases—White, Scott, Lopes 2. Sacrifice hit—Russell. Hit by pitcher—By Gullickson (Baker). Umpires—Pryor, Gregg, Runge, Rennert, Wendelstedt and West. Time—2:47. Attendance—51,273.

GAME OF WEDNESDAY, OCTOBER 14
AT LOS ANGELES (N)

Montreal	AB.	R.	H.	RBI.	PO.	A.
Raines, lf	5	0	3	1	1	0
Francona, lf	0	0	0	0	0	0
Scott, 2b	4	0	0	0	3	3
Dawson, cf	4	1	1	0	4	0
Carter, c	4	0	2	0	4	0
Parrish, 3b	4	1	1	0	0	3
White, rf	3	1	1	0	1	0
Cromartie, 1b	4	0	1	1	8	1
Speier, ss	3	0	1	0	6	3
Burris, p	4	0	0	0	0	0
Totals	35	3	10	2	27	10

Los Angeles	AB.	R.	H.	RBI.	PO.	A.
Lopes, 2b	3	0	0	0	0	3
Monday, ph	1	0	0	0	0	0
Castillo, p	0	0	0	0	0	1
Landreaux, cf	3	0	0	0	1	0
Baker, lf	4	0	2	0	2	0
Garvey, 1b	4	0	1	0	11	1
Cey, 3b	4	0	0	0	1	4
Guerrero, rf	3	0	0	0	1	1
Scioscia, c	3	0	0	0	7	0
Russell, ss	3	0	2	0	4	3
Valenzuela, p	2	0	0	0	0	1
Niedenfuer, p	0	0	0	0	0	1
Forster, p	0	0	0	0	0	0
Pena, p	0	0	0	0	0	0
Johnstone, ph	1	0	0	0	0	0
Sax, 2b	0	0	0	0	0	1
Totals	31	0	5	0	27	16

Montreal .... 0 2 0 0 0 1 0 0 0—3
Los Angeles .... 0 0 0 0 0 0 0 0 0—0

Montreal	IP.	H.	R.	ER.	BB.	SO.
Burris (Winner)	9	5	0	0	2	3

Los Angeles	IP.	H.	R.	ER.	BB.	SO.
Valenzuela (Loser)	6	7	3	3	2	4
Niedenfuer	1/3	2	0	0	0	0
Forster	1/3	0	0	0	0	1
Pena	1 1/3	1	0	0	0	0
Castillo	1	0	0	0	0	1

Game-winning RBI—Cromartie.

Errors—Baker, Speier. Double plays—Montreal 2. Left on base—Montreal 7, Los Angeles 6. Two-base hits—Cromartie, Raines. Wild pitch—Valenzuela. Umpires—Gregg, Runge, Rennert, Wendelstedt, West and Pryor. Time—2:48. Attendance —53,463.

GAME OF FRIDAY, OCTOBER 16
AT MONTREAL (N)

Los Angeles	AB.	R.	H.	RBI.	PO.	A.
Lopes, 2b	4	0	2	0	2	1
Landreaux, cf	3	0	0	0	2	0
Baker, lf	4	1	1	0	1	0
Garvey, 1b	4	0	2	0	14	1
Cey, 3b	4	0	1	1	2	8
Guerrero, rf	4	0	0	0	0	0
Scioscia, c	4	0	0	0	2	0
Russell, ss	3	0	1	0	1	3
Reuss, p	2	0	0	0	0	0
Johnstone, ph	1	0	0	0	0	0
Pena, p	0	0	0	0	0	0
Totals	33	1	7	1	24	13

Montreal	AB.	R.	H.	RBI.	PO.	A.
Raines, lf	4	0	0	0	1	0
Scott, 2b	4	0	0	0	2	4
Dawson, cf	4	1	2	0	0	0
Carter, c	3	1	1	0	5	1
Parrish, 3b	4	1	2	1	1	6
White, rf	3	1	1	3	0	0
Cromartie, 1b	3	0	0	0	15	0
Speier, ss	3	0	1	0	3	4
Rogers, p	2	0	0	0	0	1
Totals	30	4	7	4	27	16

Los Angeles .... 0 0 0 1 0 0 0 0 0—1
Montreal .... 0 0 0 0 0 4 0 0 x—4

Los Angeles	IP.	H.	R.	ER.	BB.	SO.
Reuss (Loser)	7	7	4	4	1	2
Pena	1	0	0	0	0	0

Montreal	IP.	H.	R.	ER.	BB.	SO.
Rogers (Winner)	9	7	1	1	1	5

Game-winning RBI—White.
Error—Scott. Double plays—Montreal 3. Left on

base—Los Angeles 6, Montreal 4. Home run— White. Stolen base—Lopes. Sacrifice hit—Rogers. Wild pitch—Rogers. Passed ball—Scioscia. Umpires—Runge, Rennert, Wendelstedt, West, Pryor and Gregg. Time—2:27. Attendance—54,372.

GAME OF SATURDAY, OCTOBER 17
AT MONTREAL

Los Angeles	AB.	R.	H.	RBI.	PO.	A.
Lopes, 2b	4	0	1	0	2	2
Russell, ss	3	2	0	0	2	1
Baker, lf	4	2	3	3	4	0
Garvey, 1b	5	1	2	2	5	0
Cey, 3b	3	0	2	1	0	0
Monday, rf	4	0	1	0	2	0
Landreaux, cf	0	0	0	0	1	0
Guerrero, cf-rf	4	0	0	0	1	0
Welch, p	0	0	0	0	0	0
Smith, ph	1	0	1	1	0	0
Howe, p	0	0	0	0	0	0
Scioscia	2	0	0	0	7	0
Yeager, ph-c	2	1	1	0	2	0
Hooton, p	2	0	0	0	0	1
Thomas, rf	1	1	1	0	1	0
Totals	35	7	12	7	27	4

Montreal	AB.	R.	H.	RBI.	PO.	A.
Raines, lf	4	0	0	0	0	0
Scott, 2b	4	0	1	0	2	2
Dawson, cf	4	0	0	0	3	0
Carter, c	3	1	1	0	8	0
Parrish, 3b	4	0	0	0	2	3
White, rf	3	0	1	0	3	0
Cromartie, 1b	4	0	1	1	5	1
Speier, ss	3	0	1	0	4	2
Gullickson, p	2	0	0	0	0	1
Fryman, p	0	0	0	0	0	0
Sosa, p	0	0	0	0	0	0
Lee, p	0	0	0	0	0	0
Milner, ph	1	0	0	0	0	0
Totals	32	1	5	1	27	9

Los Angeles .... 0 0 1 0 0 0 0 2 4—7
Montreal .... 0 0 0 1 0 0 0 0 0—1

Los Angeles	IP.	H.	R.	ER.	BB.	SO.
Hooton (Winner)	7 1/3	5	1	0	3	5
Welch	2/3	0	0	0	0	1
Howe	1	0	0	0	0	2

Montreal	IP.	H.	R.	ER.	BB.	SO.
Gullickson (Loser)	7 1/3	7	3	2	4	6
Fryman	1	3	4	4	1	1
Sosa	1/3	1	0	0	1	0
Lee	1/3	1	0	0	0	0

Game-winning RBI—Garvey.
Errors—Parrish, Cey. Double plays—Montreal 2. Left on base—Los Angeles 10, Montreal 8. Two-base hit—Baker. Home run—Garvey. Stolen base —Lopes. Sacrifice hits—Russell, Gullickson, Hooton, Lopes. Umpires—Rennert, Wendelstedt, West, Pryor, Gregg and Runge. Time—3:14. Attendance—54,499.

GAME OF MONDAY, OCTOBER 19
AT MONTREAL

Los Angeles	AB.	R.	H.	RBI.	PO.	A.
Lopes, 2b	4	0	1	0	3	3
Russell, ss	4	0	2	0	2	3
Baker, lf	4	0	0	0	0	0
Garvey, 1b	4	0	0	0	10	0
Cey, 3b	3	0	0	0	0	2
Monday, rf	4	2	2	1	0	0
Landreaux, cf	0	0	0	0	0	0
Guerrero, cf-rf	4	0	1	0	5	0
Scioscia, c	3	0	0	0	7	0
Valenzuela, p	3	0	0	1	0	1
Welch, p	0	0	0	0	0	0
Totals	33	2	6	2	27	9

Montreal	AB.	R.	H.	RBI.	PO.	A.
Raines, lf	4	1	1	0	2	0
Scott, 2b	3	0	0	0	4	4
Dawson, cf	4	0	0	0	4	0
Carter, c	3	0	1	0	3	1
Manuel, pr	0	0	0	0	0	0
Parrish, 3b	3	0	1	0	0	1
White, rf	3	0	0	0	2	0
Cromartie, 1b	3	0	0	0	12	0
Speier, ss	3	0	0	0	0	5
Burris, p	2	0	0	0	0	1
Wallach, ph	1	0	0	0	0	0
Rogers, p	0	0	0	0	0	0
Totals	29	1	3	0	27	12

Los Angeles	IP.	H.	R.	ER.	BB.	SO.
Valenzuela (Winner)	8⅔	3	1	1	3	6
Welch (Save)	⅓	0	0	0	0	0

Montreal	IP.	H.	R.	ER.	BB.	SO.
Burris	8	5	1	1	1	1
Rogers (Loser)	1	1	1	1	0	1

Los Angeles .... 0 0 0   0 1 0   0 0 1—2
Montreal .... 1 0 0   0 0 0   0 0 0—1

Game-winning RBI—Monday.

Error—Speier. Double plays—Los Angeles 1, Montreal 1. Left on base—Los Angeles 5, Montreal 5. Two-base hits—Raines, Parrish. Three-base hit —Russell. Home run—Monday. Stolen base— Lopes. Sacrifice hit—Scott. Wild pitch—Burris. Umpires—Wendelstedt, West, Pryor, Gregg, Runge and Rennert. Time—2:41. Attendance— 36,491.

LOS ANGELES DODGERS' BATTING AND FIELDING AVERAGES

Player—Position	G.	AB.	R.	H.	TB.	2B.	3B.	HR.	RBI.	B.A.	PO.	A.	E.	F.A.
Thomas, pr-3b-rf	2	1	2	1	1	0	0	0	0	1.000	1	0	0	1.000
Smith, ph	1	1	0	1	1	0	0	0	1	1.000	0	0	0	.000
Yeager, ph-c	1	2	1	1	1	0	0	0	0	.500	2	0	0	1.000
Monday, ph-rf	3	9	2	3	6	0	0	1	1	.333	2	0	0	1.000
Baker, lf	5	19	3	6	7	1	0	0	3	.316	10	0	1	.909
Russell, ss	5	16	2	5	7	0	1	0	1	.313	10	13	0	1.000
Garvey, 1b	5	21	2	6	9	0	0	1	2	.286	49	2	0	1.000
Cey, 3b	5	18	1	5	6	1	0	0	3	.278	5	16	1	.955
Lopes, 2b	5	18	0	5	5	0	0	0	0	.278	13	13	0	1.000
Scioscia, c	5	15	1	2	5	0	0	1	1	.133	27	1	0	1.000
Guerrero, rf-cf	5	19	1	2	5	0	0	1	2	.105	9	2	0	1.000
Landreaux, cf	5	10	0	1	2	1	0	0	0	.100	4	0	0	1.000
Welch, p	3	0	0	0	0	0	0	0	0	.000	0	0	0	.000
Howe, p	2	0	0	0	0	0	0	0	0	.000	0	0	0	.000
Pena, p	2	0	0	0	0	0	0	0	0	.000	0	0	0	.000
Castillo, p	1	0	0	0	0	0	0	0	0	.000	0	1	0	1.000
Forster, p	1	0	0	0	0	0	0	0	0	.000	0	0	0	.000
Niedenfuer, p	1	0	0	0	0	0	0	0	0	.000	0	1	0	1.000
Sax, 2b	1	0	0	0	0	0	0	0	0	.000	0	1	0	1.000
Johnstone, ph	2	2	0	0	0	0	0	0	0	.000	0	0	0	.000
Reuss, p	1	2	0	0	0	0	0	0	0	.000	0	0	0	.000
Hooton, p	2	5	0	0	0	0	0	0	0	.000	0	1	0	1.000
Valenzuela, p	2	5	0	0	0	0	0	0	1	.000	0	2	0	1.000
Totals	5	163	15	38	55	3	1	4	15	.233	132	53	2	.989

MONTREAL EXPOS' BATTING AND FIELDING AVERAGES

Player—Position	G.	AB.	R.	H.	TB.	2B.	3B.	HR.	RBI.	B.A.	PO.	A.	E.	F.A.
Carter, c	5	16	3	7	8	1	0	0	0	.438	27	3	0	1.000
White, rf	5	16	2	5	9	1	0	1	3	.313	6	0	0	1.000
Parrish, 3b	5	19	2	5	7	2	0	0	2	.263	3	13	1	.941
Raines, lf	5	21	1	5	7	2	0	0	1	.238	9	0	0	1.000
Speier, ss	5	16	0	3	3	0	0	0	0	.188	15	16	2	.939
Cromartie, 1b	5	18	0	3	4	1	0	0	2	.167	48	2	0	1.000
Scott, 2b	5	18	0	3	3	0	0	0	0	.167	12	14	1	.963
Dawson, cf	5	20	2	3	3	0	0	0	0	.150	12	0	0	1.000
Fryman, p	1	0	0	0	0	0	0	0	0	.000	0	0	0	.000
Lee, p	1	0	0	0	0	0	0	0	0	.000	0	0	0	.000
Manuel, pr	1	0	0	0	0	0	0	0	0	.000	0	0	0	.000
Reardon, p	1	0	0	0	0	0	0	0	0	.000	0	0	0	.000
Sosa, p	1	0	0	0	0	0	0	0	0	.000	0	0	0	.000
Francona, ph-lf	2	1	0	0	0	0	0	0	0	.000	0	0	0	.000
Milner, ph	1	1	0	0	0	0	0	0	0	.000	0	0	0	.000
Wallach, ph	1	1	0	0	0	0	0	0	0	.000	0	0	0	.000
Rogers, p	2	2	0	0	0	0	0	0	0	.000	0	1	0	1.000
Gullickson, p	2	3	0	0	0	0	0	0	0	.000	0	2	0	1.000
Burris, p	2	6	0	0	0	0	0	0	0	.000	0	1	0	1.000
Totals	5	158	10	34	44	7	0	1	8	.215	132	52	4	.979

LOS ANGELES DODGERS' PITCHING RECORDS

Pitcher	G.	GS.	CG.	IP.	H.	R.	ER.	BB.	SO.	HB.	WP.	W.	L.	Pct.	ERA.
Hooton	2	2	0	14⅔	11	1	0	6	7	0	0	2	0	1.000	0.00
Pena	2	0	0	2⅓	1	0	0	0	0	0	0	0	0	.000	0.00
Howe	2	0	0	2	1	0	0	0	2	0	0	0	0	.000	0.00
Castillo	1	0	0	1	0	0	0	0	1	0	0	0	0	.000	0.00
Forster	1	0	0	⅓	0	0	0	0	1	0	0	0	0	.000	0.00
Niedenfuer	1	0	0	⅓	2	0	0	0	0	0	0	0	0	.000	0.00
Valenzuela	2	2	0	14⅔	10	4	4	5	10	0	1	1	1	.500	2.45
Reuss	1	1	0	7	7	4	4	1	2	0	0	0	1	.000	5.14
Welch	3	0	0	1⅔	2	1	1	0	2	0	0	0	0	.000	5.40
Totals	5	5	0	44	34	10	9	12	25	0	1	3	2	.600	1.84

No shutouts. Save—Welch.

Game 5 hero Rick Monday (right) and winning pitcher Fernando Valenzuela celebrate their good fortune after beating the Expos.

MONTREAL EXPOS' PITCHING RECORDS

Pitcher	G.	GS.	CG.	IP.	H.	R.	ER.	BB.	SO.	HB.	WP.	W.	L.	Pct.	ERA.
Lee	1	0	0	⅓	1	0	0	0	0	0	0	0	0	.000	0.00
Sosa	1	0	0	⅓	1	0	0	1	0	0	0	0	0	.000	0.00
Burris	2	2	1	17	10	1	1	3	4	0	1	1	0	1.000	0.53
Rogers	2	1	1	10	8	2	2	1	6	0	1	1	1	.500	1.80
Gullickson	2	2	0	14⅓	12	5	4	6	12	1	0	0	2	.000	2.51
Reardon	1	0	0	1	3	3	3	0	0	0	0	0	0	.000	27.00
Fryman	1	0	0	1	3	4	4	1	1	0	0	0	0	.000	36.00
Totals	5	5	2	44	38	15	14	12	23	1	2	2	3	.400	2.86

Shutout—Burris. No saves.

COMPOSITE SCORE BY INNINGS

Los Angeles	0	2	1		1	1	0		0	5	5 — 15
Montreal	1	2	0		1	0	5		0	0	1 — 10

Game-winning RBIs—Cey, Cromartie, White, Garvey, Monday.
Sacrifice hits—Russell 2, Rogers, Gullickson, Hooton, Lopes, Scott.
Sacrifice flies—None.
Stolen bases—Lopes 5, White, Scott.
Caught stealing—Raines.
Double plays—Lopes, Russell and Garvey 2; Speier, Scott and Cromartie 2; Scott, Speier and Cromartie 2; Cey, Lopes and Garvey; Guerrero and Lopes; Russell, Lopes and Garvey; Parrish, Scott and Cromartie; Speier and Scott; Parrish, Speier and Scott; Parrish and Cromartie.
Left on bases—Los Angeles 6, 6, 6, 10, 5–33; Montreal 7, 7, 4, 8, 5–31.
Hit by pitcher—By Gullickson (Baker).
Passed ball—Scioscia.
Balks—None.
Time of games—First game, 2:47; second game, 2:48; third game, 2:27; fourth game, 3:14; fifth game, 2:41.
Attendance—First game, 51,273; second game, 53,463; third game, 54,372; fourth game, 54,499; fifth game, 36,491.
Umpires—Pryor, Gregg, Runge, Rennert, Wendelstedt and West.
Official scorers—Chris Mortensen, Torrance (Cal.) Daily Breeze; Michael Spinelli.

Oakland left fielder Rickey Henderson goes high, but can't reach Lou Piniella's three-run homer in the Yanks' Game 2 victory.

Hot Yankees Sweep Past A's

By LARRY WIGGE

While everyone was concentrating on the war of words between Billy Martin and George Steinbrenner as the Oakland A's and New York Yankees prepared to square off in the American League Championship Series, Graig Nettles quietly went about his business.

The 37-year-old Nettles started the series with a three-run double, keying the Yankees' 3-1 victory in Game 1. He went 4-for-4, including a three-run homer, to lead the Yanks in a 13-3 rout in Game 2. Then he ended the series the way he started it—with a three-run double that climaxed a 4-0 triumph and a three-game Yankee sweep.

"This series was a victory for the veterans," said Nettles. He added that it was an inside joke. But everyone knew Steinbrenner had issued a win-or-else ultimatum to the club during the A.L. East Division Series against Milwaukee. The "or else" meant that the veteran New York club would be broken up.

Nettles' 6-for-12 performance with a Championship Series-record nine RBIs was a dramatic contrast to his 1-for-17 batting mark in the division series against the Brewers.

"George made his big speech before we eliminated Milwaukee in the division series," Nettles said. "He said we'd better win or a lot of the veterans would be gone. We joked about it later."

Joke or no joke, the Yankees were laced with veteran players. Six of their eight starters were over 30 as were seven of their pitchers. Someone suggested in jest that the proud Yankee pinstripes had been erased and replaced by varicose veins.

Martin tried to pull a psyche job on the Yankees before the series, saying that his youthful A's were "awesome against left-handers." He also pointed out that the Yanks had to use their top two pitchers, Ron Guidry and Dave Righetti, to finish off the Brewers.

"If I'm only the No. 3 man in the Yankee rotation, then we must be in pretty good shape because we still have No. 1 and No. 2 waiting to pitch," growled 35-year-old Tommy John after he, Ron Davis and Goose Gossage had stymied the A's on six hits in Game 1.

The victory was secured in the first inning when Larry Milbourne stroked a one-out single, Dave Winfield and Oscar

Relief pitcher Ron Davis lost this battle in Game 1, but the Yanks won the war.

Gamble walked, and Nettles drilled an 0-2 pitch into the left-center field gap to clear the bases.

The A's held a 3-1 lead in Game 2 behind Steve McCatty after they pushed across two runs in the top of the fourth inning. But the Yanks responded with seven runs in their half and rolled to a 13-3 win.

Nettles opened the inning with a single and later set another Championship Series record by becoming the first player to get two hits in one inning. After Bob Watson flied out, Cerone was hit by a pitch and Willie Randolph stroked an RBI single. Jerry Mumphrey walked to load the bases and Dave Beard replaced McCatty on the mound for Oakland. Milbourne tied the game with a single before Winfield provided a two-run double and Lou Piniella blasted a three-run homer.

Game 3 was a pitchers battle. Oakland's Matt Keough and Righetti of New York threw zeros for the first five innings. Then Randolph broke up the scoreless tie with a two-out homer in the sixth to back the five-hit pitching by

Righetti, Davis and Gossage as the Yankees captured their 33rd A.L. pennant.

The Yankees finished off the A's in three straight games, but to borrow a line from Yogi Berra, a coach for the Yankees, "It isn't over 'til it's over." Not when the Yanks are involved at least.

A team party was held at an Oakland restaurant the night of October 15. Friends and family were present and what was billed as a celebration turned into a shoving match when Nettles' family was allegedly mistreated by some of Reggie Jackson's friends. Before order could be restored, Nettles had popped Jackson with a right hand and Mr. October was seeing stars.

It was just another chapter in the wacky world of the Yankees.

GAME OF TUESDAY, OCTOBER 13
AT NEW YORK (N)

Oakland	AB.	R.	H.	RBI.	PO.	A.
Henderson, lf	4	0	2	0	1	0
Murphy, cf	2	0	0	1	6	0
Johnson, dh	3	0	0	0	0	0
Armas, rf	4	0	1	0	2	1
Klutts, 3b	3	0	2	0	1	1
Gross, ph-3b	1	0	0	0	0	0
Moore, 1b	4	0	0	0	4	1
Newman, c	2	0	0	0	4	1
Drumright, ph	1	0	0	0	0	0
Heath, c	1	0	0	0	1	0
McKay, 2b	4	0	0	0	1	2
Picciolo, ss	3	1	1	0	3	1
Totals	32	1	6	1	23	7

New York	AB.	R.	H.	RBI.	PO.	A.
Mumphrey, cf	4	0	1	0	1	0
Milbourne, ss	4	1	3	0	2	4
Winfield, lf	3	0	0	0	2	0
Jackson, rf	3	1	0	0	1	0
Gamble, dh	2	1	0	0	0	0
Piniella, ph-dh	1	0	1	0	0	0
Nettles, 3b	3	0	1	3	0	2
Watson, 1b	3	0	1	0	8	0
Brown, pr	0	0	0	0	0	0
Revering, 1b	1	0	0	0	3	0
Cerone, c	2	0	0	0	6	0
Randolph, 2b	3	0	0	0	4	7
Totals	29	3	7	3	27	13

Oakland 0 0 0 0 1 0 0 0 0–1
New York 3 0 0 0 0 0 0 0 x–3

Oakland	IP.	H.	R.	ER.	BB.	SO.
Norris (Loser)	7⅓	6	3	3	2	4
Underwood	⅔	1	0	0	2	0

New York	IP.	H.	R.	ER.	BB.	SO.
John (Winner)	6	6	1	1	3	
Davis	1⅓	0	0	0	2	3
Gossage (Save)	1⅔	0	0	0	0	0

Game-winning RBI—Nettles.

Errors—Nettles, Henderson. Double plays—New York 2. Left on base—Oakland 7, New York 7. Two-base hits—Nettles, Henderson 2. Stolen base—Jackson. Sacrifice hit—Cerone. Umpires—Bremigan, Goetz, Neudecker, Springstead, Merrill and Voltaggio. Time—2:52. Attendance—55,740.

GAME OF WEDNESDAY, OCTOBER 14
AT NEW YORK

Oakland	AB.	R.	H.	RBI.	PO.	A.
Henderson, lf	5	0	1	1	3	0
Murphy, cf	5	0	2	0	3	0
Moore, 1b	2	0	0	0	3	2
Spencer, ph-1b	2	0	0	0	3	2
Armas, rf	4	0	0	0	1	1
Klutts, 3b	2	1	1	0	0	2
Gross, ph-3b	2	0	0	0	1	0
Heath, c	4	1	2	0	2	0
McKay, 2b	4	0	2	1	2	3
Bosetti, dh	1	1	1	0	0	0
Drumright, ph-dh	2	0	0	0	0	0
Stanley, ss	3	0	1	1	4	2
Davis, ph	1	0	0	0	0	0
Totals	37	3	11	3	22	12

New York	AB.	R.	H.	RBI.	PO.	A.
Mumphrey, cf	5	2	4	0	3	0
Milbourne, ss	5	2	2	1	0	1
Robertson, ph-ss	1	0	0	0	2	1
Winfield, lf	5	2	2	2	0	0
Jackson, rf	1	0	0	1	0	0
Piniella, rf	3	1	1	3	0	0
Brown, rf	1	1	1	0	0	0
Gamble, dh	3	1	1	1	0	0
Nettles, 3b	4	2	4	3	3	0
Rodriguez, 3b	0	0	0	0	0	0
Watson, 1b	4	0	1	1	2	0
Revering, 1b	1	0	1	0	3	1
Cerone, c	4	1	1	0	10	2
Foote, c	0	0	0	0	0	0
Randolph, 2b	5	1	2	1	2	3
Totals	42	13	19	13	27	8

Oakland 0 0 1 2 0 0 0 0 0– 3
New York 1 0 0 7 0 1 4 0 x–13

Oakland	IP.	H.	R.	ER.	BB.	SO.
McCatty (Loser)	3⅓	6	5	5	2	2
Beard	⅔	5	3	3	0	0
Jones	2	2	1	1	1	0
Kingman	⅓	3	3	3	0	0
Owchinko	1⅔	3	1	1	0	0

New York	IP.	H.	R.	ER.	BB.	SO.
May	3⅓	6	3	3	0	5
Frazier (Winner)	5⅔	5	0	0	1	5

Game-winning RBI—Winfield.

Error—Klutts. Double plays—New York 2. Left on base—Oakland 8, New York 11. Two-base hits—Mumphrey, Bosetti, Winfield, Murphy. Three-base hit—Henderson. Home runs—Piniella, Nettles. Stolen base—Winfield. Sacrifice fly—Gamble. Hit by pitcher—By McCatty (Cerone), by Jones (Nettles). Wild pitch—Frazier. Passed ball—Cerone. Umpires—Goetz, Neudecker, Springstead, Merrill, Voltaggio and Bremigan. Time—3:08. Attendance—48,497.

GAME OF THURSDAY, OCTOBER 15
AT OAKLAND (N)

New York	AB.	R.	H.	RBI.	PO.	A.
Mumphrey, cf	3	0	1	0	0	0
Milbourne, ss	4	1	1	0	0	2
Winfield, lf	5	0	0	0	2	0
Murcer, dh	3	0	1	0	0	0
Piniella, ph-dh	1	1	1	0	0	0
Gamble, rf	1	0	0	0	4	0
Foote, ph	1	0	1	0	0	0
Brown, pr-rf	0	1	0	0	0	0
Nettles, 3b	5	0	1	3	1	2
Watson, 1b	5	0	1	0	7	0
Cerone, c	4	0	1	0	7	0
Randolph, 2b	4	1	2	1	6	2
Totals	36	4	10	4	27	6

Oakland	AB.	R.	H.	RBI.	PO.	A.
Henderson, lf	2	0	1	0	2	0
Heath, lf	1	0	0	0	0	1
Murphy, cf	1	0	0	0	0	0
Bosetti, ph-cf	3	0	0	0	2	0
Johnson, dh	3	0	0	0	0	0
Armas, rf	4	0	1	0	2	0
Klutts, 3b	2	0	0	0	2	2
Gross, ph-3b	2	0	0	0	1	0
Moore, 1b	2	0	2	0	6	0
Spencer, ph-1b	1	0	0	0	1	0
McKay, 2b	3	0	1	0	4	1
Newman, c	3	0	0	0	5	0
Picciolo, ss	2	0	0	0	2	4
Drumright, ph	1	0	0	0	0	0
Stanley, ss	0	0	0	0	0	0
Totals	30	0	5	0	27	8

New York .... 0 0 0   0 0 1   0 0 3—4
Oakland .... 0 0 0   0 0 0   0 0 0—0

New York	IP.	H.	R.	ER.	BB.	SO.
Righetti (Winner)	6	4	0	0	2	4
Davis	2	0	0	0	0	1
Gossage	1	1	0	0	0	2

Oakland	IP.	H.	R.	ER.	BB.	SO.
Keough (Loser)	8⅓	7	2	1	6	4
Underwood	⅔	3	2	2	0	0

Game-winning RBI—Randolph.
Errors—Picciolo, McKay. Double plays—New York 2, Oakland 1. Left on base—New York 12, Oakland 5. Two-base hit—Nettles. Home run—Randolph. Stolen bases—Henderson 2. Sacrifice hit—Milbourne. Wild pitch—Keough. Umpires—Neudecker, Springstead, Merrill, Voltaggio, Bremigan and Goetz. Time—3:19. Attendance—47,302.

NEW YORK YANKEES' BATTING AND FIELDING AVERAGES

Player—Position	G.	AB.	R.	H.	TB.	2B.	3B.	HR.	RBI.	B.A.	PO.	A.	E.	F.A.
Brown, pr-rf	3	1	2	1	1	0	0	0	0	1.000	0	0	0	.000
Foote, c-ph	2	1	0	1	1	0	0	0	0	1.000	0	0	0	.000
Piniella, ph-dh-rf	3	5	2	3	6	0	0	1	3	.600	0	0	0	.000
Nettles, 3b	3	12	2	6	11	2	0	1	9	.500	4	4	1	.889
Mumphrey, cf	3	12	2	6	7	1	0	0	0	.500	4	0	0	1.000
Revering, 1b	2	2	0	1	1	0	0	0	0	.500	6	1	0	1.000
Milbourne, ss	3	13	4	6	6	0	0	0	1	.462	2	7	0	1.000
Randolph, 2b	3	12	2	4	5	1	0	0	2	.333	12	12	0	1.000
Murcer, dh	1	3	0	1	1	0	0	0	0	.333	0	0	0	.000
Watson, 1b	3	12	0	3	3	0	0	0	1	.250	17	0	0	1.000
Gamble, dh-rf	3	6	2	1	1	0	0	0	1	.167	4	0	0	1.000
Winfield, lf	3	13	2	2	3	1	0	0	2	.154	6	0	0	1.000
Cerone, c	3	10	1	1	1	0	0	0	0	.100	23	2	0	1.000
Davis, p	2	0	0	0	0	0	0	0	0	.000	0	0	0	.000
Gossage, p	2	0	0	0	0	0	0	0	0	.000	0	0	0	.000
Frazier, p	1	0	0	0	0	0	0	0	0	.000	0	2	0	1.000
John, p	1	0	0	0	0	0	0	0	0	.000	0	0	0	.000
May, p	1	0	0	0	0	0	0	0	0	.000	0	0	0	.000
Righetti, p	1	0	0	0	0	0	0	0	0	.000	0	1	0	1.000
Rodriguez, 3b	1	0	0	0	0	0	0	0	0	.000	0	0	0	.000
Robertson, ph-ss	1	1	0	0	0	0	0	0	0	.000	2	1	0	1.000
Jackson, rf	2	4	1	0	0	0	0	0	1	.000	1	0	0	1.000
Totals	3	107	20	36	47	5	0	2	20	.336	81	30	1	.991

OAKLAND ATHLETICS' BATTING AND FIELDING AVERAGES

Player—Position	G.	AB.	R.	H.	TB.	2B.	3B.	HR.	RBI.	B.A.	PO.	A.	E.	F.A.
Davis, ph	1	1	0	1	1	0	0	0	0	1.000	0	0	0	.000
Klutts, 3b	3	7	1	3	3	0	0	0	0	.429	3	5	1	.889
Henderson, lf	3	11	0	4	8	2	1	0	1	.364	6	0	1	.857
Heath, c-lf	3	6	1	2	2	0	0	0	0	.333	3	1	0	1.000
Stanley, ss	2	3	0	1	1	0	0	0	1	.333	4	2	0	1.000
McKay, 2b	3	11	0	3	3	0	0	0	1	.273	7	6	1	.929
Murphy, cf	3	8	0	2	3	1	0	0	1	.250	9	0	0	1.000
Moore, 1b	3	8	0	2	2	0	0	0	0	.250	13	3	0	1.000
Bosetti, dh-ph-cf	2	4	1	1	2	1	0	0	0	.250	2	0	0	1.000
Picciolo, ss	2	5	1	1	1	0	0	0	0	.200	5	5	1	.909
Armas, rf	3	12	0	2	2	0	0	0	0	.167	5	2	0	1.000
Underwood, p	2	0	0	0	0	0	0	0	0	.000	0	0	0	.000
Beard, p	1	0	0	0	0	0	0	0	0	.000	0	1	0	1.000
Jones, p	1	0	0	0	0	0	0	0	0	.000	1	0	0	1.000
Keough, p	1	0	0	0	0	0	0	0	0	.000	0	1	0	1.000
Kingman, p	1	0	0	0	0	0	0	0	0	.000	0	0	0	.000
McCatty, p	1	0	0	0	0	0	0	0	0	.000	1	1	0	1.000
Norris, p	1	0	0	0	0	0	0	0	0	.000	1	2	0	1.000
Owchinko, p	1	0	0	0	0	0	0	0	0	.000	0	1	0	1.000
Spencer, ph-1b	2	3	0	0	0	0	0	0	0	.000	4	2	0	1.000
Drumright, ph-dh	3	4	0	0	0	0	0	0	0	.000	0	0	0	.000
Gross, ph-3b	3	5	0	0	0	0	0	0	0	.000	2	0	0	1.000
Newman, c	2	5	0	0	0	0	0	0	0	.000	9	1	0	1.000
Johnson, dh	2	6	0	0	0	0	0	0	0	.000	0	0	0	.000
Totals	3	99	4	22	28	4	1	0	4	.222	75	33	4	.964

Third baseman Graig Nettles sparkled, as usual, with his glove, but let his bat do most of the damage to the A's.

NEW YORK YANKEES' PITCHING RECORDS

Pitcher	G.	GS.	CG.	IP.	H.	R.	ER.	BB.	SO.	HB.	WP.	W.	L.	Pct.	ERA.
Righetti	1	1	0	6	4	0	0	2	4	0	0	1	0	1.000	0.00
Frazier	1	0	0	5⅔	5	0	0	1	5	0	1	1	0	1.000	0.00
Davis	2	0	0	3⅓	0	0	0	2	4	0	0	0	0	.000	0.00
Gossage	2	0	0	2⅔	1	0	0	0	2	0	0	0	0	.000	0.00
John	1	1	0	6	6	1	1	1	3	0	0	1	0	1.000	1.50
May	1	1	0	3⅓	6	3	3	0	5	0	0	0	0	.000	8.10
Totals	3	3	0	27	22	4	4	6	23	0	1	3	0	1.000	1.33

Shutout—Righetti-Davis-Gossage (combined). Save—Gossage

OAKLAND ATHLETICS' PITCHING RECORDS

Pitcher	G.	GS.	CG.	IP.	H.	R.	ER.	BB.	SO.	HB.	WP.	W.	L.	Pct.	ERA.
Keough	1	1	0	8⅓	7	2	1	6	4	0	1	0	1	.000	1.08
Norris	1	1	0	7⅓	6	3	3	2	4	0	0	0	1	.000	3.68
Jones	1	0	0	2	2	1	1	1	0	1	0	0	0	.000	4.50
Owchinko	1	0	0	1⅔	3	1	1	0	0	0	0	0	0	.000	5.40
McCatty	1	1	0	3⅓	6	5	5	2	2	1	0	0	1	.000	13.50
Underwood	2	0	0	1⅓	4	2	2	2	0	0	0	0	0	.000	13.50
Beard	1	0	0	⅔	5	3	3	0	0	0	0	0	0	.000	40.50
Kingman	1	0	0	⅓	3	3	3	0	0	0	0	0	0	.000	81.00
Totals	3	3	0	25	36	20	19	13	10	2	1	0	3	.000	6.84

No shutouts or saves.

COMPOSITE SCORE BY INNINGS

New York	4	0	0	7	0	2	4	0	3 — 20
Oakland	0	0	1	2	1	0	0	0	0 — 4

Game-winning RBIs—Nettles, Winfield, Randolph.
Sacrifice hits—Cerone, Milbourne.
Sacrifice fly—Gamble.
Stolen bases—Henderson 2, Jackson, Winfield.
Caught stealing—Mumphrey.
Double plays—Nettles, Randolph and Watson 2; Milbourne, Randolph and Watson 2; Frazier, Cerone and Watson; Revering, Robertson and Revering; Picciolo and Spencer.
Left on bases—New York 7, 11, 12—30; Oakland 7, 8, 5—20.
Passed ball—Cerone.
Balks—None.
Time of games—First game, 2:52; second game, 3:08; third game, 3:19.
Attendance—First game, 55,740; second game, 48,497; third game, 47,302.
Umpires—Bremigan, Goetz, Neudecker, Springstead, Merrill and Voltaggio.
Official scorers—Red Foley, New York Daily News; Glenn Schwartz, San Francisco Examiner.

1981 WORLD SERIES

Including

Review of '81 Series

Official Play-by-Play, Each Game

Official Composite Box Score

World Series Tables — Attendance, Money, Results

Dodgers Steve Howe (left), catcher Steve Yeager and first baseman Steve Garvey celebrate their championship status.

Dodgers Trip Stumbling Yanks

By LARRY WIGGE

Giggling into a champagne bottle, Los Angeles Dodgers third baseman Ron Cey said: "I'm glad they aren't going to present that award to me posthumously."

Cey shared the Most Valuable Player Award for the 78th World Series with teammates Steve Yeager and Pedro Guerrero. But it was Cey who symbolized the get-back-on-your-feet approach the Dodgers used in coming from behind to win the National League West Division Series against Houston, the N.L. Championship Series against Montreal, and the World Series against the New York Yankees.

He had just driven home the go-ahead run in the Dodgers' 9-2 victory over New York in the sixth and deciding game of the Series. His three-run homer and sparkling diving catch of a Bobby Murcer bunt in Game 3 were also key contributions, especially after the Dodgers had dropped the first two games of the Series in New York.

Cey was down, but not out, when fireballing Yankee righthander Rich Gossage drilled him in the head with a 94 mph fastball in the eighth inning of Game 5. He suffered dizziness throughout the days that followed, but he still played.

"The most important thing to me on Sunday morning was winning Game 5 and to take the lead in the Series," Cey recalled. "But by the time I got home that night, the most important thing was being alive, sitting with my kids."

Anyone who saw the fierce collision when Gossage's bullett-like delivery met with Cey's head and saw him lying motionless in the batter's box had to think the worst. "I remember hitting the ground in slow motion. At least, it felt like slow motion," Cey said.

The Dodgers turned the tables on the Yankees, who had lost the first two games of the 1978 World Series before bouncing back with four straight victories over the Dodgers.

"I guess you could call us the Comeback Kids," Cey said of the Dodgers' first championship club since 1965. "But we haven't been kids in a long time." The Dodgers infield of Steve Garvey, Dave Lopes, Bill Russell and Cey had remained intact for seven seasons.

The title was even sweeter when you consider that Yankee third baseman

Ron Cey had to be helped from the field after taking a Goose Gossage fastball on the head.

Graig Nettles, Cey's counterpart, stole the headlines in Game 1 by spearing Garvey's line drive in the eighth inning to preserve a 5-3 victory.

"If that gets by Nettles and starts rolling around in the corner, we've got trouble," New York Manager Bob Lemon said afterward. Instead, Gossage picked up the pieces and saved the game for Ron Guidry.

The Yanks leaped to the lead in the first inning of the Series. Jerry Mumphrey singled and Lou Piniella stroked a ground-rule double with two out, bringing veteran first baseman Bob Watson to the plate. Watson lofted a three-run homer over the right-center field wall. It was his first Series at-bat.

Dodgers lefthander Jerry Reuss was driven from the mound in the third after Mumphrey's second single, a stolen base and Piniella's single. The Yankees took a 5-0 lead in the fourth when Los Angeles reliever Bobby Castillo walked four batters in succession.

Yeager touched Guidry for a home run in the fifth innning. Jay Johnstone greeted Gossage with a run-scoring single and Dusty Baker hit a sacrifice fly for two runs in the eighth before Nettles' nifty glovework ended the threat.

Tommy John, who pitched for the Dodgers in '78, combined with Gossage in limiting Los Angeles to five hits in a 3-0 Game 2 victory.

Larry Milbourne's RBI single in the fifth inning would have stood up. But, in the eighth, Watson swatted a run-scoring single and Willie Randolph produced a sacrifice fly.

"When you pitch against a club you played with, knowledge becomes a dangerous thing," said John. "You can't let yourself pitch to what you know are the hitters' weaknesses. You have to pitch your own game, as if they were any other team."

The Dodgers halted their six-game World Series losing streak to the Yankees, dating back to '78, with a 5-4 win October 23. Fernando Valenzuela, who surrendered nine hits and seven walks, went the route to gain the victory.

"I think he's the best closing pitcher in baseball," said Los Angeles Manager Tommy Lasorda. "I don't count pitches, but I knew it was more than he'd ever thrown before in his life. I knew that if I could have him around for the end, I wanted him around for the end.

"He didn't have his good stuff. But he went out there like a sharp poker player and bluffed, without having a good hand."

The Yankees were minus third baseman Nettles (swollen thumb) and whether or not he could have flagged down a couple of choppers hit by Garvey and Guerrero to tie the game, 4-4, in the fifth inning will go unanswered. Mike Scioscia's double-play grounder produced the game-winning run later in the inning.

Reggie Jackson made his initial '81 Series appearance in Game 4 and went 3-for-3, but the Yankees squandered a 4-0 cushion and lost, 8-7.

Dodgers starting pitcher Bob Welch couldn't retire a batter, yielding Randolph's triple, Milbourne's double, a walk to Dave Winfield and Jackson's single. Watson stroked a sacrifice fly off reliever Dave Goltz and Randolph clubbed a second-inning homer, with Rick Cerone's run-scoring single in the third mounting the four-run advantage.

The Dodgers scored twice in the third and closed the gap to 4-3 in the fifth. But

the Yanks moved ahead, 6-3, in the sixth. Reliever Ron Davis couldn't hold the lead, however.

Scioscia coaxed Davis for a walk and Johnstone, pinch-hitting, drove a two-run homer into the right-field seats. It was the 13th pinch-homer in Series history and the first since Bernie Carbo's memorable three-run blast for Boston in the epic sixth-game battle with Cincinnati in 1975.

But Jackson's batting heroics were overshadowed by his key defensive lapse. Jackson lost Dave Lopes' popup in the sun, the ball caromed off his chest in right field and Lopes raced to second base. Lopes then stole third and waltzed home on Bill Russell's single for a 6-6 tie.

Baker snapped an 0-for-11 slump with an infield single in the seventh. Rick Monday then hit a sinking liner to center. Bobby Brown, who had just entered the game in lieu of a benched Mumphrey, got a bad jump on the ball and came up short in his diving attempt for the catch.

John was summoned from the bullpen after George Frazier walked Guerrero to load the bases with none out. Yeager drove a sacrifice fly and, one out later, Lopes chopped a single off the hard Dodger Stadium infield for an 8-6 lead. Jackson's eighth-inning homer—his 10th career Series wallop—was too little, too late.

Yankees' Owner George Steinbrenner was fuming after the loss but New York Manager Lemon suggested: "Even George's horses lose sometimes, but he doesn't go out and shoot 'em."

Cey's co-Series MVP recipients, Guerrero and Yeager, came front and center in Game 5.

With New York's Guidry rolling into the bottom of the seventh with a 1-0 lead, the Yankees seemed on the verge of taking a 3-2 lead back to New York. Guerrero, who had struggled early in the Series, positioned himself in a crouch at the suggestion of hitting instructor Manny Mota. It worked. He belted many of Guidry's offerings into the left-field seats for a 1-1 tie. Yeager followed with a similar swat for a 2-1 victory. It was the ninth time back-to-back homers had been hit in Series play. Reuss went all the way for the Dodgers and allowed only five hits.

Game 6 was postponed by day-long rains October 27 at New York. When the Series finale was held the next evening, Yankees fans will long remember the lasting image of Tommy John shaking his head and saying, "I can't believe that!" when Lemon removed him from the game for a pinch-hitter in the fourth inning of a 1-1 game.

New York reliever Frazier suffered the dubious distinction of losing three games in a row and became the first three-game loser since Claude Williams of the 1919 Black Sox, when, with two outs and Lopes on second after a walk and sacrifice, Cey bounced a soft grounder up the middle. The ball kicked off the grass lip of the infield and skidded past second baseman Randolph.

After Baker singled Cey to third, Guerrero blasted a 410-foot, two-run triple for a 4-1 margin. He slugged a homer later in the game and wound up with five runs batted in.

"I was trying to get a run by using Murcer to pinch hit so that I could go to Goose (Gossage) in the seventh," reasoned Lemon. "John had given up six hits and Burt Hooton was pitching well for them. I didn't know if I'd get a man in scoring position the rest of the night."

"I had just held that club to one run for 13 innings," shrugged John. "All I know is I wanted to pitch."

"This makes up for 1977 and '78," said Baker.

"It's been a long time coming," said Garvey, who batted .417 in the six games and was the only player on either side with double figures (10) in the hit column.

The MVP awards were well-deserved. Guerrero hit .333 (a 7-for-13 finish after an 0-for-8 start) and drove in seven runs. Yeager provided some clutch hitting (two homers and two game-winning RBIs) after a season of virtual inactivity. And Cey hit .350, collected six RBIs and made the rally-busting catch on Murcer's foul pop in Game 4.

Game 1

**At New York
October 20**

Los Ang. (N.L.)	AB.	R.	H.	PO.	A.	E.
Lopes, 2b	3	1	0	3	1	0
Russell, ss	3	0	0	2	1	0
cJohnstone	1	0	1	0	0	0
Stewart, p	0	0	0	0	0	0
Baker, lf	2	0	1	3	0	0
Garvey, 1b	4	0	1	5	0	0
Cey, 3b	4	0	1	0	1	0
Guerrero, cf	3	0	0	3	0	0
Monday, rf	4	0	0	4	0	0
Yeager, c	3	1	1	3	0	0
dLandreaux	1	0	1	0	0	0
Reuss, p	1	0	0	0	1	0
Castillo, p	0	0	0	0	2	0
Goltz, p	0	0	0	0	0	0
aSax, ph	1	0	0	0	0	0
Niedenfuer, p	0	0	0	0	0	0
bThomas, ss	0	1	0	1	1	0
Totals	30	3	5	24	7	0

New York (A.L.).	AB.	R.	H.	PO.	A.	E.
Randolph, 2b	3	0	0	3	3	0
Mumphrey, cf	3	2	2	3	0	0
Winfield, lf	3	0	0	0	1	0
Piniella, rf	4	1	2	4	0	0
Watson, 1b	3	1	2	8	0	0
Nettles, 3b	3	0	0	1	3	0
Cerone, c	3	0	0	8	0	0
Milbourne, ss	4	1	0	0	2	0
Guidry, p	2	0	0	0	0	0
Davis, p	0	0	0	0	0	0
Gossage, p	0	0	0	0	0	0
Totals	28	5	6	27	9	0

Los Angeles............................ 0 0 0 0 1 0 0 2 0–3
New York................................ 3 0 1 1 0 0 0 0 *–5

Los Angeles	IP.	H.	R.	ER.	BB.	SO.
Reuss (L)	2⅔	5	4	4	0	2
Castillo	1	0	1	1	5	0
Goltz	⅓	0	0	0	0	0
Niedenfuer	3	1	0	0	0	0
Stewart	1	0	0	0	1	0

New York	IP.	H.	R.	ER.	BB.	SO.
Guidry (W)	7	4	1	1	2	6
Davis	0†	0	2	2	2	0
Gossage (S)	2	1	0	0	0	2

†Pitched to two batters in eighth.

Bases on balls—Off Castillo 5 (Watson, Cerone, Randolph, Mumphrey, Winfield), off Stewart 1 (Nettles), off Guidry 2 (Baker, Guerrero), off Davis 2 (Thomas, Lopes).

Strikeouts—By Reuss 2 (Winfield, Guidry), by Guidry 6 (Monday 2, Guerrero, Yeager, Reuss, Garvey), by Gossage 2 (Guerrero, Monday).

Game-winning RBI—Watson.

aFlied out for Goltz in fifth. bWalked for Niedenfuer in eighth. cSingled in one run for Russell in eighth. dGrounded out for Yeager in ninth. Runs batted in—Johnstone, Baker, Yeager, Winfield, Piniella, Watson 3. Two-base hit—Piniella. Home runs—Yeager, Watson. Stolen bases—Mumphrey, Piniella. Sacrifice hit—Guidry. Sacrifice fly—Baker. Passed ball—Cerone. Double play—Thomas and Garvey. Left on bases—Los Angeles 5, New York 6. Umpires—Barnett (A.L.) plate, Colosi (N.L.) first, Cooney (A.L.) second, Harvey (N.L.) third, Garcia (A.L.) left, Stello (N.L.) right. Time—2:32. Attendance—56,470.

FIRST INNING

Los Angeles—Lopes laced a grounder down the third-base line, but Nettles made a diving backhanded stop and threw to first for the out. Russell grounded to Milbourne. Baker popped to Randolph. No runs, no hits, no errors, none left.

New York—Randolph grounded to Lopes. Mumphrey grounded a single to the left of Lopes. Winfield struck out. Piniella cracked a ground-rule double down the right-field line, Mumphrey stopping at third. Watson drilled a home run to right field, Mumphrey and Piniella scoring ahead of him. Nettles flied to Monday. Three runs, three hits, no errors, none left.

SECOND INNING

Los Angeles—Garvey lined a single off the glove of Nettles. Cey popped to Watson. Guerrero struck out. Monday struck out. No runs, one hit, no errors one left.

New York—Cerone grounded to Russell. Milbourne hit a line drive off the right ankle of Reuss, who retrieved the ball and threw to first for the out. Guidry struck out. No runs, no hits, no errors, none left.

Graig Nettles broke the Dodgers' back with his magic glove in Game 1.

THIRD INNING

Los Angeles—Yeager struck out. Reuss struck out. Lopes grounded to Milbourne. No runs, no hits, no errors, none left.

New York—Randolph grounded to Garvey. Mumphrey singled to center. Winfield flied to Baker on the warning track. On the first pitch to Piniella, Mumphrey stole second without a throw as Yeager was unable to handle the ball. Piniella grounded a single between third and short, Mumphrey scoring. Castillo replaced Reuss on the mound for Los Angeles. With Watson batting, Piniella stole second. Watson walked. Nettles flied to Monday. One run, two hits, no errors, two left.

FOURTH INNING

Los Angeles—Russell grounded to Nettles. Baker lined a single to left. Garvey flied to Mumphrey. Cey flied to Piniella. No runs, one hit, no errors, one left.

New York—Cerone walked. Milbourne forced Cerone, Castillo to Russell. Guidry sacrificed, Castillo to Lopes, Milbourne advancing to second. Randolph walked. Mumphrey walked, loading the bases. Winfield walked, Milbourne scoring and the bases remaining loaded. Goltz replaced Castillo on the mound for Los Angeles. Piniella popped to Lopes. One run, no hits, no errors, three left.

FIFTH INNING

Los Angeles—Guerrero flied to Mumphrey. Monday grounded to Randolph. Yeager hit a towering home run to right field. Sax batted for Goltz and flied to Mumphrey. One run, one hit, no errors, none left.

New York—Niedenfuer replaced Goltz on the mound for Los Angeles. Watson lined a single to the left of Lopes. Nettles flied to Monday. Cerone popped to Russell. Milbourne forced Watson, Cey to Lopes. No runs, one hit, no errors, one left.

SIXTH INNING

Los Angeles—Lopes grounded to Randolph. Russell flied to Piniella. Baker walked. Garvey struck out. No runs, no hits, no errors, one left.

New York—Guidry lined to Guerrero. Randolph flied to Baker. Mumphrey flied to Baker. No runs, no hits, no errors, none left.

SEVENTH INNING

Los Angeles—Cey singled into the left-field corner but was thrown out trying to reach second base, Winfield to Randolph. Guerrero walked. Monday struck out. Yeager flied to Piniella. No runs, one hit, no errors, one left.

New York—Winfield fouled out to Yeager. Piniella flied to Guerrero. Watson lined to Monday. No runs, no hits, no errors, none left.

EIGHTH INNING

Los Angeles—Davis replaced Guidry on the mound for New York. Thomas batted for Niedenfuer and walked. Lopes walked, Thomas advancing to second. Gossage replaced Davis on the mound for New York. Johnstone batted for Russell and lined a single to right, Thomas scoring and Lopes advancing to third. Baker flied to Piniella, Lopes scoring after the catch. Garvey hit a line drive headed for the left-field corner, but Nettles made a sensational diving catch. Cey forced Johnstone, Nettles to Randolph. Two runs, one hit, no errors, one left.

New York—Stewart came in to pitch for Los Angeles and assumed the second position in the batting order. Thomas remained in the game to play shortstop. Nettles walked. Cerone flied to Guerrero. Milbourne grounded to Thomas, who forced Nettles at second and threw on to first for a double play. No runs, no hits, no errors, none left.

NINTH INNING

Los Angeles—Guerrero struck out. Monday was called out on strikes. Landreaux batted for Yeager and grounded to Randolph. No runs, no hits, no errors, none left.

Game 2

At New York
October 21

Los Ang. (N.L.)	AB.	R.	H.	PO.	A.	E.
Lopes, 2b	3	0	0	7	3	1
eMonday	1	0	0	0	0	0
Howe, p	0	0	0	0	0	0
Stewart, p	0	0	0	0	0	1
Russell, ss	4	0	1	0	5	0
Baker, lf	4	0	0	0	0	0
Garvey, 1b	3	0	2	6	0	0
Cey, 3b	4	0	0	0	3	0
Guerrero, rf	4	0	0	4	0	0
Landreaux, cf	3	0	0	4	0	0
Yeager, c	2	0	0	1	0	0
bJohnstone	1	0	0	0	0	0
Scioscia, c	0	0	0	1	0	0
Hooton, p	2	0	0	1	0	0
Forster, p	0	0	0	0	1	0
cSmith	1	0	1	0	0	0
dSax, 2b	0	0	0	0	0	0
Totals	32	0	4	24	12	2

New York (A.L.)	AB.	R.	H.	PO.	A.	E.
Mumphrey, cf	2	0	0	1	0	0
Milbourne, ss	4	0	1	1	3	1
Winfield, lf	4	0	0	1	0	0
Gamble, rf	2	0	0	2	0	0
fPiniella	1	0	1	0	0	0
gBrown, rf	0	1	0	0	0	0
Nettles, 3b	4	1	2	1	5	0
Watson, 1b	4	0	2	13	0	0
Cerone, c	2	0	0	7	0	0
Randolph, 2b	2	1	0	1	3	0
John, p	1	0	0	0	2	0
aMurcer	0	0	0	0	0	0
Gossage, p	1	0	0	0	0	0
Totals	27	3	6	27	13	1

Los Angeles	000	000	000—	0
New York	000	010	02*—	3

Los Angeles	IP.	H.	R.	ER.	BB.	SO.
Hooton (L)	6†	3	1	0	4	1
Forster	1	0	0	0	1	0
Howe	1/3	2	2	2	0	0
Stewart	2/3	1	0	0	1	1

New York	IP.	H.	R.	ER.	BB.	SO.
John (W)	7	3	0	0	0	4
Gossage (S)	2	1	0	0	1	3

†Pitched to two batters in seventh.

Bases on balls—Off Hooton 4 (Mumphrey, Gamble, Cerone, Randolph), off Forster 1 (Mumphrey), off Stewart 1 (Cerone), off Gossage 1 (Garvey).
Strikeouts—By Hooton 1 (Nettles), by Stewart 1 (Gossage), by John 4 (Hooton 2, Baker, Landreaux), by Gossage 3 (Monday, Cey, Guerrero).
Game-winning RBI—Milbourne.
aSacrificed for John in seventh. bFlied out for Yeager in eighth. cSingled for Forster in eighth. dRan for Smith in eighth. eStruck out for Lopes in eighth. fSingled for Gamble in eighth. gRan for Piniella in eighth and scored. Runs batted in—Milbourne, Watson, Randolph. Two-base hit—Milbourne. Sacrifice hits—John, Murcer. Sacrifice fly—Randolph. Double play—Russell, Lopes and Garvey. Left on bases—Los Angeles 6, New York 9. Umpires—Colosi (N.L.) plate, Cooney (A.L.) first, Harvey (N.L.) second, Garcia (A.L.) third, Stello (N.L.) left, Barnett (A.L.) right. Time—2:29. Attendance—56,505.

FIRST INNING

Los Angeles—Lopes flied to Mumphrey. Russell grounded to Randolph. Baker grounded to Randolph. No runs, no hits, no errors, none left.

New York—Mumphrey walked. Milbourne forced Mumphrey, Russell to Lopes. Winfield forced Milbourne, Cey to Lopes. Gamble walked, Winfield advancing to second. Nettles was called out on strikes. No runs, no hits, no errors, two left.

SECOND INNING

Los Angeles—Garvey was out trying to bunt, Nettles to Watson. Cey grounded to Nettles. Guerrero grounded to Milbourne. No runs, no hits, no errors, none left.

New York—Watson singled to right. Cerone flied to Guerrero. Randolph forced Watson, Cey to Lopes. John grounded to Lopes. No runs, one hit, no errors, one left.

THIRD INNING

Los Angeles—Landreaux bounced to John. Yeager grounded to Milbourne. Hooton struck out. No runs, no hits, no errors, none left.

New York—Mumphrey lined to Guerrero. Milbourne flied to Landreaux. Winfield grounded to Russell. No runs, no hits, no errors, none left.

FOURTH INNING

Los Angeles—Lopes grounded to Randolph. Russell grounded to Milbourne. Baker struck out. No runs, no hits, no errors, none left.

New York—Gamble popped to Lopes. Nettles singled to left-center. Watson forced Nettles, Cey to Lopes. Cerone forced Watson, Russell to Lopes. No runs, one hit, no errors, one left.

FIFTH INNING

Los Angeles—Garvey grounded a single to the left of Milbourne. Cey went out on a slow bouncer to Nettles, Garvey advancing to second. Guerrero grounded to Milbourne, whose throw to third base was obscured by Garvey's slide. Nettles could not handle the throw, Garvey was safe and Milbourne was charged with an error, Guerrero reaching first. Landreaux struck out. Yeager hit a line drive back through the box, but John knocked it down and threw to Watson, who tagged Yeager as they collided. No runs, one hit, one error, two left.

New York—Randolph hit a hard one-hopper to Lopes, who was not able to handle the chance and was charged with an error. John sacrificed, Hooton making the play unassisted as Randolph advanced to second. Mumphrey flied to Landreaux. Milbourne doubled down the left-field line, Randolph scoring. Winfield grounded to Lopes. One run, one hit, one error, one left.

SIXTH INNING

Los Angeles—Hooton struck out. Lopes grounded to Nettles. Russell lined a single between Nettles and the third-base bag. Baker forced Russell, Nettles to Randolph. No runs, one hit, no errors, one left.

New York—Gamble flied to Landreaux. Nettles flied to Guerrero. Watson grounded to Russell, who made a strong throw from deep in the hole. No runs, no hits, no errors, none left.

SEVENTH INNING

Los Angeles—Garvey lined a single over Milbourne's head. Cey flied to Gamble on the warning track. Guerrero lined to Milbourne. Landreaux lined to Winfield, who made the catch running toward the line. No runs, one hit, no errors, one left.

New York—Cerone walked. Randolph walked, Cerone advancing to second. Forster replaced Hooton on the mound for Los Angeles. Murcer batted for John and sacrificed, Forster to

Garvey, the runners advancing to second and third. Mumphrey was walked intentionally. Milbourne grounded into a double play, Russell to Lopes to Garvey. No runs, no hits, no errors, two left.

EIGHTH INNING

Los Angeles—Gossage came in to pitch for New York. Johnstone batted for Yeager and flied to Gamble. Smith batted for Forster and grounded a single between Watson and Randolph. Sax ran for Smith. Monday batted for Lopes and struck out. Russell fouled out to Nettles. No runs, one hit, no errors, one left.

New York—Howe came in to pitch for Los Angeles and assumed the first position in the batting order. Scioscia came in to catch and bat eighth and Sax remained in the game to play second base. Winfield flied to Landreaux. Piniella batted for Gamble and singled to center. Brown ran for Piniella. Nettles dropped a check-swing single into center field, Brown stopping at second. Stewart replaced Howe on the mound for Los Angeles. Watson grounded a single to the right of a diving Russell, Brown scoring and Nettles stopping at second. Before making a pitch to Cerone, Stewart attempted to pick off Nettles, but his throw was in the dirt and skipped into center field, Nettles advancing to third and Watson to second on the error. Cerone was walked intentionally. Randolph flied to Guerrero on the warning track, Nettles scoring after the catch. Gossage struck out. Two runs, three hits, one error, two left.

NINTH INNING

Los Angeles—Brown remained in the game to play right field for New York. Baker grounded to Watson. Garvey walked. Cey was called out on strikes. Guerrero was called out on strikes. No runs, no hits, no errors, one left.

Game 3

At Los Angeles
October 23

New York (N.L.)	AB.	R.	H.	PO.	A.	E.
Randolph, 2b	2	0	0	5	3	0
Mumphrey, cf	5	0	0	0	0	0
Winfield, lf	3	0	0	2	0	0
Piniella, rf	5	1	1	0	0	0
Watson, 1b	4	1	2	9	0	0
Cerone, c	4	2	2	5	1	0
Rodriguez, 3b	4	0	2	1	3	0
Milbourne, ss	2	0	2	2	4	0
Righetti, p	1	0	0	0	0	0
Frazier, p	1	0	0	0	0	0
May, p	0	0	0	0	0	0
cMurcer	1	0	0	0	0	0
Davis, p	0	0	0	0	0	0
Totals	32	4	9	24	11	0

Los Ang. (N.L.)	AB.	R.	H.	PO.	A.	E.
Lopes, 2b	4	1	2	7	3	1
Russell, ss	5	1	2	0	3	0
Baker, lf	4	0	0	2	0	0
Garvey, 1b	4	1	2	7	1	0
Cey, 3b	2	2	2	2	3	0
Guerrero, cf-rf	3	0	1	1	0	0
Monday, rf	2	0	1	2	0	0
bThomas, cf	1	0	0	0	0	0
Yeager, c	1	0	0	2	0	0
aScioscia, c	3	0	1	4	1	0
Valenzuela, p	3	0	0	0	1	0
Totals	32	5	11	27	12	1

New York .... 0 2 2 0 0 0 0 0 0—4
Los Angeles .... 3 0 0 0 2 0 0 0 *—5

New York	IP.	H.	R.	ER.	BB.	SO.
Righetti	2†	5	3	3	2	1
Frazier (L)	2‡	3	2	2	2	1
May	3	2	0	0	0	2
Davis	1	1	0	0	0	1

Los Angeles	IP.	H.	R.	ER.	BB.	SO.
Valenzuela (W)	9	9	4	4	7	6

†Pitched to two batters in third.
‡Pitched to four batters in fifth.

Bases on balls—Off Righetti 2 (Valenzuela, Cey), off Frazier 2 (Cey, Monday), off Valenzuela 7 (Randolph 3, Winfield 2, Milbourne 2). Strikeouts—By Righetti 1 (Garvey), by Frazier 1 (Guerrero), by May 2 (Baker, Guerrero), by Davis 1 (Lopes), by Valenzuela 6 (Winfield, Righetti, Cerone, Frazier, Mumphrey, Piniella). Game-winning RBI—None.

aGrounded out for Yeager in third. bHit into double play for Monday in seventh. cBunted into double play for May in eighth. Runs batted in—Watson, Cerone, Milbourne, Cey 3, Guerrero. Two-base hits—Lopes, Cerone, Watson, Guerrero. Home runs—Cey, Watson, Cerone. Caught stealing—Randolph. Sacrifice hits—Righetti, Lopes. Hit by pitcher—By Righetti (Guerrero). Double plays—Randolph and Watson; Milbourne, Randolph and Watson; Russell, Lopes and Garvey; Cey and Lopes. Left on bases—New York 9, Los Angeles 9. Umpires—Cooney (A.L.) plate, Harvey (N.L.) first, Garcia (A.L.) second, Stello (N.L.) third, Barnett (A.L.) left, Colosi (N.L.) right. Time—3:04. Attendance—56,236.

FIRST INNING

New York—Randolph walked. Mumphrey forced Randolph, Cey to Lopes. Winfield walked, Mumphrey advancing to second. Piniella grounded into a double play, Russell to Lopes to Garvey. No runs, no hits, no errors, one left.

Los Angeles—Lopes lashed a double down the right-field line. Russell pushed a bunt past the mound and toward Randolph for a single, Lopes advancing to third. Baker popped to Randolph. Garvey struck out. Cey drilled a home run to left-center, Lopes and Russell scoring ahead of him. Guerrero was hit by a pitch. Monday hit a ground ball that was bobbled by Watson, whose throw to Righetti at first base was not in time, Guerrero advancing to third on the single. Yeager popped to Watson. Three runs, four hits, no errors, two left.

SECOND INNING

New York—Watson homered to left field. Cerone nearly followed suit, lining a two-bagger off the railing to the low gate in left. Rodriguez flied to Monday, Cerone advancing to third after the catch. Milbourne singled between Garvey and Lopes, Cerone scoring. Righetti sacrificed, Garvey to Lopes, Milbourne advancing to second. Randolph walked. Mumphrey grounded to Valenzuela, who threw to Garvey for the out. Two runs, three hits, no errors, two left.

Los Angeles—Valenzuela walked. Lopes sacrificed Valenzuela to second, Cerone to Randolph. Russell grounded to Randolph, Valenzuela advancing to third. Baker popped to Watson. No runs, no hits, no errors, one left.

THIRD INNING

New York—Winfield struck out. Piniella singled to center. Watson popped to Lopes. Cerone drove a home run to left-center, Piniella scoring ahead of him. Rodriguez' bouncer over the mound was fielded by Lopes, who threw a one-hopper past Garvey. Rodriguez was credited with a single and advanced to second on Lopes' error. Milbourne was walked intentionally. Righetti struck out. Two runs, three hits, one error two left.

Los Angeles—Garvey lined a single to center. Cey walked, Garvey advancing to second. Frazier replaced Righetti on the mound for New York. Guerrero struck out. Monday flied to Winfield. Scioscia batted for Yeager and grounded to Milbourne. No runs, one hit, no errors, two left.

FOURTH INNING

New York—Scioscia remained in the game to catch for Los Angeles. Randolph grounded to Russell. Mumphrey grounded to Russell. Winfield walked. Piniella lined to Baker. No runs, no hits, no errors, one left.

Los Angeles—Valenzuela grounded to Milbourne. Lopes grounded to Rodriguez. Russell lined a single to left. Baker forced Russell, Rodriguez to Randolph. No runs, one hit, no errors, one left.

FIFTH INNING

New York—Watson lined a ground-rule double down the right-field line. Cerone struck out. Rodriguez grounded to Lopes, Watson advancing to third. Milbourne was walked intentionally. Frazier struck out. No runs, one hit, no errors, two left.

Los Angeles—Garvey singled on a high bouncer to third. Cey walked, Garvey advancing to second. Guerrero bounced a double over Rodriguez' head and down the line, Garvey scoring and Cey stopping at third. Monday was walked intentionally, loading the bases. May replaced Frazier on the mound for New York. Scioscia grounded into a double play, Randolph fielding his grounder at second base and throwing to Watson for the second out. Cey scored and Guerrero advanced to third. Valenzuela grounded to Milbourne. Two runs, two hits, no errors, one left.

SIXTH INNING

New York—Randolph walked. With Mumphrey batting, Randolph was caught stealing, Scioscia to Lopes. Mumphrey struck out. Winfield grounded to Cey. No runs, no hits, no errors, none left.

Los Angeles—Lopes lined a single to left. Russell flied to Winfield. Baker struck out. Garvey fouled out to Rodriguez. No runs, one hit, no errors, one left.

SEVENTH INNING

New York—Piniella flied to Monday. Watson flied to Baker, who made the catch against the wall. Cerone popped to Lopes in short right-center. No runs, no hits, no errors, none left.

Los Angeles—Cey lined a single to the right of Randolph. Guerrero struck out. Thomas batted for Monday and grounded into a double play, Milbourne to Randolph to Watson. No runs, one hit, no errors, none left.

EIGHTH INNING

New York—Thomas remained in the game to play center field for Los Angeles and Guerrero moved to right. Rodriguez lined a single to left. Milbourne singled on a trickler to the glove-hand side of Lopes and Rodriguez advanced to second. Murcer batted for May and, bunting for a hit, popped the ball into the air just outside the foul line midway between home and third. Cey made a diving catch and then threw to Garvey to double off Milbourne, Rodriguez remaining at second. Randolph hit a slow grounder toward the third-base bag. Cey probably could not have throw out Randolph, but he did not have to because Rodriguez tried to advance and was tagged out by Cey

when he stumbled trying to reverse field. No runs, two hits, no errors, one left.

Los Angeles—Davis came in to pitch for New York. Scioscia lined a single over Randolph's head. Valenzuela attempted to sacrifice but forced Scioscia at second, Rodriguez to Milbourne. Lopes struck out. Russell popped to Milbourne. No runs, one hit, no errors, one left.

NINTH INNING

New York—Mumphrey grounded to Lopes. Winfield flied to Guerrero. Piniella struck out. No runs, no hits, no errors, none left.

Game 4

At Los Angeles
October 24

New York (A.L.)	AB.	R.	H.	PO.	A.	E.
Randolph, 2b	5	3	2	2	0	0
Milbourne, ss	4	1	1	1	3	0
Winfield, cf-lf-cf	4	0	0	4	0	0
Jackson, rf	3	2	3	2	0	1
Gamble, lf	4	1	2	2	0	0
cBrown, cf	0	0	0	1	0	0
fPiniella, lf	1	0	0	0	0	0
Watson, 1b	3	0	1	5	0	0
Cerone, c	5	0	2	7	0	0
hRobertson	0	0	0	0	0	0
Rodriguez, 3b	4	0	2	0	3	0
gFoote	1	0	0	0	0	0
Reuschel, p	2	0	0	0	0	0
May, p	1	0	0	0	1	0
Davis, p	0	0	0	0	0	0
Frazier, p	1	0	0	0	0	0
John, p	0	0	0	0	0	0
iMurcer	1	0	0	0	0	0
Totals	39	7	13	24	7	1

Los Ang. (N.L.)	AB.	R.	H.	PO.	A.	E.
Lopes, 2b	5	2	2	5	2	0
Russell, ss	5	0	1	2	5	1
Garvey, 1b	5	1	3	5	1	0
Cey, 3b	5	0	2	1	1	0
Baker, lf	5	1	1	4	0	0
Monday, rf	3	1	1	2	0	0
Thomas, cf	1	0	0	3	0	0
Guerrero, cf-rf	3	0	2	2	1	0
Scioscia, c	1	1	0	2	0	0
eYeager, c	0	0	0	1	0	0
Welch, p	0	0	0	0	0	0
Goltz, p	0	0	0	0	0	0
aLandreaux	1	1	1	0	0	0
Forster, p	0	0	0	0	0	0
bSmith	1	0	0	0	0	0
Niedenfuer, p	0	0	0	0	0	0
dJohnstone	1	1	1	0	0	0
Howe, p	0	0	0	0	1	1
Totals	36	8	14	27	11	2

New York	2 1 1	0 0 2	0 1 0—7			
Los Angeles	0 0 2	0 1 3	2 0*—8			

New York	IP.	H.	R.	ER.	BB.	SO.
Reuschel	3⅓	6	2	2	1	2
May	1⅓	2	1	1	0	1
Davis	1	2	3	2	1	2
Frazier (L)	⅔§	2	2	2	1	0
John	2	2	0	0	0	2

Los Angeles	IP.	H.	R.	ER.	BB.	SO.
Welch	0†	3	2	2	1	0
Goltz	3	4	2	2	1	2
Forster	1	1	0	0	2	0
Niedenfuer	2	2	2	0	1	0
Howe (W)	3	3	1	1	0	1

†Pitched to four batters in first.
‡Pitched to two batters in fourth.
§Pitched to three batters in seventh.

Bases on balls—Off Reuschel 1 (Monday), off Davis 1 (Scioscia), off Frazier 1 (Guerrero), off Welch 1 (Winfield), off Goltz 1 (Watson), off Forster 2 (Randolph, Jackson), off Niedenfuer 1 (Jackson).

Strikeouts—By Reuschel 2 (Russell, Baker), by May 1 (Smith), by Davis 2 (Baker, Monday), by John 2 (Garvey, Thomas), by Goltz 2 (Rodriguez, Reuschel), by Howe 1 (Foote).

Game-winning RBI—Yeager.

aDoubled for Goltz in third. bStruck out for Forster in fourth. cRan for Gamble in sixth. dHit two-run homer for Niedenfuer in sixth. eHit sacrifice fly for Scioscia in seventh. fGrounded out for Brown in eighth. gStruck out for Rodriguez in ninth. hRan for Cerone in ninth. iReached first base safely on error in ninth. Runs batted in—Randolph, Milbourne, Jackson, Gamble, Watson 2, Cerone, Lopes 2, Russell, Cey 2, Yeager, Johnstone 2. Two-base hits—Milbourne, Landreaux, Garvey, Monday. Three-base hit—Randolph. Home runs—Randolph, Johnstone, Jackson. Stolen bases—Lopes 2, Winfield. Sacrifice hits—Milbourne, Scioscia, Howe. Sacrifice fly—Watson, Yeager. Double plays—None. Left on bases—New York 12, Los Angeles 10. Umpires—Harvey (N.L) plate, Garcia (A.L.) first, Stello (N.L.) second, Barnett (A.L.) third, Colosi (N.L.) left, Cooney (A.L.) right. Time—3:32. Attendance—56,242.

FIRST INNING

New York—Randolph lined a one-hopper to right field that bounced over Monday's head and rolled to the fence for a triple. Milbourne doubled down the right-field line, Randolph scoring. Winfield walked. Jackson lined a single to left-center, loading the bases. Goltz replaced Welch on the mound for Los Angeles. Gamble flied to Guerrero; the runners held their bases. Watson flied to Baker, Milbourne scoring after the catch. Cerone forced Jackson, Lopes unassisted. Two runs, three hits, two left.

Los Angeles—Lopes grounded to Rodriguez. Russell grounded to Rodriguez. Garvey lined a single to right-center. Cey flied to Winfield. No runs, one hit, no errors, one left.

SECOND INNING

New York—Rodriguez struck out. Reuschel was called out on strikes. Randolph unloaded a home run to right-center. Milbourne grounded to Lopes. One run, one hit, no errors, none left.

Los Angeles—Baker lined to Milbourne. Monday lined to Gamble. Guerrero blooped a single to center. Scioscia lined to Gamble. No runs, one hit, no errors, one left.

THIRD INNING

New York—Winfield grounded to Lopes. Jackson grounded a single to center. Gamble forced Jackson, Russell to Lopes. Watson walked, Gamble advancing to second. Cerone lined a single between Cey and Russell, Gamble scoring and Watson advancing to second. Rodriguez loaded the bases with a single on a slow roller that Russell backhanded in the hole. Reuschel forced Rodriguez, Russell to Lopes. One run, three hits, no errors, three left.

Los Angeles—Landreaux batted for Goltz and grounded a double along the right-field line. Lopes singled to right, Landreaux scoring. With Russell batting and the count 0-1, Lopes stole second. Russell was called out on strikes. Garvey singled on a high two-hopper to Rodriguez, Lopes advancing to third. Cey grounded out to Mil-

Jay Johnstone accepted his due after keeping the Dodgers alive in Game 4 with a pinch home run.

bourne, whose throw from deep short was taken on one hop by Watson; Lopes scored and Garvey advanced to second. Baker struck out. Two runs, three hits, no errors, one left.

FOURTH INNING

New York—Forster came in to pitch for Los Angeles. Randolph walked. Milbourne sacrificed, Cey to Lopes, Randolph advancing to second. Winfield grounded to Russell, who threw to Cey to nail Randolph trying to advance. Winfield remained at first and, with the count to Jackson 2-2, stole second. Jackson walked. Gamble loaded the bases with a single on a slow roller that Lopes took behind second. Watson forced Gamble, Russell to Lopes. No runs, one hit, no errors, three left.

Los Angeles—Monday walked. Guerrero lined a single to the right of Milbourne, Monday stopping at second. May replaced Reuschel on the mound for New York. Scioscia advanced the runners with a sacrifice, May to Randolph. Smith batted for Forster and struck out. Lopes grounded to Milbourne. No runs, one hit, no errors, two left.

FIFTH INNING

New York—Niedenfuer came in to pitch for Los Angeles. Cerone flied to Guerrero. Rodriguez popped to Russell. May fouled out to Baker. No runs, no hits, no errors, none left.

Los Angeles—Russell flied to Jackson. Garvey doubled down the left-field line. Cey lined a single to left, Garvey scoring. Davis replaced May on the mound for New York. Baker was called out on strikes. Monday struck out. One run, two hits, no errors, one left.

SIXTH INNING

New York—Randolph grounded to Russell, whose throw to Garvey was high for an error. Garvey argued that he had tagged Randolph as he slid toward first, but first base umpire Garcia disagreed. Milbourne, after failing to sacrifice, fouled out to Baker. Winfield flied to Baker in deep left, Randolph advancing to second after the catch. Jackson was walked intentionally. Gamble ripped an 0-2 pitch to center for a single, Randolph scoring and Jackson advancing to third. Watson hit a sinking liner to left-center that was trapped by Baker, Jackson scoring and Gamble advancing to third on the single. Brown ran for Gamble. Cerone flied to Monday. Two runs, two hits, one error, two left.

Los Angeles—Brown remained in the game to play center field for New York and Winfield moved to left. Guerrero flied to Brown. Scioscia walked. Johnstone batted for Niedenfuer and blasted a home run to right-center, Scioscia scoring ahead of him. Lopes hit a fly ball that Jackson lost in the sun, the ball bouncing off his chest for a two-base error. With Russell batting, and the count 0-1, Lopes stole third. Russell lined a single to left, Lopes scoring. Frazier replaced Davis on the mound for New York. Garvey flied to Winfield. Cey flied to Winfield. Three runs, two hits, one error, one left.

SEVENTH INNING

New York—Howe came in to pitch for Los Angeles. Rodriguez singled to left-center but was thrown out trying for a double, Guerrero to Russell. Frazier hit a grounder that Garvey backhanded and took to the bag for the out. Randolph flied to Monday. No runs, one hit, no errors, none left.

Los Angeles—Baker beat out a slow roller to short. Monday doubled to short right-center as Brown at first misjudged the ball and then nearly made a sliding catch; Baker stopping at third. Guerrero was walked intentionally, loading the bases. John replaced Frazier on the mound for New York. Yeager batted for Scioscia and flied to Jackson, Baker scoring after the catch. Howe advanced the runners with a sacrifice, Rodriguez to Randolph. Lopes hit a high bouncer to third for a single, Monday scoring and Guerrero advancing to third. Russell grounded to Milbourne. Two runs, three hits, no errors, two left.

EIGHTH INNING

New York—Yeager remained in the game to catch for Los Angeles. Thomas came in to play center field and Guerrero moved to right. Milbourne flied to Thomas. Winfield flied to Thomas on the track. Jackson clouted a home run to right-center. Piniella batted for Brown and bounced out, Howe to Garvey. One run, one hit, no errors, none left.

Los Angeles—Piniella remained in the game to play left field for New York and Winfield moved back to center. Garvey struck out. Cey singled to right. Baker flied to Winfield. Thomas struck out. No runs, one hit, no errors, one left.

NINTH INNING

New York—Watson grounded to Russell, whose throw was off line but snared by Garvey, who applied the tag. Cerone singled up the middle. Foote batted for Rodriguez and struck out. Robertson ran for Cerone. Murcer batted for John and reached on an error when Howe was not on the bag to take the throw from Garvey, who had fielded the grounder; Robertson stopped at second. Randolph flied to Thomas on the warning track. No runs, one hit, one error, two left.

Game 5

At Los Angeles
October 25

New York (A.L.)	AB.	R.	H.	PO.	A.	E.
Randolph, 2b	3	0	0	0	0	0
Milbourne, ss	4	0	1	1	1	0
Winfield, cf-lf	4	0	1	4	0	0
Jackson, rf	4	1	1	0	0	0
Gossage, p	0	0	0	0	0	0
Watson, 1b	3	0	0	6	0	0
Piniella, lf-rf	4	0	2	3	0	0
bBrown	0	0	0	0	0	0
Cerone, c	4	0	0	8	1	0
Rodriguez, 3b	3	0	0	2	3	0
Guidry, p	3	0	0	0	0	0
Mumphrey, cf	0	0	0	0	0	0
Totals	32	1	5	24	5	0

Los Ang. (N.L.)	AB.	R.	H.	PO.	A.	E.
Lopes, 2b	3	0	0	3	3	3
Russell, ss	4	0	0	0	7	0
Garvey, 1b	4	0	1	12	1	0
Cey, 3b	2	0	0	0	2	0
aLandreaux, cf	0	0	0	1	0	0
Baker, lf	4	0	0	2	0	0
Guerrero, rf	3	1	1	1	0	0
Yeager, c	3	1	2	7	0	0
Thomas, cf-3b	3	0	0	0	0	0
Reuss, p	2	0	0	1	2	0
Totals	28	2	4	27	15	3

New York	0 1 0	0 0 0	0 0 0–1
Los Angeles	0 0 0	0 0 0	2 0 *–2

New York	IP.	H.	R.	ER.	BB.	SO.
Guidry (L)	7	4	2	2	2	9
Gossage	1	0	0	0	1	0

Los Angeles	IP.	H.	R.	ER.	BB.	SO.
Reuss (W)	9	5	1	1	3	6

Bases on balls—Off Guidry 2 (Cey, Reuss), off Gossage 1 (Lopes), off Reuss 3 (Randolph, Watson, Rodriguez). Strikeouts—By Guidry 9 (Lopes, Reuss, Garvey 2, Cey, Baker 2, Guerrero, Thomas), by Reuss 6 (Winfield 2, Guidry 2, Jackson, Rodriguez). Game-winning RBI—Yeager. aRan for Cey in eighth. bRan for Piniella in ninth. Runs batted in—Piniella, Guerrero, Yeager. Two-base hits—Jackson, Yeager. Home runs—Guerrero, Yeager. Stolen bases—Lopes, Landreaux. Hit by pitcher—By Gossage (Cey). Double plays—Russell, Lopes and Garvey; Lopes and Garvey. Left on bases—New York 7, Los Angeles 6. Umpires—Garcia (A.L.) plate, Stello (N.L.) first, Barnett (A.L.) second, Colosi (N.L.) third, Cooney (A.L.) left, Harvey (N.L.) right. Time—2:19. Attendance—56,115.

FIRST INNING

New York—Randolph grounded out, Garvey to Reuss. Milbourne grounded to Lopes. Winfield struck out. No runs, no hits, no errors, none left.

Los Angeles—Lopes struck out. Russell popped to Rodriguez. Garvey singled to center. Cey walked, Garvey advancing to second. Baker hit a sinking liner that Piniella caught dropping to his knees. No runs, one hit, no errors, two left.

SECOND INNING

New York—Jackson cracked a line drive down the left-field line and the ball rolled into the festive bunting draped over the railing for a ground-rule double. Watson hit a grounder to the left of Lopes, who fielded it and then dropped it for an error, Jackson advancing to third. Piniella

Game 5 heroes Pedro Guerrero (left) and Steve Yeager celebrate their good fortune.

grounded a single to the right of Russell, Jackson scoring and Watson stopping at second. Cerone grounded into a double play, Russell to Lopes to Garvey, Watson advancing to third. Rodriguez grounded to Russell. One run, two hits, one error, one left.

Los Angeles—Guerrero flied to Winfield. Yeager cracked a double, the ball barely eluding Piniella's glove as it hit about a foot from the top of the wall in left-center. Thomas flied to Winfield, who made a diving catch after misjudging the ball. Reuss was called out on strikes. No runs, one hit, no errors, one left.

THIRD INNING

New York—Guidry was called out on strikes. Randolph walked. Milbourne singled to left, Randolph stopping at second. Winfield forced Milbourne, Cey to Lopes, Randolph advancing to third. Jackson struck out. No runs, one hit, no errors, two left.

Los Angeles—Lopes flied to Winfield. Russell grounded to Rodriguez. Garvey struck out. No runs, no hits, no errors, none left.

FOURTH INNING

New York—Watson walked. Piniella hit a grounder to Lopes, who fumbled it and then threw it into the Yankees' dugout. Watson advanced to third and Piniella to second as Lopes was charged with two errors. Cerone grounded to Russell; the runners held even though the infield was not in. Rodriguez was walked intentionally, loading the bases. Guidry bunted, but Watson was forced, Reuss to Yeager, the bases remaining loaded.

Randolph grounded to Garvey unassisted. No runs, no hits, two errors, three left.

Los Angeles—Cey was called out on strikes. Baker struck out. Guerrero struck out. No runs, no hits, no errors, none left.

FIFTH INNING

New York—Milbourne bounced out, Reuss to Garvey. Winfield lined a single to left. Jackson grounded into a double play, Lopes stepping on the bag and throwing to Garvey for the second out. No runs, one hit, no errors, none left.

Los Angeles—Yeager popped to Rodriguez. Thomas struck out. Reuss walked. Lopes grounded to Milbourne. No runs, no hits, no errors, one left.

SIXTH INNING

New York—Watson grounded to Russell. Piniella flied to Guerrero. Cerone flied to Baker. No runs, no hits, no errors, none left.

Los Angeles—Russell flied to Piniella, who made a running catch on the track in left center. Garvey struck out on a pitch in the dirt and was retired, Cerone to Watson. Cey grounded to Rodriguez. No runs, no hits, no errors, none left.

SEVENTH INNING

New York—Rodriguez grounded to Russell. Guidry struck out. Randolph grounded to Russell. No runs, no hits, no errors, none left.

Los Angeles—Baker struck out. Guerrero hit a home run into the left-center field bleachers. Yeager followed with a home run to a similar spot.

Thomas flied to Winfield. Reuss lined to Milbourne. Two runs, two hits, no errors, none left.

EIGHTH INNING

New York—Milbourne grounded to Cey. Winfield struck out. Jackson flied to Baker. No runs, no hits, no errors, none left.

Los Angeles—Gossage replaced Guidry on the mound for New York and assumed the fourth spot in the batting order. Mumphrey came in to play center field and batted ninth. Winfield moved to left field and Piniella to right. Lopes walked. Russell popped his bunt to Watson. Garvey flied to Piniella. Cey was beaned on the left side of the helmet by a Gossage fastball, Lopes advancing to second. Cey lay behind home plate for several minutes but left the field under his own power. Landreaux ran for Cey. With Baker batting, Lopes and Landreaux pulled off a double steal. Baker grounded to Rodriguez. No runs, no hits, no errors, two left.

NINTH INNING

New York—Landreaux remained in the game to play center field for Los Angeles and Thomas moved to third. Watson grounded to Russell. Piniella grounded a single to center. Brown ran for Piniella. Cerone flied to Landreaux. Rodriguez, after lining a foul just outside the third-base line, struck out. No runs, one hit, no errors, one left.

Game 6

At New York
October 28

Los Ang. (N.L.)	AB.	R.	H.	PO.	A.	E.
Lopes, 2b	4	2	1	1	2	1
Russell, ss	4	0	2	0	5	0
Garvey, 1b	4	1	1	9	0	0
Cey, 3b	3	1	2	1	1	0
bThomas, 3b	2	1	0	0	0	0
Baker, lf	5	2	2	2	0	0
Guerrero, cf-rf	5	1	3	6	0	0
Monday, rf	3	0	1	1	0	0
Landreaux, cf	1	0	0	1	0	0
Yeager, c	5	0	1	6	0	0
Hooton, p	2	1	0	0	0	0
Howe, p	2	0	0	0	0	0
Totals	40	9	13	27	8	1

New York (A.L.)	AB.	R.	H.	PO.	A.	E.
Randolph, 2b	3	1	2	2	2	0
Mumphrey, cf	5	0	1	2	0	0
Winfield, lf	4	0	0	2	0	0
Jackson, rf	5	0	0	3	0	0
Watson, 1b	5	0	0	10	0	0
Nettles, 3b	3	0	2	1	2	1
cRodriguez, 3b	1	1	1	0	0	0
Cerone, c	3	0	0	7	2	0
Milbourne, ss	2	0	0	0	3	1
John, p	1	0	0	0	1	0
aMurcer	1	0	0	0	0	0
Frazier, p	0	0	0	0	0	0
Davis, p	0	0	0	0	0	0
Reuschel, p	0	0	0	0	0	0
dGamble	0	0	0	0	0	0
ePiniella	1	0	1	0	0	0
May, p	0	0	0	0	0	0
fBrown	1	0	0	0	0	0
LaRoche, p	0	0	0	0	0	0
Totals	35	2	7	27	10	2

Los Angeles		000	134	010—9		
New York		001	001	000—2		

Los Angeles	IP.	H.	R.	ER.	BB.	SO.
Hooton (W)	5⅓	5	2	2	5	2
Howe (S)	3⅔	2	0	0	1	3

New York	IP.	H.	R.	ER.	BB.	SO.
John	4	6	1	1	0	2
Frazier (L)	1	4	3	3	0	1
Davis	⅓	1	3	2	2	1
Reuschel	⅔	1	1	0	2	0
May	2	1	1	1	1	2
LaRoche	1	0	0	0	0	2

Bases on balls—Off Hooton 5 (Randolph, Winfield, Milbourne 2, Cerone), off Howe 1 (Randolph), off Davis 2 (Hooton, Lopes), off Reuschel 2 (Garvey, Monday), off May 1 (Lopes).

Strikeouts—By Hooton 2 (Jackson, Cerone), by Howe 3 (Jackson, Brown, Mumphrey), by John 2 (Cey, Hooton), by Frazier 1 (Monday), by Davis 1 (Yeager), by May 2 (Howe, Landreaux), by LaRoche 2 (Howe, Lopes).

Game-winning RBI—Cey.

aFlied out for John in fourth. bDrove in one run on forceout for Cey in sixth. cRan for Nettles in sixth and scored. dAnnounced for Reuschel in sixth. eSingled in one run for Gamble in sixth. fStruck out for May in eighth. Runs batted in—Russell, Thomas, Cey, Guerrero 5, Yeager, Randolph, Piniella. Two-base hits—Nettles, Randolph. Three-base hit—Guerrero. Home runs—Randolph, Guerrero. Stolen bases—Randolph, Lopes, Russell. Caught stealing—Russell. Sacrifice hit—Russell. Double plays—None. Left on bases—Los Angeles 10, New York 12. Umpires—Stello (N.L.) plate, Barnett (A.L.) first, Colosi (N.L.) second, Cooney (A.L.) third, Harvey (N.L.) left, Garcia (A.L.) right. Time—3:09. Attendance—56,513.

FIRST INNING

Los Angeles—Lopes grounded to Nettles. Russell grounded to Randolph. Garvey lined a single to center. Cey lined a single to left, Garvey stopping at second. Baker flied to Jackson. No runs, two hits, no errors, two left.

New York—Randolph walked. With Mumphrey batting and the count 1-0, Randolph stole second. Mumphrey flied to Guerrero, who made a running catch. Winfield lined to Baker, who made a backhand catch of the sinking drive. Jackson struck out. No runs, no hits, no errors, one left.

SECOND INNING

Los Angeles—Guerrero flied to Jackson on the track. Monday grounded to Milbourne. Yeager grounded to Milbourne, but his throw to Watson was in the dirt for an error. Hooton grounded out, John to Watson. No runs, no hits, one error, one left.

New York—Watson hit a high bouncer over the bag at third, but Cey made a leaping, backhanded grab and threw a one-hopper to Garvey for the out. Nettles grounded to Lopes. Cerone grounded to Russell, whose throw was dug out by Garvey. No runs, no hits, no errors, none left.

THIRD INNING

Los Angeles—Lopes, after pushing a bunt foul up the first-base line, grounded to Nettles. Russell singled to right. With Garvey batting, Russell was caught stealing, Cerone to Randolph. Garvey flied to Mumphrey. No runs, one hit, no errors, none left.

New York—Milbourne grounded to Garvey. John flied to Guerrero. Randolph lined a home run into the left-field bleachers. Mumphrey grounded sharply past Garvey and down the line, but held up with a single when the ball caromed to Monday in short right. Winfield walked, Mumphrey advancing to second. Jackson flied to Baker. One run, two hits, no errors, two left.

FOURTH INNING

Los Angeles—Cey struck out. Baker lined a single to right-center. Guerrero lined to Winfield. Monday hit a sharp grounder that went between Watson's legs on one short hop for a single, Baker stopping at second. Yeager scorched a grounder between Nettles and Milbourne for a single, Baker scoring and Monday stopping at second. Hooton struck out. One run, three hits, no errors, two left.

New York—Watson grounded to Russell. Nettles doubled down the right-field line. Cerone struck out. Milbourne was walked intentionally. Murcer batted for John and flied to Monday on the warning track. No runs, one hit, no errors, two left.

FIFTH INNING

Los Angeles—Frazier came in to pitch for New York. Lopes bounced a single to left. Russell sacrificed, Watson unassisted, Lopes advancing to second. Garvey flied to Winfield. Cey hit a bouncer up the middle that took a tricky hop and eluded Randolph for a single, Lopes scoring. Baker blooped a single to short center, the ball falling just beyond Randolph's grasp as Cey advanced to third. Guerrero smashed a triple to left-center, Cey and Baker scoring. Monday struck out. Three runs, four hits, no errors, one left.

New York—Randolph doubled on a drive that one-hopped the wall in left. Mumphrey lined to Cey. Winfield fouled out to Yeager. Jackson grounded to Lopes. No runs, one hit, no errors, one left.

SIXTH INNING

Los Angeles—Davis replaced Frazier on the mound for New York. Yeager struck out. Hooton walked. Lopes walked, Hooton advancing to second. Russell grounded a single past the glovehand side of Nettles, Hooton scoring and Lopes stopping at second. Reuschel replaced Davis on the mound for New York. With Garvey batting and the count 1-0, Lopes and Russell pulled a double steal. Garvey was walked intentionally, loading the bases. Thomas batted for Cey and bounced a shot over the third-base bag—Nettles made a backhanded stop and forced Russell, Lopes scoring and Garvey advancing to second. Baker hit a ground ball that handcuffed Nettles for an error, loading the bases. Guerrero singled to center, Garvey and Thomas scoring, Baker advancing to third and Guerrero taking second on the throw. Monday was walked intentionally. Yeager

grounded to Milbourne. Four runs, two hits, one error, three left.

New York—Thomas remained in the game to play third base for Los Angeles; Landreaux replaced Monday and played center field with Guerrero moving to right. Watson grounded to Russell. Nettles singled to center. Rodriguez ran for Nettles. Cerone walked, Rodriguez advancing to second. Milbourne walked, loading the bases. Gamble was announced as a pinch-hitter for Reuschel, and Howe replaced Hooton on the mound for Los Angeles. Piniella batted for Gamble and singled to center, Rodriguez scoring and the bases remaining loaded. Randolph lined to Guerrero, the runners holding their bases. Mumphrey lined to Guerrero. One run, two hits, no errors, three left.

SEVENTH INNING

Los Angeles—Rodriguez remained in the game to play third base for New York and May came in to pitch. Howe struck out. Lopes walked. Russell grounded to Milbourne, Lopes advancing to second. Garvey flied to Mumphrey. No runs, no hits, no errors, one left.

New York—Winfield grounded to Russell. Jackson struck out. Watson grounded to Russell. No runs, no hits, no errors, none left.

EIGHTH INNING

Los Angeles—Thomas grounded to Randolph. Baker popped to Randolph. Guerrero smacked a home run into the left-field bleachers. Landreaux struck out. One run, one hit, no errors, none left.

New York—Rodriguez singled to left-center. Cerone flied to Guerrero. Milbourne popped to Lopes. Brown batted for May and struck out. No runs, one hit, no errors, one left.

NINTH INNING

Los Angeles—LaRoche came in to pitch for New York. Yeager flied to Jackson. Howe struck out. Lopes struck out on a blooper pitch that bounced in front of the plate and was retired, Cerone to Watson. No runs, no hits, no errors, none left.

New York—Randolph walked. Mumphrey struck out. Winfield flied to Guerrero. Jackson hit a ground ball to Lopes, but he fumbled it for his sixth error of the Series, Randolph stopping at second. Watson flied to Landreaux. No runs, no hits, one error, two left.

RESULTS OF WORLD SERIES GAMES OF 1981

Game	Where Played	Date	Winner		Winner	Loser	Att.
First	New York	Oct. 20	New York	5-3	Guidry	Reuss	56,470
Second	New York	Oct. 21	New York	3-0	John	Hooton	56,505
Third	Los Angeles	Oct. 23	Los Angeles	5-4	Valenzuela	Frazier	56,236
Fourth	Los Angeles	Oct. 24	Los Angeles	8-7	Howe	Frazier	56,242
Fifth	Los Angeles	Oct. 25	Los Angeles	2-1	Reuss	Guidry	56,115
Sixth	New York	Oct. 28	Los Angeles	9-2	Hooton	Frazier	56,513

ROSTERS OF ELIGIBLE PLAYERS FOR THE WORLD SERIES

Los Angeles Dodgers—Johnnie B. Baker, Robert E. Castillo, Ronald C. Cey, Terry J. Forster, Steven P. Garvey, David A. Goltz, Pedro Guerrero, Burt C. Hooton, Steven R. Howe, John W. Johnstone, Kenneth F. Landreaux, David E. Lopes, Robert J. Monday, Thomas E. Niedenfuer, Alejandro Pena, Jerry Reuss, William E. Russell, Stephen L. Sax, Michael L. Scioscia, C. Reginald Smith, David K. Stewart, Derrel O. Thomas, Fernando Valenzuela, Robert L. Welch, Stephen W. Yeager; Thomas C. Lasorda, manager; Romanus Basgall, Mark E. Cresse, Manuel R. Mota, Daniel L. Ozark, Ronald P. Perranoski, coaches.

New York Yankees—Rogers L. Brown, Richard A. Cerone, Ronald G. Davis, Barry C. Foote, George A. Frazier, Oscar C. Gamble, Richard M. Gossage, Ronald A. Guidry, Reginald M. Jackson, Thomas E. John, David E. LaRoche, Rudolph May, Lawrence W. Milbourne, Jerry W. Mumphrey, Bobby R. Murcer, Graig Nettles, Louis V. Piniella, William L. Randolph, Ricky E. Reuschel, David A. Revering, David A. Righetti, Andre L. Robertson, Aurelio Rodriguez, Robert J. Watson, David M. Winfield; Robert G. Lemon, manager; Joseph S. Altobelli, Lawrence P. Berra, Michael D. Ferraro, Clyde E. King, Charles R. Lau, Jeffrey A. Torborg, coaches.

LOS ANGELES DODGERS' BATTING AND FIELDING AVERAGES

Player—Position	G.	AB.	R.	H.	TB.	2B.	3B.	HR.	RBI.	BB.	IBB.	SO.	B.A.	PO.	A.	E.	F.A.
Johnstone, ph	3	3	1	2	5	0	0	1	3	0	0	0	.667	0	0	0	.000
Smith, ph	2	2	0	1	1	0	0	0	0	0	0	1	.500	0	0	0	.000
Garvey, 1b	6	24	3	10	11	1	0	0	0	2	1	5	.417	44	3	0	1.000
Cey, 3b	6	20	3	7	10	0	0	1	6	3	0	3	.350	4	11	0	1.000
Guerrero, cf-rf	6	21	2	7	16	1	1	2	7	2	1	6	.333	17	1	0	1.000
Yeager, ph-c	6	14	2	4	11	1	0	2	4	0	0	2	.286	20	0	0	1.000
Scioscia, c-ph	3	4	1	1	1	0	0	0	0	1	0	0	.250	7	1	0	1.000
Russell, ss	6	25	1	6	6	0	0	0	2	0	0	1	.240	4	26	1	.968
Monday, rf-ph	5	13	1	3	4	1	0	0	0	3	2	6	.231	9	0	0	1.000
Lopes, 2b	6	22	6	5	6	1	0	0	2	4	0	3	.227	26	14	6	.870
Landreaux, ph-cf-pr	5	6	1	1	2	1	0	0	0	0	0	2	.167	6	0	0	1.000
Baker, lf	6	24	3	4	4	0	0	0	1	1	0	6	.167	13	0	0	1.000
Forster, p	2	0	0	0	0	0	0	0	0	0	0	0	.000	0	1	0	1.000
Goltz, p	2	0	0	0	0	0	0	0	0	0	0	0	.000	0	0	0	.000
Niedenfuer, p	2	0	0	0	0	0	0	0	0	0	0	0	.000	0	0	0	.000
Stewart, p	2	0	0	0	0	0	0	0	0	0	0	0	.000	0	0	1	.000
Castillo, p	1	0	0	0	0	0	0	0	0	0	0	0	.000	0	2	0	1.000
Welch, p	1	0	0	0	0	0	0	0	0	0	0	0	.000	0	0	0	.000
Sax, ph-pr-2b	2	1	0	0	0	0	0	0	0	0	0	0	.000	0	0	0	.000
Howe, p	3	2	0	0	0	0	0	0	0	0	0	2	.000	0	1	1	.500
Reuss, p	2	3	0	0	0	0	0	0	0	1	0	2	.000	1	3	0	1.000
Valenzuela, p	1	3	0	0	0	0	0	0	0	1	0	0	.000	0	1	0	1.000
Hooton, p	2	4	1	0	0	0	0	0	0	1	0	3	.000	1	0	0	1.000
Thomas, ph-ss-cf-3b	5	7	2	0	0	0	0	0	1	1	0	2	.000	4	1	0	1.000
Totals	6	198	27	51	77	6	1	6	26	20	4	44	.258	156	65	9	.961

Johnstone singled in one run for Russell in eighth inning of first game; flied out for Yeager in eighth inning of second game; hit two-run homer for Niedenfuer in sixth inning of fourth game.

Landreaux grounded out for Yeager in ninth inning of first game; doubled for Goltz in third inning of fourth game; ran for Cey in eighth inning of fifth game.

Monday struck out for Lopes in eighth inning of second game.

Sax flied out for Goltz in fifth inning of first game; ran for Smith in eighth inning of second game.

Scioscia grounded out for Yeager in third inning of third game.

Smith singled for Forster in eighth inning of second game; struck out for Forster in fourth inning of fourth game.

Thomas walked for Niedenfuer in eighth inning of first game; hit into double play for Monday in seventh inning of third game; drove in one run on forceout for Cey in sixth inning of sixth game.

Yeager hit sacrifice fly for Scioscia in seventh inning of fourth game.

NEW YORK YANKEES' BATTING AND FIELDING AVERAGES

Player—Position	G.	AB.	R.	H.	TB.	2B.	3B.	HR.	RBI.	BB.	IBB.	SO.	B.A.	PO.	A.	E.	F.A.
Piniella, rf-ph-lf	6	16	2	7	8	1	0	0	3	0	0	1	.438	7	0	0	1.000
Rodriguez, 3b-pr	4	12	1	5	5	0	0	0	0	1	1	2	.417	3	9	0	1.000
Nettles, 3b	3	10	1	4	5	1	0	0	0	1	0	1	.400	3	10	1	.929
Jackson, rf	3	12	3	4	8	1	0	1	1	2	1	3	.333	5	0	1	.833
Gamble, rf-lf-ph	3	6	1	2	2	0	0	0	1	1	0	0	.333	4	0	0	1.000
Watson, 1b	6	22	2	7	14	1	0	2	7	3	0	0	.318	51	0	0	1.000
Milbourne, ss	6	20	2	5	7	2	0	0	3	4	3	0	.250	5	16	2	.913
Randolph, 2b	6	18	5	4	13	1	1	2	3	9	0	0	.222	13	11	0	1.000
Mumphrey, cf	5	15	2	3	3	0	0	0	0	3	1	2	.200	6	0	0	1.000
Cerone, c	6	21	2	4	8	1	0	1	3	4	1	2	.190	42	4	0	1.000
Winfield, lf-cf	6	22	0	1	1	0	0	0	1	5	0	4	.045	13	1	0	1.000
Davis, p	4	0	0	0	0	0	0	0	0	0	0	0	.000	0	0	0	.000
LaRoche, p	1	0	0	0	0	0	0	0	0	0	0	0	.000	0	0	0	.000
Robertson, pr	1	0	0	0	0	0	0	0	0	0	0	0	.000	0	0	0	.000
Brown, pr-rf-cf-ph	4	1	1	0	0	0	0	0	0	0	0	1	.000	1	0	0	1.000
Foote, ph	1	1	0	0	0	0	0	0	0	0	0	1	.000	0	0	0	.000
Gossage, p	3	1	0	0	0	0	0	0	0	0	0	1	.000	0	0	0	.000
May, p	3	1	0	0	0	0	0	0	0	0	0	0	.000	0	1	0	1.000
Righetti, p	1	1	0	0	0	0	0	0	0	0	0	1	.000	0	0	0	.000
Frazier, p	3	2	0	0	0	0	0	0	0	0	0	1	.000	0	0	0	.000
John, p	3	2	0	0	0	0	0	0	0	0	0	0	.000	0	3	0	1.000
Reuschel, p	2	2	0	0	0	0	0	0	0	0	0	1	.000	0	0	0	.000
Murcer, ph	4	0	0	0	0	0	0	0	0	0	0	0	.000	0	0	0	.000
Guidry, p	2	5	0	0	0	0	0	0	0	0	0	3	.000	0	0	0	.000
Totals	6	193	22	46	74	8	1	6	22	33	7	24	.238	153	55	4	.981

Brown ran for Piniella in eighth inning of second game and scored; ran for Gamble in sixth inning of fourth game; ran for Piniella in ninth inning of fifth game; struck out for May in eighth inning of sixth game.

Foote struck out for Rodriguez in ninth inning of fourth game.

Gamble was announced as pinch-hitter for Reuschel in sixth inning of sixth game.

Murcer sacrificed for John in seventh inning of second game; bunted into double play for May in eighth inning of third game; reached first base safely on error for John in ninth inning of fourth game; flied out for John in fourth inning of sixth game.

Piniella singled for Gamble in eighth inning of second game; grounded out for Brown in eighth inning of fourth game; singled in one run for Gamble in sixth inning of sixth game.

Robertson ran for Cerone in ninth inning of fourth game.

Rodriguez ran for Nettles in sixth inning of sixth game and scored.

LOS ANGELES DODGERS' PITCHING RECORDS

Pitcher	G.	GS.	CG.	IP.	H.	R.	ER.	HR.	BB.	IBB.	SO.	HB.	WP.	W.	L.	Pct.	ERA.
Niedenfuer	2	0	0	5	3	2	0	0	1	1	0	6	0	0	0	.000	0.00
Forster	2	0	0	2	1	0	0	0	3	1	0	0	0	0	0	.000	0.00
Stewart	2	0	0	1⅔	1	0	0	0	2	1	1	0	0	0	0	.000	0.00
Hooton	2	2	0	11⅓	8	3	2	1	9	1	3	0	0	1	1	.500	1.59
Reuss	2	2	1	11⅔	10	5	5	1	3	1	8	0	0	1	1	.500	3.86
Howe	3	0	0	7	7	3	3	1	1	0	4	0	0	1	0	1.000	3.86
Valenzuela	1	1	1	9	4	4	4	2	7	2	6	0	0	1	0	1.000	4.00
Goltz	2	0	0	3⅓	4	2	2	1	1	0	2	0	0	0	0	.000	5.40
Castillo	1	0	0	1	0	1	1	0	5	0	0	0	0	0	0	.000	9.00
Welch	1	1	0	0*	3	2	2	0	1	0	0	0	0	0	0	.000	.....
Totals	6	6	2	52	46	22	19	6	33	7	24	0	0	4	2	.667	3.29

*Pitched to four batters in first inning of fourth game.

No shutouts. Save—Howe.

NEW YORK YANKEES' PITCHING RECORDS

Pitcher	G.	GS.	CG.	IP.	H.	R.	ER.	HR.	BB.	IBB.	SO.	HB.	WP.	W.	L.	Pct.	ERA.
Gossage	3	0	0	5	2	0	0	0	2	0	5	1	0	0	0	.000	0.00
LaRoche	1	0	0	1	0	0	0	0	0	0	2	0	0	0	0	.000	0.00
John	3	2	0	13	11	1	1	0	0	0	8	0	0	1	0	1.000	0.69
Guidry	2	2	0	14	8	3	3	0	4	0	15	0	0	1	1	.500	1.93
May	3	0	0	6⅓	5	2	2	1	1	0	5	0	0	0	0	.000	2.84
Reuschel	2	1	0	3⅔	7	3	2	0	3	2	2	0	0	0	0	.000	4.91
Righetti	1	1	0	2	5	3	3	1	2	0	1	1	0	0	0	.000	13.50
Frazier	3	0	0	3⅔	9	7	7	0	3	2	2	0	0	0	3	.000	17.18
Davis	4	0	0	2⅓	4	8	6	1	5	0	4	0	0	0	0	.000	23.14
Totals	6	6	0	51	51	27	24	6	20	4	44	2	0	2	4	.333	4.24

Shutout—John-Gossage (combined). Saves—Gossage 2.

COMPOSITE SCORE BY INNINGS

Los Angeles	3	0	2	1	7	7	4	3	0	—	27
New York	5	4	5	1	1	3	0	3	0	—	22

Game-winning RBI—Yeager 2, Cey, Watson, Milbourne.

Sacrifice hits—Lopes, Scioscia, Howe, Russell, Guidry, John, Murcer, Righetti, Milbourne.

Sacrifice flies—Baker, Yeager, Randolph, Watson.

Stolen bases—Lopes 4, Landreaux, Russell, Mumphrey, Piniella, Winfield, Randolph.

Caught stealing—Russell, Randolph.

Double plays—Russell, Lopes and Garvey 3; Thomas and Garvey; Cey and Lopes; Lopes and Garvey; Randolph and Watson; Milbourne, Randolph and Watson.

Passed ball—Cerone.

Hit by pitcher—By Righetti (Guerrero), by Gossage (Cey).

Balks—None.

Bases on balls—Off Hooton 9 (Cerone 2, Milbourne 2, Randolph 2, Mumphrey, Gamble, Winfield), off Valenzuela 7 (Randolph 3, Winfield 2, Milbourne 2), off Castillo 5 (Watson, Cerone, Randolph, Mumphrey, Winfield), off Forster 3 (Mumphrey, Randolph, Jackson), off Reuss 3 (Randolph, Watson, Rodriguez), off Stewart 2 (Nettles, Cerone), off Goltz 1 (Watson), off Howe 1 (Randolph), off Niedenfuer 1 (Jackson), off Welch 1 (Winfield), off Davis 5 (Lopes 2, Thomas, Scioscia, Hooton), off Guidry 4 (Baker, Cey, Guerrero, Reuss), off Frazier 3 (Cey, Guerrero, Monday), off Reuschel 3 (Monday 2, Garvey), off Gossage 2 (Garvey, Lopes), off Righetti 2 (Valenzuela, Cey), off May 1 (Lopes).

Strikeouts—By Reuss 8 (Winfield 3, Guidry 3, Jackson, Rodriguez), by Valenzuela 6 (Winfield, Righetti, Cerone, Frazier, Mumphrey, Piniella), by Howe 4 (Brown, Foote, Jackson, Mumphrey), by Hooton 3 (Cerone, Jackson, Nettles), by Goltz 2 (Reuschel, Rodriguez), by Stewart 1 (Gossage), by Guidry 15 (Garvey 3, Guerrero 2, Monday 2, Reuss 2, Baker 2, Yeager, Lopes, Cey, Thomas), by John 8 (Hooton 3, Baker, Landreaux, Garvey, Thomas, Cey), by May 5 (Baker, Guerrero, Howe, Landreaux, Smith), by Gossage 5 (Guerrero 2, Monday 2, Cey), by Davis 4 (Lopes, Baker, Monday, Yeager), by Frazier 2 (Guerrero, Monday), by LaRoche 2 (Howe, Lopes), by Reuschel 2 (Baker, Russell), by Righetti 1 (Garvey).

Left on bases—Los Angeles 46—5, 6, 9, 10, 6, 10; New York 55—6, 9, 9, 12, 7, 12.

Time of games—First game, 2:32; second game, 2:29; third game, 3:04; fourth game, 3:32; fifth game, 2:19; sixth game, 3:09.

Attendance—First game, 56,470; second game, 56,505; third game, 56,236; fourth game, 56,242; fifth game, 56,115; sixth game, 56,513.

Umpires—Barnett (A.L.), Colosi (N.L.), Cooney (A.L.), Harvey (N.L.), Garcia (A.L.), Stello (N.L.).

Official scorers—Tracy Ringolsby, Seattle Post-Intelligencer; Red Foley, New York Daily News; Chris Mortenson, Torrance Daily Breeze.

1981 ALL-STAR GAME

Including

Review of '81 Game

Official Box Score

Official Play-by-Play

Results of Previous Games

Philadelphia's Mike Schmidt arrives home after hitting a game-winning home run against A.L. pitcher Rollie Fingers.

Deprived Fans Go Star Crazy

By LARRY WIGGE

As a record 72,086 fans streamed out of Cleveland's Municipal Stadium August 9 after the 52nd All-Star Game, they were talking baseball.

They were talking about Mike Schmidt's two-run homer in the eighth inning that gave the National League a 5-4 victory. They were talking about Gary Carter's two home runs. They were talking about Toronto pitcher Dave Stieb batting in the ninth inning because American League Manager Jim Frey didn't have any more available hitters.

It was just like old times.

For 50 days, there hadn't been much talk about trades, batting averages, earned run averages and the many other things that have made the sport an American institution. The only talk was over a bargaining table. The fans were left with re-creations of games from the past and memories of the pre-strike performances of Fernando Valenzuela, Tony Armas, Dwight Evans, Pete Rose, and others.

One segment of fans encouraged a boycott of the All-Star Game. Others suggested that the fans in attendance at Municipal Stadium bring whistles and blow them in displeasure when each player was announced. But there was no boycott and there were only a few whistles.

Had baseball surgically repaired in one evening the wound it dealt to the fans with the strike? Not likely.

Mike Schmidt said he thought of the fans during the strike. He said he thought of one fan in particular when he clouted the game-winning home run that night off Milwaukee's Rollie Fingers.

"When I think of the strike, I think of my grandmother," said Schmidt. "She lived the last two years of her life counting on hearing a Cincinnati Reds or Phillies game on the radio. She was a shut-in. I don't know what she would have done during the strike.

"Shut-ins, people like that, they're the ones I really feel sorry for. Hopefully, time will heal this wound."

The script for the All-Star Game didn't change. The Nationals won for the 10th consecutive time and the 18th in the last 19 midsummer meetings.

The N.L. tied an All-Star record with four home runs (Pittsburgh's Dave Parker, Philadelphia's Schmidt and two by Montreal's Carter). But it was Baltimore's Ken Singleton who started the power display by lining a Tom Seaver fastball over the right-center field fence, giving the Americans a 1-0 lead after two innings.

Carter knotted the count with a leadoff homer in the fifth inning, belting the first pitch over the left-field wall.

With one out in the sixth, Parker sent the N.L. ahead 2-1. But the Americans weren't about to lay down and play dead. They came back with three runs in their half of the sixth.

Consecutive singles by Singleton, Dwight Evans of Boston and Carlton Fisk of the White Sox loaded the bases against the Dodgers' Burt Hooton. Frey went to the bench for California's Fred Lynn, who delivered a single to tie the score.

A sacrifice fly by Buddy Bell of Texas gave the A.L. a 3-2 lead. Eddie Murray of Baltimore batted for California's Rod Carew and forced Lynn at second, but Ted Simmons of Milwaukee—batting for the Yankees' Willie Randolph—singled home Fisk to give the Americans a 4-2 cushion.

Carter, who was later voted the Most Valuable Player in the game, again pounced on the first pitch as he opened the seventh inning with his second straight home run. Carter was the fifth player in All-Star history to clout a pair of homers in one game.

"In the fifth, I was looking for a fastball all the way," said Carter. "I had faced Kenny Forsch in the N.L. and I know he likes to throw an inside fastball on the first pitch.

"In the seventh, I had never faced Ron Davis before but I had heard he just rears back and throws like Rich Gossage. So I was looking for another fastball and just jumped on it."

Clinging to a 4-3 lead, Frey called on Fingers to get the final six outs to preserve the victory. Instead, the righthander walked San Diego's Ozzie Smith. Fingers was given a reprieve when Smith stole second base, but overran the bag and was caught in a rundown. Fingers couldn't stand prosperity, however, as he proceeded to put another man on base, walking Pittsburgh's Mike Easler, setting the stage for Schmidt's game-winning blow.

"I think Rollie wanted the pitch low and away," Schmidt said. "He kind of hung it inside a little bit . . . If I don't remember that, I won't remember anything. You're not going to beat Rollie Fingers in that situation too often."

The only thing remaining was for Bruce Sutter of the Cardinals to finish off the A.L.

With pitchers Britt Burns, Doug Corbett and Scott McGregor the only players remaining on his bench, Frey was forced to let Stieb bat for himself against Sutter in the ninth.

"I wanted to save Tony Armas, but after Lynn pinch-hit, he (Lynn) went into the clubhouse," Frey explained. "I told Lynn I wanted him to play center and he said he had a bad knee and couldn't play."

Frey said Lynn told him he was okay before the game. Lynn insisted he injured himself sliding into second base in the sixth inning.

Stieb said he planned on pitching in the All-Star game, but he didn't plan on hitting. He had just retired the final two hitters in the eighth inning when Frey told him he would have to bat in the ninth.

For the record, Sutter struck Stieb out on three pitches. "I just saw a guy in a Toronto uniform," Sutter said. "I remember Terry Kennedy saying in the bullpen that he used to be an outfielder.

"How embarrassing would it have been to give up a home run to a pitcher?"

Probably very embarrassing. But there was plenty to talk about. Baseball was back.

NATIONALS	AB.	R.	H.	RBI.	PO.	A.
Rose (Phillies), 1b	3	0	1	0	5	0
Hooton (Dodgers), p	0	0	0	0	0	0
Ruthven (Phillies), p	0	0	0	0	0	0
kGuerrero (Dodg.), ph	1	0	0	0	0	0
Blue (Giants), p	0	0	0	0	0	0
Madlock (Pirates), 3b	1	0	0	0	0	1
Concepcion (Reds), ss	3	0	0	0	0	0
Smith (Padres), ss	0	0	0	0	1	0
Parker (Pirates), rf	3	1	1	1	1	0
Easler (Pirates), rf	1	1	0	0	0	0
Schmidt (Phillies), 3b	4	1	2	2	0	2
Ryan (Astros), p	0	0	0	0	0	0
Garner (Pirates), 2b	0	0	0	0	0	0
Foster (Reds), lf	2	0	0	0	0	0
Baker (Dodgers), lf	2	0	1	0	2	0
lRaines (Expos), lf	0	0	0	0	1	0
Dawson (Expos), cf	4	0	1	0	4	0
Carter (Expos), c	3	2	2	2	5	1
Benedict (Braves), c	1	0	0	0	3	0
Lopes (Dodgers), 2b	0	0	0	0	1	0
Trillo (Phillies), 2b	2	0	0	0	1	1
mBuckner (Cubs), ph	1	0	0	0	0	0
Sutter (Cardinals), p	0	0	0	0	0	0
Valenzuela (Dodg.), p	0	0	0	0	0	1
aYoungbl'd (Mets), ph	1	0	0	0	0	0
Seaver (Reds), p	0	0	0	0	0	2
Knepper (Astros), p	0	0	0	0	0	1
eKennedy (Padres), ph	1	0	0	0	0	0
Garvey (Dodgers), 1b	2	0	1	0	3	1
Totals	35	5	9	5	27	10

AMERICANS	AB.	R.	H.	RBI.	PO.	A.
Carew (Angels), 1b	3	0	1	0	12	0
gMurray (Orioles), 1b	2	0	0	0	2	1
Randolph (Yanks), 2b	3	0	1	0	0	5
hSimmons (Brew.), ph	1	0	1	1	0	0
iWhite (Royals), 2b	1	0	0	0	1	0
Brett (Royals), 3b	3	0	0	0	0	1
Norris (A's), p	0	0	0	0	0	0
jOliver (Rangers), ph	1	0	0	0	0	0
Davis (Yankees), p	0	0	0	0	0	0
Fingers (Brewers), p	0	0	0	0	1	0
Stieb (Blue Jays), p	1	0	0	0	1	1
Winfield (Yankees), cf	4	0	0	0	0	1
Singleton (Orioles), lf	3	2	2	1	0	0
Burleson (Angels), ss	1	0	0	0	1	3
Jackson (Yankees), rf	1	0	0	0	0	0
cEvans (Red Sox), rf	2	1	1	0	2	0
Fisk (White Sox), c	3	1	1	0	4	0
Diaz (Indians), c	1	0	0	0	2	0
Dent (Yankees), ss	2	0	2	0	0	2
fLynn (Angels), ph	1	0	1	1	0	0
Armas (A's), lf	1	0	0	0	0	0
Morris (Tigers), p	0	0	0	0	0	0
bPaciorek (Marin.), ph	1	0	1	0	0	0
Barker (Indians), p	0	0	0	0	0	0
dThomas (Brew.), ph	1	0	0	0	0	0
Forsch (Angels), p	0	0	0	0	0	0
Bell (Rangers), 3b	1	0	0	1	1	2
Totals	37	4	11	4	27	16

```
Nationals................ 000  011  120—5
Americans............... 010  003  000—4
```

Nationals	IP.	H.	R.	ER.	BB.	SO.
Valenzuela (Dodgers)	1	2	0	0	0	0
Seaver (Reds)	1	3	1	1	0	1
Knepper (Astros)	2	1	0	0	2	3
Hooton (Dodgers)	1⅔	5	3	3	0	1
Ruthven (Phillies)	⅓	0	0	0	0	0
Blue (Giants)	1	0	0	0	0	1
Ryan (Astros)	1	0	0	0	0	1
Sutter (Cardinals)	1	0	0	0	0	1

Americans	IP.	H.	R.	ER.	BB.	SO.
Morris (Tigers)	2	2	0	0	1	2
Barker (Indians)	2	0	0	0	0	1
Forsch (Angels)	1	1	1	1	0	0
Norris (A's)	1	2	1	1	0	1
Davis (Yankees)	1	1	1	1	0	1
Fingers (Brewers)	⅓	2	2	2	2	0
Stieb (Blue Jays)	1⅔	1	0	0	1	1

Winning pitcher—Blue. Losing pitcher—Fingers. Save—Sutter.

Game-winning RBI—Schmidt.

aFouled out for Valenzuela in second. bSingled for Morris in second. cWalked for Jackson in fourth. dPopped out for Barker in fourth. eGrounded out for Knepper in fifth. fSingled home one run for Dent in sixth. gGrounded out for Carew in sixth. hSingled home one run for Randolph in sixth. iRan for Simmons in sixth. jFlied out for Norris in sixth. kStruck out for Ruthven in seventh. lRan for Baker in eighth. mGrounded out for Trillo in ninth. Errors—Schmidt, Fingers. Double plays—None. Left on bases—Nationals 7, Americans 9. Two-base hits—Dent, Schmidt, Garvey. Home runs—Singleton, Carter 2, Parker, Schmidt. Stolen bases—Dawson, Smith. Caught stealing—Carew. Sacrifice fly—Bell. Wild pitch—Blue. Bases on balls—Off Morris 1 (Lopes), off Fingers 2 (Smith, Easler), off Stieb 1 (Smith), off Knepper 2 (Winfield, Evans). Strikeouts—By Morris 2 (Concepcion, Schmidt), by Barker 1 (Parker), by Norris 1 (Dawson), by Davis 1 (Guerrero), by Stieb 1 (Benedict), by Seaver 1 (Fisk), by Knepper 3 (Randolph, Brett, Carew), by Hooton 1 (Brett), by Blue 1 (Diaz), by Ryan 1

(Armas), by Sutter 1 (Stieb). Umpires—Haller (A.L.) plate, Vargo (N.L.) first base, DiMuro (A.L.) second base, Engel (N.L.) third base, Kosc (A.L.) left field, Quick (N.L.) right field. Time—2:59. Attendance—72,086. Official scorers—Ray Kelly Jr., Camden (N.J.) Courier Post; Dave Nightingale, The Sporting News; Hank Kozloski, Horvitz Newspapers Inc. (Lorain, O.). Players listed on rosters but not used: N.L.—Carlton; A.L.—Burns, Corbett, McGregor.

FIRST INNING

Nationals—Rose singled to left. Concepcion struck out. Parker grounded to Carew, Rose advancing to second. Schmidt struck out. No runs, one hit, one left.

Americans—Carew beat out a grounder to second for an infield single. With Randolph batting, Carew was caught stealing, Carter to Lopes. Randolph singled to left. Brett grounded out, Valenzuela to Rose, Randolph advancing to second. Winfield grounded to Schmidt. No runs, two hits, no errors, one left.

SECOND INNING

Nationals—Foster grounded to Brett. Dawson lashed a single off Carew's glove. With Carter batting, Dawson stole second. Carter popped to Carew. Lopes walked. Youngblood batted for Valenzuela and fouled out to Carew. No runs, one hit, no errors, two left.

Americans—Seaver came in to pitch for the Nationals. Singleton hit an 0-2 pitch over the right-field fence for a home run. Jackson tapped out, Seaver to Rose. Fisk was called out on strikes. Dent singled to right. Paciorek batted for Morris and singled past Schmidt, Dent advancing to third. Carew grounded back to Seaver, who threw to Rose for the out. One run, three hits, no errors, two left.

THIRD INNING

Nationals—Barker came in to pitch for the Americans. Rose grounded to Randolph. Concepcion grounded to Randolph. Parker struck out. No runs, no hits, no errors, none left.

Americans—Knepper replaced Seaver on the mound for the Nationals and Trillo replaced Lopes at second base. Randolph was called out on strikes. Brett was called out on strikes. Winfield walked. Singleton grounded out, Knepper to Rose. No runs, no hits, no errors, one left.

FOURTH INNING

Nationals—Schmidt grounded to Dent. Foster grounded to Randolph. Dawson grounded to Dent. No runs, no hits, no errors, none left.

Americans—Baker replaced Foster in left field for the Nationals. Evans batted for Jackson and walked. Fisk flied to Parker. Dent doubled down the left-field line, Evans stopping at third. Thomas batted for Barker and popped to Trillo. Carew struck out. No runs, one hit, no errors, two left.

FIFTH INNING

Nationals—Forsch came in to pitch for the Americans and Evans stayed in the game to play right field. Carter hit Forsch's first pitch over the left-field fence for a home run. Trillo flied to Evans. Kennedy batted for Knepper and grounded to Randolph. Rose grounded to Randolph. One run, one hit, no errors, none left.

Americans—Hooton came in to pitch for the Nationals and assumed the first spot in the batting order. Garvey replaced Rose at first base and batted ninth. Randolph grounded to Schmidt.

Brett struck out. Winfield flied to Dawson. No runs, no hits, no errors, none left.

SIXTH INNING

Nationals—Norris replaced Forsch on the mound for the Americans and assumed the third spot in the batting order. Bell replaced Brett at third base and batted ninth. Concepcion grounded to Bell. Parker slugged a home run over the right-field fence. Schmidt lined a double down the right-field line. Baker grounded to Bell, who tagged out Schmidt trying to advance. Dawson struck out. One run, two hits, no errors, one left.

Americans—Smith replaced Concepcion at shortstop and Easler replaced Parker in right field for the Nationals. Singleton singled to center. Evans singled to right, Singleton stopping at second. Fisk singled to right, loading bases. Lynn batted for Dent and singled to right, Singleton scoring and the bases remaining loaded. Bell flied to Baker, Evans scoring after the catch. Murray batted for Carew and forced Lynn, Garvey to Smith, Fisk advancing to third. Simmons batted for Randolph and singled to right, Fisk scoring and Murray stopping at second. Ruthven replaced Hooton on the mound for the Nationals. White ran for Simmons. Oliver batted for Norris and hit a fly ball to short left that Baker handled with a diving catch. Three runs, five hits, no errors, two left.

SEVENTH INNING

Nationals—Davis came in to pitch for the Americans. Murray and White remained in the game to play first base and second base, respectively. Burleson went in to play shortstop and assumed the fifth spot in the batting order; Diaz replaced Fisk at catcher and batted seventh, and Armas came in to play left field and batted eighth. Carter hit Davis' first pitch over the center-field fence to become only the fifth player ever to hit two home runs in one All-Star Game. Trillo flied to Evans. Garvey popped to Burleson. Guerrero batted for Ruthven and struck out. One run, one hit, no errors, none left.

Americans—Blue came in to pitch for the Nationals and batted first in the order; Benedict replaced Carter behind the plate and batted seventh. Winfield flied to Dawson. Burleson reached first when Schmidt mishandled his grounder for an error. With Evans batting, Burleson raced all the way to third on a wild pitch. Evans flied to Dawson, Burleson holding third. Diaz struck out. No runs, no hits, one error, one left.

EIGHTH INNING

Nationals—Fingers replaced Davis on the mound for the Americans. Smith walked. With Easler batting, Smith stole second, but when Diaz' throw went into center field, Smith was out trying to advance to third, Winfield to Bell to Burleson to Fingers. Easler walked. Schmidt blasted a home run to center, Easler scoring ahead of him. Baker singled to left. Raines ran for Baker and with Dawson batting, advanced to second on a wild pickoff throw by Fingers. Fingers threw a ball to Dawson before Stieb replaced him on the mound. Dawson grounded out, Stieb to Murray, Raines advancing to third. Benedict struck out. Two runs, two hits, one error, one left.

Americans—Ryan replaced Blue on the mound for the Nationals and Madlock replaced Schmidt at third base. Ryan assumed the fourth spot in the batting order and Madlock the first. Raines remained in the game to play left field. Armas struck out. Bell flied to Dawson. Murray grounded to Trillo. No runs, no hits, no errors, none left.

NINTH INNING

Nationals—Buckner batted for Trillo and grounded out, Murray to Stieb. Garvey doubled down the left-field line. Madlock grounded to Burleson, Garvey advancing to third. Smith walked. Easler forced Smith, Burleson to White. No runs, one hit, no errors, two left.

Americans—Sutter replaced Ryan on the mound for the Nationals and Garner came in to play second base. Sutter assumed the eighth spot in the batting order and Garner the fourth. White grounded to Madlock. Stieb struck out. Winfield flied to Raines. No runs, no hits, no errors, none left.

RESULTS OF PREVIOUS GAMES

1933—At Comiskey Park, Chicago, July 6. Americans 4, Nationals 2. Managers —Connie Mack, John McGraw. Winning pitcher—Lefty Gomez. Losing pitcher— Bill Hallahan. Attendance—47,595.

1934—At Polo Grounds, New York, July 10. Americans 9, Nationals 7. Managers—Joe Cronin, Bill Terry. Winning pitcher—Mel Harder. Losing pitcher—Van Mungo. Attendance—48,363.

1935—At Municipal Stadium, Cleveland, July 8. Americans 4, Nationals 1. Managers—Mickey Cochrane, Frankie Frisch. Winning pitcher—Lefty Gomez. Losing pitcher—Bill Walker. Attendance—69,831.

1936—At Braves Field, Boston, July 7. Nationals 4, Americans 3. Managers— Charlie Grimm, Joe McCarthy. Winning pitcher—Dizzy Dean. Losing pitcher— Lefty Grove. Attendance—25,556.

1937—At Griffith Stadium, Washington, July 7. Americans 8, Nationals 3. Managers—Joe McCarthy, Bill Terry. Winning pitcher—Lefty Gomez. Losing pitcher—Dizzy Dean. Attendance—31,391.

1938—At Crosley Field, Cincinnati, July 6. Nationals 4, Americans 1. Managers —Bill Terry, Joe McCarthy. Winning pitcher—Johnny Vander Meer. Losing pitcher—Lefty Gomez. Attendance—27,067.

1939—At Yankee Stadium, New York, July 11. Americans 3, Nationals 1. Managers—Joe McCarthy, Gabby Hartnett. Winning pitcher—Tommy Bridges. Losing pitcher—Bill Lee. Attendance—62,892.

1940—At Sportsman's Park, St. Louis, July 9. Nationals 4, Americans 0. Managers—Bill McKechnie, Joe Cronin. Winning pitcher—Paul Derringer. Losing pitcher—Red Ruffing. Attendance—32,373.

1941—At Briggs Stadium, Detroit, July 8. Americans 7, Nationals 5. Managers—Del Baker, Bill McKechnie. Winning pitcher—Ed Smith. Losing pitcher—Claude Passeau. Attendance—54,674.

1942—At Polo Grounds, New York, July 6. Americans 3, Nationals 1. Managers—Joe Cronin, Leo Durocher. Winning pitcher—Spud Chandler. Losing pitcher—Mort Cooper. Attendance—34,178.

1943—At Shibe Park, Philadelphia, July 13 (night game). Americans 5, Nationals 3. Managers—Joe McCarthy, Billy Southworth. Winning pitcher—Dutch Leonard. Losing pitcher—Mort Cooper. Attendance—31,938.

1944—At Forbes Field, Pittsburgh, July 11 (night game). Nationals 7, Americans 1. Managers—Billy Southworth, Joe McCarthy. Winning pitcher—Ken Raffensberger. Losing pitcher—Tex Hughson. Attendance—29,589.

1945—No game played.

1946—At Fenway Park, Boston, July 9. Americans 12, Nationals 0. Managers—Steve O'Neill, Charlie Grimm. Winning pitcher—Bob Feller. Losing pitcher—Claude Passeau. Attendance—34,906.

1947—At Wrigley Field, Chicago, July 8. Americans 2, Nationals 1. Managers—Joe Cronin, Eddie Dyer. Winning pitcher—Frank Shea. Losing pitcher—Johnny Sain. Attendance—41,123.

1948—At Sportsman's Park, St. Louis, July 13. Americans 5, Nationals 2. Managers—Bucky Harris, Leo Durocher. Winning pitcher—Vic Raschi. Losing pitcher—Johnny Schmitz. Attendance—34,009.

1949—At Ebbets Field, Brooklyn, July 12. Americans 11, Nationals 7. Managers—Lou Boudreau, Billy Southworth. Winning pitcher—Virgil Trucks. Losing pitcher—Don Newcombe. Attendance—32,577.

1950—At Comiskey Park, Chicago, July 11. Nationals 4, Americans 3 (14 innings). Managers—Burt Shotton, Casey Stengel. Winning pitcher—Ewell Blackwell. Losing pitcher—Ted Gray. Attendance—46,127.

1951—At Briggs Stadium, Detroit, July 10. Nationals 8, Americans 3. Managers—Eddie Sawyer, Casey Stengel. Winning pitcher—Sal Maglie. Losing pitcher—Ed Lopat. Attendance—52,075.

1952—At Shibe Park, Philadelphia, July 8. Nationals 3, Americans 2 (five innings—rain). Managers—Leo Durocher, Casey Stengel. Winning pitcher—Bob Rush. Losing pitcher—Bob Lemon. Attendance—32,785.

1953—At Crosley Field, Cincinnati, July 14. Nationals 5, Americans 1. Managers—Chuck Dressen, Casey Stengel. Winning pitcher—Warren Spahn. Losing pitcher—Allie Reynolds. Attendance—30,846.

1954—At Municipal Stadium, Cleveland, July 13. Americans 11, Nationals 9. Managers—Casey Stengel, Walter Alston. Winning pitcher—Dean Stone. Losing pitcher—Gene Conley. Attendance—68,751.

1955—At Milwaukee County Stadium, Milwaukee, July 12. Nationals 6, Americans 5 (12 innings). Managers—Leo Durocher, Al Lopez. Winning pitcher—Gene Conley. Losing pitcher—Frank Sullivan. Attendance—45,643.

1956—At Griffith Stadium, Washington, July 10. Nationals 7, Americans 3. Managers—Walter Alston, Casey Stengel. Winning pitcher—Bob Friend. Losing pitcher—Billy Pierce. Attendance—28,843.

1957—At Busch Stadium, St. Louis, July 9. Americans 6, Nationals 5. Managers—Casey Stengel, Walter Alston. Winning pitcher—Jim Bunning. Losing pitcher—Curt Simmons. Attendance—30,693.

1958—At Memorial Stadium, Baltimore, July 8. Americans 4, Nationals 3. Managers—Casey Stengel, Fred Haney. Winning pitcher—Early Wynn. Losing pitcher—Bob Friend. Attendance—48,829.

1959 (first game)—At Forbes Field, Pittsburgh, July 7. Nationals 5, Americans 4. Managers—Fred Haney, Casey Stengel. Winning pitcher—Johnny Antonelli. Losing pitcher—Whitey Ford. Attendance—35,277.

1959 (second game)—At Memorial Coliseum, Los Angeles, August 3. Americans 5, Nationals 3. Managers—Casey Stengel, Fred Haney. Winning pitcher—Jerry Walker. Losing pitcher—Don Drysdale. Attendance—55,105.

Cleveland's Municipal Stadium was ready to host the 1981 All-Star Game on July 14, but sat vacant as players and owners fought over the negotiating table. The stands were full, however, when baseball resumed August 9.

1960 (first game)—At Municipal Stadium, Kansas City, July 11. Nationals 5, Americans 3. Managers—Walter Alston, Al Lopez. Winning pitcher—Bob Friend. Losing pitcher—Bill Monbouquette. Attendance—30,619.

1960 (second game)—At Yankee Stadium, New York, July 13. Nationals 6, Americans 0. Managers—Walter Alston, Al Lopez. Winning pitcher—Vern Law. Losing pitcher—Whitey Ford. Attendance—38,362.

1961 (first game)—At Candlestick Park, San Francisco, July 11. Nationals 5, Americans 4 (10 innings). Managers—Danny Murtaugh, Paul Richards. Winning pitcher—Stu Miller. Losing pitcher—Hoyt Wilhelm. Attendance—44,115.

1961 (second game)—At Fenway Park, Boston, July 31. Americans 1, Nationals 1 (nine-inning tie, stopped by rain). Managers—Paul Richards, Danny Murtaugh. Attendance—31,851.

1962 (first game)—At District of Columbia Stadium, Washington, July 10. Nationals 3, Americans 1. Managers—Fred Hutchinson, Ralph Houk. Winning pitcher—Juan Marichal. Losing pitcher—Camilo Pascual. Attendance—45,480.

1962 (second game)—At Wrigley Field, Chicago, July 30. Americans 9, Nationals 4. Managers—Ralph Houk, Fred Hutchinson. Winning pitcher—Ray Herbert. Losing pitcher—Art Mahaffey. Attendance—38,359.

1963—At Municipal Stadium, Cleveland, July 9. Nationals 5, Americans 3. Managers—Alvin Dark, Ralph Houk. Winning pitcher—Larry Jackson. Losing pitcher—Jim Bunning. Attendance—44,160.

1964—At Shea Stadium, New York, July 7. Nationals 7, Americans 4. Managers—Walter Alston, Al Lopez. Winning pitcher—Juan Marichal. Losing pitcher—Dick Radatz. Attendance—50,850.

1965—At Metropolitan Stadium, Bloomington (Minnesota), July 13. Nationals 6, Americans 5. Managers—Gene Mauch, Al Lopez. Winning pitcher—Sandy Koufax. Losing pitcher—Sam McDowell. Attendance—46,706.

1966—At Busch Memorial Stadium, St. Louis, July 12. Nationals 2, Americans 1 (10 innings). Managers—Walter Alston, Sam Mele. Winning pitcher—Gaylord Perry. Losing pitcher—Pete Richert. Attendance—49,936.

1967—At Anaheim Stadium, Anaheim (California), July 11. Nationals 2, Americans 1 (15 innings). Managers—Walter Alston, Hank Bauer. Winning pitcher—Don Drysdale. Losing pitcher—Jim Hunter. Attendance—46,309.

1968—At Astrodome, Houston, July 9 (night). Nationals 1, Americans 0. Managers—Red Schoendienst, Dick Williams. Winning pitcher—Don Drysdale. Losing pitcher—Luis Tiant. Attendance—48,321.

1969—At Robert F. Kennedy Memorial Stadium, Washington, July 23. Nationals 9, Americans 3. Managers—Red Schoendienst, Mayo Smith. Winning pitcher—Steve Carlton. Losing pitcher—Mel Stottlemyre. Attendance—45,259.

1970—At Riverfront Stadium, Cincinnati, July 14 (night). Nationals 5, Americans 4 (12 innings). Managers—Gil Hodges, Earl Weaver. Winning pitcher—Claude Osteen. Losing pitcher—Clyde Wright. Attendance—51,838.

1971—At Tiger Stadium, Detroit, July 13 (night). Americans 6, Nationals 4. Managers—Earl Weaver, George (Sparky) Anderson. Winning pitcher—Vida Blue. Losing pitcher—Dock Ellis. Attendance—53,559.

1972—At Atlanta Stadium, Atlanta, July 25 (night). Nationals 4, Americans 3 (10 innings). Managers—Danny Murtaugh, Earl Weaver. Winning pitcher—Tug McGraw. Losing pitcher—Dave McNally. Attendance—53,107.

1973—At Royals Stadium, Kansas City, July 24 (night). Nationals 7, Americans 1. Managers—George (Sparky) Anderson, Dick Williams. Winning pitcher—Rick Wise. Losing pitcher—Bert Blyleven. Attendance—40,849.

1974—At Three Rivers Stadium, Pittsburgh, July 23 (night). Nationals 7, Americans 2. Managers—Yogi Berra, Dick Williams. Winning pitcher—Ken Brett. Losing pitcher—Luis Tiant. Attendance—50,706.

1975—At Milwaukee County Stadium, Milwaukee, July 15 (night). Nationals 6, Americans 3. Managers—Walter Alston, Alvin Dark. Winning pitcher—Jon Matlack. Losing pitcher—Jim Hunter. Attendance—51,480.

1976—At Veterans Stadium, Philadelphia, July 13 (night). Nationals 7, Americans 1. Managers—George (Sparky) Anderson, Darrell Johnson. Winning pitcher— Randy Jones. Losing pitcher—Mark Fidrych. Attendance—63,974.

1977—At Yankee Stadium, New York, July 19 (night). Nationals 7, Americans 5. Managers—Alfred (Billy) Martin, George (Sparky) Anderson. Winning pitcher—Don Sutton. Losing pitcher—Jim Palmer. Attendance—56,683.

1978—At San Diego Stadium, San Diego, July 11. Nationals 7, Americans 3. Managers—Alfred (Billy) Martin, Thomas Lasorda. Winning pitcher—Bruce Sutter. Losing pitcher—Rich Gossage. Attendance—51,549.

1979—At Kingdome, Seattle, July 17, Nationals 7, Americans 6. Managers—Chuck Tanner, Bob Lemon. Winning pitcher—Bruce Sutter. Losing pitcher—Jim Kern. Attendance—58,905.

1980—At Dodger Stadium, Los Angeles, July 8, Nationals 4, Americans 2. Managers—Chuck Tanner, Earl Weaver. Winning pitcher—Jerry Reuss. Losing pitcher—Tommy John. Attendance—56,088.

BATTING, PITCHING FEATURES

Including

No-Hit Performances

Low-Hit Pitching Performances

Top Strikeout Performances

Baseball's Top Firemen

Pitchers Winning 1-0 Games

Multi-Home Run Performances

Batters Hitting Grand Slams

Top One-Game Hitting Performances

Baseball's Top Pinch-Hitters

Homers by Parks

Award Winners

Hall of Fame Electees

Hall of Famers List, Years Selected

Len Barker was perfect for one night in 1981.

Barker Finds Perfect Formula

By LARRY WIGGE

Mrs. Tokie Lockhart of Ona, W. Va., is the 92-year-old grandmother of Cleveland Indians righthander Len Barker. When informed that her grandson had hurled the first perfect game since 1968 and only the 12th in more than 100 years of major league baseball, she said: "Tell Len I'm proud. I hope he does better next time."

All kidding aside, on May 15, 1981, Barker was as good as the gold kept at Fort Knox, where he was born in 1955. Barker's masterpiece, a 3-0 triumph over the Toronto Blue Jays, was the first perfect game since May 8, 1968, when Oakland's Catfish Hunter stymied the Minnesota Twins, 4-0.

There is no greater drama than watching a pitcher string together inning after inning of no-hit ball, much less the thrill of seeing a rare performance when someone retires 27 straight batters. Unfortunately, there were only 7,290 fans at Municipal Stadium as a misty rain gusted in off Lake Erie on a 47-degree evening in Cleveland.

According to Barker, the highest moments of tension arrived in the final inning. "My legs were quivering," he said. "I might have seemed like I was relaxed, but I wasn't. It was a mental thing. I was concentrating like crazy to keep myself together.

"It was the most unreal experience of my life . . . it was real and yet like a dream. Never before in my life have I concentrated more about each pitch and about controlling myself."

Barker's perfect game was one of three no-hitters in 1981. Nolan Ryan of the Houston Astros hurled his fifth career no-hitter, beating the Los Angeles Dodgers on September 26, 5-0. Ryan's five no-hitters set a new major league record. Montreal's Charlie Lea had the first no-hitter of the season, throttling the San Francisco Giants on May 10—just five days before Barker's perfecto.

"I was thinking about it (a no-hitter) all the way," the 6-4, 225-pound Barker said. "But you can't take it all that seriously until the last inning. You've still got three guys to go and any one of them can get a hit, a blooper, anything."

But the ninth inning was no different from any other for Barker. 1-2-3. Up and down in order.

Toronto center fielder Rick Bosetti popped up to third baseman Toby Harrah to open the ninth. Al Woods, pinch-hitting for Danny Ainge, struck out on three pitches. Then Ernie Whitt, batting for Buck Martinez, lifted a soft fly to center fielder Rick Manning.

It was the first no-hitter in the American League since Bert Blyleven (then of Texas and Barker's teammate in '81) beat the California Angels on September 22, 1977.

Barker struck out 11 batters in the game. There were only four batted balls that might have been considered more than routine plays. Shortstop Tom Veryzer had to charge Alfredo Griffin's slow roller over the mound in the first inning to nip the speedy leadoff hitter. Manning ran a long way to grab Damaso Garcia's liner to left center in the second. Second baseman Duane Kuiper threw out Bosetti on a sharp one-hopper to his right in the sixth and then went to his left on Griffin's grounder in the seventh. He needed three steps to right himself for an off-balance throw that beat Griffin by an eyelash.

"Because of the situation, it makes those plays seem better than they actually were," Kuiper said later. "Lennie was in total command."

Noted for one of the best fastballs in the A.L., Barker relied heavily on a sharp-breaking curve against the Blue Jays. He made 103 pitches and never threw three called balls to any batter, or more than five pitches out of the strike zone in a single inning.

The Indians scored all the runs Barker needed with two in the first inning on Andre Thornton's sacrifice fly and Ron Hassey's RBI single. They added a run in the eighth on Jorge Orta's home run.

The 34-year-old Ryan tossed four no-hitters in the mid-70s with the California Angels. He shackled Kansas City, 3-0, on May 15, 1973. Two months later, he performed his magic on Detroit, 6-0. On September 28, 1974, he blanked Minnesota, 4-0. No-hitter No. 4 occurred on June 1, 1975 when Nolan baffled Baltimore, 1-0. His 5-0 victory on September 26 enabled him to surpass Hall of Famer Sandy Koufax, who had four career no-hitters.

"This is something I've wanted to accomplish for a long time," Ryan said. "But I've been there too many times before (seven one-hitters) in the late innings. I was beginning to think I didn't have the stamina to get the fifth one."

But he did. Ryan walked only three batters and struck out 11. The performance lowered Ryan's league-leading ERA to 1.74.

The Alvin, Tex., native labeled this as his favorite no-hitter, not just because it was nationally televised by NBC, but rather because his wife, Ruth, his mother and other family members and close friends were in the Astrodome rooting. "This was also the first no-hitter I've pitched during a pennant race late in the season," Ryan added.

Ryan struggled early, throwing 65 pitches the first three innings and 81 pitches through the fourth, when he was continuously behind in the count and walked the three batters.

"He said after the third inning that his delivery was messed up, his back was killing him and that he just didn't feel right," Astros pitcher Dave Smith remembered. "Well, mess up my delivery, kill my back and tell me not to feel right."

After pitching coach Mel Wright walked to the mound at the start of the fourth inning and suggested that Ryan was overstriding, the hard-throwing righthander never permitted another baserunner. He retired the last 19 Dodgers batters in order.

"I let up a little in the late innings," Ryan said. "I didn't get as many strikeouts (10 in the first six innings), but I had better control."

Ryan fired three straight fastballs past pinch-hitter Reggie Smith to lead off the ninth. And he coaxed an easy grounder from Ken Landreaux before enticing Dusty Baker to ground feebly to third base.

The Dodgers had lost to Ryan only one time in nine previous decisions. He had never beaten them in two seasons with the Astros. His last victory over them came when he pitched for the New York Mets.

Ryan needed one superb defensive play, a running catch by Terry Puhl near the right-center field wall to rob Mike Scioscia of an extra-base hit in the seventh.

Following his no-hitter, Charlie Lea said, "I don't know how I'm going to celebrate. I'm just going to have to sit back and let it sink in."

Lea held the distinction of being the first French-born pitcher to toss a no-hitter after he baffled the Giants, 4-0, in the second game of a doubleheader at

Barker's Perfect Game

Toronto	AB.	R.	H.	RBI.	E.
Griffin, ss	3	0	0	0	1
Moseby, rf	3	0	0	0	0
Bell, lf	3	0	0	0	0
Mayberry, 1b	3	0	0	0	1
Upshaw, dh	3	0	0	0	0
Garcia, 2b	3	0	0	0	1
Bosetti, cf	3	0	0	0	0
Ainge, 3b	2	0	0	0	0
Woods, ph	1	0	0	0	0
Martinez, c	2	0	0	0	0
Whitt, ph	1	0	0	0	0
Totals	27	0	0	0	3

Cleveland	AB.	R.	H.	RBI.	E.
Manning, cf	4	1	1	0	0
Orta, rf	4	1	3	1	0
Hargrove, 1b	4	1	1	0	0
Thornton, dh	3	0	0	1	0
Hassey, c	4	0	1	1	0
Harrah, 3b	4	0	1	0	0
Charboneau, lf	3	0	0	0	0
Kuiper, 2b	3	0	0	0	0
Veryzer, ss	3	0	0	0	0
Totals	32	3	7	3	0

Toronto.................................. 0 0 0   0 0 0   0 0 0—0
Cleveland............................. 2 0 0   0 0 0   0 1 x—3

Toronto	IP.	H.	R.	ER.	BB.	SO.
Leal (L. 2-4)	8	7	3	1	0	5

Cleveland	IP.	H.	R.	ER.	BB.	SO.
BARKER (W. 3-1)	9	0	0	0	0	11

Game-winning RBI—Thornton.
LOB—Toronto 0, Cleveland 6. HR—Orta (2). SF —Thornton. T—2:09. A—7,290.

Perfect Game Play-by-Play

FIRST INNING—Alfredo Griffin grounded out to shortstop Tom Veryzer on a 1-and-2 count. Lloyd Moseby grounded out to Veryzer on an 1-0 count. Jorge Bell grounded out to first baseman Mike Hargrove on the first pitch.

SECOND INNING—John Mayberry flied out to center fielder Rick Manning on a 2-2 count. Willie Upshaw grounded out to second baseman Duane Kuiper on a 1-2 count. Damaso Garcia flied out to Manning on an 0-1 count.

THIRD INNING—Rick Bosetti grounded out to Veryzer on a 1-2 count. Dan Ainge grounded out to Kuiper on a 2-0 count. Buck Martinez flied out to Manning on a 1-1 count.

FOURTH INNING—Griffin flied out to right fielder Jorge Orta on a 2-2 count. Moseby struck out swinging on a 1-2 count. Bell struck out swinging on a 2-2 count.

FIFTH INNING—Mayberry struck out swinging on a 1-2 count. Upshaw fouled out to third baseman Toby Harrah on a 1-1 count. Garcia struck out swinging on a 2-2 count.

SIXTH INNING—Bosetti grounded out to Kuiper on an 0-1 count. Ainge struck out swinging on a 1-2 count. Mayberry struck out swinging on a 2-2 count.

SEVENTH INNING—Griffin grounded out to Kuiper on the first pitch. Moseby struck out swinging on a 2-2 count. Bell struck out swinging on a 2-2 count.

EIGHTH INNING—Mayberry struck out swinging on a 1-2 count. Upshaw grounded out to Kuiper on an 0-2 count. Garcia struck out swinging on a 2-2 count.

NINTH INNING—Bosetti popped out to Harrah on a 1-1 count. Al Woods, batting for Ainge, struck out swinging on an 0-2 count. Ernie Whitt, batting for Martinez, flied out to Manning on a 1-2 count.

Montreal's Olympic Stadium on May 10.

Born in Orleans, France, where his father was serving a U.S. military assignment, Charlie was a rather unlikely candidate to add his name to the no-hit honor roll. After all, he had been shelled for 16 hits in his previous 11 innings and had failed to make it past the fourth inning in two starts.

But Lea was nearly perfect for the first seven innings while facing the minimum 21 batters. Bill North coaxed the first of four walks off the 24-year-old Montreal righthander in the fourth inning, but was erased when caught stealing.

One inning later, however, Lea was in danger of losing his shutout after walking the bases loaded.

"I was tired," Lea said of his wild streak. "It's the longest outing I've had this year."

Lea walked Darrell Evans and Larry Herndon with none out. But then Milt May hit a sharp one-hopper that second baseman Rodney Scott converted into a double play. Lea walked Dave Bergman but Billy Smith flied out.

If the Expos hadn't built up a 4-0 bulge in the seventh inning on a homer by Tim Wallach, a two-run double by Scott and a run-scoring double by Andre Dawson, Montreal Manager Dick Williams might have found himself in the position of removing a no-hit pitcher because of his wildness in the eighth.

"We were watching him closely," Williams said. "If it had gotten to the stage where he simply couldn't find the plate, we might have made the change. But that's hypothetical—he regained his control. Besides, if we hadn't scored those runs, maybe he wouldn't have walked those people. There's a natural letdown. . ."

In the ninth, however, Lea got pinch-hitter Jim Wohlford on a grounder to third, struck out North after falling behind 3-0, and then got Enos Cabell on a long fly to Dawson.

Lea's No-Hitter

San Francisco	AB.	R.	H.	RBI.	E.
North, cf	3	0	0	0	0
Cabell, 1b	4	0	0	0	1
Morgan, 2b	3	0	0	0	0
Evans, 3b	2	0	0	0	0
Herndon, rf	2	0	0	0	0
May, c	3	0	0	0	0
Bergman, lf	2	0	0	0	0
Smith, ss	3	0	0	0	0
Whitson, p	2	0	0	0	0
Lavelle, p	0	0	0	0	0
Wohlford, ph	1	0	0	0	0
Totals	25	0	0	0	1

Montreal	AB.	R.	H.	RBI.	E.
Raines, lf	3	1	0	0	0
Scott, 2b	4	1	2	2	0
Dawson, cf	4	0	1	1	0
Carter, c	4	0	1	0	0
Cromartie, 1b	4	0	1	0	0
Wallach, 3b	2	1	1	1	0
Office, rf	4	1	1	0	0
Phillips, ss	4	0	0	0	0
LEA, p	1	0	0	0	0
Totals	30	4	7	4	0

San Francisco 000 000 000–0
Montreal 000 000 40x–4

San Francisco	IP.	H.	R.	ER.	BB.	SO.
Whitson (L. 0-4)	6⅔	7	4	4	2	3
Lavelle	1⅓	0	0	0	0	1

Montreal	IP.	H.	R.	ER.	BB.	SO.
LEA (W. 1-1)	9	0	0	0	4	8

Game-winning RBI—Wallach.

DP—San Francisco 1, Montreal 1. LOB—San Francisco 2, Montreal 7. 2B—Scott, Dawson. HR—Wallach (2). SB—Dawson. SH—LEA. HBP—By Whitson (Wallach), by Lavelle (Wallach). T—2:16. A—25,343.

Ryan's No-Hitter

Los Angeles	AB.	R.	H.	RBI.	E.
Lopes, 2b	3	0	0	0	0
Smith, ph	1	0	0	0	0
Landreaux, cf	3	0	0	0	0
Baker, lf	4	0	0	0	0
Garvey, 1b	2	0	0	0	0
Guerrero, 3b	3	0	0	0	0
Scioscia, c	3	0	0	0	0
Roenicke, rf	3	0	0	0	0
Thomas, ss	2	0	0	0	1
Power, p	1	0	0	0	0
Goltz, p	0	0	0	0	0
Perconte, ph	1	0	0	0	0
Forster, p	0	0	0	0	0
Johnstone, ph	1	0	0	0	0
Stewart, p	0	0	0	0	0
Howe, p	0	0	0	0	0
Totals	27	0	0	0	1

Houston	AB.	R.	H.	RBI.	E.
Puhl, rf	4	1	1	0	0
Garner, 2b	4	0	2	1	0
Scott, cf	5	1	0	0	0
Cruz, lf	4	1	3	1	0
Ashby, c	4	0	1	2	0
Howe, 3b	4	0	0	0	0
Spilman, 1b	2	0	0	0	0
Pittman, ph	1	0	1	0	0
Walling, 1b	0	1	0	0	0
Reynolds, ss	4	1	2	1	0
RYAN, p	2	0	1	0	0
Totals	34	5	11	5	0

Los Angeles 000 000 000–0
Houston 002 000 03x–5

Los Angeles	IP.	H.	R.	ER.	BB.	SO.
Power (L. 1-3)	3⅓	6	2	1	3	1
Goltz	⅔	0	0	0	0	0
Forster	3	2	0	0	1	2
Stewart	⅓	2	3	3	2	0
Howe	⅔	1	0	0	0	0

Houston	IP.	H.	R.	ER.	BB.	SO.
RYAN (W. 10-5)	9	0	0	0	3	11

Game-winning RBI—Ashby.

LOB—Los Angeles 3, Houston 12. 2B—Cruz, Reynolds. 3B—Reynolds. SB—Garner, Garvey, Thomas, Cruz. SH—RYAN. WP—RYAN, Stewart. PB—Scioscia. T—2:46. A—32,115.

Berenyi Leads Low-Hit Parade

By CARL CLARK

Cincinnati rookie Bruce Berenyi and Seattle lefthander Floyd Bannister were the only major league pitchers involved in more than one low-hit game in 1981. Berenyi pitched a one-hitter and a pair of two-hitters; Bannister tossed a pair of two-hitters.

There were 17 low-hit games in the American League—a perfect game by Len Barker of Cleveland (the first no-hitter in the league since Bert Blyleven's in 1977 and the first perfect game since Jim Hunter's in 1968), two one-hitters and 14 two-hitters. The National League had no-hitters by Montreal's Charlie Lea and Houston's Nolan Ryan, four one-hitters and 10 two-hitters.

Berenyi's first standout effort came at San Diego April 14, his first start of the season and his seventh in the big leagues. Going the distance for the first time in his major league career, Berenyi recorded a 4-0 victory, allowing singles by Terry Kennedy and Luis Salazar in the third and seventh innings, respectively. Berenyi's one-hitter came June 7 against Montreal. Andre Dawson's fourth-inning single was the Expos' only hit in a 2-0 defeat. Berenyi struck out 10 batters and walked only one. His third low-hit game (and the third of his five complete games) was against the Mets August 24. In another 2-0 victory, Berenyi gave up a leadoff single to Mookie Wilson and a fourth-inning single to Ellis Valentine.

Bannister's two-hit victims were California and Boston. The only safeties off Bannister in his 3-0 victory over the Angels April 21 were singles by Rod Carew in the first inning and Butch Hobson in the third. Dwight Evans' first-inning single and Carney Lansford's double in the ninth were the only Red Sox hits in Bannister's 2-0 win June 8.

Three A.L. hurlers took no-hitters into the ninth inning, only to see the leadoff man burst the bubble. Blyleven had Toronto stopped May 6 until Lloyd Moseby lined his first pitch of the final frame for a double. Jorge Bell followed with a run-scoring single and Blyleven settled for a 4-1 decision. Robin Yount's bloop double was Milwaukee's only hit in a 5-1 loss to the White Sox' Dennis Lamp August 25. Boston lefthander Bob Ojeda had thrown eight hitless innings against the Yankees September 11 before pinch-doubles by

Rick Cerone and Dave Winfield cut the Red Sox' lead to 2-1. Mark Clear relieved Ojeda and recorded the final three outs.

In the N.L., Pittsburgh's Jim Bibby set down Atlanta's last 27 batters in a 5-0 victory May 19 after a leadoff single by Terry Harper. The day after Ryan's September 26 no-hitter against Los Angeles, teammate Don Sutton held the Dodgers hitless until Ken Landreaux singled in the seventh inning. Sutton wound up with a two-hitter and 4-1 victory.

The season's only double low-hit game was Baltimore's 1-0 decision over Seattle September 1. Winner Steve Stone, who pitched 7⅓ innings before being relieved by Tippy Martinez, gave up both Mariner hits, singles by Julio Cruz in the fourth inning and Terry Bulling in the sixth. The Mariners' Glenn Abbott surrendered a fourth-inning double to Rich Dauer, who came around to score on ground-outs, and a sixth-inning single to Al Bumbry.

A complete list of one-hit and two-hit games follows:

AMERICAN LEAGUE
One-Hit Games

April 29—Darwin, Texas vs. Boston, 5-0—Miller, single in fifth.
Aug. 25—Lamp, Chicago vs. Milwaukee, 5-1—Yount, double in ninth.

Two-Hit Games

April 21—Bannister, Seattle vs. California, 3-0—Carew, single in first; Hobson, single in third.
April 26—Witt, California vs. Minnesota, 7-1 (first game)—Smalley, triple in fourth; Castino, homer in ninth.
April 30—Rozema, Detroit vs. Seattle, 2-0—Zisk, single in second; Auerbach, single in third.
May　6—Blyleven, Cleveland vs. Toronto, 4-1—Moseby, double in ninth; Bell, single in ninth.
May 21—Eckersley, Boston vs. Oakland, 3-0—Doyle, single in third; Armas, double in fourth.
June　8—Bannister, Seattle vs. Boston, 2-0—Evans, single in first; Lansford, double in ninth.
Sept.　1—Stone (seven and one-third innings) and T. Martinez (one and two-thirds inning), Baltimore vs. Seattle, 1-0—Cruz, single in fourth; Bulling, single in sixth.
Sept.　1—Abbott, Seattle vs. Baltimore, 0-1—Dauer, double in fourth; Bumbry, single in sixth.
Sept.　4—Zahn (five innings), California vs. Cleveland, 3-1 (stopped by rain)—Harrah, single in fifth; Bando, double in fifth.
Sept.　7—Morris, Detroit vs. Boston, 3-1—Miller, single in third; Yastrzemski, homer in seventh.

Reds Pitcher Bruce Berenyi receives congratulations from catcher Joe Nolan after stopping Montreal on one hit June 7.

Sept. 11—Righetti (seven innings) and Gossage (two innings), New York vs. Boston, 4-1—Lansford, single in fourth; Remy, single in eighth.

Sept. 12—Ojeda (eight innings) and Clear (one inning), Boston vs. New York, 2-1—Cerone, double in ninth; Winfield, double in ninth.

Sept. 19—Medich, Texas vs. Minnesota, 6-0—Butera, single in eighth; Powell, single in ninth.

Oct. 3—Stieb (eight and one-third innings), Garvin (one-third inning) and McLaughlin (one-third inning), Toronto vs. Seattle, 4-3—Anderson, homer in third; Zisk, homer in ninth.

NATIONAL LEAGUE
One-Hit Games

May 19—Bibby, Pittsburgh vs. Atlanta, 5-0—Harper, single in first.

June 7—Berenyi, Cincinnati vs. Montreal, 2-0—Dawson, single in fourth.

Aug. 27—Burris (eight innings) and Reardon (one inning), Montreal vs. Cincinnati, 12-0—Griffey, single in seventh.

Oct. 4—Soto, Cincinnati vs. Atlanta, 3-0—Chambliss, single in second.

Two-Hit Games

April 14—Berenyi, Cincinnati vs. San Diego, 4-0—Kennedy, single in third; Salazar, single in seventh.

April 15—Boggs, Atlanta vs. Houston, 0-2—Reynolds, single in seventh; Walling, single in seventh.

May 12—Niekro, Atlanta vs. Pittsburgh, 2-0—Garner, single in second; Pena, single in fifth.

Aug. 16—Niekro (seven innings) and D. Smith (two innings), Houston vs. San Diego, 3-0—Mura, single in third; Jones, double in sixth.

Aug. 24—Berenyi, Cincinnati vs. New York, 2-0—Wilson, single in first; Valentine, single in fourth.

Sept. 2—Seaver (eight innings) and Price (one inning), Cincinnati vs. Montreal, 7-0—Raines, single in third; Cromartie, double in fourth.

Sept. 3—Alexander, San Francisco vs. Chicago, 12-0—Buckner, single in first; Bonds, single in third.

Sept. 18—McWilliams, Atlanta vs. San Diego, 3-0—Jones, single in second; Kennedy, single in second.

Sept. 27—Sutton, Houston vs. Los Angeles, 4-1—Landreaux, single in seventh; Sax, homer in ninth.

Oct. 2—Rogers, Montreal vs. New York, 3-0—Taveras, single in first; Brooks, single in seventh.

Carlton Fans 15, but Strikes Out

By LARRY WIGGE

When Philadelphia southpaw Steve Carlton struck out 15 batters in the second game of a doubleheader against the New York Mets September 16, the performance brought back memories of 1969. The major leagues' top strikeout performance of 1981 was marred by the Mets' 5-4 victory.

It wasn't the first time Carlton wound up on the wrong side of the score while piling up a large number of strikeouts. Nearly 12 years to the day, On September 15, 1969, he set a major league record of 19 strikeouts (now shared by Tom Seaver) when he was a member of the St. Louis Cardinals. That game also was against the Mets and he lost, 4-3.

This time, catcher John Stearns struck the blow that turned Carlton into a loser, connecting for a two-run homer in the eighth inning to give the Mets a 5-4 victory. It was Stearns' first homer since August 18, 1979, a drought covering 197 games and 684 official at-bats.

Carlton's 15-strikeout perfromance was a Phillies' record for a lefthander. Carlton previously had shared the club high of 14 (four times) with Chris Short.

It was a year of strikeout highlights for Carlton. He surpassed Bob Gibson's National League record of 3,117 strikeouts against Montreal September 21 and finished the season with 3,148, fourth on the all-time list behind Walter Johnson (3,508), Gaylord Perry (3,336) and Nolan Ryan (3,249).

Steve Carlton . . . Strikeout artist.

There were 35 10-strikeout games in the majors in '81, 27 of those coming in the National League. Fernando Valenzuela, rookie lefthander of the Dodgers, led the N.L. with seven, while Cleveland's Len Barker topped the A.L. with three.

Barker fanned 11 Toronto batters May 15 while pitching the majors' first perfect game since 1968. Houston's Ryan struck out 11 batters when he stymied the Dodgers September 26 for his fifth career no-hitter. Ryan also extended his major league record for 10-strikeout games to 135, with four such efforts in '81.

Following is a listing of all the pitchers who achieved 10-strikeout games in 1981 with the number of times accomplished:

AMERICAN LEAGUE: Baltimore (1)—McGregor. Boston (1)—Eckersley. California—None. Chicago—None. Cleveland (4)—Barker 3, Denny. Detroit—None. Kansas City—None. Milwaukee—None. Minnesota—None. New York (1)—Righetti. Oakland (1)—Underwood. Seattle—None. Texas—None. Toronto—None.

NATIONAL LEAGUE: Atlanta—None. Chicago (1)—Krukow. Cincinnati (7)—Berenyi 4, Soto 3. Houston (4)—Ryan 4. Los Angeles (8)—Valenzuela 7, Welch. Montreal (2)—Gullickson 2. New York—None. Philadelphia (4)—Carlton 4. Pittsburgh—None. St. Louis—None. San Diego (1)—Eichelberger. San Francisco—None.

Following is a recap of Carlton's 15-strikeout game:

Date	Pitcher—Club—Opp.	Place	IP.	H.	R.	ER.	BB.	SO.	Result
Sept. 16—†	Carlton, Phillies vs. Mets	A	8	8	5	5	4	15	L-4-5

†Second game of doubleheader.

Fingers Leads Baseball Firemen

By LARRY WIGGE

The importance of relief pitching never was more evident than in the 1981 season, when a 50-day work stoppage cut short the stamina of most starting pitchers down the stretch.

Rollie Fingers of the Milwaukee Brewers was a perfect example of what a superb bullpen specialist could mean to a team. In 24 second-half appearances, Rollie posted 16 saves and five wins. He figured in 21 of the Brewers' 31 wins in the second season and led Milwaukee to its first playoff ever.

Over the course of the '81 season, Fingers logged 28 saves and six victories in relief to capture his fourth Fireman of the Year Award from THE SPORTING NEWS. The National League winner was Bruce Sutter of the St. Louis Cardinals.

Since 1960, THE SPORTING NEWS has honored the top relief pitcher in each league, with one point being awarded for each save and each relief win.

Fingers twice won the title outright when he was with the San Diego Padres (in 1977 and '78) and shared the award with Cincinnati's Tom Hume in 1980. His fourth Fireman honor is the most ever by any reliever. Mike Marshall won three titles while playing for Montreal, Los Angeles and Minnesota.

Sutter had 25 saves and three relief wins for a total of 28 points in winning his second Fireman title. He previously led the N.L. in 1979 while a member of the Chicago Cubs.

Ironically, for four days during the previous December, Fingers and Sutter were both members of the Cardinals as a result of trades engineered by St. Louis Manager-General Manager Whitey Herzog. Sutter was obtained from the Cubs, while Fingers was part of a seven-player trade with the Padres. When it became apparent that the Redbirds wouldn't be able to sign Fingers to a new contract, Herzog dispatched the moustachioed righthander to the Brewers.

Fingers outdistanced the Yankees' Rich Gossage, 34 points to 23. Amazingly, Gossage had held a six-point edge over Fingers before the 50-day strike, but the hard-throwing Yankee righthander was bothered by arm trouble and had only three saves and one win in the second half of the season.

Sutter's 28 points were two better than

Bruce Sutter . . . Tops in N.L.

Rick Camp of Atlanta and three more than Neil Allen of the Mets and Greg Minton of the Giants.

Dan Quisenberry of the Kansas City Royals dropped from 45 points and the A.L. Fireman award in 1980 to 19 points in '81. Hume, who had 34 points to share the '80 N.L. title with Fingers, had 22 points in '81.

Following is a listing of the Fireman of he Year leaders for 1981:

National League

Pitcher—Club	Saves	Relief Wins	Tot. Pts.	Pitcher—Club	Saves	Relief Wins	Tot. Pts.
Sutter, St. Louis	25	3	28	Littlefield, San Diego	2	2	4
Camp, Atlanta	17	9	26	Mahler, Atlanta	2	2	4
Allen, New York	18	7	25	Moskau, Cincinnati	2	2	4
Minton, San Francisco	21	4	25	Proly, Philadelphia	2	2	4
Hume, Cincinnati	13	9	22	Show, San Diego	3	1	4
Lucas, San Diego	13	7	20	Smith, Chicago	1	3	4
Sambito, Houston	10	5	15	Sosa, Montreal	3	1	4
Holland, San Francisco	7	6	13	Urrea, San Diego	2	2	4
Howe, Los Angeles	8	5	13	Bahnsen, Montreal	1	2	3
R. Reed, Philadelphia	8	5	13	Bradford, Atlanta	1	2	3
D. Smith, Houston	8	5	13	Boone, San Diego	2	1	3
Fryman, Montreal	7	5	12	Falcone, New York	1	2	3
McGraw, Philadelphia	10	2	12	LaCoss, Cincinnati	1	2	3
Tidrow, Chicago	9	3	12	Littell, St. Louis	2	1	3
Lyle, Philadelphia	2	9	11	Marshall, New York	0	3	3
Reardon, New York-Montreal	8	3	11	Pena, Los Angeles	2	1	3
Kaat, St. Louis	4	6	10	Boitano, San Diego	0	2	2
Price, Cincinnati	4	6	10	Christenson, Philadelphia	1	1	2
Romo, Pittsburgh	9	1	10	Cruz, Pittsburgh	1	1	2
Stewart, Los Angeles	6	4	10	Curtis, San Diego	0	2	2
LaCorte, Houston	5	4	9	Edelen, St. Louis-Cincinnati	0	2	2
Lee, Monreal	6	3	9	Goltz, Los Angeles	1	1	2
Scurry, Pittsburgh	7	2	9	Hanna, Atlanta	0	2	2
Martz, Chicago	6	2	8	Hernandez, Chicago	2	0	2
Tekulve, Pittsburgh	3	5	8	Hrabosky, Atlanta	1	1	2
Castillo, Los Angeles	5	2	7	Lee, Pittsburgh	2	0	2
Breining, San Francisco	1	5	6	Lollar, San Diego	1	1	2
Garber, Atlanta	2	4	6	D. Robinson, Pittsburgh	2	0	2
Jackson, Pittsburgh-Montreal	4	2	6	Searage, New York	1	1	2
Lavelle, San Francisco	4	2	6	Shirley, St. Louis	1	1	2
Bair, Cincinnati-St. Louis	1	4	5	Solomon, Pittsburgh	1	1	2
Niedenfuer, Los Angeles	2	3	5	Sykes, St. Louis	0	2	2

One Save—Eastwick, Chicago; Griffin, Chicago; Harris, New York; Montefusco, Atlanta; Orosco, New York; Ruhle, Houston; B. Smith, Houston.

One Relief Win—Andujar, Houston-St. Louis; Bedrosian, Atlanta; Brown, Cincinnati; Capilla, Chicago; Combe, Cincinnati; Geisel, Chicago; Jones, Pittsburgh; Leach, New York; McGlothen, Chicago; Miller, New York; Otten, St. Louis; Power, Los Angeles; Ratzer, Montreal; B. Smith, Montreal.

American League

Pitcher—Club	Saves	Relief Wins	Tot. Pts.	Pitcher—Club	Saves	Relief Wins	Tot. Pts.
Fingers, Milwaukee	28	6	34	Lopez, Detroit	3	3	6
Gossage, New York	20	3	23	Owchinko, Oakland	2	4	6
Corbett, Minnesota	17	2	19	Lopez, Detroit	3	3	6
Hoyt, Chicago	10	9	19	J. Johnson, Texas	2	3	5
Quisenberry, Kansas City	18	1	19	Koosman, Minnesota-Chicago	5	0	5
Clear, Boston	9	8	17	Stanton, Cleveland	2	3	5
Saucier, Detroit	13	4	17	Beard, Oakland	3	1	4
Aase, California	11	4	15	LaRoche, New York	4	0	4
Comer, Texas	6	8	14	Augustine, Milwaukee	2	1	3
T. Martinez, Baltimore	11	3	14	K. Brett, Kansas City	2	1	3
Farmer, Chicago	10	3	13	Clark, Seattle	2	1	3
Rawley, Seattle	8	4	12	Cleveland, Milwaukee	1	2	3
McLaughlin, Toronto	10	1	11	Frazier, New York	3	0	3
Stoddard, Baltimore	7	4	11	Hickey, Chicago	3	0	3
Burgmeier, Boston	6	4	10	Lamp, Chicago	0	3	3
Davis, New York	6	4	10	Leal, Toronto	1	2	3
Spillner, Cleveland	7	3	10	O'Connor, Minnesota	0	3	3
Stanley, Boston	0	10	10	Tobik, Detroit	1	2	3
Drago, Seattle	5	4	9	Underwood, New York-Oakland	1	2	3
Hassler, California	5	4	9	Aponte, Boston	1	1	2
Andersen, Seattle	5	3	8	Bird, New York	0	2	2
Campbell, Boston	7	1	8	Bomback, Toronto	0	2	2
Jackson, Toronto	7	1	8	Cappuzzello, Detroit	1	1	2
Martin, Kansas City	4	4	8	Galasso, Seattle	1	1	2
Stewart, Baltimore	4	4	8	Lerch, Milwaukee	0	2	2
Easterly, Milwaukee	4	3	7	Mercer, Texas	2	0	2
Jones, Oakland	3	4	7	Renko, California	1	1	2
Kern, Texas	6	1	7	Sanchez, California	2	0	2
Monge, Cleveland	4	3	7	Tudor, Boston	1	1	2

ONE SAVE—Beattie, Seattle; Hough, Texas; May, New York; McLaughlin, Oakland; Parrott, Seattle; Rothschild, Detroit; Schmidt, Texas; Schneider, Baltimore.

One Relief Win—Babcock, Texas; Berenguer, Kansas City-Toronto; Castro, New York; Cooper, Minnesota; Ford, Baltimore; Gale, Kansas City; Garvin, Toronto; Haas, Milwaukee; Heaverlo, Oakland; D. Jackson, Minnesota; Jefferson, California; Keeton, Milwaukee; Murray, Toronto; Robinson, Chicago; Schatzeder, Detroit; Splittorff, Kansas City; Trout, Chicago; Veselic, Minnesota; Wright, Kansas City.

Knepper Gets Three 1-0 Wins

By CARL CLARK

There were nine 1-0 games in the National League in 1981, and Houston's Bob Knepper was the winning pitcher in three of them.

Knepper, in his first season with the Astros after four years with San Francisco, defeated Los Angeles April 21 on a three-hitter. In his next start, against Cincinnati, Denny Walling's leadoff home run in the first inning was all the support he needed. (Home runs decided four of the majors' 1-0 games.) Knepper blanked San Diego May 27. He went the route in each game and allowed a total of 17 hits, all singles.

Fernando Valenzuela of Los Angeles, the N.L. Rookie of the Year and Cy Young Award winner, was the only other N.L. pitcher with a decision in more than one 1-0 game. Valenuela tamed Houston April 22 and New York May 8, but lost to San Diego October 1.

Detroit's Dan Petry was the only hurler to win more than one of the 19 American League 1-0 games. It took Petry 11 innings to edge Seattle May 13 and he beat Texas September 5. Petry was on the losing end of a 1-0 game against Baltimore and Dennis Martinez September 23.

Milwaukee's Mike Caldwell and Dave Stieb of Toronto each lost a pair of 1-0 games.

The longest 1-0 game of the season was the September 21 struggle between Montreal and Philadelphia. The Expos prevailed in 17 innings, seven fewer innings than the major league record (Houston over New York, 1968). Steve Carlton pitched the first 10 innings for the Phillies and struck out 10 batters as he broke Bob Gibson's N.L. career strikeout record (3,117). Ray Burris pitched the first 10 frames for the Expos. Andre Dawson drove in the deciding run with a one-out, bases-loaded grounder to third baseman Mike Schmidt, whose throw to the plate was too late to force Rodney Scott. The winning pitcher was Bryn Smith, the loser Jerry Reed. It was the first major league decision for each hurler.

The A.L.'s longest 1-0 game was Kansas City's 15-inning victory over Minnesota May 23. Paul Splittorff worked the first 11 innings for the Royals and Renie Martin the last four. Willie Wilson's two-out single scored Dan Garcia and

snapped a Royals club record of 30 consecutive scoreless innings.

The complete list of 1-0 games, including the winning and losing pitchers and the inning in which the run was scored, follows:

AMERICAN LEAGUE (19)

APRIL—

Date	Winner	Loser	Inning
12 —	McCatty, Oak.	*Redfern, Minn.	1
16 —	Garland, Clev.	*Caldwell, Milw.	2

MAY—

13 —	Petry, Det.	*Drago, Sea.	11
17†—*	Waits, Clev.	Stieb, Tor.	5
17 —	*Bannister, Sea.	*Davis, N.Y.	6
23 —	*Martin, K.C.	*Cooper, Minn.	15
30 —	*Nelson, N.Y.	Spillner, Clev.	1

JUNE—

8 —	*Erickson, Minn.	Caldwell, Milw.	7

AUGUST—

11 —	*Honeycutt, Tex.	*Righetti, N.Y.	1
14 —	*Wilcox, Det.	*May, N.Y.	3
28 —	Denny, Clev.	*Rawley, Sea.	9

SEPTEMBER—

1 —	*Stone, Balt.	Abbott, Sea.	4
5 —	Petry, Det.	*Jenkins, Tex.	2
8 —	Havens, Minn.	Stieb, Tor.	9
22 —	*Moreno, Calif.	Baumgarten, Chi.	2
23 —	D. Martinez, Balt.	Petry, Det.	9
25 —	McGregor, Balt.	John, N.Y.	5
28 —	Vuckovich, Milw.	Tanana, Bos.	7

OCTOBER—

3 —	Butcher, Tex.	Moreno, Calif.	9

NATIONAL LEAGUE (9)

APRIL—

Date	Winner	Loser	Inning
21 —	Knepper, Hou.	Reuss, L.A.	3
22 —	Valenzuela, L.A.	*Sutton, Hou.	5
26 —	Knepper, Hou.	*Soto, Cin.	1

MAY—

8 —	Valenzuela, L.A.	*Scott, N.Y.	1
26 —	*Ryan, Hou.	Eichelberger, S.D.	7
27 —	Knepper, Hou.	*Welch, S.D.	4

SEPTEMBER—

17 —	*Seaver, Cin.	*Holland, S.F.	10
21 —	*Smith, Mont.	*J. Reed, Phila.	17

OCTOBER—

1 —	*Kuhaulua, S.D.	*Valenzuela, L.A.	2

*Did not pitch complete game.

†First game of doubleheader.

O's Were Grandest of Slammers

By CARL CLARK

The Baltimore Orioles blasted five grand slams during the 1981 season, all in the second half. Lenn Sakata hit one; Doug DeCinces and Eddie Murray cracked two apiece. DeCinces' grand slam off Lamarr Hoyt accounted for all of Baltimore's runs in a shutout of the White Sox August 15. The next day, Murray, a switch-hitter, drove in six runs with a grand slam off lefthander Ross Baumgarten and a two-run homer in the ninth off righthander Ed Farmer, but the White Sox prevailed in 10 innings, 8-7.

The only National League batter with a pair of slams was the Mets' Dave Kingman. Kingman's second, off the Reds' Frank Pastore August 22, erased a 4-1, eighth-inning deficit.

Other grand slam hitters included two returning Jerrys, Grote and Hairston. Grote, a 38-year-old catcher who had not played since 1978, was used infrequently by Kansas City, playing in only 22 games. But on June 3 he drove in seven runs (he had nine all season) in the Royals' 12-9 victory over Seattle. His only home run of the season keyed an eight-run fifth inning.

The 29-year-old Hairston, who had last played in the majors with Pittsburgh in 1977, ended his four-year Mexican League exile by joining the White Sox in September. On the last day of the season, Hairston starred in a come-from-behind victory over the Twins. His grand slam in the eighth inning cut Minnesota's lead to 12-9 and his run-scoring single with two out in the ninth, his sixth RBI of the game, gave Chicago a 13-12 decision.

The only game in which two grand slams were hit was San Francisco's 15-7 victory over Cincinnati June 2. Jerry Martin homered for the Giants, Ron Oester for the Reds.

Three pitchers were touched for two slams each: Dick Ruthven of Philadelphia, Steve Rogers of Montreal and Minnesota's Don Cooper.

The complete list of grand slams, with the inning in which each was hit in parentheses, follows:

Doug DeCinces ... Two slams.

MAY—
28 —Howell, Milwaukee vs. Petry, Detroit .... (4)
JUNE—
3 —Grote, Kansas City vs. Clay, Seattle .... (5)
7 —Bell, Texas vs. Jackson, Toronto .... (8)
AUGUST—
12* —White, Kansas City vs. Schneider, Baltimore ..... (8)
15 —DeCinces, Baltimore vs. Hoyt, Chicago .... (4)
16 —Murray, Baltimore vs. Baumgarten, Chicago ..... (3)
24 —Burroughs, Seattle vs. D. Martinez, Baltimore ... (4)
27 —DeCinces, Baltimore vs. Aase, California .... (8)
SEPTEMBER—
6 —Sakata, Baltimore vs. Beard, Oakland .... (7)
7 —Murray, Baltimore vs. Garland, Cleveland .... (5)
18 —Murphy, Oakland vs. Hickey, Chicago .... (9)
23 —Allenson, Boston vs. Cleveland, Milwaukee .... (7)
OCTOBER—
4 —Hairston, Chicago vs. Cooper, Minnesota .... (8)

NATIONAL LEAGUE (14)

APRIL—
12 —Bass, San Diego vs. Griffin, San Francisco .... (3)
MAY—
9 —North, San Francisco vs. Rogers, Montreal .... (7)
25 —Kingman, New York vs. Ruthven, Philadelphia . (2)
JUNE—
2 —Martin, San Francisco vs. Bair, Cincinnati .... (4)
2 —Oester, Cincinnati vs. Whitson, San Francisco ... (5)
6 —Hernandez, St. Louis vs. Littlefield, San Diego... (8)
AUGUST—
13 —Dawson, Montreal vs. Cruz, Pittsburgh .... (7)
22 —Kingman, New York vs. Pastore, Cincinnati .... (8)
23 —Schmidt, Philadelphia vs. Knepper, Houston ...... (3)
25 —Carter, Montreal vs. Moskau, Cincinnati .... (4)
25 —Benedict, Atlanta vs. M. Davis, Philadelphia ...... (1)
31 —Hubbard, Atlanta vs. Ruthven, Philadelphia ...... (1)
SEPTEMBER—
3 —Foster, Cincinnati vs. Reed, Philadelphia .... (8)
17 —Porter, St. Louis vs. Rogers, Montreal .... (3)

*First game of doubleheader.

AMERICAN LEAGUE (20)

APRIL—
9 —Murcer, New York vs. Comer, Texas .... (7)
9 —Downing, California vs. Abbott, Seattle .... (1)
12 —Rice, Boston vs. Farmer, Chicago .... (8)
14 —Fisk, Chicago vs. Vuckovich, Milwaukee .... (4)
18 —Smalley, Minnesota vs. Travers, California .... (3)
22 —Molitor, Milwaukee vs. McLaughlin, Toronto ..... (5)
27 —Randle, Seattle vs. Cooper, Minnesota .... (10)

Burroughs Only 3-Homer Man

By LARRY WIGGE

Bespectacled outfielder Jeff Burroughs had slugged 201 career home runs in his 10-plus major league seasons. But never had he connected for three homers in one game. Never, that is, until August 14, when he became the first member of the Seattle Mariners to accomplish the feat.

Burroughs was the only player in the major leagues to hit three homers in a game in 1981. He achieved the feat in the second game of a doubleheader at Minnesota, won by the Mariners, 13-3.

The former Texas and Atlanta slugger hit his initial homer with two men aboard in the first inning. He crushed a 420-foot homer to straightaway center field in the fifth and then pounded out his third homer, a 370-foot clout, into the left-field seats in the seventh.

Gorman Thomas of the Milwaukee Brewers led the majors with four two-homer games in 1981. The National League lead was shared by Bob Horner of Atlanta and Andre Dawson of Montreal, each with three two-homer games. There were 51 multiple-homer performances in the A.L. and 36 in the N.L.

Highlights of some of the other two-homer games included: Baltimore's Eddie Murray connecting from both sides of the plate against the White Sox August 16; San Diego's Joe Lefebvre getting two homers in a game he did not start—he entered the April 30 game at Cincinnati in the seventh inning with a pinch-homer; Aurelio Rodriguez, a reserve infielder for the Yankees, homered in his first two plate appearances of the season May 10 in a game at Seattle.

Following is a list of players who had two-homer games in '81 and the number of times they did it:

AMERICAN LEAGUE: Baltimore (10) —DeCinces 3, Sakata 2, Crowley, Dauer, Lowenstein, Murray, Singleton. Boston (5)—Evans, Perez, Rice, Rudi, Stapleton. California (5)—Grich 3, Brunansky, Lynn. Chicago (3)—Luzinski 2, Fisk. Cleveland (1)—Harrah. Detroit (3)—Hebner, Parrish, Wockenfuss. Kansas City (0). Milwaukee (6)—Thomas 4, Cooper, Yount. Minnesota (1)—Jackson. New York (5)—Gamble, Nettles, Rodriguez,

Jeff Burroughs . . . Three in one.

Watson, Winfield. Oakland (3)—Armas 2, Klutts. Seattle (5)—Gray 3, Burroughs, Paciorek. Texas (2)—Bell, Putnam. Toronto (2)—Mayberry, Velez.

NATIONAL LEAGUE: Atlanta (5)— Horner 3, Benedict, Murphy. Chicago (5) —Bonds 2, Buckner, Durham, Henderson. Cincinnati (3)—Concepcion 2, Bench. Houston (1)—Howe. Los Angeles (5)—Cey, Garvey, Guerrero, Landreaux, Monday. Montreal (4)—Dawson 3, Carter. New York (4)—Kingman 2, Staub, Valentine. Philadelphia (4)—Moreland 2, Schmidt 2. Pittsburgh (1)—Easler. St. Louis (2)—Hendrick, Tenace. San Diego (1)—Lefebvre. San Francisco (1)—Clark.

A recap of Burroughs' three-homer game follows:

Date	Player–Club–Opp.	Place	AB.	R.	H.	2B.	3B.	HR.	RBI.	Result
Aug. 14†	Burroughs, Mariners vs. Twins	A	4	3	3	0	0	3	6	W 13 -3

†Second game of doubleheader.

Six A.L. Batters Get Five Hits

By CARL CLARK

The number of players collecting five or more hits in one game dropped considerably in 1981, even taking into consideration the shortened season. There were 29 such performances in 1980, but only seven in '81.

Six of the seven were turned in by American League batters—three by members of the Red Sox and one by a former member of the Boston club. The Red Sox batters were Rick Miller, A.L. batting champion Carney Lansford, and Jerry Remy; the former Sox member was the Angels' Rick Burleson, who had been the Boston shortstop for the previous seven years.

Remy collected six singles in 10 at-bats against the Mariners September 3, a contest Boston lost in 20 innings, 8-7. Remy, who extended to 36 the number of six-hit games in A.L. history, had four hits in the first nine innings—off Floyd Bannister in the first and third innings, off Mike Parrott in the seventh and off Shane Rawley in the ninth. Remy's fifth hit came in the 16th inning off Larry Andersen and he connected again in the 20th against Jerry Don Gleaton.

Rod Carew of the Angels and Cecil Cooper of the Brewers were the other A.L. batters with five hits. Each went 5-for-5, as did Miller, Lansford and Burleson.

The only National League batter to register five hits in a game was the Dodgers' Ron Cey, who had five singles in six at-bats in a 16-6 whipping of the Pirates August 26.

The major leagues' longest hitting streaks belonged to Art Howe of the Astros and Lonnie Smith of the Phillies. Howe's 23-game hitting streak ran from May 1 through May 24. During that stretch, he hit .444 (40-for-90). The streak was halted when Howe went 0-for-3 with a sacrifice against the Padres' Steve Mura, Tim Lollar and Dan Boone. Smith began his tear on August 29 and

kept it up through the completion of the regular season. In the 23 games, he batted .415 (34-for-82), scored 20 runs, had 13 extra-base hits and stole 12 bases.

The A.L.'s longest streak belonged to Bobby Grich of the Angels. Grich's string lasted from May 21 through August 19, nearly a month longer than Joe DiMaggio's 56-game streak in 1941—but because most of that time coincided with the players' strike, Grich's streak encompassed just 21 games. In that stretch, Grich posted a .440 average (33-for-75) with seven homers and 15 runs batted in.

Four members of the Texas Rangers had streaks of 17 or more games. The most remarkable of those was Bill Stein's 18-game streak, which included six of seven consecutive pinch-hits, tying an A.L. record. Stein was 24-for-44 (.545) before going hitless in three at-bats against the Twins on June 2. Other Rangers with successful runs were Billy Sample (19 games, .389), Jim Sundberg (17 games, .428) and Al Oliver (17 games, .411).

Other streaks were notable not so much for their length as for the bursts of power they contained. Richie Zisk of the Mariners went 25-for-58 (.431) in 15 games from April 18 through May 2. Zisk belted six homers, five in consecutive games. Twins rookie Dave Engle reeled off 15 games in September. Included in the 24-for-60 binge (.400) were five homers—his entire output for 82 games—and 17 RBIs. Andre Dawson hit safely in 16 consecutive games for the Expos in May, posting a .400 average (26-for-65) with six homers.

Streaks of 15 or more games were also recorded by these players: 18 games—Larry Bowa, Phillies; 17 games—Pete Rose, Phillies; 16 games—Bill Buckner, Cubs; Tommy Herr, Cardinals; Jerry Mumphrey, Yankees; Jerry Remy, Red Sox; 15 games—Dusty Baker, Dodgers; Rick Burleson, Angels; Dave Collins, Reds; Ron Oester, Reds; Broderick Perkins, Padres; Willie Wilson, Royals.

The records of all players with five or more hits in a game follow:

Date	Player—Club—Opp.	Place	AB.	R.	H.	2B.	3B.	HR.	RBI.	Result
May 11	Miller, Red Sox vs. Blue Jays	A	5	3	5	4	0	0	1	W 7-6
May 17	Lansford, Red Sox vs. Blue Jays	H	5	1	5	0	0	0	2	L 4-5
June 3	Burelson, Angels vs. Blue Jays	A	5	2	5	1	0	0	3	W 17-6
Aug. 11*	Cooper, Brewers vs Indians	A	5	3	5	1	0	2	2	W 6-1
Aug. 21	Carew, Angels vs. Indians	H	5	0	5	0	0	0	1	W 12-2
Aug. 26	Cey, Dodgers vs. Pirates	A	6	2	5	0	0	0	2	W 16-6
Sept. 3	Remy, Red Sox vs. Mariners (20 innings)	H	10	2	6	0	0	0	0	L 7-8

*Second game of doubleheader.

Jerry Remy singled six times in a 20-inning game against Seattle.

Rod Carew of the Angels and George Brett of the Royals led the majors in games with four or more hits. Each had four.

The complete list of players with four or more hits in one game follows:

AMERICAN LEAGUE: Baltimore (10) —Murray 3, Bumbry 2, Singleton 2, Bonner, Dauer, Sakata. Boston (10)—Lansford 2, Remy 2, Rice 2, Evans, Hoffman, Miller, Stapleton. California (11)—Carew 4, Burleson 3, Baylor, Ford, Grich, Hobson. Chicago (10)—Baines 2, Bernazard 2, Almon, Fisk, Lemon, Luzinski, Nordhagen, Squires. Cleveland (7)—Hargrove 2, Manning 2, Bannister, Charboneau, Dilone. Detroit (4)—Jones 2, Gibson, Kemp. Kansas City (10)—G. Brett 4, Wilson 3, Otis, Wathan, White. Milwaukee (11)— Gantner 3, Cooper 2, Howell 2, Molitor, Moore, Thomas, Yount. Minnesota (2)— Hrbek, Wilfong. New York (2)— Mumphrey 2. Oakland (10)—Henderson 3, Armas, Gross, Heath, Johnson, Murphy, Picciolo, Revering. Seattle (6)— Meyer 3, Bochte, Paciorek, Simpson. Texas (9)—Oliver 2, Rivers 2, Wills 2, Mendoza, Putnam, Sundberg. Toronto (4)—Bonnell, Cox, Garcia, Moseby.

NATIONAL LEAGUE: Atlanta (6)— Horner 3, Washington 2, Ramirez. Chicago (6)—Buckner 2, Henderson 2, Durham, Reitz. Cincinnati (5)—Concepcion 2, Foster, Griffey, Nolan. Houston (6)— Scott 2, Ashby, Cedeno, Cruz, Reynolds. Los Angeles (6)—Cey 2, Baker, Guerrero, Lopes, Sax. Montreal (4)—Dawson 2, Cromartie, Raines. New York (5)—Wilson 2, Youngblood 2, Brooks. Philadelphia (2)—McBride, Schmidt. Pittsburgh (10)—Parker 3, Foli 2, Berra, Madlock, Moreno, Nicosia, Thompson. St. Louis (4)—Hernandez 2, Oberkfell, Templeton. San Diego (3)—Kennedy, Lefebvre, Salazar. San Francisco (4)—Evans, Herndon, Ivie, Martin.

Francona, Adams Best in Pinch

By LARRY WIGGE

Montreal's rookie outfielder Terry Francona and veteran pinch-hitting specialist Glenn Adams of the Minnesota Twins were the major league leaders in pinch-hitting for 1981. Francona was 5-for-10 for a .500 average and Adams went 6-for-13 for a .462 mark. It was the second time Adams had led the American League, previously winning the pinch-hitting championship in 1977.

Mike Cubbage of the Mets paced the N.L. with 12 pinch-hits in '81, while Bob Molinaro of the White Sox and Bill Stein of the Rangers topped the A.L. with nine pinch-blows each.

Mike Lum of the Cubs became the sixth player in history to amass 100 career pinch-hits when he belted a pinch-homer against the Mets August 12. Jose Morales and Terry Crowley of the Orioles are both knocking on the door of that milestone with 99 and 96 pinch-hits, respectively.

Bobby Murcer of the Yankees and Jay Johnstone of the Dodgers led the majors with three pinch-homers apiece. Murcer led all pinch-swingers with 12 RBIs, including a grand slam on opening day (the majors' only pinch-grand slam in '81) and two three-run homers. Two of Johnstone's pinch-homers were consecutive on May 23 and 24.

Oakland's Cliff Johnson smashed his 16th career pinch-homer on May 10 against Milwaukee, tying him with Smo-

Glenn Adams . . . Tough in pinch.

key Burgess, Gates Brown and Willie McCovey for second on the all-time pinch-homer list. Jerry Lynch is the career leader with 18.

NATIONAL LEAGUE PINCH-HITTING
(Compiled by Elias Sports Bureau)

Club Pinch-Hitting

Club	AB.	H.	HR.	RBI.	Pct.	Club	AB.	H.	HR.	RBI.	Pct.
Houston	139	40	2	20	.288	Montreal	123	28	2	12	.228
Pittsburgh	176	48	5	27	.273	Cincinnati	132	30	1	18	.227
Los Angeles	158	40	6	26	.253	Philadelphia	132	30	2	17	.227
New York	184	45	2	26	.245	Chicago	158	35	5	27	.222
San Diego	171	40	4	27	.234	St. Louis	117	22	0	18	.188
Atlanta	185	43	2	24	.232	San Francisco	156	29	1	17	.186
						Totals	1831	430	32	259	.235

Individual Pinch-Hitting
(10 or More At-Bats)

Player—Club	AB.	H.	HR.	RBI.	Pct.	Player—Club	AB.	H.	HR.	RBI.	Pct.
Francona, Montreal	10	5	0	1	.500	Stargell, Pittsburgh	26	8	0	7	.308
G. Vukovich, Phila.	11	5	1	3	.455	Thompson, Pitts.	13	4	1	6	.308
Flannery, San Diego	16	6	0	1	.375	Tyson, Chicago	13	4	1	5	.308
Staub, New York	24	9	0	6	.375	Dillard, Chicago	10	3	0	1	.300
D. Davis, Phila.	14	5	0	5	.357	Trevino, New York	10	3	0	1	.300
Monday, Los Ang.	23	8	1	4	.348	Montanez, Mtl.-Pitts	31	9	1	2	.290
Milner, Pitts.-Mtl.	26	9	2	6	.346	Johnstone, Los Ang.	38	11	3	6	.289
Smith, San Fran.	12	4	0	0	.333	Iorg, St. Louis	14	4	0	8	.286
Walling, Houston	18	6	1	7	.333	Perkins, San Diego	14	4	0	6	.286
Spilman, Cin.-Hou.	29	9	0	2	.310	Porter, Atlanta	14	4	0	4	.286
Ivie, San Fran.-Hou.	13	4	0	2	.308	White, Montreal	18	5	2	5	.278

Individual Pinch-Hitting—Continued
(10 or More At-Bats)

Player—Club	AB.	H.	HR.	RBI.	Pct.	Player—Club	AB.	H.	HR.	RBI.	Pct.
Cubbage, New York	44	12	1	3	.273	Gonzalez, St. Louis..	10	2	0	0	.200
Landrum, St. Louis.	11	3	0	2	.273	Harper, Atlanta.......	15	3	1	2	.200
Sanchez, St. Louis...	11	3	0	1	.273	Woods, Houston......	15	3	0	3	.200
Bass, San Diego.......	19	5	0	3	.263	Smith, Los Angeles .	31	6	1	8	.194
Bevacqua, Pitts........	19	5	1	3	.263	Unser, Philadelphia	26	5	0	4	.192
Moreno, San Diego..	23	6	0	3	.261	Roberts, Houston	11	2	0	1	.182
Turner, San Diego ..	23	6	2	6	.261	Vail, Cincinnati	28	5	0	3	.179
Lum, Atl.-Chicago....	31	8	1	5	.258	Cruz, Chicago	17	3	1	2	.176
Asselstine, Atlanta ..	36	9	1	6	.250	Bergman, Hou.-S.F.	23	4	1	3	.174
Backman, N.Y.	12	3	0	0	.250	Jorgensen, N.Y.	29	5	1	5	.172
Morales, Chicago.....	12	3	1	5	.250	Tracy, Chicago	29	5	0	2	.172
Pittman, Houston....	16	4	0	0	.250	Gross, Philadelphia.	39	6	0	0	.154
Stennett, San Fran..	20	5	0	1	.250	Pocoroba, Atlanta....	26	4	0	2	.154
Tenace, St. Louis.....	12	3	0	1	.250	Ferguson, Los Ang..	14	2	0	1	.143
Biittner, Cincinnati.	29	7	0	5	.241	Wohlford, San Fran.	40	5	0	5	.125
Hodges, New York ..	25	6	0	3	.240	Hutton, Montreal	17	2	0	1	.118
Edwards, San Diego	17	4	0	3	.235	Landestoy, Ho.-Ci. ..	10	1	0	1	.100
Royster, Atlanta	17	4	0	2	.235	Wilson, New York ...	10	1	0	0	.100
Office, Montreal.......	13	3	0	0	.231	Thompson, Chicago.	21	2	0	1	.095
Lacy, Pittsburgh	14	3	0	1	.214	Venable, San Fran. .	12	1	0	0	.083
Linares, Atlanta	24	5	0	3	.208	B. Robinson, Pitts. ..	15	1	0	0	.067
Braun, St. Louis	25	5	0	2	.200	Evans, San Diego	16	1	0	0	.063

AMERICAN LEAGUE PINCH-HITTING
(Compiled by Sports Information Center)
Club Pinch-Hitting

Club	AB.	H.	HR.	RBI.	Pct.	Club	AB.	H.	HR.	RBI.	Pct.
New York	90	26	3	22	.289	Chicago....................	80	16	1	14	.200
Cleveland	120	32	2	28	.267	Boston.....................	58	11	1	10	.190
Kansas City..............	67	17	0	9	.254	Seattle.....................	117	22	2	13	.188
Texas	76	19	0	13	.250	Oakland...................	98	16	4	13	.163
Toronto....................	77	18	1	15	.234	Milwaukee...............	43	7	0	4	.163
Minnesota................	100	23	1	22	.230	California	54	8	0	5	.148
Detroit	109	23	1	17	.211	Totals	1208	262	18	205	.217
Baltimore	119	24	2	20	.202						

Individual Pinch-hitting
(10 or More At-Bats)

Player-Club	AB.	H.	HR.	RBI.	Pct.	Player-Club	AB.	H.	HR.	RBI.	Pct.
Adams, Minnesota...	13	6	0	5	.462	Watson, New York ..	13	3	0	2	.231
Stein, Texas	20	9	0	5	.450	Rudi, Boston	22	5	1	6	.227
Bannister, Cleve......	11	4	0	0	.364	Quirk, Kansas City .	18	4	0	3	.222
Gamble, New York..	15	5	0	2	.333	Summers, Detroit....	14	3	0	1	.214
Ayala, Baltimore	16	5	1	5	.313	Leach, Detroit	10	2	0	3	.200
Jones, Detroit...........	13	4	1	3	.308	Narron, Seattle........	15	3	0	1	.200
May, Kansas City	13	4	0	2	.308	Roenicke, Baltimore	16	3	0	0	.188
Spencer, N.Y.-Oak ..	13	4	0	1	.308	Harris, California....	19	3	0	3	.158
Goodwin, Minnesota	10	3	0	4	.300	Meyer, Seattle.........	19	3	0	2	.158
Lowenstein, Balt	10	3	0	0	.300	Phelps, Kansas City	15	2	0	1	.133
Wells, Toronto	10	3	0	4	.300	Kelly, Cleveland	24	3	0	6	.125
Crowley, Baltimore.	21	6	0	7	.286	Johnson, Oakland....	17	2	1	4	.118
Murcer, New York ..	22	6	3	12	.273	R. Jackson, Min-Det	10	1	0	1	.100
Powell, Minnesota ...	11	3	0	1	.273	Rosello, Cleveland...	10	1	0	0	.100
Molinaro, Chicago...	34	9	1	9	.265	Hebner, Detroit	11	1	0	1	.091
Gray, Seattle............	19	5	2	4	.263	Revering, Oak-N.Y.	11	1	0	1	.091
Morales, Baltimore..	19	5	1	8	.263	Hancock, Boston	12	1	0	1	.083
Cowens, Detroit.......	12	3	0	3	.250	Wockenfuss, Detroit	13	1	0	1	.077
Diaz, Cleveland........	12	3	0	4	.250	Hosley, Oakland......	14	1	1	4	.071
Poquette, Bos-Tex ...	12	3	0	3	.250	Davis, Oakland........	10	0	0	0	.000
Upshaw, Toronto.....	17	4	1	5	.235						

PINCH-HOMERS FOR 1981

NATIONAL LEAGUE: Atlanta (2)—Asselstine, Harper. Chicago (5)—Cruz, Hall, Lum, Morales, Tyson. Cincinnati (1)—Bench. Houston (2)—Bergman, Walling. Los Angeles (6)—Johnstone 3, Baker, Monday, Smith. Montreal (2)—White 2. New York (2)—Cubbage, Jorgensen. Philadelphia (2)—Schmidt, G. Vukovich. Pittsburgh (5)—Milner 2, Bevacqua, Montanez, Thompson. St. Louis (0). San Diego (4)—Lefebvre 2, Turner 2. San Francisco (1)—May.

AMERICAN LEAGUE: Baltimore (2)—Ayala, Morales. Boston (1)—Rudi. California (0). Chicago (1)—Molinaro. Cleveland (2)—Pagel, Thornton. Detroit (1)—Jones. Kansas City (0). Milwaukee (0). Minnesota (1)—Mackanin. New York (3)—Murcer 3. Oakland (4)—Gross Hosley, Johnson, Page. Seattle (2)—Gray 2. Texas (0). Toronto (1)—Upshaw.

Homers by Parks for 1981

National League

	At Atl.	At Chi.	At Cin.	At Hou.	At L.A.	At Mont.	At N.Y.	At Phil.	At Pitt.	At St.L.	At S.D.	At S.F.	Totals 1981	1980
Atlanta	37	1	5	0	6	0	3	4	0	1	2	5	64	144
Chicago	4	41	1	0	0	0	1	2	2	5	0	1	57	107
Cincinnati	6	3	26	0	8	0	5	4	2	1	6	3	64	113
Houston	6	1	5	16	4	2	0	2	3	1	3	2	45	75
Los Angeles	3	5	12	1	37	4	3	2	2	3	6	4	82	148
Montreal	4	6	5	1	3	39	9	5	3	3	3	0	81	114
New York	3	7	1	2	2	3	30	4	2	1	0	2	57	61
Philadelphia	6	5	0	1	2	1	5	41	2	5	1	0	69	117
Pittsburgh	2	2	3	2	1	4	5	2	29	4	1	0	55	116
St. Louis	1	1	1	0	2	4	4	9	4	22	2	0	50	101
San Diego	3	2	3	1	2	2	1	2	3	2	9	2	32	67
San Francisco	3	5	5	1	4	3	2	3	6	0	3	28	63	80
1981 Totals	78	79	67	25	71	62	68	80	58	48	36	47	719	....
1980 Totals	163	116	136	48	140	91	115	108	116	83	62	65	......	1243

AT ATLANTA (78): Atlanta (37)—Horner 9, Murphy 8, Linares 5, Hubbard 4, Washington 3, Benedict 2, Chambliss 2, Harper 2, Asselstine, Ramirez. **Chicago (4)**—Buckner, Cruz, Henderson, Reitz. **Cincinnati (6)**—Knight 2, Collins, Foster, Householder, Oester. **Houston (6)**—Cruz 3, Reynolds 2. Walling. **Los Angeles (3)**—Garvey 3. **Montreal (4)**—Carter, Dawson, Milner, Parrish. **New York (3)**—Kingman 2, Valentine. **Philadelphia (6)**—Aguayo, Matthews, Moreland, Schmidt, Smith, G. Vukovich. **Pittsburgh (2)**—Berra, Easler. **St. Louis (1)**—Hendrick. **San Diego (3)**—Richards 2, Lefebvre. **San Francisco (3)**—Leonard, Morgan, Wohlford.

AT CHICAGO (79): Atlanta (1)—Chambliss. **Chicago (41)**—Durham 8, Buckner 7, Cruz 4, Davis 4, Henderson 3, Waller 3, Bonds 2, Dillard 2, Lum 2, Blackwell, Hall, Morales, Reitz, Tabler, Tyson. **Cincinnati (3)**—Bair, Foster, Knight. **Houston (1)**—Cruz. **Los Angeles (5)**—Landreaux 2, Baker, Guerrero, Smith. **Montreal (6)**—Raines 2, Wallach 2, Dawson, Parrish. **New York (7)**—Brooks 2, Valentine 2, Kingman, Mazzilli, Staub. **Philadelphia (5)**—Schmidt 3, Matthews, McBride. **Pittsburgh (2)**—Moreno, Parker. **St. Louis (1)**—Hernandez. **San Diego (2)**—Lefebvre, Turner. **San Francisco (5)**—Clark 2, Evans, Leonard, Morgan.

AT CINCINNATI (67): Atlanta (5)—Horner 4, Washington. **Chicago (1)**—Durham. **Cincinnati (26)**—Foster 8, Bench 5, Concepcion 4, Oester 3, Driessen 2, Collins, Knight, Nolan, Seaver. **Houston (5)**—Cedeno, Cruz, Puhl, Reynolds, Walling. **Los Angeles (12)**—Monday 4, Baker 2, Johnstone 2, Cey, Garvey, Guerrero, Thomas. **Montreal (5)**—Dawson 2, Carter, Cromartie, Milner. **New York (1)**—Kingman. **Philadelphia**—None. **Pittsburgh (3)**—Easler, Garner, Parker. **St. Louis (1)**—Hendrick. **San Diego (3)**—Lefebvre 2, Lollar. **San Francisco (5)**—Clark 3, Leonard, Martin.

AT HOUSTON (25): Atlanta—None. **Chicago**—None. **Cincinnati**—None. **Houston (16)**—Ashby 3, Cruz 3, Howe 3, Walling 2, Cedeno, Knepper, Puhl, Pujols, Scott. **Los Angeles (1)**—Sax. **Montreal (1)**—Parrish. **New York (2)**—Kingman, Mazzilli. **Philadelphia (1)**—Schmidt. **Pittsburgh (2)**—Thompson 2. **St. Louis**—None. **San Diego (1)**—Kennedy. **San Francisco (1)**—Clark.

AT LOS ANGELES (71): Atlanta (6)—Chambliss 2, Murphy 2, Asselstine, Horner. **Chicago**—None. **Cincinnati (8)**—Foster 4, Bench, Concepcion, Driessen, O'Berry. **Houston (4)**—Knicely 2, Bergman, Cedeno. **Los Angeles (37)**—Cey 9, Garvey 5, Guerrero 5, Baker 4, Monday 4, Landreaux 3, Lopes 3, Thomas 2, Johnstone, Yeager. **Montreal (2)**—Dawson 2, Speier. **New York (2)**—Mazzilli, Youngblood. **Philadelphia (2)**—Schmidt 2. **Pittsburgh (1)**—Madlock. **St. Louis (2)**—Lezcano, Oberkfell. **San Diego (2)**—Bass, Turner. **San Francisco (4)**—Clark 2, Bergman, Morgan.

AT MONTREAL (62): Atlanta—None. **Chicago**—None. **Cincinnati**—None. **Houston (2)**—Cedeno, Cruz. **Los Angeles (4)**—Cey 2, Landreaux, Monday. **Montreal (39)**—Dawson 9, Carter 7, Cromartie 4, Parrish 3, Raines 3, Valentine 3, White 3, Manuel 2, Francona, Lee, Milner, Speier, Wallach. **New York (3)**—Kingman 3. **Philadelphia (1)**—Schmidt. **Pittsburgh (4)**—Easler, Madlock, Milner, Thompson. **St. Louis (4)**—Porter 2, Hendrick, Lezcano. **San Diego (2)**—Perkins, Salazar. **San Francisco (3)**—Cabell, Evans, North.

AT NEW YORK (68): Atlanta (3)—Hubbard, Murphy, Washington. **Chicago (1)**—Cruz. **Cincinnati (5)**—Foster 2, Collins, Driessen, Griffey. **Houston**—None. **Los Angeles (3)**—Guerrero 2, Lopes. **Montreal (9)**—Dawson 3, Carter 2, Cromartie, Hostetler, Ramos, Wallach. **New York (30)**—Kingman 11, Jorgensen 3, Staub 3, Brooks 2, Valentine 2, Wilson 2, Youngblood 2, Cubbage, Flynn, Hodges, Mazzilli, Stearns. **Philadelphia (5)**—Schmidt 3, Matthews, Moreland. **Pittsburgh (5)**—Thompson 2, Alexander, Madlock, Parker. **St. Louis (4)**—Hendrick 2, Hernandez, Porter. **San Diego (1)**—Edwards. **San Francisco (2)**—Griffin, Smith.

AT PHILADELPHIA (80): Atlanta (4)—Chambliss 2, Benedict, Perry. **Chicago (2)**—Buckner, Tyson. **Cincinnati (4)**—Foster 2, Bench, Householder. **Houston (2)**—Cruz 2. **Los Angeles (2)**—Cey, Guerrero. **Montreal (5)**—Carter 2, Dawson, Manuel, Parrish. **New York (4)**—Kingman 2, Falcone, Wilson. **Philadelphia (41)**—Schmidt 17, Maddox 5, Matthews 5, Trillo 5, Moreland 4, Boone 2, Davis, McBride, Smith. **Pittsburgh (2)**—Madlock, Thompson. **St. Louis (9)**—Hendrick 4, Hernandez, Iorg, Lezcano, Tenace. **San Diego (2)**—Jones, Lefebvre. **San Francisco (3)**—Evans 2, Clark.

AT PITTSBURGH (58): Atlanta—None. **Chicago (2)**—Cruz, Henderson. **Cincinnati (2)**—Griffey, Knight. **Houston (3)**—Cruz, Reynolds, Walling. **Los Angeles (3)**—Baker, Yeager. **Montreal (3)**—Dawson 2, Carter. **New York (2)**—Mazzilli, Staub. **Philadelphia (2)**—Schmidt, Trillo. **Pittsburgh (29)**—Thompson 8, Easler 4, Parker 4, Madlock 2, Nicosia 2, B. Robinson 2, Berra, Bevacqua, Bibby, Lacy, Milner, Montanez, Pena. **St. Louis (4)**—Hendrick 2, Porter, Tenace. **San Diego (3)**—Bass, Jones, Lefebvre. **San Francisco (6)**—Evans 2, Cabell, Herndon, May, Morgan.

AT ST. LOUIS (48): Atlanta (1)—Chambliss. **Chicago (5)**—Bonds 4, Durham. **Cincinnati (1)**—Foster. **Houston (1)**—Roberts. **Los Angeles (3)**—Garvey, Sax, Thomas. **Montreal (3)**—Carter, Dawson, Parrish. **New York (1)**—Mazzilli. **Philadelphia (5)**—Boone 2, Davis, Matthews, Schmidt. **Pittsburgh (4)**—Parker 2, Lacy, Pena. **St. Louis (22)**—Hendrick 6, Hernandez 4, Tenace 3, Lezcano 2, Porter 2, Scott 2, Gonzalez, Iorg, Templeton. **San Diego (2)**—Lefebvre, Richards. **San Francisco**—None.

AT SAN DIEGO (36): **Atlanta (2)**—Hubbard, Ramirez. **Chicago**—None. **Cincinnati (6)**—Driessen 2, Foster 2, Bench, Knight. **Houston (3)**—Cedeno, Cruz, Puhl. **Los Angeles (6)**—Guerrero 2, Baker, Landreaux, Lopes, Scioscia. **Montreal (3)**—Dawson 2, Carter. **New York**—None. **Philadelphia (1)**—Schmidt. **Pittsburgh (1)**—Thompson. **St. Louis (2)**—Hendrick, Oberkfell. **San Diego (9)**—Jones 2, Salazar 2, Bass, Bonilla, Edwards, Kennedy, Perkins. **San Francisco (3)**—Bergman, Clark, Leonard.

AT SAN FRANCISCO (47): **Atlanta (5)**—Benedict 2, Murphy 2, Horner. **Chicago (1)**—Buckner. **Cincinnati (3)**—Driessen, Foster, Oester. **Houston (2)**—Ashby, Scott. **Los Angeles (4)**—Monday 2, Scioscia, Yeager. **Montreal**—None. **New York (2)**—Kingman, Youngblood. **Philadelphia**—None. **Pittsburgh**—None. **St. Louis**—None. **San Diego (2)**—Bass, Lefebvre. **San Francisco (28)**—Clark 7, Evans 6, Herndon 4, Morgan 4, Martin 3, Bergman, Brenly, May, Stennett.

AMERICAN LEAGUE

	At Balt.	At Bos.	At Cal.	At Chi.	At Clev.	At Det.	At K.C.	At Mil.	At Min.	At N.Y.	At Oak.	At Sea.	At Tex.	At Tor.	Totals 1981	1980
Baltimore	49	0	2	3	1	8	0	2	2	6	3	7	1	4	88	156
Boston	2	52	3	2	5	2	1	6	5	2	4	2	0	4	90	162
California	9	0	48	3	2	3	2	2	3	0	8	8	3	6	97	106
Chicago	2	7	5	31	1	2	0	4	1	2	12	2	0	7	76	91
Cleveland	3	4	3	4	19	0	1	0	0	2	0	3	0	0	39	89
Detroit	3	2	2	0	2	43	1	1	4	1	1	1	3	1	65	143
Kansas City	7	6	3	0	5	5	17	2	6	0	1	5	1	3	61	115
Milwaukee	2	8	6	3	10	7	2	33	6	4	3	4	1	7	96	203
Minnesota	1	1	1	0	0	0	4	2	25	1	2	5	3	2	47	99
New York	5	4	4	6	3	7	4	4	3	47	6	5	1	1	100	189
Oakland	9	11	2	5	1	0	3	0	4	1	57	5	3	3	104	137
Seattle	1	2	0	4	2	1	7	0	9	2	2	52	5	0	89	104
Texas	0	2	4	1	1	5	1	4	4	0	2	3	21	1	49	124
Toronto	3	0	4	2	0	4	1	2	0	3	2	3	3	34	61	126
1981 Totals	96	99	87	64	52	87	44	62	72	71	103	105	45	75	1062	
1980 Totals	156	153	125	78	121	172	98	155	114	138	115	173	115	131		1844

AT BALTIMORE (96): **Baltimore (49)**—Murray 12, DeCinces 10, Singleton 5, Crowley 4, Dempsey 4, Lowenstein 4, Dwyer 3, Sakata 3, Ayala, Belanger, Bumbry, Graham. **Boston (2)**—Allenson, Rice. **California (9)**—Grich 3, Baylor 2, Campaneris, Carew, Ford, Hobson. **Chicago (2)**—Luzinski, Morrison. **Cleveland (3)**—Diaz, Hayes, Manning. **Detroit (3)**—Wockenfuss 2, Papi. **Kansas City (7)**—Hurdle 2, Otis 2, Wathan, White, Wilson. **Milwaukee (2)**—Oglivie, Thomas. **Minnesota (1)**—Ward. **New York (5)**—Winfield 2, Dent, Jackson, Nettles. **Oakland (9)**—Armas 3, Gross 2, Johnson 2, Murphy, Spencer. **Seattle (1)**—Randle. **Texas**—None. **Toronto (3)**—Bell, Moseby, Upshaw.

AT BOSTON (99): **Baltimore**—None. **Boston (52)**—Evans 15, Rice 10, Perez 7, Rudi 4, Stapleton 4, Allenson 3, Gedman 3, Yastrzemski 3, Miller 2, Lansford. **California**—None. **Chicago (7)**—Almon 2, Baines 2, Fisk, Luzinski, Morrison. **Cleveland (4)**—Charboneau, Harrah, Orta, Thornton. **Detroit (2)**—Kemp, Wockenfuss. **Kansas City (6)**—Aikens 3, McRae 2, White. **Milwaukee (8)**—Simmons 2, Bando, Gantner, Howell, Romero, Yost, Yount. **Minnesota (1)**—Smalley. **New York (4)**—Murcer, Piniella, Watson, Winfield. **Oakland (11)**—Heath 3, Johnson 2, Klutts 2, Armas, Murphy, Newman, Page. **Seattle (2)**—Cruz, Zisk. **Texas (2)**—Bell, Grubb. **Toronto**—None.

AT CALIFORNIA (87): **Baltimore (2)**—Lowenstein, Murray. **Boston (3)**—Gedman, Rice, Stapleton. **California (48)**—Baylor 10, Ford 9, Grich 7, Downing 6, Clark 4, Lynn 3, Beniquez 2, Burleson 2, Brunansky, Ferguson, Harris, Hobson, Sconiers. **Chicago (5)**—Baines 2, Luzinski 2, Morrison. **Cleveland (3)**—Diaz, Hassey, Thornton. **Detroit (2)**—Kemp, Summers. **Kansas City (3)**—Motley, Washington, White. **Milwaukee (6)**—Hisle 2, Cooper, Oglivie, Simmons, Thomas. **Minnesota (1)**—Smalley. **New York (4)**—Foote 2, Dent, Piniella. **Oakland (2)**—Armas 2. **Seattle**—None. **Texas (4)**—Putnam 2, Jones, Rivers. **Toronto (4)**—Mayberry 2, Bonnell, Velez.

AT CHICAGO (64): **Baltimore (3)**—Singleton 3. **Boston (2)**—Allenson, Lansford. **California (3)**—Grich 2, Baylor. **Chicago (31)**—Luzinski 9, Fisk 4, Lemon 4, Baines 3, Bernazard 3, Morrison 3, Nordhagen 3, Almon, Hairston. **Cleveland (4)**—Charboneau 2, Orta, Rosello. **Detroit**—None. **Kansas City**—None. **Milwaukee (3)**—Hisle, Money, Thomas. **Minnesota**—None. **New York (6)**—Jackson, Mumphrey, Murcer, Nettles, Piniella, Winfield. **Oakland (5)**—Murphy 2, Gross, McKay, Page. **Seattle (4)**—Paciorek 2, Parsons, Serna. **Texas (1)**—Grubb. **Toronto (2)**—Barfield, Bell.

AT CLEVELAND (52): **Baltimore (1)**—Ayala. **Boston (5)**—Evans 3, Lansford, Rice. **California (2)**—Baylor, Grich. **Chicago (1)**—Nordhagen. **Cleveland (19)**—Diaz 5, Harrah 3, Hargrove 2, Manning 2, Orta 2, Thornton 2, Bannister, Kelly, Pagel. **Detroit (2)**—Papi, Summers. **Kansas City (5)**—G. Brett 2, Aikens, McRae, White. **Milwaukee (10)**—Cooper 3, Howell 2, Hisle, Oglivie, Simmons, Thomas, Yount. **Minnesota**—None. **New York (3)**—Dent, Jackson, Winfield. **Oakland (1)**—Murphy. **Seattle (2)**—Burroughs, Simpson. **Texas (1)**—Sundberg. **Toronto**—None.

AT DETROIT (87): **Baltimore (8)**—DeCinces 2, Murray 2, Sakata 2, Ayala, Singleton. **Boston (2)**—Yastrzemski 2. **California (3)**—Carew, Ford, Hobson. **Chicago (2)**—Lemon, Luzinski. **Cleveland**—None. **Detroit (43)**—Parrish 8, Kemp 6, Gibson 4, Hebner 4, Whitaker 4, Wockenfuss 4, Brookens 3, Jones 2, Trammell 2, Cowens, Fahey, Jackson, Leach, Papi, Summers. **Kansas City (5)**—Aikens 2, Geronimo, Motley, Otis. **Milwaukee (7)**—Thomas 3, Cooper, Oglivie, Simmons, Yount. **Minnesota**—None. **New York (7)**—Watson 2, Dent, Foote, Piniella, Randolph, Winfield. **Oakland**—None. **Seattle (1)**—Zisk. **Texas (5)**—Bell 2, Oliver, Putnam, Rivers. **Toronto (4)**—Velez 2, Martinez, Mayberry.

AT KANSAS CITY (44): **Baltimore**—None. **Boston (1)**—Evans. **California (2)**—Baylor, Burleson. **Chicago**—None. **Cleveland (1)**—Thornton. **Detroit (1)**—Wockenfuss. **Kansas City (17)**—Aikens 4, Otis 4, White 4, G. Brett

2, McRae 2, Grote. **Milwaukee (2)**–Oglivie, Yount. **Minnesota (4)**–Engle 2, Castino, Mackanin. **New York (4)**–Mumphrey, Nettles, Watson, Winfield. **Oakland (3)**–Armas, McKay, Moore. **Seattle (7)**–Paciorek 4, Bochte 2, Gray. **Texas (1)**–Putnam. **Toronto (1)**–Mayberry.

AT **MILWAUKEE (62)**: Baltimore **(2)**–Murray, Roenicke. **Boston (6)**–Stapleton 2, Evans, Gedman, Rice, Schmidt. **California (2)**–Baylor, Grich. **Chicago (4)**–Almon, Baines, Bernazard, Nordhagen. **Cleveland**– None. **Detroit (1)**–Hebner. **Kansas City (2)**–Aikens 2. **Milwaukee (33)**–Simmons 8, Thomas 8, Cooper 5, Oglivie 3, Howell 2, Bando, Brouhard, Molitor, Money, Moore, Yost, Yount. **Minnesota (2)**–Castino, Jackson. **New York (4)**–Jackson 2, Piniella, Watson. **Oakland**–None. **Seattle**–None. **Texas (4)**–Roberts 2, Bell, Sundberg. **Toronto (2)**–Moseby, Velez.

AT **MINNESOTA (72)**: Baltimore **(2)**–Dempsey, Singleton. **Boston (5)**–Lansford, Perez, Schmidt, Stapleton, Yastrzemski. **California (3)**–Burleson, Ford, Lynn. **Chicago (1)**–Morrison. **Cleveland**–None. **Detroit (4)**–Brookens, Gibson, Kemp, Wockenfuss. **Kansas City (6)**–Hurdle 2, Aikens, G. Brett, McRae, White. **Milwaukee (6)**–Gantner, Howell, Oglivie, Simmons, Thomas, Yount. **Minnesota (25)**–Castino 3, Mackanin 3, Hatcher 3, Wilfong 3, Engle 2, Laudner 2, Smalley 2, Ward 2, Adams, Gaetti, Goodwin, Jackson, Powell. **New York (3)**–Jackson 2, Gamble. **Oakland (4)**–Armas 2, Gross, Heath. **Seattle (9)**–Burroughs 3, Zisk 3, Gray, Paciorek, Randle. **Texas (4)**–Bell, Ellis, Putnam, Rivers. **Toronto**–None.

AT **NEW YORK (71)**: Baltimore **(6)**–Dauer 2, Murray 2, Morales, Roenicke. **Boston (2)**–Perez, Stapleton. **California**–None. **Chicago (2)**–Luzinski, Morrison. **Cleveland (2)**–Charboneau, Manning. **Detroit (1)**– Gibson. **Kansas City**–None. **Milwaukee (4)**–Oglivie 2, Cooper, Yount. **Minnesota (2)**–Hrbek. **New York (47)**–Nettles 11, Jackson 7, Gamble 6, Murcer 4, Winfield 4, Dent 3, Mumphrey 3, Cerone 2, Revering 2, Foote, Milbourne, Randolph, Spencer, Watson. **Oakland (1)**–Johnson. **Seattle (2)**–Gray 2. **Texas**–None. **Toronto (3)**–Mayberry, Moseby, Upshaw.

AT **OAKLAND (103)**: Baltimore **(3)**–Murray, Roenicke, Singleton. **Boston (4)**–Hoffman, Rice, Stapleton, Yastrzemski. **California (8)**–Grich 4, Baylor, Burleson, Ford, Harris. **Chicago (12)**–Lemon 3, Baines 2, Fisk 2, Bernazard, Johnson, Luzinski, Morrison, Nordhagen. **Cleveland**–None. **Detroit (1)**–Gibson. **Kansas City (1)**–Aikens. **Milwaukee (3)**–Thomas 2, Brouhard. **Minnesota (2)**–Adams, Smalley. **New York (3)**–Foote 2, Gamble 2, Mumphrey, Spencer. **Oakland (57)**–Armas 13, Johnson 11, Murphy 7, Henderson 5, Heath 4, Picciolo 4, Gross 3, Klutts 3, Newman 2, Page 2, Hosley, McKay, Revering. **Seattle (2)**–Henderson, Zisk. **Texas (2)**–Jones, Stein. **Toronto (2)**–Bonnell, Mayberry.

AT **SEATTLE (105)**: Baltimore **(7)**–Dauer 2, Singleton 2, DeCinces, Morales, Murray. **Boston (2)**–Rice, Rudi. **California (8)**–Grich 3, Brunansky 2, Downing, Ford, Lynn. **Chicago (2)**–Luzinski, Morrison. **Cleveland (3)**–Harrah, Orta, Thornton. **Detroit (1)**–Whitaker. **Kansas City (5)**–Aikens 2, Otis 2, Washington. **Milwaukee (4)**–Yount 3, Thomas. **Minnesota (5)**–Jackson 2, Smalley 2, Smith. **New York (5)**–Rodriguez 2, Winfield 2, Jackson. **Oakland (5)**–Murphy 2, Henderson, Johnson, Revering. **Seattle (52)**–Zisk 10, Gray 9, Paciorek 7, Burroughs 5, Henderson 5, Bochte 4, Anderson 2, Bulling 2, Meyer 2, Serna 2, Auerbach, Cruz, Narron, Randle. **Texas (3)**–Bell 2, Sample. **Toronto (3)**–Mayberry, Upshaw, Whitt.

AT **TEXAS (45)**: Baltimore **(1)**–Graham. **Boston**–None. **California (3)**–Beniquez, Grich, Harris. **Chicago**–None. **Cleveland**–None. **Detroit (3)**–Parrish 2, Gibson. **Kansas City (1)**–Geronimo. **Milwaukee (1)**–Oglivie. **Minnesota (3)**–Engle, Gaetti, Goodwin. **New York (1)**–Nettles. **Oakland (3)**–Gross, McKay, Murphy. **Seattle (5)**–Meyer, Narron, Randle, Serna, Simpson. **Texas (21)**–Oliver 3, Putnam 3, Bell 2, Johnson 2, Roberts 2, Sample 2, Wills 2, Grubb, Jones, Stein, Sundberg, Wagner. **Toronto (3)**–Moseby 3.

AT **TORONTO (75)**: Baltimore **(4)**–Murray 2, Dempsey, Lowenstein. **Boston (4)**–Evans 2, Rice, Rudi. **California (6)**–Downing 2, Ott 2, Ford, Hobson. **Chicago (7)**–Luzinski 4, Bernazard, Lemon, Molinaro. **Cleveland**–None. **Detroit (1)**–Gibson. **Kansas City (3)**–Aikens, G. Brett, McRae. **Milwaukee (7)**–Oglivie 2, Thomas 2, Cooper, Molitor, Yost. **Minnesota (2)**–Castino, Powell. **New York (1)**–Gamble. **Oakland (3)**–Gross 2, Spencer. **Seattle (2)**–Burroughs, Narron. **Texas (1)**–Bell. **Toronto (34)**–Mayberry 10, Velez 7, Bell 3, Martinez 3, Moseby 3, Bonnell 2, Cox 2, Barfield, Garcia, Upshaw, Woods.

The Sporting News AWARDS

THE SPORTING NEWS MVP AWARDS

AMERICAN LEAGUE

Year	Player	Club	Points
1929	Al Simmons, Philadelphia, of		40
1930	Joseph Cronin, Washington, ss		52
1931	H. Louis Gehrig, New York, 1b		40
1932	James Foxx, Philadelphia, 1b		56
1933	James Foxx, Philadelphia, 1b		49
1934	H. Louis Gehrig, New York, 1b		51
1935	Henry Greenberg, Detroit, 1b		64
1936	H. Louis Gehrig, New York, 1b		55
1937	Charles Gehringer, Detroit, 2b		78
1938	James Foxx, Boston, 1b		305
1939	Joseph DiMaggio, N. York, of		280
1940	Henry Greenberg, Detroit, of		292
1941	Joseph DiMaggio, N. York, of		291
1942	Joseph Gordon, New York, 2b		270
1943	Spurgeon Chandler, N. Y., p		246
1944	Robert Doerr, Boston, 2b		
1945	Edward J. Mayo, Detroit, 2b		

NATIONAL LEAGUE

Player	Club	Points
No selection		
William Terry, New York, 1b		47
Charles Klein, Philadelphia, of		40
Charles Klein, Philadelphia, of		46
Carl Hubbell, New York, p		64
Jerome Dean, St. Louis, p		57
J. Floyd Vaughan, Pitts., ss		42
Carl Hubbell, New York, p		61
Joseph Medwick, St. Louis, of		70
Ernest Lombardi, Cincinnati, c		229
William Walters, Cincinnati, p		303
Frank McCormick, Cinn., 1b		274
Adolph Camilli, Brooklyn, 1b		300
Morton Cooper, St. Louis, p		263
Stanley Musial, St. Louis, of		267
Martin Marion, St. Louis, ss		
Thomas Holmes, Boston, of		

THE SPORTING NEWS PLAYER, PITCHER OF YEAR

AMERICAN LEAGUE

1948 — Louis Boudreau, Cleveland, ss
Robert Lemon, Cleveland, p
1949 — Theodore Williams, Boston, of
Ellis Kinder, Boston, p
1950 — Philip Rizzuto, New York, ss
Robert Lemon, Cleveland, p
1951 — Ferris Fain, Philadelphia, 1b
Robert Feller, Cleveland, p
1952 — Luscious Easter, Cleveland, 1b
Robert Shantz, Philadelphia, p
1953 — Albert Rosen, Cleveland, 3b
Erv (Bob) Porterfield, Wash., p
1954 — Roberto Avila, Cleveland, 2b
Robert Lemon, Cleveland, p
1955 — Albert Kaline, Detroit, of
Edward Ford, New York, p
1956 — Mickey Mantle, New York, of
W. William Pierce, Chicago, p
1957 — Theodore Williams, Boston, of
W. William Pierce, Chicago, p
1958 — Jack Jensen, Boston, of
Robert Turley, New York, p
1959 — J. Nelson Fox, Chicago, 2b
Early Wynn, Chicago, p
1960 — Roger Maris, New York, of
Charles Estrada, Baltimore, p
1961 — Roger Maris, New York, of
Edward Ford, New York, p
1962 — Mickey Mantle, New York, of
Richard Donovan, Cleveland, p
1963 — Albert Kaline, Detroit, of
Edward Ford, New York, p
1964 — Brooks Robinson, Baltimore, 3b
Dean Chance, Los Angeles, p
1965 — Pedro (Tony) Oliva, Minn., of
James Grant, Minnesota, p
1966 — Frank Robinson, Baltimore, of
James Kaat, Minnesota, p
1967 — Carl Yastrzemski, Boston, of
Jim Lonborg, Boston, p
1968 — Ken Harrelson, Boston, of
Denny McLain, Detroit, p
1969 — Harmon Killebrew, Minn., 1b-3b
Denny McLain, Detroit, p
1970 — Harmon Killebrew, Minn., 3b
Sam McDowell, Cleveland, p
1971 — Pedro (Tony) Oliva, Minn., of
Vida Blue, Oakland, p
1972 — Richie Allen, Chicago, 1b
Wilbur Wood, Chicago, p

NATIONAL LEAGUE

1948 — Stanley Musial, St. Louis, of-1b
John Sain, Boston, p
1949 — Enos Slaughter, St. Louis, of
Howard Pollet, St. Louis, p
1950 — Ralph Kiner, Pittsburgh, of
C. James Konstanty, Phila., p
1951 — Stanley Musial, St. Louis, of
Elwin Roe, Brooklyn, p
1952 — Henry Sauer, Chicago, of
Robin Roberts, Philadelphia, p
1953 — Roy Campanella, Brooklyn, c
Warren Spahn, Milwaukee, p
1954 — Willie Mays, New York, of
John Antonelli, New York, p
1955 — Edwin Snider, Brooklyn, of
Robin Roberts, Philadelphia, p
1956 — Henry Aaron, Milwaukee, of
Donald Newcombe, Brooklyn, p
1957 — Stanley Musial, St. Louis, 1b
Warren Spahn, Milwaukee, p
1958 — Ernest Banks, Chicago, ss
Warren Spahn, Milwaukee, p
1959 — Ernest Banks, Chicago, ss
Samuel Jones, San Francisco, p
1960 — Richard Groat, Pittsburgh, ss
Vernon Law, Pittsburgh, p
1961 — Frank Robinson, Cincinnati, of
Warren Spahn, Milwaukee, p
1962 — Maurice Wills, Los Angeles, ss
Donald Drysdale, Los Angeles, p
1963 — Henry Aaron, Milwaukee, of
Sanford Koufax, Los Angeles, p
1964 — Kenton Boyer, St. Louis, 3b
Sanford Koufax, Los Angeles, p
1965 — Willie Mays, San Francisco, of
Sanford Koufax, Los Angeles, p
1966 — Roberto Clemente, Pittsburgh, of
Sanford Koufax, Los Angeles, p
1967 — Orlando Cepeda, St. Louis, 1b
Mike McCormick, San Fran., p
1968 — Pete Rose, Cincinnati, of
Bob Gibson, St. Louis, p
1969 — Willie McCovey, San Fran., 1b
Tom Seaver, New York, p
1970 — Johnny Bench, Cin., c
Bob Gibson, St. Louis, p
1971 — Joe Torre, St. Louis, 3b
Ferguson Jenkins, Chicago, p
1972 — Billy Williams, Chicago, of
Steve Carlton, Philadelphia, p

PLAYER, PITCHER OF YEAR—Continued

AMERICAN LEAGUE	NATIONAL LEAGUE
1973—Reggie Jackson, Oakland, of	1973—Bobby Bonds, San Francisco, of
Jim Palmer, Baltimore, p	Ron Bryant, San Francisco, p
1974—Jeff Burroughs, Texas, of	1974—Lou Brock, St. Louis, of
Jim Hunter, Oakland, p	Mike Marshall, Los Angeles, p
1975—Fred Lynn, Boston, of	1975—Joe Morgan, Cincinnati, 2b
Jim Palmer, Baltimore, p	Tom Seaver, New York, p
1976—Thurman Munson, New York, c	1976—George Foster, Cincinnati, of
Jim Palmer, Baltimore, p	Randy Jones, San Diego, p
1977—Rod Carew, Minnesota, 1b	1977—George Foster, Cincinnati, of
Nolan Ryan, California, p	Steve Carlton, Philadelphia, p
1978—Jim Rice, Boston, of	1978—Dave Parker, Pittsburgh, of
Ron Guidry, New York, p	Vida Blue, San Francisco, p
1979—Don Baylor, California, of	1979—Keith Hernandez, St. Louis, 1b
Mike Flanagan, Baltimore, p	Joe Niekro, Houston, p
1980—George Brett, Kansas City, 3b	1980—Mike Schmidt, Philadelphia, 3b
Steve Stone, Baltimore, p	Steve Carlton, Philadelphia, p
1981—Tony Armas, Oakland, of	1981—Andre Dawson, Montreal, of
Jack Morris, Detroit, p	Fernando Valenzuela, Los Angeles, p

FIREMAN (Relief Pitcher) OF THE YEAR

Year	Player	Club	Player	Club
1960	Mike Fornieles, Boston		Lindy McDaniel, St. Louis	
1961	Luis Arroyo, New York		Stu Miller, San Francisco	
1962	Dick Radatz, Boston		Roy Face, Pittsburgh	
1963	Stu Miller, Baltimore		Lindy McDaniel, Chicago	
1964	Dick Radatz, Boston		Al McBean, Pittsburgh	
1965	Eddie Fisher, Chicago		Ted Abernathy, Chicago	
1966	Jack Aker, Kansas City		Phil Regan, Los Angeles	
1967	Minnie Rojas, California		Ted Abernathy, Cincinnati	
1968	Wilbur Wood, Chicago		Phil Regan, L.A.-Chicago	
1969	Ron Perranoski, Minnesota		Wayne Granger, Cincinnati	
1970	Ron Perranoski, Minnesota		Wayne Granger, Cincinnati	
1971	Ken Sanders, Milwaukee		Dave Giusti, Pittsburgh	
1972	Sparky Lyle, New York		Clay Carroll, Cincinnati	
1973	John Hiller, Detroit		Mike Marshall, Montreal	
1974	Terry Forster, Chicago		Mike Marshall, Los Angeles	
1975	Rich Gossage, Chicago		Al Hrabosky, St. Louis	
1976	Bill Campbell, Minnesota		Rawly Eastwick, Cincinnati	
1977	Bill Campbell, Boston		Rollie Fingers, San Diego	
1978	Rich Gossage, New York		Rollie Fingers, San Diego	
1979	Mike Marshall, Minnesota		Bruce Sutter, Chicago	
	Jim Kern, Texas			
1980	Dan Quisenberry, Kansas City		Rollie Fingers, San Diego	
			Tom Hume, Cincinnati	
1981	Rollie Fingers, Milwaukee		Bruce Sutter, St. Louis	

THE SPORTING NEWS ROOKIE AWARDS

1946—Combined selection—Delmer Ennis, Philadelphia, N. L., of
1947—Combined selection—Jack Robinson, Brooklyn, 1b
1948—Combined selection—Richie Ashburn, Philadelphia, N. L., of

Year	Player	Club	Player	Club
1949	Roy Sievers, St. Louis, of		Donald Newcombe, Brooklyn, p	
1950	Combined selection—Edward Ford, New York, A. L., p			
1951	Orestes Minoso, Chicago, of		Willie Mays, New York, of	
1952	Clinton Courtney, St. Louis, c		Joseph Black, Brooklyn, p	
1953	Harvey Kuenn, Detroit, ss		James Gilliam, Brooklyn, 2b	
1954	Robert Grim, New York, p		Wallace Moon, St. Louis, of	
1955	Herbert Score, Cleveland, p		William Virdon, St. Louis, of	
1956	Luis Aparicio, Chicago, ss		Frank Robinson, Cincinnati, of	
1957	Anthony Kubek, New York, inf-of		Edward Bouchee, Philadelphia, 1b	
	(No pitcher named)		Jack Sanford, Philadelphia, p	
1958	Albert Pearson, Washington, of		Orlando Cepeda, San Francisco, 1b	
	Ryne Duren, New York, p		Carlton Willey, Milwaukee, p	
1959	W. Robert Allison, Washington, of		Willie McCovey, San Francisco, 1b	
1960	Ronald Hansen, Baltimore, ss		Frank Howard, Los Angeles, of	
1961	Richard Howser, Kansas City, ss		Billy Williams, Chicago, of	
	Donald Schwall, Boston, p		Kenneth Hunt, Cincinnati, p	
1962	Thomas Tresh, New York, of-ss		Kenneth Hubbs, Chicago, 2b	
1963	Peter Ward, Chicago, 3b		Peter Rose, Cincinnati, 2b	
	Gary Peters, Chicago, p		Raymond Culp, Philadelphia, p	
1964	Pedro (Tony) Oliva, Minn., of		Richard Allen, Philadelphia, 3b	
	Wallace Bunker, Baltimore, p		William McCool, Cincinnati, p	
1965	Curtis Blefary, Baltimore, of		Joseph Morgan, Houston, 2b	
	Marcelino Lopez, California, p		Frank Linzy, San Francisco, p	

THE SPORTING NEWS ROOKIE AWARDS—Continued

AMERICAN LEAGUE	NATIONAL LEAGUE
Year Player Club	Player Club
1966—Tommie Agee, Chicago, of	Tommy Helms, Cincinnati, 3b
James Nash, Kansas City, p	Donald Sutton, Los Angeles, p
1967—Rod Carew, Minnesota, 2b	Lee May, Cincinnati, 1b
Tom Phoebus, Baltimore, p	Dick Hughes, St. Louis, p
1968—Del Unser, Washington, of	Johnny Bench, Cincinnati, c
Stan Bahnsen, New York, p	Jerry Koosman, New York, p
1969—Carlos May, Chicago, of	Coco Laboy, Montreal, 3b
Mike Nagy, Boston, p	Tom Griffin, Houston, p
1970—Roy Foster, Cleveland, of	Bernie Carbo, Cincinnati, of
Bert Blyleven, Minnesota, p	Carl Morton, Montreal, p
1971—Chris Chambliss, Cleveland, 1b	Earl Williams, Atlanta, c
Bill Parsons, Milwaukee, p	Reggie Cleveland, St. Louis, p
1972—Carlton Fisk, Boston, c	Dave Rader, San Francisco, c
Dick Tidrow, Cleveland, p	Jon Matlack, New York, p
1973—Al Bumbry, Baltimore, of	Gary Matthews, San Fran., of
Steve Busby, Kansas City, p	Steve Rogers, Montreal, p
1974—Mike Hargrove, Texas, 1b	Greg Gross, Houston, of
Frank Tanana, California, p	John D'Acquisto, San Francisco, p
1975—Fred Lynn, Boston, of	Gary Carter, Montreal, of-c
Dennis Eckersley, Cleveland, p	John Montefusco, San Francisco, p
1976—Butch Wynegar, Minnesota, c	Larry Herndon, San Francisco, of
Mark Fidrych, Detroit, p	Butch Metzger, San Diego, p
1977—Mitchell Page, Oakland, of	Andre Dawson, Montreal, of
Dave Rozema, Detroit, p	Bob Owchinko, San Diego, p
1978—Paul Molitor, Milwaukee, 2b	Bob Horner, Atlanta, 3b
Rich Gale, Kansas City, p	Don Robinson, Pittsburgh, p
1979—Pat Putnam, Texas, 1b	Jeff Leonard, Houston, of
Mark Clear, California, p	Rick Sutcliffe, Los Angeles, p
1980—Joe Charboneau, Cleveland, of	Lonnie Smith, Philadelphia, of
Britt Burns, Chicago, p	Bill Gullickson, Montreal, p
1981—Rich Gedman, Boston, c	Tim Raines, Montreal, of
Dave Righetti, New York, p	Fernando Valenzuela, Los Angeles, p

MAJOR LEAGUE EXECUTIVE

Year Executive Club	Year Executive Club
1936—Branch Rickey, St. Louis NL	1960—George Weiss, New York AL
1937—Edward Barrow, New York AL	1961—Dan Topping, New York AL
1938—Warren Giles, Cincinnati NL	1962—Fred Haney, Los Angeles AL
1939—Larry MacPhail, Brooklyn NL	1963—Vaughan (Bing) Devine, St.L.NL
1940—W. O. Briggs, Sr., Detroit AL	1964—Vaughan (Bing) Devine, St.L.NL
1941—Edward Barrow, New York AL	1965—Calvin Griffith, Minnesota AL
1942—Branch Rickey, St. Louis NL	1966—Lee MacPhail, Commissioner's
1943—Clark Griffith, Washington AL	Office
1944—Wm. O. DeWitt, St. Louis AL	1967—Dick O'Connell, Boston AL
1945—Philip K. Wrigley, Chicago NL	1968—James Campbell, Detroit AL
1946—Thomas A. Yawkey, Boston AL	1969—John Murphy, New York NL
1947—Branch Rickey, Brooklyn NL	1970—Harry Dalton, Baltimore AL
1948—Bill Veeck, Cleveland AL	1971—Cedric Tallis, Kansas City AL
1949—Robt. Carpenter, Phila'phia NL	1972—Roland Hemond, Chicago AL
1950—George Weiss, New York AL	1973—Bob Howsam, Cincinnati NL
1951—George Weiss, New York AL	1974—Gabe Paul, New York AL
1952—George Weiss, New York AL	1975—Dick O'Connell, Boston AL
1953—Louis Perini, Milwaukee NL	1976—Joe Burke, Kansas City AL
1954—Horace Stoneham, N. York NL	1977—Bill Veeck, Chicago AL
1955—Walter O'Malley, Brooklyn NL	1978—Spec Richardson, San Fran. NL
1956—Gabe Paul, Cincinnati NL	1979—Hank Peters, Baltimore AL
1957—Frank Lane, St. Louis NL	1980—Tal Smith, Houston NL
1958—Joe L. Brown, Pittsburgh NL	1981—John McHale, Montreal NL
1959—E. J. (Buzzie) Bavasi, L.A. NL	

MAJOR LEAGUE MANAGER

Year Manager Club	Year Manager Club
1936—Joe McCarthy, New York AL	1948—Bill Meyer, Pittsburgh NL
1937—Bill McKechnie, Boston NL	1949—Casey Stengel, New York AL
1938—Joe McCarthy, New York AL	1950—Red Rolfe, Detroit AL
1939—Leo Durocher, Brooklyn NL	1951—Leo Durocher, New York NL
1940—Bill McKechnie, Cincinnati NL	1952—Eddie Stanky, St. Louis NL
1941—Billy Southworth, St. Louis NL	1953—Casey Stengel, New York AL
1942—Billy Southworth, St. Louis NL	1954—Leo Durocher, New York NL
1943—Joe McCarthy, New York AL	1955—Walter Alston, Brooklyn NL
1944—Luke Sewell, St. Louis AL	1956—Birdie Tebbetts, Cincinnati NL
1945—Ossie Bluege, Washington AL	1957—Fred Hutchinson, St. Louis NL
1946—Eddie Dyer, St. Louis NL	1958—Casey Stengel, New York AL
1947—Bucky Harris, New York AL	1959—Walter Alston, Los Angeles NL

MAJOR LEAGUE MANAGER—Continued

Year	Manager	Club
1960	Danny Murtaugh, Pitts. NL	
1961	Ralph Houk, New York AL	
1962	Bill Rigney, Los Angeles AL	
1963	Walter Alston, Los Angeles NL	
1964	Johnny Keane, St. Louis NL	
1965	Sam Mele, Minnesota AL	
1966	Hank Bauer, Baltimore AL	
1967	Dick Williams, Boston AL	
1968	Mayo Smith, Detroit AL	
1969	Gil Hodges, New York NL	
1970	Danny Murtaugh, Pittsb'gh NL	
1971	Charlie Fox, San Francisco NL	
1972	Chuck Tanner, Chicago AL	
1973	Gene Mauch, Montreal NL	
1974	Bill Virdon, New York AL	
1975	Darrell Johnson, Boston AL	
1976	Danny Ozark, Philadelphia NL	
1977	Earl Weaver, Baltimore AL	
1978	George Bamberger, Milw'kee AL	
1979	Earl Weaver, Baltimore AL	
1980	Bill Virdon, Houston NL	
1981	Billy Martin, Oakland AL	

MAJOR LEAGUE PLAYER

Year	Player	Club
1936	Carl Hubbell, New York NL	
1937	Johnny Allen, Cleveland AL	
1938	Johnny Vander Meer, Cinn. NL	
1939	Joe DiMaggio, New York AL	
1940	Bob Feller, Cleveland AL	
1941	Ted Williams, Boston AL	
1942	Ted Williams, Boston AL	
1943	Spud Chandler, New York AL	
1944	Marty Marion, St. Louis NL	
1945	Hal Newhouser, Detroit AL	
1946	Stan Musial, St. Louis NL	
1947	Ted Williams, Boston AL	
1948	Lou Boudreau, Cleveland AL	
1949	Ted Williams, Boston AL	
1950	Phil Rizzuto, New York AL	
1951	Stan Musial, St. Louis NL	
1952	Robin Roberts, Philadelphia NL	
1953	Al Rosen, Cleveland AL	
1954	Willie Mays, New York NL	
1955	Duke Snider, Brooklyn NL	
1956	Mickey Mantle, New York AL	
1957	Ted Williams, Boston AL	
1958	Bob Turley, New York AL	
1959	Early Wynn, Chicago AL	
1960	Bill Mazeroski, Pittsburgh NL	
1961	Roger Maris, New York AL	
1962	Maury Wills, Los Angeles NL	
	Don Drysdale, Los Angeles NL	
1963	Sandy Koufax, Los Angeles NL	
1964	Ken Boyer, St. Louis NL	
1965	Sandy Koufax, Los Angeles NL	
1966	Frank Robinson, Baltimore AL	
1967	Carl Yastrzemski, Boston AL	
1968	Denny McLain, Detroit AL	
1969	Willie McCovey, San Fran. NL	
1970	Johnny Bench, Cin. NL	
1971	Joe Torre, St. Louis NL	
1972	Billy Williams, Chicago NL	
1973	Reggie Jackson, Oakland AL	
1974	Lou Brock, St. Louis NL	
1975	Joe Morgan, Cincinnati NL	
1976	Joe Morgan, Cincinnati NL	
1977	Rod Carew, Minnesota AL	
1978	Ron Guidry, New York AL	
1979	Willie Stargell, Pittsburgh NL	
1980	George Brett, Kansas City AL	
1981	Fernando Valenzuela, Los Angeles NL	

MINOR LEAGUE EXECUTIVE (HIGHER CLASSIFICATIONS)
(Restricted to Class AAA Starting in 1963)

Year	Executive	Club
1936	Earl Mann, Atlanta, Southern	
1937	Robt. LaMotte, Savannah, Sally	
1938	Louis McKenna, St. Paul, A.A.	
1939	Bruce Dudley, Louisville, A.A.	
1940	Roy Hamey, Kansas City, A.A.	
1941	Emil Sick, Seattle, PCL	
1942	Bill Veeck, Milwaukee, A.A.	
1943	Clar. Rowland, Los Angeles, PCL	
1944	William Mulligan, Seattle, PCL	
1945	Bruce Dudley, Louisville, A.A.	
1946	Earl Mann, Atlanta, Southern	
1947	Wm. Purnhage, Waterloo, I.I.I.	
1948	Ed. Glennon, Bir'ham, Southern	
1949	Ted Sullivan, Indianapolis, A.A.	
1950	Cl. (Brick) Laws, Oakland, PCL	
1951	Robert Howsam, Denver, West.	
1952	Jack Cooke, Toronto, Int.	
1953	Richard Burnett, Dallas, Texas	
1954	Edward Stumpf, Indpls., A.A.	
1955	Dewey Soriano, Seattle, PCL	
1956	Robert Howsam, Denver, A.A.	
1957	John Stiglmeier, Buffalo, Int.	
1958	Ed. Glennon, Bir'ham, Southern	
1959	Ed. Leishman, Salt Lake, PCL	
1960	Ray Winder, Little Rock, Sou.	
1961	Elten Schiller, Omaha, A.A.	
1962	Geo. Sisler, Jr., Rochester, Int.	
1963	Lewis Matlin, Hawaii, PCL	
1964	Ed. Leishman, San Diego, PCL	
1965	Harold Cooper, Columbus, Int.	
1966	John Quinn, Jr., Hawaii, PCL	
1967	Hillman Lyons, Richmond, Int.	
1968	Gabe Paul, Jr., Tulsa, PCL	
1969	Bill Gardner, Louisville, Int.	
1970	Dick King, Wichita, A.A.	
1971	Carl Steinfeldt, Jr., Roch'ter, Int.	
1972	Don Labbruzzo, Evansville, A.A.	
1973	Merle Miller, Tucson, PCL	
1974	John Carbray, Sacramento, PCL	
1975	Stan Naccarato, Tacoma, PCL	
1976	Art Teece, Salt Lake City, PCL	
1977	George Sisler, Jr., Col'bus, Int.	
1978	Willie Sanchez, Albu'que, PCL	
1979	George Sisler, Jr., Col'bus, Int.	
1980	Jim Burris, Denver, A.A.	
1981	Pat McKernan, Albuquerque, PCL	

MINOR LEAGUE EXECUTIVE (LOWER CLASSIFICATIONS)
(Separate Awards for Class AA and Class A Started in 1963)

Year	Executive	Club
1950	H. Cooper, Hutch'son, West. A.	
1951	O. W. (Bill) Hayes, T'ple, B.S.	
1952	Hillman Lyons, Danville, MOV	
1953	Carl Roth, Peoria, III	
1954	James Meaghan, Cedar R., III	
1955	John Petrakis, Dubuque, MOV	
1956	Marvin Milkes, Fresno, Calif.	
1957	Richard Wagner, L'coln, West.	

MINOR LEAGUE EXECUTIVE (LOWER CLASSIFICATIONS)
(Continued)
(Separate Awards for Class AA and Class A Started in 1963)

Year Executive   Club
1958—Gerald Waring, Macon, Sally
1959—Clay Dennis, Des Moines, III
1960—Hubert Kittle, Yakima, Northw.
1961—David Steele, Fresno, California
1962—John Quinn, Jr., S. Jose, Calif.
1963—Hugh Finnerty, Tulsa, Texas
    Ben Jewell, M. Valley, Pioneer
1964—Glynn West, B'ham, Southern
    Jas. Bayens, Rock Hill, W. Car.
1965—Dick Butler, Dallas-Ft.W., Tex.
    Ken. Blackman, Quad C., Midw.
1966—Tom Fleming, Evansville, South.
    Cappy Harada, Lodi, California
1967—Robt. Quinn, Reading, East.
    Pat Williams, Spar'burg, W. C.
1968—Phil Howser, Charlotte, South.
    Merle Miller, Burlington, Midw.
1969—Charlie Blaney, Albuq., Tex.
    Bill Gorman, Visalia, Calif.
1970—Carl Sawatski, Arkansas, Tex.
    Bob Williams, Bakersfield, Calif.

Year Executive   Club
1971—Miles Wolff, Savannah, Dixie A.
    Ed Holtz, Appleton, Midwest
1972—John Begzos, S. Antonio, Texas
    Bob Piccinini, Modesto, Calif.
1973—Dick Kravitz, Jacksonville, Sou.
    Fritz Colschen, Clinton, Midw.
1974—Jim Paul, El Paso, Texas
    Bing Russell, Portland, N'west
1975—Jim Paul, El Paso, Texas
    Cordy Jensen, Eugene, N'west
1976—Woodrow Reid, Chat'ooga, Sou.
    Don Buchheister, Ced. Rap., Mid.
1977—Jim Paul, El Paso, Texas
    Harry Pells, Quad Cities, Midw.
1978—Larry Schmittou, Nashville, Sou.
    Dave Hersh, Appleton, Midw.
1979—Bill Rigney Jr., Midland, Tex.
    Tom Romenesko, G'sboro, W.C.
1980—Frances Crockett, C'lotte, Sou.
    Tom Romenesko, G'sboro, W.C.
1981—Allie Prescott, Memphis, Sou.
    Dan Overstreet, Hagerstown, Caro.

MINOR LEAGUE MANAGER

Year Manager   Club
1936—Al Sothoron, Milwaukee, A.A.
1937—Jake Flowers, Salis'y, East. Sh.
1938—Paul Richards, Atlanta, South.
1939—Bill Meyer, Kansas City, A.A.
1940—Larry Gilbert, Nashville, South.
1941—Burt Shotton, Columbus, A.A.
1942—Eddie Dyer, Columbus, A.A.
1943—Nick Cullop, Columbus, A.A.
1944—Al Thomas, Baltimore, Int.
1945—Lefty O'Doul, San Fran., PCL
1946—Clay Hopper, Montreal, Int.
1947—Nick Cullop, Milwaukee, A.A.
1948—Casey Stengel, Oakland, PCL
1949—Fred Haney, Hollywood, PCL
1950—Rollie Hemsley, Columbus, A.A.
1951—Charlie Grimm, Milw., A.A.
1952—Luke Appling, Memphis, South.
1953—Bobby Bragan, Hollywood, PCL
1954—Kerby Farrell, Indpls., A.A.
1955—Bill Rigney, Minneapolis, A.A.
1956—Kerby Farrell, Indpls., A.A.
1957—Ben Geraghty, Wichita, A.A.
1958—Cal Ermer, Birmingham, South.

Year Manager   Club
1959—Pete Reiser, Victoria, Texas
1960—Mel McGaha, Toronto, Int.
1961—Kerby Farrell, Buffalo, Int.
1962—Ben Geraghty, Jackson'le, Int.
1963—Rollie Hemsley, Indpls., Int.
1964—Harry Walker, Jacks'vle, Int.
1965—Grady Hatton, Okla. City, PCL
1966—Bob Lemon, Seattle, PCL
1967—Bob Skinner, San Diego, PCL
1968—Jack Tighe, Toledo, Int.
1969—Clyde McCullough, Tide., Int.
1970—Tom Lasorda, Spokane, PCL
1971—Del Rice, Salt Lake City, PCL
1972—Hank Bauer, Tidewater, Int.
1973—Joe Morgan, Charleston, Int.
1974—Joe Altobelli, Rochester, Int.
1975—Joe Frazier, Tidewater, Int.
1976—Vern Rapp, Denver, A.A.
1977—Tommy Thompson, Arkan., Tex.
1978—Les Moss, Evansville, A.A.
1979—Vern Benson, Syracuse, Int.
1980—Hal Lanier, Springfield, A.A.
1981—Del Crandall, Albuquerque, PCL

MINOR LEAGUE PLAYER

Year Player   Club
1936—Jn. Vander Meer, Durham, Pied.
1937—Charlie Keller, Newark, Int.
1938—Fred Hutchinson, Seattle, PCL
1939—Lou Novikoff, Tulsa-Los A'les.
1940—Phil Rizzuto, Kansas City, A.A.
1941—John Lindell, Newark, Int.
1942—Dick Barrett, Seattle, PCL
1943—Chet Covington, Scranton, East.
1944—Rip Collins, Albany, Eastern
1945—Gil Coan, Chattanooga, South.
1946—Sibby Sisti, Indianapolis, A.A.
1947—Hank Sauer, Syracuse, Int.
1948—Gene Woodling, S. F., PCL
1949—Orie Arntzen, Albany, Eastern
1950—Frank Saucier, San Ant'o, Tex.
1951—Gene Conley, Hartford, Eastern
1952—Bill Skowron, Kans. City, A.A.
1953—Gene Conley, Toledo, A.A.
1954—Herb Score, Indianapolis, A.A.
1955—John Murff, Dallas, Texas
1956—Steve Bilko, Los Angeles, PCL
1957—Norm Siebern, Denver, A.A.
1958—Jim O'Toole, Nashville, South.

Year Player   Club
1959—Frank Howard, Victoria-Spok.
1960—Willie Davis, Spokane, PCL
1961—Howie Koplitz, Bir'ham, South.
1962—Bob Bailey, Columbus, Int.
1963—Don Buford, Indianapolis, Int.
1964—Mel Stottlemyre, Richm'd., Int.
1965—Joe Foy, Toronto, International
1966—Mike Epstein, Rochester, Int.
1967—Johnny Bench, Buffalo, Int.
1968—Merv Rettenmund, Roch'ter, Int.
1969—Danny Walton, Okla. City, A.A.
1970—Don Baylor, Rochester, Int.
1971—Bobby Grich, Rochester, Int.
1972—Tom Paciorek, Albuq'que, PCL
1973—Steve Ontiveros, Phoenix, PCL
1974—Jim Rice, Pawtucket, Int.
1975—Hector Cruz, Tulsa, A.A.
1976—Pat Putnam, Asheville, W. Car.
1977—Ken Landreaux, S.L.C., PCL-El Paso, Tex.
1978—Champ Summers, Indi'polis, A.A.
1979—Mark Bomback, Vancouver, PCL
1980—Tim Raines, Denver, A.A.
1981—Mike Marshall, Albuquerque, PCL

Baseball Writers' Association Awards
Most Valuable Player Citations
CHALMERS AWARD

AMERICAN LEAGUE			NATIONAL LEAGUE		
Year	Player Club	Points	Player Club		Points
1911	Tyrus Cobb, Detroit, of	64	Frank Schulte, Chicago, of		29
1912	Tristram Speaker, Boston, of	59	Lawrence Doyle, N. Y., 2b		48
1913	Walter Johnson, Washington, p	54	Jacob Daubert, Brooklyn, 1b		50
1914	Edward Collins, Phila., 2b	63	John Evers, Boston, 2b		50

LEAGUE AWARDS

AMERICAN LEAGUE			NATIONAL LEAGUE		
Year	Player Club	Points	Player Club		Points
1922	George Sisler, St. Louis, 1b	59	No selection		
1923	George Ruth, New York, of	64	No selection		
1924	Walter Johnson, Washington, p	55	Arthur Vance, Brooklyn, p		74
1925	Roger Peckinpaugh, Wash., ss	45	Rogers Hornsby, St. Louis, 2b		73
1926	George Burns, Cleveland, 1b	63	Robert O'Farrell, St. Louis, c		79
1927	H. Louis Gehrig, New York, 1b	56	Paul Waner, Pittsburgh, of		72
1928	Gordon Cochrane, Phila., c	53	James Bottomley, St. Louis, 1b		76
1929	No selection		Rogers Hornsby, Chicago, 2b		60

BASEBALL WRITERS' ASSOCIATION MVP AWARDS

AMERICAN LEAGUE			NATIONAL LEAGUE		
Year	Player Club	Points	Player Club		Points
1931	Robert Grove, Philadelphia, p	78	Frank Frisch, St. Louis, 2b		65
1932	James Foxx, Philadelphia, 1b	75	Charles Klein, Phila., of		78
1933	James Foxx, Philadelphia, 1b	74	Carl Hubbell, New York, p		77
1934	Gordon Cochrane, Detroit, c	67	Jerome Dean, St. Louis, p		78
1935	Henry Greenberg, Detroit, 1b	*80	Charles Hartnett, Chicago, c		75
1936	H. Louis Gehrig, New York, 1b	73	Carl Hubbell, New York, p		60
1937	Charles Gehringer, Detroit, 2b	78	Joseph Medwick, St. Louis, of		70
1938	James Foxx, Boston, 1b	305	Ernest Lombardi, Cincinnati, c		229
1939	Joseph DiMaggio, N. York, of	280	William Walters, Cincinnati, p		303
1940	Henry Greenberg, Detroit, of	292	Frank McCormick, Cinn., 1b		274
1941	Joseph DiMaggio, N. York, of	291	Adolph Camilli, Brooklyn, 1b		300
1942	Joseph Gordon, New York, 2b	270	Morton Cooper, St. Louis, p		263
1943	Spurgeon Chandler, N. Y., p	246	Stanley Musial, St. Louis, of		267
1944	Harold Newhouser, Detroit, p	236	Martin Marion, St. Louis, ss		190
1945	Harold Newhouser, Detroit, p	236	Philip Cavarretta, Chicago, 1b		279
1946	Theodore Williams, Boston, of	224	Stanley Musial, St. Louis, 1b		319
1947	Joseph DiMaggio, N. York, of	202	Robert Elliott, Boston, 3b		205
1948	Louis Boudreau, Cleveland, ss	324	Stanley Musial, St. Louis, of		303
1949	Theodore Williams, Boston, of	272	Jack Robinson, Brooklyn, 2b		264
1950	Philip Rizzuto, New York, ss	284	C. James Konstanty, Phila., p		286
1951	Lawrence Berra, New York, c	184	Roy Campanella, Brooklyn, c		243
1952	Robert Shantz, Phila., p	280	Henry Sauer, Chicago, of		226
1953	Albert Rosen, Cleveland, 3b	*336	Roy Campanella, Brooklyn, c		297
1954	Lawrence Berra, New York, c	230	Willie Mays, New York, of		283
1955	Lawrence Berra, New York, c	218	Roy Campanella, Brooklyn, c		226
1956	Mickey Mantle, N. Y., of	*336	Donald Newcombe, Brkn., p		223
1957	Mickey Mantle, New York, of	233	Henry Aaron, Milwaukee, of		239
1958	Jack Jensen, Boston, of	233	Ernest Banks, Chicago, ss		283
1959	J. Nelson Fox, Chicago, 2b	295	Ernest Banks, Chicago, ss		232½
1960	Roger Maris, New York, of	225	Richard Groat, Pittsburgh, ss		276
1961	Roger Maris, New York, of	202	Frank Robinson, Cincinnati, of		219
1962	Mickey Mantle, New York, of	234	Maurice Wills, Los Angeles, ss		209
1963	Elston Howard, New York, c	248	Sanford Koufax, Los Angeles, p		237
1964	Brooks Robinson, Balti., 3b	269	Kenton Boyer, St. Louis, 3b		243
1965	Zoilo Versalles, Minn., ss	275	Willie Mays, San Francisco, of		224
1966	Frank Robinson, Balti., of	*280	Roberto Clemente, Pitts., of		218
1967	Carl Yastrzemski, Boston, of	275	Orlando Cepeda, St. Louis, 1b		*280
1968	Dennis McLain, Detroit, p	*280	Robert Gibson, St. Louis, p		242
1969	Harmon Killebrew, Minn., 1-3b	294	Willie McCovey, San Fran., 1b		265
1970	John (Boog) Powell, Balti., 1b	234	Johnny Bench, Cincinnati, c		326
1971	Vida Blue, Oakland, p	268	Joseph Torre, St. Louis, 3b		318
1972	Richie Allen, Chicago, 1b	321	Johnny Bench, Cincinnati, c		263
1973	Reggie Jackson, Oak., of	*336	Pete Rose, Cincinnati, of		274
1974	Jeff Burroughs, Texas, of	248	Steve Garvey, Los Angeles, 1b		270
1975	Fred Lynn, Boston, of	326	Joe Morgan, Cincinnati, 2b		321½
1976	Thurman Munson, N. Y., c	304	Joe Morgan, Cincinnati, 2b		311
1977	Rod Carew, Minn., 1b	273	George Foster, Cincinnati, of		291
1978	Jim Rice, Boston, of	352	Dave Parker, Pittsburgh, of		320
1979	Don Baylor, California, of	347	Willie Stargell, Pittsburgh, 1b		216
			Keith Hernandez, St. Louis, 1b		216
1980	George Brett, Kansas City, 3b	335	Mike Schmidt, Philadelphia, 3b		*336
1981	Rollie Fingers, Milwaukee, p	319	Mike Schmidt, Philadelphia, 3b		321

*Unanimous selection.

BASEBALL WRITERS' ASSOCIATION ROOKIE AWARDS

1947—Combined selection—Jack Robinson, Brooklyn, 1b.
1948—Combined selection—Alvin Dark, Boston, N. L., ss.

Year Player Club	Votes	Player Club	Votes
1949—Roy Sievers, St. Louis, of	10	Donald Newcombe, Brkn, p	21
1950—Walter Dropo, Boston, 1b	15	Samuel Jethroe, Boston, of	11
1951—Gilbert McDougald, N. Y., 3b	13	Willie Mays, New York, of	18
1952—Harry Byrd, Philadelphia, p	9	Joseph Black, Brooklyn, p	19
1953—Harvey Kuenn, Detroit, ss	23	James Gilliam, Brooklyn, 2b	11
1954—Robert Grim, New York, p	15	Wallace Moon, St. Louis, of	17
1955—Herbert Score, Cleveland, p	18	William Virdon, St. Louis, of	15
1956—Luis Aparicio, Chicago, ss	22	Frank Robinson, Cincinnati, of	*24
1957—Anthony Kubek, N. Y., inf-of	23	John Sanford, Philadelphia, p	16
1958—Albert Pearson, Washington, of	14	Orlando Cepeda, S. Fran., 1b	*†21
1959—W. Robert Allison, Wash., of	18	Willie McCovey, San Fran., 1b	*24
1960—Ronald Hansen, Baltimore, ss	22	Frank Howard, Los Angeles, of	12
1961—Donald Schwall, Boston, p	7	Billy Williams, Chicago, of	10
1962—Thomas Tresh, New York, of-ss	13	Kenneth Hubbs, Chicago, 2b	19
1963—Gary Peters, Chicago, p	10	Peter Rose, Cincinnati, 2b	17
1964—Pedro (Tony) Oliva, Minn., of	19	Richard Allen, Philadelphia, 3b	18
1965—Curtis Blefary, Baltimore, of	12	James Lefebvre, Los Ang., 2b	13
1966—Tommie Agee, Chicago, of	16	Tommy Helms, Cincinnati, 3b	12
1967—Rod Carew, Minnesota, 2b	19	Tom Seaver, New York, p	11
1968—Stan Bahnsen, New York, p	17	Johnny Bench, Cincinnati, c	10½
1969—Lou Piniella, Kansas City, of	9	Ted Sizemore, Los Angeles, 2b	14
1970—Thurman Munson, N. Y., c	23	Carl Morton, Montreal, p	11
1971—Chris Chambliss, Cleveland, 1b	11	Earl Williams, Atlanta, c	18
1972—Carlton Fisk, Boston, c	*24	Jon Matlack, New York, p	19
1973—Al Bumbry, Baltimore, of	13½	Gary Matthews, San Fran., of	11
1974—Mike Hargrove, Texas, 1b	16½	Bake McBride, St. Louis, of	16
1975—Fred Lynn, Boston, of	23	John Montefusco, San Fran., p	12
1976—Mark Fidrych, Detroit, p	22	Butch Metzger, San Diego, p	11
		Pat Zachry, Cincinnati, p	11
1977—Eddie Murray, Balt., dh-1b	12½	Andre Dawson, Montreal, of	10
1978—Lou Whitaker, Detroit, 2b	21	Bob Horner, Atlanta, 3b	12½
1979—John Castino, Minn., 3b	7	Rick Sutcliffe, L.A., p	20
Alfredo Griffin, Tor., ss	7		
1980—Joe Charboneau, Clev., of	103	Steve Howe, L.A., p	80
1981—Dave Righetti, N. Y., p	127	Fernando Valenzuela, L. A., p	107

*Unanimous selection. †Three writers did not vote.

CY YOUNG MEMORIAL AWARD

Year Pitcher Club	Votes
1956—Donald Newcombe, Brkn	10
1957—Warren Spahn, Milwaukee	15
1958—Robert Turley, N. Y., A. L.	5
1959—Early Wynn, Chicago, A.L.	13
1960—Vernon Law, Pittsburgh	8
1961—Edward Ford, N. Y., A. L.	9
1962—Don Drysdale, L.A., N.L.	14
1963—Sanford Koufax, L.A., N.L.	*20
1964—Dean Chance, L. A., A. L.	17
1965—Sanford Koufax, L.A., N.L.	*20
1966—Sanford Koufax, L.A., N.L.	*20
1967—A. L.—Jim Lonborg, Boston	18
N. L.—M. McCormick, S. F.	18
1968—A. L.—Dennis McLain, Det.	*20
N. L.—Bob Gibson, St. L.	*20
1969—A. L.—Dennis McLain, Det.	10
Mike Cuellar, Balt	10
N. L.—Tom Seaver, N. Y.	23
1970—A. L.—Jim Perry, Minn.	†55
N. L.—Bob Gibson, St. L.	†118
1971—A. L.—Vida Blue, Oakland	†98
N. L.—Fergy Jenkins, Chi.	†97

1972—A. L.—Gaylord Perry, Cleve.	†64
N. L.—Steve Carlton, Phil.	*†120
1973—A. L.—Jim Palmer, Balt.	†88
N. L.—Tom Seaver, N. Y.	†71
1974—A. L.—Jim Hunter, Oakland	†90
N. L.—Mike Marshall, L. A.	†96
1975—A. L.—Jim Palmer, Balt.	†98
N. L.—Tom Seaver, N. Y.	†98
1976—A. L.—Jim Palmer, Balt.	†108
N. L.—Randy Jones, S. D.	†96
1977—A. L.—Sparky Lyle, N.Y.	†56½
N. L.—Steve Carlton, Phil.	†104
1978—A. L.—Ron Guidry, N.Y.	*†140
N. L.—Gaylord Perry, S.D.	†116
1979—A. L.—Mike Flanagan, Balt.	†136
N. L.—Bruce Sutter, Chi.	†72
1980—A. L.—Steve Stone, Balt.	100
N. L.—Steve Carlton, Phil.	118
1981—A. L.—Rollie Fingers, Milwaukee	126
N. L.—Fernando Valenzuela, L. A.	70

*Unanimous selection. †Point system used.

Aaron, Robinson Voted Into Hall

By LARRY WIGGE

Did Hank Aaron really have to have a unanimous vote behind him to cross the threshold of the Hall of Fame at Cooperstown, N.Y., when the ballots were counted in mid-January of 1982? Of course he didn't. No one else ever needed a perfect score to be admitted to the Hall of Fame. Not Babe Ruth, not Ty Cobb, not Christy Mathewson, not Joe DiMaggio, not Stan Musial, not Willie Mays. . . .

The fact that Aaron was left off nine of 415 ballots when he was elected to the Hall of Fame wasn't really important. Sure it would have been nice to see everyone recognize him in the voting. But what was important was that Hammerin Hank finally had been given the game's greatest honor.

An imperfect score did not erase the 755 career home runs Aaron belted during his 23-year major league career with the Milwaukee and Atlanta Braves and Milwaukee Brewers. It didn't blemish his .305 lifetime batting average, or his 3,771 career hits. He didn't have to forfeit his eight 40-homer seasons, his four home run titles, 1956 batting championship or his four RBI titles. Those figures and the many memories he left behind will last forever.

When Aaron slammed one of Al Downing's deliveries over the left-field fence in Atlanta Stadium on April 8, 1974, breaking Babe Ruth's career home run total of 714, he was hurt that some people frowned on his accomplishment because he needed 2,896 more times at bat to hit 715 homers.

"I never wanted them to forget Babe Ruth," he said. "I just wanted them to remember Henry Aaron."

His election to the Hall of Fame was the same. There was a touch of bitterness in his voice when he was asked about not getting unanimous support in the voting by the 10-year members of the Baseball Writers Association of America, but he was thoroughly pleased anyway.

"I don't think it's a disappointment, but I'd be lying if I said I didn't want to be unanimous," Aaron said after he and Frank Robinson were elected, swelling the Hall of Fame honor roll to 178 members.

"I feel for the first time that what I did has been appreciated," he continued. "It was always this player and that player and then Aaron, but now I think I'm ap-preciated. I don't know the yardstick for election, and I know I was never a politician. But if you're talking about a man's record and what I accomplished between the white lines, I can't understand why I wasn't unanimous—or why Frank Robinson or Willie Mays or Ted Williams weren't."

Only Ty Cobb in 1936 (the year the voting began) joined the game's elite with a greater voting percentage (98.2) than Aaron's 97.8. And only Ruth, Honus Wagner, Mays, Bob Feller, Williams, Musial and Mathewson were ever named on more than 90 percent of the ballots.

Aaron possessed all the talents. He could hit for average and for power. He could run (he is one of only five players to hit 30 homers and steal 30 bases in one season). And he was graceful in the field. His playing career spanned from 1953 through 1976.

Needing 75 percent of the vote, or 312 votes, Robinson received 370 votes and also was an easy winner. Aaron and Robinson were the 12th and 13th players in history to be elected to the Hall of Fame in their first year of eligibility.

High-kicking Giants' righthander Juan Marichal moved closer to election with 305 votes, just seven short of enshrinement. Minnesota Twins' slugger Harmon Killebrew was fourth with 246 votes.

Robinson, who ranks fourth on the all-time homer list with 586, played in 2,808 games from 1956 through 1976 with Cincinnati, Baltimore, Los Angeles Dodgers, California and Cleveland. He compiled a .294 lifetime batting average with 2,943 hits. And he hit more than .300 in nine seasons.

"This would have to be the greatest day in my life," proclaimed Robinson. "There's no question I would put it right at the top."

Robinson is the only player to win Most Valuable Player honors in both leagues (1961 with Cincinnati and 1966 with Baltimore). In '66 he became only the 10th player in major league history to win a Triple Crown, leading the American League in batting (.316), homers (49) and runs batted in (122).

Frank is currently the manager of the San Francisco Giants. In addition to his great playing skills, he has always been recognized for his ability to lead people. When the Cleveland Indians named him as their manager in 1975, he became the

Hank Aaron . . . 755 homers.

first black to ever manage in the majors.

Robinson said it was an honor to enter the Hall of Fame with Aaron. "It's very strange," he said. "It seems like I've been chasing him my entire career. Now I've finally caught up with him."

The complete Hall of Fame voting follows:

Henry Aaron 406, Frank Robinson 370, Juan Marichal 305, Harmon Killebrew 246, Hoyt Wilhelm 236, Don Drysdale 233, Gil Hodges 205, Luis Aparicio 174, Jim Bunning 138, Red Schoendienst 135, Nelson Fox 127, Richie Ashburn 126, Billy Williams 97, Maury Wills 91, Roger Maris 69, Tony Oliva 63, Harvey Kuenn 62, Lew Burdette 43, Orlando Cepeda 42, Elston Howard 40, Don Larsen 32, Bill Mazeroski 28, Thurman Munson 26, Roy Face 22, Vada Pinson 6, Tommy Davis 5, Dave McNally 5, Lindy McDaniel 3, Rico Petrocelli 3, Jim Brewer 2, Bill Freehan 2, Leo Cardenas 1.

The following failed to receive any votes: Gates Brown, Tommy Harper, Alex Johnson, Deron Johnson, Cleon Jones, Jim Northrup, Sonny Siebert, Tony Taylor, Cesar Tovar.

Following is a complete list of those enshrined in the Hall of Fame prior to 1982 with the vote by which each enrollee was elected:

1936—Tyrus Cobb (222), John (Honus) Wagner (215), George (Babe) Ruth (215), Christy Mathewson (205), Walter Johnson (189), named by Baseball Writers Association of America. Total ballots cast, 226.

1937—Napoleon Lajoie (168), Tristram Speaker (165), Denton (Cy) Young (153), named by the BBWAA. Total ballots cast, 201. George Wright, Morgan G. Bulkeley, Byron Bancroft Johnson, John J. McGraw, Cornelius McGillicuddy (Connie Mack), named by Centennial Commission.

1938—Grover C. Alexander (212), named by BBWAA. Total ballots, 262. Henry Chadwick, Alexander J. Cartwright, named by Centennial Commission.

1939—George Sisler (235), Edward Collins (213), William Keeler (207), Louis Gehrig, named by BBWAA. (Gehrig by special election after retirement from game was announced). Total ballots cast, 274. Albert G. Spalding, Adrian C. Anson, Charles A. Comiskey, William (Buck) Ewing, Charles Radbourn, William A. (Candy) Cummings, named by committee of old-time players and writers.

1942—Rogers Hornsby (182), named by BBWAA. Total ballots cast, 233.

1944—Judge Kenesaw M. Landis, named by committee on old timers.

1945—Hugh Duffy, Jimmy Collins, Hugh Jennings, Ed Delahanty, Fred Clarke, Mike Kelly, Wilbert Robinson, Jim O'Rourke, Dennis (Dan) Brouthers and Roger Bresnahan, named by committee on old timers.

1946—Jesse Burkett, Frank Chance, Jack Chesbro, Johnny Evers, Clark Griffith, Tom McCarthy, Joe McGinnity, Eddie Plank, Joe Tinker, Rube Waddell and Ed Walsh, named by committee on old timers.

1947—Carl Hubbell (140), Frank Frisch (136), Gordon (Mickey) Cochrane (128) and Robert (Lefty) Grove (123), named by BBWAA. Total ballots, 161.

1948—Herbert J. Pennock (94) and Harold (Pie) Traynor (93), named by BBWAA. Total ballots cast, 121.

1949—Charles Gehringer (159), named by BBWAA in runoff election. Total ballots cast, 187. Charles (Kid) Nichols and Morde-cai (Three-Finger) Brown, named by committee on old timers.

1951—Mel Ott (197) and Jimmie Foxx (179), named by BBWAA. Total ballots cast, 226.

1952—Harry Heilmann (203) and Paul Waner (195), named by BBWAA. Total ballots cast, 234.

1953—Jerome (Dizzy) Dean (209) and Al Simmons (199), named by BBWAA. Total ballots cast, 264. Charles Albert (Chief) Bender, Roderick (Bobby) Wallace, William Klem, Tom Connolly, Edward G. Barrow and William Henry (Harry) Wright, named by the new Committee on Veterans.

1954—Walter (Rabbit) Maranville (209), William Dickey (202) and William Terry (195), named by BBWAA. Total ballots cast, 252.

1955—Joe DiMaggio (223), Ted Lyons (217), Arthur (Dazzy) Vance (205) and Charles (Gabby) Hartnett (195), named by BBWAA. Total ballots cast, 251. J. Franklin (Home Run) Baker and Ray Schalk, named by Committee on Veterans.

1956—Hank Greenberg (164) and Joe Cronin (152), named by BBWAA. Total ballots cast, 193.

1957—Joseph V. McCarthy and Sam Crawford, named by Committee on Veterans.

1959—Zachariah (Zack) Wheat, named by Committee on Veterans.

1961—Max Carey and William Hamilton, named by Committee on Veterans.

1962—Bob Feller (150) and Jackie Robinson (124), named by BBWAA. Total ballots cast, 160. Bill McKechnie and Edd Roush, named by Committee on Veterans.

1963—Eppa Rixey, Edgar (Sam) Rice, Elmer Flick and John Clarkson, named by Committee on Veterans.

1964—Luke Appling (189), named by BBWAA in runoff election. Total ballots cast, 225. Urban (Red) Faber, Burleigh Grimes, Tim Keefe, Heinie Manush, Miller Huggins and John Montgomery Ward, named by Committee on Veterans.

1965—James (Pud) Galvin, named by Committee on Veterans.

1966—Ted Williams (282), named by BBWAA. Total ballots cast, 302. Casey Stengel, named by Committee on Veterans.

1967—Charles (Red) Ruffing (266), named by BBWAA in runoff election. Total ballots cast, 306. Branch Rickey and Lloyd Waner, named by Committee on Veterans.

1968—Joseph (Ducky) Medwick (240), named by BBWAA. Total ballots cast, 283. Leon (Goose) Goslin and Hazen (Kiki) Cuyler, named by Committee on Veterans.

1969—Stan (The Man) Musial (317) and Roy Campanella (270), named by BBWAA. Total ballots cast, 340. Stan Coveleski and Waite Hoyt, named by Committee on Veterans.

1970—Lou Boudreau (232), named by BBWAA. Total ballots cast, 300. Earle Combs, Jesse Haines and Ford Frick, named by Committee on Veterans.

1971—Chick Hafey, Rube Marquard, Joe Kelley, Dave Bancroft, Harry Hooper, Jake Beckley and George Weiss, named by Committee on Veterans. Satchel Paige, named by Special Committee on Negro Leagues.

1972—Sandy Koufax (344), Yogi Berra (339) and Early Wynn (301), named by BBWAA. Total ballots cast, 396. Lefty Gomez, Will Harridge and Ross Youngs, named by Committee on Veterans. Josh Gibson and Walter (Buck) Leonard, named by Special Committee on Negro Leagues.

1973—Warren Spahn (316), named by BBWAA. Total ballots cast, 380. Roberto Clemente (393), in special election by BBWAA in which 424 ballots were cast. Billy Evans, George Kelly and Mickey Welch, named by Committee on Veterans. Monte Irvin, named by Special Committee on Negro Leagues.

1974—Mickey Mantle (322) and Whitey Ford (284), named by BBWAA. Total ballots cast, 365. Jim Bottomley, Sam Thompson and Jocko Conlan, named by Committee on Veterans. James (Cool Papa) Bell, named by Special Committee on Negro Leagues.

1975—Ralph Kiner (273), named by BBWAA. Total ballots cast, 362. Earl Averill, Bucky Harris and Billy Herman, named by Committee on Veterans. William (Judy) Johnson, named by Special Committee on Negro Leagues.

1976—Robin Roberts (337) and Bob Lemon (305), named by BBWAA. Total ballots cast, 388. Roger Connor, Cal Hubbard and Fred Lindstrom, named by Committee on Veterans. Oscar Charleston, named by Special Committee on Negro Leagues.

1977—Ernie Banks (321), named by BBWAA. Total ballots cast, 383. Joe Sewell, Al Lopez and Amos Rusie, named by Committee on Veterans. Martin Dihigo and John Henry Lloyd, named by Special Committee on Negro Leagues.

1978—Eddie Mathews (301), named by BBWAA. Total ballots cast, 379. Larry MacPhail and Addie Joss, named by Committee on Veterans.

1979—Willie Mays (409), named by BBWAA. Total ballots cast, 432. Hack Wilson and Warren Giles, named by Committee on Veterans.

1980—Al Kaline (340) and Duke Snider (333), named by BBWAA. Total ballots cast, 385. Chuck Klein and Tom Yawkey, named by Committee on Veterans.

1981—Bob Gibson (337), named by BBWAA. Total ballots cast, 401. Johnny Mize and Rube Foster, named by Committee on Veterans.

BASEBALL RE-ENTRY DRAFT

MINOR LEAGUE DRAFT

MAJOR LEAGUE TRANSACTIONS

NECROLOGY

Reggie Jackson is taking his home run bat to California.

Jackson Tops Free-Agent List

By LARRY WIGGE

Reggie Jackson, Bert Campaneris, Bill Campbell and Joe Rudi were all members of the Class of '76. They were four of the 24 players who were granted total free agency and went through baseball's first reentry draft on November 4, 1976.

The same four names appeared on the 41-man list for the 1981 reentry draft. Jackson, Campaneris, Campbell and Rudi again were free agents without compensation required, but only because they were going through the reentry time tunnel for a second time. Others in the '81 draft were free to sign with another club, but compensation in the form of a player or draft choice was involved, depending on the rating system provided as part of the settlement to the 50-day players strike that began June 12, 1981.

Times have changed since arbitrator Peter Seitz' decision to grant total free agency to Andy Messersmith and Dave McNally. Two subsequent court rulings stated that all players would be totally free upon completion of their contracts.

The Basic Agreement between management and players on August 9, 1976 allowed that draft choice compensation would be obligatory from a team signing a free agent, except for those players who had signed long-term contracts prior to August, 1976. In the years that followed, it was obvious that draft choice compensation did not provide the desired immediate help that management wanted, especially when they lost a star player. Free-agent compensation became the main stumbling block which stalled negotiations and forced baseball's first mid-season strike last year.

Ratings for potential free agents were based on the performance of all players over the last two seasons. In order to secure the services of a Type A player, for instance, the signing club would have to compensate the player's former team with a draft choice. The previous club would also have the choice of a player from a pool of unprotected players after each team (excluding Boston, California, Los Angeles, Minnesota and Seattle) protected 26 players (24 if they lost a free agent) from its organization. The pool concept was a change from the direct compensation the owners originally sought in the negotiations. Two draft choices were required for the signing of a Type B player.

Jackson and New York Yankee teammate Ron Guidry were the biggest names of the '81 draft. Since there were no restrictions on the number of clubs that might select a player (except for the five aforementioned clubs granted exempt status, Guidry's selection by 18 clubs was a record for the reentry draft. Jackson was chosen by eight clubs.

Guidry agreed to a new four-year contract with the Yankees December 15 for $4.5 million. The 31-year-old lefthander had an option on a fifth year. However, the lack of movement by other free agents since the November 13 draft prompted Players' Association boss Marvin Miller to accuse the owners of collusion. Most of the signings, in fact, did not come until after the new year began.

On January 22, the California Angels signed Jackson to a three-year deal. The Phillies signed former Chicago White Sox reliever Ed Farmer six days later. Outfielder Dave Collins had previously departed Cincinnati and signed with the Yankees. Rudi left Boston to return to Oakland; catcher Tim Blackwell went from the Chicago Cubs to Montreal, and shortstop Mark Belanger signed with the Dodgers after many years in Baltimore. Pitchers Campbell and Ferguson Jenkins signed with the Cubs after being with Boston and Texas, respectively, last year. The Rangers signed pitcher Frank Tanana, who formerly was with the Red Sox, and first baseman Lamar Johnson, who was with the White Sox.

Following is a list of the 41 free-agent players in 1981 and the teams which selected them in the reentry draft. Capital letters indicate the player's former club chose to retain negotiating rights:

Type A Players

Ed Farmer (5)—Braves, WHITE SOX, Phillies, Pirates, Rangers.

Ron Guidry (18)—Braves, Orioles, Cubs, White Sox, Reds, Indians, Astros, Royals, Expos, Mets, YANKEES, A's, Phillies, Pirates, Cardinals, Giants, Rangers, Blue Jays.

Dick Tidrow (2)—White Sox, Phillies.

Type B Players

Tim Blackwell (7)—Angels, CUBS, Expos, A's, Phillies, Giants, Mariners.

Dave Collins (10)—Cubs, Royals, Dodgers, Brewers, Mets, Yankees, A's, Cardinals, Rangers, Blue Jays.

Chris Speier (0)—None.

Others

Glenn Abbott (5)—White Sox, Indians, Mets, Phillies, MARINERS.

Glenn Adams (0)—None.

Fergie Jenkins was introduced to the Chicago media by Dallas Green.

Joaquin Andujar (12)−Orioles, Cubs, Indians, Dodgers, Yankees, A's, Phillies, Pirates, CARDINALS, Giants, Mariners, Rangers.

Mark Belanger (3)−Braves, Dodgers, Cardinals.

Jeff Burroughs (0)−None.

Bert Campaneris (0)−None.

Bill Campbell (6)−Cubs, Indians, Brewers, Expos, A's, Pirates.

Dave Chalk (1)−Cardinals.

Larry Christenson (9)−Braves, Cubs, White Sox, Indians, Brewers, Expos, PHILLIES, Pirates, Giants.

Hector Cruz (0)−None.

John Denny (14)−Braves, Orioles, Angels, Cubs, White Sox, INDIANS, Expos, Mets, Yankees, A's, Phillies, Pirates, Cardinals, Giants.

Cesar Geronimo (0)−None.

Reggie Jackson (8)−Braves, Orioles, Angels, White Sox, YANKEES, Pirates, Rangers, Blue Jays.

Ron Jackson (0)−None.

Jesse Jefferson (0)−None.

Ferguson Jenkins (2)−Cubs, A's.

Lamar Johnson (2)−Rangers, Blue Jays.

Dave LaRoche (5)−Indians, Expos, YANKEES, Rangers, Blue Jays.

Pete Mackanin (2)−White Sox, Pirates.

Buck Martinez (5)−Red Sox, Giants, Mariners, Rangers, BLUE JAYS.

Rick Monday (3)−Braves, Cubs, Pirates.

Sid Monge (10)−Braves, Orioles, Red Sox, INDIANS, Royals, Expos, Yankees, Phillies, Pirates, Mariners.

John Montefusco (0)−None.

Bobby Murcer (0)−None.

Ed Ott (5)−ANGELS, A's, Phillies, Pirates, Giants.

Tom Poquette (0)−None.

Ron Reed (6)−Cubs, White Sox, Mets, Yankees, A's, PHILLIES.

Jerry Remy (6)−Orioles, RED SOX, Cubs, Brewers, A's, Giants.

Joe Rudi (5)−A's, Pirates, Cardinals, Mariners, Blue Jays.

Tony Scott (5)−Red Sox, Cubs, Indians, ASTROS, Rangers.

Reggie Smith (0)−None.

Frank Tanana (6)−RED SOX, Brewers, Phillies, Pirates, Giants, Rangers.

Jerry Turner (4)−Braves, Indians, Giants, Rangers.

Mike Vail (3)−Pirates, Cardinals, Giants.

Rick Waits (9)−Braves, Orioles, Red Sox, INDIANS, Brewers, A's, Phillies, Pirates, Rangers.

NOTE−The following players, selected by fewer than four clubs, are free to negotiate with any club: Adams, Belanger, Burroughs, Campaneris, Chalk, Cruz, Geronimo, Ron Jackson, Jefferson, Jenkins, Johnson, Mackanin, Monday, Montefusco, Murcer, Poquette, Smith, Speier, Tidrow, Vail.

Jays, Cubs Lead Way in Draft

By CARL CLARK

Ten players were selected in baseball's annual major league draft, conducted December 7 at the winter meetings in Hollywood, Fla. Players with three years in the minors who were left off the parent club's 40-man roster were eligible to be purchased by another major league club for $25,000. Each drafted player then must remain on the major league roster for the first 90 days of the season or be offered back to his former club for $12,500.

The Blue Jays and Cubs were the only clubs to take more than one player. Toronto began the proceedings by selecting Jim Gott, a pitcher in the Cardinals' organization, and opened the second round by taking outfielder Anthony Johnson from the Expos. The Cubs chose Rafael Pimentel, another pitcher in the Cardinals' chain, and Miguel Ibarra, a catcher in the Phillies' system.

The Blue Jays said that the 6-4, 200-pound Gott, 5-9 with a 3.44 earned-run average at Arkansas (Texas) in 1981, would be used in long relief. Johnson, a .319 hitter at Memphis (Southern), has exceptional speed but tends to strike out often.

Pimentel was 8-5 at Arkansas. He struck out 85 batters in 66 innings but walked 59. Ibarra batted .266 and drove in 65 runs for Reading (Eastern).

The Twins, who had selected two pitchers in each of the two previous drafts, tabbed Paul Boris, 10-6 with a 3.37 ERA for the Yankees' Columbus (International) affiliate.

Three of the players—Domingo Ramos, Jose Moreno and Rich Murray—had major league experience.

Draft choices in order of selection:

FIRST ROUND

Blue Jays —Pitcher Jim Gott from Springfield (American Association) of the Cardinals' organization.

Cubs —Pitcher Rafael Pimentel from Springfield (American Association) of the Cardinals' organization.

Twins —Pitcher Paul Boris from Columbus (International) of the Yankees' organization.

Padres —Infielder Clifton Wherry from Tucson (Pacific Coast) of the Astros' organization.

Mariners —Infielder Domingo Ramos from Syracuse (International) of the Blue Jays' organization.

Angels —Infielder Jose Moreno from Hawaii (Pacific Coast) of the Padres' organization.

Indians —First baseman-outfielder Rich Murray from Phoenix (Pacific Coast) of the Giants' organization.

Dodgers —Catcher Ramon Lora from Syracuse (International) of the Blue Jays' organization.

SECOND ROUND

Blue Jays —Outfielder Anthony Johnson from Denver (American Association) of the Expos' organization.

Cubs —Catcher Miguel Ibarra from Oklahoma City (American Association) of the Phillies' organization.

Major League Attendance for 1981

NATIONAL LEAGUE			AMERICAN LEAGUE		
	Home	Away		Home	Away
Atlanta	535,418	1,112,144	Baltimore	1,024,247	954,002
Chicago	565,637	867,495	Boston	1,060,379	1,061,602
Cincinnati	1,093,730	1,171,994	California	1,441,545	831,550
Houston	1,321,282	1,168,379	Chicago	946,651	1,068,340
Los Angeles	2,381,292	1,210,884	Cleveland	661,395	977,866
Montreal	1,534,564	965,561	Detroit	1,149,144	858,009
New York	704,244	1,006,609	Kansas City	1,279,403	1,076,624
Philadelphia	1,638,752	969,457	Milwaukee	874,292	1,144,657
Pittsburgh	541,789	989,073	Minnesota	469,090	844,101
St. Louis	1,010,247	979,212	New York	1,614,353	1,632,469
San Diego	519,161	1,019,489	Oakland	1,304,052	1,105,334
San Francisco	632,274	1,018,093	Seattle	636,276	804,473
			Texas	850,076	892,594
			Toronto	755,083	814,365
Total	12,478,390	12,478,390	Total	14,065,986	14,065,986

White Sox Deal a Winning Hand

By CARL CLARK

Once there was a time when trades were prompted primarily by a team's desire to improve itself, and by differing assessments of players' abilities. No longer. Considerations of a different nature have come to the fore. Is the player eligible for arbitration? Does he want to renegotiate his contract? When can he become a free agent? In 1981, most major trades pivoted on one or more of these questions.

How else to explain the number of quality players traded, or lost altogether, often for less than equal value? Among the prominent names were Fred Lynn, Dave Kingman, Ken Griffey, Gary Matthews, Greg Luzinski, Ellis Valentine, Rich Reuschel, Phil Garner, Steve Kemp and Cesar Cedeno.

The year's most visible speculators in the new market were the Chicago White Sox. Under the new, aggressive ownership of Jerry Reinsdorf and Eddie Einhorn, they acquired four key players in the two months immediately preceding the season. First, they signed shortstop Bill Almon, who had been released by the Mets following the 1980 campaign, in which he batted .193. Then, in the space of two weeks, Chicago added Carlton Fisk, Dennis Lamp and Greg Luzinski.

Almon in 1981 fulfilled the expectations that made him the first player selected in the June draft of 1974. He batted .301 and stole 16 bases. Lamp, obtained in a seemingly insignificant deal with the Cubs for pitcher Ken Kravec, began the season as a reliever but eventually worked his way into the starting rotation. His 2.41 earned-run average was the league's third best. Luzinski, purchased from the Phillies, paced the White Sox in home runs (21) and runs batted in (62). Fisk, who became a free agent because the Red Sox failed to offer him a new contract before the December 20 deadline, signed a five-year, $2.9 million package. The seven-time All-Star gave the White Sox the field leader they had so desperately needed.

Also lost to the Red Sox as a consequence of that clerical snafu was outfielder Fred Lynn. Moments before Lynn's grievance was to be heard by an arbitrator, the Red Sox traded him to California along with pitcher Steve Renko for outfielder Joe Rudi and pitchers Frank Tanana and Jim Dorsey. Lynn had his most dismal season in 1981; he batted .219 and failed to make the All-Star team for the first time in his seven-year career. Boston fared no better—Rudi posted a .180 average, Tanana went 4-10 and both opted for free agency at season's end.

Two other outfield sluggers were traded during spring training. Dave Kingman, who had hit 94 homers in his three seasons with the Cubs, including 48 in 1979, was traded to the Mets for outfielder Steve Henderson and cash. Kingman, who also plays first base, was prepared to sit out the season unless his $240,000-a-year contract was upgraded. The Braves traded Gary Matthews for similar reasons. Going into the final year of his pact with Atlanta, Matthews was seeking $3.5 million for five years, significantly more than the Braves were offering. Accepting somewhat less than his original demand, Matthews struck a deal with the Phillies, from whom the Braves received pitcher Bob Walk.

In late May, the Mets landed another talented outfielder, securing Ellis Valentine from the Expos for reliever Jeff Reardon and minor league outfielder Dan Norman. Valentine, however, had his first subpar season, batting just .208. Reardon, in 25 appearances for Montreal, was 2-0 with six saves and an ERA of 1.29.

Imminent free agency was the motive behind the trades of Phil Garner and Ken Griffey. The Pirates sent Garner to the Astros on August 31 for three minor league players. One of these players, Johnnie Ray, was promoted, taking Garner's second base position for the remainder of the season. In a November 4 trade of Griffey, a .308 lifetime hitter, the Reds were able to get a pair of promising pitchers from the Yankees' minor league system, Brian Ryder and Freddie Toliver.

In other noteworthy deals made after the season:

• The Indians, one week after trading second baseman Duane Kuiper to the Giants for pitcher Ed Whitson, obtained two more National League pitchers in a three-way deal with the Cardinals and Phillies. Cleveland dealt catcher Bo Diaz to the Phillies for outfielder Lonnie Smith (.324, 21 stolen bases), whom they then traded to St. Louis for Lary Sorensen and Silvio Martinez.

• The Tigers and White Sox swapped

star outfielders Steve Kemp and Chet Lemon. Kemp had taken the Tigers to arbitration two straight years and appeared to be heading that way again.

• The White Sox picked up a new first baseman in 35-year-old Tom Paciorek, who batted .326 for the Mariners but rejected their offer of a three-year, guaranteed contract. The White Sox gave up catcher Jim Essian, infielder Todd Cruz and outfielder Rod Allen.

• The Astros granted outfielder-first baseman Cesar Cedeno's long-standing request to be traded, sending him to the Reds for third baseman Ray Knight.

A chronological listing of major league deals and free-agent signings in 1981 follows:

January 7—Cubs signed pitcher Rawly Eastwick, a free agent, and assigned him to Wichita.

January 12—Braves signed pitcher Gaylord Perry, a free agent.

January 12—Reds signed first baseman Larry Biittner, a reentry free agent formerly with the Cubs.

January 15—Padres signed third baseman Kevin Bell, a free agent, and assigned him to Hawaii.

January 15—Blue Jays purchased infielder Ken Macha from Expos.

January 19—Pirates signed shortstop Larvell Blanks and outfielder Mike Anderson, free agents, and assigned them to Portland.

January 20—Pirates signed outfielder Rusty Torres, a free agent, and assigned him to Portland.

January 20—Blue Jays signed pitcher Dale Murray, a free agent, and assigned him to Syracuse.

January 21—Reds traded outfielder Cesar Geronimo to Royals for infielder German Barranca, who was assigned to Indianapolis.

January 23—Angels signed pitcher Jesse Jefferson, a reentry free agent.

January 23—Red Sox traded pitcher Steve Renko and outfielder Fred Lynn to Angels for pitchers Frank Tanana and Jim Dorsey and outfielder Joe Rudi.

January 23—Pirates re-signed first baseman-outfielder John Milner, a reentry free agent.

January 26—Angels signed pitcher Bill Travers, a reentry free agent formerly with the Brewers.

February 2—Angels signed catcher Dave Rader, a reentry free agent formerly with the Red Sox.

February 2—Angels released catcher Dave Skaggs.

February 3—Yankees re-signed first baseman Marshall Brant, a free agent, and assigned him to Columbus, O.

February 3—Blue Jays signed outfielders Bruce Boisclair and Leroy Stanton, free agents, and assigned them to Syracuse.

February 4—White Sox signed infielder Bill Almon, a free agent, and assigned him to Edmonton.

February 5—Mets released third baseman-outfielder Elliott Maddox.

February 9—Giants signed second baseman Joe Morgan, a free agent.

February 10—Orioles signed pitcher Jim Umbarger, a free agent, and assigned him to Rochester.

February 10—Angels purchased pitcher Luis Sanchez from Aguila; released pitcher John Montague.

February 10—Astros traded infielder Jimmy Sexton to A's for a player to be named; pitcher Rick Lysander was assigned to Astros' organization to complete deal, October 20.

February 11—Astros traded catcher Bruce Bochy to Mets, who assigned him to Tidewater, for players to be named; infielder Randy Rogers and catcher Stan Hough were assigned to Astros' organization to complete deal, April 3.

February 12—White Sox signed catcher Marc Hill, a free agent.

February 12—Dodgers released pitcher Doug Rau.

February 16—Cardinals conditionally purchased shortstop Rafael Santana from Yankees.

February 17—Cubs signed outfielder Jerry Morales, a free agent, and assigned him to Iowa.

February 17—Yankees signed pitcher Bill Castro, a reentry free agent formerly with the Brewers.

February 17—Blue Jays signed pitcher Dave Tomlin, a free agent, and assigned him to Syracuse.

February 18—Indians released catcher Manny Sanguillen.

February 19—Expos signed pitcher Ray Burris, a reentry free agent formerly with the Cubs.

February 23—Pirates' Portland affiliate signed pitcher Luis Tiant, a free agent.

February 26—Cubs released pitcher George Riley.

February 27—Expos released outfielder-first baseman Dan Briggs.

February 28—Cubs traded outfielder Dave Kingman to Mets for outfielder Steve Henderson and cash.

March 1—Phillies traded pitcher Randy Lerch to Brewers for outfielder Dick Davis.

March 2—A's released first baseman-outfielder Orlando Gonzalez.

March 2—Blue Jays signed pitcher John Montague, a free agent, and assigned him to Syracuse.

March 3—Cardinals signed outfielder Steve Braun, a free agent, and assigned him to Springfield.

March 4—Giants sold outfielder Terry Whitfield to Japan's Seibu Lions.

March 7—Braves traded outfielder Jeff Burroughs to Mariners for pitcher Carlos Diaz, who was assigned from Spokane to Richmond.

March 8—Cubs re-signed infielder Mick Kelleher, a reentry free agent, and assigned him to Iowa.

March 15—Indians' second baseman Jack Brohamer became free agent when his request to be traded was not honored.

March 18—White Sox signed catcher Carlton Fisk, who had become a free agent February 12 following arbitration grievance involving Red Sox' failing to meet deadline for mailing a new contract offer.

March 24—Indians signed catcher Glenn Borgmann, a reentry free agent, and assigned him to Charleston, W. Va.

March 24—Tigers purchased catcher Bill Fahey from Padres.

March 25—Braves traded outfielder Gary Matthews to Phillies for pitcher Bob Walk.

March 26—Mariners traded outfielder Rodney Craig to Indians for first baseman Wayne Cage; Craig was assigned to Charleston, W. Va., and Cage to Spokane.

March 26—Mariners released pitchers Dave Heaverlo and Rob Dressler, third baseman-outfielder Ted Cox and outfielder Willie Norwood.

March 27—A's traded pitcher Bob Lacey and pitcher Roy Moretti to Padres for pitcher Eric Mustad and infielders Kevin Bell and Tony Phillips; Moretti was assigned from West Haven to Amarillo.

March 27—Padres released pitcher Eric Rasmussen.

March 27—Twins released outfielder Bombo Rivera.

March 27—Astros released second baseman Julio Gonzalez.

March 28—White Sox traded pitcher Ken Kravec to Cubs for pitcher Dennis Lamp.

March 28—Mariners released pitcher Mike Bacsik.

March 29—Tigers released outfielder Jim Lentine.

March 30—Twins traded outfielder Ken Landreaux to Dodgers for third baseman-outfielder Mickey Hatcher, first baseman Kelly Snider and pitcher Matt Reeves; Snider and Reeves were assigned from Albuquerque to Toledo.

March 30—A's released pitcher Alan Wirth.

March 30—White Sox purchased outfielder-designated hitter Greg Luzinski from Phillies.

March 30—Phillies reacquired pitcher Carlos Arroyo from White Sox, who had purchased him conditionally, and assigned him to Oklahoma City.

March 31—Twins released pitcher Byron McLaughlin.

March 31—Mets traded pitcher Juan Berenguer to Royals for outfielder Marvell Wynne and pitcher John Skinner; Wynne was assigned from Charleston, S.C. to Jackson, and Skinner was assigned from Jacksonville to Jackson.

March 31—Mariners released catcher Dave Skaggs.

April 1—Indians traded second baseman Juan Bonilla to Padres for pitcher Bob Lacey.

April 1—Yankees traded outfielders Ruppert Jones and Joe Lefebvre and pitchers Tim Lollar and Chris Welsh to Padres for outfielder Jerry Mumphrey and pitcher John Pacella.

April 1—White Sox traded outfielder Thad Bosley to Brewers for first baseman-outfielder John Poff; Bosley was assigned to Vancouver, Poff to Edmonton.

April 1—Astros traded pitcher Ken Forsch to Angels for second baseman Dickie Thon.

April 1—Angels released pitchers Jim Barr and Dave LaRoche.

April 1—White Sox traded pitcher Mike Proly to Phils for second baseman Jay Loviglio.

April 1—Angels traded first baseman Jason Thompson to Pirates for catcher Ed Ott and pitcher Mickey Mahler.

April 1—Orioles traded shortstop Kiko Garcia to Astros for outfielder Chris Bourjos and cash; Bourjos was assigned to Rochester.

April 1—Brewers released pitcher Paul Mitchell.

April 1—Cubs traded infielder Mick Kelleher, on Iowa roster, to Tigers for cash and a player to be named; deal was later completed by a cash settlement.

April 1—Mariners released shortstop Mario Guerrero.

April 1—Rangers released designated hitter-outfielder Willie Horton.

April 1—Expos released catcher John Tamargo.

April 1—Astros reclaimed pitcher Billy Smith from Mets, who had selected Smith from Tucson in the 1980 major league draft.

April 2—Royals released infielder Jerry Terrell.

April 2—Expos released pitcher Fred Norman.

April 2—Mariners sold first baseman Wayne Cage to Japan's Hankyu Braves.

April 3—Cardinals signed second baseman Julio Gonzalez, a free agent.

April 3—Astros traded shortstop Mike Fischlin to Indians for cash or a player to be named; Fischlin was assigned to Charleston, W. Va., and outfielder

Jim Lentine was assigned to Astros' organization to complete deal, September 28.

April 3—Astros traded outfielder-first baseman Gary Rajsich to Mets for outfielder John Csefelvay; Rajsich was assigned to Tidewater and Csefelvay was assigned from Lynchburg to Columbus, Ga.

April 3—Yankees reclaimed pitcher Dave Wehrmeister from Royals, who had selected Wehrmeister from Columbus, O., in the 1980 major league draft.

April 3—Mexico City Tigers reclaimed outfielder Carlos Lopez from Cardinals, who had selected Lopez in the 1980 major league draft.

April 4—Padres released second baseman Dave Cash.

April 5—Mets purchased pitcher Dan Boitano from Brewers' Vancouver affiliate and assigned him to Tidewater.

April 6—Mariners signed third baseman Lenny Randle, a reentry free agent formerly with the Cubs.

April 6—Pirates traded pitcher Bob Owchinko to A's for cash and a player to be named; pitcher Ernie Camacho was assigned to Pirates to complete deal, April 10.

April 6—Mets traded catcher Bruce Benton to Cubs for cash or a player to be named; Benton was assigned to Iowa.

April 6—Mets traded pitcher Ed Glynn to Indians for a player to be named; pitcher Dominick Bullinger was assigned to Mets' organization to complete deal, December 14.

April 6—Red Sox released pitcher Skip Lockwood.

April 6—Mets traded pitcher Mark Bomback to Blue Jays' Syracuse affiliate for cash or a player to be named; pitcher Charlie Puleo was assigned from Syracuse to Tidewater to complete deal, April 14.

April 6—Yankees re-signed catcher Johnny Oates, a reentry free agent.

April 7—Royals signed catcher Jerry Grote, free agent.

April 7—A's signed pitcher Dave Heaverlo, a free agent, and assigned him to Tacoma.

April 7—Cardinals reclaimed catcher George Bjorkman from Giants, who had selected Bjorkman from Springfield in the 1980 major league draft.

April 7—White Sox released catcher-outfielder Ron Pruitt.

April 8—Red Sox traded pitcher Dick Drago to Mariners for pitcher Manny Sarmiento, who was assigned to Pawtucket.

April 8—Mariners signed third baseman-outfielder Ted Cox, a free agent, and assigned him to Spokane.

April 9—Yankees reclaimed pitcher Tom Filer from A's, who had selected Filer from Columbus, O., in the 1980 major league draft.

April 9—A's signed Bo McLaughlin, a free agent.

April 9—Indians signed outfielder Jim Lentine, a free agent, and assigned him to Charleston, W. Va.; released outfielder Dell Alston from same club.

April 17—Yankees signed pitcher Dave LaRoche, a free agent.

April 17—Indians signed catcher-outfielder Ron Pruitt, a free agent, and assigned him to Charleston, W. Va.

April 17—Astros signed pitcher David Clyde, a free agent, and assigned him to Columbus, Ga.

April 17—Dodgers released pitcher Don Stanhouse.

April 19—Rangers signed outfielder Bobby Bonds, a free agent, and assigned him to Wichita.

April 20—Angels released catcher Dave Rader.

April 20—Giants traded first baseman Mike Ivie to Astros for outfielder-first baseman Dave Bergman and outfielder Jeff Leonard, who was assigned to Phoenix.

April 22—Angels signed pitcher Doug Rau, a free agent, and assigned him to Redwood.

April 27—Cubs traded catcher Barry Foote to Yankees for pitcher Tom Filer and cash; Filer was assigned from Columbus, O., to Iowa.

April 28—Angels' Salt Lake City affiliate activated catcher Bob Davis, who had begun the season as a non-playing coach.

May 1—Braves released outfielder Mike Lum.

May 4—Pirates' Portland affiliate signed outfielder Willie Horton, a free agent.

May 10—Expos purchased infielder Mike Phillips from Padres.

May 10—Brewers traded catcher Buck Martinez to Blue Jays for outfielder Gil Kubski, who was assigned from Syracuse to Vancouver.

May 17—Cubs signed first baseman-oufielder Mike Lum, a free agent.

May 18—Tigers released catcher Duffy Dyer.

May 20—Yankees traded first baseman Jim Spencer and pitcher Tom Underwood to A's for first baseman Dave Revering, outfielder Mike Patterson and pitcher Chuck Dougherty; Patterson was assigned to Columbus, O., and Dougherty was assigned from San Jose to Ft. Lauderdale.

May 27—Mets released pitcher Dave Roberts.

May 29—Expos traded outfielder Ellis Valentine to Mets for pitcher Jeff Reardon, outfielder Dan Norman and a player to be named; Norman was assigned from Tidewater to Denver.

June 4—Cubs purchased outfielder Bobby Bonds from Rangers' affiliate.

June 7—Cardinals traded outfielder Tony Scott to Astros for pitcher Joaquin Andujar.

June 7—Yankees purchased pitcher George Frazier from Cardinals' Springfield affiliate and assigned him to Columbus, O.

June 8—Reds traded first baseman Harry Spilman to Astros for second baseman Rafael Landestoy.

June 10—A's purchased outfielder Rick Bosetti from Blue Jays.

June 10—Rangers released pitcher Adrian Devine.

June 12—Yankees traded pitcher Doug Bird, cash estimated at $400,000 and a player to be named to Cubs for pitcher Rick Reuschel; pitcher Mike Griffin was assigned to Cubs to complete deal, August 5.

June 15—Phillies signed outfielder-third baseman Elliott Maddox, a free agent, and assigned him to Oklahoma City.

June 20—Tigers signed outfielder Bernie Carbo, a free agent, and assigned him to Evansville.

August 3—Giants released catcher Mike Sadek.

August 4—Giants released pitcher Randy Moffitt and outfielder Billy North.

August 8—Blue Jays purchased pitcher Juan Berenguer from Royals.

August 8—Braves released catcher Bill Nahorodny.

August 11—Giants acquired utilityman Mike Turgeon from Cubs' Iowa affiliate to complete deal of December 12, 1980, in which Giants traded second baseman Joe Strain and pitcher Phil Nastu to Cubs for outfielders Jerry Martin and Jesus Figueroa and a player to be named; Turgeon was assigned to Phoenix.

August 12—Rangers purchased outfielder Tom Poquette from Red Sox.

August 13—Dodgers released catcher Joe Ferguson.

August 13—Indians released pitcher Ross Grimsley.

August 15—Cubs traded pitcher Lynn McGlothen to White Sox for cash or a player to be named.

August 18—Rangers released catcher Larry Cox.

August 19—Mets signed pitcher Mike Marshall, a free agent.

August 19—Cubs acquired second baseman Pat Tabler from Yankees for cash or a player to be named.

August 20—Pirates traded first baseman-outfielder John Milner to Expos for first baseman Willie Montanez.

August 23—Twins traded first baseman-outfielder Ron Jackson to Tigers for a player to be named; first baseman-outfielder Tim Corcoran, on Evansville roster, was assigned to Twins to complete deal, September 4.

August 24—Phillies released infielder John Vukovich.

August 25—Indians purchased pitcher Dennis Lewallyn from Rangers' Wichita affiliate.

August 27—Reds released pitcher Bill Bonham.

August 27—A's released catcher Tim Hosley.

August 30—Twins traded pitcher Jerry Koosman to White Sox for shortstop Ivan Mesa and third baseman Ronnie Perry, cash and a player to be named; Mesa and Perry were assigned from Glens Falls to Toledo, and outfielder Randy Johnson was assigned to Twins' organization to complete deal, September 2.

August 31—Dodgers released shortstop Pepe Frias.

August 31—Phillies released pitcher Nino Espinosa.

August 31—Pirates traded second baseman Phil Garner to Astros for second baseman Johnny Ray, on Tucson roster, and players to be named; outfielder Kevin Houston was assigned to Alexandria and pitcher Randy Niemann was assigned to Portland to complete deal, September 9.

September 1—Royals released catcher Jerry Grote.

September 1—Angels signed catcher Joe Ferguson, a free agent.

September 1—Pirates traded pitcher Grant Jackson to Expos for cash or a player to be named.

September 1—White Sox released pitcher Francisco Barrios.

September 3—Brewers conditionally purchased pitcher Donnie Moore from Cardinals' Springfield affiliate; returned him November 5.

September 8—Rangers purchased pitcher Bob Lacey from Indians.

September 8—Expos released first baseman Tommy Hutton.

September 8—Dodgers signed catcher Jerry Grote, a free agent.

September 9—White Sox purchased outfielder Jerry Turner from Padres.

September 10—Blue Jays signed pitcher Nino Espinosa, a free agent.

September 10—Reds traded pitcher Doug Bair to Cardinals for second baseman Neil Fiala and pitcher Joe Edelen.

September 10—White Sox purchased outfielder Jerry Hairston from Mexico City Reds.

September 25—Angels released pitcher Doug Rau.

October 5—Pirates released pitcher Luis Tiant.

October 5—Tigers released pitcher Mark Fidrych.

October 5—Braves released pitcher Gaylord Perry.

October 12—Mets released pitcher Mike Marshall.

October 13—Yankees released third baseman Eric Soderholm.

October 14—Dodgers released catcher Jerry Grote.

October 14—Cardinals released pitcher Jim Otten.

October 15—Angels released catcher Bob Davis.

October 20—Phillies traded infielder Ramon Aviles to Rangers for pitcher Dave Rajsich.

October 21—Cardinals traded pitcher Bob Sykes to Yankees for outfielder Willie McGee.

October 22—Mariners released shortstop Rick Auerbach.

October 22—Mets released pitcher Dyar Miller.

October 23—Brewers traded pitcher Buster Keeton to Astros for pitcher Pete Ladd; Keeton was assigned to Tucson, Ladd to Vancouver.

October 23—Cubs released outfielder Bobby Bonds.

October 23—Reds traded second baseman Junior Kennedy to Cubs for a player to be named.

October 23—Royals traded infielder Manny Castillo, on Omaha roster, to Mariners for a player to be named.

October 23—Red Sox traded pitcher Manny Sarmiento, on Pawtucket roster, to Pirates for a player to be named.

October 23—White Sox traded pitcher Dewey Robinson and first baseman Gary Holle, the latter on Edmonton roster, to Phillies for infielder Jose Castro, on Oklahoma City roster; Robinson and Holle were assigned to Oklahoma City.

October 26—Pirates released third baseman Kurt Bevacqua.

November 4—Reds traded outfielder Ken Griffey to Yankees for pitcher Brian Ryder, on Columbus roster, and a player to be named; pitcher Freddie Toliver was assigned to Indianapolis to complete deal, December 9.

November 14—Indians traded second baseman Duane Kuiper to Giants for pitcher Ed Whitson.

November 17—Yankees traded third baseman Aurelio Rodriguez to Blue Jays for a player to be named; catcher Mike Lebo was assigned to Columbus, O., to complete deal, December 9.

November 20—In a three-way deal, Indians traded catcher Bo Diaz to Phillies for outfielder Lonnie Smith and a player to be named, then traded Smith to Cardinals for pitchers Silvio Martinez and Lary Sorensen; Phillies assigned pitcher Scott Munninghoff to Indians' Charleston, W. Va., affiliate to complete deal, December 9.

November 24—Twins released first baseman Danny Goodwin.

November 25—Royals released pitcher Ken Brett.

November 27—White Sox traded outfielder Chet Lemon to Tigers for outfielder Steve Kemp.

November 27—Reds re-signed outfielder Mike Vail, a reentry free agent.

December 2—Dodgers re-signed outfielder Rick Monday, a reentry free agent.

December 4—A's signed outfielder Joe Rudi, a reentry free agent formerly with the Red Sox.

December 6—Blue Jays re-signed catcher Buck Martinez, a reentry free agent.

December 6—Angels purchased catcher Bob Boone from Phillies.

December 7—Cards purchased pitcher Mike Stanton from Indians.

December 7—Giants traded pitcher Allen Ripley to Cubs for pitcher Doug Capilla.

December 8—Phillies traded catcher Keith Moreland and pitchers Dan Larson and Dickie Noles to Cubs for pitcher Mike Krukow and a player to be named.

December 8—Cubs signed pitcher Fergie Jenkins, a reentry free agent formerly with the Rangers.

December 8—Cubs signed pitcher Bill Campbell, a

reentry free agent formerly with the Red Sox.

December 8—Red Sox re-signed second baseman Jerry Remy, a reentry free agent.

December 9—Dodgers traded pitcher Rick Sutcliffe and second baseman Jack Perconte to Indians for outfielder Jorge Orta, catcher Jack Fimple and pitcher Larry White.

December 9—Mariners traded outfielder-third baseman Dan Meyer to A's for pitcher Rich Bordi.

December 9—Tigers traded pitchers Dan Schatzeder and Mike Chris to Giants for outfielder Larry Herndon; Chris was assigned to Phoenix.

December 9—Astros traded outfielder Gary Woods to Cubs for outfielder Jim Tracy; Woods was assigned from Tucson to Iowa and Tracy was assigned to Tucson.

December 9—A's traded pitcher Roy Thomas to Mariners for outfielder Rusty McNealy and pitcher Tim Hallgren; Thomas was assigned to Salt Lake City.

December 9—Cardinals purchased pitcher Eric Rasmussen from Yucatan and pitcher Vicente Romo from Coatzacoalcos and assigned both to Louisville.

December 10—Cardinals traded outfielder Sixto Lezcano and a player to be named to Padres for pitcher Steve Mura and a player to be named.

December 11—Pirates traded shortstop Tim Foli to Angels for catcher Brian Harper.

December 11—Mariners traded outfielder Tom Paciorek to White Sox for shortstop Todd Cruz, catcher Jim Essian and outfielder Rod Allen.

December 11—Reds traded pitcher Scott Brown to Royals for outfielder Clint Hurdle.

December 11—Royals traded pitchers Rich Gale and Bill Laskey, the latter on Omaha roster, to Giants for outfielder Jerry Martin.

December 11—Royals re-signed outfielder Cesar Geronimo, a reentry free agent.

December 11—Dodgers signed shortstop Mark Belanger, a reentry free agent formerly with the Orioles.

December 11—Pirates traded first baseman-outfielder Doe Boyland to Giants for pitcher Tom Griffin; Boyland was assigned to Phoenix.

December 11—Mets traded shortstop Frank Taveras to Expos for pitcher Steve Ratzer and cash.

December 11—Giants re-signed second baseman Joe Morgan, a free agent.

December 11—Rangers traded pitcher Jim Kern to Mets for second baseman Doug Flynn and pitcher Dan Boitano.

December 14—Tigers released pitcher Dennis Kinney.

December 15—Yankees re-signed pitcher Ron Guidry, a reentry free agent.

December 17—Cubs released second baseman Steve Dillard and outfielder Mike Lum.

December 17—Angels purchased first baseman Craig Cacek from Pirates' Portland affiliate.

December 18—Astros traded first baseman-outfielder Cesar Cedeno to Reds for third baseman Ray Knight.

December 23—Yankees signed outfielder Dave Collins, a reentry free agent formerly with the Reds.

December 28—Twins traded outfielder Hosken Powell to Blue Jays for a player to be named; first baseman Greg Wells was assigned to Twins to complete deal, January 18, 1982.

December 28—Blue Jays traded pitcher Paul Mirabella to Cubs for a player to be named; Mirabella was assigned to Iowa.

December 29—Cardinals re-signed pitcher Joaquin Andujar, a reentry free agent.

Lindstrom, Reiser Died in 1981

By CARL CLARK

Foremost among baseball notables who died in 1981 were two of the youngest players ever to stride into the spotlight: Fred Lindstrom and Pete Reiser. Lindstrom holds the distinction of being the youngest player in World Series history. Reiser, the youngest batting champion in National League annals, won the 1941 crown before his 23rd birthday.

As an 18-year-old third baseman for John McGraw's New York Giants, Lindstrom rapped 10 hits in 30 at-bats in the 1924 Series against the Washington Senators. Four of those hits came in Game 5 against Walter Johnson. What is remembered more, however, is that with two out in the bottom of the 12th inning of Game 7 at Washington, Earl McNeely's routine grounder struck a pebble and shot over Lindstrom's head, allowing Muddy Ruel to sprint home with the deciding run. The Senators had tied the score in the eighth inning when Bucky Harris drove in two runs with the benefit of an almost identical hop.

Lindstrom played eight more seasons for the Giants. In 1928, he batted .358 with a league-leading 231 hits. Two years later, he again collected 231 hits and compiled a .379 average. The only other batters to collect more than 230 hits twice are Rogers Hornsby and George Sisler.

Switched to the outfield in 1931, partly because of chronic back ailments, Lindstrom hit over .300 for the sixth consecutive season. His passion for the game, however, began to wane when, in 1932, teammate Bill Terry was chosen to succeed McGraw as manager, a position which Lindstrom believed would be his. Upset, he asked Terry to trade him. Terry obliged, sending him to Pittsburgh.

"It was the worst mistake I ever made," Lindstrom once said. "If I just could have accepted that setback, it would have worked out all right in time. I'm sure I'd have managed some club. It was just a matter of waiting. But I fouled the whole thing up—forever."

Lindstrom spent two seasons with the Pirates, then in 1935 helped the Chicago Cubs win the N.L. pennant with his clutch hitting during a 21-game winning streak in September. He was released after a six-game setback against Detroit in the World Series, in which he collected three hits in 15 at-bats. Lindstrom began

Fred Lindstrom . . . Series hero.

the next season with Brooklyn but soon retired.

On McGraw's list of the 20 greatest players, Lindstrom ranked ninth, ahead of Sisler, Lou Gehrig, Al Simmons, Christy Mathewson and Walter Johnson. Commenting on that list some 20 years ago, Lindstrom said: "You notice one thing about McGraw's list—every one of those 20, except No. 9, has been elected to baseball's Hall of Fame. Well, maybe I'll make it someday. I hope so." His wish came true in 1976 by action of the Veterans Committee.

Lindstrom died October 4 in his hometown of Chicago. He was 75.

By the testimony of his contemporaries, Reiser would have joined Lindstrom in Cooperstown had it not been for a long series of injuries. In his first full season in the majors (1941), Reiser batted a league-leading .343 and sparked the Brooklyn Dodgers to their first pennant in 21 years. He also was the league leader in slugging percentage (.558), runs (117), doubles (39) and triples (17).

The next spring, Reiser picked up where he left off. In mid-July, the switch-hitting center fielder was batting

Pete Reiser (7) was plagued by injury problems throughout his career.

.379. He was an irresistible force, or so it seemed, until his first close encounter with an immovable object. Although he had a running start, Pistol Pete found the wall at St. Louis' Sportsman's Park unyielding. He suffered a serious concussion and a separated shoulder and tumbled to .310 that year.

After three years in the Army—where he dislocated his shoulder making a catch for Camp Lee, Va.—Reiser led the league in stolen bases in 1946 with 34 and set a major league record (later tied by Rod Carew) with seven steals of home. His .309 mark in 1947 helped the Dodgers to another pennant, but in June of that year he again crashed into a barrier.

"They thought I had reached the end," Reiser recalled. "Playing against Pittsburgh at Ebbets Field, I caromed off the center-field wall while traveling at top speed. For three days I couldn't move. Everyone thought I was paralyzed. They even called in the priest and I received the last rites of the Catholic Church."

Reiser played five more seasons—with Brooklyn in 1948, the Boston Braves in 1949-50, Pittsburgh in 1951 and Cleveland in 1952—but never hit higher than .272.

Broken ankles, a torn knee cartilage, wrenched arm muscles, ripped elbow ligaments, a broken collarbone and five severe concussions. Did Reiser regret his reckless play?

Reminiscing for Donald Honig's "Baseball When the Grass Was Real," a collection of interviews with the players of his era, Reiser said: "I remember somebody asking me one time how long I think I would have played and what my averages might have been if I hadn't played as hard as I did. If I hadn't played that way, I told him, I may never have got there to begin with . . . You slow up a half step, and it's the beginning of your last ball game. It might take a few years, but you're on your way out."

Reiser died October 25 at Palm Springs, Calif. He was 62.

Death also claimed a pair of former St.

Louis Cardinals pitchers, Wild Bill Hallahan and Paul Dean. Hallahan, 78, won many important games for the Redbirds in the early 1930s, including one in the 1930 World Series and two in the '31 Series. Dean, 67, and his brother, Dizzy, won two games apiece in the Cardinals' 1934 Series triumph over Detroit.

Others who died in 1981 included Gee Walker, standout outfielder for Detroit in the 1930s and six times a .300 hitter; Andy High, N.L. third baseman from 1922-34 who appeared in three World Series for the Cardinals; and Steve Macko, infielder for the Cubs who succumbed to cancer at age 27.

The most well-known front office personality to die in 1981 was 85-year-old Frank Lane, former general manager for the White Sox, Cardinals, Indians and Kansas City A's. Lane made more than 400 deals, including 241 trades while he ran the White Sox.

No one was safe. In 1960, Lane traded Indians home run king Rocky Colavito to Detroit for Harvey Kuenn, the American League batting champion from the previous season. Later that year, he traded his manager at Cleveland, Joe Gordon, for Tigers Manager Jimmy Dykes.

Lane said that his best trades were the ones that brought Nellie Fox and Billy Pierce to the White Sox and that his worst was sending the Cardinals' Bill Virdon to the Pirates for Bobby Del Greco and Dick Littlefield.

Longtime occupants of the press box, Dan Daniel and Bob Elson, also died. Daniel, 91, for many years a New York correspondent and columnist for THE SPORTING NEWS, received the Hall of Fame's J. G. Taylor Spink Award in 1972. Elson, 76, a broadcaster identified primarily with the White Sox, was inducted into the Hall of Fame in 1979.

An alphabetical list of baseball deaths in 1981 follows:

Robert B. Abel, 83, president of the Western International League for 10 years in the 1940s and 1950s, at Tacoma, Wash., March 14.

Edward Wilbur (Eddie) Ainsmith, 91, catcher for Washington from 1910-18, Detroit from 1919-21, the St. Louis Cardinals from 1921-23, Brooklyn in 1923 and the New York Giants in 1924, at Ft. Lauderdale, Fla., September 6; best season for the .232 lifetime hitter was 1922, when he batted .293 with 13 homers and 59 RBIs.

Horace Tanner Allen, 82, outfielder who played four games for Brooklyn in 1919, at Canton, N.C., July 5.

Don Avery, 57, administrator of minor league transactions and contracts for the National Association, at Inverness, Fla., October 9.

Samuel Thomas (Sam) Barnes, 81, second baseman in seven games for Detroit in 1921, at Montgomery, Ala., February 19.

William Lear (Bill) Bayne, 82, pitcher for the St. Louis Browns from 1919-24, Cleveland in 1928 and the Boston Red Sox in 1929-30, at St. Louis, Mo., May 22; best season for the 31-32 lifetime hurler was 1921, when he was 11-5; batted .290 in 214 at-bats.

Lester Biederman, 74, retired sports editor of the Pittsburgh Press and longtime correspondent for the THE SPORTING NEWS who covered the Pirates for 31 years, of cancer, at Ft. Myers, Fla., November 30; served as president of the Baseball Writers' Association of America in 1959.

Homer Blackburn, 77, scout for Cincinnati from 1952-58 and Houston from 1969-74, at Zelienople, Pa., August 7.

Albert Bool, 84, catcher for three major league teams, killed when he was pinned beneath a pick-up truck he had been operating on his farm near Lincoln, Neb., September 27; played 129 games with .237 batting average for Washington in 1928, Pittsburgh in 1930 and the Boston Braves in 1931.

William D. (Dick) Bowie, 57, Baltimore Orioles' scouting supervisor for the middle Atlantic states, of a heart attack, at Hagerstown, Md., September 1; he had been scouting for the Orioles since 1968.

Myrl Lincoln Brown, 83, pitcher with a 3-1 record and 5.97 ERA for Pittsburgh in 1922, at Harrisburg, Pa., February 23.

Earle Francis Brucker, Sr., 80, backup catcher for the Philadelphia Athletics from 1937-40 and 1943 and manager of Cincinnati for five games in 1952, at San Diego, Calif., May 8; batted .290 in 241 games, including .374 in 53 games in 1938; pitching coach for Athletics from 1941-49, the St. Louis Browns in 1950 and Cincinnati in 1952; managed at Ogden (Pioneer) in 1953-54; his son caught two games for the Athletics in 1948.

Lawrence E. (Larry) Brumit, Sr., 73, former president of the old Georgia-Florida League in the early 1960s, at Savannah, Ga., in early April.

Samuel Dewey (Sammy) Byrd, 74, outfielder for the New York Yankees from 1929-34 and Cincinnati in 1935-36 and later a successful golf pro, at Mesa, Ariz., May 11; he had little opportunity to play in Yankees outfield that included Babe Ruth, Earle Combs and Ben Chapman, but was a steady backup, batting .274 in 744 games; won 23 tournaments during his golf career.

Larry Claflin, 53, sports director of WITS-AM radio in Boston and a former columnist for the Boston Herald-American and correspondent for THE SPORTING NEWS, at Boston, Mass., June 21.

Gowell Sylvester Claset, 73, pitcher in eight games for the 1933 Philadelphia Athletics, at St. Petersburg, Fla., March 8; he had a 2-0 record with a 9.53 ERA.

Merrill Russell Combs, 61, a scout for Cleveland since 1975 and an American League infielder for Boston in 1947 and 1949-50, Washington in 1950 and Cleveland in 1951-52, at Riverside, Calif., July 8; in 140 games he batted .202.

Mark Connors, 22, South Atlantic League umpire, of injuries received in an automobile accident, at Asheville, N.C., July 11.

Dan Daniel, 91, a New York sportswriter for more than 60 years and for many of those years a correspondent and columnist for THE SPORTING NEWS, at Pompano Beach, Fla., July 1; Daniel's primary assignment for TSN was covering the Yankees; a former president of the Baseball Writers' Association of America and a member of baseball's rules committee, he was one of the winners of the Hall of Fame's J.G. Taylor Spink Award in 1972; although baseball was his forte, he reported on football and was one of the founders of Ring

Magazine, a boxing publication.

Paul Dee Dean, 67, who teamed with his Hall of Fame brother, Dizzy, to pitch the St. Louis Cardinals to a 1934 World Series championship over Detroit, of a heart attack, at Springdale, Ark., March 17; he pitched for the Cardinals from 1934-39, the New York Giants in 1940-41 and the St. Louis Browns in 1943, but it was in his first two seasons that he made his mark; he was 19-11 in '34, including a no-hitter against Brooklyn (two years earlier he had pitched a no-hitter for Columbus of the American Association), and 19-12 the next year; he and Dizzy each won two games in the '34 Series; after his sophomore season, Paul injured his arm and won only 12 more games in the majors, winding up 50-34 lifetime with an ERA of 3.75; after contract hassles, Paul reported to camp in 1936 fifty pounds over his playing weight; working in relief early that season, he felt a sting in his arm—he didn't win another game that season and worked in only one contest in 1937.

George Emerson Dickman, 66, pitcher for the Boston Red Sox in 1936 and from 1938-41, at New York, N.Y., April 27; his career record was 22-15; coached Princeton University from 1949-51, leading his team into the College World Series in '51.

Philip C. Dixon, 73, owner of the Oklahoma City franchise (American Association) in the early 1970s, at Tulsa, Okla., June 21.

Jerry Donovan, 73, longtime consultant to the San Francisco Giants and a former minor league president, at San Francisco, Calif., August 29; an outfielder for several Pacific Coast League teams in the 1930s, he joined the Giants in 1958 and at various times was business manager and general manager; he was president of the old Far West League for several years, beginning with its formation in 1948, and later head of the California League.

Clarence E. Eldridge, 92, an American League umpire in 1914 and later sports editor of the old Detroit Times, at Seminole, Fla., February 7.

Robert A. (Bob) Elson, 76, longtime Chicago sportscaster, at Chicago, Ill., March 10; prior to World War II, he called home games for the Cubs and White Sox, then went exclusively with the White Sox, home and road, for more than 20 years; his last year as a play-by-play man was 1970, when he called Oakland's games; handled 12 World Series and nine All-Star Games; also did games of hockey's Chicago Black Hawks and the NFL's Chicago Cardinals; inducted into the Baseball Hall of Fame in 1979.

James E. (Jim) Enright, 70, for many years a Chicago sportswriter and college basketball official, of kidney failure following a long illness, at Chicago, Ill., December 20; officiated from 1929-64 and in 1979 became the eighth official to be enshrined in the Naismith Basketball Hall of Fame in Springfield, Mass.; covered the Chicago Cubs for 20 years beginning in the mid-1940s; he also wrote a college basketball column for THE SPORTING NEWS.

Thomas Francis (Frank) Fahey, 83, a scout for 33 years until his retirement in 1977, at St. Paul, Minn., January 17; scouted for the Chicago Cubs, St. Louis Cardinals, Cleveland, Milwaukee Braves, Los Angeles Angels and Boston Red Sox.

Lynn Faris, 51, radio and television broadcaster for the Kansas City A's from 1965-67 and a TV announcer for Minnesota in 1972, at Minneapolis, Minn., October 20.

Louis Henry William (Lou) Fette, 73, a pitcher who won 20 games as a rookie for the Boston Bees in 1937, at Warrensburg, Mo., January 3; that 20-10 season, in which he led the National League in shutouts (five), was his only winning campaign;

he pitched for Boston until 1940, when he split the season with Brooklyn, then returned to his original club for five games in 1945; in 109 games, he compiled a 41-40 record with a 3.15 ERA and 14 shutouts.

James Leroy Finigan, 52, a member of the American League All-Star team as a rookie third baseman for the Philadelphia Athletics in 1954, at Quincy, Ill., May 16; he spent six years in the majors but never again approached the .302 average of his rookie season; he was the starting third baseman for the Americans in the 1955 All-Star Game, but batted only .255 that season and wound up his career at .264 in 512 games; played for the A's from 1954-56, Detroit in 1957, San Francisco in 1958 and Baltimore in 1959.

Eugene Francis Joseph (Huck) Geary, 64, shortstop for Pittsburgh in 1942-43, at Cuba, N.Y., January 27; batted .160 in 55 games.

Frank (Chick) Genovese, 66, minor league player and manager, and a scout for San Francisco from 1958 until his death, at Orlando, Fla., February 12; set American Association record in mid-1940s by playing 268 successive games in the outfield without an error; credited with the discovery of Juan Marichal.

Joseph Henry (Joe) Giebel, 89, catcher in one game for the 1913 Philadelphia Athletics, at Washington, D.C., March 17.

Grant Gillis, 80, infielder for Washington in 1927-28 and the Boston Red Sox in 1929, at Thomasville, Ala., February 4; batted .245 in 62 games.

Robert E. Lee (Bobby) Goff, 76, former major league scout and coach and minor league player, manager and executive, at Sulphur Springs, Tex., January 13; scouted for the St. Louis Browns in 1945-46 and Cleveland (for whom he coached in 1971) from 1945-70; he managed several minor league clubs and was general manager at Dallas (Texas League) in the late 1940s.

Gene Leroy Green, 47, outfielder and catcher for the St. Louis Cardinals from 1957-59, Baltimore in 1960, Washington in 1961, Cleveland in 1962-63 and Cincinnati in 1963, at St. Louis, Mo., May 23; in his two seasons as a regular, he hit .281 with 13 homers in 1958 and .280 with 18 homers in 1961; his career average was .267 in 408 games.

William Anthony (Wild Bill) Hallahan, 78, clutch lefthander for the St. Louis Cardinals in their pennant years of 1930-31 and in 1933 the starting pitcher for the National League in the first All-Star Game, at Binghamton, N.Y., July 8; he was 15-9 in 1930 and his 1-0 defeat of Brooklyn in 10 innings September 16 snapped the Robins' 11-game winning streak and put the Cardinals in first place to stay; a few weeks later, he shut out the Philadelphia Athletics in the third game of the World Series, but the A's won the Series in six games; his best season was 1931, when he led the N.L. in victories with a 19-9 record and was a World Series hero, beating the A's twice—once on a three-hit shutout—and saving the seventh-game victory for Burleigh Grimes; compiled a 102-94 slate over a 12-year career with St. Louis in 1925-26 and 1929-36, Cincinnati in 1936-37 and the Philadelphia Phillies in 1938; led the N.L. in strikeouts twice—with 177 in 1930 and 159 in 1931—and in walks three times (hence his nickname).

Andy (Bud) Harred, 55, former major league scout for Detroit, the Seattle Pilots, Milwaukee Brewers and San Diego, of a heart attack, at Fletcher, Okla., April 15.

Andrew Aird (Andy) High, 83, a National League infielder, primarily a third baseman, for Brooklyn from 1922-25, Boston from 1925-27, St. Louis from 1928-31, Cincinnati in 1932-33 and Philadelphia in 1934, at Toledo, O., February 22;

in his four years with the Cardinals, he appeared in three World Series; in the 1931 classic he had three hits in the deciding victory over Philadelphia; a .284 lifetime hitter, he managed in the minors for several years, then became a coach for the Dodgers in 1937-38; scouted for the Dodgers from 1938-42 and 1946-63; his brothers, Hugh and Charlie, were American League outfielders—Hugh for Detroit and New York from 1913-18 and Charlie for Philadelpia in 1919-20.

Harry Keller Hoch, 94, pitcher for the Philadelphia Phillies in 1908 and the St. Louis Browns in 1914-15, at Lewes, Del., October 27; pitched in 30 games, mostly in relief, and was 2-7 with a 4.35 ERA.

Stanley Ernest (Stan) Hollmig, 55, outfielder for the Philadelphia Phillies from 1949-51 and a scout for Houston since 1962, at New Braunfels, Tex., in early December; batted .255 in 81 games in 1949 and made only a handful of appearances the next two seasons.

Richard Lloyd (Dick) Hoover, 55, pitcher in two games for the 1952 Boston Braves, at Lake Placid, Fla., April 12; pitched a no-hitter for Columbus (International) against Richmond in 1955.

Walter Henry Huntzinger, 82, pitcher for the New York Giants from 1923-25 and for the St. Louis Cardinals and Chicago Cubs in 1926, at Upper Darby, Pa., August 11; posted a record of 7-8 in 60 games.

Gordon L. Jones Sr., 73, scout for Cleveland from 1948-50 and for the New York Yankees from 1951-73, at San Rafael, Calif., April 17.

Frank Joseph (Cactus) Keck, 82, pitcher for Cincinnati in 1922-23 with records of 7-6 and 3-6, at Kirkwood, Mo., February 6.

Sid C. Keener, 92, sportswriter and editor for several St. Louis newspapers from the early 1900s until 1951 and director of the Baseball Hall of Fame from 1952-63, at West Palm Beach, Fla., January 30.

Clayton Patrick (Clay) Lambert, 64, pitcher with a 2-2 record in 26 games for Cincinnati in 1946-47, at Ogden, Utah, April 3.

Frank (Trader) Lane, 85, general manager of four major league clubs and the game's most prolific trader, at Richardson, Tex., March 19; began his career in 1933 as assistant general manager for Cincinnati; after World War II, he became farm director for the New York Yankees, then served two years as president of the American Association; he became the Chicago White Sox' G.M. in 1949 and later filled the same position for the St. Louis Cardinals, Cleveland and the Kansas City A's; in the early 1970s he was director of baseball operations for Milwaukee; also was general manager for Chicago's NBA entry in the early 1960s; credited with more than 400 baseball deals, including 241 trades involving 353 players while he ran the White Sox; his most controversial moves: sending Cardinals second baseman Red Schoendienst to the New York Giants in 1956, trading Indians home run champion Rocky Colavito to Detroit in 1960 for batting champion Harvey Kuenn, and swapping his manager at Cleveland, Joe Gordon, for Detroit's manager, Jimmie Dykes.

Elmer Ellsworth Leonard, 92, pitcher for the 1911 Philadelphia Athletics, at Napa, Calif., May 27; split four decisions in five games.

Frederick Charles (Freddie) Lindstrom, 75, Hall of Fame third baseman and outfielder and the youngest player in World Series history, at Chicago, Ill., October 4; he played in the 1924 Series as an 18-year-old rookie for the New York Giants and played well, making 10 hits in 30 at-

bats—four of them in Game Five against Walter Johnson; what most people remember about his role in that Series, however, is that with two out in the bottom of the 12th inning of Game Seven at Washington, Earl McNeely's ground ball hit a pebble and shot over Lindstrom's head, allowing Muddy Ruel to race home with the deciding run; he went on to play eight more seasons with the Giants and finished up his career with Brooklyn in 1936 after stints with Pittsburgh in 1933-34 and the Chicago Cubs in 1935; seven times a .300 hitter, his best seasons were 1928, when he batted .358 and led the National League in hits with 231, and 1930, when he batted .379; managed in minors for three years and served as baseball coach at Northwestern University from 1948-62; elected to the Hall of Fame by the Veterans Committee in 1976.

George Tony Lyons, 85, pitcher for the St. Louis Cardinals in 1920 and the St. Louis Browns in 1924, at Nevada, Mo., August 12; working mostly in relief, he was 2-1 for the Cards and 3-2 for the Browns.

Steven Joseph Macko, 27, infielder for the Chicago Cubs, of cancer, at Arlington, Tex., November 15; an All-America at Baylor University, he entered pro ball with Cubs organization in 1977 and played with Chicago in parts of 1979 and 1980, hitting .250 in 25 games; injured in a collision at second base in Chicago August 5, 1980, he was taken to a hospital, where it was discovered that he had cancer; his father, Joe, is equipment manager for Texas.

Effa Manley, 81, owner of the Newark Eagles when they were the class of the Negro National League, at Los Angeles, Calif., April 18; some of the Eagles' top stars were Larry Doby, sold to Cleveland for $15,000 and Monte Irvin, sold to the New York Giants for $5,000.

Clifton Ambrose (Runt) Marr, 89, on the scene for 60 years as a scout and minor league player and manager, at Grove, Okla., August 31; scouted for the St. Louis Cardinals, New York Mets, Kansas City Athletics, Cleveland and Detroit; managed a dozen minor league clubs, all in lower classifications, and played for almost that many; offered Bob Gibson his first professional contract.

Franklin C. Matzek, 80, chronicler of the Boston Red Sox and Boston Braves for the Providence (R.I.) Journal for many years, at Sarasota, Fla., June 21.

Samuel Faulkner (Sam) McConnell, 86, third baseman in six games for the 1915 Philadelphia Athletics, at Phoenixville, Pa., June 13.

Soule James (Jim) McLeod, 72, third baseman and shortstop for Washington in 1930 and 1932 and the Philadelphia Phillies in 1933, at Little Rock, Ark., August 3; batted .203 in 92 games.

Thomas William (Tommy) Mee, 91, infielder in eight games for the 1910 St. Louis Browns, at Chicago, Ill., May 16.

Stephen Mathias (Steve) Mesner, 63, third baseman for the Chicago Cubs in 1938-39, the St. Louis Cardinals in 1941 and Cincinnati from 1943-45, at San Diego, Calif., April 6; batted .331 for Los Angeles of the Pacific Coast League in 1935 at the age of 17, but didn't live up to that promise, managing just a .252 average in 451 major league games.

John Leo O'Dowd, 90, shortstop in ten games for the 1912 New York Yankees, at Ft. Lauderdale, Fla., January 31.

Edward Joseph (Eddie) Onslow, 88, first baseman for Detroit in 1912-13, Cleveland in 1918 and Washington in 1927, at Dennison, O., May 8; the younger brother of Jack Onslow, catcher for Detroit in 1912 and the New York Giants in 1917, Eddie played in 63 games in the majors, posting a

.232 average; he was an excellent minor league player—with a .317 batting average and 430 stolen bases in 17 seasons, he was named to the International League Hall of Fame; scout for the Chicago White Sox in 1949 and the Philadelphia Athletics from 1950-53.

Raymond Francis (Ray) Oyler, 42, American League shortstop for six seasons, of a heart attack, at Bellevue, Wash., January 26; played for Detroit from 1965-68, Seattle in 1969 and California in 1970; an excellent fielder, he batted above .200 only once and his average for 542 games was .175.

Leroy Earl (Bud) Parmelee, 74, pitcher for the New York Giants from 1929-35, the St. Louis Cardinals in 1936, the Chicago Cubs in 1937 and the Philadelphia Athletics in 1939, at Monroe, Mich., August 31; prime seasons for the 59-55 lifetime hurler were 1933-35, when he was 13-8, 10-6 and 14-10, respectively.

Arthur Matthew (Art) Passarella, 71, American League umpire in 1941-42 and from 1945-53, of a heart attack, at Hemet, Calif., October 12; worked the World Series in 1945-49-52 and the All-Star Game in 1947 and 1951; after retiring from umpiring, he pursued an acting career, appearing in movies and on the television series "The Streets of San Francisco."

John Gaston Peacock, 71, backup catcher for the Boston Red Sox from 1937-44, the Philadelphia Phillies in 1944-45 and Brooklyn in 1945, at Fremont, N.C., October 17; batted .262 in 619 games.

Marino Paul Pieretti, 59, pitcher for Washington from 1945-48, the Chicago White Sox in 1948-49 and Cleveland in 1950, at San Francisco, Calif., January 30; 14-13 as a rookie, he never had another winning season and wound up with a career record of 30-38.

Anthony Francis (Tony) Piet, 74, infielder for Pittsburgh from 1931-33, Cincinnati in 1934-35, the Chicago White Sox from 1935-37 and Detroit in 1938, at Hinsdale, Ill., December 1; primarily a second baseman, his best season was 1932 when he drove in 85 runs; his batting average in 744 major league games was .277.

Alfred Pinkston, 64, winner of four consecutive Mexican League batting titles (1959-62), of a heart attack, at New Orleans, La., in March; a member of the Mexican League Hall of Fame, his .372 career batting average is the highest in the League's history.

Edward H. Prell, 76, retired Chicago Tribune sportswriter and former contributor to THE SPORTING NEWS, at Kansas City, Mo., September 1.

Harold Patrick (Pete) Reiser, 62, the youngest player to win a National League batting title, at Palm Springs, Calif., October 25; in 1941, at age 22 and in his second season in the majors, he batted .343 to spark Brooklyn to its first pennant in 21 years—that season he also led the league in slugging (.588), runs (117), doubles (39) and triples (17); his notorious encounters with outfield walls began July 19, 1942, when he ran headlong into the concrete barrier at Sportsman's Park in St. Louis; he suffered a serious concussion and was carried off the field on a stretcher, a scene which was to be repeated on 11 occasions during his career; he was batting .379 at that time, but, bothered by dizziness and headaches—ailments that would plague him the rest of his life—slipped to .310; after a three-year stint in the Army, he played three more years for the Dodgers before being traded to the Boston Braves, for whom he played two seasons before winding up his career with Pittsburgh in 1951 and Cleveland in 1952; in 1946 he led the league in stolen bases with 34 and set a record with seven steals of home, equaled only by Rod Carew in 1969; in 1947 he batted .309

and helped Brooklyn to another pennant; managed in the minors for the Dodgers' organization from 1955-59 and coached for the parent club from 1960-64; coached for the Chicago Cubs from 1965-69, California in 1970 and for the Cubs again in 1972-73.

Donald Lester Richmond, 61, third baseman for the Philadelphia Athletics in 1941 and 1946-47 and the St. Louis Cardinals in 1951, of cancer, at Elmira, N.Y., May 24; batted .211 in 56 games; managed at Batavia (New York-Pennsylvania) in 1957-58 and scouted for Cleveland in 1959 and Milwaukee in 1960-61.

Bennett Harold (Ben) Rochefort, 84, first baseman in one game for the 1914 Philadelphia Athletics, at Red Bank, N.J., April 2.

Edwin F. Schweda, 65, an outfielder who was the minors' top hitter in 1940 with a .422 mark for Lubbock of the West Texas-New Mexico League, at LaSalle, Ill., June 21.

Richard (Dick) Seay, 75, considered one of the Negro leagues' best second basemen, at Jersey City, N.J., April 6; played from 1925-47 for clubs in New York, Baltimore, Pittsburgh, Newark, Philadelphia and Brooklyn.

Danny Richard Simons, 37, former minor league infielder and a scout for the St. Louis Cardinals from 1976 until his death, in an auto accident, at Clearwater, Fla., January 21.

George Selby Smith, 79, pitcher for Detroit from 1926-29 and the Boston Red Sox in 1930, at Richmond, Va., May 26; compiled a 10-8 record with a 5.33 ERA in 132 games, almost all of them in relief.

Paul E. (Jake) Stephens, 80, star shortstop for the Pittsburgh Crawfords and Philadelphia Hillsdales of the Negro National League in the 1930s, at York, Pa., February 5.

John William Stevens, 69, assistant supervisor of umpires for the American League, at Philadelphia, Pa., September 9; he was an A.L. umpire from 1948-69 and also refereed college basketball games; umpired four World Series (1951-54-60-67) and six All-Star Games.

John Tattersall, 71, baseball historian who had tabulated the specifics on almost every home run in major league history and a contributor to THE SPORTING NEWS, at Boca Raton, Fla., May 28.

George Thompson, 55, scout for Baltimore from 1976-78 and Oakland from 1980 until he was killed by a hit-and-run driver, at Fresno, Calif., April 14.

Albert Joseph (Al) Van Camp, 76, outfielder and first baseman for Cleveland in 1928 and the Boston Red Sox in 1931-32, at Davenport, Ia., February 2; batted .261 in 141 games.

Gerald Holmes (Gee) Walker, 72, major league outfielder for 15 years and six times a .300 hitter, at Whitfield, Miss., March 20; played for Detroit from 1931-37, the Chicago White Sox in 1938-39, Washington in 1940, Cleveland in 1941 and Cincinnati from 1942-45; a .294 lifetime hitter, he batted .335 with 113 RBIs in 1937; his brother, Hub, was an outfielder for Detroit in 1931-35-45 and Cincinnati in 1936-37; managed Columbia's South Atlantic League club from 1947-49.

William Wise, 76, scout for Milwaukee from 1955-60 and St. Louis in 1969-70 and 1973-74; at Springfield, Mass., February 16.

Taft Shedron Wright, 70, American League outfielder for Washington in 1938-39, Chicago from 1940-42 and 1946-48 and Philadelphia in 1949, at Orlando, Fla., October 22; batted .311 lifetime and .337 in 1940; twice drove in more than 90 runs; managed in minors at Ottawa, Amarillo and Orlando and batted .353 as a playing manager for Orlando (Florida State) at the age of 45.

LEAGUE AND CLUB
INFORMATION

Including

Major League Directory

National League Directory

National League Team Directories

American League Directory

American League Team Directories

Major League Farm Systems

Minor League Presidents

Directory of Organized Baseball

MAJOR LEAGUES

COMMISSIONER–Bowie K. Kuhn
SECRETARY-TREASURER–Alexander H. Hadden
HEADQUARTERS–75 Rockefeller Plaza
New York, N. Y. 10019
Telephone–586-7400 (area code 212)
Teletype–710-581-4279

EXECUTIVE COUNCIL–Bowie K. Kuhn, Commissioner; Leland S. Mac-Phail, Jr., President of American League; Charles S. Feeney, President of National League; Ewing Kauffman, Allan H. Selig, Haywood C. Sullivan and Edward Bennett Williams, representatives of American League, and Daniel M. Galbreath, Robert L. Howsam, Robert A. Lurie and Ballard F. Smith, Jr., representatives of National League.

EXECUTIVE DIRECTOR OF MARKETING AND BROADCASTING–
C. J. (Tom) Villante
ADMINISTRATOR–William A. Murray
SPECIAL ASSISTANTS TO THE COMMISSIONER–
Joseph L. Reichler, Monte Irvin
DIRECTOR OF INFORMATION–Robert A. Wirz
DIRECTOR OF SECURITY–Horace J. (Harry) Gibbs
CONTROLLER–Donald C. Marr, Jr.
ASSISTANTS TO ADMINISTRATOR–George E. Pfister, Miguel A. Rodriguez
ADMINISTRATIVE ASSISTANTS–Harry Simmons, Miguel A. Rodriguez
ASSISTANT COUNSEL–Edwin M. Durso
ASSOCIATE DIRECTOR OF INFORMATION, MEDIA–Charles B. Adams
ASSISTANT DIRECTOR OF INFORMATION, PUBLICATIONS–Vince Nauss
ASSISTANT DIRECTOR OF SECURITY–Art Fuss
OFFICE MANAGER–Mary Ann Burns
BOOKKEEPER–Rita Datz

NATIONAL ASSOCIATION REPRESENTATIVES–John Johnson, President of the National Association, and members of National Association Executive Committee.

NATIONAL ASSOCIATION
OF PROFESSIONAL BASEBALL LEAGUES

PRESIDENT-TREASURER–John H. Johnson
VICE-PRESIDENT–Carl Sawatski
DIRECTOR OF PROMOTIONS–Bob Sparus
HEADQUARTERS–201 Bayshore Dr. S.E., P. O. Box A
St. Petersburg, Fla. 33731
Telephone–822-6937 (area code 813)
Teletype–810-863-0361

EXECUTIVE COMMITTEE–Carl Sawatski, Chairman, President of the Texas League; Harold M. Cooper, President of the International League, George G. MacDonald, Jr., President of the Florida State League.

National League
Organized 1876

CHARLES S. FEENEY
President and Treasurer

JOHN J. McHALE
Vice-President

PHYLLIS B. COLLINS
Secretary

BLAKE CULLEN
Administrator and Public Relations Director

KATY FEENEY
Assistant Public Relations Director

LOUIS H. KREMS
Business Manager

ROSE TROTTA
Computer Manager

JOSEPHINE TROY
Administrative Assistant

Headquarters—1 Rockefeller Plaza, New York, N. Y. 10020

Telephone—582-4213 (area code 212)

UMPIRES—Fred Brocklander, Nick Colosi, Jerry Crawford, Jerry Dale, David Davidson, Robert Engel, Bruce Froemming, Eric Gregg, Lanny Harris, H. Douglas Harvey, John Kibler, Randy Marsh, John McSherry, Ed Montague, Dave Pallone, Frank Pulli, Jim Quick, Lawrence (Dutch) Rennert, Paul Runge, Dick Stello, Terry Tata, Ed Vargo, Harry Wendelstedt, Joe West, Lee Weyer, William G. Williams.

OFFICIAL STATISTICIANS—Elias Sports Bureau, Inc., 500 5th Ave., Suite 2114, New York, N. Y. 10036. Telephone (212) 869-1530.

Players cannot be transferred from one major league club to another after June 15 to the close of the championship season except through regular waiver channels.

WAIVER PRICE, $20,000. Interleague waivers, $20,000, except for selected players and draft-excluded players.

National League President Charles S. Feeney

ATLANTA BRAVES

Chairman of the Board—William C. Bartholomay

President—R. E. (Ted) Turner III
Executive Vice-President—Allison Thornwell
Vice-President, General Manager—John Mullen
Vice-President, Player Development—Hank Aaron
Assistant to General Manager—Patrick Nugent
Director of Scouting—Paul Snyder
Manager of Broadcast Sales—Wayne Long
Director of Broadcasting—Ernie Johnson
Vice-President & Controller—Charles Sanders
Accountant—Michael Warren
Ticket Distribution Manager—Ed Newman
Ticket Manager—Andre DeLorenzo
Group Sales Manager—Larry Cancro
Director of Stadium Operations—Joe Shirley
Administrative Assistant—Mary Beth Fay
Manager—Joe Torre
Club Physician—Dr. David T. Watson
Executive Offices—P.O. Box 4064, Atlanta, Ga. 30302
Telephone—522-7630 (area code 404)

SCOUTS—Mike Arbuckle, Sam Berry, Smoky Burgess, Stu Cann, Joe Caputo, Harold Cronin, Lou Fitzgerald, Pedro Gonzalez, John Groth, Willie Harris, Gene Hassell, Herb Hippauf, Phil Holmes, Burney R. (Dickey) Martin, Bob Mavis, Rance Pless, Charles Smith, Tony Stiel, Bob Turzilli, Bob Wadsworth, Wesley Westrum, William R. Wight, Don Williams, H.F. (Red) Wooten.

PARK LOCATION—Atlanta-Fulton County Stadium, on Capitol Avenue at the junction of Interstate Highways 20, 75 and 85.

Seating capacity—52,785

FIELD DIMENSIONS—Home plate to left field at foul line, 330 feet; to center field, 402 feet; to right field at foul line, 330 feet.

CHICAGO CUBS

Chairman of the Board—Andrew J. McKenna

Executive Vice-President and General Manager—Dallas Green
Assistant to Executive Vice-President—John Cox
Director of Minor Leagues and Scouting—Gordon Goldsberry
Director of Scouting—A.B. (Vedie) Himsl
Associate Director, Minor Leagues—William Harford
Vice-President, Administration—E. R. Saltwell
Vice-President, Director of Finance and Planning—Mark McGuire
Chief Accounting Officer—Joseph A. Kirchen
Vice-President, Director of Marketing and Ad Sales—Bing Hampton
Vice-President, Director of Ticket Sales—Patty Cox Hampton
Director, Promotions and Advertising—Robert R. (Buck) Peden
Director, Speakers Bureau and Sales Manager—Mary Beth Hughes
Marketing Manager—Valentine Judge
Director, Group Sales—Frank Maloney
Ticket Manager—P. Jerome (Jerry) Foran
Director, Public Relations—Robert Ibach
Director, Publications—Peter Mead
Traveling Secretary—James Davidovich
Home Secretary—Howie Roberts
Vice-President, Director of Stadium Operations—Terry Barthelmas
Club Physician—Dr. Jacob R. Suker
Grounds Superintendent—Roy Bogren
Field Manager—Lee Elia
Executive Offices—Wrigley Field, N. Clark and Addison Streets, Chicago, Ill. 60613
Telephone—281-5050 (area code 312)

SCOUTS—Dave Bartosch, William Capps, Brandon Davis, Thomas Davis, Frank DeMoss, Walt Dixon, Gene Handley, Herman Hannah, John Hennesy, Julian Javier, Roy Johnson, Julio Navarro, Gary Nickels, John O'Neil, Evo Pusich, Jim Snyder, Eugene Thompson, Joaquin Velilla, H. D. Wilson.

PARK LOCATION—Wrigley Field, Addison Street, N. Clark Street, Waveland Avenue and Sheffield Avenue.

Seating capacity—37,272

FIELD DIMENSIONS—Home plate to left field at foul line, 355 feet; to center field, 400 feet; to right field at foul line, 353 feet.

CINCINNATI REDS

Chairman of the Board—Louis Nippert
Vice-Chairman of the Board—Robert L. Howsam
President & Chief Executive Officer—Richard Wagner
Vice-President—William J. Williams
Vice-President, Marketing—Roger Ruhl
Vice-President, Player Personnel—Sheldon Bender
Vice-President, Scouting—Joe Bowen
Business Manager—Don Tecklenburg
Treasurer—James R. Williams
Secretary—Andrew Hopple
Assistant Secretary—Henry W. Hobson Jr.
Special Assignment Scout—Ray Shore
Assistant General Manager—Woody Woodward
Assistant to Vice-President, Scouting—Larry Doughty
Director of Publicity—Jim Ferguson
Controller—D.L. Porco
Business Coordinator, Player Development—Sal Artiaga
Traveling Secretary—Doug Bureman
Director of Speakers Bureau—Gordy Coleman
Director of Stadium Operations—Doug Duennes
Director of Group Sales—Ted Williams
Director of Special Projects—Bob Kruetzkamp
Director of Season Tickets & Customer Relations—Janet Wendel
Director of Publications—John Olberding
Director of Ticket Department—Bill Stewart
Director of Broadcasting—Jim Winters
Manager—John McNamara
Club Physician—Dr. George Ballou
Executive Offices—100 Riverfront Stadium, Cincinnati, O. 45202
Telephone—421-4510 (area code 513)

SCOUTS—Larry Barton, Jr., Gene Bennett, Porter Blinn, Cam Bonifay, David Calaway, Bill Clark, Marty Daily, Larry D'Amato, Reno DeBenedetti, Elmer Gray, Edwin Howsam, Chester Montgomery, Greg Riddoch, Ed Roebuck, Fred Uhlman, George Zuraw.

PARK LOCATION—Riverfront Stadium, downtown Cincinnati, bounded by Second Street to Ohio River and from Walnut Street to Broadway.

Seating capacity—52,392

FIELD DIMENSIONS—Home plate to left field at foul line, 330 feet; to center field, 404 feet; to right field at foul line, 330 feet.

HOUSTON ASTROS

Board of Directors—John J. McMullen, Jack T. Trotter, T.H. Neyland

President and General Manager—Albert L. Rosen
Vice-President, Baseball Operations—Bob Kennedy
Administrative Asst. to the President and Traveling Secretary—Donald Davidson
Assistant to the General Manager—Andy MacPhail
Director of Minor League Operations—William J. Wood
Director of Scouting—Lynwood Stallings
Assistant, Minor League Operations and Scouting—Dan O'Brien, Jr.
Director of Public Relations—Mike Ryan
Asst. Director of Public Relations—Rick Rivers
Director of Broadcasting and Promotions—Art Elliott
Promotions, Scoreboard Operations—Paul Darst
Broadcast and Promotions Sales—Hugh Pickett
Director of Ticket Sales—Larry Serota
Manager, Season Ticket Sales—M.M. (Buddy) Hancken
Manager, Group Sales—Donna deGruyter
Administrative Asst., Major League Operations—Sandra Zimmerman
Secretary, Public Relations—Beverly Rains
Club Physicians—Drs. Harold H. Brelsford, Hatch Cummings
Public Address Announcer—J. Fred Duckett
Manager—Bill Virdon
Executive Offices—Astrodome, P.O. Box 288
Houston, Tex. 77001
Telephone—799-9500 (area code 713)
Teletype—901 991-1740
HOUSTON SPORTS ASSOCIATION, INC.
President and Chief Operating Officer—Robert G. Harter
Vice-President, Administration—E. Michael Crowley
Vice-President, Engineering—W. Gary Keller
Vice-President, Public Relations and Advertising—Ben Gillespie
Executive Vice-President, Event Sales and Management—Jimmie Fore
Director, Special Projects—Jim Weidler
Director, Service and Administration—Bill Boyd
Treasurer—A. Eugene Stoffel
Controller—Adam C. Richards
Financial Analyst—Bill Boyd
Ticket Manager—Charles T. Wall

SCOUTS—Clary Anderson, Stan Benjamin, Jack Bloomfield, Paul Florence, Ben Galante, Carl Greene, Bill Hallauer, Bob Hartsfield, Bob Kennedy, Jr., David Lakey, Gordon Lakey, Walter Matthews, Tony Pacheco, Reggie Waller, Paul Weaver, Harrison Wickel.

PARK LOCATION—Astrodome, Kirby and Interstate Loop 610

Seating capacity—45,000

FIELD DIMENSIONS—Home plate to left field at foul line, 340 feet; to center field, 406 feet; to right field at foul line, 340 feet.

LOS ANGELES DODGERS

BOARD OF DIRECTORS
Peter O'Malley, President; Harry M. Bradt, Treasurer;
Roland Seidler, Jr., Secretary; Mrs. Roland (Terry) Seidler

President—Peter O'Malley
Vice-President, Player Personnel—Al Campanis
Vice-President, Public Relations and Promotions—Fred Claire
Vice-President, Minor League Operations—William P. Schweppe
Vice-President, Marketing—Merritt Willey
Special Consultant—Walter Alston
Controller and Assistant Treasurer—Ken Hasemann
Assistant Secretary—Irene Tanji
Director, Advertising, Novelties and Souvenirs—Danny Goodman
Director, Dodgertown—Charles Blaney
Director, Stadium Operations—Bob Smith
Director, Ticket Department—Walter Nash
Director, Stadium Club and Transportation—Bob Schenz
Director, Dodger Network—David Van de Walker
Director, Scouting—Ben Wade
Director, Publicity—Steve Brener
Director, Publications—Toby Zwikel
Director, Community Relations—Don Newcombe
Community Relations—Roy Campanella
Director, Ticket Marketing—Barry Stockhamer
Director, Speakers' Bureau—Bill Shumard
Executive Pilot, Dodger 720-B Fan Jet—Captain Lewis G. Carlisle
Administrative Assistant—Ike Ikuhara
Traveling Secretary—Billy DeLury
Auditor—Michael Strange
Manager—Tom Lasorda
Club Physicians—Dr. Frank Jobe, Dr. Robert Woods
Executive Offices—Dodger Stadium, 1000 Elysian Park Avenue,
Los Angeles, Calif. 90012
Telephone—224-1500 (area code 213)

SCOUTS—Rafael Avila, Boyd Bartley, Bob Bishop, Gib Bodet, Mike Brito, Paul Duval, Jim Garland, Dick Hanlon, Dennis Haren, Gail Henley, Goldie Holt, Elvio Jimenez, Tony John, Hank Jones, John Keenan, Ron King, Ed Liberatore, Carl Lowenstine, Dale McReynolds, Tommy Mixon, John O'Neil, Regie Otero, Medardo Perez, Bill Pleis, Jerry Stephenson, Corito Varona, Guy Wellman.

PARK LOCATION—Dodger Stadium, 1000 Elysian Park Avenue.

Seating capacity—56,000

FIELD DIMENSIONS—Home plate to left field at foul line, 330 feet; to center field, 395 feet; to right field at foul line, 330 feet.

MONTREAL EXPOS

Board of Directors—Charles R. Bronfman, Lorne C. Webster,
John J. McHale, Sydney Maislin, Paul Beaudry, Hugh Hallward,
Charlemagne Beaudry, E. Leo Kolber, Melvin W. Griffin,
Louis R. Desmarais, Arnold Ludwick, Honorary Treasurer

Chairman of the Board—Charles R. Bronfman
President and Chief Executive Officer—John J. McHale
Vice-President, Baseball—Bing Devine
Director of Scouting—Danny Menendez
Director, Team Travel—Peter Durso
Director, Business Operations—Gerry Trudeau
Director of Marketing—Rene Guimond
Director of Finance—Dennis Bodin
Publicists—Monique Giroux, Richard Griffin
Coordinator of Broadcasting—Gene Kirby
Field Coordinator, Player Development—Pat Daugherty
Coordinator, Spring Training—Kevin McHale
Manager—Jim Fanning
Club Physician—Dr. Robert Brodrick
Mailing Address—P. O. Box 500, Station M, Montreal, Quebec,
Canada H1V 3P2
Telephone—253-3434 (area code 514)

SCOUTS—(special assignment)—Charlie Fox, Carroll (Whitey) Lockman, Ed
Lopat; (West Coast supervisor)—Bob Fontaine, Jr.; (regular)—Bill Adair, Terry
Boyle, Harry Bright, Cliff Ditto, Al Harper, Mercer Harris, Dick Lemay, Eddie
Lyons, Roy McMillan, Walter Millies, John (Red) Murff, Herb Newberry, Bob
Oldis, Jack Paepke, Frank Perez, Ron Piche, Harry Postove, Harry Pritikin, Jack
Warner, Jerry Zimmerman.

PARK LOCATION—Olympic Stadium, 4545 Pierre de Coubertin, Montreal,
Quebec, Canada H1V 3N7.

Seating capacity—58,838

FIELD DIMENSIONS—Home plate to left field at foul line, 325 feet; to center
field, 404 feet; to right field at foul line, 325 feet.

NEW YORK METS

Chairman of the Board—Nelson Doubleday

Directors—Nelson Doubleday, Fred Wilpon, Walter E. Freese
John W. O'Donnell, John C. Herndon, John T. Sargent
President & Chief Executive Officer—Fred Wilpon
Executive Vice-President, General Manager & Chief Operating Officer—
J. Frank Cashen
Vice-President-Administration—James Nagourney
Vice-President, Baseball Operations—James Lou Gorman
Vice-President—Alan E. Harazin
Vice-President and Controller—Harold W. O'Shaughnessy
Special Assistant to the General Manager & Team
Travel Director—Arthur Richman
Director of Scouting—Joseph McIlvaine
Ticket Manager—Bob Mandt
Director of Minor League Operations—Stephen Schryver
Director of Public Relations—Jay Horwitz
Director of Promotions—Joseph Donohue
Stadium Manager—John McCarthy
Stadium Superintendant—Samuel Nelson
Manager—George Bamberger
Club Physician—Dr. James C. Parkes II
Team Trainer—Larry Mayol
Executive Offices—William A. Shea Stadium, Roosevelt
Avenue and 126th Street, Flushing, N. Y. 11368
Telephone—672-2000 (area code 212)

SCOUTS—Ed Charles, Carmen Fusco, Dean Jongewaard, Hank Kelly, Buddy
Kerr, Dave Madison, Joe Mason, Harry Minor, Robert Minor, Julian Morgan, Roy
Partee, Carlos Pascual, Junior Roman, Terry Ryan, Bob Scheffing, Marvin Scott,
Jim Terrell, Eddy Toledo, Ollie Vanek, Bob Wellman, Len Zanke.

PARK LOCATION—William A. Shea Stadium, Roosevelt Avenue and 126th
Street, Flushing, N. Y. 11368

Ticket Information—672-3000 (area code 212)

Seating capacity—55,300

FIELD DIMENSIONS—Home plate to left field at foul line, 338 feet; to center
field, 410 feet; to right field at foul line, 338 feet.

PHILADELPHIA PHILLIES

President—Bill Giles

Partners—The Taft Baseball Co., John Drew Betz, Tri-Play Associates,
Fitz Eugene Dixon Jr., Mrs. Rochelle Levy, Robert D. Hedberg
Vice-President and General Manager—Paul Owens
Executive Vice-President—David Montgomery
Vice-President, Finance—Jerry Clothier
Vice-President, Public Relations—Larry Shenk
Secretary and Counsel—William Y. Webb
Director of Minor Leagues and Scouting—Jim Baumer
Executive Assistant—Tony Siegle
Assistant to the President—Mrs. Cathy Halpin
Ticket Manager—Ray Krise
Director of Promotions—Frank Sullivan
Director of Advertising—Tom Hudson
Traveling Secretary—Eddie Ferenz
Director of Ticket Sales—Richard Deats
Asst. Director of Minor Leagues and Scouting—Jack Pastore
Public Relations and Broadcaster—Chris Wheeler
Director of Marketing—Dennis Lehman
Director of Stadium Operations—Mike DiMuzio
Executive Secretary to Minor Leagues—Bill Gargano
Special Consultant—Pat Cassidy
Club Physician—Dr. Phillip Marone
Club Trainer—Jeff Cooper
Strength and Flexibility Instructor—Gus Hoefling
Manager—Pat Corrales
Executive Offices—Philadelphia Veterans Stadium
Mailing Address—P.O. Box 7575, Philadelphia, Pa. 19101
Telephone—463-6000 (area code 215)

SCOUTS—Special assignment scout—Hugh Alexander. Regular scouts—Ruben Amaro, Edward Bockman, George Farson, Doug Gassaway, Charles Gault, Bill Harper, Wilbur Johnson, John Jorgensen, Lou Kahn, Dick Lawlor, Anthony Lucadello, Gene Martin, Tom Oliver, Ken Parker, Bob Reasonover, Scott Reid, Joe Reilly, Tony Roig, Andy Seminick, Billy Tracy, Elmer Valo, Randy Waddill, Don Williams.

PARK LOCATION—Philadelphia Veterans Stadium, Broad Street and Pattison Avenue.

Seating capacity—65,454

FIELD DIMENSIONS—Home plate to left field at foul line, 330 feet; to center field, 408 feet; to right field at foul line, 330 feet.

PITTSBURGH PIRATES

President—Daniel M. Galbreath

Chairman of the Board—John W. Galbreath
Directors: Daniel M. Galbreath, David M. Roderick, Thomas
P. Johnson, Thomas P. Johnson, Jr., James M. Johnson, James
W. Phillips, Willard F. Rockwell, Jr., James H. Higgins
Executive Vice-President—Harding Peterson
Vice-President, Administration—Joseph M. O'Toole
Vice-President, Public Relations and Marketing—Jack Schrom
Vice-President and Secretary—Thomas P. Johnson
Assistant to Vice-President for Sales and Promotions—Olin J. DePolo
Treasurer, Assistant Secretary—Douglas G. McCormick
Assistant to the Vice-Presidents—Milt Graff
Director of Publicity—Edward A. Wade
Assistant Directors of Publicity—Sally O'Leary, Thomas Bird
Director of Scouting—Murray Cook
Director of Minor League Clubs—Branch B. Rickey III
Assistant Director of Scouting—Jon Neiderer
Assistant Director of Minor League Clubs—Tom Kayser
Director of Season and Group Sales—Steve Greenberg
Season and Group Sales Department—Mark Ferraco
Assistant Directors of Promotions—Kathy Saba, Greg Brown
Assistant to the Treasurer—Kenneth C. Curcio
Ticket Manager—Richard C. Holland
Manager—Chuck Tanner
Traveling Secretary—Charles Muse
Club Physicians—Drs. Joseph Coroso, Jack Failla
Team Trainer—Tony Bartirome
Pirates Equipment Mgr.—John Hallahan
Public Address Announcer—Art McKennan
Executive Offices—Three Rivers Stadium, P.O. Box 6415
Pittsburgh, Pa. 15212
Telephone—323-5000 (area code 412)

SCOUTS—(Special assignment scouts)—Gene Baker, Kelvin Bowles, Joe L. Brown, Bill Bryk, Pablo Cruz, Bob Dawson, George Detore, Angel Figueroa, Jerry Gardner, Pete Gebrian, Fred Goodman, Howie Haak, Bob Johnson, Carlton Keller, Jose Luna, Jim Maxwell, Jeff McKay, Steve Oleschuk, Earl Silverthorn, Bob Whalen, Lenny Yochim. (Scouting assistants)—Ronnie Ahlhorn, Ossie Alvarez, Calvin Biron, Willie Bojos, Paul Bordi, Bill Bryan, Curt Bryan, Dave Buccolo, Joe Buccolo, F. (Kid) Carr, Bill Cayavec, Frank Coimbre, Cecil Cole, Nick Creola, Chuck Faris, Ed Farnum, Mike Fitzpatrick, John Gordon, Fred Hannum, Leroy Hill, Bud Hoff, Woody Hunt, Tom Johnson, Jim Lehman, J.D. McCord, Harry Miller, Tom Myers, Sam Narron, John Nix, Boyd Odom, Ed Olivares, George Omachi, Angel Ortiz, Elmo Plaskett, Bobby Prescott, Dick Probola, Ron Rahr, Harold Ray, Doug Robbins, Andre Rodgers, Ken Saybel, George Schmidt, John Sloan, Jesse Smith, Lloyd Sorrells, Les Stewart, Cloy Sykes, John Tucker, Tom Urich, Roy Velasco, Tom Venditelli, Bill White, Bill Wigle, Jim Williams, Tom Work, Ed Zeidler, Jack Zilles.

PARK LOCATION—Three Rivers Stadium, 600 Stadium Circle.

Seating capacity—54,499

FIELD DIMENSIONS—Home plate to left field at foul line, 335 feet; to center field, 400 feet; to right field at foul line, 335 feet.

ST. LOUIS CARDINALS

Chairman of the Board, President and Chief Executive Officer—
August A Busch, Jr.

Vice-President—August A. Busch, III
Vice-President—Fred L. Kuhlmann
Vice-President—Margaret Snyder Busch
Secretary and Treasurer—John L. Hayward
Assistant Secretary—Richard Schwartz
Assistant Treasurer—H. F. Suellentrop
General Manager-Manager—Whitey Herzog
Executive Assistant-Baseball—Joe McDonald
Director of Administration—Joe McShane
Senior Vice-President—Stan Musial
Director of Public Relations—Jim Toomey
Assistant Director of Public Relations—Robin Monsky
Executive Assistant-Business—Gary Blase
Traveling Secretary—C. J. Cherre
Director of Player Development—Lee Thomas
Director of Scouting—Fred McAlister
Director of Tickets and Operations—Mike Bertani
Director of Promotions—Marty Hendin
Director of Sales—Joe Cunningham
Director of Operations, Minor Leagues—Paul Fauks
Club Physician—Dr. Stan London
Executive Offices—Busch Memorial Stadium, 250 Stadium
Plaza, St. Louis, Mo. 63102
Telephone—421-3060 (area code 314)

SCOUTS—Ted Baker, James Belz, Vern Benson, Red Brown, Wilfredo Calvino, Walker Cress, Roberto Diaz, Cecil Espy, Steve Flores, Joe Frazier, Ray Goodman, Rich Hacker, James Holden, Darren Holt, Roland Johnson, James Johnston, Marty Keough, Henry Krause, Thornton Lee, Tom McCormack, Ben McLure, Martin Maier, Frank Matthews, Virgil Melvin, Mo Mozzali, Jerry Oswald, Mike Roberts, William Sayles, Larry Schultz, Bart Shelly, George Silvey, John Skurski, Hal Smith, Eddie Taylor, Charles (Tim) Thompson.

PARK LOCATION—Busch Memorial Stadium, Broadway, Walnut Street, Stadium Plaza and Spruce Street.

Seating capacity—50,100

FIELD DIMENSIONS—Home plate to left field at foul line, 330 feet; to center field, 414 feet; to right field at foul line, 330 feet.

SAN DIEGO PADRES

Board of Directors—Ray A. Kroc, Chairman; Joan Kroc, Ballard F. Smith, Jr.

President and Treasurer—Ballard F. Smith, Jr.
Senior Vice-President, Business Operations—Elten F. Schiller
Vice-President, Baseball Operations—Jack McKeon
Administrative Assistant—Rhoda Polley
Vice-President, Chief Financial Officer—Dick Freeman
Accounting Dept. Supervisor—Sondra Welch
Vice-President, Marketing—John Worcester
Director of Player Development—Bob Cluck
Director of Scouting—Sandy Johnson
Major League Scout, Special Assignments—Dick Hager
Administrator, Minor Leagues and Scouting—Tom Romenesko
Director of Public Relations—Bob Chandler
Assistants—Be Barnes, Bruce Rowe
Director of Broadcasting—Jerry Coleman
Director of Group Sales—Tom Mulcahy
Director of Promotions—Andy Strasberg
Director of Ticket Sales—J. C. Crouch
Traveling Secretary—John Mattei
Manager—Dick Williams
Club Physician—Scripps Clinic
Executive Offices—P.O. Box 2000, San Diego, Calif. 92120
Telephone—283-4494 (area code 714)

SCOUTS—Supervisors: Ken Bracey, Joe Cusick, Denny Galehouse, Dick Hager, Al Heist, Jim Marshall, Luis Rosa, Brad Sloan. Regular scouts: Aquiles Angulo, Dave Bartosch, Jose Casino, Billy Castell, Grisha Davida, Bill Earnhart, Tony Garcia, Donald Hennelly, John Herbold, Tom Hinkle, Edgar Jewell, Jay Lowers, Clyde McCullough, Bill McKeon, Kelly McKeon, Bob Polewski, Bob Warner, Hank Zacharias.

PARK LOCATION—San Diego Stadium, 9949 Friars Road

Seating capacity—51,309

FIELD DIMENSIONS—Home plate to left field at foul line, 330 feet; to center field, 420 feet; to right field at foul line, 330 feet.

SAN FRANCISCO GIANTS

President—Robert A. Lurie
Vice-President, Baseball Operations—Thomas F. Haller
Vice-President, Business Operations—Patrick J. Gallagher
Vice-President, Administration—Corey Busch
Field Director of Player Personnel and Development—Bob Fontaine
Director of Minor League Operations—John S. Schwarz
Asst. Vice-President, Baseball Operations-Traveling Sec.—Ralph E. Nelson, Jr.
Asst. Field Director of Player Personnel and Development—Robert L. Miller
Director of Publicity—Duffy Jennings
Director of Community and Public Relations—Stu Smith
Director of Marketing—Laurence M. Baer
Director of Stadium Operations—Don Foreman
Ticket Manager—Arthur Schulze
Accounting Manager—Ron Mosher
Director of Sales—Bob Gaillard
Group Sales Manager—Kathleen O'Brien
Speakers Bureau—Joe Orengo
Community Representative—Ben Moore
Team Photographer—Dennis Desprois
Manager—Frank Robinson
Executive Offices—Candlestick Park, San Francisco, Calif. 94124
Telephone—468-3700 (area code 415)

SCOUTS—John D. (Dutch) Anderson, Mark Conkin, Morris A. (Dutch) Deutsch, Jack DiGrace, Saturnino Escalera, Robert Folkins, Grady Hatton, Carl Hubbell, Richard G. (Richie) Klaus, Harvey Koepf, Andrew Korenek, Jim Lyke, Horacio Martinez, Romano Mascetti, Marty Miller, Dennis Mizzi, William Parese, Hugh Poland, Veto Ramirez, Del Rice, Walter Ripley, Hank Sauer, Richard Wilson, Tom Zimmer.

PARK LOCATION—Candlestick Point, Bayshore Freeway.

Seating capacity—58,000

FIELD DIMENSIONS—Home plate to left field at foul line, 335 feet; to center field, 410 feet; to right field at foul line, 335 feet.

American League
Organized 1900

LELAND S. MacPHAIL, Jr.
President

JOSEPH E. CRONIN
Chairman

CALVIN R. GRIFFITH, JOHN E. FETZER, GENE AUTRY
Vice-Presidents

ROBERT O. FISHEL
Secretary and
Assistant to the President

DONALD C. MARR, Jr.
Controller

RICHARD BUTLER
Supervisor of Umpires

ROBERT F. HOLBROOK
Special Assistant

STEPHANIE VARDAVAS
Manager, Waivers & Player Records Department

PHYLLIS MERHIGE
Assistant Public Relations Director

TESS BASTA, ROBERT GRIM, JEANNE BILL
Administrators

Headquarters—280 Park Avenue, New York, N. Y. 10017

Telephone—682-7000 (area code 212)

ASSISTANT SUPERVISORS OF UMPIRES—Larry Napp, Henry Soar.

UMPIRES—Lawrence Barnett, Nicholas Bremigan, Joseph Brinkman, Alan Clark, Terrance Cooney, Derryl Cousins, Donald Denkinger, Lou DiMuro, James Evans, Dale Ford, Richard Garcia, Russell Goetz, William Haller, Ted Hendry, Kenneth Kaiser, Greg Kosc, William Kunkel, George Maloney, Larry McCoy, James McKean, Durwood Merrill, Jerome Neudecker, Stephen Palermo, Dallas Parks, David Phillips, Michael Reilly, John (Rocky) Roe, John Shulock, Martin Springstead, Vic Voltaggio.

OFFICIAL STATISTICIANS—Sports Information Center, 1776 Heritage Drive, No. Quincy, Mass. 02171. Telephone—(617) 328-4674.

Players cannot be transferred from one major league to another after June 15 to close of the championship season except through regular waiver channels.

WAIVER PRICE, $20,000. Interleague waivers, $20,000, except for selected players and draft-excluded players.

American League President Leland S. MacPhail Jr.

BALTIMORE ORIOLES

Chairman of the Board—Edward Bennett Williams
President—Jerold C. Hoffberger
Executive Vice-President, General Manager—Henry J. Peters
Vice-President, Stadium Operations—Jack Dunn III
Vice-President, Finance—Joseph P. Hamper, Jr.
Treasurer—Gerald T. Gabrys
Secretary, General Counsel—Lawrence Lucchino
Directors—Edward Bennett Williams, Joseph P. DiMaggio, Jack Dunn III,
Gerald T. Gabrys, Charles H. Hoffberger, Jerold C. Hoffberger,
Zanvyl Kreiger, Lawrence Lucchino, Henry J. Peters, Peter P. Weidenbruch, Jr.
Special Assistant to the General Manager—James J. Russo
Public Relations Director—Robert W. Brown
Traveling Secretary—Philip E. Itzoe
Director, Player Development and Scouting—Thomas A. Giordano
Director of Business Affairs—Robert R. Aylward
Director of Sales—Jon Richardson
Promotions and Community Relations Director—Walter R. Freeman
Ticket Office Manager—Timothy Geraghty
Assistant Public Relations Director—John C. Blake
Assistant Director, Player Development and Scouting—John J. McCall
Miami Coordinator—Ralph A. Morcroft
Assistant Ticket Manager—Joseph B. Codd
Assistant Sales and Assistant Promotions Director—Drew M. Sheinman
Washington Area Representative—Dave Dinerman
Assistant Washington Area Representative—Joe Felperin
Consultant, President, Orioles Foundation—Herbert E. Armstrong
Manager—Earl S. Weaver
Club Physician—Dr. Leonard Wallenstein
Executive Offices—Memorial Stadium, Baltimore, Md. 21218
Telephone—243-9800 (area code 301)

SCOUTS—Jack Baker, Joe Bowman, Dan Cressman, Ray Crone, Ed Crosby, Joe DeLucca, Jim Driscoll, Jim Freitas, Jim Gilbert, Myron Hayworth, Len Johnston, George Lauzerique, Bill Lohr, Frank McGowan, Earl McKenzie, Paul McNeal, Domenic Napolitano, Lance Nichols, Lamar North, James Pamlayne, Frank Piet, Chichi Rodriguez, Jim Russo, Jack Sanford, Caesar Sinabaldi, John Stokoe, William Teed, Tommy Thompson, Herman Welsh, Bill Werle.

PARK LOCATION—Memorial Stadium, 33rd Street, Ellerslie Avenue, 36th Street and Ednor Road.

Seating capacity—52,696.

FIELD DIMENSIONS—Home plate to left field at foul line, 309 feet; at center field, 410 feet; to right field at foul line, 309 feet.

BOSTON RED SOX

President—Jean R. Yawkey

Executive Vice-President, General Manager—Haywood C. Sullivan
Executive Vice-President, Administration—Edward G. LeRoux, Jr.
Treasurer—James M. Olivier, Jr.
Secretary—Joseph H. LaCour
V. P., Director Player Development—Edward F. Kenney
Director, Scouting—Edward M. Kasko
Traveling Secretary—John J. Rogers
Director, Public Relations—George Sullivan
Director, Publicity—Richard L. Bresciani
Director, Marketing—James P. Healey
Director of Group Sales—Leslie Cargill
Assistant Publicity Director—John E. McCarthy
Executive Assistant—Joseph F. McDermott
Assistant Treasurer—John J. Reilly
Director, Tickets—Arthur J. Moscato
Superintendent, Grounds & Maintenance—Joseph Mooney
Field Manager—Ralph G. Houk
Club Physician—Dr. Arthur M. Pappas
Executive Offices—24 Yawkey Way, Boston, Mass. 02215
Telephone—267-9440 (area code 617)

SCOUTS—Milton Bolling, Ray Boone, Wayne Britton, George Digby, Howard (Danny) Doyle, Bill Enos, Larry Flynn, Earl Johnson, Charles Koney, Wilfrid (Lefty) Lefebvre, Don Lenhardt, Tommy McDonald, Felix Maldonado, Frank Malzone, Sam Mele, Ramon Naranjo, Willie Paffen, Edward Scott, Matt Sczesny, Joe Stephenson, Larry Thomas, Charlie Wagner.

PARK LOCATION—Fenway Park, Yawkey Way, Lansdowne Street and Ipswich Street.

Seating capacity—33,536.

FIELD DIMENSIONS—Home plate to left field at foul line, 315 feet; to center field, 420 feet; to right field at foul line, 302 feet; average right field distance, 382 feet.

CALIFORNIA ANGELS
President and Chairman of the Board—Gene Autry

Executive Vice-President—E.J. Bavasi
Assistant to the Chairman of the Board—Arthur E. Patterson
Vice-President and Chief Administrative Officer—Mike Port
Director Public Relations and Promotions—Tom Seeberg
Director of Accounting—Jim Kaczmarek
Director Scouting—Larry Himes
Minor League Administrator—Bill Bavasi
Director Ticket Department—Carl Gordon
Director Group Sales—Lynn Kirchmann Biggs
Director Stadium Operations—Jean (Corky) Lippert
Traveling Secretary—Frank Sims
Assistant Director Public Relations—Tim Mead
Assistant Ticket Director—Bob Terzes
Stadium Operations—Kevin Uhlich
Film Coordinator and Special Statistics—George Goodale
Medical Director—Dr. Robert K. Kerlan
Orthropedist—Dr. Lewis Yocum
Trainers—Rick Smith, Ned Bergert
Manager—Gene Mauch
Executive Offices—Anaheim Stadium, 2000 State College Blvd.,
Anaheim Calif. 92806
Telephone—937-6700 (area code 714) or 625-1123 (area code 213)

SCOUTS—Edmundo Borrome, Vince Capece, Joe Carpenter, Lloyd Christopher, Lou Cohenour, Alex Cosmidis, Pompeyo Davillo, Bob Gardner, Al Goldis, Steve Gruwell, Harry Hayes, Rick Ingalls, Nick Kamzic, Joe Maddon, Vic Power, Philip Rizzo, Lou Snipp, George Zabala.

PARK LOCATION—Anaheim Stadium, 2000 State College Blvd.

Seating capacity—65,158

FIELD DIMENSIONS—Home plate to left field at foul line, 333 feet; to center field, 404 feet; to right field at foul line, 333 feet.

CHICAGO WHITE SOX

Chairman, Board of Directors—Jerry M. Reinsdorf
President—Eddie M. Einhorn
Executive Vice-President, General Manager—Roland A. Hemond
Executive Vice-President—Howard C. Pizer
Vice-President, Marketing—Michael D. McClure
Vice-President, Broadcasting and Special Projects—Laureen Ong Fadil
Vice-President, Baseball Administration—Jack Gould
Treasurer—Leo M. Breen
Assistant General Manager—David Dombrowski
Director of Player Development—Bob Winkles
Assistant to Vice-President, Marketing—Stephen M. Schanwald
Director of Public Relations—Charles A. Shriver
Director of Ticket Sales—Russell G. Williams
Director of Broadcast Sales—Edwin M. Doody
Controller—Timothy L. Buzard
Traveling Secretary—Glen Rosenbaum
Ticket Manager—Robert K. Devoy
Season Ticket Coordinator—Millie Johnson
Director of Promotions—George M. Koch
Assistant Director of Public Relations—Kenneth M. Valdiserri
Assistant, Public Relations—Daniel P. Evans
Administrative Assistant, Baseball Operations—William E. Smith, Jr.
General Counsel—Allan B. Muchin
Trainer—Herman Schneider
Assistant Trainer—Brandt McFarlin
Team Physicians—Drs. Richard D. Corzatt, James B. Boscardin, Hugo Cuadros
Manager—Tony LaRussa
Equipment/Club House Mgr., White Sox—Willie Thompson
Equipment/Club House Mgr., Visitors—John MacNamara
Director of Park Operations—David M. Schaffer
Groundskeepers—Gene and Roger Bossard
P.A. Announcer—Bob Finnegan
Organist—Nancy Faust
Executive Offices—Comiskey Park, Dan Ryan at 35th Street, Chicago, Ill. 60616
Telephone—924-1000 (area code 312)

SCOUTS—Advance: Loren Babe. Special Assignment: Jerry Krause, Fred Shaffer. Supervisors: Gary Johnson, Walt Widmayer. Regular: John Boles, James Busby, Angel Vasquez (Castro), Roger Ferguson, Sam Hairston, Bennie Huffman, Joseph Ingalls, Bart Johnson, Leo Labossiere, Marv Lane, Dario Lodigiani, Terry Logan, Larry Monroe, Fern Paredes, Silvano Quezada, Mark Serrais, Duane Shaffer, George Sobek, Lynn Squires, Ken Stauffer, Stan Zielinski.

PARK LOCATION—Comiskey Park, Dan Ryan at 35th Street, Chicago, Ill. 60616

Seating capacity—44,492.

FIELD DIMENSIONS—Home plate to left field at foul line, 352 feet; to center field, 445 feet; to right field at foul line, 352 feet.

CLEVELAND INDIANS

President and Chief Executive Officer—Gabe Paul

Chairman of the Board—F.J. (Steve) O'Neill
Directors—F.J. O'Neill, C.C. Tippit, Dudley S. Blossom, III, Alva T. Bonda,
Walter Laich, Gabe Paul, Arnold Pinkney, Phillip Seghi, Maurice Stonehill
Secretary-Treasurer—Dudley S. Blossom III
Vice-President and General Manager—Phillip D. Seghi
Vice-President, Player Development and Scouting—Bob Quinn
Secretary and Club Legal Counsel—Armond D. Arnson
Manager—Dave Garcia
Traveling Secretary—Mike Seghi
Director of Public Relations—Bob DiBiasio
Director of Marketing—Joann Klonowski
Director of Sales—Tom Pulchinski
Director of Stadium Operations—Dan Zerbey
Ticket Director—Jerry Waring
Controller—Jason Rosenthal
Public Relations—Bob Feller
Special Assistant to General Manager—Dan Carnevale
Asst. Public Relations Director—Pete Spudich
Minor League Administrator—Joe Pavia
Asst. Farm Director—Phil Thomas
Trainer—Jim Warfield
Club Physicians—Drs. William Wilder, Earl Brightman
Club Dentist—Dr. Marvin Schermer
Equipment Manager—Cy Buynak
Groundskeeper—Marshall Bossard
Executive Offices—Cleveland Stadium, Cleveland, Ohio 44114
Telephone—861-1200 (area code 216)

SCOUTS—Special assignment scout—Dan Carnevale. Regular scouts—Hector
Acevedo, Jack Cassini, Al Daniels, Phil English, Red Gaskill, Leon Hamilton, Luis
Isaac, Don Kohler, Frank Lucchesi, Bobby Malkmus, Jim Miller, Dave Oliver,
Larry Quirico, Woody Smith, Gary Sutherland, Al Unser, Jack Vallely, Gene Wood-
ling.

PARK LOCATION—Cleveland Stadium, Boudreau Blvd.

Seating capacity—74,208

FIELD DIMENSIONS—Home plate to left field at foul line, 320 feet; to center
field, 400 feet; to right field at foul line, 320 feet.

DETROIT TIGERS

Owner & Chairman of the Board—John E. Fetzer

President & General Manager—James A. Campbell
Vice-President/Finance & Secretary-Treasurer—Alexander C. Callam
Vice-President/Operations—William E. Haase
Vice-President/Baseball—William R. Lajoie
Director of Public Relations—Dan Ewald
Director of Ticket Sales—Jerry Bucholtz
Box Office Treasurer—William H. Willis
Director of Stadium Operations—Ralph E. Snyder
Field Director/Player Development—Walter A. Evers
Administrator, Player Development—David Miller
Scouting Director—John Young
Traveling Secretary—Bill Brown
Assistant Director of Public Relations—Bob Miller
Asst. Dir. of Public Relations/Special Events—Lew Matlin
Asst. Dir. of Public Relations/Community Affairs—Vince Desmond
Executive Secretary/Baseball—Alice Sloane
Executive Secretary/Operations—Hazel McLane
Consultants—Richard B. Ferrell, Edward G. Katalinas
Asst. Director of Stadium Operations—Frank Feneck
Manager—Sparky Anderson
Club Physician—Clarence S. Livingood M.D.
Orthopaedic Consultant—Robert A. Teitge M.D.
Executive Offices—Tiger Stadium, Detroit, Mich. 48216
Telephone—962-4000 (area code 313)

SCOUTS—Ray Bellino, Wayne Blackburn, George Bradley, Joe Henderson, Roger Jongewaard, Joe Lewis, Orlando Pena, Jax Robertson, William Schudlich. Scouting consultants—Frank Skaff, Jack Tighe.

PARK LOCATION—Tiger Stadium, Michigan Avenue, Cochrane Avenue, Kaline Drive and Trumbull Avenue.

Seating capacity—52,806

FIELD DIMENSIONS—Home plate to left field at foul line, 340 feet; to center field, 440 feet; to right field at foul line, 325 feet.

KANSAS CITY ROYALS

Board of Directors

Joe Burke, William Deramus III, Charles Hughes, Ewing Kauffman, Mrs. Ewing Kauffman, Earl Smith.

Chairman of the Board—Ewing Kauffman
President—Joe Burke
Executive Vice-President and General Manager—John Schuerholz
Vice-President, Administration—Spencer (Herk) Robinson
Vice-President, Controller—Dale Rohr
Vice-President and Legal Counsel—Phil Koury
Director of Public Relations—Dean Vogelaar
Director of Marketing and Broadcasting—Bryan Burns
Traveling Secretary/Lancer Coordinator—Bill Beck
Assistant Director of Publications—Will Rudd
Director of Scouting and Player Development—Dick Balderson
Assistant Director of Scouting and Player Development—Dean Taylor
Director of Ticket Operations—Tom Pfannenstiel
Director of Season Ticket Sales—Joe Grigoli
Season Ticket Coordinator—Chris Rice
Director of Group Sales/Special Events—Rush Limbaugh
Manager—Dick Howser
Club Physician—Dr. Paul Meyer
Accountant—Ken Willeke
Director of Event Personnel—Chris Muehlbach
Stadium Engineer—George Humphrey
Stadium Maintenance Coordinator—Bob Frank
Equipment Manager—Al Zych
Groundskeeper—George Toma
Executive Offices—Royals Stadium, Harry S Truman Sports Complex
Mailing Address—P.O. Box 1969, Kansas City, Mo. 64141
Telephone—921-8000 (area code 816)

SCOUTS—Carl Blando, Al Diez, Tom Ferrick, Rosey Gilhousen, Ken Gonzales, Guy Hansen, Ron Hopkins, Al Kubski, Art Lilly, George Noga, Earl Rapp, Rich Schlenker, Jerry Stephens, Red Whitsett, Art Stewart (part time).

PARK LOCATION—Royals Stadium, Harry S Truman Sports Complex.

Seating capacity—40,628.

FIELD DIMENSIONS—Home plate to left field at foul line, 330 feet; to center field, 410 feet; to right field at foul line, 330 feet.

MILWAUKEE BREWERS

President, Chief Executive Officer, Director—Allan H. (Bud) Selig
Executive Vice-President, General Manager—Harry Dalton
Vice-President, Marketing—Richard Hackett
Vice-President, Administration—Thomas J. Ferguson
Vice-President, Broadcast Operations—William Haig
Vice-President, Finance—Richard Hoffmann
Vice-President, Stadium Operations—Gabe Paul Jr.
Assistant General Manager—Walter Shannon
Special Assistants to the General Manager—Dee Fondy, Sal Bando
Special Assignments Scout—Ray Scarborough
Director of Player Procurement—Ray Poitevint
Coordinator of Minor League Operations—Bruce Manno
Administrative Assistant for Scouting and Player Development—Dan Duquette
Coordinator of Player Development—Herman Starrette
Director of Publicity—Tom Skibosh
Assistant Director of Stadium Operations and Advertising—Jack Hutchinson
Ticket Sales Director—Tim Trovato
Director of the Speakers Bureau—John Counsell
Assistant Director of Publicity—Mario Ziino
Ticket Office Manager—John Barnes
Director of Ticket Office Computer Operations—Alice Boettcher
Director of Special Events—Mark Paget
Manager—Bob Rodgers
Club Physician—Dr. Paul Jacobs
Trainers—Freddie Frederico, John Adam
Superintendent of Grounds and Maintenance—Harry Gill
Assistant Groundskeeper—Gary Vandenberg
Equipment Manager—Bob Sullivan
P.A. Announcer—Bob Betts
Organist—Frank Charles
Executive Offices—Milwaukee Brewers Baseball Club
Milwaukee County Stadium, Milwaukee, Wis. 53214
Telephone—933-1818 (area code 414)

SCOUTS—Scouting supervisors: Julio Blanco-Herrera, Nelson Burbrink, Felix Delgado, Tom Gamboa, Roland LeBlanc, Walter Youse. Regular Scouts: Fred Beene, Tom Bourque, Ken Califano, Gerry Craft, Dick Elrig, Charles Fitzgerald, Dick Foster, Hy Gomberg, Gene Kerns, Billy Moffitt, Willie Moore, Johnny Neun, Tim Nordbrook, Ken Richardson, Ray Scarborough, Lee Sigman, Harry Smith, Milt Sobel, Sam Suplizio, Paul Tretiak, Jerry Weinstein.

PARK LOCATION—Milwaukee County Stadium, S. 46th St. off Bluemound Rd.

Seating capacity—53,192.

FIELD DIMENSIONS—Home plate to left field at foul line, 315 feet; to center field, 402 feet; to right field at foul line, 315 feet.

MINNESOTA TWINS

Chairman of Board, President—Calvin R. Griffith

Vice-President—Mrs. Thelma Griffith Haynes
Executive Vice-President—Clark Griffith
Executive Vice-President—Bruce G. Haynes
Director—H. Gabriel Murphy
Director—Eugene V. Young
Director—Wheelock Whitney
Executive Vice-President—Howard T. Fox, Jr.
Vice-President—Williams S. Robertson
Vice-President—James K. Robertson
Vice-President-Farm Director—George Brophy
Assistant Farm Director—Jim Rantz
Controller—Jack Alexander
Director of Public Relations—Tom Mee
Director of Sales—Gil Lansdale
Stadium Superintendent—Richard Ericson
Manager—Billy Gardner
Club Physicians—Dr. Leonard J. Michienzi and Dr. Harvey O'Phelan
Executive Offices—Hubert H. Humphrey Metrodome, 501 Chicago Ave. South,
Minneapolis, Minn. 55415
Telephone—375-1366 (area code 612)

SCOUTS—Floyd Baker, Dave Boswell, Spud Chandler, Ellis Clary, Edward Dunn, Jesse Flores, Jr., Jesse Flores, Sr., Angelo Giuliani, Tom Hull, Lee Irwin, Hank Izquierdo, William Messmann, Marvin Olson, Spencer (Red) Robbins, Stanley Rogers, Herb Stein.

PARK LOCATION—Hubert H. Humphrey Metrodome, 501 Chicago Ave. South.

Seating capacity—54,000.

FIELD DIMENSIONS—Home plate to left field at foul line, 343 feet; to center field, 408 feet; to right field at foul line, 327 feet.

NEW YORK YANKEES

Principal Owner—George M. Steinbrenner III
Limited Partners—Harold Bowman, Lester Crown, John Z. DeLorean, Michael
Friedman, Marvin Goldklang, Barry Halper, Leonard L. Kleinman,
Harvey Leighton, Daniel McCarthy, Harry Nederlander, Robert
Nederlander, William J. O'Neill, William Rose, Edward
Rosenthal, Jack Satter, Charlotte Witkind.
President—Lou Saban
Executive Vice-President—Cedric Tallis
Manager—Bob Lemon
Administrative Vice-President—Eugene J. McHale
Vice-President, General Counsel—Edwin T. Broderick
Vice-President, Baseball Operations—Bill Bergesch
Vice-President—Ed Weaver
Treasurer-Controller—David Weidler
Director of Player Development—Bill Livesay
Director of Scouting—Bobby Hofman
Traveling Secretary—Bill Kane
Administrative Assistant—Gerry Murphy
Director of Media Relations—Irv Kaze
Director of Publications—David Szen
Director of Public Relations—John Fugazy
Public Relations Assistants—Betsy Leesman, Bob Pelegrino
Stadium Manager—Patrick Kelly
Director of Promotions—Bruce Weinstein
Executive Director of Ticket Operations—Frank Swaine
Ticket Director—Michael Rendine
Assistant Ticket Director—Jim Hodge
Director, Customer Services and Asst. Stadium Manager—Jim Naples
Assistant Director of Player Development—Dale Weeks
Assistant Director of Scouting—Bob Kalaf
Director of Group Sales—Frank McCormick
Director of Speakers Bureau, Publicity Asst.—Joe D'Ambrosio
Director of Accounting—Alan Friedman
Stadium Superintendent—Jimmy Esposito
Spring Training Coordinator—Marsh Samuel
Team Photographer—John Woodward
Director, Yankee Alumni Association—Jim Ogle
Club Physician—Dr. John J. Bonamo
P.A. Announcer—Bob Sheppard
Organist—Eddie Layton
Executive Offices—Yankee Stadium, Bronx, N.Y. 10451
Telephone—293-4300 (area code 212)
Ticket Information—293-6000 (area code 212)

SCOUTS—Advance Scout: Clyde King. Luis Arroyo, Hank Bauer, Joe Begani,
Howard Cassidy, Harry Craft, Al Cuccinello, Joe DiCarlo, Henry Dotterer, Fred
Ferreira, Whitey Ford, Jack Gillis, Tom Greenwade, Jim Gruzdis, Roy Hamey, Jim
Hegan, Gary Hughes, John Kennedy, Dave Lemanczyk, Don Lindeberg, Jack
Llewellyn, Gene Michael, Jim Naples, Sr., Bob Nieman, Frank O'Rourke, Meade
Palmer, Gust Poulos, Stan Sanders, Russ Sehon, Robert Shaw, Birdie Tebbets, Stan
Williams.

PARK LOCATION—Yankee Stadium, E. 161st St. and River Ave., Bronx, N.Y.
10451.

Seating Capacity—57,545.

FIELD DIMENSIONS—Home plate to left field at foul line, 312 feet; to center
field, 417 feet; to right field at foul line, 310 feet.

OAKLAND A's

President—Roy Eisenhardt

Executive Vice-President—Walter J. Haas
Field Manager, Director of Player Development—Billy Martin
Vice-President, Baseball Administration—Carl A. Finley
Vice-President, Business Operations—Andy Dolich
Vice-President, Finance—James Lawrence
Vice-President and General Counsel—Richard (Sandy) Alderson
Director of Scouting and Minor League Personnel—Dick Wiencek
Director, Minor League Operations—Walt Jocketty
Traveling Secretary, Director of Press Relations—Mickey Morabito
Director of Marketing and Merchandising—Roger Moskowitz
Director of Sales and Telecommunications—David Rubinstein
Director of Media Relations—Rick Moxley
Director of Publications—Daniel Orum
Administrative Assistant, Baseball Administration-Legal—Olive Kanewske
Executive Assistant—Sharon Jones
Director of Special Projects—Earl Robinson
Director of Youth Programs, Speakers Bureau—Craig Amerkhanian
Assistant Press Relations—Enzo DeMonte
Administrative Assistant—Pam Bruder
Director of Stadium Operations—Jorge Costa
Director of Ticket Operations—Raymond Krise, Jr.
Assistant to Director of Ticket Operations—Barbara Beggs
Assistant Ticket Manager—Shelly Russo
Administrative Assistants—Julie Delk, Ann Vargas
Equipment Manager—Frank Ciensczyk
Trainer—Joe Romo
Club Physician—Dr. Thomas E. Richmond
Visiting Clubhouse Manager—Steve Vucinich
Executive Offices—Oakland-Alameda County Coliseum, Oakland, Calif. 94621
Telephone—638-4900 (area code 415)

SCOUTS—Albert Elliott, Jr., Frank Franchi, Grady Fuson, Fred Hatfield, Harmon Killebrew, Edwin Mathews, Mel Nelson, Camilo Pascual, James Perry, Charles Silvera, Ed Stevens, Gary Wiencek, Del Wilber.

PARK LOCATION—Oakland-Alameda County Coliseum, Nimitz Freeway and Hegenberger Road.

Seating capacity—50,255.

FIELD DIMENSIONS—Home plate to left field at foul line, 330 feet; to center field, 400 feet; to right field at foul line, 330 feet.

SEATTLE MARINERS

Principal Owner—George L. Argyros

Limited Partners—Stanley Golub, Danny Kaye, Walter Schoenfeld, Lester M. Smith
President—Daniel F. O'Brien
Director of Player Development—Hal Keller
Vice-President, Sales and Marketing—Bill Long
Director of Marketing—Jeff Odenwald
Director of Sales—Gary Mounger
Director of Team Travel—Lee Pelekoudas
Director of Stadium Operations—Craig Barrick
Director of Ticket Services—Lamar Vernon
Director of Public Relations—Randy Adamac
Manager—Rene Lachemann
Manager of Publicity—Bob Porter
Manager of Promotions—Steve Krause
Manager of Broadcast Operations—Melody Tucker
Manager of Community Relations—Jeff Klein
Manager of Stadium Entertainment—Randy Stearns
Manager of Corporate Sales—Mark Bloomquist
Controller—Brian Beggs
Office Manager—Janet Croft
Vault Manager—Doug Hopkins
Trainer—Gary Nicholson
Club Physicians—Drs. Ernie Burgess, Larry Pedegana, James Thombold
Club Dentist—Dr. Richard Leshgold
Club Attorney—Irwin Treiger
Home Clubhouse—Henry Genzale
Visiting Clubhouse—Fred Genzale
Executive Offices—P.O. Box 4100
Seattle, Washington 98104
Telephone—628-3555 (area code 206)

SCOUTS—Bob Harrison, Bill Kearns, Jeff Malinoff, Marty Martinez, Whitey Piurek, Rip Tutor, Steve Vrablik.

PARK LOCATION—Kingdome, 201 South King Street, Seattle, Washington

Seating Capacity—59,438

FIELD DIMENSIONS—Home plate to left field at foul line, 316 feet; to center field, 410 feet; to right field at foul line, 316 feet.

TEXAS RANGERS

Chairman of the Board, President, Chief Executive Officer—Eddie Chiles

Vice Chairman, General Counsel, Secretary—Dee J. Kelly
Executive Vice-President, Baseball Operations—Eddie Robinson
Assistant to the Executive Vice-President, Baseball Operations—Paul Richards
Executive Vice-President, Business Operations—Samuel G. Meason
Vice-President—Amon G. Carter Jr.
Vice-President, Marketing—James T. Medick
Directors—Dee J. Kelly, Amon G. Carter Jr., Mack Rankin,
William H. Seay, Charles S. Sharp
Treasurer—Charles F. Wangner
Executive Director, Texas Rangers Network—Roy Parks
Director of Player Procurement and Development—Joe Klein
Asst. Director of Player Procurement and Development—Tom Grieve
Director of Media Relations—Burton Hawkins
Director of Public Relations—Allan Charnish
Director of Advertising and Promotions—Harry Campbell
Director of Ticket Management—Mary Ann Bosher
Director of Security—John Welaj
Director of Maintenance and Crowd Control—Matt Stolley
Director of Team Sports Marketing—Phil Small
Traveling Secretary—Dan Schimek
Manager—Don Zimmer
Administrative Assistant and Director of Speakers Bureau—Bobby Bragan
Administrative Assistant—Wayne Krivsky
Physical Fitness Consultant—Dr. Eugene Coleman
Physical Fitness Instructor—Mike Fitzsimmons
Medical Director—Dr. B. J. Mycoskie
Field Superintendent—John Oliveria
Public Address Announcer—Mitch Carr
Executive Offices—Arlington Stadium, P.O. Box 1111,
1500 Copeland Road, Arlington, Tex. 76010
Telephone—273-5222 (area code 817)

SCOUTS—Harley Anderson, Lee Anthony, Joseph Branzell, Jackie Brathwaite
Paddy Cottrell, Dick Gernert, Orlando Gomez, Cesar Guttierez, Andy Hancock, Sid
Hudson, Stan Jakubowski, Joseph Lewis, Joseph Marchese, Don Nichols, Cotton
Nix, Connie Ryan, Rick Schroeder, Fred Velasquez.

PARK LOCATION—Arlington Stadium, 1500 Copeland Road, Arlington, Tex.

Seating capacity—41,284.

FIELD DIMENSIONS—Home plate to left field at foul line, 330 feet; to center
field, 400 feet; to right field at foul line, 330 feet.

TORONTO BLUE JAYS

Board of Directors—L. G. Greenwood, N. E. Hardy, J. P. Robarts,
R. Howard Webster, P. N. T. Widdrington
Chairman of the Board—R. Howard Webster
Vice-President, Business Operations—Paul Beeston
Vice-President, Baseball Operations—Pat Gillick
Executive Coordinator, Baseball Operations—Bobby Mattick
Director, Public Relations—Howard Starkman
Director, Operations—Ken Erskine
Director, Ticket Operations—George Holm
Administrator, Player Personnel—Elliott Wahle
Trainer-Director, Team Travel—Ken Carson
Director, Group Sales—Mike Nash
Director, Player Development—Billy Smith
Director, Canadian Scouting—Bob Prentice
Assistant Director, Public Relations—Herb Morell
Assistant Director, Operations—Gord Ash
Assistant Director, Ticket Operations—Len Frejlich
Director, Security—Fred Wootton
Equipment Manager—Jeff Ross
Coordinator, Promotions & Group Services—Maureen Haffey
Supervisor, Grounds—Dave Hamilton
Manager—Bobby Cox
Team Physician—Dr. Ron Taylor
Executive Offices—Exhibition Stadium, Exhibition Place,
Toronto, Ontario
Mailing Address—Box 7777, Adelaide St. P. O., Toronto, Ont. M5C 2K7
Telephone—595-0077 (area code 416)

SCOUTS—Robert Engle, Joe Ford, Epy Guerrero, Jim Hughes, Al LaMacchia (senior scouting supervisor), Larry Maxie, Wayne Morgan, Paul Ricciarini, Don Welke, Bob Wilbur, Tim Wilken, Dave Yoakum, Bob Zuk (senior scouting supervisor).

PARK LOCATION—Exhibition Stadium on the grounds of Exhibition Place. Entrances to Exhibition Place via Lakeshore Boulevard, Queen Elizabeth Way Highway and Dufferin and Bathurst Streets.

Seating capacity—43,737

FIELD DIMENSIONS—Home plate to left field at foul line, 330 feet; to center field, 400 feet; to right field at foul line, 330 feet.

FERNANDO VALENZUELA
● LOS ANGELES DODGERS ●
MAJOR LEAGUE
PLAYER OF THE YEAR

JOHN McHALE
● MONTREAL EXPOS ●
MAJOR LEAGUE EXECUTIVE

BILLY MARTIN
● OAKLAND A's ●
MAJOR LEAGUE MANAGER

DEL CRANDALL
● ALBUQUERQUE ●
MINOR LEAGUE MANAGER

PAT McKERNAN
● ALBUQUERQUE ●
MINOR LEAGUE EXECUTIVE
IN CLASS AAA

MIKE MARSHALL
● ALBUQUERQUE ●
MINOR LEAGUE PLAYER

ALLIE PRESCOTT
● MEMPHIS ●
MINOR LEAGUE EXECUTIVE
IN CLASS AA

𝕿𝖍𝖊 𝕾𝖕𝖔𝖗𝖙𝖎𝖓𝖌 𝕹𝖊𝖜𝖘

NO. **1**

MEN

of

1981

DAN OVERSTREET
● HAGERSTOWN ●
MINOR LEAGUE EXECUTIVE
IN CLASS A

Major League Players Association

1370 Avenue of the Americas
Suite 2602
New York, N.Y. 10019
Telephone—(212) 581-8484

Marvin J. Miller—Executive Director
Donald Fehr—General Counsel
Peter Rose—Associate Counsel
Staff—Marlene Blake, Millie Ciuro and John Hess

EXECUTIVE BOARD

Doug DeCinces—American League Representative
Phil Garner—National League Representative
Mark Belanger—Pension Committee
Steve Rogers—Pension Committee
Plus all remaining player representatives

NATIONAL LEAGUE PLAYER REPRESENTATIVES

Phil Niekro—Atlanta Braves
To Be Announced—Chicago Cubs
To Be Announced—Cincinnati Reds
Joe Niekro—Houston Astros
Jerry Reuss—Los Angeles Dodgers
Steve Rogers—Montreal Expos
Rusty Staub—New York Mets
Dick Ruthven—Philadelphia Phillies
Kent Tekulve—Pittsburgh Pirates
Keith Hernandez—St. Louis Cardinals
Gary Lucas—San Diego Padres
Gary Lavelle—San Francisco Giants

AMERICAN LEAGUE PLAYER REPRESENTATIVES

Scott McGregor—Baltimore Orioles
Tom Burgmeier—Boston Red Sox
Don Baylor—California Angels
To Be Announced—Chicago White Sox
To Be Announced—Cleveland Indians
Milt Wilcox—Detroit Tigers
Dan Quisenberry—Kansas City Royals
Ted Simmons—Milwaukee Brewers
Roger Erickson—Minnesota Twins
To Be Announced—New York Yankees
Jeff Newman—Oakland A's
Bruce Bochte—Seattle Mariners
Jon Matlack—Texas Rangers
Al Woods—Toronto Blue Jays

Presidents of Minor Leagues for '82

CLASS AAA

American Association—Joe Ryan, P. O. Box 382, Wichita, Kan. 67201

International League—Harold Cooper, Box 608, Grove City, Ohio 43123

Mexican League—Roberto Avila, Angel Pola No. 16, Col. del Periodista, Mexico 10, D. F., Mexico

Pacific Coast League—Bill Cutler, 2101 E. Broadway Rd., Tempe, Ariz. 85282

CLASS AA

Eastern League—Charles Eshbach, Box 318, Bristol, Conn. 06010

Southern League—Jimmy Bragan, 235 Main St., Suite 200, Trussville, Ala. 35173

Texas League—Carl Sawatski, 1501 N. University, Suite 412, Little Rock, Ark. 72207

CLASS A

California League—Joe Gagliardi, 1060 Willow, San Jose, Calif. 95125

Carolina League—Jim Mills, 219 W. Chatham St., Apex, N.C. 27502

Florida State League—George MacDonald, Jr., P. O. Box 414, Lakeland, Fla. 33802

Midwest League—William K. Walters, P. O. Box 444, Burlington, Ia. 52601

New York-Pennsylvania League—Vincent M. McNamara, 220 Brookside Drive, Buffalo, N. Y. 14220.

Northwest League—Bob Freitas, 1840 Tabor Street, Eugene, Ore. 97401

South Atlantic League—John H. Moss, P. O. Box 49, Kings Mountain, N. C. 28086

ROOKIE CLASSIFICATION

Appalachian League—Bill Halstead, 157 Carson Lane, Bristol, Va. 24201

Gulf Coast League—Thomas J. Saffell, 420 Golden Gate Point, Apt. 18, Sarasota, Fla. 33577

Pioneer League—Ralph C. Nelles, P. O. Box 1144, Billings, Mont. 59103

Major League Farm Systems for 1982

AMERICAN LEAGUE

BALTIMORE (5): AAA–Rochester. AA–Charlotte. A–Hagerstown, Miami. Rookie–Bluefield.

BOSTON (5): AAA–Pawtucket. AA–Bristol, Conn. A–Elmira, Winston-Salem, Winter Haven.

CALIFORNIA (5): AAA–Spokane. AA–Holyoke. A–Danville, Redwood, Salem.

CHICAGO (5): AAA–Edmonton. AA–Glens Falls. A–Appleton, Niagara Falls. Rookie–Sarasota.

CLEVELAND (4): AAA–Charleston, W. Va. AA–Chattanooga. A–Batavia, Waterloo.

DETROIT (5): AAA–Evansville. AA–Birmingham. A–Lakeland, Macon. Rookie–Bristol, Va.

KANSAS CITY (6): AAA–Omaha. AA–Jacksonville. A–Fort Myers, Charleston, S. C. Rookie–Sarasota, Butte.

MILWAUKEE (3): AAA–Vancouver. AA–El Paso. A–Beloit.

MINNESOTA (5): AAA–Toledo. AA–Orlando. A–Visalia, Wisconsin Rapids. Rookie–Elizabethton.

NEW YORK (7): AAA–Columbus, O. AA–Nashville. A–Ft. Lauderdale, Greensboro, Oneonta. Rookie–Bradenton, Paintsville.

OAKLAND (6): AAA–Tacoma. AA–West Haven. A–Idaho Falls, Madison, Medford, Modesto.

SEATTLE (4): AAA–Salt Lake City. AA–Lynn. A–Bellingham, Wausau.

TEXAS (4): AAA–Denver. AA–Tulsa. A–Burlington. Rookie–Sarasota.

TORONTO (6): AAA–Syracuse. AA–Knoxville. A–Florence, Kinston. Rookie–Bradenton, Medicine Hat.

NATIONAL LEAGUE

ATLANTA (5): AAA–Richmond. AA–Savannah. A–Anderson, Durham. Rookie–Bradenton.

CHICAGO (5): AAA–Iowa. AA–Midland. A–Geneva, Quad Cities. Rookie–Sarasota.

CINCINNATI (6): AAA–Indianapolis. AA–Waterbury. A–Cedar Rapids, Eugene, Tampa. Rookie–Billings.

HOUSTON (5): AAA–Tucson. AA–Columbus, Ga. A–Asheville, Auburn. Rookie–Sarasota.

LOS ANGELES (5): AAA–Albuquerque. AA–San Antonio. A–Lodi, Vero Beach. Rookie–Lethbridge.

MONTREAL (6): AAA–Wichita. AA–Memphis. A–Jamestown, West Palm Beach. Rookie–Calgary, San Jose.

NEW YORK (6): AAA–Tidewater. AA–Jackson. A–Little Falls, Lynchburg, Shelby. Rookie–Kingsport.

PHILADELPHIA (6): AAA–Oklahoma City. AA–Reading. A–Bend, Peninsula, Spartanburg. Rookie–Helena.

PITTSBURGH (5): AAA–Portland. AA–Buffalo. A–Alexandria, Greenwood. Rookie–Bradenton.

ST. LOUIS (6): AAA–Louisville. AA–Arkansas. A–Erie, Gastonia, St. Petersburg. Rookie–Johnson City.

SAN DIEGO (6): AAA–Hawaii. AA–Amarillo. A–Reno, Salem, Walla Walla. Rookie–Bradenton.

SAN FRANCISCO (5): AAA–Phoenix. AA–Shreveport. A–Clinton, Fresno. Rookie–Great Falls.

OFFICIAL MINOR LEAGUE AVERAGES

Including

Official Averages of All Class AAA, Class AA, Class A and Rookie Leagues

National Association President John Johnson.

American Association

CLASS AAA

Leading Batter
MIKE RICHARDT
Wichita

League President
JOE RYAN

Leading Pitcher
LARRY PASHNICK
Evansville

CHAMPIONSHIP WINNERS IN PREVIOUS YEARS

1902—Indianapolis	.683
1903—St. Paul	.657
1904—St. Paul	.646
1905—Columbus	.658
1906—Columbus	.615
1907—Columbus	.584
1908—Indianapolis	.601
1909—Louisville	.554
1910—Minneapolis	.637
1911—Minneapolis	.600
1912—Minneapolis	.636
1913—Milwaukee	.599
1914—Milwaukee	.590
1915—Minneapolis	.597
1916—Louisville	.605
1917—Indianapolis	.588
1918—Kansas City	.589
1919—St. Paul	.610
1920—St. Paul	.701
1921—Louisville	.583
1922—St. Paul	.641
1923—Kansas City	.675
1924—St. Paul	.578
1925—Louisville	.635
1926—Louisville	.629
1927—Toledo	.601
1928—Indianapolis	.593
1929—Kansas City	.665
1930—Louisville	.608
1931—St. Paul	.623
1932—Minneapolis	.595
1933—Columbus°	.604
Minneapolis	.562
1934—Minneapolis	.570
Columbus°	.556
1935—Minneapolis	.591

1936—Milwaukee†	.584
1937—Columbus†	.584
1938—St. Paul	.596
Kansas City (2nd)‡	.556
1939—Kansas City	.695
Louisville (4th)‡	.490
1940—Kansas City	.625
Louisville (4th)‡	.500
1941—Columbus†	.621
1942—Kansas City	.549
Columbus (3rd)‡	.532
1943—Milwaukee	.596
Columbus (3rd)‡	.532
1944—Milwaukee	.667
Louisville (3rd)‡	.574
1945—Milwaukee	.604
Louisville (3rd)‡	.545
1946—Louisville†	601
1947—Kansas City	.608
Milwaukee (3rd)‡	.513
1948—Indianapolis	.649
St. Paul (3rd)‡	.558
1949—St. Paul	.608
Indianapolis (2nd)‡	.604
1950—Minneapolis	.584
Columbus (3rd)‡	.549
1951—Milwaukee†	.623
1952—Milwaukee	.656
Kansas City (2nd)‡	.578
1953—Toledo	.584
Kansas City (2nd)‡	.571
1954—Indianapolis	.625
Louisville (2nd)‡	.556
1955—Minneapolis†	.597
1956—Indianapolis†	.597
1957—Wichita	.604
Denver (2nd)‡	.584

1958—Charleston	.589
Minneapolis (3rd)‡	.536
1959—Louisville§	.599
Omaha§	.516
Minneapolis (2nd)‡	.586
1960—Denver	.571
Louisville (2nd)‡	.556
1961—Indianapolis	.573
Louisville (2nd)‡	.533
1962—Indianapolis	.605
Louisville (4th)‡	.486
1963-1968—Did not operate.	
1969—Omaha	.607
1970—Omaha°	.529
Denver	.504
1971—Indianapolis	.604
Denver°	.521
1972—Wichita	.621
Evansville°	.593
1973—Iowa	.610
Tulsa°	.504
1974—Indianapolis	.578
Tulsa°	.567
1975—Evansville°	.566
Denver	.596
1976—Denver°	.632
Omaha	.574
1977—Omaha	.563
Denver°	.522
1978—Indianapolis	.578
Omaha°	.489
1979—Evansville°	.574
Oklahoma City	.533
1980—Denver	.676
Springfield°	.551

*Won playoff (East vs. West). †Won championship and four-team playoff. ‡Won four-team playoff. §Respective Eastern and Western division winners.

STANDING OF CLUBS AT CLOSE OF SEASON
EAST DIVISION

Club	Evan.	Spfd.	Ind.	Iowa	Oma.	Den.	O.C.	Wich.	W.	L.	T.	Pct.	G.B.
Evansville (Tigers)	....	11	15	16	8	9	7	7	73	63	0	.537	....
Springfield (Cardinals)	13	....	10	14	4	6	9	10	66	70	0	.485	7
Indianapolis (Reds)	9	14	....	12	4	5	9	9	62	74	0	.456	11
Iowa (Cubs)	8	10	12	....	2	11	4	6	53	82	0	.393	19½

WEST DIVISION

Club	Evan.	Spfd.	Ind.	Iowa	Oma.	Den.	O.C.	Wich.	W.	L.	T.	Pct.	G.B.
Omaha (Royals)	8	12	12	14	....	12	11	10	79	57	0	.581	....
Denver (Expos)	7	10	11	5	12	....	16	15	76	60	0	.559	3
Oklahoma City (Phillies)	9	7	7	12	13	8	....	13	69	67	0	.507	10
Wichita (Rangers)	9	6	7	9	14	9	11	....	65	70	0	.481	13½

Iowa club represented Des Moines, Ia.

Major league affiliations in parentheses.

Playoff—Denver defeated Omaha, four games to none.

Regular Season Attendance—Denver, 555,806; Evansville, 113,167; Indianapolis, 205,220; Iowa, 124,371; Oklahoma City, 191,502; Omaha, 196,924; Springfield, 120,537; Wichita, 122,371. Total—1,629,898. Playoffs, 32,314. No all-star game.

Managers: Denver—Felipe Alou; Evansville—Jim Leyland; Indianapolis—Jim Beauchamp; Iowa—Randy Hundley, Roy Hartsfield; Oklahoma City—Jim Snyder; Omaha—Joe Sparks; Springfield—Tommy Thompson; Wichita—Rich Donnelly.

All-Star Team: 1B—Hostetler, Denver; 2B—Richardt, Wichita; 3B—Castillo, Omaha; SS—Sandberg, Oklahoma City; OF—Briggs, Denver; Dernier, Oklahoma City; Francona, Denver; Householder, Indianapolis; Utility—Gates, Denver; Matuszek, Oklahoma City; C—Bjorkman, Springfield; Van Gorder, Indianapolis; DH—Jones, Wichita; P—Jones, Omaha; Lewallyn, Wichita; Schattinger, Omaha; Smith, Denver; Manager—Sparks, Omaha.

(Compiled by Ed Williams, League Statistician, Shawnee, Okla.)

CLUB BATTING

Club	Pct.	G.	AB.	R.	OR.	H.	TB.	2B.	3B.	HR.	RBI.	GW.	SH.	SF.	HP.	BB.	Int. BB.	SO.	SB.	CS.	LOB.
Denver	.287	136	4483	733	666	1285	1921	239	44	103	670	67	54	38	26	534	42	623	104	49	978
Wichita	.277	135	4271	615	718	1181	1701	169	27	99	567	58	57	44	30	544	19	588	152	65	996
Okla. City	.274	136	4419	582	647	1211	1779	210	44	90	628	63	37	44	22	498	46	620	171	61	923
Springfield	.273	136	4476	658	602	1221	1899	209	23	141	604	59	33	29	40	496	33	807	96	52	972
Omaha	.268	136	4393	617	552	1178	1747	209	39	94	571	70	58	41	25	493	33	601	104	62	958
Evansville	.263	136	4361	624	585	1146	1663	194	16	97	568	64	64	39	28	586	33	668	78	44	1013
Indianapolis	.262	136	4470	575	598	1173	1697	174	28	98	519	55	78	36	19	468	53	725	103	37	1008
Iowa	.251	135	4309	567	703	1081	1591	187	31	87	501	49	51	30	31	504	32	742	98	64	904

INDIVIDUAL BATTING
(Leading Qualifiers for Batting Championship—367 or More Plate Appearances)

°Bats lefthanded. †Switch-hitter.

Player and Club	Pct.	G.	AB.	R.	H.	TB.	2B.	3B.	HR.	RBI.	GW.	SH.	SF.	HP.	BB.	Int. BB.	SO.	SB.	CS.
Richardt, Michael, Wichita	.354	90	350	53	124	169	17	2	8	60	9	1	7	2	30	3	27	10	3
Francona, Terry, Denver°	.352	93	355	53	125	163	17	9	1	58	7	3	5	1	16	0	22	7	3
Roof, Eugene, Springfield†	.348	96	322	64	112	170	19	3	11	44	6	3	1	7	54	3	50	17	6
Castillo, Manuel, Omaha†	.335	136	543	79	182	251	31	4	10	91	9	4	5	0	44	10	25	2	8
Fiala, Neil, Springfield	.323	130	461	71	149	185	16	4	4	32	4	10	3	4	61	4	46	16	7
Hostetler, David, Denver	.318	125	440	91	140	249	14	7	27	103	8	0	5	4	66	4	89	3	2
Jones, Robert, Wichita°	.315	117	352	53	111	192	15	3	20	72	11	0	7	3	56	3	75	9	5
Matuszek, Leonard, Okla. City°	.315	129	463	87	146	240	27	2	21	91	6	2	3	0	76	22	57	14	3
Briggs, Dan, Denver°	.314	133	493	83	155	263	34	4	22	110	10	1	3	5	55	7	93	6	1
Mills, Bradley, Denver°	.314	118	427	65	134	206	34	1	12	66	2	4	6	2	38	7	34	2	3

Departmental Leaders: G—E.M. Castillo, 136; AB—E.M. Castillo, 543; R—Dernier, 105; H—E.M. Castillo, 182; TB—Briggs, 263; 2B—Gates, 36; 3B—Francona, 9; HR—Bjorkman, 28; RBI—Briggs, 110; GWRBI—Householder, B. Jones, 11; SH—Chappas, 20; SF—L. D. Johnson, 8; HP—Fletcher, 9; BB—Gulliver, 87; SO—Calise, 132; SB—Dernier, 72; CS—Rohn, 17.

(All Players—Listed Alphabetically)

Player and Club	Pct.	G.	AB.	R.	H.	TB.	2B.	3B.	HR.	RBI.	GW.	SH.	SF.	HP.	BB.	Int. BB.	SO.	SB.	CS.
Alfaro, Jesus, Iowa	.250	123	352	43	88	137	17	7	6	54	7	2	3	3	54	1	61	5	4
Altamirano, Porfirio, Okla. City	.500	29	2	0	1	1	0	0	0	0	0	0	0	0	0	0	0	0	0
Angelini, Norman, Denver°	.000	61	2	0	0	0	0	0	0	0	0	0	0	0	0	0	2	0	0
Aranzamendi, Jorge, Springfield	.256	22	43	6	11	16	2	0	1	4	0	1	0	1	0	0	9	1	0
Arroyo, Carlos, Okla. City°	.000	17	1	0	0	0	0	0	0	0	0	0	0	0	0	0	1	0	0
Bargar, Greg, Denver	.333	26	6	3	2	4	0	1	0	2	1	1	0	0	0	0	2	0	0
Barnes, William, Indianapolis	.263	36	118	10	31	42	6	1	1	11	0	1	0	1	9	4	10	1	1
Barranca, German, Indianapolis°	.284	125	482	68	137	180	22	3	5	34	3	5	2	1	42	6	62	22	9
Barrow, Melvin, Wichita	.303	32	76	8	23	23	0	0	0	9	0	3	0	1	5	0	13	5	1
Bazan, Pedro, Iowa°	.333	1	3	0	1	1	0	0	0	0	0	0	0	0	1	0	0	0	0
Benton, Alfred, Iowa	.202	70	203	25	41	69	8	1	6	20	0	1	1	2	15	2	35	2	1
Bialas, David, Springfield	.233	99	317	53	74	107	3	0	10	33	3	3	3	3	43	0	57	4	4
Bjorkman, George, Springfield	.254	107	323	69	82	182	14	1	28	66	5	1	1	2	72	4	86	2	4
Bogener, Terry, Wichita	.309	89	243	49	75	125	19	5	7	37	5	5	5	1	6	21	0	26	3	3
Bonaparte, Elijah, Okla. City°	.292	88	267	41	78	109	12	5	3	38	2	0	4	1	21	7	38	11	2
Bonds, Bobby, Wichita	.244	35	127	18	31	54	5	0	6	25	3	0	4	2	19	1	26	3	1
Bonham, William, Indianapolis	.143	4	7	0	1	1	0	0	0	2	0	2	0	0	0	0	3	0	0
Briggs, Dan, Denver°	.314	133	493	83	155	263	34	4	22	110	10	°1	3	5	55	7	93	6	1
Brito, Jose, Indianapolis	.075	25	40	1	3	3	0	0	0	1	0	1	0	0	1	0	15	0	0
Brown, Darrell, Evansville†	.270	101	430	53	116	142	17	3	1	30	4	5	1	3	12	2	46	30	6
Brown, Scott, Indianapolis	.000	51	11	0	0	0	0	0	0	0	0	0	0	0	2	0	7	0	0
Brummer, Glenn, Springfield	.234	26	77	12	18	25	2	1	1	8	2	0	1	6	0	16	0	1
Buckner, James, Omaha°	.118	14	34	2	4	5	1	0	0	4	1	0	2	0	4	1	3	0	0
Burton, Jeffrey, Iowa	.150	7	20	4	3	3	0	0	0	2	0	0	0	0	5	0	7	0	1
Calise, Michael, Springfield	.234	115	444	55	104	198	14	1	26	87	8	3	5	2	30	7	132	2	1
Capra, Nick, Wichita	.261	123	398	74	104	140	16	4	4	38	2	8	6	0	76	0	61	41	15
Carbo, Bernardo, Evansville°	.190	19	42	7	8	11	0	0	1	5	0	0	1	0	9	0	9	0	0

Player and Club	Pct.	G.	AB.	R.	H.	TB.	2B.	3B.	HR.	RBI.	GW.	SH.	SF.	HP.	BB.	Int. BB.	SO.	SB.	CS.
Carrion, Leonel, Denver	.250	1	4	0	1	2	1	0	0	0	0	0	0	0	0	0	0	0	0
Castillo, E. Manuel, Omaha†	.335	136	543	79	182	251	31	4	10	91	9	4	5	0	44	10	25	2	8
Castillo, Martin, Evansville	.265	120	396	63	105	183	23	2	17	68	6	6	3	6	68	4	81	8	2
Castro, Jose, Okla. City	.303	122	406	68	123	193	27	5	11	76	8	4	7	2	46	1	64	3	3
Chappas, Harry, Denver†	.222	126	424	65	94	121	16	4	1	34	3	20	2	3	65	5	70	24	7
Combe, Geoffrey, Indianapolis	.000	11	3	0	0	0	0	0	0	0	0	0	0	0	0	0	0	0	0
Concepcion, Onix, Omaha	.256	118	438	62	112	149	15	2	6	57	6	6	6	4	36	0	41	32	8
Corcoran, Timothy, Evansville°	.298	106	336	48	100	143	17	1	8	63	9	2	5	1	60	3	37	3	1
Corey, Mark, Springfield	.304	52	184	22	56	92	16	1	6	23	1	2	2	1	19	1	38	3	4
Cruz, Henry, Evansville°	.296	64	206	25	61	89	10	0	6	30	1	0	2	2	27	3	21	2	2
Davis, Odie, Wichita	.164	20	55	5	9	10	1	0	0	4	0	0	0	0	7	0	11	1	1
Dawley, William, Indianapolis	.289	26	45	3	13	16	0	0	1	7	0	3	0	1	0	0	15	0	0
DeJohn, Mark, Evansville†	.238	127	395	42	94	121	10	1	5	43	4	12	4	1	35	2	57	3	3
Dernier, Robert, Okla. City	.302	127	497	105	150	205	26	7	5	34	4	3	1	3	69	1	44	72	14
DeSa, Joseph, Springfield°	.292	132	497	60	145	215	30	2	12	73	7	0	5	7	67	9	66	4	3
Detherage, Robert, Omaha	.230	89	248	31	57	82	5	1	6	34	5	7	1	0	17	0	51	5	5
Dotson, Eugene, Springfield	.280	112	400	61	112	187	29	2	14	57	9	0	2	3	33	1	89	7	3
Dues, Hal, Denver	.000	20	6	0	0	0	0	0	0	0	0	0	0	0	0	0	3	0	0
Duran, Daniel, Wichita°	.241	10	29	1	7	11	1	0	1	3	0	0	0	0	0	0	6	0	0
Earley, William, Iowa	.667	29	3	0	2	2	0	0	0	0	0	0	0	0	0	0	0	0	0
Engle, Ricky, Denver°	.000	39	6	4	0	0	0	0	0	0	0	3	0	0	1	0	1	0	0
Esasky, Nicholas, Indianapolis	.265	121	423	55	112	193	22	4	17	62	7	2	1	5	46	5	110	1	1
Farkas, Ronald, Indianapolis°	.309	86	259	29	80	102	12	2	2	29	5	5	3	0	40	3	43	0	1
Ferrer, Sergio, Indianapolis°	.211	43	71	7	15	17	2	0	0	3	0	4	1	0	13	0	16	0	3
Ferris, Robert, Omaha	.095	8	21	1	2	3	1	0	0	1	0	0	0	0	5	0	7	0	0
Fiala, Neil, Springfield°	.323	130	461	71	149	185	16	4	4	32	4	10	3	4	61	4	46	16	7
Fidrych, Mark, Evansville	.000	25	0	1	0	0	0	0	0	0	0	0	0	0	0	0	0	0	0
Fierro, Javier, Iowa	.097	13	31	1	3	3	0	0	0	1	0	0	0	0	1	0	4	0	0
Filer, Thomas, Iowa	.500	21	6	0	3	4	1	0	0	2	1	0	0	0	0	0	2	0	0
Filkins, Leslie, Evansville°	.287	97	286	51	82	129	15	1	10	55	7	1	2	1	35	5	54	0	1
Fletcher, Scott, Iowa	.255	119	458	66	117	163	26	4	4	33	3	7	2	9	51	2	72	24	7
Foley, Thomas, Indianapolis°	.233	103	347	47	81	115	12	2	6	27	3	7	1	2	27	3	27	6	1
Followell, Vernon, Evansville†	.171	28	82	7	14	17	3	0	0	2	1	3	0	1	11	0	10	0	3
Francona, Terry, Denver°	.352	93	355	53	125	163	17	9	1	58	7	3	5	1	16	0	22	7	3
Franklin, Glen, Oklahoma City°	.250	34	96	14	24	33	5	2	0	10	1	2	2	1	9	0	11	6	6
Garcia, Daniel, Omaha°	.278	88	277	37	77	99	8	4	2	27	4	7	1	5	53	5	41	17	7
Garbey, Barbaro, Evansville	.083	4	12	4	1	1	0	0	0	0	0	0	0	1	0	0	4	0	0
Gates, Eddie, Evansville	.263	94	232	33	61	107	13	0	11	51	5	2	1	2	42	1	58	0	0
Gates, Michael, Denver°	.309	127	498	91	154	207	36	4	3	57	7	8	4	2	52	4	50	13	6
Gaudet, James, Omaha	.230	46	139	18	32	45	7	0	2	13	3	0	2	0	21	0	20	0	0
Geisel, David, Iowa°	.000	28	1	0	0	0	0	0	0	0	0	0	0	0	0	0	1	0	0
Gonzales, Daniel, Wichita°	.303	42	152	24	46	71	5	1	6	23	5	0	0	0	12	1	6	2	1
Grant, Thomas, Iowa°	.272	91	298	37	81	113	12	1	6	39	7	10	2	2	41	2	53	2	4
Green, David, Springfield	.270	106	430	66	116	178	26	3	10	67	5	1	3	2	24	0	83	23	9
Gulliver, Glenn, Evansville°	.265	121	366	67	97	139	15	3	7	41	3	3	3	1	87	4	33	9	14
Gustavson, Duane, Omaha	.250	3	4	0	1	1	0	0	0	1	0	0	0	0	0	0	2	0	0
Hale, John, Denver°	.329	55	155	27	51	81	7	1	7	26	2	0	1	0	24	0	46	2	4
Hampton, Raphael, Evansville	.257	134	440	64	113	147	12	2	6	43	4	12	2	4	60	1	81	15	2
Hayes, William, Iowa	.247	83	267	33	66	111	13	1	10	42	2	5	1	4	18	3	49	3	3
Heath, Kelly, Omaha	.240	111	387	52	93	133	21	5	3	37	5	4	3	4	42	1	34	13	4
Herring, Paul, Indianapolis	.262	45	122	8	32	34	2	0	0	9	1	3	2	1	8	1	25	0	1
Hicks, Joseph, Iowa	.240	125	363	47	87	153	16	1	16	50	2	8	2	4	53	3	87	3	4
Holt, Roger, Wichita†	.262	125	420	51	110	137	15	0	4	49	3	18	3	4	49	1	39	9	8
Hood, Donald, Omaha°	.000	33	0	1	0	0	0	0	0	0	0	0	0	0	0	0	0	0	0
Hostetler, David, Denver	.318	125	440	91	140	249	14	7	27	103	8	0	5	4	66	4	89	3	2
Householder, Paul, Indianapolis†	.300	124	453	72	136	224	19	6	19	77	11	2	6	1	50	12	72	33	8
Howell, Jay, Iowa	.000	23	2	0	0	0	0	0	0	0	0	0	0	0	0	0	1	0	0
Ireland, Timothy, Omaha	.260	126	450	65	117	169	23	4	7	59	9	7	5	3	63	1	48	8	11
Isales, Orlando, Oklahoma City	.251	93	319	43	80	109	15	1	4	44	4	1	1	3	30	0	37	3	7
James, Robert, Denver	.000	20	3	0	0	0	0	0	0	0	0	0	0	0	0	0	1	0	0
Johnson, Anthony, Denver	.186	14	43	4	8	11	1	1	0	4	0	0	2	0	2	0	4	2	0
Johnson, Bobby, Wichita	.263	109	354	46	93	173	18	1	20	27	5	0	1	2	44	0	104	4	4
Johnson, Larry, Evansville	.262	101	290	42	76	123	18	1	9	32	6	5	8	1	25	3	28	2	5
Johnson, Ronald, Omaha	.246	88	297	36	73	116	20	1	7	41	4	1	3	5	40	1	50	0	2
Johnson, Wallace, Denver†	.298	59	215	39	64	85	13	4	0	16	2	2	0	2	25	1	15	15	3
Jones, Robert, Evansville°	.315	117	352	53	111	192	15	3	20	72	11	0	7	3	56	3	75	9	5
Keatley, Gregory, Omaha	.237	78	241	27	57	83	7	2	5	21	2	6	2	0	19	0	48	0	2
Kelly, William, Indianapolis	.116	27	43	1	5	5	0	0	0	1	0	3	0	0	2	0	12	0	0
Kenaga, Jeffrey, Evansville°	.262	22	61	4	16	18	2	0	0	3	0	0	0	1	5	1	13	0	0
Kennedy, Kevin, Springfield	.130	9	23	2	3	4	1	0	0	0	0	0	0	0	3	0	3	0	0
Kerrigan, Joseph, Indianapolis	.083	54	12	0	1	1	0	0	0	0	0	2	0	0	0	0	5	0	0
Krug, Gary, Iowa°	.312	70	205	31	64	89	7	0	6	35	6	0	2	0	13	4	20	1	1
Kusick, Craig, Evansville	.250	54	160	40	40	67	12	0	5	16	3	0	2	1	41	0	38	3	1
Lahti, Jeffrey, Indianapolis	.273	51	22	1	6	8	0	1	0	2	0	0	0	1	2	0	7	0	0
Larson, Daniel, Oklahoma City	.000	31	2	2	0	0	0	0	0	0	0	0	0	0	0	0	1	0	0
Leach, Richard, Evansville°	.409	13	44	8	18	29	5	0	2	16	2	1	1	1	10	0	5	0	1
Leibrandt, Charles, Indianapolis	.241	28	54	5	13	15	2	0	0	5	0	9	0	0	2	0	16	0	0
Lezcano, Carlos, Iowa	.217	57	175	15	38	54	2	4	2	18	1	2	1	0	22	2	41	7	3
Lisi, Riccardo, Wichita	.258	103	326	49	84	128	11	0	11	47	7	0	2	5	45	3	37	9	5
Lockwood, Claude, Denver	.000	24	2	0	0	0	0	0	0	0	0	0	0	0	0	0	1	0	0
Lopez, Juan, Evansville	.254	122	409	41	104	130	16	2	2	41	4	12	3	1	39	3	59	2	3
MacPherson, Bruce, Denver	.000	13	3	0	0	0	0	0	0	0	0	0	0	0	0	0	2	0	0
Maddox, Elliott, Oklahoma City	.259	58	158	21	41	54	10	0	1	13	2	2	0	1	26	2	22	0	3
Mahlberg, Gregory, Indianapolis	.229	48	105	8	24	36	6	0	2	12	2	0	0	0	16	2	11	0	0
Matuszek, Leonard, Oklahoma City°	.315	129	463	87	146	240	27	2	21	91	6	2	3	0	76	22	57	14	3
McCormack, Donald, Oklahoma City°	.229	116	402	52	92	146	15	3	11	75	10	3	4	0	44	2	66	5	1
McClain, Joe, Iowa	.000	19	4	0	0	0	0	0	0	0	0	0	0	0	0	0	1	0	0
McDonald, Manuel, Oklahoma City°	.256	121	386	51	99	126	12	6	1	47	4	5	3	2	26	1	25	12	4
Mendoza, Michael, Iowa	.000	16	1	0	0	0	0	0	0	0	0	0	0	0	0	0	0	0	0
Menees, Eugene, Indianapolis	.212	77	170	15	36	43	5	1	0	10	2	3	2	0	21	1	16	0	0
Mills, Bradley, Denver°	.314	118	427	65	134	206	34	1	12	66	2	4	6	2	38	7	34	2	3

Player and Club	Pct.	G.	AB.	R.	H.	TB.	2B.	3B.	HR.	RBI.	GW.	SH.	SF.	HP.	BB.	Int. BB.	SO.	SB.	CS.
Milner, Eddie, Indianapolis°	.287	127	453	69	130	165	14	6	3	42	8	4	2	1	55	1	43	26	8
Miscik, Dennis, Oklahoma City°	.000	26	3	0	0	0	0	0	0	0	0	1	0	0	0	0	0	0	0
Motley, Darryl, Omaha	.288	109	410	63	118	200	18	5	18	64	7	5	3	2	24	6	58	8	4
Munninghoff, Scott, Oklahoma City	.000	28	1	0	0	0	0	0	0	0	0	1	0	0	0	0	1	0	0
Mutz, Thomas, Denver°	.221	59	145	15	32	48	7	0	3	19	0	1	1	1	11	2	19	0	0
Nandin, Robert, Evansville†	.188	24	48	9	9	10	1	0	0	3	0	0	0	0	6	0	5	1	0
Neuenschwander, Douglas, Ind	.000	22	8	0	0	0	0	0	0	0	0	1	0	0	0	0	1	0	0
Noles, Dickie, Oklahoma City	.000	23	1	0	0	0	0	0	0	0	0	0	0	0	0	0	0	0	0
Norman, Daniel, Denver	.272	73	239	46	65	117	13	3	11	38	6	0	2	2	27	1	36	13	3
Norman, Nelson, Wichita†	.246	115	349	37	86	93	7	0	0	31	1	11	4	1	26	0	40	3	2
Norris, James, Wichita°	.267	124	401	64	107	148	16	5	5	46	3	4	5	1	84	5	14	17	7
O'Keeffe, Richard, Indianapolis°	.171	36	35	2	6	7	1	0	0	6	1	4	0	0	0	0	12	0	0
Orensky, Herbert, Oklahoma City°	.224	30	76	6	17	28	6	1	1	5	2	0	0	1	11	0	16	1	0
Paris, Kelly, Springfield†	.267	90	292	38	78	108	10	1	6	31	3	3	1	1	26	2	48	4	3
Parker, Mark, Iowa°	.167	26	6	0	1	1	0	0	0	1	0	0	0	0	1	0	3	0	0
Patchin, Steven, Evansville	.250	40	88	10	22	40	3	0	5	19	3	0	1	0	11	1	21	0	0
Pate, Robert, Denver	.283	38	120	20	34	40	3	0	1	19	2	0	0	1	24	0	13	5	3
Penniall, David, Springfield	.254	62	205	27	52	86	14	1	6	27	3	1	2	4	15	1	35	6	3
Perkins, Craig, Denver	.292	14	24	3	7	11	1	0	1	4	0	0	0	0	6	1	3	0	0
Phelps, Kenneth, Omaha°	.333	19	66	9	22	47	8	1	5	21	2	0	0	0	12	1	9	0	0
Quintana, Luis, Denver°	.571	51	7	1	4	5	1	0	0	0	0	0	0	0	0	0	0	0	0
Ramos, Richard, Denver	.000	21	1	0	0	0	0	0	0	0	0	0	0	0	1	0	1	0	0
Rasmussen, James, Oklahoma City	.000	22	2	0	0	0	0	0	0	0	0	0	0	0	0	0	0	0	0
Ratzer, Stephen, Denver	1.000	41	1	0	1	1	0	0	0	1	0	0	0	0	1	0	0	0	0
Reece, Robert, Denver	.357	10	14	2	5	6	1	0	0	1	0	1	1	0	4	1	4	0	1
Reelhorn, Jonathon, Oklahoma City	.500	46	2	0	1	2	1	0	0	1	0	0	0	0	0	0	1	0	0
Richardt, Michael, Wichita	.354	90	350	53	124	169	17	2	8	60	9	1	7	2	30	3	27	10	3
Rivera, Jesus, Omaha	.259	126	429	73	111	188	25	2	16	60	7	2	1	7	77	7	88	4	5
Rodriguez, Luis, Oklahoma City	.263	74	251	32	66	94	10	3	4	34	2	3	4	1	19	1	38	5	6
Rohn, Daniel, Iowa°	.266	131	488	73	130	182	23	4	7	43	2	2	4	0	74	1	45	17	17
Roof, Eugene, Springfield†	.348	96	322	65	112	170	19	3	11	44	6	3	1	7	54	3	50	17	6
Rooney, Patrick, Denver	.212	55	179	23	38	75	7	3	8	29	2	0	2	1	12	4	32	1	1
Rosinski, Brian, Iowa°	.242	94	298	38	72	108	16	1	6	36	3	6	1	2	40	4	71	4	5
Ryal, Mark, Omaha°	.211	6	19	2	4	4	0	0	0	1	1	1	1	0	0	0	6	0	0
Sample, William, Wichita	.357	3	14	2	5	6	1	0	0	2	0	0	1	2	0	1	1	0	1
Sandberg, Ryne, Oklahoma City	.293	133	519	78	152	206	17	5	9	62	7	5	5	2	48	1	94	32	10
Santana, Rafael, Springfield	.500	2	8	3	4	8	1	0	1	2	0	0	0	0	0	0	0	1	0
Schmidt, David, Wichita	.000	12	3	0	0	0	0	0	0	0	0	0	0	0	0	0	3	0	0
Segelke, Herman, Iowa	.000	38	4	0	0	0	0	0	0	1	0	0	1	0	1	0	2	0	0
Semall, Paul, Iowa	.000	53	3	1	0	0	0	0	0	0	0	0	0	0	0	0	0	0	0
Sheridan, Patrick, Omaha	.298	86	315	49	94	140	15	8	5	31	3	5	0	1	32	0	61	12	5
Slaught, Donald, Omaha	.296	22	71	10	21	31	4	0	2	8	2	3	0	1	4	0	7	3	1
Smith, Bryn, Denver	.125	29	8	0	1	1	0	0	0	0	0	2	0	1	0	1	5	0	0
Smith, Christopher, Denver†	.303	38	132	22	40	54	9	1	1	17	3	0	2	2	22	1	15	1	2
Smith, Keith, Springfield	.210	22	81	6	17	20	3	0	0	4	0	0	0	1	4	0	9	3	1
Stephans, Russell, Omaha	.333	2	3	0	1	1	0	0	0	0	0	0	0	0	0	0	1	0	0
Stockstill, David, Iowa°	.176	22	51	5	9	13	1	0	1	4	1	3	2	0	7	0	10	0	0
Strain, Joseph, Iowa	.222	11	27	4	6	7	1	0	0	1	1	0	0	0	5	0	4	0	0
Suter, Burke, Oklahoma City	.000	25	1	0	0	0	0	0	0	0	0	0	0	0	0	0	0	0	0
Tabler, Patrick, Iowa	.306	63	222	41	68	105	13	3	6	37	2	1	3	3	25	1	40	2	3
Tamargo, John, Denver†	.263	20	38	1	10	11	1	0	0	3	1	0	0	0	4	1	6	0	1
Thomas, Randall, Springfield	.240	110	341	42	82	111	8	3	5	43	3	6	0	2	36	1	35	3	3
Thompson, Scot, Iowa°	.267	69	277	35	74	90	10	0	2	29	4	1	2	0	20	2	23	11	4
Tisdale, Freddie, Springfield°	.308	5	13	1	4	5	1	0	0	2	0	0	0	0	0	0	2	0	0
Tolleson, Wayne, Wichita†	.261	107	375	58	98	124	9	4	3	38	0	6	1	0	44	0	56	36	8
Turgeon, Michael, Iowa†	.216	102	328	39	71	93	13	0	3	24	4	1	2	1	44	3	64	3	5
Twitty, Jeffrey, Omaha°	.000	43	1	0	0	0	0	0	0	0	0	0	0	0	0	0	1	0	0
Ujdur, Gerald, Evansville	.000	26	1	0	0	0	0	0	0	0	0	0	0	0	0	0	1	0	0
Ulrich, Jeffrey, Oklahoma City	.140	21	57	1	8	9	1	0	0	5	0	1	1	0	3	0	11	0	0
Van Gorder, David, Indianapolis	.250	123	432	50	108	174	21	0	15	66	5	2	5	1	38	7	58	0	1
Virgil, Osvaldo, Oklahoma City	.229	83	275	41	63	111	11	2	11	44	4	1	2	5	41	4	59	1	0
Vukovich, George, Oklahoma City°	.302	62	232	40	70	113	15	2	8	48	8	1	7	0	29	4	34	6	2
Walker, Duane, Indianapolis°	.282	130	450	80	127	208	22	1	19	80	2	6	6	1	58	5	78	12	3
Waller, Tyrone, Iowa	.263	55	213	29	56	90	8	4	6	29	3	2	1	1	13	2	46	14	2
Washington, LaRue, Denver	.241	46	145	25	35	48	10	0	1	12	4	0	0	0	28	1	19	8	4
Werner, Donald, Wichita	.272	83	246	23	67	94	13	1	4	26	4	1	3	2	24	2	43	0	0
Whitehouse, Leonard, Wichita°	1.000	24	1	0	1	3	0	1	0	0	0	0	0	0	0	0	0	0	0
Wieghaus, Thomas, Denver	.241	124	345	48	83	110	13	1	4	50	7	8	2	0	49	2	33	2	5
Wilson, Glenn, Evansville	.243	10	37	5	9	17	2	0	2	7	2	0	0	0	3	0	7	0	0
Winslow, Daniel, Springfield	.133	7	15	0	2	2	0	0	0	1	0	0	0	0	2	0	3	0	0
Wolfe, Lawrence, Indianapolis	.264	72	254	37	67	95	5	1	7	30	5	2	5	3	33	3	46	0	9
Wortham, Richard, Denver	.667	16	3	2	2	2	0	0	0	1	0	0	0	0	0	0	0	0	0
Young, Kip, Indianapolis	.176	29	51	7	9	13	1	0	1	3	0	7	0	0	3	0	15	0	0

The following pitchers had no plate appearances primarily through use of designated hitters, listed alphabetically by club, games in parentheses:

DENVER—Campbell, David (10); Mueller, Willard (1); Shimp, Tommy (18).

EVANSVILLE—Bailey, Howard (17); Burns, Michael (11); Cappuzzello, George (8); Chris, Michael (16); Gumpert, David (1); Kinney, Dennis (46); Pashnick, Larry (25); Rothschild, Lawrence (56); Rucker, David (35); Seoane, Manuel (6); Underwood, Patrick (26); Weaver, Roger (23).

IOWA—Hernandez, Guillermo (19); Moore, Edmund (6); Myrick, Robert (12); Perlman, Jonathan (16); Wilkes, Gregory (25).

OKLAHOMA CITY—Brusstar, Warren (46); Davis, Mark (13); Faulk, Mitchell (4).

OMAHA—Chamberlain, Craig (21); Christenson, Gary (32); Cram, Gerald (2); Creel, Steven (6); Fischer, Daniel (22); Hammaker, C. Atlee (21); Jones, Michael (20); Laskey, William (23); Paschall, William (20); Schattinger, Jeffrey (59).

SPRINGFIELD—Chamberlain, Thomas (26); Citarella, Ralph (1); Davis, Christopher (28); DeLeon, Luis (52); Edelen, Benny (17); Frazier, George (21); Jorn, David (9); LaPoint, David (25); Littell, Mark (4); Little, Jeffrey (47); Martin, John (5); Moore, Donnie (21); Rincon, Andrew (8); Strelitz, Leonard (2); Stuper, John (28); Thomas, William (5).

WICHITA—Bruhert, Michael (4); Butcher, John (24); Crutcher, David (11); Devine, Adrian (11); Farr, James (24); Figueroa, Eduardo (6); Jakobowski, Stanley (2); Kainer, Donald (25); Kern, James (2); Lazorko, Jack (8); Lewallyn, Dennis (52); Mercer, Mark (46); Nielsen, Steven (6); Rajsich, David (36); Wilson, Gary (36).

GRAND SLAM HOME RUNS—Green 3; Esasky 2; Alfaro, Bjorkman, Briggs, Carbo, Manny Castillo, Marty Castillo, E. Gates, M. Gates, Hayes, Hostetler, Leach, McCormack, Motley, D. Norman, Wieghaus, 1 each.

AWARDED FIRST BASE ON INTERFERENCE—Paris 4 (Gaudet 2, Mutz, L.D. Johnson), Hicks 2 (Bjorkman, L.D. Johnson), Bialas (Benton), Buckner (Bjorkman), Esasky (Bjorkman), Filkins (Keatley), Lopez (Mutz), D. Norman (Marty Castillo), Norris (Patchin), Rosinski (Bjorkman) and Sandberg (Van Gorder).

CLUB FIELDING

Club	Pct.	G.	PO.	A.	E.	DP.	PB.	Club	Pct.	G.	PO.	A.	E.	DP.	PB.
Wichita	.974	135	3323	1477	127	139	11	Springfield	.970	136	3447	1463	152	140	11
Omaha	.972	136	3473	1392	140	127	4	Okla. City	.969	136	3411	1492	156	130	16
Evansville	.970	136	3454	1578	153	145	25	Denver	.969	136	3456	1480	160	119	7
Indianapolis	.970	136	3477	1439	152	123	7	Iowa	.966	135	3410	1458	173	132	13

Triple Play—None.

INDIVIDUAL FIELDING
FIRST BASEMEN

° Throws lefthanded.

Player and Club	Pct.	G.	PO.	A.	E.	DP.	Player and Club	Pct.	G.	PO.	A.	E.	DP.
Arenzamendi, Springfield	1.000	1	12	2	0	2	Krug, Iowa°	.980	32	229	16	5	22
Barnes, Indianapolis	.993	31	250	23	2	20	Kusick, Evansville	.977	29	243	14	6	29
Bialas, Springfield	.970	4	31	1	1	4	Leach, Evansville°	.986	13	129	16	7	9
Briggs, Denver°	.985	17	126	6	2	6	Mahlberg, Indianapolis	.972	6	34	1	1	1
Marty Castillo, Evansville	.984	12	59	4	1	5	MATUSZEK, Okla. City	.995	129	1146	101	6	114
Corcoran, Evansville°	.983	75	596	41	11	58	McCormack, Okla. City	.917	4	20	2	2	1
Cruz, Evansville°	.978	20	165	13	4	22	McDonald, Okla. City	1.000	3	45	6	0	1
DeSa, Springfield°	.992	132	1182	104	11	124	Norris, Wichita°	.992	96	818	60	7	81
Duran, Wichita°	1.000	7	47	3	0	8	Patchin, Evansville	1.000	8	49	4	0	8
Farkas, Indianapolis	.995	44	350	27	2	40	Perkins, Denver	1.000	1	3	0	0	1
Ferris, Omaha	1.000	6	47	0	0	2	Phelps, Omaha°	.989	18	169	15	2	19
Garcia, Omaha	.969	25	168	19	6	15	Tamargo, Denver	1.000	1	4	0	0	1
Herring, Indianapolis	.944	2	17	0	1	1	Tisdale, Springfield	1.000	1	10	1	0	1
Hicks, Iowa	.988	118	930	47	12	101	Turgeon, Iowa	1.000	2	21	2	0	1
Hostetler, Denver	.989	123	1104	66	13	92	Van Gorder, Indianapolis	.900	3	7	2	1	1
Ireland, Omaha	1.000	11	85	4	0	5	Vukovich, Okla. City	1.000	1	12	0	0	0
B. Johnson, Wichita	.978	17	125	7	3	11	Werner, Wichita	1.000	1	3	0	0	0
L.D. Johnson, Evansville	.941	3	15	1	1	0	Glenn Wilson, Evansville	1.000	1	1	0	0	0
R. Johnson, Omaha	.985	82	723	52	12	62	Wolfe, Indianapolis	.994	61	479	46	3	45
R. Jones, Wichita°	.996	25	214	11	1	25							

SECOND BASEMEN

Player and Club	Pct.	G.	PO.	A.	E.	DP.	Player and Club	Pct.	G.	PO.	A.	E.	DP.
Barranca, Indianapolis	.989	108	228	305	6	63	W. Johnson, Denver	.964	39	71	116	7	23
D. Brown, Evansville	.818	3	2	7	2	1	Lopez, Evansville	.968	116	243	330	19	89
Manny Castillo, Omaha	1.000	1	0	2	0	1	McDonald, Okla. City	1.000	2	3	5	0	1
Castro, Okla. City	.964	101	187	272	17	55	Menees, Indianapolis	.985	32	55	77	2	18
Chappas, Denver	1.000	1	4	5	0	0	Mills, Denver	1.000	1	1	0	0	0
DeJohn, Evansville	1.000	8	17	23	0	7	Nandin, Evansville	.913	4	9	12	2	3
Farkas, Indianapolis	.900	3	4	5	1	1	Richardt, Wichita	.988	36	72	97	2	16
Ferrer, Indianapolis	1.000	2	1	0	0	1	Rodriguez, Okla. City	1.000	1	1	2	0	2
FIALA, Springfield	.984	129	294	386	11	97	Rohn, Iowa	.979	84	189	276	10	63
Followell, Evansville	.889	7	19	21	5	5	Sandberg, Okla. City	.943	17	43	56	6	13
Franklin, Okla. City	.942	26	42	55	6	9	Strain, Iowa	.929	3	7	6	1	1
M. Gates, Denver	.980	101	207	237	9	47	Tabler, Iowa	.984	52	110	141	4	41
Gulliver, Evansville	.964	11	15	12	1	2	R. Thomas, Springfield	1.000	15	20	15	0	5
Heath, Omaha	.980	99	207	277	10	55	Tolleson, Wichita	1.000	5	16	12	0	5
Holt, Wichita	.981	101	232	335	11	83	Washington, Denver	1.000	5	16	12	0	4
Ireland, Omaha	.974	40	91	94	5	2							

THIRD BASEMEN

Player and Club	Pct.	G.	PO.	A.	E.	DP.	Player and Club	Pct.	G.	PO.	A.	E.	DP.
Alfaro, Iowa	.893	86	47	128	21	9	Ireland, Omaha	1.000	1	2	3	0	0
Aranzamendi, Springfield	.839	17	3	23	5	2	Lopez, Evansville	1.000	2	1	3	0	0
Barranca, Indianapolis	.882	8	3	12	2	0	McDonald, Okla. City	.915	68	51	143	18	11
Bialas, Springfield	.897	66	47	92	16	8	Mills, Denver	.952	117	84	236	16	20
Calise, Springfield	.872	19	10	24	5	4	Nandin, Evansville	1.000	2	3	0	0	0
Mn. CASTILLO, Omaha	.959	135	116	286	17	31	N. Norman, Wichita	.667	4	0	2	1	0
Marty Castillo, Evansville	.940	60	41	100	9	10	Paris, Springfield	.841	22	14	39	10	7
Castro, Okla. City	.900	8	8	10	2	1	Richardt, Wichita	.918	25	13	54	6	3
Corey, Springfield	.000	1	0	0	2	0	Rodriguez, Okla. City	.905	63	59	131	20	12
O. Davis, Wichita	.964	19	19	34	2	9	Rohn, Iowa	1.000	4	5	2	0	0
DeJohn, Evansville	1.000	1	1	3	0	0	Santana, Springfield	.500	1	0	1	1	1
Esasky, Indianapolis	.896	120	99	220	37	25	C. Smith, Denver	.818	4	3	6	2	0
Ferrer, Indianapolis	.667	2	1	1	1	0	R. Thomas, Springfield	.893	31	16	59	9	2
Fierro, Iowa	.944	6	5	12	1	2	Tolleson, Wichita	.974	71	49	139	5	13
M. Gates, Denver	.925	16	15	22	3	3	Turgeon, Iowa	.891	47	35	87	15	8
Gulliver, Evansville	.940	91	75	193	17	17	Waller, Iowa	.923	7	2	10	1	1
Hale, Denver	.667	2	1	1	1	0	Washington, Denver	.000	1	0	0	2	0
Holt, Wichita	.897	27	10	42	6	4	Wolfe, Indianapolis	.857	11	8	16	4	3

SHORTSTOPS

Player and Club	Pct.	G.	PO.	A.	E.	DP.	Player and Club	Pct.	G.	PO.	A.	E.	DP.
Alfaro, Iowa	.921	16	24	69	8	9	Heath, Omaha	.909	3	5	5	1	2
Aranzamendi, Springfield	.952	5	7	13	1	2	Ireland, Omaha	.947	52	103	166	15	35
Barranca, Indianapolis	.667	3	4	4	4	0	Lopez, Evansville	.857	2	3	3	1	1
Castro, Okla. City	.905	3	7	12	2	3	McDonald, Okla. City	.938	19	41	49	6	10
Chappas, Denver	.945	121	165	352	30	61	Menees, Indianapolis	1.000	15	3	28	0	2
Concepcion, Omaha	.936	84	126	211	23	41	Nandin, Evansville	1.000	2	1	2	0	1
DeJOHN, Evansville	.974	118	193	380	15	93	N. Norman, Wichita	.944	109	182	306	29	75
Farkas, Indianapolis	.953	30	29	53	4	6	Paris, Springfield	.921	69	105	198	26	42
Ferrer, Indianapolis	.915	16	20	34	5	5	Rodriguez, Okla. City	1.000	1	1	0	0	0
Fletcher, Iowa	.952	119	222	337	28	88	Sandberg, Okla. City	.972	117	186	340	15	64
Foley, Indianapolis	.942	100	175	267	27	61	Santana, Springfield	.800	2	1	7	2	2
Followell, Evansville	.960	19	30	67	4	7	R. Thomas, Springfield	.962	69	124	202	13	52
M. Gates, Denver	.949	17	18	38	3	9	Tolleson, Wichita	.932	36	30	107	10	14
Gulliver, Evansville	.929	4	2	11	1	1	Washington, Denver	.865	12	12	20	5	2

CATCHERS

Player and Club	Pct.	G.	PO.	A.	E.	DP.	PB.	Player and Club	Pct.	G.	PO.	A.	E.	DP.	PB.
Bazan, Iowa	1.000	1	4	0	0	0	1	McCormack, Oklahoma City	.981	84	419	42	9	4	5
Benton, Iowa	.966	64	353	40	14	3	8	Mutz, Denver	.948	39	113	14	7	3	1
Bjorkman, Springfield	.977	104	537	61	14	3	9	Orensky, Oklahoma City	.870	6	18	2	3	2	1
Brummer, Springfield	.976	26	153	13	4	1	1	Patchin, Evansville	.952	10	19	1	1	0	1
Marty Castillo, Evansville	.968	67	293	45	11	5	21	Reece, Denver	1.000	9	27	2	0	0	0
Gaudet, Omaha	.978	45	249	14	6	3	1	Slaught, Omaha	.970	19	91	7	3	0	2
Gustavson, Omaha	1.000	2	4	0	0	0	0	Stephans, Omaha	1.000	2	7	0	0	0	0
Hayes, Iowa	.977	74	344	39	9	2	4	Ulrich, Oklahoma City	.973	19	96	14	3	2	3
B. Johnson, Omaha	.979	71	333	47	8	2	6	VAN GORDER, Ind	.991	121	705	73	7	8	3
L.D. Johnson, Evansville	.973	79	368	29	11	5	3	Virgil, Oklahoma City	.983	35	201	28	4	9	7
Keatley, Omaha	.982	77	346	44	7	6	2	Werner, Wichita	.989	74	333	29	4	4	5
Kennedy, Springfield	1.000	9	37	2	0	0	1	Wieghaus, Denver	.985	119	621	87	11	12	6
Mahlberg, Indianapolis	.991	25	95	12	1	0	4	Winslow, Springfield	1.000	3	5	1	0	0	0

OUTFIELDERS

Player and Club	Pct.	G.	PO.	A.	E.	DP.	Player and Club	Pct.	G.	PO.	A.	E.	DP.
Alfaro, Iowa	1.000	1	1	0	0	0	Ireland, Omaha	1.000	8	11	1	0	0
Barnes, Indianapolis	.800	4	4	0	1	0	Isales, Oklahoma City	.987	91	135	13	2	5
Barranca, Indianapolis	1.000	2	2	0	0	0	A. Johnson, Denver	.923	10	11	1	1	0
Barrow, Wichita	.963	22	23	3	1	1	L.D. Johnson, Evansville	1.000	5	3	0	0	0
Bialas, Springfield	.973	21	36	0	1	0	W. Johnson, Denver	1.000	2	1	0	0	0
Bjorkman, Springfield	1.000	1	1	0	0	0	R. Jones, Wichita°	.992	71	118	8	1	1
Bogener, Wichita°	1.000	43	68	8	0	2	Kenaga, Evansville	.935	22	28	1	2	0
Bonaparte, Oklahoma City°	.925	75	111	7	9	2	Lezcano, Iowa	.972	56	96	7	3	0
Bonds, Wichita	.967	21	27	2	1	0	Lisi, Wichita	.968	96	203	6	7	2
Briggs, Denver°	.973	119	272	14	8	4	Maddox, Oklahoma City	.986	44	67	3	1	0
D. BROWN, Evansville	.988	98	250	7	3	0	Mahlberg, Indianapolis	.909	5	10	0	1	0
Buckner, Omaha°	1.000	5	22	0	0	0	McDonald, Oklahoma City	.930	24	39	1	3	0
Burton, Iowa	.833	5	5	0	1	0	Milner, Indianapolis°	.984	121	228	12	4	2
Capra, Wichita	.971	121	226	6	7	1	Motley, Omaha	.986	101	201	7	3	1
Carrion, Denver	1.000	1	2	0	0	0	Munninghoff, Oklahoma City	.500	1	1	0	1	0
Corcoran, Evansville°	.980	33	48	0	1	0	D. Norman, Denver	.981	59	100	2	2	0
Corey, Springfield	1.000	46	61	0	0	0	Norris, Wichita°	.956	27	40	3	2	1
Cruz, Evansville	1.000	4	4	0	0	0	Pate, Denver	.950	35	56	1	3	0
Dernier, Oklahoma City	.985	126	317	7	5	4	Penniall, Springfield	1.000	57	102	4	0	1
DeSa, Springfield°	1.000	1	3	0	0	0	Richardt, Wichita	1.000	1	1	0	0	0
Detherage, Omaha	.966	85	185	11	7	2	Rivera, Omaha	.975	82	151	7	4	0
Dotson, Springfield	.978	103	169	7	4	0	Rodriguez, Oklahoma City	.000	1	0	0	1	0
Duran, Wichita	.500	1	1	0	1	0	Roof, Springfield	.970	81	126	3	4	0
Farkas, Indianapolis	.923	8	11	1	1	0	Rooney, Denver	.978	52	85	3	2	2
Filkins, Evansville°	.958	91	130	6	6	0	Rosinski, Iowa	.973	89	135	3	4	0
Francona, Denver	.982	92	158	7	3	1	Ryal, Omaha°	1.000	6	9	1	0	1
Franklin, Oklahoma City	1.000	5	6	0	0	0	Sample, Wichita	1.000	3	9	0	0	0
Garcia, Omaha°	.992	62	120	1	1	0	Sheridan, Omaha	.984	80	193	2	3	2
Garbey, Evansville	1.000	4	7	0	0	0	C. Smith, Denver	1.000	12	15	0	0	0
E. Gates, Evansville	.982	48	54	1	1	1	K. Smith, Springfield	1.000	9	17	0	0	0
Gaudet, Omaha	1.000	2	2	1	0	1	Stockstill, Iowa	1.000	15	18	3	0	1
Gonzales, Wichita	1.000	34	42	3	0	0	Thompson, Iowa°	.968	69	177	3	6	0
Grant, Iowa	.980	91	187	10	4	1	Tisdale, Springfield	1.000	2	1	0	0	0
Green, Springfield	.985	106	251	12	4	1	Tolleson, Wichita	1.000	3	1	1	0	0
Gulliver, Evansville	1.000	14	14	0	0	0	Turgeon, Iowa	.975	53	75	3	2	1
Hale, Denver	.983	30	56	2	1	1	Vukovich, Oklahoma City	.989	59	87	8	1	1
Hampton, Evansville	.979	134	214	15	5	2	Walker, Indianapolis°	.973	129	213	3	6	2
Herring, Indianapolis	1.000	32	57	2	0	0	Waller, Iowa	.970	50	119	10	4	1
Hicks, Iowa	1.000	2	4	0	0	0	Washington, Denver	.953	18	40	1	2	1
Householder, Indianapolis	.979	124	315	10	7	2	Glenn Wilson, Evansville	1.000	10	15	2	0	0

PITCHERS

Player and Club	Pct.	G.	PO.	A.	E.	DP.	Player and Club	Pct.	G.	PO.	A.	E.	DP.
Altamirano, Oklahoma City	.778	29	8	13	6	4	Butcher, Denver	.923	24	11	13	2	1
Angelini, Denver°	.964	61	5	22	1	1	Campbell, Denver	1.000	10	0	3	0	0
Arroyo, Oklahoma City°	1.000	17	2	10	0	2	Cappuzzello, Evansville	.917	8	2	9	1	1
Bailey, Evansville	.963	17	4	22	1	5	C. Chamberlain, Omaha	1.000	21	3	13	0	0
Bargar, Oklahoma City°	.864	23	5	14	3	1	T. Chamberlain, Springfield	.979	26	12	34	1	4
Bonham, Indianapolis	1.000	4	1	3	0	0	Chris, Evansville	.941	16	4	12	1	2
Brito, Indianapolis	.750	25	4	11	5	1	Christenson, Omaha°	1.000	32	7	13	0	2
S. Brown, Indianapolis	1.000	51	2	7	0	0	Citarella, Springfield	1.000	1	0	3	0	0
Bruhert, Wichita	1.000	4	0	3	0	1	Combe, Indianapolis	1.000	11	2	5	0	0
Brusstar, Oklahoma City	1.000	46	6	20	0	1	Cram, Omaha	1.000	2	2	1	0	0
Burns, Evansville	.889	11	2	6	1	0	Creel, Omaha	.875	6	2	5	1	0

OFFICIAL BASEBALL GUIDE

PITCHERS—Continued

Player and Club	Pct.	G.	PO.	A.	E.	DP.	Player and Club	Pct.	G.	PO.	A.	E.	DP.
Crutcher, Wichita	1.000	11	2	4	0	0	Mendoza, Iowa	.800	16	3	5	2	0
C. Davis, Springfield	.933	28	4	10	1	0	Mercer, Wichita°	.917	46	4	18	2	1
M. Davis, Oklahoma City°	1.000	13	1	8	0	2	Miscik, Oklahoma City°	1.000	26	4	15	0	0
Dawley, Indianapolis	.967	26	8	21	1	0	D. Moore, Springfield	1.000	21	7	20	0	1
DeLeon, Springfield	1.000	52	3	13	0	1	E. Moore, Iowa	1.000	6	1	2	0	0
Devine, Wichita	1.000	11	0	2	0	0	Munninghoff, Oklahoma City	.971	24	8	26	1	5
Dotson, Springfield	1.000	1	1	0	0	0	Neuenschwander, Indianapolis	.857	22	3	3	1	1
Dues, Denver	.885	20	8	15	3	0	Nielsen, Wichita	1.000	6	0	2	0	0
Earley, Iowa	.929	29	14	38	4	0	Noles, Oklahoma City	.947	22	4	14	1	2
Edelen, Springfield	.964	16	10	17	1	4	O'Keeffe, Indianapolis°	.905	36	3	16	2	3
Engle, Denver°	.938	31	7	38	3	4	Parker, Iowa	1.000	26	10	23	0	3
Farr, Wichita	.966	24	9	19	1	3	Paschall, Omaha	.931	20	9	18	2	3
Fidrych, Evansville	.944	24	6	11	1	1	Pashnick, Evansville	.960	25	20	28	2	1
Figueroa, Wichita	1.000	6	1	4	0	0	Perlman, Iowa	.880	16	2	20	3	1
Filer, Iowa	1.000	21	7	26	0	1	Quintana, Denver°	.781	51	4	21	7	0
Fischer, Omaha	.889	22	5	19	3	0	Rajsich, Wichita°	.889	36	5	11	2	0
Frazier, Springfield	1.000	21	3	4	0	0	Ramos, Denver	.929	21	1	12	1	0
Geisel, Iowa°	1.000	28	1	3	0	0	Rasmussen, Oklahoma City	.966	22	11	17	1	1
Gumpert, Evansville	1.000	1	0	1	0	0	Ratzer, Denver	.962	41	11	14	1	1
Hammaker, Omaha°	.967	21	4	25	1	3	Reelhorn, Oklahoma City	.857	46	6	18	4	1
Hernandez, Iowa°	1.000	18	3	17	0	1	Rincon, Springfield	1.000	8	2	6	0	2
Hood, Omaha°	.840	30	4	17	4	2	Rothschild, Evansville	.947	56	8	10	1	0
Howell, Iowa	.897	23	7	28	4	2	Rucker, Evansville	.960	35	6	18	1	0
James, Denver	.833	20	4	11	3	0	Schattinger, Omaha	1.000	59	3	15	0	3
M. Jones, Omaha°	.857	20	2	16	3	1	Schmidt, Wichita	.950	12	8	11	1	0
Jorn, Springfield	1.000	9	3	7	0	1	Segelke, Iowa	.875	38	7	14	3	0
Kainer, Wichita	.964	25	10	17	1	3	Semall, Iowa	.850	53	2	15	3	2
Kelly, Indianapolis	.966	27	11	17	1	2	Seoane, Evansville	.750	6	2	1	1	0
Kerrigan, Indianapolis	1.000	54	7	21	0	1	Shimp, Denver	.917	17	2	9	1	0
Kinney, Indianapolis°	1.000	40	4	9	0	2	B. Smith, Denver	.965	29	11	44	2	4
Lahti, Indianapolis	.917	50	5	28	3	0	Stuper, Springfield	1.000	28	9	32	0	3
LaPoint, Springfield°	.879	25	7	22	4	1	Suter, Oklahoma City°	.964	25	8	19	1	3
Larson, Oklahoma City	1.000	25	12	22	0	2	W. Thomas, Springfield	1.000	5	2	1	0	0
Laskey, Omaha	.955	23	7	14	1	2	Twitty, Omaha°	1.000	43	3	6	0	1
Lazorko, Wichita	1.000	8	0	2	0	0	UJDUR, Evansville	1.000	25	17	31	0	3
Leibrandt, Indianapolis°	.943	25	9	41	3	0	Underwood, Evansville°	.972	26	7	28	1	1
Lewallyn, Indianapolis	1.000	52	5	14	0	2	Weaver, Evansville	1.000	23	13	25	0	0
Littell, Springfield	1.000	4	0	2	0	0	Whitehouse, Wichita	.962	20	6	19	1	1
Little, Springfield°	.955	47	7	14	1	2	Wilkes, Iowa	.875	25	3	4	1	0
Lockwood, Denver	1.000	24	0	9	0	1	Gary Wilson, Wichita	.909	31	7	13	2	1
MacPherson, Denver	1.000	13	4	8	0	0	Wortham, Denver°	.857	16	3	9	2	0
Martin, Springfield°	1.000	5	2	8	0	0	Young, Indianapolis	.904	29	15	32	5	5
McClain, Iowa	1.000	19	6	12	0	0							

The following players had no recorded accepted chances at the positions indicated; therefore, are not listed in the fielding averages for those particular positions: Barnes, 3b; Benton, 3b; Briggs, p; Carbo, of; Chappas, p; Detherage, p; Edelen, 3b; Faulk, p; Fiala, ss, c; Fierro, of; Jakobowski, p; A. Johnson, ss; L.D. Johnson, 3b; Kern, p; Lopez, 1b; Maddox, 3b; Mahlberg, 3b; Matuszek, 3b; Menees, 3b; Mueller, p; Mutz, of; Myrick, p; Noles, of; Norris, p; Rohn, of; Strelitz, p; Winslow, of.

CLUB PITCHING

Club	ERA.	G.	CG.	ShO.	Sv.	IP.	H.	R.	ER.	HR.	HB.	BB.	Int. BB.	SO.	WP.	Bk.
Omaha	3.68	136	37	8	34	1157⅔	1123	552	474	84	15	466	18	643	29	11
Evansville	3.78	136	30	15	31	1151⅓	1175	585	484	93	28	441	48	537	45	9
Indianapolis	3.92	136	13	3	35	1159	1118	598	505	91	19	529	58	748	38	16
Springfield	3.94	136	34	10	24	1149	1171	602	503	121	32	463	23	678	57	16
Oklahoma City	4.38	136	26	10	29	1137	1220	647	553	90	32	531	44	673	56	12
Denver	4.40	136	26	4	29	1152	1170	666	563	91	38	585	26	713	57	16
Iowa	4.83	135	24	8	17	1136⅔	1253	703	610	108	34	582	35	657	59	16
Wichita	5.22	135	23	4	32	1107⅔	1246	718	643	131	23	526	39	625	51	8

PITCHERS' RECORDS

(Leading Qualifiers for Earned-Run Average Leadership — 109 or More Innings)

°Throws lefthanded.

Pitcher—Club	W.	L.	Pct.	ERA.	G.	GS.	CG.	GF.	ShO.	Sv.	IP.	H.	R.	ER.	HR.	HB.	BB.	Int. BB.	SO.	WP.
Pashnick, Evansville	9	10	.474	2.89	25	25	7	0	4	0	165	154	66	53	18	3	49	3	64	7
Leibrandt, Indianapolis°	9	7	.563	2.93	25	25	5	0	1	0	169	149	76	55	9	4	75	3	101	6
M. Jones, Omaha°	11	7	.611	2.95	20	20	7	0	1	0	134	102	55	44	8	1	79	0	101	0
B. Smith, Denver	15	5	.750	3.05	29	24	9	2	0	1	183	166	80	62	13	8	42	1	127	6
LaPoint, Springfield°	13	9	.591	3.19	25	24	9	0	2	0	172	160	83	61	15	1	66	0	129	10
Larson, Oklahoma City	14	7	.667	3.49	25	25	8	0	1	0	178	163	76	69	15	2	83	5	112	3
Paschall, Omaha	9	7	.563	3.53	20	19	8	0	1	0	135	132	57	53	14	1	25	2	68	3
Hammaker, Omaha°	11	5	.688	3.64	21	21	8	0	1	0	146	147	70	59	13	1	40	1	63	2
C. Chamberlain, Omaha	6	7	.462	3.72	21	19	4	0	1	0	133	110	64	55	12	2	73	1	58	2
Engle, Denver°	6	7	.462	3.74	31	21	5	3	1	0	154	137	73	64	5	0	69	0	78	6

Departmental Leaders: G—Angelini, 61; GS—Underwood, Young, Earley, 25; CG—B. Smith, 9; ShO—Pashnick, 4; W—B. Smith, 15; L—Earley, 16; Sv—Lewallyn, 25; Pct.—B. Smith, .750; IP—B. Smith, 108⅔; H—Kainer, 192; R—Kainer, 115; ER—Kainer, 102; HR—Kainer, 29; BB—Earley, 90; Int.BB—Reelhorn, 16; SO—LaPoint, 129; HB—T. Chamberlain, 10; WP—Filer, 11.

(All Pitchers—Listed Alphabetically)

Pitcher—Club	W.	L.	Pct.	ERA.	G.	GS.	CG.	GF.	ShO.	Sv.	IP.	H.	R.	ER.	HR.	HB.	BB.	Int. BB.	SO.	WP.
Altamirano, Oklahoma City	10	6	.625	4.74	29	18	1	6	0	1	133	163	86	70	10	3	42	3	88	3
Angelini, Denver°	10	7	.588	3.18	61	0	0	30	0	4	99	99	52	35	5	3	46	8	67	5
Arroyo, Oklahoma City°	0	3	.000	4.76	17	1	0	7	0	0	34	40	22	18	4	0	15	1	15	1
Bailey, Evansville	2	7	.222	5.02	17	14	1	1	0	0	86	101	61	48	4	1	41	2	56	5
Bargar, Denver	5	6	.455	6.03	23	14	0	5	0	0	91	108	63	61	10	4	58	3	58	5

Pitcher—Club	W.	L.	Pct.	ERA.	G.	GS.	CG.	GF.	ShO.	Sv.	IP.	H.	R.	ER.	HR.	HB.	BB.	Int. BB.	SO.	WP.
Bonham, Indianapolis	1	1	.500	4.29	4	4	0	0	0	0	21	16	10	10	2	0	13	0	13	2
Briggs, Denver°	0	0	.000	0.00	1	0	0	0	0	0	1	0	0	0	0	1	2	0	0	0
Brito, Indianapolis	6	11	.353	4.89	25	22	1	0	0	0	116	114	77	63	11	2	77	3	91	7
S. Brown, Indianapolis	6	5	.545	2.28	51	3	0	35	0	13	87	59	23	22	3	1	42	6	86	1
Bruhert, Wichita	0	1	.000	10.00	4	1	0	2	0	0	9	17	11	10	1	0	11	4	1	1
Brusstar, Oklahoma City	3	2	.600	2.81	46	0	0	36	0	14	93	93	36	29	2	2	31	7	47	5
Burns, Evansville	2	1	.667	2.43	11	5	1	3	1	0	37	36	10	10	2	0	16	1	23	2
Butcher, Wichita	8	10	.444	5.63	24	24	5	0	1	0	136	171	100	85	19	2	60	2	87	7
Campbell, Denver	0	0	.000	4.91	10	0	0	5	0	1	11	10	8	6	1	2	11	1	5	0
Cappuzzello, Evansville°	4	0	1.000	1.76	8	5	1	0	0	0	46	41	15	9	4	0	13	1	27	0
C. Chamberlain, Omaha	6	7	.462	3.72	21	19	4	0	1	0	133	110	64	55	12	2	73	1	58	2
T. Chamberlain, Springfield	5	7	.417	4.43	26	20	2	4	0	0	126	150	79	62	19	10	52	2	54	8
Chappas, Denver	0	0	.000	3.00	1	0	0	0	0	0	3	2	1	1	0	0	2	0	1	0
Chris, Evansville°	2	2	.500	6.46	16	4	0	5	0	1	39	52	34	28	6	1	38	4	21	2
Christenson, Omaha°	4	2	.667	3.90	32	0	0	14	0	3	60	64	30	26	3	0	34	2	49	3
Citarella, Springfield	0	0	.000	3.86	1	1	0	0	0	0	7	7	3	3	2	1	2	0	2	1
Combe, Indianapolis	2	0	.000	1.89	11	0	0	9	0	3	19	16	5	4	0	0	11	3	10	1
Cram, Omaha	0	1	.000	7.20	2	1	0	1	0	0	5	7	5	4	1	1	2	0	2	0
Creel, Omaha	4	1	.800	4.26	6	6	1	0	1	0	38	35	19	18	1	1	13	0	29	0
Crutcher, Wichita	2	2	.500	3.12	11	3	0	3	0	0	26	23	15	9	0	1	16	0	14	1
C. Davis, Springfield	3	3	.500	4.16	28	5	1	13	0	0	80	92	43	37	11	1	19	3	39	5
M. Davis, Oklahoma City°	5	2	.714	3.88	13	13	1	0	0	0	65	66	34	28	6	0	47	2	56	4
Dawley, Indianapolis	6	8	.429	4.94	26	23	2	2	0	0	133	141	77	73	12	1	69	3	109	3
DeLeon, Springfield	8	7	.533	2.55	52	0	0	39	0	9	99	73	34	28	8	6	35	5	96	1
Detherage, Omaha	0	0	.000	0.00	1	0	0	0	0	0	2	0	0	0	0	0	0	0	0	0
Devine, Wichita	0	1	.000	7.71	11	0	0	4	0	0	14	18	14	12	2	0	12	1	6	1
Dotson, Springfield	0	0	.000	0.00	1	0	0	1	0	0	2	0	0	0	0	0	0	0	2	0
Dues, Denver	5	6	.455	6.73	20	18	3	0	0	0	91	113	75	68	12	1	60	1	47	7
Earley, Iowa°	4	16	.200	4.85	29	26	5	0	0	0	154	164	94	83	19	5	90	5	75	5
Edelen, Springfield	9	1	.900	3.56	16	16	3	0	1	0	96	90	42	38	8	5	35	1	45	3
Engle, Denver°	6	7	.462	3.74	31	21	5	3	1	0	154	137	73	64	5	5	69	0	78	6
Farr, Wichita	10	9	.526	5.17	24	23	4	0	0	0	141	171	89	81	13	4	44	3	76	4
Faulk, Oklahoma City	0	0	.000	5.63	4	0	0	4	0	2	8	10	6	5	1	1	4	0	5	1
Fidrych, Evansville	6	3	.667	5.75	24	9	2	8	0	0	83	111	58	53	10	6	27	2	26	6
Figueroa, Wichita	2	1	.667	7.83	6	6	0	0	0	0	23	32	23	20	5	0	18	0	10	1
Filer, Iowa	4	9	.308	4.79	21	18	3	0	1	0	109	123	64	58	14	2	57	2	61	11
Fischer, Omaha	7	8	.467	5.03	22	21	2	0	0	0	127	161	80	71	9	3	38	1	65	2
Frazier, Springfield	1	2	.333	3.19	21	0	0	16	0	5	31	35	14	11	1	0	11	0	28	3
Geisel, Iowa°	1	2	.333	4.50	28	1	0	15	0	1	38	38	24	19	2	0	31	2	43	2
Gumpert, Evansville	0	0	.000	4.50	1	0	0	0	0	0	4	5	2	2	0	2	1	3	0	0
Hammaker, Omaha°	11	5	.688	3.64	21	21	8	0	1	0	146	147	70	59	13	1	40	1	63	2
Hernandez, Iowa°	4	5	.444	3.89	18	8	2	8	0	2	74	84	39	32	5	3	27	0	41	2
Hood, Omaha°	4	3	.571	3.69	30	7	0	9	0	0	95	80	50	39	6	3	53	1	48	11
Howell, Iowa	5	10	.333	3.75	23	22	2	0	0	0	144	141	74	60	12	5	62	4	90	4
Jakubowski, Wichita	0	0	.000	5.14	2	0	0	2	0	0	7	8	4	4	2	0	3	0	6	0
James, Denver	1	2	.333	5.68	20	15	0	0	0	0	57	43	43	36	4	1	69	0	46	3
M. Jones, Omaha°	11	7	.611	2.95	20	20	7	0	1	0	134	102	55	44	8	1	79	0	101	0
Jorn, Springfield	2	3	.400	7.24	9	9	1	0	1	0	41	52	34	33	8	1	14	1	16	1
Kainer, Wichita	6	14	.300	5.67	25	25	4	0	1	0	162	192	115	102	29	1	73	7	87	4
Kelly, Indianapolis	4	4	.500	5.48	27	19	2	1	0	0	115	157	78	70	16	3	32	5	53	2
Kern, Wichita	0	0	.000	0.00	2	2	0	0	0	0	6	2	0	0	0	0	5	0	6	0
Kerrigan, Indianapolis	4	8	.333	2.97	54	0	0	32	0	12	88	76	34	29	4	2	39	10	57	1
Kinney, Evansville°	6	4	.600	2.03	46	0	0	24	0	12	71	64	27	16	4	2	33	11	45	3
Lahti, Indianapolis	6	6	.500	2.97	50	0	0	29	0	5	100	78	38	33	6	2	31	8	70	4
LaPoint, Springfield°	13	9	.591	3.19	25	24	9	0	2	0	172	160	83	61	15	1	66	0	129	10
Larson, Oklahoma City	14	7	.667	3.49	25	25	8	0	1	0	178	163	76	69	15	2	83	5	112	3
Laskey, Omaha	10	8	.556	3.91	23	22	7	1	1	0	138	136	67	60	10	0	52	3	87	0
Lazorko, Wichita	1	0	1.000	2.77	8	0	0	6	0	0	13	14	4	4	0	2	8	0	9	0
Leibrandt, Indianapolis°	9	7	.563	2.93	25	25	5	0	1	0	169	149	76	55	9	4	75	3	101	6
Lewallyn, Wichita	8	5	.615	3.44	52	0	0	44	0	25	68	68	27	26	3	0	31	7	45	3
Littell, Springfield	1	2	.333	3.79	4	4	0	0	0	0	19	20	13	8	6	1	10	0	6	0
Little, Springfield°	6	7	.462	3.87	47	3	2	25	0	10	114	98	57	49	6	2	65	4	99	9
Lockwood, Denver	2	5	.286	5.10	24	0	0	17	0	4	30	39	20	17	2	2	18	3	26	2
MacPherson, Denver	3	3	.500	4.11	13	6	1	2	0	0	46	39	24	21	4	3	14	0	16	2
Martin, Springfield	2	2	.500	1.46	5	5	3	0	1	0	37	26	8	6	1	0	9	0	25	0
McClain, Iowa	6	7	.462	5.35	19	19	1	0	0	0	111	112	72	66	8	1	77	1	82	9
Mendoza, Iowa	1	2	.333	6.84	16	0	0	9	0	2	25	35	27	19	5	1	11	1	19	1
Mercer, Wichita°	10	8	.556	5.26	46	6	1	21	0	4	101	99	67	59	9	3	55	9	60	4
Miscik, Oklahoma City°	6	8	.429	5.53	26	20	4	2	1	0	114	129	77	70	13	2	49	2	74	8
D. Moore, Springfield	8	6	.571	3.42	21	13	6	3	1	0	108	115	49	41	12	3	31	1	47	3
E. Moore, Iowa	1	0	1.000	3.46	6	0	0	3	0	1	13	13	5	5	1	1	8	1	6	1
Mueller, Denver	0	0	.000	0.00	1	0	0	1	0	1	2	1	0	0	0	0	1	0	2	0
Munninghoff, Okla. City	5	6	.455	6.12	24	15	1	2	0	0	97	122	78	66	9	3	58	1	33	7
Myrick, Iowa°	0	0	.000	17.25	12	0	0	6	0	0	12	35	23	23	0	0	6	1	5	2
Neuenschwander, Ind.	4	3	.571	3.73	22	1	0	8	0	1	41	38	27	17	3	0	23	8	32	0
Nielsen, Wichita	0	0	.000	13.20	6	1	0	3	0	0	15	33	24	22	5	1	7	2	6	2
Noles, Oklahoma City	6	6	.500	3.29	22	13	6	5	1	3	104	85	45	38	8	7	46	4	82	3
Norris, Oklahoma City	0	0	.000	4.50	1	0	0	1	0	0	2	1	1	1	0	0	1	0	0	0
O'Keeffe, Indianapolis°	6	7	.462	4.72	36	13	0	7	0	1	103	100	63	54	12	3	59	4	58	7
Parker, Iowa	10	8	.556	4.36	26	25	9	1	4	0	159	170	86	77	15	4	54	1	76	5
Paschall, Omaha	9	7	.563	3.53	20	19	8	0	0	0	135	132	57	53	14	1	25	2	68	3
Pashnick, Evansville	9	10	.474	2.89	25	25	7	0	4	0	165	154	66	53	18	3	49	3	64	7
Perlman, Iowa	2	7	.222	6.39	16	9	1	4	0	0	62	74	53	44	5	5	37	4	16	3
Quintana, Denver°	7	2	.778	4.80	51	4	1	12	0	2	105	116	64	56	9	2	50	2	90	5
Rajsich, Wichita°	6	5	.545	4.24	36	6	1	18	0	3	85	82	45	40	10	2	30	2	60	8
Ramos, Denver	6	5	.545	4.01	21	12	3	3	1	1	83	92	42	37	8	0	25	1	44	1
Rasmussen, Oklahoma City	7	10	.412	5.45	22	20	2	2	0	1	114	137	81	69	7	4	51	3	55	8
Ratzer, Denver	7	3	.700	3.42	41	3	0	26	0	13	71	85	32	27	4	2	21	4	33	1
Reelhorn, Oklahoma City	10	11	.476	4.37	46	0	0	41	0	7	103	114	55	50	7	7	57	16	43	5
Rincon, Springfield	1	3	.250	6.55	8	8	0	0	0	0	22	32	16	16	3	1	14	2	17	1
Rothschild, Evansville	8	5	.615	3.27	56	0	0	37	0	15	77	62	32	28	4	5	29	9	81	1
Rucker, Evansville°	7	4	.636	3.76	35	0	0	22	0	3	67	60	30	28	4	2	42	7	36	4

Pitcher—Club	W.	L.	Pct.	ERA.	G.	GS.	CG.	GF.	ShO.	Sv.	IP.	H.	R.	ER.	HR.	HB.	BB.	Int. BB.	SO.	WP.
Schattinger, Omaha	8	4	.667	2.65	59	0	0	41	0	23	78	76	29	23	3	0	33	3	40	4
Schmidt, Wichita	2	5	.286	4.86	12	12	4	0	0	0	87	90	47	47	9	1	26	2	49	2
Segelke, Iowa	5	7	.417	5.97	38	7	1	13	1	1	107	141	81	71	15	5	47	3	65	5
Semall, Iowa	8	6	.571	3.00	53	0	0	39	0	13	93	78	35	31	2	1	45	6	65	6
Seoane, Evansville	0	2	.000	2.70	6	0	0	6	0	0	10	10	6	3	0	0	5	0	8	0
Shimp, Denver	3	3	.500	6.84	17	4	0	2	0	0	50	63	41	38	7	3	26	0	40	3
B. Smith, Denver	15	5	.750	3.05	29	24	9	2	0	1	183	166	80	62	13	8	42	1	127	6
Strelitz, Springfield	0	2	.000	14.14	2	2	0	0	0	0	7	16	12	11	3	0	1	0	4	0
Stuper, Springfield	6	14	.300	4.92	28	22	6	0	0	0	161	175	101	88	18	0	85	4	59	9
Suter, Oklahoma City	3	6	.333	3.93	25	11	3	5	1	1	94	98	51	41	8	1	48	0	63	8
Thomas, Springfield	1	2	.333	3.81	5	4	1	1	0	0	26	30	14	11	0	0	14	0	10	3
Twitty, Omaha°	5	4	.556	2.96	43	0	0	32	0	8	67	73	26	22	4	2	21	4	33	2
Ujdur, Evansville	7	10	.412	4.09	25	25	6	0	2	0	163	170	94	74	9	2	60	3	88	8
Underwood, Evansville°	9	8	.529	3.98	26	26	6	0	0	0	165	158	86	73	19	3	44	3	90	5
Weaver, Evansville	11	7	.611	3.85	23	23	6	0	3	0	138	151	64	59	3	3	44	1	69	2
Whitehouse, Wichita°	6	5	.545	3.86	20	15	3	1	0	0	105	106	51	45	12	2	39	0	59	3
Wilkes, Iowa	2	3	.400	5.50	25	0	0	13	0	0	36	45	26	22	2	1	30	4	13	3
Wilson, Wichita	4	4	.500	6.39	31	11	1	7	0	0	107	119	81	76	11	4	87	0	44	10
Wortham, Denver°	6	6	.500	4.79	16	15	4	1	0	0	77	57	48	41	7	1	71	2	33	11
Young, Indianapolis	10	12	.455	4.04	29	26	3	0	1	0	167	174	90	75	13	1	58	5	68	4

BALKS—Hammaker, Howell, 6 each; James 4; Reelhorn, Altamirano and Kelly, 3 each; Underwood, Cappuzzello and Butcher, 2 each.

COMBINATION SHUTOUTS—Shimp-B. Smith, B. Smith-Ratzer, Denver; Cappuzzello-Kinney-Rothschild-Chris, Weaver-Kinney, Ujdur-Kinney-Rothschild, Pashnick-Kinney-Rothschild, Ujdur-Kinney, Evansville; Young-S. Brown, Indianapolis; Howell-Semall, Filer-Semall, Iowa; Larson-Noles 2, Munninghoff-Brusstar, M. Davis-Rasmussen, M. Davis-Brusstar, M. Davis-Reelhorn, Oklahoma City; Fisher-Christenson, M. Jones-Schattinger, Omaha; LaPoint-DeLeon, Littell-DeLeon, T. Chamberlain-Frazier, Moore-Frazier, Springfield; Wilson-Devine, Kern-Wilson-Mercer-Lewallyn, Wichita.

NO-HIT GAMES—Mike Jones (9 innings), Omaha, defeated Iowa, 2-0, April 27; Larry Pashnick (9 innings), Evansville, defeated Iowa, 1-0, August 19.

International League

CLASS AAA

Leading Batter
WADE BOGGS
Pawtucket

League President
HAROLD COOPER

Leading Pitcher
BOB OJEDA
Pawtucket

CHAMPIONSHIP WINNERS IN PREVIOUS YEARS

1884—Trenton ... .520	1926—Toronto ... .657	Rochester (4th)† ... .497
1885—Syracuse ... .584	1927—Buffalo ... .667	1956—Toronto ... .566
1886—Utica ... .646	1928—Rochester ... .549	Rochester (2nd)† ... .553
1887—Toronto ... .644	1929—Rochester ... .613	1957—Toronto ... .575
1888—Syracuse ... .723	1930—Rochester ... .629	Buffalo (2nd)† ... .571
1889—Detroit ... .649	1931—Rochester ... .601	1958—Montreal‡ ... .588
1890—Detroit ... .617	1932—Newark ... .649	1959—Buffalo ... .582
1891—Buffalo (reg. season) ... .727	1933—Newark ... .622	Havana (3rd)† ... .523
Buffalo (supplem'l) ... .680	Buffalo (4th)† ... .494	1960—Toronto‡ ... .649
1892—Providence ... .615	1934—Newark ... .608	1961—Columbus ... .597
Binghamton° ... .667	Toronto (3rd)† ... .559	Buffalo (3rd)† ... .559
1893—Erie ... .606	1935—Montreal ... .597	1962—Jacksonville ... .610
1894—Providence ... .696	Syracuse (2nd)† ... .565	Atlanta (3rd)† ... .539
1895—Springfield ... .687	1936—Buffalo‡ ... .610	1963—Syracuse x ... .533
1896—Providence ... .602	1937—Newark‡ ... .717	Indianapolis† ... .562
1897—Syracuse ... .632	1938—Newark‡ ... .684	1964—Jacksonville ... .589
1898—Montreal ... .586	1939—Jersey City ... .582	Rochester (4th)† ... .532
1899—Rochester ... .624	Rochester (2nd)† ... .556	1965—Columbus ... .582
1900—Providence ... .616	1940—Rochester ... .611	Toronto (3rd)† ... .556
1901—Rochester ... .642	Newark (2nd)† ... .594	1966—Rochester ... .565
1902—Toronto ... .669	1941—Newark ... .649	Toronto (2nd-tied)† ... .558
1903—Jersey City ... .642	Montreal (2nd)† ... .584	1967—Richmond ... .574
1904—Buffalo ... .657	1942—Newark ... .601	Toledo (3rd)† ... .525
1905—Providence ... .638	Syracuse (3rd)† ... .513	1968—Toledo ... .565
1906—Buffalo ... .607	1943—Toronto ... .625	Jacksonville (4th)† ... .514
1907—Toronto ... .619	Syracuse (3rd)† ... .536	1969—Tidewater ... .563
1908—Baltimore ... .593	1944—Baltimore‡ ... .553	Syracuse (3rd)† ... .536
1909—Rochester ... .596	1945—Montreal ... .621	1970—Syracuse‡ ... .600
1910—Rochester ... .601	Newark (2nd)† ... .582	1971—Rochester‡ ... .614
1911—Rochester ... .645	1946—Montreal‡ ... .649	1972—Louisville ... .563
1912—Toronto ... .595	1947—Jersey City ... .610	Tidewater (3rd)† ... .545
1913—Newark ... .625	Syracuse (3rd)† ... .575	1973—Charleston ... .586
1914—Providence ... .617	1948—Montreal‡ ... .614	Pawtucket y† ... .534
1915—Buffalo ... .632	1949—Buffalo ... .584	1974—Memphis ... .613
1916—Buffalo ... .586	Montreal (3rd)† ... .545	Rochester x‡ ... .611
1917—Toronto ... .604	1950—Rochester ... .609	1975—Tidewater‡ ... .610
1918—Toronto ... .693	Baltimore (3rd)† ... .556	1976—Rochester ... .638
1919—Baltimore ... .671	1951—Montreal‡ ... .617	Syracuse (2nd)† ... .590
1920—Baltimore ... .719	1952—Montreal ... .629	1977—Pawtucket ... .571
1921—Baltimore ... .717	Rochester (3rd)† ... .619	Charleston (2nd)† ... .557
1922—Baltimore ... .689	1953—Rochester ... .630	1978—Charleston ... .607
1923—Baltimore ... .677	Montreal (2nd)† ... .586	Richmond (4th)† ... .511
1924—Baltimore ... .709	1954—Toronto ... .630	1979—Columbus‡ ... .612
1925—Baltimore ... .633	Syracuse (4th)§ ... .510	1980—Columbus‡ ... .593
	1955—Montreal ... .617	

°Won split-season playoff. †Won four-team playoff. ‡Won championship and four-team playoff. §Defeated Havana in game to decide fourth place, then won four-team playoff. xLeague was divided into Northern, Southern divisions. yLeague divided into American, National divisions. (NOTE—Known as Eastern League in 1884, New York State League in 1885, International League in 1886-87, International Association in 1888, International League in 1889-90, Eastern Association in 1891, and Eastern League from 1892 until 1912.)

STANDING OF CLUBS AT CLOSE OF SEASON, SEPTEMBER 2

Club	Col.	Rich.	Tide.	Roch.	Char.	Paw.	Syr.	Tol.	W.	L.	T.	Pct.	G.B.
Columbus (Yankees)	....	11	12	11	15	12	15	12	88	51	0	.633	......
Richmond (Braves)	9	....	11	11	14	11	14	13	83	56	0	.597	5
Tidewater (Mets)	7	9	....	13	7	10	12	12	70	68	0	.507	17½
Rochester (Orioles)	9	8	7	....	10	9	12	14	69	70	0	.496	19
Charleston (Indians)	5	6	12	10	....	9	11	14	67	72	0	.482	21
Pawtucket (Red Sox)	8	9	10	11	11	....	9	9	67	73	0	.479	21½
Syracuse (Blue Jays)	5	6	8	8	9	11	....	13	60	80	0	.429	28½
Toledo (Twins)	8	7	8	6	6	11	7	....	53	87	0	.379	35½

Major League affiliations in parentheses.

Tidewater club represented Norfolk and Portsmouth, Va.

Playoffs—Columbus defeated Rochester, three games to two; Richmond defeated Tidewater, three games to two; Columbus was leading Richmond, two games to one, when final series was ended early because of rain (Columbus was awarded Governor's Cup).

Regular-Season Attendance—Charleston, 99,537; Columbus, 527,124; Pawtucket, 191,859; Richmond, 218,208; Rochester, 349,341; Syracuse, 198,097; Tidewater, 135,001; Toledo, 170,359. Total, 1,924,525. Playoffs, 34,999. No all-star game.

Managers: Charleston—Cal Emery, Frank Lucchesi; Columbus—Frank Verdi; Pawtucket—Joe Morgan; Richmond—Eddie Haas; Rochester—Doc Edwards; Syracuse, Bob Humphreys; Tidewater—Jack Aker; Toledo—Cal Ermer.

All-Star Team: 1B—Wells, Syracuse; 2B—Giles, Tidewater; 3B—Ripken, Rochester; SS—Robertson, Columbus; OF—Bowen, Pawtucket; Butler, Richmond; Rajsich, Tidewater; C—Bando, Charleston; DH—Balboni, Columbus; P—Murray, Syracuse; Ojeda, Pawtucket; Manager—Haas, Richmond.

(Compiled by Leonard Alley and Don Leigers, League Statisticians, Richmond, Va.)

CLUB BATTING

Club	Pct.	G.	AB.	R.	OR.	H.	TB.	2B.	3B.	HR.	RBI.	GW.	SH.	SF.	HP.	BB.	Int. BB.	SO.	SB.	CS.	LOB.
Charleston	.267	139	4414	638	630	1178	1704	177	38	91	573	58	61	35	27	618	35	771	137	61	1011
Columbus	.266	139	4659	738	604	1240	2064	214	44	174	696	81	46	33	40	557	32	866	47	42	984
Syracuse	.266	140	4737	616	646	1259	1760	224	44	63	550	54	40	34	38	471	49	668	141	52	1029
Richmond	.254	139	4492	604	544	1142	1672	157	38	99	541	76	45	31	28	646	38	812	127	68	1077
Pawtucket	.254	140	4746	544	551	1206	1823	212	27	117	494	61	55	26	33	489	41	813	107	64	1036
Tidewater	.254	138	4423	547	558	1123	1638	187	29	90	501	60	70	31	27	435	40	644	178	95	881
Rochester	.248	139	4744	614	598	1174	1813	206	35	121	563	60	61	34	36	574	34	822	125	67	1046
Toledo	.247	140	4431	510	678	1095	1594	186	23	89	467	47	72	33	25	409	25	658	116	56	877

INDIVIDUAL BATTING
(Leading Qualifiers for Batting Championship—378 or More Plate Appearances)

°Bats lefthanded.　†Switch-hitter.

Player and Club	Pct.	G.	AB.	R.	H.	TB.	2B.	3B.	HR.	RBI.	GW.	SH.	SF.	HP.	BB.	Int. BB.	SO.	SB.	CS.
Boggs, Wade, Pawtucket°	.3353	137	498	67	167	229	41	3	5	60	8	2	2	2	89	14	41	4	4
Butler, Brett, Richmond°	.3348	125	466	93	156	192	19	4	3	36	4	1	1	2	103	9	63	44	16
Hayes, Von, Charleston°	.314	105	382	58	120	181	19	6	10	73	6	4	4	3	55	6	56	34	7
Beamon, Charles, Syracuse°	.300	139	536	77	161	246	34	3	15	95	10	0	6	5	58	18	71	23	2
Ashford, Thomas, Columbus	.300	132	504	81	151	250	32	8	17	86	5	6	4	3	65	6	61	7	5
Tevlin, Creighton, Syracuse°	.297	117	427	62	127	159	18	4	2	40	8	4	3	3	45	1	30	8	4
Flores, Gilberto, Tidewater	.296	113	419	57	124	153	13	2	4	31	3	6	0	1	49	2	53	43	12
Estes, Frank, Toledo°	.293	117	403	42	118	158	18	5	4	54	7	4	2	1	23	1	35	10	5
Wells, Gregory, Syracuse	.292	112	435	70	127	215	20	4	20	71	7	1	5	4	40	8	51	15	4
Washington, Ronald, Toledo	.289	138	544	84	157	245	27	8	15	54	5	10	5	3	32	3	99	37	15

Departmental Leaders: G—Beamon, 139; AB—Washington, 544; R—Butler, 93; H—Boggs, 167; TB—Ashford, 250; 2B—Boggs, 41; 3B—Cannon, 11; HR—Balboni, 33; RBI—Balboni, 98; GWRBI—Brant, 15; SH—Fischlin, 15; SF—Beamon, Brant, Laribee, Lentine, Norrid, Ramos, 6; BB—Butler, 103; IBB—Beamon, 18; HP—Valdez, 10; SO—Balboni, 146; SB—Williams, 51; CS—Williams, 18.

(All Players—Listed Alphabetically)

Player and Club	Pct.	G.	AB.	R.	H.	TB.	2B.	3B.	HR.	RBI.	GW.	SH.	SF.	HP.	BB.	Int. BB.	SO.	SB.	CS.
Anderson, Karl, Charleston	.000	16	1	0	0	0	0	0	0	0	0	1	0	0	0	0	1	0	0
Ashford, Thomas, Columbus	.300	132	504	81	151	250	32	8	17	86	5	6	4	3	65	6	61	7	5
Backman, Wally, Tidewater†	.153	21	59	6	9	14	3	1	0	6	0	1	0	0	10	1	8	2	2
Baker, David, Syracuse°	.240	116	367	38	88	119	13	0	6	40	4	4	1	4	53	10	73	2	1
Baker, Ricky, Charleston†	.257	78	269	43	69	81	6	3	0	28	4	5	2	1	28	0	49	20	6
Balboni, Stephen, Columbus	.247	125	434	68	107	231	21	2	33	98	13	0	3	6	55	5	146	0	0
Bando, Christopher, Charleston†	.306	96	320	47	98	151	16	2	11	45	3	1	1	1	54	8	34	5	1
Barrett, Martin, Pawtucket	.265	88	343	36	91	110	12	2	1	28	3	9	1	1	31	0	17	9	8
Barton, Kenneth, Charleston†	.263	57	198	19	52	62	10	0	0	27	4	0	2	1	26	0	27	3	1
Beamon, Charles, Syracuse°	.300	139	536	77	161	246	34	3	15	95	10	0	6	5	58	18	71	23	2
Beltre, Sergio, Tidewater	.177	51	158	15	28	44	6	2	2	42	2	2	0	2	11	0	37	4	3
Bochy, Bruce, Tidewater	.227	85	269	23	61	100	11	2	8	38	2	3	2	1	22	3	47	0	3
Boggs, Wade, Pawtucket°	.335	137	498	67	167	229	41	3	5	60	8	2	2	2	89	14	41	4	4
Boitano, Danny, Tidewater	.000	40	3	0	0	0	0	0	0	0	0	0	0	0	1	0	2	0	0
Bonner, Robert, Rochester	.229	84	301	19	69	90	10	1	3	35	1	8	2	2	9	0	39	10	6
Borgmann, Glenn, Charleston	.217	11	23	0	5	6	1	0	0	1	0	1	0	0	7	1	3	0	0
Bourjos, Christopher, Rochester	.249	58	197	30	49	74	7	3	4	16	2	2	1	4	13	0	17	3	1
Bowen, Samuel, Pawtucket	.243	131	445	65	108	211	14	4	27	64	6	6	0	2	74	3	123	5	4
Brant, Marshall, Columbus	.261	121	456	80	119	215	19	1	25	95	15	0	6	9	73	2	117	1	0
Brown, Rogers, Columbus†	.329	40	152	28	50	80	6	3	6	27	4	0	0	0	13	5	26	8	5
Brown, Thomas, Syracuse	.000	7	1	0	0	0	0	0	0	0	0	0	0	0	0	0	0	0	0
Bucci, Michael, Charleston	.204	92	245	36	50	54	4	0	0	19	2	5	4	3	33	1	31	5	6
Butler, Brett, Richmond°	.335	125	466	93	156	192	19	4	3	36	4	1	1	2	103	9	63	44	16
Cadahia, Aurelio, Toledo	.208	31	53	6	11	14	3	0	0	3	0	2	1	0	3	0	2	0	0
Callahan, Patrick, Columbus	.235	21	51	6	12	15	1	1	0	4	0	0	0	0	5	0	15	0	2
Cannon, Joseph, Charleston	.231	134	463	54	107	163	19	11	5	50	2	2	3	4	31	8	97	23	10
Charboneau, Joseph, Charleston	.217	14	46	6	10	11	1	0	0	3	0	0	1	0	6	0	7	0	0
Chapman, Kelvin, Syracuse	.226	128	513	77	116	156	25	3	3	45	3	5	3	6	58	0	60	28	12
Chapman, Nathan, Columbus°	.207	9	29	0	6	7	1	0	0	0	0	3	0	0	1	0	5	1	0
Chauncey, Keathel, Toledo°	.263	106	278	38	73	111	12	1	8	35	3	4	4	2	37	0	48	8	6

Player and Club	Pct.	G.	AB.	R.	H.	TB.	2B.	3B.	HR.	RBI.	GW.	SH.	SF.	HP.	BB.	Int. BB.	SO.	SB.	CS.
Chism, Thomas, Rochester°	.255	100	302	37	77	126	11	1	12	44	7	1	2	5	38	2	46	1	1
Christensen, James, Toledo	.188	19	48	5	9	17	2	0	2	7	1	0	1	0	5	0	6	0	0
Cipot, Edwin, Toledo°	.231	72	199	21	46	71	11	1	4	27	1	0	2	2	27	3	31	1	2
Coleman, David, Columbus	.231	61	160	23	37	57	2	0	6	16	1	0	1	2	21	0	39	0	0
Corey, Mark, Rochester	.239	23	67	15	16	27	4	2	1	5	1	0	1	1	18	1	26	1	2
Craig, Rodney, Charleston†	.256	23	78	14	20	31	3	1	2	5	2	1	0	0	8	0	14	7	3
Cuellar, Robert, Charleston	.000	42	1	1	0	0	0	0	0	0	0	0	0	0	0	0	0	0	0
Cuervo, Edward, Tidewater†	.333	1	3	1	1	4	0	0	1	1	0	0	0	0	1	0	0	0	0
Curry, Steven, Richmond	.189	68	206	15	39	61	7	0	5	19	2	4	2	2	25	0	54	0	4
Davis, Odie, Charleston	.214	66	103	24	37	46	6	0	1	13	2	5	0	2	17	0	39	1	5
Davis, Steven, Syracuse	.282	50	149	19	42	54	7	1	1	15	3	4	0	0	16	1	26	3	1
Dooner, Glenn, Toledo	.000	59	1	0	0	0	0	0	0	0	0	0	0	0	0	0	1	0	0
Eaton, Tom, Rochester	.216	115	371	42	80	95	10	1	1	26	5	11	1	2	62	0	41	16	12
Espino, Juan, Columbus	.233	80	253	22	59	92	8	2	7	32	4	3	0	2	19	0	36	0	1
Estes, Frank, Toledo°	.293	117	403	42	118	158	18	5	4	54	7	4	2	1	23	1	35	10	5
Faedo, Leonardo, 64-Char.-43-Tol..	.250	107	348	41	87	129	15	3	7	44	2	6	2	1	14	1	38	1	2
Fernandez, Octavio, Syracuse†	.278	31	115	13	32	45	6	2	1	9	0	2	1	2	7	0	15	9	5
Fischlin, Michael, Charleston	.238	136	463	83	110	153	14	7	5	43	4	15	2	5	89	0	97	40	13
Fitzgerald, Michael, Tidewater	.155	24	58	9	9	14	2	0	1	3	2	1	1	0	5	0	13	2	0
Flores, Gilberto, Tidewater	.296	113	419	57	124	153	13	2	4	31	3	6	0	1	49	2	53	43	12
Funderburk, Mark, Toledo	.223	119	394	47	88	158	14	1	18	52	2	1	1	3	27	4	71	2	1
Gaff, Brent, Tidewater	.000	23	1	0	0	0	0	0	0	0	0	0	0	0	0	0	0	0	0
Gardenhire, Ronald, Tidewater	.254	125	414	52	105	144	17	8	2	40	3	6	4	2	28	1	61	28	12
Gardner, Vassie, Charleston	.281	26	96	14	27	41	4	2	2	10	0	1	0	0	7	0	23	4	5
Gedman, Richard, Pawtucket°	.296	25	81	8	24	33	3	0	2	11	0	0	0	1	9	3	11	0	1
Giles, Brian, Tidewater	.268	121	400	60	107	151	17	3	7	40	1	8	3	1	49	5	70	16	12
Graham, Lee, Pawtucket°	.218	133	472	50	103	127	22	1	0	30	0	9	2	1	47	4	55	33	13
Gulden, Bradley, Columbus°	.295	73	237	37	70	142	13	4	17	42	4	1	2	2	24	3	41	1	3
Hale, John, Rochester°	.220	35	118	14	26	51	6	2	5	16	2	1	1	0	15	1	35	0	2
Hammond, Steven, Richmond°	.274	87	310	31	85	113	20	1	2	40	5	1	2	3	23	2	37	2	0
Harer, Wayne, Columbus†	.270	111	397	68	107	138	15	5	2	34	7	6	1	1	67	3	41	11	7
Harris, Greg, Tidewater	.000	8	2	0	0	0	0	0	0	0	0	0	0	0	0	0	2	0	0
Harper, Terry, Richmond	.227	10	44	3	10	19	3	0	2	4	1	0	0	1	2	0	9	0	1
Hart, Michael, 88-Roch.-19-Tol.†	.259	107	313	53	81	129	12	3	10	33	3	2	4	1	87	4	73	4	4
Haslerig, William, Tidewater°	.234	37	124	10	29	35	6	0	0	12	2	1	1	1	4	0	37	6	4
Hayes, Von, Charleston°	.314	105	382	58	120	181	19	6	10	73	6	4	4	3	55	6	56	34	7
Hazewood, Drungo, Rochester	.094	18	64	5	6	9	0	0	1	6	0	1	1	0	5	0	22	0	0
Hernandez, Pedro, Syracuse	.256	84	262	27	67	90	14	3	1	28	3	5	0	3	16	0	45	2	4
Herz, Steven, Toledo	.225	119	342	37	77	98	18	0	1	27	4	12	5	7	21	2	36	2	1
Howard, Michael, Tidewater†	.278	120	418	56	116	166	22	5	6	33	4	7	3	1	48	6	62	23	17
Huppert, David, 47-Roc—21-Tol.	.182	68	176	22	32	46	6	1	2	12	1	6	0	4	35	0	48	1	1
Johnson, Randall, Richmond	.281	126	470	78	132	196	20	4	12	72	9	12	3	1	52	1	45	1	1
Johnston, Gregory, Toledo°	.235	112	405	39	95	141	13	3	9	42	7	1	1	1	33	2	76	9	3
Jurak, Edward, Pawtucket	.300	23	90	13	27	37	3	2	1	9	1	0	0	3	11	0	14	1	0
Keller, Charles, Richmond	.191	98	314	37	60	132	6	0	22	60	9	1	2	2	65	3	91	0	1
Kennedy, Kevin, Rochester	.183	24	71	5	13	15	2	0	0	5	1	1	1	0	4	0	12	0	0
Koza, David, Pawtucket	.268	104	410	44	110	192	26	1	18	54	11	1	4	2	20	1	71	2	2
Krenchicki, Wayne, Rochester°	.179	16	56	5	10	10	0	0	0	4	2	1	0	0	6	2	8	3	0
Kubski, Gilbert, Syracuse°	.242	18	66	11	16	27	6	1	1	4	0	0	0	0	5	0	13	1	0
LaFrancois, Roger, Pawtucket°	.230	95	309	26	71	104	13	1	6	16	3	3	1	3	15	5	54	3	1
Landis, Craig, Richmond	.238	83	261	41	62	94	11	0	7	24	4	1	0	6	51	4	43	5	3
Laribee, Russell, Pawtucket°	.212	92	325	36	69	119	11	0	13	46	5	1	6	3	42	2	87	11	7
Lentine, James, Charleston	.279	134	451	60	126	174	23	5	5	59	4	9	6	3	69	3	48	9	9
Lickert, John, Pawtucket	.091	15	33	2	3	7	1	0	1	3	0	0	1	0	6	0	7	1	0
Littleton, Larry, Charleston	.276	91	275	41	76	119	12	2	9	34	2	4	1	2	42	0	69	2	2
Logan, Daniel, Rochester°	.255	130	440	53	112	195	14	0	23	73	7	3	5	1	68	8	85	0	0
LoGrande, Angelo, Charleston	.287	130	470	51	135	193	17	1	13	66	11	1	3	4	32	3	102	2	2
Lora, Ramon, Syracuse	.310	80	274	32	85	120	13	5	4	41	4	3	1	2	12	1	41	5	1
MacDonald, Ronald, Tidewater	.263	129	449	49	118	168	17	3	9	55	10	8	4	6	45	4	54	2	2
Machemer, David, Toledo	.283	72	187	21	53	67	12	1	0	17	1	3	3	2	20	2	17	3	2
Mankowski, Phil, Tidewater°	.251	55	199	18	50	72	4	0	6	30	4	1	0	2	18	3	20	3	2
Miller, Michael, Richmond†	.146	24	41	2	6	6	0	0	0	2	0	2	0	0	4	0	10	0	0
Norman, Daniel, Tidewater	.247	40	150	23	37	59	8	1	4	21	2	0	1	2	7	0	23	10	2
Norrid, Timothy, Charleston°	.250	104	292	34	73	116	14	4	7	39	3	2	6	1	24	3	32	0	1
Ongarato, Michael, Pawtucket	.240	110	325	47	78	129	18	3	9	31	2	5	3	1	24	1	56	5	2
Orosco, Jesse, Tidewater	.000	47	3	0	0	0	0	0	0	0	0	0	0	0	1	0	1	0	0
Pacella, John, Columbus	.000	31	2	0	0	0	0	0	0	0	0	0	0	0	0	0	0	0	0
Pagel, Karl, Charleston°	.272	114	323	62	88	163	13	1	20	67	10	1	2	0	81	9	102	3	0
Pasley, Kevin, Syracuse	.375	10	32	5	12	14	2	0	0	0	0	0	0	0	0	0	2	0	0
Patterson, Michael, Columbus°	.253	94	320	53	81	152	18	4	15	54	3	1	2	1	29	2	77	10	4
Perlozzo, Samuel, Tidewater	.207	33	82	10	17	20	0	0	1	4	2	4	0	1	9	2	9	2	1
Petralli, Eugene, Syracuse†	.265	45	151	17	40	51	11	0	0	16	0	0	0	0	16	1	11	1	1
Porter, Robert, Richmond°	.260	48	169	23	44	65	5	2	4	19	1	1	1	1	24	2	36	7	5
Pruitt, Ronald, Charleston	.295	40	105	17	31	47	5	1	3	13	2	3	0	1	32	0	13	2	0
Putman, Eddy, Rochester	.289	14	45	11	13	22	3	0	2	8	0	1	1	0	11	0	10	0	0
Quetti, Russell, Pawtucket	.121	18	33	4	4	8	1	0	1	1	0	1	0	0	5	0	12	0	0
Rajsich, Gary, Tidewater°	.277	74	253	47	70	155	11	1	24	56	4	1	3	3	28	7	52	6	2
Ramos, Domingo, Syracuse	.256	96	320	42	82	96	4	5	0	31	3	6	6	1	39	0	30	12	4
Rayford, Floyd, Rochester	.248	96	311	50	77	132	18	2	11	45	2	2	5	6	34	1	86	2	3
Ripken, Calvin, Jr., Rochester	.288	114	437	74	126	234	31	4	23	75	11	1	1	2	66	6	85	0	2
Robertson, Andre, Columbus	.259	123	402	55	104	145	13	6	9	49	8	7	5	2	13	0	70	4	4
Ruiz, Manuel, Richmond	.247	88	291	34	72	94	8	4	2	27	5	9	4	1	34	1	32	4	4
Runge, Paul, Richmond	.230	134	426	49	98	155	20	5	9	41	10	6	4	0	53	1	98	3	6
Saferight, Harry, 46-Rich—33-Roc.°	.218	79	257	21	56	68	4	1	2	22	4	0	2	2	32	5	37	0	1
Schmidt, David, Pawtucket	.194	63	191	20	37	72	8	0	9	25	5	1	1	1	39	0	62	2	2
Schmitz, Daniel, Columbus°	.278	111	356	65	99	122	16	2	1	28	2	11	2	1	54	2	31	0	5
Seibert, Kurt, Toledo	.237	97	245	21	58	68	8	1	0	17	3	12	3	2	25	0	34	5	4
Shelby, John, Rochester†	.264	76	326	42	86	132	21	8	3	32	1	5	2	0	16	0	55	18	6
Showalter, William, Columbus°	.189	14	37	6	7	11	1	0	1	3	0	1	0	0	3	0	0	0	0
Sinatro, Matthew, Richmond	.235	121	430	43	101	136	13	2	6	53	9	3	4	5	42	0	58	18	13
Smith, Garry, Columbus	.239	90	238	25	57	89	11	0	7	26	3	3	1	0	12	0	40	1	0
Smith, Keith, 33 Roc.—32 Tide	.215	65	163	16	35	51	8	1	2	21	5	2	2	1	9	0	11	6	3

Player and Club	Pct.	G.	AB.	R.	H.	TB.	2B.	3B.	HR.	RBI.	GW.	SH.	SF.	HP.	BB.	Int. BB.	SO.	SB.	CS.
Smith, Kenneth, Richmond°	.268	129	478	64	128	182	9	6	11	60	11	3	2	2	57	4	114	22	6
Smithson, Mike, Pawtucket	.000	37	1	0	0	0	0	0	0	0	0	0	0	0	0	0	1	0	0
Snider, Kelly, Toledo°	.248	105	359	42	89	139	14	0	12	43	6	3	1	0	49	2	50	2	0
Sofield, Richard, Toledo°	.208	22	72	8	15	20	2	0	1	4	0	0	0	1	12	0	12	2	1
Stegman, David, Columbus	.291	90	227	42	66	101	15	1	6	24	3	3	2	4	35	2	38	3	5
Stenholm, Richard, Columbus°	.220	79	186	28	41	78	5	1	10	38	3	0	1	3	25	1	29	0	0
Stroughter, Stephen, Toledo°	.247	27	73	9	18	30	6	0	2	9	0	0	1	0	8	1	12	0	1
Sweet, Ricky, Tidewater†	.277	128	462	58	128	172	30	1	4	55	5	8	3	2	55	3	36	14	9
Tabler, Patrick, Columbus	.296	52	179	41	53	106	14	3	11	33	4	1	3	4	27	1	43	0	1
Tevlin, Creighton, Syracuse°	.297	117	427	62	127	159	18	4	2	40	8	4	3	3	45	1	30	8	4
Thompson, Marvin, Syracuse	.270	124	440	54	119	154	22	2	3	55	7	1	4	0	53	1	62	9	3
Thompson, Tommy, Richmond°	.000	6	4	0	0	0	0	0	0	0	0	0	0	0	1	0	1	0	0
Valdez, Julio, Pawtucket†	.258	112	384	45	99	132	7	4	6	27	3	3	3	10	18	0	54	6	7
Valle, John, Rochester	.249	91	301	45	75	119	15	1	9	39	7	4	4	1	41	5	54	5	3
Vega, Jesus, 54 Tol.—51 Tide.	.258	105	365	44	94	127	13	1	6	35	3	3	2	0	33	4	51	20	9
Walker, Cleotha, Pawtucket†	.277	138	535	50	148	230	21	5	17	68	9	9	3	0	49	8	110	24	12
Walker, John, Toledo†	.217	125	391	40	85	111	9	1	5	35	5	13	2	0	43	4	56	27	10
Washington, LaRue, Rochester	.225	64	227	21	51	79	18	2	2	25	2	2	1	1	16	2	35	7	4
Washington, Ronald, Toledo	.289	138	544	84	157	245	27	8	15	54	5	10	5	3	32	3	99	37	15
Wells, Gregory, Syracuse	.292	112	435	70	127	215	20	4	20	71	7	1	5	4	40	8	51	15	4
Werth, Dennis, Columbus	.341	16	41	8	14	22	3	1	1	7	2	0	0	0	16	0	11	0	0
Whisenton, Larry, Richmond°	.271	129	446	71	121	192	14	9	13	72	4	1	4	1	89	8	98	21	8
Whitmer, Daniel, Syracuse	.204	66	186	18	38	51	10	0	1	11	0	3	1	4	22	0	41	0	0
Wilkins, Eric, Charleston	.000	10	1	0	0	0	0	0	0	0	0	0	0	0	0	0	0	0	0
Williams, Dallas, Rochester°	.283	127	523	69	148	198	17	3	9	48	1	10	1	4	38	0	45	51	18
Wilson, James, Pawtucket	.247	67	271	22	67	83	11	1	1	26	5	5	2	1	10	0	38	1	1
Winterfeldt, Todd, Tidewater	.211	86	237	26	50	77	9	0	6	27	8	9	2	1	21	0	33	2	4
Young, Michael, Rochester°	.333	1	3	0	1	1	0	0	0	0	0	0	0	0	0	0	1	0	0

The following pitchers had no plate appearances primarily through use of designated hitters, listed alphabetically by club, games in parentheses.

CHARLESTON—Brennan, Thomas (25); Collins, Donald (6); Fuson, Robin (1); Glaser, Gordon (39); Glynn, Edward (42); Grimsley, Ross (4); Hrynko, Lawrence (26); Lacey, Robert (2); Nuismer, Jack (15); Paxton, Michael (21); Pietroburgo, Robert (41); Puryear, Nathaniel (17); Wihtol, Alexander (21).

COLUMBUS—Boris, Paul (35); Bruhert, Michael (21); Castro, William (17); Cochran, Gregory (5); Filer, Thomas (1); Frazier, George (27); Griffin, Michael (17); Lewis, James (54); Lewis, Timothy (5); McGaffigan, Andrew (17); Mitchell, Paul (7); Nelson, Eugene (5); Righetti, David (7); Ryder, Brian (31); Taylor, Steven (1); Wehrmeister, David (24).

PAWTUCKET—Aponte, Luis (51); Denman, Brian (1); Dorsey, James (27); Finch, Joel (28); Howard, Michael (5); Hurst, Bruce (31); MacWhorter, Keith (28); Ojeda, Robert (25); Parks, Daniel (29); Rainey, Charles (4); Remmerswaal, Wilhelmus (20); Sarmiento, Manuel (47).

RICHMOND—Acker, James (21); Alvarez, Jose (39); Bedrosian, Stephen (26); Brizzolara, Anthony (25); Cowley, Joe (18); Dayley, Kenneth (31); Diaz, Carlos (35); Edge, Claude (34); Matula, Richard (16); McWilliams, Larry (29); O'Brien, Daniel (16); Walk, Robert (4).

ROCHESTER—Boddicker, Michael (30); Carey, Brooks (29); Ford, David (1); Grilli, Stephen (Syracuse) (32); Jones, Larry (38); Luebber, Stephen (21); Ramirez, Daniel (8); Rowe, Thomas (28); Schneider, Jeffrey (46); Snell, Nathaniel (15); Speck, Clifford (27); Torrez, Pete (28); Umbarger, James (40); Welchel, Donald (8).

SYRACUSE—Baker, Steven (30); Barlow, Michael (10); Bomback, Mark (1); Fore, Charles (15); Huffman, Philip (28); Kucek, John (30); McCall Larry (13); McLaughlin, Colin (14); Mirabella, Paul (22); Murray, Dale (5?); Schrom, Kenneth (42); Tomlin, David (38); Willis, Michael (5); Wright, James (24).

TIDEWATER—Anderson, Richard (37); Daly, Mark (5); Davis, Ted (8); Dixon, Thomas (27); Dye, Scott (19); Leach, Terry (15); Leary, Timothy (6); Lynch, Edward (15); Mendoza, Michael (6); Puleo, Charles (26); Searage, Ray (18); Semprini, John (14); VonOhlen, David (10).

TOLEDO—Bastian, Jose (2); Felton, Terry (32); Hannahs, Gerald (24); Hodge, Eddie (29); Jackson, Darrel (2); Kinnunen, Michael (50); MacPherson, Bruce (8); Mapel, Steven (12); Sarmiento, Wilfredo (48); Veselic, Robert (29); Williams, Richard (27).

GRAND SLAM HOME RUNS—Keller, Pagel, Whisenton, 2 each; Balboni, Bonner, Bowen, Christensen, Coleman, Faedo, Hart, Hayes, Johnson, Koza, Logan, Patterson, Robertson, Shelby, Snider, Walker, C., 1 each.

AWARDED FIRST BASE ON INTERFERENCE—Baker, D., 3 (Gedman, Herz, LaFrancois); Koza (Borgmann); Norman (Herz); Saferight (Whitmer); Tabler (Gedman); Wells (Gedman).

CLUB FIELDING

Club	Pct.	G.	PO.	A.	E.	DP.	PB.
Syracuse	.976	140	3646	1541	130	147	26
Rochester	.974	139	3792	1729	146	152	8
Columbus	.974	139	3664	1500	110	111	9
Tidewater	.973	138	3566	1593	144	150	18
Pawtucket	.971	140	3760	1659	161	124	7
Charleston	.970	139	3496	1612	157	127	13
Richmond	.970	139	3602	1503	157	125	11
Toledo	.970	140	3536	1531	159	129	15

Triple Play—Charleston.

INDIVIDUAL FIELDING

FIRST BASEMEN

° Throws lefthanded.

Player and Club	Pct.	G.	PO.	A.	E.	DP.
Snider, Toledo°	.997	76	675	48	2	55
Brant, Columbus	.997	69	625	46	2	45
LOGAN, Rochester°	.9947	126	1235	86	7	13
MacDonald, Tidewater	.9946	112	1050	73	6	118
Valle, Rochester	.994	25	147	11	1	10
Keller, Richmond	.993	17	138	4	1	16
Rajsich, Tidewater°	.993	15	129	13	1	11
Wells, Syracuse	.992	108	1001	79	9	96
Vega, 31 Toledo–13 Tidewater	.992	44	427	20	4	34
Norrid, Charleston	.992	41	240	20	2	19
Smith, Richmond	.990	127	1060	84	12	94
Beamon, Syracuse°	.990	34	275	29	3	37
Koza, Pawtucket	.989	100	978	78	12	82
Pagel, Charleston	.988	54	448	37	6	31
LoGrande, Charleston	.987	66	565	26	8	48
Estes, Toledo°	.985	34	298	21	5	27
Boggs, Pawtucket	.983	35	279	19	5	23
Balboni, Columbus	.980	74	631	55	14	50

(Fewer Than Ten Games)

Player and Club	Pct.	G.	PO.	A.	E.	DP.
Pruitt, Charleston	1.000	8	62	8	9	8
Ongarato, Pawtucket†	1.000	7	53	2	0	1
Chism, Rochester°	1.000	7	45	3	0	3
Werth, Columbus	1.000	3	24	1	0	2
Hayes, Charleston	1.000	6	17	0	0	1
Harer, Columbus°	1.000	1	11	0	0	1
Sweet, Tidewater	1.000	1	7	1	0	0
Herz, Columbus	1.000	1	2	0	0	0
LaFrancois, Pawtucket	.986	10	67	6	1	5
Hale, Rochester	.667	2	2	0	1	0

SECOND BASEMEN

Player and Club	Pct.	G.	PO.	A.	E.	DP.
Krenchicki, Rochester	1.000	12	22	47	9	6
Faedo, Charleston	.987	41	93	135	3	26
EATON, Rochester	.986	112	207	354	8	75
Washington, Rochester	.982	22	47	62	2	20
Seibert, Toledo	.981	84	202	211	8	46
Schmitz, Columbus	.981	69	90	216	6	24
Machemer, Toledo	.981	39	72	81	3	24
Winterfeldt, Tidewater	.981	20	31	72	2	14
Chapman, Syracuse	.980	128	292	404	14	83
Gardenhire, Tidewater	.979	27	60	78	3	16
Barrett, Pawtucket	.978	87	186	254	10	48
Giles, Tidewater	.974	69	184	228	11	54
Ruiz, Richmond	.972	79	179	240	12	52
S. Davis, Syracuse	.972	14	27	42	2	10
Perlozzo, Tidewater	.968	28	54	96	5	15
C. Walker, Pawtucket	.967	56	97	164	9	32
Bucci, Charleston	.957	23	45	45	4	12
Curry, Richmond	.954	59	106	142	12	20
O. Davis, Charleston	.950	56	99	185	15	32
Ashford, Columbus	.950	45	60	91	8	18
Fischlin, Charleston	.950	22	56	76	7	17
J. Walker, Toledo	.946	21	59	63	7	18
Barton, Charleston	.939	14	26	36	4	11
Tabler, Columbus	.937	44	57	106	11	13
Christensen, Toledo	.932	17	28	40	5	4

(Fewer Than Ten Games)

Player and Club	Pct.	G.	PO.	A.	E.	DP.
Backman, Tidewater	1.000	2	3	7	0	2
Wilson, Pawtucket	1.000	1	4	2	0	0
Cuervo, Tidewater	1.000	1	2	3	0	1
Bonner, Rochester	.935	5	9	20	2	2
Ramos, Syracuse	.933	3	5	9	1	2
Miller, Richmond	.857	4	6	6	2	1
Ongarato, Pawtucket	.750	2	1	2	1	1

THIRD BASEMEN

Player and Club	Pct.	G.	PO.	A.	E.	DP.
Hammond, Richmond	1.000	12	4	25	0	3
Gardenhire, Tidewater	.973	19	6	31	1	3
Schmitz, Columbus	.963	17	6	20	1	1
Mankowski, Tidewater	.958	48	28	85	5	8
S. Davis, Syracuse	.957	21	15	29	2	25
Rayford, Rochester	.954	49	30	94	6	10
Ripken, Rochester	.952	85	74	204	14	25
D. BAKER, Syracuse	.947	114	66	203	15	22
Johnson, Richmond	.946	125	110	225	19	30
Hayes, Charleston	.941	103	79	222	19	18
R. Washington, Toledo	.940	125	102	271	24	28
Ashford, Columbus	.939	100	73	158	15	14
Bucci, Charleston	.936	39	30	87	8	11
Boggs, Pawtucket	.934	101	80	219	21	18
Winterfeldt, Tidewater	.932	48	29	81	8	8
Coleman, Columbus	.918	29	15	41	5	3
Sweet, Tidewater	.917	29	16	39	5	4
Wilson, Pawtucket	.909	45	36	74	11	5
L. Washington, Rochester	.885	13	6	17	3	2
Tabler, Columbus	.864	11	9	10	3	2

(Fewer Than Ten Games)

Player and Club	Pct.	G.	PO.	A.	E.	DP.
Krenchicki, Rochester	1.000	5	5	9	0	3
Backman, Tidewater	1.000	5	4	10	0	0
Ramos, Syracuse	1.000	7	3	7	0	0
Miller, Richmond	1.000	4	0	7	0	0
Ruiz, Richmond	1.000	2	3	3	0	2
Norrid, Charleston	1.000	3	2	3	0	0
Perlozzo, Tidewater	1.000	1	2	0	0	0
Brant, Columbus	1.000	1	1	1	0	0
Howard, Tidewater	1.000	3	1	1	0	0
Bando, Charleston	1.000	3	0	1	0	0
Thompson, Syracuse	1.000	2	0	1	0	0
C. Walker, Pawtucket	1.000	1	0	1	0	0
Hernandez, Syracuse	.929	8	4	9	1	1
Machemer, Toledo	.824	9	2	12	3	1

SHORTSTOPS

Player and Club	Pct.	G.	PO.	A.	E.	DP.
Fernandez, Syracuse	.980	31	69	80	3	26
ROBERTSON, Columbus	.971	122	210	362	17	66
Washington, Rochester	.970	31	45	81	4	13
S. Davis, Syracuse	.970	15	25	40	2	12
Wilson, Pawtucket	.970	13	24	40	2	7
Schmitz, Columbus	.963	33	40	63	4	8
Ripken, Rochester	.960	35	54	116	7	18
Giles, Tidewater	.958	53	83	156	13	28
Ramos, Syracuse	.955	81	150	232	18	54
Bonner, Rochester	.949	79	155	272	23	64
Runge, Richmond	.948	132	191	450	35	67
Valdez, Pawtucket	.947	110	173	327	28	57
Fischlin, Charleston	.939	117	168	357	24	58
Faedo, 23 Char.-43 Tol.	.939	66	92	186	18	35
Hernandez, Syracuse	.935	21	37	64	7	11
Gardenhire, Tidewater	.933	81	140	264	29	61
J. Walker, Toledo	.932	88	117	282	19	36
Jurak, Pawtucket	.923	23	39	81	10	16
Miller, Richmond	.863	13	16	28	7	6

(Fewer Than Ten Games)

Player and Club	Pct.	G.	PO.	A.	E.	DP.
Winterfeldt, Tidewater	1.000	2	2	7	0	2
Coleman, Columbus	1.000	1	1	4	0	0
Rayford, Rochester	1.000	1	1	0	0	0
Backman, Tidewater	.963	6	5	21	1	4
Bucci, Charleston	.962	7	8	17	1	2
R. Washington, Toledo	.957	6	11	16	1	3
Seibert, Toledo	.882	4	6	9	2	1
Ruiz, Richmond	.857	3	3	3	1	0
Krenchicki, Rochester	.750	1	1	2	1	1

OUTFIELDERS

Player and Club	Pct.	G.	PO.	A.	E.	DP.
Ongarato, Pawtucket	1.000	84	123	9	0	1
G. Smith, Columbus°	1.000	85	117	2	0	0
Valle, Rochester	1.000	56	107	1	0	0
Bucci, Charleston	1.000	26	28	0	0	0
Wilson, Pawtucket	1.000	15	20	0	0	0
Laribee, Pawtucket	1.000	15	19	0	0	0
LENTINE, Charleston	.9952	132	197	12	1	0
Harer, Columbus°	.9950	101	191	7	1	2
Butler, Richmond°	.990	125	286	15	3	3
Howard, Tidewater	.989	114	259	12	3	1
Cannon, Syracuse	.988	129	336	6	4	1
Thompson, Syracuse	.987	118	215	11	3	2
Beltre, Syracuse	.986	44	65	6	1	0
Hart, 71 Roc.-16 Tol.	.984	87	250	2	4	0
Patterson, Columbus	.984	90	183	7	3	1
Gardner, Charleston	.984	26	59	2	1	0
Estes, Toledo°	.984	30	55	5	1	1
Norman, Tidewater	.983	38	56	2	1	0
Johnston, Toledo°	.982	110	152	8	3	2
Graham, Pawtucket°	.981	133	255	9	5	3
Hammond, Richmond	.981	73	147	6	3	1
Littleton, Charleston	.980	91	189	9	4	3
Hale, Rochester	.980	26	49	2	1	0
Sofield, Toledo	.980	21	44	4	1	1
Cipot, Toledo°	.978	57	83	7	2	1
Stegman, Columbus	.977	82	128	2	3	2
Coleman, Columbus	.977	26	42	1	1	0
Craig, Charleston	.974	23	38	0	1	0
Strouhter, Toledo	.972	20	34	1	1	0

OUTFIELDERS —Continued

Player and Club	Pct.	G.	PO.	A.	E.	DP.
Shelby, Rochester	.970	76	189	8	6	4
K. Smith, 16 Roc.-26 Tid.	.970	42	65	0	2	0
C. Walker, Pawtucket	.969	82	112	13	4	1
Bowen, Pawtucket	.967	118	195	12	7	0
Whisenton, Richmond°	.964	127	205	11	8	1
Brown, Columbus	.964	40	78	3	3	1
Bourjos, Rochester	.961	44	71	1	3	0
Beamon, Syracuse°	.960	11	23	1	1	0
Williams, Rochester°	.958	123	239	11	11	2
Chauncey, Toledo°	.958	80	126	11	6	2
Pagel, Charleston°	.953	24	22	1	1	0
Rajsich, Tidewater°	.952	42	59	0	3	0
Flores, Tidewater	.951	109	186	8	10	3
Norrid, Charleston	.951	31	39	0	2	0
Porter, Richmond°	.951	24	38	1	2	0
Barton, Charleston	.950	32	37	1	2	0
Hernandez, Syracuse	.948	45	89	2	5	2
R. Baker, Charleston	.945	74	149	7	9	4
Landis, Richmond	.941	65	93	2	6	0
Funderburk, Toledo	.940	103	166	5	11	2
Stenholm, Columbus°	.940	32	45	2	3	1
Kubski, Syracuse	.920	17	29	0	2	0
Haslerig, Tidewater	.927	35	48	3	4	0
Showalter, Columbus°	.917	12	11	0	1	0
Vega, Tidewater	.914	17	31	1	3	0
Lora, Syracuse	.909	17	20	0	2	0
Winterfeldt, Tidewater	.895	16	16	1	2	1
Werth, Columbus	.846	11	11	0	2	0
Hazewood, Rochester	.920	18	23	0	2	0

(Fewer Than Ten Games)

Player and Club	Pct.	G.	PO.	A.	E.	DP.
Harper, Richmond	1.000	10	22	0	0	0
Machemer, Toledo	1.000	10	9	1	0	0
Pruitt, Charleston	1.000	3	3	0	0	0
Charbonneau, Charleston	1.000	1	3	0	0	0
K. Smith, Richmond	1.000	3	2	0	0	0
Ruiz, Richmond	1.000	1	1	0	0	0
Smithson, Pawtucket	1.000	1	1	0	0	0
Young, Rochester	1.000	1	1	0	0	0
Corey, Rochester	.967	9	29	0	1	0
R. Washington, Toledo	.944	8	17	0	1	0
Chapman, Columbus°	.923	9	10	2	1	0

CATCHERS

Player and Club	Pct.	G.	PO.	A.	E.	DP.	PB.
Lickert, Pawtucket	1.000	14	75	11	0	0	1
Putman, Rochester	1.000	11	48	6	0	0	0
Whitmer, Syracuse	.997	65	299	42	1	7	9
Schmidt, Pawtucket	.992	42	237	18	2	1	3
Keller, Richmond	.992	16	116	4	1	1	2
Pruitt, Charleston	.991	19	92	14	1	4	1
Bochy, Tidewater	.990	59	253	35	3	3	9
Cadahia, Toledo	.989	23	84	6	1	1	2
LaFRANCOIS, Pawtucket	.988	78	433	60	6	6	3
Sinatro, Richmond	.986	120	738	78	12	9	8
Fitzgerald, Tidewater	.985	22	124	9	2	2	1
Espino, Columbus	.984	78	434	53	8	5	6
Gulden, Columbus	.983	56	362	39	7	5	2
Sweet, Tidewater	.982	70	399	41	8	9	8
Herz, Toledo	.981	110	508	65	11	10	11
Bando, Charleston	.979	92	414	50	10	6	5
Norrid, Charleston	.979	38	121	17	3	0	5
Saferight, 11 Ric.-33 Roc.	.977	44	238	18	6	3	2
Rayford, Rochester	.974	42	177	12	5	3	2
Callahan, Columbus°	.974	18	95	18	3	1	1
Petralli, Syracuse	.973	41	188	30	6	4	5
Huppert, 45 Roc.-21 Tol.	.970	66	374	46	13	7	6
Gedman, Pawtucket	.969	24	176	20	6	1	0
Lora, Syracuse	.967	40	182	21	8	1	10
Kennedy, Rochester	.962	23	91	11	4	0	1

(Fewer Than Ten Games)

Player and Club	Pct.	G.	PO.	A.	E.	DP.	PB.
Werth, Columbus	1.000	2	10	2	0	0	0
Thompson, Richmond	1.000	1	6	0	0	0	0
Borgmann, Charleston	.983	10	51	6	1	1	2
Pasley, Syracuse	.964	9	51	3	2	1	?

PITCHERS

Player and Club	Pct.	G.	PO.	A.	E.	DP.
VESELIC, Toledo	1.000	48	10	29	0	2
Paxton, Charleston	1.000	21	16	17	0	1
Carey, Rochester°	1.000	29	4	29	0	4
Huffman, Syracuse	1.000	27	10	20	0	2
Torrez, Rochester°	1.000	28	4	25	0	0
Jones, Rochester	1.000	38	5	23	0	3
R. Anderson, Tidewater	1.000	37	3	22	0	2
Cuellar, Charleston	1.000	40	7	17	0	2
Orosco, Tidewater°	1.000	47	6	17	0	1
K. Anderson, Charleston	1.000	16	9	12	0	1
Aponte, Pawtucket	1.000	51	6	15	0	2
Hannahs, Toledo°	1.000	24	0	21	0	1
Boris, Columbus	1.000	55	6	14	0	1
W. Sarmiento, Toledo	1.000	29	4	16	0	1
Fore, Syracuse	1.000	15	7	11	0	0
Schrom, Syracuse	1.000	42	8	9	0	0
Lynch, Tidewater	1.000	15	3	13	0	0
Hrynko, Charleston	1.000	26	7	8	0	0
Leach, Tidewater	1.000	15	5	10	0	0
Edge, Richmond	1.000	34	3	12	0	0
McCall, Syracuse	1.000	13	7	7	0	1
Smithson, Pawtucket	1.000	34	5	8	0	1
Griffin, Columbus	1.000	17	3	10	0	0
Frazier, Columbus	1.000	27	1	11	0	0
Dye, Tidewater	1.000	19	5	6	0	1
Puryear, Charleston	1.000	17	4	6	0	0
Snell, Rochester	1.000	15	1	9	0	0
Semprini, Tidewater	1.000	14	1	6	0	1
Searage, Tidewater°	1.000	18	0	6	0	1
Boddicker, Rochester	.986	30	25	45	1	0
Wehrmeister, Columbus	.978	24	16	28	1	1
Hurst, Pawtucket	.977	31	12	31	1	1
Dayley, Richmond°	.974	31	17	21	1	2
Acker, Richmond	.974	21	8	30	1	1
Dixon, Tidewater	.973	27	12	24	1	2
Puleo, Tidewater	.971	26	7	27	1	2
Murray, Syracuse	.970	52	6	26	1	3
Ojeda, Pawtucket°	.966	25	8	48	2	4
Parks, Pawtucket	.959	29	20	51	3	5
Williams, Toledo	.959	27	17	30	2	2
Felton, Toledo	.957	32	11	11	1	0
Kinnunen, Toledo°	.957	50	4	18	1	0
Pietroburgo, Charleston°	.957	42	3	19	1	1
Brizzolara, Richmond	.956	25	16	27	2	1
Matula, Richmond	.955	16	7	14	1	1
Dooner, Toledo	.952	59	4	16	1	1
Speck, Rochester	.950	27	5	14	1	2
Glaser, Charleston	.947	39	20	34	3	0
Umberger, Rochester°	.947	41	5	31	2	0
Bruhert, Columbus	.947	21	9	9	1	1
Castro, Columbus	.941	17	9	7	1	1
M. Sarmiento, Pawtucket	.941	47	7	9	1	1
McGaffigan, Columbus	.941	17	7	9	1	0
McWilliams, Richmond°	.939	29	4	42	3	2
Brennan, Charleston	.939	25	9	22	2	0
Hodge, Toledo°	.939	29	3	28	2	0
J. Lewis, Columbus	.936	54	13	31	3	0
Finch, Pawtucket	.936	27	12	32	3	2
McLaughlin, Syracuse	.933	14	3	11	1	1
Gaff, Richmond	.930	23	10	30	3	3
MacWhorter, Pawtucket	.929	28	17	22	3	1
Luebber, Rochester	.929	21	1	12	1	1
Schneider, Rochester°	.929	46	0	13	1	1
Mirabella, Syracuse°	.926	22	8	17	2	0
S. Baker, Syracuse	.923	30	12	24	3	0
Grilli, 3 Syracuse-29 Rochester	.923	32	5	7	1	0
Nuismer, Charleston	.923	15	4	8	1	1
Cowley, Richmond	.923	18	3	9	1	1
Rowe, Rochester	.906	28	9	39	5	3
Kucek, Syracuse	.905	30	6	13	2	0
Pacella, Columbus	.900	27	10	17	3	1
Diaz, Richmond°	.900	35	3	6	1	0

PITCHERS—Continued

Player and Club	Pct.	G.	PO.	A.	E.	DP.	Player and Club	Pct.	G.	PO.	A.	E.	DP.
Ryder, Columbus	.893	31	9	16	3	1	Glynn, Charleston°	.833	42	4	11	3	1
Boitano, Tidewater	.889	40	5	11	2	2	Tomlin, Syracuse°	.833	38	1	14	3	2
Wihtol, Charleston	.882	21	5	10	2	1	Mapel, Toledo	.786	12	1	10	3	2
Wright, Syracuse	.875	24	8	20	4	1	Remmerswaal, Pawtucket	.778	20	3	4	2	0
Bedrosian, Richmond	.872	26	12	22	5	0	Dorsey, Pawtucket	.772	27	6	11	5	1
Alvarez, Richmond	.864	39	2	17	3	1	O'Brien, Richmond	.500	16	0	2	2	0

(Fewer Than Ten Games)

Player and Club	Pct.	G.	PO.	A.	E.	DP.	Player and Club	Pct.	G.	PO.	A.	E.	DP.
Cochran, Columbus	1.000	5	5	8	0	1	Bastian, Toledo	1.000	2	0	2	0	0
T. Brown, Syracuse	1.000	7	4	8	0	2	Thurberg, Tidewater	1.000	4	0	1	0	0
Willis, Syracuse°	1.000	5	4	5	0	0	Hart, Rochester	1.000	1	0	1	0	0
Walk, Richmond	1.000	4	3	5	0	1	Harris, Tidewater	.875	8	5	9	2	2
Leary, Tidewater	1.000	6	2	6	0	0	Ramirez, Rochester	.875	8	4	3	1	0
VonOhlen, Tidewater°	1.000	10	2	6	0	1	Rainey, Pawtucket	.857	4	0	6	1	0
Barlow, Syracuse	1.000	10	5	2	0	0	Righetti, Columbus°	.846	7	2	7	2	0
MacPherson, Toledo	1.000	8	1	5	0	0	Mitchell, Columbus	.833	7	1	4	1	1
Grimsley, Charleston°	1.000	4	0	6	0	0	Daly, Tidewater°	.833	5	1	4	1	0
Davis, Tidewater	1.000	8	2	3	0	0	Nelson, Columbus	.833	5	1	4	1	0
Mendoza, Tidewater	1.000	6	0	4	0	0	Collins, Charleston°	.833	6	0	5	1	0
Bomback, Syracuse	1.000	1	2	1	0	0	Wilkins, Charleston	.800	10	3	5	2	0
Taylor, Columbus	1.000	1	2	1	0	0	Welchel, Rochester	.500	8	2	1	1	0
Jackson, Toledo°	1.000	2	1	1	0	0	T. Lewis, Columbus°	.000	5	0	0	1	0
Howard, Pawtucket	1.000	5	1	1	0	0	Lacey, Charleston°	.000	2	0	0	1	0

The following players do not have any recorded accepted chances at the positions indicated; therefore, are not listed in the fielding averages for those particular positions: Chism, p; Cuellar, of; Davis, O., ss; Denman, p; Estes, p; Faedo, of; Filer, p; Fitzgerald, of; Ford, p; Fuson, p; Gulden, of; Howard, ss; Johnston, p; Koza, of; LaFrancois, of; Norrid, 2b; Smith, p; Tevlin, 1b; p; Vega, 3b; Walker, J., 3b; Washington, L., of.

CLUB PITCHING

Club	ERA.	G.	CG.	ShO.	Sv.	IP.	H.	R.	ER.	HR.	HB.	BB.	Int. BB.	SO.	WP.	Bk.
Pawtucket	3.30	140	29	6	31	1253⅓	1115	551	459	104	43	549	62	894	53	13
Richmond	3.41	139	35	11	32	1200⅔	1064	546	455	81	35	575	12	846	47	11
Tidewater	3.60	138	42	11	23	1188⅔	1073	558	476	95	34	533	39	738	38	10
Rochester	3.76	139	31	10	26	1264	1230	598	528	124	27	523	43	735	68	10
Columbus	3.88	139	18	9	42	1221⅓	1175	604	526	110	31	535	48	863	51	10
Syracuse	4.23	140	25	5	28	1215⅓	1217	646	571	122	25	517	21	698	51	6
Charleston	4.24	139	34	9	17	1165⅓	1234	630	549	104	29	436	36	645	80	6
Toledo	4.43	140	34	7	18	1178⅔	1309	678	580	104	30	531	33	635	42	10

PITCHERS' RECORDS

(Leading Qualifiers for Earned-Run Average Leadership — 112 or More Innings)

°Throws lefthanded.

Pitcher—Club	W.	L.	Pct.	ERA.	G.	GS.	CG.	GF.	ShO.	Sv.	IP.	H.	R.	ER.	HR.	HB.	BB.	Int. BB.	SO.	WP.
OJEDA, Pawtucket°	12	9	.571	2.13	23	23	8	1	0	0	173	136	52	41	11	3	73	8	113	4
Bedrosian, Richmond	10	10	.500	2.69	26	25	8	1	1	0	184	143	76	55	5	8	99	2	144	2
Hurst, Pawtucket°	12	7	.632	2.87	32	23	7	0	3	0	157	143	68	50	9	3	71	3	99	6
Gaff, Tidewater	9	5	.643	2.94	23	21	7	0	0	0	147	150	54	48	7	6	64	4	59	3
Mirabella, Syracuse°	11	7	.611	3.06	22	21	9	1	1	0	153	150	91	80	21	5	43	2	57	6
Wehrmeister, Columbus	11	3	.786	3.11	24	19	2	2	0	1	136	117	53	47	10	7	48	1	83	4
Dayley, Richmond°	13	8	.619	3.33	31	31	4	0	1	0	200	180	82	74	14	3	117	0	162	6
Dorsey, Pawtucket	4	10	.286	3.35	27	21	4	4	1	2	137	116	59	51	12	1	70	6	97	2
Carey, Rochester°	10	9	.526	3.37	29	28	7	0	2	0	195	168	86	73	30	0	82	7	107	7
Boris, Columbus	10	6	.625	3.37	55	1	0	31	0	9	131	127	60	49	12	3	47	15	102	3

Departmental Leaders: G—Dooner, 59; GS—Dayley, 31; CG—Brennan, Dixon, 11; ShO—Brennan, 6; W—Dayley, McWilliams, 13; L—Hodge, 17; Sv.—Murray, 16; Pct.—Wehrmeister, .786; IP—Dayley, 200; H—Williams, 210; R—Ryder, 101; ER—McWilliams, Ryder, 86; HR—Carey, 30; BB—Dayley, 117; IBB—Boris, 15; HB—Parks, 11; SO—Dayley, 162; WP—Puryear, 18.

(All Pitchers—Listed Alphabetically)

Pitcher—Club	W.	L.	Pct.	ERA.	G.	GS.	CG.	GF.	ShO.	Sv.	IP.	H.	R.	ER.	HR.	HB.	BB.	Int. BB.	SO.	WP.
Acker, Richmond	8	7	.533	4.19	21	21	7	0	0	0	118	112	63	55	6	1	74	0	72	5
Alvarez, Richmond	7	5	.583	2.15	39	0	0	25	0	8	71	51	29	17	5	6	31	4	61	4
Aponte, Pawtucket	7	5	.583	1.94	51	0	0	39	0	15	79	58	26	17	5	4	31	8	67	2
K. Anderson, Charleston	9	3	.750	2.42	16	12	7	1	0	0	93	71	31	25	4	2	28	3	48	5
R. Anderson, Tidewater	3	5	.375	3.34	37	0	0	17	0	3	89	68	34	33	3	1	45	9	41	2
Baker, Syracuse	8	14	.364	4.56	30	26	5	2	1	0	160	170	94	81	13	3	77	0	79	9
Barlow, Syracuse°	0	2	.000	0.78	10	0	0	9	0	1	23	22	4	2	1	0	10	2	12	2
Bastian, Toledo	0	0	.000	18.00	2	0	0	0	0	0	2	4	4	4	0	0	3	0	3	1
Bedrosian, Richmond	10	10	.500	2.69	26	25	8	1	1	0	184	143	76	55	5	8	99	2	144	2
Boddicker, Rochester	10	10	.500	4.20	30	29	8	1	3	0	182	182	91	85	20	3	66	4	109	6
Boitano, Tidewater	5	6	.455	3.74	40	4	1	22	1	7	65	56	37	27	8	2	30	4	43	3
Bomback, Syracuse	1	0	1.000	3.00	1	1	1	0	0	0	9	5	5	3	1	0	2	0	8	0
Boris, Columbus	10	6	.625	3.37	55	1	0	31	0	9	131	127	60	49	12	3	47	15	102	3
Brennan, Charleston	11	8	.579	3.92	25	25	11	0	6	0	156	163	77	68	11	6	24	2	64	7
Brizzolara, Richmond	10	3	.769	3.57	25	19	3	3	2	0	141	138	62	56	13	2	44	2	59	3
Brown, Pawtucket	1	2	.333	7.26	7	5	1	0	0	0	31	43	25	25	4	0	11	0	17	3
Bruhert, Columbus	6	3	.667	3.00	21	5	2	5	0	0	60	59	25	20	3	1	15	1	17	0
Carey, Rochester°	10	9	.526	3.37	29	28	7	0	2	0	195	168	86	73	30	0	82	7	107	7
Castro, Columbus	8	1	.889	4.56	17	12	0	4	0	1	73	92	41	37	6	1	20	1	40	3
Chism, Rochester°	0	0	.000	6.75	4	0	0	3	0	0	4	4	3	3	0	0	3	0	2	0
Cochran, Columbus	1	2	.333	6.00	5	5	1	0	0	0	21	21	16	14	1	0	17	0	12	3
Collins, Charleston°	0	2	.000	8.64	6	5	0	0	0	0	25	41	31	24	7	0	13	1	17	2
Cowley, Richmond	3	2	.600	2.80	18	1	1	12	0	5	45	33	15	14	3	2	16	1	39	3
Cuellar, Charleston	6	7	.462	4.65	40	4	5	0	16	0	1	89	100	55	46	8	3	48	5	55	12

Pitcher—Club	W.	L.	Pct.	ERA.	G.	GS.	CG.	GF.	ShO.	Sv.	IP.	H.	R.	ER.	HR.	HB.	BB.	Int. BB.	SO.	WP.
Daly, Tidewater°	0	3	.000	3.60	5	0	0	2	0	0	10	10	7	4	0	0	6	2	7	0
Davis, Tidewater	0	1	.000	4.29	8	3	0	1	0	0	21	20	12	10	1	1	7	0	11	0
Dayley, Richmond°	13	8	.619	3.33	31	31	4	0	1	0	200	180	82	74	14	3	117	1	162	6
Denman, Pawtucket	0	0	.000	4.50	1	0	0	1	0	0	2	1	1	1	0	0	0	0	3	0
Diaz, Richmond°	3	3	.500	2.81	35	0	0	25	0	11	48	32	17	15	5	2	20	1	29	2
Dixon, Tidewater	9	11	.450	4.07	27	27	11	0	0	0	177	149	93	80	16	5	93	4	113	5
Dooner, Toledo	3	5	.375	4.08	59	0	0	45	0	11	106	124	58	48	9	7	38	9	45	1
Dorsey, Pawtucket	4	10	.286	3.35	27	21	4	4	1	2	137	116	59	51	12	1	70	6	97	2
Dye, Tidewater	4	4	.500	4.80	19	7	1	4	0	0	75	91	45	40	6	3	30	2	42	5
Edge, Richmond	7	1	.875	2.95	34	0	0	25	0	7	64	40	24	21	6	0	34	1	53	7
Estes, Toledo°	0	0	.000	0.00	2	0	0	1	0	0	2	1	0	0	0	2	0	1	0	
Felton, Toledo	7	11	.389	4.19	32	16	6	8	1	1	131	127	71	61	13	3	76	3	99	6
Filer, Columbus	0	1	.000	15.00	1	1	0	0	0	0	3	6	5	5	0	0	4	0	3	1
Finch, Pawtucket	6	7	.462	3.74	27	16	1	3	0	0	137	133	63	57	12	4	59	5	81	5
Ford, Rochester	1	0	1.000	1.50	1	1	0	0	0	0	6	6	1	1	0	0	1	0	1	0
Fore, Syracuse	3	6	.333	6.04	15	14	4	1	0	0	70	83	49	47	6	2	33	1	32	2
Frazier, Columbus	4	1	.800	3.20	27	0	0	22	0	9	59	58	23	21	0	2	12	1	50	1
Fuson, Charleston°	0	0	.000	9.00	1	0	0	1	0	0	1	2	1	1	0	0	1	0	2	0
Gaff, Tidewater	9	5	.643	2.94	23	21	7	0	0	0	147	150	54	48	7	6	64	4	59	3
Glaser, Tidewater	9	10	.474	4.61	39	24	7	10	1	0	164	183	91	84	20	5	35	6	48	3
Glynn, Charleston°	4	6	.400	3.55	42	0	0	26	0	8	71	50	34	28	3	0	42	5	70	6
Griffin, Columbus	3	1	.750	2.44	17	1	0	13	0	6	48	39	14	13	1	2	16	3	34	0
Grilli, 3 Syr.-29 Roch.	4	5	.444	6.26	32	0	0	16	0	2	46	63	35	32	7	4	19	3	34	0
Grimsley, Charleston°	1	1	.500	3.27	4	4	0	0	0	0	22	25	10	8	0	0	6	0	9	3
Hannahs, Toledo°	4	11	.267	5.24	25	20	0	4	0	0	115	133	83	67	10	2	76	2	68	9
Harris, Tidewater	4	0	1.000	2.06	7	7	2	0	0	0	48	37	14	11	0	0	16	1	26	2
Hart, Rochester	0	0	.000	0.00	1	0	0	0	0	0	1	0	0	0	0	0	0	0	0	0
Hodge, Toledo°	8	17	.320	4.53	29	25	10	1	1	0	163	173	92	82	19	5	60	4	84	7
Howard, Pawtucket	0	1	.000	15.00	5	2	0	2	0	0	9	15	15	15	3	0	8	1	11	1
Hrynko, Charleston	1	3	.250	3.56	27	0	0	18	0	3	48	49	24	19	5	1	19	3	29	1
Huffman, Syracuse	5	9	.357	5.50	27	18	1	4	0	0	131	150	91	80	21	5	43	2	57	6
Hurst, Pawtucket°	12	7	.632	2.87	32	23	7	0	3	0	157	143	68	50	9	3	71	3	99	6
Jackson, Toledo°	0	0	.000	2.25	2	2	0	0	0	0	8	8	2	2	0	1	1	0	6	0
Johnston, Toledo°	0	0	.000	0.00	1	0	0	1	0	0	1	0	0	0	0	0	0	0	1	0
Jones, Rochester	9	9	.500	3.77	38	18	4	11	1	3	160	154	80	67	15	2	79	6	108	15
Kinnunen, Toledo°	4	4	.500	5.50	50	1	0	31	0	4	72	94	53	44	7	1	35	4	36	4
Kucek, Syracuse	4	4	.500	3.06	30	6	0	6	0	0	100	77	46	34	7	0	54	3	80	4
Lacey, Charleston°	1	0	1.000	1.13	2	1	1	1	0	1	8	8	1	1	0	0	2	0	5	0
Leach, Tidewater	5	2	.714	2.72	15	8	4	4	1	0	76	63	27	23	8	1	19	3	42	1
Leary, Tidewater	1	3	.250	3.71	6	6	1	0	0	0	34	27	16	14	2	4	27	0	15	3
J. Lewis, Columbus	8	7	.533	4.98	54	7	2	37	0	13	150	147	89	83	19	2	65	11	100	6
T. Lewis, Columbus°	0	0	.000	5.14	5	1	0	1	0	0	7	8	4	4	1	0	10	0	6	2
Luebber, Rochester	5	5	.500	1.80	21	0	0	15	0	5	45	31	11	9	1	1	16	7	32	1
Lynch, Tidewater	7	6	.538	3.91	15	15	6	0	3	0	99	93	46	43	12	3	29	0	54	2
MacPherson, Toledo	1	4	.200	5.00	8	8	1	0	0	0	36	40	25	20	2	1	16	2	12	1
MacWhorter, Pawtucket	7	10	.412	4.43	28	23	5	3	1	0	132	124	77	65	10	8	57	5	96	8
Mapel, Toledo	2	7	.222	4.03	12	12	3	0	1	0	76	87	38	34	9	1	30	1	36	1
Matula, Richmond	7	4	.636	2.97	16	11	4	4	1	1	94	100	41	31	4	3	32	0	37	3
McCall, Syracuse	4	5	.444	4.50	13	13	2	0	0	0	82	85	41	41	9	2	25	0	34	0
McGaffigan, Columbus	8	6	.571	3.23	17	17	4	0	1	0	103	85	45	37	14	0	37	4	57	5
McLaughlin, Syracuse	3	5	.375	7.08	14	14	1	0	0	0	61	62	54	48	5	1	57	0	49	7
McWilliams, Richmond°	13	10	.565	4.35	29	28	8	1	3	0	178	174	98	86	13	7	79	1	157	9
Mendoza, Tidewater	0	0	.000	7.50	6	0	0	3	0	0	12	16	10	10	4	0	5	0	4	1
Mirabella, Syracuse°	11	7	.611	3.06	22	21	9	1	1	0	153	150	63	52	14	3	53	0	79	2
Mitchell, Columbus	1	4	.200	4.20	7	6	1	1	0	0	30	40	20	14	2	0	13	1	19	3
Murray, Syracuse	5	4	.556	1.85	52	0	0	41	0	16	78	57	23	16	5	1	28	5	57	3
Nelson, Columbus	4	0	1.000	2.53	5	4	0	1	0	1	32	25	9	9	3	0	14	0	37	0
Nuismer, Charleston	5	4	.556	2.97	15	5	2	0	2	0	91	99	37	30	3	1	36	2	62	1
O'Brien, Richmond	0	2	.000	6.43	16	0	0	8	0	0	35	43	32	25	5	1	18	0	20	2
Ojeda, Pawtucket°	12	9	.571	2.13	25	23	8	1	0	0	173	136	52	41	11	3	73	8	113	4
Orosco, Tidewater°	9	5	.643	3.31	46	10	0	24	0	8	87	80	39	32	7	3	32	4	81	3
Pacella, Columbus	11	9	.550	4.47	27	26	3	0	2	0	155	149	84	77	14	5	91	4	135	15
Parks, Pawtucket	9	12	.429	3.38	29	28	4	0	0	0	181	168	80	68	13	11	80	8	105	11
Paxton, Charleston	6	9	.400	4.62	21	19	5	0	0	0	115	138	64	59	12	2	27	1	48	2
Pietroburgo, Charleston°	9	9	.500	4.00	42	9	1	18	0	2	126	134	62	56	14	1	47	6	84	11
Puleo, Tidewater	12	9	.571	3.46	26	26	9	0	3	0	169	132	74	65	16	5	73	1	133	3
Puryear, Charleston°	1	2	.333	5.69	17	3	0	5	0	0	49	53	34	31	3	2	52	0	32	18
Rainey, Pawtucket	1	1	.500	3.15	4	4	0	0	0	0	20	23	8	7	2	0	6	0	16	1
Ramirez, Rochester	1	3	.250	4.17	8	8	0	0	0	0	41	32	19	19	6	1	19	0	26	1
Remmerswaal, Pawtucket	0	2	.000	5.93	20	0	0	12	0	0	41	53	31	27	5	1	22	3	25	3
Righetti, Columbus°	5	0	1.000	1.00	7	7	2	0	2	0	45	30	8	5	1	1	26	2	50	1
Rowe, Rochester	8	9	.471	4.34	28	28	8	0	1	0	174	180	94	84	15	3	72	5	93	11
Ryder, Columbus	8	7	.533	4.93	31	27	1	2	0	2	157	160	101	86	20	5	97	4	113	3
M. Sarmiento, Pawtucket	7	5	.583	2.34	47	0	0	29	0	10	96	71	27	25	9	4	27	8	99	0
W. Sarmiento, Toledo	3	5	.375	4.78	48	1	0	14	0	2	111	127	68	59	11	2	48	2	73	5
Schneider, Rochester°	5	1	.833	2.35	46	0	0	34	0	12	69	58	19	18	4	3	35	5	61	6
Schrom, Syracuse	4	6	.400	3.72	42	3	0	29	0	6	104	86	44	43	10	4	41	1	72	4
Searage, Tidewater°	2	0	1.000	2.33	18	0	0	8	0	3	27	29	10	7	0	0	13	1	23	1
Semprini, Tidewater	0	2	.000	3.00	14	0	0	10	0	2	18	13	7	6	0	1	15	2	17	3
Smith, Columbus	0	0	.000	0.00	2	0	0	2	0	0	4	3	0	0	0	1	1	0	3	0
Smithson, Pawtucket	2	4	.333	3.86	34	0	0	17	0	4	91	74	44	39	12	4	45	7	82	10
Snell, Rochester	1	3	.250	2.63	15	2	0	4	0	1	41	33	14	12	4	0	7	1	20	1
Speck, Columbus	6	3	.667	3.79	27	10	1	6	0	0	76	81	35	32	10	2	37	2	51	4
Taylor, Columbus	0	0	.000	12.60	1	0	0	0	0	0	5	9	7	7	3	1	2	0	2	1
Tevlin, Syracuse°	0	0	.000	9.00	1	0	0	1	0	0	2	4	2	2	0	0	0	0	1	0
Thurberg, Tidewater	0	2	.000	8.00	4	2	0	0	0	0	9	9	11	8	1	1	18	0	9	1
Tomlin, Syracuse°	2	3	.400	3.63	38	0	0	17	0	5	57	67	25	23	8	1	19	3	36	5
Torrez, Rochester°	2	4	.333	3.63	28	0	0	6	0	1	62	63	28	25	4	0	19	1	27	2
Umbarger, Rochester°	6	9	.400	4.18	41	15	3	9	0	2	157	179	85	73	7	6	65	2	59	10
Veselic, Toledo	11	11	.500	4.16	29	28	6	1	1	0	171	181	93	79	15	6	81	4	94	3
VonOhlen, Tidewater°	0	4	.000	5.76	10	2	0	1	0	0	25	30	22	16	4	0	11	2	18	0
Walk, Richmond	2	1	.667	2.45	4	3	0	0	0	0	22	18	7	6	2	0	11	0	13	2

Pitcher—Club	W.	L.	Pct.	ERA.	G.	GS.	CG.	GF.	ShO.	Sv.	IP.	H.	R.	ER.	HR.	HB.	BB.	Int. BB.	SO.	WP.
Wehrmeister, Columbus	11	3	.786	3.11	24	19	2	2	0	1	136	117	53	47	10	7	48	1	83	4
Welchel, Rochester...................	1	1	.500	2.25	8	0	0	4	0	0	12	9	5	3	1	2	4	0	7	0
Wihtol, Charleston....................	4	5	.444	4.97	22	9	0	8	0	2	76	78	49	42	8	2	30	1	51	6
Wilkins, Charleston...................	0	3	.000	7.84	10	8	0	1	0	0	31	40	30	27	6	4	26	1	21	6
Williams, Toledo.......................	10	12	.455	3.91	27	27	8	0	1	0	184	210	91	80	9	1	65	2	77	4
Willis, Syracuse°	1	3	.250	5.85	5	2	0	0	0	0	20	21	13	13	3	0	9	1	9	0
Wright, Syracuse......................	8	9	.471	3.76	24	17	1	1	0	0	127	122	59	53	15	3	54	3	75	4

BALKS—Gaff, 5; Dayley, Edge, 4 each; Boddicker, Mirabella, Schneider, 3 each; Boris, Carey, Dooner, Dorsey, Hannahs, Hurst, Lewis, J., McGaffigan, McWilliams, Ojeda, Orosco, Parks, Pietroburgo, Ryder, Sarmiento, M., Umbarger, Wihtol, Williams, 2 each; Aponte, Collins, Diaz, Dixon, Dye, Felton, Lynch, MacWhorter, Mapel, McLaughlin, Nelson, Nuismer, Pacella, Sarmiento, W., Schrom, Smithson, Tevlin, Veselic, 1 each.

COMBINATION SHUTOUTS—Castro-Lewis, Wehrmeister-Griffin, Righetti-Lewis-Boris, Wehrmeister-Lewis, Columbus; MacWhorter-Smithson-Sarmiento, Pawtucket; Dayley-Edge, Bedrosian-Diaz, Brizzolara-Cowley, Richmond; Jones-Schneider, Snell-Luebber, Ramirez-Umbarger, Rochester; Wright-Murray, Wright-Schrom, McLaughlin-Barlow, Syracuse; Orosco-Boitano, Harris-Searage, Gaff-Orosco, Tidewater; Jackson-Hodge; Williams-Dooner, Toledo.

NO-HIT GAME—None.

Mexican League

CLASS AAA

Leading Batter
WILLIE NORWOOD
Reynosa

Leading Pitcher
VICENTE ROMO
Coatzacoalcos

CHAMPIONSHIP WINNERS IN PREVIOUS YEARS

1955—Mexico City Tigers° .... .539	1966—Mexico City Tigers‡ .... .614	1974—Jalisco .... .627
1956—Mexico City Reds .... .692	Mexico City Reds .... .571	Mexico City Reds x .... .551
1957—Yucatan .... .567	1967—Jalisco .... .607	1975—Tampico x .... .541
Mex. C. Reds (2nd)† .... .550	1968—Mexico City Reds .... .586	Cordoba .... .649
1958—Nuevo Laredo .... .625	1969—Reynosa .... .591	1976—Mexico City Reds x .... .543
1959—Poza Rica............................ .575	1970—Aguila§ .... .580	Union Laguna .... .547
Mex. C. Reds (3rd)† .... .507	Mexico City Reds .... .607	1977—Mexico City Reds .... .623
1960—Mexico City Tigers .... .538	1971—Jalisco§ .... .558	Nuevo Laredo x .... .507
1961—Veracruz .... .575	Saltillo .... .593	1978—Aguascalientes x .... .589
1962—Monterrey .... .592	1972—Saltillo .... .636	Union Laguna .... .523
1963—Puebla .... .606	Cordoba§ .... .541	1979—Saltillo .... .704
1964—Mexico City Reds .... .586	1973—Saltillo .... .656	Puebla x .... .628
1965—Mexico City Tigers .... .590	Mexico City Reds x .... .590	1980—No champion .... y

°Defeated Nuevo Laredo, two games to none, in playoff for pennant. †Won four-team playoff. ‡Won split-season playoff. §League divided into Northern, Southern divisions; won two-team playoff. xLeague divided into Northern, Southern zones; sub-divided into Eastern, Western divisions, won eight-team playoff. yA players strike on July 1 forced the cancellation of the regular season and playoff schedule.

STANDING OF CLUBS AT CLOSE OF SEASON,
NORTHERN ZONE
EASTERN DIVISION

Club	MR	Cam.	Yuc.	PR	Sal.	CJ	UL	Chi.	NL	Rey.	Mon.	Ags.	W.	L.	T.	Pct.	G.B.
Nuevo Laredo	3	5	4	5	5	7	7	11	....	11	10	7	75	50	1	.600	....
Reynosa	3	3	4	5	6	8	5	13	3	....	4	8	62	64	1	.492	13½
Monterrey	3	4	4	7	4	5	5	9	4	8	....	6	59	69	0	.461	17½
Aguascalientes	3	2	2	6	5	7	4	8	7	5	8	....	57	70	2	.449	19

WESTERN DIVISION

Club	MT	Ctz.	Tab.	Agu.	Sal.	CJ	UL	Chi.	NL	Rey.	Mon.	Ags.	W.	L.	T.	Pct.	G.B.
Saltillo..................................	3	3	3	5	....	5	9	10	8	8	10	8	72	52	2	.581	....
Ciudad Juarez	3	5	3	5	9	....	8	10	6	6	9	7	71	57	0	.556	3
Union Laguna	4	3	3	4	5	5	....	10	7	8	9	10	68	58	1	.540	5
Chihuahua	1	4	5	2	2	4	3	....	3	1	5	6	36	90	1	.286	37

SOUTHERN ZONE
EASTERN DIVISION

Club	MT	Ctz.	Tab.	Agu.	MR	Cam.	Yuc.	PR	NL	Rey.	Mon.	Ags.	W.	L.	T.	Pct.	G.B.
Mexico City Reds...................	8	7	7	9	....	7	6	11	5	5	5	5	75	47	5	.615	....
Campeche	10	6	7	10	6	....	5	11	2	5	4	5	71	50	3	.587	3½
Yucatan	7	7	12	8	4	9	....	9	2	4	4	6	72	51	3	.585	3½
Poza Rica	4	7	1	6	3	3	5	....	3	3	1	2	38	87	0	.304	38½

WESTERN DIVISION

Club	MT	Ctz.	Tab.	Agu.	MR	Cam.	Yuc.	PR	Sal.	CJ	UL	Chi.	W.	L.	T.	Pct.	G.B.
Mexico City Tigers	....	6	9	7	5	4	7	8	5	5	3	6	65	56	3	.537	....
Coatzacoalcos	8	....	3	10	6	5	6	7	5	3	5	4	62	60	3	.508	3½
Tabasco.................................	4	8	....	7	7	5	2	10	3	5	5	3	59	59	3	.500	4½
Aguila	4	4	6	....	4	3	6	8	3	3	4	6	51	73	4	.411	15½

Tabasco club represented Villahermosa.

Union Laguna club represented Gomez Palacio and Torreon.

(Compiled by Ana Luisa Perea de Silva, League Statistician, Mexico, D.F.)

CLUB BATTING

Club	Pct.	G.	AB.	R.	OR.	H.	TB.	2B.	3B.	HR.	RBI.	GW.	SH.	SF.	HP.	BB.	Int. BB.	SO.	SB.	CS.	LOB.
Mexico City Reds.....	.294	127	4192	574	471	1231	1564	171	42	26	506	66	58	55	38	45	70	377	88	61	987
Mexico City Tigers ...	.285	124	3984	516	499	1134	1479	155	32	42	459	56	56	30	25	336	44	441	50	41	819
Saltillo	.283	126	4025	521	450	1140	1514	146	45	46	449	64	70	30	36	390	44	520	105	49	891
Ciudad Juarez........	.279	128	4013	518	453	1120	1447	141	42	34	446	61	43	33	37	373	42	524	105	54	841
Union Laguna	.276	127	4016	519	439	1109	1478	144	39	49	459	59	70	40	27	322	44	622	98	50	852
Campeche	.273	124	3950	432	389	1080	1297	118	18	21	386	61	97	30	34	330	59	466	86	34	908
Yucatan	.272	126	3967	490	442	1078	1364	141	23	33	423	60	73	33	26	488	56	443	121	59	967
Aguascalientes	.272	129	4207	518	567	1143	1574	162	43	61	465	51	47	30	26	407	32	694	76	58	893
Nuevo Laredo..........	.268	126	3975	470	382	1067	1367	106	34	42	413	68	65	29	22	344	44	531	56	48	827
Reynosa	.266	127	3999	469	466	1065	1430	153	31	50	435	57	68	25	30	412	30	535	89	41	979
Monterrey	.264	128	3962	447	470	1045	1330	120	24	39	390	52	93	36	44	371	30	473	63	37	885
Tabasco	.257	121	3779	430	395	971	1227	118	36	22	383	53	87	27	42	332	36	475	58	43	800
Chihuahua	.247	127	3899	358	622	963	1254	108	36	37	300	29	72	22	25	341	27	545	35	32	851
Poza Rica	.238	125	3803	322	492	906	1111	96	26	19	274	30	56	23	26	328	37	512	45	35	826
Aguila	.236	128	3977	346	436	940	1183	116	20	29	308	46	66	27	28	340	35	564	41	41	841
Coatzacoalcos	.236	125	3911	442	399	922	1229	128	31	39	386	53	88	32	39	424	40	613	34	30	830

INDIVIDUAL BATTING

(Leading Qualifiers for Batting Championship—351 or More Plate Appearances)

°Bats lefthanded.   †Switch-hitter.

Player and Club	Pct.	G.	AB.	R.	H.	TB.	2B.	3B.	HR.	RBI.	GW.	SH.	SF.	HP.	BB.	Int. BB.	SO.	SB.	CS.
Norwood, Willie, Reynosa	.365	101	367	69	134	205	23	3	14	65	12	0	7	6	29	8	49	24	9
Rodriguez, Roberto, Mex. C. Reds° ...	.363	115	454	67	165	200	13	8	2	49	4	4	1	0	56	14	22	9	6
Scott, George, Mexico City Tigers ...	.355	116	411	68	146	228	24	2	18	81	11	1	4	4	50	9	53	4	2
Biagini, Gregory, Ciudad Juarez†	.348	127	402	82	140	234	27	8	17	90	13	1	6	0	92	24	70	7	7
Duncan, Taylor, Mexico City Tigers ...	.340	115	412	59	140	182	19	1	7	58	9	2	3	2	51	4	30	5	4
Nettles, Morris, Campeche°	.332	113	416	71	138	160	13	3	1	33	8	5	0	3	59	12	67	22	7
Olivares, Oswaldo, Union Laguna°	.328	112	405	79	133	190	15	15	4	43	3	3	5	2	68	7	34	24	11
Navarrete, Juan, Saltillo°	.325	105	378	60	123	148	17	4	0	28	10	7	2	5	42	3	26	31	5
Collins, James, Saltillo°	.323	123	446	73	144	208	25	12	5	48	5	1	7	5	45	10	40	19	8
Joshua, Von, Yucatan°	.322	123	456	62	147	209	22	5	10	87	11	1	9	2	43	10	76	6	2
Defreites, Arturo, Tabasco	.321	111	418	66	134	185	18	3	9	48	7	1	0	2	34	4	67	8	5
Negron, Miguel, Nuevo Laredo°	.320	124	490	61	157	196	16	7	3	38	5	6	4	0	25	8	27	12	9
James, Arthur, Ciudad Juarez°	.319	120	430	70	137	179	23	5	3	49	11	0	3	1	31	0	40	4	4
Sommers, Jesus, Mexico City Reds	.316	119	430	63	136	175	22	4	5	44	5	2	4	5	41	3	44	8	4
Mora, Andres, Saltillo.......................	.316	124	437	65	138	230	17	3	23	93	9	6	4	6	56	14	53	3	2
Dyes, Andrew, Union Laguna	.316	124	414	74	131	213	22	3	18	87	9	0	7	8	45	17	72	12	6
Paredes, Jesus, Nuevo Laredo	.315	113	384	52	121	145	12	3	2	39	4	3	4	3	39	3	41	11	3

Departmental Leaders: G—F. Rodriguez, 129; AB—F. Rodriguez, 504; R—Obradovich, 84; H—R. Rodriguez, 165; TB—Biagini, 234; 2B—Biagini, 37; 3B—Olivares, 15; HR—Mora, 23; RBI—Mora, 93; GWRBI—Biagini, 13; SH—F. Lara, P. Mendoza, 18; SF—W. Howard, W. Llenas, 10; BB—Hairston, 122; HP—P. Ruiz, 13; SO—J. Pierce, 94; SB—Alston, 37; CS—Alston, 19.

(All Players—Listed Alphabetically)

Player and Club	Pct.	G.	AB.	R.	H.	TB.	2B.	3B.	HR.	RBI.	GW.	SH.	SF.	HP.	BB.	Int. BB.	SO.	SB.	CS.
Abarca Aceves, David, Aguas............	.325	16	40	2	13	15	2	0	0	4	0	0	0	1	2	0	10	0	1
Acuna, Clemente, Campeche	.273	84	264	31	72	79	5	1	0	21	4	13	1	5	9	0	30	4	2
Alcaraz, Luis, Poza Rica...................	.230	91	243	16	56	68	6	0	2	21	2	4	3	1	42	6	54	2	1
Alonso, Hermilo, Poza Rica...............	.232	86	220	16	51	54	3	0	0	4	1	2	0	0	14	0	12	2	3
Alexander, Roberto, Aguascalientes ..	.203	21	64	5	13	17	4	0	0	2	0	1	0	0	7	0	11	0	3
Alston, Wendell, Yucatan°	.279	96	323	79	90	110	6	4	2	27	5	4	1	2	91	4	29	37	19
Alvarado, Luis, Mexico City Reds	.241	109	365	42	88	111	13	2	2	38	2	8	6	2	26	1	24	5	6
Alvarado, Natanael, Mex. C. Reds.....	.279	117	433	44	121	154	14	5	3	53	10	5	6	11	33	3	52	7	8
Alvarez, Jose, Union Laguna	.133	8	15	2	2	2	0	0	0	1	0	0	0	0	0	0	2	0	0
Alvarez, Juan, Aguascalientes	.297	117	411	43	122	168	16	3	8	56	5	4	3	2	34	5	73	15	7
Alvarez, Jorge, Ciudad Juarez	.286	10	28	0	8	10	0	1	0	1	0	0	0	0	3	0	3	0	0
Alvarez, Manuel, Mexico City Reds° ..	.263	75	232	33	61	84	13	2	2	31	7	6	3	0	36	5	41	2	1
Arano, Samuel, Coatzacoalcos°	.114	17	35	1	4	4	0	0	0	0	0	0	0	0	4	0	4	0	1
Arano, Wilfredo, Mexico City Tigers ..	.063	11	16	1	1	2	1	0	0	0	0	1	0	0	0	0	2	0	0
Arias, Rodolfo, Aguascalientes	.100	30	80	5	8	10	2	0	0	3	1	3	1	0	2	1	16	0	0
Arratia, Javier, Union Laguna	.000	1	0	1	0	0	0	0	0	0	0	0	0	0	0	0	0	0	0
Arrieta, Jorge, Ciudad Juarez	.222	16	36	4	8	8	0	0	0	0	0	0	0	1	1	0	7	0	0
Arzate, Martin, Nuevo Laredo	.213	57	136	13	29	34	1	2	0	11	1	6	0	1	3	0	15	1	0
Ayala, Juan, Monterrey	.083	15	36	3	3	4	1	0	0	3	1	0	0	0	2	0	11	0	0
Bautista, Antonio, Campeche	.250	33	112	13	28	32	2	1	0	8	1	5	0	4	8	1	15	1	2
Barrera, Nelson, Nuevo Laredo.........	.265	117	423	54	112	153	13	2	8	52	11	6	1	3	44	11	80	5	1
Batista, Rafael, Union Laguna°	.281	106	370	61	104	159	23	1	10	64	11	0	6	5	47	9	67	3	3
Beare, Gary, Nuevo Laredo...............	1.000	1	1	0	1	1	0	0	0	0	0	0	0	0	1	0	0	0	0
Bellacetin, Juan, Yucatan°	.311	87	222	37	69	75	4	1	0	16	2	2	2	0	50	1	14	5	0
Benitez, Jose, Saltillo	.200	94	275	20	55	72	8	3	1	24	2	9	3	4	18	1	52	2	3
Benitez, Jose, Chihuahua	.216	63	204	15	44	64	2	0	6	28	2	4	2	1	14	0	48	1	0
Bernal, Cosme, Aguascalientes..........	.192	78	245	28	47	66	10	3	1	17	0	2	0	1	29	0	57	4	5
Bernhardt, Juan, Campeche...............	.307	121	449	40	138	170	15	1	5	63	7	9	7	3	21	9	33	14	4
Biagini, Gregory, Ciudad Juarez†	.348	127	402	82	140	234	27	8	17	90	13	1	6	0	92	24	70	7	7
Bobadilla, Manuel, Ciudad Juarez.....	.264	109	314	33	83	98	12	0	1	27	3	10	4	6	30	1	38	5	4
Bojorquez, Jose, Coatzacoalcos	.267	108	345	37	92	130	12	1	8	40	5	3	5	2	40	11	70	2	0
Buckner, James, Campeche	.267	23	75	6	20	21	1	0	0	6	1	5	1	0	6	4	11	4	0
Burke, Norberto, Reynosa	.197	80	208	29	41	51	4	0	2	16	2	6	2	0	24	0	56	1	1
Blanks, Larvell, Coatzacoalcos	.276	49	196	25	54	70	11	1	1	19	5	1	1	1	15	1	26	4	3
Briones, Antonio, Ciudad Juarez	.274	128	489	62	134	153	8	4	1	36	5	7	4	2	35	2	33	34	13
Brown, Curtis, Mexico City Tigers.....	.299	24	87	9	26	31	5	0	0	8	1	1	1	0	8	0	6	3	1
Cabrera, Jorge, Coatzacoalcos..........	.217	10	23	5	5	5	0	0	0	0	0	0	0	0	4	1	5	0	0
Canedo, Donald, Mexico City Reds	.270	67	137	10	37	46	4	1	1	12	2	3	1	0	14	2	34	1	5
Carreno, Luis, Campeche	.270	24	74	11	20	21	1	0	0	4	0	3	0	0	9	2	12	4	2
Carter, Tim, Poza Rica°	.273	18	44	3	12	12	0	0	0	2	0	1	0	1	1	7	0	0	
Castaneda, Jose, Coatzacoalcos	.000	1	0	1	0	0	0	0	0	0	0	0	0	0	0	0	0	0	0
Castelan, Miguel, Union Laguna°	.087	31	46	3	4	5	1	0	0	4	0	0	0	0	2	0	13	1	0
Castellanos, Rodolfo, Coatzacoalcos .	.000	3	1	0	0	0	0	0	0	0	0	0	0	0	0	0	1	0	0

Player and Club	Pct.	G.	AB.	R.	H.	TB.	2B.	3B.	HR.	RBI.	GW.	SH.	SF.	HP.	BB.	Int. BB.	SO.	SB.	CS.
Castillo, Juan, Coatzacoalcos	.043	19	23	2	1	1	0	0	0	0	0	0	0	1	2	0	5	0	0
Castillejos, Jose, Mexico City Tigers	.000	1	1	0	0	0	0	0	0	0	0	0	0	0	0	0	0	0	0
Castro, Alberto, Tabasco	.333	17	15	3	5	7	2	0	0	3	0	0	0	0	0	0	0	0	0
Castro, Antonio, Mexico City Tigers °	.252	114	357	43	90	120	11	5	3	43	7	4	2	0	48	10	38	8	2
Castro, Jose, Aguila	.052	35	58	1	3	4	1	0	0	2	0	3	1	1	3	0	15	1	0
Cazares, Francisco, M.C. Tigers	.000	0	0	0	0	0	0	0	0	0	0	0	0	0	0	0	0	0	0
Cerda, Benjamin, Aguila	.255	99	329	17	84	91	7	0	0	30	5	2	3	3	24	4	23	1	2
Cervantes, Eduardo, Nuevo Laredo	.247	99	352	48	87	101	10	2	0	14	2	10	1	3	47	1	49	1	5
Chavarria, Miguel, Union Laguna	.250	91	252	27	63	74	11	0	0	26	3	5	1	1	17	0	49	11	2
Chavez, Francisco, M.C. Tigers	.250	16	40	3	10	10	0	0	0	1	0	1	0	0	4	0	11	2	2
Chavez, Guadalupe, Saltillo	.267	67	217	25	58	66	8	0	0	15	3	10	2	1	27	3	29	3	3
Chavez Soto, Guadalupe, Un. Laguna	.000	4	3	0	0	0	0	0	0	0	0	0	0	0	0	0	1	0	0
Chavez, Juan de Dios, Chihuahua	.239	125	473	38	113	140	12	3	3	28	1	13	0	1	32	1	62	4	6
Chavez, Jose, Nuevo Laredo	.208	58	149	10	31	38	2	1	1	10	4	6	1	2	21	2	32	5	5
Collins, James, Saltillo°	.323	123	446	73	144	208	25	12	5	48	5	1	7	5	45	10	40	19	8
Collins, Silvester, Coatzacoalcos	.228	81	311	32	71	92	11	2	2	34	6	6	2	1	14	2	57	4	2
Contreras, Juan, Union Laguna	.202	95	272	16	55	60	1	2	0	19	2	8	3	0	13	0	52	9	4
Corcino, Frank, Aguila	.222	14	18	3	4	4	0	0	0	2	0	0	1	0	4	0	4	0	0
Cordova, Ignacio, Monterrey	.364	4	11	0	4	4	0	0	0	2	0	0	0	0	2	0	4	0	0
Cotes, Eugenio, Saltillo	.311	100	376	70	117	178	17	10	8	39	5	1	0	3	30	2	52	32	8
Cruz, Domingo, Yucatan	.299	86	294	39	88	107	9	2	2	23	6	10	3	3	23	0	27	4	2
Daut, Manuel, Monterrey	.232	55	138	11	32	36	2	1	0	10	1	3	1	3	7	0	27	3	2
Davalillo, Victor, Aguascalientes°	.307	40	153	21	47	69	10	3	2	14	1	1	0	0	13	1	19	0	1
Davila, Luis, Ciudad Juarez	.294	108	384	52	113	140	16	4	1	53	4	7	4	5	18	1	50	10	6
Defreites, Arturo, Tabasco	.321	111	418	66	134	185	18	3	9	48	7	1	0	2	34	4	67	8	5
Deliza, Juan, Union Laguna	.314	112	411	63	129	148	12	2	1	49	7	7	3	4	23	0	30	10	5
Delgado, Alberto, Chi.°	.208	75	231	18	48	70	6	2	4	24	1	3	2	1	33	3	34	1	1
Delgado, Paez, Javier, Campeche	.230	23	74	9	17	20	3	0	0	8	1	0	1	1	5	1	16	2	0
Delgado Espinosa, Manuel, Chi°	.240	68	196	15	47	52	5	0	0	11	1	4	1	1	23	1	26	2	1
Del Moral, Jose, Aguila	.231	48	182	13	42	59	6	1	3	21	2	0	1	0	8	5	18	6	2
Diaz, Alberto, Chihuahua	.285	89	288	31	82	98	12	2	0	30	4	8	1	3	25	0	27	4	4
Diaz, Arsenio, Chihuahua	.211	89	304	33	64	104	16	0	8	37	6	3	6	4	38	5	54	2	2
Diaz, Cesar, Campeche	.000	4	0	2	0	0	0	0	0	0	0	0	0	0	0	0	0	0	0
Diaz, Jesus, Reynosa	.120	18	25	0	3	4	1	0	0	3	1	0	0	0	3	0	3	0	1
Dixon, James, Poza Rica	.000	3	6	1	0	0	0	0	0	0	0	0	0	0	0	0	2	0	0
Duncan, Taylor, Mexico City Tigers	.340	115	412	59	140	182	19	1	7	58	9	2	3	2	51	4	30	5	4
Duarte, Luis, Aguila	.200	20	60	4	12	13	1	0	0	4	2	0	0	0	8	0	17	0	0
Duran, Gerardo, Chihuahua	.179	37	106	9	19	31	2	2	2	11	1	1	3	0	7	0	26	0	1
Dyes, Andrew, Union Laguna	.316	124	414	74	131	213	22	3	18	87	9	0	7	8	45	17	72	12	6
Elizondo, Fernando, Aguila	.179	128	420	27	75	90	3	3	2	20	4	13	3	2	25	0	64	3	2
Escobar, Rene, Campeche	.000	1	3	0	0	0	0	0	0	0	0	1	0	0	0	0	2	0	0
Esparza, Julio, Poza Rica	.234	106	329	16	77	86	7	1	0	17	3	3	0	0	26	0	33	1	2
Espino, Hector, Monterrey	.292	95	319	40	93	118	13	0	4	46	5	2	8	5	41	7	14	0	1
Espinosa Ramos, Ernesto, M.C. Tig°.	.231	51	143	13	33	33	0	0	0	5	2	1	0	5	9	0	22	2	0
Esqueda, Carlos, Yucatan	.143	6	14	0	2	2	0	0	0	0	0	2	0	0	0	0	5	0	0
Estrada, Francisco, Campeche	.252	112	389	29	98	107	7	1	0	34	5	10	2	2	36	4	23	1	3
Faudoa, Victor, Mexico City Tigers°	.243	53	111	8	27	28	1	0	0	4	0	0	0	2	17	6	16	0	1
Felix, Fernando, Monterrey	.200	24	85	8	17	26	4	1	1	4	3	0	2	0	4	0	12	0	0
Felix, Victor, Aguila	.239	91	309	44	74	89	10	1	1	9	0	9	1	0	47	1	42	4	7
Ferrer, Sergio, Tabasco	.318	22	88	16	28	32	4	0	0	8	2	0	1	1	7	0	4	3	1
Figueroa, Leobardo, Ciudad Juarez	.275	88	291	38	80	94	5	3	1	21	0	4	2	11	39	1	16	11	7
Firoba, Dan, Nuevo Laredo	.237	97	291	25	69	85	3	2	3	38	7	9	6	5	11	1	59	1	1
Flores, Mario, Monterrey	.243	86	226	28	55	73	2	5	2	18	6	11	1	4	14	0	47	6	6
Ford, Lambert, Tabasco	.286	56	189	25	54	70	9	2	1	24	4	5	0	0	23	2	12	2	2
Ford, Theodore, Reynosa	.291	119	399	38	116	156	19	3	5	59	9	2	4	2	67	5	40	1	2
Fraga, Ramiro, Saltillo	.167	4	6	0	1	1	0	0	0	0	0	0	0	0	1	0	1	0	0
Gamez, Rigoberto, Capeche	.218	28	55	6	12	17	0	1	1	7	4	4	1	0	6	0	18	1	0
Gamundi, Timoteo, Poza Rica	.244	108	352	36	86	97	3	4	0	16	2	10	1	4	48	0	60	14	8
Garcia, Humberto, Reynosa	.168	49	161	13	27	31	4	0	0	8	1	3	2	0	10	0	39	0	2
Garr, Ralph, Mexico City Tigers°	.265	11	34	2	9	11	2	0	0	0	0	0	0	0	2	1	5	0	0
Gaytan, Ricardo, Aguila	.140	17	43	1	6	6	0	0	0	1	1	1	0	0	0	0	10	0	1
Gomez, Alejandro, Nuevo Laredo	.208	94	269	23	56	69	2	4	1	20	1	5	1	0	4	0	29	3	4
Gomez, Graciano, Coatzacoalcos	.224	86	299	24	67	78	9	1	0	20	2	10	3	4	7	0	26	1	2
Gonzalez, Arturo, Chihuahua	.135	83	170	22	23	28	0	1	1	11	2	3	0	2	22	1	49	2	1
Gonzalez, Efrain, Union Laguna	.241	89	249	15	60	76	5	1	3	21	5	7	4	1	8	0	31	0	2
Gonzalez, Fernando, M.C. Reds	.307	38	140	18	43	52	9	0	0	16	0	4	2	0	4	0	11	0	0
Gonzalez, Jesus, Coatzacoalcos	.276	124	471	56	130	161	11	7	2	34	3	13	3	1	29	0	44	4	4
Gonzalez, Jorge, Poza Rica	.182	27	99	12	18	19	1	0	0	0	0	1	0	1	4	1	8	0	0
Gonzalez, Joseph, Aguascalientes	.287	115	380	43	109	143	12	5	4	31	4	4	6	6	46	8	77	7	8
Gonzalez, Mario, Yucatan	.500	5	2	2	1	1	0	0	0	0	0	0	0	0	0	0	0	1	0
Gonzalez, Noe, Aguascalientes	.280	34	100	9	28	34	1	1	1	12	1	2	1	1	9	0	23	0	1
Gonzalez, Wenceslao, Monterrey	.199	76	191	9	38	57	7	0	4	16	3	2	0	2	27	3	46	1	0
Guerra, Adrian, Nuevo Laredo	.246	115	386	52	95	139	12	4	8	49	9	6	3	0	67	11	52	3	7
Guerrero, Leobardo, Yucatan	.234	114	402	52	94	118	13	4	1	22	2	10	0	3	30	2	30	27	11
Guillermo, Leonardo, Saltillo	.167	43	60	8	10	10	0	0	0	3	1	0	0	0	8	0	16	0	0
Gutierrez, Felipe, Poza Rica	.224	46	147	11	33	41	2	3	0	9	2	4	2	4	7	0	20	0	5
Gutierrez, Gerardo, MC Tigers	.176	10	17	1	3	3	0	0	0	0	1	0	0	0	4	0	5	0	0
Gutierrez, Porfirio, Ciudad Juarez	.000	1	0	0	0	0	0	0	0	0	0	0	0	0	0	0	0	0	0
Guzman, Andres, Coatzacoalcos	.206	72	209	15	43	53	7	0	1	20	4	7	2	3	14	3	39	0	0
Guzman, Marco, Mexico City Reds	.250	74	232	30	58	78	11	3	1	21	1	2	0	3	21	0	31	5	4
Grandy, Eric, Aguascalientes	.293	83	294	42	86	108	10	6	0	30	6	4	4	3	33	2	52	8	9
Greene, Altar, Coatzacoalcos°	.270	113	344	51	93	142	17	4	8	48	5	2	3	4	106	9	64	5	2
Hairston, Jerry, Mexico City Reds	.296	123	399	74	118	160	14	8	7	73	10	4	9	1	122	24	33	24	15
Heras, Roberto, Saltillo	.221	56	131	12	29	38	4	1	1	13	1	5	1	1	4	0	29	0	0
Henderson, Joseph, Aguascalientes° .	.211	16	38	4	8	19	0	1	3	11	2	0	0	0	3	1	9	0	0
Henderson, Michael, Monterrey†	.354	31	113	16	40	50	7	0	1	7	3	2	0	1	10	1	9	3	4
Hernandez, Eduardo, Aguila	.176	39	74	5	13	15	2	0	0	2	0	1	0	0	7	2	6	0	0
Hernandez, Jorge, Campeche	.247	50	166	15	41	58	7	2	2	17	5	2	0	1	9	0	22	1	0
Hernandez, Jose, Coatzacoalcos	.331	45	166	16	55	78	10	2	3	24	2	1	1	0	12	1	19	1	1
Hernandez, Juan, Union Laguna	.296	119	449	65	133	172	12	9	3	33	1	12	4	0	40	0	84	16	11
Hernandez, Miguel, Coatzacoalcos	.219	84	228	24	50	59	5	2	0	14	2	12	1	3	27	0	30	3	3
Hernandez, Pedro, Ciudad Juarez	.287	31	94	6	27	34	7	0	0	13	1	1	0	0	3	1	9	1	0

Player and Club	Pct.	G.	AB.	R.	H.	TB.	2B.	3B.	HR.	RBI.	GW.	SH.	SF.	HP.	BB.	Int. BB.	SO.	SB.	CS.
Hernandez, Raul, Yucatan	.200	14	20	4	4	0	0	0	0	0	0	2	0	0	2	0	2	0	0
Hernandez, Rodolfo, Reynosa	.216	53	171	14	37	52	7	1	2	21	3	3	1	1	15	0	12	1	1
Hernandez, Salvador, M.C. Tigers	.260	97	289	39	75	82	4	0	1	27	1	8	2	4	26	0	28	1	5
Herrera, Ricardo, Mexico City Reds	.259	12	27	4	7	8	1	0	0	2	0	0	0	0	0	0	4	1	1
Hill, Scott, Monterrey	.218	19	55	5	12	19	1	0	2	8	1	1	0	0	1	0	11	0	0
Howard, Wilbur, Yucatan	.303	117	449	54	136	173	20	4	3	67	7	6	10	1	35	8	37	21	14
James, Arthur, Ciudad Juarez°	.319	120	430	70	137	179	23	5	3	49	11	0	3	1	31	0	40	4	4
Javier, Ignacio, Tabasco	.298	91	299	37	89	122	19	1	4	29	3	8	2	12	19	3	22	6	5
Jimenez, Leopoldo, Monterrey	.221	41	86	8	19	29	4	0	2	8	0	4	0	2	8	0	16	2	1
Jimenez, Sergio, Tabasco	.500	1	2	0	1	1	0	0	0	0	0	0	0	0	0	0	0	0	0
Joshua, Von, Yucatan°	.322	123	456	62	147	209	22	5	10	87	11	1	9	2	43	10	76	6	2
Juarez, Marcelo, Monterrey	.306	128	484	55	148	164	5	4	1	44	4	9	6	5	29	1	21	11	4
Lara, Francisco, Campeche	.300	113	410	32	123	138	13	1	0	40	5	18	3	8	17	4	17	9	0
Lara, Francisco, Mexico City Tigers	.211	9	19	1	4	5	1	0	0	2	0	1	0	0	0	0	3	1	1
Lazo, Esteban, Poza Rica	.000	3	3	0	0	0	0	0	0	0	0	0	0	0	1	0	1	0	0
Leal, Jose, Reynosa°	.264	76	201	24	53	78	6	5	3	22	0	4	0	1	12	1	49	1	2
Leon, Richard, Yucatan°	.284	123	426	43	121	146	17	1	2	45	7	4	4	4	52	16	50	2	3
Limon, Arturo, Poza Rica	.185	67	119	12	22	25	3	0	0	6	1	3	0	0	4	0	15	1	0
Limon, Jose, Aguila	.000	1	1	0	0	0	0	0	0	0	0	0	0	0	0	0	0	0	0
Liranzo, Rafael, Union Laguna	.217	23	83	12	18	22	4	0	0	13	4	4	1	1	2	0	4	1	0
Lizarraga, Alejandro, M.C. Reds	.300	110	406	54	122	149	18	3	1	51	9	7	3	6	12	0	19	13	5
Llanes, Ramon, Monterrey	.125	10	16	2	2	3	1	0	0	1	0	1	0	0	1	0	8	0	0
Llenas, Winston, Mexico City Reds	.282	122	440	62	124	171	26	3	5	61	11	3	10	3	51	15	55	1	4
Lopez, Carlos, Tabasco	.298	60	208	32	62	87	8	4	3	28	5	3	4	1	23	6	25	13	9
Lopez, Almanza, Jaime, Chihuahua°	.280	85	271	27	76	105	9	7	2	18	4	1	1	1	40	6	32	1	4
Lopez Felix, Jaime, Monterrey°	.343	95	306	31	105	122	15	1	0	32	6	7	0	0	16	2	15	5	2
Lopez, Raul, Chihuahua°	.202	41	114	7	23	26	1	1	0	10	1	9	1	0	9	1	19	0	0
Lopez, Victor, Campeche	.211	96	299	22	63	71	5	0	1	22	1	5	3	1	31	2	51	1	0
Lora Marino, Luis, Campeche°	.271	118	432	59	117	152	21	4	2	47	9	5	6	2	49	12	58	14	6
Low, Gabriel, Aguascalientes	.500	1	2	1	1	2	1	0	0	1	0	0	0	0	0	0	0	0	0
Lugo, Gabrie, Reynosa	.280	109	379	22	106	136	14	2	4	43	3	3	1	4	23	3	37	2	1
Lugo, Pedro, Poza Rica	.223	25	83	5	19	20	1	0	0	4	1	1	1	1	3	0	7	0	0
Luna, Jose, Poza Rica	.091	11	22	0	2	3	1	0	0	0	0	1	0	0	0	0	9	0	0
Macias, Gerardo, Chihuahua	.333	4	9	0	3	3	0	0	0	0	0	0	0	0	2	1	1	0	0
Madero, Carlos, Coatzacoalcos	.279	35	86	6	24	29	2	0	1	11	0	3	0	0	3	0	14	0	0
Marquez, Francisco, Yucatan	.224	121	406	29	91	124	15	0	6	49	5	4	3	6	25	2	64	2	1
Marquez, Prudencio, Poza Rica	.250	2	4	1	1	1	0	0	0	0	0	0	0	0	0	0	1	0	0
Martin, Gene, Poza Rica°	.295	91	298	32	88	137	16	3	9	45	3	2	4	2	48	19	33	0	0
Martin, Jared, Tabasco°	.285	31	116	16	33	38	3	1	0	8	0	6	0	0	10	0	4	4	3
Martinez, Jesus, Poza Rica	.158	40	76	3	12	16	2	1	0	10	0	1	0	0	10	0	23	1	0
Martinez, Francisco, Coatzacoalcos	.214	24	56	2	12	12	0	0	0	2	0	3	0	4	2	0	7	0	0
Martinez, Gabriel, Chihuahua	.000	1	1	0	0	0	0	0	0	0	0	0	0	0	0	0	0	0	0
Martinez, Reynaldo, Aguila	.242	87	281	24	68	91	15	1	2	21	1	8	1	2	15	0	53	6	3
McDonald, James, Aguila°	.303	77	274	24	83	111	11	1	5	35	9	1	0	0	34	15	23	3	5
Mejia, Alfredo, Aguila	.286	6	14	0	4	5	1	0	0	0	0	0	0	0	2	0	2	0	0
Mejia, Carlo, Mexico City Tigers	.277	86	235	20	65	77	12	0	0	23	3	6	0	5	17	1	17	1	0
Mendez, Roberto, Aguila	.265	123	426	49	113	130	15	1	0	18	3	9	2	9	53	0	53	4	2
Mendoza, Luis, Ciudad Juarez	.249	102	325	33	81	99	5	5	1	31	3	2	3	1	35	2	28	5	3
Mendoza, Margarito, Chihuahua	.199	46	176	8	35	2	0	0	0	9	2	2	1	0	8	0	32	2	1
Mendoza, Porfirio, Coatzacoalcos	.202	121	376	40	76	85	7	1	0	26	4	18	1	2	28	0	48	7	9
Mendoza, Saul, Yucatan	.244	118	361	35	88	107	15	2	0	41	6	16	2	2	81	5	33	4	1
Millan, Felix, Mexico City Reds	.306	106	385	62	118	144	15	4	1	32	4	10	2	4	43	3	15	14	2
Molina, Jose, Aguila	.213	85	235	15	50	60	7	0	1	18	2	6	2	3	21	1	48	1	2
Monasterio, Juan, Poza Rica	.298	112	399	42	119	147	13	6	1	40	4	3	2	3	22	3	26	11	6
Monroy, Hugo, Chihuahua	.259	21	58	2	15	19	4	0	0	6	0	1	1	1	1	1	12	0	1
Moore, Alvin, Reynosa	.307	26	88	10	27	45	4	1	4	21	2	0	0	0	12	3	7	0	1
Mora, Andres, Saltillo	.316	124	437	65	138	230	17	3	23	93	9	6	4	6	56	14	53	3	2
Moreno, Jesus, Aguila	.000	1	0	1	0	0	0	0	0	0	0	0	0	0	0	0	0	0	0
Munoz, Eduardo, Reynosa	.302	90	338	62	102	147	20	5	5	43	7	2	2	3	33	1	34	11	2
Najera, David, Mexico City Tigers	.267	6	15	3	4	4	0	0	0	2	0	1	0	0	2	0	1	0	1
Navarrete, Juan, Saltillo°	.325	105	378	60	123	148	17	4	0	28	10	7	2	5	42	3	26	31	5
Negron, Conrado, Poza Rica	.211	64	190	9	40	47	7	0	0	21	6	0	1	2	3	0	38	1	0
Negron, Miguel, Nuevo Laredo°	.320	124	490	61	157	196	16	7	3	38	5	6	4	0	25	8	27	12	9
Nettles, Morris, Campeche°	.332	113	416	71	138	160	13	3	1	33	8	5	0	3	59	12	67	22	7
Norwood, Willie, Reynosa	.365	101	367	69	134	205	23	3	14	65	12	0	7	6	29	8	49	24	9
Nunez, Arturo, Aguila	.091	18	33	2	3	3	0	0	0	0	0	0	0	0	0	0	10	0	0
Nunez, Jose, Campeche	.210	30	62	6	13	14	1	0	0	1	0	2	0	0	5	0	9	0	0
Obradovich, James, Aguascalientes°	.278	126	439	84	122	208	21	4	19	77	12	1	4	3	77	8	81	5	5
Olivares, Oswaldo, Union Laguna°	.328	112	405	79	133	190	15	15	4	43	3	5	2	2	68	7	34	24	11
Orozco, Arturo, Tabasco	.240	118	392	43	94	124	13	1	5	51	9	3	7	3	54	6	75	2	0
Orozco, Victor, Yucatan	.444	5	9	1	4	5	1	0	0	0	0	0	0	0	0	0	1	0	0
Ortega, Angel, Reynosa	.211	15	38	5	8	0	0	0	0	6	1	0	1	6	0	8	1	0	
Ortiz, Alejandro, Nuevo Laredo	.198	41	101	12	20	25	0	1	1	11	1	0	2	1	7	1	14	0	0
Ortiz, Alfredo, Tabasco°	.250	25	28	1	7	7	0	0	0	5	1	0	0	0	6	1	4	0	0
Ortiz, Jose, Tabasco	.284	119	398	32	113	127	12	1	0	34	5	6	5	3	22	4	44	1	0
Osuna, Elpidio, Ciudad Juarez	.198	64	192	18	38	45	7	0	0	24	4	4	1	1	32	5	37	1	0
Page, Michael, Chihuahua°	.059	5	17	1	1	1	0	0	0	0	0	0	0	0	5	0	4	0	0
Palacios, Catarino, Saltillo	.250	9	24	1	6	6	0	0	0	0	0	1	0	1	0	1	6	0	1
Paredes, Alfonso, Aguascalientes	.190	15	58	2	11	11	0	0	0	4	0	2	1	0	2	0	9	1	2
Paredes, Jesus, Nuevo Laredo	.315	113	384	52	121	145	12	3	2	39	8	3	3	4	39	3	41	11	3
Paredes, Raul, Campeche	.273	60	165	24	45	47	2	0	0	6	1	4	0	1	6	1	12	3	2
Pena, Manuel, Chihuahua°	.000	1	1	0	0	0	0	0	0	0	0	0	0	0	0	0	0	0	0
Pena, Ricardo, Union Laguna	.200	7	20	4	4	5	1	0	0	2	0	0	0	0	3	0	2	2	0
Peraza Canul, Jose, Yucatan	.200	15	25	1	5	5	0	0	0	3	0	0	0	0	0	0	3	0	0
Perez, Alfredo, Saltillo	.261	111	376	35	98	114	6	5	0	50	7	4	0	3	36	3	60	3	6
Perry, Kenneth, Nuevo Laredo	.277	19	65	8	18	23	2	0	1	13	2	0	2	0	4	0	10	1	0
Pierce, Jack, Coatzacoalcos	.265	124	422	52	112	189	19	2	18	78	7	0	9	7	69	16	94	2	0
Pisker, Donald, Aguascalientes°	.296	42	159	23	47	78	13	3	4	27	1	0	1	0	18	1	51	1	2
Quintero, Victor, Saltillo	.243	112	362	27	88	106	9	3	0	33	5	5	3	2	25	2	42	8	0
Quinonez, Ventura, Tabasco	.183	97	301	27	55	62	3	2	0	12	3	12	0	2	13	0	38	5	2
Ramirez, Gregorio, Union Laguna°	.177	8	17	3	3	4	1	0	0	0	0	0	0	0	3	0	8	0	0
Ramirez, Manuel, Monterrey	.291	126	430	50	125	157	12	4	4	48	4	11	9	5	37	0	32	4	6

Player and Club	Pct.	G.	AB.	R.	H.	TB.	2B.	3B.	HR.	RBI.	GW.	SH.	SF.	HP.	BB.	Int. BB.	SO.	SB.	CS.
Ramirez, Milton, Campeche	.268	42	138	19	37	40	3	0	0	16	2	3	3	0	10	1	5	2	2
Ramirez, Orlando, Chihuahua	.312	122	429	54	134	186	13	6	9	46	5	5	1	2	49	3	41	9	5
Rendon, Josue, Aguascalientes	.267	30	90	11	24	30	3	0	1	10	2	2	0	0	9	0	22	1	2
Reyes, Pedro, Aguascalientes	.201	106	329	18	66	75	6	0	1	19	1	12	2	3	9	0	44	4	4
Rios, Armando, Campeche	.136	21	59	2	8	8	0	0	0	3	1	2	0	1	4	0	18	0	1
Rios, Carlos, Mexico City Tigers	.283	116	428	41	121	139	11	2	1	40	5	7	2	1	12	1	36	1	4
Rivers, Carlos, Yucatan	.247	126	434	47	107	143	14	2	6	32	3	9	1	3	29	4	72	8	4
Rivero, Gener, Reynosa	.262	125	381	35	100	114	6	4	0	23	4	14	2	3	41	0	21	9	3
Robles, Humberto, Ciudad Juarez	.181	46	116	13	21	26	2	0	1	8	1	1	2	0	9	0	26	1	1
Robles, Sergio, Mexico City Reds	.291	69	234	24	68	78	5	1	1	26	5	6	6	0	6	0	15	0	1
Rodriguez, Arturo, Monterrey	.125	6	16	2	2	2	0	0	0	1	0	0	0	0	2	0	2	1	0
Rodriguez I., Francisco, Ags	.300	129	504	69	151	189	21	4	3	40	8	7	4	0	35	1	40	10	2
Rodriguez, Guillermo, Coatzacoalcos	.245	49	106	6	26	34	4	2	0	15	4	1	0	1	4	1	21	0	1
Rodriguez, Juan, Reynosa	.230	105	287	36	66	80	10	2	0	20	1	8	1	3	28	0	26	10	5
Rodriguez Clayton, Leonardo, Mon.†	.224	115	362	41	81	99	13	1	1	26	1	14	4	1	43	3	71	7	3
Rodriguez, Pilar, Yucatan	.000	1	0	0	0	0	0	0	0	0	0	0	0	0	1	0	0	0	0
Rodriguez, Roberto, Mexico C. Reds°	.363	115	454	67	165	200	13	8	2	49	4	4	1	0	56	14	22	9	6
Rodriguez, Rodolfo, Saltillo°	.310	118	423	71	131	164	22	4	1	33	4	9	3	2	64	1	25	5	3
Rojas, Olegario, Mexico City Tigers	.000	3	2	2	0	0	0	0	0	0	0	0	0	0	0	0	0	0	0
Romo, Jose, Coatzacoalcos	.198	85	247	22	49	85	12	3	6	34	5	3	4	2	24	1	56	0	0
Romero, Pedro, Poza Rica	.086	42	58	8	5	5	0	0	0	0	0	0	0	2	0	0	9	0	1
Rosado, Luis, Poza Rica	.283	95	321	31	91	118	13	4	2	37	5	3	8	1	20	4	31	3	2
Rosales, Arturo, Ciudad Juarez	.279	97	333	48	93	126	10	4	5	31	4	2	1	3	13	2	65	17	5
Rosario, Angel, Coatzacoalcos°	.239	108	368	64	88	118	16	4	2	28	6	9	1	1	65	7	47	4	2
Rosas, Clemente, Reynosa	.263	93	315	21	83	111	10	0	6	31	1	4	2	1	19	3	39	0	1
Rubio, Arturo, Tabasco	.239	64	188	22	45	52	3	2	0	19	2	8	0	4	14	3	7	1	4
Ruiz, Porfirio, Monterrey	.237	104	308	40	73	112	12	3	7	44	7	4	4	13	32	4	39	2	1
Saiz, Francisco, Poza Rica°	.199	85	267	20	53	61	6	1	0	9	0	6	1	2	35	1	28	3	3
Salas, Cesareo, Ciudad Juarez	.077	7	13	1	1	1	0	0	0	0	0	0	0	0	2	0	5	0	0
Salazar, Ronaldo, Union Laguna	.273	112	363	42	99	133	16	3	4	47	5	8	4	3	31	2	32	4	8
Sanchez, Armando, Mexico City Reds	.000	10	4	1	0	0	0	0	0	0	0	0	0	0	0	0	2	0	0
Sanchez, Jorge, Reynosa	.243	46	103	17	25	33	2	3	0	9	1	2	0	1	16	0	25	8	1
Sanchez, Juan, Union Laguna	.235	67	166	12	39	50	4	2	1	16	1	4	1	1	3	0	35	0	0
Salcido, Teodoro, Aguila	.342	27	79	8	27	30	1	1	0	7	0	0	2	0	12	0	17	1	2
Sandoval, Francisco, Aguila	.000	1	1	0	0	0	0	0	0	0	0	0	0	0	0	0	0	0	0
Santana, Blas, Saltillo	.266	107	399	43	106	140	13	6	3	45	6	5	0	1	12	0	26	5	8
Sauceda, Victor, Chihuahua	.208	101	365	30	76	97	11	2	2	24	1	8	2	8	8	0	68	3	6
Scott, George, Mexico City Tigers	.355	116	411	68	146	228	24	2	18	81	11	1	4	4	50	9	53	4	2
Serna, Joel, Saltillo	.282	117	415	50	117	166	16	3	9	49	7	6	7	2	40	8	91	2	7
Serna, Paul, Nuevo Laredo	.291	78	282	31	82	105	13	2	2	31	7	5	1	1	9	0	30	8	4
Serratos, Ramon, Aguascalientes	.231	92	320	42	74	85	5	3	0	19	4	3	4	2	53	1	44	18	8
Silverio, Tomas, Mexico City Tigers°	.271	61	192	29	52	58	2	2	0	14	0	0	0	0	37	8	15	1	0
Sommers, Jesus, Mexico City Reds	.316	119	430	63	136	175	22	4	3	55	4	2	4	5	41	3	44	8	4
Soto, Carlos, Nuevo Laredo	.311	108	366	50	114	161	15	1	10	57	7	2	3	2	37	4	40	0	5
Soto, Gregorio, Tabasco	.263	68	179	23	47	61	10	2	0	14	2	3	1	1	15	1	25	4	3
Soto, Jorge, Monterrey	.500	3	4	0	2	2	0	0	0	0	0	0	0	0	0	0	2	0	0
Stepa, Ramon, Nuevo Laredo	.328	52	177	17	58	70	3	3	1	21	3	1	1	0	14	2	28	4	2
Stillman, Roy, Campeche	.174	14	46	3	8	10	0	1	0	6	1	1	0	0	6	1	11	0	1
Suarez, Miguel, Mexico City Tigers°	.303	123	502	67	152	173	17	2	0	34	2	11	3	1	23	4	24	7	5
Tiburcio, Zeferino, Poza Rica	.184	93	299	24	55	81	12	1	4	27	3	2	1	2	20	0	77	3	2
Torres, Nemesio, Monterrey	.248	128	447	53	111	125	4	2	2	23	2	16	0	3	31	1	30	3	5
Trevino, Ted, Tabasco	.218	117	371	28	81	98	9	4	0	39	3	8	3	3	36	2	48	0	0
Tyrone, Wayne, Monterrey	.227	45	150	19	34	49	4	1	3	22	2	4	1	0	21	2	21	3	0
Valdez, Baltazar, Chihuahua	.309	35	110	11	34	43	4	1	1	9	1	4	1	0	5	1	8	0	0
Valle, Guadalupe, Ciudad Juarez	.297	117	387	41	115	141	14	6	0	42	9	2	2	3	19	1	65	7	3
Valle, Hector, Chihuahua	.000	1	3	0	0	0	0	0	0	0	0	0	0	0	0	0	0	0	0
Vazquez, Efrain, Aguascalientes†	.340	71	250	34	85	135	14	6	8	47	3	1	1	4	26	4	22	0	1
Vazquez, Nicolas, Mexico City Tigers	.260	117	420	45	109	137	16	3	2	46	8	3	5	17	0	32	3	4
Vega, Abelardo, Ciudad Juarez	.275	43	138	15	38	56	5	2	3	18	3	1	1	2	10	2	25	2	1
Vega, Ramon, Aguascalientes	.240	35	75	7	18	24	2	2	0	7	1	1	1	2	0	8	0	1	
Velarde, Roman, Tabasco	.209	86	244	21	51	66	3	3	2	22	2	11	0	5	14	2	39	0	3
Villaescusa, Fernando, Yucatan	.278	27	72	8	20	25	5	0	0	5	2	1	0	0	3	0	3	2	2
Villagomez, David, Aguila	.297	123	428	53	127	178	15	6	8	44	8	5	5	32	3	64	5	7	
Villalobos, Lauro, Chihuahua	.271	64	199	9	54	64	2	4	0	8	0	4	0	0	6	0	17	2	1
Villarreal, Roberto, Reynosa	.224	75	228	37	51	62	8	0	1	9	1	8	0	2	30	0	43	16	7
Villegas, David, Campeche	.000	1	2	0	0	0	0	0	0	0	0	0	0	0	0	0	0	0	0
Villela, Carlos, Union Laguna	.277	125	444	51	123	148	11	7	0	31	4	11	1	1	17	2	76	16	4
Villela, Rigoberto, Chihuahua	.266	125	433	40	115	147	12	1	6	40	2	6	0	4	35	3	35	1	0
Westmoreland, Claude, Mex. C. T.	.250	119	400	69	100	173	24	8	11	73	11	0	7	3	45	7	90	13	7
Whiting, Don, Monterrey°	.275	92	276	42	76	113	20	1	5	37	4	4	2	4	61	9	36	11	2
Williams, James, Aguascalientes°	.189	10	37	2	7	8	1	0	0	3	0	0	0	2	0	5	0	0	
Yepez, Francisco, Poza Rica	.250	43	124	12	31	37	2	2	0	8	1	5	0	0	14	2	13	2	2
Zamora, Roberto, Aguascalientes	.211	83	256	26	54	72	8	5	0	29	1	7	1	1	17	0	53	2	1
Zavala, Marcos, Tabasco	.232	90	271	26	63	80	6	1	3	33	5	8	1	2	15	0	58	1	0
Zuniga, Rafael, Coatzacoalcos	.238	83	240	23	57	64	1	3	0	21	3	4	1	6	11	0	40	1	2

TWO CLUBS—Alvarado, Luis (14 Monterrey, 95 Mexico City Reds); Alvarez, Manuel (55 Reynosa, 20 Mexico City Reds); Bojorquez, Jose (90 Union Laguna, 18 Coatzacoalcos); Blanks, Larvell (5 Mexico City Tigers, 44 Coatzacoalcos); Cabrera, Jorge (2 Aguascalientes, 8 Coatzacoalcos); Castro, Antonio (29 Yucatan, 85 Mexico City Tigers); Collins, James (55 Chihuahua, 68 Saltillo); Defreites, Arturo (24 Reynosa, 61 Aguascalientes, 26 Tabasco); Delgado Espinosa, Manuel (77 Ciudad Juarez, 51 Chihuahua); Diaz, Albino (47 Saltillo, 42 Chihuahua); Diaz, Arsenio (45 Campeche, 44 Chihuahua); Duncan, Taylor (29 Yucatan, 86 Mexico City Tigers); Espino, Hector (29 Mexico City Reds, 66 Monterrey); Espinosa Ramos, Ernesto (47 Poza Rica, 4 Mexico City Tigers); Garcia, Humberto (16 Nuevo Laredo, 33 Reynosa); Gonzalez, Fernando (20 Poza Rica, 18 Mexico City Reds); Gonzalez, Noe (5 Mexico City Tigers, 29 Aguascalientes); Gonzalez, Wenceslao (10 Chihuahua, 66 Monterrey); Guzman, Andres (35 Reynosa, 37 Coatzacoalcos); Grandy, Eric (58 Tabasco, 25 Aguascalientes); Heras, Roberto (19 Mexico City Tigers, 37 Saltillo); Joshua, Von (31 Mexico City Tigers, 92 Yucatan); Leon, Richard (33 Mexico City Tigers, 90 Yucatan); Limon, Arturo (47 Mexico City Reds, 20 Poza Rica); Lopez Almanza, Jaime (1 Aguascalientes, 9 Campeche, 75 Chihuahua); Lopez Felix, Jaime (3 Coatzacoalcos, 97 Monterrey); Lopez, Victor (26 Chihuahua, 70 Campeche); Madero, Carlos (4 Mexico City Reds, 25 Poza Rica, 6 Coatzacoalcos); Mejia, Carlo (22 Yucatan, 57 Mexico City Tigers); Mendoza, Margarito (19 Saltillo, 46 Chihuahua); Negron, Conrado (39 Aguascalientes, 25 Poza Rica); Olivares, Oswaldo (53 Tabasco, 59 Union Laguna); Rios, Armando (6 Aguascalientes, 15 Campeche); Salazar, Ronaldo (22 Nuevo Laredo, 90 Union Laguna); Santana, Blas (75 Aguascalientes, 32 Saltillo); Silverto, Tomas (29 Chihuahua, 32 Mexico City Tigers); Zamora, Roberto (32 Mexico City Tigers, 51 Aguascalientes).

GRAND SLAM HOME RUNS—Benitez, Norwood, 2 each; Biagini, Collins, Dyes, Guerra, Madero, Martin, Ramirez, Romo, Serna, Villela, Zavala, 1 each.

AWARDED FIRST BASE ON INTERFERENCE—Navarrete 3 (Sanchez 2, Alvarez); Alcaraz 2 (Hernandez, Westmoreland); Benitez (Sanchez); Bernhardt (Daut); Hairston (Westmoreland); Lopez (Gaytan); Marquez (Trevino); Mendoza (Guzman); Orozco (Robles), 1 each.

CLUB FIELDING

Club	Pct.	G.	PO.	A.	E.	DP.	PB.	Club	Pct.	G.	PO.	A.	E.	DP.	PB.
Ciudad Juarez	.979	128	3150	1358	96	96	12	Union Laguna	.973	127	3093	1408	126	122	18
Aguila	.978	128	3201	1491	108	106	24	Campeche	.972	124	3123	1324	129	107	11
Saltillo	.976	126	3171	1509	114	110	7	Reynosa	.972	127	3177	1358	132	94	12
Aguascalientes	.976	129	3288	1586	119	131	10	Mexico City Reds	.971	127	3261	1478	140	93	11
Yucatan	.975	126	3159	1382	116	96	16	Mexico City Tigers	.970	124	3099	1392	138	94	25
Nuevo Laredo	.975	126	3186	1410	119	137	25	Monterrey	.968	128	3168	1428	151	126	27
Coatzacoalcos	.974	125	3219	1435	122	71	10	Tabasco	.965	121	3015	1366	158	114	10
Poza Rica	.973	125	3009	1328	119	99	9	Chihuahua	.962	127	3087	1391	177	117	23

Triple Plays—Aguila, Monterrey, Poza Rica, Saltillo, Leach.

INDIVIDUAL FIELDING

°Throws lefthanded.

FIRST BASEMEN

Player and Club	Pct.	G.	PO.	A.	E.	DP.	Player and Club	Pct.	G.	PO.	A.	E.	DP.
Sommers, Mexico City Reds	1.000	15	131	3	0	9	Biagini, Ciudad Juarez	.990	115	960	61	10	78
J. Hernandez, Campeche	1.000	10	93	7	0	6	Mora, Saltillo	.989	119	1092	74	13	99
Osuna, Ciudad Juarez	1.000	10	88	8	0	6	Diaz, Chihuahua	.988	51	404	22	5	32
McDonald, Aguascalientes	1.000	10	63	3	0	6	Lugo, Reynosa	.988	84	696	46	9	53
Duarte, Aguascalientes	1.000	10	54	5	0	6	Batista, Union Laguna°	.987	69	591	32	8	62
Bojorquez, Coatzacoalcos	.997	45	373	20	1	35	Pierce, Coatzacoalcos	.987	124	1177	57	16	74
Delgado, Aguascalientes°	.997	37	347	17	1	23	Llenas, Mexico City Reds	.987	16	149	3	2	9
Defreites, Tabasco	.997	31	306	17	1	24	J.A. Lopez, Chihuahua°	.987	30	280	16	4	22
Bernhardt, Campeche	.997	36	297	19	1	43	A. Martinez, Poza Rica	.986	11	66	5	1	11
Cerda, Aguascalientes	.997	64	587	32	2	45	Grandy, Tabasco	.985	54	508	25	8	42
V. Lopez, Campeche	.996	60	481	35	2	46	Lopez, Felix, Monterrey°	.985	40	309	15	5	23
Guerra, Nuevo Laredo	.995	46	387	22	2	40	Mendoza, Chihuahua	.985	14	125	3	2	11
Scott, Mexico City Tigers	.995	81	782	35	4	50	Obradovich, Aguascalientes°	.984	121	1182	66	20	107
Barrera, Nuevo Laredo	.995	22	194	8	1	27	C. Soto, Nuevo Laredo	.984	56	481	17	8	43
Tyrone, Monterrey	.994	40	332	25	2	35	Dyes, Union Laguna	.983	20	160	9	3	16
R. Lopez, Chihuahua°	.994	39	333	18	2	31	Tiburcio, Poza Rica	.981	69	543	34	11	52
Millan, Mexico City Reds	.994	72	656	20	4	42	Faudoa, Mexico City Tigers°	.980	12	93	4	2	7
Garcia, Reynosa	.994	38	317	13	2	26	G. Soto, Tabasco	.980	32	325	13	7	32
LEON, Yucatan°	.994	104	885	49	6	73	Burke, Reynosa	.972	16	96	8	3	3
C. Rodriguez, Monterrey	.993	18	135	6	1	16	Negron, Poza Rica	.972	27	225	15	7	18
Espino, Monterrey	.992	67	581	55	5	66	Rosado, Poza Rica	.971	11	99	3	2	3
Martin, Poza Rica°	.992	28	238	12	2	19	Delgado, Chihuahua°	.968	14	112	9	4	9
Duncan, Mexico City Tigers	.990	30	294	14	3	30							

(Fewer Than Ten Games)

Player and Club	Pct.	G.	PO.	A.	E.	DP.	Player and Club	Pct.	G.	PO.	A.	E.	DP.
Mejia, Mexico City Tigers	1.000	7	60	1	0	8	Abarca, Aguascalientes	1.000	1	6	0	0	0
Brown, Mexico City Tigers	1.000	5	35	3	0	2	Rosario, Coatzacoalcos	1.000	1	5	1	0	1
Villalobos, Chihuahua	1.000	4	21	4	0	3	Heras, Saltillo	1.000	1	5	0	0	0
Ortiz, Tabasco°	1.000	4	25	0	0	3	Contreras, Union Laguna	1.000	2	3	0	0	0
W. Gonzalez, Monterrey	1.000	6	20	1	0	3	R. Hernandez, Reynosa	1.000	1	1	0	0	0
Robles, Ciudad Juarez	1.000	4	20	1	0	3	Davalillo, Aguascalientes°	.989	8	83	3	1	8
Castro, Tabasco	1.000	2	18	0	0	0	Joshua, Yucatan°	.987	8	73	2	1	4
Villaescusa, Yucatan	1.000	4	14	0	0	1	Alvarez, Mexico City Reds	.970	8	60	5	2	5
Olivares, Tabasco°	1.000	3	14	0	0	0	Serna, Saltillo	.970	5	61	4	2	4
Saiz, Poza Rica°	1.000	1	12	2	0	0	Castro, Mexico City Tigers°	.969	5	29	2	1	2
Westmoreland, Mex City Tigers	1.000	2	11	0	0	3	C. Lopez, Tabasco	.958	4	22	1	1	4
Ortega, Reynosa	1.000	1	9	1	0	1	Stillman, Campeche	.949	5	33	4	2	4
Velarde, Tabasco	1.000	1	10	0	0	0	Perez, Saltillo	.931	3	26	1	2	4
G. Rodriguez, Coatzacoalcos	1.000	1	8	1	0	0	E. Hernandez, Aguascalientes	.929	3	13	0	1	1
Arrieta, Ciudad Juarez	1.000	4	8	0	0	1	Madero, Poza Rica°	.889	1	8	0	1	1
R. Rodriguez, Mexico City Reds	1.000	2	7	0	0	0	Lora, Campeche°	.857	1	6	0	1	1

Triple Plays—Mora, Tyrone, Tiburcio.

SECOND BASEMEN

Player and Club	Pct.	G.	PO.	A.	E.	DP.	Player and Club	Pct.	G.	PO.	A.	E.	DP.
Alvarado, Mexico City Reds	1.000	17	30	45	0	5	Chavez, Chihuahua	.971	125	291	317	18	64
Chavez, Mexico City Tigers	1.000	13	19	26	0	1	Bernhardt, Campeche	.971	36	77	91	5	13
MENDEZ, Aguascalientes	.989	123	309	308	7	69	J. Rodriguez, Reynosa	.971	99	221	244	14	42
Villela, Union Laguna	.985	125	296	350	10	81	Ortiz, Tabasco	.970	119	303	314	19	76
Alcaraz, Poza Rica	.984	67	146	166	5	36	Reyes, Aguascalientes	.969	106	292	305	19	75
Navarrete, Saltillo	.983	78	183	222	7	46	Mejia, Mexico City Tigers	.969	30	67	56	4	11
S. Hernandez, Mex City Tigers	.979	96	251	254	11	56	N. Gonzalez, Aguascalientes	.968	19	47	44	3	6
R. Hernandez, Reynosa	.978	21	46	44	2	10	J. Gonzalez, Coatzacoalcos	.964	59	126	144	10	28
J. Hernandez, Campeche	.978	50	122	144	6	36	Nunez, Campeche	.960	29	52	45	4	13
F. Gonzalez, Mexico City Reds	.977	24	64	65	3	16	Blanks, Coatzacoalcos	.960	40	90	125	9	13
Serna, Saltillo	.977	51	126	128	6	31	Alonso, Poza Rica	.959	32	76	66	6	14
Millan, Mexico City Reds	.977	21	58	67	3	13	Cervantes, Nuevo Laredo	.954	98	273	268	26	80
Limon, Poza Rica	.976	24	39	43	2	7	Carreno, Campeche	.953	11	38	23	3	10
Torres, Monterrey	.976	128	331	307	16	81	F. Martinez, Coatzacoalcos	.939	23	36	56	6	11
Alexander, Aguascalientes	.975	14	31	48	2	8	Perry, Nuevo Laredo	.935	19	46	40	6	9
Guerrero, Yucatan	.975	110	299	321	16	64	Villaescusa, Yucatan	.932	15	36	33	5	5
Alvarado, Mexico City Reds	.973	75	192	202	11	37	Burke, Reynosa	.927	13	16	22	3	3
Briones, Ciudad Juarez	.972	128	312	342	19	80	Lugo, Reynosa	.894	13	17	25	5	6

SECOND BASEMEN—Continued

(Fewer Than Ten Games)

Player and Club	Pct.	G.	PO.	A.	E.	DP.	Player and Club	Pct.	G.	PO.	A.	E.	DP.
Acuna, Campeche	1.000	7	22	22	0	4	Alvarez, Mexico City Reds	1.000	1	0	2	0	0
Zuniga, Coatzacoalcos	1.000	7	16	12	0	0	Castro, Tabasco	1.000	1	1	0	0	0
Contreras, Union Laguna	1.000	5	12	12	0	5	Quintero, Saltillo	1.000	1	0	1	0	0
Esqueda, Yucatan	1.000	4	7	11	0	3	Serna, Nuevo Laredo	.986	9	35	36	1	9
Moore, Reynosa	1.000	4	8	6	0	2	Corcino, Aguascalientes	.957	5	8	14	1	2
V. Lopez, Campeche	1.000	3	6	7	0	2	Fraga, Saltillo	.929	2	6	7	1	4
Barrera, Nuevo Laredo	1.000	2	10	3	0	2	Cabrera, Coatzacoalcos	.921	9	18	17	3	3
Velarde, Tabasco	1.000	5	4	8	0	3	Yepez, Poza Rica	.900	9	12	15	3	2
Alston, Yucatan	1.000	2	5	7	0	1	Castro, Aguascalientes	.900	5	1	8	1	2
Sanchez, Mexico City Reds	1.000	4	6	4	0	0	A. Gonzalez, Chihuahua	.857	4	8	4	2	1
Rosario, Coatzacoalcos	1.000	3	2	7	0	1	Lazo, Poza Rica	.800	2	1	3	1	0
Rios, Mexico City Tigers	1.000	2	4	1	0	0	Jimenez, Monterrey	.500	2	1	1	2	0

Triple Plays—Torres, Serna

THIRD BASEMEN

Player and Club	Pct.	G.	PO.	A.	E.	DP.	Player and Club	Pct.	G.	PO.	A.	E.	DP.
Ortiz, Nuevo Laredo	1.000	12	13	21	0	2	Bautista, Campeche	.938	33	27	63	6	3
Serna, Saltillo	.983	60	47	130	3	13	Zamora, Aguascalientes	.937	64	68	154	15	16
RIVERA, Yucatan	.978	126	119	287	9	21	Bojorquez, Coatzacoalcos	.937	31	27	47	5	9
Yepez, Poza Rica	.974	13	15	22	1	1	Rios, Mexico City Tigers	.936	11	13	31	3	2
Moore, Reynosa	.973	16	8	28	1	0	Ramirez, Monterrey	.927	125	134	288	33	33
Bobadilla, Ciudad Juarez	.970	97	73	189	8	15	Vega, Ciudad Juarez	.927	33	24	52	6	1
Cerda, Aguila	.970	22	17	47	2	3	J. Hernandez, Campeche	.921	15	20	38	5	4
Duncan, Mexico City Tigers	.967	85	64	198	9	6	Velarde, Tabasco	.921	81	63	157	19	11
Gomez, Nuevo Laredo	.965	38	29	80	4	17	Zavala, Tabasco	.918	53	41	82	11	6
Quintero, Saltillo	.964	33	19	61	3	8	A. Gonzalez, Chihuahua	.913	64	50	107	15	7
Alonso, Poza Rica	.963	44	35	95	5	6	Deliza, Union Laguna	.909	34	30	71	10	5
Del Moral, Aguila	.962	21	14	36	2	0	Diaz, Chihuahua	.906	16	21	37	6	4
Llenas, Mexico City Reds	.961	27	17	56	3	7	Alvarez, Mexico City Reds	.906	63	43	121	17	6
Bernhardt, Campeche	.959	41	41	75	5	8	Delgado, Campeche	.898	19	14	39	6	3
Santana, Saltillo	.957	103	94	261	16	17	Salazar, Union Laguna	.898	72	66	128	22	14
Gutierrez, Poza Rica	.957	46	48	85	6	8	Sommers, Mexico City Reds	.898	74	62	131	22	10
Barrera, Nuevo Laredo	.956	90	74	189	12	23	Carreno, Campeche	.885	11	9	14	3	2
Vazquez, Aguascalientes	.956	66	56	140	9	8	Limon, Poza Rica	.875	23	10	18	4	1
J. Gonzalez, Coatzacoalcos	.954	67	51	114	8	6	V. Lopez, Campeche	.872	11	11	23	5	1
Zuniga, Coatzacoalcos	.953	59	41	100	7	3	Castro, Aguila	.869	21	13	40	8	3
Burke, Reynosa	.951	48	36	81	6	6	R. Hernandez, Reynosa	.848	22	10	29	7	2
Alvarado, Mexico City Reds	.944	10	4	13	1	2	Villalobos, Chihuahua	.844	26	18	47	12	7
Monasterio, Poza Rica	.940	14	19	28	3	1	Valdez, Chihuahua	.829	30	24	34	12	2

(Fewer Than Ten Games)

Player and Club	Pct.	G.	PO.	A.	E.	DP.	Player and Club	Pct.	G.	PO.	A.	E.	DP.
Alvarez, Aguascalientes	1.000	5	2	13	0	0	Tyrone, Monterrey	1.000	1	0	2	0	0
Chavez, Mexico City Tigers	1.000	4	8	7	0	1	Ruiz, Monterrey	1.000	1	0	1	0	0
Acuna, Campeche	1.000	5	6	7	0	0	Villela, Chihuahua	1.000	1	0	1	0	0
Scott, Mexico City Reds	1.000	5	1	11	0	1	Jimenez, Monterrey	.900	5	2	7	1	0
Alvarado, Mexico City Reds	1.000	4	4	6	0	0	Rosado, Poza Rica	.875	2	3	4	1	0
N. Gonzalez, Aguascalientes	1.000	4	1	9	0	0	Tiburcio, Poza Rica	.850	8	6	11	3	1
Lugo, Reynosa	1.000	3	5	4	0	0	Rios, Aguila	.833	4	2	3	1	0
Biagini, Ciudad Juarez	1.000	3	2	6	0	0	Salas, Ciudad Juarez	.833	4	0	5	1	0
Brown, Mexico City Tigers	1.000	2	1	7	0	0	Navarrete, Saltillo	.833	2	0	5	1	0
Corcino, Aguila	1.000	7	3	4	0	0	Alexander, Aguascalientes	.800	6	2	6	2	0
Benitez, Saltillo	1.000	2	1	1	0	0	F. Gonzalez, Mexico City Reds	.789	4	3	12	4	0
Castro, Tabasco	1.000	2	1	1	0	0	Westmoreland, Mex. City Tigers	.765	5	3	10	4	1

Triple Plays—Santana 2; Gutierrez, Ramirez, 1 each.

SHORTSTOPS

Player and Club	Pct.	G.	PO.	A.	E.	DP.	Player and Club	Pct.	G.	PO.	A.	E.	DP.
ESPARZA, Poza Rica	.981	100	141	316	9	55	Deliza, Union Laguna	.959	78	133	260	17	48
Bobadilla, Ciudad Juarez	.979	12	15	31	1	3	O. Ramirez, Chihuahua	.958	122	221	421	28	77
Ituarte, Aguascalientes	.975	129	206	492	18	81	Mendoza, Yucatan	.955	115	148	345	23	46
Baeza, Saltillo	.972	67	117	269	11	45	Jimenez, Monterrey	.955	18	13	29	2	2
Zavala, Tabasco	.972	20	11	24	1	2	Navarrete, Saltillo	.952	23	44	74	6	16
Serna, Nuevo Laredo	.971	68	118	218	10	54	Yepez, Poza Rica	.951	19	34	64	5	15
Rivero, Reynosa	.971	125	191	408	18	57	Canedo, Mexico City Reds	.950	58	76	154	12	22
Contreras, Nuevo Laredo	.969	47	65	154	7	29	M. Ramirez, Campeche	.943	42	70	128	12	31
Anderson, Monterrey	.969	30	59	95	5	17	Rios, Campeche	.940	16	24	39	4	12
Quintero, Saltillo	.964	37	73	117	7	17	Quinonez, Tabasco	.939	97	136	313	29	56
Gomez, Nuevo Laredo	.964	56	76	168	9	29	Herrera, Mexico City Reds	.938	12	20	25	3	5
Elizondo, Aguila	.962	128	238	454	27	72	Acuna, Campeche	.933	65	114	194	22	27
Alvarado, Mexico City Reds	.962	91	147	337	19	38	Rios, Mexico City Tigers	.930	102	174	328	38	39
Ferrer, Tabasco	.962	22	33	94	5	16	Blanks, Coatzacoalcos	.921	13	16	42	5	4
Valle, Ciudad Juarez	.962	117	191	390	23	67	Flores, Monterrey	.911	76	125	244	36	39
Mendoza, Coatzacoalcos	.959	121	209	421	27	54							

(Fewer Than Ten Games)

Player and Club	Pct.	G.	PO.	A.	E.	DP.	Player and Club	Pct.	G.	PO.	A.	E.	DP.
Zamora, Mexico City Tigers	1.000	5	9	20	0	2	Sanchez, Mexico City Reds	1.000	1	2	2	0	1
Guerrero, Yucatan	1.000	4	6	9	0	3	Alvarado, Mexico City Reds	1.000	1	1	3	0	0
J. Gonzalez, Coatzacoalcos	1.000	4	7	8	0	2	Salas, Ciudad Juarez	1.000	1	0	3	0	0
N. Gonzalez, Aguascalientes	1.000	7	3	10	0	2	M. Gonzalez, Yucatan	1.000	2	0	2	0	1
J. Hernandez, Campeche	1.000	3	1	8	0	3	Castro, Tabasco	1.000	1	1	1	0	0
Bernhardt, Campeche	1.000	2	4	5	0	1	Lazo, Poza Rica	1.000	1	0	2	0	0
J. Rodriguez, Reynosa	1.000	2	5	3	0	0	Corcino, Aguila	1.000	1	1	0	0	0
Burke, Reynosa	1.000	2	5	3	0	1	Najera, Mexico City Tigers	.952	5	9	11	1	4

SHORTSTOPS —Continued

(Fewer Than Ten Games)

Player and Club	Pct.	G.	PO.	A.	E.	DP.	Player and Club	Pct.	G.	PO.	A.	E.	DP.
Limon, Poza Rica	.939	8	10	21	2	1	Pena, Union Laguna	.875	6	14	14	4	2
F. Gonzalez, Mexico City Reds	.933	9	13	29	3	4	Ortiz, Nuevo Laredo	.875	4	3	4	1	0
Barrera, Nuevo Laredo	.929	7	11	15	2	4	Llanes, Monterrey	.867	5	7	19	4	4
J. Hernandez, Union Laguna	.923	3	5	7	1	1	A. Gonzalez, Chihuahua	.842	6	3	13	3	2
Villaescusa, Yucatan	.900	8	11	16	3	3	Esqueda, Yucatan	.000	2	0	0	1	0
Mejia, Mexico City Tigers	.891	8	15	26	5	1							

Triple Play—Elizondo.

OUTFIELDERS

Player and Club	Pct.	G.	PO.	A.	E.	DP.	Player and Club	Pct.	G.	PO.	A.	E.	DP.
ROSARIO, Coatzacoalcos	1.000	100	182	5	0	0	Howard, Yucatan	.981	107	240	12	5	2
ROSALES, Ciudad Juarez	1.000	92	173	5	0	0	Villagomez, Aguascalientes	.980	122	275	22	6	2
Romo, Coatzacoalcos	1.000	49	79	6	0	0	Bernal, Aguascalientes	.980	71	139	5	3	0
Stepa, Nuevo Laredo	1.000	41	76	4	0	2	Rubio, Tabasco	.979	53	89	6	2	1
Alvarado, Mexico City Reds	1.000	45	77	4	0	0	Cotes, Saltillo	.979	82	171	16	4	1
Paredes, Campeche	1.000	40	73	7	0	0	Lizarraga, Mexico City Reds	.979	108	224	10	5	4
Grandy, Aguascalientes	1.000	27	63	2	0	0	Gamundi, Poza Rica	.978	108	247	17	6	2
Buckner, Campeche	1.000	22	51	1	0	1	Alston, Yucatan	.978	92	137	7	4	0
Castelan, Union Laguna°	1.000	18	35	1	0	0	McDonald, Aguascalientes°	.977	65	120	6	3	1
Salazar, Union Laguna	1.000	18	31	3	0	2	Perez, Saltillo	.976	76	114	10	3	2
Delgado, Aguascalientes°	1.000	17	26	1	0	0	Gomez, Coatzacoalcos	.976	77	120	2	3	0
Jimenez, Monterrey	1.000	12	24	0	0	0	Bellacetin, Yucatan°	.976	46	76	4	2	1
G. Rodriguez, Coatzacoalcos	1.000	14	19	0	0	0	Dyes, Union Laguna	.974	107	183	7	5	3
R. Hernandez, Yucatan	1.000	10	19	0	0	0	Liranzo, Union Laguna	.974	23	35	3	1	0
Carter, Poza Rica°	1.000	12	18	0	0	0	Lora, Campeche°	.974	102	246	18	7	4
Davalillo, Aguascalientes°	1.000	10	16	1	0	0	Saloido, Aguascalientes	.974	15	32	5	1	0
Williams, Aguascalientes°	1.000	10	10	3	0	0	J. Lopez, Chihuahua	.973	39	68	4	2	0
Diaz, Chihuahua	1.000	10	10	1	0	0	Cruz, Yucatan	.973	40	66	5	2	1
Hill, Monterrey	1.000	18	10	0	0	0	Romero, Poza Rica	.971	23	31	3	1	0
James, Ciudad Juarez°	.995	116	189	2	1	2	Pisker, Aguascalientes°	.971	17	34	0	1	0
Paredes, Nuevo Laredo	.995	93	180	8	1	0	Olivares, Union Laguna	.971	109	223	13	7	1
Chavarria, Union Laguna	.992	67	120	6	1	2	Monasterio, Poza Rica°	.970	97	214	10	7	2
R. Rodriguez, Mexico City Reds	.992	112	227	11	2	0	R. Espinosa, Poza Rica	.970	39	61	3	2	0
Suarez, Mexico City Tigers°	.991	123	209	13	2	3	Guerra, Nuevo Laredo	.968	56	87	5	3	0
Ford, Tabasco°	.990	54	102	2	1	0	Defreites, Aguascalientes	.968	69	115	6	4	0
R. Martinez, Aguascalientes	.990	54	94	2	1	0	Diaz, Chihuahua	.968	84	170	9	6	0
C. Rodriguez, Monterrey†	.989	95	173	14	2	2	Nettles, Campeche°	.967	111	197	11	7	1
Vazquez, Mexico City Tigers	.989	97	176	9	2	1	Negron, Nuevo Laredo°	.967	118	228	9	8	0
Collins, Saltillo°	.988	120	242	11	3	1	Silverio, Mexico City Tigers°	.967	58	143	5	5	0
Greene, Coatzacoalcos	.988	50	75	5	1	0	Del Moral, Aguascalientes	.964	31	51	3	2	0
Munoz, Reynosa	.987	73	143	11	2	2	Serratos, Aguascalientes	.963	53	78	0	3	0
J. Gonzalez, Aguascalientes	.986	115	280	12	4	3	Javier, Tabasco	.963	90	170	11	7	1
Sauceda, Chihuahua	.986	97	210	9	3	0	Norwood, Reynosa	.962	75	167	8	7	0
Ciudad Juarez, Monterrey	.986	128	267	12	4	2	Leal, Reynosa°	.960	61	90	7	4	2
Rod. Rodriguez, Saltillo°	.986	94	132	7	2	1	Davila, Ciudad Juarez	.956	77	142	11	7	1
Chavez, Nuevo Laredo°	.985	41	65	2	1	0	J. Hernandez, Union Laguna	.956	108	198	18	10	1
Whiting, Monterrey°	.985	89	122	9	2	2	Brown, Mexico City Tigers	.955	11	19	2	1	0
Saiz, Poza Rica°	.985	66	122	6	2	2	Rendon, Aguascalientes	.953	24	35	6	2	0
Arzate, Nuevo Laredo	.985	46	57	7	1	0	Ayala, Monterrey	.952	15	18	2	1	0
Lara, Campeche	.984	97	176	5	3	2	Robles, Ciudad Juarez	.944	30	31	3	2	0
Jorge Gonzalez, Poza Rica	.984	26	58	2	1	0	Zavala, Tabasco	.941	26	30	2	2	1
C. Lopez, Tabasco	.983	54	114	2	2	0	G. Soto, Tabasco	.935	19	28	1	2	1
Hairston, Mexico City Reds	.983	123	334	11	6	4	F. Felix, Monterrey	.930	24	40	0	3	0
Villela, Chihuahua	.982	104	204	20	4	3	A. Martinez, Poza Rica	.929	12	13	0	1	0
Collins, Coatzacoalcos	.982	78	160	7	3	0	Sanchez, Reynosa	.927	39	37	1	3	0
Joshua, Yucatan°	.982	95	205	16	4	2	Delgado, Chihuahua°	.919	27	31	3	3	0
Castro, Mexico City Tigers°	.982	98	207	12	4	1	Guillermo, Saltillo	.913	20	19	2	2	0
Villarreal, Reynosa	.982	73	105	3	2	1	Martin, Tabasco°	.906	30	45	3	5	1
Figueroa, Ciudad Juarez	.982	77	105	2	2	0	Ortega, Reynosa	.895	10	16	1	2	0
V. Felix, Aguascalientes	.982	85	149	11	3	2	Quintero, Saltillo	.882	11	15	0	2	0
Ford, Reynosa	.981	62	99	5	2	1	Paredes, Aguascalientes	.870	14	19	1	3	0

(Fewer Than Ten Games)

Player and Club	Pct.	G.	PO.	A.	E.	DP.	Player and Club	Pct.	G.	PO.	A.	E.	DP.
Garcia, Reynosa	1.000	7	12	1	0	0	Limon, Mexico City Reds	1.000	3	2	0	0	0
E. Hernandez, Aguascalientes	1.000	7	9	1	0	0	Bernhardt, Campeche	1.000	2	2	0	0	0
Leon, Mexico City Tigers°	1.000	4	10	0	0	0	Daut, Monterrey	1.000	2	2	0	0	0
Ramirez, Union Laguna°	1.000	8	7	0	0	0	Contreras, Union Laguna	1.000	1	2	0	0	0
J. Lopez Felix, Monterrey	1.000	7	7	0	0	0	Bojorquez, Union Laguna	1.000	1	0	1	0	0
Arano, Mexico City Tigers	1.000	6	7	0	0	0	Jimenez, Tabasco	1.000	1	1	0	0	0
Madero, Poza Rica	1.000	3	6	1	0	0	Arano, Coatzacoalcos°	.909	8	8	2	1	0
M.A. Guzman, Mex City Reds	1.000	4	6	0	0	0	Alonso, Poza Rica	.800	3	4	0	1	0
Faudoa, Mexico City Tigers°	1.000	6	4	0	0	0	Tiburcio, Poza Rica	.750	5	6	0	2	0
P. Hernandez, Ciudad Juarez	1.000	4	4	0	0	0	Page, Chihuahua	.667	5	5	1	3	0
N. Gonzalez, Aguascalientes	1.000	3	3	1	0	0	A. Rodriguez, Monterrey	.667	6	1	1	1	0
J. Hernandez, Campeche	1.000	3	4	0	0	0	Cordova, Monterrey	.500	3	1	0	1	0
Garr, Mexico City Tigers°	1.000	1	3	0	0	0	Dixon, Poza Rica	.500	2	1	0	1	0
Ortiz, Nuevo Laredo	1.000	5	2	0	0	0							

Triple Plays—Martinez, Monasterio.

CATCHERS

Player and Club	Pct.	G.	PO.	A.	E.	DP.	PB.	Player and Club	Pct.	G.	PO.	A.	E.	DP.	PB.
J. Diaz, Reynosa	1.000	16	36	10	0	1	1	P. Hernandez, Ciudad Juarez	.993	25	135	9	1	0	5
Castillo, Coatzacoalcos	1.000	19	28	7	0	0	0	Lugo, Poza Rica	.991	25	99	15	1	1	2
Luna, Poza Rica	1.000	11	33	1	0	0	0	L. Mendoza, Ciudad Juarez	.991	102	585	60	6	5	6
RUIZ, Monterrey	.993	98	399	58	3	11	9	Rosas, Reynosa	.990	91	518	60	6	5	8

CATCHERS —Continued

Player and Club	Pct.	G.	PO.	A.	E.	DP.	PB.	Player and Club	Pct.	G.	PO.	A.	E.	DP.	PB.
Molina, Aguascalientes	.989	83	309	44	4	4	9	Duran, Chihuahua	.976	35	141	21	4	3	2
C. Soto, Nuevo Laredo	.989	37	164	9	2	0	5	E. Gonzalez, Union Laguna ...	.975	87	380	57	11	6	3
Estrada, Campeche	.988	107	512	73	7	5	7	Marquez, Yucatan	.977	121	529	60	14	3	14
M. Hernandez, Coatzacoalcos	.987	84	480	69	7	0	5	Mendoza, Chihuahua	.976	40	136	28	4	4	6
Gaytan, Aguascalientes	.987	16	66	12	1	1	4	A. Guzman, Coatzacoalcos	.974	70	351	60	11	3	8
Monroy, Chihuahua	.987	18	61	13	1	1	6	Robles, Mexico City Reds	.973	66	225	30	7	5	4
Arias, Aguascalientes	.985	30	116	17	2	1	4	M.A. Guzman, Mex City Reds	.971	68	268	36	9	4	7
Firoba, Nuevo Laredo	.984	97	417	67	8	16	20	Vega, Aguascalientes	.968	34	75	15	3	0	1
Sanchez, Union Laguna	.983	62	205	31	4	6	15	Heras, Saltillo	.965	49	147	18	6	0	3
Gamez, Campeche	.983	21	51	8	1	1	4	Westmoreland, M City Tigers	.965	111	446	76	19	6	22
Benitez, Saltillo	.983	91	451	60	9	7	4	Benitez, Chihuahua	.961	56	244	30	11	4	10
Rosado, Poza Rica	.982	82	325	59	7	8	9	Canul, Yucatan	.966	11	19	3	1	0	1
Daut, Monterrey	.981	50	216	39	5	7	18	Nunez, Aguascalientes	.930	17	34	6	3	1	6
Alvarez, Aguascalientes	.979	108	438	80	11	13	9	Madero, Coatzacoalcos	.928	19	56	8	5	0	0
Trevino, Tabasco	.979	115	487	65	12	6	10								

(Fewer Than Ten Games)

Player and Club	Pct.	G.	PO.	A.	E.	DP.	PB.	Player and Club	Pct.	G.	PO.	A.	E.	DP.	PB.
J. Hernandez, Campeche	1.000	5	26	5	0	1	0	Valle, Chihuahua	1.000	1	1	3	0	0	0
Mejia, Aguascalientes	1.000	5	20	5	0	0	0	Zamora, Aguascalientes	1.000	1	2	1	0	0	0
Orozco, Tabasco	1.000	8	20	3	0	0	0	Guerra, Nuevo Laredo	1.000	1	3	0	0	0	0
Duarte, Aguascalientes	1.000	4	19	2	0	0	0	Barrera, Nuevo Laredo	1.000	1	2	0	0	0	0
Gutierrez, Mexico City Tigers	1.000	3	15	2	0	0	1	Palacios, Saltillo	1.000	1	1	0	0	0	0
Orozco, Yucatan	1.000	5	15	0	0	0	1	Alvarez, Ciudad Juarez	.971	6	30	3	1	0	1
Castro, Tabasco	1.000	8	6	2	0	0	0	Lara, Mexico City Tigers	.963	7	26	0	1	0	1
Bobadilla, Ciudad Juarez	1.000	1	5	1	0	0	0	Villela, Chihuahua	.500	1	1	0	1	0	0
Marquez, Poza Rica	1.000	2	4	1	0	0	0	Negron, Aguascalientes		1	0	0	0	0	1

PITCHERS

Player and Club	Pct.	G.	PO.	A.	E.	DP.	Player and Club	Pct.	G.	PO.	A.	E.	DP.
BEARE, Nuevo Laredo	1.000	26	12	50	0	5	Higueras, Ciudad Juarez	.977	28	7	35	1	1
Kuk Lee, Poza Rica	1.000	34	7	43	0	1	McEnaney, Tabasco°	.975	19	4	35	1	1
Brunet, Aguila	1.000	29	3	47	0	2	Ibarra, Reynosa	.974	29	6	32	1	1
Henderson, Aguascalientes	1.000	22	11	34	0	2	Leon, Mexico City Reds	.972	25	10	25	1	3
Rivera, Yucatan	1.000	22	7	24	0	2	Pollorena, Saltillo	.971	26	7	27	1	2
Dominguez, Mexico City Tigers	1.000	23	6	22	0	2	Jimenez, Aguila	.969	12	3	28	1	2
Silva, Union Laguna	1.000	31	3	24	0	4	Camper, Monterrey	.968	28	3	27	1	1
Low, Aguascalientes	1.000	30	9	18	0	1	C. Sosa, Union Laguna	.968	29	2	28	1	3
Franco, Poza Rica	1.000	22	4	23	0	1	Branch, Chihuahua	.968	29	6	24	1	2
Dominguez, Mexico City Reds°	1.000	29	2	24	0	0	E. Lopez, Poza Rica	.967	22	6	23	1	1
D. Ochoa, Coatzacoalcos	1.000	34	5	20	0	2	Salinas, Mexico City Reds	.966	28	10	47	2	3
J. Ochoa, Union Laguna	1.000	28	9	16	0	1	Colorado, Coatzacoalcos	.966	30	2	54	2	0
Arano, Mexico City Reds	1.000	26	8	16	0	0	Juarez, Aguascalientes	.964	28	10	44	2	2
Garcia, Nuevo Laredo	1.000	24	4	20	0	4	R. Garcia, Saltillo	.964	33	5	22	1	0
Castillejos, Mexico City Tigers	1.000	39	6	17	0	0	A. Gonzalez, Monterrey	.961	30	11	38	2	2
Jimenez, Campeche°	1.000	35	5	18	0	1	Sutton, Nuevo Laredo	.961	26	10	63	3	6
A. Soto, Saltillo	1.000	47	4	18	0	2	Equer, Monterrey°	.960	31	6	42	2	1
Segui, Reynosa	1.000	22	5	17	0	0	Limon, Aguila	.960	50	3	21	1	0
Cordova, Aguila	1.000	31	4	17	0	2	Perez, Campeche	.960	16	7	17	1	1
L. Guzman, Coatzacoalcos	1.000	13	4	17	0	0	Moreno, Aguascalientes	.958	20	2	21	1	1
R. Guzman, Union Laguna	1.000	42	7	12	0	0	Rondon, Yucatan	.955	29	13	29	2	1
Moret, Union Laguna°	1.000	13	2	17	0	2	Ramirez, Reynosa°	.952	32	3	17	1	1
Miranda, Coatzacoalcos	1.000	23	3	13	0	0	Barr, Aguascalientes	.952	15	5	15	1	0
Montague, Aguascalientes	1.000	10	5	11	0	0	Sauceda, Mexico City Tigers	.950	54	4	15	1	1
Maytorena, Union Laguna	1.000	34	2	13	0	2	Orozco, Campeche	.950	21	5	14	1	0
Preciado, Mexico City Reds	1.000	30	3	12	0	0	G. Solis, Monterrey	.950	20	5	14	1	0
Vazquez, Mexico City Reds	1.000	26	2	13	0	0	R. Garcia, Ciudad Juarez	.947	26	12	24	2	1
Posadas, Poza Rica	1.000	25	4	11	0	0	Kekich, Ciudad Juarez°	.947	22	11	25	2	3
Valenzuela, Aguascalientes°	1.000	27	3	10	0	2	J. L. Garcia, Tabasco	.947	33	4	14	1	1
Garduza, Poza Rica	1.000	16	1	12	0	0	C. Diaz, Campeche	.944	30	8	43	3	3
Heredia, Monterrey	1.000	21	2	10	0	0	Vidana, Reynosa	.944	23	3	14	1	1
Enriquez, Ciudad Juarez	1.000	13	3	9	0	1	Arratia, Union Laguna	.944	14	3	14	1	0
Renteria, Ciudad Juarez	1.000	13	3	9	0	0	Valdez, Chihuahua	.941	32	6	10	1	0
Abarca, Aguascalientes	1.000	16	2	9	0	0	Gutierrez, Ciudad Juarez	.941	21	3	13	1	2
Santos, Aguila	1.000	13	3	8	0	0	Purata, Aguila°	.941	17	5	11	1	0
Aguilar, Monterrey	1.000	25	2	8	0	2	R. Ochoa, Tabasco	.939	16	3	28	2	0
Buentello, Reynosa	1.000	35	2	8	0	2	J. Martinez, Monterrey	.938	22	8	22	2	0
A. Hernandez, Nuevo Laredo	1.000	28	1	9	0	1	Ant. Pulido, Campeche	.938	59	3	12	1	1
H. Lopez, Yucatan	1.000	28	5	5	0	0	Alf. Pulido, Mexico City Reds°	.935	31	5	24	2	1
Brueggeman, Ciudad Juarez	1.000	21	3	7	0	1	Villanueva, Mexico City Tigers°	.933	30	4	24	2	1
Chavez, Union Laguna	1.000	16	3	7	0	1	Acosta, Coatzacoalcos	.933	21	4	24	2	0
Jones, Mexico City Tigers°	1.000	10	0	10	0	0	R. Rodriguez, Poza Rica	.933	32	8	6	1	0
Palacios, Tabasco	1.000	18	2	7	0	0	J. Guzman, Poza Rica	.933	16	1	13	1	1
R. Martinez, Saltillo	1.000	20	1	7	0	1	Menendez, Saltillo	.931	30	3	24	2	1
Alvarez, Chihuahua	1.000	14	1	7	0	0	Mundo, Chihuahua	.929	30	5	34	3	0
Velazquez, Monterrey	1.000	15	4	1	0	0	Vidana, Chihuahua	.929	16	4	22	2	2
Delfin, Coatzacoalcos	1.000	39	2	3	0	0	Corona, Nuevo Laredo°	.923	28	2	11	1	1
Delgadillo, Aguascalientes	1.000	21	0	5	0	0	F. Lopez, Campeche	.923	12	5	7	1	0
Tejeda, Coatzacoalcos°	1.000	21	1	3	0	0	Rios, Reynosa	.919	25	10	24	3	2
Franco, Nuevo Laredo	1.000	19	0	3	0	1	Rogers, Tabasco	.918	33	10	46	5	3
J. Martinez, Yucatan°	1.000	16	1	2	0	0	De Los Santos, Union Laguna°	.912	18	6	25	3	0
Castro, Tabasco	1.000	11	1	2	0	0	Barojas, Mexico City Reds	.913	50	6	36	4	4
Holguin, Ciudad Juarez°	1.000	16	0	2	0	0	Divison, Reynosa	.909	21	3	17	2	0
J. Rodriguez, Mexico City Reds°	1.000	11	1	1	0	0	McLaughlin, Nuevo Laredo	.909	21	5	15	2	0
Romo, Coatzacoalcos	.983	29	14	45	1	2	G. Martinez, Chihuahua	.908	32	19	40	6	7
E. Escarrega, Campeche	.983	28	13	44	1	2	M. A. Rodriguez, Chihuahua	.906	34	6	23	3	1
Ortiz, Tabasco°	.982	28	6	49	1	3	F. Martinez, Nuevo Laredo	.905	21	3	16	2	1
Paul, Ciudad Juarez°	.980	23	8	40	1	2	Saldivar, Poza Rica	.900	18	3	15	2	0
Solis, Saltillo	.978	24	13	31	1	2	Madrigal, Mexico City Tigers	.900	27	4	14	2	0

PITCHERS—(Continued)

Player and Club	Pct.	G.	PO.	A.	E.	DP.	Player and Club	Pct.	G.	PO.	A.	E.	DP.
Beltran, Chihuahua	.900	20	2	7	1	0	J. Solis, Nuevo Laredo	.867	46	2	11	2	0
Lagunas, Yucatan	.900	10	0	9	1	1	Saucedo, Yucatan	.857	19	4	8	2	0
Casas, Mexico City Tigers	.895	28	2	15	2	0	R. Morales, Reynosa	.857	13	4	8	2	1
Monteagudo, Aguila	.889	22	2	22	3	2	A. Rodriguez, Reynosa	.857	22	1	5	1	0
Pena, Chihuahua°	.889	33	3	5	1	0	Perez, Tabasco°	.857	21	1	5	1	1
Cazares, Yucatan	.889	10	0	8	1	0	M. Morales, Aguila	.846	26	1	10	2	2
Beltran, Union Laguna	.886	21	9	22	4	3	D. Villegas, Campeche	.842	43	4	12	3	0
P. Rodriguez, Yucatan	.886	51	11	20	4	0	H. Madrigal, Tabasco	.833	28	5	20	5	2
Rasmussen, Yucatan	.885	19	3	20	3	1	Gaxiola, Aguila	.833	14	4	16	4	1
Cazares, Mexico City Tigers	.882	24	5	10	2	2	Dimas, Ciudad Juarez	.833	22	0	5	1	1
Villegas, Mexico City Tigers	.880	25	4	18	3	0	Lugo, Aguascalientes	.826	46	2	17	4	0
Bass, Aguila	.880	11	3	19	3	1	Sandate, Mexico City Reds°	.815	20	3	19	5	1
Bane, Saltillo°	.879	38	9	42	7	0	Nava, Yucatan	.800	13	1	3	1	0
Carranza, Coatzacoalcos	.879	24	9	20	4	1	G. Hernandez, Nuevo Laredo	.800	10	0	4	1	0
Lance, Monterrey	.878	26	12	24	5	1	Baruch, Poza Rica	.667	31	0	2	1	0
J. Pena, Yucatan	.875	28	4	31	5	1	Guerrero, Monterrey	.667	11	0	2	1	0
F. Garcia, Chihuahua	.875	21	0	7	1	1	Estrada, Mexico City Reds	.500	10	0	2	2	0

(Fewer Than Ten Games)

Player and Club	Pct.	G.	PO.	A.	E.	DP.	Player and Club	Pct.	G.	PO.	A.	E.	DP.
Hughes, Mexico City Tigers	1.000	5	2	13	0	1	Pineda, Poza Rica	1.000	8	0	2	0	0
Kobel, Yucatan	1.000	8	0	14	0	0	Peralta, Coatzacoalcos	1.000	4	0	2	0	0
Pole, Mexico City Tigers	1.000	9	2	10	0	0	Venzor, Reynosa	1.000	4	0	2	0	0
Chavez, Yucatan	1.000	8	1	11	0	1	Mota, Poza Rica	1.000	3	0	2	0	0
Nipp, Ciudad Juarez	1.000	8	1	9	0	1	Trinidad, Reynosa°	1.000	6	1	0	0	0
Cervantes, Aguascalientes	1.000	8	2	8	0	0	Abreu, Aguila	1.000	4	0	1	0	0
Torres, Saltillo	1.000	8	1	7	0	0	Granillo, Aguascalientes°	1.000	4	0	1	0	0
Rincon, Mexico City Tigers	1.000	6	2	4	0	1	Torrealba, Saltillo	1.000	4	0	1	0	0
Nieto, Yucatan	1.000	7	1	4	0	1	Ruiz, Aguascalientes	1.000	3	0	1	0	0
Williams, Chihuahua°	1.000	7	0	5	0	3	Valle, Campeche	1.000	2	1	0	0	0
F. Soto, Campeche	1.000	6	0	5	0	0	Sandoval, Aguila	1.000	1	0	1	0	0
Espinosa, Aguascalientes	1.000	8	1	3	0	2	Rabouin, Aguila	.909	4	3	7	1	0
Ponce, Tabasco	1.000	8	1	3	0	0	E. Rodriguez, Monterrey	.875	6	1	6	1	1
Castaneda, Saltillo°	1.000	6	0	4	0	0	Hallgreen, Reynosa	.857	9	2	4	1	0
Urrea, Saltillo	1.000	8	0	3	0	0	Borbon, Reynosa	.857	3	3	3	1	1
Moreno, Aguascalientes	1.000	5	1	2	0	0	Esparza, Campeche	.833	8	2	3	1	1
P. Escarrega, Mex. City Tigers	1.000	4	0	3	0	0	Bonfils, Poza Rica°	.818	5	2	7	2	0
Arroyo, Mexico City Tigers°	1.000	4	0	3	0	0	Palomares, Reynosa	.750	8	1	2	1	0
Madden, Tabasco	1.000	3	0	3	0	0	C. Guzman, Campeche	.667	8	0	2	1	0
Guerra, Nuevo Laredo	1.000	1	0	3	0	1	Preciado, Tabasco	.667	4	0	2	1	0

CLUB PITCHING

Club	ERA.	G.	CG.	ShO.	Sv.	IP.	H.	R.	ER.	HR.	HB.	BB.	Int. BB.	SO.	WP.	Bk.
Coatzacoalcos	2.32	125	58	22	11	1073	961	399	277	22	28	316	38	665	30	7
Nuevo Laredo	2.64	126	60	23	14	1062	995	382	311	49	26	335	44	503	32	1
Campeche	2.70	124	30	13	31	1041	985	389	312	40	29	344	45	523	31	4
Tabasco	2.81	121	62	12	9	1005	1040	395	314	29	23	299	43	462	22	1
Aguila	2.99	128	44	17	20	1067	1030	436	355	23	38	385	56	467	45	5
Yucatan	3.10	126	49	21	21	1053	1045	442	363	42	39	346	30	502	42	3
Monterrey	3.14	128	57	14	9	1056	1067	470	368	44	41	381	44	535	45	3
Union Laguna	3.19	127	36	16	23	1031	988	439	365	39	25	398	13	543	28	3
Mexico City Reds	3.23	127	42	12	21	1087	1107	471	390	35	25	313	30	427	49	5
Ciudad Juarez	3.35	128	74	16	9	1050	1080	453	391	34	28	337	16	714	28	4
Saltillo	3.37	126	52	16	16	1057	1095	450	396	35	28	325	53	567	28	3
Reynosa	3.39	127	48	20	6	1059	1031	466	399	37	22	420	20	663	47	2
Mexico City Tigers	3.42	124	30	13	24	1033	1019	499	392	29	36	443	49	441	42	4
Poza Rica	3.75	125	46	10	8	1003	1049	492	418	39	30	453	77	413	26	12
Aguascalientes	4.06	129	38	8	15	1096	1243	567	495	41	33	412	47	443	50	5
Chihuahua	4.32	127	38	8	9	1029	1179	622	494	51	54	481	65	467	60	1

PITCHERS' RECORDS

(Leading Qualifiers for Earned-Run Average Leadership—104 or More Innings)

°Throws lefthanded.

Pitcher—Club	W.	L.	Pct.	ERA.	G.	GS.	CG.	GF.	ShO.	Sv.	IP.	H.	R.	ER.	HR.	HB.	BB.	Int. BB.	SO.	WP.
Romo, Coatzacoalcos	16	6	.727	1.40	29	27	21	1	7	1	219	161	50	34	4	4	55	7	159	11
Limon, Aguila	6	4	.600	1.55	50	1	0	49	0	19	110	86	23	19	0	0	35	5	72	2
McLaughlin, Nuevo Laredo	12	5	.706	1.58	21	21	11	0	3	0	142	116	32	25	6	1	44	3	108	7
Sutton, Nuevo Laredo	17	7	.708	1.63	26	25	21	1	7	0	204	168	52	37	5	8	62	5	59	4
Rogers, Tabasco	16	10	.615	1.66	33	23	21	10	3	5	212	187	54	39	4	6	45	17	126	0
R. Garcia, Ciudad Juarez	20	5	.800	1.83	26	26	24	0	5	0	212	176	58	43	4	5	42	2	187	12
Paul, Ciudad Juarez°	12	7	.632	1.95	25	23	22	14	1	4	171	149	43	37	4	3	17	1	103	0
Ant. Pulido, Campeche	9	5	.643	2.04	59	0	0	51	0	27	106	84	27	24	0	3	27	6	81	4
Ortiz, Tabasco	12	11	.522	2.08	28	25	18	2	4	1	182	180	56	42	5	5	41	6	65	0
Colorado, Coatzacoalcos	14	10	.583	2.08	30	22	17	3	5	0	199	179	60	46	2	3	20	7	140	0
Segui, Reynosa	14	6	.700	2.08	22	22	19	0	5	0	182	145	52	42	4	1	35	1	147	5

Departmental Leaders: G—Pulido, 59; GS—Diaz, C., 30; CG—Garcia, 24; ShO—Romo, Brunet, Sutton, 7; W—Garcia, 20; L—Martinez, 18; Sv—Pulido, 27; Pct.—Barojas, Garcia, .800; IP—Romo, 219; H—Juarez, 213; R—Martinez, 111; ER—Martinez, 92; HR—Escarrega, 11; BB—Martinez, 102; IBB—Rogers, 17; HB—Martinez, 15; SO—Garcia, 187; WP—Martinez, 15.

(All Pitchers—Listed Alphabetically)

Pitcher—Club	W.	L.	Pct.	ERA.	G.	GS.	CG.	GF.	ShO.	Sv.	IP.	H.	R.	ER.	HR.	HB.	BB.	Int. BB.	SO.	WP.
Abarca Aceves, Ags	4	6	.400	4.64	16	12	2	3	0	0	66	78	40	34	2	0	36	5	27	4
Abreu, Aguila	0	0	.000	9.00	4	2	0	0	0	0	5	6	8	5	0	3	5	0	3	3
Acosta, Coatzacoalcos	4	10	.286	2.71	21	21	3	0	2	0	113	123	47	34	3	9	36	5	49	1
Aguilar, Monterrey	2	5	.286	4.65	35	1	0	28	0	3	62	71	37	32	2	4	21	4	19	5

Pitcher—Club	W.	L.	Pct.	ERA.	G.	GS.	CG.	GF.	ShO.	Sv.	IP.	H.	R.	ER.	HR.	HB.	BB.	Int. BB.	SO.	WP.
Alvarado, Mexico C. Reds	0	0	.000	0.00	1	0	0	1	0	0	1	0	0	0	0	0	0	0	0	0
Alvarez, Chihuahua	3	6	.333	4.13	14	9	3	2	0	0	61	71	33	28	5	2	43	8	29	3
Antunez, Mexico C. Reds°	0	0	.000	0.00	3	0	0	2	0	0	3	2	0	0	0	0	2	0	1	0
Arano, Mexico City Reds	14	5	.737	2.93	26	26	14	0	4	0	181	180	66	59	5	1	29	4	50	9
Armas, Coatzacoalcos	0	0	.000	0.00	3	0	0	3	0	0	3	2	0	0	0	0	0	0	2	0
Arratia, Union Laguna	5	3	.625	5.19	14	12	1	2	1	0	52	69	39	30	3	3	27	1	17	1
Arrieta, Mexico C. Tigers	0	0	.000	9.00	1	0	0	0	0	0	2	2	2	2	0	0	4	0	1	0
Arroyo, Mexico City Reds	1	1	.500	6.00	4	1	0	0	0	0	9	12	9	6	0	0	4	1	5	2
Bane, Saltillo°	14	11	.560	3.24	38	25	9	5	3	0	189	180	79	68	7	5	69	7	139	2
Bass, Aguila	6	4	.600	2.25	11	11	4	0	2	0	68	60	22	17	2	0	37	2	34	1
Barojas, Mexico City Reds	12	3	.800	3.04	50	3	0	34	0	13	98	81	40	33	0	4	41	9	42	5
Barr, Aguascalientes	9	4	.692	4.05	15	14	5	0	2	0	100	103	49	45	2	3	43	2	37	10
Baruch, Coatzacoalcos	1	4	.200	2.93	31	2	1	21	0	2	85	84	34	28	0	5	33	6	49	3
Beare, Nuevo Laredo	17	8	.680	2.67	26	26	12	0	4	0	192	156	63	57	9	6	62	7	117	3
Belman, Coatzacoalcos	0	0	.000	0.00	1	0	0	1	0	0	1	1	0	0	0	0	0	0	0	0
E. Beltran, Union Laguna	5	2	.714	2.11	21	16	5	4	1	0	111	100	31	26	0	3	44	1	66	3
M. Beltran, Chihuahua	2	3	.400	2.91	20	1	0	15	0	2	34	32	13	11	1	1	13	4	28	1
Benzor, Reynosa	0	1	.000	12.60	4	0	0	1	0	0	5	10	9	7	0	0	2	1	1	0
Bonfils, Poza Rica°	2	1	.667	3.09	5	5	3	0	0	0	32	34	18	11	0	1	14	1	23	1
Borbon, Reynosa	0	3	.000	4.50	3	2	1	1	0	0	18	21	10	9	0	3	3	0	8	1
Branch, Chihuahua	5	15	.250	3.86	29	21	10	6	2	3	140	167	69	60	6	6	57	6	92	8
Brueggeman, Ciudad Juarez	3	2	.600	6.39	21	0	0	17	0	5	38	57	27	27	1	3	17	3	21	1
Brunet, Aguila	13	12	.520	2.57	29	29	14	0	7	0	216	206	75	62	4	2	77	13	126	14
Buentello, Aguila	4	3	.571	2.36	35	0	0	27	0	6	61	55	20	16	2	3	15	2	32	0
Camper, Monterrey	6	16	.273	4.83	28	25	9	1	1	1	149	175	92	80	8	6	42	7	69	0
Carranza, Coatzacoalcos°	5	6	.455	2.77	24	18	2	2	2	0	130	109	54	40	3	1	69	8	104	5
Casas, Mexico City Tigers	6	4	.600	2.52	28	8	4	5	1	0	93	93	38	26	1	4	38	6	37	3
Cazarez, Mex. C. Tigers	3	9	.250	3.66	24	12	5	2	1	0	86	85	49	35	0	3	62	7	33	7
Castillejos, MC Tigers	9	8	.529	4.13	39	12	3	19	0	4	120	127	59	55	7	1	25	6	50	1
Castaneda, Saltillo°	0	1	.000	8.57	6	4	0	0	0	0	21	26	22	20	1	1	20	0	16	4
Cazares, Yucatan	1	4	.200	5.91	10	7	0	0	0	0	35	50	32	23	2	0	18	0	17	2
Castro, Tabasco	0	2	.000	4.26	11	1	0	7	0	0	19	24	10	9	2	1	5	1	14	0
Cervantes, Aguascalientes	1	3	.250	2.93	8	5	3	3	0	0	43	35	16	14	2	1	19	2	18	2
C. Chavez, Yucatan	0	5	.000	3.75	8	6	0	0	0	0	36	43	20	15	1	1	9	2	7	2
G. Chavez, Union Laguna	2	0	1.000	3.55	16	0	0	11	0	0	38	39	21	15	0	0	21	1	22	3
Colbert, Reynosa	0	1	.000	5.00	3	1	0	0	0	0	9	7	8	5	0	2	5	1	5	1
Colorado, Coatzacoalcos	14	10	.583	2.08	30	22	17	3	5	0	199	179	60	46	2	3	20	7	140	0
Cordova, Aguila	5	11	.313	3.66	31	17	1	12	0	2	128	156	61	52	5	2	31	6	36	1
Davalillo, Aguascalientes	0	0	.000	27.00	1	0	0	1	0	0	1	5	3	3	0	0	1	0	0	0
Delfin, Coatzacoalcos	4	5	.444	3.41	39	1	2	20	0	3	74	70	34	28	2	1	25	2	41	4
Delgadillo, Aguascalientes	1	1	.500	5.35	21	1	0	13	0	2	37	50	22	22	0	0	19	1	21	1
De Los Santos, U. Laguna°	5	8	.385	3.43	18	15	5	1	3	1	97	83	42	37	2	0	45	0	72	3
Diaz, Campeche	14	10	.583	2.30	30	30	6	0	1	0	192	179	66	49	8	7	61	7	78	3
Dimas, Ciudad Juarez	4	3	.571	2.57	22	0	0	19	0	4	35	34	12	10	3	1	14	2	14	1
Division, Reynosa	7	3	.700	3.06	21	10	4	4	0	3	100	97	36	34	2	2	35	5	55	3
Dominguez, Mexico C. Reds°	10	8	.556	3.68	29	25	5	4	3	1	137	145	65	56	3	1	42	2	86	6
Durazo, Nuevo Laredo	0	0	.000	4.50	2	0	0	2	0	0	2	3	1	1	0	2	1	0	1	0
Enriquez, Ciudad Juarez	2	2	.500	4.67	13	2	0	8	0	1	27	27	17	14	2	2	14	1	11	1
E. Escarrega, Campeche	13	9	.591	2.71	28	28	15	0	2	0	196	191	68	59	11	4	50	7	104	1
P. Escarrega, MC Tigers	0	0	.000	9.00	4	0	0	1	0	0	6	10	6	6	0	1	5	2	4	0
Esparza, Campeche	2	4	.333	3.50	8	5	0	2	0	1	36	46	22	14	2	2	9	1	19	2
Espinosa, Aguascalientes	0	1	.000	5.06	8	1	0	1	0	0	16	20	12	9	0	1	13	3	2	0
Esquer, Monterrey°	15	7	.682	2.40	31	28	15	2	3	1	199	183	70	53	10	6	74	5	125	14
Estrada Ley, MC Reds	0	2	.000	7.29	10	1	0	2	0	0	21	28	22	17	0	3	14	0	10	6
D. Franco, Nuevo Laredo	1	2	.333	3.53	19	1	0	10	0	0	51	67	25	20	2	0	15	5	26	4
F. Franco, Poza Rica	6	9	.400	3.96	22	20	6	2	1	0	116	111	62	51	7	3	73	7	37	4
Feola Corona, N. Laredo°	1	5	.167	4.50	20	9	1	4	0	1	54	63	36	27	0	2	31	1	25	4
Gamundi, Poza Rica	0	0	.000	0.00	1	0	0	1	0	0	1	0	0	0	0	0	0	0	0	0
F. Garcia, Chihuahua	0	0	.000	3.98	21	1	1	8	0	0	52	60	34	23	2	2	35	4	19	5
J.L. Garcia, Tabasco	3	4	.429	2.47	33	0	0	22	0	3	68	60	29	25	1	1	48	6	45	6
L. Garcia, Nuevo Laredo	0	0	.000	2.57	3	0	0	3	0	0	7	7	2	2	0	0	3	1	3	0
R. Garcia, Ciudad Juarez	20	5	.800	1.83	26	26	24	0	5	0	212	176	58	43	4	5	42	2	187	12
Rog. Garcia, Saltillo	10	6	.625	3.50	33	12	2	11	0	1	139	137	60	54	6	7	49	9	79	5
T. Garcia, Reynosa	0	0	.000	9.00	1	0	0	1	0	0	2	4	2	2	0	1	0	1	0	0
V. Garcia, Nuevo Laredo	13	5	.722	2.90	24	24	8	0	2	0	155	150	58	50	10	1	41	1	53	3
Garduza, Poza Rica	4	8	.333	4.61	16	14	3	2	0	0	80	84	44	41	3	4	36	1	25	0
Gaxiola, Aguila	3	6	.333	3.12	14	12	2	1	0	0	75	79	38	26	6	3	35	4	26	2
Gonzalez, Monterrey	14	13	.519	2.30	30	28	14	1	2	1	215	202	79	55	4	5	68	8	144	4
Granillo, Aguascalientes	2	0	1.000	2.25	4	1	0	2	0	0	12	8	4	3	1	0	2	1	9	0
Guerra, Nuevo Laredo	0	0	.000	0.00	1	0	0	0	0	0	5	4	0	0	0	0	4	0	2	0
Guerrero, Monterrey	0	0	.000	2.63	11	0	0	9	0	0	24	22	8	7	1	1	8	1	9	2
Gutierrez, Ciudad Juarez	2	6	.250	4.90	21	7	3	6	0	0	79	96	48	43	4	1	38	1	51	4
G. Guzman, Campeche	0	0	.000	4.09	8	0	0	6	0	0	11	20	7	5	0	0	9	0	1	1
J.R. Guzman, Poza Rica	2	3	.400	4.43	16	7	2	5	1	0	63	61	36	31	4	4	39	5	37	3
L.F. Guzman, Coatzacoalcos	4	5	.444	3.04	13	12	4	1	1	0	80	79	36	27	3	1	16	1	45	4
R. Guzman, Nuevo Laredo	8	7	.533	2.93	42	8	3	25	2	8	126	113	51	41	6	1	40	4	87	7
Hallgreen, Reynosa	2	3	.400	4.40	9	9	0	0	0	0	45	48	26	22	2	0	22	0	28	2
Henderson, Aguascalientes	10	8	.556	2.73	22	22	8	0	1	0	158	160	57	48	5	4	44	8	72	5
A. Hernandez, N. Laredo	1	7	.125	4.17	28	0	0	17	0	6	41	44	22	19	3	0	21	9	31	2
G. Hernandez, N. Laredo	1	2	.333	5.82	10	1	0	6	0	0	17	21	12	11	3	0	9	3	12	2
Heredia, Monterrey	2	3	.400	2.81	21	5	1	10	1	1	64	55	31	20	2	2	32	5	20	3
Higueras, Ciudad Juarez°	16	9	.640	3.10	28	28	14	0	5	0	203	207	81	70	5	4	69	5	157	2
Holguin, Ciudad Juarez°	1	2	.333	7.00	16	2	0	10	0	0	36	45	29	28	1	1	24	1	19	5
Hughes, Mexico C. Tigers	0	2	.000	5.67	5	4	1	0	0	0	27	32	21	17	1	1	14	2	15	3
Ibarra, Reynosa	7	14	.333	3.18	29	27	7	1	3	0	184	181	80	65	8	3	97	4	124	11
G. Jimenez, Campeche	7	6	.538	2.85	35	18	2	7	0	1	117	115	47	37	2	1	37	5	68	3
J. Jimenez, Aguila	4	8	.333	2.93	12	12	6	0	0	0	86	93	35	28	1	2	14	4	9	0
Jones, Mexico C. Tigers°	0	5	.000	4.83	10	7	0	2	0	2	41	49	28	22	2	1	12	2	12	2
Juarez, Aguascalientes	10	12	.455	3.05	28	26	10	2	2	1	195	213	76	66	6	5	51	5	69	5
Kekich, Ciudad Juarez°	7	11	.389	4.04	22	22	10	0	0	0	147	160	82	66	3	3	79	2	102	2
Kobel, Yucatan °	4	1	.800	1.80	8	8	4	0	3	0	60	43	14	12	1	0	2	0	36	1
Kuk Lee, Poza Rica	18	11	.621	2.36	34	24	19	10	5	3	198	183	56	52	7	6	57	11	76	2

Pitcher—Club	W.	L.	Pct.	ERA.	G.	GS.	CG.	GF.	ShO.	Sv.	IP.	H.	R.	ER.	HR.	HB.	BB.	Int. BB.	SO.	WP.
Lagunas, Yucatan	2	1	.667	2.25	10	10	1	0	1	0	36	32	12	9	2	1	5	2	13	1
Lance, Monterrey	10	13	.435	3.10	26	23	12	3	4	0	148	149	67	51	5	9	52	5	83	6
M. Leon, Mexico City Reds	14	9	.609	3.65	25	25	8	0	1	0	148	165	67	60	8	5	37	3	46	6
R. Leon, Mex. C. Tigers°	0	0	.000	9.00	1	0	0	1	0	0	1	1	1	1	0	0	2	0	0	0
Limon, Aguascalientes	6	4	.600	1.55	50	1	0	49	0	19	110	86	23	19	0	0	35	5	72	2
E. Lopez, Poza Rica	4	15	.211	3.31	22	20	6	1	2	0	136	160	61	50	8	3	35	15	37	1
F. Lopez, Campeche	4	5	.444	3.77	12	12	2	0	1	0	62	70	33	26	4	2	26	4	28	4
H. Lopez, Yucatan	5	0	1.000	4.32	28	3	0	13	0	0	50	58	26	24	1	0	29	3	29	2
Low, Aguascalientes	5	5	.500	3.71	30	10	3	12	1	0	114	121	56	47	5	5	42	4	62	10
Lucero, Mexico C. Tigers	0	0	.000	0.00	1	0	0	0	0	0	1	1	1	0	0	0	1	0	0	1
Lugo, Aguascalientes	5	9	.357	3.70	46	5	1	33	1	8	112	125	51	46	6	2	53	8	39	3
Macias, Chihuahua	1	0	1.000	6.75	5	2	0	3	0	0	8	12	9	6	1	0	12	1	5	1
Madden, Tabasco	0	2	.000	8.18	3	3	0	0	0	0	11	9	10	10	0	0	15	0	7	1
E. Madrigal, MC Tigers°	8	8	.500	4.71	27	20	1	1	1	1	107	113	69	56	2	4	55	5	49	2
H. Madrigal, Tabasco	9	10	.474	3.79	28	25	9	2	2	0	145	180	77	61	4	5	35	5	61	6
Mariscal, Tabasco°	0	0	.000	13.50	2	0	0	1	0	0	2	7	3	3	1	0	0	3	0	0
F. Martinez, N. Laredo°	5	4	.556	2.82	21	14	5	1	0	0	102	109	38	32	7	1	23	3	34	0
G. Martinez, Chihuahua	8	18	.308	4.48	32	28	10	2	1	1	185	205	111	92	5	15	102	10	86	15
J. Martinez, Yucatan°	2	1	.667	6.35	16	2	0	9	0	0	34	47	25	24	3	0	14	2	10	1
J.L. Martinez, Monterrey	7	10	.412	2.50	22	18	10	2	2	0	126	115	41	35	2	5	50	4	56	6
R. Martinez, Saltillo	0	3	.000	4.59	20	2	0	9	0	0	49	57	29	25	0	0	25	5	17	4
McDonald, Aguila°	0	0	.000	0.00	1	0	0	1	0	0	1	0	0	0	0	0	0	0	0	0
McEnaney, Tabasco°	12	5	.706	2.11	19	18	10	1	2	0	132	129	40	31	5	0	19	0	61	1
McLaughlin, Nuevo Laredo	12	5	.706	1.58	21	21	11	0	3	0	142	116	32	25	6	1	44	3	108	7
Maytorena, Union Laguna	5	8	.385	3.11	34	6	2	26	0	10	84	74	32	29	3	2	20	1	45	0
Menendez, Saltillo	15	9	.625	2.84	30	28	14	2	3	0	190	197	71	60	7	2	53	7	69	3
Miranda, Coatzacoalcos°	6	6	.500	2.74	23	9	3	6	1	1	92	69	33	28	1	3	44	2	37	3
Montague, Aguascalientes	2	3	.400	4.19	10	7	4	3	1	1	58	69	31	27	3	0	12	1	18	1
Monteagudo, Aguila	5	14	.263	2.63	22	19	12	2	2	1	139	125	58	54	2	7	45	9	50	6
Mota, Poza Rica	0	3	.000	10.80	3	3	0	0	0	0	10	24	16	12	2	0	6	2	4	0
M. Morales, Aguila	2	2	.500	3.21	26	1	0	15	0	0	73	78	35	26	2	3	23	4	27	6
R. Morales, Reynosa	3	5	.375	5.25	13	8	2	2	1	0	48	53	29	28	4	0	27	0	29	5
C. Moreno, Aguascalientes	0	4	.000	10.89	5	3	0	0	0	0	19	29	27	23	2	6	12	0	9	2
J. Moreno, Aguascalientes	7	10	.412	2.77	20	20	4	0	2	0	111	111	49	34	2	8	39	6	48	3
Moret, Union Laguna°	9	4	.692	3.42	13	13	9	0	1	0	93	71	30	25	3	1	27	0	47	2
Mundo, Chihuahua	5	12	.294	4.81	30	18	4	5	2	0	116	137	76	62	8	10	62	16	42	5
Nava, Yucatan	0	0	.000	4.09	13	0	1	7	0	0	33	37	18	15	0	1	7	0	10	1
Nieto, Yucatan	1	0	1.000	7.20	7	0	0	2	0	0	10	17	9	8	0	0	10	0	1	2
Nipp, Ciudad Juarez	2	4	.333	4.58	8	8	5	0	1	0	55	75	29	28	3	1	20	0	31	0
D. Ochoa, Coatzacoalcos	8	7	.533	3.08	34	10	5	18	3	5	108	107	50	37	1	3	24	4	67	1
J. Ochoa, Union Laguna	8	4	.667	3.12	28	9	1	10	0	1	130	141	49	45	5	5	36	1	23	1
R. Ochoa, Tabasco	5	7	.417	2.25	16	16	3	0	0	0	104	92	34	26	1	0	35	2	34	5
C. Orozco, Campeche	0	0	.000	9.00	1	0	0	0	0	0	2	3	2	2	0	0	2	0	0	0
J. Orozco, Campeche	8	3	.727	2.50	21	11	2	5	2	0	90	71	25	25	1	2	28	3	34	1
Ortiz, Tabasco°	12	11	.522	2.08	28	25	18	2	4	1	182	180	56	42	5	5	41	6	65	0
Palacios, Tabasco	1	4	.200	3.67	18	4	0	4	0	0	54	66	31	22	2	4	23	1	16	1
Palomares, Reynosa	1	0	1.000	5.73	8	2	0	3	0	0	11	14	8	7	1	0	11	0	5	0
Paul, Ciudad Juarez°	12	7	.632	1.95	23	22	14	1	4	0	171	149	43	37	4	3	17	1	103	0
Paredes, Campeche	0	0	.000	......	1	1	0	0	0	0	0	1	1	1	0	0	0	0	0	0
J. Pena, Coatzacoalcos	12	10	.545	3.62	28	25	6	2	1	1	159	167	76	64	9	13	66	3	75	10
M. Pena, Chihuahua°	0	4	.000	5.49	33	2	1	13	0	0	59	80	44	36	5	3	27	0	30	9
Peralta, Coatzacoalcos	0	1	.000	6.75	4	1	0	2	0	1	4	7	4	3	0	0	2	0	2	0
C.J. Perez, Campeche	4	3	.571	2.77	16	12	2	2	0	1	78	67	29	24	3	2	27	2	45	6
C. Perez, Tabasco°	1	3	.250	4.15	21	4	1	5	0	0	52	66	26	24	2	1	18	5	20	0
Pineda, Poza Rica	0	1	.000	5.63	8	2	0	2	0	0	16	17	13	10	0	1	18	0	7	3
Pollorena, Saltillo	14	9	.609	2.84	26	26	13	0	3	0	184	198	67	58	6	2	34	6	112	2
Pole, Mex City Tigers	5	2	.714	1.36	9	6	4	2	2	0	53	48	11	8	0	0	9	2	26	1
Ponce, Tabasco°	0	1	.000	6.00	8	0	0	3	0	0	12	19	9	8	1	0	5	0	5	0
Posadas, Poza Rica	0	13	.000	5.74	25	13	3	8	0	0	94	109	64	60	5	2	59	6	28	4
Alf. Pulido, MC Reds°	5	6	.455	3.07	31	17	7	6	2	0	126	121	46	43	8	2	25	1	46	1
Ant. Pulido, Campeche	9	5	.643	2.04	59	0	0	51	0	27	106	84	27	24	0	3	27	6	81	4
Purata, Poza Rica°	0	10	.000	4.97	17	10	1	4	0	0	58	75	42	32	2	1	23	4	33	2
I. Preciado, MC Reds	5	2	.714	2.34	30	0	0	14	0	2	77	76	27	20	3	3	21	2	33	1
J. Preciado, Tabasco	0	0	.000	19.80	4	2	0	0	0	0	5	12	12	11	0	0	8	0	2	1
Pruneda, Mex City Reds	0	1	.000	7.20	2	0	0	0	0	0	5	3	4	4	0	1	5	0	2	0
Quintero, Reynosa	0	1	.000	7.50	4	3	0	0	0	0	6	5	5	5	0	0	6	1	3	0
Rabouin, Aguascalientes	1	3	.250	4.68	4	4	1	0	1	0	25	22	14	13	0	1	16	3	23	2
J. Ramirez, Aguascalientes	4	5	.444	3.29	32	9	2	5	1	0	63	59	23	23	3	1	46	1	26	0
M. Ramirez, Aguila	0	0	.000	6.00	2	0	0	2	0	0	3	5	2	2	0	0	1	0	1	0
Rasmussen, Aguila°	12	6	.667	2.30	19	18	12	1	4	0	145	130	47	37	3	4	36	4	70	5
Renteria, Ciudad Juarez	4	7	.364	4.50	13	11	4	2	0	1	64	74	34	32	4	6	15	0	28	0
Reyes, Monterrey	0	0	.000	......	1	0	0	0	0	0	2	1	1	0	0	0	0	0	0	0
Rincon, Mex City Tigers	0	1	.000	5.14	6	4	0	1	0	0	14	23	15	8	1	1	10	0	5	1
H. Rios, Reynosa	11	10	.524	2.81	25	24	11	1	3	0	160	154	66	50	4	1	56	3	92	7
P. Rios, Monterrey	0	0	.000	0.00	1	0	0	1	0	0	1	0	0	0	0	0	0	0	0	0
Rivera, Yucatan	7	9	.438	6.42	22	18	4	2	1	1	101	134	79	72	4	8	44	4	35	3
A. Rodriguez, Reynosa	2	0	1.000	4.70	22	0	0	12	0	0	46	43	25	24	2	5	25	1	39	6
E. Rodriguez, Monterrey	1	5	.167	5.92	6	6	2	0	0	0	38	45	31	25	3	5	15	1	19	1
J.M. Rodriguez, MC Reds°	1	0	1.000	7.36	11	0	0	7	0	2	11	18	11	9	0	2	4	0	5	0
M.A. Rodriguez, Chihuahua	4	14	.222	4.24	34	19	3	10	0	1	121	150	82	57	4	5	45	7	50	4
P. Rodriguez, Yucatan	7	9	.438	2.53	51	0	0	47	0	20	103	99	36	29	4	9	39	8	58	4
R. Rodriguez, Poza Rica	0	2	.000	3.54	32	3	1	22	0	2	84	77	39	33	2	1	42	10	58	2
Rogers, Tabasco	16	10	.615	1.66	33	23	21	10	3	5	212	187	54	39	4	6	45	17	126	0
Romero, Yucatan	0	0	.000	18.00	1	0	0	0	0	0	1	5	6	4	1	0	2	0	0	2
Romo, Coatzacoalcos	16	6	.727	1.40	29	27	21	1	7	1	219	161	50	34	4	5	55	7	159	11
Rondon, Yucatan	17	8	.680	2.12	29	28	17	1	6	0	208	173	57	49	6	4	63	3	108	7
Ruiz, Aguascalientes	0	0	.000	14.40	3	0	0	1	0	0	5	14	8	8	1	0	1	0	3	1
Saldivar, Poza Rica	1	7	.125	3.46	18	4	1	7	0	1	65	69	29	25	3	1	40	9	14	4
Salinas, Mex City Reds	11	9	.550	3.02	28	27	9	0	3	0	179	193	70	60	5	0	41	3	86	6
Sandate, Mex City Reds°	6	7	.462	3.10	20	19	5	0	0	0	125	132	64	43	5	2	31	2	50	8
Sandoval, Aguascalientes	0	0	.000	4.50	1	0	0	0	0	0	4	3	3	2	0	0	0	0	1	1
Santos, Aguascalientes	1	3	.250	4.40	13	6	0	4	0	0	43	42	23	21	0	3	21	2	16	2

Pitcher—Club	W.	L.	Pct.	ERA.	G.	GS.	CG.	GF.	ShO.	Sv.	IP.	H.	R.	ER.	HR.	HB.	BB.	Int. BB.	SO.	WP.
Sauceda, Mex City Tigers	6	4	.600	2.45	54	0	0	35	0	16	88	82	33	24	2	5	36	7	27	8
Saucedo, Yucatan	3	4	.429	6.06	19	6	2	5	0	0	52	78	48	35	8	3	14	2	29	0
Segui, Reynosa	14	6	.700	2.08	22	22	19	0	5	0	182	145	52	42	4	1	35	1	147	5
Silva, Union Laguna	10	12	.455	3.55	31	20	4	5	2	0	142	131	66	56	9	9	67	1	85	4
G. Solis, Monterrey	4	4	.500	3.55	20	7	1	10	1	2	71	85	36	28	9	3	16	1	12	2
J. Solis, Nuevo Laredo	7	5	.583	2.85	46	3	2	28	2	10	101	94	42	32	6	5	25	6	44	3
M. Solis, Saltillo	11	9	.550	3.53	24	24	11	0	2	0	153	161	68	60	4	7	34	10	70	5
Sosa, Union Laguna	11	9	.550	3.33	29	28	6	1	2	0	146	154	71	54	6	1	67	3	68	4
A. Soto, Saltillo	8	3	.727	2.33	47	0	0	39	0	15	81	73	23	21	1	1	30	8	43	1
F. Soto, Campeche	0	0	.000	3.18	6	5	0	1	0	0	17	22	8	6	0	1	10	0	5	1
Sutton, Nuevo Laredo	17	7	.708	1.63	26	25	21	1	7	0	204	168	52	37	5	8	62	5	59	4
Tejeda, Coatzacoalcos	1	0	1.000	3.71	21	0	0	10	0	0	34	31	17	14	1	1	16	2	17	0
Torrealba, Saltillo°	0	0	.000	6.00	4	0	0	2	0	0	6	14	6	4	0	0	6	1	3	1
Torres, Saltillo	1	2	.333	4.00	8	5	0	0	0	0	36	33	18	16	0	4	22	2	13	3
Trinidad, Reynosa	0	1	.000	12.00	6	0	0	0	0	0	3	4	4	4	0	0	2	0	1	0
Urrea, Saltillo	0	0	.000	3.60	8	0	0	6	0	0	10	13	4	4	1	0	4	0	4	0
Valdez, Chihuahua	1	4	.200	4.37	32	3	0	19	0	1	101	109	57	49	6	3	41	4	26	4
Valenzuela, Aguascalientes°	2	3	.400	4.68	27	2	1	10	0	1	50	56	30	26	3	2	26	1	21	5
Valle, Campeche°	0	0	.000	18.00	2	0	0	1	0	0	1	3	2	2	1	0	1	0	1	0
Vazquez, Mex City Reds	1	2	.333	3.25	26	1	0	12	0	2	61	56	27	22	3	0	35	1	24	3
Velazquez, Monterrey	0	0	.000	4.14	15	0	0	6	0	1	37	42	20	17	2	1	15	2	10	2
A. Vidana, Reynosa	5	2	.714	3.74	23	1	0	12	0	1	65	66	33	27	1	0	22	1	28	3
M. Vidana, Chihuahua	4	5	.444	4.27	16	11	2	3	1	1	78	78	43	37	4	3	22	3	36	5
Villanueva, MC Tigers°	9	7	.563	2.89	40	21	6	8	0	0	137	132	59	44	3	6	49	3	56	4
D. Villegas, Campeche	10	5	.667	2.57	43	2	1	19	0	1	133	113	52	38	7	5	57	10	59	5
Ra. Villegas, MC Tigers	9	3	.750	2.67	25	12	4	4	1	1	118	93	45	35	5	2	43	3	68	2
Ro. Villegas, Tabasco	0	0	.000	3.86	3	0	0	2	0	0	7	9	4	3	0	0	2	0	3	1
Williams, Chihuahua°	1	3	.250	5.85	7	4	0	1	0	0	20	28	17	13	2	0	10	0	4	0

Balks—Kuk Lee, 5; Higueras, Peralta, 3 each; Bonfils, Camper, De Los Santos, Purata, Santos, Tejeda, Valenzuela, Villanueva, 2 each; Alvarez, Bane, Bass, Barojas, Baruch, Carranza, Casas, Castaneda, Delgadillo, Gaxiola, Granillo, G. Guzman, Heredia, Juarez, Kekich, M. Leon, E. Lopez, E. Madrigal, J.L. Martinez, M. Morales, Nava, Orozco, Palomares, J. Pena, Posades, Pulido, I. Preciado, Rogers, Salinas, Sandate, Saucedo, C. Sosa, Sutton, Vazquez, D. Villegas, 1 each.

COMBINATION SHUTOUTS—Diaz-Pulido 2, Orozco-Pulido, Perez-F. Orozco, Soto-Jimenez, Perez-Pulido, Orozco-Jimenez-Pulido, Campeche; Pena-P. Rodriguez 3, Rondon-P. Rodriguez, Kobel-P. Rodriguez, Yucatan; V. Garcia-J. Solis, Beare-F. Martinez-J. Solis, McLaughlin-Sutton, McLaughlin-J. Solis, McLaughlin-A. Hernandez, Nuevo Laredo; Dominguez-Castillejos, Dominguez-Sauceda, E. Madrigal-Sauceda, R. Villegas-Sauceda, R. Villegas-Pole-Jones, Mexico City Tigers; Maytorena-A. Hernandez, Beltran-De Los Santos, J. Ochoa-R. Guzman, Beltran-Silva, Union Laguna; Morales-Vidana, Segui-Buentello, Rios-Vidana, Ramirez-Buentello, Reynosa; Solis-A. Soto, Bane-A. Soto, Pollorena-A. Soto, R. Garcia-A. Soto, Saltillo; Santos-Morales-J. Limon, Monteagudo-J. Limon, Moreno-J. Limon, Aguila; M. Rodriguez-Branch, Camper-Alvarez-M. Rodriguez, Chihuahua; Sandate-Barojas, Salinas-Barojas, Mexico City Reds; E. Lopez-Baruch, Poza Rica; Palacios-Rogers, Tabasco; Carranza-Delfin, Coatzacoalcos; Kekich-Brueggeman, Ciudad Juarez; A. Gonzalez-Aguilar, Monterrey.

NO-HIT GAMES—De Los Santos, Union Laguna, defeated Chihuahua, 4-0, March 29; Menendez, Saltillo, defeated Reynosa, 2-0, April 12; Garcia, Ciudad Juarez, defeated Coatzacoalcos, 3-0, May 17; Beare, Nuevo Laredo, defeated Mexico City Reds, 2-0, May 25.

PERFECT GAME—Garcia, Nuevo Laredo, defeated Ciudad Juarez, 1-0, April 26.

Pacific Coast League

CLASS AAA

**Leading Batter
MIKE MARSHALL
Albuquerque**

**League President
BILL CUTLER**

**Leading Pitcher
BOB STODDARD
Spokane**

CHAMPIONSHIP WINNERS IN PREVIOUS YEARS

1903—Los Angeles .... .630	1932—Portland............................ .587	1961—Tacoma.............................. .630
1904—Tacoma............................ .589	1933—Los Angeles .... .610	1962—San Diego .... .604
Tacoma§................................ .571	1934—Los Angeles z...................... .786	1963—Spokane............................ .620
Los Angeles§...................... .571	Los Angeles z...................... .689	Oklahoma City a .... .632
1905—Tacoma............................ .583	1935—Los Angeles .... .648	1964—Arkansas........................... .609
Los Angeles° .... .604	San Francisco° .... .608	San Diego a...................... .576
1906—Portland............................ .657	1936—Portland‡ .... .549	1965—Oklahoma City a .... .628
1907—Los Angeles .... .608	1937—Sacramento........................ .573	Portland............................ .547
1908—Los Angeles .... .585	San Diego (3rd)† .... .545	1966—Seattle a .... .561
1909—San Francisco .... .623	1938—Los Angeles .... .590	Tulsa.................................. .578
1910—Portland............................ .567	Sacramento (3rd)†............ .537	1967—San Diego a....................... .574
1911—Portland............................ .589	1939—Seattle .... .589	Spokane............................ .541
1912—Oakland .... .591	Sacramento (4th)† .... .500	1968—Tulsa a .... .642
1913—Portland............................ .559	1940—Seattle‡ .... .629	Spokane............................ .586
1914—Portland............................ .574	1941—Seattle‡ .... .598	1969—Tacoma a........................... .589
1915—San Francisco .... .570	1942—Sacramento........................ .590	Eugene.............................. .603
1916—Los Angeles .... .601	Seattle (3rd)† .... .539	1970—Spokane a .... .644
1917—San Francisco .... .561	1943—Los Angeles .... .710	Hawaii.............................. .671
1918—Vernon.............................. .569	S. Francisco (2nd)† .... .574	1971—Salt Lake City.................... .534
Los Angeles (2nd) x........... .548	1944—Los Angeles .... .586	Tacoma............................ .545
1919—Vernon.............................. .613	S. Francisco (3rd)† .... .509	1972—Albuquerque .... .622
1920—Vernon.............................. .556	1945—Portland............................ .622	Eugene.............................. .534
1921—Los Angeles .... .574	S. Francisco (4th)† .... .525	1973—Tucson .... .583
1922—San Francisco .... .638	1946—San Francisco‡ ....``` .628	Spokane a.......................... .563
1923—San Francisco .... .617	1947—Los Angeles†† .... .567	1974—Spokane a.......................... .549
1924—Seattle .... .545	1948—Oakland‡ .... .606	Albuqerque........................ .535
1925—San Francisco .... .643	1949—Hollywood‡ .... .583	1975—Salt Lake City.................... .556
1926—Los Angeles .... .599	1950—Oakland .... .590	Hawaii a............................ .611
1927—Oakland .... .615	1951—Seattle‡ .... .593	1976—Salt Lake City.................... .625
1928—San Francisco° .... .630	1952—Hollywood .... .606	Hawaii a............................ .531
Sacramento§§...................... .626	1953—Hollywood .... .589	1977—Phoenix a .... .579
San Francisco§§.................. .626	1954—San Diego y........................ .604	Hawaii.............................. .541
1929—Mission .... .643	1955—Seattle .... .552	1978—Tacoma b........................... .584
Hollywood° .... .592	1956—Los Angeles .... .637	Albuquerque b.................... .557
1930—Los Angeles .... .576	1957—San Francisco .... .601	1979—Albuquerque .... .581
Hollywood° .... .650	1958—Phoenix .... .578	Salt Lake City c.................. .541
1931—Hollywood .... .626	1959—Salt Lake City.................... .552	1980—Albuquerque° .... .578
San Francisco° .... .608	1960—Spokane .... .601	Hawaii.............................. .539

°Won split-season playoff. †Won four-team playoff. ‡Won pennant and four-team playoff. §Tied for second-half title with Tacoma winning playoff. §§Tied for second-half title, with Sacramento winning playoff. ††Ended regular season in tie with San Francisco and won one-game playoff for pennant, then won four-club playoff. xWon playoff from first-place Vernon and awarded championship. yDefeated Hollywood in one-game playoff for pennant. zWon both halves, no playoff. aLeague was divided into Northern, Southern divisions in 1963, 1969-70-71, and Eastern, Western divisions in 1964 through 1968 and 1972 through 1977, won two-team playoff. bLeague divided into Eastern and Western divisions, Tacoma and Albuquerque declared co-champions following cancellation of four-team playoff due to continuing rain and wet grounds. cWon second-half title and defeated Hawaii in four-team playoff.

STANDING OF CLUBS AT CLOSE OF FIRST HALF, JUNE 21

NORTHERN DIVISION

Club	W.	L.	T.	Pct.	G.B.
Hawaii (Padres)	35	31	0	.530	....
Portland (Pirates)	34	33	0	.507	1½
Tacoma (A's)	35	34	0	.507	1½
Edmonton (White Sox)	31	33	0	.484	3
Spokane (Mariners)	31	37	0	.456	5
Vancouver (Brewers)	27	34	0	.443	5½

SOUTHERN DIVISION

Club	W.	L.	T.	Pct.	G.B.
Albuquerque (Dodgers)	46	22	0	.676	....
Phoenix (Giants)	35	32	0	.522	10½
Tucson (Astros)	30	39	0	.435	16½
Salt Lake City (Angels)	28	37	0	.431	16½

STANDING OF CLUBS AT CLOSE OF SECOND HALF, AUGUST 30

NORTHERN DIVISION

Club	W.	L.	T.	Pct.	G.B.
Tacoma (A's)	43	27	0	.614	....
Portland (Pirates)	38	32	0	.543	5
Hawaii (Padres)	37	34	0	.521	6½
Edmonton (White Sox)	31	41	0	.431	13
Vancouver (Brewers)	29	42	0	.408	14½
Spokane (Mariners)	25	47	0	.347	19

SOUTHERN DIVISION

Club	W.	L.	T.	Pct.	G.B.
Albuquerque (Dodgers)	48	16	0	.750	....
Phoenix (Giants)	34	31	0	.523	14½
Salt Lake City (Angels)	35	34	0	.507	15½
Tucson (Astros)	27	43	0	.386	24

COMPOSITE STANDING OF CLUBS AT CLOSE OF SEASON, AUGUST 30

NORTHERN DIVISION

Club	Tac.	Haw.	Port.	Edm.	Van.	Spo.	Alb.	Phx.	SLC.	Tuc.	W.	L.	T.	Pct.	G.B.
Tacoma (A's)	....	9	12	15	13	11	3	5	3	7	78	61	0	.561	....
Hawaii (Padres)	12	....	11	9	12	13	4	2	5	4	72	65	0	.526	5
Portland (Pirates)	10	11	....	10	13	14	2	4	3	5	72	65	0	.526	5
Edmonton (White Sox)	7	12	9	....	15	12	0	3	2	2	62	74	0	.456	14½
Vancouver (Brewers)	8	7	9	6	....	13	0	5	3	5	56	76	0	.424	18½
Spokane (Mariners)	11	9	7	10	8	....	2	3	2	4	56	84	0	.400	22½

SOUTHERN DIVISION

Club															
Albuquerque (Dodgers)	5	4	6	7	7	6	....	16	18	25	94	38	0	.712	....
Phoenix (Giants)	2	6	4	5	1	5	11	....	14	21	69	63	0	.523	25
Salt Lake City (Angels)	5	3	4	6	5	6	10	15	....	9	63	71	0	.470	32
Tucson (Astros)	1	4	3	6	2	4	6	10	21	....	57	82	0	.410	40½

Hawaii club represented Honolulu, Hawaii.

Major league affiliations in parentheses.

Playoffs—Tacoma defeated Hawaii, two games to one; Albuquerque defeated Tacoma, three games to none, for League Championship.

Regular-Season Attendance—Albuquerque, 244,464; Edmonton, 187,501; Hawaii, 157,918; Phoenix, 240,832; Portland, 192,214; Salt Lake City, 205,353; Spokane, 227,050; Tacoma, 244,083; Tucson, 188,488; Vancouver, 127,161. Total, 1,995,064. Playoffs, 26,079.

Managers: Albuquerque—Del Crandall; Edmonton—Gordy Lund; Hawaii—Doug Rader; Phoenix—Rocky Bridges; Portland—Pete Ward; Salt Lake City—Moose Stubing; Spokane—Rene Lachemann; Tacoma—Ed Nottle; Tucson—Jimmy Johnson; Vancouver—Lee Sigman.

All-Star Team: 1B—Moore, Albuquerque; 2B—Loviglio, Edmonton; 3B—Rush, Vancouver; SS—Sexton, Tacoma; OF—Davis, Tacoma; Henderson, Spokane; Wiggins, Hawaii; C—Kearney, Tacoma; DH—Holle, Edmonton; P—Barnes, Edmonton; Long, Portland; Manager—Nottle, Tacoma.

(Compiled by William J. Weiss, League Statistician, San Mateo, Calif.)

CLUB BATTING

Club	Pct.	G.	AB.	R.	OR.	H.	TB.	2B.	3B.	HR.	RBI.	GW.	SH.	SF.	HP.	BB.	Int. BB.	SO.	SB.	CS.	LOB.
Albuquerque	.325	132	4288	875	604	1393	2003	214	72	84	774	81	79	73	31	642	29	520	281	982	115
Phoenix	.303	132	4476	686	710	1355	1924	198	58	85	634	69	26	46	36	461	18	619	166	970	53
Salt Lake City	.290	134	4529	770	850	1314	2020	243	47	123	705	60	38	45	28	567	24	616	65	962	40
Tucson	.283	139	4658	746	811	1320	1994	284	78	78	679	52	37	62	34	530	7	602	150	981	60
Edmonton	.283	136	4444	667	733	1258	1907	193	48	120	606	52	36	38	32	498	10	625	183	966	71
Portland	.277	137	4308	654	631	1192	1775	222	47	89	592	65	51	49	19	522	12	538	118	927	51
Tacoma	.276	139	4470	706	590	1232	1825	191	45	104	628	61	92	44	33	608	27	771	212	968	98
Hawaii	.267	137	4503	627	617	1204	1773	195	64	82	572	64	25	58	24	426	21	644	170	892	69
Spokane	.265	140	4425	627	705	1173	1739	232	41	84	557	47	35	51	44	512	10	596	131	929	75
Vancouver	.256	132	4168	470	577	1067	1517	180	36	66	423	47	36	36	21	373	11	682	172	824	73

INDIVIDUAL BATTING

(Leading Qualifiers for Batting Championship — 378 or More Plate Appearances)

°Bats lefthanded.   †Switch-hitter.

Player and Club	Pct.	G.	AB.	R.	H.	TB.	2B.	3B.	HR.	RBI.	GW.	SH.	SF.	HP.	BB.	Int. BB.	SO.	SB.	CS.
Marshall, Michael, Albuquerque	.373	128	467	114	174	315	25	7	34	137	17	2	6	9	57	3	80	21	8
Sconiers, Daryl, Salt Lake City°	.354	108	410	91	145	224	24	8	13	74	5	0	1	2	55	9	65	2	2
Davis, Charles, Phoenix†	.350	88	334	76	117	202	16	6	19	75	8	0	2	3	46	4	54	40	12
Harper, Brian, Salt Lake City	.350	134	549	99	192	339	45	9	28	122	11	0	9	2	33	0	2		
Ray, John, Tucson†	.349	131	525	111	183	268	50	10	5	83	6	1	7	1	46	0	23	19	5
Perconte, John, Albuquerque	.346	127	448	107	155	196	26	6	1	58	6	14	8	3	85	3	45	45	12
Law, Rudy, Albuquerque°	.335	107	397	75	133	167	16	9	0	39	6	7	3	0	48	1	27	56	17
Maldonado, Candido, Albuquerque	.335	126	460	96	154	275	40	4	21	104	11	4	13	7	50	2	104	13	14
Brunansky, Thomas, Salt Lake City	.332	96	343	61	114	217	17	10	22	81	4	4	2	3	57	1	74	6	7
Holle, Gary, Edmonton	.327	108	370	70	121	219	16	2	26	88	4	1	3	5	40	1	48	8	5

Departmental Leaders: G—Maler, 139; AB—Lubratich, 551; R—Marshall, 114; H—Harper, 192; TB—Harper, 339; 2B—Ray, 50; 3B—Cypret, 13; HR—Marshall, 34; RBI—Marshall, 137; GWRBI—Marshall, 17; SH—Mize, 16; SF—Roenicke, 16; BB—Roenicke, 110; HP—Maler, 11; SO—Moore, 140; SB—Wiggins, 73; CS—K. Allen, 23.

(All Players—Listed Alphabetically)

Player and Club	Pct.	G.	AB.	R.	H.	TB.	2B.	3B.	HR.	RBI.	GW.	SH.	SF.	HP.	BB.	Int. BB.	SO.	SB.	CS.
Alexander, Matthew, Portland†	.324	27	108	13	35	42	1	3	0	8	0	2	0	0	10	0	12	11	4
Allen, James, Spokane	.197	22	61	3	12	15	3	0	0	8	2	0	2	0	10	0	6	2	2
Allen, Kim, Spokane	.286	109	402	87	115	157	20	2	6	27	5	5	1	0	66	0	22	50	23
Allen, Roderick, Edmonton	.294	109	388	47	114	178	25	3	11	52	4	0	1	6	28	0	69	9	3
Alvarez, John, Hawaii	.266	84	289	39	77	110	8	2	7	41	3	0	3	1	24	1	34	5	2
Anderson, Michael, Portland	.193	39	119	15	23	34	5	0	2	14	0	3	1	0	22	0	26	0	0

Player and Club	Pct.	G.	AB.	R.	H.	TB.	2B.	3B.	HR.	RBI.	GW.	SH.	SF.	HP.	BB.	Int. BB.	SO.	SB.	CS.
Ashby, Gary, Hawaii°	.233	70	219	21	51	65	6	1	2	15	1	1	1	0	17	1	32	5	2
Augustine, David, Portland	.282	92	294	45	83	123	21	2	5	27	3	1	1	3	31	1	36	3	0
Barrios, Jose, Phoenix	.314	129	491	92	154	254	23	10	19	96	10	1	12	0	58	1	102	5	2
Bass, Kevin, Vancouver	.257	97	339	40	87	113	10	5	2	30	3	6	3	2	43	0	36	29	12
Beall, Robert, Portland†	.268	62	82	19	22	28	3	0	1	13	2	1	0	1	34	0	18	1	1
Bell, Kevin, Tacoma	.250	129	420	66	105	180	19	4	16	65	5	4	7	1	73	5	89	4	2
Bertoni, Jeffrey, Salt Lake City	.240	127	458	78	110	157	13	8	6	55	6	10	4	6	44	1	78	8	3
Beswick, James, Hawaii†	.237	128	460	50	109	164	17	7	8	56	10	4	4	0	40	1	112	10	9
Bevacqua, Kurt, Portland	.250	14	52	6	13	14	1	0	0	5	0	0	1	0	5	0	10	0	1
Bishop, Michael, Salt Lake City	.277	133	470	73	130	202	21	3	15	91	8	1	10	2	86	3	74	1	1
Bodie, Keith, Tucson	.221	77	213	34	47	64	10	2	1	17	2	3	0	3	21	0	46	13	6
Bohnet, Robert, Salt Lake City	.314	11	35	9	11	14	3	0	0	2	0	1	0	0	10	0	11	0	0
Bosley, Thaddis, Vancouver°	.320	34	122	15	39	48	5	2	0	14	0	1	0	0	12	0	12	10	3
Botting, Ralph, Salt Lake City°	.000	23	1	0	0	0	0	0	0	0	0	0	0	0	0	0	1	0	0
Boyland, Dorian, Portland°	.310	68	210	31	65	92	11	5	2	28	3	2	1	2	34	4	28	17	6
Brenly, Robert, Phoenix	.292	76	257	42	75	113	11	3	7	41	2	0	2	1	29	1	37	2	1
Brouhard, Mark, Vancouver	.288	16	59	10	17	26	2	2	1	5	1	0	0	1	7	0	9	7	3
Brown, Steven, Salt Lake City	.400	27	5	0	2	2	0	0	0	0	0	0	0	0	0	0	0	0	0
Brunansky, Thomas, Salt Lake City	.332	96	343	61	114	217	17	10	22	81	4	4	2	3	57	1	74	6	7
Bryant, Derek, Tacoma	.303	121	412	57	125	174	24	5	5	50	4	9	6	1	59	1	47	11	10
Budaska, Mark, Tacoma†	.294	58	187	37	55	96	7	2	10	42	5	2	1	4	50	3	55	12	6
Cacek, Craig, Portland	.287	116	369	64	106	178	26	2	14	65	6	2	7	3	75	1	20	4	1
Calvert, Mark, Phoenix	.000	18	2	0	0	0	0	0	0	0	0	0	1	0	0	0	1	0	0
Carnes, Scott, Salt Lake City	.271	94	288	42	78	99	12	3	1	30	2	5	3	2	37	0	53	7	3
Castillo, Anthony, Hawaii	.264	79	280	27	74	111	15	2	6	41	4	0	3	0	7	0	48	4	1
Caughey, Wayne, Albuquerque°	.314	103	287	51	90	100	5	1	1	38	2	6	2	1	42	4	22	15	6
Cias, Darryl, Tacoma	.193	20	57	5	11	14	3	0	0	6	0	0	0	1	3	0	9	0	0
Clark, Roy, Spokane	.251	96	303	40	76	109	17	5	2	31	3	4	2	1	29	0	36	1	7
Colbern, Michael, Edmonton	.267	64	202	28	54	87	8	2	7	16	1	1	0	1	9	0	40	1	2
Cox, Jeffrey, Tacoma	.281	97	317	64	89	107	11	2	1	30	2	12	2	7	66	0	29	31	10
Cox, Ted, Spokane	.149	25	87	4	13	16	1	1	0	8	1	0	0	1	6	0	14	1	1
Crow, Donald, Albuquerque	.286	107	329	47	94	109	11	2	0	54	3	12	2	2	37	0	29	8	6
Cruz, Todd, Edmonton	.259	8	27	2	7	12	0	1	1	3	1	1	0	0	0	0	2	0	0
Cypret, Gregory, Tucson	.307	132	498	64	153	231	40	13	4	81	7	3	8	1	52	0	38	1	4
Davis, Charles, Phoenix†	.350	88	334	76	117	202	16	6	19	75	8	0	2	3	46	4	54	40	12
Davis, Michael, Tacoma°	.287	133	515	84	148	206	28	6	6	71	11	12	7	4	49	4	68	36	19
Davis, Robert, Salt Lake City	.237	89	334	41	79	123	24	1	6	47	6	3	5	1	25	1	37	0	0
Dempsey, Patrick, Tacoma	.209	45	139	11	29	35	4	1	0	8	0	1	1	1	9	0	18	1	1
De Simone, Gerald, Hawaii†	.250	13	52	10	13	28	2	5	1	10	1	1	2	0	6	0	7	2	1
Doyle, Brian, Tacoma°	.173	21	52	10	9	11	2	0	0	3	1	3	0	1	9	0	4	0	3
Drumright, Keith, Tacoma°	.228	28	79	4	18	22	4	0	0	7	0	2	1	0	7	0	4	1	2
Edler, David, Spokane	.254	66	224	31	57	84	9	0	6	30	6	6	4	3	32	1	52	6	4
Edwards, Marshall, Vancouver°	.373	12	51	6	19	26	3	2	0	3	0	1	0	0	1	0	2	5	3
Estrada, Manuel, Spokane	.250	108	344	45	86	121	20	3	3	44	2	6	6	5	46	0	41	15	8
Figueroa, Jesus, Phoenix°	.421	20	38	6	16	20	4	0	0	6	1	0	1	1	2	0	2	0	1
Flammang, Christopher, Spokane°	.198	31	101	9	20	28	6	1	0	6	2	1	0	0	7	1	15	3	7
Flannery, John, Edmonton	.227	26	75	7	17	18	1	0	0	3	0	1	0	1	5	0	3	1	0
Flannery, Timothy, Hawaii°	.282	21	78	16	22	27	3	1	0	10	1	4	1	0	11	0	10	2	0
Flinn, John, Vancouver	.000	31	2	0	0	0	0	0	0	0	0	0	0	0	0	0	1	0	0
Fobbs, Larry, Albuquerque	.320	90	272	49	87	122	15	4	4	42	6	5	4	2	33	2	24	11	8
Foley, Marvis, Edmonton°	.296	99	294	48	87	138	14	2	11	43	6	4	5	0	48	1	36	2	0
Foley, William, Vancouver	.267	25	75	10	20	31	2	0	3	9	0	1	1	9	0	23	0	0	
Fowler, Don, Tacoma	.000	16	0	0	0	0	0	0	0	0	0	1	0	0	1	0	0	0	0
Gates, Joseph, Edmonton°	.256	86	289	45	74	127	11	6	10	43	6	2	0	2	36	4	31	18	5
Gelfarb, Stephen, Tacoma°	.209	52	172	17	36	53	3	1	4	17	1	1	4	1	12	0	31	4	2
Gonzalez, Fernando, Salt Lake City	.274	24	95	12	26	41	6	0	3	11	1	0	0	3	0	7	2	0	
Grandas, Robert, Tacoma	.188	11	32	7	6	13	1	0	2	6	1	1	0	0	2	0	6	0	0
Gray, Lorenzo, Edmonton	.208	35	101	17	21	28	3	2	0	5	0	1	0	3	14	0	13	5	0
Gross, George, Tucson	.178	47	146	20	26	34	6	1	0	14	1	4	1	2	12	0	13	7	3
Gulden, Bradley, Spokane°	.275	15	51	9	14	25	5	0	2	9	0	0	1	0	5	1	5	1	1
Gwosdz, Douglas, Hawaii	.264	66	201	36	53	91	12	1	8	28	4	3	3	5	23	0	48	5	3
Hargesheimer, Alan, Phoenix	.000	20	2	0	0	0	0	0	0	0	0	0	0	0	0	0	1	0	0
Hargis, Gary, Portland	.293	57	167	25	49	64	9	0	2	28	1	2	1	0	3	0	15	4	0
Harper, Brian, Salt Lake City	.350	134	549	99	192	339	45	9	28	122	11	0	9	2	39	2	33	0	2
Harris, John, Salt Lake City°	.306	12	49	6	15	27	5	2	1	11	1	0	1	0	3	0	2	0	0
Hart, Michael, Spokane°	.277	105	357	51	99	144	19	4	6	48	2	2	2	2	64	0	43	6	7
Heep, Daniel, Tucson°	.337	78	285	55	96	162	23	5	11	60	6	0	5	5	47	2	19	3	6
Henderson, David, Spokane	.279	80	272	47	76	137	23	1	12	50	2	1	7	4	47	2	56	3	2
Henderson, Michael, Vancouver†	.231	19	52	7	12	14	2	0	0	3	0	0	1	0	11	0	7	1	1
Hilton, David, Portland	.279	118	402	52	112	146	19	3	3	40	5	4	5	0	31	1	36	8	3
Holle, Gary, Edmonton	.327	108	370	70	121	219	16	2	26	88	4	1	3	5	40	1	48	8	5
Holton, Brian, Albuquerque	.000	26	1	0	0	0	0	0	0	0	0	0	0	0	0	0	0	0	0
Horton, Willie, Portland	.302	104	368	50	111	189	25	1	17	75	8	0	8	3	26	1	61	1	1
Jones, Thomas, Phoenix	.304	17	69	7	21	29	4	2	0	11	1	0	0	0	8	1	0	0	
Kearney, Robert, Tacoma	.252	86	278	38	70	96	13	2	3	29	1	13	2	1	23	0	42	9	1
Klutts, Gene, Spokane	.393	9	28	3	11	18	2	1	1	4	1	1	0	0	2	0	7	0	0
Knicely, Alan, Tucson	.306	138	490	81	150	246	32	5	18	96	1	4	1	73	3	73	0	1	
Kubski, Gilbert, Vancouver°	.278	83	284	44	79	113	17	4	3	28	5	5	1	2	35	0	45	9	2
Kusick, Craig, Hawaii	.272	43	125	20	34	62	9	2	5	22	1	0	1	0	27	1	21	3	1
Lake, Steven, Vancouver	.230	109	348	27	80	102	14	1	2	38	7	4	4	0	5	0	41	2	0
Lancellotti, Richard, Hawaii°	.253	132	482	67	122	212	23	5	19	84	8	0	14	2	52	8	46	8	5
Law, Rudy, Albuquerque°	.335	107	397	75	133	167	16	9	0	39	6	7	3	0	48	1	27	56	17
Law, Vance, Portland	.277	88	310	55	86	133	14	9	5	43	7	5	1	1	47	0	41	8	4
Lee, Terrence, Vancouver°	.235	71	213	14	50	75	8	1	5	29	5	0	2	0	14	2	51	1	2
Leonard, Jeffrey, Phoenix	.401	47	187	38	75	119	17	3	7	45	5	0	0	3	14	1	20	18	1
Littlejohn, Dennis, Phoenix	.270	31	100	8	27	30	3	0	0	6	0	0	1	0	17	1	18	0	3
Loman, Douglas, Vancouver°	.248	62	214	23	53	83	8	2	6	19	3	2	2	4	23	2	31	5	3
Loucks, Scott, Tucson	.271	88	339	60	92	122	11	5	3	22	2	1	3	1	36	0	65	35	9
Loviglio, John, Edmonton	.299	113	461	71	138	204	23	5	11	57	7	4	2	2	40	0	39	40	10
Lubratich, Steven, Salt Lake City	.298	132	551	100	164	233	30	0	13	68	5	4	3	3	48	0	36	4	7
Mahler, Michael, Salt Lake City†	.000	24	0	0	0	0	0	0	0	0	0	0	0	0	1	0	0	0	0
Maldonado, Candido, Albuquerque	.335	126	460	96	154	275	40	9	21	104	11	4	13	7	50	2	104	13	14

Player and Club	Pct.	G.	AB.	R.	H.	TB.	2B.	3B.	HR.	RBI.	GW.	SH.	SF.	HP.	BB.	Int. BB.	SO.	SB.	CS.
Maler, James, Spokane	.305	139	518	84	158	260	29	8	19	99	9	0	3	11	36	1	62	10	4
Mangual, Jose, Salt Lake City	.264	108	326	63	86	142	21	1	11	46	6	4	2	3	73	4	75	22	11
Marshall, Michael, Albuquerque	.373	128	467	114	174	315	25	7	34	137	17	2	6	9	57	3	80	21	8
McHenry, Vance, Spokane	.237	109	350	43	83	102	8	4	1	27	1	5	4	4	21	1	36	12	7
Mercado, Orlando, Spokane	.215	95	312	32	67	104	21	2	4	31	3	1	3	6	27	0	55	4	2
Michael, Steven, Vancouver°	.273	3	11	2	3	6	0	0	1	1	0	0	0	0	2	0	4	0	0
Mitchell, Robert, Portland	.294	128	446	68	131	163	17	3	3	40	4	6	4	0	42	1	33	42	20
Mitchell, Robert, Albuquerque°	.311	104	341	68	106	136	17	5	1	63	8	6	7	0	58	11	37	14	5
Mize, Paul, Tacoma	.218	87	284	46	62	75	7	3	0	31	4	16	1	4	49	2	53	11	6
Moffitt, Scott, Salt Lake City	.257	102	327	45	84	106	11	1	3	35	3	6	2	2	30	2	35	7	1
Moore, David, Albuquerque	.000	28	1	1	0	0	0	0	0	0	0	0	0	0	0	0	0	0	0
Moore, Kelvin, Tacoma	.327	134	508	93	166	291	24	4	31	109	15	1	4	4	50	5	140	19	8
Moreno, Jose, Hawaii†	.305	107	393	73	120	200	25	11	11	70	10	0	6	4	41	4	32	30	10
Mueller, Willard, Vancouver	.000	33	2	0	0	0	0	0	0	0	0	0	0	0	0	0	2	0	0
Mullins, Francis, Edmonton	.244	77	238	46	58	92	8	1	8	27	1	1	1	4	36	1	54	7	4
Murray, Richard, Phoenix	.326	94	359	52	117	176	15	4	12	69	7	0	3	1	29	1	70	2	4
Nettles, James, Tacoma°	.241	108	344	42	83	113	10	4	4	45	3	4	3	1	48	4	61	3	8
Nyman, Christopher, Edmonton	.297	128	461	79	137	217	24	4	16	90	8	0	9	4	66	0	64	26	12
Olmsted, Alan, Hawaii	.000	26	1	0	0	0	0	0	0	0	0	0	0	0	0	0	0	0	0
Ortiz, Adalberto, Portland	.269	105	346	49	93	127	14	7	2	46	11	4	2	0	25	0	33	5	2
Page, Mitchell, Tacoma°	.328	71	250	46	82	149	12	2	17	68	6	1	3	0	36	1	51	14	11
Pankovits, James, Tucson	.282	122	450	83	127	200	34	9	7	64	4	4	6	1	53	1	67	18	9
Parsons, Casey, Spokane°	.295	41	149	23	44	63	11	1	2	13	1	3	2	2	16	2	25	4	2
Patterson, Larry, Spokane	.295	55	173	19	51	69	8	2	2	20	3	0	2	0	26	0	19	0	0
Pechek, Wayne, Salt Lake City°	.300	55	203	42	61	71	8	1	0	23	0	0	2	4	40	0	14	6	2
Pena, Adalberto, Tucson	.261	135	468	69	122	191	24	12	7	66	8	10	7	7	47	0	93	25	8
Pentz, Eugene, Phoenix	.000	41	2	0	0	0	0	0	0	0	0	0	0	0	0	0	1	0	0
Perconte, John, Albuquerque°	.346	127	448	107	155	196	26	6	1	58	6	14	8	3	85	3	45	45	12
Perez, Julio, Edmonton°	.277	56	191	24	53	67	10	2	0	18	2	2	0	0	15	1	16	2	3
Pettini, Joseph, Phoenix	.244	21	86	13	21	26	5	0	0	5	0	0	0	0	3	0	15	10	0
Phillips, Anthony, Tacoma†	.364	4	11	1	4	5	1	0	0	2	0	0	0	0	0	0	0	0	1
Pisker, Donald, Salt Lake City°	.205	26	83	8	17	24	4	0	1	9	1	0	1	0	16	1	19	0	0
Pittman, Joseph, Tucson	.348	6	23	4	8	13	0	1	1	5	1	0	0	0	6	0	2	3	1
Poff, John, Edmonton°	.278	108	363	54	101	151	15	4	9	53	3	1	6	1	47	0	45	2	2
Ramirez, Mario, Hawaii	.251	118	411	51	103	145	13	7	5	49	3	4	6	1	34	0	76	10	8
Ransom, Jeffrey, Phoenix†	.232	108	358	45	83	112	12	4	3	39	6	1	4	1	39	0	72	1	3
Ray, John, Tucson†	.349	131	525	111	183	268	50	10	5	83	6	1	7	1	46	0	23	19	5
Reed, Curtis, Hawaii°	.278	101	367	44	102	138	19	4	3	41	5	3	3	2	39	2	66	2	2
Rex, Michael, Phoenix	.323	132	469	69	158	208	24	4	6	54	8	4	7	9	52	3	33	10	1
Reynolds, Donald, Spokane	.283	68	237	34	67	87	12	1	2	23	3	1	1	3	36	0	33	0	1
Richards, David, Albuquerque°	.316	39	98	10	31	36	1	2	0	14	0	6	1	0	4	0	8	2	3
Roberts, David, Phoenix°	.143	17	35	3	5	8	0	0	1	4	0	0	0	0	3	0	9	0	0
Rodriguez, Ivan, Vancouver°	.199	120	356	30	71	88	15	1	0	21	3	2	2	2	32	0	67	6	8
Rodriguez, Jose, Portland	.246	26	61	12	15	19	4	0	0	2	0	2	0	1	10	0	15	5	1
Roenicke, Ronald, Albuquerque†	.316	126	411	100	130	216	23	9	15	94	9	3	16	3	110	8	55	25	15
Romero, Ramon, Edmonton	.375	28	96	13	36	46	4	0	2	12	1	4	1	0	6	0	8	2	3
Rosario, Simon, Tucson	.255	95	341	38	87	120	10	4	5	39	0	1	6	2	15	0	36	3	1
Rowland, Michael, Phoenix	.000	25	6	0	0	0	0	0	0	0	0	0	0	0	1	0	3	0	0
Runnells, Thomas, Phoenix†	.274	131	467	40	128	143	11	2	0	51	3	10	6	3	33	1	30	13	6
Rush, Lawrence, Vancouver	.277	125	451	56	125	211	19	5	19	71	6	1	2	4	31	0	94	35	10
Ryan, Craig, Vancouver°	.264	51	182	24	48	89	11	0	10	31	1	0	2	1	20	3	37	1	1
Sandt, Thomas, Portland	.100	6	10	0	1	1	0	0	0	1	0	0	0	0	1	0	3	0	1
Schaefer, Douglas, Phoenix	.200	27	5	0	1	1	0	0	0	1	0	0	0	0	1	0	4	0	0
Schuster, Mark, Vancouver°	.256	124	406	43	104	152	26	2	6	36	1	5	5	0	44	2	67	7	3
Sconiers, Daryl, Salt Lake City°	.354	108	410	91	145	224	24	8	13	74	5	0	1	2	55	9	65	2	2
Seaman, Kim, Hawaii°	.667	30	3	0	2	3	1	0	0	0	0	0	0	0	0	0	1	0	0
Sexton, Jimmy, Tacoma	.319	103	385	75	123	167	16	8	4	35	3	8	2	2	60	2	54	56	9
Sigman, Lee, Vancouver†	.000	3	2	0	0	0	0	0	0	0	1	1	0	0	1	0	1	0	0
Smith, Bobby Glenn, Vancouver°	.290	87	317	41	92	131	14	8	3	22	4	1	2	1	20	0	45	26	11
Smith, James, Portland	.251	129	386	53	97	153	16	5	10	51	3	14	5	1	33	0	57	2	1
Smith, Kelly, Phoenix	.225	24	71	6	16	18	0	1	0	5	0	1	0	0	11	0	6	2	2
Smith, Steven, Hawaii	.224	88	299	32	67	81	11	0	1	26	6	0	2	1	21	0	26	4	6
Soto, Thomas, Vancouver	.236	103	314	24	74	94	14	0	2	29	4	3	7	1	21	0	31	5	2
Spencer, Thomas, Tucson	.114	14	44	5	5	6	1	0	0	1	0	0	1	0	3	0	4	0	1
Stegman, David, Hawaii	.302	14	53	5	16	27	2	3	1	12	1	0	3	0	5	0	6	0	1
Stember, Jeffrey, Phoenix	.500	25	2	0	1	1	0	0	0	0	0	0	0	0	0	0	1	0	0
Stimac, Craig, Hawaii	.303	74	277	39	84	121	12	5	5	34	3	0	2	4	17	2	42	8	3
Stroughter, Stephen, Spokane°	.282	87	308	42	87	145	14	4	12	61	2	0	9	2	22	1	41	0	0
Sularz, Guy, Phoenix	.324	132	515	86	167	206	17	8	2	56	7	4	7	8	46	1	37	24	8
Sutherland, Leonardo, Edmonton°	.277	123	466	63	129	167	19	8	1	43	6	6	4	1	45	1	67	51	18
Taveras, Alejandro, Albuquerque	.433	13	30	6	13	14	1	0	0	5	0	2	1	0	7	0	2	2	2
Thomas, Franklin, Vancouver	.253	85	296	43	75	92	8	0	3	30	4	4	1	2	36	0	57	14	10
Thomas, Vernon, Edmonton	.258	85	256	28	66	94	6	5	4	33	2	6	2	3	28	1	58	8	3
Tolman, Timothy, Tucson	.322	137	479	85	154	240	28	8	14	99	9	2	9	5	89	0	45	14	3
Torres, Alfredo, Portland	.267	55	135	16	36	55	7	3	2	32	3	1	2	0	8	0	25	1	1
Torres, Rosendo, Portland†	.257	133	443	81	114	213	28	4	21	74	2	2	6	4	85	3	66	6	4
Turgeon, Michael, Phoenix†	.276	15	58	8	16	21	3	1	0	9	2	0	0	1	6	0	16	2	0
Venable, McKinley, Phoenix°	.285	104	428	81	122	190	24	10	8	48	8	3	1	4	41	2	51	33	8
Vessey, Thomas, Tucson	.162	40	99	7	16	21	2	0	1	8	1	1	1	4	5	0	21	0	0
Walters, Michael, Salt Lake City	.000	47	1	0	0	0	0	0	0	0	0	0	0	0	0	0	0	0	0
Walton, Reginald, Spokane	.271	48	177	24	48	73	6	2	5	22	1	0	2	2	15	0	31	10	7
Wantz, Douglas, Vancouver	.241	31	79	11	19	23	2	1	0	2	0	0	1	0	6	0	17	4	0
Weiss, Gary, Albuquerque°	.294	115	388	82	114	158	18	7	4	60	7	5	4	2	60	4	52	30	8
Wiedenbauer, Thomas, Tucson°	.205	83	263	30	54	76	13	3	1	25	3	3	3	1	24	0	52	9	4
Wiggins, Alan, Hawaii†	.302	133	513	97	155	188	17	8	0	33	3	5	4	4	62	1	33	73	15
Wiggins, James, Phoenix†	.306	39	108	13	33	45	9	0	1	13	1	1	0	1	28	1	17	2	0
Williams, Dan, Edmonton°	.271	60	166	25	45	62	6	1	3	20	0	1	1	1	34	0	28	1	2
Williams, Michael, Phoenix†	.333	28	6	1	2	2	0	0	0	0	0	0	0	0	1	0	2	0	1
Wilson, Michael, Albuquerque	.315	96	330	68	104	145	15	10	0	64	6	7	5	2	51	1	27	40	10
Wright, David, Albuquerque°	.571	29	7	2	4	7	1	1	0	0	0	0	0	0	0	0	0	0	0
Zouras, Michael, Albuquerque	.190	6	21	1	4	7	0	0	1	2	0	0	1	0	0	0	6	0	0

The following pitchers had no plate appearances primarily through use of designated hitters, listed alphabetically by club, games in parentheses:

ALBUQUERQUE—Keefe, Kevin (22); Patterson, David (38); Pena, Alejandro (38); Power, Ted (27); Rondon, Gilbert (4); Shirley, Steven (37); Strom, Brent (7); Swiacki, William (25).

EDMONTON—Agosto, Juan (48); Atkinson, William (36); Barnes, Richard (27); Barr, James (10); Contreras, Arnaldo (11); Eduardo, Hector (13); Geiger, Burwell (26); Hoffman, Guy (20); Murillo, Ramon (18); Patterson, Reginald (20); Robinson, Dewey (25); Teutsch, Mark (45); Vasquez, Dennis (4).

HAWAII—Armstrong, Michael (22); Chiffer, Floyd (42); Fireovid, Stephen (25); Hamm, Timothy (10); Kuhaulua, Fred (29); Pickert, Gary (24); Show, Eric (34); Stablein, George (16); Tellmann, Thomas (25).

PHOENIX—Hinrichs, Phillip (38); Pisel, Ronald (5); Tucker, Michael (21); Tufts, Robert (30).

PORTLAND—Alcala, Santo (28); Camacho, Ernie (18); Cliburn, Stewart (6); Cruz, Victor (9); Cuen, Eleno (19); Farr, Steven (4); Guante, Cecilio (19); Jones, Odell (24); Lee, Mark (49); Long, Robert (26); Mohorcic, Dale (40); Perez, Pascual (5); Tiant, Luis (21).

SALT LAKE CITY—D'Acquisto, John (18); Eaton, Craig (46); Ferris, Robert (26); Frost, David (5); Knapp, Christian (14); Martinez, Alfredo (12); Moreno, Angel (3); Rau, Douglas (2); Sanchez, Luis (6); Schuler, David (34); Steirer, Ricky (28).

SPOKANE—Allard, Brian (2); Anderson, Richard (7); Beattie, James (18); Biercevicz, Gregory (25); Black, Harry (4); Coleman, Joseph (15); Finch, Steven (20); Galasso, Robert (15); Gleaton, Jerry Don (13); Musselman, Ronald (43); Rawley, Shane W. (3); Stein, W. Randolph (10); Stoddard, Robert L. (19); Stranski, H. Scott (26); Vande Berg, Edward J. (49); Welborn, Sammye (34); Wirth, Alan (33).

TACOMA—Abraham, Brian (21); Beard, David (42); Bordi, Richard (27); Buice, DeWayne (2); Figueroa, Eduardo (13); Hamilton, David (4); Heaverlo, David (17); Heimueller, Gorman (6); Holdsworth, Frederick (20); Lysander, Richard (25); Minetto, Craig (22); Mustad, Eric (46); Souza, Mark (23); Thomas, Roy (36).

TUCSON—Aponte, Ricardo (20); Clyde, David (19); Ladd, Peter (47); Leatherwood, Delrick (6); Leland, Stanley (5); MacDonald, James (29); Meredith, Ronald (34); Miggins, Mark (34); Moore, Balor (28-10 with Vancouver); Niemann, Randy (10); Pladson, Gordon (22); Roberge, Bertrand (50); Smith, Billy (10); Taylor, Steven (12).

VANCOUVER—Ako, Gerald (12); Anderson, Michael (11); Bernard, Dwight (49); Cocanower, James (26); DiPino, Frank (27); Hartzell, Paul (13); Jones, Douglas (11); Keeton, Rickey (2); Olsen, Richard (25); Porter, Charles (27); Quinones, Rene (8); Quiros, Gustavo (20); Replogle, Andrew (1).

GRAND SLAM HOME RUNS—Marshall 3; Brunansky, Holle, Moreno, J. Smith, 2 each; R. Allen, Alvarez, Ashby, Beswick, Lancellotti, Loviglio, Lubratich, Maldonado, Mullins, Poff, Sconiers, Tolman, R. Torres, 1 each.

AWARDED FIRST BASE ON INTERFERENCE—Bertoni 8 (Gwosdz 2, Knicely 2, Ortiz 2, M. Foley, Lake); Castillo 2 (R. Davis, Dempsey); Anderson (Gulden); Brenly (Harper); Brunansky (L. Patterson); Flammang (Dempsey); R.D. Mitchell (Harper); Page (M. Foley); Ray (R. Davis); Schuster (Ortiz).

CLUB FIELDING

Club	Pct.	G.	PO.	A.	E.	DP.	PB.	Club	Pct.	G.	PO.	A.	E.	DP.	PB.
Portland	.979	137	3388	1269	102	94	17	Phoenix	.972	132	3396	1568	145	148	20
Edmonton	.973	136	3390	1640	138	128	12	Tacoma	.969	139	3594	1613	169	142	9
Hawaii	.973	137	3526	1590	143	134	7	Salt Lake City	.966	134	3457	1549	178	133	11
Albuquerque	.972	132	3342	1485	137	157	16	Spokane	.965	140	3482	1432	179	139	14
Vancouver	.972	132	3308	1490	139	112	26	Tucson	.962	139	3567	1625	205	158	18

Triple Plays—Albuquerque, Spokane, Tucson, Vancouver.

INDIVIDUAL FIELDING

°Throws lefthanded.

FIRST BASEMEN

Player and Club	Pct.	G.	PO.	A.	E.	DP.	Player and Club	Pct.	G.	PO.	A.	E.	DP.
Ashby, Hawaii°	.991	66	525	28	5	48	Kusick, Hawaii	.994	22	154	9	1	17
Barrios, Phoenix	.984	47	401	35	7	45	Lancellotti, Hawaii°	.991	26	219	12	2	23
Beall, Portland°	1.000	32	167	10	0	14	Littlejohn, Phoenix	1.000	2	24	0	0	2
Bishop, Salt Lake City	.986	30	269	10	4	28	Maler, Spokane	.986	135	1123	93	17	115
Boyland, Portland°	.989	64	541	23	6	24	Marshall, Albuquerque	.992	126	1127	54	9	136
Budaska, Tacoma°	.962	3	22	3	1	2	Moffitt, Salt Lake City	1.000	2	16	2	0	0
Cacek, Portland	.981	59	364	53	8	37	Moore, Tacoma°	.985	132	1203	85	19	118
Castillo, Hawaii	.986	8	69	3	1	7	Murray, Phoenix	.986	87	821	52	12	86
Caughey, Albuquerque	1.000	4	20	0	0	0	Nyman, Edmonton	.991	117	1105	68	11	98
Cox, Spokane	1.000	1	10	0	0	2	Roenicke, Albuquerque°	1.000	6	41	2	0	4
Crow, Albuquerque	1.000	1	2	0	0	0	Rush, Vancouver	1.000	7	50	5	0	6
Davis, Tacoma°	1.000	1	3	1	0	1	Ryan, Vancouver	.950	2	18	1	1	0
Doyle, Tacoma	1.000	1	11	3	0	2	SCHUSTER, Vancouver°	.994	123	1054	91	7	93
Edler, Spokane	1.000	1	11	0	0	1	Sconiers, Salt Lake City°	.993	95	866	36	6	80
Gelfarb, Tacoma°	.979	5	43	4	1	1	Stimac, Hawaii	.993	27	268	18	2	20
Gross, Tucson	.984	12	119	3	2	7	Stroughter, Spokane	1.000	3	27	2	0	4
Gwosdz, Hawaii	1.000	1	1	0	0	1	Sularz, Phoenix	1.000	2	8	0	0	0
Harper, Salt Lake City	.985	13	120	8	2	13	Tolman, Tucson	.992	60	601	41	5	62
Harris, Salt Lake City°	1.000	1	11	0	0	0	A. Torres, Portland	.750	1	2	1	1	0
Heep, Tucson°	.984	70	617	43	11	82	Williams, Edmonton	1.000	21	155	14	0	16
Holle, Edmonton°	1.000	3	25	0	0	1	Zouras, Albuquerque	.857	1	5	1	1	0

Triple Play—Maler.

SECOND BASEMEN

Player and Club	Pct.	G.	PO.	A.	E.	DP.	Player and Club	Pct.	G.	PO.	A.	E.	DP.
K. Allen, Spokane	.969	37	73	116	6	20	Moreno, Hawaii	.973	50	129	156	8	36
Carnes, Salt Lake City	.933	6	10	18	2	2	Mullins, Edmonton	1.000	2	3	0	0	0
Clark, Spokane	.952	22	43	57	5	14	Pankovits, Tucson	.943	13	24	26	3	9
Cox, Tacoma	.969	86	179	266	14	68	Perconte, Albuquerque	.963	123	286	321	23	103
De Simone, Hawaii	.973	13	31	42	2	12	Perez, Edmonton	1.000	1	0	1	0	0
Doyle, Tacoma	.970	16	18	46	2	4	Phillips, Tacoma	1.000	2	4	5	0	2
Drumright, Tacoma	1.000	13	24	38	0	10	Ray, Tucson	.973	130	309	369	19	101
Estrada, Spokane	.971	85	189	241	13	61	Rex, Phoenix	.975	131	281	371	17	105
Flannery, Edmonton	.985	14	33	32	1	10	Runnells, Phoenix	.900	3	6	3	1	0
Flannery, Hawaii	.982	21	47	62	2	13	Sandt, Portland	1.000	3	3	1	0	0
Fobbs, Albuquerque	1.000	12	20	38	0	13	Sexton, Tacoma	.969	24	37	58	3	12
Gates, Edmonton	.979	20	42	52	2	15	Smith, Portland	1.000	1	2	2	0	0
Hargis, Portland	.991	30	45	64	1	10	Smith, Hawaii	.973	55	143	144	8	34
Henderson, Vancouver	.986	13	31	39	1	10	Soto, Edmonton	.981	41	97	110	4	21
Hilton, Portland	1.000	1	0	1	0	0	Stimac, Hawaii	1.000	1	0	1	0	0
Law, Portland	.979	78	143	191	7	30	Sularz, Phoenix	1.000	1	0	2	0	0
Lee, Vancouver	1.000	5	1	4	0	0	Taveras, Albuquerque	1.000	3	6	6	0	2
Loviglio, Edmonton	.979	107	220	330	12	69	Thomas, Vancouver	.974	84	183	222	11	41
LUBRATICH, Salt Lake City	.984	131	325	407	12	103	Wiggins, Hawaii	.846	1	5	6	2	2
Mitchell, Portland	.969	42	56	100	5	12	Wilson, Albuquerque	.833	1	1	4	1	0
Mize, Tacoma	.930	10	33	20	4	6							

Triple Plays—Allen, Perconte, Ray, Thomas.

THIRD BASEMEN

Player and Club	Pct.	G.	PO.	A.	E.	DP.	Player and Club	Pct.	G.	PO.	A.	E.	DP.
J. Allen, Spokane	.868	17	17	20	7	1	Gray, Edmonton	.929	33	33	71	8	8
K. Allen, Spokane	.625	2	4	1	3	0	Hargis, Portland	.800	4	0	4	1	0
Alvarez, Hawaii	.956	77	58	180	11	16	HILTON, Portland	.966	115	98	188	10	21
Augustine, Portland	1.000	2	3	3	0	1	Klutts, Tacoma	1.000	2	1	4	0	0
Bell, Tacoma	.949	129	109	283	21	27	Law, Portland	1.000	1	2	3	0	0
Bertoni, Salt Lake City	.940	58	42	115	10	14	Lee, Vancouver	.968	10	5	25	1	0
Bevacqua, Portland	.973	14	12	24	1	1	Loucks, Tucson	1.000	1	0	1	0	0
Bishop, Salt Lake City	.930	54	31	102	10	15	Lubratich, Salt Lake City	1.000	1	2	0	0	0
Bodie, Tucson	1.000	1	1	0	0	0	Mitchell, Portland	.969	42	56	100	5	12
Brenly, Phoenix	.800	4	2	2	1	0	Mize, Tacoma	1.000	1	1	0	0	0
Carnes, Salt Lake City	.778	6	4	10	4	0	Moreno, Hawaii	.900	18	21	42	7	3
Castillo, Hawaii	.800	1	2	2	1	0	Mullins, Edmonton	.833	2	0	5	1	1
Caughey, Albuquerque	.970	91	62	200	8	20	Nyman, Edmonton	.800	2	1	3	1	0
Clark, Spokane	.937	41	38	66	7	8	Pankovits, Tucson	.794	26	13	37	13	4
Cox, Tacoma	.900	4	2	7	1	0	Patterson, Spokane	.750	1	0	3	1	0
Cox, Spokane	.923	18	26	22	4	4	Perez, Edmonton	.941	20	13	51	4	3
Cypret, Tucson	.934	109	102	281	27	32	Pittman, Tucson	.941	5	5	11	1	1
Drumright, Tacoma	.941	7	1	15	1	2	Romero, Edmonton	.909	20	14	46	6	7
Edler, Spokane	.920	58	53	85	12	2	Rush, Vancouver	.954	94	80	213	14	17
Estrada, Spokane	.929	8	3	10	1	1	Smith, Hawaii	.867	9	9	17	4	1
Flannery, Edmonton	.000	1	0	0	1	0	Soto, Vancouver	.978	40	25	62	2	8
Fobbs, Albuquerque	.920	59	25	113	12	14	Stimac, Hawaii	.888	37	24	87	14	6
Foley, Edmonton	.889	4	0	8	1	1	Sularz, Phoenix	.965	132	105	313	15	32
Gates, Edmonton	.918	64	61	119	16	9	Zouras, Albuquerque	.917	4	2	9	1	2
Gonzalez, Salt Lake City	.928	23	11	53	5	7							

Triple Plays—Edler, Fobbs, Rush.

SHORTSTOPS

Player and Club	Pct.	G.	PO.	A.	E.	DP.	Player and Club	Pct.	G.	PO.	A.	E.	DP.
Augustine, Portland	.500	2	0	1	1	0	Pankovits, Tucson	.846	6	11	11	4	4
Bertoni, Salt Lake City	.955	63	94	203	14	29	Pena, Tucson	.946	135	224	464	39	101
Carnes, Salt Lake City	.950	79	95	246	18	49	Perez, Edmonton	.975	37	57	100	4	14
Caughey, Albuquerque	1.000	2	4	5	0	2	Pettini, Phoenix	.970	17	28	70	3	15
Clark, Spokane	.934	26	32	67	7	16	Phillips, Tacoma	1.000	2	4	5	0	0
Cruz, Edmonton	.980	8	15	34	1	6	Ramirez, Hawaii	.970	118	192	390	18	74
Estrada, Spokane	.957	7	7	15	1	4	Ransom, Phoenix	1.000	1	2	0	0	0
Flannery, Edmonton	.893	11	20	47	8	8	Rodriguez, Vancouver	.956	119	214	326	25	65
Fobbs, Albuquerque	.886	15	14	56	9	10	Romero, Edmonton	.974	9	13	25	1	3
Gray, Edmonton	1.000	1	0	1	0	0	Runnells, Phoenix	.959	115	213	389	26	82
Hargis, Portland	1.000	3	5	8	0	1	Sexton, Tacoma	.949	67	101	233	18	50
Henderson, Vancouver	.933	3	4	10	1	2	SMITH, Portland	.980	128	208	287	10	54
Law, Portland	.959	12	23	24	2	4	Smith, Hawaii	.949	22	43	68	6	18
Loviglio, Edmonton	.875	6	11	10	3	1	Soto, Vancouver	.967	17	25	62	3	4
McHenry, Spokane	.940	109	172	312	31	82	Taveras, Albuquerque	.973	10	17	19	1	3
Mize, Tacoma	.955	74	136	225	17	40	Thomas, Vancouver	.800	2	1	3	1	0
Mullins, Edmonton	.974	73	122	252	10	51	Weiss, Albuquerque	.960	110	184	364	23	80

Triple Plays—Pena, Rodriguez, Taveras.

OUTFIELDERS

Player and Club	Pct.	G.	PO.	A.	E.	DP.	Player and Club	Pct.	G.	PO.	A.	E.	DP.
Alexander, Portland	.980	27	46	2	1	1	Henderson, Vancouver	1.000	1	1	0	0	0
K. Allen, Spokane	.978	63	127	5	3	0	Holle, Edmonton°	1.000	1	1	0	0	0
Allen, Edmonton	.975	109	144	12	4	1	Jones, Phoenix	.944	17	31	3	2	0
Anderson, Portland	.927	39	50	1	4	0	Knicely, Tucson	.932	26	36	5	3	0
Ashby, Hawaii	1.000	2	3	0	0	0	Kubski, Vancouver	.945	69	116	5	7	0
Augustine, Portland	.970	89	175	17	6	7	Lancellotti, Hawaii°	.984	93	185	5	3	1
Barrios, Phoenix	.955	38	61	3	3	1	Law, Albuquerque°	.970	71	158	5	5	2
Bass, Vancouver	.964	96	175	14	7	2	Leonard, Phoenix	.979	43	90	2	2	0
Beall, Portland°	1.000	2	1	0	0	0	Loman, Vancouver°	.983	62	166	5	3	0
Bertoni, Salt Lake City	.966	13	27	1	1	0	Loucks, Tucson	.971	71	158	6	5	0
Beswick, Hawaii	.973	128	309	15	9	3	Maldonado, Albuquerque	.968	114	221	21	8	5
Bishop, Salt Lake City	1.000	14	16	0	0	0	Mangual, Salt Lake City	.940	59	76	2	5	2
Bodie, Tucson	.979	74	132	5	3	2	Mercado, Spokane	1.000	1	1	0	0	0
Bohnet, Salt Lake City	.950	11	19	0	1	0	Michael, Vancouver°	1.000	3	6	0	0	0
Bosley, Vancouver°	.938	34	75	0	5	0	Mitchell, Portland	.975	83	156	3	4	1
Brenly, Phoenix	.951	24	36	3	2	1	Mitchell, Albuquerque	1.000	92	250	8	0	1
Brouhard, Vancouver	1.000	13	33	3	0	0	Mize, Tacoma	1.000	3	1	0	0	0
Brunansky, Salt Lake City	.981	96	250	14	5	1	Moffitt, Salt Lake City	.973	101	212	6	6	3
Bryant, Tacoma	.974	118	219	4	6	1	Moreno, Hawaii	.945	38	65	4	4	1
Budaska, Tacoma°	.935	53	97	4	7	2	Nettles, Tacoma°	.951	78	128	8	7	2
Cacek, Portland	1.000	30	28	0	0	0	Nyman, Edmonton	1.000	4	5	0	0	0
Colbern, Edmonton	1.000	1	1	0	0	0	Page, Tacoma	1.000	6	11	0	0	0
Cox, Tacoma	1.000	2	4	0	0	0	Pankovits, Tucson	.958	28	45	1	2	0
Davis, Phoenix	.968	86	175	7	6	0	Parsons, Spokane	1.000	36	76	2	0	1
Davis, Tacoma°	.976	121	283	6	7	2	Patterson, Spokane	1.000	2	2	0	0	0
Dempsey, Tacoma	.000	1	0	0	1	0	Pechek, Salt Lake City°	.888	51	81	6	11	0
Edler, Spokane	.500	1	1	0	1	0	Pisker, Salt Lake City°	.964	25	51	2	2	0
Edwards, Vancouver°	.950	11	18	1	1	0	Poff, Edmonton°	.983	106	161	15	3	1
Estrada, Spokane	1.000	1	1	1	0	0	Ransom, Phoenix	1.000	4	8	0	0	0
Figueroa, Phoenix	.833	14	10	0	2	0	Reed, Hawaii	1.000	16	10	0	0	0
Flammang, Spokane°	1.000	26	44	2	0	2	Reynolds, Spokane	1.000	66	115	7	0	0
Gelfarb, Tacoma°	.965	45	80	3	3	1	Rodriguez, Portland	.980	23	50	0	1	0
Grandas, Tacoma	.900	7	8	1	1	0	Roenicke, Albuquerque°	.979	99	176	12	4	3
Gross, Tucson	.889	21	24	0	3	0	Rosario, Spokane	.938	59	88	2	6	0
Hargis, Portland	1.000	17	28	2	0	0	Runnells, Phoenix	.955	14	21	0	1	0
Harper, Salt Lake City	.965	45	79	3	3	0	Rush, Vancouver	.949	26	36	1	2	1
Harris, Salt Lake City°	.929	12	12	1	1	0	Ryan, Vancouver	.962	29	47	3	2	0
Hart, Spokane	.988	96	237	7	3	2	Sandt, Portland	1.000	1	1	0	0	0
Heep, Tucson°	.950	10	18	1	1	0	Schaefer, Phoenix	.800	1	4	0	1	0
Henderson, Spokane	.981	67	146	7	3	0	Sigman, Vancouver	1.000	1	2	0	0	0

OUTFIELDERS—Continued

Player and Club	Pct.	G.	PO.	A.	E.	DP.
Smith, Vancouver°	.958	64	108	5	5	0
Smith, Phoenix	.952	24	57	3	3	0
Spencer, Tucson	.969	12	29	2	1	0
Stegman, Hawaii	1.000	14	25	2	0	0
Stroughter, Spokane	.953	27	40	1	2	0
Sutherland, Edmonton	.973	122	272	11	8	5
Thomas, Edmonton	1.000	78	126	6	0	0
Tolman, Tucson	.966	68	134	8	5	1
A. Torres, Portland	1.000	9	11	0	0	0
R. TORRES, Portland	.997	131	298	10	1	3
Turgeon, Phoenix	1.000	15	36	3	0	1
Venable, Phoenix	.989	104	263	6	3	1
Walton, Spokane	.984	42	61	2	1	0
Wiedenbauer, Tucson	.959	76	177	12	8	2
Wiggins, Hawaii	.980	131	229	20	5	3
Wiggins, Phoenix°	.919	39	65	3	6	1
Williams, Edmonton°	1.000	5	4	0	0	0
Wilson, Albuquerque	.988	42	80	1	1	0
Wright, Albuquerque°	.750	1	3	0	1	0

Triple Play—Mitchell (Albuquerque).

CATCHERS

Player and Club	Pct.	G.	PO.	A.	E.	DP.	PB.
Bishop, Salt Lake City	.900	6	32	4	4	0	1
Brenly, Phoenix	.967	38	139	36	6	1	8
Carnes, Salt Lake City	1.000	1	2	1	0	0	0
Castillo, Hawaii	.974	70	338	37	10	4	2
Cias, Tacoma	.989	17	83	3	1	1	2
Colbern, Edmonton	.976	60	251	37	7	4	5
CROW, Albuquerque	.990	104	455	62	5	10	12
Davis, Salt Lake City	.972	81	424	68	14	4	6
Dempsey, Tacoma	.963	42	178	30	8	0	5
Foley, Edmonton	.977	86	401	73	11	2	7
Foley, Vancouver	.988	21	73	8	1	0	6
Gulden, Spokane	.889	6	37	3	5	2	1
Gwosdz, Hawaii	.978	62	321	42	8	5	4
Harper, Salt Lake City	.927	50	222	19	19	2	4
Kearney, Tacoma	.984	86	487	73	9	5	2
Knicely, Tucson	.980	120	513	76	12	3	15
Lake, Vancouver	.989	105	502	102	7	8	16
Littlejohn, Phoenix	.978	10	41	4	1	1	0
Mercado, Spokane	.975	89	445	60	13	8	10
Nyman, Edmonton	1.000	1	1	0	0	0	0
Ortiz, Portland	.978	104	606	76	15	11	8
Patterson, Spokane	.976	48	231	16	6	3	3
Ransom, Phoenix	.975	90	388	73	12	7	12
Richards, Albuquerque	.967	38	134	14	5	2	2
Sigman, Vancouver	1.000	1	1	0	0	0	0
Stimac, Hawaii	.960	12	46	2	2	0	1
A. Torres, Portland	.981	36	174	34	4	2	9
Vessey, Tucson	.954	40	126	20	7	2	2
Wantz, Vancouver	.952	20	75	4	4	0	4
Zouras, Albuquerque	1.000	1	1	1	0	0	0

Triple Plays—Crow, Lake.

PITCHERS

Player and Club	Pct.	G.	PO.	A.	E.	DP.
Abraham, Tacoma°	1.000	21	1	3	0	0
Agosto, Edmonton°	.909	48	7	33	4	2
Ako, Vancouver	.889	12	4	4	1	1
Alcala, Portland	1.000	28	3	17	0	0
Allard, Spokane	.833	2	2	3	1	0
Anderson, Vancouver°	1.000	11	2	10	0	1
Anderson, Spokane	.500	7	1	1	0	0
Aponte, Tucson	1.000	20	0	5	0	0
Armstrong, Hawaii	1.000	22	0	2	0	0
Atkinson, Edmonton	.977	36	10	33	1	4
Barnes, Edmonton	.971	26	6	27	1	2
Barr, Edmonton	.941	10	6	10	1	1
Beall, Portland°	1.000	13	5	5	0	0
Beard, Tacoma	1.000	42	5	14	0	0
Beattie, Spokane	.923	18	12	24	3	1
Bernard, Vancouver	.938	49	7	8	1	1
Biercevicz, Spokane	.933	25	7	21	2	2
Black, Spokane°	1.000	4	1	2	0	1
Bordi, Tacoma	.935	27	17	26	3	2
Botting, Salt Lake City°	1.000	23	1	16	0	1
Brown, Salt Lake City	.957	26	11	55	3	3
Calvert, Phoenix	.973	18	14	22	1	1
Camacho, Portland	.900	18	6	3	1	0
Chiffer, Hawaii	.929	42	5	8	1	0
Cliburn, Hawaii	1.000	6	2	2	0	2
Clyde, Tucson°	.920	19	2	21	2	0
Cocanower, Vancouver	.891	26	6	35	5	4
Coleman, Spokane	1.000	15	3	2	0	0
Contreras, Edmonton	1.000	11	6	4	0	1
Cruz, Portland	1.000	9	3	2	0	0
Cuen, Portland	.941	19	7	9	1	0
D'Acquisto, Salt Lake City	.917	18	4	7	1	0
DiPino, Vancouver°	1.000	27	3	12	0	0
Eaton, Salt Lake City	.931	46	11	16	2	2
Eduardo, Edmonton	.875	13	2	12	2	0
Farr, Portland	1.000	4	0	5	0	0
Ferris, Salt Lake City	.919	26	6	28	3	0
Figueroa, Tacoma	.882	13	7	8	2	1
Finch, Spokane	.947	20	14	22	2	6
Fireovid, Hawaii	.976	25	8	32	1	2
Flinn, Vancouver	.857	31	9	15	4	0
Fowler, Tacoma	.893	16	6	19	3	0
Frost, Salt Lake City	.571	5	0	4	3	0
Galasso, Spokane	1.000	15	1	9	0	1
Geiger, Edmonton	.818	26	2	7	2	0
Gleaton, Spokane°	.870	13	3	17	3	1
Guante, Portland	.950	19	4	15	1	0
Hamilton, Tacoma°	.500	4	0	1	1	0
Hamm, Hawaii	.955	10	4	17	1	2
Hargesheimer, Phoenix	.957	20	7	15	1	0
Hartzell, Vancouver	.769	13	5	10	4	0
Heaverlo, Tacoma	.667	17	2	2	2	0
Heimueller, Tacoma°	.882	6	2	13	2	0
Hinrichs, Phoenix	.947	38	4	14	1	2
Hoffman, Edmonton°	1.000	20	7	22	0	1
Holdsworth, Tacoma	.962	20	6	19	1	0
Holton, Albuquerque	.918	26	11	34	4	0
Jones, Vancouver	1.000	11	6	11	0	1
Jones, Portland	.963	23	8	18	1	1
Keefe, Albuquerque	.941	22	3	13	1	0
Keeton, Vancouver	1.000	2	1	1	0	1
Knapp, Salt Lake City	1.000	14	5	5	0	1
Kuhaulua, Hawaii°	.929	29	3	23	2	2
Kusick, Hawaii	1.000	1	0	1	0	0
Ladd, Tucson	.909	47	1	9	1	0
Leatherwood, Tucson	1.000	6	2	4	0	0
Lee, Portland	.867	49	5	8	2	0
Leland, Tucson	.875	5	0	7	1	0
Long, Portland	1.000	26	17	10	0	2
Lysander, Tacoma	.950	25	15	23	2	2
MacDonald, Tacoma	.977	29	11	32	1	1
Mahler, Salt Lake City°	.926	23	5	20	2	1
Martinez, Salt Lake City	.800	12	1	3	1	0
Meredith, Tucson°	.935	34	12	17	2	0
Miggins, Tucson°	.828	34	10	43	11	2
Minetto, Tacoma°	1.000	22	1	5	0	0
Mohorcic, Portland	.941	40	5	11	1	0
Moore, Vancouver-Tucson	.897	28	4	22	3	3
Moore, Albuquerque	.933	27	6	22	2	1
Moreno, Salt Lake City°	1.000	3	2	2	0	0
Mueller, Vancouver	.950	31	7	12	1	2
Murillo, Edmonton	.955	18	6	15	1	1
Musselman, Spokane	.957	43	5	17	1	0
Mustad, Tacoma	1.000	46	7	22	0	1
Niemann, Spokane	.929	10	0	13	1	0
Olmsted, Hawaii°	1.000	26	7	23	0	3
Olsen, Vancouver	.931	25	12	15	2	0
Patterson, Albuquerque	1.000	38	4	7	0	1
Patterson, Edmonton	1.000	20	9	20	0	1
Pena, Albuquerque	.813	38	1	12	3	1
Pentz, Phoenix	1.000	41	2	6	0	0
Perez, Phoenix	.818	5	4	5	2	0
Pickert, Hawaii°	1.000	24	1	5	0	0
Pisel, Phoenix	1.000	5	4	3	0	0
Pladson, Tucson	.947	22	7	11	1	2
Porter, Vancouver	.950	27	10	28	2	0
Power, Albuquerque	.833	27	6	29	7	3
Quinones, Vancouver	.625	8	1	4	3	2
Quiros, Vancouver	1.000	20	5	15	0	0
Rau, Salt Lake City°	1.000	2	1	2	0	0
Roberge, Tucson	.960	50	5	19	1	1
Roberts, Phoenix°	1.000	6	3	2	0	0
Robinson, Edmonton	1.000	25	8	7	0	0
Rondon, Albuquerque	1.000	4	0	1	0	0
ROWLAND, Phoenix	1.000	25	7	30	0	0
Sanchez, Salt Lake City	1.000	6	1	3	0	0
Schaefer, Phoenix	.889	25	8	16	3	1
Schuler, Salt Lake City°	.933	34	2	12	1	0
Seaman, Hawaii°	1.000	30	6	13	0	1
Shirley, Albuquerque°	1.000	37	1	4	0	0
Show, Hawaii	.952	34	4	16	1	0
Smith, Tucson	1.000	10	4	8	0	0
Souza, Tacoma°	1.000	23	3	9	0	1
Stablein, Hawaii	1.000	16	4	16	0	0

PITCHERS—Continued

Player and Club	Pct.	G.	PO.	A.	E.	DP.
Stein, Spokane	1.000	10	2	4	0	0
Steirer, Salt Lake City	.958	28	8	15	1	3
Stember, Phoenix	.920	25	5	18	2	1
Stoddard, Spokane	.917	19	11	22	3	2
Stranski, Spokane	.833	26	9	21	6	0
Strom, Tucson°	1.000	7	0	3	0	0
Swiacki, Albuquerque	.963	25	4	22	1	2
Taylor, Tucson	.800	12	3	5	2	0
Tellmann, Hawaii	.963	25	11	41	2	0
Teutsch, Edmonton	.923	45	6	18	2	0
Thomas, Tacoma	.969	36	16	15	1	1
Tiant, Portland	.919	21	9	25	3	1
Tucker, Phoenix	.962	21	8	17	1	1
Tufts, Phoenix°	1.000	30	4	19	0	0
Vande Berg, Spokane°	.941	49	4	12	1	1
Vasquez, Edmonton	1.000	4	1	1	0	0
Walters, Salt Lake City	.963	47	2	24	1	4
Welborn, Spokane	.824	34	7	7	3	2
Williams, Edmonton°	1.000	3	0	1	0	0
Williams, Phoenix°	.882	26	9	21	4	1
Wirth, Spokane	.947	33	3	15	1	1
Wright, Albuquerque°	.935	27	8	21	2	0

The following players do not have any recorded accepted chances at the positions indicated; therefore, are not listed in the fielding averages for those particular positions: Buice, p; Carnes, of; Caughey, of; Colbern, 3b; Moffitt, 3b; Murray, of; Pechek, 1b; Pettini, of; Pittman, of; Rawley, p; Replogle, p; Schuster, of; Sigman, p; Soto, of; Wantz, of.

CLUB PITCHING

Club	ERA.	G.	CG.	ShO.	Sv.	IP.	H.	R.	ER.	HR.	HB.	BB.	Int. BB.	SO.	WP.	Bk.
Tacoma	3.81	139	35	9	30	1198	1188	590	507	107	21	486	19	702	52	6
Hawaii	4.03	137	33	8	25	1175⅓	1269	617	526	70	23	434	11	644	80	5
Vancouver	4.14	132	20	10	22	1102⅔	1106	577	507	57	30	541	4	593	65	6
Albuquerque	4.25	132	31	3	41	1114	1165	604	526	100	29	507	16	547	44	6
Portland	4.43	137	36	11	30	1129⅓	1179	631	556	90	43	479	29	731	49	8
Spokane	4.46	140	29	4	30	1160⅔	1228	705	575	96	28	538	14	655	64	7
Phoenix	4.85	132	24	4	34	1132	1263	710	610	102	34	542	23	518	67	4
Edmonton	4.93	136	23	3	31	1130	1227	733	619	117	24	563	20	597	44	8
Tucson	5.07	139	32	4	17	1189	1430	811	670	87	33	557	21	600	75	5
Salt Lake City	5.83	134	23	4	21	1152⅓	1452	850	746	89	37	492	12	627	56	7

PITCHERS' RECORDS

(Leading Qualifiers for Earned-Run Average Leadership—112 or More Innings)

°Throws lefthanded.

Pitcher—Club	W.	L.	Pct.	ERA.	G.	GS.	CG.	GF.	ShO.	Sv.	IP.	H.	R.	ER.	HR.	HB.	BB.	Int. BB.	SO.	WP.
Stoddard, Spokane	10	4	.714	2.90	19	19	3	0	0	0	121	117	47	39	6	2	41	0	70	7
Long, Portland	15	3	.833	2.98	26	20	4	3	2	1	157	122	56	52	12	10	59	1	97	1
Thomas, Tacoma	12	8	.600	3.05	36	18	7	12	2	1	165	137	61	56	18	0	49	2	111	9
Beattie, Edmonton	6	9	.400	3.15	18	17	7	1	0	0	120	115	60	42	7	6	48	1	70	10
Fireovid, Hawaii	11	7	.611	3.17	25	25	5	0	0	0	162	173	77	57	6	1	55	3	57	11
Patterson, Portland	10	8	.556	3.31	20	20	6	0	1	0	136	111	63	50	11	6	71	1	80	6
Holton, Albuquerque	16	6	.727	3.44	26	26	9	0	0	0	191	215	94	73	23	5	51	1	73	5
Olsen, Vancouver	9	7	.563	3.51	25	25	4	0	1	0	146	124	64	57	8	3	77	0	67	7
Jones, Portland	12	6	.667	3.53	23	23	9	0	1	0	153	138	73	60	6	6	68	3	135	13
Power, Albuquerque	18	3	.857	3.56	27	26	8	0	1	0	187	165	84	74	13	6	103	0	111	10

Departmental Leaders: G—Roberge, 50; GS—MacDonald, 28; CG—Bordi, MacDonald, 15; ShO—Tellmann, 5; W—Power, 18; L—MacDonald, 16; Sv—Pena, 22; Pct.—Power, .857; IP—MacDonald, 192; R—M. Williams, 145; ER—M. Williams, 127; HR—Alcala, 24; BB—Power, 103; IBB—Stember, 13; HB—Long, 10; SO—O. Jones, 135; WP—Cocanower, 18.

(All Pitchers—Listed Alphabetically)

Pitcher—Club	W.	L.	Pct.	ERA.	G.	GS.	CG.	GF.	ShO.	Sv.	IP.	H.	R.	ER.	HR.	HB.	BB.	Int. BB.	SO.	WP.
Abraham, Tacoma°	4	2	.667	2.86	21	1	0	12	0	1	44	36	16	14	3	0	23	2	25	0
Agosto, Edmonton°	7	10	.412	3.90	48	4	2	25	0	7	120	128	61	52	8	2	49	3	57	4
Ako, Vancouver	1	3	.250	3.66	12	0	0	3	0	1	32	34	15	13	3	1	10	0	9	1
Alcala, Portland	7	13	.350	4.39	27	26	6	1	1	1	164	174	89	80	24	5	57	2	94	4
Allard, Spokane	1	1	.500	1.29	2	2	2	0	1	0	14	9	2	2	0	0	2	0	11	0
Anderson, Vancouver°	0	2	.000	3.77	11	2	1	4	0	0	43	42	25	18	0	0	31	0	22	10
Anderson, Spokane	0	3	.000	16.20	7	1	0	4	0	0	10	20	21	18	2	0	9	0	7	4
Aponte, Tucson	1	3	.250	6.55	20	2	0	6	0	0	44	63	36	32	5	5	20	1	9	4
Armstrong, Hawaii	5	2	.714	1.50	22	0	0	21	0	6	36	21	7	6	4	1	12	0	39	1
Atkinson, Edmonton	8	8	.500	5.48	36	16	3	13	0	2	151	158	108	92	21	5	68	3	64	8
Barnes, Edmonton°	13	8	.619	4.75	26	26	3	0	0	0	163	181	100	86	15	3	82	1	80	7
Barr, Edmonton	4	5	.444	4.87	10	10	2	0	0	0	61	74	41	33	4	0	21	2	18	2
Beall, Portland°	0	0	.000	6.43	13	0	0	11	0	0	28	38	21	20	4	2	10	1	12	2
Beard, Tacoma	11	11	.500	4.26	42	12	3	27	0	10	129	132	67	61	14	0	51	2	114	3
Beattie, Spokane	6	9	.400	3.15	18	17	7	1	0	0	120	115	60	42	7	6	48	1	70	10
Bernard, Vancouver	3	5	.375	3.35	49	0	0	44	0	11	51	45	23	19	2	1	29	1	42	5
Biercevicz, Spokane	6	10	.375	6.00	25	22	6	1	0	0	126	150	100	84	20	4	57	1	53	6
Black, Spokane°	1	0	1.000	4.50	4	0	0	1	0	0	8	12	4	4	1	0	2	0	4	2
Bordi, Tacoma	9	11	.450	3.68	27	27	15	0	2	0	191	197	98	78	12	4	66	0	101	5
Botting, Salt Lake City°	3	5	.375	7.29	23	12	2	6	0	0	100	121	94	81	20	6	53	0	48	8
Brown, Salt Lake City	11	13	.458	5.44	26	26	6	0	0	0	187	239	123	113	10	5	48	1	76	5
Buice, Tacoma	1	0	1.000	0.00	2	0	0	1	0	0	3	0	0	0	0	0	3	0	2	0
Calvert, Phoenix	7	4	.636	4.46	18	17	2	0	0	0	101	100	59	50	4	1	53	4	31	13
Camacho, Portland	2	3	.400	4.74	18	0	0	9	0	0	38	45	24	20	2	1	22	1	31	6
Chiffer, Hawaii	4	5	.444	3.44	42	0	0	39	0	14	68	63	33	26	5	3	22	3	51	7
Cliburn, Portland	0	1	.000	9.53	6	2	1	0	0	0	17	32	18	18	2	0	6	0	7	1
Clyde, Tucson°	4	10	.286	6.85	19	19	2	0	0	0	109	150	100	83	4	0	67	2	59	13
Cocanower, Vancouver	6	12	.333	5.65	26	25	0	1	0	0	137	144	95	86	6	3	102	0	78	18
Coleman, Spokane	1	0	1.000	4.38	15	1	0	8	0	1	39	44	19	19	3	4	9	1	24	4
Contreras, Edmonton	4	3	.571	5.44	11	9	0	1	0	0	48	69	36	29	3	2	28	0	29	0
Cruz, Portland	2	1	.667	4.13	9	3	0	4	0	2	24	25	11	11	1	0	5	1	19	2
Cuen, Portland	3	8	.273	6.55	19	14	1	4	0	0	77	88	60	56	6	3	37	2	36	2
D'Acquisto, Salt Lake City	5	10	.333	8.32	18	18	2	0	0	0	92	119	97	85	1	5	88	0	66	8
DiPino, Vancouver°	3	5	.375	4.33	27	5	0	14	0	4	81	83	45	39	7	0	39	1	81	2
Eaton, Salt Lake City	3	2	.600	6.07	46	1	0	28	0	5	83	115	63	56	5	0	32	1	48	0
Eduardo, Edmonton	2	7	.222	8.67	13	12	0	0	0	0	55	61	56	53	9	1	54	1	38	5
Farr, Portland	0	3	.000	7.83	4	4	0	0	0	0	23	39	28	20	3	1	12	0	19	0
Ferris, Salt Lake City	8	9	.471	5.13	26	23	6	2	0	0	144	171	95	82	8	2	51	2	70	5
Figueroa, Tacoma	5	4	.556	3.34	13	10	0	1	0	0	62	56	27	23	1	0	26	1	23	4
Finch, Spokane	6	9	.400	5.05	20	19	1	0	0	0	107	119	73	60	9	1	42	0	66	10

Pitcher—Club	W.	L.	Pct.	ERA.	G.	GS.	CG.	GF.	ShO.	Sv.	IP.	H.	R.	ER.	HR.	HB.	BB.	Int. BB.	SO.	WP.
Fireovid, Hawaii	11	7	.611	3.17	25	25	5	0	0	0	162	173	77	57	6	1	55	3	57	11
Flinn, Vancouver	7	6	.538	4.02	31	7	0	10	0	1	85	82	44	38	6	5	27	0	55	5
Fowler, Tacoma	7	6	.538	3.21	16	16	3	0	0	0	87	80	39	31	8	4	45	3	35	1
Frost, Salt Lake City	1	2	.333	8.61	5	5	0	0	0	0	23	35	27	22	1	2	7	1	14	2
Galasso, Spokane	1	2	.333	1.80	15	0	0	12	0	6	25	17	6	5	0	1	12	1	23	1
Geiger, Edmonton	3	3	.500	3.95	26	0	0	18	0	3	57	58	30	25	5	0	36	3	44	5
Gleaton, Spokane°	5	7	.417	4.15	13	13	7	0	1	0	91	104	53	42	4	0	39	0	57	1
Guante, Portland	6	6	.500	5.37	19	17	3	0	1	0	104	110	64	62	10	5	58	3	70	4
Hamilton, Tacoma°	0	0	.000	7.00	4	0	0	0	0	0	9	16	7	7	0	0	5	0	5	0
Hamm, Hawaii	3	3	.500	3.60	10	10	2	0	0	0	75	83	38	30	4	1	17	1	40	2
Hargesheimer, Phoenix	6	8	.429	3.66	20	20	2	0	1	0	118	127	58	48	9	8	41	0	64	7
Hartzell, Vancouver	3	9	.250	5.59	13	13	1	0	0	0	66	85	45	41	5	2	24	0	29	3
Heaverlo, Tacoma	2	1	.667	2.74	17	0	0	14	0	8	23	30	10	7	1	0	9	2	10	0
Heimueller, Tacoma°	3	3	.500	3.89	6	6	1	0	0	0	37	36	16	16	2	2	22	0	16	1
Hinrichs, Phoenix	5	4	.556	5.10	39	0	0	27	0	6	83	104	55	47	4	3	31	6	37	7
Hoffman, Edmonton°	4	6	.400	4.30	20	20	4	0	0	0	111	117	70	53	5	0	60	2	71	1
Holdsworth, Tacoma	8	7	.533	4.26	20	19	2	1	0	0	114	122	68	54	14	3	52	0	64	6
Holton, Albuquerque	16	6	.727	3.44	26	26	9	0	0	0	191	215	94	73	23	5	51	1	73	5
Jones, Vancouver	5	3	.625	3.04	11	10	2	1	0	0	80	79	29	27	6	4	22	0	38	2
Jones, Portland	12	6	.667	3.53	23	23	9	0	1	0	153	138	73	60	6	6	68	3	135	13
Keefe, Albuquerque	6	3	.667	5.88	22	8	0	5	0	2	72	83	50	47	5	2	50	1	27	0
Keeton, Vancouver	0	0	.000	2.00	2	1	0	0	0	0	9	9	2	2	0	0	6	0	1	1
Knapp, Salt Lake City	1	4	.200	8.08	14	8	1	3	1	0	49	69	45	44	9	5	20	0	35	5
Kuhaulua, Hawaii°	10	10	.500	4.17	29	18	7	6	1	2	162	188	83	75	9	1	51	1	85	3
Kusick, Hawaii	0	0	.000	9.00	1	0	0	1	0	0	1	1	1	1	1	0	0	0	1	0
Ladd, Tucson	5	4	.556	3.38	47	2	0	34	0	6	96	90	43	36	8	1	44	6	68	5
Leatherwood, Tucson	0	3	.000	2.05	6	3	0	2	0	0	22	25	11	5	1	0	10	0	5	0
Lee, Portland	6	9	.400	4.07	48	1	0	41	0	20	73	75	39	33	3	4	38	7	50	2
Leland, Tucson	1	4	.200	7.36	5	5	0	0	0	0	22	38	23	18	2	1	12	0	11	2
Long, Portland	15	3	.833	2.98	26	20	4	3	2	1	157	122	56	52	12	10	59	1	97	1
Lysander, Tacoma	9	3	.750	3.97	25	25	2	0	0	0	161	159	80	71	13	3	53	3	91	10
MacDonald, Tucson	11	16	.407	4.92	29	28	15	0	1	0	192	242	133	105	20	6	67	2	77	5
Mahler, Salt Lake City°	10	4	.714	4.96	23	21	3	0	1	0	127	164	75	70	11	3	47	1	63	7
Martinez, Salt Lake City	3	3	.500	9.75	12	7	1	1	0	0	48	64	59	52	4	0	41	0	31	2
Meredith, Tucson°	7	6	.538	5.45	34	16	3	9	0	1	132	166	93	80	15	8	63	3	70	4
Miggins, Tucson°	10	9	.526	4.91	34	20	5	5	1	0	163	186	106	89	11	4	79	2	79	7
Minetto, Tacoma°	1	2	.333	4.50	22	2	1	9	0	2	46	57	29	23	5	0	19	2	20	1
Mohorcic, Portland	5	3	.625	4.35	40	1	0	24	0	5	93	103	54	45	8	6	41	4	39	8
Moore, 10 Van-18 Tuc°	2	5	.286	5.83	28	10	1	9	0	0	88	107	67	57	4	2	55	1	38	6
Moore, Albuquerque	12	5	.706	5.15	27	23	2	1	0	0	138	148	85	79	19	6	65	1	65	5
Moreno, Salt Lake City°	1	0	1.000	4.76	3	3	1	0	0	0	17	11	9	9	1	0	13	0	14	1
Mueller, Vancouver	5	3	.625	1.78	31	2	0	21	0	5	81	67	20	16	2	0	44	0	52	2
Murillo, Edmonton	4	7	.364	5.87	18	17	2	0	1	0	92	102	68	60	13	4	45	0	52	3
Musselman, Spokane	1	8	.111	3.76	43	1	0	30	0	10	67	69	31	28	6	2	27	5	25	1
Mustad, Tacoma	5	1	.833	4.27	46	2	1	15	0	3	99	95	53	47	13	6	45	1	67	8
Niemann, Tucson°	4	2	.667	4.89	10	10	1	0	0	0	57	68	40	31	3	1	38	0	39	4
Olmsted, Hawaii°	8	9	.471	5.95	26	20	2	3	0	0	124	166	92	82	6	3	48	0	44	16
Olsen, Vancouver	9	7	.563	3.51	25	25	4	0	1	0	146	124	64	57	8	3	77	0	67	7
Patterson, Albuquerque	7	1	.875	4.24	38	0	0	20	0	8	85	97	45	40	7	3	30	3	49	4
Patterson, Edmonton	10	8	.556	3.31	20	20	6	0	1	0	136	111	63	50	11	6	71	1	80	6
Pena, Albuquerque	2	5	.286	1.61	38	0	0	37	0	22	56	36	12	10	0	1	21	4	40	0
Pentz, Phoenix	3	4	.429	4.38	41	0	0	33	0	14	74	82	38	36	11	1	42	2	51	2
Perez, Portland	1	2	.333	4.94	5	5	1	0	0	0	31	40	19	17	1	2	14	2	11	1
Pickert, Hawaii°	3	3	.500	5.44	24	6	0	8	0	1	81	73	61	49	8	2	55	0	60	17
Pisel, Phoenix	0	1	.000	4.50	5	1	0	2	0	1	18	16	10	9	0	0	15	0	6	1
Pladson, Tucson	3	12	.200	6.77	22	15	3	4	1	1	101	129	83	76	4	2	53	1	55	12
Porter, Vancouver	7	10	.412	3.79	27	17	7	5	1	0	140	142	67	59	1	4	40	1	54	5
Power, Albuquerque	18	3	.857	3.56	27	26	8	0	1	0	187	165	84	74	13	6	103	0	111	10
Quinones, Vancouver	2	1	.667	5.34	8	5	1	2	1	0	32	22	20	19	2	3	32	0	14	0
Quiros, Vancouver	3	6	.333	5.42	20	10	1	6	1	0	73	91	48	44	7	3	21	0	30	3
Rau, Salt Lake City°	1	1	.500	4.50	2	2	0	0	0	0	10	14	8	5	1	0	3	0	4	1
Rawley, Spokane°	0	0	.000	0.00	3	1	0	1	0	1	6	3	0	0	0	0	3	0	3	1
Replogle, Vancouver	0	0	.000	4.50	1	1	0	0	0	0	2	3	2	1	0	0	4	0	1	0
Roberge, Tucson	5	4	.556	3.62	50	0	0	38	0	9	87	85	43	35	4	2	32	4	62	10
Roberts, Phoenix°	0	0	.000	2.40	6	0	0	6	0	0	15	16	4	4	0	0	3	0	7	2
Robinson, Edmonton	1	4	.200	4.50	25	0	0	24	0	10	46	48	24	23	7	0	14	2	37	2
Rondon, Albuquerque	1	1	.500	9.00	4	0	0	1	0	0	7	6	7	7	1	0	8	0	3	0
Rowland, Phoenix	15	7	.682	3.99	25	25	9	0	1	0	176	189	90	78	21	2	42	1	84	2
Sanchez, Salt Lake City	0	0	.000	7.88	6	0	0	5	0	0	8	12	7	7	1	0	7	0	7	1
Schaefer, Phoenix	3	5	.375	6.61	25	10	1	7	0	1	94	109	87	69	14	1	69	2	29	12
Schuler, Salt Lake City°	4	5	.444	4.76	34	1	0	20	0	4	68	100	45	36	7	1	22	3	35	3
Seaman, Hawaii°	6	8	.429	5.29	30	13	1	11	0	2	114	138	74	67	11	0	47	2	79	10
Shirley, Albuquerque°	5	3	.625	2.37	37	0	0	30	0	9	57	56	24	15	3	0	31	2	36	9
Show, Hawaii	7	3	.700	2.54	34	5	2	16	1	1	85	67	30	24	4	4	35	0	70	6
Sigman, Vancouver	0	0	.000	0.00	1	0	0	1	0	0	2	3	0	0	0	0	0	0	1	0
Smith, Tucson	5	2	.714	2.96	10	10	2	0	1	0	76	72	34	25	4	2	15	0	30	3
Souza, Tacoma°	1	2	.333	5.90	23	1	0	12	0	5	29	35	19	19	3	0	17	1	18	2
Stablein, Hawaii	3	4	.429	3.76	15	15	4	0	0	0	91	107	43	38	2	3	39	1	51	4
Stein, Spokane	1	1	.500	3.00	10	2	0	5	0	1	21	20	9	7	0	1	8	0	16	0
Steirer, Salt Lake City	5	7	.417	4.58	28	7	1	9	1	0	116	133	73	59	5	6	37	2	65	4
Stember, Phoenix	7	9	.438	6.44	25	17	2	6	0	2	116	131	94	83	12	9	90	13	63	10
Stoddard, Spokane	10	4	.714	2.90	19	19	3	0	0	0	121	117	47	39	6	2	41	0	70	7
Stranski, Spokane	5	15	.250	5.22	26	25	4	0	0	0	157	163	116	91	20	7	101	1	75	7
Strom, Albuquerque°	2	0	1.000	8.53	7	2	0	3	0	0	19	32	20	18	4	0	6	0	3	0
Swiacki, Albuquerque	11	5	.688	5.47	25	23	5	2	0	0	148	186	102	90	16	7	50	2	28	2
Taylor, Tucson	1	6	.143	5.44	12	8	0	1	0	0	43	60	32	26	4	0	29	0	12	2
Tellmann, Hawaii	12	11	.522	3.63	25	25	9	0	5	0	176	189	78	71	10	4	53	0	67	5
Teutsch, Edmonton	2	4	.333	5.54	45	1	0	32	0	9	78	101	61	48	14	1	26	2	23	2
Thomas, Tacoma	12	8	.600	3.05	36	18	7	12	2	1	165	137	61	56	18	0	49	2	111	9
Tiant, Portland	13	7	.650	3.82	21	21	11	0	2	0	146	150	75	62	8	1	49	2	111	3
Tucker, Phoenix	6	7	.462	3.68	21	14	2	6	0	2	110	118	48	45	9	4	30	2	41	1
Tufts, Phoenix°	9	2	.818	1.70	30	2	1	21	1	8	69	59	22	13	2	1	29	2	38	4

Pitcher—Club	W.	L.	Pct.	ERA.	G.	GS.	CG.	GF.	ShO.	Sv.	IP.	H.	R.	ER.	HR.	HB.	BB.	Int. BB.	SO.	WP.
Vande Berg, Spokane°	4	3	.571	3.77	49	2	0	23	0	9	62	62	33	26	3	3	29	2	49	2
Vasquez, Edmonton	0	1	.000	10.29	4	1	0	1	0	0	7	10	8	8	1	0	3	0	1	0
Walters, Salt Lake City	7	6	.538	2.85	47	0	0	38	0	12	79	83	32	25	5	2	23	1	52	2
Welborn, Spokane	3	3	.500	5.93	34	5	0	13	0	1	82	105	63	54	11	1	49	1	52	3
Williams, Edmonton°	0	0	.000	12.60	3	0	0	0	0	0	5	9	7	7	1	0	5	0	3	0
Williams, Phoenix°	8	12	.400	7.28	26	26	5	0	1	0	157	210	145	127	16	4	96	1	67	6
Wirth, Spokane	5	9	.357	4.63	33	10	0	10	0	1	105	99	68	54	4	1	55	1	50	8
Wright, Albuquerque°	14	6	.700	4.24	27	24	7	2	0	0	155	141	81	73	8	1	90	2	112	9

BALKS—B. Moore, Souza, 4 each; Barnes, D'Acquisto, 3 each; Alcala, Brown, Fireovid, Guante, Hamm, Hinrichs, Pena, Stoddard, Stranski, Wirth, 2 each; Agosto, Ako, Barr, Biercevicz, Bordi, Calvert, Cocanower, Cuen, Eduardo, Geiger, Hargesheimer, Heimueller, Kuhaulua, Lee, Mahler, Meredith, Mohorcic, D. Moore, Murillo, Niemann, Olsen, D. Patterson, Perez, Pladson, Power, Roberge, Schuler, 1 each.

COMBINATION SHUTOUTS—Moore-Pena, Power-Patterson, Albuquerque; Atkinson-Robinson, Edmonton; Hamm-Chiffer, Hawaii; Alcala-Lee, Jones-Camacho-Lee, Jones-Mohorcic, Long-Cruz, Portland; Mahler-Walters, Salt Lake City; Stoddard-Vande Berg, Wirth-Galasso, Spokane; Beard-Heaverlo, Fowler-Abraham, Fowler-Heaverlo, Holdsworth-Abraham, Lysander-Minetto-Beard, Tacoma; Meredith-Roberge, Tucson; Cocanower-Flinn, Hartzell-Bernard, Hartzell-Flinn, Olsen-Flinn-DiPino, Quiros-Bernard, Vancouver.

NO-HIT GAMES—Tiant, Portland, defeated Spokane, 2-0, April 18 (seven innings); Smith, Tucson, defeated Vancouver, 4-0, June 2 (six innings); Stablein, Hawaii, defeated Tacoma, 6-1, June 13; Quinones, Vancouver, defeated Edmonton, 3-0, June 16 (seven innings).

Eastern League

CLASS AA

Leading Batter
ED JURAK
Bristol

League President
CHARLES ESHBACH

Leading Pitcher
BRIAN DENMAN
Bristol

CHAMPIONSHIP WINNERS IN PREVIOUS YEARS

1923—Williamsport .661	1944—Hartford .723	1963—Charleston .593
1924—Williamsport .654	Binghamton (4th)‡ .474	1964—Elmira .586
1925—York§ .583	1945—Utica .615	1965—Pittsfield .607
Williamsport§ .583	Albany (3rd)‡ .564	1966—Elmira .633
1926—Scranton .627	1946—Scranton† .691	1967—Binghamton z .586
1927—Harrisburg .630	1947—Utica† .652	Elmira .532
1928—Harrisburg .603	1948—Scranton† .636	1968—Pittsfield .604
1929—Binghamton .597	1949—Albany .664	Reading (2nd)‡ .579
1930—Wilkes-Barre .572	Binghamton (4th)‡ .500	1969—York .640
1931—Harrisburg .597	1950—Wilkes-Barre‡ .652	1970—Waterbury a .560
1932—Wilkes-Barre .561	1951—Wilkes-Barre .612	Reading a .553
1933—Binghamton .690	Scranton (2nd)† .562	1971—Three Rivers .569
1934—Binghamton .694	1952—Albany .603	Elmira b .561
Williamsport° .603	Binghamton (2nd)‡ .562	1972—West Haven b .600
1935—Scranton .657	1953—Reading .682	Three Rivers .559
Binghamton° .580	Binghamton (2nd)‡ .636	1973—Reading b .551
1936—Scranton° .609	1954—Wilkes-Barre .576	Pittsfield .551
Elmira .629	Albany (3rd)‡ .540	1974—Thetford Mines (2nd)c .536
1937—Elmira† .622	1955—Reading .613	Pittsfield (2nd) .496
1938—Binghamton .622	Allentown (2nd)‡ .565	1975—Reading .613
Elmira (3rd)‡ .522	1956—Schenectady† .609	Bristol° .587
1939—Scranton† .571	1957—Binghamton .607	1976—Three Rivers .601
1940—Scranton .568	Reading (3rd)‡ .529	West Haven d .576
Binghamton (2nd)‡ .554	1958—Lancaster x .568	1977—West Haven e .623
1941—Wilkes-Barre .630	Binghamton (6th)‡ .493	Three Rivers .551
Elmira (3rd)‡ .514	1959—Springfield† .607	1978—Reading .642
1942—Albany .600	1960—Williamsport y .551	Bristol° .580
Scranton (2nd)‡ .593	Springfield (3rd)y .496	1979—West Haven f .597
1943—Scranton .630	1961—Springfield .612	1980—Holyoke° .561
Elmira (2nd)‡ .568	1962—Williamsport .593	Waterbury .540
	Elmira (2nd)‡ .514	

°Won split-season playoff. †Won championship and four-team playoff. ‡Won four-team playoff. §Tied for pennant, York winning playoff. xLeague was divided into Northern, Southern divisions and played a split season; Lancaster over-all season leader. yPlayoff finals canceled after one game because of rain with Williamsport and Springfield declared playoff co-champions. zLeague was divided into Eastern, Western divisions; Binghamton won playoff. aTied for pennant, Waterbury winning playoff. bLeague was divided into American, National divisions; won playoff. cLeague was divided into American and National divisions; won four-team playoff. dLeague was divided into Northern, Southern divisions, won playoff. eLeague was divided into New England and Canadian-American divisions, won playoff. fWon both halves of split season (no playoffs). (NOTE—Known as New York-Pennsylvania League prior to 1938.)

STANDING OF CLUBS AT CLOSE OF FIRST HALF, JUNE 22

NORTHERN DIVISION

Club	W.	L.	T.	Pct.	G.B.
Glens Falls (White Sox)	41	27	0	.603	....
Holyoke (Angels)	37	32	0	.536	4½
Lynn (Mariners)	30	39	0	.435	11½
Buffalo (Pirates)	23	46	0	.333	18½

SOUTHERN DIVISION

Club	W.	L.	T.	Pct.	G.B.
Reading (Phillies)	42	28	0	.609	....
West Haven (A's)	40	30	1	.571	2
Bristol (Red Sox)	37	31	0	.544	4
Waterbury (Reds)	26	43	1	.377	15½

STANDING OF CLUBS AT CLOSE OF SECOND HALF, SEPTEMBER 1

NORTHERN DIVISION

Club	W.	L.	T.	Pct.	G.B.
Glens Falls (White Sox)	42	25	0	.627	....
Buffalo (Pirates)	33	35	0	.485	9½
Lynn (Mariners)	32	37	0	.464	11
Holyoke (Angels)	31	38	0	.449	12

SOUTHERN DIVISION

Club	W.	L.	T.	Pct.	G.B.
Bristol (Red Sox)	42	27	0	.609	....
Reading (Phillies)	34	35	0	.493	8
West Haven (A's)	31	37	0	.456	10½
Waterbury (Reds)	29	40	0	.420	13

COMPOSITE STANDING OF CLUBS AT CLOSE OF SEASON, SEPTEMBER 1

Club	G.F.	Bri.	Rea.	W.H.	Holy.	Lynn.	Buff.	Wat.	W.	L.	T.	Pct.	G.B.
Glens Falls (White Sox)	....	10	14	10	10	12	15	12	83	52	0	.615	....
Bristol (Red Sox)	8	....	11	11	14	12	12	11	79	58	0	.577	5
Reading (Phillies)	6	9	....	12	14	11	10	14	76	63	0	.547	9
West Haven (A's)	8	9	8	....	7	10	13	16	71	67	1	.514	13½
Holyoke (Angels)	10	6	5	13	....	12	12	10	68	70	0	.493	16½
Lynn (Mariners)	7	8	9	10	8	....	9	11	62	76	0	.449	22½
Buffalo (Pirates)	5	7	10	7	8	10	....	9	56	81	0	.409	28
Waterbury (Reds)	8	9	6	4	9	9	10	....	55	83	1	.399	29½

Major League affiliations in parentheses.

Playoffs—Bristol defeated Reading, two games to none; Bristol defeated Glens Falls, three games to two, for League Championship.

Regular-Season Attendance—Bristol, 77,066; Buffalo, 83,464; Glens Falls, 101,567; Holyoke, 80,117; Lynn, 38,468; Reading, 117,050; Waterbury, 67,609; West Haven, 55,552. Total, 620,893. Playoff, 10,750. No all-star game.

Managers: Bristol, Tony Torchia; Buffalo, John Lipon; Glens Falls, Jim Mahoney; Holyoke, Jim Saul; Lynn, Bobby Floyd; Reading, Ron Clark; Waterbury, George Scherger; West Haven, Bob Didier.

All-Star Team: 1B—Gregory Walker, Glens Falls; 2B—Thomas Lawless, Waterbury; 3B—Edward Jurak, Bristol; SS—Julio Franco, Reading; OF—Michael Brown, Holyoke; Luis Rois, Glens Falls; Randall Johnson, Glens Falls; C—Miguel Ibarra, Reading; DH—Ronald Kittle, Glens Falls; Utility—Joseph Bruno, Reading; LHP—Gorman Heimueller, West Haven; RHP—Brian Denman, Bristol; MVP—Ronald Kittle, Glens Falls; Manager of Year—Jim Mahoney, Glens Falls.

(Compiled by Howe News Bureau, Boston, Mass.)

CLUB BATTING

Club	Pct.	G.	AB.	R.	OR.	H.	TB.	2B.	3B.	HR.	RBI.	GW.	SH.	SF.	HP.	BB.	Int. BB.	SO.	SB.	CS.	LOB.
Reading	.275	139	4494	675	617	1234	1717	175	52	68	589	67	46	43	35	536	37	729	145	99	975
Glens Falls	.273	135	4381	756	641	1196	1985	200	26	179	675	72	29	31	46	572	42	756	36	32	968
Holyoke	.265	138	4440	626	611	1177	1698	189	43	82	563	62	33	40	43	497	32	760	151	62	955
Buffalo	.252	137	4388	616	709	1105	1806	197	30	148	556	47	47	32	27	563	31	864	100	62	929
West Haven	.252	139	4210	589	603	1060	1535	191	25	78	503	56	65	43	44	522	25	679	227	116	837
Bristol	.251	137	4279	621	504	1076	1518	193	30	63	538	66	59	40	39	666	43	813	114	62	1004
Lynn	.243	138	4253	530	562	1035	1504	165	23	86	481	53	53	30	46	586	39	785	119	90	946
Waterbury	.236	139	4332	524	690	1022	1460	168	33	68	466	47	91	37	47	593	49	783	166	47	1046

INDIVIDUAL BATTING

(Leading Qualifiers for Batting Championship—378 or More Plate Appearances)

°Bats lefthanded.   †Switch-hitter.

Player and Club	Pct.	G.	AB.	R.	H.	TB.	2B.	3B.	HR.	RBI.	GW.	SH.	SF.	HP.	BB.	Int. BB.	SO.	SB.	CS.
Jurak, Edward, Bristol†	.340	87	297	63	101	129	19	3	1	25	4	2	2	3	64	4	36	9	4
Kittle, Ronald, Glens Falls	.326	109	389	97	127	270	17	3	40	103	10	0	1	7	60	7	107	0	1
Walker, Gregory, Glens Falls°	.321	135	508	117	163	266	33	2	22	86	9	2	3	9	72	9	85	1	2
Brown, Michael, Holyoke	.321	135	499	64	160	219	25	8	6	83	11	1	6	6	60	3	56	15	7
Hamric, Russell, Reading	.307	129	524	80	161	204	20	4	5	66	10	9	8	5	34	1	67	20	16
Gentile, James, Bristol°	.302	118	367	60	111	165	20	5	8	59	4	2	2	2	62	6	66	12	7
Franco, Julio, Reading	.301	139	532	70	160	207	17	3	8	74	13	5	6	5	52	2	60	27	14
Sherow, Dennis, West Haven	.292	141	387	54	113	146	18	3	3	44	5	3	5	5	29	0	75	35	7
Lawless, Thomas, Waterbury	.291	136	522	77	152	216	20	10	4	50	7	6	1	1	67	1	69	60	16
Rois, Luis, Glens Falls	.291	131	498	73	145	246	27	4	22	89	9	2	6	4	14	2	74	12	9

Departmental Leaders: G—Franco, 139; AB—Franco, 532; R—Walker, 117; H—Walker, 163; TB—Kittle, 270; 2B—Walker, 33; 3B—Sanchez, 17; HR—Kittle, 40; RBI—Kittle, 103; GWRBI—R. Johnson, 16; SH—Garrett, 21; SF—Hamric, Pearsey, Redus, 8; BB—Chambers, 91; HP—Phillips, 10; SO—Frobel, 147; SB—Lawless, 60; CS—Woodard, 23.

(All Players—Listed Alphabetically)

Player and Club	Pct.	G.	AB.	R.	H.	TB.	2B.	3B.	HR.	RBI.	GW.	SH.	SF.	HP.	BB.	Int. BB.	SO.	SB.	CS.
Adams, Ricky, Holyoke	.262	120	446	85	117	164	11	3	10	48	5	5	2	2	41	3	43	21	11
Aldrich, Russell, Waterbury°	.246	132	414	55	102	165	23	5	10	53	9	10	1	4	49	7	65	1	0
Aponte, Edwin, Lynn	.198	61	207	14	41	51	7	0	1	19	2	3	2	1	13	1	20	1	2
Arline, James, Waterbury°	.107	34	28	0	3	5	2	0	0	1	0	0	0	0	4	0	8	0	1
Baez, Jessie, Lynn	.188	22	64	5	12	15	0	0	1	8	0	0	0	5	13	0	13	2	0
Barnes, William, Bristol	.256	96	363	45	93	128	17	0	6	49	7	3	3	4	33	6	29	15	4
Bennett, James, West Haven°	.259	84	247	38	64	117	15	1	12	40	3	0	4	2	27	4	48	5	2
Bienek, Vincent, Glens Falls	.274	119	401	73	110	196	17	3	21	64	4	5	4	2	74	3	96	2	4
Bisceglia, David, Waterbury	.118	22	34	3	4	5	1	0	0	6	0	2	0	0	8	0	6	0	0
Blanco, Geronimo, Buffalo	.133	8	15	0	2	2	0	0	0	1	0	0	0	0	0	0	1	0	0
Boddy, William, Waterbury	.087	20	46	4	4	5	1	0	0	0	0	0	0	0	10	0	12	1	0
Borucki, Raymond, Reading	.258	137	469	63	121	155	14	4	4	54	3	4	5	3	54	2	47	5	5
Brooks, Craig, Bristol°	.315	50	143	28	45	80	5	3	8	37	7	0	3	2	42	7	37	3	0
Brown, Michael, Holyoke	.321	135	499	64	160	219	25	8	6	83	11	1	6	6	60	3	56	15	7
Bruno, Joseph, Reading°	.287	137	516	88	148	203	27	5	6	54	6	8	7	2	75	7	39	22	20

Player and Club	Pct.	G.	AB.	R.	H.	TB.	2B.	3B.	HR.	RBI.	GW.	SH.	SF.	HP.	BB.	Int. BB.	SO.	SB.	CS.
Bryant, Erwin, Bristol	.263	125	433	67	114	142	23	1	1	26	3	13	4	4	73	3	53	10	7
Buckle, Larry, Waterbury	.094	29	32	1	3	3	0	0	0	0	0	2	0	0	0	0	16	0	0
Bustabad, Juan, Bristol°	.265	79	306	46	81	98	3	4	2	38	1	9	2	1	36	1	49	25	11
Carlucci, Richard, Waterbury°	.350	37	40	2	14	15	1	0	0	4	0	3	0	0	1	0	7	0	0
Cato, J. Keefe, Waterbury	.000	8	9	1	0	0	0	0	0	0	0	0	2	0	0	1	0	3	0	0
Chambers, Albert, Lynn°	.269	134	446	71	120	208	20	4	20	77	12	3	2	6	91	9	113	8	12
Christmas, Steven, Waterbury°	.263	126	395	40	104	146	21	0	7	63	6	4	6	3	51	11	35	1	1
Cias, Darryl, West Haven	.314	66	153	23	48	77	6	1	7	29	3	4	2	1	32	2	21	6	7
Clark, Christopher, Holyoke†	.272	116	375	47	102	149	20	0	9	53	5	4	4	1	54	7	36	3	4
Cliburn, Stanley, Buffalo	.253	62	198	18	50	74	7	1	5	24	1	2	4	0	17	2	23	0	0
Cliburn, Stewart, Buffalo	.000	29	1	0	0	0	0	0	0	0	0	0	0	0	0	0	1	0	0
Colbert, Richard, Bristol	.199	108	286	40	57	97	16	0	8	42	4	3	2	1	62	3	86	4	5
Conner, Jeffrey, Holyoke°	.000	26	3	0	0	0	0	0	0	0	0	0	0	0	1	0	0	0	0
Crist, Clark, Lynn	.236	82	237	27	56	67	11	0	0	15	1	9	0	0	27	1	40	2	4
Crone, William, Lynn	.256	124	445	70	114	140	21	1	1	29	3	10	2	0	69	2	72	26	12
Culbert, Aurdie, West Haven	.245	37	94	7	23	31	2	0	2	10	2	0	1	1	18	2	27	0	2
Culmer, Wilfred, Reading	.282	120	411	58	116	172	16	5	10	53	7	0	0	4	50	3	99	3	4
De La Rosa, Bienvenido, Buffalo°	.238	68	214	24	51	70	13	3	0	9	1	2	1	0	28	1	41	15	5
DeLeon, Jose, Buffalo	.000	25	2	0	0	0	0	0	0	0	0	0	0	0	0	0	1	0	0
Dempsey, Patrick, West Haven	.297	36	128	22	38	52	10	2	0	21	2	0	0	0	15	0	27	7	5
Diaz, Mario, Lynn	.201	106	314	16	63	76	8	1	1	22	3	7	6	1	16	0	42	1	1
Dowless, Michael, Waterbury	.178	30	45	3	8	13	2	0	1	7	1	7	0	0	7	0	20	0	0
Duglenski, Peter, Waterbury°	.257	17	35	2	9	10	1	0	0	4	0	0	0	1	6	1	10	0	1
Durrman, James, West Haven°	.241	49	116	6	28	31	3	0	0	6	2	2	0	0	18	1	6	2	1
Eddins, Glenn, Bristol	.183	108	345	31	63	93	12	0	6	43	7	5	3	4	28	0	68	0	0
Estepa, Ramon, Lynn	.228	44	158	16	36	47	6	1	1	8	1	0	0	0	16	1	31	3	3
Feliz, L. Adolfo, Waterbury	.189	92	185	17	35	43	6	1	0	13	0	5	2	3	14	2	37	1	3
Flammang, J. Christopher, Lynn°	.239	72	234	29	56	87	6	2	7	24	1	2	2	2	37	7	47	5	5
Foley, Rick, Holyoke	.667	30	3	2	2	3	1	0	0	1	0	0	0	0	1	0	0	0	0
Foote, Michael, Waterbury	.204	66	196	14	40	48	4	2	0	10	1	4	3	3	26	3	64	0	0
Fournier, Bruce, West Haven°	.246	112	313	33	77	128	19	1	10	39	2	1	1	4	52	5	35	9	8
Franco, Julio, Reading	.301	139	532	70	160	207	17	3	8	74	13	5	6	5	52	2	60	27	14
Frobel, Douglas, Buffalo°	.251	135	479	72	120	227	17	3	28	78	3	2	1	5	55	4	147	8	5
Fucci, Dominic, Glens Falls°	.242	57	161	26	39	63	4	1	6	25	4	0	2	2	30	2	44	1	3
Garrett, Bobby, West Haven	.230	117	330	46	76	94	11	2	1	25	6	21	1	0	34	1	43	24	9
Garrett, Lynn, West Haven	.258	107	329	41	85	113	11	4	3	39	3	5	7	1	35	2	48	15	9
Gause, Ernest, Waterbury°	.143	21	14	1	2	2	0	0	0	0	0	0	0	0	0	0	2	0	0
Gelfarb, Stephen, West Haven°	.303	75	267	46	81	119	14	0	8	45	5	2	4	5	18	3	44	12	6
Gentile, Gene, Bristol	.302	118	367	60	111	165	20	5	8	59	4	2	2	2	62	6	66	12	7
Gilbert, Dennis, Holyoke	.226	108	323	48	73	135	14	3	14	48	3	4	2	0	48	2	91	2	2
Gilbert, Mark, Waterbury†	.247	105	360	60	89	129	15	5	5	31	1	6	2	3	71	5	47	26	8
Gray, Lorenzo, Glens Falls	.271	58	218	47	59	84	9	2	4	26	3	4	1	3	33	1	21	4	1
Hamric, Russell, Reading	.307	129	524	80	161	204	20	4	5	66	10	9	8	5	34	1	67	20	16
Hargis, Gary, Buffalo	.239	30	109	13	26	30	4	0	0	5	0	0	2	2	10	1	2	1	1
Harrigan, David, Reading	.167	16	42	3	7	8	1	0	0	2	0	1	0	1	4	0	17	1	2
Harris, Frank, West Haven	.000	17	0	0	0	0	0	0	0	0	0	0	0	0	0	0	0	0	0
Harris, Tracy, Lynn	.500	28	2	1	1	1	0	0	0	0	0	0	0	0	0	0	1	0	0
Harvey, Steven, Reading	.253	33	83	11	21	31	1	0	3	9	0	2	1	0	4	1	22	1	1
Hayes, Ben, Waterbury	.000	30	9	0	0	0	0	0	0	0	0	1	0	0	1	0	4	0	0
Heimueller, Gorman, West Haven°	.000	28	1	0	0	0	0	0	0	0	0	0	0	0	0	0	1	0	0
Hill, Marc, Glens Falls	.429	2	7	1	3	3	0	0	0	3	0	0	0	0	2	0	0	0	0
Hobbs, Rodney, Lynn	.232	129	457	64	106	161	18	5	9	40	4	7	1	6	79	1	80	28	20
Holland, John, Buffalo	.250	98	324	51	81	157	19	0	19	53	5	3	3	6	27	3	66	1	3
Hudgens, David, West Haven°	.184	42	114	10	21	41	6	1	4	12	0	1	0	1	10	0	31	0	3
Hulett, Timothy, Glens Falls	.227	134	437	59	99	158	27	1	10	55	3	1	4	3	66	2	87	0	3
Ibarra, Miguel, Reading†	.266	132	433	73	115	169	28	4	6	65	8	3	6	1	84	9	64	2	5
Incaviglia, Tony, Buffalo	.272	130	437	70	119	203	28	1	18	64	10	4	4	1	80	3	117	6	8
Johnson, Randall, Glens Falls°	.255	115	400	80	102	214	14	1	32	99	16	1	4	5	75	12	82	1	0
Jones, Jeffery, Waterbury	.181	48	127	19	23	39	5	1	3	16	1	2	2	5	25	3	49	2	0
Jones, Kenneth, Waterbury	.191	31	47	5	9	9	0	0	0	1	0	4	0	3	0	11	0	0
Jurak, Edward, Bristol	.340	87	297	63	101	129	19	3	1	25	4	2	2	3	64	4	36	9	4
Keedy, C. Patrick, Holyoke	.245	107	367	45	90	126	14	2	6	34	5	4	1	5	26	3	85	16	8
King, Kevin, Lynn†	.188	31	96	8	18	28	2	1	2	19	2	1	1	0	7	1	42	2	0
Kittle, Ronald, Glens Falls	.326	109	389	97	127	270	17	3	40	103	10	0	1	7	60	7	107	0	1
Kraus, Jeffrey, Waterbury	.259	115	367	37	95	115	8	0	4	35	3	3	6	2	55	0	64	0	4
Krueger, William, West Haven°	.000	18	3	0	0	0	0	0	0	0	0	1	0	0	1	0	2	1	0
Lawless, Thomas, Waterbury	.291	136	522	77	152	216	20	10	8	50	7	6	1	1	67	1	69	60	16
Lesley, Bradley, Waterbury	.100	26	10	1	1	1	0	0	0	1	0	0	0	0	1	0	3	0	0
Lickert, John, Bristol	.270	102	371	44	100	136	15	3	5	57	6	4	3	7	32	3	29	2	5
Lombarski, Thomas, Reading°	.243	128	416	61	101	147	6	5	10	64	9	4	4	7	54	7	70	15	8
Macauley, J. Andrew, Buffalo†	.205	116	371	58	76	114	13	5	5	31	4	7	1	0	60	6	59	9	5
Merulla, Tony, Buffalo°	.254	116	342	50	87	154	17	1	16	46	5	1	2	5	58	4	58	2	4
Mesa, Ivan, Glens Falls	.240	126	499	75	120	154	18	2	4	29	2	3	4	6	55	2	31	9	6
Meyer, Scott, West Haven	.260	125	384	54	100	168	21	1	15	72	6	3	4	6	43	1	67	8	7
Miller, Darrell, Holyoke	.264	126	443	61	117	191	26	9	10	62	6	2	2	8	41	3	90	14	5
Miscik, Robert, Buffalo	.196	45	143	13	28	43	4	1	3	17	2	4	1	0	26	0	28	3	2
Moloney, William, Bristol°	.000	42	1	0	0	0	0	0	0	0	0	0	0	0	0	0	0	0	0
Morris, Donald, West Haven	.177	39	96	12	17	21	1	0	1	5	1	3	1	1	15	0	21	2	3
Morrison, Perry, Holyoke	.000	34	3	1	0	0	0	0	0	0	0	0	0	0	0	0	3	0	0
Nanni, Tito, Lynn°	.249	116	361	46	90	127	14	1	7	40	6	5	4	6	70	7	72	20	13
Nelson, James, Lynn	.272	90	246	33	67	98	8	1	7	32	4	2	2	3	36	1	29	1	4
Neuenschwander, Douglas, Wtby	.000	30	8	1	0	0	0	0	0	0	0	0	0	0	0	0	2	0	0
Nocciolo, Mark, Lynn	.265	99	317	47	84	121	16	3	5	40	5	0	3	5	47	0	55	3	1
O'Keeffe, Richard, Waterbury°	.167	5	6	0	1	1	0	0	0	0	0	0	1	0	0	0	1	0	0
Orensky, Herbert, Reading°	.296	79	250	45	74	108	21	5	1	38	4	3	2	1	52	2	47	4	3
Pasillas, J. Andrew, Glens Falls	.276	66	214	27	59	85	14	0	4	28	4	4	0	1	15	0	23	0	0
Pautt, Juan, Bristol	.255	96	341	45	87	118	20	1	3	39	7	1	5	4	45	1	61	5	0
Pearsey, Leslie, Holyoke	.282	130	478	64	135	219	29	2	17	82	13	1	8	8	46	8	91	6	4
Peltz, Peter, Glens Falls	.284	65	204	27	58	80	5	7	1	20	2	0	2	1	36	1	39	2	0
Perry, Ronald, Glens Falls	.256	46	164	19	42	62	5	0	5	21	2	2	0	2	15	0	18	4	0
Pettis, Gary, Holyoke†	.266	120	421	77	112	147	8	9	3	36	3	4	2	4	86	3	93	55	12
Phillips, K. Anthony, West Haven†	.247	131	461	79	114	172	25	3	9	64	8	3	7	10	67	3	69	40	13

Player and Club	Pct.	G.	AB.	R.	H.	TB.	2B.	3B.	HR.	RBI.	GW.	SH.	SF.	HP.	BB.	Int. BB.	SO.	SB.	CS.
Polidor, Gustavo, Holyoke	.248	130	479	46	119	148	17	3	2	47	4	6	2	3	31	0	62	5	4
Presley, James, Lynn	.257	64	210	32	54	87	7	1	8	36	4	1	4	6	24	1	52	4	4
Pyle, Scott, West Haven	.210	116	262	52	55	77	15	2	1	18	2	6	3	4	56	0	64	18	11
Quade, Michael, Buffalo	.219	63	215	28	47	53	6	0	0	21	0	6	0	1	32	0	40	9	1
Redus, Gary, Waterbury	.249	138	477	71	119	213	26	4	20	75	6	2	8	1	82	8	108	48	5
Rincones, Hector, Waterbury	.190	49	137	8	26	31	3	1	0	8	0	2	0	2	12	1	21	0	2
Rios, Carlos, Buffalo	.285	106	351	43	100	130	13	1	5	38	4	5	4	3	23	0	23	17	12
Rock, Robert, Buffalo	.000	18	1	0	0	0	0	0	0	0	0	0	0	0	0	0	0	0	0
Rodriguez, Eduardo, Holyoke	.234	85	282	39	66	76	8	1	0	16	2	2	4	1	15	0	54	11	4
Rodriguez, Jose, Buffalo	.277	67	235	36	65	131	11	8	13	34	4	0	1	1	27	0	68	12	8
Rois, Luis, Glens Falls	.291	131	498	73	145	246	27	4	22	89	9	2	6	4	14	2	74	12	9
Rojas, Luis, West Haven	.100	6	10	1	1	4	0	0	1	1	0	0	0	0	0	0	3	0	0
Rommel, Richard, Holyoke	.000	32	1	0	0	0	0	0	0	0	0	0	0	0	0	0	1	0	0
Salazar, Terrell, Buffalo	.265	66	200	29	53	81	9	2	5	22	1	0	2	1	17	2	23	4	3
Sanchez, Alejandro, Reading	.275	138	495	77	136	228	19	17	13	76	4	1	2	5	28	2	132	34	11
Sandberg, Charles, Bristol°	.198	47	106	16	21	27	6	0	0	14	2	0	2	1	43	3	36	0	0
Sarrett, Daniel, Waterbury	.000	4	10	0	0	0	0	0	0	0	0	0	0	0	2	0	0	0	0
Scherrer, William, Waterbury°	.118	51	17	0	2	2	0	0	0	1	0	3	0	0	4	0	4	0	0
Schoppee, David, Bristol	1.000	56	1	0	1	2	1	0	0	0	0	0	0	0	0	0	0	0	0
Seilheimer, Ricky, Glens Falls°	.259	80	263	32	68	99	10	0	7	25	3	5	0	1	25	1	44	0	3
Serna, Paul, Lynn	.255	13	51	7	13	19	4	1	0	3	1	0	0	0	5	0	4	0	1
Sheaffer, Danny, Bristol	.000	8	12	0	0	0	0	0	0	1	0	0	1	0	0	0	3	0	0
Sherow, Dennis, West Haven	.292	117	387	54	113	146	18	3	3	44	5	3	5	5	29	0	75	35	7
Smith, Ronald, Reading	.212	50	132	16	28	33	2	0	1	18	0	4	0	1	15	0	18	1	2
Soreca, Vincent, Reading	.178	13	45	4	8	13	2	0	1	2	1	0	0	0	1	0	21	0	0
Straker, Lester, Waterbury	.000	21	8	3	0	0	0	0	0	0	0	2	0	0	4	0	4	0	0
Sullivan, Michael, Waterbury	.167	9	6	0	1	1	0	0	0	0	0	.3	0	0	0	0	2	0	0
Torres, A. Raymundo, Glens Falls	.111	11	18	3	2	5	0	0	1	2	1	0	0	0	0	0	5	0	0
Town, Randall, Waterbury	.151	32	53	7	8	10	2	0	0	3	1	6	1	0	3	0	17	0	0
Tyler, David, Bristol	1.000	21	1	1	1	1	0	0	0	0	1	0	0	0	0	0	0	0	0
Valle, David, Lynn	.258	93	318	38	82	131	16	0	11	54	2	0	2	8	36	2	48	3	5
Vargas, Hediberto, Buffalo	.274	125	419	65	115	219	23	3	25	84	6	2	4	3	71	4	109	7	3
Viltz, Escamillo, Waterbury†	.262	39	122	13	32	44	6	3	0	13	1	5	1	5	6	1	14	2	0
Waag, William, Buffalo	.256	96	332	46	85	118	13	1	6	29	1	9	2	1	40	0	50	5	2
Walker, Anthony Bruce, Waterbury	.091	17	22	2	2	2	0	0	0	0	0	0	0	1	5	0	3	1	0
Walker, Gregory, Glens Falls°	.321	135	508	117	163	266	33	2	22	86	9	2	3	9	72	9	85	1	2
Walker, Tony Dwayne, Waterbury	.218	76	188	32	41	59	4	1	4	20	3	1	1	9	44	0	44	8	2
Washington, Keith, Reading†	.260	61	146	26	38	39	1	0	0	14	2	2	2	0	29	1	26	10	8
Watkins, James, Bristol°	.236	115	331	41	78	97	12	2	1	30	5	7	1	0	39	4	69	13	6
Weirum, Robert, West Haven	.261	39	88	5	23	30	5	1	0	8	2	0	0	1	8	0	13	2	0
White, Michael, Lynn	.260	118	407	53	106	161	17	4	10	55	7	3	1	4	47	5	79	13	4
Whittemore, Reginald, Bristol	.227	124	375	52	85	137	12	2	12	58	4	4	2	5	64	4	124	12	2
Wilson, James, Bristol	.244	66	217	26	53	69	10	0	2	21	5	3	5	2	19	0	23	1	4
Woodard, Michael, West Haven°	.225	133	427	59	96	114	9	3	1	25	4	10	3	2	43	1	34	41	23
Young, Kenneth, Bristol†	.225	108	346	61	78	127	19	6	6	47	6	6	3	3	57	4	73	18	11

The following pitchers had no plate appearances primarily through use of designated hitters, listed alphabetically by club, games in parentheses:

BRISTOL—Birrell, Robert (1); Burtt, Dennis (27); Denman, Brian (25); Fredlund, Jay (18); Howard, Michael (13); Johnson, Clinton (32); Kane, Kevin (13); King, Jerome (25); Shields, Stephen (29).

BUFFALO—Barez, Angel (23); Britt, Douglas (34); Calderon, Jose (49); Carvajal, Crucito (24); Farr, Steven (29); Guante, Cecilio (10); Hamner, Peter (12); Ricelli, Frank (2); Taylor, John (17); Thibodeaux, Keith (11); Tunnel, Byron (12); Vasquez, Rafail (44); Warthen, Daniel (10); Wiltbank, Benjamin (14); Winn, James (12); Zaske, Lloyd (4).

GLENS FALLS—Barnicle, Theodore (1); Bradley, Leonard (47); Desjarlais, Keith (14); Edwards, Larry (27); Estrada, Luis (6); Evans, Randy (3); Fallon, Robert (26); Geiger, Burwell (12); Johnson, Charles (27); Maitland, Michael (20); Mullen, Thomas (6); Siwy, James (16); Vasquez, Dennis (35); Wieters, Richard (31); Withrow, Michael (2).

HOLYOKE—Brown, Curtis (32); Dugger, Lawrence (20); Duran, David (18); Mooneyham, William (25); Rasmussen, Dennis (24); Yandle, John (28).

LYNN—Best, Karl (13); Black, Harry (22); Cahill, Mark (5); Floyd, Robert (1); Georger, Joseph (34); Harrison, Robert (20); Krueger, Steven (41); Moore, Michael (13); Murray, Jed (43); Randolph, Robert (5); Simond, Robert (5); Smith, David (50); Stottlemyre, Jeffrey (22); Welborn, Sammye (6); Young, Matthew (14).

READING—Alicea, Miguel (38); Burroughs, Darren (27); Bystrom, Martin (2); Cabassa, Carlos (43); Carman, Donald (28); Cepeda, Orlando (4); Culver, George (2); Faulk, Kelly (48); Goff, Wallace (24); Hart, Thomas (24); Prior, Daniel (7); Reed, Jerry (56); Smith, Leroy (27); Wright, James (20).

WEST HAVEN—Abeyta, Manny (4); Abraham, Brian (34); Atherton, Keith (28); Bradley, Bert (30); Buice, DeWayne (58); Codiroli, Christopher (21); Constock, Keith (35); Conroy, Timothy (14); Cort, Barry (3); Hensley, Charles (5); Holloway, Rick (1); Krajewski, Christopher (12); Mantsch, Ronald (16); Souza, Mark (31); Tronerud, Ricky (33).

GRAND SLAM HOME RUNS—Meyer, 4; Johnson, R., 3; Kittle, 2; Barnes, Clark, Colbert, Flammang, Hulett, Incaviglia, Lawless, Nanni, Pasillas, Pearsey, Valle, Walker, White, 1 each.

AWARDED FIRST BASE ON INTERFERENCE—Salazar 3 (Bisceglia 2, Christmas); Barnes (Ibarra); Durrmann (Colbert); Flammang (Christmas); Fournier (Pasillas); Rojas (Colbert); Sanchez (Miller).

CLUB FIELDING

Club	Pct.	G.	PO.	A.	E.	DP.	PB.
Reading	.973	139	3528	1536	139	129	25
Waterbury	.972	139	3488	1446	144	118	20
Glens Falls	.968	135	3379	1621	165	157	5
Lynn	.968	138	3474	1598	167	110	28
Holyoke	.966	138	3476	1516	177	139	13
Bristol	.964	137	3492	1449	184	99	15
West Haven	.964	139	3458	1540	187	128	15
Buffalo	.959	137	3475	1390	210	116	18

Triple Plays—Bristol, West Haven.

INDIVIDUAL FIELDING

FIRST BASEMEN

°Throws lefthanded.

Player and Club	Pct.	G.	PO.	A.	E.	DP.	Player and Club	Pct.	G.	PO.	A.	E.	DP.
Adams, Holyoke	1.000	4	32	4	0	5	Bienek, Glens Falls°	1.000	1	3	0	0	0
Aldrich, Waterbury	.996	77	655	18	3	73	Borucki, Reading	.993	17	127	8	1	9
Barnes, Waterbury	1.000	3	7	0	0	0	Christmas, Waterbury	1.000	4	11	1	0	0

FIRST BASEMEN—Continued

Player and Club	Pct.	G.	PO.	A.	E.	DP.
Clark, Holyoke°	.800	1	4	0	1	2
Colbert, Bristol	1.000	10	69	4	0	6
Culbert, West Haven	.991	28	205	17	2	19
Eddins, Bristol	1.000	1	2	0	0	0
Estepa, Lynn	.978	4	42	2	1	1
Flammang, Lynn°	.987	18	146	7	2	12
Fournier, West Haven	.984	44	344	25	6	31
Frobel, Buffalo	.982	64	540	55	11	39
Fucci, Glens Falls°	1.000	7	58	8	0	13
Gelfarb, West Haven°	.984	75	668	51	12	60
Keedy, Holyoke	1.000	1	8	0	0	1
Krueger, West Haven°	1.000	2	3	0	0	0
LOMBARSKI, Reading	.997	125	1099	84	4	114
Meyer, West Haven	1.000	1	6	0	0	0
Miller, Holyoke	.991	14	108	5	1	11
Morrison, Holyoke	1.000	2	6	1	0	0
Nelson, Lynn	.981	12	98	5	2	8
Nocciolo, Holyoke	.984	5	27	0	1	4
Pearsey, Holyoke	.994	118	1105	80	7	97
Redus, Waterbury	.982	68	522	29	10	36
Sandberg, Bristol°	.991	32	193	18	2	19
Soreca, Reading	1.000	1	1	0	0	0
Valle, Lynn	1.000	2	12	5	0	2
Vargas, Buffalo	.997	75	648	42	2	59
Walker, Glens Falls	.992	129	1215	77	11	134
Weirum, West Haven	1.000	2	2	0	0	0
White, Lynn	.980	108	1021	74	22	81
Whittemore, Bristol	.989	107	834	40	10	54
Young, Bristol	1.000	12	98	6	0	5

Triple Play—Whittemore.

SECOND BASEMEN

Player and Club	Pct.	G.	PO.	A.	E.	DP.
Adams, Holyoke	.984	103	175	301	8	71
Aponte, Lynn	1.000	1	5	1	0	0
Barnes, Waterbury	1.000	1	0	2	0	0
Bryant, Bristol	.963	125	270	361	24	62
Colbert, Bristol	.938	3	7	8	1	1
Crist, Lynn	.948	12	23	32	3	8
CRONE, Lynn	.989	114	232	317	6	60
Estepa, Lynn	1.000	1	1	0	0	0
Feliz, Waterbury	.912	9	13	18	3	4
Hamric, Reading	.978	129	294	380	15	89
Hargis, Buffalo	.968	21	49	41	3	12
Hulett, Glens Falls	.979	132	332	415	16	112
Jurak, Bristol	1.000	3	3	4	0	1
Keedy, Holyoke	.667	1	1	1	1	1
Lawless, Waterbury	.979	134	323	379	15	82
Macauley, Buffalo	.918	29	64	71	12	14
Pasillas, Glens Falls	1.000	1	2	5	0	1
Peltz, Glens Falls	.867	2	6	7	2	2
Pyle, West Haven	.981	28	48	55	2	16
Quade, Buffalo	1.000	4	7	3	0	1
Rodriguez, Holyoke	.951	42	78	97	9	19
Serna, Lynn	1.000	13	18	34	0	4
Scheaffer, Bristol	1.000	1	1	2	0	1
Smith, Reading	.977	11	23	20	1	4
Waag, Buffalo	.978	93	171	263	10	51
Wilson, Bristol	1.000	11	15	23	0	3
Woodard, West Haven	.967	129	249	299	19	77

Triple Plays—Bryant, Woodard.

THIRD BASEMEN

Player and Club	Pct.	G.	PO.	A.	E.	DP.
Aldrich, Waterbury	1.000	19	11	25	0	1
Aponte, Lynn	.916	57	37	116	14	7
Barnes, Waterbury	.954	93	104	183	14	18
BORUCKI, Reading	.968	120	88	242	11	20
Colbert, Bristol	1.000	1	0	1	0	0
Crist, Lynn	.954	17	4	37	2	1
Crone, Lynn	.750	2	0	3	1	0
Eddins, Bristol	.904	103	66	169	25	13
Feliz, Waterbury	.800	11	5	11	4	1
Fournier, West Haven	.936	66	36	154	13	14
Gray, Glens Falls	.927	57	37	116	12	17
Hulett, Glens Falls	1.000	2	1	7	0	1
Incaviglia, Buffalo	.904	71	61	117	19	13
Jurak, Bristol	.884	30	26	50	10	6
Keedy, Holyoke	.930	103	54	238	22	25
Macauley, Buffalo	.868	22	12	34	7	4
Miscik, Buffalo	.870	45	29	85	17	9
Nelson, Lynn	.778	4	2	5	2	0
Pearsey, Holyoke	1.000	6	5	8	0	0
Peltz, Glens Falls	.926	35	23	90	9	7
Perry, Glens Falls	.900	43	25	92	13	9
Presley, Lynn	.935	64	49	110	11	6
Pyle, West Haven	.897	79	41	150	22	14
Quade, Buffalo	1.000	1	1	3	0	1
Rodriguez, Holyoke	.921	32	13	69	7	7
Smith, Reading	.900	22	16	38	6	5
Viltz, Waterbury	.908	21	23	36	6	6
Weirum, West Haven	.836	32	14	47	12	8
Whittemore, Bristol	.667	1	0	2	1	0
Wilson, Bristol	.950	12	14	24	2	5

Triple Play—Eddins.

SHORTSTOPS

Player and Club	Pct.	G.	PO.	A.	E.	DP.
Adams, Holyoke	.947	10	13	23	2	4
Bustabad, Bristol	.947	79	110	229	19	31
Crist, Lynn	.961	42	59	112	7	26
DIAZ, Lynn	.964	105	163	318	18	60
Eddins, Bristol	1.000	1	2	3	0	0
Feliz, Waterbury	.921	34	39	77	10	11
Foote, Waterbury	.931	62	89	168	19	42
Franco, Reading	.958	139	246	437	30	89
Gray, Glens Falls	1.000	1	1	4	0	1
Jurak, Bristol	.922	56	85	140	19	22
Macauley, Buffalo	.938	49	71	141	14	23
Mesa, Glens Falls	.955	126	230	426	31	103
Peltz, Glens Falls	.946	11	15	38	3	6
Perry, Glens Falls	1.000	1	0	2	0	1
Phillips, West Haven	.947	130	200	391	33	67
Polidor, Holyoke	.947	129	192	375	32	71
Pyle, West Haven	.886	14	14	25	5	4
Quade, Buffalo	.833	1	5	0	1	0
Rincones, Waterbury	.937	43	72	107	12	14
Rios, Buffalo	.928	94	164	236	31	47
Smith, Reading	1.000	4	0	2	0	0
Viltz, Waterbury	.950	14	35	41	4	12
Wilson, Bristol	1.000	3	6	14	0	2

Triple Play—Pyle.

OUTFIELDERS

Player and Club	Pct.	G.	PO.	A.	E.	DP.
Adams, Holyoke	.875	4	2	5	1	2
Aldrich, Waterbury	1.000	29	26	1	0	0
Barnes, Waterbury	.800	5	4	0	1	0
Bennett, West Haven°	.949	69	89	4	5	1
Bienek, Glens Falls°	.940	116	166	7	11	0
Blanco, Buffalo	1.000	7	10	2	0	0
Brooks, Bristol	1.000	12	21	0	0	0
Brown, Holyoke	.955	134	182	9	9	3
Bruno, Reading°	.974	136	328	13	9	3
Chambers, Lynn°	.953	124	178	5	9	0
Clark, Holyoke	.969	38	59	3	2	0
Colbert, Bristol	1.000	47	69	2	0	1
Culmer, Reading	.915	93	127	12	13	1
Delarosa, Buffalo°	.950	64	91	4	5	0
Duglenski, Waterbury°	1.000	14	14	1	0	0
Estepa, Lynn	.972	35	63	7	2	1
Flammang, Lynn°	.936	35	57	1	4	0
Frobel, Buffalo	.915	67	84	2	8	1
Fucci, Glens Falls°	.980	29	47	2	1	0
Garrett, West Haven	.988	108	164	5	2	1
Garrett, West Haven	.971	104	128	7	4	1
Gentile, Bristol°	.943	117	172	9	11	1
Gilbert, Holyoke	.973	103	203	11	6	3
Gilbert, Waterbury	.973	101	201	16	6	2
Hargis, Buffalo	.929	9	12	1	1	1
Harvey, Reading	.936	24	27	2	2	0

OUTFIELDERS —Continued

Player and Club	Pct.	G.	PO.	A.	E.	DP.
Hobbs, Lynn	.949	88	143	5	8	0
Hudgens, West Haven°	.944	21	34	0	2	0
Incaviglia, Buffalo	.925	60	70	4	6	0
Johnson, Glens Falls°	.974	109	179	5	5	0
Jones, Waterbury	.963	45	75	3	3	0
King, Lynn	.886	22	29	2	4	0
Kittle, Glens Falls	.903	20	28	0	3	0
KRAUS, Waterbury	.995	109	175	6	1	1
Lickert, Bristol	1.000	4	4	0	0	0
Macauley, Buffalo	.833	11	14	1	3	0
Merulla, Buffalo	.933	13	13	1	1	0
Miller, Holyoke	.958	50	87	5	4	1
Morris, West Haven	.946	38	51	2	3	0
Nanni, Waterbury°	.959	114	203	6	9	1
Pautt, Bristol	.936	95	155	5	11	0
Peltz, Glens Falls	1.000	1	0	1	0	0
Pettis, Holyoke	.984	100	237	5	4	3
Quade, Buffalo	.987	60	145	4	2	1
Redus, Waterbury	.974	76	145	5	4	1
Rios, Buffalo	1.000	3	3	0	0	0
Rodriguez, Buffalo	.980	66	140	5	3	0
Rois, Glens Falls	.952	131	244	15	13	4
Salazar, Buffalo	.961	47	68	5	3	2
Sanchez, Reading	.939	140	216	13	15	5
Sheaffer, Bristol	1.000	2	1	0	0	0
Sherow, West Haven	.983	117	219	12	4	3
Torres, Glens Falls	1.000	11	8	0	0	0
Vargas, Buffalo	.933	33	40	2	3	1
A. Walker, Waterbury	.900	9	9	0	1	0
T. Walker, Waterbury	1.000	71	132	7	0	0
Washington, Reading	1.000	58	91	3	0	1
Watkins, Bristol	.987	113	208	23	3	3
Whittemore, Bristol	.974	28	34	3	1	0
Wilson, Bristol	.987	45	71	5	1	3

CATCHERS

Player and Club	Pct.	G.	PO.	A.	E.	DP.	PB.
Baez, Lynn	.994	21	141	14	1	5	3
Bisceglia, Waterbury	.958	18	60	8	3	1	1
Boddy, Waterbury	.979	19	79	14	2	0	4
Christmas, Waterbury	.982	118	594	95	13	9	15
Cias, West Haven	.990	62	342	36	4	8	5
Cliburn, Buffalo	.983	41	316	23	6	3	4
Colbert, Bristol	.971	45	268	33	9	2	3
Dempsey, West Haven	.964	31	199	13	8	1	4
Durrman, West Haven	.988	37	214	29	3	3	5
Harrigan, Reading	1.000	10	56	5	0	1	3
Harrison, Lynn	1.000	1	2	0	0	0	0
Hill, Glens Falls	1.000	1	6	1	0	0	0
Holland, Buffalo	.977	82	452	66	12	12	7
Ibarra, Reading	.983	93	511	79	10	5	14
Lickert, Bristol	.980	95	600	83	14	10	12
Merulla, Buffalo	.976	21	115	9	3	3	7
Meyer, West Haven	.992	32	115	8	1	1	1
Miller, Holyoke	.949	52	312	40	19	3	7
Nelson, Lynn	.993	43	233	33	2	2	10
Nocciolo, Holyoke	.968	90	520	53	19	13	6
Orensky, Reading	.971	33	188	13	6	1	8
Pasillas, Glens Falls	.992	65	339	40	3	2	1
Sarrett, Waterbury	.917	2	9	2	1	1	0
Seilheimer, Glens Falls	.964	73	334	36	14	6	4
Sheaffer, Bristol	1.000	3	15	1	0	1	0
Soreca, Reading	1.000	8	35	7	0	0	0
VALLE, Lynn	.988	81	445	56	6	5	15

PITCHERS

Player and Club	Pct.	G.	PO.	A.	E.	DP.
Abraham, West Haven°	.917	34	3	8	1	0
Alicea, Reading	.938	38	5	10	1	0
Arline, Waterbury°	1.000	20	5	3	0	0
Atherton, West Haven	.922	27	16	31	4	5
Barez, Buffalo	.800	23	4	16	5	2
Best, Lynn	.800	13	5	11	4	1
Black, Lynn°	.957	22	1	21	1	1
Bradley, West Haven	1.000	30	2	11	0	2
Bradley, Glens Falls	1.000	47	5	21	0	1
Britt, Buffalo	.875	34	1	6	1	0
Brown, Holyoke	.958	32	7	16	1	2
Buckle, Waterbury	.958	29	4	19	1	1
Buice, West Haven	.926	58	12	13	2	0
Burroughs, Reading°	.895	27	3	14	2	0
Burtt, Bristol	.860	27	12	31	7	0
Cabassa, Reading°	.941	43	4	12	1	0
Cahill, Lynn	.800	5	1	3	1	0
Calderon, Buffalo	.800	49	5	7	3	1
Carlucci, Waterbury	1.000	35	5	24	0	2
Carman, Reading°	.943	28	4	29	2	1
Carvajal, Buffalo	.500	24	1	2	3	1
Cato, Waterbury	1.000	8	5	6	0	0
Cepeda, Reading	1.000	4	1	0	0	0
Christmas, Waterbury	1.000	1	3	0	0	0
Cliburn, Buffalo	1.000	28	9	23	0	0
Codiroli, West Haven	1.000	21	4	9	0	0
Comstock, West Haven	.962	35	2	23	1	0
Conner, Holyoke	.886	26	7	24	4	1
Conroy, West Haven°	.529	14	2	7	8	0
Cort, West Haven	.500	3	1	1	2	0
De Leon, Buffalo	.903	25	9	19	3	0
Denman, Bristol	.946	25	12	23	2	2
Desjarlais, Glens Falls	.962	14	11	14	1	2
Dowless, Waterbury	.864	28	2	17	3	1
Dugger, Holyoke	.900	20	2	7	1	0
Duran, Holyoke	1.000	18	5	8	0	3
Edwards, Glens Falls°	.957	27	15	29	2	4
Estrada, Glens Falls	.875	6	1	6	1	2
Evans, Glens Falls	.667	3	0	4	2	0
Fallon, Glens Falls	.862	26	3	22	4	2
Farr, Buffalo	.960	29	5	19	1	1
Faulk, Reading	.923	48	4	20	2	2
Floyd, Lynn	1.000	1	1	0	0	0
Foley, Holyoke	.981	29	12	40	1	2
Fredlund, Bristol	.889	18	2	14	2	0
Gause, Waterbury	.667	21	1	1	1	0
Geiger, Glens Falls	1.000	12	1	7	0	0
Georger, Lynn	.961	33	16	58	3	6
Gilbert, Waterbury	1.000	2	0	1	0	0
Goff, Reading°	.917	24	2	9	1	1
Guante, Buffalo	1.000	10	0	2	0	0
Hamner, Buffalo	.571	12	2	2	3	0
Harris, West Haven	1.000	17	0	6	0	0
Harris, Lynn	.848	28	9	41	9	2
Harrison, Lynn	1.000	19	2	14	0	1
Hart, Reading	.923	24	11	25	3	5
Hayes, Waterbury	1.000	30	1	3	0	0
Heimueller, West Haven°	.976	28	6	34	1	0
Hensley, West Haven°	1.000	5	1	6	0	0
Howard, Bristol	.864	13	5	14	3	0
Johnson, Glens Falls	.961	27	11	38	2	3
Johnson, Bristol	.957	32	8	14	1	0
Jones, Waterbury	.950	24	11	27	2	4
Kane, Bristol	1.000	13	2	9	0	0
King, Bristol	.946	25	11	24	2	1
Krajewski, West Haven	.800	12	4	0	1	0
Krueger, Lynn	1.000	41	2	9	0	1
Krueger, West Haven°	1.000	11	1	12	0	1
Lesley, Waterbury	1.000	26	1	11	0	1
Maitland, Glens Falls°	1.000	20	7	20	0	2
Mantsch, West Haven	1.000	16	2	9	0	1
Moloney, Bristol°	1.000	42	4	22	0	0
Mooneyham, Holyoke	.773	25	5	12	5	2
Moore, Lynn	.952	13	2	18	1	0
Morrison, Holyoke	.833	32	5	5	2	0
Mullen, Glens Falls	1.000	6	3	4	0	0
Murray, Lynn	.914	43	5	27	3	2
Neuenschwander, Waterbury	1.000	29	2	10	0	1
O'Keeffe, Waterbury°	1.000	4	3	7	0	0
Prior, Reading	1.000	7	0	5	0	0
Randolph, Lynn	1.000	5	1	6	0	0
Rasmussen, Holyoke°	.911	24	3	38	4	1
Reed, Reading	.966	56	3	25	1	1
Rock, Buffalo	1.000	18	7	5	0	1
Rommel, Holyoke	.900	32	3	6	1	2
Scherrer, Waterbury°	.889	50	2	14	2	1
Schoppee, Bristol	.944	56	12	22	2	1
Shields, Bristol	.818	29	4	5	2	0
Simond, Lynn°	.667	5	1	1	1	0
Siwy, Glens Falls	.944	16	10	24	2	3
Smith, Lynn	.913	50	4	17	2	2
Smith, Reading	.938	27	13	17	2	2
Souza, West Haven°	.800	31	1	7	2	0
Stottlemyre, Lynn	.959	22	11	36	2	3
Straker, Waterbury	1.000	19	1	6	0	0
Sullivan, Waterbury	1.000	8	0	2	0	0
Taylor, Buffalo	1.000	17	3	9	0	1
Thibodeaux, Buffalo	1.000	11	1	3	0	0
TOWN, Waterbury	1.000	28	10	42	0	2
Tronerud, West Haven	.939	33	15	31	3	4
Tunnel, Buffalo	.955	12	6	15	1	0
Tyler, Bristol	1.000	17	1	9	0	1
Vasquez, Glens Falls	.958	35	5	18	1	2
Vasquez, Buffalo	.897	41	13	22	4	1

PITCHERS —Continued

Player and Club	Pct.	G.	PO.	A.	E.	DP.	Player and Club	Pct.	G.	PO.	A.	E.	DP.
Warthen, Buffalo°	.714	10	2	3	2	0	Withrow, Glens Falls	1.000	2	0	1	0	0
Welborn, Lynn	.750	6	2	4	2	0	Wright, Reading	.944	20	5	12	1	0
Wieters, Glens Falls	.900	31	8	19	3	2	Yandle, Holyoke°	.912	28	4	27	3	0
Wiltbank, Buffalo	1.000	13	9	5	0	2	Young, Lynn°	.938	14	5	25	2	3
Winn, Buffalo	.929	12	3	10	1	1	Zaske, Buffalo	1.000	4	0	2	0	0

The following players do not have any recorded accepted chances at the positions indicated; therefore, are not listed in the fielding averages for those particular positions: Barnicle, p; Birrell, p; Bystrom, p; Cias, of; Crone, ss, of; Culver, p; Fournier, p; Holloway, p; Ibarra, 3b; K. Jones, of; Lickert, 1b; Macauley, p; Merulla, p; Meyer, 3b; Nelson, of; Presley, 2b; Rojas, of; Ricelli, p; Sandberg, p; D. Smith, of; Tronerud, of; Watkins; p; Weirum, of; Wiltbank, of; Young, of.

CLUB PITCHING

Club	ERA.	G.	CG.	ShO.	Sv.	IP.	H.	R.	ER.	HR.	HB.	BB.	Int. BB.	SO.	WP.	Bk.
Bristol	3.14	137	38	16	25	1164	1018	504	406	66	41	530	53	840	62	7
Lynn	3.55	138	34	12	26	1158	1128	562	457	71	37	487	32	786	62	10
West Haven	3.78	139	16	10	33	1152⅔	1113	603	484	112	40	560	38	830	77	14
Holyoke	3.85	138	44	11	20	1158⅔	1089	611	496	92	30	574	30	795	76	12
Reading	4.07	139	28	13	36	1176	1113	617	532	108	47	588	34	752	90	8
Glens Falls	4.17	138	28	5	38	1126⅓	1156	641	522	90	39	514	22	629	44	9
Buffalo	4.56	137	9	5	25	1158⅓	1142	709	587	119	54	689	35	834	66	17
Waterbury	4.61	139	15	5	20	1162⅔	1146	690	595	114	39	593	55	703	64	10

PITCHERS' RECORDS

(Leading Qualifiers for Earned-Run Average Leadership — 112 or More Innings)

° Throws lefthanded.

Pitcher—Club	W.	L.	Pct.	ERA.	G.	GS.	CG.	GF.	ShO.	Sv.	IP.	H.	R.	ER.	HR.	HB.	BB.	Int. BB.	SO.	WP.
Denman, Bristol	15	3	.833	2.44	25	24	13	0	2	0	188	172	65	51	12	4	51	5	109	5
King, Bristol	12	10	.545	2.73	25	24	9	1	3	0	175	126	69	53	9	11	87	2	168	6
Burtt, Bristol	10	8	.556	2.81	27	27	6	0	3	0	170	134	77	53	9	9	80	2	108	9
Georger, Lynn	11	8	.579	2.95	33	19	4	3	0	0	165	144	67	54	10	4	80	2	116	9
DeLeon, Buffalo	12	6	.667	3.11	25	25	2	0	0	0	159	136	72	55	14	3	94	0	158	7
Burroughs, Reading°	9	6	.600	3.38	27	24	8	0	5	0	152	142	69	57	13	7	66	1	100	10
Yandle, Holyoke°	5	8	.385	3.44	28	17	8	7	2	2	136	131	63	52	11	3	42	0	70	3
Harris, Lynn	15	9	.625	3.48	28	25	8	1	1	0	168	162	92	65	8	5	87	1	90	6
Murray, Lynn	3	6	.333	3.50	43	8	0	18	0	8	127	123	54	49	11	4	38	5	85	6
Hart, Reading	9	10	.474	3.52	24	24	4	0	1	0	151	144	69	59	12	8	66	2	108	11

Departmental Leaders: G—Buice, 58; GS—Carman, 28; CG—Denman, 13; ShO—Burroughs, 5; W—Edwards, Harris, Foley, Denman, 15; L—Shields, 14; Sv—Schoppee, 22; Pct.—Moloney, .909; IP—Denman, 188; H—Foley, 184; R—Fallon, 112; ER—Dowless, 88; HR—Conner, 20; BB—Mooneyham, 131; IBB—Schoppee, Shields, 10; SO—King, 168; WP—Rasmussen, 18.

(All Pitchers—Listed Alphabetically)

Pitcher—Club	W.	L.	Pct.	ERA.	G.	GS.	CG.	GF.	ShO.	Sv.	IP.	H.	R.	ER.	HR.	HB.	BB.	Int. BB.	SO.	WP.
Abeyta, West Haven	0	1	.000	7.31	4	4	1	0	0	0	16	19	13	13	4	1	8	0	4	0
Abraham, West Haven°	6	2	.750	1.15	34	3	0	25	0	14	56	33	9	7	0	4	19	0	48	2
Alicea, Reading	3	3	.500	3.71	38	0	0	12	0	2	85	95	45	35	11	0	35	6	49	6
Arline, Waterbury°	1	3	.250	5.14	20	1	0	9	0	1	42	36	28	24	7	3	29	4	30	2
Atherton, West Haven	11	13	.458	3.60	27	27	4	0	0	0	175	174	83	70	13	6	64	2	116	7
Barez, Buffalo	4	8	.333	6.08	23	23	2	0	1	0	114	108	82	77	17	12	92	0	91	7
Barnicle, Glens Falls°	0	0	.000	12.00	1	1	0	0	0	0	3	5	4	4	2	0	1	0	2	0
Best, Lynn	4	4	.500	3.80	13	13	1	0	1	0	71	73	37	30	7	1	31	1	50	2
Birrell, Bristol°	0	0	.000	4.50	1	1	0	0	0	0	2	2	1	1	0	0	1	0	2	2
Black, Lynn°	2	6	.250	3.00	22	11	2	5	1	2	87	78	38	29	12	1	23	3	86	3
Bradley, West Haven	4	5	.444	5.83	30	3	0	4	0	0	54	61	41	35	8	3	27	4	38	3
Bradley, Glens Falls	10	3	.769	2.80	47	0	0	42	0	16	91	86	30	28	2	3	34	6	56	4
Britt, Buffalo°	1	5	.167	4.17	34	0	0	20	0	1	41	42	29	19	7	7	29	3	22	2
C. Brown, Holyoke	5	3	.625	1.48	32	0	0	31	0	8	67	55	15	11	5	0	19	6	32	3
Buckle, Waterbury	3	9	.250	6.32	29	15	1	7	0	0	104	123	82	73	12	5	63	5	53	10
Buice, West Haven	8	3	.727	2.09	58	1	0	42	0	15	82	75	24	19	6	2	41	9	88	7
Burroughs, Reading°	9	6	.600	3.38	27	24	8	0	5	0	152	142	69	57	13	7	66	1	100	10
Burtt, Bristol	10	8	.556	2.81	27	27	6	0	3	0	170	134	77	53	9	9	80	2	108	9
Bystrom, Reading	0	0	.000	4.50	2	2	0	0	0	0	4	5	2	2	0	1	1	0	2	1
Cabassa, Reading°	4	2	.667	3.98	43	0	0	20	0	7	61	58	30	27	7	4	43	8	36	3
Cahill, Lynn	0	2	.000	9.00	5	5	0	0	0	0	16	27	18	16	0	1	15	0	7	1
Calderon, Buffalo°	4	5	.444	4.08	49	2	0	25	0	7	86	83	52	39	11	5	65	4	69	7
Carlucci, Waterbury	5	6	.455	3.90	35	15	1	6	0	2	127	120	63	55	11	4	49	4	74	4
Carman, Reading°	12	13	.480	4.04	28	28	9	0	4	0	176	167	93	79	15	6	75	1	105	11
Carvajal, Buffalo	0	3	.000	3.79	24	0	0	14	0	1	38	37	24	16	1	1	20	2	17	1
Cato, Waterbury	2	3	.400	5.29	8	6	0	1	0	0	34	34	22	20	4	0	18	1	25	4
Cepeda, Reading	0	1	.000	6.92	4	0	0	1	0	0	13	16	13	10	4	3	4	1	6	1
Christmas, Waterbury	0	0	.000	6.00	1	0	0	1	0	0	3	3	2	2	1	0	2	0	1	0
Stew. Cliburn, Buffalo	5	8	.385	4.34	28	9	2	13	0	3	85	77	45	41	10	4	35	7	53	2
Codiroli, Holyoke	3	2	.600	2.70	21	5	2	4	0	0	50	35	25	15	4	2	25	2	47	3
Comstock, West Haven	8	7	.533	4.10	35	22	1	2	0	0	145	123	76	66	18	1	80	4	133	13
Conner, Holyoke°	11	13	.458	3.69	26	26	10	0	2	0	183	169	90	75	20	4	62	4	91	9
Conroy, West Haven°	2	6	.250	6.00	14	13	0	0	0	0	57	59	50	38	4	4	43	2	51	10
Cort, West Haven	0	0	.000	4.50	3	1	0	1	0	0	6	10	4	3	0	0	2	0	2	0
Culver, Reading	0	1	.000	13.50	2	0	0	2	0	0	2	3	4	3	1	0	3	0	1	0
DeLeon, Buffalo	12	6	.667	3.11	25	25	2	0	0	0	159	136	72	55	14	3	94	0	158	7
Denman, Bristol	15	3	.833	2.44	25	24	13	0	2	0	188	172	65	51	12	4	51	5	109	5
Desjarlais, Glens Falls	8	3	.727	3.42	14	13	4	0	0	0	92	78	39	35	6	2	52	2	52	5
Dowless, Waterbury	6	13	.316	5.28	28	27	4	1	1	1	150	161	96	88	16	4	68	2	98	3
Dugger, Holyoke	5	3	.625	5.04	20	9	1	7	0	0	75	62	51	42	8	3	63	2	68	8
Duran, Holyoke°	5	6	.455	3.35	18	9	3	5	0	1	94	92	42	35	7	1	31	4	33	4
Edwards, Glens Falls°	15	7	.682	4.16	27	25	5	2	0	0	158	171	86	73	17	5	70	0	72	4
Estrada, Glens Falls	2	3	.400	6.19	6	6	1	0	1	0	32	38	24	22	2	0	19	0	10	5
Evans, Glens Falls	2	0	1.000	3.00	3	3	0	0	0	0	18	18	10	6	2	2	9	0	13	0
Fallon, Glens Falls°	11	9	.550	5.40	26	26	4	0	0	0	135	155	112	81	9	7	78	2	81	10

OFFICIAL BASEBALL GUIDE

Pitcher—Club	W.	L.	Pct.	ERA.	G.	GS.	CG.	GF.	ShO.	Sv.	IP.	H.	R.	ER.	HR.	HB.	BB.	Int. BB.	SO.	WP.
Farr, Buffalo	8	3	.727	3.74	29	12	0	8	0	3	106	102	50	44	8	1	48	3	82	3
Faulk, Reading	10	4	.714	3.84	48	0	0	31	0	10	82	65	40	35	7	1	34	4	48	6
Floyd, Lynn	0	0	.000	2.25	1	0	0	1	0	0	4	1	1	1	0	0	1	0	2	0
Foley, Holyoke	15	7	.682	4.42	29	27	10	1	2	0	177	184	102	87	17	5	81	0	109	11
Fournier, West Haven	0	0	.000	36.00	1	0	0	1	0	0	2	8	8	8	2	0	4	0	1	0
Fredlund, Bristol	2	4	.333	3.90	18	12	0	2	0	0	60	44	31	26	1	3	43	3	43	5
Gause, Waterbury°	4	0	1.000	3.35	21	1	1	9	0	0	51	36	21	19	4	2	24	4	32	2
Geiger, Glens Falls	1	0	1.000	1.08	12	0	0	12	0	6	25	13	3	3	2	0	8	0	21	0
Georger, Lynn	11	8	.579	2.95	33	19	4	3	0	0	165	144	67	54	10	4	80	2	116	9
Gilbert, Waterbury	0	0	.000	5.40	2	0	0	2	0	0	5	5	5	3	1	0	5	0	1	2
Goff, Reading°	7	6	.538	4.18	24	16	1	1	0	0	97	84	50	45	7	1	59	0	73	12
Guante, Buffalo	1	1	.500	0.64	10	0	0	10	0	3	14	8	3	1	0	1	9	1	17	1
Hamner, Buffalo	2	3	.400	6.50	12	0	0	6	0	1	18	26	21	13	4	2	8	2	16	1
Harris, West Haven	4	4	.500	4.60	17	6	0	6	0	1	45	47	31	23	9	2	22	1	20	4
Harris, Lynn	15	9	.625	3.48	28	25	8	1	1	0	168	162	92	65	8	5	87	1	90	6
Harrison, Lynn	3	1	.750	4.28	19	3	2	8	0	0	61	70	32	29	4	5	15	2	26	3
Hart, Reading	9	10	.474	3.52	24	24	4	0	1	0	151	144	69	59	12	8	66	2	108	11
Hayes, Waterbury	2	5	.286	3.24	30	0	0	16	0	6	50	40	21	18	6	2	20	5	50	2
Heimueller, West Haven°	9	4	.692	2.33	28	13	2	7	1	0	108	94	40	28	10	5	50	1	73	8
Hensley, West Haven°	1	2	.333	4.85	5	4	1	1	0	0	26	32	15	14	4	1	8	0	13	0
Holloway, West Haven	0	0	.000	0.00	1	0	0	1	0	0	1	0	0	0	0	0	1	0	1	0
Howard, Bristol	4	4	.500	3.21	13	13	2	0	1	0	70	63	33	25	4	5	30	3	59	3
Ch. Johnson, Glens Falls	10	13	.435	4.53	27	26	4	1	0	1	167	179	99	84	13	7	82	3	123	3
Johnson, Bristol	8	6	.571	4.38	32	15	1	8	0	1	117	131	67	57	13	3	59	5	78	8
Jones, Waterbury	9	8	.529	3.95	24	24	4	0	1	0	139	119	78	61	10	5	93	5	60	8
Kane, Bristol	5	3	.625	3.75	13	6	1	3	0	0	48	47	22	20	4	0	18	2	32	2
King, Bristol	12	10	.545	2.73	25	24	9	1	3	0	175	126	69	53	9	11	87	2	168	6
Krajewski, West Haven	0	0	.000	4.33	12	2	0	8	0	0	27	28	15	13	1	1	9	1	14	3
Krueger, Lynn°	1	3	.250	2.77	41	2	0	22	0	2	52	49	16	16	1	3	26	7	43	3
Krueger, West Haven°	3	6	.333	3.57	11	11	1	0	0	0	68	74	36	27	4	1	31	0	36	2
Lesley, Waterbury	4	1	.800	2.60	26	0	0	16	0	4	45	45	17	13	1	2	15	2	37	1
Macauley, Buffalo	0	0	.000	0.00	1	0	0	1	0	0	2	1	0	0	0	0	0	0	0	0
Maitland, Glens Falls	8	3	.727	3.86	20	13	1	5	0	1	84	81	52	36	11	1	39	1	41	3
Mantsch, West Haven	1	0	1.000	5.03	16	1	0	3	0	0	34	41	23	19	5	2	12	2	10	1
Merulla, Buffalo	0	0	.000	54.00	1	0	0	1	0	0	1	2	6	6	0	0	7	0	0	0
Moloney, Bristol°	10	1	.909	1.80	42	0	0	17	0	0	80	61	21	16	1	0	25	8	54	1
Mooneyham, Holyoke	9	11	.450	4.53	25	25	5	0	1	0	135	124	90	68	4	6	131	4	155	15
Moore, Lynn	6	5	.545	3.64	13	13	6	0	2	0	94	83	42	38	4	5	34	1	81	14
Morrison, Holyoke	3	3	.500	3.25	32	1	1	20	0	2	83	77	34	30	9	1	27	3	76	4
Mullen, Glens Falls	0	2	.000	8.50	6	2	0	2	0	0	18	23	18	17	4	1	11	0	10	1
Murray, Lynn	3	6	.333	3.50	43	8	0	18	0	8	126	123	54	49	11	4	38	5	85	6
Neuenschwander, Waterbury	5	4	.556	4.96	29	0	0	24	0	3	49	41	30	27	7	3	28	5	40	3
O'Keeffe, Waterbury°	1	1	.500	4.50	4	3	0	1	0	0	16	14	9	8	2	1	12	1	5	1
Prior, Reading	0	0	.000	5.29	7	0	0	1	0	0	17	14	10	10	3	0	12	0	7	0
Randolph, Lynn	3	2	.600	2.83	5	5	2	0	2	0	35	23	13	11	4	0	10	0	32	3
Rasmussen, Holyoke°	8	12	.400	3.98	24	24	6	0	1	0	156	134	95	69	9	6	99	3	125	18
Reed, Reading	5	4	.556	3.26	56	0	0	43	0	17	80	80	34	29	7	1	29	8	62	6
Ricelli, Buffalo	0	0	.000	9.00	2	0	0	1	0	0	3	2	3	3	0	0	8	0	2	3
Rock, Buffalo	1	6	.143	8.50	18	2	0	8	0	1	36	37	44	34	5	0	29	4	15	6
Rommel, Holyoke	2	4	.333	4.42	32	0	0	23	0	7	55	61	29	27	2	1	19	4	36	1
Sandberg, Bristol	0	0	.000	12.00	1	0	0	0	0	0	3	5	4	4	1	0	2	0	0	0
Scherrer, Waterbury°	5	9	.357	4.31	50	10	1	24	0	1	119	121	70	57	10	2	62	5	89	6
Schoppee, Bristol	8	3	.727	1.76	56	0	0	48	0	22	92	71	21	18	0	0	42	10	70	4
Shields, Bristol°	5	14	.263	4.64	29	15	6	8	0	2	126	136	75	65	10	2	65	10	87	13
Simond, Lynn°	0	1	.000	3.75	5	1	0	0	0	0	12	13	12	5	0	1	10	1	7	1
Siwy, Glens Falls	11	4	.733	3.85	16	15	8	1	1	1	110	125	57	47	9	5	19	0	45	1
Smith, Lynn	4	7	.364	3.81	50	0	0	42	0	13	59	72	32	25	1	2	35	5	34	3
L. Smith, Reading	11	8	.579	4.42	27	27	4	0	2	0	161	123	92	79	13	10	97	0	117	14
Souza, West Haven°	1	2	.333	3.77	31	1	0	13	0	1	31	29	19	13	5	0	20	5	21	1
Stottlemyre, Lynn	5	12	.294	4.34	22	19	6	1	1	0	110	124	60	53	5	2	34	1	53	2
Straker, Waterbury	1	5	.167	6.40	19	6	0	6	0	2	45	50	35	32	3	1	34	4	33	5
Sullivan, Waterbury	0	4	.000	4.65	8	6	0	1	0	0	31	44	19	16	2	1	16	1	23	3
Taylor, Buffalo	1	7	.125	8.31	17	7	0	2	0	1	39	44	43	36	5	5	48	0	31	5
Thibodeaux, Buffalo	2	2	.500	2.25	11	5	1	1	0	0	44	40	12	11	3	1	19	1	29	0
Town, Waterbury	7	12	.368	4.71	28	25	3	1	1	0	151	154	92	79	17	4	55	7	52	8
Tronerud, West Haven	10	10	.500	3.86	33	22	4	5	0	2	170	171	91	73	15	5	94	5	114	13
Tunnel, Buffalo	5	5	.500	4.44	12	12	0	0	0	0	71	76	38	35	6	3	37	0	45	2
Tyler, Bristol	0	2	.000	4.35	17	0	0	11	0	0	31	24	15	15	2	4	24	3	30	4
Vasquez, Glens Falls	5	2	.714	3.36	35	3	0	23	0	11	91	81	45	34	5	2	38	5	50	3
Vasquez, Buffalo°	4	8	.333	3.98	41	15	1	13	1	4	147	165	79	65	15	3	42	6	83	0
Warthen, Buffalo°	0	1	.000	11.45	10	0	0	6	0	0	11	11	16	14	0	2	16	0	12	3
Watkins, Bristol	0	0	.000	9.00	1	0	0	1	0	0	2	2	3	2	0	0	3	0	0	0
Welborn, Lynn	2	1	.667	0.00	6	0	0	3	0	1	17	6	1	0	0	1	10	0	17	0
Wieters, Glens Falls	0	3	.000	4.50	31	2	1	17	0	2	100	99	60	50	6	4	51	2	52	5
Wiltbank, Buffalo	4	4	.500	5.51	13	13	1	0	0	0	67	75	44	41	8	1	52	0	44	6
Winn, Buffalo	2	5	.286	4.57	12	12	0	0	0	0	65	60	40	33	4	2	23	1	44	9
Withrow, Glens Falls	0	0	.000	6.00	2	0	0	2	0	0	3	4	2	2	0	0	3	0	1	0
Wright, Reading	6	5	.545	5.87	20	18	2	0	0	0	95	117	66	62	8	5	64	3	38	9
Yandle, Holyoke°	5	8	.385	3.44	28	17	8	7	2	2	136	131	63	52	11	3	42	0	70	3
Young, Lynn°	3	9	.250	4.00	14	14	3	0	0	0	81	80	47	36	4	2	38	3	57	6
Zaske, Buffalo	0	1	.000	3.60	4	0	0	0	0	0	10	10	6	4	1	1	8	1	4	1

BALKS—Mooneyham, 5; Barez, Black, Fallon, K. Jones, Souza, Yandle, 3 each; Atherton, Burtt, Calderon, Carman, Comstock, DeLeon, Desjarlais, Georger, Hamner, Hart, Randolph, Rasmussen, Thibodeaux, Wright, 2 each; Abraham, Arline, Britt, Burroughs, Carjaval, Cliburn, Denman, Dowless, Evans, Foley, Fredlund, Gause, F. Harris, T. Harris, Hayes, Heimueller, Ch. Johnson, Kane, Krajewski, S. Krueger, Maitland, Mantsch, Moore, Morrison, Murray, O'Keeffe, Shields, Siwy, L. Smith, Straker, Taylor, Town, Tronerud, Tyler, Winn, 1 each.

COMBINATION SHUTOUTS—Burtt-King, Burtt-Schoppee, Howard-Moloney-Schoppee, Howard-Schoppee, Johnson-Fredlund-Kane, King-Johnson, King-Schoppee, Bristol; Wiltbank-Taylor, Winn-Thibodeaux, Buffalo; Edwards-Bradley, Evans-Geiger, Fallon-Geiger, Glens Falls; Duran-Brown, Mooneyham-Brown, Rasmussen-Morrison, Holyoke; Black-Harris-Welborn, Murray-Smith, Stottlemyre-Murray-Krueger-Smith, Young-Murray, Lynn; Bystrom-Alicea-Reed, Reading; Carlucci-Lesley, Jones-Lesley-Hayes-Gause, Waterbury; Abraham-Bradley-Heimueller, Abraham-Buice, Atherton-Abraham, Atherton-Abraham-Buice, Comstock-Mantsch-Buice, Heimueller-Buice 2, Hensley-Tronerud, Krueger-Krajewski, West Haven.

NO-HIT GAMES—Denman, Bristol, defeated West Haven, July 6; Hart, Reading, defeated Lynn, July 22, first game (seven innings).

Southern League

CLASS AA

Leading Batter
KEVIN RHOMBERG
Chattanooga

League President
JIMMY BRAGAN

Leading Pitcher
MARK ROSS
Columbus

CHAMPIONSHIP WINNERS IN PREVIOUS YEARS

1904—Macon	.598
1905—Macon	.625
1906—Savannah	.637
1907—Charleston	.620
1908—Jacksonville	.694
1909—Chattanooga°	.738
Augusta	.702
1910—Columbus	.588
1911—Columbus°	.681
Columbia	.710
1912—Jacksonville°	.679
Columbus	.632
1913—Savannah°	.754
Savannah	.593
1914—Savannah°	.667
Albany	.650
1915—Macon	.588
Columbus°	.686
1916—Augusta°	.617
Columbia	.631
1917—Charleston	.741
Columbia°	.667
1918—Did not operate.	
1919—Columbia	.585
1920—Columbia	.633
1921—Columbia	.642
1922—Charleston	.625
1923—Charlotte°	.653
Macon	.580
1924—Augusta	.612
1925—Spartanburg	.620
1926—Greenville	.662
1927—Greenville	.622
1928—Asheville	.664
1929—Asheville	.605
Knoxville°	.634
1930—Greenville°	.620
Macon	.643

1931-35—Did not operate.	
1936—Jacksonville	.652
Columbus°	.650
1937—Columbus	.572
Savannah (3rd)†	.565
1938—Savannah	.574
Macon (2nd)†	.570
1939—Cclumbus	.601
Au justa (2nd)†	.597
1940—Savannah	.627
Columbus (2nd)†	.583
1941—Macon	.643
Columbia (2nd)†	.636
1942—Charleston	.620
Macon (2nd)†	.585
1943-45—Did not operate.	
1946—Columbus	.568
Augusta (4th)†	.547
1947—Columbus	.575
Savannah (2nd)†	.563
1948—Charleston	.572
Greenville (3rd)†	.549
1949—Macon‡	.623
1950—Macon‡	.588
1951—Montgomery	.607
1952—Columbia	.649
Montgomery (3rd)†	.558
1953—Jacksonville	.679
Savannah (2nd)†	.571
1954—Jacksonville	.593
Savannah (2nd)†	.571
1955—Columbia	.636
Augusta (3rd)†	.543
1956—Jacksonville‡	.621
1957—Augusta	.636
Charlotte (2nd)†	.562
1958—Augusta	.550
Macon (3rd)†	.500

1959—Knoxville	.557
Gastonia (4th)†	.504
1960—Columbia	.597
Savannah (3rd)†	.561
1961—Asheville	.635
1962—Savannah	.662
Macon (3rd)†	.576
1963—Augusta°	.661
Lynchburg	.662
1964—Lynchburg	.579
1965—Columbus	.572
1966—Mobile	.629
1967—Birmingham	.604
1968—Asheville	.614
1969—Charlotte	.579
1970—Columbus	.569
1971—Did not operate as league — clubs were members of Dixie Association.	
1972—Asheville	.583
Montgomery§	.561
1973—Montgomery§	.580
Jacksonville	.559
1974—Jacksonville	.565
Knoxville§	.533
1975—Orlando	.587
Montgomery§	.545
1976—Montgomery x	.591
Orlando	.540
1977—Montgomery x	.628
Jacksonville	.522
1978—Knoxville x	.611
Savannah	.500
1979—Columbus	.587
Nashville x	.576
1980—Memphis	.576
Charlotte x	.500

°Won split-season playoff. †Won four-club playoff. ‡Won championship and four-club playoff. §League was divided into Eastern and Western divisions; won playoff. xLeague was divided into Eastern and Western divisions and played split-season. Playoff winner.

STANDING OF CLUBS AT CLOSE OF FIRST HALF, JUNE 20

EASTERN DIVISION

Club	W.	L.	T.	Pct.	G.B.
Orlando (Twins)	42	27	0	.609	......
Charlotte (Orioles)	37	35	0	.514	6½
Columbus (Astros)	34	34	2	.500	7½
Jacksonville (Royals)	34	36	1	.486	8½
Savannah (Braves)	34	37	0	.479	9

WESTERN DIVISION

Club	W.	L.	T.	Pct.	G.B.
Memphis (Expos)	42	29	0	.592	......
Nashville (Yankees)	38	32	0	.543	3½
Birmingham (Tigers)	33	39	1	.458	9½
Chattanooga (Indians)	30	36	1	.455	9½
Knoxville (Blue Jays)	26	45	1	.366	16

STANDING OF CLUBS AT CLOSE OF SECOND HALF, SEPTEMBER 1

EASTERN DIVISION

Club	W.	L.	T.	Pct.	G.B.
Savannah (Braves)	36	33	0	.5217	......
Charlotte (Orioles)	37	34	0	.5211	......
Orlando (Twins)	37	36	0	.507	1
Jacksonville (Royals)	31	41	0	.431	6½
Columbus (Astros)	29	44	0	.397	9

WESTERN DIVISION

Club	W.	L.	T.	Pct.	G.B.
Nashville (Yankees)	43	30	0	.589	......
Birmingham (Tigers)	38	31	0	.551	3
Knoxville (Blue Jays)	37	35	0	.514	5½
Chattanooga (Indians)	37	39	0	.487	7½
Memphis (Expos)	35	37	0	.486	7½

COMPOSITE STANDING OF CLUBS AT CLOSE OF SEASON, SEPTEMBER 1

Club	Nash.	Orl.	Mem.	Char.	Bir.	Sav.	Chat.	Jax.	Col.	Knox.	W.	L.	T.	Pct.	G.B.
Nashville (Yankees)	....	10	6	13	9	8	6	7	12	10	81	62	0	.566	......
Orlando (Twins)	6	....	10	10	7	7	12	10	10	7	79	63	0	.556	1½
Memphis (Expos)	10	6	....	9	9	7	9	8	8	11	77	66	0	.538	4
Charlotte (Orioles)	3	6	7	....	8	11	11	5	13	10	74	69	0	.517	7
Birmingham (Tigers)	7	7	7	8	....	6	7	13	8	8	71	70	1	.504	9
Savannah (Braves)	8	9	9	5	9	....	7	8	7	8	70	70	0	.500	9½
Chattanooga (Indians)	9	4	6	5	9	9	....	9	5	11	67	75	1	.472	13½
Jacksonville (Royals)	9	6	8	10	3	7	7	....	7	8	65	77	1	.458	15½
Columbus (Astros)	4	6	8	3	8	7	11	9	....	7	63	78	2	.447	17
Knoxville (Blue Jays)	6	9	5	6	8	8	5	8	8	....	63	80	1	.441	18

Major league affiliations in parentheses.

Playoffs—Orlando defeated Savannah, three games to one; Nashville defeated Memphis, three games to none; Orlando defeated Nashville, three games to one, for League Championship.

Regular-Season Attendance—Birmingham, 220,219; Charlotte, 204,546; Chattanooga, 149,017; Columbus, 109,135; Jacksonville, 126,384; Knoxville, 70,807; Memphis, 307,007; Nashville, 550,676; Orlando, 69,391; Savannah, 104,254. Total, 1,911,436. Playoff, 26,281. All-star game, 5,366.

Managers: Birmingham, Roy Majtyka; Charlotte, Mark Wiley; Chattanooga, Woody Smith; Columbus, Matt Galante; Jacksonville, Gene Lamont; Knoxville, Duane Larson replaced by Larry Hardy; Memphis, Larry Bearnarth; Nashville, Carl Merrill; Orlando, Tom Kelly; Savannah, Andy Gilbert.

All-Star Team: 1B—Michael Laga, Birmingham; 2B—Kevin Rhomberg, Chattanooga; 3B—Gary Gaetti, Orlando; SS—Bryan Little, Memphis; OF—Albert Hall, Savannah; Donald Mattingly, Nashville; Randall Bush, Orlando; and (tie) Willie McGee, Nashville; Larry Ray, Columbus; C—Timothy Laudner, Orlando; DH—Willie Royster, Charlotte; LHP—Thomas Gorman, Memphis; RHP—James Werly, Nashville; MVP—Tim Laudner, Orlando; Pitcher of Year—James Werly, Nashville; Manager of Year—Tom Kelly, Orlando.

(Compiled by Howe News Bureau, Boston, Mass.)

CLUB BATTING

Club	Pct.	G.	AB.	R.	OR.	H.	TB.	2B.	3B.	HR.	RBI.	GW.	SH.	SF.	HP.	BB.	Int. BB.	SO.	SB.	CS.	LOB.
Birmingham	.275	142	4786	691	1317	1971	205	43	121	625	60	50	39	22	438	22	686	139	65	986
Memphis	.273	143	4727	749	714	1291	1945	189	39	129	656	57	28	49	27	646	30	793	182	105	1013
Nashville	.269	143	4743	744	574	1276	1813	211	58	70	650	64	60	42	40	592	26	704	205	82	1081
Chattanooga	.267	143	4591	660	713	1225	1832	211	45	102	579	45	51	36	39	526	35	882	194	77	977
Savannah	.265	140	4405	617	622	1168	1823	183	29	138	543	54	46	34	34	478	30	757	158	64	932
Knoxville	.264	144	4725	600	702	1249	1794	204	55	77	541	50	47	36	31	409	26	816	124	61	948
Charlotte	.263	143	4725	703	648	1244	1944	205	27	147	643	65	36	42	38	519	27	885	181	76	977
Columbus	.261	143	4634	661	729	1208	1724	193	58	69	581	54	49	38	24	549	41	758	162	84	987
Orlando	.257	142	4551	750	671	1171	1901	183	23	167	693	67	44	54	46	622	20	794	90	58	940
Jacksonville	.246	143	4528	566	652	1113	1593	170	35	80	514	48	46	31	34	507	20	793	169	70	979

INDIVIDUAL BATTING

(Leading Qualifiers for Batting Championship—389 or More Plate Appearances)

°Bats lefthanded. †Switch-hitter.

Player and Club	Pct.	G.	AB.	R.	H.	TB.	2B.	3B.	HR.	RBI.	GW.	SH.	SF.	HP.	BB.	Int. BB.	SO.	SB.	CS.
Rhomberg, Kevin, Chattanooga	.366	141	511	104	187	242	24	14	1	55	1	2	3	4	84	9	59	74	17
Slaught, Donald, Jacksonville	.335	96	379	45	127	170	21	2	6	44	6	5	0	3	32	1	44	13	11
McGee, Willie, Nashville†	.322	100	388	77	125	176	20	5	7	63	7	6	4	1	24	1	46	24	7
Jones, Christopher, Columbus°	.320	143	535	102	171	235	25	9	7	65	7	4	5	1	78	8	88	37	14
Mattingly, Donald, Nashville°	.316	141	547	74	173	237	35	4	7	98	10	1	9	2	64	7	55	4	2
Hall, Albert, Savannah†	.308	133	487	83	150	213	28	10	5	27	4	3	5	7	64	5	44	60	17
Rodriguez, Victor, Charlotte	.306	138	553	68	169	220	22	1	9	65	8	7	3	1	37	0	51	5	4
Wilson, Glenn, Birmingham	.306	124	496	77	152	242	24	6	18	82	5	1	3	2	23	2	56	7	4
Fry, Jerry, Memphis	.303	120	435	73	132	224	18	1	24	72	9	1	1	1	49	4	73	4	0
Kenaga, Jeffrey, Birmingham°	.301	99	376	57	113	187	20	3	16	64	4	3	3	4	26	2	47	2	4

Departmental Leaders: G—Little, C. Jones, 143; AB—Younger, 588, R—Wilborn, 106; H—Rhomberg, 187; TB—Laga, 293; 2B—Mattingly, 35; 3B—Rhomberg, 14; HR—Laudner, 42; RBI—Ray, 107; GWRBI—Laudner, 14; SH—DeLeon, 15; SF—Mattingly, Simunic, Ulger, 9; BB—Nixon, 110; IBB—Perry, 12; HP—Bush, 12; SO—Hall, 128; SB—Rhomberg, 74; CS—Hall, Rhomberg, 17.

(All Players—Listed Alphabetically)

Player and Club	Pct.	G.	AB.	R.	H.	TB.	2B.	3B.	HR.	RBI.	GW.	SH.	SF.	HP.	BB.	Int. BB.	SO.	SB.	CS.
Adams, W. Craig, Chattanooga	.253	117	383	49	97	151	22	1	10	45	3	6	3	4	44	1	95	12	9
Alvarez, Roberto, Chattanooga	.229	84	240	35	55	71	9	2	1	17	1	3	3	4	20	0	35	4	0
Anderson, Karl, Chattanooga	.000	25	2	0	0	0	0	0	0	0	0	0	0	0	0	0	1	0	0
Atkinson, James, Columbus°	.224	99	317	36	71	107	8	2	8	42	1	2	2	2	45	1	43	3	1
Baker, Kenneth, Birmingham°	.310	60	171	22	53	74	8	2	3	19	0	1	0	17	0	14	3	1
Baker, Ricky, Chattanooga†	.294	49	197	39	58	81	10	2	3	14	1	4	1	0	26	1	24	21	13
Barfield, Jesse, Knoxville	.261	141	524	83	137	235	24	13	16	70	8	0	7	4	59	2	111	25	11
Bazan, Pedro, Orlando°	.125	11	24	2	3	4	1	0	0	4	0	2	0	0	1	0	6	0	0

Player and Club	Pct.	G.	AB.	R.	H.	TB.	2B.	3B.	HR.	RBI.	GW.	SH.	SF.	HP.	BB.	Int. BB.	SO.	SB.	CS.
Beltran, Julio, Columbus	.197	19	66	8	13	14	1	0	0	2	0	0	0	0	2	0	6	2	3
Benson, Steve, Columbus	.289	107	350	56	101	160	18	7	9	52	0	4	4	0	48	1	34	25	9
Biancalana, Roland, Jacksonville†	.210	132	385	47	81	98	7	2	2	27	4	11	2	3	51	0	78	25	9
Booker, Roderick, Orlando°	.257	111	331	56	85	99	8	3	0	33	1	2	2	1	58	1	44	10	7
Borchers, Rick, Chattanooga°	.000	36	1	0	0	0	0	0	0	0	0	0	0	0	0	0	0	0	0
Botelho, Derek, Jacksonville	.000	8	2	0	0	0	0	0	0	0	0	0	0	0	0	0	1	0	0
Bowman, Donald, Charlotte	.238	139	500	67	119	208	21	4	20	82	8	3	7	8	46	3	84	8	3
Bozich, Gary, Birmingham	.190	19	63	11	12	17	1	2	0	6	0	0	0	1	9	0	10	4	0
Brown, Darrell, Birmingham	.212	19	66	8	14	16	0	1	0	3	0	0	0	0	2	0	7	5	1
Buckner, James, Jacksonville°	.264	45	148	29	39	60	9	3	2	22	5	0	3	0	20	2	11	8	1
Budner, Scott, Charlotte°	.000	26	1	0	0	0	0	0	0	0	0	0	0	0	0	0	0	0	0
Bush, R. Randall, Orlando°	.290	136	482	98	140	238	26	3	22	94	11	1	8	12	85	3	93	14	10
Cadahia, Aurelio, Orlando	.224	18	49	3	11	15	4	0	0	10	0	1	2	0	5	0	1	0	0
Callahan, Patrick, Nashville	.277	83	282	30	78	106	13	6	1	35	2	1	2	3	27	0	49	2	2
Campbell, Mark, Columbus	.235	65	200	29	47	67	10	2	2	20	3	2	2	0	27	2	28	3	4
Carrasquel, Emilio, Birmingham	.233	30	86	8	20	22	2	0	0	9	0	2	0	2	14	0	15	0	1
Carrion, Leonel, Memphis	.289	105	342	49	99	154	24	2	9	58	3	0	7	4	60	4	61	9	4
Castillo, M. Carmelo, Chattanooga	.281	119	441	63	124	186	17	6	11	58	3	0	2	3	33	0	65	25	5
Cecchetti, George, Chattanooga°	.255	131	440	64	112	207	22	2	23	83	7	3	1	9	64	8	98	8	3
Chaney, Bruce, Birmingham	.102	21	49	4	5	6	1	0	0	3	0	3	0	0	3	0	15	3	0
Chapman, Nathan, Nashville°	.284	123	475	70	135	200	21	7	10	75	8	5	6	6	40	1	57	20	10
Colletti, Manuel, Orlando†	.201	97	239	39	48	51	3	0	0	16	1	10	2	2	58	1	39	6	4
Cornell, Jeffrey, Jacksonville†	.000	26	1	0	0	0	0	0	0	0	0	0	0	0	0	0	1	0	0
Cox, Ted, Knoxville	.306	59	193	34	59	109	15	1	11	50	4	0	4	0	27	3	36	4	2
Crowley, Raymond, Memphis°	.212	39	104	17	22	43	3	0	6	16	0	0	3	1	31	1	36	1	1
Csefalvay, John, Columbus°	.176	36	102	12	18	27	1	1	2	10	2	0	0	0	13	3	26	3	1
David, Andre, Orlando°	.234	133	475	57	111	164	13	5	10	54	4	4	4	8	49	2	54	14	6
Dayett, Brian, Nashville	.269	112	338	53	91	166	15	3	18	62	8	1	5	2	60	1	51	4	11
DeJesus, Alex, Memphis	.208	30	77	9	16	29	2	1	3	8	1	2	0	0	12	0	26	1	0
DeLeon, Luis, Chattanooga†	.235	130	429	42	101	123	13	3	1	38	5	15	2	2	26	2	69	11	6
Dempsey, Peter, Knoxville	.247	140	518	68	128	220	26	9	16	77	9	3	2	9	26	4	119	4	4
Denman, John, Charlotte	.235	105	340	48	80	122	14	2	8	34	1	4	0	2	39	0	98	24	11
Dennis, Eduardo, Knoxville	.235	89	277	24	65	76	9	1	0	19	2	4	0	3	9	0	32	7	9
Derryberry, Timothy, Charlotte°	.246	94	280	45	69	117	12	0	12	53	5	0	1	10	46	4	51	0	1
Dilks, Derrin, Memphis°	.500	12	2	0	1	2	1	0	0	0	0	0	0	0	0	0	1	0	0
Doran, William, Columbus†	.281	124	427	83	120	166	17	7	5	56	6	6	4	4	74	4	48	18	11
Dotson, Lawrence, Chattanooga°	.261	47	157	17	41	52	2	3	1	16	2	1	3	1	5	0	19	4	3
Douglas, Stephen, Orlando	.294	132	513	87	151	201	25	2	7	54	3	6	3	3	61	1	67	18	10
Dumouchelle, Patrick, Charlotte	.500	5	16	4	8	12	2	1	0	1	0	0	0	0	0	0	4	2	0
Ereu, William, Knoxville	.198	41	121	10	24	28	0	2	0	9	0	4	0	0	4	0	16	1	2
Fabrizio, Kurt, Charlotte°	.105	6	19	0	2	3	1	0	0	1	0	0	0	0	2	0	2	0	0
Followell, Vernon, Birmingham†	.278	92	334	45	93	118	13	3	2	28	2	2	0	0	34	1	38	3	1
Francona, Terry, Memphis°	.348	41	161	20	56	66	8	1	0	18	1	0	1	0	7	3	18	0	3
Franklin, Glen, Memphis°	.253	88	324	56	82	134	12	2	12	43	4	3	5	2	34	2	46	32	11
Fry, Jerry, Memphis°	.303	120	435	73	132	224	18	1	24	72	9	1	1	1	49	4	73	4	0
Fuentes, Michael, Memphis	.231	3	13	0	3	4	1	0	0	0	0	0	0	0	0	0	6	0	0
Gaetti, Gary, Orlando	.277	137	495	92	137	250	19	2	30	93	12	1	4	3	58	0	105	15	9
Garbey, Barbaro, Birmingham	.286	107	391	56	112	155	17	4	6	55	9	1	5	1	37	1	41	8	10
Gardner, Vassie, Chattanooga	.332	67	244	35	81	113	10	5	4	35	4	0	2	1	27	1	43	15	18
Glass, Timothy, Chattanooga	.217	62	189	28	41	79	6	1	10	25	2	3	1	1	28	1	81	0	11
Gleissner, James, Jacksonville	.194	13	31	2	6	9	3	0	0	4	0	0	0	0	3	0	11	0	30
Glynn, Eugene, Memphis	.210	113	276	46	58	71	3	2	2	23	0	2	2	0	45	0	36	11	19
Grace, Michael, Savannah	.153	26	59	9	9	14	0	1	1	5	1	0	0	0	7	0	10	0	0
Grout, Ronald, Savannah	.243	135	482	57	117	210	27	0	22	90	10	1	4	3	56	1	96	0	0
Guerra, Randall, Nashville°	.197	30	66	12	13	25	0	0	4	13	0	0	0	0	9	1	13	0	1
Hall, Albert, Savannah†	.308	133	487	83	150	213	28	10	5	27	4	3	5	7	64	5	44	60	17
Hallberg, Lance, Orlando	.224	128	451	61	101	167	15	0	17	68	3	2	7	4	50	0	106	1	3
Hanggie, Dan, Nashville†	.175	22	40	2	7	8	1	0	0	5	0	0	1	1	6	0	5	0	0
Hardy, William C., Birmingham	.239	15	46	8	11	12	1	0	0	3	0	2	1	2	3	0	9	0	1
Havens, Bradley, Orlando°	.000	11	1	0	0	0	0	0	0	0	0	0	0	0	0	0	1	0	0
Hazewood, Drungo, Charlotte	.282	105	340	63	96	170	13	2	19	55	8	0	1	1	80	3	97	17	8
Heimer, Todd, Chattanooga°	.000	25	1	0	0	0	0	0	0	0	0	0	0	0	0	0	0	0	0
Hernandez, Tobias, Knoxville	.182	4	11	1	2	4	0	1	0	3	0	1	0	0	2	0	1	0	0
Hicks, Joseph, Jacksonville	.212	43	146	14	31	38	5	1	0	15	0	1	0	0	9	1	18	8	5
Hinson, Gary, Birmingham	.176	7	17	2	3	6	0	0	1	1	1	1	0	0	1	0	4	1	0
Hodgson, Paul, Knoxville	.286	97	336	42	96	134	11	3	7	40	1	5	4	0	43	1	57	1	3
Hogg, David, Jacksonville	.222	95	284	44	63	103	11	1	9	33	1	2	1	4	61	3	61	2	2
Hough, Stanley, Columbus	.215	60	177	15	38	57	8	1	3	27	2	3	1	1	19	0	32	0	2
Hunsaker, Frank, Birmingham	.263	42	137	18	36	51	6	0	3	28	3	2	1	1	14	0	19	0	1
Hyman, Donald, Orlando	.208	10	24	4	5	5	0	0	0	2	0	0	0	0	1	0	8	0	0
Ingle, Randy, Savannah	.206	119	383	44	79	113	8	1	8	32	2	5	1	0	27	0	79	2	2
Ivie, Lonnie, Charlotte	.000	2	2	0	0	0	0	0	0	0	0	0	0	0	0	0	1	0	0
Jabalera, Francisco, Columbus°	.266	134	503	64	134	155	9	6	0	31	2	9	1	5	49	3	63	48	16
Jacobs, Ronald, Columbus	.236	94	309	30	73	84	11	0	0	24	3	4	1	0	31	0	42	2	2
Jacoby, Brook, Savannah	.292	140	507	59	148	254	28	3	24	82	6	1	3	5	37	5	105	0	4
Johnson, Anthony, Memphis	.319	92	335	55	107	143	14	2	6	42	2	1	3	2	46	1	75	36	13
Johnson, Howard, Birmingham†	.266	138	488	84	130	238	28	7	22	83	8	6	7	0	75	6	93	19	10
Johnson, Roy, Memphis°	.264	130	477	83	126	219	19	10	18	90	8	0	3	4	56	5	89	16	12
Johnson, Wallace, Memphis†	.363	28	102	15	37	49	9	0	1	18	1	1	1	0	11	0	10	8	3
Jones, Christopher, Columbus°	.320	143	503	102	171	235	25	9	7	65	7	4	5	1	78	8	88	37	14
Jones, Ricky, Charlotte	.261	134	479	66	125	179	17	2	11	56	3	2	8	2	25	1	72	12	4
Kelly, D. Patrick, Knoxville	.274	30	106	7	29	36	7	0	0	10	0	0	0	1	7	0	31	1	2
Kenaga, Jeffrey, Birmingham°	.301	99	376	57	113	187	20	3	16	64	4	3	3	4	26	2	47	2	4
Knight, Timothy, Nashville°	.202	31	94	14	19	30	4	2	1	13	0	2	0	0	18	2	14	0	1
Kromy, Ted, Columbus	.000	31	1	0	0	0	0	0	0	0	0	0	0	0	0	0	0	0	0
Laga, Michael, Birmingham°	.289	142	547	89	158	293	28	7	31	86	13	1	8	5	49	5	113	2	1
Laudner, Timothy, Orlando	.284	130	433	87	123	272	21	1	42	104	14	1	7	4	63	7	90	3	0
Leeper, David, Jacksonville°	.269	67	227	19	61	74	7	0	2	21	4	2	2	3	12	2	35	9	4
Little, R. Bryan, Memphis†	.293	143	553	98	162	186	15	3	1	46	3	10	5	5	92	1	46	28	16
Livingstone, Stuart, Memphis	.500	37	2	1	1	1	0	0	0	0	0	0	0	0	0	0	1	0	0
Lowry, Dwight, Birmingham°	.154	19	52	3	8	10	2	0	0	4	0	0	0	0	7	1	7	0	0
Luethy, Dave, Jacksonville	.222	8	18	2	4	6	2	0	0	2	0	0	0	0	2	0	4	0	0

Player and Club	Pct.	G.	AB.	R.	H.	TB.	2B.	3B.	HR.	RBI.	GW.	SH.	SF.	HP.	BB.	Int. BB.	SO.	SB.	CS.
Malkin, John, Chattanooga	.237	31	76	4	18	33	6	0	3	13	1	1	2	0	6	0	14	0	1
Manrique, Fred, Knoxville	.279	115	469	62	131	173	15	6	5	42	5	7	4	4	21	1	68	7	7
Mariano, Robert, Nashville°	.222	44	108	16	24	35	6	1	1	9	0	2	1	1	19	0	22	0	2
Mattingly, Donald, Nashville	.316	141	547	74	173	237	35	4	7	98	10	1	9	2	64	7	55	4	2
McCann, Francis, Jacksonville	.266	134	463	75	123	201	15	9	15	70	9	1	7	1	66	4	80	20	6
McGee, Willie, Nashville†	.322	100	388	77	125	176	20	5	7	63	7	6	4	1	24	1	46	24	7
Medina, Valentin, Columbus	.273	73	245	27	67	84	10	2	1	28	2	2	3	2	5	0	55	2	1
Miller, Michael, Savannah†	.000	2	1	1	0	0	0	0	0	0	0	0	0	0	0	0	0	0	0
Milner, Brian, Knoxville	.231	112	385	31	89	115	14	3	2	35	3	4	1	0	19	0	96	3	0
Mizerock, John, Columbus°	.229	11	35	6	8	10	2	0	0	2	0	0	0	0	4	0	8	0	0
Morley, Michael, Jacksonville	.500	18	2	0	1	1	0	0	0	0	0	0	0	0	0	0	1	0	0
Moronko, Jeffrey, Chattanooga	.256	126	442	67	113	157	24	1	6	51	4	4	5	4	48	4	82	14	7
Mulligan, Robert, Orlando°	.000	15	1	0	0	0	0	0	0	0	0	0	0	0	0	0	0	0	0
Naehring, Mark, Charlotte	.256	127	414	63	106	168	25	2	11	53	7	4	8	3	74	2	84	2	3
Nandin, Richard, Birmingham†	.279	87	262	37	73	88	10	1	1	25	2	9	4	1	41	3	29	9	9
Neal, E. Earl, Charlotte	.281	100	366	50	103	159	16	2	12	63	4	2	2	3	25	4	63	4	10
Nixon, Otis, Nashville†	.251	127	407	89	102	115	9	2	0	20	1	6	1	3	110	0	101	72	15
Norko, Thomas, Knoxville	.250	4	12	1	3	3	0	0	0	2	0	1	0	0	0	0	4	0	0
Owen, Lawrence, Savannah	.229	90	279	30	64	93	8	3	5	23	4	2	2	1	24	0	42	0	0
Pasley, Kevin, Knoxville	.281	86	302	31	85	112	13	1	4	33	6	0	2	0	13	2	22	2	1
Patterson, Steven, Jacksonville	.125	18	56	5	7	12	1	2	0	4	0	0	0	0	6	0	14	0	0
Perry, Gerald, Savannah°	.277	137	476	71	132	213	18	3	19	84	7	2	7	0	69	12	95	22	12
Peterson, Erik, Nashville	.226	85	235	31	53	85	12	1	6	43	8	5	1	4	24	2	39	4	2
Poldberg, Brian, Nashville	.211	57	152	16	32	44	5	2	1	22	1	3	0	4	16	0	14	0	0
Poole, Stine, Birmingham	.253	100	316	42	80	137	19	1	12	49	4	2	0	1	17	0	69	1	2
Ramie, Vernon, Knoxville°	.286	122	374	44	107	154	18	4	7	60	3	2	5	0	81	8	82	4	3
Ray, Larry, Columbus°	.253	136	505	72	128	242	33	9	21	107	11	0	4	5	49	9	128	5	4
Reece, Robert, Memphis	.243	25	74	8	18	25	1	0	2	3	0	1	0	0	5	0	7	0	0
Reed, Jeffrey, Orlando°	.250	3	4	0	1	1	0	0	0	0	0	0	0	0	1	0	0	0	0
Rende, Salvatore, Chattanooga°	.228	134	486	69	111	222	28	4	25	93	7	2	6	1	65	8	114	4	2
Rey, Everett, Chattanooga	.268	93	250	29	67	89	11	1	3	28	3	6	2	2	29	0	60	2	1
Reynolds, Michael, Savannah°	.261	48	88	18	23	34	6	1	1	6	3	1	0	0	19	2	15	3	1
Rhomberg, Kevin, Chattanooga	.366	141	511	104	187	242	24	14	1	55	1	2	3	4	84	9	59	74	17
Robbins, Wesley, Nashville	.238	48	168	25	40	60	11	3	1	18	1	1	3	3	16	1	24	2	1
Roberts, Steven, Orlando	.250	1	4	0	1	1	0	0	0	0	0	0	0	0	0	0	0	0	0
Rodriguez, Luis, Memphis	.266	43	177	25	47	69	5	1	5	19	1	3	0	0	9	0	26	8	4
Rodriguez, Victor, Charlotte	.306	138	553	68	169	220	22	1	9	65	8	7	3	1	37	0	51	5	4
Rogers, Randall, Columbus	.170	37	106	9	18	20	2	0	0	9	2	5	2	1	21	1	20	0	2
Rooney, Pat, Memphis	.306	9	36	4	11	21	2	1	2	6	2	0	1	0	1	0	9	2	0
Royster, Willie, Charlotte	.265	138	562	98	149	268	22	2	31	88	9	2	4	6	35	4	120	53	11
Ryal, Mark, Jacksonville°	.267	123	457	50	122	183	15	2	14	69	7	2	3	1	23	4	78	14	2
Serum, Gary, Orlando	1.000	45	1	0	1	1	0	0	0	0	0	0	0	0	0	0	0	0	0
Shannon, Kevin, Nashville	.134	28	67	7	9	11	2	0	0	5	0	0	1	1	11	0	16	0	0
Shelby, John, Charlotte†	.235	62	251	40	59	84	11	4	2	21	3	5	1	0	27	1	38	24	11
Shines, Anthony, Memphis†	.220	119	359	50	79	124	7	4	10	42	6	1	4	1	46	4	52	14	12
Showalter, W. Nathaniel Nashville°	.264	90	307	46	81	110	17	6	0	38	6	6	2	3	46	3	16	3	3
Silverio, Luis, Jacksonville	.245	19	53	5	13	19	3	0	1	6	0	0	1	0	11	0	14	6	4
Simons, Neil, Columbus°	.246	74	264	31	65	97	7	5	5	28	1	1	3	1	27	4	30	2	3
Simunic, Douglas, Memphis	.262	138	481	73	126	192	20	2	14	80	10	1	9	5	66	4	113	8	11
Skeens, George, Orlando	.125	20	56	3	7	12	2	0	1	5	1	0	1	1	6	0	18	0	1
Slaught, Donald, Jacksonville	.335	96	379	45	127	170	21	2	6	44	6	5	0	3	32	1	44	13	11
Smith, Thomas, Charlotte†	.193	16	57	8	11	17	4	1	0	5	2	2	0	0	7	1	9	0	1
Stenhouse, Michael, Memphis°	.272	118	397	64	108	189	25	7	14	72	6	2	4	2	74	1	62	4	6
Stephans, Russell, Jacksonville	.167	4	12	1	2	2	0	0	0	1	0	0	0	0	1	0	0	0	0
Stieb, Steve, Savannah	.214	28	84	13	18	34	2	1	4	13	0	0	2	0	4	0	20	1	0
Strucher, Mark, Columbus	.239	138	482	70	115	185	25	3	13	85	9	0	7	3	68	5	90	4	5
Teegarden, Robert, Nashville	.265	17	49	5	13	22	2	2	1	10	0	0	0	1	8	0	12	0	0
Teufel, Timothy, Orlando°	.248	128	416	69	103	185	21	5	17	60	7	6	5	2	45	2	80	4	1
Thompson, Milton, Savannah°	.274	140	493	92	135	169	18	2	4	31	3	11	2	1	89	2	112	46	11
Thompson, Tommy, Savannah°	.250	18	52	5	13	22	3	0	2	5	0	0	0	8	0	3	4	0	0
Tomski, Jeffrey, Chat-Sav	.167	63	132	16	22	29	7	0	0	9	2	3	0	3	27	0	29	0	1
Tovar, Raul, Jacksonville	.228	97	289	22	66	77	9	1	0	23	2	7	1	6	27	0	44	8	3
Turner, Ira, Jacksonville	.241	98	336	41	81	128	12	7	7	40	2	1	1	6	25	0	99	25	9
Ullger, Scott, Orlando	.269	138	483	86	130	217	23	2	20	87	10	8	9	6	77	3	72	2	6
Vargas, Leonel, Savannah	.265	140	499	73	132	252	20	2	32	76	4	3	5	5	37	1	88	14	9
Villaescusa, J. Fernando, Orlando°	.091	5	11	0	1	1	0	0	0	0	0	0	0	0	0	0	0	0	0
Villaman, Rafael, Nashville°	.250	132	424	62	106	133	17	2	2	28	1	9	1	2	32	2	69	24	9
Walker, W. Keith, Knoxville°	.232	50	69	5	16	26	7	0	1	9	0	0	1	0	3	0	15	0	0
Weaver, James, Orlando°	.211	17	57	6	12	17	2	0	1	9	0	0	0	0	4	0	9	3	1
Webster, Mitchell, Knoxville†	.294	140	554	89	163	204	26	6	1	42	5	10	2	5	45	3	56	52	12
Wellman, Brad, Jacksonville	.263	135	498	72	131	178	25	2	6	47	2	9	4	4	47	0	68	14	6
Werth, Dennis, Nashville	.279	13	43	9	12	15	0	0	1	8	2	0	1	1	13	0	12	3	2
Westendorf, Phil, Jacksonville	.196	28	92	5	18	23	5	0	0	7	2	0	1	0	2	0	23	0	0
Wherry, Clifton, Columbus	.280	93	328	46	92	121	14	6	1	35	4	9	1	1	34	1	60	11	7
Whitfield, Robert, Charlotte	.222	84	270	25	60	71	9	1	0	21	1	3	4	1	27	1	44	7	4
Wieser, Dan, Jacksonville	.199	105	331	52	66	104	12	1	8	37	3	4	3	0	64	2	64	14	7
Wilborn, Thaddeus, Nashville†	.295	140	553	106	163	235	21	12	9	85	9	12	4	2	49	2	89	43	14
Williams, Larry, Jacksonville	.000	17	1	0	0	0	0	0	0	0	0	0	0	0	0	0	1	0	0
Wilson, Glenn, Birmingham	.306	124	496	77	152	242	24	6	18	82	5	1	3	2	23	2	56	7	4
Wood, Andre, Knoxville	.243	136	474	68	115	165	19	5	7	40	4	6	4	5	50	2	70	13	5
Woodard, Darrell, Birmingham†	.249	103	301	38	75	89	7	2	1	26	4	11	1	2	29	0	26	25	4
Young, Michael, Charlotte°	.320	75	275	58	88	146	16	3	12	45	6	2	3	1	45	3	67	23	5
Younger, Stanley, Birmingham°	.287	139	588	82	169	210	18	4	5	51	4	4	5	0	37	1	74	47	15
Zuvella, Paul, Savannah	.299	138	485	61	145	199	17	2	11	68	9	14	5	10	31	2	42	10	8

The following pitchers had no plate appearances primarily through use of designated hitters, listed alphabetically by club, games in parentheses.

BIRMINGHAM—Beecroft, Michael (15); Chris, Michael (14); Collins, Donald (including Chattanooga) (15); Dacko, Mark (27); Garcia, Dave (7); George, William (including Charlotte) (24); Gumpert, David (11); Josephson, Paul (16); Lackey, John (15); Mathis, Ronald (23); O'Connor, Nicholas (6); Pole, Richard (7); Quealey, Steven (including Columbus) (47); Richards, Kevin (4); Robbins, Bruce (10); Ruiz, August (58); Seoane, Manuel (15); Smith, Jack (31); Steffen, David (1); Travel, Ralph (including Knoxville) (14); Williams, Mark (4).

CHARLOTTE—Arias, Juan (45); Boyd, Randy (15); Davis, George (28); Edwards, Allen (12); Gonzalez, Julian (16); Graven, Timothy (26);

Hook, Edwin (1); Maples, Timothy (16); Norris, Timothy (15); Olivares, Francisco (4); Smith, Mark (25); Snell, Nathaniel (8); Speck, Clifford (12); Swaggerty, William (35); Welchel, Donald (22).

CHATTANOOGA—Anthony, Dane (16); Bohnet, John (27); Bullinger, Matthews (8); Burden, John (5); Fuson, Robin (26); Heaton, Neal (11); Marleski, Steven (42); Nuisher, Jack (13); Owens, Thomas (12); Roche, Stephen (8); Romero, Ramon (19); White, Larry (27); Wilkins, Eric (1).

COLUMBUS—Aponte, Ricardo (21); Bonine, Eddie (23); Brown, Lawrence (24); Cacciatore, Paul (5); Clyde, David (10); Heathcock, Jeffrey (16); Hessler, John (16); Johnson, David (4); Leland, Stanley (22); Melson, Gary (4); O'Brien, Daniel (7); Paris, Zacarias (29); Perry, Patrick (27); Peterson, Gregory (18); Ross, Mark (64); Wilkes, Gregory (12).

JACKSONVILLE—Creel, Keith (20); DiLorenzo, Christopher (10); Dubee, Richard (34); Fischer, Daniel (3); Hanslovan, Jeffrey (27); Pippin, Craig (26); Potestio, Douglas (11); St. Claire, Daniel (20); Vanderbush, Walter (12); Voyles, Curtis (32); Wills, Frank (27).

KNOXVILLE—Baker, James (13); Brown, Thomas (3); Cuellar, Miguel (41); Eichhorn, Mark (30); Elam, Scott (17); Flores, Jesse (5); Fore, Charles (14); Lukish, Thomas (18); McCall, Larry (11); McLaughlin, Colin (16); Robertson, Jay (43); Santana, Rafael (16); Senteney, Steve (46); Wright, Ken (13).

MEMPHIS—Abone, Joseph (29); Anderson, Scott (6); Bargar, Gregory (10); Caldwell, Ronnie (16); Chapin, Peter (2); Fadhel, Antonio (12); Gorman, Thomas (52); Murphy, John (24); Palmer, David (1); Sattler, William (28); Schuler, Mark (25); Shimp, Tommy Joe (17); Tenenini, Robert (40); Westray, Kenneth (2); Wortham, Richard (5); Yanus, Raymond (27).

NASHVILLE—Boxberger, Rodney (23); Elston, Guy (1); Filson, Peter (14); Kaufman, Curt (44); Ledduke, Daniel (25); Lewis, Timothy (7); Morgan, Michael (26); Ricci, Frank (39); Slagle, Roger (25); Smith, Kenneth (1); Taylor, Jeffrey (17); Taylor, Steven (12); Werly, James (28); Wever, Stefan (9).

ORLANDO—Barr, Timothy (5); Broersma, Eric (8); Gleckel, Scott (33); Green, Steven (47); Hobbs, John (41); Konopa, Robert (15); Mapel, Steven (16); Reyes, Jose (37); Viola, Frank (17).

SAVANNAH—Acker, James (10); Cole, Timothy (27); Cowley, Joseph (11); Field, Gregory (27); Hamer, Michael (1); Hatcher, Charles (2); Jones, Craig (24); McMurtry, Joe (28); Morogiello, Daniel (43); Patterson, Scott (13); Pettaway, Felix (42); Shields, William (27); Smith, Michael (3).

GRAND-SLAM HOME RUNS—R. Johnson, 3; Laudner, Perry, Peterson, Ray, Teufel, 2 each; Bush, Carrion, David, Dempsey, Doran, Fry, Gaetti, Glynn, Hallberg, Hazewood, Jacoby, H. Johnson, R. Jones, McCann, McGee, Neal, Poole, Ryal, Simunic, Strucher, Weaver, Wilborn, Wilson, Zuvella, 1 each.

AWARDED FIRST BASE ON INTERFERENCE—Wellman 7 (Laudner 2, Owen 2, Callahan, Shannon, Tomski); C. Jones, 2 (Derryberry, Gleissner); Castillo (Pasley); Chapman (Simunic); Dempsey (Thompson); Nixon (Malkin); Ramie (Simunic); Strucher (Callahan).

CLUB FIELDING

Club	Pct.	G.	PO.	A.	E.	DP.	PB.	Club	Pct.	G.	PO.	A.	E.	DP.	PB.
Birmingham	.970	142	3651	1510	159	106	22	Memphis	.963	143	3736	1574	205	119	24
Charlotte	.969	143	3713	1551	171	145	19	Chattanooga	.962	143	3596	1599	207	124	30
Columbus	.968	143	3638	1622	172	145	13	Savannah	.962	140	3434	1531	195	107	15
Orlando	.967	142	3633	1657	178	139	12	Jacksonville	.961	143	3601	1410	204	116	9
Knoxville	.963	144	3672	1598	203	124	20	Nashville	.961	143	3673	1493	209	119	26

INDIVIDUAL FIELDING

°Throws lefthanded.

FIRST BASEMEN

Player and Club	Pct.	G.	PO.	A.	E.	DP.	Player and Club	Pct.	G.	PO.	A.	E.	DP.
Atkinson, Jacksonville	.986	55	459	27	7	39	Laga, Birmingham°	.983	142	1193	105	23	91
Bowman, Charlotte	.987	124	1078	70	15	119	Laudner, Orlando	1.000	2	9	1	0	1
Bush, Orlando°	1.000	3	14	0	0	1	Mattingly, Nashville°	.990	90	758	64	8	69
Campbell, Columbus	.917	6	39	5	4	6	McCann, Jacksonville	.970	21	150	10	5	11
Carrion, Memphis	1.000	1	9	0	0	1	Milner, Knoxville	.800	1	3	1	1	0
Cecchetti, Chattanooga°	.980	45	410	38	9	29	Pasley, Knoxville	.985	26	250	17	4	21
Cox, Knoxville	.995	18	174	10	1	13	Perry, Savannah	.986	137	1221	86	18	94
Crowley, Memphis°	1.000	1	3	0	0	0	Peterson, Nashville	.968	24	146	7	5	13
DeJesus, Memphis	.982	28	206	16	4	10	Poldberg, Nashville	1.000	1	12	0	0	1
Derryberry, Charlotte	1.000	4	13	0	0	3	Ramie, Savannah	.979	5	44	2	1	4
Fabrizio, Charlotte°	1.000	3	16	0	0	2	Rende, Chattanooga°	.983	98	908	70	17	74
Francona, Memphis°	.961	5	46	3	2	2	Shines, Memphis	.986	77	582	52	9	53
Fry, Memphis	.976	7	38	3	1	5	Showalter, Nashville°	.970	19	151	10	5	6
Gaetti, Orlando	1.000	3	21	2	0	0	Simunic, Memphis	.953	13	97	5	5	6
Glass, Chattanooga	.955	5	20	1	1	4	Slaught, Jacksonville	1.000	4	32	0	0	2
Grout, Savannah	1.000	3	24	3	0	2	Stenhouse, Memphis	.993	35	282	20	2	32
Guerra, Nashville°	1.000	20	176	10	0	14	STRUCHER, Columbus	.988	137	1230	103	16	122
Hallberg, Orlando	.986	118	1065	82	16	111	Turner, Jacksonville	.970	39	310	15	10	24
Hodgson, Knoxville	.988	97	832	54	11	72	Ullger, Orlando°	.975	21	179	12	5	13
Hogg, Jacksonville	1.000	5	34	3	0	4	Walker, Knoxville°	.917	2	10	1	1	0
Hough, Columbus	1.000	1	14	0	0	1	Werth, Nashville	1.000	2	14	1	0	3
Hunsaker, Birmingham	1.000	1	5	0	0	0	Westendorf, Jacksonville	.995	27	202	13	1	26
Hyman, Orlando	1.000	1	2	1	0	0	Whitfield, Charlotte	.993	19	142	3	1	8

SECOND BASEMEN

Player and Club	Pct.	G.	PO.	A.	E.	DP.	Player and Club	Pct.	G.	PO.	A.	E.	DP.
Alvarez, Chattanooga	.974	18	31	44	2	9	Nandin, Birmingham	.964	45	78	108	7	20
Benson, Columbus	.970	17	25	40	2	5	Peterson, Nashville	.950	12	18	20	2	7
Bozich, Birmingham	.980	9	20	30	1	3	Reynolds, Savannah	.958	17	25	43	3	3
Campbell, Columbus	.968	12	25	35	2	7	Rhomberg, Chattanooga	.967	129	281	335	21	73
Carrion, Memphis	1.000	1	0	1	0	0	Robbins, Nashville	.946	10	13	22	2	5
Colletti, Orlando	.964	21	45	61	4	10	Rodriquez, Memphis	.969	43	105	141	8	26
Dennis, Knoxville	.936	6	9	20	2	5	Rodriquez, Charlotte	.975	128	337	357	18	90
Doran, Columbus	.973	121	263	355	17	102	Teufel, Orlando	.972	126	312	376	20	92
Ereu, Knoxville	.950	4	5	14	1	1	Villaescusa, Orlando	1.000	3	4	6	0	1
Franklin, Memphis	.954	48	109	141	12	37	Villaman, Nashville	.970	111	206	308	16	64
Glynn, Memphis	.955	42	87	106	9	17	Wellman, Jacksonville	.985	130	279	357	23	77
Grace, Savannah	.949	9	13	24	2	4	Whitfield, Charlotte	.976	15	36	44	2	9
Ingle, Savannah	.963	119	254	366	24	65	Wieser, Jacksonville	1.000	11	18	26	0	4
Johnson, Memphis	.900	16	38	52	10	8	Wilborn, Nashville	.942	26	41	56	6	14
Luethy, Jacksonville	1.000	1	2	0	0	1	Wood, Knoxville	.970	135	310	441	23	77
McCann, Jacksonville	.941	4	10	6	1	2	WOODARD, Birmingham	.989	99	176	275	5	54

THIRD BASEMEN

Player and Club	Pct.	G.	PO.	A.	E.	DP.	Player and Club	Pct.	G.	PO.	A.	E.	DP.
Alvarez, Chattanooga	.929	40	30	75	8	3	Booker, Orlando	.500	1	0	1	1	0
Atkinson, Jacksonville	.912	18	14	38	5	4	Campbell, Columbus	.913	7	7	14	2	0
Benson, Columbus	.910	40	27	64	9	9	Carrion, Memphis	.667	3	1	3	2	0

THIRD BASEMEN—Continued

Player and Club	Pct.	G.	PO.	A.	E.	DP.
Chaney, Birmingham	1.000	1	2	3	0	0
Colletti, Orlando	1.000	14	9	22	0	1
Cox, Knoxville	.917	11	10	12	2	4
Dayett, Nashville	.920	80	48	125	15	8
DeJesus, Memphis	.000	1	0	0	0	0
Dempsey, Knoxville	.922	132	119	246	31	25
Dennis, Knoxville	.000	1	0	0	0	0
Ereu, Knoxville	.800	4	2	6	2	0
Franklin, Memphis	.879	26	14	44	8	3
Fry, Memphis	.893	51	43	90	16	7
Gaetti, Orlando	.926	131	122	281	32	23
Glynn, Memphis	.877	62	36	92	18	10
Grace, Savannah	.810	6	3	14	4	2
Hanggie, Nashville	.850	19	1	16	3	2
Hinson, Birmingham	1.000	1	0	1	0	0
Jacoby, Savannah	.917	137	99	232	30	18
Johnson, Birmingham	.925	138	103	218	26	16
Luethy, Jacksonville	1.000	5	3	8	0	1
Mariano, Nashville	.978	42	19	71	2	9
McCann, Jacksonville	.970	79	85	139	7	18
Medina, Columbus	.927	67	48	104	12	12
Moronko, Chattanooga	.936	110	89	249	23	18
NAEHRING, Charlotte	.961	124	101	266	15	30
Nandin, Birmingham	.750	4	0	6	2	0
Patterson, Jacksonville	.900	9	4	14	2	1
Peterson, Nashville	.925	32	21	53	6	7
Rogers, Columbus	.888	37	21	90	14	9
Shines, Memphis	.893	28	24	51	9	7
Smith, Charlotte	1.000	2	1	1	0	0
Tomski, Chattanooga	.500	1	1	0	1	0
Ullger, Orlando	1.000	5	4	9	0	0
Whitfield, Charlotte	.956	25	24	41	3	1
Wieser, Jacksonville	.898	38	30	58	10	2

SHORTSTOPS

Player and Club	Pct.	G.	PO.	A.	E.	DP.
Beltran, Columbus	.902	19	26	48	8	10
Benson, Columbus	.966	36	46	96	5	15
Biancalana, Jacksonville	.924	132	208	374	48	60
Booker, Orlando	.939	102	145	303	29	61
Bozich, Birmingham	.833	9	7	18	5	4
Chaney, Birmingham	.976	19	30	52	2	14
Colletti, Orlando	.964	55	52	164	8	32
DeLeon, Chattanooga	.939	130	181	371	36	59
Dempsey, Knoxville	1.000	8	13	24	0	7
Dennis, Knoxville	.963	25	35	69	4	8
Followell, Birmingham	.964	91	156	293	17	52
Glynn, Memphis	1.000	1	1	2	0	1
Grace, Savannah	.923	2	5	7	1	1
Jones, Charlotte	.938	131	175	402	38	75
LITTLE, Memphis	.964	143	237	399	24	73
Luethy, Jacksonville	.667	1	1	1	1	0
Manrique, Knoxville	.916	115	161	330	45	62
Mariano, Nashville	.800	2	0	8	2	1
Moronko, Chattanooga	.953	19	28	53	4	7
Nandin, Birmingham	.935	34	49	94	10	12
Nixon, Nashville	.907	124	198	348	56	51
Villaescusa, Orlando	1.000	2	2	5	0	1
Villaman, Nashville	.918	23	30	60	8	11
Wellman, Nashville	.900	4	7	11	2	1
Wherry, Columbus	.976	93	165	313	12	73
Whitfield, Charlotte	.928	14	27	50	6	13
Wieser, Jacksonville	.949	13	14	23	2	4
Zuvella, Savannah	.947	138	220	406	35	61

OUTFIELDERS

Player and Club	Pct.	G.	PO.	A.	E.	DP.
Adams, Chattanooga	.955	110	199	11	10	3
Alvarez, Chattanooga	1.000	2	3	1	0	0
Baker, Birmingham°	1.000	52	93	5	0	0
Baker, Chattanooga	.920	49	75	5	7	0
Barfield, Knoxville	.980	141	270	23	6	3
Benson, Columbus	.889	5	7	1	1	0
Bowman, Charlotte	1.000	16	19	4	0	0
Brown, Birmingham	1.000	18	29	0	0	0
Buckner, Jacksonville°	.939	29	44	2	3	0
R. Bush, Orlando°	.971	114	160	7	5	3
Campbell, Columbus	1.000	7	12	0	0	0
Carrion, Memphis	.957	93	145	12	7	3
Castillo, Chattanooga	.943	113	236	13	15	1
Cecchetti, Chattanooga°	.957	79	146	9	7	5
Chapman, Nashville°	.950	122	235	13	13	0
Colletti, Orlando	1.000	4	7	0	0	0
Cox, Knoxville	.964	16	25	2	1	1
Csefalvay, Columbus	.926	21	22	3	2	1
David, Orlando°	.968	126	253	17	9	1
Dayett, Nashville	1.000	4	7	0	0	0
Denman, Charlotte	.963	97	170	11	7	2
Dennis, Knoxville	.984	40	55	8	1	1
Dotson, Chattanooga	1.000	32	37	5	0	2
Douglas, Orlando	.981	120	250	12	5	2
Dumouchelle, Charlotte	1.000	5	8	0	0	0
Ereu, Knoxville	.944	16	16	1	1	0
Francona, Memphis°	.952	36	56	4	3	0
Franklin, Memphis	1.000	9	7	1	0	0
Garbey, Birmingham	.956	72	106	3	5	0
Gardner, Chattanooga	.961	58	95	4	4	1
Glynn, Memphis	1.000	4	7	0	0	0
Guerra, Nashville°	1.000	1	2	0	0	0
Hall, Savannah	.965	132	263	16	10	7
Hardy, Birmingham	.929	9	13	0	1	0
Hazewood, Charlotte	.972	97	166	8	5	1
Hernandez, Knoxville	1.000	1	1	0	0	0
Hicks, Jacksonville	.940	42	76	2	5	0
Jabalera, Columbus°	.946	123	265	13	16	4
Jacoby, Savannah	.800	3	4	0	1	0
A. Johnson, Memphis	.977	85	164	3	4	1
R. Johnson, Memphis°	.969	126	340	8	11	1
W. Johnson, Memphis	1.000	4	6	0	0	0
JONES, Columbus°	.989	126	178	9	2	2
Kenaga, Birmingham	.978	33	40	4	1	0
Knight, Nashville°	.980	29	47	1	1	1
Leeper, Jacksonville	.946	63	117	6	7	2
Mattingly, Nashville°	.959	55	88	5	4	1
McGee, Nashville	.973	87	203	10	6	6
Milner, Knoxville	.600	4	3	0	2	0
Neal, Charlotte	.965	80	155	8	6	2
Norko, Knoxville	1.000	4	1	0	0	0
Pasley, Columbus	1.000	1	2	0	0	0
Poole, Birmingham	1.000	2	1	0	0	0
Ramie, Knoxville	.964	88	129	5	5	0
Ray, Columbus	.944	95	128	6	8	1
Rende, Chattanooga°	1.000	1	6	0	0	0
Reynolds, Savannah	1.000	9	15	0	0	0
Roberts, Orlando	1.000	1	1	0	0	0
Rooney, Memphis	.944	9	16	1	1	0
Ryal, Jacksonville°	.957	119	237	8	11	1
Shelby, Charlotte	.925	57	120	3	10	0
Shines, Memphis	1.000	3	6	0	0	0
Showalter, Nashville°	.964	33	50	4	2	1
Silverio, Jacksonville	1.000	15	34	2	0	0
Simons, Columbus°	.972	58	132	6	4	1
Smith, Charlotte	1.000	11	18	2	0	0
Stenhouse, Memphis	.970	79	125	6	4	1
Teegarden, Nashville	.857	7	6	0	1	0
Thompson, Savannah	.968	140	226	17	8	3
Tovar, Jacksonville	.976	91	187	12	5	1
Turner, Jacksonville	.926	51	72	3	6	0
Ullger, Orlando	.989	54	85	6	1	0
Vargas, Savannah	.949	140	222	22	13	4
Weaver, Orlando°	.917	15	21	1	2	0
Webster, Knoxville°	.970	140	317	7	10	1
Wieser, Jacksonville	.931	43	61	6	5	1
Wilborn, Knoxville	.961	108	191	4	8	2
Wilson, Birmingham	.984	123	292	18	5	4
Woodard, Birmingham	1.000	1	2	0	0	0
Young, Charlotte	.975	73	190	5	5	3
Younger, Birmingham°	.957	134	193	9	9	0

CATCHERS

Player and Club	Pct.	G.	PO.	A.	E.	DP.	PB.
Bazan, Orlando	.909	7	17	3	2	0	1
Cadahia, Orlando	1.000	11	57	8	0	0	2
Callahan, Nashville	.978	68	448	39	11	3	12
Campbell, Columbus	1.000	3	5	0	0	0	0
Carrasquel, Birmingham	.983	30	216	18	4	1	2
Derryberry, Charlotte	.942	16	75	6	5	2	8
Glass, Chattanooga	.889	4	7	1	1	0	1
Gleissner, Jacksonville	.951	10	54	4	3	1	0
Hanggie, Nashville	1.000	3	6	1	0	0	1
Hogg, Jacksonville	.983	59	316	34	6	3	5
Hough, Columbus	.965	41	223	26	9	4	5
Hunsaker, Birmingham	.994	26	145	13	1	0	2
Hyman, Orlando	1.000	6	38	4	0	1	0
Ivie, Charlotte	1.000	2	5	0	0	0	0
Jacobs, Columbus	.986	94	556	82	9	8	7
Kelly, Knoxville	.934	9	52	5	4	0	2
Laudner, Orlando	.979	114	622	65	15	11	7
Lowry, Birmingham	.975	17	108	11	3	0	2
Malkin, Chattanooga	.976	28	140	19	4	4	6
MILNER, Knoxville	.992	102	539	72	5	8	14

CATCHERS —Continued

Player and Club	Pct.	G.	PO.	A.	E.	DP.	PB.
Mizerock, Columbus	.979	11	80	11	2	1	1
Owen, Savannah	.958	85	450	77	23	6	11
Pasley, Knoxville	.967	38	194	38	8	4	4
Poldberg, Nashville	.973	52	257	35	8	2	8
Poole, Birmingham	.972	85	509	54	16	8	16
Reece, Memphis	.984	21	113	10	2	0	2
Reed, Orlando	1.000	2	4	1	0	0	0
Rey, Chattanooga	.961	93	424	44	19	4	17
Royster, Charlotte	.976	131	780	100	22	8	11
Shannon, Nashville	.987	27	142	14	2	1	0
Shines, Memphis	.971	15	61	5	2	2	3
Simunic, Memphis	.986	117	651	105	11	8	19
Skeens, Orlando	.947	15	48	6	3	1	2
Slaught, Jacksonville	.983	74	450	61	9	4	4
Stephans, Jacksonville	1.000	4	27	3	0	0	0
Stieb, Savannah	.983	28	153	20	3	0	1
Thompson, Savannah	.944	17	77	7	5	2	1
Tomski, Chat-Sav	.968	60	235	39	9	2	8
Werth, Nashville	1.000	12	75	5	0	0	5

PITCHERS

Player and Club	Pct.	G.	PO.	A.	E.	DP.
Acker, Savannah	1.000	10	11	25	0	0
Anderson, Chattanooga	1.000	25	5	10	0	2
Anderson, Memphis	1.000	4	0	1	0	0
Anthony, Chattanooga	.952	16	8	12	1	0
Aponte, Columbus	1.000	21	7	5	0	0
Arias, Charlotte	1.000	45	4	10	0	0
Baker, Knoxville	1.000	13	5	12	0	1
Bargar, Memphis	1.000	9	4	14	0	0
Barr, Orlando	1.000	5	1	6	0	1
Beecroft, Birmingham	1.000	15	6	7	0	0
BOHNET, Chattanooga°	1.000	27	9	33	0	1
Bonine, Columbus	.943	22	9	24	2	2
Borchers, Chattanooga	.959	36	8	39	2	4
Botelho, Jacksonville	1.000	7	2	5	0	0
Boxberger, Nashville	.967	23	6	23	1	3
Boyd, Charlotte°	1.000	15	0	2	0	0
Broersma, Orlando	1.000	8	5	2	0	0
Brown, Columbus	.955	23	8	13	1	1
Brown, Knoxville	1.000	3	1	1	0	0
Budner, Charlotte°	.941	25	3	29	2	4
Bullinger, Chattanooga°	1.000	8	0	2	0	0
Burden, Chattanooga	1.000	5	2	0	0	0
Cacciatore, Columbus	.875	5	1	6	1	1
Caldwell, Memphis	.882	11	7	8	2	0
Chapin, Memphis	.000	2	0	0	1	0
Chris, Birmingham°	1.000	14	3	27	0	0
Clyde, Columbus°	.938	10	6	9	1	0
Cole, Savannah°	.964	27	5	22	1	1
Collins, Chat-Birm	.750	15	0	9	3	1
Cornell, Jacksonville	.926	26	13	12	2	1
Cowley, Savannah	.950	11	9	10	1	1
Creel, Jacksonville	.897	20	9	17	3	1
Cuellar, Knoxville	.923	41	10	14	2	2
Dacko, Birmingham	.943	27	14	19	2	0
Davis, Charlotte	.929	28	3	23	2	0
Dilks, Memphis°	.923	12	3	9	1	0
DiLorenzo, Jacksonville	.571	10	0	4	3	0
Dubee, Jacksonville	.957	33	7	15	1	0
Edwards, Charlotte	1.000	12	3	4	0	1
Eichhorn, Knoxville	.906	30	13	35	5	2
Elam, Knoxville	.733	17	4	7	4	0
Fadhel, Memphis	.833	12	4	6	2	1
Field, Savannah	1.000	27	12	28	0	3
Filson, Nashville°	.944	14	3	14	1	1
Fischer, Jacksonville	1.000	3	0	9	0	0
Flores, Knoxville	1.000	5	0	1	0	0
Fore, Knoxville	1.000	14	1	14	0	3
Fuson, Chattanooga	1.000	26	11	14	0	1
Garcia, Birmingham	1.000	7	0	1	0	0
George, Char-Birm°	1.000	24	1	19	0	0
Glecker, Orlando°	.902	33	13	24	4	1
Gonzalez, Charlotte°	.889	16	3	5	1	0
Gorman, Memphis°	.857	52	7	17	4	3
Graven, Charlotte°	1.000	26	4	4	0	2
Green, Orlando	.923	47	9	15	2	3
Guerra, Nashville°	.500	7	0	1	1	0
Gumpert, Birmingham	1.000	11	13	11	0	0
Hanslovan, Jacksonville°	.333	27	1	0	2	0
Hatcher, Savannah	1.000	2	0	1	0	0
Havens, Orlando°	.941	11	0	16	1	0
Heathcock, Columbus	1.000	16	11	16	0	0
Heaton, Chattanooga°	1.000	11	2	10	0	0
Heimer, Chattanooga°	.929	25	3	10	1	2
Hessler, Columbus	.909	16	6	14	2	1
Hobbs, Orlando°	.800	41	5	19	6	4
Hook, Charlotte	1.000	1	1	0	0	0
Johnson, Columbus°	1.000	4	0	2	0	0
Jones, Savannah	.964	24	8	19	1	0
Josephson, Birmingham	1.000	16	1	6	0	1
Kaufman, Nashville	.917	44	4	7	1	0
Konopa, Orlando°	.882	15	3	12	2	2
Kromy, Orlando	.927	30	11	27	3	1
Lackey, Birmingham	.947	15	10	8	1	2
Ledduke, Nashville	1.000	25	2	12	0	3
Leland, Columbus	.960	22	6	18	1	0
Lewis, Nashville°	1.000	7	1	2	0	0
Livingstone, Memphis	.923	37	6	6	1	0
Lukish, Knoxville	1.000	18	1	2	0	0
Mapel, Orlando	.972	16	16	19	1	1
Maples, Charlotte	.909	16	2	8	1	1
Mathis, Birmingham	.909	23	9	11	2	0
McCall, Knoxville	.889	11	4	4	1	0
McLaughlin, Knoxville	.893	16	9	16	3	1
McMurtry, Savannah	.912	28	16	46	6	5
Melson, Columbus	1.000	4	0	2	0	0
Morgan, Nashville	.959	26	10	37	2	1
Morley, Jacksonville°	1.000	17	8	17	0	1
Morogiello, Savannah°	.933	43	5	9	1	1
Mulligan, Orlando°	1.000	14	4	16	0	0
Murphy, Memphis°	1.000	24	3	17	0	0
Narleski, Chattanooga	.966	42	6	22	1	0
Norris, Charlotte	.889	15	6	10	2	1
Nuismer, Chattanooga	.947	13	6	12	1	1
O'Brien, Columbus	1.000	7	1	2	0	1
O'Connor, Birmingham	1.000	6	2	0	0	0
Oliveras, Charlotte	1.000	4	0	1	0	1
Owen, Savannah	1.000	1	6	1	0	0
Owens, Chattanooga	.857	12	0	6	1	0
Paris, Columbus	.915	29	13	30	4	1
Patterson, Savannah	1.000	13	11	8	0	2
Perry, Columbus	.941	27	4	12	1	2
Petersen, Columbus°	1.000	17	10	15	0	1
Pettaway, Savannah	.917	42	3	8	1	1
Pippin, Jacksonville	1.000	26	1	2	0	0
Pole, Birmingham	1.000	7	1	3	0	0
Potestio, Jacksonville	.875	11	3	11	2	1
Queasey, Col-Birm	.955	47	8	13	1	2
Reyes, Orlando	1.000	37	3	11	0	2
Ricci, Nashville	.923	39	4	8	1	0
Richards, Nashville	.000	4	0	0	1	0
Robbins, Birmingham°	.818	10	1	8	2	0
Robertson, Knoxville	.842	43	8	8	3	0
Roche, Chattanooga	1.000	8	1	2	0	0
Romero, Chattanooga°	1.000	19	2	5	0	1
Ross, Columbus	.964	63	4	23	1	3
Ruiz, Birmingham°	1.000	58	12	26	0	0
Santana, Savannah	.900	16	5	13	2	1
Sattler, Memphis	.911	28	11	30	4	0
Schuler, Memphis	.889	25	2	6	1	1
Senteney, Knoxville	.813	46	10	16	6	1
Seoane, Birmingham	.500	15	0	2	2	0
Serum, Orlando	.952	45	6	14	1	2
Shields, Savannah	1.000	27	5	9	0	0
Shimp, Memphis	1.000	17	3	8	0	0
Slagle, Nashville	.949	18	8	29	2	0
Smith, Birmingham°	.962	31	6	19	1	1
Smith, Charlotte	.926	25	11	14	2	3
Snell, Charlotte	1.000	8	4	9	0	0
Speck, Charlotte	.889	12	1	7	1	0
St. Claire, Jacksonville	1.000	20	0	2	0	0
Swaggerty, Charlotte	1.000	35	1	13	0	1
J. Taylor, Nashville	.950	17	6	13	1	1
S. Taylor, Nashville	.818	12	3	6	2	0
Tenenini, Memphis	1.000	40	7	19	0	2
Treuel, Knox-Birm	.800	14	0	4	1	1
Vanderbush, Jacksonville	.889	12	4	4	1	0
Viola, Orlando°	.967	17	9	20	1	0
Voyles, Jacksonville	.867	32	2	11	2	2
Walker, Knoxville°	.946	30	8	27	2	1
Welchel, Charlotte	.931	22	10	17	2	5
Werly, Nashville	.914	28	13	19	3	3
Westray, Memphis°	1.000	2	0	1	0	0
Wever, Nashville	.889	9	4	12	2	1
White, Chattanooga	.900	27	20	34	6	3
Wilkes, Columbus	.833	12	6	4	2	0
Wilkins, Chattanooga	1.000	1	0	2	0	0
Williams, Jacksonville	.875	16	0	7	1	0
Williams, Birmingham	1.000	4	1	2	0	0
Wills, Jacksonville	.927	27	10	28	3	1
Wortham, Memphis°	1.000	5	0	1	0	0
Wright, Nashville	.870	13	2	18	3	1
Yanus, Memphis	.971	27	9	25	1	3

The following players do not have any recorded accepted chances at the positions indicated; therefore, are not listed in the fielding averages for those particular positions: Benson, p; Crowley, 3b, of; DeJesus, 3b; Dennis, p; Doran, ss; Elston, p; Fuentes, of; Grace, of; Hamer, p; Hinson, 1b; Hogg, p; Hough, p; Malkin, 3b; Mariano, 2b; Palmer, p; Poole, 3b; Robbins, of; K. Smith, p; Mi. Smith, p; Steffen, p.

CLUB PITCHING

Club	ERA.	G.	CG.	ShO.	Sv.	IP.	H.	R.	ER.	HR.	HB.	BB.	Int. BB.	SO.	WP.	Bk.
Nashville	3.26	143	54	9	21	1224⅓	1102	574	443	77	32	535	29	882	58	13
Savannah	3.95	140	52	9	17	1144⅔	1096	622	502	120	38	534	25	694	47	4
Charlotte	3.99	143	43	5	26	1237⅔	1304	648	549	108	20	499	24	792	56	6
Jacksonville	4.05	143	46	11	20	1200⅓	1171	652	540	111	38	552	30	784	63	8
Orlando	4.14	142	23	3	34	1211	1312	671	557	104	21	477	41	727	63	10
Memphis	4.19	143	24	8	29	1245⅓	1271	714	580	119	33	498	29	798	78	13
Knoxville	4.26	144	27	2	23	1224	1266	702	579	115	26	539	24	756	81	13
Chattanooga	4.35	143	38	10	22	1198⅔	1190	713	579	111	38	556	25	701	48	11
Birmingham	4.53	142	27	7	25	1217	1260	716	613	127	43	557	18	913	69	7
Columbus	4.58	143	32	8	25	1212⅔	1290	729	617	108	46	539	32	821	50	11

PITCHERS' RECORDS
(Leading Qualifiers for Earned-Run Average Leadership — 115 or More Innings)

°Throws lefthanded.

Pitcher—Club	W.	L.	Pct.	ERA.	G.	GS.	CG.	GF.	ShO.	Sv.	IP.	H.	R.	ER.	HR.	HB.	BB.	Int. BB.	SO.	WP.
Ross, Columbus	8	10	.444	2.25	64	0	0	59	0	22	116	103	35	29	3	5	32	12	70	3
Werly, Nashville	13	11	.542	2.59	28	28	18	0	1	0	222	184	91	64	10	6	88	1	193	11
Creel, Jacksonville	12	7	.632	2.72	20	20	10	0	4	0	149	106	52	45	13	2	44	4	105	4
McMurtry, Savannah	15	11	.577	2.76	28	28	13	0	2	0	202	168	87	62	13	4	95	3	111	7
Sattler, Memphis	11	6	.647	2.76	28	22	7	1	1	0	163	136	67	50	12	7	45	1	94	8
Welchel, Charlotte	13	7	.650	2.91	22	22	11	0	0	0	161	161	76	52	11	0	63	0	90	9
Slagle, Nashville	9	5	.643	3.02	18	18	10	0	1	0	134	124	52	45	9	2	29	1	78	2
Bonine, Columbus	11	7	.611	3.07	22	20	5	1	2	0	132	119	55	45	10	4	43	3	120	1
Ruiz, Birmingham°	5	3	.625	3.15	58	0	0	35	0	4	123	112	54	43	7	3	62	3	106	9
Bohnet, Chattanooga°	13	7	.650	3.38	27	27	6	0	3	0	168	169	80	63	14	4	52	0	94	9

Departmental Leaders: G—Ross, 64; GS—Eichhorn, Paris, 29; CG—Werly, 18; ShO—Creel, 4; GF—Ross, 59; W—McMurtry, 15; L—Cole, 15; Sv—Gorman, Ross, 22; Pct.—Filson, Tenenini, .833; IP—Werly, 122; H—Davis, 215; ER—Eichhorn, 112; ER—Paris, 92; HR—Eichhorn, 23; BB—Cornell, 114; IBB—Ross, 12; HB—Cole, 11; SO—Werly, 193; WP—Robertson, Wills, 15.

(All Pitchers—Listed Alphabetically)

Pitcher—Club	W.	L.	Pct.	ERA.	G.	GS.	CG.	GF.	ShO.	Sv.	IP.	H.	R.	ER.	HR.	HB.	BB.	Int. BB.	SO.	WP.
Abone, Memphis	9	10	.474	4.24	29	25	7	2	2	0	170	183	98	80	19	5	49	3	72	2
Acker, Savannah	5	5	.500	2.69	10	10	6	0	0	0	77	57	34	23	9	3	34	0	37	3
Anderson, Chattanooga	2	3	.400	3.11	25	1	0	18	0	8	55	41	25	19	2	3	28	2	35	9
Anderson, Memphis	0	0	.000	6.00	4	0	0	1	0	0	6	6	6	4	1	0	6	0	4	0
Anthony, Chattanooga	4	2	.667	5.37	16	5	1	6	0	0	62	61	41	37	7	3	33	0	42	2
Aponte, Columbus	2	5	.286	3.88	21	3	0	4	0	1	65	73	32	28	3	2	23	1	28	2
Arias, Charlotte	5	7	.417	3.92	45	0	0	28	0	8	101	97	52	44	5	2	38	3	84	6
Baker, Knoxville	5	5	.500	3.56	13	13	3	0	1	0	86	85	42	34	6	1	29	1	42	4
Bargar, Memphis	5	2	.714	3.60	9	9	2	0	1	0	65	58	29	26	2	3	27	1	52	3
Barr, Columbus	1	3	.250	5.40	7	5	0	0	0	0	30	38	20	18	1	0	13	0	19	0
Beecroft, Birmingham	3	6	.333	5.48	15	14	1	0	0	0	69	73	52	42	8	7	58	1	48	8
Benson, Columbus	0	0	.000	0.00	1	0	0	1	0	0	2	2	0	0	0	0	2	0	0	0
Bohnet, Chattanooga°	13	7	.650	3.38	27	27	6	0	3	0	168	169	80	63	14	4	52	0	94	9
Bonine, Columbus	11	7	.611	3.07	22	20	5	1	2	0	132	119	55	45	10	4	43	3	120	1
Borchers, Chattanooga°	5	11	.313	3.66	36	15	7	10	1	0	150	155	79	61	13	6	71	2	61	6
Botelho, Jacksonville	2	2	.500	1.95	7	5	2	2	1	1	37	27	9	8	2	0	4	0	15	0
Boxberger, Nashville	4	9	.308	4.54	23	18	4	3	0	0	109	114	74	55	7	8	72	4	62	13
Boyd, Charlotte°	1	1	.500	2.63	15	0	0	8	0	2	24	20	8	7	1	0	12	1	32	2
Broersma, Orlando	2	4	.333	4.81	8	7	0	1	0	0	43	44	29	23	7	1	22	1	41	0
Brown, Columbus	1	5	.167	8.17	23	5	0	8	0	0	76	111	83	69	8	3	42	2	39	5
Brown, Knoxville	1	0	1.000	1.13	3	0	0	1	0	0	8	7	1	1	0	1	0	0	3	1
Budner, Charlotte°	5	6	.455	4.77	25	18	6	5	1	0	132	159	72	70	10	4	42	1	82	11
Bullinger, Chattanooga	0	0	.000	5.00	8	0	0	3	0	1	9	10	9	5	1	0	5	0	5	0
Burden, Chattanooga	0	0	.000	6.75	5	0	0	4	0	0	8	14	9	6	0	4	1	0	0	0
Cacciatore, Columbus	0	4	.000	8.25	5	5	0	0	0	0	24	33	29	22	5	1	20	0	7	2
Caldwell, Memphis	4	4	.500	5.43	11	11	1	0	0	0	63	66	42	38	9	2	38	3	50	11
Chapin, Memphis	0	0	.000	3.27	2	2	0	0	0	0	11	8	6	4	1	1	11	0	9	3
Chris, Birmingham°	5	5	.500	4.15	14	14	3	0	0	0	89	82	46	41	11	2	69	0	77	5
Clyde, Columbus°	6	0	1.000	0.76	10	7	2	2	2	0	59	41	8	5	1	0	16	2	51	2
Cole, Savannah°	8	15	.348	4.63	27	27	7	0	3	0	169	166	107	87	21	11	101	2	95	7
Collins, Chat.-Birm.	6	5	.545	5.37	15	11	0	2	0	1	62	75	43	37	7	4	39	1	52	2
Cornell, Jacksonville	8	9	.471	3.58	26	26	8	0	1	0	166	141	76	66	8	7	114	6	106	8
Cowley, Savannah	6	0	1.000	2.74	11	7	4	4	0	1	69	47	22	21	8	2	16	1	56	0
Creel, Jacksonville	12	7	.632	2.72	20	20	10	0	4	0	149	106	52	45	13	2	44	4	105	4
Cuellar, Knoxville	6	3	.667	4.66	41	0	0	25	0	5	87	89	53	45	6	1	38	5	42	3
Dacko, Birmingham	13	7	.650	4.45	27	27	7	0	0	0	168	177	96	83	19	4	56	0	115	5
Davis, Charlotte	14	10	.583	3.47	28	28	6	0	2	0	187	215	86	72	14	0	65	2	119	7
Dilks, Memphis°	1	7	.125	4.08	12	12	1	0	0	0	75	65	42	34	10	1	49	0	63	11
DiLorenzo, Jacksonville	0	3	.000	5.45	10	3	0	2	0	1	33	38	24	20	4	2	19	1	22	1
Dubee, Jacksonville	8	6	.571	4.04	33	7	2	18	0	5	107	134	65	48	10	3	26	5	61	1
Edwards, Charlotte	3	6	.333	5.94	12	7	1	3	0	0	47	56	40	31	6	0	22	1	30	0
Eichhorn, Knoxville	10	14	.417	3.98	30	29	9	0	1	0	192	202	112	85	23	3	57	2	99	10
Elam, Knoxville	6	4	.600	3.60	17	13	2	2	0	0	90	85	45	36	5	1	55	2	81	14
Elston, Nashville	0	0	.000	9.00	1	0	0	0	0	0	2	5	2	2	0	0	2	0	1	0
Fadhel, Memphis	2	2	.500	3.33	12	8	0	3	0	0	46	39	27	17	0	3	30	1	30	2
Field, Savannah	11	10	.524	4.19	27	27	8	0	2	0	172	198	98	80	18	8	64	4	101	8
Filson, Nashville°	10	2	.833	1.82	14	13	7	1	3	1	99	73	30	20	3	3	28	1	77	3
Fischer, Jacksonville	2	0	1.000	1.17	3	3	2	0	0	0	23	16	4	3	0	0	6	1	9	0
Flores, Knoxville	1	0	1.000	6.00	5	0	0	0	0	0	12	12	8	8	1	1	6	0	5	0
Fore, Knoxville	3	8	.273	3.64	14	14	0	0	0	0	99	102	53	40	13	2	35	1	60	3
Fuson, Chattanooga	7	8	.467	4.93	26	19	4	6	0	0	115	122	78	63	10	2	59	1	79	4
Garcia, Chattanooga	0	1	.000	11.00	7	0	0	2	0	0	9	20	13	11	0	2	12	1	7	4
George, Char.-Birm.°	6	5	.545	4.33	24	13	2	6	0	0	108	105	59	52	14	2	68	3	68	3
Gleckel, Orlando°	10	7	.588	3.65	33	20	5	6	1	4	165	170	77	67	9	1	47	6	94	3
Gonzalez, Charlotte°	2	5	.000	4.20	16	3	0	2	0	0	45	45	24	21	2	0	27	1	38	6
Gorman, Memphis	12	9	.571	3.07	52	0	0	46	0	22	91	82	39	31	9	3	30	5	91	7
Graven, Charlotte°	0	3	.000	4.91	26	0	0	10	0	3	22	28	12	12	3	1	8	1	7	0
Green, Orlando	7	6	.538	4.97	47	6	2	36	0	8	96	129	61	53	7	2	26	8	22	1

Pitcher—Club	W.	L.	Pct.	ERA.	G.	GS.	CG.	GF.	ShO.	Sv.	IP.	H.	R.	ER.	HR.	HB.	BB.	Int. BB.	SO.	WP.
Guerra, Nashville	0	0	.000	1.13	7	0	0	6	0	0	8	4	1	1	0	1	4	1	8	0
Gumbert, Birmingham	6	3	.667	4.14	11	11	3	0	1	0	74	78	39	34	8	3	16	0	25	0
Hamer, Savannah	0	0	.000	9.00	1	0	0	1	0	0	1	3	1	1	0	0	0	0	0	0
Hanslovan, Jacksonville°	2	1	.667	5.11	27	0	0	13	0	3	44	53	30	25	2	0	25	1	29	5
Hatcher, Savannah	0	0	.000	0.00	2	0	0	2	0	0	4	1	0	0	0	0	1	0	1	0
Havens, Orlando°	6	2	.750	3.53	11	11	1	0	0	0	74	81	38	29	10	0	20	1	58	1
Heathcock, Columbus	4	7	.364	4.63	16	15	7	0	0	0	101	104	57	52	6	3	35	0	59	2
Heaton, Chattanooga°	4	4	.500	3.97	11	11	4	0	0	0	77	61	42	34	13	0	27	1	50	2
Heimer, Chattanooga°	1	3	.250	6.39	25	0	0	14	0	4	62	69	51	44	6	4	55	1	40	5
Hessler, Columbus	4	4	.500	4.83	16	13	3	1	0	0	82	86	52	44	9	5	63	0	70	8
Hobbs, Orlando°	11	7	.611	4.08	41	9	1	13	0	0	139	119	75	63	11	7	85	5	120	11
Hogg, Jacksonville	0	0	.000	13.50	1	0	0	0	0	0	2	5	3	3	0	0	0	0	1	0
Hook, Charlotte	0	0	.000	9.00	1	0	0	1	0	0	1	1	1	1	0	0	1	0	0	0
Hough, Columbus	0	0	.000		1	0	0	1	0	0	2	0	0	0	0	0	0	0	0	0
Johnson, Columbus°	0	1	.000	10.50	4	1	0	2	0	0	6	8	8	7	3	0	2	0	6	0
Jones, Savannah	6	8	.429	4.15	24	23	5	1	1	0	141	133	79	65	10	2	75	1	94	8
Josephson, Birmingham	3	1	.750	5.03	16	1	0	9	0	1	34	39	20	19	6	0	15	2	19	1
Kaufman, Nashville	9	5	.643	2.88	44	1	0	33	0	12	78	62	28	25	5	2	33	11	77	4
Konopa, Orlando°	5	5	.500	5.27	15	12	2	0	0	0	70	74	46	41	9	0	22	1	47	6
Kromy, Orlando	10	9	.526	3.92	30	28	6	0	1	0	170	180	96	74	14	3	79	5	59	11
Lackey, Birmingham	5	7	.417	6.98	15	14	0	1	0	0	80	86	67	62	12	4	32	0	35	5
Ledduke, Nashville	1	10	.091	4.84	25	9	0	9	0	2	93	104	64	50	6	0	49	2	65	2
Leland, Columbus	5	10	.333	5.54	22	21	3	1	0	0	112	127	86	69	13	5	65	2	49	6
Lewis, Nashville°	0	0	.000	3.38	7	0	0	4	0	0	24	24	15	9	2	1	11	0	15	3
Livingstone, Memphis	2	1	.667	4.94	37	1	0	23	0	2	62	83	43	34	10	1	10	0	25	3
Lukish, Knoxville	0	2	.000	1.73	18	0	0	17	0	6	26	18	11	5	3	0	11	1	28	1
Mapel, Orlando	10	4	.714	3.60	16	16	1	0	0	0	100	109	54	40	10	1	31	2	55	1
Maples, Charlotte	6	6	.500	5.23	16	14	4	0	0	0	86	87	51	50	12	5	41	3	50	4
Mathis, Birmingham	8	8	.500	4.57	23	23	5	0	2	0	134	129	79	68	11	3	53	0	125	7
McCall, Knoxville	2	3	.400	4.67	11	4	1	3	0	0	54	48	28	28	10	1	10	0	30	1
McLaughlin, Knoxville	5	8	.385	4.92	16	16	3	0	0	0	86	77	54	47	5	5	73	1	81	9
McMurtry, Savannah	15	11	.577	2.76	28	28	13	0	2	0	202	168	87	62	13	4	95	3	111	7
Melson, Columbus	0	4	.000	10.20	4	2	1	0	0	0	15	22	20	17	3	1	9	0	11	1
Morgan, Nashville	8	7	.533	4.42	26	26	7	0	0	0	169	164	97	83	16	2	83	0	100	12
Morley, Jacksonville°	5	10	.333	3.72	17	17	4	0	0	0	109	95	57	45	8	2	59	3	54	3
Morogiello, Savannah°	5	4	.556	4.23	43	0	0	29	0	7	66	78	39	31	8	2	35	6	50	1
Mulligan, Orlando°	5	6	.455	3.43	14	13	3	0	0	0	84	91	39	32	5	1	30	2	45	1
Murphy, Memphis°	10	10	.500	4.91	24	23	2	0	1	0	132	147	81	72	13	1	55	1	91	3
Narleski, Chattanooga	9	10	.474	4.57	42	12	4	22	0	6	130	130	74	66	15	2	55	8	56	2
Norris, Charlotte	3	3	.500	5.40	15	10	2	2	0	1	65	85	47	39	12	2	27	0	29	2
Nuismer, Chattanooga	5	5	.500	4.56	13	13	3	0	1	0	79	83	46	40	3	0	27	1	55	0
O'Brien, Columbus	0	0	.000	10.50	7	0	0	4	0	0	12	21	15	14	3	1	7	1	4	1
O'Connor, Birmingham	0	3	.000	14.40	6	3	0	2	0	0	10	18	23	16	2	0	12	0	13	1
Oliveras, Charlotte	0	2	.000	5.63	4	1	0	3	0	0	16	23	10	10	5	0	5	2	10	0
Owens, Chattanooga	2	4	.333	5.06	12	6	1	3	1	0	48	40	30	27	8	2	26	1	37	4
Palmer, Memphis	0	0	.000		1	1	0	0	0	0	0	0	0	1	0	0	1	0	0	0
Paris, Columbus	11	9	.550	4.36	29	29	6	0	0	0	190	184	105	92	15	10	76	1	166	5
Patterson, Savannah	5	8	.385	4.40	13	13	8	0	0	0	94	94	56	46	15	1	36	0	55	0
Perry, Columbus	3	1	.750	6.35	27	0	0	17	0	1	51	54	40	36	7	1	38	1	35	4
Petersen, Columbus	4	6	.400	5.52	17	14	1	1	0	0	93	112	64	57	12	2	33	4	60	5
Pettaway, Savannah	4	6	.400	5.37	42	1	1	34	0	8	62	64	40	37	6	3	26	3	57	9
Pippin, Jacksonville	1	2	.333	8.74	26	0	0	22	0	3	34	47	40	33	10	1	18	1	16	4
Pole, Birmingham	1	0	1.000	3.00	7	0	0	7	0	3	18	15	7	6	1	0	6	3	18	0
Potestio, Jacksonville	3	7	.300	5.13	11	11	3	0	1	0	72	89	50	41	6	3	27	1	33	4
Quealey, Col-Birm	8	3	.727	2.27	47	0	0	37	0	13	99	86	30	25	13	4	35	1	85	5
Reyes, Orlando	3	1	.750	4.72	37	0	0	27	0	2	82	96	48	43	10	5	37	3	67	11
Ricci, Nashville	8	9	.471	3.53	39	5	2	25	0	4	97	83	49	38	9	1	48	5	94	4
Richards, Birmingham	0	0	.000	30.00	4	0	0	2	0	0	3	9	10	10	1	0	6	0	2	0
Robbins, Birmingham°	3	2	.600	3.79	10	10	2	0	1	0	57	51	29	24	3	0	27	0	60	4
Robertson, Knoxville	3	5	.375	4.64	43	1	0	34	0	4	64	66	38	33	7	0	28	0	43	15
Roche, Chattanooga	1	1	.500	7.94	8	0	0	4	0	0	17	21	17	15	3	1	17	4	7	0
Romero, Chattanooga°	2	2	.500	5.21	19	1	0	15	0	3	19	23	11	11	0	1	11	3	16	1
Ross, Columbus	8	10	.444	2.25	64	0	0	59	0	22	116	103	35	29	3	5	32	12	70	3
Ruiz, Birmingham°	5	3	.625	3.15	58	0	0	35	0	4	123	112	54	43	7	3	62	3	106	9
Santana, Knoxville	3	6	.333	4.95	16	13	0	3	0	0	80	97	50	44	9	0	46	1	49	2
Sattler, Memphis	11	6	.647	2.76	28	22	7	1	1	0	163	136	67	50	12	7	45	1	94	8
Schuler, Memphis	1	2	.333	5.17	25	0	0	14	0	1	47	47	32	27	8	0	16	2	36	2
Senteney, Knoxville	10	5	.667	3.14	46	1	0	26	0	7	106	87	50	37	6	3	43	3	93	9
Seoane, Birmingham°	0	4	.000	7.71	15	1	0	9	0	3	21	43	27	18	3	0	11	0	12	4
Serum, Orlando	4	5	.444	5.37	45	0	0	36	0	20	62	69	41	37	2	0	32	6	51	4
Shields, Savannah	4	3	.571	5.01	27	4	0	15	0	1	79	74	52	44	12	2	45	5	33	4
Shimp, Memphis	2	3	.400	6.19	17	4	0	8	0	1	48	50	36	33	6	0	26	2	40	3
Slagle, Nashville	9	5	.643	3.02	18	18	10	0	1	0	134	124	52	45	9	2	29	1	78	2
Smith, Birmingham	6	10	.375	4.43	31	18	5	7	2	1	132	152	73	65	11	7	38	2	90	7
Smith, Nashville	0	1	.000	9.00	1	0	0	0	0	0	1	1	1	1	0	0	1	0	1	0
Smith, Charlotte	8	6	.571	4.03	25	25	8	0	0	0	163	165	90	73	16	3	58	2	113	2
Smith, Savannah	1	0	1.000	5.63	3	0	0	2	0	0	8	13	7	5	0	0	6	0	4	0
Snell, Charlotte	1	2	.333	2.61	8	3	3	2	1	0	38	32	14	11	3	1	10	0	19	0
Speck, Charlotte	1	0	1.000	2.73	12	0	0	6	0	2	33	29	11	10	1	0	11	0	24	0
St. Claire, Jacksonville	1	2	.333	3.21	20	0	0	20	0	2	28	20	10	10	4	1	9	1	27	0
Steffen, Birmingham	0	0	.000	9.00	1	0	0	0	0	0	1	1	1	1	0	1	1	0	0	1
Swaggerty, Charlotte	8	5	.615	2.02	35	0	0	30	0	10	49	35	15	11	1	0	19	5	26	4
J. Taylor, Nashville°	5	1	.833	2.43	17	6	1	7	1	2	63	55	26	17	2	2	25	2	31	1
S. Taylor, Nashville	9	1	1.000	2.70	12	10	1	1	0	0	60	51	22	18	5	1	32	0	41	1
Tenenini, Memphis	10	2	.833	4.17	40	0	0	17	0	1	95	109	62	44	5	2	32	8	45	1
Treuel, Knox-Birm	0	2	.000	8.50	14	0	0	6	0	0	18	25	20	17	5	4	12	2	8	1
Vanderbush, Jacksonville	3	4	.429	3.44	12	8	2	2	0	1	55	48	29	21	3	2	30	1	41	8
Viola, Orlando°	5	4	.556	3.43	17	15	2	0	0	0	97	112	47	37	9	0	33	1	50	9
Voyles, Jacksonville	6	6	.500	4.66	32	10	0	17	0	4	85	88	54	44	11	4	47	2	46	7
Walker, Knoxville°	6	10	.375	4.88	30	25	5	3	0	1	153	189	98	83	14	3	66	5	65	5
Welchel, Charlotte	13	7	.650	2.91	22	22	11	0	0	0	161	161	76	52	11	0	63	0	90	9
Werly, Nashville	13	11	.542	2.59	28	28	18	0	1	0	222	184	91	64	10	6	88	1	193	11

Pitcher—Club	W.	L.	Pct.	ERA.	G.	GS.	CG.	GF.	ShO.	Sv.	IP.	H.	R.	ER.	HR.	HB.	BB.	Int. BB.	SO.	WP.
Westray, Memphis°	1	0	1.000	7.20	2	0	0	0	0	0	5	9	4	4	0	0	4	0	3	3
Wever, Nashville	5	2	.714	2.05	9	9	4	0	1	0	66	54	22	15	2	3	30	1	39	2
White, Chattanooga	10	12	.455	3.51	27	27	8	0	2	0	172	158	93	67	11	9	65	0	101	3
Wilkes, Columbus	2	5	.286	3.67	12	8	4	2	0	0	54	61	31	22	4	1	24	3	32	3
Wilkins, Chattanooga	0	0	.000	6.00	1	1	0	0	0	0	6	6	6	4	0	0	5	0	3	1
Williams, Jacksonville	3	4	.429	5.95	16	6	2	1	0	0	65	65	45	43	14	2	33	0	45	3
Williams, Birmingham	1	2	.333	3.60	4	4	1	0	0	0	30	24	12	12	1	1	8	1	20	1
Wills, Jacksonville	9	14	.391	3.98	27	27	11	0	1	0	192	199	104	85	16	9	91	3	174	15
Wortham, Memphis°	1	0	1.000	8.00	5	5	0	0	0	0	18	15	17	16	1	1	28	0	8	8
Wright, Knoxville	2	6	.250	5.35	13	13	1	0	0	0	69	84	45	41	4	2	35	2	32	3
Yanus, Memphis	6	8	.429	4.38	27	20	4	4	1	2	148	168	82	72	13	3	41	2	85	6

BALKS—White, 5; Borchers, Cacciatore, Dilks, Morgan, 4 each; Creel, Eichhorn, Ledduke, Paris, Sattler, Walker, Wills, 3 each; Boxberger, Kromy, Mapel, Maples, McLaughlin, Reyes, J. Smith, Ma. Smith, 2 each; Abone, Aponte, Arias, Bonine, Broersma, Caldwell, Cuellar, Edwards, Elam, Field, Filson, Garcia, Havens, Hobbs, Jones, Kaufman, Konopa, Lackey, Leland, Mathis, McCall, Melson, Morogiello, Murphy, O'Connor, Owens, Pettaway, Pippin, Robbins, Romero, Santana, S. Taylor, Tenenini, Voyles, Werly, Wortham, Wright, Yanus, 1 each.

COMBINATION SHUTOUTS—Collins-Quealey, Birmingham; George-Swaggerty, Charlotte; Fuson-Anderson, Narleske-Heimer, Chattanooga; Bonine-Ross, Clyde-Ross, Heathcock-Ross, Leland-Ross, Columbus; Cornell-Voyles, Morley-St. Clair, Vanderbush-Voyles, Jacksonville; Sattler-Gorman, Yanus-Gorman, Memphis; J. Taylor,-Kaufman, Nashville; Gleckel-Serum, Kromy-Serum, Orlando; Jones-Morogiello, Savannah.

NO-HIT GAME—Cornell, Jacksonville, defeated Nashville, May 16.

Texas League

Leading Batter
STEVE SAX
San Antonio

League President
CARL SAWATSKI

Leading Pitcher
TIM HAMM
Amarillo

CHAMPIONSHIP WINNERS IN PREVIOUS YEARS

1888—Dallas ..... .671	1924—Fort Worth ..... .689	1955—Dallas ..... .581
1889—Houston ..... .551	Fort Worth ..... .763	Shreveport (3rd)§ ..... .540
1890—Galveston ..... .705	1925—Fort Worth ..... .711	1956—Houston‡ ..... .623
1892—Houston ..... .741	Fort Worth y ..... .653	1957—Dallas ..... .662
Houston ..... .613	1926—Dallas ..... .574	Houston (2nd)§ ..... .630
1895—Dallas ..... .754	1927—Wichita Falls ..... .654	1958—Fort Worth ..... .582
Fort Worth° ..... .750	1928—Houston° ..... .679	Cor. Christi (3rd)§ ..... .507
1896—Fort Worth ..... .757	Wichita Falls ..... .731	1959—Victoria ..... .589
Houston° ..... .679	1929—Dallas° ..... .588	Austin (2nd)§ ..... .548
Galveston ..... .548	Wichita Falls ..... .620	1960—Rio Grande Valley ..... .590
1897—San Antonio† ..... .657	1930—Wichita Falls ..... .697	Tulsa (3rd)° ..... .528
Galveston† ..... .717	Fort Worth° ..... .632	1961—Amarillo ..... .643
1898—League disbanded.	1931—Houston°° ..... .625	San Antonio (3rd)§ ..... .532
1899—Galveston ..... .632	Houston ..... .734	1962—El Paso ..... .571
Galveston ..... .762	1932—Beaumont° ..... .640	Tulsa (2nd)§ ..... .550
1900-01—Did not operate.	Dallas ..... .727	1963—San Antonio ..... .564
1902—Corsicana ..... .866	1933—Houston ..... .623	Tulsa (3rd)§ ..... .529
Corsicana ..... .682	San Antonio (4th)§ ..... .523	1964—San Antonio‡ ..... .607
1903—Paris-Waco ..... .615	1934—Galveston‡ ..... .579	1965—Tulsa ..... .574
Dallas° ..... .648	1935—Oklahoma City‡ ..... .590	Albuquerque xx ..... .550
1904—Corsicana° ..... .615	1936—Dallas ..... .604	1966—Arkansas ..... .579
Fort Worth ..... .800	Tulsa (3rd)§ ..... .519	1967—Albuquerque ..... .557
1905—Fort Worth ..... .545	1937—Oklahoma City ..... .635	1968—Arkansas ..... .586
1906—Fort Worth ..... .677	Fort Worth (3rd)§ ..... .535	El Paso xx ..... .562
Cleburne x ..... .609	1938—Beaumont ..... .635	1969—Amarillo ..... .593
1907—Austin ..... .629	1939—Houston ..... .606	Memphis xx ..... .504
1908—San Antonio ..... .664	Fort Worth (4th)§ ..... .540	1970—Albuquerque°° ..... .615
1909—Houston ..... .601	1940—Houston‡ ..... .652	Memphis ..... .507
1910—Dallas† ..... .586	1941—Houston ..... .673	1971—Did not operate as league— clubs
Houston† ..... .586	Dallas (4th)§ ..... .519	were members of Dixie Association.
1911—Austin ..... .575	1942—Beaumont ..... .605	1972—Alexandria ..... .600
1912—Houston ..... .626	Shreveport (2nd)§ ..... .576	El Paso xx ..... .557
1913—Houston ..... .620	1943-44-45—Did not operate.	1973—San Antonio ..... .590
1914—Houston† ..... .671	1946—Fort Worth ..... .656	Memphis xx ..... .558
Waco† ..... .671	Dallas (2nd)§ ..... .591	1974—Victoria xx ..... .581
1915—Waco ..... .592	1947—Houston‡ ..... .623	El Paso ..... .555
1916—Waco ..... .587	1948—Fort Worth‡ ..... .601	1975—Lafayette xxx ..... .558
1917—Dallas ..... .600	1949—Fort Worth ..... .649	Midland xxx ..... .604
1918—Dallas ..... .584	Tulsa (2nd)§ ..... .584	1976—Amarillo xx ..... .600
1919—Shreveport° ..... .677	1950—Beaumont ..... .595	Shreveport ..... .515
Fort Worth ..... .651	San Antonio (4th)§ ..... .513	1977—El Paso ..... .600
1920—Fort Worth ..... .703	1951—Houston‡ ..... .619	Arkansas a ..... .485
Fort Worth ..... .750	1952—Dallas ..... .571	1978—El Paso a ..... .593
1921—Fort Worth ..... .691	Shreveport (3rd)§ ..... .522	Jackson ..... .567
Fort Worth ..... .662	1953—Dallas‡ ..... .571	1979—Arkansas a ..... .571
1922—Fort Worth ..... .694	1954—Shreveport ..... .559	Midland ..... .563
Fort Worth ..... .711	Houston (2nd)§ ..... .553	1980—Arkansas a ..... .596
1923—Fort Worth ..... .632		San Antonio ..... .544

°Won split-season playoff. †No playoff for title. ‡Finished first and won four-club playoff. §Won four-club playoff. xTitle to Cleburne by default. yTied with Dallas in second half and won playoff for championship. zFort Worth disbanded. °°Tied with Beaumont at end of first half and won title in best-of-five series played as part of second half schedule. xxLeague divided into Eastern, Western divisions; won two-team playoff. xxxLeague divided into Eastern, Western divisions; declared co-champions when playoffs were not completed. aLeague divided into Eastern and Western divisions and played split-season; won playoffs. NOTE—Championship awarded to winner of four-team playoff, 1933-51; first-place team and playoff winner co-champions, 1952-64.

STANDING OF CLUBS AT CLOSE OF FIRST HALF, JUNE 20

EASTERN DIVISION

Club	W.	L.	T.	Pct.	G.B.
Jackson (Mets)	39	27	0	.590	....
Shreveport (Giants)	36	30	0	.545	3
Tulsa (Rangers)	32	25	0	.479	7½
Arkansas (Cardinals)	25	39	0	.390	13

WESTERN DIVISION

Club	W.	L.	T.	Pct.	G.B.
San Antonio (Dodgers)	36	29	0	.553	....
El Paso (Angels)	37	31	0	.544	½
Amarillo (Padres)	35	33	0	.515	2½
Midland (Cubs)	26	42	0	.382	11½

STANDING OF CLUBS AT CLOSE OF SECOND HALF, SEPTEMBER 2

EASTERN DIVISION

Club	W.	L.	T.	Pct.	G.B.
Tulsa (Rangers)	36	30	0	.545	....
Shreveport (Giants)	32	37	0	.464	5½
Jackson (Mets)	29	39	0	.426	8
Arkansas (Cardinals)	27	41	0	.397	10

WESTERN DIVISION

Club	W.	L.	T.	Pct.	G.B.
Amarillo (Padres)	42	26	0	.618	....
San Antonio (Dodgers)	40	28	0	.588	2
Midland (Cubs)	36	31	0	.537	5½
El Paso (Brewers)	28	38	0	.424	13

COMPOSITE STANDING OF CLUBS AT CLOSE OF SEASON, SEPTEMBER 2

EASTERN DIVISION

Club	Tul.	Jack.	Shrv.	Ark.	S.A.	Amar.	EIP.	Mid.	W.	L.	T.	Pct.	G.B.
Tulsa (Rangers)	...	11	18	21	1	6	6	5	68	65	0	.511	....
Jackson (Mets)	19	...	13	19	5	5	4	3	68	66	0	.507	½
Shreveport (Giants)	14	19	...	16	2	5	5	7	68	67	0	.504	1
Arkansas (Cardinals)	11	13	15	...	3	4	4	2	52	80	0	.394	15½

WESTERN DIVISION

Club	Tul.	Jack.	Shrv.	Ark.	S.A.	Amar.	EIP.	Mid.	W.	L.	T.	Pct.	G.B.
San Antonio (Dodgers)	9	5	8	4	...	14	18	18	76	57	0	.571	....
Amarillo (Padres)	4	5	5	6	18	...	18	21	77	59	0	.566	½
El Paso (Brewers)	3	6	5	6	14	14	...	17	65	69	0	.485	11½
Midland (Cubs)	5	7	3	8	14	11	14	...	62	73	0	.459	15

Arkansas club represented Little Rock, Ark.

Major league affiliations in parentheses.

Playoffs—Jackson defeated Tulsa, two games to one; San Antonio defeated Amarillo, two games to one; Jackson defeated San Antonio, four games to none for championship.

Regular-Season Attendance—Amarillo, 89,476; Arkansas, 202,604; El Paso, 210,398; Jackson, 112,511; Midland, 105,294; San Antonio, 134,668; Shreveport, 46,930; Tulsa, 155,845. Total, 1,057,726. Playoffs, 10,337. All-Star game, 4,202.

Managers: Amarillo—Eddie Watt; Arkansas—Galen Pitts; El Paso—Tony Muser; Jackson—Dave Johnson; Midland—Roy Hartsfield, George Enright; San Antonio—Don (Ducky) LeJohn; Shreveport—Jack Mull; Tulsa—Tom Burgess.

All-Star Team: 1B—Stan Davis, El Paso; 2B—Steve Sax, San Antonio; 3B—Tom O'Malley, Shreveport; SS—Willie Lozado, El Paso; OF—Gotay Mills, Arkansas; Dale Holeman, San Antonio; Mark Bradley, San Antonio; Mel Hall, Midland; Utility—Marty Scott, Tulsa; David Sax, San Antonio; C—Ron Tingley, Amarillo; Mike Fitzgerald, Jackson; DH—John Evans, El Paso; P—Rich Rodas, San Antonio; Alan Fowlkes, Shreveport; Rick Ownbey, Jackson; John Semprini, Jackson; Mark Dempsey, Shreveport; Tom Niedenfuer, San Antonio; Dave Dravecky, Amarillo; Manager—Don (Ducky) LeJohn, San Antonio.

(Compiled by Ed Williams, League Statistician, Shawnee, Okla.)

CLUB BATTING

Club	Pct.	G.	AB.	R.	OR.	H.	TB.	2B.	3B.	HR.	RBI.	GW.	SH.	SF.	HP.	BB.	Int. BB.	SO.	SB.	CS.	LOB.
San Antonio	.297	133	4568	775	682	1358	2081	228	30	145	698	67	40	38	30	468	21	686	114	40	966
Midland	.281	135	4557	755	771	1279	1963	239	38	123	687	51	44	38	29	518	29	801	83	52	962
El Paso	.280	134	4532	712	736	1271	1921	213	37	121	641	61	49	34	33	478	21	854	127	65	925
Amarillo	.276	136	4375	667	595	1206	1735	192	44	83	567	68	66	37	26	599	20	808	142	70	1015
Tulsa	.266	133	4366	592	577	1155	1680	184	43	85	541	64	58	41	34	473	30	722	141	70	919
Shreveport	.266	135	4385	547	563	1165	1677	192	34	84	475	59	28	30	31	460	31	780	130	68	945
Jackson	.259	134	4547	532	554	1176	1565	190	29	47	471	62	45	35	33	366	34	803	95	49	930
Arkansas	.239	132	4146	504	606	992	1403	158	29	65	452	45	38	24	27	430	20	714	91	70	820

INDIVIDUAL BATTING

(Leading Qualifiers for Batting Championship—367 or More Plate Appearances)

*Bats lefthanded.   †Switch-hitter.

Player and Club	Pct.	G.	AB.	R.	H.	TB.	2B.	3B.	HR.	RBI.	GW.	SH.	SF.	HP.	BB.	Int. BB.	SO.	SB.	CS.
Sax, Stephen, San Antonio	.346	115	485	94	168	221	23	3	8	52	3	4	2	5	40	2	32	34	8
Holman, Dale, San Antonio*	.333	130	507	95	169	246	29	3	14	86	5	2	7	2	72	4	83	7	4
Upton, Jack, Midland	.328	127	479	95	157	247	36	3	16	84	9	7	6	1	58	1	67	3	2
Hall, Melvin, Midland*	.319	131	533	98	170	286	34	5	24	95	10	6	6	3	50	5	117	18	14
Bradley, Mark, San Antonio	.316	129	472	98	149	243	26	4	20	89	4	5	5	4	83	2	85	28	10
Gladden, Daniel, Shreveport	.314	124	472	81	148	213	23	9	8	44	5	4	4	4	50	5	58	52	26
Evans, Johnny, El Paso	.313	124	422	94	132	232	25	3	23	107	12	0	5	9	93	5	73	2	1
Davis, Stanley, El Paso*	.312	129	497	90	155	266	28	7	23	109	8	1	6	0	36	5	89	14	5
Connally, Fritzie, Midland	.308	94	344	61	106	163	21	0	12	57	3	3	0	4	33	2	48	3	1
Cowger, Tracy, Tulsa	.306	114	382	53	117	167	23	3	7	40	4	7	0	1	35	0	60	13	9

Departmental Leaders; G—Lansford, Wright, 133; AB—Irvine, 563; R—Hall, Bradley, 98; H—Hall, 170; TB—Hall, 286; 2B—Upton, 36; 3B—Tingley, 10; HR—Brock, 32; RBI—S. Davis, 109; GWRBI—Evans, Hernandez, 12; SH—Lozado, 12; SF—Gooch, 9; BB—Evans, 93; HP—Evans, Ball, 9; SO—Lansford 142; SB—Gladden, 52; CS—Gladden, 26.

(All Players—Listed Alphabetically)

Player and Club	Pct.	G.	AB.	R.	H.	TB.	2B.	3B.	HR.	RBI.	GW.	SH.	SF.	HP.	BB.	Int. BB.	SO.	SB.	CS.
Adduci, James, Arkansas*	.275	40	131	16	36	65	8	3	5	14	1	0	0	1	11	1	29	4	1
Alexander, Patrick, Shreveport	.261	35	23	5	6	6	0	0	0	1	0	2	0	0	2	0	9	0	0
Alvarez, John, Amarillo	.311	29	106	24	33	60	5	2	6	24	2	1	1	0	17	0	12	1	0
Amelung, Edward, San Antonio*	.133	4	15	1	2	2	0	0	0	1	0	0	0	0	4	0	0	0	0
Anicich, Michael, Jackson	.216	47	148	17	32	51	10	0	3	17	1	0	3	1	13	0	28	1	0
Apodaca, Robert, Jackson	.000	6	4	0	0	0	0	0	0	0	0	0	0	0	0	0	2	0	0

Player and Club	Pct.	G.	AB.	R.	H.	TB.	2B.	3B.	HR.	RBI.	GW.	SH.	SF.	HP.	BB.	Int. BB.	SO.	SB.	CS.
Aranzamendi, Jorge, Arkansas	.200	60	155	19	31	34	3	0	0	11	1	2	0	1	20	1	32	5	6
Baker, Gregory, Shreveport	.253	125	400	43	101	141	15	2	7	38	4	1	2	1	44	2	77	3	6
Ball, Robert, Tulsa	.237	124	469	74	111	144	10	7	3	36	1	5	4	9	61	2	93	42	13
Barba, Michael, Amarillo	.000	31	0	1	0	0	0	0	0	0	0	0	0	0	0	0	0	0	0
Barrow, Melvin, Tulsa	.311	33	119	20	37	53	8	1	2	17	3	1	2	0	13	1	17	7	0
Bauman, Brad, Shreveport	.095	10	21	1	2	3	1	0	0	1	0	0	0	0	2	0	6	0	1
Beltre, Sergio, Jackson	.212	48	165	17	35	46	4	2	1	18	1	1	1	0	15	1	42	5	1
Bendorf, Jerry, San Antonio	.310	14	58	10	18	21	3	0	0	12	2	1	0	0	8	0	9	1	0
Beyers, Tom, San Antonio°	.300	118	487	66	146	201	20	7	7	59	7	3	1	4	20	2	24	10	4
Bilardello, Dann, San Antonio	.053	6	19	0	1	1	0	0	0	1	0	1	1	0	1	0	9	0	0
Bittiger, Jeffrey, Jackson	.200	4	5	1	1	1	0	0	0	0	0	0	0	0	0	0	1	0	0
Bradley, Mark, San Antonio	.316	129	472	98	149	243	26	4	20	89	4	5	5	4	83	2	85	28	10
Brock, Gregory, San Antonio°	.295	128	499	86	147	274	25	3	32	106	10	1	5	1	46	3	67	3	1
Burchett, Kerry, Arkansas	.000	20	9	0	0	0	0	0	0	0	0	1	0	0	0	0	3	0	0
Burton, Jeffrey, Midland	.342	13	38	8	13	15	2	0	0	2	1	1	0	0	3	0	7	0	0
Cain, Aaron, Amarillo	.294	109	347	62	102	125	14	3	1	39	5	4	2	3	52	1	55	19	4
Carter, Joseph, Midland	.269	67	249	42	67	103	15	3	5	35	1	1	1	2	8	1	30	12	2
Castro, Frank, Amarillo	.274	59	201	27	55	78	9	1	4	31	3	3	0	3	19	1	41	0	3
Citarella, Ralph, Arkansas	.182	31	11	0	2	2	0	0	0	1	0	1	0	0	0	0	4	0	0
Connally, Fritzie, Midland	.308	94	344	61	106	163	21	0	12	57	3	3	0	4	33	2	48	3	1
Cowger, Tracy, Tulsa	.306	114	382	53	117	167	23	3	7	40	4	7	0	1	35	0	60	13	9
Cuervo, Edward, Jackson†	.243	115	411	40	100	140	8	4	8	42	4	2	4	2	17	2	86	8	5
Cummings, Robert, Shreveport	.228	70	241	19	55	80	13	0	4	22	3	0	0	1	12	0	56	0	0
Daly, Mark, Amarillo°	.000	32	5	0	0	0	0	0	0	0	0	0	0	0	0	0	4	0	0
Davis, Michael, Jackson	.271	122	431	56	117	178	29	1	10	62	8	2	3	2	35	1	50	6	4
Davis, Stanley, El Paso°	.312	129	497	90	155	266	28	7	23	109	8	1	6	0	36	5	89	14	5
Davis, Ted, Jackson	.000	24	4	0	0	0	0	0	0	0	0	0	0	0	0	0	1	0	0
Delaney, Dennis, Arkansas	.229	78	236	22	54	68	9	1	1	18	3	4	1	4	22	0	30	0	3
Dempsey, Mark, Shreveport	.161	27	31	3	5	5	0	0	0	2	0	3	1	0	2	0	9	0	0
DeSimone, Gerald, Amarillo†	.271	113	424	57	115	163	21	3	7	44	6	7	2	0	62	6	61	18	10
Diaz, Michael, Midland	.264	110	390	56	103	156	19	2	10	60	4	5	2	4	36	0	64	4	0
Doyle, Jeffrey, Arkansas°	.265	132	479	73	127	188	24	8	7	71	5	4	5	3	57	3	39	6	4
Duff, David, Jackson	.149	17	47	0	7	8	1	0	0	5	1	2	0	1	5	0	8	0	0
Duncan, Lindon, Tulsa	.204	20	54	10	11	17	1	1	1	3	1	4	0	0	17	0	12	3	0
Dunn, James, Shreveport	.276	44	29	4	8	12	1	0	1	4	0	2	0	0	0	0	4	0	1
Evans, Johnny, El Paso	.313	124	422	94	132	232	25	3	23	107	12	0	5	9	93	5	73	2	1
Fierro, Javier, Midland	.287	94	373	58	107	148	17	3	6	42	3	2	4	1	43	1	39	4	4
Fisher, Glenn, Shreveport	.105	26	19	0	2	2	0	0	0	2	1	0	0	1	0	0	8	1	0
Fitzgerald, Michael, Jackson	.312	66	218	28	68	98	14	2	4	29	5	1	3	4	24	1	44	1	1
Fowlkes, Alan, Shreveport	.175	32	40	3	7	10	0	0	1	4	1	0	0	0	0	0	15	0	0
Gaff, Brent, Jackson	.182	7	11	3	2	2	0	0	0	0	0	1	0	0	2	0	1	0	0
Garrelts, Scott, Shreveport	.000	14	11	0	0	0	0	0	0	0	0	0	0	0	1	0	4	0	0
Gausepohl, Daniel, Amarillo	.269	96	320	44	86	131	13	4	8	33	3	6	2	2	60	1	62	13	2
Gil, Carlos, Midland	.000	6	0	1	0	0	0	0	0	0	0	0	0	0	0	0	0	0	0
Gladden, Daniel, Shreveport	.314	124	472	81	148	213	23	9	8	44	5	4	4	4	50	5	58	52	26
Glinatsis, Michael, San Antonio	.125	19	8	1	1	1	0	0	0	0	0	2	0	0	0	0	4	0	0
Gooch, Ronald, Tulsa	.248	128	500	68	124	160	16	4	4	56	4	8	9	2	54	0	82	5	12
Gotay, Ruben, Arkansas	.000	8	7	0	0	0	0	0	0	0	0	0	0	0	0	0	2	0	0
Gott, James, Arkansas	.000	28	9	1	0	0	0	0	0	0	0	0	0	0	1	0	7	0	0
Grant, Thomas, Midland°	.349	48	189	34	66	119	13	5	10	39	0	0	2	0	33	4	33	5	3
Gutierrez, Julian, Arkansas	.211	46	152	11	32	38	3	0	1	14	0	1	1	1	12	1	28	2	3
Gwynn, Anthony, Amarillo°	.462	23	91	22	42	66	8	2	4	19	4	1	1	1	5	1	7	5	1
Hagen, Kevin, Arkansas	.053	27	19	1	1	1	0	0	0	0	0	1	0	0	0	0	11	0	0
Hall, Melvin, Midland°	.319	131	533	98	170	286	34	5	24	95	10	6	6	3	50	5	117	18	14
Hansen, Jon, El Paso	.309	68	259	31	80	123	15	2	8	40	3	0	1	1	15	0	43	4	3
Haslerig, Jacob, Jackson°	.295	69	220	33	65	102	12	5	5	24	1	0	2	2	20	3	49	9	6
Hernandez, Leonardo, San Antonio	.298	131	497	90	148	263	34	3	25	91	12	3	6	4	33	0	74	8	5
Hershister, Orel, San Antonio	.000	42	6	0	0	0	0	0	0	0	0	0	0	0	0	0	3	0	0
Holman, Dale, San Antonio°	.333	130	507	95	169	246	29	3	14	86	5	2	7	2	72	4	83	7	4
Holman, Scott, Jackson	.125	23	16	1	2	2	0	0	0	1	0	0	0	0	1	0	6	0	0
Irvine, Edward, El Paso	.288	132	563	91	162	206	24	4	4	42	3	11	1	2	31	0	71	48	21
Jirschele, Michael, Tulsa	.251	121	379	53	95	129	10	6	4	43	5	10	1	4	25	0	67	19	2
Johnson, David, Arkansas	.200	20	5	0	1	1	0	0	0	0	0	1	0	0	1	0	3	0	0
Johnson, Jerry, Amarillo	.253	86	281	42	71	99	23	1	1	29	3	9	3	3	50	1	38	7	3
Johnson, Jerry, Arkansas	.167	21	12	0	2	2	0	0	0	1	0	2	0	0	0	0	6	0	0
Jones, Charles, San Antonio	.000	21	6	0	0	0	0	0	0	0	0	0	0	0	0	0	4	0	0
Jones, Ross, San Antonio	.266	129	444	75	118	154	17	2	5	43	5	9	2	3	43	0	94	6	4
Jorn, David, Arkansas	.111	17	9	1	1	1	0	0	0	0	0	1	0	0	0	0	4	0	0
Kable, David, Arkansas°	.267	124	415	57	111	196	15	5	20	68	3	1	3	3	67	4	130	4	3
Keener, Jeffrey, Arkansas°	.000	30	1	0	0	0	0	0	0	0	0	0	0	0	0	0	0	0	0
Klimas, Philip, Tulsa	.303	97	353	41	107	156	18	2	9	58	11	2	1	2	36	3	57	1	1
Koenigsfield, Ronald, El Paso	.173	28	104	16	18	22	1	0	1	8	0	1	1	0	16	0	21	4	0
Kornfeld, Craig, Midland	.248	53	210	33	52	69	6	4	1	19	1	3	1	0	15	1	21	2	8
Kutcher, Randy, Shreveport	.285	77	249	36	71	104	13	4	4	20	2	4	1	1	23	1	62	22	5
Lane, Jerry, El Paso	.287	51	167	20	48	69	13	1	2	23	3	1	1	0	6	1	20	2	0
Lansford, Joseph, Amarillo	.237	133	464	67	110	209	20	2	25	86	6	3	7	1	85	3	142	1	1
LaVigne, Randall, Midland	.273	119	417	78	114	176	18	7	10	69	8	4	5	4	41	5	91	9	7
Leach, Terry, Jackson	.182	8	11	0	2	2	0	0	0	0	0	1	0	1	0	0	5	0	0
Lohuis, Mark, Shreveport	.000	31	3	0	0	0	0	0	0	0	0	0	0	0	0	0	1	0	0
Loman, Douglas, El Paso°	.306	71	271	50	83	125	17	2	7	42	6	1	4	4	32	4	35	5	6
Lowry, Michael, Jackson	.182	24	22	0	4	4	0	0	0	0	0	1	0	0	2	0	10	0	0
Lozado, William, El Paso	.252	127	456	58	115	163	17	5	7	49	3	12	4	5	33	1	104	22	6
Malden, Christopher, San Antonio	.000	28	8	1	0	0	0	0	0	0	0	1	0	0	0	0	4	0	0
Manning, Allen, El Paso	.262	122	405	53	106	142	11	5	5	38	7	7	2	3	55	0	114	5	5
Marsden, Stephen, Amarillo	.400	5	5	0	2	2	0	0	0	2	0	0	0	0	0	0	1	0	0
Martinez, Carmelo, Midland	.296	116	392	65	116	203	22	1	21	84	4	4	4	6	56	5	73	5	2
McCauley, Stanley, Arkansas	.159	35	107	9	17	26	3	0	2	10	2	0	0	1	14	0	24	0	0
McDonald, Russell, San Antonio	.000	32	4	0	0	0	0	0	0	0	0	0	0	0	0	0	0	0	0
McMullen, Ricky, Jackson	.269	13	52	4	14	15	1	0	0	6	1	0	1	0	2	0	7	2	1
Miller, Lemmie, San Antonio	.333	2	6	4	2	4	0	1	0	0	0	0	0	0	2	0	2	2	0
Miller, Thomas, Jackson°	.000	26	3	0	0	0	0	0	0	0	0	0	0	0	0	0	1	0	0
Mills, Rhadames, Arkansas	.289	127	485	79	140	186	22	6	4	43	5	4	1	3	47	2	68	39	21

Player and Club	Pct.	G.	AB.	R.	H.	TB.	2B.	3B.	HR.	RBI.	GW.	SH.	SF.	HP.	BB.	Int. BB.	SO.	SB.	CS.
Mitchell, James, Midland°	.206	65	199	23	41	62	10	1	3	27	0	0	3	0	26	1	35	3	2
Moore, Donald, Arkansas†	.239	41	155	17	37	57	6	1	4	25	1	1	2	1	13	2	33	0	2
Moore, Stephen, Jackson†	.270	119	441	72	119	151	17	6	1	24	0	3	2	0	57	7	65	21	13
Morgan, William, Midland	.212	25	66	8	14	21	2	1	1	6	0	1	0	1	10	0	15	1	0
Moyer, Gregory, Shreveport	.154	35	13	1	2	2	0	0	0	2	0	0	0	1	1	0	4	0	0
Murphy, Daniel, Tulsa°	.255	14	51	6	13	25	1	1	3	13	3	1	1	0	2	1	11	0	1
Niedenfuer, Thomas, San Antonio	.000	36	1	0	0	0	0	0	0	0	0	1	0	0	0	0	0	0	0
Nieto, Thomas, Arkansas	.179	62	184	12	33	41	2	0	2	19	5	3	2	5	13	0	33	1	0
Nobles, James, San Antonio	.000	35	1	0	0	0	0	0	0	0	0	1	0	0	0	0	0	0	0
O'Brien, Peter, Tulsa°	.285	110	382	57	109	185	19	3	17	78	5	3	7	0	56	6	87	3	2
Ojeda, Luis, Arkansas	.269	28	104	16	28	36	8	0	0	4	1	0	0	4	10	2	2	2
O'Malley, Thomas, Shreveport°	.289	123	467	50	135	188	23	6	6	53	8	0	3	2	32	5	51	2	4
Owen, Dave, Midland†	.215	80	247	40	53	63	8	1	0	23	4	4	0	0	48	0	73	10	4
Ownbey, Richard, Jackson	.148	21	27	0	4	4	0	0	0	0	0	1	0	0	2	0	9	0	0
Pagel, David, Midland°	.223	47	179	30	40	55	5	2	2	19	0	2	1	0	28	0	38	2	2
Pastors, Gregory, Jackson	.230	89	270	28	62	80	7	1	3	25	6	7	0	1	30	1	59	5	2
Pedrique, Alfredo, Jackson	.240	115	379	39	91	100	9	0	0	25	3	7	3	7	22	2	33	4	3
Perdue, Doran, Shreveport°	.299	120	391	64	117	147	14	5	2	38	4	3	2	3	61	4	58	24	11
Pimentel, Rafael, Arkansas	.000	50	1	0	0	0	0	0	0	0	0	0	0	0	0	0	0	0	0
Pisel, Ronald, Shreveport	.000	15	10	0	0	0	0	0	0	0	0	0	0	0	0	0	1	0	0
Poe, Richard, Jackson°	.288	106	364	41	105	122	15	1	0	50	9	3	5	0	41	9	40	0	1
Pratt, Louis, Arkansas	.000	7	6	0	0	0	0	0	0	0	0	0	0	0	0	0	4	0	0
Purpura, Daniel, Amarillo	.263	96	323	48	85	101	9	2	1	36	3	10	1	1	58	2	61	9	13
Pyburn, Jeffrey, Amarillo	.285	130	512	86	146	202	20	6	8	53	9	8	4	1	62	0	77	37	12
Quick, Ronald, Shreveport†	.149	28	74	7	11	12	1	0	0	5	1	3	1	0	7	0	13	1	0
Rabb, John, Shreveport	.276	102	355	51	98	166	16	2	16	58	7	0	3	7	26	2	88	8	2
Reynolds, Larry, Tulsa†	.285	70	228	26	65	79	10	2	0	18	2	3	2	0	19	1	28	20	6
Reynolds, Ronn, Jackson	.235	88	272	16	64	84	12	1	2	30	1	4	4	5	28	2	59	0	0
Riggins, Mark, Arkansas	.143	51	7	1	1	1	0	0	0	0	0	0	0	0	0	0	3	0	0
Riggleman, James, Arkansas	.241	37	133	17	32	44	7	1	1	15	2	0	2	2	16	1	29	3	0
Rodas, Richard, San Antonio°	.083	26	12	0	1	1	0	0	0	0	0	0	0	0	2	0	7	0	0
Rodriguez, Jose, Jackson°	.000	15	1	0	0	0	0	0	0	0	0	0	0	0	0	0	0	0	0
Roman, Louis, Arkansas°	.235	78	251	22	59	66	4	0	1	19	1	3	0	0	14	1	29	6	6
Rotherford, James, Shreveport	.274	111	369	34	101	164	16	1	15	56	6	4	5	1	23	3	65	0	0
Russell, Joseph, Tulsa	.000	1	1	0	0	0	0	0	0	0	0	0	0	0	2	0	0	0	0
Santana, Rafael, Arkansas	.233	110	326	34	76	96	14	3	0	19	3	1	0	1	24	1	43	2	2
Sax, David, San Antonio	.308	62	221	43	68	97	13	2	4	31	1	0	1	1	32	0	25	2	0
Sax, Stephen, San Antonio	.346	115	485	94	168	221	23	3	8	52	3	4	2	5	40	2	32	34	8
Schroeder, William, El Paso	.260	95	335	41	87	156	20	2	15	61	6	5	2	3	25	0	118	2	2
Schultz, Greg, San Antonio	.279	57	165	21	46	52	6	0	0	14	3	0	2	4	14	1	22	9	2
Scott, Donald, Tulsa†	.236	114	385	44	91	126	16	2	5	41	5	6	3	3	42	6	78	4	6
Scott, Martin, Tulsa	.270	92	285	50	77	119	9	3	9	38	6	4	2	2	44	2	30	2	6
Semprini, John, Jackson	.000	34	2	0	0	0	0	0	0	0	0	0	0	0	0	0	2	0	0
Shepston, Michael, Midland	.243	53	152	15	37	44	7	0	0	17	1	0	3	3	17	0	25	2	0
Shoebridge, Terence, El Paso	.223	57	188	13	42	57	6	0	3	20	3	5	1	0	18	0	32	0	0
Simmons, Wayne, Midland†	.111	7	27	2	3	4	1	0	0	2	0	1	0	0	0	0	3	0	1
Simond, Robert, Jackson°	.227	22	22	1	5	5	0	0	0	1	0	0	0	0	1	0	10	0	0
Sisk, Douglas, Jackson	.500	14	2	0	1	1	0	0	0	1	1	0	0	0	0	0	0	0	0
Skinner, John, Jackson°	.000	6	3	0	0	0	0	0	0	0	0	0	0	0	0	0	3	0	0
Skorochocki, John, El Paso°	.280	119	446	64	125	154	12	1	5	38	0	4	4	2	33	1	56	11	10
Skube, Robert, El Paso°	.284	114	398	89	113	200	23	5	18	59	6	1	1	4	82	3	74	8	6
Slettvet, Douglas, Amarillo	.273	25	77	9	21	26	2	0	1	11	4	0	2	0	11	1	28	0	1
Smith, David, Jackson	.000	24	1	0	0	0	0	0	0	0	0	0	0	0	0	0	1	0	0
Sobbe, William, San Antonio°	.271	28	96	11	26	31	5	0	0	12	1	1	0	0	5	2	10	0	0
Steels, James, Amarillo°	.285	127	485	58	138	185	28	5	3	59	4	5	6	4	22	1	65	11	9
Stevenson, John, Amarillo	.255	111	365	48	93	113	11	3	1	43	6	2	2	3	44	2	61	13	10
Stockstill, David, Tulsa°	.276	61	221	28	61	103	12	0	10	36	4	0	5	0	25	3	26	0	1
Stovall, Jerry, Shreveport†	.000	25	5	0	0	0	0	0	0	0	0	0	0	0	1	0	1	0	0
Szymarek, Stanley, Shreveport	.262	88	267	42	70	131	20	1	13	45	7	1	2	3	61	2	78	6	5
Thurberg, Thomas, Jackson	.200	28	20	0	4	5	1	0	0	2	1	0	0	3	0	8	0	0
Tillman, Kerry, Jackson	.278	122	464	66	129	176	21	4	6	59	11	4	1	1	24	2	92	29	5
Tingley, Ronald, Amarillo	.288	116	379	72	109	177	9	10	13	60	10	7	4	4	52	0	98	8	1
Tisdale, Freddie, Arkansas°	.258	101	333	42	86	148	21	1	13	57	7	1	3	1	37	0	43	5	7
Tracy, James, Midland°	.274	22	73	8	20	29	3	0	2	7	2	0	0	0	13	3	22	0	0
Tucker, Michael, Shreveport	.286	11	7	1	2	3	1	0	0	1	0	0	0	0	0	0	3	0	0
Turco, Steve, Arkansas°	.176	79	176	24	31	34	0	0	1	14	4	2	0	0	32	2	35	9	7
Upton, Jack, Midland	.328	127	479	95	157	247	36	3	16	80	4	9	7	6	58	1	67	3	2
Valley, Charles, El Paso†	.238	48	21	2	5	6	1	0	0	5	1	0	1	0	3	1	4	0	0
Violette, John, Jackson	.000	4	3	0	0	0	0	0	0	0	0	0	0	0	0	0	1	0	0
Von Ohlen, David, Jackson°	.167	11	6	0	1	1	0	0	0	0	0	0	0	0	0	0	3	0	0
Wabeke, Douglas, Shreveport	.286	102	287	36	82	110	15	2	3	35	3	1	1	2	38	0	23	5	0
Wallace, Brooks, Tulsa	.263	12	38	4	10	12	2	0	0	6	2	1	0	0	1	0	10	0	0
White, Myron, San Antonio°	.329	73	234	38	77	127	13	2	11	41	8	2	1	1	27	2	42	4	1
Wickensheimer, Clint, San Antonio	.000	22	4	0	0	0	0	0	0	0	0	1	0	0	1	0	2	0	0
Wiggins, David, Shreveport°	.229	50	157	24	36	52	8	1	2	13	5	0	2	0	22	1	30	3	4
Winfield, Steven, Arkansas	.000	10	4	0	0	0	0	0	0	0	0	0	0	0	0	0	1	0	0
Winslow, Daniel, Arkansas	.191	39	115	16	22	30	5	0	1	13	0	2	2	0	11	1	15	3	2
Wojcik, James, Shreveport°	.223	47	157	16	35	44	4	1	1	13	2	0	2	2	12	1	24	2	1
Wright, George, Tulsa	.260	133	489	58	127	205	29	8	11	58	8	3	4	5	41	5	64	22	11
Wynne, Marvell, Jackson°	.286	127	497	69	142	187	29	2	4	50	8	5	5	6	20	3	73	4	7
Zayas, Felipe, Arkansas	.294	37	109	14	32	42	4	0	2	16	1	0	2	0	14	0	16	0	1
Zicardi, John, Shreveport°	.247	98	287	26	71	82	8	0	1	18	0	0	1	3	39	4	32	2	2
Zouras, Michael, San Antonio	.224	89	308	41	69	139	13	0	19	58	6	2	5	1	38	3	80	0	1

The following pitchers had no plate appearances primarily through use of designated hitters, listed alphabetically by club, games in parentheses:

AMARILLO—Ballard, Byron (20); Church, Sydney (35); Dixon, Troy (26); Dravecky, David (30); Hamm, Timothy (17); Hawkins, Andrew (27); Johnson, Donald (8); Majer, Joseph (2); Miller, Randall (12); Thurmond, Mark (27); Wyrick, Courtney (23).

ARKANSAS—Rincon, Andrew (2).

EL PASO—Ako, Gerald (19); Candiotti, Thomas (21); Cook, Grover (18); Jenkins, Jerry (6); Jones, Douglas (15); Koontz, James (41); Kranitz, Richard (14); Madden, Michael (22); Montgomery, Larry (30); Park, Chel Sun (11); Quinones, Rene (10); Swift, Weldon (18); Torres, Anthony (26).

MIDLAND—Blyth, Robert (44); Churchill, Norman (37); Clark, Randall (29); Clarke, Timothy (1); King, Michael (14); Lefferts, Craig (26); Mack, Henry (20); McClain, Joe (10); Millner, Timothy (26); Moore, Edmund (7); Nastu, Phillip (36); Nowlin, Mark (1); Perlman, Jonathan (12); Spino, Thomas (13); Thompson, Michael (14); Wright, Michael (12).

SAN ANTONIO—Madden, Morris (4); Thorp, Bradley (3); Wheelock, Gary (9); Wise, Brett (2).

TUSLA—Carney, Ronald (22); Crutcher, David (21); Darling, Ronald (14); Fossas, Anthony (38); Henke, Thomas (15); Hudson, Anthony (6); Hughes, Gregory (19); Lamson, Charles (6); Lazorko, Jack (47); Leach, Martin (2); Long, Dennis (35); Nielsen, Steven (16); Richards, Kevin (17); Roberts, Michael (34); Schmidt, David (3); Terrell, Walter (27).

GRAND SLAM HOME RUNS—Kable, Rothford, 2 each; Alvarez, Cain, S. Davis, Evans, Gooch, D. Holman, Irvine, Kornfeld, Lansford, Mitchell, D. Moore, Murphy, Schroeder, M. Scott, Skorochocki, Wabeke, Wright, Zayas, Zouras, 1 each.

AWARDED FIRST BASE ON INTERFERENCE—S. Davis, (Sobbe, Rotherford, Reynolds), Pyburn (Schroeder 2, Shoebridge), Cuervo (Rabb, Winslow, D. Scott), 3 each; Adduci (Cummings 2), Pedrique (D. Scott, Rabb), White (D. Scott, Slettvet), Wojcik (Tingley, D. Scott), 2 each; Skube (Zayas), 1.

CLUB FIELDING

Club	Pct.	G.	PO.	A.	E.	DP.	PB.	Club	Pct.	G.	PO.	A.	E.	DP.	PB.
San Antonio	.971	133	3427	1377	142	106	36	Shreveport	.967	135	3443	1493	170	95	21
Tulsa	.970	133	3433	1576	157	122	32	Midland	.966	135	3448	1566	175	117	13
Arkansas	.969	132	3311	1545	153	136	15	Amarillo	.962	136	3454	1565	198	149	33
Jackson	.969	134	3565	1583	165	139	14	El Paso	.960	134	3491	1463	204	128	14

Triple Plays—Arkansas 2, Amarillo 1.

INDIVIDUAL FIELDING

°Throws lefthanded.

FIRST BASEMEN

Player and Club	Pct.	G.	PO.	A.	E.	DP.	Player and Club	Pct.	G.	PO.	A.	E.	DP.
Anicich, Jackson	.987	40	347	31	5	36	O'Brien, Tulsa°	.990	103	973	95	11	86
Beltre, Jackson	1.000	2	18	3	0	2	Pastors, Jackson	1.000	5	37	1	0	3
Brock, San Antonio	.992	128	1071	90	9	88	POE, Jackson°	.993	91	783	66	6	71
Connally, Midland	1.000	7	56	3	0	6	Rothford, Shreveport	.990	90	814	47	9	46
Cummings, Shreveport	1.000	3	12	0	0	1	M. Scott, Tulsa	.982	7	52	2	1	2
S. Davis, El Paso	.983	64	486	44	9	53	Steels, Amarillo°	.923	2	9	3	1	0
Evans, El Paso	.991	67	605	51	6	57	Tillman, Jackson	.938	2	14	1	1	1
Fitzgerald, Jackson	.974	7	34	4	1	4	Tingley, Amarillo	1.000	2	22	0	0	4
D. Holman, San Antonio	1.000	4	34	2	0	6	Tisdale, Arkansas	.991	25	206	14	2	23
Kable, Arkansas°	.993	109	1064	56	8	106	Tracy, Midland	1.000	6	47	2	0	5
Klimas, Tulsa	.979	29	261	19	6	19	Upton, Midland	.992	122	1088	99	9	73
Lansford, Amarillo	.990	133	1283	61	13	137	Valley, El Paso°	1.000	9	46	4	0	6
Martinez, Midland	.944	1	15	2	1	0	Zicardi, Shreveport°	.992	61	464	38	4	31
McCauley, Arkansas	1.000	3	10	2	0	1	Zouras, San Antonio	1.000	2	7	0	0	2

Triple Plays—Kable, Lansford.

SECOND BASEMEN

Player and Club	Pct.	G.	PO.	A.	E.	DP.	Player and Club	Pct.	G.	PO.	A.	E.	DP.
Bendorf, San Antonio	1.000	12	37	24	0	8	Owen, Midland	1.000	8	11	14	0	4
Cain, Amarillo	.875	2	1	6	1	0	Pastors, Jackson	.969	26	52	71	4	12
Cuervo, Jackson	.968	103	247	321	19	63	Pedrique, Jackson	1.000	1	0	1	0	0
DeSimone, Amarillo	.976	99	199	329	13	75	Perdue, Shreveport	.965	62	107	167	10	28
DOYLE, Arkansas	.979	120	246	403	14	88	Purpura, Amarillo	.958	17	29	63	4	14
Fierro, Midland	.976	71	156	212	9	48	Santana, Arkansas	1.000	2	1	5	0	1
Gooch, Tulsa	.975	128	294	399	18	80	S. Sax, San Antonio	.970	114	255	298	17	69
Gutierrez, Arkansas	.927	13	23	28	4	6	Schultz, San Antonio	.962	11	27	23	2	7
J. Johnson, Amarillo	.960	22	46	74	5	15	D. Scott, Tulsa	1.000	3	9	10	0	2
Koenigsfield, El Paso	.952	28	56	82	7	16	Simmons, Midland	.889	2	4	4	1	2
Kornfeld, Midland	.966	53	132	148	10	26	Skorochocki, El Paso	.944	76	159	177	20	63
Lane, El Paso	.959	43	75	89	7	21	Turco, Arkansas	.900	2	5	4	1	2
Martinez, Midland	1.000	3	5	5	0	0	Wabeke, Shreveport	.961	60	99	148	10	21
McMullen, Jackson	.942	12	22	43	4	12	Wallace, Tulsa	1.000	2	3	5	0	0
Mitchell, Midland	1.000	3	8	4	0	0	Wojcik, Shreveport	.957	26	50	85	6	12

Triple Plays—Doyle 2, DeSimone.

THIRD BASEMEN

Player and Club	Pct.	G.	PO.	A.	E.	DP.	Player and Club	Pct.	G.	PO.	A.	E.	DP.
Alvarez, Amarillo	.958	29	20	48	3	6	Mitchell, Midland	.932	22	19	50	5	3
Aranzamendi, Arkansas	.959	19	11	31	2	0	D. Moore, Arkansas	.918	36	29	61	8	5
Connally, Midland	.958	87	73	179	11	11	S. Moore, Jackson	.667	3	2	2	2	0
Cowger, Tulsa	.893	35	19	81	12	4	Ojeda, Arkansas	.936	28	22	51	5	3
M. DAVIS, Jackson	.965	118	96	238	12	32	O'Malley, Shreveport	.957	122	94	237	15	16
Doyle, Arkansas	.976	13	10	30	1	2	Pastors, Jackson	.929	18	6	20	2	3
Fitzgerald, Jackson	1.000	3	5	6	0	1	Perdue, Shreveport	1.000	1	0	1	0	1
Gausepohl, Amarillo	1.000	1	1	0	0	0	Purpura, Amarillo	.933	57	39	127	12	18
Gutierrez, Arkansas	.949	13	10	27	2	3	Riggleman, Arkansas	.909	6	10	20	3	2
Hernandez, San Antonio	.938	128	107	271	25	24	Santana, Arkansas	1.000	5	2	8	0	1
D. Holman, San Antonio	1.000	1	1	0	0	0	Schultz, San Antonio	1.000	4	3	5	0	0
Jirschele, Tulsa	.903	13	6	22	3	3	D. Scott, Tulsa	.955	26	21	43	3	5
J. Johnson, Amarillo	.886	43	27	74	13	8	Skorochocki, El Paso	.900	15	15	21	4	2
Klimas, Tulsa	.949	64	48	120	9	19	Turco, Arkansas	.875	7	2	12	2	1
Manning, El Paso	.942	122	100	276	23	23	Wabeke, Shreveport	.900	26	14	40	6	3
Martinez, Midland	.829	30	21	71	19	5	Wallace, Tulsa	1.000	1	2	1	0	0
McCauley, Arkansas	.909	13	9	21	3	2							

SHORTSTOPS

Player and Club	Pct.	G.	PO.	A.	E.	DP.	Player and Club	Pct.	G.	PO.	A.	E.	DP.
Bendorf, San Antonio	1.000	2	0	6	0	1	Jirschele, Tulsa	.943	106	146	365	31	64
Cain, Amarillo	.931	11	10	17	2	1	R. Jones, San Antonio	.929	129	185	328	39	65
DeSimone, Amarillo	.942	9	20	29	3	6	Kutcher, Shreveport	.947	76	112	212	18	33
Duncan, Tulsa	.946	20	39	49	5	4	Lozado, El Paso	.930	127	235	367	45	79
Fierro, Midland	.958	24	41	73	5	15	Owen, Midland	.917	64	98	191	26	28
Gladden, Shreveport	1.000	1	0	3	0	0	Pagel, Midland	.951	47	72	124	10	27

SHORTSTOPS—Continued

Player and Club	Pct.	G.	PO.	A.	E.	DP.
Pastors, Jackson	.913	35	37	79	11	9
Pedrique, Jackson	.937	112	184	323	34	68
Perdue, Shreveport	.914	38	41	98	13	9
Purpura, Amarillo	.878	22	33	53	12	11
Quick, Shreveport	.929	24	31	60	7	10
SANTANA, Arkansas	.955	102	151	337	23	79
Schultz, San Antonio	.909	2	3	7	1	2

Player and Club	Pct.	G.	PO.	A.	E.	DP.
Simmons, Midland	.842	5	5	11	3	1
Skorochocki, El Paso	.923	9	8	16	2	5
Stevenson, Amarillo	.906	111	152	360	53	74
Turco, Arkansas	.920	41	69	114	16	20
Wabeke, Shreveport	1.000	4	6	7	0	2
Wallace, Tulsa	.949	10	10	27	2	2

Triple Plays—Santana, Purpura, Turco.

CATCHERS

Player and Club	Pct.	G.	PO.	A.	E.	DP.	PB.
Bauman, Shreveport	.972	9	32	3	1	1	2
Bilardello, San Antonio	.973	6	34	2	1	0	2
Castro, Amarillo	.952	28	159	19	9	1	7
Cowger, Tulsa	.980	47	259	31	6	2	5
Cuervo, Jackson	1.000	1	7	0	0	0	1
Cummings, Shreveport	.973	44	223	31	7	2	12
Delaney, Arkansas	.982	55	295	40	6	3	4
Diaz, Midland	.977	106	593	75	16	4	8
Duff, Jackson	1.000	17	71	19	0	3	4
Fitzgerald, Jackson	.994	47	297	42	2	4	3
Mitchell, Midland	1.000	1	1	2	0	0	5
Nieto, Arkansas	.975	53	270	37	8	0	6
Rabb, Shreveport	.970	82	532	42	18	6	4

Player and Club	Pct.	G.	PO.	A.	E.	DP.	PB.
R. Reynolds, Jackson	.979	83	493	67	12	4	6
Rothford, Shreveport	.969	11	59	5	2	0	3
Russell, Tulsa	1.000	1	4	0	0	0	0
D. Sax, San Antonio	.981	25	196	16	4	2	8
Schroeder, El Paso	.982	80	511	49	10	3	6
D. Scott, Tulsa	.971	90	470	58	16	6	27
Shepston, Midland	.969	36	171	19	6	0	5
Shoebridge, El Paso	.982	57	381	44	8	6	8
Slettvet, Arkansas	.975	14	72	6	2	0	4
Sobbe, San Antonio	.970	26	140	24	5	1	3
Tingley, Amarillo	.983	96	584	47	11	3	22
Winslow, Arkansas	.979	30	171	15	4	4	5
ZOURAS, San Antonio	.985	81	454	64	8	0	23

OUTFIELDERS

Player and Club	Pct.	G.	PO.	A.	E.	DP.
Adduci, Arkansas°	.983	39	55	3	1	0
Alexander, Shreveport°	1.000	2	1	0	0	0
Amelung, San Antonio°	1.000	4	9	0	0	0
Aranzamendi, Arkansas	1.000	25	27	2	0	2
Baker, Shreveport	.971	121	194	10	6	3
Ball, Tulsa	.967	120	189	19	7	2
Barrow, Tulsa	.970	33	60	5	2	0
Beltre, Jackson	.943	43	79	4	5	1
BEYERS, San Antonio°	.992	109	240	2	2	0
Bradley, San Antonio	.980	128	240	10	5	1
Burton, Midland	.857	11	12	0	2	0
Cain, Amarillo	.982	65	101	7	2	3
Carter, Midland	.965	65	100	10	4	1
Cowger, Tulsa	.939	18	28	3	2	1
Cuervo, Jackson	1.000	3	6	0	0	0
S. Davis, El Paso	1.000	4	4	0	0	0
Delaney, Arkansas	1.000	1	1	0	0	0
Fitzgerald, Jackson	1.000	6	8	0	0	0
Gausepohl, Amarillo	.963	93	164	17	7	2
Gladden, Shreveport	.987	120	211	9	3	0
Grant, Midland	.978	48	77	12	2	3
Gutierrez, Arkansas	.889	6	8	0	1	0
Gwynn, Amarillo°	1.000	21	41	1	0	0
Hall, Midland°	.975	128	302	14	8	5
Hansen, El Paso	.938	66	126	11	9	1
Haslerig, Jackson	.918	55	88	2	8	1
D. Holman, San Antonio	.984	118	224	15	4	2
Irvine, El Paso	.950	132	292	11	16	3
J. Johnson, Amarillo	1.000	3	4	1	0	0
Lane, El Paso	1.000	1	1	0	0	0
LaVigne, Midland	.981	118	185	20	4	1
Loman, El Paso°	.937	71	118	15	9	0
Martinez, Midland	.846	20	20	2	4	0
McCauley, Arkansas	.966	18	27	1	1	0
L. Miller, San Antonio	1.000	1	3	0	0	0

Player and Club	Pct.	G.	PO.	A.	E.	DP.
Mills, Arkansas	.969	127	267	13	9	1
Mitchell, Midland	1.000	1	1	0	0	0
S. Moore, Jackson	.962	103	142	9	6	1
Morgan, Midland	1.000	7	11	1	0	0
Murphy, Tulsa°	1.000	4	6	0	0	0
Pagel, Midland	1.000	1	1	0	0	0
Pastors, Jackson	1.000	2	1	0	0	0
Perdue, Shreveport	.938	18	29	1	2	0
Poe, Jackson°	.941	14	14	2	1	1
Pyburn, Amarillo	.971	118	167	3	5	0
Rabb, Shreveport	1.000	3	1	0	0	0
L. Reynolds, Tulsa	.969	55	85	9	3	1
Riggleman, Arkansas	.960	31	46	2	2	1
Roman, Arkansas°	.974	77	108	6	3	0
D. Sax, San Antonio	.973	18	35	1	1	0
D. Scott, Tulsa	1.000	19	18	2	0	0
Skorochocki, El Paso	.923	20	23	1	2	0
Skube, El Paso°	.955	114	170	19	9	0
Steels, Amarillo°	.967	115	197	11	7	2
Stockstill, Tulsa	.960	29	45	3	2	0
Szymarek, Shreveport	.953	85	129	13	7	3
Tillman, Jackson	.975	74	112	7	3	2
Tingley, Amarillo	1.000	1	1	0	0	0
Tisdale, Arkansas	.953	48	54	7	3	0
Tracy, Midland	1.000	16	26	0	0	0
Turco, Arkansas	.933	20	14	0	1	0
Valley, El Paso°	1.000	1	1	0	0	0
White, San Antonio°	1.000	25	48	1	0	1
Wiggins, Shreveport°	.959	46	68	3	3	0
Wojcik, Shreveport	.909	6	7	3	1	0
G. Wright, Tulsa	.977	130	286	8	7	2
Wynne, Jackson	.980	124	267	21	6	3
Zayas, Arkansas	.974	30	36	1	1	0
Zicardi, Shreveport°	.946	34	33	2	2	4

PITCHERS

Player and Club	Pct.	G.	PO.	A.	E.	DP.
Ako, El Paso	1.000	19	1	3	0	0
Alexander, Shreveport°	.912	34	9	43	5	0
Apodaca, Jackson	.833	6	4	1	1	0
Ballard, Amarillo	.947	20	11	25	2	1
Barba, Amarillo	.824	30	2	12	3	1
Bittiger, Jackson	1.000	4	2	4	0	0
Blyth, Midland	1.000	44	7	12	0	0
Burchett, Amarillo	.926	20	2	3	2	1
Candiotti, El Paso	1.000	21	16	26	0	0
Carney, Tulsa°	1.000	22	6	13	0	0
Church, Amarillo°	.947	35	6	12	1	1
Churchill, Midland°	.903	37	13	15	3	0
Citarella, Arkansas	1.000	31	9	18	0	1
Clark, Midland	.900	29	14	31	5	2
Cook, El Paso	.800	18	4	16	5	0
Crutcher, Tulsa	.958	21	10	13	1	1
Daly, Amarillo	.882	32	3	12	2	1
Darling, Tulsa	.947	13	6	12	1	2
T. Davis, Jackson	.939	24	6	25	2	1
Dempsey, Shreveport	.976	26	13	28	1	1
Dixon, Amarillo	.973	26	10	26	1	3
Dravecky, Amarillo°	.921	30	14	21	3	3
Dunn, Shreveport	.941	35	9	23	2	1

Player and Club	Pct.	G.	PO.	A.	E.	DP.
Fisher, Shreveport	.966	26	6	22	1	1
Fossas, Tulsa°	1.000	38	5	14	0	0
Fowlkes, Shreveport	.961	32	14	35	2	0
Gaff, Jackson	.905	7	4	15	2	0
Garrelts, Shreveport	.955	14	6	15	1	0
Gil, Midland	1.000	5	1	5	0	0
Glinatsis, San Antonio	1.000	19	5	19	0	0
Gotay, Arkansas	.800	8	2	2	1	0
Gott, Arkansas	.857	28	8	22	5	3
Hagen, Arkansas	.922	27	8	39	4	1
Hamm, Amarillo	.875	17	2	26	4	2
Hawkins, Amarillo	.977	27	12	31	1	5
Henke, Tulsa	.667	15	0	2	1	0
Hershister, San Antonio	.857	42	11	13	4	0
S. Holman, Jackson	.917	20	11	11	2	0
Hudson, Tulsa	1.000	6	1	7	0	0
Hughes, Tulsa	.955	19	8	13	1	1
Jenkins, El Paso	1.000	6	3	3	0	0
Dave Johnson, Arkansas°	1.000	20	4	18	0	1
Don Johnson, Amarillo°	1.000	8	2	5	0	0
J.D. Johnson, Arkansas	1.000	21	4	24	0	1
C. Jones, San Antonio	1.000	21	6	15	0	0
D. Jones, El Paso	1.000	15	2	14	0	1

PITCHERS—Continued

Player and Club	Pct.	G	PO	A	E	DP
Jorn, Arkansas	1.000	17	2	11	0	1
Keener, Arkansas	.778	30	3	4	2	0
King, Midland	.905	14	6	13	2	1
Koontz, El Paso	.920	41	5	18	2	1
Kranitz, El Paso	.857	14	6	12	3	2
Lamson, Tulsa°	1.000	6	0	2	0	0
Lazorko, Tulsa	.966	47	6	22	1	4
M. Leach, Tulsa°	.667	2	0	2	1	0
T. Leach, Jackson	.929	8	3	10	1	0
Lefferts, Midland	.980	26	12	38	1	2
Lohuis, Shreveport	.905	31	8	11	2	0
Long, Tulsa	.923	35	4	8	1	3
Lowry, Jackson	.938	24	13	17	2	1
Mack, Midland	1.000	20	3	12	0	0
Mike Madden, El Paso°	.966	22	8	20	1	3
Morris Madden, San Antonio	1.000	4	0	3	0	0
Majer, Amarillo	1.000	2	1	0	0	0
Malden, San Antonio	.958	27	5	18	1	0
Marsden, San Antonio	.950	10	6	13	1	1
McClain, Midland	.833	10	4	6	2	1
McDonald, San Antonio	.905	32	13	25	4	1
R. Miller, Amarillo	.875	12	0	7	1	0
T. Miller, Jackson°	.917	25	0	11	1	1
Millner, Midland	.933	26	4	10	1	1
Montgomery, El Paso	.926	30	8	17	2	0
E. Moore, Midland	1.000	7	0	2	0	0
Moyer, Shreveport	.963	35	6	20	1	2
Nastu, Midland	.913	36	8	13	2	1
Niedenfuer, San Antonio	1.000	36	4	14	0	3
Nielsen, Tulsa	1.000	16	11	19	0	1
Nobles, San Antonio°	.889	35	3	13	2	0
Nowlin, Midland	1.000	1	0	1	0	0
Ownbey, Jackson	.875	20	8	20	4	1
Park, El Paso	.929	11	3	10	1	1
Perlman, Midland	.909	12	13	17	3	1
Pimentel, Arkansas	.857	50	1	5	1	0
Pisel, Shreveport	.875	15	8	13	3	0
Pratt, Arkansas°	1.000	7	1	3	0	1
Quinones, El Paso	.667	10	1	1	1	0
Richards, Tulsa	.958	17	8	15	1	0
Riggins, Arkansas°	1.000	51	6	21	0	3
Rincon, Arkansas	1.000	2	1	1	0	0
Roberts, Tulsa	.962	34	11	14	1	0
Rodas, San Antonio	.978	26	10	34	1	0
Rodriguez, Jackson°	1.000	15	2	3	0	0
Schmidt, Tulsa	1.000	3	4	1	0	1
Semprini, Jackson	1.000	34	6	7	0	1
Shepston, Midland	1.000	1	0	1	0	0
Simond, Jackson°	.962	22	18	33	2	6
Sisk, Jackson	.857	14	1	5	1	0
Skinner, Jackson°	1.000	6	3	1	0	0
Smith, Jackson	.867	24	3	10	2	1
Spino, Midland°	.952	13	3	17	1	0
Stovall, Shreveport	.938	25	1	14	1	2
Swift, El Paso	.960	18	9	15	1	1
TERRELL, Tulsa	1.000	27	16	35	0	1
Thompson, Midland°	1.000	14	8	20	0	2
Thorp, San Antonio	.667	3	1	1	1	0
Thurberg, Jackson	.889	28	8	16	3	3
Thurmond, Amarillo°	.958	27	9	37	2	1
Torres, El Paso	.952	26	8	12	1	1
Tucker, Shreveport	.857	11	0	6	1	0
Valley, El Paso°	.960	36	5	19	1	1
Violette, Jackson	1.000	4	2	4	0	0
Von Ohlen, Jackson°	1.000	11	4	6	0	1
Wheelock, San Antonio	1.000	9	1	1	0	0
Wickensheimer, San Antonio	.833	22	9	16	5	2
Winfield, Arkansas	.500	10	1	3	4	0
Wise, San Antonio	1.000	2	0	2	0	0
M.Wright, Midland°	1.000	12	0	8	0	0
Wyrick, Amarillo	1.000	22	4	3	0	0

The following players do not have any recorded accepted chances at the positions indicated; therefore, are not listed in the fielding averages for those particular positions: Bauman, p; Clarke, p; Cuerro, 3b; Gausepohl, p; Gladden, 2b; Lane, p, ss; D. Moore, of; Owen, 3b; Schroeder, of; Schultz, 1b, of; Skorochocki, 1b; Stockstill, 1b; Zouras, 3b.

CLUB PITCHING

Club	ERA	G	CG	ShO	Sv	IP	H	R	ER	HR	HB	BB	Int. BB	SO	WP.	Bk.
Jackson	3.42	134	23	19	24	1188⅓	1096	554	451	71	29	542	30	807	66	8
Tulsa	3.62	133	21	9	28	1144⅓	1124	577	460	84	33	480	47	700	81	3
Amarillo	3.63	136	61	12	22	1151⅓	1196	595	464	94	13	376	20	779	49	8
Shreveport	3.69	135	30	5	31	1147⅔	1169	563	471	76	33	418	9	817	80	9
Arkansas	4.22	132	24	9	16	1103⅔	1122	606	518	71	47	473	33	716	81	10
San Antonio	4.48	133	35	8	23	1142⅓	1225	682	568	116	27	511	28	781	98	4
El Paso	4.70	134	20	5	23	1163⅔	1351	736	608	108	24	461	25	837	74	8
Midland	5.05	135	31	5	22	1149⅓	1319	771	645	133	31	531	14	731	76	9

PITCHERS' RECORDS
(Leading Qualifiers for Earned-Run Average Leadership—109 or More Innings)

°Throws lefthanded.

Pitcher—Club	W.	L.	Pct.	ERA	G.	GS.	CG.	GF.	ShO.	Sv.	IP.	H.	R.	ER.	HR.	HB.	BB.	Int. BB.	SO.	WP.
Hamm, Amarillo	9	6	.600	2.27	17	15	11	2	1	1	123	126	51	31	10	0	17	0	78	2
Dravecky, Amarillo°	15	5	.750	2.67	30	19	11	6	4	2	172	157	69	51	11	2	45	3	141	4
Ownbey, Jackson	10	7	.588	2.77	20	20	2	0	2	0	133	110	49	41	4	4	62	1	125	8
Fowlkes, Shreveport	14	10	.583	2.79	32	25	13	2	1	0	203	186	81	63	14	4	51	3	152	6
Candiotti, El Paso	7	6	.538	2.80	21	14	6	7	1	0	119	137	51	37	8	3	27	4	68	6
Simond, Jackson°	6	7	.462	2.87	22	19	5	0	2	0	135	123	54	43	2	0	49	1	58	7
Terrell, Tulsa	15	7	.682	3.10	27	26	5	0	3	0	174	158	74	60	12	2	63	3	234	14
Thurmond, Amarillo°	12	5	.706	3.26	27	27	10	0	2	0	193	202	86	70	10	1	56	1	128	4
Gott, Arkansas	5	9	.357	3.44	28	19	4	2	0	0	131	133	68	50	5	6	65	1	93	16
Fisher, Shreveport	8	6	.571	3.71	26	21	3	3	0	1	126	139	61	52	9	1	46	0	112	6

Departmental Leaders: G—Riggins, 51; GS—Hawkins, Thurmond, 27; CG—Hawkins, 14; ShO—Dravecky, 4; W—Dempsey, Dravecky, Terrell, 15; L—Dixon, Lefferts, 12; Sv—Hershiser, 15; Pct.—Niedenfuer, .813; IP—Fowlkes, 203; H—Hawkins, 209; R—R. Clark, 119; ER—Hawkins, 93; HR—R. Clark, 22; BB—Thurberg, 79; IBB—Pimentel, 9; HB—Hagen, 9; SO—Fowlkes, 152; WP—Burchett, 20.

(All Pitchers—Listed Alphabetically)

Pitcher—Club	W.	L.	Pct.	ERA	G.	GS.	CG.	GF.	ShO.	Sv.	IP.	H.	R.	ER.	HR.	HB.	BB.	Int. BB.	SO.	WP.
Ako, El Paso	2	1	.667	6.80	19	1	0	14	0	1	45	81	42	34	9	1	5	1	25	3
Alexander, Shreveport°	3	9	.250	4.26	34	16	3	16	0	2	152	175	85	72	8	3	57	1	76	7
Apodaca, Jackson	1	3	.250	7.56	6	5	0	1	0	0	25	39	28	21	3	0	14	0	14	3
Ballard, Amarillo	7	6	.538	4.39	20	20	6	0	0	0	123	131	73	60	16	4	33	1	67	4
Barba, Amarillo	4	5	.444	3.07	30	1	0	16	0	5	44	42	32	15	3	0	26	1	23	5
Bauman, Shreveport	0	0	.000	0.00	1	0	0	1	0	0	1	1	0	0	0	0	0	0	0	0
Bittiger, Jackson	2	1	.667	1.09	4	4	1	0	1	0	33	24	4	4	1	0	8	0	27	0
Blyth, Midland	9	5	.643	3.36	44	1	0	32	0	10	75	70	34	28	6	4	33	4	78	6
Burchett, Arkansas	6	11	.353	4.57	20	20	2	0	0	0	126	140	71	64	8	6	40	3	76	20
Candiotti, El Paso	7	6	.538	2.80	21	14	6	7	1	0	119	137	51	37	8	3	27	4	68	6
Carney, Tulsa°	4	6	.400	4.33	22	12	1	5	0	1	81	69	46	39	9	2	63	1	43	7
Church, Amarillo°	3	4	.429	3.71	35	0	0	21	0	7	34	37	20	14	2	1	24	5	34	2
Churchill, Midland°	7	11	.389	5.43	37	12	2	12	0	2	121	145	86	73	17	5	40	0	68	9
Citarella, Arkansas	8	9	.471	3.82	31	16	4	12	2	2	125	120	57	53	6	1	37	2	81	3

Pitcher—Club	W.	L.	Pct.	ERA.	G.	GS.	CG.	GF.	ShO.	Sv.	IP.	H.	R.	ER.	HR.	HB.	BB.	Int. BB.	SO.	WP.
Clark, Midland	8	10	.444	5.07	29	21	6	4	0	0	158	171	118	89	22	4	76	1	71	9
Clarke, Midland	0	0	.000	3.00	1	0	0	0	0	0	3	3	1	1	0	0	1	0	0	0
Cook, El Paso	6	5	.545	3.89	18	18	3	0	0	0	104	118	60	45	10	2	49	1	63	6
Crutcher, Tulsa	4	3	.571	3.90	21	6	1	6	0	1	67	70	34	29	5	1	40	2	37	6
Daly, 20 Jac-12 Am°	5	6	.455	3.35	32	2	1	17	1	3	78	82	40	29	6	0	43	6	58	8
Darling, Tulsa	4	2	.667	4.44	13	13	2	0	2	0	71	72	43	35	4	2	33	2	53	6
T. Davis, Jackson	1	7	.125	3.40	24	16	1	5	1	0	106	114	63	40	4	2	43	5	60	4
Dempsey, Shreveport	15	7	.682	3.76	26	26	7	0	1	0	165	178	83	69	14	5	58	1	136	6
Dixon, Amarillo	9	12	.429	3.96	26	25	8	0	2	0	157	170	93	69	13	3	62	1	82	13
Dravecky, Amarillo°	15	5	.750	2.67	30	19	11	6	4	2	172	157	69	51	11	2	45	3	141	4
Dunn, Shreveport	5	8	.385	3.60	35	10	1	19	0	12	105	99	49	42	7	4	44	1	79	8
Fisher, Shreveport	8	6	.571	3.71	26	21	3	3	0	1	126	139	61	52	9	1	46	0	112	6
Fossas, Tulsa	5	6	.455	4.16	38	12	1	7	1	2	106	113	65	49	4	3	44	2	57	4
Fowlkes, Shreveport	14	10	.583	2.79	32	25	13	2	1	0	203	186	81	63	14	4	51	3	152	6
Gaff, Jackson	5	1	.833	2.53	7	7	5	0	2	0	57	48	18	16	5	0	13	1	27	1
Garrelts, Shreveport	3	8	.273	4.44	14	13	1	0	0	0	71	56	43	35	2	4	43	0	73	19
Gausepohl, Amarillo	0	0	.000	0.00	1	0	0	0	0	0	1	0	0	0	0	0	0	0	1	0
Gil, Midland	0	5	.000	6.75	5	5	0	0	0	0	16	22	19	12	1	1	15	0	8	4
Glinatsis, San Antonio	5	5	.500	3.45	19	16	5	0	0	0	107	114	52	41	12	2	37	1	40	13
Gotay, Arkansas	2	6	.250	6.13	8	8	2	0	2	0	47	52	38	32	8	1	22	1	46	2
Gott, Arkansas	5	9	.357	3.44	28	19	4	2	0	0	131	133	68	50	5	6	65	1	93	16
Hagen, Arkansas	8	11	.421	3.98	27	26	5	0	1	0	165	179	95	73	10	9	69	3	66	9
Hamm, Amarillo	9	6	.600	2.27	17	15	11	2	1	1	123	126	51	31	10	0	17	0	78	2
Hawkins, Amarillo	11	10	.524	4.19	27	27	14	0	2	0	200	209	100	93	15	1	48	1	144	4
Henke, Tulsa	4	3	.571	3.94	15	0	0	9	0	1	32	31	16	14	2	2	14	4	37	1
Hershiser, San Antonio	7	6	.538	4.68	42	4	3	30	1	15	102	94	54	53	12	5	50	5	95	14
Holman, Jackson	4	9	.308	3.85	20	20	2	0	1	0	110	106	57	47	6	8	71	1	43	3
Hudson, Tulsa	2	3	.400	4.11	6	6	1	0	0	0	35	34	23	16	1	5	21	0	23	3
Hughes, Tulsa	8	6	.571	3.51	19	16	1	0	0	0	95	99	47	37	5	1	47	2	61	10
Jenkins, El Paso	1	0	1.000	7.50	6	0	0	4	0	0	18	22	15	15	3	1	11	1	5	2
Dave Johnson, Arkansas°	1	2	.333	4.02	20	4	1	1	1	0	56	58	29	25	6	3	21	2	27	3
Don Johnson, Amarillo°	0	0	.000	10.89	8	1	0	2	0	0	19	36	23	23	5	0	10	0	14	2
J. Johnson, Arkansas	8	10	.444	4.67	21	21	4	0	0	0	129	130	68	67	7	4	45	1	80	8
C. Jones, San Antonio	7	6	.538	6.17	21	16	4	3	0	0	89	109	75	61	13	3	65	2	60	10
D. Jones, El Paso	5	7	.417	5.80	15	15	3	0	1	0	90	121	67	58	6	1	28	1	62	2
Jorn, Arkansas	2	2	.500	2.00	17	9	0	3	0	0	72	60	22	16	2	1	23	2	31	3
Keener, Arkansas	0	3	.000	1.93	30	0	0	24	0	2	42	29	16	9	2	7	15	3	42	3
King, Midland°	4	2	.667	7.06	14	13	1	0	0	0	65	76	60	51	11	0	70	0	43	10
Koontz, El Paso	5	6	.455	3.79	41	0	0	31	0	6	102	116	54	43	7	3	44	7	81	4
Kranitz, El Paso	2	7	.222	6.21	14	10	1	2	1	0	58	62	54	40	9	4	56	0	53	7
Lamson, Tulsa°	1	0	1.000	4.50	6	0	0	1	0	0	10	11	5	5	2	0	6	1	8	0
Lane, El Paso	0	0	.000	12.00	1	0	0	1	0	0	3	7	4	4	0	1	1	0	3	1
Lazorko, Tulsa	4	8	.333	3.36	47	0	0	37	0	12	67	54	31	25	6	5	23	8	36	4
M. Leach, Tulsa	0	0	.000	5.00	2	1	0	1	0	1	9	11	8	5	1	2	0	5	1	
T. Leach, Jackson	5	1	.833	1.71	8	7	2	1	1	0	58	47	14	11	2	2	12	1	43	0
Lefferts, Midland	12	12	.500	4.14	26	25	11	1	3	0	185	203	95	85	21	3	36	2	135	1
Lohuis, Shreveport	4	2	.667	3.11	31	0	0	22	0	3	55	50	24	19	3	3	26	0	51	4
Long, Tulsa	4	3	.571	2.33	35	0	0	30	0	7	54	58	14	14	5	1	19	7	22	4
Lowry, Jackson	6	11	.353	4.36	24	23	3	1	1	0	126	132	67	61	16	1	64	2	73	13
Mack, Tulsa	4	5	.444	4.24	20	9	1	6	0	2	68	58	35	32	3	1	54	0	55	6
Mike Madden, El Paso	6	8	.429	5.69	22	22	2	0	0	0	125	154	94	79	13	1	40	0	140	13
Mo. Madden, San Antonio°	0	3	.000	13.91	4	4	0	0	0	0	11	22	17	17	3	0	14	0	6	2
Majer, Amarillo	0	0	.000	22.50	2	0	0	2	0	0	2	7	5	5	0	0	1	0	2	1
Malden, San Antonio	7	7	.500	4.57	27	21	4	2	0	0	130	151	77	66	13	2	43	1	79	10
Marsden, San Antonio	4	4	.500	3.26	10	10	3	0	2	0	69	66	34	25	3	0	18	0	39	3
McClain, Midland	3	4	.429	4.43	10	10	4	0	0	0	69	72	37	34	7	2	31	1	54	4
McDonald, San Antonio	6	6	.500	4.83	32	14	2	10	0	1	123	149	85	66	12	1	49	4	60	3
R. Miller, Amarillo	2	1	.667	2.25	12	0	0	6	0	1	20	14	11	5	2	0	18	4	19	0
T. Miller, Jackson°	2	3	.400	5.40	25	1	0	11	0	2	55	56	36	33	3	1	28	0	39	6
Millner, Midland	2	3	.400	4.22	26	0	0	13	0	1	49	57	29	23	4	2	28	4	40	7
Montgomery, El Paso	6	6	.500	4.62	30	7	1	13	0	2	113	136	63	58	6	1	31	3	44	4
E. Moore, Midland	0	1	.000	5.14	7	0	0	7	0	2	7	9	4	4	0	0	5	1	4	0
Moyer, Shreveport	7	8	.467	3.99	35	10	1	13	0	3	115	132	60	51	5	3	41	2	68	7
Nastu, Midland°	6	5	.545	5.36	36	4	0	20	0	4	94	125	65	56	13	3	51	0	72	3
Niedenfuer, San Antonio	13	3	.813	1.80	36	0	0	27	0	5	90	61	19	18	3	2	34	4	95	9
Nielsen, Tulsa	5	4	.556	3.94	16	14	4	0	0	0	96	103	46	42	7	2	23	1	35	6
Nobles, San Antonio°	4	4	.500	6.75	35	0	0	15	0	2	76	91	71	57	10	3	57	4	66	15
Nowlin, Midland	0	0	.000	0.00	1	0	0	1	0	0	1	0	0	0	0	0	0	0	1	0
Ownbey, Jackson	10	7	.588	2.77	20	20	2	0	2	0	133	110	49	41	8	4	62	1	125	8
Park, El Paso	3	3	.500	5.77	11	11	1	0	0	0	53	74	40	34	4	1	17	1	27	2
Perlman, Midland	1	4	.200	7.60	12	11	2	1	0	1	58	90	62	49	5	4	22	0	29	7
Pimentel, Arkansas	8	5	.615	4.23	50	0	0	36	0	10	66	53	34	31	3	3	59	9	85	5
Pisel, Shreveport	5	6	.455	5.35	15	14	1	0	0	0	79	94	55	47	9	4	33	1	39	13
Pratt, Arkansas°	0	2	.000	9.00	7	4	0	1	0	0	23	25	25	23	2	1	20	0	17	4
Quinones, El Paso	1	3	.250	2.70	10	0	0	9	0	2	20	18	9	6	1	0	16	2	19	3
Richards, Jackson	5	5	.500	3.22	17	13	3	2	0	0	95	80	50	34	13	3	36	3	69	10
Riggins, Arkansas°	4	6	.400	5.87	51	3	2	27	1	1	89	109	62	58	11	2	46	5	53	4
Rincon, Arkansas	0	2	.000	6.75	2	2	0	0	0	0	8	11	6	6	0	0	1	1	6	0
Roberts, Tulsa	2	4	.333	2.94	34	4	0	13	0	2	95	97	37	31	4	3	19	8	56	1
Rodas, San Antonio	14	6	.700	4.14	26	26	10	0	3	0	185	193	100	85	15	4	60	4	148	11
Rodriguez, Jackson°	0	2	.000	1.73	15	0	0	7	0	1	26	20	9	5	0	0	6	1	13	0
Schmidt, Tulsa	1	1	.500	1.88	3	3	2	0	0	0	24	17	5	5	1	0	6	0	17	1
Semprini, Jackson	7	3	.700	2.09	34	0	0	29	0	12	56	35	15	13	1	2	27	5	71	6
Shepston, Midland	0	0	.000	36.00	1	0	0	1	0	0	2	9	8	8	1	0	0	0	0	0
Simond, Jackson°	6	7	.462	2.87	22	19	5	0	2	0	135	123	54	43	2	0	49	1	58	7
Sisk, Jackson	3	0	1.000	3.60	14	0	0	12	0	4	25	23	11	10	0	1	12	4	15	0
Skinner, Jackson	0	0	.000	5.54	6	1	0	1	0	0	13	11	11	8	1	1	17	1	2	1
D. Smith, Jackson	4	4	.500	4.50	24	0	0	15	0	0	56	55	32	28	5	2	25	3	42	4
Spino, Midland°	0	5	.000	8.10	13	10	0	1	0	0	50	71	56	45	11	0	32	0	23	3
Stovall, Shreveport	1	3	.250	3.38	25	0	0	19	0	5	48	46	19	18	4	1	13	0	18	4
Swift, El Paso	6	5	.545	6.50	18	18	2	0	0	0	90	100	75	65	9	3	65	0	57	12
Terrell, Tulsa	15	7	.682	3.10	27	26	5	0	3	0	174	158	74	60	12	2	63	3	123	14

Pitcher—Club	W.	L.	Pct.	ERA.	G.	GS.	CG.	GF.	ShO.	Sv.	IP.	H.	R.	ER.	HR.	HB.	BB.	Int. BB.	SO.	WP.
Thompson, Midland°	6	1	.857	3.60	14	14	4	0	1	0	100	112	45	40	9	0	17	0	28	0
Thorp, San Antonio	0	1	.000	3.60	3	0	0	2	0	0	5	7	3	2	0	0	4	1	4	0
Thurberg, Jackson	6	5	.545	4.76	28	13	2	9	0	0	121	118	83	64	13	4	79	3	106	9
Thurmond, Amarillo°	12	5	.706	3.26	27	27	10	0	2	0	193	202	86	70	10	1	56	1	128	4
Torres, El Paso	5	7	.417	4.35	26	17	1	7	0	2	122	124	74	59	15	1	42	2	110	3
Tucker, Shreveport	3	0	1.000	1.00	11	0	0	10	0	5	27	13	3	3	1	1	6	0	13	0
Valley, El Paso°	10	5	.667	2.79	36	1	0	26	0	10	100	81	34	31	8	0	29	2	80	6
Violette, Jackson	1	3	.250	4.71	4	4	0	0	0	0	21	20	14	11	2	0	10	0	8	2
Von Ohlen, Jackson°	4	0	1.000	0.93	11	0	0	9	0	3	29	20	3	3	0	1	4	1	24	0
Wheelock, San Antonio	2	0	1.000	2.50	9	0	0	8	0	0	18	16	5	5	2	2	5	0	7	3
Wickensheimer, San Antonio	7	6	.538	4.87	22	22	4	0	0	0	133	152	90	72	18	3	75	2	80	5
Winfield, Arkansas	0	2	.000	3.96	10	0	0	2	0	1	25	23	15	11	1	3	10	0	13	1
Wise, San Antonio	0	0	.000	0.00	2	0	0	1	0	0	4	0	0	0	0	0	0	0	2	0
M. Wright, Midland°	0	0	.000	5.00	12	0	0	5	0	0	27	26	17	15	2	1	20	1	22	7
Wyrick, Amarillo	1	2	.333	3.81	22	0	0	14	0	5	26	25	11	11	3	1	12	0	23	2

BALKS—Hagen, Hamm, 4 each; Citarella, Dempsey, Fowlkes, Rodriguez, 3 each; Alexander, Clark, Fossas, D. Jones, King, Lefferts, Spino, Thurberg, 2 each; Cook, Dixon, Garrelts, Gotay, J. Johnson, C. Jones, D. Jones, Keener, Koontz, Mike Madden, McDonald, Millner, Montgomery, Nobles, Ownbey, Rodas, Rodriguez, Simond, Swift, Thurmond, Torrez, Terrell, Violette, 1 each.

COMBINATION SHUTOUTS—Jackson-Pratt-Pimentel, Jorn-Keener, Arkansas; Park-Valley, Swift-Valley, El Paso; Ownbey-Daly, Simond-Sisk, Ownbey-Semprini 2, Lowry-Semprini, Leach-Semprini 2, Thurberg-Sisk, Jackson; Lefferts-Milner-Blyth, Midland; Malden-Niedenfuer, Rodas-Niedenfuer, San Antonio; Garrelts-Moyer, Garrelts-Dunn, Fisher-Alexander, Shreveport; Hughes-Lazorko, Carney-Lazorko, Nielsen-Lazorko, Tulsa.

NO-HIT GAMES—None.

California League

CLASS A

CHAMPIONSHIP WINNERS IN PREVIOUS YEARS

1914—Fresno .571	1958—Fresno° .639	1970—Bakersfield .667
1915—Modesto .857	Bakersfield .672	Bakersfield .671
1916-40—Did not operate.	1959—Bakersfield .592	1971—Visalia§ .583
1941—Fresno .643	Modesto§ .643	Fresno .500
S. Barbara (2nd)° .597	1960—Reno .614	1972—Modesto§ .547
1942—Santa Barbara† .642	Reno .657	Bakersfield .629
1943-44-45—Did not operate.	1961—Reno .743	1973—Lodi§ .657
1946—Stockton‡ .600	Reno .643	Bakersfield .571
1947—Stockton‡ .679	1962—San José§ .686	1974—Fresno§ .607
1948—Fresno .607	Reno .587	San José .579
S. Barbara (3rd)° .529	1963—Modesto .589	1975—Reno .614
1949—Bakersfield .612	Stockton§ .687	Reno .614
San José (4th)° .543	1964—Fresno .638	1976—Salinas .650
1950—Ventura .607	Fresno .600	Reno§ .547
Modesto (2nd)° .586	1965—San José .586	1977—Salinas .564
1951—Santa Barbara† .599	Stockton§ .614	Lodi§ .579
1952—Fresno‡ .629	1966—Modesto .577	1978—Visalia§ .698
1953—San José‡ .664	Modesto .671	Lodi .607
1954—Modesto† .623	1967—San José§ .676	1979—San José§ .636
1955—Stockton .733	Modesto .586	Reno .525
Fresno§ .718	1968—San José .629	1980—Stockton§ .638
1956—Fresno‡ .650	Fresno§ .623	Visalia .507
1957—Visalia x .622	1969—Stockton§ .600	
Salinas (4th)° .504	Visalia .614	

°Won four-club playoff. †League disbanded June 28. ‡Won championship and four-club playoff. §Won split-season playoff. xWon both halves of split-season.

STANDING OF CLUBS AT CLOSE OF FIRST HALF, JUNE 21

Club	W.	L.	T.	Pct.	G.B.	Club	W.	L.	T.	Pct.	G.B.
Visalia (Twins)	44	26	0	.629	......	Redwood (Angels)	35	35	0	.500	9
Reno (Padres)	37	32	0	.536	6½	Modesto (A's)	30	38	0	.441	13
Fresno (Giants)	37	33	0	.529	7	Lodi (Dodgers)	30	40	0	.429	14
San Jose (Co-op)	36	34	0	.514	8	Stockton (Brewers)	29	40	0	.420	14½

STANDING OF CLUBS AT CLOSE OF SECOND HALF, AUGUST 30

Club	W.	L.	T.	Pct.	G.B.	Club	W.	L.	T.	Pct.	G.B.
Reno (Padres)	44	26	0	.629	......	Modesto (A's)	37	33	0	.529	7
Lodi (Dodgers)	43	27	0	.614	1	Redwood (Angels)	31	39	0	.443	13
Visalia (Twins)	43	27	0	.614	1	Fresno (Giants)	26	44	0	.371	18
Stockton (Brewers)	39	31	0	.557	5	San Jose (Co-op)	17	53	0	.243	27

COMPOSITE STANDING OF CLUBS AT CLOSE OF SEASON, AUGUST 30

Club	Vis.	Reno	Lodi	Sto.	Mod.	Red.	Fr.	S.J.	W.	L.	T.	Pct.	G.B.
Visalia (Twins)	....	10	11	14	14	10	12	16	87	53	0	.621	......
Reno (Padres)	10	....	13	14	10	11	11	12	81	58	0	.583	5½
Lodi (Dodgers)	9	7	....	8	17	13	10	9	73	67	0	.521	14
Stockton (Brewers)	6	6	12	....	8	12	13	11	68	71	0	.489	18½
Modesto (A's)	6	9	3	11	....	14	11	13	67	71	0	.486	19
Redwood (Angels)	10	9	7	8	6	....	14	12	66	74	0	.471	21
Fresno (Giants)	8	9	10	7	9	6	....	14	63	77	0	.450	24
San Jose (Co-op)	4	8	11	9	7	8	6	....	53	87	0	.379	34

Major league affiliations in parentheses.

Playoffs—Visalia defeated Stockton, two games to one; Lodi defeated Reno, two games to none. Lodi defeated Visalia, three games to two.

Regular-Season Attendance—Fresno, 89,666; Lodi, 61,271; Modesto, 65,675; Redwood, 66,466; Reno, 100,947; San Jose, 99,701; Stockton, 106,170; Visalia, 44,576. Total, 634,472. Playoffs, 11,965. No all-star game.

Managers: Fresno —Wayne Cato; Lodi—Terry Collins; Modesto—Keith Lieppman; Redwood—Chris Cannizzaro; Reno—Jack Maloof; San Jose—Fred Hatfield; Stockton—Duane Espy; Visalia—Dick Phillips.

All-Star Team: 1B—Hrbek, Visalia; 2B—Christensen, Visalia; 3B—Francis, Redwood; Jacobson, Modesto; SS—Rivera, Lodi; OF—Hinshaw, Reno; Deer, Fresno; Casey, Reno; James, Stockton; C—Madison, Visalia; DH—Brewer, Lodi; P—Romanick, Redwood; Williams, Fresno; Hardwick, Reno; Voigt, Visalia; Couches, Reno; Manager—Collins, Lodi.

(Compiled by William J. Weiss, League Statistician, San Mateo, Calif.)

CLUB BATTING

Club	Pct.	G.	AB.	R.	OR.	H.	TB.	2B.	3B.	HR.	RBI.	GW.	SH.	SF.	HP.	BB.	Int. BB.	SO.	SB.	CS.	LOB.
Visalia	.301	140	4768	889	672	1434	2055	202	40	113	760	73	43	53	28	647	27	674	246	93	1090
Reno	.298	139	4650	986	838	1387	2135	187	54	151	882	67	56	57	46	710	34	850	146	69	1041
Lodi	.294	140	4771	798	774	1404	2065	216	38	123	710	63	55	51	40	454	26	683	197	72	1013
Redwood	.265	140	4551	655	720	1204	1635	182	36	59	564	52	74	40	41	534	14	765	188	85	1044
Stockton	.263	139	4387	634	644	1153	1567	167	32	61	560	58	49	39	30	561	31	728	316	115	924
Fresno	.263	140	4596	687	764	1207	1786	190	31	109	581	56	49	39	22	530	21	847	186	76	958
Modesto	.262	138	4372	664	774	1147	1595	196	24	68	575	56	72	43	42	680	27	712	218	104	1025
San Jose	.251	140	4432	607	734	1114	1559	168	44	63	520	45	61	43	40	607	27	980	242	90	1016

INDIVIDUAL BATTING
(Leading Qualifiers for Batting Championship — 378 or More Plate Appearances)

°Bats lefthanded.   †Switch-hitter.

Player and Club	Pct.	G.	AB.	R.	H.	TB.	2B.	3B.	HR.	RBI.	GW.	SH.	SF.	HP.	BB.	Int. BB.	SO.	SB.	CS.
Hrbek, Kent, Visalia°	.379	121	462	119	175	291	25	5	27	111	9	1	9	4	59	7	59	12	5
Brewer, Anthony, Lodi	.371	118	434	86	161	241	22	5	16	85	6	4	8	2	43	4	56	17	12
Hinshaw, George, Reno°	.371	128	510	113	189	298	20	7	25	131	14	6	6	7	55	8	91	24	11
Christensen, James, Visalia	.370	104	411	101	152	250	27	1	23	84	5	3	3	1	57	1	43	16	5
Madison, Scott, Visalia†	.342	133	459	109	157	273	32	3	26	110	12	3	5	3	91	5	53	19	2
Harper, Therron, Modesto	.328	121	427	59	140	182	18	0	8	72	11	4	7	1	52	3	38	10	13
McNealy, Robert, San Jose°	.322	128	450	100	145	192	22	8	3	48	6	5	2	1	84	2	72	63	15
Scherger, Joseph, Reno	.319	114	401	74	128	225	23	10	18	93	6	5	5	4	58	5	67	3	4
Santos, Edgardo, Lodi	.318	129	513	100	163	265	21	6	23	94	10	3	5	6	27	4	62	40	7
Garcia, Steven, Reno°	.316	111	433	120	137	165	17	4	1	44	7	10	3	8	61	0	44	31	8

Departmental Leaders: G—Hunter, Krauss, Lulay, 137; AB—Hunter, 549; R—Garcia, 120; H—Hinshaw, 189; TB—Hinshaw, 298; 2B—Madison, 32; 3B—Brackenridge, Scherger, 10; HR—Deer, 33; RBI—Hinshaw, 131; SH—Krauss, 17; SF—Hrbek, Watanabe, 9; BB—Casey, 99; HP—Woods, 12; SO—Deer, 146; SB—McNealy, 63; CS—Sheehy, 22.

(All Players—Listed Alphabetically)

Player and Club	Pct.	G.	AB.	R.	H.	TB.	2B.	3B.	HR.	RBI.	GW.	SH.	SF.	HP.	BB.	Int. BB.	SO.	SB.	CS.
Adams, Dwight, Modesto†	.248	123	444	74	110	157	21	4	6	55	2	5	8	4	60	1	96	49	19
Allen, Robert, Lodi	.241	97	282	40	68	81	5	4	0	27	1	7	3	0	36	1	35	10	2
Alonzo, Raymond, Stockton°	.275	126	429	66	118	187	25	4	12	67	6	3	5	5	55	11	50	51	15
Anderson, Thomas, Fresno°	.238	133	441	69	105	195	20	5	20	66	7	3	3	2	61	3	96	6	6
Austin, Richard, Visalia	.297	109	390	45	116	150	17	1	5	57	6	1	2	2	27	2	45	8	6
Bagiotti, Aldo, Redwood	.250	31	88	13	22	27	5	0	0	8	1	1	0	1	20	1	24	3	2
Bailey, Robert, Lodi	.293	70	205	30	60	75	6	0	3	30	2	2	5	2	24	0	18	2	2
Bass, Ricki, Stockton	.157	15	51	6	8	8	0	0	0	3	0	1	1	0	11	0	10	4	1
Bathe, William, San Jose	.254	51	177	20	45	68	9	1	4	22	0	3	1	0	14	1	58	5	1
Bilardello, Dann, Lodi	.307	105	352	72	108	194	19	2	21	80	7	1	4	1	36	1	55	1	3
Bohnet, Robert, Redwood	.300	97	323	53	97	148	16	4	9	53	3	1	7	2	59	1	67	2	4
Brackenridge, Lyle, Visalia	.289	136	471	83	136	182	20	10	2	77	9	1	6	2	91	1	98	30	17
Brainard, Bartley, Stockton	.260	27	73	6	19	21	0	1	0	12	1	1	1	0	5	0	16	5	3
Braun, Barton, Redwood	.000	23	1	0	0	0	0	0	0	0	0	0	0	0	0	0	0	0	0
Brewer, Anthony, Lodi	.371	118	434	86	161	241	22	5	16	85	6	4	8	2	43	4	56	17	12
Brock, Joseph, Redwood	.200	36	90	9	18	25	2	1	1	12	1	1	2	1	11	0	24	2	2
Brown, Christopher, Fresno	.289	85	291	37	84	123	11	2	8	44	4	4	2	3	20	1	44	9	7
Byrum, Terry, Mod. 5-S.J. 34°	.241	39	112	8	27	42	7	1	2	15	1	0	1	1	20	3	24	2	2
Camacho, James, San Jose	.261	57	199	25	52	74	6	2	4	27	1	2	1	0	19	1	29	2	2
Campbell, Steven, Modesto	.136	31	59	7	8	12	1	0	1	9	1	0	2	1	10	0	12	2	2
Cardwell, David, Fresno	.238	110	332	39	79	103	13	1	3	36	5	6	3	1	18	0	68	18	6
Casey, Patrick, Reno	.310	126	432	105	134	233	15	6	24	107	8	1	6	4	99	2	102	11	8
Christensen, James, Visalia	.370	104	411	101	152	250	27	1	23	84	5	3	3	1	57	1	43	16	5
Christianson, David, Reno°	.282	116	386	86	109	179	15	2	17	86	8	4	3	4	84	5	85	1	1
Codiroli, Michael, San Jose	.365	44	137	36	50	64	3	4	1	16	2	2	0	4	37	1	15	23	10
Colburn, Thomas, Modesto†	.189	36	106	10	20	30	7	0	1	16	3	3	0	0	21	0	31	2	1
Colby, Charles, San Jose°	.260	74	231	27	60	86	11	3	3	27	4	0	2	4	19	2	32	7	0
Cole, Audie, Lodi	.260	74	231	27	60	86	11	3	3	27	4	0	2	4	19	2	32	7	0
Crow, Edward, San Jose°	.216	17	37	7	8	8	0	0	0	1	0	0	0	0	8	2	4	3	1
Cruz, Juan, San Jose	.198	95	258	26	51	58	5	1	0	20	2	9	2	3	38	0	49	21	6
Davenport, Gary, Fresno	.194	30	108	13	21	34	6	2	1	8	1	0	1	1	9	0	21	2	3
Dawson, Gary, San Jose	.254	103	401	40	102	130	12	5	2	52	4	3	3	5	27	3	87	23	8
Deer, Robert, Fresno	.286	135	479	86	137	268	24	4	33	107	14	0	4	2	70	10	146	18	7
de Leon, Orlando, Lodi	.000	33	0	1	0	0	0	0	0	0	0	0	0	0	0	0	0	0	0
Diaz, Roberto, Stockton	.000	33	1	0	0	0	0	0	0	0	0	0	0	0	0	0	1	0	0
Downs, Kirk, Stockton	.250	66	204	26	51	59	4	2	0	16	0	3	0	1	25	0	41	18	7
Duran, Richard, Stockton	.261	67	222	43	58	87	8	0	7	42	3	1	2	2	43	2	41	0	0
Durrman, James, Modesto°	.311	36	103	15	32	43	9	1	0	12	1	1	1	1	13	1	10	3	3
Eakes, Steven, Redwood	.187	40	91	6	17	20	1	1	0	11	1	2	1	1	8	0	12	4	6
Eakin, Gordon, Modesto	.194	9	31	5	6	7	1	0	0	1	0	1	0	0	6	0	5	0	1
Estepan, Rafael, Fresno	.293	107	376	52	110	155	16	1	9	51	8	6	2	1	18	0	42	6	1
Evans, Pride, Reno	.273	7	22	3	6	7	1	0	0	4	0	1	1	0	3	0	5	2	1
Favata, Salvatore, Stockton	.255	85	333	58	85	108	11	3	2	31	1	6	1	6	33	2	37	49	9
Felder, Michael, Stockton†	.269	91	338	66	91	110	8	1	3	30	3	5	1	1	38	0	42	41	8
Fick, Charles, San Jose	.225	73	204	24	46	74	11	1	5	36	1	3	4	1	38	3	55	1	3
Francis, Harry, Redwood	.279	136	459	91	128	194	24	3	12	62	12	5	7	4	67	0	79	17	8
Gallego, Michael, Modesto	.272	60	202	38	55	70	9	3	0	23	3	1	2	2	31	0	31	9	3
Garcia, Steven, Reno°	.316	111	433	120	137	165	17	4	1	44	7	10	3	8	61	0	44	31	8
Gauntlett, Todd, Lodi	.314	104	341	47	107	158	11	2	12	55	5	5	1	0	34	2	35	3	1
Gibson, Steven, Stockton	.000	16	2	0	0	0	0	0	0	0	0	0	0	0	0	0	2	0	0
Gilmartin, Daniel, Stockton	.182	17	33	0	6	6	0	0	0	2	0	1	0	0	7	0	12	0	0
Gomez, Marcos, Stockton	.171	14	41	5	7	10	1	1	0	5	0	1	0	0	1	0	10	1	1
Gomez, Randall, Fresno	.306	105	399	59	122	153	14	4	3	43	0	4	5	1	40	1	35	7	3
Gonzalez, Orlando, Stockton	.213	18	47	5	10	11	1	0	0	6	1	1	0	0	6	0	6	5	3
Gundelfinger, Matthew, Redwood	.218	72	238	31	52	81	11	0	6	27	1	6	0	2	44	0	59	8	0
Guzman, Hector, Lodi†	.222	59	189	24	42	48	2	2	0	13	1	3	1	1	23	0	40	16	7
Hansen, Jon, Stockton	.295	31	105	19	31	48	8	0	3	19	2	1	0	0	11	1	13	1	2
Harper, Therron, Modesto	.328	121	427	59	140	182	18	0	8	72	11	4	7	1	52	3	38	10	13
Heimach, William, Fresno†	.267	130	484	71	129	153	14	2	2	41	3	4	3	1	65	0	60	22	13
Hernandez, Nicolas, Stockton	.234	29	77	13	18	24	0	0	2	9	2	3	0	0	12	0	19	3	0
Hill, Donald, Modesto†	.195	46	149	21	29	50	3	0	6	22	1	5	2	0	24	2	26	9	2
Hines, Bruce, San Jose†	.214	54	117	21	25	31	4	1	0	9	0	2	0	0	27	0	35	11	2
Hinshaw, George, Reno°	.371	128	510	113	189	298	20	7	25	131	14	6	6	7	55	8	91	24	11
Hotchkiss, John, San Jose	.275	67	222	26	61	81	5	0	5	23	0	1	1	2	23	1	56	7	4
Hrbek, Kent, Visalia°	.379	121	462	119	175	291	25	5	27	111	9	1	9	4	59	7	59	12	5
Hudgens, David, San Jose°	.260	59	208	28	54	79	6	2	5	28	2	0	5	3	19	2	56	3	1
Hudson, Lance, San Jose†	.225	64	138	23	31	42	6	1	1	12	1	3	2	1	14	0	30	14	4
Hunt, Ronald, Redwood	.290	129	452	73	131	193	22	5	10	74	8	2	1	7	39	2	56	10	5
Hunter, Marion, Redwood	.259	137	549	70	142	159	9	4	0	55	4	6	6	3	42	1	77	48	17
Ireland, Billy, Reno	.267	42	120	10	32	40	4	2	0	16	0	1	3	1	6	0	6	0	0
Jacobson, Kevin, Modesto	.288	118	386	65	111	144	17	2	4	53	7	3	6	7	52	1	28	3	8

Player and Club	Pct.	G.	AB.	R.	H.	TB.	2B.	3B.	HR.	RBI.	GW.	SH.	SF.	HP.	BB.	Int. BB.	SO.	SB.	CS.
Jamerson, Donald, Fresno°	.000	36	0	0	0	0	0	0	0	0	0	0	0	0	0	0	0	1	0
James, Dion, Stockton°	.304	124	451	70	137	166	17	3	2	49	7	2	5	1	62	4	43	45	16
Johnson, Donald, San Jose°	.205	61	185	25	38	61	6	1	5	20	2	1	0	2	16	1	38	6	2
Johnson, Steven, Reno	.245	124	436	82	107	156	15	5	8	58	0	3	2	6	68	0	105	31	13
Junker, Lance, Frenso	.287	38	129	23	37	63	8	0	6	17	1	4	0	1	12	0	15	5	1
Kaczmarski, Randy, Reno	.308	93	351	83	108	146	14	0	8	58	3	9	5	0	42	1	51	11	3
Killebrew, Cameron, San Jose	.098	15	41	4	4	7	0	0	1	3	0	0	0	2	9	0	21	0	0
Kingsolver, Kurtis, Stockton	.260	115	342	55	89	133	18	1	8	55	8	4	4	3	80	0	78	36	14
Koenigsfeld, Ronald, Stockton	.206	102	355	44	73	103	10	4	4	40	3	2	3	1	33	2	60	6	5
Krauss, Timothy, Redwood°	.254	137	484	66	123	156	23	2	2	48	4	17	4	8	61	1	61	21	10
Kubit, Joseph, Visalia	.239	22	67	11	16	25	3	3	0	12	2	0	0	1	7	0	16	1	1
Kutcher, Randy, Fresno	.273	41	161	28	44	67	10	2	3	26	1	0	2	2	9	0	24	18	5
Kyzer, Richard, Visalia	.236	98	296	38	70	80	7	0	1	34	3	7	3	1	36	3	34	3	3
Lachowetz, Anthony, Lodi	.317	57	164	38	52	85	5	2	8	33	0	0	1	0	39	3	44	14	2
Lais, John, San Jose°	.370	13	27	6	10	13	1	1	0	4	0	0	1	0	4	1	5	1	1
Lane, Jerry, Stockton	.207	25	87	7	18	25	4	0	1	8	0	0	0	1	4	2	12	1	2
Lemon, Leo, Redwood	.266	118	414	55	110	125	8	2	1	25	2	11	1	4	38	0	80	40	13
Levi, Stanley, Stockton°	.356	76	261	49	93	122	12	4	3	34	5	3	3	2	29	0	30	11	11
Liddle, Steven, Redwood	.302	47	126	22	38	59	8	2	3	28	5	3	2	1	14	0	21	2	0
Liska, Anthony, Fresno	.111	4	9	1	1	1	0	0	0	0	0	0	0	0	1	0	2	0	0
Lulay, Douglas, Reno°	.289	137	526	102	152	229	26	9	11	90	4	6	8	4	50	3	83	16	8
Madison, Scott, Visalia†	.342	133	459	109	157	273	32	3	26	110	12	3	5	3	91	5	53	19	2
Manderfield, Steven, Stockton°	.000	24	0	0	0	0	0	0	0	0	0	0	0	0	0	0	1	0	0
Mann, Leo, Lodi	.125	4	8	1	1	2	1	0	0	0	0	0	0	0	0	0	1	0	0
Martin, Michael, Reno°	.310	112	384	83	119	221	14	2	28	93	10	5	2	5	79	8	79	6	1
Martin, Hollis, Lodi	.161	16	31	3	5	6	1	0	0	3	0	0	1	1	4	0	8	1	0
May, Larry, Visalia	.500	29	2	0	1	1	0	0	0	0	0	0	0	0	0	0	1	0	0
McAbee, Monte, Modesto°	.303	107	353	64	107	189	23	1	19	76	7	9	4	5	80	6	46	8	9
McFarlen, Randy, Stockton†	.155	25	71	4	11	14	0	0	1	8	0	0	2	1	1	0	27	1	0
McInerny, Daniel, Modesto°	.208	19	53	6	11	15	2	1	0	6	0	0	1	2	5	2	7	3	0
McMullen, Ricky, Reno	.202	27	104	20	21	26	5	0	0	10	2	1	1	0	14	0	9	3	1
McNealy, Robert, San Jose°	.322	128	450	100	145	192	22	8	3	48	6	5	2	1	84	2	72	63	15
Meier, David, Visalia	.337	71	273	53	92	131	12	0	9	50	8	1	3	0	34	0	28	8	3
Murphy, Roderick, Modesto	.231	46	130	18	30	40	2	1	2	14	2	3	0	1	17	1	18	12	2
Murray, William, Lodi	.273	4	11	4	3	4	1	0	0	0	0	0	0	0	2	0	5	0	0
Noce, Paul, Reno	.269	37	134	29	36	50	1	2	3	22	1	0	3	0	15	0	33	2	1
Ornest, Maury, Stockton†	.236	95	326	34	77	122	21	3	6	36	4	1	1	1	40	4	111	15	9
Painton, Timothy, Redwood°	.265	54	132	20	35	49	6	1	2	18	2	1	1	2	19	3	22	4	0
Parr, Robert, Fresno	.241	103	295	44	71	100	12	1	5	33	4	4	5	3	33	1	65	11	6
Pederson, Stuart, Lodi°	.368	56	182	47	67	107	14	1	8	35	3	3	4	3	23	5	27	6	0
Pilla, Antonio, Visalia	.284	112	398	79	113	146	10	7	3	54	5	3	2	8	86	2	87	27	8
Purpura, Daniel, Reno	.312	27	93	23	29	38	3	3	0	16	0	2	2	1	26	1	13	4	5
Pyznarski, Timothy, Modesto	.225	53	160	32	36	55	4	0	5	18	1	5	0	1	42	0	45	2	1
Quick, Ronald, Fresno†	.200	39	105	21	21	29	3	1	1	11	1	1	2	0	16	0	18	4	3
Ransom, Eugene, San Jose†	.138	30	65	8	9	13	2	1	0	5	0	1	0	1	9	0	21	7	0
Reece, Thad, San Jose°	.259	47	139	18	36	46	8	1	0	6	0	5	0	0	26	0	17	7	5
Reid, Jessie, Fresno°	.246	124	426	68	105	129	15	3	1	40	1	2	3	0	77	0	85	34	10
Rivera, German, Lodi	.266	128	478	78	127	201	31	2	13	71	10	5	5	8	28	1	57	12	3
Robinson, Thomas, Lodi°	.172	37	87	11	15	18	3	0	0	7	0	1	0	2	12	2	12	4	1
Rodriguez, Michael, San Jose	.091	6	22	0	2	3	1	0	0	1	0	0	1	0	1	0	4	0	1
Rojas, Luis, San Jose	.187	37	107	10	20	30	5	1	1	11	1	0	1	0	15	0	25	1	3
Romero, Albert, Redwood	.255	48	153	18	39	49	5	1	1	16	0	2	3	0	9	0	29	1	2
Rossi, Joseph, Lodi	.293	107	358	44	105	139	21	2	3	38	4	8	2	2	27	0	84	19	8
Rudolph, Wayne, Modesto†	.297	126	465	76	138	173	28	2	1	47	1	8	2	4	69	3	40	55	12
Ryan, Duffy, Redwood	.265	60	170	20	45	73	9	2	5	29	2	0	2	0	16	0	25	1	2
Saatzer, Michael, Redwood°	.000	27	1	0	0	0	0	0	0	0	0	0	0	0	0	0	1	0	0
Santos, Edgardo, Lodi	.318	129	513	100	163	265	21	6	23	94	10	3	5	6	27	4	62	40	7
Schellin, Jay, Modesto	.200	38	90	12	18	24	3	0	1	9	2	0	2	1	22	1	24	7	2
Scherger, Joseph, Reno	.319	114	401	74	128	225	23	10	18	93	6	5	5	4	58	5	67	3	4
Schexnayder, Wade, Redwood	.233	34	103	11	24	37	4	3	1	12	0	0	0	1	8	0	30	2	3
Sheehy, Mark, Lodi	.307	122	492	86	151	196	26	2	5	49	6	11	5	4	45	1	48	42	22
Smith, Clay, Lodi°	.228	50	145	19	33	45	3	3	1	15	1	1	1	0	16	0	30	1	0
Smith, Gregory, Lodi°	.295	68	217	33	64	98	12	2	6	40	3	0	3	1	12	0	22	2	1
Smith, Kelly, Fresno	.233	46	146	22	34	42	4	2	0	8	1	2	1	0	27	1	28	16	3
Smith, Michael, Reno†	.000	27	2	0	0	0	0	0	0	0	0	0	0	0	0	0	1	0	0
Soprano, Joseph, Modesto	.278	106	352	47	98	146	16	4	8	51	2	5	3	7	39	1	68	10	8
Spillane, Paul, San Jose	.303	27	76	9	23	37	3	1	3	10	0	3	1	0	7	0	10	0	1
Spiroff, George, Fresno	.299	43	144	15	43	70	12	0	5	21	1	2	0	2	28	0	9	0	0
Sproesser, Mark, Redwood	.290	133	431	65	125	161	22	4	2	53	5	9	2	4	49	4	48	11	5
Spurlin, Robert, Fresno	.206	37	102	16	21	24	3	0	0	5	0	5	1	0	17	0	19	7	2
Stein, Raymond, Visalia°	.283	81	237	37	67	83	8	1	2	31	2	4	3	0	31	1	20	5	5
Stockley, Paul, Modesto°	.230	115	374	39	86	108	18	2	0	34	0	5	1	2	24	0	99	12	6
Stowe, Dennis, Modesto	.179	10	28	0	5	7	2	0	0	6	2	1	1	0	0	0	3	0	0
Strawberry, Michael, Lodi	.231	35	52	7	12	16	1	0	1	7	0	1	1	1	4	0	12	0	1
Sutherland, Matthew, Fresno°	.000	24	0	1	0	0	0	0	0	0	0	0	0	0	0	0	0	0	0
Tanabe, Collin, Stockton	.000	2	6	0	0	0	0	0	0	0	0	0	0	0	0	0	2	0	1
Tettleton, Mickey, Modesto†	.246	48	138	28	34	52	3	0	5	19	2	2	0	0	46	3	33	2	2
Thomas, Jimmy, Reno	.256	95	309	53	79	121	14	2	8	55	4	2	7	2	51	1	73	2	2
Tillman, Kenneth, Redwood	.250	61	120	14	30	47	5	0	4	21	1	4	0	2	5	0	25	7	4
Tipton, Jeffery, San Jose	.216	73	222	30	48	98	10	2	12	34	6	2	2	0	25	0	52	0	1
Tirado, Julio, Visalia°	.406	8	32	5	13	19	3	0	1	8	1	0	0	0	3	0	5	4	0
Waller, Kevin, San Jose°	.248	82	222	36	55	66	6	1	1	22	4	3	2	1	27	2	28	13	6
Wantz, Douglas, Stockton	.154	6	13	0	2	2	0	0	0	1	0	0	0	2	3	0	3	0	0
Ward, Randall, Fresno°	.243	48	136	18	33	62	3	1	8	22	2	1	0	1	29	2	42	1	0
Watanabe, Curt, Stockton	.281	135	455	60	128	162	18	5	2	69	10	9	9	3	57	2	55	16	7
Weaver, James, Visalia°	.283	81	300	53	85	128	12	5	7	44	3	1	5	2	32	3	54	25	13
Weirum, Robert, San Jose	.297	70	256	28	76	106	14	2	4	36	2	7	4	2	27	4	39	6	1
Whiting, Don, Stockton°	.359	19	64	8	23	39	1	0	5	18	2	0	1	0	7	1	9	4	1
Wilkinson, Ronald, Visalia†	.257	130	505	65	130	156	17	3	1	48	5	13	7	1	44	1	43	53	14
Williams, Joseph, Modesto	.266	60	158	16	42	56	7	2	1	19	5	2	1	0	33	0	30	9	4
Williams, Kevin, Visalia	.239	131	465	70	111	140	9	1	6	40	3	6	4	1	46	1	87	36	8
Woods, Victor, San Jose	.246	121	378	46	93	133	16	6	4	60	10	5	8	12	69	0	138	24	10

Player and Club	Pct.	G.	AB.	R.	H.	TB.	2B.	3B.	HR.	RBI.	GW.	SH.	SF.	HP.	BB.	Int. BB.	SO.	SB.	CS.
Young, Selwyn, Modesto	188	53	154	31	29	33	2	1	0	12	2	6	2	4	31	1	19	10	8
Zambrana, Luis, Redwood	.222	59	126	19	28	32	2	1	0	14	0	2	1	1	23	1	27	5	1
Ziccardi, John, Fresno⁰	.303	12	33	4	10	15	2	0	1	3	1	0	0	1	4	1	3	1	1

The following pitchers had no plate appearances, primarily through use of designated hitters, listed alphabetically by club, games in parentheses:

FRESNO—Anderson, Kelly (18); Bangert, Gregory (13); Buckmier, James (28); Christianson, Alec (11); Gallo, Bernard (18); Goodchild, Christopher (25); Lusted, Charles (8); Pierce, Daniel (11); Sensenbrenner, David (14); Stadler, Jeffrey (30); Stovall, Jerry (14); Wilcox, Steven (10); Williams, Frank (27).

LODI—Alexander, Roberto (26); Borbon, Ernesto (27); Cordova, Rocky (3); Cozzolino, Paul (32); Daniel, David (54); Dente, Frank (29); Felt, Richard (25); Klawitter, Thomas (28); Lund, Frederick (11); Nunez, Mario (41); Terry, Glenn (24).

MODESTO—Altobelli, Michael (28); Arnold, Rick (4); Bradley, Bert (27); Conroy, Timothy (8); Ferguson, Mark (24); Gosse, John (17); Harris, Frank (4); Hensley, Charles (19); Holloway, Richard (7); Jensen, Ron (21); Krueger, William (16); Mantsch, Ronald (25); Mine, Gregory (2); Retzer, Edwin (28); Rodriguez, Ricardo (11); Van Marter, Donald (34); Vavrock, Robert (6); Warren, Michael (22); Wood, Robert (4); Young, Curtis (5).

REDWOOD—Bankowski, Kris (14); Bastian, Robert (20); Brown, Curtis (5); Buckley, Brian (55); Burroughs, David (3); Crisler, Joel (7); Humphry, Brandt (4); Kibbe, Jay (31); Rau, Douglas (3); Roen, Thomas (45-SJ 9-Red 36); Romanick, Ronald (28); Schneider, Thomas (16); Smith, Jeffrey (34); Sylvia, Ronald (29); Travers, William (1); Venezia, Michael (25).

RENO—Balderston, Joseph (9); Biko, Thomas (27); Blamey, Patrick (6); Bryant, Neil (29); Conroy, Steven (38); Couchee, Michael (53); Duffy, Brian (25); Gerhardt, Russell (5); Hardwick, Willie (25); Kain, Martin (3); Macias, Robert (4); Mahoski, Michael (27); Moretti, Roy (33); Peterson, Rodney (5); White, John (14).

SAN JOSE—Cary, Jeff (22); Codiroli, Christopher (14); Cyburt, Philip (11); DeHart, Gregory (13); Dougherty, Charles (8); Free, Michael (4); Hallgren, Tim (13); Kolotka, Charles (4); Krajewski, Christopher (2); Lynes, Michael (27); Marietta, Louis (30); McDonald, Mark (20); Moore, Robert (30-Mod 6-SJ 24); Odekirk, Richard (13); Palica, Wayne (22); Puckett, Brian (10); Rathjen, Dennis (25); Tillema, John (25); Tuchalski, Bruce (3); Weatherman, David (6); Wright, Mitchell (2).

STOCKTON—Anderson, Michael (26); Bain, Paul (1); Beene, Andrew (19); Biggus, Bengie (25); Burns, Daniel (4); Dinkins, Charles (18); Donovan, Michael (1); Gibson, Robert (49); Grier, David (20); Kranitz, Richard (11); Park, Chel Sun (14); Parrott, Stephen (24).

VISALIA—Angulo, Kenneth (26); Arrington, Samuel (24); Belanger, Lee (34); Francingues, Kenneth (18); Krueger, Kirby (16); Mulligan, Robert (20); Pettibone, Harry (27); Reeves, Mathew (12); Ruzek, Don (7); Snider, Eric (22-Fr 13-Vis 9); Tirella, Michael (8); Voigt, Paul (27).

GRAND-SLAM HOME RUNS—Casey, Hinshaw, Madison, Martin, Soprano, 2 each; Adams, Bathe, Cardwell, Christianson, Duran, Garcia, Hrbek, Hunt, Kaczmarski, Kutcher, Lachowetz, Levi, McAbee, Noce, Parr, Pilla, Ryan, Santos, Scherger, Thomas, Waller, Weaver, 1 each.

AWARDED FIRST BASE ON INTERFERENCE—Bilardello 5 (Martin 2, Bathe, Harper, Spiroff); Gundelfinger 5 (Madison 2, Martin, Tettleton, Tipton); Kyzer 3 (Kingsolver 2, Harper); Reid 2 (Austin, Tettleton); Brackenridge (Gomez); Favata (Ryan); Heimach (Colburn); Lulay (Hernandez); Rojas (Harper); Rossi (Martin); Scherger (Kingsolver); Spurlin (Schexnayder); Stein (Ryan); Whiting (Spiroff).

CLUB FIELDING

Club	Pct.	G.	PO.	A.	E.	DP.	PB.	Club	Pct.	G.	PO.	A.	E.	DP.	PB.
Visalia	.964	140	3617	1491	192	109	23	Modesto	.957	138	3509	1499	225	121	43
Lodi	.961	140	3573	1798	217	148	26	Fresno	.953	140	3568	1651	257	126	21
Stockton	.960	139	3505	1557	210	95	46	Reno	.951	139	3531	1608	266	122	19
Redwood	.958	140	3536	1414	219	116	30	San Jose	.947	140	3519	1467	277	98	20

Triple Play—Visalia.

INDIVIDUAL FIELDING

⁰Throws lefthanded.

FIRST BASEMEN

Player and Club	Pct.	G.	PO.	A.	E.	DP.	Player and Club	Pct.	G.	PO.	A.	E.	DP.
Alonzo, Stockton⁰	.983	94	844	42	15	55	James, Stockton⁰	1.000	2	12	1	0	1
T. Anderson, Fresno⁰	.987	118	1044	102	15	83	Johnson, San Jose⁰	.978	35	256	17	6	18
Bailey, Lodi	.977	36	355	27	9	43	Kingsolver, Stockton	1.000	1	11	0	0	0
Bohnet, Redwood	.985	29	190	6	3	14	Kubit, Visalia	.769	2	10	0	3	0
Brock, Redwood	.954	11	58	4	3	5	Kyzer, Visalia	1.000	13	119	4	0	12
Brown, Fresno	1.000	3	24	1	0	2	Lais, San Jose⁰	.987	9	75	3	1	2
Casey, Reno	1.000	2	8	0	0	1	Lane, Stockton	1.000	1	16	1	0	1
Christianson, Reno⁰	.983	114	952	74	18	91	Madison, Visalia	1.000	1	4	0	0	0
Cole, Lodi	.983	58	485	32	9	26	Martin, Reno	1.000	1	5	0	0	4
Crow, San Jose⁰	1.000	1	2	0	0	0	McAbee, Modesto⁰	.9897	99	900	61	10	71
Duran, Stockton	.977	32	286	15	7	20	Painton, Redwood⁰	1.000	2	6	0	0	1
Eakin, Modesto	1.000	1	14	0	0	0	Reid, Fresno⁰	.931	3	25	2	2	7
Fick, San Jose	.967	21	165	11	6	13	Robinson, Lodi	1.000	2	22	0	0	1
Francis, Redwood	.962	3	24	1	1	3	G. Smith, Lodi	.990	66	628	36	7	64
Gilmartin, Stockton	.938	7	25	5	2	0	Tettleton, Modesto	1.000	1	3	0	0	0
Gundelfinger, Redwood	.988	71	635	32	8	49	Thomas, Reno	.994	19	153	12	1	9
Harper, Modesto	.986	17	131	14	2	11	Tirado, Visalia⁰	.982	8	50	4	1	5
Hernandez, Stockton	1.000	3	25	0	0	1	Ward, Fresno	.977	18	157	15	4	23
HRBEK, Visalia	.9899	120	1034	53	11	84	Whiting, Stockton⁰	1.000	7	55	7	0	5
Hudgens, San Jose⁰	.974	40	317	22	9	24	Williams, Modesto	.996	25	208	19	1	23
Hunt, Redwood	.969	41	264	15	9	22	Woods, San Jose	.968	51	373	14	13	26
Hunter, Redwood	.889	1	8	0	1	2	Ziccardi, Fresno⁰	.951	4	37	2	2	1
Ireland, Reno	.973	12	64	7	2	5							

Triple Play—Hrbek.

SECOND BASEMEN

Player and Club	Pct.	G.	PO.	A.	E.	DP.	Player and Club	Pct.	G.	PO.	A.	E.	DP.
Allen, Lodi	.964	7	13	14	1	2	Gilmartin, Stockton	.750	2	0	3	1	0
Cardwell, Fresno	1.000	2	2	6	0	0	Guzman, Lodi	1.000	2	2	2	0	0
Christensen, Visalia	.959	103	225	261	21	53	Heimach, Fresno	.9711	125	291	348	19	73
Colby, San Jose	.909	3	11	9	2	2	Hines, San Jose	.906	37	74	81	16	17
Cruz, San Jose	.961	16	38	35	3	5	Hudson, San Jose	.900	32	60	48	12	9
Davenport, Fresno	.974	8	16	22	1	8	Hunter, Redwood	1.000	5	6	8	0	0
Downs, Stockton	1.000	1	3	3	0	1	Ireland, Reno	.970	6	13	19	1	5
Eakin, Modesto	1.000	3	3	6	0	0	Jacobson, Modesto	.926	8	12	13	2	3
Evans, Reno	.938	7	16	14	2	3	Kaczmarski, Reno	.947	9	33	21	3	6
Favata, Stockton	.966	82	153	245	14	39	Koenigsfeld, Stockton	1.000	2	2	2	0	0
Felder, Stockton	.964	55	111	160	10	23	KRAUSS, Redwood	.9713	137	315	395	21	83
Gallego, Modesto	.957	59	127	161	13	38	Kutcher, Fresno	1.000	3	4	2	0	0
Garcia, Reno	.958	91	245	252	22	58	Kyzer, Visalia	.969	32	74	83	5	19

SECOND BASEMEN—Continued

Player and Club	Pct.	G.	PO.	A.	E.	DP.
Mann, Lodi	1.000	3	3	3	0	0
Martin, Lodi	1.000	1	2	0	0	1
McMullen, Reno	.947	27	65	77	8	13
Murphy, Modesto	.954	19	51	52	5	12
Murray, Lodi	1.000	4	11	10	0	4
Pilla, Visalia	1.000	6	16	12	0	4
Quick, Fresno	.920	!2	23	23	4	4
Ransom, San Jose	.943	26	54	45	6	4

Player and Club	Pct.	G.	PO.	A.	E.	DP.
Reece, San Jose	.966	44	78	119	7	21
Robinson, Lodi	.946	18	46	42	5	13
Sheehy, Lodi	.970	114	322	362	21	92
Sproesser, Redwood	1.000	3	4	1	0	0
Stockley, Modesto	.893	6	9	16	3	2
Wilkinson, Visalia	1.000	1	2	0	0	0
S. Young, Modesto	.959	47	92	118	9	26

Triple Play—Christensen.

THIRD BASEMEN

Player and Club	Pct.	G.	PO.	A.	E.	DP.
Allen, Lodi	.927	74	47	157	16	14
Austin, Visalia	1.000	1	0	2	0	0
Bohnet, Redwood	.889	5	2	6	1	0
Brown, Fresno	.904	65	62	155	23	12
Byrum, Mod-San Jose	.750	6	5	7	4	1
Davenport, Fresno	.941	7	6	10	1	2
Eakin, Modesto	1.000	1	0	2	0	0
Estepan, Fresno	.892	76	54	161	26	10
Francis, Redwood	.914	133	118	210	31	24
Gauntlett, Lodi	.875	8	2	19	3	4
Gilmartin, Stockton	.750	2	0	3	1	0
Gomez, Fresno	1.000	1	0	3	0	0
Hotchkiss, San Jose	.957	67	51	103	7	8
Hudson, San Jose	.750	1	1	2	1	0
Ireland, Reno	.857	9	7	17	4	2
Jacobson, Modesto	.930	111	83	224	23	19
Koenigsfeld, Stockton	1.000	3	2	8	0	0

Player and Club	Pct.	G.	PO.	A.	E.	DP.
Kutcher, Fresno	1.000	1	0	2	0	0
Kyzer, Visalia	.857	3	0	6	1	0
Lulay, Reno	.900	131	95	267	40	21
Meier, Visalia	.912	17	8	23	3	1
Pyznarski, Modesto	.850	18	7	27	6	2
Quick, Fresno	1.000	2	0	3	0	1
Rivera, Lodi	.934	65	63	190	18	17
Robinson, Lodi	1.000	3	3	6	0	0
Rodriguez, San Jose	.000	1	0	0	1	0
Sproesser, Redwood	.889	11	3	21	3	2
Spurlin, Fresno	1.000	1	0	1	0	0
Stockley, Modesto	.906	17	18	40	6	5
Thomas, Reno	.667	1	1	1	1	0
Watanabe, Stockton	.919	135	104	247	31	7
Weirum, San Jose	.943	70	53	147	12	6
WILKINSON, Visalia	.954	123	75	279	17	21

SHORTSTOPS

Player and Club	Pct.	G.	PO.	A.	E.	DP.
Allen, Lodi	.955	14	22	42	3	9
Camacho, San Jose	.910	56	112	170	28	28
Cardwell, Fresno	.884	91	110	262	49	40
Cruz, San Jose	.900	77	135	224	40	32
Davenport, Fresno	.919	16	27	41	6	9
Downs, Stockton	.947	32	50	111	9	15
Eakes, Redwood	.925	35	29	82	9	10
Eakin, Modesto	.900	4	9	9	2	2
Garcia, Reno	.939	19	41	52	6	11
Gilmartin, Stockton	.000	2	0	0	1	0
Gonzalez, Stockton	.903	13	18	38	6	8
Guzman, Lodi	.888	57	79	159	30	26
Hill, Modesto	.853	33	44	84	22	14
Hinshaw, Reno	.429	1	1	2	4	0
Hudson, San Jose	.867	18	29	43	11	10
Hunter, Redwood	.963	11	10	16	1	3
Ireland, Reno	.842	3	4	12	3	0

Player and Club	Pct.	G.	PO.	A.	E.	DP.
Jacobson, Modesto	1.000	1	0	1	0	0
Kaczmarski, Reno	.905	68	105	201	32	36
KOENIGSFELD, Stockton	.951	98	154	316	24	42
Kutcher, Fresno	.880	25	44	73	16	11
Kyzer, Visalia	.936	18	25	48	5	4
Mann, Lodi	.667	1	1	1	1	0
Martin, Lodi	.941	15	10	22	2	2
Meier, Visalia	.896	24	27	59	10	7
Murphy, Modesto	.919	17	30	49	7	6
Noce, Reno	.884	26	28	94	16	11
Pilla, Visalia	.933	103	150	311	33	48
Purpura, Reno	.963	25	48	109	6	23
Quick, Fresno	.942	20	19	62	5	13
Rivera, Lodi	.936	65	94	229	22	42
Sproesser, Redwood	.904	111	156	278	46	52
Stockley, Modesto	.948	94	155	286	24	53
S. Young, Modesto	1.000	1	0	1	0	0

OUTFIELDERS

Player and Club	Pct.	G.	PO.	A.	E.	DP.
Adams, Modesto	.947	108	208	7	12	1
Allen, Lodi	1.000	1	1	0	0	0
Bass, Stockton	.909	15	20	0	2	0
Bathe, San Jose	.800	3	7	1	2	0
Bohnet, Redwood	.987	59	71	5	1	1
Brackenridge, Visalia	.960	135	223	14	10	2
Brainard, Stockton	1.000	2	0	1	0	0
Brewer, Lodi	.970	80	88	8	3	1
Brock, Redwood	.957	21	21	1	1	0
Brown, Fresno	1.000	4	3	0	0	0
Byrum, Modesto-San Jose	.929	7	11	2	1	0
Campbell, Modesto	1.000	29	35	1	0	1
Casey, Reno	.936	82	114	18	9	0
M. Codiroli, San Jose°	.980	42	93	4	2	2
Colby, San Jose	1.000	1	3	1	0	0
Cole, Lodi	.909	11	9	1	1	0
Crow, San Jose°	.769	4	10	0	3	0
Dawson, San Jose	.910	103	147	5	15	0
Deer, Fresno	.974	132	211	14	6	1
Downs, Stockton	.889	32	52	4	7	0
Favata, Stockton	1.000	3	5	1	0	0
Felder, Stockton	.955	32	61	2	3	1
Gilmartin, Stockton	1.000	1	1	0	0	0
Gomez, Stockton	1.000	6	7	1	0	0
Gomez, Fresno	1.000	2	1	0	0	0
Hansen, Stockton	.932	29	40	1	3	0
Harper, Modesto	.909	8	9	1	1	0
Hines, San Jose	.857	4	6	0	1	0
Hinshaw, Reno	.952	127	201	16	11	2
Hudgens, San Jose°	1.000	1	2	0	0	0
Hunter, Redwood	.956	128	207	8	10	2
Ireland, Reno	1.000	7	5	0	0	0
JAMES, Stockton°	.988	123	238	9	3	2
Johnson, San Jose°	.500	1	1	0	1	0
Johnson, Reno	.948	121	318	8	18	3

Player and Club	Pct.	G.	PO.	A.	E.	DP.
Junker, Fresno	.922	34	46	1	4	0
Kingsolver, Stockton	.786	11	11	0	3	0
Koenigsfeld, Stockton	1.000	1	1	0	0	0
Kubit, Visalia	.966	17	24	4	1	0
Kutcher, Fresno	.913	8	18	3	2	1
Kyzer, Visalia	.950	22	17	2	1	0
Lachowetz, Lodi	.967	53	80	8	3	0
Lane, Stockton	1.000	2	5	2	0	1
Lemon, Redwood	.955	118	242	12	12	3
Levi, Stockton°	.976	71	111	9	3	1
McFarlen, Stockton	1.000	6	5	0	0	0
McInerny, Modesto°	.857	7	5	1	1	1
McNealy, San Jose°	.945	119	228	14	14	1
Meier, Visalia	1.000	18	30	3	0	0
Murphy, Modesto	1.000	1	1	0	0	0
Ornest, Stockton	.943	90	172	10	11	3
Painton, Redwood°	1.000	48	48	4	0	0
Parr, Fresno	.973	95	166	11	5	3
Pederson, Lodi°	.989	50	84	8	1	3
Pyznarski, Modesto	.943	36	64	2	4	0
Reid, Fresno°	.972	118	197	11	6	2
Rojas, San Jose	.938	36	55	5	4	1
Rossi, Lodi	.981	103	189	13	4	1
Rudolph, Modesto°	.985	121	185	6	3	0
Santos, Lodi	.941	121	202	22	14	2
Schellin, Modesto	.906	33	56	2	6	1
Scherger, Reno	.988	90	157	7	2	1
C. Smith, Lodi	1.000	10	12	0	0	0
K. Smith, Fresno	.992	45	101	10	1	1
Soprano, Modesto	.979	87	133	10	3	2
Sproesser, Redwood	.900	4	9	0	1	0
Stein, Visalia°	.959	56	117	1	5	0
Stowe, Modesto	1.000	9	10	2	0	1
Strawberry, Lodi	.857	30	12	0	2	0
Tettleton, Modesto	1.000	7	8	0	0	0

OUTFIELDERS—Continued

Player and Club	Pct.	G.	PO.	A.	E.	DP.
Tillman, Redwood	.929	48	48	4	4	1
Tipton, San Jose	.833	3	5	0	1	0
Waller, San Jose	.991	70	110	6	1	2
Ward, Fresno	1.000	4	5	1	0	1
Weaver, Visalia°	.967	70	110	7	4	2

Player and Club	Pct.	G.	PO.	A.	E.	DP.
Whiting, Stockton°	1.000	4	10	0	0	0
Williams, Visalia	.954	130	301	8	15	1
Woods, San Jose	.944	49	81	3	5	0
Zambrana, Redwood	.961	54	69	4	3	1

CATCHERS

Player and Club	Pct.	G.	PO.	A.	E.	DP.	PB.
Austin, Visalia	.980	68	384	65	9	3	10
Bagiotti, Redwood	.964	25	111	21	5	0	10
Bailey, Lodi	.962	17	63	13	3	1	1
Bathe, San Jose	.978	40	227	41	6	4	5
Bilardello, Lodi	.964	42	203	39	9	2	10
Brainard, Stockton	.983	23	105	8	2	0	6
Colburn, Modesto	.983	28	153	19	3	2	3
Durrman, Modesto	.973	29	165	15	5	0	6
Fick, San Jose	.972	38	186	26	6	0	7
Gauntlett, Lodi	.981	92	459	118	11	11	15
Gilmartin, Stockton	.914	5	28	4	3	0	3
Gomez, Fresno	.963	91	518	79	23	6	10
Harper, Modesto	.964	45	262	29	11	3	20
Hernandez, Stockton	.964	24	117	15	5	3	12
Kingsolver, Stockton	.980	99	561	91	13	5	22
Liddle, Redwood	.976	47	285	44	8	5	5

Player and Club	Pct.	G.	PO.	A.	E.	DP.	PB.
Liska, Fresno	1.000	4	8	0	0	0	2
MADISON, Visalia	.982	83	538	66	11	4	13
Martin, Reno	.963	104	582	91	26	3	12
McFarlen, Stockton	1.000	1	1	1	0	0	0
Romero, Redwood	.962	26	134	18	6	2	0
Ryan, Redwood	.975	39	237	35	7	3	6
Schexnayder, Redwood	.994	24	145	17	1	0	9
Spillane, San Jose	.961	22	111	12	5	3	3
Spiroff, Fresno	.969	34	168	17	6	2	4
Spurlin, Fresno	.950	20	83	12	5	1	5
Tanabe, Stockton	.857	1	6	0	1	0	0
Tettleton, Modesto	.948	39	224	31	14	3	14
Thomas, Reno	.974	43	192	35	6	0	7
Tipton, San Jose	.979	50	284	37	7	4	5
Wantz, Stockton	.957	6	18	4	1	0	3
Williams, Modesto	.953	8	37	4	2	1	0

PITCHERS

Player and Club	Pct.	G.	PO.	A.	E.	DP.
Alexander, Lodi	.881	26	14	23	5	1
Altobelli, Modesto	.867	28	5	8	2	0
K. Anderson, Fresno	1.000	17	6	7	0	0
Anderson, Stockton°	.750	26	2	16	6	0
Angulo, Visalia	.850	26	3	14	3	0
Arnold, Modesto	.000	4	0	0	1	0
Arrington, Visalia	.921	24	9	26	3	1
Bain, Stockton	1.000	1	1	0	0	0
Balderston, Reno	.909	9	5	5	1	1
Bangert, Fresno°	.813	13	3	10	3	0
Bankowski, Redwood°	1.000	14	3	4	0	1
Bastian, Redwood	.957	20	9	13	1	0
Beene, Stockton	.900	19	5	13	2	0
Belanger, Visalia°	.950	34	1	18	1	0
Biggus, Stockton	.929	25	17	35	4	1
Biko, Reno°	.977	27	12	31	1	3
Blamey, Reno	1.000	6	2	1	0	0
Borbon, Lodi°	1.000	27	4	30	0	1
Bradley, Modesto	1.000	27	5	13	0	1
Braun, Redwood	1.000	23	2	9	0	0
Brown, Redwood	.500	5	0	2	2	0
Bryant, Fresno	.930	29	6	34	3	1
Buckley, Redwood	.900	55	4	5	1	0
Buckmier, Fresno	.909	28	15	35	5	1
Burns, Stockton	.800	4	1	3	1	1
Cary, San Jose	1.000	22	1	9	0	1
Christianson, Fresno	1.000	11	1	3	0	1
C. Codiroli, San Jose	.875	14	0	7	1	0
Conroy, Reno°	1.000	38	3	15	0	2
Conroy, Modesto°	.857	8	3	3	1	1
Couchee, Reno	.917	53	10	23	3	2
Cozzolino, Lodi	.929	32	3	10	1	0
Crisler, Redwood	1.000	7	2	10	0	0
Cyburt, San Jose°	.870	11	1	19	3	0
Daniel, Lodi	1.000	54	2	12	0	2
De Hart, San Jose	1.000	13	1	3	0	1
de Leon, Lodi	.947	30	6	12	1	0
Dente, Lodi	.879	29	7	22	4	4
Diaz, Stockton	.958	33	5	18	1	0
Dinkins, Stockton°	1.000	18	3	4	0	0
Dougherty, San Jose°	1.000	8	1	11	0	1
Duffy, Reno°	.878	25	3	33	5	1
Felt, Lodi°	.952	25	4	36	2	0
Ferguson, Modesto	.929	24	3	10	1	0
Francingues, Visalia	1.000	18	3	5	0	1
Free, San Jose	1.000	4	1	0	0	0
Gallo, Fresno°	1.000	18	2	1	0	0
Gerhardt, Reno°	.800	5	1	3	1	0
R. Gibson, Stockton	.833	49	4	11	3	0
S. Gibson, Stockton	1.000	16	3	6	0	0
Gilmartin, Stockton	1.000	3	0	1	0	1
Goodchild, Fresno	1.000	25	8	12	0	0
Gosse, Modesto°	1.000	17	0	6	0	1
Grier, Stockton	.917	20	5	17	2	0
Hallgren, San Jose	1.000	13	5	17	0	0
Hardwick, Reno	.862	25	9	16	4	1
Harris, Modesto	1.000	4	1	0	0	0
Hensley, Modesto°	.943	19	4	29	2	1
Holloway, Modesto	.600	7	1	2	2	0
Humphry, Redwood	1.000	4	1	1	0	0
Jamerson, Fresno	.842	34	7	9	3	0
Jensen, Modesto°	.958	21	5	18	1	1

Player and Club	Pct.	G.	PO.	A.	E.	DP.
Kain, Reno	1.000	3	1	0	0	0
Kibbe, Redwood	.956	31	14	31	2	2
Klawitter, Lodi°	.951	27	8	50	3	2
Kolotka, San Jose	.800	4	2	6	2	1
Krajewski, San Jose	.800	2	1	3	1	0
Kranitz, Stockton	.684	11	3	10	6	1
Krueger, Visalia	1.000	16	3	3	0	0
Krueger, Modesto°	.903	16	5	23	3	3
Lund, Lodi	.875	11	5	2	1	1
Lusted, Fresno	.900	8	5	13	2	2
LYNES, San Jose°	1.000	27	7	32	0	1
Macias, Reno	1.000	4	3	4	0	0
Mahoski, Reno	1.000	27	7	6	0	0
Manderfield, Stockton°	.868	24	5	28	5	2
Mantsch, Modesto	1.000	25	1	6	0	1
Marietta, San Jose	.978	30	15	30	1	4
May, Visalia	.969	27	7	24	1	1
McDonald, San Jose	.778	20	1	6	2	1
Mine, Modesto	1.000	2	0	1	0	0
Moore, Modesto-San Jose	.887	30	14	33	6	1
Moretti, Reno	.923	33	5	7	1	1
Mulligan, Visalia°	1.000	20	0	8	0	0
Nunez, Lodi	.941	41	5	11	1	0
Odekirk, San Jose°	1.000	13	0	6	0	1
Palica, San Jose	.895	22	10	7	2	1
Park, Stockton	.867	14	2	11	2	1
Parrott, Stockton	.900	24	9	18	3	2
Peterson, Reno	1.000	5	1	0	0	0
Pettibone, Visalia	.818	27	9	27	8	1
Pierce, Fresno	1.000	11	1	7	0	0
Puckett, San Jose	1.000	10	1	1	0	0
Reeves, Visalia°	.600	12	1	2	2	0
Retzer, Modesto	.956	28	16	27	2	0
Rodriguez, Modesto	.941	11	7	9	1	1
Roen, San Jose-Redwood°	.857	45	0	12	2	1
Romanick, Redwood	.911	28	10	31	4	1
Ruzek, Visalia	1.000	7	5	8	0	0
Saatzer, Redwood	.941	27	7	9	1	2
Schneider, Redwood	.600	16	2	1	2	0
Sensenbrenner, Fresno°	.800	14	0	4	1	0
Smith, Redwood	.938	34	5	10	1	0
Smith, Reno°	.800	27	2	10	3	0
Snider, Fresno-Visalia	.889	22	2	6	1	0
Stadler, Fresno	.857	30	12	18	5	3
Stovall, Fresno	.750	14	0	3	1	0
Sutherland, Fresno°	.951	23	14	25	2	1
Sylvia, Redwood°	.959	29	18	29	2	4
Terry, Stockton	.889	24	3	5	1	0
Tillema, San Jose	.813	25	1	12	3	0
Tirella, Stockton	1.000	8	0	3	0	0
Van Marter, Modesto	.938	34	1	14	1	1
Venezia, Redwood	.818	25	3	6	2	0
Voigt, Visalia	.873	27	12	36	7	2
Waller, San Jose	1.000	6	0	1	0	0
Warren, Modesto	.792	22	7	12	5	1
Weatherman, San Jose	1.000	6	0	8	0	0
White, Reno	.905	14	8	11	2	3
Wilcox, Fresno	1.000	10	3	3	0	0
Williams, Modesto	.934	27	17	40	4	1
Wood, Modesto	.000	4	0	0	1	0
Wright, San Jose	1.000	2	0	1	0	0
C. Young, Modesto°	1.000	5	2	6	0	0

The following players do not have any recorded accepted chances at the positions indicated; therefore, are not listed in the fielding averages for those particular positions: Bailey, of; Burroughs, p; Cardwell, 3b; Cordova, p; Donovan, p; Duran, of; Estepan, of; Francis, of; Heimach, of; Hill, 1b; Kaczmarski, p; Rathjen, p; Rau, p; Schexnayder, 3b; Travers, p; Tuchalski, p; Vavrock, p; Watanabe, of; Williams, 3b, of; Ziccardi, of.

CLUB PITCHING

Club	ERA.	G.	CG.	ShO.	Sv.	IP.	H.	R.	ER.	HR.	HB.	BB.	Int. BB.	SO.	WP.	Bk.
Stockton	3.98	139	40	11	22	1168⅓	1218	644	516	79	25	461	7	807	73	8
Visalia	4.12	140	52	9	20	1205⅔	1309	672	552	91	31	465	19	877	48	12
Redwood	4.33	140	26	7	23	1178⅔	1168	720	567	82	33	637	60	868	50	7
San Jose	4.36	140	38	7	16	1173	1205	734	568	88	31	582	18	742	84	14
Modesto	4.68	138	27	2	24	1169⅔	1211	774	609	102	46	616	45	812	79	22
Fresno	4.75	140	44	4	11	1189⅓	1272	764	627	91	45	610	23	716	78	10
Lodi	4.85	140	23	6	26	1191	1257	774	642	101	46	755	19	678	96	14
Reno	4.97	139	17	7	30	1177	1410	838	650	113	32	597	16	739	89	7

PITCHERS' RECORDS
(Leading Qualifiers for Earned-Run Average Leadership — 112 or More Innings)

*Throws lefthanded.

Pitcher—Club	W.	L.	Pct.	ERA.	G.	GS.	CG.	GF.	ShO.	Sv.	IP.	H.	R.	ER.	HR.	HB.	BB.	Int. BB.	SO.	WP.
Romanick, Redwood	15	10	.600	2.91	28	28	11	0	3	0	207	173	88	67	10	4	76	5	178	6
Manderfield, Stockton°	7	8	.467	3.00	24	24	5	0	0	0	153	167	74	51	8	1	67	1	111	15
Jensen, Modesto	6	5	.545	3.23	21	16	2	0	0	0	120	113	63	43	4	0	65	3	89	10
Voigt, Visalia	16	7	.696	3.23	27	27	10	0	0	0	184	195	91	66	10	7	62	3	143	9
Grier, Stockton	11	6	.647	3.28	20	19	8	0	2	0	140	159	60	51	10	3	23	0	69	2
Williams, Fresno	14	9	.609	3.37	27	25	14	0	1	0	187	170	81	70	12	13	85	3	170	10
Bastian, Redwood	6	5	.545	3.50	20	19	3	0	1	0	121	113	54	47	9	2	34	3	79	0
Lynes, San Jose°	9	14	.391	3.61	27	26	6	1	3	0	162	183	88	65	15	2	50	1	73	10
Arrington, Visalia	12	7	.632	3.64	24	23	14	1	4	0	168	185	83	68	9	9	66	3	98	4
Hensley, Modesto°	8	8	.500	3.71	19	19	4	0	0	0	136	153	75	56	10	6	57	6	83	4

Departmental Leaders: G—Buckley, 55; GS—Marietta, 29; CG—Arrington, Marietta, Williams, 14; ShO—Arrington, 4; W—Voigt, 16; L—Moore, 15; Sv—Couchee, 16; Pct.—Hardwick, .833; IP—Romanick, 207; H—Biko, 218; R—Marietta, May, 129; ER—May, 112; HR—May, 22; BB—Hardwick, 121; IBB—Kibbe, 10; HB—Williams, 13; SO—Romanick, 178; WP—Felt, 26.

(All Pitchers—Listed Alphabetically)

Pitcher—Club	W.	L.	Pct.	ERA.	G.	GS.	CG.	GF.	ShO.	Sv.	IP.	H.	R.	ER.	HR.	HB.	BB.	Int. BB.	SO.	WP.
Alexander, Lodi	9	12	.429	5.20	26	26	5	0	1	0	168	175	117	97	16	9	86	0	90	11
Altobelli, Modesto	2	2	.500	7.42	28	2	0	16	0	1	57	70	59	47	11	5	40	2	40	2
K. Anderson, Fresno	1	1	.500	3.86	17	0	0	15	0	0	28	26	16	12	4	1	20	3	17	3
Anderson, Stockton°	4	6	.400	3.53	26	6	3	9	0	0	97	78	49	38	6	3	50	2	63	5
Angulo, Visalia	11	7	.611	4.00	26	21	10	2	3	2	162	169	85	72	13	2	79	3	135	9
Arnold, Modesto	1	1	.500	10.50	4	0	0	3	0	0	6	9	8	7	0	0	6	0	2	1
Arrington, Visalia	12	7	.632	3.64	24	23	14	1	4	0	168	185	83	68	9	9	66	3	98	4
Bain, Stockton	0	0	.000	9.00	1	0	0	1	0	0	3	6	3	3	0	0	1	0	2	0
Balderston, Modesto	4	2	.667	6.79	9	9	1	0	0	0	53	70	48	40	11	2	33	1	33	3
Bangert, Fresno°	2	8	.200	7.33	13	12	3	1	0	0	70	86	71	57	10	2	38	0	41	4
Bankowski, Redwood°	0	0	.000	5.40	14	0	0	8	0	2	15	16	11	9	3	1	15	6	5	1
Bastian, Redwood	6	5	.545	3.50	20	19	3	0	1	0	121	113	54	47	9	2	34	3	79	0
Beene, Stockton	3	5	.375	2.57	19	10	1	3	1	0	63	62	25	18	2	1	35	1	74	5
Belanger, Visalia°	6	2	.750	3.04	34	0	0	24	0	5	80	72	35	27	3	3	33	3	65	6
Biggus, Stockton	9	10	.474	5.47	25	24	7	0	1	0	153	193	113	93	14	2	49	0	78	13
Biko, Reno°	12	9	.571	4.73	27	25	7	0	1	0	173	218	114	91	15	3	57	3	93	11
Blamey, Reno	0	1	.000	42.75	6	0	0	3	0	0	4	11	20	19	4	0	16	0	1	1
Borbon, Lodi°	8	10	.444	5.83	27	26	1	1	0	0	139	161	107	90	14	5	88	0	68	2
Bradley, Modesto	7	4	.636	2.42	27	0	0	25	0	7	52	41	15	14	3	1	21	6	43	0
Braun, Redwood	2	1	.667	3.73	23	0	0	17	0	2	41	47	23	17	2	0	17	4	27	2
Brown, Redwood°	1	0	1.000	6.00	5	0	0	4	0	1	9	10	6	6	0	0	2	1	2	0
Bryant, Reno°	10	8	.556	4.94	29	22	3	1	0	0	155	165	106	85	11	1	88	0	103	13
Buckley, Redwood	9	5	.643	3.10	55	3	0	41	0	12	87	54	41	30	7	1	63	4	92	3
Buckmier, Fresno	10	9	.526	4.12	28	28	11	0	1	0	188	187	99	86	16	5	101	2	107	5
Burns, Stockton	2	1	.667	3.60	4	4	0	0	0	0	20	21	11	8	1	0	8	0	8	0
Burroughs, Redwood°	0	0	.000	9.00	3	0	0	2	0	0	2	2	2	2	0	0	4	0	1	1
Cary, San Jose°	0	2	.000	4.02	22	1	0	14	0	3	47	49	26	21	4	1	27	2	35	1
Christianson, Fresno	0	1	.000	6.58	11	0	0	5	0	1	26	32	23	19	3	3	8	0	16	1
C. Codiroli, San Jose	3	2	.600	1.54	14	3	1	10	0	5	35	23	8	6	1	0	24	1	26	2
Conroy, Reno°	6	3	.667	4.44	38	1	0	20	0	3	71	70	49	35	8	2	48	1	49	4
Conroy, Modesto°	1	3	.250	7.85	8	8	0	0	0	0	39	50	37	34	7	1	23	0	46	5
Cordova, Stockton	0	0	.000	3.60	3	0	0	2	0	0	5	1	2	2	0	1	8	0	3	1
Couchee, Reno	7	5	.583	4.63	53	0	0	50	0	16	68	73	41	35	5	3	23	5	44	3
Cozzolino, Lodi	4	7	.364	5.12	32	13	0	12	0	1	102	110	65	58	8	6	69	3	77	9
Crisler, Redwood	3	3	.500	4.95	7	7	1	0	0	0	40	42	24	22	1	2	29	2	18	4
Cyburt, San Jose°	1	6	.143	3.63	11	11	2	0	1	0	72	68	41	29	8	0	34	0	48	6
Daniel, Lodi	6	2	.750	3.58	54	0	0	46	0	12	78	71	44	31	8	1	45	5	45	5
De Hart, San Jose	2	1	.667	7.65	13	1	0	4	0	0	20	17	20	17	1	2	26	2	16	2
de Leon, Lodi	2	3	.400	4.35	30	1	0	11	0	2	89	105	45	43	10	6	39	1	46	4
Dente, Lodi	14	6	.700	4.33	29	16	3	6	1	1	131	153	80	63	4	3	72	2	50	13
Diaz, Stockton	3	1	.750	4.06	33	0	0	22	0	7	82	86	43	37	8	1	16	0	36	2
Dinkins, Stockton°	3	3	.500	6.00	18	1	0	5	0	1	39	47	33	26	1	0	16	0	30	5
Donovan, Stockton	0	0	.000	9.00	1	0	0	1	0	0	2	3	2	2	0	0	1	0	3	0
Dougherty, San Jose°	3	3	.500	3.80	8	8	0	0	0	0	45	46	24	19	4	1	9	0	21	2
Duffy, Reno°	6	10	.375	4.32	25	16	0	7	0	1	125	165	84	60	11	3	61	0	79	7
Felt, Lodi°	10	9	.526	4.68	25	25	6	0	3	0	150	137	88	78	8	1	114	0	84	26
Ferguson, Modesto	3	5	.375	6.88	24	9	1	6	0	0	68	91	60	52	9	3	36	2	28	5
Francingues, Visalia	2	0	1.000	3.16	18	0	0	14	0	7	37	32	14	13	2	0	14	1	33	1
Free, San Jose	0	1	.000	15.43	4	0	0	3	0	0	7	14	16	12	5	1	4	1	7	2
Gallo, Fresno°	4	3	.571	5.91	18	2	0	8	0	0	35	36	25	23	3	1	21	0	27	2
Gerhardt, Reno°	0	0	.000	6.75	5	0	0	5	0	1	12	20	20	9	3	0	6	0	5	1
R. Gibson, Stockton	6	8	.429	3.00	49	0	0	46	0	14	66	61	31	22	3	1	38	0	67	7
S. Gibson, Stockton	2	3	.400	3.56	16	2	0	4	0	0	43	39	22	17	3	3	22	0	18	6
Gilmartin, Stockton	0	0	.000	4.50	3	1	0	2	0	0	4	5	4	2	0	2	3	0	3	0

Pitcher—Club	W.	L.	Pct.	ERA.	G.	GS.	CG.	GF.	ShO.	Sv.	IP.	H.	R.	ER.	HR.	HB.	BB.	Int. BB.	SO.	WP.
Goodchild, Fresno	4	6	.400	5.65	25	16	1	4	0	0	102	113	78	64	5	7	55	2	57	17
Gosse, Modesto°	2	4	.333	4.50	17	0	0	13	0	3	28	28	15	14	1	0	8	0	25	1
Grier, Stockton	11	6	.647	3.28	20	19	8	0	2	0	140	159	60	51	10	3	23	0	69	2
Hallgren, San Jose	7	1	.875	2.21	13	13	5	0	1	0	102	84	31	25	6	2	24	1	59	2
Hardwick, Reno	15	3	.833	4.53	25	25	2	0	1	0	157	166	111	79	8	11	121	2	117	25
Harris, Modesto	0	0	.000	2.25	4	0	0	2	0	1	4	4	4	1	0	0	2	0	3	0
Hensley, Modesto°	8	8	.500	3.71	19	19	4	0	0	0	136	153	75	56	10	6	57	6	83	4
Holloway, Modesto	2	1	.667	3.13	7	3	0	3	0	0	23	21	12	8	0	1	13	2	12	3
Humphry, Redwood	1	0	1.000	3.60	4	0	0	1	0	0	5	4	2	2	0	0	2	0	3	0
Jamerson, Fresno	4	5	.444	3.69	34	4	0	18	0	2	83	70	51	34	1	2	63	6	45	8
Jensen, Modesto°	6	5	.545	3.23	21	16	2	0	0	0	120	113	63	43	4	0	65	3	89	10
Kaczmarski, Reno	0	0	.000	0.00	1	0	0	1	0	0	2	0	0	0	0	0	1	0	1	0
Kain, Reno	2	0	1.000	2.70	3	0	0	2	0	0	10	8	4	3	1	0	3	0	2	0
Kibbe, Redwood	10	14	.417	5.66	31	23	7	3	1	1	170	185	127	107	18	1	92	10	115	5
Klawitter, Lodi°	11	7	.611	4.50	27	25	7	0	1	0	162	150	102	81	11	3	110	0	100	6
Kolotka, San Jose	0	4	.000	6.55	4	4	1	0	0	0	22	37	27	16	4	0	13	0	11	2
Krajewski, San Jose	0	2	.000	11.00	2	2	0	0	0	0	9	15	14	11	3	1	6	0	5	1
Kranitz, Stockton	6	4	.600	3.30	11	11	7	0	2	0	79	59	40	29	6	4	39	0	88	4
Krueger, Visalia	5	2	.714	4.20	16	2	0	11	0	1	45	52	22	21	3	2	15	1	35	2
Krueger, Modesto°	3	5	.375	3.67	16	13	5	3	1	0	98	87	49	40	3	4	52	3	76	8
Lund, Lodi	2	1	.667	6.43	11	1	0	2	0	0	28	39	27	20	4	3	15	2	12	5
Lusted, Fresno	3	4	.429	3.00	8	8	5	0	0	0	60	60	23	20	2	2	14	1	43	4
Lynes, San Jose°	9	14	.391	3.61	27	26	6	1	3	0	162	183	88	65	15	2	50	1	73	10
Macias, Reno	3	1	.750	2.10	4	4	3	0	1	0	30	30	12	7	7	0	5	0	23	0
Mahoski, Reno	4	3	.571	5.25	27	9	1	11	1	4	84	107	58	49	16	0	27	1	34	3
Manderfield, Stockton°	7	8	.467	3.00	24	24	5	0	0	0	153	167	74	51	8	1	67	1	111	15
Mantsch, Modesto	3	2	.600	2.30	25	0	0	17	0	8	43	37	14	11	1	4	11	3	19	2
Marietta, San Jose	11	14	.440	4.24	30	29	14	0	1	0	191	200	129	90	11	7	82	2	113	6
May, Visalia	10	11	.476	5.63	27	27	6	0	1	0	179	215	129	112	22	3	69	1	129	11
McDonald, San Jose	3	3	.500	2.49	20	2	0	10	0	1	65	51	28	18	1	2	40	0	43	9
Mine, Modesto	0	1	.000	12.00	2	2	0	0	0	0	6	9	8	8	1	0	8	0	3	0
Moore, 6 Mod-24 San Jose	9	15	.375	5.12	30	26	9	1	1	0	190	176	122	108	8	8	115	3	169	23
Moretti, Reno	5	1	.833	3.54	33	0	0	16	0	4	56	63	32	22	3	0	32	1	45	4
Mulligan, Visalia°	6	1	.857	2.35	20	1	1	18	0	4	46	37	14	12	1	1	11	1	27	0
Nunez, Lodi	5	5	.500	4.39	41	3	1	27	0	7	84	85	49	41	12	3	57	5	67	10
Odekirk, San Jose°	0	3	.000	7.20	13	3	0	6	0	0	30	41	31	24	4	1	20	1	9	2
Palica, San Jose	2	3	.400	4.36	22	7	0	13	0	1	66	74	37	32	4	1	32	4	35	4
Park, Stockton	5	7	.417	4.22	14	14	5	0	1	0	96	97	50	45	6	2	26	1	84	5
Parrott, Stockton	7	9	.438	5.20	24	23	4	1	2	0	128	135	83	74	11	2	67	1	73	4
Peterson, Reno	1	1	.500	3.60	5	4	0	0	0	0	15	14	9	6	1	1	7	0	8	3
Pettibone, Visalia	14	8	.636	4.33	27	27	10	0	1	0	187	211	105	90	18	2	61	3	139	2
Pierce, Fresno	0	0	.000	8.63	11	1	0	4	0	1	24	35	24	23	2	3	18	0	4	4
Puckett, San Jose	0	4	.000	7.20	10	0	0	8	0	3	15	12	16	12	2	1	13	1	4	3
Rathjen, San Jose	0	0	.000	13.50	3	0	0	2	0	0	2	4	3	3	0	0	1	0	1	1
Rau, Redwood°	1	0	1.000	0.82	3	3	0	0	0	0	11	6	1	1	0	0	2	0	14	0
Reeves, Visalia°	1	3	.250	5.02	12	4	1	6	0	1	43	46	31	24	4	1	24	0	25	1
Retzer, Modesto	8	10	.444	5.18	28	23	7	4	0	0	158	148	115	91	15	6	97	5	134	6
Rodriguez, Modesto	2	5	.286	5.29	11	10	2	0	0	0	63	68	51	37	4	1	28	2	28	8
Roen, 9 SJ-36 Redwood°	4	4	.500	5.12	45	0	0	18	0	1	51	41	34	29	2	2	62	5	38	9
Romanick, Redwood	15	10	.600	2.91	28	28	11	0	3	0	207	173	88	67	10	4	76	5	178	6
Ruzek, Visalia	3	4	.429	4.38	7	7	0	0	0	0	37	45	29	18	4	0	5	0	15	0
Saatzer, Redwood	1	10	.091	5.81	27	16	1	4	0	0	93	112	81	60	5	6	92	5	67	2
Schneider, Redwood	0	1	.000	4.29	16	0	0	3	0	0	21	27	17	10	1	2	24	1	10	4
Sensenbrenner, Fresno°	3	3	.500	7.03	14	3	0	3	0	0	32	47	28	25	2	0	30	0	23	3
Smith, Redwood	5	4	.556	3.62	34	5	0	15	0	4	77	70	46	31	10	0	32	5	64	4
Smith, Reno°	3	6	.333	6.95	27	12	0	5	0	1	92	141	82	71	7	2	40	2	56	6
Snider, 13 Fresno-9 Vis	3	1	.750	3.98	22	1	0	15	0	1	52	51	26	23	4	2	20	1	41	2
Stadler, Fresno	2	10	.167	5.67	30	13	3	15	0	2	119	139	92	75	13	5	58	3	57	10
Stovall, Fresno	3	2	.600	3.27	14	0	0	13	0	4	22	23	9	8	0	0	5	2	15	2
Sutherland, Fresno°	10	10	.500	4.21	23	23	7	0	1	0	154	175	98	72	11	0	69	0	62	3
Sylvia, Redwood	7	13	.350	5.08	29	27	3	0	1	0	172	199	120	97	11	9	87	6	128	11
Terry, Lodi°	2	5	.286	6.87	24	3	0	10	0	0	55	70	48	42	6	2	52	1	36	4
Tillema, San Jose	3	5	.375	3.52	25	0	0	17	0	3	46	44	26	18	0	2	20	1	39	4
Tirella, Visalia°	0	1	.000	12.27	8	0	0	4	0	0	11	20	16	15	0	0	16	0	8	1
Travers, Redwood°	0	0	.000	0.00	1	0	0	0	0	0	1	1	1	0	0	0	0	0	0	0
Tuchalski, San Jose	0	0	.000	15.00	3	0	0	2	0	0	3	6	5	5	1	0	1	0	2	0
Van Marter, Modesto	7	6	.538	5.92	34	5	0	17	0	2	76	97	66	50	13	4	34	4	47	7
Vavrock, Modesto	1	0	1.000	4.50	6	0	0	2	0	1	10	13	6	5	0	0	6	3	8	1
Venezia, Redwood	1	6	.143	5.70	25	9	0	4	0	0	71	83	53	45	5	3	32	3	39	2
Voigt, Visalia	16	7	.696	3.23	27	27	10	0	0	0	184	195	91	66	10	7	62	3	143	9
Waller, San Jose	0	0	.000	15.75	6	0	0	6	0	0	8	13	14	14	2	1	7	0	3	2
Warren, Modesto	9	6	.600	4.17	22	20	5	1	1	0	123	110	76	57	18	8	74	3	91	7
Weatherman, San Jose	0	3	.000	4.86	6	6	0	0	0	0	37	47	27	20	3	0	14	1	21	2
White, Reno	3	5	.375	4.68	14	12	0	1	0	0	73	89	48	38	6	4	29	0	46	3
Wilcox, Fresno	1	5	.167	9.28	10	5	0	2	0	0	32	49	38	33	5	0	15	0	19	2
Williams, Fresno	14	9	.609	3.37	27	25	14	0	1	0	187	170	81	70	12	13	85	3	170	10
Wood, Modesto	0	0	.000	6.30	4	2	0	1	0	1	10	11	9	7	1	0	6	0	2	1
Wright, San Jose	0	1	.000	9.00	2	0	0	0	0	0	3	6	3	3	0	0	4	0	2	0
C. Young, Modesto°	2	1	.667	3.48	5	4	1	0	0	0	31	28	15	12	0	0	16	0	14	2

BALKS—W. Krueger, 6; Retzer, 4; Angulo, Belanger, Cozzolino, Dente, Jensen, Klawitter, Nunez, Williams, 3 each; Altobelli, Anderson, Bangert, Biko, Borbon, Buckmier, S. Conroy, Cyburt, K. Krueger, Marietta, Romanick, Snider, Van Marter, Weatherman, 2 each; Bryant, Burns, Cary, T. Conroy, Diaz, Dougherty, Goodchild, Grier, Harris, Lynes, Macias, Manderfield, Mantsch, McDonald, Palica, Park, Parrott, Pierce, Puckett, Rodriguez, Roen, Ruzek, Saatzer, Schneider, J. Smith, M. Smith, Venezia, Voigt, Waller, Warren, 1 each.

COMBINATION SHUTOUTS—Goodchild-Stovall, Fresno; Kibbe-Buckley, Redwood; Biko-Couchee, Hardwick-Conroy, White-Couchee, Reno; Manderfield-S. Gibson-Dinkins-R. Gibson, Park-Diaz, Stockton.

NO-HIT GAME—Kranitz, Stockton, defeated San Jose, 7-0, August 30.

Carolina League

CLASS A

CHAMPIONSHIP WINNERS IN PREVIOUS YEARS

1945—Danville		.681
1946—Greensboro		.599
	Raleigh (2nd)†	.563
1947—Burlington		.613
	Raleigh (3rd)†	.574
1948—Raleigh		.592
	Martinsville (2nd)†	.570
1949—Danville		.601
	Burlington (4th)†	.500
1950—Winston-Salem°		.693
1951—Durham		.600
	Wins-Salem (2nd)†	.583
1952—Raleigh		.581
	Reidsville (4th)†	.536
1953—Raleigh		.593
	Danville (2nd)†	.572
1954—Fayetteville°		.628
1955—HP-Thomasville		.580
	Danville (2nd)†	.533
1956—HP-Thomasville		.591
	Fayetteville (4th)†	.523
1957—Durham		.632
	HP-Thomasville		.622
1958—Danville		.576
	Burlington (4th)†	.511

1959—Raleigh		.600
	Wilson (2nd)†	.550
1960—Greensboro‡		.636
	Burlington		.586
1961—Wilson		.594
1962—Durham		.636
	Wilson		.600
	Kinston (2nd)†	.593
1963—Kinston§		.538
	Greensboro§		.590
	Wilson (2nd)†	.535
1964—Kinston§		.572
	Winston-Salem§†	.590
1965—Peninsula§		.597
	Durham§		.580
	Tidewater†		.528
1966—Kinston§		.547
	Winston-Salem§	.586
	Rocky Mount†		.533
1967—Durham x (West.)		.536
	Raleigh (East.)		.542
1968—Salem (West.)		.607
	Ral-Dur (East.)		.597
	HP-Thom. y (W.)		.493

1969—Rocky M (East.)		.569
	Salem (West.)		.542
	Ral-Dur z (East.)		.560
1970—Winston-Salem‡		.586
	Burlington		.597
1971—Peninsula‡		.647
	Kinston		.623
1972—Salem‡		.657
	Burlington		.632
1973—Lynchburg		.588
	Winston-Salem‡		.557
1974—Salem		.671
	Salem		.582
1975—Rocky Mount		.667
	Rocky Mount		.614
1976—Winston-Salem		.618
	Winston-Salem		.551
1977—Lynchburg		.591
	Peninsula‡		.556
1978—Peninsula		.696
	Lynchburg‡		.614
1979—Winston-Salem a		.607
1980—Peninsula‡		.714
	Durham		.600

°Won championship and four-club playoff. †Won four-club playoff. ‡Won split-season playoff. §League was divided into Eastern, Western divisions. xWon eight-club, two-division playoff. yWon eight-club, two-division playoff against Raleigh-Durham. zWon eight-club, two-division playoff against Burlington. aWon both halves of split-season (no playoffs).

STANDING OF CLUBS AT CLOSE OF FIRST HALF, JUNE 18

NORTHERN DIVISION

Club	W.	L.	T.	Pct.	G.B.
Hagerstown (Co-op)	37	31	0	.544	....
Alexandria (Pirates)	33	34	0	.493	3½
Lynchburg (Mets)	32	38	0	.457	6
Salem (Padres)	26	44	0	.371	12

SOUTHERN DIVISION

Club	W.	L.	T.	Pct.	G.B.
Kinston (Blue Jays)	42	28	0	.600	....
Durham (Braves)	40	28	0	.588	1
Winston-Salem (Red Sox)	34	35	0	.493	7½
Peninsula (Phillies)	30	36	0	.455	10

STANDING OF CLUBS AT CLOSE OF SECOND HALF, SEPTEMBER 1

NORTHERN DIVISION

Club	W.	L.	T.	Pct.	G.B.
Salem (Padres)	40	30	0	.571	....
Lynchburg (Mets)	39	31	0	.557	1
Hagerstown (Co-op)	33	37	0	.471	7
Alexandria (Pirates)	29	41	0	.414	11

SOUTHERN DIVISION

Club	W.	L.	T.	Pct.	G.B.
Peninsula (Phillies)	41	29	0	.585	....
Winston-Salem (Red Sox)	38	32	0	.543	3
Durham (Braves)	30	40	0	.429	11
Kinston (Blue Jays)	30	40	0	.429	11

COMPOSITE STANDING OF CLUBS AT CLOSE OF SEASON, SEPTEMBER 1

Club	Pen.	W.-S.	Kin.	Dur.	Hag.	Lyn.	Sal.	Alex.	W.	L.	T.	Pct.	G.B.
Peninsula (Phillies)	....	12	9	9	8	13	12	8	71	65	0	.522	....
Winston-Salem (Red Sox)	8	....	10	13	10	10	11	10	72	67	0	.518	½
Kinston (Blue Jays)	11	10	....	11	12	9	11	8	72	68	0	.514	1
Durham (Braves)	11	6	9	....	9	7	15	13	70	68	0	.507	2
Hagerstown (Co-op)	11	10	8	10	....	12	9	10	70	68	0	.507	2
Lynchburg (Mets)	7	10	11	13	8	....	7	15	71	68	0	.507	2
Salem (Padres)	8	9	9	5	11	13	....	13	71	69	0	.507	2
Alexandria (Pirates)	9	10	12	7	10	5	9	....	62	75	0	.453	9½

Major league affiliations in parentheses.

Peninsula represented Hampton, Va.

Playoffs—Hagerstown defeated Salem for Northern Division championship. Peninsula defeated Kinston for Southern Division championship. Hagerstown defeated Peninsula, three games to none, for League Championship.

Regular-Season Attendance—Alexandria, 40,659; Durham, 151,905; Hagerstown, 145,335; Kinston, 40,183; Lynchburg, 51,960; Peninsula, 66,261; Salem, 72,125; Winston-Salem, 72,132. Total, 640,560. Playoff, 5,028. All-star game, 4,011.

Managers: Alexandria, Mike Toomey; Durham, Al Gallagher; Hagerstown, Grady Little; Kinston, John McLaren; Lynchburg, Gene Dusan; Peninsula, Bill Dancy; Salem, Glenn Ezell; Winston-Salem, Buddy Hunter.

All-Star Team: 1B (tie)—Michael Anicich, Lynchburg; John Schaive, Alexandria; 2B—Larry Jeltz, Peninsula; 3B—Thomas Hayes, Durham; SS (tie)—Octavio Fernandez, Kinston; Jose Oquendo, Lynchburg; OF—Brad Komminsk, Durham; Gerald Davis, Salem; Paul Croft, Hagerstown; C-Marc Sullivan, Winston-Salem; DH—David Rivera, Hagerstown; LHP—Randy Ford, Kinston; RHP—Michael Brown, Winston-Salem; MVP—Brad Komminsk, Durham; Pitcher of Year—Michael Brown, Winston-Salem. Manager of Year—Grady Little, Hagerstown.

(Compiled by Howe News Bureau, Boston, Mass.)

CLUB BATTING

Club	Pct.	G.	AB.	R.	OR.	H.	TB.	2B.	3B.	HR.	RBI.	GW.	SH.	SF.	HP.	BB.	Int. BB.	SO.	SB.	CS.	LOB.
Hagerstown	.276	138	4543	752	716	1254	2011	209	40	156	658	46	25	33	32	577	40	910	142	82	961
Lynchburg	.262	140	4610	704	680	1207	1736	203	43	80	609	57	38	42	56	611	28	936	146	60	1072
Durham	.255	138	4572	700	655	1165	1779	198	16	128	607	59	33	32	54	645	32	878	184	62	1084
Kinston	.254	140	4548	589	635	1157	1575	153	41	61	508	55	38	37	39	485	29	837	116	53	1008
Alexandria	.252	137	4540	631	610	1144	1645	181	31	86	545	54	57	26	48	487	34	876	145	54	1006
Peninsula	.248	136	4314	609	538	1069	1556	188	19	87	518	56	51	38	26	509	23	941	159	77	894
Winston-Salem	.246	139	4677	708	762	1151	1723	197	30	105	635	59	26	32	44	655	43	985	168	57	1054
Salem	.239	140	4560	699	796	1091	1713	163	33	131	624	61	24	27	46	713	30	987	126	53	1087

INDIVIDUAL BATTING

(Leading Qualifiers for Batting Championship—378 or More Plate Appearances)

°Bats lefthanded.   †Switch-hitter.

Player and Club	Pct.	G.	AB.	R.	H.	TB.	2B.	3B.	HR.	RBI.	GW.	SH.	SF.	HP.	BB.	Int. BB.	SO.	SB.	CS.
Komminsk, Brad, Durham	.322	132	459	108	148	278	27	2	33	104	9	0	4	8	110	8	101	35	12
Davis, Gerald, Salem	.306	138	431	114	132	264	24	3	34	103	6	2	3	14	161	5	98	12	6
Tyner, Matthew, Hagerstown	.301	108	386	70	116	231	18	2	31	77	8	1	3	2	52	4	78	4	1
Evans, Duane, Lynchburg°	.295	103	336	56	99	153	19	1	11	61	3	1	4	8	46	6	90	3	1
Schaive, John, Alexandria	.290	126	476	66	138	213	33	3	12	69	9	4	2	6	35	3	59	7	1
Butler, William, Hagerstown	.289	91	329	59	95	151	21	4	9	48	4	6	4	5	34	1	36	9	6
Rivera, David, Hagerstown	.288	130	479	88	138	214	27	5	13	67	4	0	2	2	65	3	91	20	8
Stefero, John, Hagerstown°	.287	111	338	69	97	192	16	2	25	82	5	2	3	0	78	9	88	4	0
Rodriguez, Angel, Alexandria	.285	102	365	59	104	160	17	0	13	62	10	1	2	6	22	1	51	1	2
Wotus, Ronald, 83 Hager-51 Alex	.283	134	487	72	138	178	20	4	4	63	4	4	2	4	63	4	32	7	10

Departmental Leaders: G—Davis, 138; AB—Perez, 526; R—Davis, 114; H—Komminsk, Perez, 148; TB—Komminsk, 278; 2B—Schaive, 33; 3B—Beane, Pavlik, 9; HR—Davis, 34; RBI—Komminsk, 104; GWRBI—Perez, Rodriguez, 10; SH—Belliard, 12; SF—Beane, Burgess, 8; BB—Davis, 161; HP—Davis, 14; SO—Greer, 183; SB—Burgess, 68; CS—Belliard, Burgess, Jeltz, 15.

(All Players—Listed Alphabetically)

Player and Club	Pct.	G.	AB.	R.	H.	TB.	2B.	3B.	HR.	RBI.	GW.	SH.	SF.	HP.	BB.	Int. BB.	SO.	SB.	CS.
Ackley, John, Winston-Salem	.222	4	9	2	2	3	1	0	0	0	0	0	0	0	2	0	3	0	0
Agapay, Felix, Peninsula°	.200	12	25	2	5	7	2	0	0	3	0	0	0	0	12	2	7	2	2
Anicich, Michael, Lynchburg	.310	63	239	60	74	140	13	1	17	51	9	0	1	3	30	2	44	0	1
Baugh, Darrell, Peninsula	.272	80	279	34	76	93	14	0	1	19	1	5	2	2	17	1	30	9	3
Beane, William, Lynchburg	.268	114	403	47	108	166	13	9	9	59	3	3	8	6	36	1	125	19	8
Belliard, Rafael, Alexandria†	.216	127	472	58	102	118	6	5	0	33	1	12	3	6	26	1	92	42	15
Blanco, Geronimo, Alexandria	.271	109	347	45	94	119	13	0	4	39	2	5	3	5	31	3	40	20	5
Bockhorn, Glen, Durham	.243	94	333	50	81	140	14	0	15	48	4	0	1	4	40	1	65	0	0
Brummer, Thomas, Winston-Salem°	.262	71	214	30	56	78	14	1	2	25	5	0	0	0	35	3	36	3	2
Burgess, Gus, Winston-Salem°	.282	135	510	102	144	206	27	7	7	74	7	4	8	4	81	7	92	68	15
Burton, Jeffrey, Alexandria	.250	27	100	10	25	43	6	0	4	16	0	0	0	0	8	0	36	2	1
Butler, William, Hagerstown	.289	91	329	59	95	151	21	4	9	48	4	6	4	5	34	1	36	9	6
Cannon, Timothy, Salem†	.175	32	57	10	10	14	2	1	0	4	0	0	0	0	14	1	21	2	0
Castillo, Juan, Kinston	.172	84	215	25	37	46	3	3	0	17	2	2	1	3	16	0	71	6	2
Castro, Edgar, Salem°	.243	86	247	23	60	80	9	1	3	27	1	1	0	1	57	4	52	1	0
Chamberlain, William, Lynchburg	.268	57	190	21	51	66	9	0	2	29	3	0	2	3	14	1	40	0	2
Cooper, Gary, Lynchburg	.211	134	478	76	101	128	12	3	3	37	6	5	2	6	70	2	126	41	11
Corman, David, Hagerstown	.266	99	293	40	78	100	13	0	3	33	1	3	1	5	49	0	49	11	12
Crafort, Samuel, Kinston°	.143	11	14	3	2	2	0	0	0	0	0	0	0	0	3	0	5	0	0
Crawford, James, Peninsula	.252	81	214	30	54	82	9	2	5	31	1	5	2	1	30	0	68	9	6
Croft, Paul, Hagerstown	.282	117	439	95	124	214	18	6	20	60	3	1	3	8	49	2	133	42	14
Darkis, William, Peninsula	.243	44	136	19	33	64	6	2	7	23	3	0	1	2	14	1	49	6	3
Davis, Gerald, Salem	.306	138	431	114	132	264	24	3	34	103	6	2	3	14	161	5	98	12	6
Dees, Gregory, Hagerstown°	.347	23	75	14	26	47	3	0	6	19	2	1	0	0	8	0	15	0	0
DeLano, Alexander, Lynchburg	.278	116	381	54	106	152	23	4	5	50	4	2	1	4	53	2	90	7	6
De La Rosa, Bienvenido, Alexandria°	.243	42	152	24	37	48	6	1	1	12	2	3	0	2	16	0	22	13	3
Duff, David, Lynchburg	.268	66	205	28	55	76	10	1	3	33	1	2	2	4	27	0	22	3	2
Elliott, Mark, Lynchburg°	.195	56	118	21	23	32	6	0	1	13	3	2	2	1	22	0	17	6	2
Enos, David, Peninsula†	.258	86	233	29	60	76	6	2	2	26	3	7	6	0	35	1	48	7	8
Ereu, William, Kinston	.262	28	107	9	28	30	2	0	0	5	1	3	1	2	3	0	14	7	5
Escobar, Jose, Kinston	.250	56	192	22	48	56	5	0	1	16	0	1	2	3	15	0	19	5	3
Etchebarren, Raymond, Salem	.290	63	241	36	70	97	12	0	5	35	4	0	2	1	23	0	22	3	3
Evans, Duane, Lynchburg°	.295	103	336	56	99	153	19	1	11	61	3	1	4	8	46	6	90	3	1
Fabrizio, Kurt, Hagerstown°	.278	85	295	48	82	145	12	3	15	59	3	1	4	0	40	5	49	0	2
Felt, John, Hagerstown°	.200	116	380	41	76	139	16	1	15	52	6	3	3	4	53	3	122	1	4
Fernandez, Antonio, Kinston†	.318	75	280	57	89	114	10	6	1	13	1	7	0	2	49	2	20	15	7
Fiori, Joseph, Alexandria	.179	58	151	21	27	33	0	0	2	12	1	5	1	0	22	0	33	2	1
Ford, Kenneth, Alexandria	.260	82	285	42	74	107	11	2	6	36	3	1	1	7	23	0	61	12	2
Frash, Roger, Lynchburg°	.268	119	440	68	118	174	22	5	8	41	3	4	2	7	55	7	87	7	6
Frierson, Mike, Hagerstown†	.210	34	100	15	21	27	2	2	0	5	1	1	0	0	7	0	18	6	1
Fryer, Paul, Peninsula	.260	128	439	59	114	172	17	4	11	57	1	1	1	1	30	1	97	11	4
Garcia, Michael, Durham	.270	98	315	41	85	95	7	0	1	31	1	6	1	1	28	1	37	15	6
Garnett, Bradley, Alexandria°	.175	13	40	4	7	11	2	1	0	2	1	1	0	1	4	0	18	0	0
Gill, Frank, Winston-Salem°	.248	113	428	68	106	133	14	5	1	30	4	3	2	1	30	3	29	25	11
Gomez, Jose, Salem°	.125	17	32	4	4	11	1	0	2	5	0	0	0	1	7	0	11	0	0
Greer, Brian, Salem	.200	136	456	79	91	185	11	4	25	89	8	1	3	6	106	2	183	21	1
Grubbs, Kevin, Winston-Salem	.000	32	1	0	0	0	0	0	0	0	0	0	0	0	0	0	0	0	0
Gutierrez, Joaquin, Win-Salem	.249	137	507	56	126	153	14	5	1	45	7	4	1	6	43	0	80	9	3
Hagman, Keith, Durham°	.269	128	435	57	117	177	20	2	12	68	8	2	7	3	63	7	28	2	2
Harrigan, David, Peninsula	.198	75	273	35	54	104	13	2	11	40	6	0	2	3	20	1	86	1	2
Harvey, Steven, Peninsula	.214	81	313	34	67	86	13	0	2	39	5	3	3	1	10	0	50	14	5
Hayes, Thomas, Durham	.263	118	403	80	106	175	27	0	14	62	7	4	1	5	79	2	88	15	8
Headford, Grant, Hagerstown	.268	47	157	24	42	54	6	0	2	10	1	0	0	5	13	0	36	0	2
Hearn, Edward, Hagerstown	.303	101	317	61	96	159	29	2	10	44	4	1	2	4	47	5	71	8	2
Hernandez, Tobias, Kinston	.267	82	236	27	63	77	9	1	1	27	5	7	1	2	14	0	37	3	0
Herrick, Neal, Hagerstown°	.309	57	194	25	60	85	11	1	4	26	2	1	0	0	19	1	35	2	4
Hollins, Paul, Alexandria°	.155	26	84	11	13	23	3	2	1	12	0	1	2	0	11	3	21	1	0
Hunter, Jeffrey, Winston-Salem°	.238	123	424	67	101	176	14	2	19	72	5	0	4	1	59	3	107	4	2
Huppert, David, Hagerstown	.500	1	2	0	1	1	0	0	0	0	0	0	0	0	0	0	1	0	0

Player and Club	Pct.	G.	AB.	R.	H.	TB.	2B.	3B.	HR.	RBI.	GW.	SH.	SF.	HP.	BB.	Int. BB.	SO.	SB.	CS.
Ireland, Billy, Salem	.200	14	30	5	6	7	1	0	0	3	0	1	0	0	3	1	3	0	0
Jablonski, Raymond, Alexandria	.189	15	37	3	7	7	0	0	0	4	0	2	0	0	4	0	6	0	0
Jeltz, Larry, Peninsula†	.232	133	482	81	112	136	18	0	2	32	2	8	2	1	93	0	103	38	15
Komminsk, Brad, Durham	.322	132	459	108	148	278	27	2	33	104	9	0	4	8	110	8	101	35	12
Kuvinka, Scott, 70 Alex-44 Hagers	.261	114	398	62	104	164	16	1	14	54	5	1	1	3	39	4	66	7	3
Lansford, Phillip, Kinston	.261	103	341	38	89	118	13	5	2	30	3	1	2	3	31	1	66	6	4
Lebo, Michael, Kinston°	.232	78	250	22	58	101	11	4	8	29	3	0	1	1	23	4	61	0	0
Lee, Eddie Joe, Winston-Salem	.185	92	254	42	47	76	8	0	7	24	2	3	1	8	45	2	70	20	9
Leggatt, Richard, Alexandria	.000	32	1	0	0	0	0	0	0	0	0	0	0	0	0	0	0	0	0
Lindsey, Jon, Peninsula°	.231	110	360	33	83	102	13	0	2	34	3	6	6	2	26	0	47	8	10
Lyons, Stephen, Winston-Salem	.242	64	252	43	61	94	9	3	6	40	3	2	2	2	44	2	55	19	6
Masterson, Thomas, Alexandria	.412	5	17	4	7	9	2	0	0	2	0	1	0	0	3	1	4	0	0
McClendon, Lloyd, Lynchburg	.251	103	363	55	91	136	12	6	7	57	4	3	5	7	60	1	68	3	0
McGehee, C. Connor, Alexandria°	.241	123	448	68	108	159	17	5	8	53	7	6	5	0	64	10	119	20	8
Melendez, Francisco, Peninsula°	.135	32	74	6	10	13	3	0	0	6	0	2	0	0	12	0	23	3	1
Miscik, Robert, Alexandria	.302	67	225	38	68	96	13	3	3	25	0	4	2	3	40	2	41	9	1
Moore, Alvin, Durham	.281	121	437	61	123	196	25	0	16	73	7	1	0	8	55	3	69	12	4
Moreno, Jamie, Salem	.158	8	19	1	3	3	0	0	0	3	0	0	0	1	2	0	3	0	0
Murray, Steven, Salem	.238	133	466	97	111	170	16	5	11	49	6	1	2	11	123	4	124	34	10
Nemeth, Joseph, Peninsula°	.221	52	145	23	32	44	3	0	3	18	2	1	0	1	38	2	33	3	0
Nichols, Carl, Hagerstown	.272	38	81	8	22	29	4	0	1	6	1	1	0	0	12	1	19	3	4
Norko, Thomas, Kinston	.196	67	204	25	40	63	9	1	4	22	4	1	2	1	27	1	58	2	3
Oddo, Ronald, Winston-Salem°	.189	36	106	14	20	21	1	0	0	7	0	2	0	0	22	0	9	0	1
Oquendo, Jose, Lynchburg	.249	124	393	59	98	118	8	6	0	38	4	5	1	2	71	2	61	38	14
Palmer, Robert, Hagerstown	.228	45	127	18	29	42	7	0	2	15	2	0	2	0	21	2	37	2	2
Palmieri, John, Peninsula°	.000	29	1	0	0	0	0	0	0	0	0	0	0	0	0	0	0	0	0
Pardo, Alberto, Hagerstown†	.316	21	76	11	24	32	3	1	1	7	0	0	3	0	10	1	9	1	0
Parent, Mark, Salem	.235	123	438	44	103	143	16	3	6	47	8	4	1	1	37	2	91	10	6
Paula, Julio, Kinston†	.266	69	222	24	59	71	3	3	1	23	3	1	4	3	33	1	32	5	2
Pavlik, John, Hagerstown†	.225	128	435	67	98	177	19	9	14	59	6	3	4	2	51	5	140	23	11
Payano, Vidal, Durham	.270	14	37	3	10	10	0	0	0	2	0	2	1	0	4	1	11	1	3
Pena, Jorge, Salem	.093	22	43	4	4	4	0	0	0	0	0	1	0	1	7	0	10	0	0
Perez, Benjamin, Kinston	.281	137	526	75	148	169	10	4	1	53	5	10	4	2	46	3	40	16	8
Perez, George, Salem°	.267	126	513	72	137	180	15	5	6	52	10	0	2	2	36	1	92	12	10
Pruitt, R. Lee, Winston-Salem†	.257	132	463	77	119	194	27	0	16	86	5	1	6	2	91	12	105	2	0
Pulley, Martin, Kinston	.227	58	141	11	32	42	5	1	1	13	0	1	1	3	18	0	24	0	0
Pustorino, Frederick, Lynchburg†	.162	21	37	9	6	7	1	0	0	2	0	0	1	0	16	0	8	0	1
Quade, G. Michael, Alexandria	.280	49	168	31	47	65	5	2	3	25	4	1	0	0	37	1	34	7	4
Quinones, Luis, Salem†	.224	123	455	64	102	141	10	4	7	37	3	5	2	2	36	4	52	18	8
Raley, Terry, Kinston†	.155	27	84	12	13	22	6	0	1	4	1	1	0	0	10	0	16	4	0
Ramos, Wolfgangh, Winston-Salem	.258	87	341	38	88	122	12	2	6	34	5	2	1	4	14	1	63	3	2
Rigby, Kevin, Durham°	.233	16	43	4	10	13	3	0	0	3	0	0	0	0	9	2	5	0	0
Rittweger, William, Lynchburg	.244	121	480	63	117	149	19	2	3	44	7	4	5	1	40	1	63	5	2
Rivera, David, Hagerstown	.288	130	479	88	138	214	27	5	13	67	4	0	2	2	65	3	91	20	8
Rodriguez, Angel, Alexandria	.285	102	365	59	104	160	17	0	13	62	10	1	2	6	22	1	51	1	2
Ronk, Jeffrey, Salem	.233	33	116	15	27	40	7	0	2	16	2	2	1	0	20	0	16	3	2
Rudd, Ronald, 26 Hag-82 Dur°	.256	108	383	59	98	125	11	2	4	35	2	1	4	1	62	3	78	29	10
Salava, Randy, Peninsula°	.275	94	295	50	81	138	14	2	13	43	5	3	1	0	43	3	80	12	8
Sauer, Jack, Winston-Salem	.226	26	31	5	7	10	1	1	0	5	0	0	0	1	14	0	6	3	1
Scanlon, Kenneth, Durham	.198	117	343	38	68	81	9	2	0	25	1	6	1	2	61	1	65	11	1
Schaive, John, Alexandria	.290	126	476	66	138	213	33	3	12	69	9	4	2	6	35	3	59	7	1
Schnoor, Charles, Lynchburg	.213	74	197	21	42	53	9	1	0	13	2	7	1	2	30	0	53	6	4
Shepherd, Ronald, Kinston	.235	135	486	71	114	183	15	3	16	66	7	1	5	6	47	5	147	16	7
Silverman, Robert, Kinston	.279	99	369	49	103	136	15	0	6	52	8	0	5	3	27	4	37	14	2
Snaith, Andrew, Alexandria	.251	95	299	34	75	98	12	4	1	24	1	4	1	3	27	1	57	2	1
Soreca, Vincent, Peninsula	.179	23	78	7	14	20	3	0	1	5	0	2	0	0	5	0	27	0	0
Sosa, Miguel, Durham	.276	118	479	63	132	213	22	4	17	70	9	1	7	7	8	1	94	18	6
Stefero, John, Hagerstown°	.287	111	338	69	97	192	16	2	25	82	5	2	3	0	78	9	88	4	0
Stevens, Anthony, Winston-Salem	.233	79	266	36	62	118	14	0	14	61	6	0	1	1	38	2	92	1	1
Stieb, Steven, Durham	.157	25	51	4	8	11	3	0	0	1	0	1	0	3	6	0	16	0	0
Strawberry, Darryl, Lynchburg	.255	123	420	84	107	180	22	6	13	78	7	1	4	6	82	5	105	31	8
Styons, Raymond, Alexandria	.213	104	362	54	77	163	16	2	22	69	6	2	3	2	35	1	98	2	1
Sullivan, Marc, Winston-Salem	.268	120	406	67	109	174	21	1	14	64	4	1	3	8	66	6	98	4	0
Sutton, L. Ricardo, Kinston	.253	126	430	61	109	166	20	5	9	64	9	0	3	3	60	1	100	11	7
Swoope, C. William, Alexandria	.313	19	64	11	20	32	3	0	3	6	0	0	1	4	0	0	11	0	0
Tarver, Laschelle, Lynchburg°	.455	5	22	3	10	12	2	0	0	3	0	1	0	0	2	0	1	2	2
Teller, Jeems, Winston-Salem	.205	40	117	18	24	37	4	0	3	15	2	0	1	0	25	1	40	5	2
Thompson, Michael, Hagerstown°	.000	10	1	0	0	0	0	0	0	0	0	0	0	0	0	0	0	0	0
Thompson, Timothy, Kinston°	.277	130	451	57	125	179	17	5	9	74	3	2	5	2	62	7	90	6	3
Thompson, Tommy, Durham°	.318	50	151	25	48	72	9	0	5	23	2	1	2	2	27	1	13	2	0
Timko, Andrew, Hagerstown°	.263	47	194	17	51	64	6	2	1	23	1	2	1	0	10	1	11	3	4
Tyler, David, Winston-Salem	.000	20	1	0	0	0	0	0	0	0	0	0	0	0	0	0	1	0	0
Tyner, Matthew, Lynchburg	.301	108	386	70	116	231	18	2	31	77	8	1	3	2	52	4	78	4	1
Ulrich, Jeffery, Peninsula	.307	40	114	23	35	55	5	0	5	24	5	2	1	6	9	0	15	1	2
Valdez, Angel, Salem	.172	68	232	17	40	47	5	1	0	17	0	2	2	0	12	0	42	4	2
Vaulman, Paul, Hagerstown†	.000	14	1	0	0	0	0	0	0	0	0	0	0	0	0	0	0	0	0
Vuksan, Jeffrey, Durham	.167	37	108	11	18	27	3	0	2	8	1	2	0	2	7	0	29	0	1
Washington, Keith, Peninsula†	.277	53	202	39	56	63	3	2	0	14	2	2	4	0	19	1	41	21	2
Willard, Gerald, Peninsula°	.260	107	334	43	87	142	17	1	12	60	6	3	5	2	49	5	66	6	4
Williams, Harold, Durham	.173	77	202	31	35	67	9	1	7	23	2	1	1	2	30	1	69	7	2
Wilson, Parker, Winston-Salem	.228	104	347	43	79	128	16	3	9	53	4	4	3	5	46	1	99	2	2
Wood, Joseph, Salem°	.270	111	422	60	114	164	18	4	8	68	7	2	6	3	34	5	69	4	4
Woodward, James, Lynchburg	.264	102	386	55	102	122	15	1	1	37	4	3	4	1	27	0	62	16	1
Wotus, Ronald, 83 Hagers-51 Alex	.283	134	487	72	138	178	20	4	4	63	4	4	2	4	63	4	32	7	10

The following pitchers had no plate appearances primarily through use of designated hitters, listed alphabetically by club, games in parentheses:

ALEXANDRIA—Acker, Larry (7); Adkins, Robert (23); Burke, Timothy (23); Carvajal, Crucito (16); Cyburt, Philip (6); Dodd, Lance (10); Hamner, Peter (31); Johnson, Michael (24); Keenan, Kerry (17); Krawczyk, Raymond (8); Powell, Charles (8); Ray, Arthur (26); Ricelli, Frank (1); Taylor, Johnny (19); Zamba, Michael (22); Zaske, Lloyd (21).

DURHAM—Behenna, Richard (29); Coatney, Rick (11); Dedmon, Jeffrey (28); Fuller, Timothy (9); Germer, Glen (34); Gibson, James (47); Lamson, Charles (4); Lucia, Daniel (12); North, Roy (23); Patterson, Scott (13); Payne, Michael (29); Reiter, Gary (41); Smith, Michael (23); Thompkins, James (10).

HAGERSTOWN—Anthony, Dane (14); Boyd, Randy (4); Brown, Mark (10); Carcella, Kevin (3); Chiti, Dominic (5); Dixon, Kenneth (9); Edwards, Allen (18); Gonzalez, Julian (12); Hoke, Leon (3); Hook, Edwin (22); Huey, John (14); Jones, Kirk (7); Leach, Ron (25); Marston, Anderson (5); McCullock, Alec (38-25 with Alexandria); Minnick, Donald (13); Moore, Edmund (19); Norris, Timothy (10); Ramirez, Allan (5); Richard, Todd (11); Rock, Robert (19-8 with Alexandria); Romero, Ramon (17); Smith, Freddie (4); Thibodeaux, Keith (17); Wright, Michael (21).

KINSTON—Baker, James (15); Beckman, Bernie (19); Carter, Tyson (27); Flores, Jesse (5); Ford, Randy (29); Gill, John (32); Howard, Dennis (27); Leal, Carlos (33); Lukish, Thomas (32); Phillips, Junior (41); Stemberger, Brian (60); Wright, Ken (13).

LYNCHBURG—Begue, Roger (42); Bettendorf, Jeffrey (24); Bittiger, Jeffrey (24); Faust, Clifford (52); Ibarguen, Stephen (33); Johnson, Jody (4); Kolbe, Brian (6); Kuntz, Eric (25); Rech, Edward (4); Rodriguez, Jose (5); Shockley, Lee (5); Sisk, Douglas (36); Skinner, John (3); Smith, David (28); Spicer, Kevin (12); Sunderlage, Jeffrey (10); Tibbs, Jay (15); Violette, John (28); Wilmet, Paul (8).

PENINSULA—Baller, Jay (27); Cepeda, Orlando (43); Decker, Martin (55); Downs, Kelly (25); Dunnegan, Steven (26); Mitchell, David (26); Money, Kyle (24); Prior, Daniel (28); Thomas, Dennis (31); Warner, Fred (12).

SALEM—Britt, Michael (15); Coffman, James (55); Figueroa, Ismael (21); Gerhardt, William (28); Johnson, Donald (11); Krzanik, Andrew (24); Long, William (14); Lovekamp, Scott (26); Malinski, Patrick (39); Schefsky, Steven (10); Smith, Wesley (6); Stone, Steven (27); Williams, Fred (14); Wilson, Philip (31).

WINSTON-SALEM—Baum, Mark (29); Bowlin, Allan (26); Brown, Michael (21); Clinton, Kevin (15); Dale, Charles (40); Garrett, Steven (27); Gering, Scott (34); Hill, Ronnie (23); Hulbert, Alvin (11); McCarthy, Thomas (28); Mecerod, George (23); Pecka, Keith (35).

GRAND SLAM HOME RUNS—Greer, 4; Hunter, Pavlik, Rivera, Stevens, Styons, Thompson, 2 each; Anicich, Burton, Bockhorn, Butler, Davis, Dees, Fryer, Harrigan, Herrick, Kuvinka, Lindsey, McGehee, Murray, Palmer, Shepherd, Teller, Willard, Wilson, 1 each.

AWARDED FIRST BASE ON INTERFERENCE—Jablonski (Pustorino); Lindsey (Hernandez); Pavlik (Rodriguez).

CLUB FIELDING

Club	Pct.	G.	PO.	A.	E.	DP.	PB.	Club	Pct.	G.	PO.	A.	E.	DP.	PB.
Alexandria	.963	137	3507	1456	190	114	49	Peninsula	.957	136	3451	1338	213	112	20
Kinston	.961	140	3552	1512	207	101	28	Winston-Salem	.955	139	3676	1541	245	112	21
Lynchburg	.961	140	3580	1553	206	115	30	Hagerstown	.952	138	3499	1403	249	101	24
Durham	.960	138	3562	1536	213	124	27	Salem	.948	140	3568	1472	275	143	21

Triple Plays—Salem 2, Peninsula.

INDIVIDUAL FIELDING
FIRST BASEMEN

*Throws lefthanded.

Player and Club	Pct.	G.	PO.	A.	E.	DP.	Player and Club	Pct.	G.	PO.	A.	E.	DP.
Anicich, Lynchburg	.986	55	458	21	7	39	Lansford, Kinston	.988	85	684	50	9	56
Castillo, Kinston	1.000	4	24	0	0	1	Lebo, Kinston	.985	10	62	3	1	3
Castro, Salem*	.984	73	595	31	10	56	Melendez, Peninsula*	.964	23	146	13	6	14
Chamberlain, Lynchburg	.953	15	118	4	6	8	Nemeth, Peninsula*	.989	40	348	18	4	34
Elliott, Lynchburg	.900	2	9	0	1	0	Palmer, Hagerstown	.985	8	60	4	1	4
Enos, Peninsula	.972	8	63	6	2	3	Pavlik, Hagerstown*	.984	57	453	33	8	34
Evans, Lynchburg	.989	58	502	28	6	43	Pruitt, Winston-Salem	1.000	5	24	2	0	2
Fabrizio, Hagerstown*	.983	82	604	42	11	50	Sauer, Winston-Salem	1.000	9	30	3	0	1
Frash, Lynchburg*	.984	20	162	17	3	17	SCHAIVE, Alexandria	.991	124	1098	88	11	92
Garnett, Alexandria*	.973	10	68	4	2	6	Stevens, Winston-Salem	.986	42	320	23	5	34
Gomez, Salem*	.935	8	41	2	3	5	Styons, Salem	.986	72	570	44	9	56
Hagman, Durham*	.988	123	1121	70	14	97	Sullivan, Winston-Salem	1.000	1	3	0	0	0
Hearn, Peninsula	.979	73	538	25	12	48	Thompson, Kinston*	.983	52	449	20	8	28
Hunter, Winston-Salem	.990	99	858	73	9	69	Williams, Durham	.980	26	192	8	4	20
Kuvinka, Alexandria	.971	5	31	2	1	5	Wotus, Alexandria	1.000	2	6	0	0	0

Triple Plays—Enos, Gomez, Styons.

SECOND BASEMEN

Player and Club	Pct.	G.	PO.	A.	E.	DP.	Player and Club	Pct.	G.	PO.	A.	E.	DP.
Butler, Hagerstown	.908	27	54	65	12	13	Payano, Durham	.889	4	6	18	3	0
Corman, Hagerstown	.952	91	202	231	22	54	Perez, Kinston	.967	58	104	158	9	23
Enos, Peninsula	1.000	5	9	12	0	0	Quade, Alexandria	.976	11	11	30	1	3
Ereu, Kinston	.900	3	6	3	1	0	Quinones, Salem	1.000	4	6	5	0	1
Escobar, Kinston	.946	10	10	25	2	4	Raley, Kinston	.929	13	30	35	5	8
Etchebarren, Salem	.986	40	80	130	3	29	Ramos, Winston-Salem	.926	56	110	139	20	33
Fiori, Alexandria	.962	49	108	143	10	24	Rigby, Durham	1.000	3	1	1	0	0
Frierson, Hagerstown	.918	22	42	47	8	6	RITTWEGER, Lynchburg	.965	120	273	334	22	82
Garcia, Durham	.982	51	60	102	3	18	Ronk, Salem	.925	19	46	53	8	12
Gill, Winston-Salem	.952	60	136	178	16	34	Scanlon, Durham	.960	109	207	316	22	66
Hayes, Durham	1.000	1	3	1	0	0	Schnoor, Lynchburg	.988	19	37	48	1	2
Jeltz, Peninsula	.964	132	293	369	25	84	Snaith, Alexandria	.954	87	152	244	19	46
Kuvinka, Hagerstown	1.000	4	15	5	0	1	Valdez, Salem	.925	67	148	174	26	34
Murray, Salem	1.000	1	3	0	0	0	Wood, Salem	.931	16	28	39	5	9
Nichols, Hagerstown	1.000	1	8	1	0	0	Woodward, Lynchburg	.927	9	19	32	4	4
Oddo, Winston-Salem	.892	33	65	67	16	10	Wotus, Hag-Alex	.968	8	14	16	1	4
Paula, Kinston	.948	65	142	167	17	29							

Triple Play—Wood.

THIRD BASEMEN

Player and Club	Pct.	G.	PO.	A.	E.	DP.	Player and Club	Pct.	G.	PO.	A.	E.	DP.
Anicich, Lynchburg	1.000	1	1	0	0	0	Etchebarren, Salem	.864	16	14	37	8	5
Blanco, Alexandria	.900	7	11	7	2	1	Fryer, Peninsula	.901	127	103	223	36	26
Burton, Alexandria	.824	13	3	11	3	0	Garcia, Durham	.949	35	27	65	5	4
Butler, Hagerstown	.798	31	19	52	18	3	Gutierrez, Winston-Salem	.778	3	2	5	2	0
Castillo, Kinston	.833	4	0	5	1	1	HAYES, Durham	.905	104	61	207	28	18
Chamberlain, Lynchburg	.852	24	14	32	8	1	Hunter, Winston-Salem	.863	14	13	31	7	6
Davis, Salem	.728	24	21	38	22	6	Ireland, Salem	.800	2	2	2	1	0
Dees, Hagerstown	.921	19	18	40	5	6	Kuvinka, Alex-Hag	.929	26	16	49	5	2
Elliott, Lynchburg	.667	3	2	4	3	0	Lansford, Kinston	1.000	2	1	1	0	0
Enos, Peninsula	.941	16	9	23	2	2	McClendon, Lynchburg	.870	8	4	16	3	1
Ereu, Kinston	1.000	5	4	6	0	1	Miscik, Alexandria	.936	66	49	112	11	10

THIRD BASEMEN—Continued

Player and Club	Pct.	G.	PO.	A.	E.	DP.
Norko, Kinston	.934	54	30	83	8	11
Perez, Kinston	.914	77	51	152	19	15
Quade, Alexandria	.959	17	12	35	2	1
Raley, Kinston	.929	6	5	8	1	1
Ramos, Winston-Salem	.877	30	16	41	8	3
Rivera, Hagerstown	.867	7	7	6	2	0
Ronk, Salem	.913	12	13	29	4	1
Scanlon, Durham	.800	3	1	11	3	1
Schnoor, Lynchburg	.946	33	18	52	4	5

Player and Club	Pct.	G.	PO.	A.	E.	DP.
Snaith, Alexandria	.857	6	3	3	1	2
Stefero, Hagerstown	1.000	1	0	1	0	0
Stemberger, Kinston	1.000	1	1	0	0	0
Tyner, Hagerstown	.854	51	44	73	20	3
Williams, Durham	1.000	2	1	1	0	0
Wilson, Winston-Salem	.894	99	77	185	31	10
Wood, Salem	.901	89	93	172	29	23
Woodward, Lynchburg	.874	91	57	178	34	19
Wotus, Hag-Alex	.950	53	47	86	7	6

Triple Play—Davis.

SHORTSTOPS

Player and Club	Pct.	G.	PO.	A.	E.	DP.
Belliard, Alexandria	.949	127	205	330	29	73
Butler, Hagerstown	.879	27	44	72	16	12
Enos, Peninsula	.922	35	40	78	10	10
Ereu, Kinston	.955	18	38	46	4	10
Escobar, Kinston	.933	45	65	129	14	23
Etchebarren, Salem	.833	3	3	7	2	1
Fernandez, Kinston	.948	74	121	227	19	30
Fiori, Alexandria	.944	4	5	12	1	1
Garcia, Durham	.889	1	2	6	1	1
Gutierrez, Winston-Salem	.922	134	205	423	53	74
Hayes, Durham	.938	14	22	53	5	10
Hernandez, Kinston	1.000	2	5	5	0	0
Kuvinka, Hagerstown	1.000	1	1	1	0	1
Lindsey, Peninsula	.896	108	145	294	51	55
Lyons, Winston-Salem	.929	5	9	17	2	5

Player and Club	Pct.	G.	PO.	A.	E.	DP.
Nichols, Hagerstown	.500	2	0	1	1	1
Oddo, Winston-Salem	1.000	1	2	5	0	0
OQUENDO, Lynchburg	.961	124	169	390	23	61
Payano, Durham	.875	10	11	24	5	6
Pena, Salem	.909	21	20	40	6	5
Perez, Kinston	.917	5	6	5	1	0
Quinones, Salem	.910	120	202	336	53	77
Ronk, Salem	.909	2	4	6	1	2
Scanlon, Durham	.893	6	4	21	3	4
Schnoor, Lynchburg	.923	23	36	60	8	16
Sosa, Durham	.897	111	128	315	51	68
Timko, Hagerstown	.942	46	68	126	12	22
Wood, Salem	.850	3	5	12	3	1
Wotus, Hag-Alex	.943	75	111	204	19	30

Triple Plays—Lindsey, Pena.

OUTFIELDERS

Player and Club	Pct.	G.	PO.	A.	E.	DP.
Agapay, Peninsula	.826	9	19	0	4	0
Baugh, Peninsula	.955	79	142	7	7	0
Beane, Lynchburg	.956	112	233	8	11	1
Blanco, Alexandria	.904	88	116	6	13	1
Bockhorn, Durham	1.000	4	10	0	0	0
Burgess, Winston-Salem°	.921	135	250	8	22	3
Burton, Alexandria	.909	15	20	0	2	0
Cannon, Salem	.968	20	30	0	1	0
Castillo, Kinston	.970	69	88	10	3	2
Cooper, Durham	.955	133	242	10	12	2
Crafort, Kinston	1.000	8	8	0	0	0
Crawford, Peninsula	.928	57	74	3	6	1
Croft, Hagerstown	.940	104	165	6	11	3
Darkis, Peninsula	.970	42	61	4	2	0
Davis, Salem	.942	77	119	11	8	2
DeLano, Lynchburg	.928	77	99	4	8	0
De La Rosa, Alexandria°	.954	36	60	2	3	0
Elliott, Lynchburg	.952	45	57	2	3	1
Enos, Peninsula	.913	20	18	3	2	0
Ereu, Kinston	.750	2	3	0	1	0
Felt, Alexandria	.959	110	169	16	8	4
Fiori, Alexandria	1.000	2	4	0	0	0
Ford, Alexandria	.956	46	60	5	3	2
Frash, Lynchburg°	.972	94	130	8	4	1
Frierson, Hagerstown	1.000	7	6	0	0	0
Garnett, Alexandria°	1.000	3	1	0	0	0
Gill, Winston-Salem	.988	46	75	5	1	0
GREER, Salem	.983	136	278	15	5	5
Harvey, Peninsula	.971	81	156	9	5	4
Headford, Hagerstown	.955	34	42	0	2	0
Hernandez, Kinston	.667	8	4	0	2	0
Herrick, Hagerstown	.990	54	94	5	1	0
Hollins, Alexandria	.936	22	27	2	2	1
Komminsk, Durham	.942	122	154	7	10	0
Kuvinka, Alex-Hag	.971	22	29	4	1	1

Player and Club	Pct.	G.	PO.	A.	E.	DP.
Lansford, Kinston	.923	20	23	1	2	2
Lebo, Kinston	1.000	7	15	0	0	0
Lee, Winston-Salem	.952	81	135	5	7	1
Lyons, Winston-Salem	.957	59	128	6	6	1
McGehee, Alexandria°	.936	72	155	6	11	0
Melendez, Peninsula°	1.000	5	8	0	0	0
Moore, Durham	.968	89	142	7	5	1
Murray, Salem	.960	132	251	16	11	5
Nichols, Hagerstown	.917	8	10	1	1	1
Norko, Kinston	.800	12	8	0	2	0
Palmer, Hagerstown	1.000	2	1	0	0	0
Pavlik, Hagerstown°	.964	70	152	9	6	0
Perez, Salem°	.928	60	71	6	6	1
Pruitt, Winston-Salem	.955	80	103	2	5	1
Quade, Alexandria	1.000	22	39	1	0	0
Rigby, Durham	1.000	1	1	0	0	0
Rivera, Peninsula	.961	106	166	7	7	1
Rodriguez, Alexandria	1.000	2	8	0	0	0
Rudd, Hag-Dur.	.967	85	112	5	4	3
Salava, Peninsula	.954	88	115	10	6	3
Sauer, Winston-Salem	1.000	6	1	0	0	0
Shepherd, Kinston	.960	134	280	9	12	3
Silverman, Kinston	.913	71	106	9	11	1
Stefero, Hagerstown	1.000	1	2	2	0	0
Stevens, Winston-Salem	1.000	1	7	1	0	0
Strawberry, Lynchburg°	.933	120	173	8	13	2
Sullivan, Winston-Salem	1.000	2	1	0	0	0
Sutton, Kinston	.960	118	207	7	9	2
Swoope, Alexandria	.800	10	8	0	2	0
Tarver, Lynchburg°	1.000	5	10	0	0	0
Teller, Winston-Salem	.958	38	45	1	2	1
Tyner, Hagerstown	.946	23	33	2	2	0
Washington, Peninsula	.966	53	112	2	4	0
Williams, Durham	.857	22	10	2	2	0

CATCHERS

Player and Club	Pct.	G.	PO.	A.	E.	DP.	PB.
Ackley, Winston-Salem	.958	3	21	2	1	0	0
Blanco, Alexandria	.900	4	16	2	2	0	3
Bockhorn, Durham	.978	71	491	50	12	4	18
Brummer, Winston-Salem	.992	23	117	11	1	0	4
Burton, Alexandria	.917	2	11	0	1	0	2
Duff, Lynchburg	.989	61	387	51	5	2	6
Ford, Alexandria	.979	27	163	24	4	1	13
Garnett, Alexandria°	1.000	1	5	2	0	0	0
Harrigan, Peninsula	.983	50	369	24	7	3	3
Hernandez, Kinston	.978	65	373	69	10	9	8
Huppert, Hagerstown	1.000	1	4	2	0	0	0
Jablonski, Alexandria	1.000	15	85	13	0	0	3
Kuvinka, Alexandria	.987	11	65	9	1	2	3
Lebo, Kinston	.967	53	279	44	11	2	11
Masterson, Alexandria	1.000	5	51	6	0	2	3
McClendon, Lynchburg	.972	71	433	58	14	2	17
Moreno, Salem	.979	7	37	9	1	1	2
Nichols, Hagerstown	.992	24	113	18	1	2	7

Player and Club	Pct.	G.	PO.	A.	E.	DP.	PB.
Palmer, Hagerstown	.990	29	188	18	2	3	2
Pardo, Hagerstown	.957	10	37	7	2	2	2
Parent, Salem	.965	119	694	87	28	16	16
Pruitt, Winston-Salem	.969	10	58	5	2	2	2
Pulley, Kinston	.990	44	248	38	3	2	9
Pustorino, Lynchburg	.992	21	107	13	1	3	7
Rodriguez, Alexandria	.978	80	519	63	13	8	21
Soreca, Peninsula	.995	22	164	24	1	4	4
Stefero, Hagerstown	.978	93	628	71	16	10	13
Stieb, Durham	.975	19	107	10	3	0	0
Styons, Salem	.985	22	119	16	2	2	3
SULLIVAN, Winston-Salem	.984	113	788	114	15	6	15
Swoope, Alexandria	1.000	2	9	0	0	0	1
Thompson, Durham	1.000	25	204	29	0	2	2
Ulrich, Peninsula	.980	23	135	15	3	2	5
Vuksan, Durham	.977	35	200	16	5	0	7
Willard, Peninsula	.991	50	319	28	3	3	8

Triple Play—Soreca.

PITCHERS

Player and Club	Pct.	G.	PO.	A.	E.	DP.
Adkins, Alexandria	.895	23	5	12	2	0
Anthony, Hagerstown	.968	14	12	18	1	3
Baker, Kinston	.912	15	7	24	3	1
Baller, Peninsula	.900	27	8	10	2	0
Baum, Winston-Salem	.813	29	6	7	3	1
Beckman, Kinston°	.800	19	0	4	1	0
Begue, Lynchburg	1.000	42	3	7	0	0
Behenna, Durham	.944	29	16	51	4	4
Bettendorf, Lynchburg	1.000	24	10	16	0	1
Bittiger, Lynchburg	1.000	24	3	20	0	0
Blanco, Alexandria	1.000	2	0	1	0	0
Bowlin, Winston-Salem°	.964	26	5	22	1	1
Boyd, Hagerstown°	1.000	4	0	1	0	0
Britt, Salem	.867	15	3	10	2	1
Brown, Hagerstown	.833	10	0	5	1	1
BROWN, Winston-Salem	1.000	21	11	25	0	1
Burke, Alexandria	.932	23	12	29	3	0
Carcella, Hagerstown	.500	3	0	1	1	0
Carter, Kinston	.905	27	10	28	4	2
Carvajal, Alexandria°	.857	16	0	6	1	0
Cepeda, Peninsula	.923	43	2	10	1	0
Clinton, Winston-Salem	.941	15	7	9	1	1
Coatney, Durham	1.000	11	1	4	0	0
Coffman, Salem	.958	55	11	12	1	4
Cyburt, Alexandria°	1.000	6	0	1	0	0
Dale, Winston-Salem	1.000	40	2	11	0	1
Decker, Peninsula	.909	55	4	6	1	2
Dedmon, Durham	.909	28	9	21	3	2
Dixon, Hagerstown	1.000	9	1	4	0	0
Dodd, Alexandria	.917	10	2	9	1	0
Downs, Peninsula	.889	25	11	13	3	1
Dunnegan, Alexandria	.957	26	15	29	2	2
Edwards, Hagerstown	.923	17	6	18	2	2
Faust, Lynchburg°	.947	52	5	13	1	0
Figueroa, Salem°	1.000	21	2	10	0	1
Flores, Kinston	.900	16	3	6	1	0
Ford, Kinston°	.997	29	13	30	1	1
Fuller, Durham	1.000	9	1	10	0	0
Garrett, Winston-Salem	.933	27	3	11	1	0
Gerhardt, Salem	.750	28	2	4	2	0
Gering, Winston-Salem	1.000	34	10	15	0	1
Germer, Durham	1.000	34	1	10	0	0
Gibson, Durham°	.952	46	5	15	1	0
Gill, Kinston	1.000	31	4	11	0	2
Gonzalez, Hagerstown°	1.000	12	1	9	0	0
Grubbs, Winston-Salem	.952	32	4	16	1	0
Hamner, Alexandria	1.000	31	7	13	0	0
Hill, Winston-Salem°	.889	23	1	7	1	0
Hoke, Hagerstown	.667	3	0	2	1	0
Hook, Hagerstown	.829	22	5	24	6	0
Howard, Kinston	.906	26	4	25	3	1
Huey, Hagerstown	.650	14	6	7	7	0
Hulbert, Winston-Salem	.667	11	1	1	1	0
Ibarguen, Lynchburg	.923	33	7	17	2	1
Johnson, Lynchburg°	.909	4	2	8	1	1
Johnson, Alexandria	.964	24	13	14	1	1
Johnson, Salem°	1.000	11	4	11	0	0
Jones, Hagerstown	1.000	7	1	0	0	0
Keenan, Alexandria	1.000	17	2	6	0	0
Kolbe, Lynchburg	1.000	6	1	2	0	0
Krawczyk, Alexandria	.700	8	2	5	3	0
Krzanik, Salem	.929	24	9	17	2	2
Kuntz, Lynchburg	.956	25	10	33	2	1

Player and Club	Pct.	G.	PO.	A.	E.	DP.
Lamson, Durham°	1.000	4	2	1	0	0
Leach, Hagerstown°	.765	25	2	11	4	0
Leal, Kinston	.929	33	7	19	2	0
Leggatt, Alexandria°	.920	31	8	15	2	1
Long, Salem	1.000	14	9	10	0	1
Lovekamp, Salem	.833	26	14	16	6	1
Lucia, Durham	1.000	12	0	6	0	0
Lukish, Kinston	.923	32	4	8	1	0
Malinski, Salem	1.000	39	2	8	0	0
Marston, Hagerstown	1.000	5	1	0	0	0
McCarthy, Winston-Salem	.926	28	8	17	2	0
McCullock, Alex-Hag	.867	38	3	10	2	1
Mecerod, Winston-Salem	.959	23	14	33	2	0
Minnick, Hagerstown°	.857	13	1	11	2	0
Mitchell, Peninsula	1.000	22	3	5	0	1
Money, Peninsula	.929	24	4	22	2	1
Moore, Hagerstown	1.000	19	3	15	0	1
Norris, Hagerstown	1.000	10	3	10	0	0
North, Durham	.958	23	9	14	1	1
Palmieri, Peninsula°	.917	28	10	23	3	3
Patterson, Durham	.933	13	4	10	1	0
Payne, Durham	.958	29	12	11	1	1
Pecka, Winston-Salem°	.929	35	2	11	1	0
Phillips, Kinston	.880	41	6	16	3	1
Powell, Alexandria°	1.000	8	0	2	0	0
Prior, Peninsula	1.000	28	0	11	0	0
Ramirez, Hagerstown	.333	5	0	1	2	0
Ray, Alexandria	.907	26	19	30	5	3
Rech, Lynchburg°	1.000	4	0	3	0	0
Reiter, Durham°	.938	41	3	12	1	1
Ricelli, Alexandria°	1.000	1	0	1	0	0
Richard, Peninsula°	.800	11	0	4	1	1
Rivera, Hagerstown	1.000	1	0	1	0	0
Rock, Alex-Hag	.867	19	3	10	2	1
Rodriguez, Lynchburg°	1.000	5	0	2	0	0
Romero, Peninsula	.667	17	1	3	2	0
Schefsky, Salem	.800	10	1	7	2	1
Shockley, Lynchburg	1.000	5	1	5	0	0
Sisk, Lynchburg	.905	36	6	13	2	2
Smith, Lynchburg	.850	28	6	11	3	2
Smith, Hagerstown	1.000	4	0	3	0	0
Smith, Durham	.955	23	4	17	1	1
Spicer, Lynchburg°	1.000	12	4	10	0	0
Stemberger, Kinston	.909	59	5	15	2	1
Stieb, Durham	1.000	5	2	2	0	2
Stone, Durham	.952	27	10	30	2	2
Sunderlage, Lynchburg°	1.000	10	1	6	0	1
Taylor, Alexandria	.714	19	2	3	2	0
Thibodeaux, Hagerstown	1.000	17	4	10	0	1
Thomas, Peninsula	.960	31	8	16	1	0
Thompkins, Durham	.000	10	0	0	1	0
Thompson, Hagerstown°	1.000	10	0	3	0	0
Tibbs, Lynchburg	.905	15	6	13	2	1
Tyler, Winston-Salem	1.000	20	3	4	0	1
Vaulman, Lynchburg°	1.000	14	0	4	0	0
Violette, Lynchburg	.929	28	7	6	1	0
Warner, Peninsula°	1.000	12	0	3	0	0
Williams, Salem°	.909	14	1	9	1	1
Wilson, Salem	.900	30	7	11	2	1
Wright, Hagerstown	.900	21	0	9	1	0
Wright, Kinston	.952	13	9	11	1	3
Zamba, Alexandria	.833	22	2	8	2	1
Zaske, Alexandria	.923	21	2	22	2	1

The following players had no recorded accepted chances at the positions indicated; therefore, are not listed in the fielding averages for those particular positions: Castro, of; Chamberlain, of; Chiti, p; Crawford, 2b; Dees, 2b; Greer, p; Hayes, of; Herrick, p; Mitchell, of; Quade, p; Sauer, p; Skinner, p; Silverman, 2b; W. Smith, p; Thompson, 2b; Ulrich, of; H. Williams, p; Wilmet, p.

CLUB PITCHING

Club	ERA.	G.	CG.	ShO.	Sv.	IP.	H.	R.	ER.	HR.	HB.	BB.	Int. BB.	SO.	WP.	Bk.
Peninsula	3.29	136	25	9	28	1150⅓	1008	538	421	92	59	478	18	963	65	10
Alexandria	3.84	137	31	6	18	1169	1036	610	499	85	37	612	25	908	86	9
Kinston	3.88	140	33	14	29	1184	1159	635	510	98	36	560	31	869	63	5
Durham	3.99	138	27	13	19	1187⅓	1139	655	526	109	48	545	20	996	95	10
Lynchburg	4.10	140	17	9	34	1193⅓	1196	680	544	102	43	574	37	904	96	9
Hagerstown	4.29	138	32	3	32	1166⅓	1112	716	556	113	42	689	46	940	61	15
Winston-Salem	4.45	139	32	12	21	1225⅓	1229	762	606	100	47	710	49	971	96	13
Salem	4.59	140	22	9	25	1189⅓	1359	796	606	135	33	514	32	799	85	18

PITCHERS' RECORDS
(Leading Qualifiers for Earned-Run Average Leadership—112 or More Innings)

°Throws lefthanded.

Pitcher—Club	W.	L.	Pct.	ERA.	G.	GS.	CG.	GF.	ShO.	Sv.	IP.	H.	R.	ER.	HR.	HB.	BB.	Int. BB.	SO.	WP.
Brown, Winston-Salem	14	4	.778	1.49	21	21	12	0	6	0	145	94	32	24	9	3	39	5	144	3
Thomas, Peninsula	8	2	.800	2.58	31	13	2	5	1	2	129	113	51	37	9	1	43	2	94	4
Hook, Hagerstown	10	6	.625	2.90	22	22	6	0	1	0	146	139	70	47	9	8	75	3	92	7
Downs, Peninsula	13	7	.650	2.98	25	25	9	0	2	0	175	176	79	58	16	3	35	0	124	8

Pitcher—Club	W.	L.	Pct.	ERA.	G.	GS.	CG.	GF.	ShO.	Sv.	IP.	H.	R.	ER.	HR.	HB.	BB.	Int. BB.	SO.	WP.
Kuntz, Lynchburg	9	9	.500	3.02	25	22	4	2	0	1	149	143	76	50	9	7	69	9	97	9
Ray, Alexandria	12	6	.667	3.09	26	26	7	0	2	0	169	117	72	58	11	4	88	2	135	13
Ford, Kinston°	12	10	.545	3.13	29	28	8	0	3	0	187	162	73	65	14	3	79	3	154	4
Palmieri, Peninsula°	8	8	.500	3.13	28	22	3	2	0	1	138	101	62	48	6	5	91	1	136	12
Mecerod, Winston-Salem	10	6	.625	3.15	23	23	8	0	2	0	157	142	79	55	8	5	64	2	110	12
Burke, Alexandria	8	10	.444	3.44	23	23	6	0	0	0	149	139	67	57	5	7	48	1	111	10

Departmental Leaders: G—Stemberger, 59; GS—Ford, 28; CG—Brown, 12; ShO—Brown, 6; W—Brown, 14; L—Carter, 15; Sv—Decker, 18; Pct.—Baker, .917; IP—Behenna, 196; H—Stone, 188; R—Carter, 108; ER—McCarthy, 85; HR—Stone, 20; BB—McCarthy, 99; IBB—Grubbs, 12; HB—Baller, 19; SO—Bittiger, 168; WP—Clinton, 22.

(All Pitchers—Listed Alphabetically)

Pitcher—Club	W.	L.	Pct.	ERA.	G.	GS.	CG.	GF.	ShO.	Sv.	IP.	H.	R.	ER.	HR.	HB.	BB.	Int. BB.	SO.	WP.
Acker, Alexandria°	0	2	.000	7.50	7	0	0	3	0	1	6	11	9	5	2	0	5	0	3	1
Adkins, Alexandria	3	8	.273	6.19	23	17	5	1	0	0	112	124	85	77	9	2	51	1	69	8
Anthony, Hagerstown	6	5	.545	4.19	14	14	4	0	0	0	88	99	55	41	10	0	32	1	52	4
Baker, Kinston	11	1	.917	2.46	15	14	6	0	1	0	95	72	31	26	3	2	36	1	87	4
Baller, Peninsula°	9	14	.391	3.92	27	27	6	0	1	0	147	119	85	64	14	19	78	0	166	15
Baum, Winston-Salem	5	5	.500	6.21	29	17	2	3	0	1	100	107	91	69	14	11	67	0	93	9
Beckman, Kinston	0	1	.000	7.20	19	0	0	12	0	1	20	32	24	16	2	3	13	1	15	6
Begue, Lynchburg	4	4	.500	2.64	42	0	0	29	0	7	58	46	23	17	6	6	15	2	54	4
Behenna, Durham	13	12	.520	3.63	29	27	9	2	2	1	196	182	92	79	19	12	76	0	162	6
Bettendorf, Lynchburg	10	9	.526	6.28	24	24	0	0	0	0	109	129	86	76	15	4	68	0	68	11
Bittiger, Lynchburg	11	7	.611	3.94	24	24	3	0	1	0	137	121	72	60	12	1	79	0	168	6
Blanco, Alexandria	0	0	.000	11.25	2	0	0	2	0	0	4	7	5	5	1	0	1	0	1	1
Bowlin, Winston-Salem°	7	8	.467	4.32	26	26	3	0	1	0	127	138	93	61	10	2	78	5	92	9
Boyd, Hagerstown°	1	0	1.000	1.13	4	0	0	3	0	1	8	9	3	1	0	0	0	0	3	0
Britt, Salem	2	8	.200	4.98	15	15	1	0	0	0	94	125	70	52	9	7	19	2	41	3
Brown, Hagerstown	1	0	1.000	2.14	10	0	0	3	0	0	21	19	7	5	1	1	8	2	16	1
Brown, Winston-Salem	14	4	.778	1.49	21	21	12	0	6	0	145	94	32	24	9	3	39	5	144	3
Burke, Alexandria	8	10	.444	3.44	23	23	6	0	0	0	149	139	67	57	5	7	48	1	111	10
Carcella, Hagerstown	0	1	.000	11.57	3	1	0	2	0	0	7	10	9	9	1	0	8	1	8	1
Carter, Kinston	7	15	.318	4.59	27	26	3	1	2	0	155	169	108	79	19	6	83	1	119	16
Carvajal, Alexandria	4	2	.667	2.25	16	0	0	10	0	2	32	28	10	8	2	0	10	1	23	1
Cepeda, Peninsula	3	3	.500	2.81	43	0	0	23	0	0	64	65	34	20	4	3	26	4	43	2
Chiti, Hagerstown°	0	2	.000	15.75	5	0	0	4	0	1	4	8	8	7	3	0	5	1	4	0
Clinton, Winston-Salem	4	6	.400	5.16	15	15	4	0	1	0	89	72	57	51	5	5	72	0	90	22
Coatney, Durham	0	1	.000	6.52	11	4	0	1	0	0	29	35	25	21	4	1	18	1	25	2
Coffman, Salem	10	6	.625	3.67	55	1	0	48	0	11	108	119	56	44	7	0	54	9	98	10
Cyburt, Alexandria	0	1	.000	5.14	6	1	0	3	0	0	7	6	4	4	0	0	7	0	6	1
Dale, Winston-Salem	4	6	.400	4.22	40	0	0	30	0	8	81	78	41	38	10	3	34	5	60	1
Decker, Peninsula	3	5	.375	2.09	55	0	0	49	0	18	82	50	24	19	4	5	36	8	108	4
Dedmon, Durham	7	8	.467	4.31	28	27	6	0	3	0	165	178	97	79	19	7	50	0	115	16
Dixon, Hagerstown	3	5	.375	2.91	9	9	5	0	1	0	65	44	25	21	5	1	30	1	73	3
Dodd, Alexandria	2	2	.500	5.54	10	7	2	1	0	0	39	24	27	24	0	0	51	0	37	8
Downs, Peninsula	13	7	.650	2.98	25	25	9	0	2	0	175	176	79	58	16	3	35	0	124	8
Dunnegan, Peninsula	10	13	.435	3.53	26	26	3	0	2	0	171	158	79	67	11	6	62	1	114	4
Edwards, Hagerstown	4	5	.444	3.46	17	14	2	3	1	2	91	97	56	35	7	1	48	3	58	2
Faust, Hagerstown°	1	3	.250	3.55	52	0	0	28	0	7	71	75	33	28	4	2	40	5	45	3
Figueroa, Salem°	1	5	.167	6.10	21	8	0	4	0	0	59	84	59	40	8	0	31	1	42	6
Flores, Kinston	3	5	.375	5.29	16	7	1	3	0	2	63	66	45	37	11	0	33	1	62	9
Ford, Kinston°	12	10	.545	3.13	29	28	8	0	3	0	187	162	73	65	14	3	79	3	154	4
Fuller, Durham	3	3	.500	4.14	9	8	0	0	0	0	50	53	29	23	5	3	16	0	27	3
Garrett, Winston-Salem	4	3	.571	4.00	27	2	0	13	0	3	54	69	30	24	2	3	21	0	27	6
Gerhardt, Salem	1	4	.200	5.74	28	2	0	13	0	1	69	78	50	44	16	1	26	3	49	6
Gering, Winston-Salem	9	6	.600	4.01	34	12	3	7	1	1	139	125	71	62	9	7	82	7	83	7
Germer, Durham	3	4	.429	3.98	34	0	0	23	0	4	43	36	23	19	4	4	37	6	39	12
Gibson, Durham°	9	7	.563	4.29	46	3	1	31	0	5	105	97	64	50	7	3	58	5	108	16
Gill, Kinston	1	2	.333	4.84	31	9	0	10	0	1	80	81	52	43	10	0	47	1	33	4
Gonzalez, Hagerstown°	5	5	.500	3.86	12	12	5	0	0	0	77	63	38	33	7	4	50	0	94	2
Greer, Salem	0	0	.000	0.00	1	0	0	1	0	0	1	1	2	0	0	0	3	0	1	0
Grubbs, Winston-Salem	5	4	.556	4.39	32	0	0	11	0	1	80	92	53	39	6	1	46	12	52	3
Hamner, Alexandria	6	4	.600	1.29	31	0	0	24	0	9	63	38	12	9	0	1	15	1	66	2
Herrick, Hagerstown	0	1	.000	9.00	3	0	0	3	0	0	3	8	3	3	0	0	1	0	1	0
Hill, Winston-Salem°	1	2	.333	9.18	23	4	0	10	0	0	49	86	56	50	9	0	47	4	29	7
Hoke, Hagerstown	0	1	.000	1.29	3	0	0	1	0	1	7	7	4	1	0	0	2	1	4	0
Hook, Hagerstown	10	6	.625	2.90	22	22	6	0	1	0	146	139	70	47	9	8	75	3	92	7
Howard, Kinston	4	9	.308	3.50	26	21	8	2	2	0	139	122	68	54	6	3	72	6	107	5
Huey, Hagerstown	2	5	.286	4.71	14	12	1	1	0	0	63	69	48	33	9	1	37	2	48	6
Hulbert, Winston-Salem	0	1	.000	4.50	11	0	0	4	0	0	14	5	11	7	1	1	20	3	17	2
Ibarguen, Lynchburg	7	3	.700	3.82	33	11	1	6	1	2	125	102	73	53	7	9	73	3	103	13
Johnson, Alexandria	8	9	.471	4.41	24	24	3	0	0	0	143	139	83	70	17	14	77	2	83	7
Johnson, Salem°	3	2	.600	4.59	11	6	1	0	1	0	51	61	32	26	3	2	16	3	40	1
Johnston, Lynchburg°	1	2	.333	3.24	4	4	0	0	0	0	25	26	13	9	2	0	12	1	21	1
Jones, Hagerstown	0	1	.000	11.57	7	0	0	4	0	1	7	10	10	9	1	1	7	0	4	1
Keenan, Alexandria	1	4	.200	2.33	17	0	0	10	0	1	27	19	8	7	0	0	20	5	33	2
Kolbe, Lynchburg	2	0	1.000	2.45	6	0	0	3	0	0	11	8	3	3	0	0	7	1	10	2
Krawczyk, Alexandria	2	4	.333	4.89	8	8	2	0	0	0	46	48	32	25	5	2	14	0	41	4
Krzanik, Salem	6	12	.333	3.99	24	22	7	1	2	0	149	148	89	66	12	3	48	2	98	9
Kuntz, Lynchburg	9	9	.500	3.02	25	22	4	2	0	1	149	143	76	50	9	7	69	9	97	9
Lamson, Durham°	0	0	.000	5.40	4	0	0	1	0	0	10	15	9	6	0	0	5	0	5	1
Leach, Hagerstown°	3	5	.375	4.13	25	10	2	9	0	2	96	73	55	44	15	2	60	0	76	3
Leal, Kinston	7	6	.538	4.63	33	11	3	4	1	0	105	105	66	54	12	2	62	3	67	2
Leggatt, Alexandria	3	3	.500	2.97	31	9	1	7	0	2	106	95	50	35	7	2	40	3	87	4
Long, Salem	9	2	.818	2.79	14	13	4	0	3	0	87	81	31	27	6	2	28	1	80	8
Lovekamp, Salem	10	9	.526	4.13	26	25	2	1	0	0	159	165	105	73	16	1	76	0	121	11
Lucia, Durham	2	3	.400	3.67	12	0	0	3	0	1	27	30	15	11	3	1	16	0	22	4
Lukish, Kinston	10	2	.833	1.87	32	0	0	24	0	11	53	46	15	11	3	3	17	3	50	1
Malinski, Salem	6	5	.545	4.96	39	0	0	31	0	8	69	97	59	38	12	2	22	6	27	1
Marston, Hagerstown	0	0	.000	21.60	5	0	0	1	0	1	5	12	13	12	3	2	6	0	4	0
McCarthy, Winston-Salem	3	7	.300	7.29	28	18	0	2	0	0	105	123	99	85	9	6	99	1	75	10

Pitcher—Club	W.	L.	Pct.	ERA.	G.	GS.	CG.	GF.	ShO.	Sv.	IP.	H.	R.	ER.	HR.	HB.	BB.	Int. BB.	SO.	WP.
McCullock, Alex-Hag	3	5	.375	4.71	38	0	0	24	0	1	65	68	40	34	6	2	32	3	38	1
Mecerod, Winston-Salem	10	6	.625	3.15	23	23	8	0	2	0	157	142	79	55	8	5	64	2	110	12
Minnick, Hagerstown°	3	6	.333	5.88	13	9	1	0	0	0	52	56	48	34	8	3	37	3	65	6
Mitchell, Peninsula	4	0	1.000	4.13	22	1	0	9	0	0	48	30	23	22	7	5	28	0	38	8
Money, Peninsula	6	7	.462	4.21	24	22	2	1	1	0	126	140	66	59	15	6	38	1	84	8
Moore, Hagerstown	4	2	.667	1.98	19	0	0	10	0	7	41	23	10	9	0	1	27	5	23	1
Norris, Hagerstown	7	1	.875	3.05	10	8	2	2	0	0	62	54	28	21	6	2	28	1	35	2
North, Durham	6	11	.353	4.71	23	23	0	0	0	0	126	127	89	66	16	3	64	0	105	11
Palmieri, Peninsula°	8	8	.500	3.13	28	22	3	2	0	1	138	101	62	48	6	5	91	1	136	12
Patterson, Durham	9	0	1.000	2.11	13	13	5	0	3	0	98	74	27	23	7	5	42	1	89	5
Payne, Durham	6	6	.500	5.23	29	17	2	4	0	1	105	107	76	61	12	2	65	0	84	5
Pecka, Winston-Salem°	3	5	.375	5.71	35	1	0	11	0	3	41	57	32	26	4	0	22	1	45	4
Phillips, Kinston	3	8	.273	3.86	41	14	2	12	0	4	126	138	70	54	9	6	36	1	70	6
Powell, Alexandria	0	1	.000	4.91	8	0	0	1	0	0	11	6	7	6	1	0	15	0	12	1
Prior, Peninsula	5	5	.500	3.57	28	0	0	16	0	7	53	39	27	21	2	5	29	1	43	0
Quade, Alexandria	0	0	.000	18.00	1	0	0	1	0	0	1	3	2	2	0	1	1	0	0	0
Ramirez, Hagerstown	2	1	.667	7.36	5	5	0	0	0	0	22	26	21	18	1	0	19	0	19	2
Ray, Alexandria	12	6	.667	3.09	26	26	7	0	2	0	169	117	72	58	11	4	88	2	135	13
Rech, Lynchburg°	1	3	.250	8.53	4	4	0	0	0	0	19	29	20	18	4	1	8	0	12	4
Reiter, Durham°	5	6	.455	3.60	41	5	0	22	0	3	100	88	56	40	7	1	60	6	98	3
Ricelli, Alexandria°	0	0	.000	27.00	1	0	0	0	0	0	1	3	3	3	0	0	4	0	3	0
Richard, Hagerstown°	0	1	.000	7.04	11	0	0	4	0	0	23	22	29	18	0	3	32	2	19	5
Rivera, Hagerstown	0	0	.000	0.00	1	0	0	1	0	0	2	3	0	0	0	0	2	0	1	0
Rock, Alex-Hag	3	5	.375	5.33	19	5	0	10	0	3	49	54	38	29	4	1	37	6	29	4
Rodriguez, Lynchburg°	1	1	.500	6.75	5	1	0	4	0	2	8	10	6	6	1	0	2	0	10	0
Romero, Hagerstown°	1	3	.250	2.48	17	0	0	17	0	10	29	18	9	8	1	1	15	3	32	1
Sauer, Winston-Salem	0	0	.000	6.00	1	0	0	1	0	0	3	6	2	2	2	0	1	0	2	0
Schefsky, Salem	4	4	.500	6.13	10	9	1	1	1	0	47	59	38	32	5	3	31	1	34	5
Shockley, Lynchburg	1	1	.500	4.32	5	4	0	1	0	0	25	29	14	12	5	0	3	0	20	4
Sisk, Lynchburg	3	2	.600	3.25	36	1	0	18	0	7	83	78	35	30	4	2	32	3	61	3
Skinner, Lynchburg	0	1	.000	4.50	3	1	0	1	0	0	6	2	4	3	0	0	10	0	4	4
Smith, Lynchburg	5	2	.714	2.36	28	0	0	18	0	5	61	59	25	16	1	3	26	2	41	5
Smith, Hagerstown	0	1	.000	6.50	4	4	0	0	0	0	18	18	13	13	2	1	12	0	8	0
Smith, Durham	7	7	.500	2.82	23	11	4	12	3	4	99	81	35	31	3	5	24	1	93	6
Smith, Salem	2	0	1.000	0.69	6	0	0	6	0	3	13	7	1	1	0	2	3	0	21	1
Spicer, Lynchburg	4	3	.571	4.05	12	12	2	0	1	0	60	54	32	27	6	4	41	1	41	10
Stemberger, Kinston	9	6	.600	3.99	59	0	0	39	0	9	88	94	48	39	6	5	36	7	64	2
Stieb, Durham	0	0	.000	3.60	5	0	0	4	0	0	10	13	4	4	1	0	2	0	5	0
Stone, Salem	11	9	.550	4.01	27	27	6	0	2	0	173	188	97	77	20	5	66	1	88	13
Sunderlage, Lynchburg°	0	3	.000	5.88	10	1	0	3	0	0	26	30	18	17	3	2	12	3	9	2
Taylor, Alexandria	3	2	.600	4.37	19	0	0	11	0	0	35	29	21	17	5	2	42	3	42	7
Thibodeaux, Hagerstown	7	4	.636	5.54	17	12	4	0	0	0	91	80	59	56	11	4	60	3	90	4
Thomas, Peninsula	8	2	.800	2.58	31	13	2	5	1	2	129	113	51	37	9	1	43	2	94	4
Thompkins, Durham	0	0	.000	4.09	10	0	0	6	0	0	22	20	11	10	2	1	9	1	18	5
Thompson, Hagerstown°	0	0	.000	2.25	10	0	0	8	0	1	16	14	6	4	1	0	6	1	19	0
Tibbs, Lynchburg	2	7	.222	6.88	15	15	1	0	0	0	72	89	65	55	11	0	34	1	41	6
Tyler, Winston-Salem	3	4	.429	2.79	20	0	0	15	0	4	42	35	15	13	2	0	18	4	52	1
Vaulman, Hagerstown°	4	0	1.000	2.17	14	0	0	10	0	2	29	29	11	7	1	0	11	1	19	3
Violette, Lynchburg	8	8	.500	3.79	28	16	6	8	0	2	126	139	70	53	11	2	36	5	67	9
Warner, Peninsula°	2	1	.667	3.18	12	0	0	6	0	0	17	17	8	6	4	1	12	0	13	0
Williams, Salem°	0	6	.000	6.40	14	9	0	3	0	0	45	56	44	32	5	3	27	1	26	4
Williams, Durham	0	0	.000	13.50	2	0	0	2	0	0	2	3	3	3	0	0	3	0	1	0
Wilmet, Lynchburg	1	1	.500	4.91	8	0	0	2	0	1	22	27	12	12	1	0	7	1	32	0
Wilson, Salem	1	2	.333	7.48	30	3	0	8	0	1	65	90	63	54	16	2	64	2	33	7
Wright, Hagerstown°	3	3	.500	6.23	21	2	0	8	0	2	39	36	31	27	5	4	34	5	49	4
Wright, Kinston	5	3	.625	3.95	13	10	2	0	2	0	73	72	35	32	3	3	46	3	41	4
Zamba, Alexandria	3	2	.600	1.91	22	2	2	9	1	0	47	39	18	10	5	1	19	3	38	2
Zaske, Alexandria	5	9	.357	4.42	21	19	3	1	1	0	110	105	64	54	11	0	72	1	75	10

BALKS—Hook, 4; Bowlin, Britt, Gerhardt, Krzanik, McCarthy, 3 each; Carvajal, Coffman, Dedmon, Downs, Gibson, Gonzalez, Grubbs, Long, Malinski, Mecerod, Minnick, Money, Palmieri, Patterson, Payne, Ray, Stemberger, Thomas, Tibbs, Violette, 2 each; Adkins, Behenna, Bettendorf, Brown, Carter, Dodd, Dunnegan, Faust, Figueroa, Fuller, Garrett, Hill, Howard, Huey, Ibarguen, M. Johnson, Jones, Leach, Leal, Lovekamp, Moore, Powell, Prior, Rech, Richard, Schefsky, Spicer, Taylor, Thibodeaux, Vaulman, 1 each.

COMBINATION SHUTOUTS—Johnson-Acker-Hamner, Leggatt-Hamner, Alexandria; Dedmon-Smith, Fuller-Reiter, Durham; Carter-Phillips-Gill, Ford-Stemberger, Ford-Stemberger-Beckman, Kinston; Bettendorf-Sisk-Faust, Bittiger-Faust, Bittiger-Sisk, Bittiger-Smith, Kuntz-Faust, Violette-Begue, Lynchburg; Money-Thomas, Money-Warner, Peninsula; Schefsky-Coffman, Salem; Bowlin-Tyler, Winston-Salem.

PERFECT GAME—Ibarguen, Lynchburg, defeated Alexandria, 10-0, August 15 (six innings).

Florida State League

CLASS A

CHAMPIONSHIP WINNERS IN PREVIOUS YEARS

1919—Sanford°	.605
Orlando°	.703
1920—Tampa	.654
Tampa	.722
1921—Orlando	.635
1922—St. Petersburg	.503
St. Petersburg	.618
1923—Orlando	.667
Orlando	.678
1924—Lakeland	.695
Lakeland	.683
1925—St. Petersburg	.667
Tampa†	.696
1926—Sanford	.647
Sanford	.623
1927—Orlando†	.600
Miami	.661
1928-35—Did not operate.	
1936—Gainesville	.542
St. Augustine (4th)†	.492
1937—Gainesville§	.616
1938—Leesburg	.626
Gainesville (2nd)‡	.615
1939—Sanford§	.787
1940—Daytona Beach	.619
Orlando (4th)‡	.507
1941—St. Augustine	.659
Leesburg (4th)‡	.488
1942-45—Did not operate.	
1946—Orlando§	.681
1947—St. Augustine	.625
Gainesville (2nd)‡	.584

1948—Orlando	.643
Daytona B'ch (2nd)‡	.616
1949—Gainesville	.635
St. Augustine (3rd)‡	.556
1950—Orlando	.629
DeLand (3rd)‡	.590
1951—DeLand§	.643
1952—DeLand x	.704
Palatka (3rd)‡	.569
1953—Daytona Beach†	.657
DeLand	.703
1954—Jacksonville Beach	.629
Lakeland†	.594
1955—Orlando	.671
Orlando	.643
1956—Cocoa	.614
Cocoa	.671
1957—Palatka	.629
Tampa†	.681
1958—St. Petersburg	.732
St. Petersburg	.681
1959—Tampa	.591
St. Petersburg†	.612
1960—Lakeland	.731
Palatka†	.614
1961—Tampa†	.710
Sarasota	.696
1962—Sarasota	.689
Fort Lauderdale†	.623
1963—Sarasota	.645
Sarasota	.667
1964—Fort Lauderdale†	.629
St. Petersburg	.594

1965—Fort Lauderdale	.627
Fort Lauderdale	.634
1966—Leesburg†	.781
St. Petersburg	.700
1967—St. Petersburg y	.691
Orlando	.638
1968—Miami	.613
Orlando z	.579
1969—Miami a	.606
Orlando	.606
1970—Miami b	.662
St. Petersburg	.600
1971—Miami b	.667
Daytona Beach	.586
1972—Miami c	.562
Daytona Beach	.606
1973—St. Petersburg d	.575
West Palm Beach	.580
1974—West Palm Beach d	.598
Ft. Lauderdale	.626
1975—St. Petersburg d	.652
Miami	.581
1976—Tampa	.559
Lakeland d	.536
1977—Lakeland d	.616
West Palm Beach	.583
1978—Lakeland	.565
Miami§	.539
1979—Ft. Lauderdale	.643
Winter Haven e	.577
1980—Daytona Beach	.628
Ft. Lauderdale d	.606

°Split-season playoff abandoned after each team won three games. †Won split-season playoff. ‡Won four-club playoff. §Won championship and four-club playoff. xWon both halves of split season.

yLeague divided into Eastern and Western divisions with split season. St. Petersburg and Orlando won both halves of split season; St. Petersburg won playoff.

zLeague divided into Eastern and Western divisions. Miami won regular-season pennant on basis of highest won-lost percentage. Orlando won four-club playoff involving first two teams in each division.

aLeague divided into Southern and Central divisions. Miami won playoff between division leaders. (NOTE—Pennant awarded to playoff winner in 1936.)

bLeague divided into Eastern and Western divisions. Miami won regular-season pennant on basis of highest won-loss percentage, and also won four-club playoff involving first two teams in each division.

cLeague divided into Eastern and Western divisions. Won four-club playoff involving first two teams in each division.

dLeague divided into Northern and Southern divisions. Won four-club playoff involving first two teams in each division.

eLeague divided into Northern and Southern divisions. Same two clubs won both halves; won playoffs.

STANDING OF CLUBS AT CLOSE OF FIRST HALF, JUNE 17

NORTHERN DIVISION

Club	W.	L.	T.	Pct.	G.B.
Tampa° (Reds)	44	26	0	.629	......
Lakeland° (Tigers)	43	27	0	.614	1
St. Petersburg (Cardinals)	33	36	0	.478	10½
Daytona Beach (Astros)	30	39	0	.435	13½
Winter Haven (Red Sox)	28	42	0	.400	16

SOUTHERN DIVISION

Club	W.	L.	T.	Pct.	G.B.
Fort Myers (Royals)	43	26	0	.623	......
Fort Lauderdale (Yankees)	40	30	0	.571	3½
West Palm Beach (Expos)	33	37	0	.471	10½
Miami (Orioles)	27	42	0	.391	16
Vero Beach (Dodgers)	27	43	0	.386	16½

°Tampa and Lakeland finished first half of split season tied for first place. Tampa defeated Lakeland in one-game playoff.

STANDING OF CLUBS AT CLOSE OF SECOND HALF, AUGUST 29

NORTHERN DIVISION

Club	W.	L.	T.	Pct.	G.B.
Daytona Beach (Astros)	38	28	0	.576	......
St. Petersburg (Cardinals)	36	27	0	.571	½
Tampa (Reds)	35	28	1	.556	1½
Winter Haven (Red Sox)	34	35	0	.493	5½
Lakeland (Tigers)	26	37	0	.413	10½

SOUTHERN DIVISION

Club	W.	L.	T.	Pct.	G.B.
Fort Lauderdale (Yankees)	41	23	0	.641	......
Vero Beach (Dodgers)	36	30	1	.545	6
West Palm Beach (Expos)	32	34	1	.485	10
Fort Myers (Royals)	29	32	1	.475	10½
Miami	17	50	0	.254	25½

COMPOSITE STANDING OF CLUBS AT CLOSE OF SEASON, AUGUST 29

Club	FtL.	Tam.	FtM.	St.P.	Lak.	Day.	WPB.	VeB.	WiH.	Mia.	W.	L.	T.	Pct.	G.B.
Fort Lauderdale (Yankees)	....	9	9	6	7	6	8	11	10	15	81	53	0	.604	......
Tampa (Reds)	3	....	3	11	13	9	9	9	13	9	79	54	1	.594	1½
Fort Myers (Royals)	9	4	....	7	6	6	13	8	8	11	72	58	1	.554	7
St. Petersburg (Cardinals)	4	9	4	....	9	12	8	6	7	10	69	63	0	.523	11
Lakeland (Tigers)	5	7	6	8	....	9	6	8	12	8	69	64	0	.519	11½
Daytona Beach (Astros)	4	10	6	8	9	....	6	8	10	7	68	67	0	.504	13½
West Palm Beach (Expos)	12	3	7	4	4	6	....	11	7	11	65	71	1	.478	17
Vero Beach (Dodgers)	9	2	12	5	4	4	7	....	7	13	63	73	1	.463	19
Winter Haven (Red Sox)	2	7	4	13	8	10	5	5	....	8	62	77	0	.446	21½
Miami (Orioles)	5	3	7	1	4	5	9	7	3	....	44	92	0	.324	38

Major league affiliations in parentheses.

Playoffs—Daytona Beach defeated Tampa, two games to none. Fort Myers defeated Fort Lauderdale, two games to none. Daytona Beach defeated Fort Myers, three games to one for League Championship.

Regular-Season Attendance—Daytona Beach, 70,194; Fort Lauderdale, 56,507; Fort Myers, 59,150; Lakeland, 43,490; Miami, 46,885; St. Petersburg, 116,477; Tampa, 61,758; Vero Beach, 91,732; West Palm Beach, 165,656; Winter Haven, 21,133. Total, 732,982. Playoffs, 5,399. No All-Star game.

Managers: Daytona Beach, Carlos Alfonso; Fort Lauderdale, Doug Holmquist; Fort Myers, Brian Murphy; Lakeland, Ted Brazell; Miami, Minnie Mendoza; Tampa, Jim Lett; Vero Beach, Stan Wasiak; West Palm Beach, Bob Bailey; Winter Haven, Rac Slider.

All-Star Team: 1B—Robert Gerris, Fort Myers; 2B—Paul Hundhammer, Winter Haven; 3B—Danilo Tartabull, Tampa; SS—Julio Beltran, Daytona; Utility—Rex Hudler, Fort Lauderdale; OF—Wallace Davis, Fort Myers; Bruce Fields, Lakeland; Edward Amelung, Vero Beach; Michael Young, Miami; C—Joel Lepel, West Palm Beach; Jeffrey Hall, Winter Haven; DH—Michael Brewer, Fort Myers; LHP—Kenneth Westray, West Palm Beach; Nicholas Fiorillo, Tampa; RHP—Albert Nipper, Winter Haven, Mark Williams, Lakeland; MVP—Danilo, Tartabull, Tampa; Manager of Year—Brian Murphy, Fort Myers.

(Compiled by Howe News Bureau, Boston, Mass.)

CLUB BATTING

Club	Pct.	G.	AB.	R.	OR.	H.	TB.	2B.	3B.	HR.	RBI.	GW.	SH.	SF.	HP.	BB.	Int. BB.	SO.	SB.	CS.	LOB.
Daytona Beach	.275	135	4252	644	584	1170	1573	172	42	49	547	56	31	43	44	474	30	740	226	80	899
Fort Lauderdale	.270	134	4208	579	421	1136	1518	160	42	46	519	46	60	44	53	553	41	581	80	45	1041
Vero Beach	.263	137	4510	597	695	1184	1516	143	60	23	504	48	49	46	21	524	34	702	149	69	1004
St. Petersburg	.257	132	4123	554	535	1058	1395	149	43	34	486	54	57	36	34	486	37	601	106	47	945
West Palm Beach	.256	137	4414	555	602	1128	1550	149	30	71	470	46	35	28	28	498	29	652	129	68	981
Tampa	.256	134	4190	576	522	1073	1466	167	59	36	490	64	71	41	32	523	42	833	110	48	970
Fort Myers	.256	131	4173	574	501	1067	1479	152	43	58	489	61	45	50	21	526	31	712	145	32	981
Lakeland	.254	133	4235	560	530	1077	1525	178	39	64	490	64	43	34	19	533	26	846	93	56	977
Winter Haven	.249	139	4568	585	636	1137	1457	165	31	31	501	46	67	56	31	649	43	814	138	58	1165
Miami	.244	136	4284	495	693	1044	1348	146	46	22	425	39	36	34	17	501	30	738	174	52	949

INDIVIDUAL BATTING
(Leading Qualifiers for Batting Championship—378 or More Plate Appearances)

°Bats lefthanded.   †Switch-hitter.

Player and Club	Pct.	G.	AB.	R.	H.	TB.	2B.	3B.	HR.	RBI.	GW.	SH.	SF.	HP.	BB.	Int. BB.	SO.	SB.	CS.
Tartabull, Danilo, Tampa	.310	127	422	86	131	221	28	10	14	81	10	3	4	2	90	8	77	11	6
Ferris, Robert, Fort Myers	.301	105	346	62	104	171	21	2	14	66	8	1	6	1	68	6	81	2	2
Davis, Wallace, Fort Myers	.300	126	464	89	139	215	17	10	13	70	9	1	5	3	54	2	99	44	3
Gayden, Huey, Fort Lauderdale°	.300	121	414	61	124	134	8	1	0	38	3	8	4	5	55	3	25	12	8
Amelung, Edward, Vero Beach°	.297	136	522	84	155	224	17	14	8	75	4	1	7	0	56	12	51	22	6
Fields, Bruce, Lakeland°	.297	103	377	54	112	135	14	3	1	37	7	3	0	3	49	4	54	29	15
Clements, Wesley, Daytona	.296	129	415	72	123	204	20	2	19	83	14	1	6	4	69	6	106	6	5
Cruz, Jose, West Palm Beach°	.296	109	351	45	104	138	14	7	2	38	3	1	5	5	38	5	28	9	7
Hall, Jeffrey, Winter Haven	.295	123	508	43	150	211	27	2	10	84	3	1	4	0	14	2	87	1	1
Hundhammer, Paul, Winter Haven†	.292	103	390	66	114	160	22	6	4	56	9	7	2	3	76	1	58	13	10

Departmental Leaders: G—Amelung, 136; AB—Amelung, 522; R—Davis, 89; H—Amelung, 155; TB—Amelung, 224; 2B—Tartabull, 28; 3B—Amelung, 14; HR—Clements, 19; RBI—Brewer, Hall, 84; GWRBI—Clements, 14; SH—Duncan, 16; SF—Salas, Zell, 10; BB—Dodson, 95; HP—Robles, 13; SO—Pratt, Rollin, 121; SB—Beltran, 69; CS—Beltran, 20.

(All Players—Listed Alphabetically)

Player and Club	Pct.	G.	AB.	R.	H.	TB.	2B.	3B.	HR.	RBI.	GW.	SH.	SF.	HP.	BB.	Int. BB.	SO.	SB.	CS.
Adduci, James, St. Petersburg°	.271	92	321	44	87	134	12	7	7	45	4	1	3	2	46	6	78	4	3
Albano, Ralph, Miami†	.140	31	93	7	13	16	1	1	0	5	0	1	1	0	5	0	29	0	0
Amelung, Edward, Vero Beach°	.297	136	522	84	155	224	17	14	8	75	4	1	7	0	56	12	51	22	6
Anderson, David, Vero Beach	.270	65	200	44	54	64	8	1	0	18	1	6	3	1	49	0	34	15	2
Auten, James, West Palm Beach	.260	120	408	43	106	139	15	0	6	46	7	4	3	3	35	3	55	4	4
Ayer, Jonathon, St. Petersburg	.249	125	406	60	101	140	13	4	6	43	6	5	2	4	47	6	44	9	2
Banes, David, Fort Lauderdale	.268	112	365	50	98	142	20	3	6	49	2	5	4	3	29	4	70	6	2
Bard, Paul, Vero Beach	.237	89	278	34	66	91	17	4	0	32	3	3	2	4	23	0	68	1	2
Barker, Stanley, Lakeland°	.184	23	76	7	14	21	2	1	1	6	0	1	2	0	5	0	18	2	0
Bass, Fredrick, Vero Beach	.233	26	86	7	20	24	4	0	0	15	3	0	2	2	2	0	9	1	0
Batter, Ronald, Ft. Myers-WPB	.201	58	134	20	27	29	0	1	0	5	0	3	0	0	32	1	30	3	0
Beltran, Julio, Daytona Beach	.273	103	366	58	100	117	6	4	1	33	2	1	2	5	44	2	56	69	20
Bendorf, Jerry, Vero Beach	.345	25	84	11	29	32	3	0	0	11	1	4	1	2	7	0	8	2	4
Bennett, Brad, Fort Lauderdale°	.214	97	281	45	60	73	7	3	0	19	0	1	1	1	39	5	36	10	5
Boddy, William, Tampa	.326	36	86	15	28	32	2	1	0	10	2	3	1	0	18	1	10	3	0
Boncore, Steven, Vero Beach	.209	29	86	10	18	19	1	0	0	8	0	1	1	1	21	0	16	0	0
Borges, George, West Palm Beach	.283	41	92	9	26	36	4	3	0	8	0	0	1	1	4	1	8	0	1
Bowman, Bruss, Miami°	.148	7	27	1	4	5	1	0	0	1	0	0	0	0	5	0	8	2	0
Bream, Sidney, Vero Beach°	.327	70	260	35	85	110	12	5	1	47	7	2	3	0	31	4	31	0	5
Brewer, Michael, Fort Myers	.288	128	459	69	132	214	16	9	16	84	10	0	8	2	53	10	68	37	3
Brown, Mark, Miami†	.000	17	3	0	0	0	0	0	0	0	0	0	0	0	0	0	2	0	0
Bryant, Michael, Winter Haven	.210	67	224	26	47	62	7	1	2	19	2	1	5	2	25	0	54	3	2
Buckle, Larry, Tampa	.147	4	7	1	1	1	0	0	0	1	0	0	0	0	0	0	1	0	0
Buffamoyer, David, Fort Lauderdale	.244	62	160	14	39	49	7	0	1	20	1	0	3	4	26	1	23	1	0
Bullock, Eric, Daytona Beach°	.500	1	2	1	1	2	1	0	0	1	0	0	0	0	1	0	0	0	0
Bustabad, Juan, Winter Haven°	.286	44	175	30	50	57	5	1	0	10	0	3	1	0	21	1	22	11	4
Butterfield, Brian, Fort Lauderdale	.286	94	259	31	74	85	7	2	0	27	2	8	1	1	28	0	28	3	3
Campbell, R. Thomas, Lakeland	.182	7	11	1	2	2	0	0	0	1	0	0	1	0	4	0	1	0	0

Player and Club	Pct.	G.	AB.	R.	H.	TB.	2B.	3B.	HR.	RBI.	GW.	SH.	SF.	HP.	BB.	Int. BB.	SO.	SB.	CS.
Carl, Jeffrey, West Palm Beach	.284	66	243	36	69	116	11	3	10	33	6	0	0	0	31	2	76	4	2
Carrasquel, Emilio, Lakeland	.257	54	187	26	48	59	11	0	0	18	2	3	0	0	18	3	29	0	0
Carroll, Michael, West Palm Beach	.229	65	192	29	44	54	5	1	1	11	0	4	1	1	23	0	32	8	2
Chaney, Bruce, Lakeland	.253	58	170	18	43	53	6	2	0	12	1	7	1	0	15	0	31	12	4
Chinn, Greg, Vero Beach	.189	26	53	6	10	14	1	0	1	7	0	0	1	0	18	0	14	1	0
Ciampa, Michael, Winter Haven°	.255	114	423	74	108	126	11	2	1	35	2	7	1	1	61	10	36	40	13
Cicatiello, Gary, St. Petersburg°	.294	6	17	2	5	7	0	1	0	2	0	1	0	0	2	0	0	0	0
Clements, Wesley, Daytona Beach	.296	129	415	72	123	204	20	2	19	83	14	1	6	4	69	6	106	6	5
Cole, Donald, Miami	.000	17	0	1	0	0	0	0	0	0	0	0	0	0	0	0	0	0	0
Craig, Randall, Fort Lauderdale†	.289	114	349	45	101	137	12	6	4	52	6	1	7	7	50	2	61	6	1
Cruz, Jose, West Palm Beach°	.296	109	351	45	104	138	14	7	2	38	3	1	5	5	38	5	28	9	7
Csefalvay, John, Daytona Beach°	.322	71	242	42	78	118	17	4	5	40	5	2	3	2	29	3	34	10	1
Cusack, David, Miami	.234	54	167	18	39	59	10	2	2	25	3	0	3	3	34	1	33	4	2
D'Aloia, James, Fort Lauderdale	.143	18	21	4	3	3	0	0	0	0	0	1	0	1	1	0	1	0	1
D'Onofrio, Gary, Daytona Beach	.230	115	366	49	84	111	16	1	3	44	4	6	5	6	53	3	42	4	6
Davis, Wallace, Fort Myers	.300	126	464	89	139	215	17	10	13	70	9	1	5	3	54	2	99	44	3
Dawes, Steven, West Palm Beach	.182	18	55	3	10	10	0	0	0	4	0	2	0	0	5	1	4	0	0
Deaza, Manuel, Fort Myers	.233	90	318	26	74	82	8	0	0	19	1	1	1	1	7	0	51	8	3
Debus, Jon, Vero Beach	.242	121	425	50	103	141	19	5	3	54	2	1	5	2	47	1	86	5	3
Dees, Gregory, Miami°	.271	46	170	16	46	56	8	1	0	18	1	2	0	0	18	2	48	2	1
DeJesus, Alex, West Palm Beach	.186	14	43	2	8	8	0	0	0	1	0	0	1	0	4	0	7	0	0
DeJiulio, Frank, Tampa°	.235	42	17	3	4	5	1	0	0	0	0	2	0	0	3	0	4	0	0
DeLeon, John, Miami	.210	66	181	19	38	51	5	1	2	14	1	0	1	1	23	0	68	8	1
Del Monte, John, St. Petersburg°	.243	33	103	18	25	32	2	1	1	12	3	3	0	0	16	0	17	2	1
DeSanto, Thomas, Winter Haven	.000	20	0	1	0	0	0	0	0	0	0	0	0	0	0	0	0	0	0
Dewey, Duane, Fort Myers	.231	87	238	29	55	73	6	3	2	32	4	5	2	3	39	0	65	5	4
Dillard, Ronald, Miami	.255	82	322	50	82	95	3	5	0	23	0	6	2	2	38	3	43	40	8
Doak, Leon, Fort Myers	.212	62	184	25	39	61	5	4	3	33	4	5	7	2	31	0	50	5	1
Dodd, Thomas, Fort Lauderdale	.240	12	25	5	6	9	0	0	1	1	0	0	0	1	9	0	10	2	1
Dodson, Patrick, Winter Haven°	.252	127	413	54	104	139	17	3	4	42	4	0	5	0	95	10	118	2	1
Doerrer, Robert, West Palm Beach	.194	64	170	15	33	37	4	0	0	2	0	2	0	3	19	0	29	7	0
Dummar, George, Miami°	.206	21	63	3	13	13	0	0	0	8	0	0	1	1	6	0	16	0	0
Dumouchelle, Patrick, Miami	.250	127	424	56	106	150	18	7	4	61	2	0	8	1	58	1	54	13	5
Duncan, Timothy, West Palm Beach	.198	112	374	36	74	75	1	0	0	21	3	16	4	3	37	1	65	12	6
Eldridge, Terry, West Palm Beach°	.152	32	46	6	7	8	1	0	0	5	0	0	0	8	1	5	1	1	1
Ferris, Robert, Fort Myers	.301	105	346	62	104	171	21	2	14	66	8	1	6	1	68	6	81	2	2
Fields, Bruce, Lakeland°	.297	103	377	54	112	135	14	3	1	37	7	3	0	3	49	4	54	29	15
Filkins, Randy, Fort Lauderdale	.200	6	10	2	2	3	1	0	0	3	0	0	0	0	5	0	5	0	0
Fiorillo, Nicholas, Tampa°	.159	22	44	2	7	8	1	0	0	3	1	4	0	0	3	0	8	0	0
Fisher, Keith, Lakeland	.200	25	80	4	16	16	0	0	0	4	0	3	0	0	7	0	12	1	0
Foote, Michael, Tampa	.252	68	246	42	62	80	11	2	1	18	2	5	0	1	42	0	65	5	1
Foussianes, George, Lakeland	.245	120	376	66	92	154	19	5	11	46	10	3	1	4	81	2	87	3	4
Freeman, Clements, Tampa°	.167	25	6	0	1	1	0	0	0	0	0	1	0	0	0	0	2	0	0
Fuentes, Michael, West Palm Beach	.291	67	223	43	65	118	6	1	15	45	5	2	3	1	38	2	57	6	2
Gainey, Telmanch, Daytona Beach	.248	114	347	40	86	131	11	8	6	38	4	3	2	3	35	2	111	41	7
Gaunce, David, Fort Myers	.125	9	16	1	2	2	0	0	0	1	0	1	0	1	4	0	5	0	0
Gayden, Huey, Fort Lauderdale°	.300	121	414	61	124	134	8	1	0	38	3	8	4	5	55	3	25	12	8
Geren, Robert, St. Petersburg	.222	64	167	15	37	48	9	1	0	13	1	2	1	0	13	0	32	0	2
Gleissner, James, Fort Myers	.143	3	7	0	1	2	1	0	0	1	0	0	0	0	0	0	0	0	0
Glenn, James, Winter Haven	.264	125	447	67	118	139	12	3	1	50	8	6	6	6	78	4	64	44	11
Gloyd, Timothy, West Palm Beach	.282	49	177	28	50	62	7	1	1	15	2	1	2	0	24	0	35	22	10
Goldetsky, Larry, West Palm Beach	.167	14	18	0	3	3	0	0	0	4	1	1	1	0	5	0	5	0	0
Gonzales, Jose, St. Petersburg	.268	128	463	54	124	143	15	2	0	40	4	6	0	3	24	0	69	12	11
Good, James, Lakeland	.214	41	126	14	27	40	8	1	1	10	0	2	0	0	4	0	32	0	0
Granger, L. Randall, Miami	.313	40	144	25	45	56	7	2	0	18	1	1	1	0	21	1	23	21	0
Griggs, David, Miami†	.260	18	50	6	13	16	3	0	0	6	0	1	0	0	12	0	8	0	0
Guerra, Randall, Fort Lauderdale°	.267	82	255	29	68	100	12	1	6	44	4	1	6	1	47	5	32	0	0
Gutierrez, Felipe, Vero Beach	.203	17	59	7	12	14	2	0	0	2	0	2	0	0	1	0	10	0	0
Guzman, Hector, Vero Beach†	.082	26	61	8	5	5	0	0	0	2	1	2	1	0	5	0	13	1	1
Guzman, Ruben, Tampa	.272	118	390	58	106	144	16	5	4	38	8	4	4	6	19	1	75	19	9
Hall, Jeffrey, Winter Haven	.295	123	508	43	150	211	27	2	10	84	3	1	4	0	14	2	87	1	1
Hanggie, Daniel, Fort Lauderdale†	.263	28	80	10	21	31	2	1	2	5	1	1	0	0	16	5	10	0	0
Hardy, William C., Lakeland	.307	86	303	45	93	118	12	5	1	31	5	3	3	1	24	2	21	11	10
Harvey, Randall, Lakeland°	.273	125	433	54	118	180	21	4	11	66	11	1	4	1	56	2	102	2	4
Hastings, Joseph, Lakeland	.150	6	20	2	3	3	0	0	0	0	0	0	0	0	3	0	5	0	0
Hayes, Ben, Tampa	.000	32	6	0	0	0	0	0	0	1	0	1	0	0	1	0	2	0	1
Hench, R. William, Fort Lauderdale	.280	94	318	45	89	118	18	1	3	39	6	12	1	1	26	2	31	4	3
Herrick, Neal, Miami	.201	57	174	24	35	45	3	2	1	10	0	3	1	1	24	0	37	5	1
Hibner, David, Lakeland	.188	65	176	24	33	63	5	2	7	21	3	0	0	3	25	0	89	4	0
Hicks, Robert, St. Petersburg	.148	20	54	9	8	11	0	0	1	7	0	0	1	5	0	0	19	1	1
Hinson, Gary, Lakeland	.238	89	324	42	77	105	17	1	3	33	2	8	3	0	56	2	56	9	4
Hoeksema, David, West Palm Beach	.218	97	317	35	69	102	14	5	3	35	4	4	4	1	29	1	29	4	3
Holt, David, Winter Haven°	.269	62	208	24	56	71	12	0	1	25	3	4	1	2	31	4	32	2	0
Horn, Byron, Lakeland°	.255	40	110	25	28	35	3	2	0	4	0	1	0	0	23	1	6	5	3
Houston, Kevin, Daytona Beach°	.250	108	364	51	91	125	11	7	3	47	7	1	2	2	25	2	75	17	11
Howard, David, Tampa	.286	79	234	35	67	93	9	4	3	25	1	1	2	2	30	0	53	12	4
Howser, Thomas, Fort Lauderdale	.167	9	6	4	1	1	0	0	0	0	0	0	0	0	0	0	3	0	0
Hubert, Guy, Lakeland	.179	14	28	3	5	5	0	0	0	2	0	0	0	0	2	0	4	0	0
Hudler, Rex, Fort Lauderdale	.297	79	259	35	77	96	11	1	2	26	1	3	1	3	13	0	31	6	5
Hundhammer, Paul, Winter Haven†	.292	103	390	66	114	160	22	6	4	56	9	7	2	3	76	3	58	13	10
Ivie, Lonnie, Miami	.210	40	105	7	22	25	3	0	0	7	1	4	0	1	7	0	16	5	1
Jefferson, Michael, West Haven	.167	26	96	10	16	18	2	0	0	0	0	0	0	0	7	0	21	2	1
Johnson, Rodney, Tampa	.217	93	203	22	44	54	4	3	0	18	3	9	3	4	51	2	16	5	1
Johnson, Rondin, Fort Myers°	.217	107	424	49	92	114	16	3	0	29	5	7	3	1	28	2	62	16	5
Jordan, Timothy, Fort Lauderdale°	.323	20	62	11	20	28	2	3	0	10	1	0	1	0	8	0	6	1	1
Kenyon, Robert, Vero Beach	.000	26	0	0	0	0	0	0	0	0	0	0	0	0	0	0	0	1	0
Kirsch, Paul, Tampa°	.257	126	443	46	114	130	12	2	0	52	4	5	4	1	42	3	27	14	3
Klosicki, Daniel, Tampa	.125	45	24	6	3	4	1	0	0	1	0	2	0	0	2	0	7	0	0
Knight, Timothy, Fort Lauderdale°	.270	82	241	35	65	95	8	5	4	37	3	2	4	4	28	2	42	5	3
Kripner, Michael, Tampa	.226	106	328	37	74	103	13	5	2	39	8	4	4	4	42	2	92	6	5
Labastidas, Mario, Miami	.188	44	144	8	27	29	2	0	0	11	1	1	0	0	5	0	15	2	0
Lachowetz, Anthony, Vero Beach	.179	30	95	13	17	21	4	0	0	10	1	1	3	1	21	1	28	2	2

Player and Club	Pct.	G.	AB.	R.	H.	TB.	2B.	3B.	HR.	RBI.	GW.	SH.	SF.	HP.	BB.	Int. BB.	SO.	SB.	CS.
Landrum, T. William, Tampa	.160	17	25	2	4	4	0	0	0	0	0	2	0	0	2	0	7	0	0
Lanning, David, Vero Beach°	.237	63	207	19	49	56	3	2	0	16	0	1	1	1	29	2	17	2	6
Leach, Don, Winter Haven	.221	69	195	27	43	56	4	3	1	17	2	3	3	6	41	2	60	1	0
Lepel, Joel, West Palm Beach°	.281	115	360	45	101	144	19	0	8	39	0	0	3	3	51	3	29	1	4
Leppert, Stephen, Tampa†	.260	110	339	54	88	100	8	2	0	20	2	7	2	3	48	10	67	8	5
Lindberg, Ronald, Lakeland	.222	110	342	47	76	104	17	1	3	34	2	4	4	2	57	3	56	5	4
Little, Ronald, Tampa°	.262	133	458	58	120	168	20	11	2	59	9	2	7	1	30	5	102	14	7
Lochner, David, Tampa°	.256	21	43	3	11	11	0	0	0	5	0	1	1	0	3	0	8	0	0
Luethy, David, Fort Myers	.194	39	98	14	19	31	7	1	1	7	2	1	1	1	20	0	16	0	0
Malespin, Gustavo, Winter Haven	.212	108	363	40	77	102	11	1	4	48	3	9	8	0	49	1	38	1	0
Mann, Leon, Vero Beach	.212	81	274	31	58	73	7	4	0	17	2	6	3	0	27	0	38	10	4
Marchand, Rene, West Palm Beach	.333	2	3	0	1	1	0	0	0	0	0	0	0	0	0	0	0	0	0
Mariano, Robert, Fort Lauderdale°	.300	63	200	29	60	79	13	0	2	22	3	3	2	2	32	0	21	1	1
Martin, Jeffrey, Winter Haven	.226	78	279	24	63	85	12	2	2	33	6	7	2	4	40	2	52	2	2
Martin, R. Hollis, Vero Beach	.201	59	149	17	30	33	3	0	0	10	3	6	2	0	12	0	39	2	4
Mastro, Steven, Lakeland†	.157	18	51	3	8	8	0	0	0	4	0	0	1	0	11	1	8	0	2
Matzen, Mark, Tampa	.294	16	34	5	10	11	1	0	0	4	0	0	0	1	6	1	7	0	0
McCauley, Stanley, St. Petersburg	.251	52	171	19	43	60	11	3	0	23	1	1	2	1	24	1	25	0	1
McCorkle, Robert, Daytona Beach	.222	5	9	0	2	3	1	0	0	3	0	0	0	0	1	0	4	0	0
McDaniel, Kevin, West Palm Beach	.000	5	2	1	0	0	0	0	0	0	0	0	0	0	0	0	0	0	0
McKnight, James, Daytona Beach	.295	100	292	35	86	96	8	1	0	32	1	3	3	1	15	1	20	7	7
Medina, Valentin, Daytona Beach	.383	47	149	30	57	78	12	3	1	28	0	2	1	2	10	0	29	11	2
Miller, David, Miami†	.138	28	87	9	12	17	2	0	1	4	0	0	0	0	10	0	23	1	0
Miller, Lemmie, Vero Beach	.326	68	270	52	88	113	10	3	3	35	6	2	0	1	30	1	34	30	11
Mizerock, John, Daytona Beach°	.220	92	304	36	67	81	11	0	1	42	8	0	4	1	41	6	42	3	3
Moore, Donald, St. Petersburg†	.265	80	283	35	75	117	18	3	6	55	8	0	6	1	36	3	28	0	0
Moore, Mark, Tampa†	.111	51	9	3	1	1	0	0	0	1	0	0	0	0	4	0	3	0	0
Murelli, Donald, Miami	.282	20	71	9	20	24	2	1	0	9	3	0	0	0	5	0	10	2	0
Murphy, Robert, Tampa°	.100	25	30	3	3	3	0	0	0	2	0	4	0	0	8	0	15	1	0
Nealeigh, Rodney, WP Beach°	.277	131	470	58	130	154	11	2	3	41	5	6	3	4	49	1	31	20	9
Nichols, Carl, Miami	.194	16	31	1	6	6	0	0	0	3	0	1	1	0	3	0	5	0	0
Nieves, Tito, West Palm Beach	.279	80	165	36	46	62	5	1	3	16	1	1	0	1	36	0	35	6	6
Palmer, Michael, Fort Myers	.251	99	319	49	80	109	15	4	2	32	3	3	5	3	44	6	55	5	2
Pardo, Alberto, Miami†	.216	91	291	25	63	87	9	3	3	32	4	6	3	0	35	5	45	2	1
Patterson, Steven, Fort Myers	.288	92	309	42	89	106	8	0	3	32	5	4	4	0	47	0	46	3	2
Pellack, James, West Palm Beach°	.273	120	392	52	107	152	12	3	9	54	4	3	0	1	55	7	67	17	4
Peralta, Luis, Miami	.000	17	1	0	0	0	0	0	0	0	0	0	0	0	0	0	0	0	0
Pettibone, James, Tampa	.083	25	36	3	3	3	0	0	0	1	0	3	0	1	2	0	14	0	0
Phillip, Daniel, Lakeland°	.212	20	52	4	11	15	1	0	1	6	0	0	0	0	5	0	8	0	2
Porter, Denny, Fort Myers°	.289	30	83	14	24	31	2	1	1	7	1	0	2	0	14	0	14	0	0
Portes, Carlos, Tampa	.179	24	56	2	10	14	2	1	0	4	0	0	0	2	1	5	2	1	
Pratt, Crestwell, Tampa	.283	122	410	62	116	187	23	9	10	81	11	1	7	3	54	4	121	6	3
Proulx, Patrick, St. Petersburg	.252	81	238	36	60	65	5	0	0	27	4	5	1	2	35	0	32	4	1
Quinones, Rene, West Palm Beach†	.244	111	328	25	80	93	11	1	0	35	3	2	2	1	13	0	47	6	5
Raimondo, Pasquale, Vero Beach	.395	19	81	13	32	37	3	1	0	10	1	0	0	1	4	0	6	6	0
Ramos, Wolfgangh, Winter Haven	.205	26	88	8	18	20	2	0	0	10	1	3	2	0	12	1	17	1	1
Reyes, Gilberto, Vero Beach	.207	21	58	3	12	18	3	0	1	6	0	0	1	0	4	0	20	0	0
Reynolds, Robert, Vero Beach	.277	132	502	62	139	176	9	11	2	49	5	3	5	0	44	3	77	32	9
Riche, Timothy, Miami°	.202	25	84	9	17	19	2	0	0	2	0	0	0	0	6	0	11	2	5
Rincones, Hector, Tampa	.211	62	194	15	41	50	7	1	0	21	3	2	2	3	12	3	23	2	1
Robbins, Wesley, Fort Lauderdale	.361	32	97	18	35	54	7	3	2	14	2	2	1	3	9	1	11	7	3
Roberson, Eli, Lakeland	.000	6	14	1	0	0	0	0	0	0	0	0	0	0	0	0	2	0	0
Robinson, Bruce, Fort Lauderdale°	.333	5	21	4	7	10	0	0	1	4	0	0	0	0	2	0	1	0	0
Robles, Ruben, Daytona Beach	.283	109	339	60	96	127	12	2	5	39	2	4	3	13	23	1	86	10	6
Roeder, Stephen, West Palm Beach	.183	37	104	13	19	26	2	1	1	7	1	1	0	0	7	0	29	12	3
Rollin, Rondal, Lakeland	.268	107	370	51	99	169	16	6	14	55	6	0	2	1	25	2	121	4	1
Roman, Luis, St. Petersburg°	.316	43	158	27	50	62	2	5	0	12	1	4	1	0	18	3	15	6	3
Rudolph, Jeffrey, Fort Lauderdale	.238	66	122	23	29	47	6	0	4	20	2	2	0	1	23	0	37	1	2
Russell, Jeffrey, Tampa	.212	22	52	2	11	18	5	1	0	3	0	3	0	0	2	0	11	0	0
Sadey, Richard, Miami	.183	37	93	7	17	20	1	1	0	7	1	1	0	2	17	0	30	0	2
Salas, Mark, St. Petersburg°	.243	100	321	26	78	97	9	2	2	52	5	5	10	1	23	4	25	9	4
Sanchez, Jose, St. Petersburg	.111	9	9	1	1	1	0	0	0	0	0	0	0	0	0	0	3	0	0
Sanders, Clemente, Miami	.283	60	191	26	54	83	9	4	4	30	5	0	2	0	24	2	30	4	3
Sarrett, Daniel, Tampa	.143	5	7	0	1	1	0	0	0	1	0	0	1	0	1	1	1	0	0
Sayler, Barry, St. Petersburg	.239	49	134	18	32	38	4	1	0	15	2	6	0	8	11	0	28	0	2
Scheetz, Michael, Miami	.053	7	19	3	1	1	0	0	0	0	0	1	0	0	5	0	6	0	0
Schoeller, Michael, Lake-Miami°	.280	117	400	47	112	150	16	5	4	61	10	1	9	2	49	5	44	4	3
Scranton, James, Fort Myers	.214	107	355	37	76	90	6	1	2	32	3	6	3	1	24	0	31	9	4
Shannon, Kevin, Fort Lauderdale†	.182	66	159	13	29	32	3	0	0	10	2	2	1	5	21	0	20	1	0
Shines, Anthony, West Palm Beach†	.231	8	26	4	6	15	0	0	3	6	2	0	0	0	4	1	3	0	0
Simcox, Larry, Daytona Beach	.383	19	60	11	23	31	6	1	0	10	0	1	1	0	10	0	2	0	0
Simons, Neil, Daytona Beach°	.325	53	166	32	54	77	10	5	1	21	0	0	5	0	25	1	20	7	3
Smith, Gregory, Vero Beach°	.273	60	227	34	62	93	9	5	4	24	2	0	1	1	21	5	30	2	2
Smith, Jeffrey, Lakeland	.286	113	399	45	114	157	19	3	6	60	8	3	5	1	39	3	81	4	1
Smith, Philander, Daytona Beach	.368	17	68	14	25	34	4	1	1	9	0	0	0	1	4	0	5	7	2
Smith, Thomas, Miami†	.262	24	65	9	17	26	4	1	1	6	0	0	1	0	5	0	6	2	1
Sobbe, William, Vero Beach°	.314	55	175	14	55	61	4	1	0	23	3	2	3	0	28	2	19	4	2
Sullivan, David, Daytona Beach	.258	76	248	43	64	75	8	0	1	25	2	0	4	2	44	1	36	4	3
Tartabull, Danilo, Tampa	.310	127	422	86	131	221	28	10	14	81	10	3	4	2	90	8	77	11	6
Teegarden, Robert, Fort Lauderdale	.274	88	277	42	76	124	7	10	7	49	4	2	0	8	58	10	51	5	3
Thomas, Marc, Daytona Beach	.176	34	108	14	19	23	4	0	0	10	1	1	0	0	11	0	24	10	0
Thomas, W. Richard, Vero Beach	.239	75	226	27	54	64	4	3	0	24	3	6	1	2	35	1	40	4	5
Threatt, Anthony, Tampa	.000	8	1	0	0	0	0	0	0	0	0	0	0	0	0	0	0	0	0
Thrower, Arnold, St. Petersburg†	.267	85	281	35	75	87	4	4	0	21	3	3	1	1	26	4	22	33	8
Timko, Andrew, Miami°	.282	85	330	41	93	99	6	0	0	17	2	1	3	1	26	4	22	12	6
Tinkler, Jack, St. Petersburg	.444	3	9	1	4	4	0	0	0	2	0	0	0	0	1	0	0	0	0
Townley, Robin, Fort Myers	.279	89	290	34	81	103	13	3	1	30	3	5	2	3	40	0	33	8	3
Tutt, Johnny, Miami	.291	40	141	21	41	52	4	2	1	16	2	2	2	1	11	0	16	18	2
Upshaw, John, Lakeland	.500	3	6	1	3	3	0	0	0	1	0	0	0	0	0	0	0	0	0
Vanslyke, Andrew, St. Petersburg°	.220	94	282	42	62	82	11	3	1	25	1	3	1	3	47	7	55	10	2
Vejar, Matthew, Fort Lauderdale°	.229	83	227	24	52	68	9	2	1	30	4	2	5	2	28	1	24	4	3
Villaescusa, Juan, Vero Beach°	.235	48	132	15	31	33	0	1	0	9	0	0	0	2	9	2	14	6	1

| | | | | | | | | | | | | | | | | Int. | | | |
Player and Club	Pct.	G.	AB.	R.	H.	TB.	2B.	3B.	HR.	RBI.	GW.	SH.	SF.	HP.	BB.	BB.	SO.	SB.	CS.
Walker, Anthony Bruce, Tampa.........	.300	18	40	11	12	19	3	2	0	3	0	1	0	0	5	0	8	2	1
Weems, William, Daytona Beach°......	.298	96	302	44	90	105	9	3	0	30	5	3	2	2	29	2	19	18	4
Whitfield, N. Jerome, W Palm Beach	.194	67	211	25	41	69	8	1	6	23	2	0	0	2	14	1	37	2	5
Wilkerson, Martin, Fort Myers	.245	45	147	18	36	49	11	1	0	11	2	0	0	0	27	4	10	0	0
Williams, Jaime, Daytona Beach	.229	46	105	12	24	35	5	0	2	12	1	3	0	0	5	0	29	2	0
Williams, Jeffrey, Miami°	.215	113	382	38	82	107	15	5	0	36	3	3	1	1	36	2	64	10	8
Wise, Brett, Vero Beach	.000	39	0	1	0	0	0	0	0	0	0	0	0	0	0	0	0	0	0
Wolters, Michael, St. Petersburg......	.267	118	408	72	109	154	22	1	7	49	4	11	3	3	66	2	66	13	4
Young, Michael, Miami°	.345	63	235	32	81	121	19	6	3	34	6	1	2	2	35	5	48	17	4
Zayas, Felipe, St. Petersburg...........	.275	86	298	40	82	113	12	5	3	43	7	1	4	5	46	1	43	3	2
Zell, Brian, Winter Haven°	.257	114	385	55	99	136	20	7	1	51	0	0	10	3	62	2	90	6	6

The following pitchers had no plate appearances primarily through use of designated hitters, listed alphabetically by club, games in parentheses:

DAYTONA BEACH—Brown, Lawrence (10); Cacciatorre, Paul (5); Calhoun, Jeffrey (21); Elsee, Kenneth (19); Gardner, Kenneth (23); Hawk, Thomas (15); Heathcock, Jeffrey (11); Hernandez, Manuel (13); Jackson, Larry (10); Meckes, Timothy (53); Morris, Jeffrey (9); Mundie, Donald (1); Penate, Miguel (39); Perry, Patrick (9); Regalado, Jose (12); Squilla, Joseph (27); Turner, Mark (2); Yan, Roberto (41).

FORT LAUDERDALE—Browning, Michael (17); Callahan, Benjamin (25); Christianson, Clay (26); Collins, Joseph (1); Dougherty, Charles (15); Fauland, Herbert (37); Filson, Peter (11); Fontenot, Ray (8); Gallegos, Matthew (1); Lein, Christopher (30); Nelson, Gene (2); Nurthen, John (28); Patterson, Gilbert (7); Silva, Mark (1); Smith, Kenneth (38); Wever, Stefan (12).

FORT MYERS—Botelho, Derek (8); Cecil, Timothy (17); Cooper, Junior (16); Cvejdlik, Kent (5); Harsh, Nicholas (6); Huismann, Mark (14); Jackman, Mark (18); Johnson, Abner (10); Krauss, Ronald (7); Morley, Michael (4); Pippin, Graig (21); Potestio, Douglas (14); Raine, Steven (9); Shaw, Theodore (14); St. Clair, Daniel (22); Timlin, Timothy (29); Vanderbush, Walter (18); Williams, Larry (8); Yuhas, Vincent (24).

LAKELAND—Beecroft, Michael (5); Collyer, Richard (14); Fellows, Mark (24); Garner, Walter (29); Gibson, Paul (20); Gumpert, David (14); Josephson, Paul (22); Kelly, Bryan (2); Lackey, John (6); Leisure, Phil (27); Miller, William (12); Moncrief, Homer (22); Nail, Charles (6); Nutter, Gary (42); O'Neal, Randall (13); Trevel, Ralph (3); Untisz, Michael (11); Williams, Mark (22).

MIAMI—Alvarez, Evelio (Ft. Myers) (25); Arnold, Tony (16); Clark, Irwin (26); Cratch, Richard (6); Dixon, Kenneth (12); Dolby, William (6); Ferroni, Frank (8); Gold, Brett (14); Gray, David (11); Hoke, Leon (51); Johnson, Scott (26); Kreymborg, Michael (11); Maples, Timothy (13); Olivares, Francisco (19); Ramirez, Allan (3); Smith, Freddie (23); Wadley, Anthony (6); Willsher, Christopher (26).

ST. PETERSBURG—Alba, Gibson (6); Arigoni, Scott (19); Collins, Donald (24); Davis, Russell (11); Dozier, Thomas (15); Gotay, Ruben (13); Horton, Ricky (28); Johnson, David (Daytona Beach) (12); Kish, Robert (7); Neely, Alex (28); Pratt, Louis (6); Robbins, Robin (40); Russell, Robert (6); Sanford, Edmund (4); Silva, Freddie (10); Taveras, Luis (1); Thomas, William (21); Weaver, Earl (25); Williams, Raymond (12).

VERO BEACH—Bryant, Franklin (27); Forer, Daniel (13); Franco, John (13); Hammond, Arthur (34); Madden, Morris (22); O'Malley, Michael (3); Oroz, Felix (27); Perry, Stephen (19); Reade, Curtis (36); Rennicke, Dean (5); Slezack, Robert (8); Sutcliffe, Terry (27); Tennant, Michael (2); Thorp, Bradley (23).

WEST PALM BEACH—Anderson, Scott (21); Blows, Louis (7); Cates, Timothy (24); Chaplin, Peter (27); Chesser, Brandon (8); Fadhel, Antonio (10); Glasscock, Larry (24); Grapenthin, Richard (31); Groves, Larry (33); Palmer, David (3); Schuler, Mark (19); Staffon, Gregory (15); Taylor, Jeffrey (26); Torres, Miguel (20); Westray, Kenneth (25); Winfield, Steven (St. Petersburg) (26).

WINTER HAVEN—Baldwin, Oscar (34); Bolton, Thomas (24); Boyd, Dennis (28); Cote, Brice (30); Cooke, Richard (31); Greco, George (27); Hayford, Donald (3); Herman, Tyrone (35); Johnson, Mitchell (32); Nipper, Albert (29); Plainte, Brandon (20); Weinbrecht, Mark (24).

GRAND-SLAM HOME RUNS—Amelung, Brewer, Carl, Clements, Csefalvay, Dewey, Hench, Hibner, Hoeksema, Lepel, Pardo, Robles, Smith, Whitfield, 1 each.

AWARDED FIRST BASE ON INTERFERENCE—Van Slyke 6 (Holt 2, Leach 2, Dewey, Good); Chaney 3 (Sullivan, Sarrett, Bard); Adduci 2 (Pardo, Leach); Ivie (Shines), Amelung (Kripner).

CLUB FIELDING

Club	Pct.	G.	PO.	A.	E.	DP.	PB.	Club	Pct.	G.	PO.	A.	E.	DP.	PB.
St. Petersburg............	.974	132	3246	1488	128	117	11	Winter Haven	.962	139	3586	1643	204	130	20
Fort Lauderdale	.966	134	3344	1502	170	110	12	Tampa	.958	134	3348	1377	205	92	29
Lakeland	.966	133	3335	1522	172	126	26	Miami	.957	136	3377	1312	210	115	23
Fort Myers	.965	131	3264	1416	169	106	18	Vero Beach	.957	137	3542	1535	226	135	28
West Palm Beach	.963	137	3471	1486	193	138	20	Daytona Beach	.955	135	3299	1458	222	113	20

INDIVIDUAL FIELDING

°Throws lefthanded.

FIRST BASEMEN

Player and Club	Pct.	G.	PO.	A.	E.	DP.	Player and Club	Pct.	G.	PO.	A.	E.	DP.
Bowman, Miami°	.984	7	54	8	1	2	McKnight, Daytona Beach	.962	12	50	1	2	1
Bream, Vero Beach°	.985	70	613	45	10	66	Mizerock, Daytona Beach	1.000	2	13	1	0	2
Carroll, West Palm Beach°......	.985	61	491	29	8	45	Moore, St. Petersburg	.990	80	743	47	8	69
Clements, Daytona Beach	.982	125	1048	68	21	91	Nealeigh, West Palm Beach°	.993	54	369	34	3	29
Craig, Ft. Lauderdale	.988	64	537	21	7	48	Nichols, Miami	.813	4	12	1	3	2
DeJesus, West Palm Beach......	1.000	6	23	1	0	3	Porter, Ft. Myers	.932	7	51	4	4	2
DeLeon, Miami	.983	50	386	13	7	37	Reyes, Vero Beach	.981	8	48	4	1	5
DODSON, Winter Haven°	.989	121	1134	76	13	100	Robbins, Ft. Lauderdale	1.000	2	5	0	0	0
Dummar, Miami°	.995	21	170	10	1	15	Roeder, West Palm Beach	1.000	1	2	0	0	0
Dumouchelle, Miami	.982	16	102	4	2	10	Rudolph, Ft. Lauderdale	1.000	3	19	0	0	2
Ferris, Ft. Myers	.988	103	831	84	11	72	Salas, St. Petersburg................	1.000	1	0	1	0	0
Good, Lakeland	1.000	1	6	1	0	1	Sanders, Miami	.976	20	154	7	4	16
Guerra, Ft. Lauderdale°	.995	75	709	56	4	48	Scheetz, Miami	.967	4	27	2	1	2
Hanggie, Ft. Lauderdale	1.000	1	1	0	0	0	Schoeller, Lakeland-Miami	.985	31	245	11	4	15
Harvey, Lakeland°	.979	109	1017	73	24	94	Shines, West Palm Beach	1.000	1	12	0	0	0
Holt, Winter Haven	.985	22	181	14	3	7	Smith, Vero Beach	.988	60	463	41	6	44
Johnson, Tampa	.994	20	159	5	1	10	Smith, Lakeland	.978	18	131	5	3	8
Jordan, Ft. Lauderdale°	1.000	1	11	0	0	1	Smith, Miami	1.000	5	32	4	0	3
Kirsch, Tampa°	.987	119	960	60	13	76	Sullivan, Daytona Beach	1.000	7	61	5	0	4
Lanning, Vero Beach	1.000	1	1	0	0	0	Townley, Ft. Myers	.995	25	195	10	1	11
Leach, Winter Haven	1.000	1	2	0	0	0	Villaescusa, Vero Beach	1.000	4	16	2	0	3
Luethy, Ft. Myers	1.000	1	3	1	0	0	Whitfield, West Palm Beach	.981	44	294	20	6	45
Marchand, West Palm Beach ...	1.000	1	3	0	0	0	Williams, Daytona Beach	.944	4	16	1	1	3
McCauley, St. Petersburg	.985	52	481	35	8	38	Wolters, St. Petersburg	1.000	2	2	2	0	0

SECOND BASEMEN

Player and Club	Pct.	G.	PO.	A.	E.	DP.
Albano, Miami	.946	26	52	52	6	15
Bendorf, Vero Beach	.962	24	57	69	5	15
Butterfield, Ft. Lauderdale	.963	83	152	211	14	39
Chaney, Lakeland	.902	15	24	31	6	7
D'Aloia, Ft. Lauderdale	.862	5	6	19	4	2
D'Onofrio, Daytona Beach	.970	107	194	296	15	57
Dawes, West Palm Beach	.970	12	24	40	2	8
Deaza, Ft. Myers	1.000	2	2	4	0	0
Dillard, Miami	.949	77	170	221	21	50
Doerrer, West Palm Beach	.976	64	122	166	7	45
Dumouchelle, Miami	.948	30	74	73	8	12
Gloyd, West Palm Beach	.938	27	46	75	8	17
Goldetsky, West Palm Beach	.889	10	10	14	3	2
Gutierrez, Vero Beach	.878	17	41	31	10	8
Guzman, Vero Beach	.881	12	19	18	5	2
Hanggie, Ft. Lauderdale	1.000	1	0	3	0	1
Hench, Ft. Lauderdale	1.000	10	17	19	0	2
Hinson, Lakeland	.976	83	188	267	11	50
Hoeksema, West Palm Beach	.960	18	34	38	3	10
Horn, Lakeland	.946	37	59	116	10	15
Houston, Daytona Beach°	1.000	1	1	0	0	0
Howser, Ft. Lauderdale	1.000	5	3	6	0	0
Hudler, Ft. Lauderdale	.963	52	82	151	9	32
Hundhammer, Winter Haven	.975	103	239	347	15	61
Johnson, Tampa	1.000	17	36	49	0	9
JOHNSON, Ft. Myers	.979	102	181	337	11	48
Leppert, Tampa	.959	59	150	156	13	34
Lindberg, Lakeland	.944	7	5	12	1	1
Luethy, Ft. Myers	1.000	7	12	10	0	2
Malespin, Winter Haven	.925	7	13	24	3	2
Mann, Vero Beach	.976	62	149	171	8	45
Martin, Winter Haven	.927	7	17	21	3	6
McDaniel, West Palm Beach	1.000	1	1	1	0	0
McKnight, Daytona Beach	.974	29	49	63	3	10
Murelli, Miami	.950	6	5	14	1	0
Patterson, Ft. Myers	1.000	23	43	67	0	9
Portes, Tampa	.924	16	27	34	5	3
Proulx, St. Petersburg	.972	61	121	160	8	40
Quinones, West Palm Beach	.968	40	60	90	5	20
Raimondo, Vero Beach	.949	18	34	41	4	7
Ramos, Winter Haven	.955	23	59	90	7	18
Robbins, Ft. Lauderdale	.947	7	14	22	2	2
Sadey, Miami	1.000	1	0	1	0	0
Smith, Daytona Beach	.981	11	22	30	1	5
Tartabull, Tampa	.950	46	92	96	10	20
Thrower, St. Petersburg	.981	80	172	233	8	47
Tinkler, St. Petersburg	1.000	3	13	9	0	2
Villaescusa, Vero Beach	.976	16	44	37	2	12
Weems, Daytona Beach	1.000	5	5	5	0	1
Wolters, St. Petersburg	1.000	1	3	4	0	2

THIRD BASEMEN

Player and Club	Pct.	G.	PO.	A.	E.	DP.
Albano, Miami	1.000	5	6	7	0	0
Ayer, St. Petersburg	.979	17	17	30	1	4
Bass, Vero Beach	.889	13	9	23	4	3
Bendorf, Vero Beach	1.000	1	1	3	0	0
Butterfield, Ft. Lauderdale	.833	2	1	4	1	0
Carl, West Palm Beach	.911	61	44	100	14	14
Chaney, Lakeland	.854	13	11	24	6	2
Cusack, Miami	.907	17	14	25	4	2
Dawes, West Palm Beach	1.000	9	1	16	0	2
Deaza, Ft. Myers	.879	79	55	104	22	5
Debus, Vero Beach	.901	88	59	150	23	10
Dees, Miami	.843	42	34	52	16	4
Dumouchelle, Miami	.912	28	18	44	6	4
Duncan, Winter Haven	.826	15	11	27	8	2
Ferris, Ft. Myers	1.000	1	10	0	0	0
Foussianes, Lakeland	.929	119	90	213	23	15
Gloyd, West Palm Beach	.895	24	10	24	4	2
Hench, Ft. Lauderdale	.919	82	45	148	17	14
Hinson, Lakeland	1.000	1	8	8	0	0
Hoeksema, West Palm Beach	.955	15	6	15	1	4
Hudler, Ft. Lauderdale	1.000	2	0	2	0	0
Johnson, Tampa	.942	28	31	50	5	1
Lanning, Vero Beach	.924	41	25	60	7	8
Leach, Winter Haven	.727	6	1	7	3	0
Leppert, Tampa	.883	32	12	56	9	4
Luethy, Ft. Myers	.750	2	1	2	1	0
Malespin, Winter Haven	.938	59	42	94	9	10
Mann, Vero Beach	1.000	1	1	0	0	0
Mariano, Ft. Lauderdale	.926	61	25	124	12	4
Martin, Winter Haven	.915	63	43	119	15	11
McKnight, Daytona Beach	.927	26	16	35	4	4
Medina, Daytona Beach	.863	47	29	91	19	5
Miller, Miami	.906	22	10	38	5	1
Nichols, Miami	1.000	1	0	2	0	1
Nieves, West Palm Beach	.786	17	9	13	6	2
Patterson, Ft. Myers	.824	19	9	19	6	1
Proulx, St. Petersburg	1.000	5	2	9	0	1
Ramos, Winter Haven	1.000	3	0	2	0	0
Roeder, West Palm Beach	.878	30	21	51	10	4
Sadey, Miami	.829	28	28	35	13	5
Shines, West Palm Beach	.813	6	7	6	3	1
Tartabull, Tampa	.879	78	58	152	29	9
Weems, Daytona Beach	.907	73	32	133	17	11
Wilkerson, Ft. Myers°	.941	36	25	54	5	5
WOLTERS, St. Petersburg	.954	114	78	233	15	25

SHORTSTOPS

Player and Club	Pct.	G.	PO.	A.	E.	DP.
Anderson, Vero Beach	.934	64	109	218	23	42
Banes, Ft. Lauderdale	.917	105	172	322	45	63
Beltran, Daytona Beach	.899	98	124	277	45	40
Bustabad, Winter Haven	.958	44	73	155	10	25
Butterfield, Ft. Lauderdale	.769	6	5	15	6	1
Chaney, Lakeland	.966	26	50	65	4	17
D'Aloia, Ft. Lauderdale	1.000	7	1	7	0	0
D'Onofrio, Daytona Beach	.903	8	13	15	3	6
Deaza, Ft. Myers	1.000	1	0	1	0	0
Dillard, Miami	.931	6	8	19	2	4
Doerrer, West Palm Beach	1.000	1	1	0	0	0
Dumouchelle, Miami	1.000	1	1	2	0	0
Duncan, Winter Haven	.916	96	169	324	45	59
Foote, Tampa	.912	68	98	232	32	35
Gallegos, Ft. Lauderdale	1.000	1	0	1	0	0
Gloyd, West Palm Beach	.872	9	12	22	5	5
Gonzales, St. Petersburg	.946	126	171	387	32	63
Guzman, Vero Beach	1.000	2	3	4	0	1
Hoeksema, West Palm Beach	.939	69	103	203	20	41
Hubert, Lakeland	.925	13	12	25	3	2
Hudler, Ft. Lauderdale	.914	28	21	85	10	11
Johnson, Tampa	.938	3	5	10	1	1
Johnson, Ft. Myers	.571	2	2	2	3	2
Labastidas, Miami	.933	44	83	126	15	23
Leppert, Tampa	.867	4	5	8	2	1
LINDBERG, Lakeland	.961	103	172	338	21	55
Luethy, Ft. Myers	.903	30	40	62	11	7
Mann, Vero Beach	.938	17	24	52	5	10
Mariano, Ft. Lauderdale	1.000	1	0	1	0	0
Martin, Vero Beach	.919	53	79	160	21	25
McKnight, Daytona Beach	.930	26	22	58	6	12
Nichols, Miami	.750	1	0	3	1	0
Proulx, St. Petersburg	.960	10	10	38	2	7
Quinones, West Palm Beach	.951	68	98	213	16	38
Ramos, Winter Haven	1.000	1	1	4	0	1
Rincones, Tampa	.926	62	79	184	21	26
Scranton, Ft. Myers	.949	107	206	346	30	65
Simcox, Daytona Beach	.911	19	18	54	7	4
Smith, Miami	.667	3	4	0	2	0
Timko, Miami	.957	85	149	251	18	44
Villaescusa, Vero Beach	.913	20	32	52	8	9

OUTFIELDERS

Player and Club	Pct.	G.	PO.	A.	E.	DP.
Adduci, St. Petersburg°	.964	92	185	4	7	0
Amelung, Vero Beach°	.952	135	237	22	13	2
Auten, West Palm Beach	.972	116	162	10	5	1
Ayer, St. Petersburg	.979	104	219	11	5	1
Barker, Lakeland°	.974	19	38	0	1	0
Bennett, Fort Lauderdale°	.991	77	104	2	1	1
Brewer, Fort Myers	.961	121	209	12	9	5
Bryant, West Haven	.978	53	83	4	2	2
Carl, West Palm Beach	1.000	7	10	1	0	0
Carroll, West Palm Beach°	1.000	3	2	0	0	0
Chinn, Vero Beach	1.000	7	7	0	0	0
Ciampa, Winter Haven°	.980	113	240	9	5	2
Clements, Daytona Beach	1.000	1	1	0	0	0
Cruz, West Palm Beach	.949	76	124	5	7	0
Csefalvay, Daytona Beach°	.973	58	66	6	2	2
Cusack, Miami	.903	17	28	0	3	0
D'Onofrio, Daytona Beach	1.000	1	3	1	0	0
Davis, Fort Myers	.953	112	239	5	12	3
Deaza, Fort Myers	1.000	3	2	0	0	0
Debus, Vero Beach	.974	21	33	4	1	0
DeLeon, Miami	.895	7	15	2	2	0
DelMonte, St. Petersburg°	.986	33	67	1	1	0

OUTFIELDERS —Continued

Player and Club	Pct.	G.	PO.	A.	E.	DP.	Player and Club	Pct.	G.	PO.	A.	E.	DP.
Doak, Fort Myers	.977	30	40	3	1	0	Nieves, West Palm Beach	.917	29	20	2	2	0
Dodd, Fort Lauderdale	.909	12	10	0	1	0	Palmer, Fort Myers	.983	87	165	6	3	3
Dumouchelle, Miami	.952	46	96	3	5	1	Pellack, West Palm Beach°	.930	44	64	2	5	0
Eldridge, West Palm Beach	.960	30	24	0	1	0	Pratt, Tampa	.948	120	173	9	10	0
FIELDS, Lakeland	.983	100	225	11	4	3	Reynolds, Vero Beach	.982	131	368	20	7	6
Filkins, Fort Lauderdale	1.000	5	6	1	0	0	Riche, Miami°	.884	24	36	2	5	0
Fuentes, West Palm Beach	.985	67	127	5	2	2	Robbins, Fort Lauderdale	.962	19	25	0	1	0
Gainey, Daytona Beach°	.978	96	127	7	3	0	Roberson, Lakeland	.800	4	3	1	1	0
Gayden, Fort Lauderdale°	.965	119	215	6	8	1	Robles, Daytona Beach	.959	108	197	14	9	2
Glenn, Winter Haven	.981	109	201	8	4	0	Roeder, West Palm Beach	1.000	6	6	0	0	0
Granger, Miami°	.954	40	78	4	4	0	Rollin, Lakeland	.963	94	155	2	6	1
Guzman, Tampa	.970	101	160	4	5	2	Roman, St. Petersburg°	.951	43	75	3	4	1
Hall, Winter Haven	.981	58	92	9	2	2	Sadey, Miami	1.000	6	5	0	0	0
Hardy, Lakeland	.960	81	134	9	6	4	Sayler, St. Petersburg	1.000	2	1	0	0	0
Herrick, Miami	.971	56	91	9	3	2	Schoeller, Lakeland	1.000	3	2	0	0	0
Hibner, Lakeland	.980	60	91	7	2	2	Simons, Daytona Beach°	.948	54	87	4	5	0
Hicks, St. Petersburg	1.000	16	17	0	0	0	Smith, Lakeland	.964	47	54	0	2	0
Houston, Daytona Beach°	.934	88	102	11	8	4	Smith, Miami	1.000	11	31	1	0	1
Howard, Tampa	.969	59	94	1	3	1	Sutcliffe, Vero Beach	1.000	1	0	2	0	0
Hudler, Fort Lauderdale	1.000	1	1	0	0	0	Teegarden, Fort Lauderdale	.982	85	99	9	2	1
Ivie, Miami	1.000	1	1	0	0	0	Thomas, Daytona Beach	1.000	12	16	1	0	1
Jefferson, Winter Haven	.911	26	37	4	4	0	Thomas, Vero Beach	.943	38	47	3	3	1
Kirsch, Tampa°	1.000	4	12	0	0	0	Townley, Fort Myers	.966	51	107	7	4	0
Knight, Fort Lauderdale°	.980	80	140	6	3	1	Tutt, Miami	.990	40	95	4	1	0
Lachowetz, Vero Beach	.963	25	50	2	2	0	Van Slyke, St. Petersburg	.973	93	168	10	5	2
Little, Tampa°	.965	131	290	9	11	2	Vejar, Fort Lauderdale	.947	57	68	4	4	0
Malespin, Winter Haven	.909	39	78	2	8	0	Walker, Tampa	1.000	13	21	0	0	0
Mann, Vero Beach	1.000	1	6	0	0	0	Weems, Daytona Beach	1.000	8	3	1	0	0
Mastro, Lakeland	1.000	17	23	3	0	0	Whitfield, West Palm Beach	.500	2	1	0	1	0
McKnight, Daytona Beach	1.000	15	17	1	0	0	Williams, Miami°	.944	110	257	12	16	2
Miller, Miami	1.000	6	12	0	0	0	Young, Miami	.993	63	135	7	1	3
Miller, Vero Beach	.950	67	104	10	6	1	Zayas, St. Petersburg	1.000	29	33	3	0	0
Mizerock, Daytona Beach	1.000	1	1	0	0	0	Zell, Winter Haven	.963	34	48	4	2	0
Nealeigh, West Palm Beach°	.970	93	154	6	5	2							

CATCHERS

Player and Club	Pct.	G.	PO.	A.	E.	DP.	PB.	Player and Club	Pct.	G.	PO.	A.	E.	DP.	PB.
Bard, Vero Beach	.973	79	418	56	13	7	9	Matzen, Tampa°	1.000	11	46	2	0	0	5
Batter, Ft.My-WPB	.985	58	299	28	5	4	5	McCorkle, Daytona Beach	1.000	1	3	0	0	0	1
Boddy, Tampa	.981	31	191	16	4	2	11	MIZEROCK, Daytona Beach	.993	81	501	49	4	6	13
Boncore, Vero Beach	.954	27	148	19	8	1	6	Nichols, Miami	.926	6	22	3	2	0	0
Borges, West Palm Beach	.989	37	171	16	2	2	5	Nieves, West Palm Beach	1.000	7	5	0	0	0	1
Buffamoyer, Fort Lauderdale	.985	40	182	11	3	1	5	Pardo, Miami	.987	78	396	41	6	3	12
Campbell, Lakeland	.957	6	18	4	1	0	3	Phillip, Lakeland	1.000	16	54	8	0	0	2
Carrasquel, Lakeland	.983	54	307	44	6	5	10	Porter, Fort Myers	1.000	6	4	0	0	0	0
Dewey, Fort Myers	.984	85	439	45	8	7	11	Reyes, Vero Beach	.962	6	23	2	1	0	4
Dumouchelle, Miami	1.000	1	3	0	0	0	0	Robinson, Fort Lauderdale	1.000	2	7	0	0	0	0
Fisher, Lakeland	.970	22	112	19	4	6	1	Rudolph, Fort Lauderdale	.987	62	282	23	4	2	4
Gaunce, Fort Myers	.981	9	42	9	1	0	2	Salas, St. Petersburg	.972	89	387	65	13	6	8
Geren, St. Petersburg	.987	51	204	24	3	0	3	Sarrett, Tampa	.957	5	19	3	1	0	1
Gleissner, Fort Myers	1.000	3	15	2	0	0	0	Sayler, St. Petersburg	1.000	5	20	5	0	0	0
Good, Lakeland	.970	36	143	16	5	1	8	Schoeller, Miami	.984	11	51	10	1	1	4
Griggs, Miami	.942	16	55	10	4	1	4	Shannon, Fort Lauderdale	.991	66	310	35	3	4	3
Hall, Winter Haven	.974	51	263	35	8	4	9	Shines, West Palm Beach	.667	1	5	1	3	0	2
Hastings, Lakeland	.917	6	39	5	4	1	1	Sobbe, Vero Beach	.970	37	199	25	7	3	9
Holt, Winter Haven	.973	39	196	19	6	4	4	Sullivan, Daytona Beach	.981	50	343	21	7	3	3
Ivie, Miami	.976	37	170	29	5	1	3	Townley, Fort Myers	1.000	2	1	0	0	0	0
Kripner, Tampa	.986	96	580	44	9	2	12	Upshaw, Lakeland	.818	3	9	0	2	0	1
Leach, Winter Haven	.980	59	299	36	7	7	7	Williams, Daytona Beach	.984	19	59	2	1	0	3
Lepel, West Palm Beach	.989	112	668	76	8	13	12								

PITCHERS

Player and Club	Pct.	G.	PO.	A.	E.	DP.	Player and Club	Pct.	G.	PO.	A.	E.	DP.
Alvarez, Miami-Fort Myers	.943	25	6	27	2	1	Cooke, Winter Haven°	.941	31	4	12	1	1
Anderson, West Palm Beach	1.000	17	1	4	0	0	Cooper, Fort Myers	.909	16	5	15	2	1
Arigoni, St. Petersburg°	.947	19	1	17	1	1	Cote, Winter Haven	.944	29	5	12	1	0
Arnold, Miami	1.000	6	0	5	0	0	Cratch, Miami	1.000	6	0	1	0	0
Baldwin, Winter Haven	.923	34	0	12	1	0	Cvejdlik, Fort Myers	1.000	5	4	5	0	0
Beecroft, Lakeland	.250	5	1	0	3	0	Davis, St. Petersburg	1.000	11	2	6	0	0
Bolton, Winter Haven°	1.000	24	4	17	0	1	DeJiulio, Tampa	.909	42	2	8	1	0
Botelho, Fort Myers	1.000	8	3	4	0	1	DeSanto, Winter Haven	.632	19	3	9	7	0
Boyd, Winter Haven	.977	28	8	35	1	3	Dixon, Miami	1.000	11	4	5	0	0
Brown, Daytona Beach	.944	10	3	14	1	1	Dolby, Miami	1.000	6	1	1	0	0
Brown, Miami	.923	17	3	9	1	1	Dougherty, Fort Lauderdale°	1.000	15	2	9	0	0
Browning, Fort Lauderdale	1.000	17	2	6	0	0	Dozier, St. Petersburg	1.000	15	2	2	0	0
Bryant, Vero Beach	.882	27	5	10	2	0	Elsee, Daytona Beach	.882	19	5	10	2	0
Buckle, Tampa	.833	4	2	8	2	1	Fadhel, West Palm Beach	1.000	10	4	12	0	2
Cacciatorre, Daytona Beach	1.000	5	0	2	0	0	Fauland, Fort Lauderdale°	1.000	37	5	21	0	1
Calhoun, Daytona Beach°	.688	21	5	17	10	1	Fellows, Lakeland	.949	24	7	30	2	1
Callahan, Fort Lauderdale	1.000	25	12	24	0	2	Ferroni, Miami°	1.000	8	1	6	0	1
Cates, West Palm Beach	.926	24	8	17	2	2	Filson, Fort Lauderdale°	1.000	11	2	9	0	0
Cecil, Fort Myers	.917	17	8	3	1	0	Fiorillo, Tampa°	.875	22	1	20	3	0
Chapin, West Palm Beach	.911	27	16	25	4	2	Fontenot, Fort Lauderdale°	.875	8	0	7	1	0
Chesser, West Palm Beach	.941	8	7	9	1	0	Forer, Vero Beach°	.000	13	0	0	1	0
Christianson, Fort Lauderdale	.975	26	11	28	1	3	Franco, Vero Beach°	.950	13	2	17	1	1
Clark, Miami°	.875	26	1	6	1	0	Freeman, Tampa°	.778	25	0	7	2	0
Cole, Miami°	1.000	16	1	8	0	1	Gardner, Daytona Beach	.849	23	9	19	5	0
Collins, St. Petersburg	.979	24	10	37	1	2	Garner, Lakeland	.870	29	5	15	3	3
Collyer, Lakeland°	.909	14	2	8	1	0	Gibson, Lakeland°	.929	20	5	8	1	1

PITCHERS—Continued

Player and Club	Pct.	G.	PO.	A.	E.	DP.
Glasscock, West Palm Beach*	1.000	24	1	5	0	1
Gold, Miami	.800	14	3	5	2	2
Gotay, St. Petersburg	1.000	13	4	4	0	0
Grapenthin, West Palm Beach	.893	31	4	21	3	1
Gray, Miami	.750	11	1	2	1	0
Greco, Winter Haven*	.950	27	4	15	1	1
Groves, West Palm Beach	.850	33	6	11	3	0
Gumpert, Lakeland	.962	14	10	15	1	0
Hammond, Vero Beach*	1.000	34	1	7	0	0
Harsh, Fort Myers	.867	6	6	7	2	2
Hawk, Daytona Beach	.727	15	1	7	3	0
Hayes, Tampa	.933	32	6	8	1	1
Heathcock, Daytona Beach	.917	11	5	17	2	4
Herman, Winter Haven	.962	35	5	20	1	1
Hernandez, Daytona Beach	.778	13	2	12	4	1
Hoke, Miami	1.000	51	0	11	0	0
Horton, St. Petersburg*	.964	28	4	23	1	0
Huismann, Fort Myers	.889	14	2	6	1	0
Jackman, Fort Myers*	.889	18	2	6	1	0
Jackson, Daytona Beach	.727	10	1	7	3	0
Johnson, Fort Myers	1.000	10	5	9	0	1
Johnson, St.P.-Day. Beach*	1.000	12	2	2	0	0
Johnson, Winter Haven	.833	32	3	17	4	0
Johnson, Miami*	.968	26	5	25	1	3
Josephson, Lakeland	.909	22	1	9	1	0
Kelly, Lakeland	1.000	2	0	2	0	1
Kenyon, Vero Beach	.957	24	9	13	1	1
Kish, St. Petersburg	1.000	7	1	1	0	0
Klosicki, Tampa	.950	45	15	23	2	2
Krauss, Fort Myers*	.800	7	0	4	1	0
Kreymborg, Miami	1.000	11	0	1	0	0
Lackey, Lakeland	1.000	6	2	9	0	0
Landrum, Tampa	.955	17	4	17	1	0
Lein, Fort Lauderdale	.946	30	17	36	3	2
Leisure, Lakeland*	1.000	27	2	12	0	0
Lochner, Tampa*	.889	20	2	14	2	2
Madden, Vero Beach*	.954	21	4	37	2	1
Maples, Miami	1.000	13	1	10	0	1
McKnight, Daytona Beach	1.000	1	0	2	0	0
Meckes, Daytona Beach	.931	53	6	21	2	1
Miller, Lakeland	1.000	12	4	5	0	2
Moncrief, Lakeland	.963	22	4	22	1	2
Moore, Tampa*	1.000	51	3	15	0	0
Morley, Fort Myers*	.800	4	0	4	1	0
Morris, Daytona Beach*	1.000	9	1	2	0	0
Mundie, Daytona Beach	1.000	1	1	3	0	0
Murphy, Tampa*	.900	25	5	22	3	2
Nail, Lakeland	.800	6	1	3	1	0
Neely, St. Petersburg	.833	28	1	4	1	0
Nelson, Fort Lauderdale	1.000	2	4	0	0	0
Nipper, Winter Haven	.980	29	15	33	1	1
Nurthen, Fort Lauderdale	1.000	28	8	18	0	2
Nutter, Lakeland	1.000	42	3	19	0	1
O'Malley, Vero Beach*	.000	3	0	0	1	0
O'Neal, Lakeland	.944	13	3	14	1	1
Oliveras, Miami	.933	19	4	10	1	0
Oroz, Vero Beach*	.934	27	14	43	4	3
Palmer, West Palm Beach	1.000	3	1	4	0	0
Patterson, Fort Lauderdale	.889	7	3	13	2	0
Pellack, West Palm Beach*	1.000	2	0	1	0	0
Penate, Daytona Beach	.946	39	8	27	2	2
Peralta, Miami	1.000	17	3	4	0	0
Perry, Vero Beach	.750	19	1	2	1	0
Perry, Daytona Beach*	.833	9	1	4	1	0
Pettibone, Tampa	.833	25	2	18	4	1
Pippin, Fort Myers	.900	21	5	4	1	0
Plainte, Winter Haven*	.952	20	6	14	1	0
Potestio, Fort Myers	.900	14	10	26	4	0
Pratt, St. Petersburg*	1.000	6	1	1	0	0
Raine, Fort Myers	.900	9	1	8	1	0
Ramirez, Miami	1.000	3	1	1	0	0
Reade, Vero Beach	.960	36	11	13	1	1
Regalado, Daytona Beach	.957	12	5	17	1	1
Rennicke, Vero Beach	.833	5	1	4	1	0
Robbins, St. Petersburg	1.000	40	3	18	0	2
Russell, Tampa	1.000	22	8	37	0	1
Russell, St. Petersburg	1.000	6	3	5	0	0
Sanford, St. Petersburg	1.000	4	0	6	0	0
Schuler, West Palm Beach	1.000	19	2	4	0	0
Shaw, Fort Myers	.842	14	4	12	3	1
Silva, St. Petersburg	1.000	10	3	5	0	1
Slezack, Vero Beach	1.000	8	1	0	0	0
Smith, Miami	.963	23	7	19	1	2
Smith, Fort Lauderdale	.857	38	0	6	1	1
Squilla, Daytona Beach*	1.000	27	1	8	0	0
St. Clair, Fort Myers	.833	22	0	5	1	0
Staffon, West Palm Beach	.790	15	5	10	4	1
Sutcliffe, Vero Beach	.917	26	15	18	3	3
Taylor, West Palm Beach*	.926	26	5	20	2	1
Tennant, Vero Beach	1.000	2	0	1	0	0
Thomas, St. Petersburg	.871	21	8	19	4	0
Thorp, Vero Beach	.867	23	7	19	4	2
Timlin, Fort Myers	1.000	29	7	8	0	1
Torres, West Palm Beach	.813	20	5	8	3	0
Treuel, Lakeland	1.000	3	0	1	0	0
Turner, Daytona Beach*	.000	2	0	0	1	0
Untisz, Lakeland	1.000	11	1	7	0	0
Vanderbush, Fort Myers	.964	18	8	19	1	3
Wadley, Miami	1.000	5	1	3	0	0
Weaver, St. Petersburg	1.000	25	12	19	0	0
Weinbrecht, Winter Haven*	.864	24	6	13	3	0
Westray, West Palm Beach*	.909	25	6	34	4	2
Wever, Fort Lauderdale	.933	12	3	11	1	0
Williams, Fort Myers	1.000	8	3	11	0	0
WILLIAMS, Lakeland	1.000	22	18	32	0	3
Williams, St. Petersburg	1.000	12	0	1	0	0
Willsher, Miami	.913	25	9	12	2	1
Winfield, W.P.B.-St.P.	1.000	26	2	4	0	0
Wise, Vero Beach	.929	38	2	11	1	0
Yan, Daytona Beach	.913	41	5	16	2	5
Yuhas, Fort Myers	.921	24	12	23	3	2

The following players do not have any recorded accepted chances at the positions indicated; therefore, are not listed in the fielding averages for those particular positions: Banes, 2b; Blows, p; Borges, 3b; Bryant, ss; Chaney, p; Clements, 3b; Collins, p; Dumouchelle, p; Geren, p; Gloyd, of; Goldetsky, 3b, of; Guerra, p; Guzman, 3b; Harvey, p; Hayford, p; Hibner, 1b; R. Johnson, of; Leach, of; Malespin, p; McDaniel, ss, 3b; Nichols, of; Roeder, ss; Rudolph, p, 2b, 3b, ss, of; Sadey, p; Salas, p; Sanchez, of; M. Silva, p; T. Smith, 3b; Taveras, p; Threatt, p; Thrower, of.

CLUB PITCHING

Club	ERA.	G.	CG.	ShO.	Sv.	IP.	H.	R.	ER.	HR.	HB.	BB.	Int. BB.	SO.	WP.	Bk.
Fort Lauderdale	2.63	134	48	12	16	1114⅔	971	421	325	37	22	378	29	731	49	21
Tampa	3.09	134	23	13	30	1116	993	522	383	36	33	510	39	792	79	21
Fort Myers	3.27	131	33	11	20	1088	1018	501	395	45	25	487	41	696	35	17
Lakeland	3.52	133	41	15	18	1111⅔	1099	530	434	29	30	458	31	631	73	14
Daytona Beach	3.73	135	22	14	21	1099⅔	1134	584	455	36	37	515	45	854	85	25
Winter Haven	3.74	139	27	11	17	1195⅓	1261	636	496	50	28	569	26	731	97	20
St. Petersburg	3.80	132	38	16	15	1082	1072	535	457	39	30	469	29	544	65	10
West Palm Beach	3.86	137	30	7	28	1157	1094	602	496	51	38	668	45	871	93	7
Vero Beach	4.10	137	29	3	22	1180⅔	1247	695	537	48	26	654	31	726	81	26
Miami	4.26	136	20	4	22	1125⅔	1185	693	533	63	31	559	27	641	62	13

PITCHERS' RECORDS

(Leading Qualifiers for Earned-Run Average Leadership—112 or More Innings)

*Throws lefthanded.

Pitcher—Club	W.	L.	Pct.	ERA.	G.	GS.	CG.	GF.	ShO.	Sv.	IP.	H.	R.	ER.	HR.	HB.	BB.	Int. BB.	SO.	WP.
Nipper, Winter Haven	14	8	.636	1.70	29	26	15	2	4	1	212	191	59	40	3	2	60	4	139	15
Fiorillo, Tampa*	11	6	.647	1.98	22	22	6	0	2	0	141	122	49	31	3	5	72	1	120	13
Russell, Tampa	10	4	.714	2.01	22	21	5	0	2	0	143	109	51	32	1	3	48	1	92	3
Williams, Lakeland	11	4	.733	2.15	22	22	8	0	5	0	155	135	47	37	3	4	33	2	57	7
Potestio, Fort Myers	6	6	.500	2.23	14	14	11	0	1	0	113	102	38	28	4	2	30	3	68	2
Lein, Fort Lauderdale	11	11	.500	2.25	30	21	13	5	2	1	172	163	60	43	10	1	29	2	80	5
Christianson, Fort Lauderdale	16	7	.696	2.28	26	25	14	0	2	0	178	158	59	45	7	5	46	4	98	10
Callahan, Fort Lauderdale	17	8	.680	2.50	25	24	10	0	2	0	180	144	69	50	4	4	66	4	121	2
Thomas, St. Petersburg	9	10	.474	2.65	21	21	9	0	3	0	139	121	52	41	2	2	42	1	50	5
Lochner, Tampa*	9	3	.750	2.79	20	19	2	0	1	0	116	96	42	36	2	0	34	2	91	7

Departmental Leaders: G—Meckes, 53; GS—Boyd, 28; CG—Nipper, 15; ShO—Williams, 5; W—Callahan, 17; L—S. Johnson, 14; Sv—Hoke, Meckes, 13; Pct.—Lochner, 750; IP—Nipper, 212; H—Boyd, 195; R—Sutcliffe, 104; ER—Oroz, 84; HR—Boyd, 11; BB—Westray, 102; IBB—Westray, 13; SO—Westray, 171; HB—Pettibone, 11; WP—Westray, M. Johnson, 18.

(All Pitchers—Listed Alphabetically)

Pitcher—Club	W.	L.	Pct.	ERA.	G.	GS.	CG.	GF.	ShO.	Sv.	IP.	H.	R.	ER.	HR.	HB.	BB.	Int. BB.	SO.	WP.
Alba, St. Petersburg°	0	0	.000	8.10	6	0	0	4	0	0	10	18	10	9	0	1	8	0	4	1
Alvarez, Miami-Fort Myers	8	4	.667	3.00	25	15	6	6	0	2	132	128	58	44	4	2	42	7	64	2
Anderson, West Palm Beach	1	2	.333	3.89	17	2	0	7	0	1	37	28	18	16	2	2	33	2	40	8
Arigoni, St. Petersburg	7	5	.583	3.32	19	19	5	0	1	0	103	112	48	38	4	1	31	1	61	3
Arnold, Miami	2	1	.667	1.23	6	3	0	2	0	0	22	21	4	3	0	0	3	0	8	0
Baldwin, Winter Haven	2	3	.400	2.29	34	0	0	23	0	3	59	63	27	15	1	3	24	3	35	3
Beecroft, Lakeland	0	2	.000	9.90	5	3	0	1	0	0	10	13	18	11	1	1	15	0	6	7
Blows, West Palm Beach	0	2	.000	4.85	7	1	0	1	0	1	13	14	8	7	0	1	9	2	7	0
Bolton, Winter Haven°	2	9	.182	4.50	24	16	0	3	0	0	92	125	62	46	5	3	41	2	47	7
Botelho, Fort Myers	2	3	.400	1.62	8	4	1	3	1	1	39	25	10	7	3	0	9	2	32	0
Boyd, Winter Haven	14	8	.636	3.63	28	28	6	0	2	0	186	195	90	75	11	2	54	0	154	17
Brown, Daytona Beach	5	3	.625	3.14	10	9	3	0	1	0	63	71	28	22	2	3	23	5	56	7
Brown, Miami	3	3	.500	3.40	17	1	1	9	0	1	53	47	25	20	4	0	21	1	35	3
Browning, Fort Lauderdale	1	1	.500	3.46	17	0	0	14	0	1	26	22	10	10	1	0	12	2	21	2
Bryant, Vero Beach	2	7	.222	4.28	27	10	0	8	0	2	80	88	59	38	4	2	61	3	47	6
Buckle, Tampa	1	2	.333	1.93	4	4	1	0	1	0	28	21	9	6	1	2	9	2	19	2
Cacciatorre, Daytona Beach	0	4	.000	9.50	5	4	0	1	0	0	18	26	23	19	1	3	10	0	6	7
Calhoun, Daytona Beach°	6	6	.500	3.73	21	20	5	1	3	0	111	106	55	46	3	2	71	3	94	10
Callahan, Fort Lauderdale	17	8	.680	2.50	25	24	10	0	2	0	180	144	69	50	4	4	66	4	121	2
Cates, West Palm Beach	7	5	.583	3.70	24	11	3	5	0	2	107	87	56	44	6	7	50	4	72	7
Cecil, Fort Myers	3	2	.600	2.87	17	0	0	11	0	2	47	38	18	15	2	1	11	3	21	1
Chaney, Lakeland	0	0	.000	0.00	1	0	0	1	0	0	1	1	0	0	0	0	0	0	0	0
Chapin, West Palm Beach	14	8	.636	3.25	27	23	7	3	1	1	166	160	79	60	5	4	92	4	116	14
Chesser, West Palm Beach	5	1	.833	2.53	8	7	3	1	1	0	57	50	21	16	1	0	20	4	27	0
Christianson, Fort Lauderdale	16	7	.696	2.28	26	25	14	0	4	0	178	158	59	45	7	5	46	4	98	10
Clark, Miami°	2	5	.286	3.90	26	0	0	9	0	2	30	28	17	13	1	1	18	2	30	1
Cole, Miami°	0	5	.000	7.95	16	7	0	5	0	0	43	55	53	38	4	0	45	1	18	2
Collins, St. Petersburg	8	5	.615	3.64	24	24	7	0	1	0	146	143	61	59	6	1	55	2	61	12
Collins, Fort Lauderdale	0	0	.000	3.00	1	0	0	1	0	0	3	2	2	1	0	0	3	0	2	0
Collyer, Lakeland°	3	3	.500	5.29	14	2	0	1	0	1	34	38	26	20	4	1	24	1	19	5
Cooke, Winter Haven°	7	2	.778	3.15	31	0	0	19	0	5	60	60	25	21	1	0	23	2	28	3
Cooper, Fort Myers	4	2	.667	3.71	16	12	3	1	0	1	85	89	40	35	4	2	33	4	39	0
Cote, Winter Haven	3	7	.300	3.29	29	8	2	12	0	0	93	96	47	34	4	3	58	5	40	5
Cratch, Miami	1	3	.250	8.14	6	4	1	1	0	0	21	34	23	19	0	1	6	0	10	5
Cvejdlik, Fort Myers	1	2	.333	3.18	5	5	1	0	0	0	34	38	17	12	0	1	7	0	7	1
Davis, St. Petersburg	1	4	.200	6.83	11	5	0	0	0	0	29	35	24	22	2	2	26	2	18	1
DeJiulio, Tampa	5	3	.625	3.23	42	5	0	12	0	2	92	81	46	33	8	2	47	6	71	4
DeSanto, Winter Haven	1	9	.100	5.88	19	10	0	3	0	0	72	74	58	47	8	5	69	0	40	17
Dixon, Miami	1	8	.111	4.35	11	11	3	0	0	0	60	57	41	29	4	1	42	2	40	1
Dolby, Miami	0	1	.000	8.31	6	0	0	5	0	1	13	19	14	12	3	0	10	0	2	4
Dougherty, Fort Lauderdale°	7	3	.700	2.16	15	12	2	1	0	0	75	78	26	18	3	0	25	2	37	3
Dozier, St. Petersburg	2	2	.500	5.59	15	2	0	3	0	0	37	38	23	23	3	0	21	3	13	2
Dumouchelle, Miami	0	0	.000	36.00	1	0	0	0	0	0	1	3	4	4	0	0	2	0	0	0
Elsee, Daytona Beach	3	8	.273	5.63	19	13	0	2	0	0	72	90	60	45	1	2	52	3	46	11
Fadhel, West Palm Beach	4	4	.500	2.39	10	5	3	2	1	0	49	33	15	13	0	4	21	0	34	0
Fauland, Fort Lauderdale°	1	2	.333	2.25	37	3	0	20	0	3	64	55	23	16	1	0	28	2	35	3
Fellows, Lakeland	8	10	.444	4.78	24	23	5	0	0	0	130	142	81	69	3	1	57	3	60	12
Ferroni, Miami°	1	2	.333	6.00	8	5	0	3	0	0	24	26	18	16	1	1	24	0	5	7
Filson, Fort Lauderdale°	7	1	.875	1.99	11	10	4	1	1	1	68	56	20	15	0	0	20	0	68	2
Fiorillo, Tampa°	11	6	.647	1.98	22	22	6	0	2	0	141	122	49	31	3	5	72	1	120	13
Fontenot, Fort Lauderdale	1	4	.200	5.60	8	8	0	0	0	0	45	50	34	28	2	1	31	1	37	9
Forer, Vero Beach	1	0	1.000	6.75	13	0	0	3	0	0	12	23	16	9	2	2	11	1	8	3
Franco, Vero Beach°	7	4	.636	3.53	13	11	3	1	0	0	79	78	41	31	2	2	41	2	60	5
Freeman, Tampa°	5	0	1.000	2.00	20	0	0	20	0	9	43	26	2	0	0	0	9	4	38	2
Gardner, Daytona Beach	6	10	.375	3.33	23	22	3	1	2	0	138	146	64	51	6	6	39	5	109	3
Garner, Lakeland	4	4	.500	3.56	29	7	4	8	0	3	91	79	42	36	5	3	58	7	89	4
Geren, St. Petersburg	0	0	.000	9.00	1	0	0	0	0	0	1	2	1	1	0	0	0	0	0	0
Gibson, Lakeland°	4	3	.571	2.95	20	3	2	9	0	0	64	64	25	21	1	4	21	2	38	4
Glasscock, West Palm Beach°	1	3	.250	1.24	24	0	0	14	0	5	29	24	9	4	0	1	21	2	33	3
Gold, Miami	2	9	.182	4.91	14	12	3	2	0	0	77	94	52	42	3	3	30	1	33	6
Gotay, St. Petersburg	3	5	.375	4.57	13	12	2	0	0	0	63	65	42	32	2	5	45	1	55	4
Grapenthin, West Palm Beach	5	4	.556	4.50	31	3	0	19	0	5	80	96	47	40	5	5	22	3	44	5
Gray, Miami	1	1	.500	5.63	11	0	0	3	0	0	32	33	25	20	5	2	18	3	7	3
Greco, Winter Haven°	7	2	.778	4.79	27	0	0	16	0	3	47	58	28	25	2	1	29	2	38	1
Groves, West Palm Beach	2	8	.200	3.77	33	10	2	17	0	2	105	111	56	44	6	0	43	5	42	4
Guerra, Fort Lauderdale	0	1	.000	4.50	3	0	0	2	0	0	2	1	1	1	0	0	2	0	0	1
Gumpert, Lakeland	8	5	.615	2.50	14	14	8	0	3	0	108	97	33	30	2	2	26	1	75	2
Hammond, Vero Beach°	2	2	.500	1.38	34	1	0	21	0	6	52	40	12	8	0	2	20	1	46	3
Harsh, Fort Myers	5	1	.833	2.79	6	6	0	0	0	0	42	44	19	13	2	1	20	1	29	2
Harvey, Fort Myers	0	0	.000	6.75	2	1	0	1	0	0	4	5	3	3	0	0	2	0	2	0
Hawk, Daytona Beach	0	2	.000	8.31	15	2	0	7	0	1	26	34	28	24	1	1	26	2	17	4
Hayes, Tampa	5	2	.714	1.83	32	0	0	26	0	12	54	36	13	11	1	1	25	3	53	4
Hayford, Winter Haven	0	1	.000	0.00	3	0	0	3	0	0	3	3	1	0	0	0	3	0	2	0
Heathcock, Daytona Beach	9	0	1.000	1.27	11	11	2	0	0	0	85	67	20	12	0	2	21	2	77	2
Herman, Winter Haven	4	10	.286	4.91	35	11	2	10	0	1	110	118	71	60	5	4	57	2	52	3
Hernandez, Daytona Beach	6	5	.545	3.42	13	12	2	0	0	0	79	67	36	30	1	6	34	2	61	1
Hoke, Miami	4	6	.400	2.47	51	0	0	44	0	13	62	59	24	17	2	0	20	3	55	4
Horton, St. Petersburg°	7	3	.700	4.41	28	15	2	8	1	2	100	101	52	49	6	1	49	2	66	7
Huismann, Fort Myers	3	1	.750	3.43	14	0	0	11	0	2	21	15	9	8	1	2	16	5	19	1
Jackman, Fort Myers°	2	1	.667	3.41	18	0	0	7	0	2	29	27	14	11	2	0	16	4	16	0
Jackson, Daytona Beach	4	2	.667	3.35	10	6	1	0	0	0	43	34	19	16	2	1	16	1	35	1
Johnson, Fort Myers	0	1	.000	6.08	10	7	1	1	0	0	40	45	32	27	1	0	35	3	20	2
Johnson, St. Pete-Day Beach°	2	1	.667	5.25	12	1	0	4	0	0	24	29	17	14	2	1	13	2	23	2
Johnson, Winter Haven	4	8	.333	3.97	32	16	0	9	0	3	118	130	73	52	2	1	58	5	79	18
Johnson, Miami°	5	14	.263	4.95	26	26	0	0	0	0	140	164	96	77	8	2	87	1	68	8
Josephson, Lakeland	5	2	.714	2.61	22	0	0	12	0	1	38	37	15	11	1	3	9	2	21	0

Pitcher—Club	W.	L.	Pct.	ERA.	G.	GS.	CG.	GF.	ShO.	Sv.	IP.	H.	R.	ER.	HR.	HB.	BB.	Int. BB.	SO.	WP.
Kelly, Lakeland	1	1	.500	2.45	2	2	1	0	1	0	11	10	3	3	0	0	7	0	8	0
Kenyon, Vero Beach	4	5	.444	5.60	24	9	2	8	0	0	82	111	64	51	6	1	36	1	34	6
Kish, St. Petersburg	0	1	.000	7.80	7	0	0	2	0	1	15	19	15	13	0	2	10	1	4	1
Klosicki, Tampa	8	6	.571	3.13	45	4	1	16	0	2	112	101	55	39	2	4	47	5	47	5
Krauss, Fort Myers°	2	3	.400	4.22	7	7	0	0	0	0	32	25	18	15	2	0	44	0	13	2
Kreymborg, Miami	0	0	.000	7.11	11	0	0	3	0	0	19	37	18	15	3	0	10	1	13	0
Lackey, Lakeland	1	3	.250	3.32	6	6	3	0	1	0	38	38	17	14	1	1	11	2	12	1
Landrum, Tampa	6	8	.429	3.80	17	16	3	1	1	0	83	87	44	35	6	1	22	2	52	5
Lein, Fort Lauderdale	11	11	.500	2.25	30	21	13	5	2	1	172	163	60	43	10	1	29	2	80	5
Leisure, Lakeland°	2	2	.500	3.39	27	3	0	8	0	0	69	73	35	26	1	1	26	2	40	4
Lochner, Tampa°	9	3	.750	2.79	20	19	2	0	1	0	116	96	42	36	2	0	34	2	91	7
Madden, Vero Beach°	6	12	.333	3.70	21	21	8	0	0	0	146	148	76	60	5	4	79	2	108	12
Malespin, Winter Haven	0	0	.000	0.00	1	0	0	1	0	0	2	1	0	0	0	0	1	0	1	0
Maples, Miami	4	5	.444	3.03	13	13	1	0	0	0	86	57	35	29	6	5	38	0	69	2
McKnight, Daytona Beach	0	0	.000	3.00	1	0	0	1	0	0	3	2	1	1	0	0	2	0	2	0
Meckes, Daytona Beach	6	9	.400	3.04	53	0	0	48	0	13	77	67	35	26	1	5	40	8	79	10
Miller, Lakeland	3	2	.600	5.27	12	7	0	4	0	0	41	50	27	24	0	2	24	1	27	5
Moncrief, Lakeland	9	6	.600	3.74	22	20	4	2	1	0	125	119	64	52	0	3	64	2	66	5
Moore, Tampa°	7	3	.700	4.04	51	0	0	29	0	5	78	86	46	35	3	3	45	11	58	6
Morley, Fort Myers°	2	0	1.000	1.35	4	4	0	0	0	0	20	17	8	3	1	0	9	1	10	1
Morris, Daytona Beach	0	0	.000	4.74	9	2	0	5	0	0	19	20	11	10	2	0	10	0	21	2
Mundie, Daytona Beach	0	1	.000	14.40	1	1	0	0	0	0	5	11	9	8	2	0	1	0	3	0
Murphy, Tampa	6	8	.429	4.54	25	20	2	2	0	0	105	109	73	53	5	1	67	2	58	15
Nail, Lakeland	1	4	.200	6.95	6	6	0	0	0	0	22	32	20	17	1	0	16	0	15	3
Neely, St. Petersburg	6	4	.600	2.11	28	0	0	22	0	4	64	55	18	15	1	2	24	4	51	2
Nelson, Fort Lauderdale	0	0	.000	5.40	2	2	0	0	0	0	10	9	6	6	1	0	5	0	8	2
Nipper, West Haven	14	8	.636	1.70	29	26	15	2	4	1	212	191	59	40	3	2	60	4	139	15
Nurthen, Fort Lauderdale	5	6	.455	3.62	28	10	3	15	2	2	102	92	45	41	4	5	32	4	66	5
Nutter, Lakeland	4	5	.444	1.66	42	0	0	37	0	8	76	64	16	14	1	3	37	4	52	12
O'Malley, Vero Beach	0	0	.000	5.40	3	0	0	1	0	0	5	6	3	3	0	0	9	0	1	1
O'Neal, Lakeland	4	5	.444	2.87	13	11	6	1	2	0	69	59	27	22	3	1	18	0	31	0
Oliveras, Miami	6	5	.545	3.83	19	18	4	0	0	0	108	103	55	46	5	6	48	1	80	3
Oroz, Vero Beach	10	9	.526	4.32	27	27	8	0	2	0	175	178	101	84	10	3	98	4	77	6
Palmer, West Palm Beach	0	0	.000	0.82	3	3	0	0	0	0	11	9	1	1	0	1	5	0	7	0
Patterson, Fort Lauderdale	1	4	.200	3.20	7	7	0	0	0	0	45	31	22	16	2	3	29	1	28	0
Pellack, West Palm Beach	0	0	.000	54.00	2	0	0	1	0	0	1	4	6	6	0	1	3	0	0	0
Penate, Daytona Beach	6	8	.429	2.83	39	14	4	14	1	2	127	136	66	40	4	1	57	7	79	9
Peralta, Miami	2	2	.500	1.64	17	0	0	11	0	2	33	26	7	6	2	1	10	2	24	2
Perry, Vero Beach	2	3	.400	6.30	19	4	0	8	0	3	50	57	38	35	0	1	44	1	38	5
Perry, Daytona Beach°	2	0	1.000	2.70	9	0	0	3	0	1	20	11	6	6	0	1	7	0	22	0
Pettibone, Tampa	6	9	.400	5.38	25	23	3	1	0	0	117	115	90	70	4	11	79	2	82	13
Pippin, Fort Myers	0	3	.000	3.48	21	1	0	17	0	0	31	28	12	12	2	0	17	1	30	3
Plainte, West Haven°	3	8	.273	3.84	20	14	2	5	0	0	82	80	43	35	4	1	32	0	32	4
Potestio, Fort Myers	6	6	.500	2.23	14	14	11	0	1	0	113	102	38	28	4	2	30	3	68	2
Pratt, St. Petersburg	1	2	.333	9.90	6	1	0	2	0	0	10	17	17	11	0	1	13	1	10	3
Raine, Fort Myers	1	4	.200	6.43	9	5	0	2	0	0	21	23	17	15	1	0	19	0	26	0
Ramirez, Miami	0	1	.000	2.77	3	2	0	0	0	0	13	10	8	4	1	0	8	0	10	0
Reade, Vero Beach	1	6	.143	2.57	36	5	0	21	0	2	84	69	35	24	1	6	52	3	67	10
Regalado, Daytona Beach	5	6	.455	3.22	12	12	1	0	0	0	67	75	34	24	1	1	26	2	33	4
Rennicke, Vero Beach	3	2	.600	4.85	5	4	0	0	0	0	26	33	17	14	1	1	10	0	13	2
Robbins, St. Petersburg	5	4	.556	2.88	40	0	0	33	0	6	72	56	23	23	2	3	31	3	33	5
Rudolph, Fort Lauderdale	0	0	.000	9.00	3	0	0	3	0	1	5	8	5	5	0	1	3	0	3	0
Russell, Tampa	10	4	.714	2.01	22	21	5	0	2	0	143	109	51	32	1	3	48	1	92	3
Russell, St. Petersburg	0	3	.000	6.58	6	4	1	1	0	0	26	30	20	19	4	0	11	0	9	4
Sadey, Miami	0	0	.000	0.00	1	0	0	1	0	0	1	0	0	0	0	0	0	0	1	0
Sanford, St. Petersburg	3	1	.750	0.67	4	4	3	0	1	0	27	23	6	2	0	1	8	0	14	0
Schuler, West Palm Beach	2	2	.500	2.06	19	0	0	15	0	6	35	30	10	8	3	0	14	3	28	5
Shaw, Fort Myers	7	1	.875	2.09	14	13	2	1	1	0	86	66	29	20	4	1	49	1	60	4
Silva, St. Petersburg	3	3	.500	4.02	10	7	1	0	1	0	47	45	22	21	0	0	31	4	16	4
Silva, Fort Lauderdale	1	0	1.000	0.00	1	0	0	0	0	0	1	0	0	0	0	0	0	0	0	0
Slezack, Vero Beach	1	1	.500	2.84	8	1	0	3	0	0	19	17	11	6	0	0	17	0	20	4
Smith, Miami	3	8	.273	5.14	23	12	1	4	0	0	91	116	69	52	3	2	30	2	36	7
Smith, Fort Lauderdale	6	2	.750	1.89	38	0	0	24	0	7	57	47	14	12	1	1	18	6	47	1
Squilla, Daytona Beach	1	0	1.000	6.94	27	0	0	11	0	0	35	53	30	27	2	0	29	1	26	7
St. Clair, Fort Myers	7	0	1.000	0.77	22	0	0	21	0	9	35	19	4	3	1	0	11	1	37	0
Staffon, West Palm Beach	5	6	.455	5.91	15	13	1	0	0	0	67	52	51	44	0	3	77	0	49	9
Sutcliffe, Vero Beach	6	8	.429	5.13	27	22	3	3	0	0	144	175	104	82	7	1	64	2	76	7
Taveras, St. Petersburg	0	0	.000	27.00	1	0	0	0	0	0	1	3	3	3	0	0	3	0	1	0
Taylor, West Palm Beach°	8	10	.444	4.50	26	26	4	0	2	0	152	146	87	76	10	5	99	3	140	15
Tennant, Vero Beach	0	0	.000	9.00	2	0	0	0	0	0	6	8	9	6	1	0	10	0	4	1
Thomas, St. Petersburg	9	10	.474	2.65	21	21	9	0	3	0	139	121	52	41	2	2	42	1	50	5
Thorp, Vero Beach	11	10	.524	3.97	23	22	5	1	0	0	145	148	76	64	7	0	73	6	62	7
Threatt, Tampa	0	0	.000	3.60	7	0	0	4	0	0	5	4	2	2	0	0	6	0	11	0
Timlin, Fort Myers	4	9	.308	4.62	29	4	1	17	0	2	78	78	56	40	2	4	51	5	36	6
Torres, West Palm Beach	4	5	.444	5.91	20	9	2	8	0	1	70	78	63	46	7	2	47	0	53	2
Treuel, Lakeland	0	0	.000	27.00	3	0	0	1	0	1	2	7	6	6	0	0	0	0	0	1
Turner, Daytona Beach°	0	0	.000	9.00	2	0	0	0	0	0	3	6	3	3	1	0	2	0	3	1
Untisz, Lakeland	1	3	.250	6.75	11	3	0	6	0	2	24	36	25	18	2	0	10	2	13	1
Vanderbush, Fort Myers	6	2	.750	3.17	18	8	1	5	1	1	71	60	30	25	3	4	42	1	75	3
Wadley, Miami	0	0	.000	3.38	5	2	0	3	0	0	16	20	11	6	1	1	9	0	3	0
Weaver, St. Petersburg	10	9	.526	4.02	25	17	8	1	3	0	130	144	68	58	5	2	37	1	38	6
Weinbrecht, West Haven	1	2	.333	6.90	24	10	0	6	0	1	60	67	52	46	4	3	60	1	44	4
Westray, West Palm Beach	7	9	.438	3.52	25	24	5	1	0	1	161	155	78	63	6	0	102	13	171	18
Wever, Fort Lauderdale	7	3	.700	2.02	22	12	2	0	0	0	81	55	25	18	1	1	29	1	80	4
Williams, Fort Myers	4	2	.667	2.02	8	8	0	0	0	1	58	53	19	13	2	0	7	0	26	1
Williams, Lakeland	11	4	.733	2.15	22	22	8	0	5	0	155	135	47	37	3	4	33	2	57	7
Williams, St. Petersburg	1	2	.333	3.38	12	0	0	11	0	1	16	16	15	6	1	1	6	1	8	1
Willsher, Miami	3	12	.200	4.08	25	15	3	5	0	1	119	122	72	54	5	4	61	3	65	3
Winfield, W.P.B.-St.P.	3	2	.600	2.84	26	1	0	18	0	4	57	42	20	18	1	7	24	1	37	6
Wise, Vero Beach	6	4	.600	2.64	38	0	0	30	0	9	75	68	28	22	3	1	29	5	65	3
Yan, Daytona Beach	7	2	.778	3.13	41	6	1	17	1	4	95	90	42	33	5	2	40	3	67	5
Yuhas, Fort Myers	8	7	.533	4.15	24	23	4	1	2	0	130	152	75	60	6	6	38	3	97	5

BALKS—Oroz, 12; DeSanto, 7; Nurthen, 6; Calhoun, Klosicki, 5 each; Landrum, Moncrief, Wever, 4 each; Buckle, Cates, Christianson, Clark, DeJiulio, Franco, Garner, Harsh, Jackson, M. Johnson, Yan, 3 each; L. Brown, Bryant, Collyer, Dixon, Filson, Gold, Greco, Hernandez, Meckes, Patterson, Perry, Plainte, Regalado, Shaw, Staffon, Timlin, L. Williams, Wise, 2 each; Alba, Arigoni, Arnold, Blows, Bolton, Boyd, Browning, Cacciatorre, Callahan, Cecil, Cooper, Cote, Cvejdlik, Elsee, Fauland, Freeman, Gibson, Gotay, Gumpert, Hammond, Hawk, Hayes, Heathcock, Herman, Hoke, Horton, Jackman, A. Johnson, Kelly, Kenyon, Lackey, Lein, Lochner, Madden, Morris, Murphy, Neely, Nipper, O'Malley, O'Neal, Olivares, Peralta, Pettibone, Pratt, Robbins, J. Russell, R. Russell, F. Silva, F. Smith, Squilla, St. Clair, Sutcliffe, Taveras, Taylor, Vanderbush, Weinbrecht, Willsher, Yuhas, 1 each.

COMBINATION SHUTOUTS—Brown-Penate, Elsee-Penate, Gardner-Meckes, Heathcock-Meckes, Hernandez-Meckes, Yan-Meckes, Daytona Beach; Dougherty-Nurthen, Fontenot-Smith, Wever-Fauland-Smith-Nurthen, Fort Lauderdale; Cooper-St. Clair-Jackman-Timlin, Potestio-St. Clair, Vanderbush-Cecil, Yuhas-Huisman, Fort Myers; Moncrief-Nutter, Moncrief-Untisz, Lakeland; Arnold-Hoke, Ferroni-Hoke, Johnson-Willsher, Smith-Peralta, Miami; Collins-Horton, Davis-Horton, Davis-Dozier-Williams, Gotay-Neely, Horton-Neely, St. Petersburg; DeJiulio-Freeman, Fiorillo-Hayes, Fiorillo-DeJiulio-Threatt, Landrum-Moore, Murphy-Hayes, Russell-Freeman, Tampa; Madden-Hammond, Vero Beach; Chesser-Anderson, Staffon-Glasscock-Schuler, West Palm Beach; Bolton-Weinbrecht, Boyd-Baldwin, Boyd-Johnson, Johnson-Cooke, Plainte-Johnson, Winter Haven.

NO-HIT GAMES—Vanderbush, Fort Myers, defeated Daytona Beach, June 9, first game (seven innings); Botelho, Fort Myers, defeated Miami, June 17, first game (seven innings); Nurthen, Fort Lauderdale, defeated Miami, August 11, second game (seven innings); O'Neal, Lakeland, defeated Winter Haven, August 23, first game (seven innings).

Midwest League

CLASS A

CHAMPIONSHIP WINNERS IN PREVIOUS YEARS

1947—Belleville .... .667	1960—Waterloo .... .629	1971—Appleton .... .642
Belleville .... .672	Waterloo .... .677	Quad Cities a .... .548
1948—West Frankfort° .... .708	1961—Waterloo .... .613	1972—Appleton .... .598
1949—Centralia .... .627	Quincy z .... .594	Danville a .... .584
Paducah (4th)† .... .454	1962—Dubuque z .... .667	1973—Wisconsin Rapids a .... .562
1950—Centralia‡ .... .675	Waterloo .... .625	Danville .... .537
1951—Paris§ .... .700	1963—Clinton .... .710	1974—Appleton .... .593
Danville (4th)† .... .432	Clinton .... .629	Danville a .... .517
1952—Danville x .... .685	1964—Clinton .... .667	1975—Waterloo a .... .727
Decatur (3rd)† .... .584	Fox Cities z .... .667	Quad Cities .... .624
1953—Decatur° .... .576	1965—Burlington .... .667	1976—Waterloo a .... .600
1954—Decatur .... .587	Burlington .... .677	Cedar Rapids .... .595
Danville (2nd)‡ .... .528	1966—Fox Cities z .... .689	1977—Waterloo .... .580
1955—Dubuque° .... .587	Cedar Rapids .... .762	Burlington a .... .511
1956—Paris y .... .656	1967—Wisconsin Rapids .... .685	1978—Appleton a .... .708
Dubuque .... .603	Appleton z .... .587	Burlington .... .500
1957—Decatur y .... .683	1968—Decatur .... .656	1979—Waterloo .... .600
Clinton .... .623	Quad Cities z .... .648	Quad Cities a .... .579
1958—Michigan City .... .623	1969—Appleton .... .648	1980—Waterloo a .... .610
Waterloo z .... .613	Appleton .... .690	Quad Cities .... .532
1959—Waterloo .... .613	1970—Quincy z .... .691	
Waterloo .... .613	Quad Cities .... .581	

°Won championship and four-club playoff. †Won four-club playoff. ‡Playoff finals canceled because of bad weather. §Won both halves of split-season. xWon first half of split-season and tied Paris for second-half title. yWon first-half title and four-team playoff. zWon split-season playoff. aLeague divided into Northern and Southern divisions and played split-season. Playoff winner. (NOTE—Known as Illinois State League in 1947-48 and Mississippi-Ohio Valley League from 1949 through 1955.)

STANDING OF CLUBS AT CLOSE OF FIRST HALF, JUNE 19

NORTHERN DIVISION

Club	W.	L.	T.	Pct.	G.B.
Wausau (Mariners)	41	23	1	.641	....
Waterloo (Indians)	40	26	0	.606	2
Wisconsin Rapids (Twins)	36	29	1	.554	5½
Appleton (White Sox)	29	36	0	.446	12½

SOUTHERN DIVISION

Club	W.	L.	T.	Pct.	G.B.
Cedar Rapids° (Reds)	37	29	0	.561	....
Quad Cities° (Cubs)	37	29	0	.561	....
Burlington (Indians)	21	45	0	.318	16
Clinton (Giants)	21	45	0	.318	16

STANDING OF CLUBS AT CLOSE OF SECOND HALF, SEPTEMBER 1

NORTHERN DIVISION

Club	W.	L.	T.	Pct.	G.B.
Wausau (Mariners)	43	25	0	.632	....
Waterloo (Indians)	41	29	0	.586	3
Wisconsin Rapids (Twins)	32	36	0	.471	11
Appleton (White Sox)	25	44	0	.362	18½

SOUTHERN DIVISION

Club	W.	L.	T.	Pct.	G.B.
Quad Cities (Cubs)	40	29	0	.580	....
Burlington (Indians)	33	36	0	.478	7
Clinton (Giants)	31	35	0	.470	7½
Cedar Rapids (Reds)	28	39	0	.418	11

°Cedar Rapids and Quad Cities finished first half of split season tied. Cedar Rapids defeated Quad Cities on July 2 to win first-half Southern Division Championship.

COMPOSITE STANDING OF CLUBS AT CLOSE OF SEASON, SEPTEMBER 1

Club	Wau.	Wat.	Q.C.	W.R.	C.R.	Apl.	Bur.	Cln.	W.	L.	T.	Pct.	G.B.
Wausau (Mariners)	....	11	12	13	10	15	9	14	84	48	0	.636	....
Waterloo (Indians)	13	....	5	15	9	18	14	7	81	55	0	.596	5
Quad Cities (Cubs)	4	11	....	9	13	10	14	16	77	58	0	.570	8½
Wisconsin Rapids (Twins)	9	9	7	....	11	14	9	9	68	65	0	.511	16½
Cedar Rapids (Reds)	6	7	10	5	....	8	16	13	65	68	0	.489	19½
Appleton (White Sox)	7	6	6	10	8	....	8	9	54	80	0	.403	31
Burlington (Brewers)	7	2	10	7	8	8	....	12	54	81	0	.400	31½
Clinton (Giants)	2	9	8	6	9	7	11	....	52	80	0	.394	32

Quad Cities represented Davenport and Bettendorf, Ia., and Moline and Rock Island, Ill.

Major league affiliations in parentheses.

Playoffs—Wausau defeated Waterloo, two games to one; Quad Cities defeated Cedar Rapids, two games to one. Wausau defeated Quad Cities, two games to none, for League Championship.

Regular-Season Attendance—Appleton, 66,780; Burlington, 62,127; Cedar Rapids, 89,824; Clinton, 67,940; Quad Cities, 134,142; Waterloo, 80,355; Wausau, 58,116; Wisconsin Rapids, 43,509. Total, 602,793. Playoff, 6,829. All-star game, 2,822.

Managers: Appleton, Sam Ewing; Burlington, Terry Bevington; Cedar Rapids, Randy Davidson; Clinton, Wendall Kim; Quad Cities, Rich Morales; Waterloo, Gomer Hodge; Wausau, Bill Plummer; Wisconsin Rapids, Ken Staples.

All-Star Team: 1B—Kenneth Foster, Wisconsin Rapids; 2B—Harold Reynolds, Wausau; 3B—Randy Ready, Burlington; SS—Darnell Coles, Wausau; OF—Henry Cotto, Quad Cities; James Eisenreich, Wisconsin Rapids; Edwin Saavedra, Waterloo; C—John Fimple, Waterloo; DH—Kevin King, Wausau; LHP, Starter—Richard Adair, Wausau; RHP, Starter—Edwin Nunez, Wausau; LHP, Reliever—Raymond Gallo, Burlington; RHP, Reliever—Conrad Everett, Wisconsin Rapids; MVP—Edwin Saavedra, Waterloo; Manager—Gomer Hodge, Wausau.

(Compiled by Howe News Bureau, Boston, Mass.)

CLUB BATTING

Club	Pct.	G.	AB.	R.	OR.	H.	TB.	2B.	3B.	HR.	RBI.	GW.	SH.	SF.	HP.	BB.	Int. BB.	SO.	SB.	CS.	LOB.
Wausau	.274	133	4259	768	552	1168	1833	198	16	145	658	70	61	30	44	577	20	809	237	111	878
Waterloo	.265	136	4389	695	600	1163	1756	194	27	115	598	49	78	44	45	560	33	907	215	87	965
Wisconsin Rapids	.251	134	4253	671	628	1069	1565	164	13	102	576	53	84	38	41	628	22	783	112	53	1003

Club	Pct.	G.	AB.	R.	OR.	H.	TB.	2B.	3B.	HR.	RBI.	GW.	SH.	SF.	HP.	BB.	Int. BB.	SO.	SB.	CS.	LOB.
Burlington	.247	135	4259	553	707	1052	1547	145	19	104	482	44	54	28	35	470	17	814	173	100	890
Quad Cities	.243	135	4279	569	547	1038	1444	133	39	65	486	61	38	37	41	527	22	966	166	63	936
Clinton	.239	132	4155	537	617	991	1281	154	23	30	467	42	32	31	37	566	17	772	135	68	944
Appleton	.230	134	4300	498	584	987	1363	157	42	45	421	44	52	31	33	491	31	883	106	57	948
Cedar Rapids	.222	133	4225	484	540	938	1350	147	23	73	416	49	52	22	33	513	24	891	96	42	954

INDIVIDUAL BATTING

(Leading Qualifiers for Batting Championship—367 or More Plate Appearances)

°Bats lefthanded.   †Switch-hitter.

Player and Club	Pct.	G.	AB.	R.	H.	TB.	2B.	3B.	HR.	RBI.	GW.	SH.	SF.	HP.	BB.	Int. BB.	SO.	SB.	CS.
Saavedra, Edwin, Waterloo	.336	125	453	87	152	240	25	3	19	85	7	6	6	5	62	8	53	36	7
Eisenreich, James, Wis Rapids°	.311	134	489	101	152	248	27	0	23	99	11	5	7	0	84	7	70	9	4
Ready, Randy, Burlington	.308	110	367	74	113	181	17	0	17	56	4	6	3	3	85	2	54	7	6
Calderon, Ivan, Wausau	.306	117	402	79	123	204	19	1	20	62	4	2	2	4	39	2	96	26	12
Torres, A. Raymundo, Appleton	.306	106	369	57	113	186	21	8	12	63	6	0	5	5	44	5	63	21	11
Reynolds, Harold, Wausau†	.296	127	493	98	146	208	23	3	11	59	3	12	4	2	56	1	47	69	20
Cotto, Henry, Quad Cities	.292	128	493	80	144	174	15	6	1	46	6	1	4	5	59	4	62	52	16
Gruber, Kelly, Waterloo	.290	127	458	64	133	208	25	4	14	59	8	10	2	6	24	4	85	15	7
Fimple, John, Waterloo	.288	108	371	53	107	162	21	2	10	76	9	3	8	7	50	1	77	2	5
Walker, Glen, Wausau	.283	119	441	80	125	251	21	0	35	111	13	4	3	8	37	3	103	7	7

Departmental Leaders: G—Eisenreich, 134; AB—Piggott, 507; R—Moses, 102; H—Eisenreich, Saavedra, 152; TB—Walker, 251; 2B—Eisenreich, 27; 3B—T. Johnson, 9; HR—Walker, 35; RBI—Walker, 111; GWRBI—Walker, 13; SH—Methven, Moses, Suarez, 13; SF—Fimple, 8; BB—Moses, 103; HP—Walsh, 10; SO—Cataline, 171; SB—Reynolds, 69; CS—Moses, 21.

(All Players—Listed Alphabetically)

Player and Club	Pct.	G.	AB.	R.	H.	TB.	2B.	3B.	HR.	RBI.	GW.	SH.	SF.	HP.	BB.	Int. BB.	SO.	SB.	CS.
Adams, Jeffery, Cedar Rapids	.058	22	52	1	3	3	0	0	0	0	0	0	0	0	2	0	19	0	0
Adams, Manuel, Clinton†	.252	58	202	22	51	66	6	0	3	30	3	0	0	4	33	5	39	3	2
Adams, Patrick, Appleton	.211	46	161	11	34	41	3	2	0	6	1	3	0	2	8	1	43	0	0
Aieallo, Talbot, Wisconsin Rapids	.179	10	39	6	7	13	3	0	1	4	0	0	0	2	0	0	12	0	0
Allen, Shane, Quad Cities	.189	74	233	20	44	58	9	1	1	16	1	5	2	0	20	0	48	2	2
Aponte, Edwin, Wausau	.267	66	240	35	64	89	5	1	6	30	4	4	2	2	22	0	23	4	9
Asbell, John, Waterloo	.000	7	1	0	0	0	0	0	0	0	0	0	0	0	0	0	1	0	0
Austin, Terry, Quad Cities	.245	113	387	54	95	134	10	4	7	39	6	4	0	4	49	1	99	13	7
Baez, Jesse, Wausau	.264	41	110	18	29	33	1	0	1	12	1	2	1	2	24	0	6	3	0
Bass, Ricki, Burlington	.277	124	447	87	124	169	16	4	7	37	3	5	2	4	81	2	45	43	14
Bazan, Pedro, Quad Cities°	.250	51	160	12	40	45	5	0	0	7	2	2	1	2	16	1	23	0	1
Blume, David, Wausau°	.276	74	210	31	58	84	11	0	5	28	2	3	1	0	39	0	49	3	3
Bowden, Mark, Cedar Rapids°	.167	10	6	1	1	1	0	0	0	0	0	0	1	0	0	0	4	0	0
Buchanan, Robert, Cedar Rapids°	.212	26	52	8	11	13	2	0	0	1	0	4	0	0	5	0	8	0	0
Buckley, Michael, Quad Cities	.201	113	339	39	68	82	6	1	2	25	3	4	1	5	33	0	77	9	6
Buggs, Michael, Appleton	.169	57	178	19	30	44	6	1	2	14	0	3	1	2	26	1	48	3	2
Burton, Jeffrey, Quad Cities	.281	24	89	15	25	43	4	1	4	18	3	0	0	1	12	1	29	1	2
Calderon, Ivan, Wausau	.306	117	402	79	123	204	19	1	20	62	4	2	2	4	39	2	96	26	12
Carlson, Brad, Wisconsin Rapids	.212	11	33	1	7	9	2	0	0	4	0	0	0	0	6	0	13	0	1
Castillo, Juan, Burlington†	.247	110	365	36	90	118	8	4	4	34	3	8	2	2	23	1	70	16	11
Cataline, Daniel, Quad Cities	.219	126	434	66	95	163	14	3	16	60	9	3	2	6	50	3	171	11	7
Chandler, Kenneth, Wisconsin Rapids	.226	100	332	39	75	137	15	1	15	61	7	5	3	3	33	2	119	5	1
Chelette, John, Wausau°	.213	41	127	18	27	36	6	0	1	13	2	1	1	1	15	1	16	4	2
Cochran, Arnold, Waterloo	.053	10	19	1	1	1	0	0	0	1	0	0	0	0	2	0	6	0	0
Cole, Michael, Wisconsin Rapids°	.249	114	414	75	103	120	8	3	1	22	2	9	2	9	63	2	52	32	14
Coles, Darnell, Wausau	.274	111	354	53	97	150	20	3	9	48	6	5	5	6	42	1	67	9	8
Connally, Fritzie, Quad Cities	.314	32	105	23	33	55	10	0	4	23	4	1	3	0	30	0	10	6	1
Contreras, Henry, Burlington	.125	21	48	5	6	6	0	0	0	2	0	1	0	2	2	0	13	0	0
Corbett, Raymond, Cedar Rapids	.267	99	326	40	87	122	21	1	4	35	5	3	2	5	45	0	63	4	0
Cotto, Henry, Quad Cities	.292	128	493	80	144	174	15	6	1	46	6	1	4	5	59	4	62	52	16
Crist, Clark, Wausau	.238	6	21	4	5	10	2	0	1	4	1	0	0	1	1	3	3	0	0
Davidsmeier, Daniel, Burlington	.272	68	250	34	68	99	10	0	7	33	7	5	2	4	28	0	29	11	8
Dekraai, Bradley, Burlington	.240	8	25	5	6	11	2	0	1	1	0	0	0	1	1	0	3	1	1
Diaz, Enrique, Wausau	.266	118	403	61	107	168	17	1	14	59	6	3	3	4	54	1	94	18	6
Doby, Larry, Appleton†	.231	24	78	10	18	25	2	1	1	11	3	1	2	1	16	2	26	0	1
Donofrio, Larry, Appleton	.207	80	241	29	50	82	12	1	6	25	3	4	1	2	36	2	72	2	3
Dotson, Lawrence, Waterloo°	.290	62	231	40	67	88	9	3	2	32	3	6	1	1	18	0	24	7	3
Drzayich, Emil, Cedar Rapids°	.229	125	467	51	107	171	22	0	14	59	5	0	2	2	37	8	56	0	2
Duarte, Luis, Waterloo	.205	44	127	15	26	33	5	1	0	19	1	0	3	1	14	0	20	1	0
Dugas, Shanie, Waterloo°	.258	119	392	69	101	189	17	1	23	83	3	1	4	3	74	5	109	14	2
Edmonds, Stanley, Wausau°	.258	55	182	33	47	75	12	2	4	28	6	2	0	0	20	1	30	7	2
Eisenreich, James, Wisconsin Rap.°	.311	134	489	101	152	248	27	0	23	99	11	5	7	0	84	7	70	9	4
Elkin, Ricky, Waterloo	.200	12	15	0	3	3	0	0	0	1	0	1	0	0	1	0	6	0	0
Ellison, Darold, Waterloo	.000	8	10	1	0	0	0	0	0	1	0	1	0	0	6	0	4	0	0
Ender, Scott, Cedar Rapids	.172	24	58	3	10	10	.0	0	1	7	1	1	1	0	4	0	11	0	0
Epperson, Charles, Appleton†	.244	35	119	8	29	39	7	0	1	19	1	1	1	0	12	0	30	1	0
Erickson, Donald, Clinton°	.208	76	264	24	55	78	10	2	3	28	4	1	2	1	15	2	64	1	2
Espy, Cecil, Appleton†	.201	72	273	37	55	64	2	2	1	19	0	8	0	1	30	2	54	11	3
Ficklin, Winston, Waterloo†	.268	24	56	10	15	19	1	0	1	7	1	1	1	0	8	0	19	3	1
Figueroa, Richard, Clinton	.224	77	241	30	54	68	6	1	2	32	4	1	1	1	30	0	31	8	1
Fimple, John, Waterloo	.288	108	371	53	107	162	21	2	10	76	9	3	8	7	50	1	77	2	5
Flores, James, Wisconsin Rapids†	.275	75	258	48	71	80	9	0	0	23	4	9	2	2	62	3	34	9	5
Foster, Kenneth, Wisconsin Rapids	.281	122	434	64	122	177	10	0	15	85	4	2	3	5	58	4	50	10	5
Frazier, Kenneth, Appleton	.193	35	88	5	17	22	3	1	0	7	0	2	1	0	10	0	12	1	1
Freeburg, Larry, Cedar Rapids	.034	16	29	0	1	2	1	0	0	0	0	2	0	0	1	0	13	0	0
Gallagher, David, Waterloo	.234	127	435	55	102	135	22	1	3	34	4	12	4	3	38	2	67	12	10
Garcia, A. Leonardo, Appleton°	.261	107	395	55	103	132	14	6	1	38	6	4	4	1	22	5	47	20	11
George, Leo, Quad Cities°	.250	5	12	3	3	7	1	0	1	3	1	0	0	0	3	0	4	0	0
Gertz, Michael, Waterloo°	.252	88	282	37	71	110	16	1	7	32	2	4	4	3	38	3	102	12	5
Golden, Ike, Appleton°	.176	27	68	5	12	13	1	0	0	4	2	0	1	0	2	11	0	31	0	0
Gomez, Arthur, Clinton	.000	26	4	0	0	0	0	0	0	0	0	0	0	0	0	0	2	0	0
Gomez, Marcos, Burlington†	.103	11	29	2	3	6	0	0	1	1	0	1	0	0	4	0	7	1	2
Gonzales, Orlando, Burlington	.248	94	298	31	74	107	9	0	8	28	2	4	5	2	18	0	62	9	5

Player and Club	Pct.	G.	AB.	R.	H.	TB.	2B.	3B.	HR.	RBI.	GW.	SH.	SF.	HP.	BB.	Int. BB.	SO.	SB.	CS.
Gruber, Kelly, Waterloo	.290	127	458	64	133	208	25	4	14	59	8	10	2	6	24	4	85	15	7
Hall, David, Cedar Rapids	.257	122	435	49	112	166	11	2	13	58	8	1	3	0	44	3	95	11	3
Hanley, John, Appleton	.240	44	121	13	29	50	4	1	5	19	1	1	2	2	23	2	28	1	0
Henderson, Joseph, Clinton°	.174	55	195	21	34	47	6	2	1	22	0	1	0	0	22	0	63	1	1
Hernandez, Nicholas, Burlington	.250	2	4	0	1	1	0	0	0	1	0	0	1	1	0	0	0	0	0
Higgins, Mark, Burlington	.122	28	90	7	11	11	0	0	0	2	0	0	1	2	7	0	34	2	4
Hill, Anthony, Appleton	.167	53	174	23	29	34	5	0	0	10	2	4	1	2	17	0	37	11	2
Hill, D. Clay, Wausau°	.220	33	91	10	20	29	6	0	1	11	3	4	0	0	11	0	18	0	2
Hinds, Kevin, Cedar Rapids	.208	36	144	18	30	39	9	0	0	7	1	1	1	2	16	0	27	4	1
Hoenstine, David, Cedar Rapids	.227	106	286	47	65	75	8	1	0	21	5	4	2	3	86	0	33	16	9
Hollenbach, Charleton, Cedar Rap.°	.000	16	19	2	0	0	0	0	0	2	0	2	0	0	8	0	13	0	0
Holmes, Stanley, Wisconsin Rapids	.291	54	182	27	53	88	12	1	7	38	2	2	1	1	26	0	35	0	0
Housey, Joseph, Quad Cities	.000	21	3	0	0	0	0	0	0	0	0	0	0	0	0	0	2	0	0
Hyman, Donald, Quad Cities	.188	41	133	10	25	34	6	0	1	12	0	2	4	0	11	1	31	1	0
Jackson, Larry, Cedar Rapids	.667	6	6	0	4	7	3	0	0	4	0	2	0	0	2	0	2	0	0
Johnson, James, Clinton	.268	118	448	70	120	149	23	3	0	38	2	2	4	3	47	3	84	42	13
Johnson, Thomas, Quad Cities	.236	129	441	56	104	159	10	9	9	59	10	3	5	4	57	3	131	23	9
Jones, Eric, Waterloo	.232	28	82	16	19	31	2	2	2	11	0	4	0	2	16	0	28	13	2
Jones, Jeffery, Cedar Rapids	.232	79	246	52	57	118	6	2	17	50	5	3	2	6	69	1	95	18	2
Jones, Ronnie, Burlington†	.199	39	151	14	30	33	3	0	0	9	2	3	0	0	15	0	47	8	7
Jordan, J. Steven, Burlington	.260	29	77	4	20	27	1	0	2	10	1	2	0	0	5	0	15	1	0
Junker, Lance, Clinton	.268	67	235	33	63	77	9	1	1	24	1	2	3	3	39	1	36	13	3
Kent, Wesley, Appleton	.211	97	342	36	72	107	17	0	6	27	3	0	3	1	29	5	133	2	1
Kepshire, Kurt, Cedar Rapids°	.167	39	18	2	3	5	2	0	0	1	0	2	0	0	2	0	9	0	0
King, Kevin, Wausau†	.306	56	193	43	59	120	13	0	16	52	4	0	1	2	32	2	57	4	5
Kirby, Charles, Burlington	.264	33	91	8	24	28	2	1	0	12	0	1	0	0	10	0	17	6	8
Kyles, Stanley, Quad Cities	.000	9	2	0	0	0	0	0	0	0	0	0	0	1	0	0	1	0	0
Lenti, Michael, Clinton	.214	81	201	34	43	62	5	4	2	18	1	0	0	3	44	0	33	13	1
Lesley, Bradley, Cedar Rapids	.250	22	4	0	1	1	0	0	0	1	0	2	0	0	0	0	0	0	0
Liska, Anthony, Clinton	.235	4	17	1	4	6	2	0	0	0	0	0	0	0	0	0	5	0	0
Littman, Jerome, Clinton°	.295	69	207	28	61	77	11	1	1	23	1	0	0	2	43	1	44	8	9
Locascio, Lawrence, Waterloo	.246	22	65	7	16	26	2	1	2	8	1	2	1	1	5	0	9	1	2
Lomastro, Gerardo, Wis. Rapids	.275	69	229	42	63	110	8	0	13	39	2	2	4	3	22	1	65	4	1
Lowery, Steven, Cedar Rapids	.000	11	1	0	0	0	0	0	0	0	0	1	0	0	0	0	0	0	0
Malkin, John, Waterloo	.242	56	194	30	47	93	8	1	12	34	1	2	2	3	20	4	40	1	4
McCain, Michael, Wis. Rapids°	.246	67	232	37	57	87	8	2	6	30	4	8	0	1	34	0	45	1	2
McKay, Karl, Burlington	.143	40	119	4	17	17	0	0	0	6	0	3	0	1	14	1	34	6	5
McKinney, Gregory, Cedar Rapids°	.172	85	215	16	37	67	5	2	7	22	1	0	0	1	34	2	89	3	3
Meier, Scott, Appleton	.204	53	137	9	28	35	5	1	0	12	3	2	1	0	26	0	36	2	0
Methven, Marlin, Waterloo†	.256	130	454	88	116	155	17	2	6	37	3	13	4	2	98	1	83	31	17
Michael, Steven, Burlington°	.274	96	332	50	91	155	19	0	15	61	7	1	2	1	48	6	62	7	5
Miglio, John, Quad Cities°	.000	35	2	0	0	0	0	0	0	0	0	0	0	0	0	0	0	0	0
Miley, David, Cedar Rapids°	.195	38	118	9	23	31	5	0	1	11	2	0	1	0	14	1	16	0	0
Miller, Gerald, Burlington	.229	126	424	60	97	161	8	1	18	64	6	4	5	4	47	0	100	21	8
Minaya, Omar, Wausau	.148	25	54	11	8	12	1	0	1	9	0	0	2	0	10	0	18	3	1
Monroe, Gary, Quad Cities	.000	3	3	1	0	0	0	0	0	0	0	0	0	0	0	0	3	0	0
Morales, Joe, Burlington†	.192	53	151	10	29	34	5	0	0	11	0	3	1	0	27	1	35	4	5
Morris, Angel, Burlington	.000	1	1	0	0	0	0	0	0	0	0	0	0	0	0	0	0	0	0
Morse, Michael, Appleton	.262	126	458	67	120	164	16	5	6	48	8	3	3	5	56	0	62	12	7
Moses, John, Wausau†	.280	123	429	102	120	159	24	3	3	48	7	13	2	3	103	4	67	50	21
Myles, Rick, Cedar Rapids°	.188	21	32	2	6	10	1	0	1	6	1	2	0	0	0	0	9	0	0
Nagle, Michael, Appleton°	.172	56	198	11	34	34	0	0	0	9	1	3	0	2	14	0	16	1	5
Nalley, Jerry, Waterloo	.268	43	127	17	34	58	3	0	7	22	3	0	3	1	10	1	28	9	3
Nix, David, Appleton°	.221	28	68	8	15	18	1	1	0	6	0	0	0	0	10	0	4	0	1
Nixon, R. Donell, Wausau	.284	59	204	35	58	84	7	2	5	26	3	1	0	1	28	0	31	20	9
O'Connell, Mark, Clinton	.120	11	25	3	3	3	0	0	0	0	0	1	0	0	9	0	7	0	0
Ortega, Kirk, Clinton	.240	48	154	14	37	49	6	0	2	19	2	1	0	5	15	1	31	2	2
Pacho, Juan, Waterloo	.211	24	57	7	12	14	2	0	0	2	0	1	1	1	3	0	10	1	1
Pagel, David, Quad Cities°	.211	57	180	21	38	60	8	1	4	28	2	2	1	1	26	0	27	3	2
Palica, John, Wisconsin Rapids†	.233	131	451	61	105	168	24	3	11	67	9	11	6	2	49	1	77	15	5
Parker, Joel, Burlington	.000	5	5	1	0	0	0	0	0	0	0	0	0	0	1	0	3	0	0
Payne, James, 57 Wis Rap-57 QC	.278	114	360	58	100	130	16	4	2	47	4	3	5	4	65	1	78	24	9
Peyton, Byron, Cedar Rapids	.224	23	67	6	15	16	1	0	0	3	0	0	0	1	10	0	18	0	1
Piggott, Russell, Quad Cities	.264	133	507	64	134	188	15	6	9	65	7	0	3	1	42	3	78	11	4
Ponce, Carlos, Burlington	.269	130	487	70	131	215	25	7	15	62	5	1	2	7	23	2	74	23	6
Porter, Eric, Wisconsin Rapids	.200	2	5	1	1	1	0	0	0	1	0	0	0	1	1	0	3	0	0
Porte, Carlos, Cedar Rapids	.263	71	281	30	74	94	8	3	2	20	4	3	1	2	10	0	36	5	3
Presley, James, Wausau	.279	57	208	48	58	104	10	0	12	53	3	1	1	7	34	3	60	9	2
Price, William, Wisconsin Rapids	.182	41	148	18	27	32	2	0	1	9	1	3	0	0	8	0	34	3	1
Proctor, Kenneth, Wisconsin Rapids	.153	31	59	8	9	13	1	0	1	2	0	3	1	1	10	0	14	1	0
Pryce, Kenneth, Quad Cities	.333	26	3	0	1	1	0	0	0	0	0	0	0	0	1	0	1	0	0
Raines, Michael, Cedar Rapids	.273	45	11	2	3	3	0	0	0	1	0	1	0	0	1	0	1	0	0
Randolph, John, Wisconsin Rapids°	.213	14	47	1	10	10	0	0	0	4	0	1	0	0	4	0	5	2	0
Ready, Randy, Cedar Rapids	.308	110	367	74	113	181	17	0	17	56	4	6	3	3	85	2	54	7	6
Reed, Jeffrey, Wisconsin Rapids°	.234	106	312	63	73	99	12	1	4	34	1	7	0	4	86	1	36	4	4
Reynolds, Harold, Wausau†	.296	127	493	98	146	208	23	3	11	59	3	12	4	2	56	1	47	69	20
Robertson, Gary, Wisconsin Rapids°	.143	13	28	3	4	5	1	0	0	0	0	0	0	1	3	0	5	0	0
Robinette, Gary, Appleton	.237	59	211	25	50	66	10	3	0	26	3	3	0	1	21	1	28	1	1
Robinson, Ronald, Cedar Rapids	.184	24	49	4	9	9	0	0	0	1	0	6	0	0	6	0	17	0	0
Romero (A.), Ramon, Appleton†	.214	63	187	18	40	49	4	1	1	14	0	5	3	0	28	1	28	3	4
Rothey, Mark, Cedar Rapids°	.333	35	18	2	6	6	0	0	0	2	0	0	0	0	0	0	3	0	0
Saavedra, Edwin, Waterloo	.336	125	453	87	152	240	25	3	19	85	7	6	6	5	62	8	53	36	7
Samuel, Michael, Burlington	.128	20	47	4	6	6	0	0	0	1	0	0	0	0	8	0	16	1	0
Scarpace, Kenneth, Cedar Rapids°	.242	123	463	56	112	161	22	6	5	44	7	2	5	3	30	3	60	13	8
Schoendienst, Kevin, Quad Cities°	.224	66	147	17	33	38	5	0	0	15	3	3	3	1	36	2	44	9	1
Schulze, Donald, Quad Cities	.000	17	5	1	0	0	0	0	0	0	0	0	0	0	1	0	4	0	0
Seats, Dennis, Cedar Rapids	.241	34	87	14	21	26	0	1	1	5	0	1	0	2	18	2	10	7	1
Seeger, Mark, Appleton	.196	69	199	18	39	51	9	0	1	18	2	3	1	1	24	0	46	2	3
Simmons, D. Wayne, Quad Cities†	.500	2	6	0	3	3	0	0	0	0	0	0	0	0	0	0	0	1	0
Smith, Donald, Wisconsin Rapids	.258	33	93	14	24	29	5	0	0	4	1	3	2	2	3	0	14	1	2
Smith, Thomas, Quad Cities	.000	25	1	0	0	0	0	0	0	0	0	0	0	0	0	0	0	0	0
Snyder, Bryan A., Clinton°	.273	42	143	15	39	46	4	0	1	19	4	1	1	5	14	0	39	0	4

Player and Club	Pct.	G.	AB.	R.	H.	TB.	2B.	3B.	HR.	RBI.	GW.	SH.	SF.	HP.	BB.	Int. BB.	SO.	SB.	CS.
Sodders, Michael, Wisconsin Rapids .	.179	23	78	6	14	22	2	0	2	15	1	0	3	0	8	0	21	0	0
Sorel, Michael, Cedar Rapids	.194	103	335	31	65	87	9	5	1	19	1	5	1	2	27	2	64	5	5
Spurlin, Robert, Clinton	.200	50	135	13	27	33	4	1	0	16	0	6	6	1	20	0	18	1	1
Storer, Kevin, Appleton	.273	5	11	0	3	4	1	0	0	1	0	1	1	1	2	0	2	0	0
Su'a, Murphy, Burlington	.240	125	437	46	105	153	17	2	9	49	4	6	2	1	22	2	89	6	5
Suarez, A. Nelson, Wisconsin Rapids .	.211	59	204	21	43	53	4	0	2	14	1	13	2	3	23	1	34	5	3
Suarez, Luis, Wisconsin Rapids	.000	25	2	1	0	0	0	0	0	0	0	0	0	0	0	0	1	0	0
Swaggerty, F. Glenn, Quad Cities	.000	26	7	0	0	0	0	0	0	0	0	0	0	0	0	0	0	0	0
Tarnow, Greg, Quad Cities	.174	11	23	2	4	4	0	0	0	0	0	1	0	0	2	0	8	0	0
Taylor, Dwight, Waterloo°	.216	49	153	25	33	37	4	0	0	13	0	6	0	1	24	0	43	23	4
Taylor, John, Clinton	.169	32	83	15	14	20	3	0	1	5	1	2	0	2	29	1	22	0	2
Taylor, Michael, Waterloo°	.272	120	397	73	108	154	15	5	7	41	3	6	0	4	49	4	93	34	11
Tenney, Mickey, Quad Cities	.239	20	46	8	11	12	1	0	0	4	1	1	0	0	7	0	9	2	0
Terry, Scott, Cedar Rapids	.194	113	351	32	68	92	9	5	3	31	3	2	1	4	39	2	94	10	4
Toerner, Sean, Clinton	.258	123	438	63	113	163	23	3	7	73	5	1	6	2	55	0	66	10	9
Torres, A. Raymundo, Appleton	.306	106	369	57	113	186	21	8	12	63	6	0	5	5	44	5	63	21	11
Torve, Kelvin, Clinton°	.261	57	211	27	55	68	10	0	1	27	3	0	2	0	21	2	26	7	4
Ungs, Darrell, Wisconsin Rapids	.500	12	4	1	2	2	0	0	0	0	0	0	0	0	0	0	0	0	0
Vaji, Mark, Quad Cities°	.000	26	1	0	0	0	0	0	0	0	0	0	0	0	0	0	1	0	0
Varano, Michael, Wausau	.000	6	8	1	0	0	0	0	0	0	0	0	0	0	3	0	6	0	0
Walker, Glen, Wausau	.283	119	441	80	125	251	21	0	35	111	13	4	3	8	37	3	103	7	7
Wall, David, Appleton°	.187	27	91	9	17	25	2	3	0	9	1	0	2	0	10	2	13	1	1
Walsh, James, Quad Cities	.243	98	304	43	74	101	9	3	4	36	2	0	5	10	46	2	67	5	1
Webb, Dennis, Quad Cities°	.355	14	31	9	11	15	0	2	0	4	0	0	0	3	0	2	4	0
Weissmann, Craig, Quad Cities	.000	8	2	0	0	0	0	0	0	0	0	0	0	0	1	0	1	0	0
Wesley, Thomas, Cedar Rapids	.143	26	49	6	7	12	2	0	1	5	0	1	0	0	3	0	26	0	0
Wilson, David, Clinton	.252	115	404	47	102	137	14	3	5	44	4	4	3	1	45	0	80	4	1
Wood, Johnson, Burlington	.429	14	14	1	6	9	3	0	0	2	0	0	0	0	1	0	5	0	0
Yampierre, Eddie, Wausau	.191	37	89	7	17	17	0	0	0	5	2	4	0	1	7	0	18	1	2
Yobs, David, Appleton°	.303	65	221	30	67	100	15	6	2	23	0	2	1	1	26	2	36	12	1
Young, Matt, Clinton	.237	89	253	41	60	66	6	0	0	23	4	4	1	4	47	0	37	17	9
Zacher, Todd, Clinton°	.188	59	207	31	39	44	3	1	0	19	3	3	1	0	28	1	33	4	3

The following pitchers had no plate appearances primarily through use of designated hitters, listed alphabetically by club, games in parentheses:

APPLETON—Anderson, Jesse (22); Barnard, Jeffrey (12); Desjarlais, Keith (12); Eduardo, Hector (8); Evans, Randy (3); Flannery, Kevin (38); Geiger, Burwell (3); Mullen, Thomas (33); Murillo, Ramon (1); Naumann, Richard (18); Ortega, Daniel (9); Pastrovich, Steven (26); Patterson, Reginald (1); Platel, Mark (23); Riley, George (7); Schuckert, Wayne (20); Schumacher, Roy (38); Siwy, James (8); Sutton, James (7); Welch, Dennis (1); Withrow, Michael (9).

BURLINGTON—Crews, Timothy (21); Donovan, Michael (4); Effrig, Mark (20); Gallo, Raymond (40); Gibson, Steven (4); Harris, Craig (11); Herberholz, Craig (10); Lepson, Mark (7); McClure, Robert (4); McCoy, Kevin (23); Morris, David (15); Norwood, Steven (7); Pone, Vincent (22); Schroeck, Robert (19); Smith, Gene (41); Stibora, Thomas (15); Vasquez, Jesse (12); Villegas, Michael (16).

CLINTON—Banach, Joseph (7); Bangert, Gregory (15); Bautista, Ramone (2); Brecht, Michael (11); Chue, Jose (24); D'Amore, Louis (24); Felt, Jerald (6); Gallo, Bernard (16); McLaughlin, Thomas (20); McSparran, Gregory (13); Oliver, Bruce (25); Schafer, Dennis (31); Smay, Kevin (31); Wilhelmi, David (27); Young, Gary (10).

QUAD CITIES—Gerlach, James (41); Kaufman, Ronald (7); King, Michael (11); Lockie, Randall (1); Millner, Timothy (18); Renwick, Richard (6); Schiewe, Mark (2); Shoemaker, Martin (4); Soff, Raymond (32); Wilkins, Mark (8).

WATERLOO—Bajus, Mark (2); Bullinger, Matthews (30); Burden, John (6); Burns, Thomas (2); Cushing, Stephen (9); Dixon, Michael (17); Elpin, Ralph (6); Hoban, John (8); Hyrnko, Lawrence (17); Jeffcoat, Michael (25); Lintz, Rickey (55); Owens, Thomas (16); Pope, Gregory (4); Puryear, Nathaniel (14); Roche, Stephen (24); Romero, Ramon (8); Schwarber, Michael (32); Silvas, Brian (11); Thompson, Richard (28).

WAUSAU—Adair, Richard (19); Batten, Mark (10); Brennan, Thomas (37); Cahill, Mark (20); Cary, Jeff (14); Dukes, Kevin (14); Hudson, Robert (14); Hunger, Christopher (24); Kinley, Wayne (6); McKenzie, Donald (5); Nunez, Edwin (25); Pedersen, Mark (34); Snyder, Brian (27); Steger, Kevin (29); Stottlemyre, Jeffrey (6).

WISCONSIN RAPIDS—Arney, Jeffrey (11); Broersma, Eric (6); Everett, Conrad (30); Giordano, Michael (15); Guerrero, Anthony (22); Harris, Larry (12); Henderson, Craig (6); Krueger, Kirby (11); Ortiz, Jorge (16); Pena, Adriano (26); Wardle, Curtis (16); Weibel, Randy (18); Wright, Mark (13); Yett, Richard (25).

GRAND SLAM HOME RUNS—Foster, Holmes, LoMastro, 2 each; Adams, Cataline, Chandler, Coles, Dugas, Eisenreich, Ficklin, T. Johnson, McCain, Ready, Sodders, Su'a, 1 each.

AWARDED FIRST BASE ON INTERFERENCE—Piggott 3 (Golden, Meier, Su'a); Wilson 3 (Pagel 2, Blume); Payne 2 (Ortega, Taylor); Proctor 2 (Adams, Fimple); Austin (Elkin); Blume (Taylor); Price (Taylor); Torres (Fimple).

CLUB FIELDING

Club	Pct.	G.	PO.	A.	E.	DP.	PB.	Club	Pct.	G.	PO.	A.	E.	DP.	PB.
Wisconsin Rapids	.961	134	3395	1445	197	104	22	Clinton	.956	132	3287	1464	221	107	19
Cedar Rapids	.960	133	3404	1458	202	98	25	Quad Cities	.956	135	3429	1568	229	116	29
Waterloo	.959	136	3505	1537	218	110	49	Burlington	.955	135	3356	1410	223	103	34
Wausau	.957	133	3384	1528	219	117	31	Appleton	.954	134	3434	1437	235	107	33

Triple Plays—Wisconsin Rapids, Wausau.

INDIVIDUAL FIELDING
FIRST BASEMEN

°Throws lefthanded.

Player and Club	Pct.	G.	PO.	A.	E.	DP.	Player and Club	Pct.	G.	PO.	A.	E.	DP.
Adams, Clinton	1.000	14	128	10	0	9	Hoenstine, Cedar Rapids	1.000	2	3	0	0	0
Adams, Appleton	.993	46	408	21	3	29	Johnson, Clinton	.983	64	550	35	10	48
Blume, Wausau	.980	5	46	4	1	6	Johnson, Quad Cities	.979	113	1002	79	23	94
Buckley, Quad Cities	1.000	1	4	0	0	0	Jordan, Burlington	1.000	1	1	0	0	0
Carlson, Wisconsin Rapids	1.000	4	31	1	0	1	Kent, Appleton	.978	87	758	40	18	64
Chandler, Wisconsin Rapids	.925	5	36	1	3	1	Malkin, Waterloo	.996	27	209	15	1	19
Connally, Quad Cities	.996	22	235	13	1	12	Michael, Burlington°	.968	8	60	1	2	6
Dekraai, Burlington	1.000	1	2	0	0	0	Miller, Burlington	1.000	1	3	1	0	0
Diaz, Wausau	.982	104	959	62	19	86	Nalley, Waterloo	.926	5	24	1	2	1
DRZAYICH, Cedar Rapids°	.991	124	1139	63	11	81	Nixon, Wausau	.988	27	244	9	3	13
Durate, Waterloo	.987	20	136	13	2	12	Ponce, Burlington	.979	130	1111	58	25	90
Ellison, Waterloo	.966	8	52	5	2	6	Robertson, Wisconsin Rapids	1.000	3	11	0	0	2
Fimple, Appleton	1.000	2	12	2	0	0	Schoendienst, Quad Cities	1.000	1	8	1	0	1
Foster, Wisconsin Rapids	.987	121	976	47	14	79	Sodders, Wisconsin Rapids	1.000	8	58	3	0	3
Gertz, Waterloo°	.988	86	763	38	10	57	Torve, Clinton	.993	57	538	41	4	40
Hanley, Appleton	1.000	1	0	1	0	0	Wesley, Cedar Rapids	.980	14	94	5	2	3
Triple Plays—Diaz, Foster.							Yobs, Appleton°	.941	3	15	1	1	1

SECOND BASEMEN

Player and Club	Pct.	G.	PO.	A.	E.	DP.
CASTILLO, Burlington	.967	104	244	284	18	60
Chelette, Wausau	.900	9	19	26	5	1
Cole, Wisconsin Rapids	.946	111	283	259	31	52
Crist, Wausau	1.000	1	1	1	0	0
Dugas, Waterloo	.857	3	7	11	3	2
Ficklin, Waterloo	.857	4	3	3	1	1
Gonzales, Burlington	.970	20	52	45	3	7
Hill, Appleton	.944	37	89	95	11	21
Hinds, Cedar Rapids	.936	36	73	116	13	20
Hoenstine, Cedar Rapids	.904	15	32	34	7	5
Kirby, Burlington	.978	9	24	20	1	4
Lenti, Clinton	.950	11	18	20	2	4
Littman, Clinton	.947	3	6	12	1	2
McCain, Wisconsin Rapids	.962	28	38	63	4	14
Methven, Waterloo	.957	129	292	350	29	62
Morales, Burlington	1.000	2	6	6	0	3
Nagle, Appleton	.988	54	108	133	3	19
Nix, Appleton	.909	16	42	38	8	9
Nixon, Wausau	1.000	1	6	0	0	0
Pacho, Waterloo	.964	8	12	15	1	2
Payne, Quad Cities	1.000	3	6	7	0	1
Piggott, Quad Cities	.954	127	259	400	32	72
Porte, Cedar Rapids	.951	71	140	173	16	34
Price, Wisconsin Rapids	1.000	4	12	10	0	2
Reynolds, Wausau	.960	124	258	383	27	82
Romero, Appleton	.963	16	33	45	3	10
Seats, Cedar Rapids	.667	1	2	2	2	0
Seeger, Appleton	.941	20	31	64	6	11
Smith, Wisconsin Rapids	1.000	1	2	3	0	2
Sorel, Cedar Rapids	1.000	11	18	25	0	5
Tenney, Quad Cities	.889	5	6	10	2	0
Toerner, Clinton	.953	119	255	326	29	61
Walker, Wausau	1.000	1	1	2	0	0
Webb, Quad Cities	.897	7	12	14	3	2
Zacher, Clinton	1.000	3	6	4	0	1

Triple Play—Reynolds.

THIRD BASEMEN

Player and Club	Pct.	G.	PO.	A.	E.	DP.
Allen, Quad Cities	.888	57	42	93	17	5
Aponte, Wausau	.943	66	31	133	10	10
Bazan, Quad Cities	1.000	1	0	1	0	0
Chelette, Wausau	.889	8	6	10	2	0
Cochran, Waterloo	.875	6	3	4	1	0
Connally, Quad Cities	.939	8	5	26	2	1
Crist, Wausau	.800	1	0	4	1	0
Dekraai, Burlington	.833	2	0	5	1	0
Diaz, Wausau	.857	3	1	5	1	0
Duarte, Waterloo	.879	13	6	23	4	1
Dugas, Waterloo	.928	110	65	218	22	15
Epperson, Appleton	.804	21	13	24	9	1
Ficklin, Waterloo	.800	9	0	12	3	0
Gallagher, Wateroo	.750	1	0	3	1	0
Gonzales, Burlington	.885	13	7	16	3	4
Hall, Cedar Rapids	.909	101	73	225	30	10
Henderson, Clinton	.895	55	52	127	21	14
Hill, Appleton	.857	8	7	11	3	2
Hoenstine, Cedar Rapids	.905	28	17	59	8	4
Kirby, Burlington	.897	12	5	21	3	2
Lenti, Clinton	.836	20	16	30	9	2
Littman, Clinton	1.000	3	3	5	0	0
Malkin, Waterloo	.769	5	2	8	3	0
McCain, Wisconsin Rapids	.917	47	38	72	10	8
Morales, Burlington	1.000	5	4	3	0	1
Nalley, Waterloo	1.000	1	0	2	0	0
Nix, Appleton	.875	3	2	5	1	1
Pagel, Quad Cities	.900	4	3	6	1	1
Payne, WR-Quad Cities	.913	87	57	142	19	10
Presley, Wausau	.938	57	32	105	9	5
Proctor, Wisconsin Rapids	.870	27	13	34	7	1
Randolph, Wisconsin Rapids	.880	10	7	15	3	1
READY, Burlington	.932	105	72	216	21	22
Reynolds, Wausau	1.000	1	0	3	0	0
Robertson, Wisconsin Rapids	.933	7	3	11	1	0
Robinette, Appleton	.915	58	52	120	16	8
A. Romero, Appleton	.961	33	31	67	4	5
Schoendienst, Quad Cities	.963	35	16	36	2	6
Seats, Cedar Rapids	.750	4	1	8	3	1
Seeger, Appleton	.913	10	7	14	2	0
Smith, Wisconsin Rapids	1.000	6	4	12	0	0
Sodders, Wisconsin Rapids	.625	3	1	4	3	1
Storer, Appleton	1.000	5	2	6	0	0
Suarez, Wisconsin Rapids	1.000	1	0	1	0	0
Tenney, Quad Cities	.875	2	2	5	1	1
Varano, Wausau	1.000	1	1	1	0	0
Webb, Quad Cities	1.000	1	0	1	0	0
Wesley, Cedar Rapids	1.000	1	10	1	0	1
Zacher, Clinton	.943	56	39	127	10	11

Triple Plays—Presley, Proctor.

SHORTSTOPS

Player and Club	Pct.	G.	PO.	A.	E.	DP.
BUCKLEY, Quad Cities	.933	112	179	362	39	70
Chelette, Wausau	.895	20	23	71	11	10
Coles, Wausau	.904	111	154	335	52	66
Crist, Wausau	.895	4	6	11	2	3
Davidsmeier, Burlington	.940	68	73	226	19	36
Dekrai, Burlington	.790	4	4	11	4	3
Dugas, Waterloo	.923	8	6	18	2	2
Flores, Wisconsin Rapids	.951	75	108	219	17	34
Gonzales, Burlington	.981	12	18	33	1	6
Gruber, Waterloo	.910	125	180	389	56	62
Hoenstine, Cedar Rapids	1.000	3	5	5	0	0
Littman, Clinton	.986	20	21	48	1	6
Morales, Burlington	.918	35	47	109	14	16
Morse, Appleton	.911	125	179	354	52	65
Nagle, Appleton	.889	3	3	5	1	0
Nix, Appleton	1.000	2	2	2	0	0
Pacho, Waterloo	.897	12	12	23	4	5
Pagel, Quad Cities	.895	5	6	11	2	0
Payne, WR-Quad Cities	.873	18	20	42	9	9
Peyton, Quad Cities	.964	21	27	53	3	9
Price, Wisconsin Rapids	.921	36	50	102	13	16
Romero, Appleton	.931	9	11	16	2	2
Samuel, Burlington	.861	19	24	44	11	5
Schoendienst, Quad Cities	1.000	3	2	10	0	2
Seats, Cedar Rapids	.879	22	23	57	11	10
Simmons, Quad Cities	.786	2	5	6	3	1
Smith, Wisconsin Rapids	.865	26	29	61	14	8
Sorel, Cedar Rapids	.906	90	115	260	39	42
Tenney, Quad Cities	.981	11	10	42	1	3
Wilson, Clinton	.923	114	155	313	39	55

OUTFIELDERS

Player and Club	Pct.	G.	PO.	A.	E.	DP.
Adams, Clinton	.911	19	39	2	4	0
Allen, Quad Cities	1.000	6	3	1	0	0
Austin, Quad Cities	.950	105	164	6	9	0
Bass, Burlington	.969	124	214	4	7	0
Blume, Wausau	1.000	1	1	0	0	0
Buggs, Appleton	.936	48	78	9	6	1
Burton, Quad Cities	.980	23	45	5	1	0
Calderon, Wausau	.961	106	130	17	6	2
Carlson, Wisconsin Rapids	1.000	1	1	1	0	0
Cataline, Quad Cities	.883	112	120	8	17	1
Chandler, Wisconsin Rapids	.667	1	2	0	1	0
Cotto, Quad Cities	.954	127	249	23	13	5
Doby, Appleton	1.000	4	4	1	0	0
Dotson, Waterloo	1.000	18	31	1	0	0
Edmonds, Wausau	1.000	34	48	1	0	1
Eisenreich, Wis Rapids°	.972	134	295	17	9	2
Erickson, Clinton°	.971	39	67	1	2	0
Espy, Appleton	.967	72	143	5	5	3
Ficklin, Waterloo	1.000	5	4	0	0	0
Figueroa, Clinton	.962	57	72	4	3	2
Frazier, Clinton	1.000	5	4	0	0	0
Gallagher, Waterloo	.976	124	224	19	6	7
Garcia, Appleton°	.949	102	192	13	11	2
Gomez, Appleton	.952	11	19	1	1	1
Hall, Cedar Rapids	1.000	17	12	3	0	1
Hanley, Appleton	.944	15	16	1	1	0
Higgins, Burlington	.857	19	18	0	3	0
Hill, Wausau	1.000	4	9	0	0	0
Hoenstine, Cedar Rapids	.976	35	40	1	1	1
Holmes, Wisconsin Rapids°	1.000	37	39	1	0	0
Johnson, Clinton	.946	53	103	2	6	2
Jones, Waterloo°	.915	26	41	2	4	0
Jones, Cedar Rapids	.945	74	113	8	7	3
Jones, Burlington	.890	37	61	4	8	0
Junker, Clinton	.965	67	132	4	5	0
King, Wausau°	.952	21	19	1	1	0
Lenti, Clinton	.957	35	44	0	2	0
Littman, Clinton	.957	17	22	0	1	0
Lomastro, Wisconsin Rapids	.958	47	66	2	3	0
McKay, Burlington	.963	12	26	0	1	0
McKinney, Cedar Rapids	.932	63	88	8	7	1
Michael, Burlington°	.942	85	152	9	10	1

OUTFIELDERS—Continued

Player and Club	Pct.	G.	PO.	A.	E.	DP.
Miller, Burlington	.927	123	191	11	16	1
Minaya, Wausau	.914	20	29	3	3	1
Morales, Burlington	1.000	4	6	0	0	0
Moses, Wausau°	.977	120	204	10	5	2
Nalley, Waterloo	1.000	11	6	0	0	0
Nixon, Wausau	1.000	1	2	0	0	0
O'Connell, Clinton	1.000	8	8	0	0	0
Palica, Wisconsin Rapids°	.961	131	230	18	10	10
Parker, Burlington	1.000	4	3	0	0	0
Reynolds, Wausau	1.000	2	1	0	0	0
Saavedra, Waterloo	.964	112	178	11	7	2
SCARPACE, Cedar Rapids°	.991	121	196	16	2	5
Seeger, Appleton	.958	28	42	4	2	0
Snyder, Clinton°	.972	39	65	5	2	1
Su'a, Burlington	1.000	2	9	1	0	0
Suarez, Wisconsin Rapids	.967	58	76	11	3	2
D. Taylor, Waterloo°	.966	42	51	6	2	1
M. Taylor Waterloo	.971	87	127	5	4	1
Terry, Cedar Rapids	.968	101	147	5	5	2
Torres, Appleton	.955	96	186	7	9	0
Walker, Wausau	.982	99	147	12	3	5
Wall, Appleton	1.000	6	9	0	0	0
Walsh, Quad Cities	.958	43	67	2	3	0
Yobs, Appleton°	.946	41	66	4	4	2
Young, Clinton	.964	84	123	10	5	2

CATCHERS

Player and Club	Pct.	G.	PO.	A.	E.	DP.	PB.
Adams, Cedar Rapids	.991	14	109	1	1	0	1
Baez, Wausau	.982	40	243	24	5	1	4
Bazan, Quad Cities	.997	49	270	34	1	2	6
Blume, Wausau	.973	53	333	22	10	3	10
Chandler, Wisconsin Rapids	.989	58	356	72	5	8	11
Contreras, Burlington	.947	17	65	6	4	0	1
CORBETT, Cedar Rapids	.993	90	659	65	5	11	20
Donofrio, Appleton	.974	75	480	71	15	6	19
Duarte, Waterloo	.957	4	20	2	1	0	3
Elkin, Waterloo	.929	12	51	1	4	0	2
Fimple, Waterloo	.987	97	664	90	10	6	36
Frazier, Clinton	.927	19	101	13	9	3	6
George, Quad Cities	.882	3	14	1	2	0	3
Golden, Appleton	.970	21	104	24	4	3	4
Hanley, Appleton	1.000	2	9	2	0	1	1
Hernandez, Burlington	1.000	2	9	0	0	0	1
Hill, Wausau	.994	27	136	17	1	3	8
Hyman, Quad Cities	.986	39	240	34	4	2	2
Jordan, Burlington	.902	8	35	2	4	0	3
Liska, Clinton	.958	3	21	2	1	0	0
Locascio, Waterloo	.979	19	135	7	3	2	5
Malkin, Waterloo	.984	14	107	13	2	1	3
Meier, Appleton	.979	50	245	36	6	2	9
Miley, Cedar Rapids	.973	34	228	27	7	2	4
Ortega, Clinton	.965	45	251	49	11	2	6
Pagel, Quad Cities	.973	46	278	40	9	3	16
Porter, Wisconsin Rapids	1.000	2	13	1	0	0	1
Reed, Wisconsin Rapids	.989	81	547	93	7	9	10
Spurlin, Clinton	.953	50	227	36	13	2	2
Su'a, Burlington	.980	116	740	78	17	6	29
Tarnow, Quad Cities	.949	11	50	6	3	0	2
Taylor, Clinton	.946	27	147	28	10	3	5
Yampierre, Wausau	.979	36	221	12	5	1	9

Triple Plays—Baez, Chandler.

PITCHERS

Player and Club	Pct.	G.	PO.	A.	E.	DP.
Anderson, Appleton	.821	22	6	17	5	1
Arney, Wisconsin Rapids	.800	11	1	3	1	0
Asbell, Waterloo	1.000	7	7	0	3	
Bajus, Waterloo°	1.000	2	0	1	0	0
Banach, Clinton°	.857	7	0	6	1	0
Bangert, Clinton°	.955	15	3	18	1	4
Barnard, Appleton	.923	12	4	8	1	1
Batten, Wausau	1.000	10	1	5	0	0
Bowden, Cedar Rapids°	.857	10	1	5	1	0
Brecht, Clinton°	1.000	11	4	24	0	1
Brennan, Wausau°	.900	37	2	7	1	3
Broersma, Wisconsin Rapids	1.000	6	1	3	0	0
Buchanan, Cedar Rapids°	.925	25	3	46	4	1
Bullinger, Waterloo°	.778	30	0	7	2	0
Burden, Waterloo	1.000	6	3	2	0	0
Burns, Wausau°	1.000	2	0	2	0	0
Cahill, Wausau	.931	20	7	20	2	1
Cary, Wausau	1.000	14	0	2	0	1
Chue, Clinton	.960	24	8	16	1	2
Crews, Burlington	.926	21	1	24	2	1
Cushing, Waterloo°	1.000	9	0	3	0	0
D'Amore, Clinton	.867	24	5	8	2	0
Desjarlais, Appleton	.957	12	8	14	1	1
Dixon, Waterloo°	.938	17	3	12	1	1
Donovan, Burlington	1.000	4	0	1	0	0
Dukes, Wausau°	.769	14	2	8	3	0
Eduardo, Appleton	.917	8	1	10	1	1
Effrig, Burlington	.923	20	5	7	1	1
Elpin, Waterloo	1.000	6	3	6	0	1
Ender, Cedar Rapids	1.000	24	5	26	0	1
Evans, Appleton	.500	3	0	1	1	0
Everett, Wisconsin Rapids	.875	30	2	5	1	1
Felt, Clinton	1.000	6	1	1	0	0
Flannery, Appleton	.931	38	2	25	2	0
Freeburg, Cedar Rapids	1.000	16	4	15	0	0
Gallo, Clinton°	1.000	16	4	10	0	1
Gallo, Burlington°	.889	40	4	20	3	1
Geiger, Appleton	1.000	3	1	3	0	0
Gerlach, Quad Cities	.870	41	6	14	3	0
Gibson, Burlington	1.000	4	0	2	0	0
Giordano, Wisconsin Rapids	.944	15	2	15	1	0
Gomez, Clinton	1.000	24	1	8	0	0
Guerrero, Wisconsin Rapids°	.971	22	4	30	1	1
Harris, Burlington	.941	11	5	11	1	1
Harris, Wisconsin Rapids	.857	12	3	9	2	1
Henderson, Wisconsin Rapids°	1.000	6	3	10	0	1
Herberholz, Burlington	1.000	10	4	7	0	1
Hoban, Waterloo	.750	8	2	4	2	0
Hollenbach, Cedar Rapids°	1.000	16	4	19	0	1
Housey, Quad Cities	.968	21	11	19	1	1
Hudson, Wausau	.870	22	15	32	7	0
Hunger, Wausau	.759	23	5	17	7	1
Hyrnko, Waterloo	.950	17	4	15	1	1
Jackson, Cedar Rapids	1.000	6	0	5	0	0
Jeffcoat, Waterloo°	.971	25	10	23	1	0
Kaufman, Quad Cities	.800	7	0	4	1	0
Kepshire, Cedar Rapids	.909	39	3	17	2	0
King, Quad Cities°	.933	11	6	8	1	0
Kinley, Wausau	1.000	6	0	3	0	0
Krueger, Wisconsin Rapids	.962	11	6	19	1	2
Kyles, Quad Cities	.667	8	1	3	2	1
Lepson, Burlington	1.000	7	1	1	0	0
Lintz, Waterloo	.891	55	8	33	5	2
Lockie, Quad Cities	1.000	1	0	1	0	0
Lowery, Cedar Rapids	1.000	11	1	4	0	0
McClure, Burlington°	1.000	4	0	1	0	0
McCoy, Burlington	.941	23	8	24	2	1
McKenzie, Wausau	.800	5	0	4	1	0
McLaughlin, Clinton	.895	20	7	10	2	1
McSparran, Clinton	1.000	13	3	5	0	2
Miglio, Quad Cities°	.957	35	6	16	1	2
Millner, Quad Cities°	1.000	18	1	5	0	0
Morris, Burlington	.917	15	4	7	1	2
Mullen, Appleton	.957	33	7	15	1	0
Murillo, Appleton	1.000	1	1	0	0	0
Myles, Cedar Rapids°	.944	19	3	31	2	0
Naumann, Appleton°	1.000	18	0	8	0	0
Norwood, Burlington	1.000	7	0	8	0	0
Nunez, Wausau	.882	25	12	33	6	3
Oliver, Clinton	.875	25	12	16	4	3
Ortega, Appleton	.750	9	1	5	2	0
Ortiz, Wisconsin Rapids°	.800	15	1	3	1	1
Owens, Waterloo	.917	16	5	17	2	0
Pastrovich, Appleton	.911	26	15	26	4	0
Pedersen, Wausau	.917	34	0	11	1	2
Pena, Wisconsin Rapids°	.800	26	0	16	4	0
Platel, Appleton	.846	23	7	15	4	0
Pone, Burlington	.778	22	4	10	4	1
Pope, Waterloo	1.000	4	1	0	0	0
Pryce, Quad Cities	.917	26	11	11	2	2
Puryear, Waterloo	.958	14	7	16	1	2
Raines, Cedar Rapids	.833	45	5	15	4	2
Renwick, Quad Cities	.667	6	0	2	1	0
Riley, Appleton°	1.000	7	3	8	0	0
Robinson, Cedar Rapids	.941	24	9	39	3	2
Roche, Waterloo	.947	24	12	24	2	1
Romero, Waterloo°	.800	8	2	6	2	1
Rothey, Cedar Rapids°	.750	35	2	16	6	0
Schafer, Clinton	.936	31	6	23	2	0
Schiewe, Quad Cities	1.000	2	0	1	0	1
Schroeck, Burlington°	.889	19	4	28	4	0
Schuckert, Appleton°	.917	20	1	10	1	1
Schulze, Quad Cities	.923	17	7	29	3	5
Schumacher, Appleton	.800	38	2	6	2	1
Schwarber, Waterloo	.889	32	9	23	4	1
Shoemaker, Quad Cities	1.000	4	1	2	0	0

PITCHERS—Continued

Player and Club	Pct.	G.	PO.	A.	E.	DP.	Player and Club	Pct.	G.	PO.	A.	E.	DP.
Silvas, Waterloo	.833	11	2	3	1	0	Ungs, Wisconsin Rapids	.889	11	2	22	3	0
Siwy, Appleton	.895	8	2	15	2	0	Yaji, Quad Cities°	.889	26	6	34	5	1
SMAY, Clinton	1.000	31	7	25	0	1	Vasquez, Burlington	1.000	12	1	1	0	0
Smith, Burlington	.864	41	3	16	3	1	Villegas, Burlington	.905	16	4	15	2	1
Smith, Quad Cities	1.000	25	13	18	0	1	Wardle, Wisconsin Rapids°	.882	16	2	13	2	3
Snyder, Wausau°	.857	27	4	14	3	1	Weibel, Wisconsin Rapids	1.000	18	3	11	0	1
Soff, Quad Cities	.857	32	2	4	1	0	Weissmann, Quad Cities	.800	8	1	3	1	0
Steger, Wausau	.902	29	10	27	4	3	Wilhelmi, Clinton	.862	27	12	38	8	0
Stibora, Burlington°	.714	15	0	5	2	0	Wilkins, Quad Cities	1.000	8	2	6	0	0
Stottlemyre, Wausau	1.000	6	8	13	0	1	Withrow, Appleton	.929	9	5	8	1	1
Suarez, Wisconsin Rapids	.931	24	3	24	2	0	Wood, Burlington	.909	10	3	7	1	0
Sutton, Appleton	.833	7	1	4	1	1	Wright, Wisconsin Rapids	1.000	13	2	4	0	0
Swaggerty, Quad Cities	.914	26	7	25	3	1	Yett, Wisconsin Rapids	.828	25	4	20	5	1
Thompson, Waterloo	.895	28	11	23	4	2	Young, Clinton	1.000	10	1	2	0	1

The following players do not have any accepted recorded chances at the positions indicated; therefore, are not listed in the fielding averages for those particular positions: Bautista, p; Calderon, ss; Chelette, of; Hanley, p; Kirby, ss; Lenti, 1b; Lesley, p; Miley, 1b; Miller, p; Monroe, of; Pagel, of; Patterson, p; Randolph, of; Schoendienst, of; Su'a, 3b; Welch, p; Yampierre, of.

CLUB PITCHING

Club	ERA.	G.	CG.	ShO.	Sv.	IP.	H.	R.	ER.	HR.	HB.	BB.	Int. BB.	SO.	WP.	Bk.
Quad Cities	3.26	135	31	14	29	1143	1038	547	414	55	43	519	16	813	102	9
Wausau	3.31	133	37	7	21	1128	999	552	415	101	47	462	20	898	62	3
Cedar Rapids	3.39	133	35	15	24	1134⅔	1010	540	427	95	21	482	17	952	70	3
Appleton	3.58	134	16	8	27	1144⅔	1033	584	455	68	42	561	25	807	88	6
Waterloo	3.78	136	22	10	28	1168⅓	1058	600	490	89	40	607	33	936	100	7
Clinton	3.98	132	25	7	20	1095⅔	1020	617	484	70	40	573	20	723	88	18
Wisconsin Rapids	4.03	134	54	6	25	1131⅔	1104	628	506	104	31	586	20	880	90	14
Burlington	4.64	135	29	4	21	1118⅔	1144	707	576	97	45	542	35	816	70	7

PITCHERS' RECORDS
(Leading Qualifiers for Earned-Run Average Leadership — 109 or More Innings)

°Throws lefthanded.

Pitcher—Club	W.	L.	Pct.	ERA.	G.	GS.	CG.	GF.	ShO.	Sv.	IP.	H.	R.	ER.	HR.	HB.	BB.	Int. BB.	SO.	WP.
Pryce, Quad Cities	8	5	.615	1.98	26	13	7	8	2	1	132	118	35	29	8	3	16	2	102	3
Robinson, Cedar Rapids	10	8	.556	2.24	24	24	7	0	3	0	169	136	58	42	13	1	55	1	165	8
Nunez, Wausau	16	3	.842	2.47	25	25	13	0	0	0	186	143	61	51	14	6	58	1	205	6
Lintz, Waterloo	11	5	.688	2.56	55	1	0	35	0	9	109	93	45	31	11	3	50	13	73	8
Adair, Wausau°	13	4	.765	2.73	19	19	8	0	4	0	135	109	56	41	14	1	58	2	112	9
Swaggerty, Quad Cities	11	7	.611	2.78	26	22	3	3	0	0	139	118	50	43	6	2	53	2	53	12
Gallo, Burlington°	8	7	.533	2.84	40	9	1	24	1	10	114	93	47	36	5	3	37	2	101	8
Cahill, Wausau	11	3	.786	2.95	20	20	5	0	1	0	119	118	61	39	9	6	37	0	63	3
Hudson, Wausau	13	7	.650	3.02	22	21	5	0	1	0	140	131	64	47	5	9	48	1	93	3
Ender, Cedar Rapids	8	9	.471	3.09	24	24	8	0	4	0	169	126	66	58	16	4	56	1	140	13

Departmental Leaders: G—Lintz, 55; GS—Wilhelmi, 27; CG—Nunez, 13; ShO—Adair, Ender, 4; W—Nunez, 16; L—Guerrero, 14; Sv—Everett, 18; Pct.—Bullinger, .846; IP—Nunez, 185; H—Wilhelmi, 180; R—Wilhelmi, 106; ER—Wilhelmi, 88; HR—Crews, Ender, Hunger, 16; BB—Suarez, 88; IBB—Lintz, 13; HB—Wilhelmi, 14; SO—Nunez, 205; WP—D'Amore, 20.

(All Pitchers—Listed Alphabetically)

Pitcher—Club	W.	L.	Pct.	ERA.	G.	GS.	CG.	GF.	ShO.	Sv.	IP.	H.	R.	ER.	HR.	HB.	BB.	Int. BB.	SO.	WP.
Adair, Wausau°	13	4	.765	2.73	19	19	8	0	4	0	135	109	56	41	14	1	58	2	112	9
Anderson, Cedar Rapids	7	9	.438	3.85	22	22	3	0	0	0	131	118	78	56	8	5	63	1	106	11
Arney, Wisconsin Rapids	0	2	.000	4.00	11	3	0	4	0	0	27	24	19	12	1	2	23	1	30	4
Asbell, Waterloo	0	3	.000	9.69	7	1	0	2	0	0	13	20	23	14	1	0	18	1	14	8
Bajus, Waterloo	0	1	.000	1.29	2	1	0	0	0	0	7	3	3	1	0	0	6	0	7	0
Banach, Clinton°	0	4	.000	8.67	7	7	0	0	0	0	27	37	34	26	2	2	21	1	13	5
Bangert, Clinton°	7	6	.538	3.18	15	15	5	0	0	0	99	86	51	35	7	1	47	1	86	8
Barnard, Appleton	3	3	.500	4.05	12	9	1	2	0	1	60	58	37	27	4	2	34	0	33	8
Batten, Wausau	3	3	.500	5.52	10	2	0	1	0	0	31	35	23	19	3	1	10	1	19	2
Bautista, Clinton	0	0	.000	0.00	2	0	0	2	0	0	3	4	2	0	1	0	1	0	2	0
Bowden, Cedar Rapids°	2	0	1.000	2.63	10	3	0	3	0	1	24	30	15	7	1	2	14	1	18	1
Brecht, Clinton°	5	4	.556	2.63	11	11	4	0	0	0	72	60	23	21	2	0	21	0	54	7
Brennan, Wausau°	4	3	.571	3.00	37	2	0	23	0	5	66	50	28	22	7	4	30	4	48	1
Broersma, Wisconsin Rapids	3	1	.750	3.09	6	4	1	1	1	0	35	23	13	12	3	3	19	0	48	3
Buchanan, Cedar Rapids	10	11	.476	3.21	25	25	9	0	3	0	171	174	81	61	13	1	64	1	125	8
Bullinger, Waterbury°	11	2	.846	1.17	30	0	0	22	0	7	46	29	15	6	2	3	17	2	45	4
Burden, Waterloo	0	0	.000	4.76	6	2	0	3	0	0	17	13	13	9	1	2	11	0	22	1
Burns, Waterloo	0	0	.000	18.00	2	0	0	0	0	0	2	2	4	4	0	0	4	0	2	0
Cahill, Wausau	11	3	.786	2.95	20	20	5	0	1	0	119	118	61	39	9	6	37	0	63	3
Cary, Wausau	1	1	.500	6.00	14	0	0	9	0	1	18	24	16	12	3	3	6	1	19	1
Chue, Clinton	1	5	.167	4.66	24	1	0	15	0	4	56	49	32	29	4	0	32	4	39	3
Crews, Burlington	10	4	.714	4.19	21	20	8	1	1	0	144	148	82	67	16	1	27	2	98	4
Cushing, Waterloo°	1	0	1.000	5.21	9	3	0	2	0	0	19	18	13	11	4	0	21	0	16	4
D'Amore, Clinton	1	5	.167	4.13	24	3	0	12	0	3	72	62	50	33	1	0	63	0	74	20
Desjarlais, Appleton	3	6	.333	3.12	12	12	3	0	0	0	78	68	38	27	4	3	26	0	50	3
Dixon, Waterloo°	4	6	.400	4.33	17	10	2	1	1	0	79	71	44	38	11	3	48	1	72	7
Donovan, Burlington	0	2	.000	4.09	4	2	1	1	0	0	11	9	5	5	1	0	6	2	10	0
Dukes, Waterloo	3	3	.500	3.38	14	1	0	10	0	2	32	25	15	12	3	4	17	2	40	0
Eduardo, Appleton	3	4	.429	2.74	8	8	1	0	0	0	46	28	19	14	3	5	35	1	46	3
Effrig, Burlington	2	1	.667	2.35	20	2	0	15	0	4	46	32	16	12	2	2	27	1	31	2
Elpin, Waterloo	2	2	.500	1.91	6	4	2	2	1	0	33	25	9	7	2	1	10	1	19	1
Ender, Cedar Rapids	8	9	.471	3.09	24	24	8	0	4	0	169	126	66	58	16	4	56	1	140	13
Evans, Appleton	1	1	.500	6.00	3	2	0	0	0	0	9	6	7	6	0	0	7	0	2	0
Everett, Wisconsin Rapids	5	2	.714	1.40	30	0	0	26	0	18	45	29	10	7	2	0	23	4	63	1
Felt, Clinton	0	1	.000	4.85	6	1	0	4	0	0	13	13	7	7	2	0	8	0	10	0
Flannery, Appleton	5	6	.455	2.83	38	0	0	30	0	10	89	82	35	28	3	4	31	3	74	7
Freeburg, Cedar Rapids	3	11	.214	4.12	16	16	2	0	1	0	94	67	45	43	7	3	54	0	89	7
Gallo, Clinton°	3	3	.500	1.85	16	3	1	9	0	1	39	25	9	8	1	1	24	1	38	3

Pitcher—Club	W.	L.	Pct.	ERA.	G.	GS.	CG.	GF.	ShO.	Sv.	IP.	H.	R.	ER.	HR.	HB.	BB.	Int. BB.	SO.	WP.
Gallo, Burlington°	8	7	.533	2.84	40	9	1	24	1	10	114	93	47	36	5	3	37	2	101	8
Geiger, Appleton	0	1	.000	3.60	3	0	0	2	0	1	10	7	6	4	1	0	8	3	9	0
Gerlach, Quad Cities	7	5	.583	1.67	41	0	0	34	0	8	70	43	29	13	3	4	21	4	59	4
Gibson, Burlington	0	1	.000	10.80	4	2	0	1	0	0	5	4	6	6	2	0	4	0	2	1
Giordano, Wisconsin Rapids	4	3	.571	3.09	15	9	4	4	1	2	70	78	28	24	9	2	14	1	56	5
Gomez, Clinton	0	3	.000	4.66	24	0	0	20	0	1	29	25	17	15	2	0	19	4	27	2
Guerrero, Wisconsin Rapids°	8	14	.364	5.18	22	22	5	0	0	0	132	152	96	76	14	3	80	1	89	12
Hanley, Appleton	0	0	.000	0.00	1	0	0	1	0	0	1	0	0	0	0	0	3	0	1	1
Harris, Burlington	1	7	.125	4.80	11	11	3	0	0	0	60	70	40	32	4	7	35	1	23	6
Harris, Wisconsin Rapids	5	5	.500	5.13	12	10	4	1	1	0	72	71	46	41	9	1	41	0	69	5
Henderson, Wisconsin Rapids°	2	4	.333	4.85	6	6	2	0	0	0	39	38	29	21	5	0	17	0	27	9
Herberholz, Burlington	2	2	.500	6.53	10	7	0	0	0	0	40	45	32	29	4	3	18	1	25	2
Hoban, Waterloo	1	1	.500	11.57	8	3	0	2	0	0	14	23	19	18	3	0	11	1	10	0
Hollenbach, Cedar Rapids°	8	2	.800	2.72	16	10	5	3	0	0	76	70	26	23	4	0	25	1	39	2
Housey, Quad Cities	8	9	.471	3.81	21	21	6	0	2	0	118	121	69	50	6	8	35	0	67	7
Hudson, Wausau	13	7	.650	3.02	22	21	5	0	1	0	140	131	64	47	5	9	48	1	93	3
Hunger, Wausau	7	7	.500	3.75	23	15	3	3	1	0	108	104	56	45	16	1	38	1	86	1
Hyrnko, Waterloo	5	1	.833	1.22	17	0	0	16	0	8	37	23	8	5	2	0	12	2	26	2
Jackson, Cedar Rapids	1	4	.200	8.38	6	6	1	0	0	0	29	33	32	27	7	0	19	0	19	0
Jeffcoat, Waterloo°	10	8	.556	3.86	25	25	3	0	1	0	147	151	71	63	9	2	78	5	109	9
Kaufman, Quad Cities	0	0	.000	3.60	7	0	0	2	0	1	20	14	9	8	3	1	6	0	18	0
Kepshire, Cedar Rapids	7	5	.583	4.32	39	3	1	18	0	3	98	98	63	47	14	3	32	2	94	5
King, Quad Cities°	1	3	.250	5.14	11	11	2	0	1	0	49	41	29	28	3	3	41	0	42	7
Kinley, Waterloo	0	0	.000	6.92	6	1	0	4	0	0	13	21	13	10	2	1	5	0	3	1
Krueger, Wisconsin Rapids	3	6	.333	3.58	11	10	7	0	1	0	78	83	44	31	5	0	25	2	38	3
Kyles, Quad Cities	0	2	.000	12.00	8	6	0	1	0	0	18	29	29	24	3	1	16	0	12	4
Lepson, Burlington	0	5	.000	8.28	7	5	0	0	0	0	25	38	29	23	2	3	17	1	19	1
Lesley, Cedar Rapids	4	1	.800	0.79	22	0	0	19	0	12	34	14	4	3	1	1	12	1	51	4
Lintz, Waterloo	11	5	.688	2.56	55	1	0	35	0	9	109	93	45	31	11	3	50	13	73	8
Lockie, Quad Cities	0	0	.000	0.00	1	0	0	1	0	0	4	2	0	0	0	1	0	0	1	0
Lowery, Cedar Rapids	0	1	.000	3.68	11	2	0	5	0	0	22	20	11	9	2	0	11	1	19	0
McClure, Burlington	0	2	.000	9.64	4	4	0	0	0	0	14	19	15	15	5	1	11	0	11	3
McCoy, Burlington	7	10	.412	5.12	23	23	4	0	0	0	137	148	96	78	12	2	71	3	82	3
McKenzie, Wausau	0	3	.000	9.60	5	3	0	1	0	0	15	16	17	16	3	1	13	0	5	2
McLaughlin, Clinton	7	10	.412	4.33	20	18	3	2	0	0	108	99	68	52	7	4	70	0	67	9
McSparran, Clinton	1	4	.200	3.79	13	7	0	1	0	1	57	56	26	24	4	2	21	0	31	1
Miglio, Quad Cities°	4	1	.800	2.74	35	0	0	12	0	4	69	53	29	21	3	2	45	0	54	12
Miller, Burlington	0	0	.000	12.60	2	0	0	2	0	0	5	9	9	7	1	0	5	0	3	1
Millner, Quad Cities	3	2	.600	4.20	18	2	0	8	0	1	45	43	27	21	0	2	32	3	45	7
Morris, Burlington	0	1	.000	5.50	15	1	0	7	0	0	36	47	29	22	2	1	33	3	26	1
Mullen, Appleton	3	5	.375	2.00	33	0	0	25	0	7	90	64	26	20	2	2	30	6	82	6
Murillo, Appleton	0	0	.000	2.25	1	1	0	0	0	0	4	2	1	1	0	0	2	0	6	0
Myles, Cedar Rapids°	6	6	.500	3.50	19	19	2	0	1	0	108	96	50	42	6	3	57	2	75	7
Naumann, Appleton°	4	6	.400	4.50	18	1	0	14	0	0	34	27	20	17	5	1	29	2	20	6
Norwood, Burlington	0	4	.000	5.75	7	6	0	0	0	0	36	41	30	23	0	3	25	3	23	3
Nunez, Wausau	16	3	.842	2.47	25	25	13	0	4	0	186	143	61	51	14	6	58	1	205	6
Oliver, Clinton	7	4	.636	4.19	25	12	2	9	1	0	101	89	62	47	8	7	53	1	74	6
Ortega, Appleton°	2	2	.500	4.62	9	8	0	0	0	0	37	34	26	19	2	1	32	0	21	4
Ortiz, Wisconsin Rapids°	2	1	.667	1.44	15	0	0	12	0	2	25	15	7	4	1	1	10	0	17	2
Owens, Waterloo	8	3	.727	3.41	16	16	1	0	0	0	103	80	42	39	7	6	54	0	84	9
Pastrovich, Appleton	7	4	.636	3.34	26	13	3	5	0	1	124	133	57	46	9	6	35	1	75	4
Patterson, Appleton	0	0	.000	1.80	1	1	0	0	0	0	5	2	1	1	0	0	0	0	2	0
Pedersen, Wausau	2	4	.333	6.50	34	2	0	19	0	5	54	58	44	39	14	1	36	1	25	13
Pena, Wisconsin Rapids°	8	6	.571	3.98	26	15	5	7	0	0	129	129	68	57	6	1	71	1	96	4
Platel, Appleton	3	12	.200	4.41	23	17	3	3	1	0	102	98	67	50	5	5	70	1	57	14
Pone, Burlington	1	10	.091	4.66	22	10	3	4	0	0	85	77	56	44	9	5	68	7	91	10
Pope, Waterloo	0	0	.000	15.00	4	0	0	1	0	0	6	12	11	10	1	0	7	0	5	0
Pryce, Quad Cities	8	5	.615	1.98	26	13	7	8	2	1	132	118	35	29	8	3	16	2	102	3
Puryear, Waterloo	5	4	.556	3.91	14	13	3	0	1	0	92	59	49	40	4	1	58	0	91	17
Raines, Cedar Rapids	4	2	.667	3.12	45	1	0	32	0	6	75	72	36	26	4	2	38	2	59	10
Renwick, Quad Cities	2	1	.667	3.94	6	2	0	0	0	0	16	15	7	7	1	2	8	0	16	3
Riley, Appleton°	0	3	.000	3.60	7	5	0	2	0	1	30	30	13	12	3	0	13	0	27	2
Robinson, Cedar Rapids	10	8	.556	2.24	24	24	7	0	3	0	169	136	58	42	13	1	55	1	165	8
Roche, Waterloo	8	4	.667	3.73	24	17	4	6	0	1	123	137	61	51	6	6	45	2	55	3
Romero, Waterloo°	0	2	.000	5.21	8	2	0	3	0	0	19	19	12	11	3	2	13	0	14	2
Rothey, Cedar Rapids°	2	8	.200	5.24	35	0	0	18	0	2	67	74	53	39	7	1	45	4	59	5
Schafer, Clinton	5	8	.385	3.15	31	17	4	7	1	2	137	130	62	48	9	5	45	4	71	3
Schiewe, Quad Cities	0	0	.000	3.00	2	0	0	1	0	0	6	7	2	2	0	0	6	0	1	3
Schroeck, Burlington°	9	8	.529	3.72	19	19	4	0	0	0	133	121	64	55	13	4	52	1	89	10
Schuckert, Appleton°	4	8	.333	5.82	20	18	0	1	0	0	85	89	61	55	9	2	61	1	59	8
Schulze, Quad Cities	8	5	.615	2.31	17	16	6	1	1	0	105	89	33	27	1	7	51	1	61	4
Schumacher, Appleton	2	6	.250	3.89	38	0	0	28	0	6	88	85	50	38	5	3	44	3	67	10
Schwarber, Waterloo	8	7	.533	3.84	32	18	4	8	1	2	150	136	76	64	12	5	72	3	151	4
Shoemaker, Quad Cities	1	0	1.000	0.90	4	0	0	0	0	0	10	10	4	1	0	0	2	0	4	0
Silvas, Waterloo	2	0	1.000	3.48	11	4	0	5	0	0	31	32	15	12	1	1	17	0	12	7
Siwy, Appleton	5	0	1.000	1.96	8	8	1	0	0	0	55	47	17	12	3	1	12	2	32	0
Smay, Clinton	5	8	.385	4.27	31	10	1	19	0	4	97	88	63	46	10	4	57	1	67	4
Smith, Burlington	7	7	.500	3.60	41	2	0	22	0	3	85	106	44	34	7	4	22	1	59	2
Smith, Quad Cities	12	8	.600	3.41	25	21	5	2	2	2	132	130	74	50	9	4	61	0	104	9
Snyder, Wausau°	3	1	.750	1.48	27	4	1	17	0	7	67	34	21	11	2	2	37	2	77	5
Soff, Quad Cities	3	0	1.000	3.71	32	0	0	20	0	6	51	49	27	21	2	0	24	2	39	6
Steger, Wausau	6	5	.545	3.84	29	12	1	9	0	1	103	105	63	44	5	2	51	2	77	11
Stibora, Burlington°	1	3	.250	11.16	15	1	0	10	0	1	25	34	39	31	5	2	30	2	18	5
Stottlemyre, Wausau	2	1	.667	1.54	6	6	1	0	0	0	41	26	14	7	1	5	18	2	26	4
Suarez, Wisconsin Rapids	5	5	.500	4.18	24	14	6	4	0	0	114	114	59	53	13	3	88	2	79	11
Sutton, Appleton	0	0	.000	2.14	7	0	0	4	0	0	21	18	5	5	1	0	6	1	9	0
Swaggerty, Quad Cities	11	7	.611	2.78	26	22	3	3	0	0	139	118	50	43	6	2	53	2	53	12
Thompson, Waterloo	5	6	.455	4.13	28	16	3	6	0	1	122	112	67	56	9	5	55	2	109	14
Ungs, Wisconsin Rapids	5	5	.500	5.35	11	10	4	1	0	0	74	88	54	44	9	4	22	0	46	4
Vaji, Quad Cities°	7	8	.467	3.31	26	20	2	5	0	4	117	106	63	43	2	2	75	1	99	16
Vasquez, Burlington	0	1	.000	3.27	12	0	0	9	0	1	11	11	8	4	1	0	9	1	11	4
Villegas, Burlington	5	5	.500	4.28	16	10	5	3	0	1	80	71	44	38	4	2	26	2	71	2

Pitcher—Club	W.	L.	Pct.	ERA.	G.	GS.	CG.	GF.	ShO.	Sv.	IP.	H.	R.	ER.	HR.	HB.	BB.	Int. BB.	SO.	WP.
Wardle, Wisconsin Rapids°	4	3	.571	3.23	16	6	4	5	0	0	53	49	27	19	3	0	32	0	41	9
Weibel, Wisconsin Rapids	2	1	.667	3.35	18	0	0	9	0	2	43	30	16	16	6	3	29	3	38	3
Weissmann, Quad Cities	0	2	.000	6.55	8	1	0	3	0	1	22	31	20	16	4	0	14	0	17	3
Welch, Appleton	0	0	.000	0.00	1	0	0	1	0	0	3	2	0	0	0	0	1	0	1	0
Wilhelmi, Clinton	10	13	.435	4.74	27	27	5	0	2	0	167	180	106	88	9	14	81	1	56	12
Wilkins, Quad Cities	2	0	1.000	4.29	8	0	0	3	0	0	21	19	11	10	1	1	13	1	19	2
Withrow, Appleton	2	3	.400	3.56	9	9	1	0	0	0	43	35	20	17	1	2	19	0	29	1
Wood, Burlington	1	1	.500	5.19	10	1	0	7	0	1	26	21	16	15	2	2	19	2	23	2
Wright, Wisconsin Rapids	0	1	.000	6.39	13	0	0	6	0	1	31	36	25	22	4	3	15	3	22	2
Yett, Wisconsin Rapids	12	6	.667	3.68	25	25	12	0	1	0	164	147	87	67	14	5	77	2	121	13
Young, Clinton	0	2	.000	2.37	10	0	0	7	0	4	19	17	5	5	1	0	10	2	14	1

BALKS—Kyles, 4; Guerrero, Krueger, Oliver, Thompson, 3 each; Bangert, Brecht, Chue, Dixon, Dukes, McSparran, Pastrovich, Pone, Schroeck, Schulze, Vaji, Wilhelmi, 2 each; Asbell, Banach, D'Amore, Eduardo, Effrig, Everett, Gomez, L. Harris, Henderson, Herberholz, Jackson, King, Lepson, Lesley, McLaughlin, Mullen, Myles, Nunez, Platel, Puryear, Riley, Smay, Suarez, Ungs, Weibel, Wright, Yett, 1 each.

COMBINATION SHUTOUTS—Anderson-Mullen, Barnard-Flannery, Pastrovich-Schumacher, Schuckert-Mullen, Schuckert-Schumacher, Withrow-Flannery, Withrow-Flannery-Mullen, Appleton; Harris-Crews, Schroek-Smith, Burlington; Buchanan-Lesley, Hollenbach-Kepshire, Myles-Lesley-Raines, Cedar Rapids; Brecht-Chue, Brecht-D'Amore, McSparran-Smay, Clinton; Housey-Miglio, Smith-Gerlach, Swaggerty-Gerlach, Vaji-Kaufman, Vaji-Smith, Vaji-Swaggerty, Quad Cities; Owens-Hrynko 2, Owens-Lintz, Jeffcoat-Schwarber, Schwarber-Silvas, Waterloo; Ungs-Everett, Wisconsin Rapids.

NO-HIT GAME—Bangert, Clinton, defeated Burlington, 4-1, April 20, second game (seven innings).

NY-Pennsylvania League

CLASS A

CHAMPIONSHIP WINNERS IN PREVIOUS YEARS

1939—Olean° .631	1954—Corning° .621	1968—Auburn .645
1940—Olean° .625	1955—Hamilton° .656	Oneonta (2nd)° .558
1941—Jamestown .618	1956—Wellsville° .617	1969—Oneonta .662
Bradford (2nd)† .549	1957—Wellsville .632	1970—Auburn .623
1942—Jamestown° .672	Erie (2nd)† .598	1971—Oneonta .662
1943—Lockport .591	1958—Wellsville .556	1972—Niagara Falls .686
Wellsville (3rd)† .532	Geneva (2nd)† .548	1973—Auburn .667
1944—Lockport .608	1959—Wellsville† .635	1974—Oneonta .768
Jamestown (2nd)† .565	1960—Erie .643	1975—Newark .688
1945—Batavia° .677	Wellsville (2nd)† .535	Newark .714
1946—Jamestown‡ .672	1961—Geneva .616	1976—Elmira .727
Batavia‡ .672	Olean (4th)† .512	Elmira .703
1947—Jamestown° .690	1962—Jamestown .580	1977—Oneonta y .671
1948—Lockport° .603	Auburn (3rd)† .521	Batavia .600
1949—Bradford° .635	1963—Auburn .585	1978—Oneonta .729
1950—Hornell .653	Batavia (3rd)† .485	Geneva z .718
Olean (2nd)† .568	1964—Auburn§ .622	1979—Geneva .725
1951—Olean .622	1965—Binghamton .677	Oneonta z .618
Hornell (3rd)† .568	Binghamton .607	1980—Oneonta y .662
1952—Hamilton .659	1966—Auburn x .620	Geneva .649
Jamestown (2nd)† .643	Binghamton .646	
1953—Jamestown° .704	1967—Auburn .667	

°Won championship and four-club playoff. †Won four-club playoff. ‡Jamestown and Batavia declared co-champions; Batavia defeated Jamestown in final of four-club playoff. §Won championship and two-club playoff. xWon split-season playoff. yLeague divided into Eastern and Western Divisions; won playoff. zLeague divided into Wrigley and Yawkey Divisions; won playoff. (NOTE—Known as Pennsylvania-Ontario-New York League from 1939 through 1956.)

STANDING OF CLUBS AT CLOSE OF SEASON, SEPTEMBER 3

EASTERN DIVISION

Club	W.	L.	T.	Pct.	G.B.
Oneonta (Yankees)	48	25	0	.658	
Utica (Independent)	39	31	0	.557	7½
Little Falls (Mets)	31	39	1	.443	15½
Elmira (Red Sox)	25	48	0	.342	23

WESTERN DIVISION

Club	W.	L.	T.	Pct.	G.B.
Jamestown (Expos)	48	26	0	.649	
Erie (Cardinals)	44	30	0	.595	4
Geneva (Cubs)	41	34	0	.547	7½
Batavia (Indians)	16	59	0	.213	32½

COMPOSITE STANDINGS OF CLUBS AT CLOSE OF SEASON, SEPTEMBER 3

Club	Ont.	Jmt.	Erie	Utica	Gen.	L.F.	Elm.	Bat.	W.	L.	T.	Pct.	G.B.
Oneonta (Yankees)	..	3	4	9	6	7	13	6	48	25	0	.658	....
Jamestown (Expos)	4	..	7	3	9	4	7	14	48	26	1	.649	½
Erie (Cardinals)	4	8	..	4	8	3	7	10	44	30	0	.595	4½
Utica (Independent)	5	5	4	..	5	8	8	4	39	31	0	.557	7½
Geneva (Cubs)	2	5	6	3	..	7	5	13	41	34	0	.547	8
Little Falls (Mets)	7	4	4	3	1	..	7	5	31	39	1	.443	15½
Elmira (Red Sox)	1	1	1	6	2	7	..	7	25	48	0	.342	23
Batavia (Indians)	2	0	4	3	3	3	1	..	16	59	0	.213	33

Major league affiliations in parentheses.

Playoff—Oneonta, Eastern Division champion, defeated Jamestown, Western Division champion, two games to one.

Regular Season Attendance—Batavia, 24,841; Elmira, 49,556; Erie, 76,063; Geneva, 24,403; Jamestown, 44,931; Little Falls, 23,516; Oneonta, 39,075; Utica, 19,146. Total, 301,531. Playoff, 2,298. No all-star game.

Managers: Batavia, Dave Oliver; Elmira, Dick Berardino; Erie, Sonny Ruberto; Geneva, Bob Hartsfield; Jamestown, Pat Dougherty; Little Falls, Gene Dusan; Oneonta, Art Mazmanian; Utica, Jim Gattis.

All-Star Team: 1B—Rene Marchand, Jamestown; 2B—John Damon, Jamestown; 3B—William Lyons, Erie; SS—Michael Harris, Erie; Reserve Infielder—David Rosenhahn, Geneva; OF—Francisco Batista, Erie; Willie Cooley, Jamestown; Scott Holliday, Little Falls; Randy Washington, Batavia; C—Scott Bradley, Oneonta; Robert Gilles, Little Falls; DH—David Malpeso, Elmira; LHP—Phil Deriso, Batavia; Michael Flinn, Utica; RHP—John Adams, Erie; Gregory Dunn, Erie; Manager—Pat Daugherty, Jamestown.

(Compiled by Howe News Bureau, Boston, Mass.)

CLUB BATTING

Club	Pct.	G.	AB.	R.	OR.	H.	TB.	2B.	3B.	HR.	RBI.	GW.	SH.	SF.	HP.	BB.	Int. BB.	SO.	SB.	CS.	LOB.
Utica	.286	70	2286	443	335	653	1018	112	11	77	372	34	27	18	15	354	13	397	121	37	493
Erie	.281	74	2569	467	363	722	1030	110	12	58	399	33	24	24	22	347	24	385	77	26	580
Jamestown	.271	75	2550	418	345	692	988	102	28	46	355	38	10	27	20	315	13	429	103	20	567
Oneonta	.265	73	2362	409	326	625	926	112	33	41	341	40	31	28	19	345	38	467	159	19	533
Little Falls	.255	71	2272	355	420	579	900	82	13	71	309	21	19	17	20	364	13	492	88	37	533
Geneva	.247	75	2488	414	376	614	935	117	15	58	347	33	21	19	18	371	19	515	79	25	565
Elmira	.238	73	2335	338	459	555	829	107	10	49	294	20	47	12	18	342	15	478	29	9	549
Batavia	.230	75	2447	282	502	563	799	84	16	40	246	10	20	16	25	250	12	462	46	20	505

INDIVIDUAL BATTING
(Leading Qualifiers for Batting Championship—205 or More Plate Appearances)

°Bats lefthanded. †Switch-hitter.

Player and Club	Pct.	G.	AB.	R.	H.	TB.	2B.	3B.	HR.	RBI.	GW.	SH.	SF.	HP.	BB.	Int. BB.	SO.	SB.	CS.
Romano, Thomas, Utica	.337	66	243	49	82	155	14	4	17	53	5	1	3	21	1	25	20	5	
Damon, John, Jamestown	.337	70	270	57	91	125	14	7	2	40	1	0	2	1	49	4	27	33	3
Lyons, William, Erie	.327	73	269	63	88	129	19	2	6	65	12	2	4	4	54	3	24	16	2
Washington, Randy, Batavia	.327	66	226	41	74	134	11	8	11	48	4	1	2	1	27	0	52	4	0
Moss, Barry, Utica†	.325	68	252	50	82	135	15	1	12	51	2	1	3	2	42	2	30	6	2
Guin, Gregory, Erie°	.324	71	259	67	84	136	20	1	10	56	8	1	5	1	62	4	35	2	0
Dennis, Roberto, Oneonta	.322	59	202	36	65	88	12	1	3	29	2	1	2	0	7	1	23	24	0
Gomez, Alfonso, Utica	.317	61	208	41	66	120	11	2	13	40	3	0	1	3	27	2	38	10	1
Gilles, Robert, Little Falls	.317	57	183	39	58	124	9	0	19	51	3	1	4	2	40	1	50	1	1
Hughes, John, Oneonta°	.309	58	178	28	55	92	11	1	8	38	5	3	3	1	40	6	33	1	0

Departmental Leaders: G—Hatcher, Rosenhahn, Weislak, 75; AB—Cooley, 304; R—Guin, 67; H—Damon, 91; TB—Romano, 155; 2B—Guin, 20; 3B—Washington, 8; HR—Gilles, 19; RBI—Lyons, 65; GWRBI—Lyons, 12; SH—Marcano, 8; SF—Dawes, 7; BB—Guin, 62; HP—Hatcher, 8; SO—Holliday, 73; SB—Damon, 33; CS—Renfroe, 7.

(All Players—Listed Alphabetically)

Player and Club	Pct.	G.	AB.	R.	H.	TB.	2B.	3B.	HR.	RBI.	GW.	SH.	SF.	HP.	BB.	Int. BB.	SO.	SB.	CS.
Albright, Gilbert, Utica	.248	50	137	21	34	56	7	0	5	18	3	6	1	0	10	0	20	2	0
Albright, Henry, Utica	.260	29	73	12	19	25	6	0	0	6	0	0	0	1	9	2	18	1	2
Alcala, Jesus, Oneonta	.114	19	35	6	4	4	0	0	0	1	0	0	0	0	3	1	7	1	0
Aldridge, William, Jamestown	.000	1	4	0	0	0	0	0	0	0	0	0	0	0	0	0	0	0	0
Allen, Shane, Geneva	.289	33	128	17	37	47	10	0	0	22	1	1	1	0	7	0	20	2	0
Alomar, Victor, Elmira°	.237	28	76	9	18	24	2	2	0	7	0	3	1	0	7	0	13	1	0
Alpert, George, Batavia°	.214	67	252	24	54	75	7	1	4	23	1	0	4	1	19	5	49	2	3
Archie, Richard, Utica†	.067	11	15	1	1	2	1	0	0	0	0	0	0	0	3	0	1	0	0
Arfstrom, Joseph, Elmira†	.286	51	161	22	46	69	9	1	4	21	0	1	1	0	19	2	22	1	1
Batista, Francisco, Erie	.293	74	287	41	84	117	17	2	4	54	4	2	6	4	25	4	53	15	4
Beal, Anthony, Elmira	.181	51	127	16	23	28	5	0	0	7	1	2	1	1	16	0	32	10	1
Benzinger, Todd, Elmira†	.241	41	141	21	34	52	10	1	2	8	0	2	0	0	20	1	32	4	0
Berroa, Eduardo, Elmira†	.238	30	80	9	19	27	6	1	0	9	2	3	0	1	9	0	29	0	0
Biagini, Robert, Elmira	.167	22	42	3	7	7	0	0	0	5	1	0	0	0	7	0	10	0	0
Blocker, Terry, Little Falls°	.341	36	135	28	46	77	8	1	7	16	3	0	0	0	8	0	18	14	2
Bone, Patrick, Oneonta†	.246	42	65	11	16	27	5	0	2	6	1	0	0	0	7	0	32	3	0
Bradley, Scott, Oneonta°	.308	71	276	48	85	122	17	4	4	54	7	3	6	0	22	7	15	7	0
Brito, Bernardo, Batavia	.207	12	29	1	6	6	0	0	0	2	0	1	0	1	2	0	9	0	0
Brooks, F. Trey, Geneva	.246	69	252	28	62	73	6	1	1	27	3	0	1	1	32	1	30	7	4
Burrell, Kevin, Elmira	.208	28	72	6	15	24	6	0	1	10	0	1	0	0	1	0	21	0	2
Carpenter, William, Elmira	.250	61	168	16	42	56	8	0	2	28	4	6	1	1	30	3	42	0	1
Castiglia, Patrick, Elmira°	.244	62	180	36	44	81	7	0	10	36	3	7	4	0	44	3	42	0	1
Cochran, Arnold, Batavia	.187	34	107	9	20	30	4	0	2	13	1	0	1	2	9	1	36	0	0
Collins, P. Scott, Batavia	.255	26	94	15	24	36	3	0	3	8	0	1	0	0	10	0	8	5	1
Cooley, Willie, Jamestown	.280	71	304	56	85	111	13	2	3	28	1	0	1	1	31	3	53	22	6
Cordova, Antonio, Geneva	.253	59	217	32	55	95	14	1	8	39	3	1	3	1	19	2	41	6	3
Czeszewski, Larry, Little Falls	.250	7	20	4	5	8	1	1	0	3	0	0	0	0	1	0	2	0	0
D'Aloia, James, Oneonta	.250	60	152	22	38	51	7	0	2	25	6	6	1	1	18	0	12	12	1
Damon, John, Jamestown	.337	70	270	57	91	125	14	7	2	40	1	0	2	1	49	4	27	33	3
Darling, Edward, Oneonta†	.228	25	79	10	18	21	3	0	0	9	0	0	1	0	14	2	24	0	1
Dawes, Steven, Jamestown	.261	67	253	34	66	81	13	1	0	39	5	1	7	3	23	0	20	7	0
DeMatties, Stephen, Little Falls°	.203	50	128	18	26	46	2	0	6	22	1	0	1	1	28	1	41	2	1
Denby, Darryl, Little Falls†	.281	52	146	16	41	51	6	2	0	11	3	1	2	1	19	1	38	9	4
Dennis, Roberto, Oneonta	.322	59	202	36	65	88	12	1	3	29	2	1	2	0	7	1	23	24	0
Despaux, C. Frederick, Oneonta	.255	51	98	22	25	45	5	3	3	16	3	2	1	4	19	4	23	10	1
Donovan, Dennis, Oneonta	.000	4	2	1	0	0	0	0	0	0	0	0	0	0	0	0	1	1	0
Dotson, W. Hardy, Jamestown	.228	58	180	23	41	59	6	3	2	17	1	2	1	1	16	0	28	4	0
Eiland, William, Utica†	.244	56	180	23	44	59	3	0	4	26	2	5	3	1	24	0	55	7	5
Eldridge, Terry, Jamestown°	.255	40	106	18	27	39	4	4	0	10	0	0	0	0	20	1	27	5	2
Elkin, Rick, Batavia	.107	17	28	2	3	6	1	1	0	1	0	1	0	0	2	0	11	0	0
Erickson, Steven, Utica	.306	23	49	8	15	26	3	1	2	12	1	0	1	0	8	0	14	0	0
Federici, Richard, Erie°	.309	21	81	13	25	29	4	0	0	6	2	1	0	0	5	0	11	2	0
Felice, Jason, Little Falls	.276	35	98	16	27	39	3	3	1	14	0	0	2	0	9	1	14	1	0
Ficklin, Winston, Batavia†	.167	10	18	1	3	4	1	0	0	3	0	0	0	1	4	0	6	0	2
Fisher, Charles, Elmira	.194	33	93	11	18	24	3	0	1	6	1	1	0	4	14	0	30	1	0
Franks, Michael, Little Falls	.000	2	3	0	0	0	0	0	0	0	0	0	0	0	2	0	0	0	0
Gaeta, Anthony, Utica	.286	8	14	3	4	4	0	0	0	2	1	0	0	0	1	0	4	0	0
Galarraga, Andres, Jamestown	.260	47	154	24	40	71	5	4	6	26	5	1	1	4	15	2	44	0	0
Garton, Edward, Little Falls	.188	54	170	21	32	55	6	1	5	25	2	3	0	2	22	4	23	2	0
Gattis, James, Utica	.391	43	133	24	52	86	11	1	7	39	3	0	1	1	13	1	14	8	1
George, Leo, Geneva	.260	57	208	43	54	98	12	1	10	28	3	2	1	1	29	1	60	4	1
Gilles, Robert, Little Falls	.317	57	183	39	58	124	9	0	19	51	3	1	4	2	40	1	50	1	1
Gomez, Alfonso, Utica	.317	61	208	41	66	120	11	2	13	40	3	0	1	3	27	2	38	10	1
Gonzales, Peter, Elmira†	.194	30	72	9	14	15	1	0	0	7	1	0	0	0	16	1	25	0	0
Gonzalez, James, Little Falls	.125	10	16	1	2	4	0	1	0	1	0	0	0	2	3	0	5	0	0
Guin, Gregory, Erie°	.324	71	259	67	84	136	20	1	10	56	8	1	5	1	62	4	35	2	0
Harris, Kenneth, Little Falls	.191	44	131	28	25	31	3	0	1	11	1	0	2	0	17	1	13	6	3
Harris, Michael, Erie	.241	67	291	44	70	87	6	1	3	28	0	2	1	1	15	1	38	13	4
Hatcher, William, Geneva	.280	75	289	57	81	114	15	3	4	40	4	4	2	8	36	2	41	13	1
Henry, Mark, Jamestown	.192	20	73	8	14	21	4	0	1	10	2	0	0	0	7	1	11	1	1
Hertzler, Paul, Elmira	.309	44	123	24	38	47	3	0	2	12	2	1	0	1	23	0	9	4	3
Holden, Gary, Batavia	.212	24	66	9	14	21	2	1	1	5	0	0	0	1	9	0	20	0	0
Holliday, Scott, Little Falls	.255	61	196	36	50	91	8	0	11	41	3	0	2	0	49	1	73	10	6
Howard, J. Christopher, Elmira†	.226	56	177	26	40	61	9	3	2	15	1	5	2	1	25	0	38	0	1
Huber, Randy, Jamestown	.000	26	1	0	0	0	0	0	0	0	0	0	0	0	0	0	1	0	0
Hughes, John, Oneonta°	.309	58	178	28	55	92	11	1	8	38	5	3	3	1	40	6	33	1	0
Hunt, James, Erie	.297	60	195	43	58	92	6	2	8	27	1	1	0	3	39	2	21	3	1
Jackson, John, Little Falls	.237	34	114	16	27	36	4	1	1	15	1	0	2	1	18	0	24	1	3
James, Richard, Erie	.275	68	262	46	72	103	6	4	7	36	3	2	2	1	31	1	32	7	4
Jefferson, Michael, Elmira	.269	24	52	6	14	17	3	0	0	5	0	2	0	2	8	0	13	2	1
Jewett, Gregory, Oneonta	.278	8	18	4	5	6	1	0	0	4	1	0	0	0	1	0	9	1	0

Player and Club	Pct.	G.	AB.	R.	H.	TB.	2B.	3B.	HR.	RBI.	GW.	SH.	SF.	HP.	BB.	Int. BB.	SO.	SB.	CS.
Johnston, Kevin, Elmira°	.184	23	49	9	9	15	3	0	1	8	1	0	0	0	10	0	15	0	1
Jones, Eric, Batavia	.194	57	160	28	31	55	5	2	5	20	1	1	2	2	28	1	43	7	4
Jose, Manuel, Elmira†	.200	4	5	3	1	1	0	0	0	0	0	0	0	0	3	0	0	0	0
Jurena, Mark, Utica	.250	2	4	0	1	2	1	0	0	2	0	1	0	0	1	0	0	0	0
Kempton, Gary, Oneonta	.207	41	111	14	23	38	1	1	4	10	0	1	1	2	13	0	33	4	1
Kwiecinski, Michael, Jamestown	.276	36	105	20	29	54	6	2	5	14	1	2	1	1	11	0	27	3	1
Lauziere, Michael, Jamestown°	.319	17	47	7	15	22	1	0	2	5	0	0	0	6	0	15	1	0
Lemon, Ricky, Jamestown°	.255	34	106	14	27	48	6	0	5	16	1	0	0	0	6	0	15	1	0
Licata, Joseph, Little Falls	.218	34	87	17	19	27	2	0	2	6	0	1	0	2	13	0	19	2	1
Locascio, Lawrence, Batavia	.232	18	56	3	13	15	2	0	0	5	0	1	0	2	2	0	8	0	0
Lorenz, Jerome, Utica	.276	70	239	54	66	96	9	0	7	42	4	3	3	1	49	0	45	14	5
Lyons, William, Erie	.327	73	269	63	88	129	19	2	6	65	12	2	4	4	54	3	24	16	2
Mackie, Bart, Batavia	.186	34	59	2	11	14	0	0	1	4	0	0	0	2	7	0	15	0	0
Malpeso, David, Elmira	.292	67	250	53	73	125	14	1	12	50	3	0	0	2	20	1	35	0	0
Marcano, Jose, Little Falls†	.274	58	186	34	51	59	4	2	0	10	2	8	0	3	42	0	35	10	5
Marchand, Rene, Jamestown	.304	70	257	37	78	110	13	2	5	49	7	1	6	0	28	1	28	3	2
Martin, Roger, Erie	.500	4	4	0	2	3	1	0	0	1	0	0	1	0	0	0	0	0	0
Martin, Samuel, Batavia†	.116	34	86	7	10	11	1	0	0	6	0	3	1	0	6	0	11	1	2
Martinez, Ray, Batavia°	.240	56	192	24	46	69	12	1	3	14	0	2	0	2	14	1	27	1	0
Matute, J. Joaquin, Elmira	.083	5	12	0	1	1	0	0	0	1	0	0	1	0	0	0	3	0	0
McNealy, Derwin, Oneonta°	.273	68	187	35	51	78	6	3	5	27	1	6	3	0	27	3	43	18	6
Meleski, Mark, Elmira°	.191	40	89	11	17	27	2	1	2	11	0	2	0	0	20	0	15	1	0
Menzhuber, Charles, Erie i°	.376	23	109	27	41	60	8	1	3	17	0	1	1	1	6	0	21	7	1
Merchant, John, Batavia	.250	60	196	22	49	70	6	0	5	26	0	1	0	1	17	0	38	1	2
Mesa, Jose, Elmira	.250	3	4	1	1	1	0	0	0	0	0	0	0	0	3	0	1	0	0
Miller, Scott, Geneva°	.227	37	119	23	27	56	7	2	6	22	0	0	1	0	37	3	36	1	2
Miller, Steven, Utica	.213	27	47	7	10	10	0	0	0	1	0	2	0	1	4	0	11	0	1
Miller, Timothy, Batavia	.216	36	102	13	22	23	1	0	0	3	0	2	1	1	24	0	16	5	0
Monroe, Gary, Geneva	.189	18	74	6	14	15	1	0	0	11	0	2	0	1	7	1	12	2	2
Morrison, Bruce, Oneonta	.143	9	28	2	4	4	0	0	0	1	0	0	0	0	3	0	8	0	0
Moscat, Fernando, Little Falls	.251	61	215	20	54	66	7	1	1	24	0	4	1	2	11	0	44	13	6
Moss, Barry, Utica†	.325	68	252	50	82	135	15	1	12	51	2	1	3	2	42	2	30	6	2
Murphy, Roderick, Utica	.260	58	204	56	53	78	10	0	5	27	1	1	0	0	51	0	42	29	5
Nagel, Thomas, Batavia	.143	5	14	0	2	2	0	0	0	1	0	0	0	0	1	0	0	0	0
Nalley, Jerry, Batavia	.278	15	36	3	10	12	2	0	0	2	0	2	0	0	5	0	3	0	0
Navoa, Milciades, Batavia	.302	50	162	15	49	57	8	0	0	6	1	2	1	2	11	0	19	11	4
Nay, Len, Jamestown°	.250	31	88	15	22	36	2	0	4	14	2	1	1	0	11	0	19	6	0
Nieves, Adalberto, Batavia	.167	35	72	10	12	14	2	0	0	4	0	1	0	1	6	0	20	0	0
Norment, Michael, Jamestown	.210	69	210	32	44	53	3	0	2	25	3	1	2	5	43	1	50	6	2
Nyman, Matthew, Geneva	.229	16	48	6	11	20	3	0	2	5	0	0	0	0	4	0	21	0	0
O'Regan, Daniel, Oneonta°	.296	61	186	29	55	97	16	7	4	32	1	0	1	0	32	3	50	8	0
Pacho, Juan, Batavia	.198	33	106	7	21	24	3	0	0	8	1	0	0	2	7	1	8	1	0
Pagliarulo, Michael, Oneonta†	.216	72	245	32	53	76	9	4	2	28	1	2	3	0	38	8	47	13	1
Perodin, Ronald, Utica†	.237	48	152	27	36	41	5	0	0	12	2	2	0	1	23	1	23	15	5
Picchioni, Joseph, Utica	.219	20	32	8	7	8	1	0	0	4	3	1	1	0	7	0	10	3	1
Pickett, Richard, Little Falls°	.000	8	3	0	0	0	0	0	0	0	0	0	0	0	0	0	2	0	0
Powers, Mac, Geneva†	.071	4	14	2	1	1	0	0	0	0	0	0	0	1	0	0	5	0	0
Prosper, Michael, Little Falls°	.280	27	50	5	14	16	2	0	0	3	0	0	0	0	11	0	6	0	0
Purcell, Trent, Little Falls°	.202	35	84	7	17	29	3	0	3	8	0	0	0	0	9	1	11	3	0
Rabassa, Pedro, Utica°	.263	39	99	17	26	30	2	1	0	8	1	1	0	1	20	1	21	3	2
Raeside, John, Little Falls	.293	54	198	31	58	94	9	0	9	30	0	0	2	0	25	2	35	9	3
Reddish, Michael, Oneonta	.167	2	6	0	1	1	0	0	0	1	1	0	0	0	1	0	3	0	0
Rehbaum, Christopher, Batavia°	.248	62	202	28	50	76	7	2	5	34	1	0	2	1	29	2	40	5	1
Remo, Jeffrey, Geneva	.205	51	146	25	30	52	7	0	5	20	1	2	2	2	28	1	50	2	1
Renfroe, Steven, Oneonta	.251	57	167	28	42	69	9	3	4	26	8	2	3	4	12	1	39	9	7
Roath, Steven, Erie°	.170	22	47	7	8	13	2	0	1	4	0	2	0	0	10	2	11	1	1
Rodriguez, Efrain, Oneonta	.308	50	146	27	45	56	5	3	0	19	1	1	3	2	21	2	22	15	0
Roman, Miguel, Batavia	.114	17	35	1	4	4	0	0	0	1	0	0	0	3	0	12	0	0
Romano, Thomas, Utica	.337	66	243	49	82	155	14	4	17	53	5	1	3	3	21	1	25	20	5
Rosenhahn, David, Geneva	.276	75	294	59	81	134	16	2	11	53	4	0	1	1	38	1	41	10	1
Rutledge, Jeffery, Geneva	.252	70	250	45	63	99	12	0	8	39	5	5	3	1	43	0	54	7	3
Sanchez, Orlando, Erie	.357	6	14	1	5	5	0	0	0	4	1	1	0	1	4	0	2	0	1
Scafa, Stephen, Oneonta†	.229	54	131	46	30	40	4	3	0	12	2	3	0	4	53	0	32	28	1
Seaman, Steven, Elmira	.266	36	79	10	21	23	2	0	0	9	0	2	1	1	16	0	11	1	0
Seid, Bruce, Geneva	.200	8	25	3	5	9	2	1	0	4	1	0	0	0	4	1	1	2	1
Severino, Ramon, Elmira†	.000	5	5	0	0	0	0	0	0	0	0	0	0	0	1	0	4	0	0
Sheaffer, Danny, Elmira	.288	62	198	39	57	90	9	0	8	29	1	3	0	1	23	1	38	2	0
Smith, P. Keith, Oneonta†	.200	19	50	8	10	11	1	0	0	3	0	1	0	1	14	0	11	4	0
Southern, Mitchell, Erie°	.215	62	214	35	46	69	8	0	5	31	2	2	1	2	30	3	45	3	1
Stryffeler, Daniel, Erie°	.295	67	258	46	76	101	7	0	6	35	0	3	1	1	39	3	34	5	4
Tanner, Edwin, Batavia†	.235	48	149	17	35	41	6	0	0	9	0	1	2	2	8	1	11	3	1
Tarnow, Greg, Geneva	.197	31	61	4	12	14	0	1	0	3	1	1	0	1	7	1	26	2	1
Thomas, David, Utica	.000	20	1	0	0	0	0	0	0	0	0	0	0	0	0	0	0	0	0
Thomas, Deron, Erie†	.191	44	157	16	30	41	5	0	2	19	0	4	1	2	13	0	29	2	2
Tobin, Patrick, Geneva†	.184	55	163	24	30	42	5	2	1	13	2	1	1	2	37	4	39	4	0
Tramble, Otis, Geneva	.259	52	158	34	41	48	5	1	0	16	4	1	1	2	31	1	24	17	5
Vann, Jesse, Little Falls	.248	39	109	18	27	47	5	0	5	18	2	1	1	1	38	0	39	5	2
Varano, Michael, Elmira	.222	6	18	2	4	4	0	0	0	4	0	1	0	1	0	1	2	0	0
Walck, Craig, Elmira	.221	52	145	16	32	51	7	0	4	15	0	3	0	2	27	2	18	0	0
Walker, Steve, Elmira†	.143	27	42	5	6	7	1	0	0	3	1	3	0	2	4	0	10	4	0
Washington, Randy, Batavia	.327	66	226	41	74	134	11	8	11	48	4	1	2	1	27	0	52	4	0
Weems, Charles, Erie	.271	36	118	17	32	44	1	1	3	16	0	0	1	1	11	1	28	1	1
Weislak, Kenneth, Jamestown	.279	75	269	49	75	111	9	3	7	50	7	0	5	2	25	0	48	3	0
Weppner, Daniel, Elmira	.000	1	2	0	0	0	0	0	0	0	0	0	0	0	1	0	0	0	0
Williams, Ralph, Geneva	.238	21	42	6	10	18	2	0	2	5	1	1	0	2	0	14	0	0
Wing, Robert, Utica°	.270	64	204	42	55	85	13	1	5	29	3	2	1	0	41	3	26	3	2

The following pitchers had no plate appearances primarily through use of designated hitters, listed alphabetically by club, games in parentheses:

BATAVIA—Asbell, John (3); Bajus, Mark (7); Burns, Thomas (19); Clark, Dane (3); Cosgrove, Robert (18); Cushing, Stephen (12); Deriso, Phillip (18); Dixon, Michael (9); Doyle, Richard (15); Elpin, Ralph (12); Johnson, Wayne (14); Poindexter, Michael (16); Richard, Todd (9); Ramon, Jose (20); Silvas, Brian (10).

ELMIRA—Araujo, Anazario (16); Davis, Charles (14); Ellsworth, Steven (1); Gnacinski, Paul (18); Gonzalez, Gilberto (11); Key, John (7); Lockhart, Bruce (13); Santiago, Johnnie (21); Scheller, David (15); Silva, Jesus (5); Sorenson, John (3); Wareham, David (14); Weston, William (16); Woodward, Robert (12).

ERIE—Adams, John (16); Alba, Gibson (16); Dunn, Gregory (13); Finnegan, William (5); Kish, Robert (8); Larosa, William (9); Maldanado, Ovidio (15); Milligan, Brent (15); North, Jay (12); Parmenter, Walter (25); Pittman, Michael (17); Taveris, Luis (1); Young, Scott (16).

GENEVA—Adamczak, James (10); Andrews, Jeffrey (18); Banks, Darryl (10); Black, Allen (4); Brahms, Russell (29); Chestnut, Troy (13); Kaufman, Ronald (4); Kyles, Stanley (12); Lockie, Randall (16); Schilling, Robert (14); Shoemaker, Martin (2); Smith, Scott (18); Webb, Stanley (10); Weissmann, Craig (10).

JAMESTOWN—Brodeur, Claude (6); Chesser, Brandon (1); Gilbreath, Ronnie (13); Graves, Robert (1); Johnson, Gregory (21); Pope, Gregory (9—includes 3 with Batavia); Powers, Michael (16); Scott, Charles (14); Skorupa, Elliot (6); St. Claire, Randy (13); St. John, William (15); Staffon, Gregory (9); Yenser, Steven (14).

LITTLE FALLS—Arnold, Gail (15); Foust, Algernon (15); Fuller, Leo (25); Graves, Joseph (13); Harlander, Michael (6); Latham, William (13); Magdziuk, Donald (1); Merlack, Scott (20); O'Beirne, Michael (8); Slaton, Steven (13); Vaughn, Wayne (1); Wick, Jeff (6); Wilmet, Paul (20).

ONEONTA—Brooks, Robert (15); Demaria, George (6); Dewitt, Don (11); Hernandez, Carlos (11); Herrera, Henry (2); Livesay, Michael (3); Mikesell, Lawrence (13); Niemic, David (6); Quirk, Kevin (27); Shiflett, Mark (12); Szymczak, David (17); Tewksbury, Robert (14); Wex, Gary (11); Williams, Stanley (10).

UTICA—Christiansen, John (10); Cicotte, Gregory (3); Delett, Douglas (9); Flinn, Michael (14); Gainer, Keith (17—includes 4 with Batavia); Klacza, Kenneth (8); Klutcharch, Steven (18); Powers, Daniel (8); Uhey, Jackie (13); Umdenstock, Robert (15); Vaulman, Paul (12).

GRAND SLAM HOME RUNS—Cochran, Cordova, Erickson, DeMatties, Hatcher, Holliday, Hunt, Lyons, Malpeso, Merchant, Rehbaum, Rosenhahn, 1 each.

AWARDED FIRST BASE ON INTERFERENCE—Beal (Gilles); D'Aloia (Nieves).

CLUB FIELDING

Club	Pct.	G.	PO.	A.	E.	DP.	PB.	Club	Pct.	G.	PO.	A.	E.	DP.	PB.
Oneonta	.966	73	1871	900	98	75	11	Little Falls	.954	71	1801	705	122	48	19
Jamestown	.965	75	1969	876	103	74	15	Geneva	.953	75	1949	901	140	66	23
Erie	.960	74	1956	851	117	78	14	Elmira	.951	73	1835	771	135	43	14
Utica	.959	70	1778	836	111	56	19	Batavia	.945	75	1909	812	157	63	34

INDIVIDUAL FIELDING

*Throws lefthanded

FIRST BASEMEN

Player and Club	Pct.	G.	PO.	A.	E.	DP.	Player and Club	Pct.	G.	PO.	A.	E.	DP.
Benzinger, Elmira	.988	11	80	4	1	2	Merchant, Batavia	.991	28	198	18	2	21
Brooks, Geneva	1.000	2	11	0	0	1	Miller, Geneva	.988	23	236	11	3	21
Castiglia, Elmira*	.983	61	474	47	9	37	Morrison, Oneonta	1.000	8	64	3	0	12
Darling, Oneonta	.992	24	221	16	2	17	Moscat, Little Falls	1.000	1	0	1	0	0
Federici, Erie*	.947	4	36	0	2	2	Moss, Utica	.976	20	148	13	4	12
Gaeta, Utica	1.000	3	29	1	0	3	Nalley, Batavia	1.000	7	43	0	0	2
Galarraga, Jamestown	1.000	10	73	3	0	10	Rabassa, Utica	1.000	1	7	2	0	0
Guin, Erie	.999	70	688	41	1	60	Raeside, Little Falls	.978	21	168	6	4	14
Hertzler, Jamestown*	1.000	5	19	2	0	1	Renfroe, Oneonta	.983	16	107	8	2	11
Holliday, Little Falls	.985	18	121	7	2	6	Rosenhahn, Geneva	.965	12	75	8	3	8
Hughes, Oneonta	.988	35	312	22	4	27	Tobin, Geneva	.989	44	428	21	5	33
Lorenz, Utica	1.000	2	11	2	0	0	Vann, Little Falls	.991	36	301	18	3	22
Malpeso, Elmira	.909	4	19	1	2	0	Varano, Elmira	.949	6	37	0	2	2
Marchand, Jamestown*	.991	67	606	51	6	56	Weppner, Elmira*	1.000	1	8	0	0	1
Martinez, Batavia*	.976	47	396	16	10	30	Wing, Utica*	.987	53	493	36	7	34

SECOND BASEMEN

Player and Club	Pct.	G.	PO.	A.	E.	DP.	Player and Club	Pct.	G.	PO.	A.	E.	DP.
Albright, Utica	.946	10	14	21	2	5	Martin, Batavia	1.000	2	4	6	0	0
Archie, Utica	.889	3	7	1	1	1	Meleski, Elmira	.960	13	20	28	2	3
Brooks, Geneva	.961	66	130	239	15	38	Menzhuber, Erie	.952	4	9	11	1	2
Collins, Geneva	.966	20	40	45	3	9	Miller, Batavia	.903	6	15	13	3	3
D'Aloia, Oneonta	1.000	5	7	11	0	2	Moscat, Little Falls	.967	48	108	128	8	23
Damon, Jamestown	.968	68	152	240	13	49	Nagel, Batavia	1.000	2	8	10	0	1
Dawes, Ja	.971	6	14	19	1	2	Navoa, Batavia	.910	44	82	100	18	21
Ficklin, Batavia	.790	3	9	6	4	2	Pacho, Batavia	.893	8	9	16	3	3
Franks, Little Falls	1.000	2	2	3	0	0	Picchioni, Utica	.800	2	3	1	1	0
Garton, Little Falls	1.000	5	7	8	0	0	Raeside, Little Falls	.939	22	37	55	6	8
Gattis, Utica	1.000	1	0	1	0	0	Rodriguez, Oneonta	.984	37	79	107	3	22
Gomez, Utica	.959	54	86	149	10	19	Rutledge, Geneva	.971	4	8	25	1	4
Howard, Elmira	.953	56	99	125	11	18	Scafa, Oneonta	.976	43	87	118	5	29
Jose, Elmira	1.000	3	3	5	0	0	Seid, Geneva	.957	3	6	16	1	0
Licata, Little Falls	1.000	1	1	1	0	0	Thomas, Erie	.940	42	86	118	13	24
Lorenz, Utica	.983	12	25	31	1	9	Tobin, Geneva	1.000	2	4	2	0	1
Lyons, Erie	.981	29	65	90	3	23	Walker, Elmira	.816	20	18	22	9	4
Marcano, Little Falls	.826	7	9	10	4	1	Weislak, Jamestown	1.000	1	2	3	0	1

THIRD BASEMEN

Player and Club	Pct.	G.	PO.	A.	E.	DP.	Player and Club	Pct.	G.	PO.	A.	E.	DP.
Albright, Utica	.800	3	1	3	1	0	Lyons, Erie	.967	36	23	95	4	7
Allen, Geneva	.846	8	3	8	2	1	Matute, Elmira	.800	5	7	5	3	2
Bone, Oneonta	.000	1	0	0	2	0	Menzhuber, Erie	.667	2	1	1	1	0
Cochran, Batavia	.878	30	23	49	10	5	Miller, Batavia	.917	25	22	55	7	7
Collins, Batavia	.750	3	6	3	3	0	Moscat, Little Falls	.955	14	4	17	1	0
Damon, Jamestown	1.000	1	0	1	0	0	Moss, Utica	.852	10	8	15	4	2
Dawes, Jamestown	.875	3	0	7	1	0	Pagliarulo, Oneonta	.930	72	40	159	15	9
Ficklin, Batavia	.500	2	0	1	1	0	Rodriguez, Oneonta	1.000	3	0	7	0	1
Galarraga, Jamestown	1.000	3	3	2	0	2	Rosenhahn, Geneva	.916	67	44	131	16	4
Garton, Little Falls	.891	50	46	85	16	10	Rutledge, Geneva	1.000	6	6	3	0	0
Gattis, Utica	.842	7	1	15	3	1	Seaman, Elmira	.949	30	24	51	4	2
Harris, Little Falls	.950	9	4	15	1	0	Seid, Geneva	1.000	1	0	1	0	1
James, Erie	.847	36	27	56	15	8	Tanner, Batavia	.900	18	8	37	5	0
Licata, Little Falls	.905	9	5	14	2	0	Walck, Elmira	.919	49	47	77	11	5
Lorenz, Utica	.969	54	38	118	5	5	Weislak, Jamestown	.938	70	52	128	12	7

SHORTSTOPS

Player and Club	Pct.	G.	PO.	A.	E.	DP.
Albright, Utica	.912	11	16	46	6	6
Alcala, Oneonta	.919	16	16	41	5	5
Bone, Oneonta	1.000	1	4	0	0	1
Carpenter, Elmira	.929	60	88	148	18	20
Collins, Batavia	.769	3	4	6	3	0
D'Aloia, Oneonta	.943	53	62	152	13	21
Dawes, Jamestown	.953	53	66	175	12	41
Harris, Little Falls	.863	23	20	49	11	10
Harris, Erie	.921	67	106	222	28	43
James, Erie	1.000	1	0	1	0	0
Kwiecinski, Jamestown	.886	22	33	60	12	12
Licata, Little Falls	1.000	1	2	1	0	0
Lorenz, Utica	.957	7	8	14	1	2
Lyons, Erie	.891	8	13	28	5	9
Marcano, Little Falls	.950	50	80	150	12	25
Martin, Batavia	.941	31	50	93	9	15
Meleski, Elmira	.944	25	31	54	5	11
Moscat, Little Falls	.917	4	2	9	1	0
Murphy, Batavia	.925	58	83	189	22	30
Nagel, Batavia	1.000	1	3	3	0	0
Pacho, Batavia	.953	29	42	79	6	17
Rodriguez, Oneonta	.889	2	2	6	1	0
Rutledge, Geneva	.922	62	113	208	27	40
Seaman, Elmira	.933	5	5	9	1	0
Smith, Oneonta	.921	19	30	52	7	11
Tanner, Batavia	.918	22	22	68	8	9
Tramble, Geneva	.859	17	24	37	10	7
Weislak, Jamestown	1.000	2	2	4	0	1

OUTFIELDERS

Player and Club	Pct.	G.	PO.	A.	E.	DP.
Aldridge, Jamestown	1.000	1	3	0	0	0
Allen, Geneva	.920	20	21	2	2	0
Alomar, Elmira	.971	22	30	4	1	0
Alpert, Batavia°	.959	55	111	5	5	2
Arfstrom, Elmira	.932	48	77	5	6	1
BATISTA, Erie	.977	75	161	9	4	4
Beal, Elmira	.943	50	76	6	5	0
Benzinger, Elmira	.983	31	51	5	1	0
Berroa, Elmira	.976	26	41	0	1	0
Blocker, Little Falls°	.918	35	72	6	7	0
Bone, Oneonta	.968	35	28	2	1	1
Bradley, Oneonta	1.000	3	8	0	0	0
Brito, Batavia	1.000	1	2	0	0	0
Cooley, Jamestown	.948	70	133	12	8	3
Cordova, Geneva	.850	58	80	5	15	1
Denby, Little Falls	.919	51	88	3	8	1
Dennis, Oneonta	.935	52	69	3	5	0
Despaux, Oneonta	.923	49	45	3	4	3
Dotson, Jamestown°	.927	55	73	3	6	1
Eiland, Utica	.965	51	77	6	3	0
Eldridge, Jamestown	.940	29	43	4	3	0
Federici, Erie°	1.000	4	4	0	0	0
Felice, Little Falls	.936	34	40	4	3	1
Fisher, Elmira	.939	29	44	2	3	1
Galarraga, Jamestown	1.000	5	5	0	0	0
George, Geneva	.923	10	11	1	1	1
Gonzales, Elmira°	.790	22	28	2	8	0
Guin, Erie°	1.000	1	5	2	0	0
Harris, Little Falls	1.000	4	8	1	0	0
Hatcher, Geneva	.930	75	138	7	11	2
Henry, Jamestown	.917	16	21	1	2	0
Hertzler, Jamestown°	.973	31	35	1	1	0
Holden, Batavia	.938	11	14	1	1	0
Holliday, Little Falls	1.000	40	53	3	0	1
Jackson, Little Falls	.956	30	42	1	2	0
Jefferson, Elmira	1.000	22	24	2	0	0
Jewett, Oneonta	.833	6	5	0	1	0
Johnston, Elmira°	.952	18	20	0	1	0
Jones, Batavia°	.947	42	67	4	4	1
Jurena, Utica	1.000	1	1	0	0	0
Lauziere, Jamestown	.800	10	10	2	3	0
Lemon, Jamestown°	.886	18	31	0	4	0
Licata, Little Falls	.920	20	22	1	2	0
Malpeso, Elmira	.000	2	0	0	1	0
McNealy, Oneonta°	.953	67	119	2	6	0
Menzhuber, Erie	.889	10	13	3	2	1
Miller, Geneva	.929	9	13	0	1	0
Monroe, Geneva	.936	18	29	0	2	0
Moss, Utica	.984	40	59	2	1	1
Nalley, Batavia	1.000	3	6	0	0	0
Nay, Jamestown	1.000	15	16	1	0	0
Nyman, Geneva	.929	12	13	0	1	0
O'Regan, Oneonta°	.953	53	58	3	3	2
Perodin, Utica	.942	43	62	3	4	4
Picchioni, Utica	1.000	11	8	0	0	0
Powers, Geneva°	1.000	4	7	0	0	0
Prosper, Little Falls°	.920	22	22	1	2	0
Purcell, Little Falls	.862	18	22	3	4	0
Rabassa, Utica°	.947	17	17	1	1	0
Reddish, Oneonta	1.000	2	3	0	0	0
Rehbaum, Batavia°	.895	51	72	5	9	1
Renfroe, Oneonta	.952	21	19	1	1	1
Roath, Erie°	1.000	20	23	2	0	1
Roman, Batavia	.950	14	19	0	1	0
Romano, Utica	.915	63	113	5	11	0
Rutledge, Geneva	1.000	1	2	1	0	0
Sanchez, Erie	1.000	2	4	0	0	0
Severino, Elmira	1.000	2	1	0	0	0
Southern, Erie°	.914	54	68	6	7	1
Stryffeler, Erie	.957	65	84	4	4	0
Tramble, Geneva	.921	26	33	2	3	1
Washington, Batavia	.934	62	107	6	8	3
Weems, Erie	.800	5	8	0	2	0

CATCHERS

Player and Club	Pct.	G.	PO.	A.	E.	DP.	PB.
ALBRIGHT, Utica	.989	50	243	23	3	1	10
Biagini, Elmira	.955	8	19	2	1	0	1
Bradley, Oneonta	.975	51	315	40	9	2	4
Burrell, Elmira	.961	21	86	13	4	1	3
Czeszewski, Little Falls	.978	7	42	2	1	0	3
Dematties, Little Falls	.955	3	19	2	1	0	0
Elkin, Oneonta	.952	17	62	17	4	2	4
Erickson, Utica	.932	20	63	5	5	0	4
Galarraga, Jamestown	1.000	12	73	10	0	2	2
George, Geneva	.976	4	32	9	1	1	5
Gilles, Little Falls	.981	55	359	43	8	5	11
Gonzalez, Little Falls	.980	8	48	2	1	0	2
Hughes, Oneonta	1.000	1	3	0	0	0	2
Hunt, Erie	.978	55	345	46	9	6	13
Kempton, Oneonta	.994	25	138	21	1	0	7
Lauziere, Jamestown	1.000	2	0	1	0	0	0
Locascio, Batavia	.966	18	130	14	5	1	3
Mackie, Batavia	.974	34	134	18	4	2	10
Malpeso, Elmira	.917	23	105	16	11	0	5
Mesa, Erie	1.000	2	10	0	0	0	1
Miller, Utica	.992	26	109	14	1	1	5
Nieves, Batavia	.956	35	158	16	8	1	17
Norment, Jamestown	.986	69	455	46	7	5	13
Purcell, Little Falls	1.000	8	19	3	0	0	3
Remo, Geneva	.979	50	295	26	7	1	11
Sheaffer, Elmira	.981	40	220	35	5	2	5
Tarnow, Geneva	.986	30	117	23	2	2	5
Weems, Erie	1.000	21	126	19	0	4	0
Williams, Geneva	1.000	9	40	7	0	3	2

PITCHERS

Player and Club	Pct.	G.	PO.	A.	E.	DP.
Adams, Erie	.909	16	13	17	3	0
Alba, Erie°	.800	16	0	4	1	0
Andrews, Geneva	1.000	18	0	7	0	0
Araujo, Batavia	.500	16	0	1	1	0
Arnold, Little Falls	.929	15	5	8	1	1
Asbell, Batavia	.800	3	2	2	1	0
Bajus, Batavia°	1.000	7	0	3	0	0
Banks, Geneva	.778	10	1	6	2	1
Black, Geneva	1.000	4	2	3	0	0
Brahms, Geneva°	1.000	20	1	8	0	0
Brodeur, Jamestown°	1.000	6	0	1	0	0
Brooks, Oneonta	1.000	15	4	5	0	0
Burns, Batavia	.800	19	7	13	5	3
Chesser, Jamestown	1.000	1	0	1	0	0
Chestnut, Geneva	.947	13	3	15	1	0
Christiansen, Utica	.500	10	0	1	1	0
Cicotte, Utica	1.000	3	0	1	0	0
Cosgrove, Batavia°	.800	18	0	4	1	0
Cushing, Batavia°	.857	12	2	4	1	1
Davis, Elmira	1.000	14	6	12	0	0
Delett, Utica	.857	9	3	3	1	0
DeMaria, Oneonta	1.000	6	2	2	0	0
Deriso, Batavia°	.949	18	11	26	2	1
DeWitt, Oneonta	1.000	11	2	10	0	1
Dixon, Batavia°	1.000	9	1	7	0	1
Doyle, Batavia	.875	15	4	10	2	0

PITCHERS—Continued

Player and Club	Pct.	G.	PO.	A.	E.	DP.	Player and Club	Pct.	G.	PO.	A.	E.	DP.
Dunn, Erie	.941	13	3	13	1	1	Pope, Bat-James	1.000	9	2	2	0	0
Ellsworth, Elmira	1.000	1	0	1	0	0	Powers, Utica	.778	7	1	6	2	1
Elpin, Batavia	1.000	12	3	4	0	0	Powers, Jamestown	.750	16	0	3	1	0
Finnegan, Erie	1.000	5	1	1	0	0	Quirk, Oneonta	.857	27	5	7	2	0
Flinn, Utica°	.943	14	6	27	2	1	Richard, Batavia°	.667	9	1	1	1	0
Foust, Little Falls	1.000	15	2	4	0	0	Roman, Batavia	1.000	20	3	8	0	0
Fuller, Little Falls	.750	25	2	4	2	0	Santiago, Elmira	1.000	21	6	7	0	0
Gainer, Bat-Utica	.929	17	3	10	1	0	Scheller, Elmira°	1.000	15	4	6	0	0
Gilbreath, Jamestown	1.000	13	4	18	0	0	Schilling, Geneva	.952	14	6	14	1	3
Gnacinski, Elmira	.919	18	10	24	3	0	Scott, Jamestown	.963	14	10	16	1	1
Gonzalez, Elmira	.875	11	2	12	2	0	Shiflett, Oneonta°	.941	12	0	16	1	0
Graves, Little Falls	1.000	13	3	10	0	0	Silva, Elmira	1.000	5	1	3	0	0
Harlander, Little Falls	1.000	6	3	2	0	1	Silvas, Batavia	1.000	10	2	3	0	1
Hernandez, Oneonta°	1.000	11	1	15	0	0	Skorupa, Jamestown	1.000	6	1	0	0	0
Huber, Jamestown	.909	26	4	6	1	0	Slaton, Little Falls	.900	13	4	5	1	0
Johnson, Jamestown	1.000	21	3	9	0	1	Smith, Geneva	.917	18	4	7	1	0
Johnson, Batavia°	1.000	14	2	8	0	3	Sorenson, Elmira	1.000	3	1	1	0	0
Kaufman, Geneva	.667	4	0	2	1	1	St. Claire, Jamestown	.875	13	3	4	1	1
Key, Elmira	1.000	7	3	1	0	0	St. John, Jamestown°	.923	15	1	11	1	1
Kish, Erie	.769	8	2	8	3	0	Staffon, Jamestown	.750	9	2	10	4	1
Klacza, Utica	1.000	8	3	4	0	0	Szymczak, Oneonta	.957	17	5	17	1	1
Klutcharch, Utica	.933	18	3	11	1	0	Taveris, Erie	1.000	1	1	0	0	0
Kyles, Geneva	.958	12	5	18	1	1	TEWKSBURY, Oneonta°	1.000	14	6	25	0	0
LaRosa, Erie	1.000	9	1	0	0	0	Thomas, Utica	.947	20	8	10	1	0
Latham, Little Falls°	.909	13	3	7	1	1	Uhey, Utica	.969	13	9	22	1	1
Lockhart, Elmira°	.909	13	3	7	1	1	Umdenstock, Utica	.893	15	10	15	3	0
Lockie, Geneva	.778	16	1	6	2	0	Vaulman, Utica°	.929	12	2	11	1	0
Magdziuk, Little Falls	1.000	1	0	1	0	0	Wareham, Elmira	.905	14	6	13	2	1
Maldanado, Erie	.857	15	8	4	2	0	Webb, Geneva	1.000	10	4	6	0	0
Merlack, Little Falls°	.556	20	2	3	4	0	Weissmann, Geneva	.889	10	2	6	1	0
Mikesell, Oneonta°	.867	13	1	12	2	0	Weston, Elmira	1.000	16	2	6	0	0
Milligan, Erie°	.962	15	7	18	1	4	Wex, Oneonta	.917	11	1	10	1	0
Niemic, Oneonta	.500	6	1	0	1	0	Wick, Little Falls°	1.000	6	1	2	0	0
North, Erie	.875	12	2	12	2	1	Williams, Oneonta	1.000	10	2	4	0	0
O'Beirne, Little Falls	1.000	8	0	3	0	0	Wilmet, Little Falls	.800	20	2	2	1	0
Parmenter, Erie	.909	25	3	7	1	2	Woodward, Elmira	1.000	12	9	9	0	0
Pickett, Little Falls°	.600	8	1	2	2	0	Yenser, Jamestown	.929	14	19	20	3	1
Pittman, Erie°	1.000	17	3	8	0	0	Young, Erie	.857	16	7	5	2	1
Poindexter, Batavia	1.000	16	5	6	0	0							

The following players had no recorded accepted chances at the positions indicated; therefore, are not listed in the fielding averages for those particular positions: Archie, of; Clark, p; D'Aloia, 3b; DeMatties, p; Despaux, p; Donovan, of; Eiland, 3b; Gomez, of; Graves, R., p; Herrera, p; Livesay, p; Malpeso, 3b; Nagel, 3b; Rehbaum, p; Seaman, 2b; Shoemaker, p; Varano, 3b; Vaughn, p; Walck, ss.

CLUB PITCHING

Club	ERA.	G.	CG.	ShO.	Sv.	IP.	H.	R.	ER.	HR.	HB.	BB.	Int. BB.	SO.	WP.	Bk.
Oneonta	3.62	73	21	9	12	623⅔	563	326	251	42	23	343	13	433	53	4
Jamestown	3.76	75	20	10	16	656⅓	610	345	274	39	20	337	15	492	47	0
Geneva	3.81	75	15	4	7	649⅔	610	376	275	44	27	297	14	463	53	5
Utica	3.94	70	20	5	4	592⅔	582	335	259	62	18	277	5	402	25	8
Erie	4.15	74	20	6	11	652	592	363	301	80	18	297	17	471	38	8
Little Falls	4.84	71	15	2	7	600⅓	631	420	323	56	23	368	35	465	42	6
Elmira	5.17	73	10	0	9	611⅔	719	459	351	45	13	346	35	411	32	5
Batavia	5.25	75	9	2	5	636⅔	696	502	371	72	19	423	13	488	68	3

PITCHERS' RECORDS

(Leading Qualifiers for Earned-Run Average Leadership – 61 or More Innings)

° Throws lefthanded.

Pitcher—Club	W.	L.	Pct.	ERA.	G.	GS.	CG.	GF.	ShO.	Sv.	IP.	H.	R.	ER.	HR.	HB.	BB.	Int. BB.	SO.	WP.
Uhey, Utica	7	1	.875	2.65	13	13	6	0	0	0	102	97	47	30	13	2	22	0	51	3
Szymczak, Oneonta	6	2	.750	2.76	17	10	5	4	2	0	88	73	29	27	4	1	40	1	44	4
Klutcharch, Utica	5	6	.455	2.82	18	5	2	11	0	2	67	56	29	21	3	1	15	0	56	1
Adams, Erie	7	4	.636	2.97	16	11	5	2	0	0	97	68	38	32	6	3	35	6	107	10
Yenser, Jamestown	7	4	.636	3.03	14	14	4	0	1	0	98	83	42	33	5	1	39	2	50	9
Flinn, Utica°	8	2	.800	3.04	14	11	4	3	1	0	83	80	31	28	6	1	36	0	55	1
Scott, Jamestown	10	2	.833	3.14	14	14	7	0	3	0	106	90	44	37	3	2	39	0	77	6
Woodward, Elmira	4	3	.571	3.39	12	11	3	0	0	0	77	77	38	29	3	3	23	2	47	2
Tewksbury, Oneonta	7	3	.700	3.40	14	14	6	0	1	0	90	85	43	34	8	2	37	2	62	5
Schilling, Geneva	6	3	.667	3.51	14	14	4	0	0	0	100	85	49	39	11	3	30	0	85	5

Departmental Leaders: G—Quirk, 27; GS—Arnold, Milligan, 15; CG—Scott, 7; ShO—Gilbreath, 4; W—Scott, 10; L—Burns, 11; Sv—Huber, 10; Pct.—Dunn, Thomas, Uhey, .875; IP—Scott, 106; H—Milligan, 105; R—Burns, 71; ER—Burns, 56; HR—Roman, 15; HB—Banks, Graves, Wilmet, 6; BB—St. John, 71; IBB—Santiago, 9; SO—Adams, 107; WP—Burns, 15.

(All Pitchers—Listed Alphabetically)

Pitcher—Club	W.	L.	Pct.	ERA.	G.	GS.	CG.	GF.	ShO.	Sv.	IP.	H.	R.	ER.	HR.	HB.	BB.	Int. BB.	SO.	WP.
Adamczak, Geneva	3	0	1.000	3.46	10	3	1	5	0	0	39	41	19	15	2	1	18	2	26	2
Adams, Erie	7	4	.636	2.97	16	11	5	2	2	0	97	68	38	32	6	3	35	6	107	10
Alba, Erie	1	2	.333	5.73	16	4	0	5	0	2	44	42	31	28	6	2	34	1	48	4
Andrews, Geneva	7	2	.778	2.08	18	0	0	15	0	0	39	26	23	9	3	3	17	0	23	3
Araujo, Elmira	1	0	1.000	4.34	16	0	0	9	0	1	29	41	18	14	2	0	12	1	24	0
Arnold, Little Falls	4	3	.571	4.66	15	15	2	0	0	0	87	96	57	45	10	1	60	1	76	4
Asbell, Batavia	0	1	.000	7.50	3	1	0	2	0	1	12	18	10	10	2	0	4	1	6	0
Bajus, Batavia	0	1	.000	1.80	7	3	0	2	0	0	20	17	5	4	1	0	10	0	22	1
Banks, Geneva	1	5	.167	6.12	10	10	1	0	0	0	50	46	38	34	4	6	42	1	28	6
Black, Geneva	1	0	1.000	5.25	4	0	0	3	0	0	12	10	7	7	1	1	5	0	7	0
Brahms, Geneva	3	5	.375	3.33	20	2	1	11	0	2	54	49	25	20	6	1	27	5	55	6

Pitcher—Club	W.	L.	Pct.	ERA.	G.	GS.	CG.	GF.	ShO.	Sv.	IP.	H.	R.	ER.	HR.	HB.	BB.	Int. BB.	SO.	WP.
Brodeur, Jamestown	0	1	.000	9.00	6	1	0	3	0	0	11	14	11	11	4	0	9	0	17	0
Brooks, Oneonta	5	3	.625	2.37	15	4	2	5	1	0	57	53	21	15	4	1	14	1	15	9
Burns, Batavia	0	11	.000	6.81	19	12	1	4	0	0	74	80	71	56	8	1	59	1	62	15
Chesser, Jamestown	1	0	1.000	1.29	1	1	0	0	0	0	7	7	1	1	0	0	1	0	6	1
Chestnut, Geneva	3	4	.429	3.99	13	13	3	0	1	0	70	68	48	31	5	3	35	1	49	8
Christiansen, Utica	1	1	.500	5.63	10	0	0	7	0	0	16	15	12	10	4	1	14	0	12	0
Cicotte, Utica	0	2	.000	7.00	3	2	0	1	0	0	9	15	8	7	1	1	10	0	3	1
Clark, Batavia	0	0	.000	13.50	3	0	0	2	0	0	2	4	3	3	1	0	2	0	3	1
Cosgrove, Batavia	0	3	.000	3.34	18	1	0	15	0	0	35	39	20	13	2	0	22	0	34	3
Cushing, Batavia	0	2	.000	5.40	12	4	0	4	0	0	30	21	29	18	1	1	36	0	28	9
Davis, Elmira	4	4	.500	4.39	14	11	2	1	0	0	80	84	51	39	6	2	39	4	67	3
Delett, Utica	1	2	.333	7.83	9	4	1	1	0	0	23	31	27	20	4	1	14	0	15	3
DeMaria, Oneonta	0	0	.000	9.00	6	1	0	2	0	0	12	18	12	12	3	1	11	0	7	2
Deriso, Batavia	6	7	.462	3.98	18	14	3	2	1	0	95	96	57	42	5	1	47	2	60	1
Despaux, Oneonta	0	0	.000	14.40	2	0	0	1	0	0	5	4	8	8	2	0	10	0	5	2
DeWitt, Oneonta	2	3	.400	4.40	11	5	1	3	1	1	43	40	33	21	4	4	22	1	18	3
Dixon, Batavia	2	5	.286	4.14	9	7	3	2	0	0	50	54	35	23	3	2	26	0	43	3
Doyle, Batavia	2	6	.250	4.97	15	12	1	2	1	1	58	68	49	32	11	2	38	0	36	4
Dunn, Erie	7	1	.875	4.08	13	13	3	0	2	0	75	50	42	34	8	4	54	0	84	1
Ellsworth, Elmira	0	1	.000	18.00	1	1	0	0	0	0	1	0	2	2	0	0	2	0	0	1
Elpin, Batavia	2	2	.500	3.29	12	3	0	7	0	1	41	44	28	15	3	1	19	0	31	4
Finnegan, Erie	1	1	.500	13.50	5	0	0	2	0	0	8	10	12	12	1	1	9	0	5	2
Flinn, Utica	8	2	.800	3.04	14	11	4	3	1	0	83	80	31	28	6	1	36	0	55	1
Foust, Little Falls	1	0	1.000	8.10	15	1	1	5	0	0	30	36	28	27	2	0	37	0	26	6
Fuller, Little Falls	5	4	.556	4.40	25	0	0	18	0	1	43	49	36	21	3	0	32	8	19	6
Gainer, 4 Batavia-13 Utica	0	2	.000	4.70	17	3	0	8	0	0	44	49	28	23	6	2	23	2	28	3
Gilbreath, Jamestown	5	6	.455	3.69	13	13	6	0	4	0	95	102	46	39	4	5	28	2	55	0
Gnacinski, Elmira	4	7	.364	4.61	18	13	2	5	0	1	80	93	56	41	5	1	40	2	58	3
Gonzalez, Elmira	3	5	.375	5.58	11	6	2	4	0	0	50	60	39	31	4	0	29	2	33	2
Graves, Little Falls	1	5	.167	5.77	13	9	3	4	0	1	64	75	48	41	2	6	35	5	41	8
Graves, Jamestown	0	1	.000	31.50	1	1	0	0	0	0	2	6	7	7	3	0	1	0	2	0
Harlander, Little Falls	1	3	.250	8.25	6	3	0	1	0	0	24	34	26	22	4	0	14	0	20	0
Hernandez, Oneonta	4	2	.667	4.50	11	10	2	0	1	0	50	46	33	25	4	3	56	1	53	8
Herrera, Oneonta	0	0	.000	0.00	2	0	0	1	0	0	2	2	4	0	0	0	3	0	2	0
Huber, Jamestown	6	1	.857	2.79	26	0	0	23	0	10	42	27	13	13	0	1	26	5	42	1
Johnson, Jamestown	2	3	.400	2.63	21	0	0	12	0	5	41	26	18	12	1	1	26	3	32	3
Johnson, Batavia	0	6	.000	6.43	14	5	0	2	0	0	42	54	43	30	5	4	33	0	34	6
Kaufman, Geneva	0	0	.000	2.77	4	1	0	1	0	0	13	11	6	4	0	0	12	1	14	2
Key, Elmira	2	3	.400	7.36	7	5	0	1	0	0	22	26	23	18	1	0	22	1	17	0
Kish, Erie	3	2	.600	2.60	8	6	4	2	0	0	52	43	21	15	3	1	17	1	26	4
Klacza, Utica	2	2	.500	4.26	8	2	0	5	0	1	19	14	10	9	2	2	11	1	10	1
Klutcharch, Utica	5	6	.455	2.82	18	5	2	11	0	2	67	56	29	21	3	1	15	0	56	1
Kyles, Geneva	1	8	.111	4.57	12	12	1	0	0	0	61	66	46	31	4	2	38	1	24	6
LaRosa, Erie	2	1	.667	9.00	9	0	0	6	0	0	10	20	11	10	1	1	7	2	5	2
Latham, Little Falls	5	5	.500	3.89	13	13	1	0	0	0	88	91	52	38	11	3	38	7	70	3
Livesay, Oneonta	0	0	.000	15.75	3	0	0	0	0	0	4	7	9	7	0	1	5	0	4	0
Lockhart, Elmira	2	3	.400	4.81	13	6	0	5	0	0	43	52	34	23	7	0	27	5	22	1
Lockie, Geneva	2	2	.500	2.09	16	0	0	12	0	3	43	38	19	10	1	0	13	2	24	2
Magdziuk, Little Falls	0	1	.000	14.40	1	1	0	0	0	0	5	12	8	8	2	0	2	0	0	0
Maldanado, Erie	5	2	.714	4.50	15	9	0	2	0	0	62	66	40	31	14	1	24	1	33	1
Merlack, Little Falls	2	4	.333	6.87	20	4	0	8	0	2	38	37	41	29	3	2	43	7	37	4
Mikesell, Oneonta	6	2	.750	3.68	13	11	0	1	0	0	71	68	36	29	6	3	37	0	53	7
Milligan, Erie	6	5	.545	4.81	15	15	5	0	0	0	101	105	66	54	14	2	45	0	42	4
Niemic, Oneonta	0	0	.000	3.75	6	0	0	4	0	0	12	13	7	5	1	3	5	0	6	1
North, Erie	4	2	.667	4.20	12	7	0	3	0	0	60	62	32	28	8	0	19	1	24	2
O'Beirne, Little Falls	2	6	.250	4.60	8	6	3	0	0	0	45	52	32	23	6	0	14	0	31	2
Parmenter, Erie	4	5	.444	3.50	25	0	0	21	0	7	36	33	16	14	4	0	8	2	14	0
Pickett, Little Falls	2	1	.667	3.30	8	2	1	1	0	0	30	31	15	11	4	0	13	1	24	0
Pittman, Erie	1	0	1.000	2.73	17	0	0	5	0	1	33	24	13	10	1	1	23	2	22	3
Poindexter, Batavia	2	7	.222	5.32	16	10	1	4	0	0	71	73	52	42	6	3	48	0	39	9
Pope, 3 Batavia-6 Jamestown	0	2	.000	7.77	9	4	0	4	0	0	22	26	26	19	10	0	20	2	13	1
Powers, Utica	0	3	.000	9.69	7	4	0	1	0	0	26	44	34	28	4	3	12	0	12	0
Powers, Jamestown	3	0	1.000	4.60	16	1	0	5	0	0	43	42	23	22	6	0	22	1	38	4
Quirk, Oneonta	7	2	.778	2.57	27	0	0	25	0	7	42	30	18	12	0	0	24	4	31	1
Rehbaum, Batavia	0	0	.000	45.00	2	0	0	1	0	0	1	4	5	5	0	0	3	0	1	1
Richard, Batavia	0	2	.000	13.85	9	0	0	4	0	0	13	23	25	20	1	0	22	3	14	0
Roman, Batavia	0	3	.000	6.38	20	1	0	4	0	0	55	63	45	39	15	1	27	2	46	8
Santiago, Elmira	1	6	.143	5.53	21	1	0	13	0	3	57	71	44	35	5	2	39	9	38	3
Scheller, Elmira	0	3	.000	9.29	15	3	0	9	0	2	31	49	39	32	2	0	30	4	20	4
Schilling, Geneva	6	3	.667	3.51	14	14	4	0	0	0	100	85	49	39	11	3	30	0	85	5
Scott, Jamestown	10	2	.833	3.14	14	14	7	0	3	0	106	90	44	37	3	2	39	0	77	6
Shiflett, Oneonta	1	4	.200	4.15	12	7	1	2	1	1	52	45	30	24	4	1	35	1	55	3
Shoemaker, Geneva	0	0	.000	0.00	2	0	0	2	0	0	4	1	0	0	0	0	1	0	2	0
Silva, Elmira	0	0	.000	6.38	5	5	0	0	0	0	24	25	20	17	4	1	15	0	14	2
Silvas, Batavia	2	2	.500	2.65	10	0	0	8	0	2	17	17	8	5	1	2	12	4	24	0
Skorupa, Jamestown	0	0	.000	9.00	6	2	0	2	0	1	12	15	12	12	0	1	13	0	5	4
Slaton, Little Falls	0	3	.333	5.64	13	12	1	0	1	0	67	72	52	42	7	2	42	1	55	5
Smith, Jamestown	5	2	.714	4.50	18	3	1	10	0	2	64	68	37	32	2	1	23	0	42	4
Sorenson, Elmira	0	0	.000	6.75	3	0	0	2	0	0	4	3	7	3	0	0	10	0	5	0
St. Claire, Jamestown	4	1	.800	1.94	13	3	1	6	1	0	51	53	22	11	0	0	17	0	36	1
St. John, Jamestown	8	4	.667	4.71	15	14	2	0	0	0	86	86	57	45	6	5	71	0	73	9
Staffon, Jamestown	2	2	.500	4.14	9	9	0	0	0	0	50	46	37	23	3	4	36	0	49	9
Szymczak, Oneonta	6	2	.750	2.76	17	10	5	4	2	2	88	73	29	27	4	1	40	1	44	4
Taveris, Erie	0	0	.000	0.00	1	1	0	0	0	0	1	0	0	0	0	0	1	0	1	0
Tewksbury, Oneonta	7	3	.700	3.40	14	14	6	0	1	0	90	85	43	34	8	2	37	2	62	5
Thomas, Utica	7	1	.875	2.78	20	3	1	12	0	1	55	37	21	17	6	1	28	1	45	3
Uhey, Utica	7	1	.875	2.65	13	13	6	0	0	0	102	97	47	30	13	2	22	0	51	3
Umdenstock, Utica	6	4	.600	4.13	15	14	3	0	0	0	96	88	55	44	10	4	64	1	72	5
Vaughn, Little Falls	0	0	.000	0.00	1	0	0	1	0	0	1	2	0	0	0	0	1	1	0	0
Vaulman, Utica	2	5	.286	3.69	12	9	3	2	0	0	61	64	36	25	4	0	32	0	48	4
Wareham, Elmira	2	6	.250	4.50	14	9	1	4	0	0	68	77	46	34	1	1	35	4	34	5
Webb, Geneva	4	1	.800	1.88	10	7	3	1	1	0	48	42	17	10	3	2	5	1	40	2

Pitcher—Club	W.	L.	Pct.	ERA.	G.	GS.	CG.	GF.	ShO.	Sv.	IP.	H.	R.	ER.	HR.	HB.	BB.	Int. BB.	SO.	WP.
Weissmann, Geneva	5	2	.714	5.50	10	10	0	0	0	0	54	59	42	33	2	4	31	0	44	7
Weston, Elmira	2	5	.286	6.60	16	2	0	10	0	2	45	61	42	33	5	3	23	1	32	6
Wex, Oneonta	5	1	.833	2.39	11	5	2	2	0	0	49	36	17	13	1	2	24	0	41	7
Wick, Little Falls	4	1	.800	1.85	6	5	3	0	1	0	39	24	11	8	0	3	12	0	32	1
Williams, Oneonta	5	3	.625	3.56	10	6	1	3	0	1	48	43	26	19	1	1	20	2	37	1
Wilmet, Little Falls	2	2	.500	1.85	20	0	0	18	0	3	39	20	14	8	2	6	27	4	34	3
Woodward, Elmira	4	3	.571	3.39	12	11	3	0	0	0	77	77	38	29	3	3	23	2	47	2
Yenser, Jamestown	7	4	.636	3.03	14	14	4	0	1	0	98	83	42	33	5	1	39	2	50	9
Young, Erie	3	5	.375	4.07	16	8	3	6	0	1	73	69	41	33	14	2	21	1	61	5

BALKS—D. Powers, 4; Dunn, 3; Adams, Flinn, Fuller, Gonzalez, North, Schilling, Wilmet, 2 each; Araujo, Burns, Chestnut, Deriso, Doyle, Hernandez, Kyles, Latham, Milligan, Shiflett, Silva, Tewksbury, Thomas, Vaulman, Webb, Wex, Wick, Woodward, 1 each.

COMBINATION SHUTOUTS—Dunn-Alba, North-Parmenter, Erie; Schilling-Webb, Weissmann-Shoemaker, Geneva; St. John-Johnson, Jamestown; Mikesell-Quirk, Oneonta; Flinn-Christiansen, Thomas-Klutcharch, Uhey-Thomas, Umdenstock-Klacza-Christiansen, Utica.

NO-HIT GAME—Dunn, Erie, defeated Batavia, 11-1, August 3.

Northwest League

CLASS A

CHAMPIONSHIP WINNERS IN PREVIOUS YEARS

1901—Portland .... .675	1941—Spokane .... .669	1964—Eugene .... .636
1902—Butte .... .608	1942—Vancouver .... .594	Yakima° .... .611
1903—Butte .... .578	1943-45—Did not operate.	1965—Lewiston .... .667
1904—Boise .... .625	1946—Wenatchee .... .622	Tri-City° .... .681
1905—Vancouver .... .586	1947—Vancouver .... .566	1966—Tri-City .... .679
Everett° .... .667	1948—Spokane .... .614	1967—Medford .... .607
1906—Tacoma .... .600	1949—Yakima .... .660	1968—Tri-City .... .600
1907—Aberdeen .... .625	Vancouver (2nd)† .... .615	1969—Rogue Valley .... .633
1908—Vancouver .... .578	1950—Yakima .... .613	1970—Lewiston a .... .538
1909—Seattle .... .653	1951—Spokane .... .655	Coos Bay-No. Bend .... .563
1910—Spokane .... .596	1952—Victoria .... .631	1971—Tri-City a .... .625
1911—Vancouver .... .628	1953—Salem .... .635	Bend .... .538
1912—Seattle .... .600	Spokane° .... .590	1972—Lewiston a .... .675
1913—Vancouver .... .600	1954—Vancouver° .... .636	Walla Walla .... .513
1914—Vancouver .... .632	Lewiston .... .629	1973—Walla Walla b .... .638
1915—Seattle .... .564	1955—Salem .... .646	Portland .... .563
1916—Spokane .... .622	Eugene° .... .639	1974—Bellingham .... .619
1917—Great Falls .... .592	1956—Yakima .... .691	Eugene c .... .571
1918—Seattle .... .588	Yakima .... .619	1975—Portland .... .545
1919—Seattle .... .590	1957—Eugene .... .576	Eugene d .... .684
1920—Victoria .... .600	Wenatchee° .... .647	1976—Portland .... .556
1921—Yakima .... .710	1958—Lewiston .... .621	Walla Walla d .... .639
Yakima .... .660	Yakima° .... .594	1977—Bellingham e .... .618
1922—Calgary§ .... .600	1959—Salem .... .623	Portland .... .667
1923-36—Did not operate.	Yakima° .... .563	1978—Grays Harbor f .... .671
1937—Wenatchee .... .603	1960—Yakima .... .638	Eugene .... .514
Tacoma° .... .627	Yakima .... .562	1979—Central Oregon d .... .606
1938—Yakima .... .583	1961—Lewiston° .... .621	Walla Walla .... .571
Bellingham (2nd)† .... .511	Yakima .... .600	1980—Bellingham g .... .643
1939—Wenatchee .... .601	1962—Wenatchee° .... .574	Eugene g .... .529
Tacoma (2nd)† .... .533	Tri-City .... .580	
1940—Spokane .... .587	1963—Lewiston .... .594	
Tacoma (4th)† .... .500	Yakima° .... .613	

°Won split-season playoff. †Won four-club playoff. §League disbanded June 18. aLeague divided into Northern and Southern divisions, declared champion under league rules. bLeague divided into Eastern and Western divisions, declared champion under league rules. cLeague divided into Eastern and Western divisions; won two-team playoff. dLeague divided into Northern and Southern divisions; won two-team playoff. eLeague divided into Affiliate and Independent divisions; won two-team playoff. fDeclared league champion after winning one-game playoff. g Declared co-champion after winning one game. Balance of playoff canceled due to rain and wet grounds. (NOTE—Known as Pacific Northwest League 1901-02, Pacific National League 1903-04, Northwestern League 1905-18, Pacific Coast International League 1919-22 and Western International League 1937-54.)

STANDING OF CLUBS AT CLOSE OF SEASON, SEPTEMBER 4
NORTHERN DIVISION

Club	Bell.	Bend.	W.W.	Med.	Sal.	Eug.	W.	L.	T.	Pct.	G.B.
Bellingham (Mariners)	....	8	9	9	6	7	39	31	0	.557	....
Bend (Phillies)	6	....	9	6	3	7	31	39	0	.443	8
Walla Walla (Padres)	5	5	....	3	9	7	29	41	0	.414	10

SOUTHERN DIVISION

Club	Bell.	Bend.	W.W.	Med.	Sal.	Eug.	W.	L.	T.	Pct.	G.B.
Medford (A's)	5	8	11	....	7	11	42	28	0	.600	....
Salem (Angels)	8	11	5	7	....	5	36	34	0	.514	6
Eugene (Reds)	7	7	7	3	9	....	33	37	0	.471	9

Bend represented Bend, Ore.

Major league affiliations in parentheses.

Playoff—Medford defeated Bellingham, two games to one.

Regular-Season Attendance—Bellingham, 21,390; Bend, 28,909; Eugene, 85,073; Medford, 54,243; Salem, 30,174; Walla Walla, 19,719. Total, 239,508. Playoffs, 5,432. All-Star game, 3,081.

Managers: Bellingham, Jeff Scott; Bend, P. J. Carey; Walla Walla, Bill Bryk; Medford, Brad Fisher; Salem, Rick Ingalls; Eugene, Greg Riddock.

All-Star Team: 1B—Smith, Bellingham; 2B—Seats, Eugene; 3B—Conklin, Bellingham; SS—Kiefer, Medford; OF—Davis, Eugene; Bradley, Bellingham; Coughlon, Medford; Nelson, Bellingham; C—Worden, Salem; Mitchell, Medford; Wilson, Bellingham; P—Hunter, Bend; Langston, Bellingham; Manager—Fisher, Medford.

(Compiled by William J. Weiss, League Statistician, San Mateo, Calif.)

CLUB BATTING

Club	Pct.	G.	AB.	R.	OR.	H.	TB.	2B.	3B.	HR.	RBI.	GW.	SH.	SF.	HP.	BB.	Int. BB.	SO.	SB.	CS.	LOB.
Salem	.264	70	2318	370	361	613	857	97	18	37	315	34	35	18	20	345	9	459	60	39	561
Eugene	.257	70	2350	395	370	605	806	71	26	26	332	26	27	18	16	372	10	503	139	33	576
Medford	.256	70	2274	404	338	582	824	113	21	29	325	36	50	26	20	416	12	458	150	54	541
Bend	.253	70	2372	371	421	599	850	105	19	46	309	34	20	14	21	322	5	444	75	33	509
Bellingham	.247	70	2270	364	353	560	813	91	12	46	309	24	7	20	12	317	1	610	134	38	537
Walla Walla	.232	70	2363	377	438	549	845	109	17	51	318	23	13	18	26	398	13	593	100	37	551

INDIVIDUAL BATTING

(Leading Qualifiers for Batting Championship—189 or More Plate Appearances)

°Bats lefthanded. †Switch-hitter.

Player and Club	Pct.	G.	AB.	R.	H.	TB.	2B.	3B.	HR.	RBI.	GW.	SH.	SF.	HP.	BB.	Int. BB.	SO.	SB.	CS.
Gwynn, Anthony, Walla Walla°	.331	42	178	46	59	109	12	1	12	37	2	0	1	0	23	0	21	17	3
Davis, Eric, Eugene	.322	62	214	67	69	120	10	4	11	39	1	2	0	1	57	0	59	40	7
Coughlon, Kevin, Medford†	.321	66	243	38	78	117	19	1	6	48	7	1	4	1	35	2	33	11	4
Howard, Bernardo, Bend†	.311	65	238	57	74	111	14	4	5	39	1	0	3	1	51	1	59	17	3
Copeland, Thomas, Medford°	.307	64	218	53	67	95	17	4	1	39	2	4	4	1	59	1	14	4	7
Bradley, Philip, Bellingham	.301	53	193	38	58	83	12	5	1	20	3	0	0	4	33	0	35	20	1
Ysambert, Sergio, Bend	.298	49	191	26	57	81	10	1	4	20	4	0	0	2	13	0	55	21	2
Strom, Phillip, Medford	.297	44	148	21	44	68	8	2	4	31	3	1	4	1	36	1	32	2	4
Smelko, Mark, Salem†	.296	53	189	30	56	77	11	2	2	30	4	0	1	3	32	2	24	2	1
Seats, Dennis, Eugene	.291	68	247	46	72	87	8	2	1	45	6	0	6	2	49	2	25	24	5

Departmental Leaders: G—Conklin, Gillaspie, Hoppie, Wesley, 69; AB—Wesley, 280; R—Davis, 67; H—Coughlon, 78; TB—Conklin, 131; 2B—Coughlon, 19; 3B—Wesley, 7; HR—Conklin, 15; RBI—Conklin, 57; GWRBI—Coughlon, Smith, B.D. 7; SH—Saverino, 11; SF—Seats, 6; BB—Hoppie, 63; HP—Evans, Langie, 6; SO—Wesley, 85; SB—Davis, 40; CS—Hoppie, 11.

(All Players—Listed Alphabetically)

Player and Club	Pct.	G.	AB.	R.	H.	TB.	2B.	3B.	HR.	RBI.	GW.	SH.	SF.	HP.	BB.	Int. BB.	SO.	SB.	CS.
Abate, George, Salem	.220	34	100	18	22	27	2	0	1	14	0	1	0	2	23	0	19	2	3
Adams, Jeffery, Eugene	.115	10	26	1	3	4	1	0	0	3	0	1	2	0	2	1	6	0	0
Amador, Bruce, Medford†	.253	53	174	35	44	64	9	1	3	30	4	4	2	1	38	3	40	13	8
Ashman, Michael, Medford°	.247	64	231	27	57	70	11	1	0	30	3	4	2	0	28	1	37	5	1
Aulenback, James, Bellingham	.207	29	82	10	17	24	1	0	2	9	0	1	0	1	10	0	23	1	1
Barbee, Andrew, Eugene	.296	31	108	19	32	38	6	0	0	20	1	1	2	1	20	0	18	6	1
Blood, Jeffrey, Walla Walla	.224	32	85	7	19	27	6	1	0	9	0	0	1	2	13	1	30	4	0
Boni, Joel, Medford†	.234	37	77	21	18	22	4	0	0	8	3	5	0	1	20	0	27	14	4
Booker, Gregory, Walla Walla	.188	31	64	8	12	24	0	0	4	15	2	0	1	0	8	0	18	1	0
Bradley, Philip, Bellingham	.301	53	193	38	58	83	12	5	1	20	3	0	0	4	33	0	35	20	1
Brodsky, Howard, Bellingham°	.119	33	84	8	10	12	2	0	0	7	1	0	1	1	17	0	27	4	1
Brooks, Michael, Salem	.284	49	162	32	46	69	6	1	5	20	2	2	2	1	17	0	36	3	1
Burroughs, David, Salem°	.000	13	1	0	0	0	0	0	0	0	0	0	0	0	0	0	0	0	0
Canavan, James, Eugene°	.000	19	7	0	0	0	0	0	0	0	1	0	0	1	0	0	6	0	0
Cannon, Timothy, Walla Walla†	.219	65	178	27	39	65	7	2	5	21	1	1	2	3	29	1	52	26	5
Colbert, Ernest, Bend†	.000	1	2	0	0	0	0	0	0	0	0	0	0	0	0	0	2	0	0
Colburn, Thomas, Medford†	.200	7	20	2	4	7	0	0	1	5	0	1	0	0	5	0	5	1	0
Conklin, Graham, Bellingham	.286	69	252	40	72	131	10	2	15	57	5	1	2	3	30	0	57	6	6
Copeland, Thomas, Medford°	.307	64	218	53	67	95	17	4	1	39	2	4	4	1	59	1	14	4	7
Coughlon, Kevin, Medford	.321	66	243	38	78	117	19	1	6	48	7	1	4	1	35	2	33	11	4
Crow, Edward, Medford	.000	3	6	1	0	0	0	0	0	0	0	0	0	0	1	0	2	0	1
Cruz, Eduardo, Bellingham	.160	33	75	10	12	13	1	0	0	4	0	4	1	1	7	0	19	1	1
Davis, Eric, Eugene	.322	62	214	67	69	120	10	4	11	39	1	2	0	1	57	0	59	40	7
Davisson, Jay, Bend	.000	18	1	0	0	0	0	0	0	0	0	0	0	0	0	0	0	0	0
Eakes, Steven, Salem	.333	5	12	2	4	4	0	0	0	2	0	0	0	0	3	0	2	0	0
Edmonds, Stanley, Bellingham°	.235	7	17	3	4	6	2	0	0	1	1	0	0	0	2	0	3	1	1
Evans, Pride, Walla Walla	.275	40	149	28	41	58	10	2	1	24	1	1	1	6	13	0	29	11	2
Fenton, Donald, Eugene	.000	19	3	0	0	0	0	0	0	0	0	0	0	0	1	0	1	0	0
Ferguson, Michael, A., Eugene	.045	14	22	1	1	1	0	0	0	1	0	0	0	0	1	0	5	0	0
Foley, John, Eugene	.279	50	154	39	43	49	2	2	0	15	1	1	0	0	31	1	23	16	5
Funk, Bryan, Eugene°	.000	23	7	1	0	0	0	0	0	0	0	0	0	0	1	0	1	0	0
Garza, Lonnie, Salem†	.212	52	151	24	32	37	3	1	0	11	1	8	1	2	24	0	42	20	7
Gillaspie, Mark, Walla Walla†	.262	69	233	51	61	117	16	2	12	44	3	0	3	3	60	3	72	2	4
Gomez, Luis, Bend	.298	46	151	18	45	63	13	1	1	22	1	0	0	1	14	0	42	2	1
Gonzalez, Felipe, Bend	.200	9	25	2	5	5	0	0	0	5	0	0	1	0	2	0	5	0	0
Groninger, Gehret, Eugene	.091	4	11	1	1	1	0	0	0	2	0	0	0	0	3	0	3	1	0
Gwynn, Anthony, Walla Walla°	.331	42	178	46	59	109	12	1	12	37	2	0	1	0	23	0	21	17	3
Harrison, Ronnie, Medford°	.178	32	90	10	16	26	5	1	1	7	0	2	2	1	5	0	17	3	1
Heidenreich, Curtis, Eugene	.200	16	25	1	5	5	0	0	0	0	0	0	1	2	0	0	13	0	0
Hennell, John, Walla Walla°	.280	67	246	34	69	108	18	0	7	42	6	1	5	1	41	3	35	1	2
Hill, Clay, Bellingham°	.250	3	12	1	3	4	1	0	0	2	0	0	0	0	2	0	2	1	0
Hooker, Elton, Medford†	.210	29	81	15	17	19	0	1	0	7	3	4	1	1	12	0	23	8	1
Hoppie, Bryan, Bend	.201	69	254	54	51	72	9	3	2	18	0	1	3	5	63	0	66	37	11
Howard, Bernardo, Bend†	.311	65	238	57	74	111	14	4	5	39	1	0	3	1	51	1	59	17	3
Hubbard, Tyson, Eugene	.037	12	27	1	1	4	0	0	1	1	0	0	0	0	0	0	9	0	0
Hume, Timothy, Eugene	.119	39	59	7	7	8	1	0	0	7	0	0	1	0	14	0	25	4	2
Johnson, Kenneth, Medford	.111	3	9	2	1	1	0	0	0	0	0	0	0	0	2	0	3	1	0
Johnson, Mark, Bend	.176	32	102	12	18	33	3	0	4	16	1	0	2	0	13	0	19	2	0
Keiser, Kent, Bend°	.282	67	255	35	72	92	11	0	3	28	4	2	2	0	30	0	55	11	3
Kiefer, Steven, Medford	.245	55	192	38	47	76	7	5	4	22	2	2	2	2	24	0	47	14	6
Kiesling, Larry, Walla Walla	.189	55	159	28	30	43	5	1	2	16	2	0	1	1	28	0	43	4	4
Kincanon, William, Eugene†	.000	8	17	0	0	0	0	0	0	1	0	0	0	0	0	0	6	0	0
Kordeck, David, Walla Walla	.088	32	68	8	6	9	0	0	1	4	0	0	0	0	9	0	39	1	0
Kruk, John, Walla Walla°	.242	63	157	31	38	51	10	0	1	13	0	2	0	1	56	1	45	7	4
Lamar, Daniel, Eugene	.211	48	161	13	34	48	6	1	2	19	0	3	1	2	11	2	29	0	1
Langie, Louis, Walla Walla	.216	67	213	37	46	65	4	6	1	20	1	1	0	6	30	0	71	13	3
Layton, Thomas, Eugene°	.125	18	8	1	1	1	0	0	0	2	0	0	0	0	7	0	3	0	0
Lowery, Edward, Bend	.209	65	225	30	47	72	9	2	4	28	4	0	2	0	30	0	49	4	1
Macias, Gerardo, Eugene°	.000	13	2	0	0	0	0	0	0	0	0	0	0	0	0	0	2	0	0
Maggio, Douglas, Bend	.266	42	143	13	38	45	7	0	0	15	0	0	0	0	6	0	27	1	1
Maroney, Kevin, Eugene	.000	1	1	0	0	0	0	0	0	0	0	0	0	0	0	0	0	0	0
McAfee, Bret, Bellingham	.196	54	199	30	39	42	3	0	0	7	3	1	1	1	15	0	43	5	3
Meier, Howard, Bellingham	.272	56	180	36	49	66	10	2	1	22	1	6	1	0	38	0	17	10	3
Meraz, Frank, Bellingham	.283	49	159	29	45	67	8	1	4	27	3	0	0	4	15	1	38	6	2
Metil, William, Eugene°	.282	55	174	33	49	62	5	4	0	12	2	4	0	0	17	0	24	11	4
Miley, Julian, Eugene°	.294	40	136	24	40	48	2	0	2	29	1	2	1	2	26	2	8	0	0
Mitchell, Scot, Medford	.207	63	198	38	41	67	9	1	5	24	2	7	1	1	46	1	67	8	3
Montero, Dany, Bend†	.241	45	137	23	33	53	4	2	4	19	1	1	0	14	0	45	11	4
Morris, David, Salem	.249	59	205	28	51	72	9	0	4	27	4	1	2	4	34	1	43	2	1
Myers, David, Bellingham	.230	64	204	24	47	63	11	1	1	23	1	4	2	2	28	0	34	4	0
Nelson, Ricky, Bellingham°	.284	56	197	35	56	79	5	0	6	37	6	0	3	0	24	4	29	3	2

Player and Club	Pct.	G.	AB.	R.	H.	TB.	2B.	3B.	HR.	RBI.	GW.	SH.	SF.	HP.	BB.	Int. BB.	SO.	SB.	CS.
Oberbruner, James, Walla Walla	.000	26	3	1	0	0	0	0	0	0	0	0	0	0	0	0	0	0	0
Ochoa, Orlando, Eugene	.059	17	17	3	1	1	0	0	0	1	0	0	0	0	3	0	10	0	0
O'Hara, Patrick, Medford	.250	14	16	4	4	4	0	0	0	2	0	0	0	1	1	0	6	0	0
Oppenheimer, Juan, Bellingham	.263	25	76	9	20	27	4	0	1	14	1	0	0	2	13	0	15	1	1
Painton, Timothy, Salem°	.167	6	18	2	3	6	0	0	1	4	0	0	0	0	3	0	2	0	0
Patterson, Steven, Walla Walla	.150	56	167	14	25	33	5	0	1	10	1	5	1	0	24	0	65	0	1
Peyton, Byron, Eugene	.348	16	46	9	16	18	0	1	0	6	2	1	1	1	13	0	6	4	0
Pierce, Don, Bellingham†	.234	43	124	23	29	38	7	1	0	7	1	2	0	2	19	0	28	6	5
Piller, Thomas, Eugene	.178	36	107	9	19	31	4	1	2	17	3	1	1	0	18	0	55	1	0
Quinones (Parras), Edwin, Bell.†	.191	21	47	3	9	11	2	0	0	5	1	1	0	0	7	0	13	0	0
Randall, James, Salem†	.281	43	160	28	45	70	7	0	6	29	2	0	1	0	26	0	20	3	7
Ransom, Eugene, Medford†	.276	54	170	38	47	58	8	0	1	13	3	7	1	1	35	0	25	31	7
Riley, Thomas, Eugene°	.266	57	199	28	53	58	3	1	0	18	2	3	0	3	21	1	18	5	1
Romero, Albert, Salem	.292	8	24	6	7	10	3	0	0	4	0	0	1	0	3	0	5	0	0
Ronk, Jeffrey, Walla Walla	.370	31	119	22	44	57	8	1	1	20	3	0	1	1	28	2	14	5	5
Rufkahr, Ben, Bend	.143	43	119	19	17	24	2	1	1	10	1	1	0	0	20	0	53	8	5
Salgueiro, Miguel, Eugene	.000	17	7	0	0	0	0	0	0	0	0	0	0	0	0	0	3	0	0
Sanchez, Rafael, Bellingham	.067	9	15	3	1	1	0	0	0	1	0	0	0	0	1	0	3	0	0
San Filippo, James, Medford	.267	5	15	2	4	6	0	1	0	5	0	0	1	0	2	1	4	1	0
Santiago, Edgar, Salem	.280	11	25	3	7	7	0	0	0	2	0	0	0	0	2	0	5	0	0
Saverino, Michael, Salem	.220	46	141	17	31	38	5	1	0	21	3	11	0	2	22	0	27	5	4
Schellin, Jay, Medford	.218	46	124	19	27	44	6	1	3	17	2	5	2	3	17	0	31	16	0
Schu, Richard, Bend	.267	68	258	41	69	85	10	0	2	42	4	1	5	1	35	0	53	15	5
Seats, Dennis, Eugene	.291	68	247	46	72	87	8	2	1	45	6	0	6	2	49	2	25	24	5
Shumock, Craig, Walla Walla	.203	54	182	19	37	51	3	1	3	27	1	0	0	1	19	2	27	7	2
Slettvet, Douglas, Walla Walla	.000	3	1	0	0	0	0	0	0	0	0	0	0	0	0	0	1	0	0
Smelko, Mark, Salem†	.296	53	189	30	56	77	11	2	2	30	4	0	1	3	32	2	24	2	1
Smith, Brick, Bellingham	.289	60	204	48	59	102	10	0	11	47	7	0	2	0	44	0	34	5	3
Smith, Byron, Medford	.218	25	55	6	12	15	3	0	0	6	0	2	0	2	14	0	16	1	0
Smith, John, Medford	.271	42	129	16	35	42	5	1	0	20	2	0	0	2	21	2	19	2	1
Stalp, Joseph, Eugene	.394	16	33	4	13	16	3	0	0	7	0	0	1	0	2	0	8	1	1
Stephens, Darryl, Salem°	.283	62	223	38	63	84	10	1	3	34	6	2	1	3	21	1	33	2	1
Stout, Timothy, Eugene	.256	56	180	29	46	56	6	2	0	26	3	3	2	0	38	0	36	10	1
Strom, Phillip, Medford	.297	44	148	21	44	68	8	2	4	31	3	1	4	1	36	1	32	2	4
Stromer, Richard, Salem	.262	61	202	36	53	78	8	1	5	30	3	0	4	0	47	1	48	5	3
Suarez, Brian, Bend	.269	67	271	41	73	114	13	5	6	42	3	1	1	2	26	0	80	5	2
Sundberg, Richard, Salem	.241	21	54	5	13	15	2	0	0	8	1	3	0	1	8	0	9	0	0
Towey, Curtis, Bellingham	.000	7	3	0	0	0	0	0	0	0	0	0	0	0	0	0	3	0	0
Valdes, Dennis, Salem	.288	35	104	16	30	40	3	2	1	9	1	4	0	0	20	1	22	3	0
Walker, Anthony, Eugene	.379	18	58	16	22	28	1	1	1	4	1	3	0	1	12	1	12	7	2
Wedel, Mark, Walla Walla	.144	47	160	16	23	28	5	0	0	16	0	2	1	1	17	0	31	1	2
Wesley, Thomas, Eugene	.271	69	280	37	76	120	12	7	6	56	3	1	0	2	20	0	85	8	3
White, Brooks, Eugene	.067	16	15	4	1	2	1	0	0	1	0	0	0	2	0	4	1	0
Williams, Frederick, Walla Walla°	.000	13	1	0	0	0	0	0	0	0	0	0	0	0	0	0	0	0	0
Wilson, Ricky, Bellingham	.204	48	147	14	30	44	2	0	4	19	0	0	1	0	19	0	21	1	3
Worden, William, Salem	.288	59	208	41	60	106	13	6	7	37	1	0	3	1	24	1	51	2	3
Wright, Paul, Salem	.235	34	115	15	27	34	4	0	1	16	2	2	0	1	8	0	29	1	2
Young, Selwyn, Medford†	.244	27	78	18	19	23	2	1	0	11	0	1	0	1	15	0	10	15	6
Ysambert, Sergio, Bend	.298	49	191	26	57	81	10	1	4	20	4	0	0	2	13	0	55	21	2
Zambrana, Luis, Salem	.281	58	224	29	63	83	11	3	1	17	4	1	2	0	28	2	42	10	6

The following pitchers had no plate appearances primarily through the use of designated hitters, listed alphabetically by club, games in parentheses:

BELLINGHAM—Dixon, Ronn (22); Elridge, Jeffrey (14); Guetterman, Lee (13); Hayes, Terry (15); Holland, Donald (13); Kinley, Wayne (1); Koenig, Kalvin (22); LaBounty, David (13); Langston, Mark (13); Martin, Victor (30); Parent, Eric (12); Rodriguez, Anthony (8).

BEND—Childress, Rodney (25); Gaynor, Richard (33); Giovacchini, Steven (9); Hunter, Brian (13); Hutchinson, DeWayne (11); Irions, Billy (16); Knight, Larry (14); McAnally, John (16); Rodriguez, Yonis (13); Seiler, David (14).

MEDFORD—Bailey, James (3); Feeley, James (7); Gale, John (14); Heckman, Thomas (13); Herron, Anthony (25); Jarrett, Mark (17); Kobernus, Jeffrey (17); Kolotka, Charles (9); Mine, Gregory (12); Tuchalski, Bruce (3); Vavrock, Robert (13); Vela, John (9); Weatherman, David (7); Young, Curtis (8).

SALEM—Ahern, Jeffrey (12); Bankowski, Kris (24); Halicki, Kevin (13); Jones, Lee (20); Kammeyer, Timothy (14); Long, Edelano (14); McMahon, John (13); Robins, Gary (5); Sadd, Robert (7); Schwab, Kenneth (2); Skaggs, Jackie (5); Stearns, Anthony (18); Talia, Michael (2).

WALLA WALLA—Balderston, Joseph (5); Giacomazzi, James (16); Grame, Paul (14); Kain, Martin (22); Ochal, Mark (15); Purchatzke, Lee (12); Smith, Wesley (20); Stein, James (17).

GRAND SLAM HOME RUNS—Booker, Bradley, Conklin, Evans, Gillaspie, Hennell, Piller, Stephens, Stromer, Wesley, 1 each.

AWARDED FIRST BASE ON INTERFERENCE—Foley 4 (Gonzalez, Johnson, Mitchell, Patterson); Howard 2 (Lamar 2); Keiser 2 (Lamar, Wilson); Lowery 2 (Aulenback, Mitchell); Bradley (Mitchell); Crow (Maggio); Hennell (Gonzalez); Kiesling (Wilson); Kordeck (Colburn); Maggio (Wilson); Rufkahr (Worden); Wilson (Adams).

CLUB FIELDING

Club	Pct.	G.	PO.	A.	E.	DP.	PB.	Club	Pct.	G.	PO.	A.	E.	DP.	PB.
Salem	.957	70	1809	695	112	49	12	Eugene	.943	70	1814	766	156	48	15
Bellingham	.952	70	1787	756	128	54	17	Bend	.941	70	1817	793	163	70	23
Medford	.952	70	1861	800	135	57	21	Walla Walla	.939	70	1872	780	172	45	30

Triple Play—Walla Walla.

INDIVIDUAL FIELDING

°Throws lefthanded.

FIRST BASEMEN

Player and Club	Pct.	G.	PO.	A.	E.	DP.	Player and Club	Pct.	G.	PO.	A.	E.	DP.
Ashman, Medford	.985	54	488	29	8	30	Randall, Salem°	.977	5	39	3	1	3
Booker, Walla Walla	1.000	3	22	2	0	2	Smelko, Salem	1.000	9	56	4	0	4
Foley, Eugene°	.994	33	291	17	2	17	B. Smith, Bellingham	.984	58	510	35	9	38
HENNELL, Walla Walla°	.988	66	609	38	8	37	J. Smith, Medford	.976	7	40	0	1	4
Howard, Bend	.990	10	92	4	1	11	Stephens, Salem°	.981	59	491	25	10	36
Kruk, Walla Walla°	1.000	4	34	1	0	2	Strom, Medford	.970	14	121	9	4	18
Lamar, Eugene	.972	12	100	5	3	8	Suarez, Bend	.983	60	549	32	10	49
Montero, Bend	1.000	1	1	0	0	0	Wesley, Eugene	.973	30	267	19	8	19
Oppenheimer, Bellingham	.946	14	100	6	6	10							

Triple Play—Hennell.

SECOND BASEMEN

Player and Club	Pct.	G.	PO.	A.	E.	DP.
Abate, Salem	.961	31	56	66	5	10
AMADOR, Medford	.940	50	110	155	17	30
Brooks, Salem	.923	21	42	54	8	11
Cannon, Walla Walla	1.000	1	1	1	0	0
Cruz, Bellingham	.913	33	47	48	9	9
Evans, Walla Walla	.899	30	69	83	17	18
Hoppie, Bend	.934	67	161	192	25	47
Hume, Eugene	.750	4	3	0	1	1
McAfee, Bellingham	.923	47	70	122	16	22
Metil, Eugene	1.000	5	7	13	0	1
Ronk, Walla Walla	.945	14	32	37	4	9
Saverino, Salem	.980	27	44	52	2	11
Schu, Bend	.750	6	8	4	4	2
Seats, Eugene	.908	66	147	170	32	28
Towey, Bellingham	.889	1	5	3	1	1
Wedel, Walla Walla	.947	31	54	88	8	9
S. Young, Medford	.892	23	37	46	10	12

THIRD BASEMEN

Player and Club	Pct.	G.	PO.	A.	E.	DP.
Brooks, Salem	.955	8	12	9	1	0
Conklin, Bellingham	.907	69	48	128	18	7
Evans, Walla Walla	.000	1	0	0	1	0
Howard, Bend	.810	17	13	34	11	1
Hume, Eugene	.667	6	1	1	1	0
Keiser, Bend	.857	2	0	6	1	0
Kiefer, Medford	1.000	2	1	6	0	0
Kiesling, Walla Walla	.784	22	19	39	16	2
Metil, Eugene	.856	37	21	68	15	4
Miley, Eugene	.500	1	0	1	1	0
Montero, Bend	.833	3	3	2	1	0
Piller, Eugene	.883	32	20	63	11	2
Quinones, Bellingham	1.000	3	1	1	0	0
Ransom, Medford	.906	52	49	106	16	7
Riley, Eugene	1.000	5	2	7	0	0
Ronk, Walla Walla	.915	14	15	28	4	5
San Filippo, Medford	.700	5	6	8	6	0
Santiago, Salem	1.000	7	5	11	0	0
Schu, Bend	.894	50	39	121	19	11
Shumock, Walla Walla	.810	32	18	46	15	1
B. Smith, Medford	.878	21	10	33	6	4
STROMER, Salem	.938	60	52	113	11	12
Wedel, Walla Walla	.958	6	7	16	1	2
White, Eugene	1.000	1	0	2	0	0

SHORTSTOPS

Player and Club	Pct.	G.	PO.	A.	E.	DP.
Boni, Medford	.964	25	29	77	4	11
Brooks, Salem	1.000	4	8	5	0	1
Eakes, Salem	1.000	5	8	8	0	0
Evans, Walla Walla	.714	1	2	3	2	1
Garza, Salem	.915	49	71	122	18	17
Hoppie, Bend	1.000	3	2	10	0	1
Hume, Eugene	.909	10	9	41	5	8
Johnson, Medford	.667	3	3	5	4	1
Kiefer, Medford	.933	49	67	169	17	31
Langie, Walla Walla	.882	64	93	213	41	26
Lowery, Bend	.925	64	111	187	24	39
McAfee, Bellingham	.850	11	12	22	6	3
MYERS, Bellingham	.963	64	105	180	11	37
Peyton, Eugene	.982	14	14	41	1	7
Riley, Eugene	.894	50	73	147	26	17
Ronk, Walla Walla	.903	9	12	16	3	1
Saverino, Salem	.925	21	21	53	6	9
Schu, Bend	.952	4	8	12	1	4
Wedel, Walla Walla	1.000	2	2	3	0	0

Triple Play—Langie.

OUTFIELDERS

Player and Club	Pct.	G.	PO.	A.	E.	DP.
Barbee, Eugene	.953	30	39	2	2	0
Blood, Walla Walla	1.000	12	16	2	0	0
BRADLEY, Bellingham	.990	51	94	3	1	0
Brodsky, Bellingham	1.000	14	15	1	0	1
Cannon, Walla Walla	.913	54	80	4	8	0
Copeland, Medford°	.950	63	105	10	6	2
Coughlon, Medford	.982	65	104	6	2	0
Crow, Medford°	1.000	3	2	0	0	0
Davis, Eugene	.963	61	94	11	4	3
Edmonds, Bellingham	1.000	3	1	1	0	1
Foley, Eugene°	.917	9	11	0	1	0
Gillaspie, Walla Walla	.968	48	60	1	2	0
Gomez, Bend	.918	42	41	4	4	2
Gwynn, Walla Walla°	.963	41	76	2	3	0
Harrison, Medford	.875	29	32	3	5	0
Hill, Bellingham	1.000	1	2	1	0	0
Hooker, Medford°	.903	29	27	1	3	0
Hume, Eugene	1.000	2	2	0	0	0
Keiser, Bend	.934	60	82	3	6	1.
Kiesling, Walla Walla	.960	25	19	5	1	1
Kruk, Walla Walla°	.975	54	74	4	2	1
Lamar, Eugene	.750	5	3	0	1	0
Meraz, Bellingham	.957	36	61	5	3	1
Meier, Bellingham	.973	43	66	5	2	0
Metil, Eugene	1.000	6	5	1	0	0
Montero, Bend	.973	37	33	3	1	1
Morris, Salem	.924	53	82	3	7	1
Nelson, Bellingham	.949	35	49	7	3	2
Painton, Bellingham°	.889	5	8	0	1	0
Pierce, Bellingham	.831	40	50	4	11	1
Randall, Salem°	.931	39	63	4	5	0
Rufkahr, Bend	.951	39	53	5	3	0
Schellin, Medford	1.000	44	68	1	0	0
Seats, Eugene	.500	1	1	0	1	0
Shumock, Walla Walla	.750	7	2	4	2	0
Smelko, Salem	.944	51	70	4	4	0
Stout, Eugene	.949	51	70	4	4	0
Valdes, Salem	1.000	24	29	1	0	0
Walker, Eugene	.958	15	22	1	1	0
Wesley, Bend	.877	40	51	6	8	1
White, Eugene	1.000	2	2	0	0	0
Wright, Salem	.971	30	33	1	1	0
Ysambert, Bend	.963	48	74	4	3	1
Zambrana, Salem	.971	58	92	9	3	2

CATCHERS

Player and Club	Pct.	G.	PO.	A.	E.	DP.	PB.
Adams, Eugene	.952	9	55	5	3	0	2
Aulenback, Bellingham	.968	29	185	28	7	1	6
Colburn, Medford	.953	7	51	10	3	0	0
Gonzalez, Bend	.918	7	43	2	4	0	2
Groninger, Eugene	.950	4	18	1	1	0	2
Hill, Bellingham	1.000	2	14	2	0	1	0
Johnson, Bend	.950	27	188	23	11	0	6
Kordeck, Walla Walla	.940	29	150	8	10	0	13
Lamar, Eugene	.975	27	175	23	5	1	7
Maggio, Bend	.971	42	288	45	10	3	15
Miley, Eugene	.971	37	273	29	9	2	4
Mitchell, Medford	.973	63	453	51	14	1	17
O'Hara, Medford	.923	9	23	1	2	1	3
Patterson, Walla Walla	.969	56	371	38	13	2	17
Romero, Salem	.950	3	18	1	1	0	1
Sanchez, Bellingham	1.000	6	7	0	0	0	2
Sundberg, Salem	.994	21	136	18	1	0	2
WILSON, Bellingham	.981	48	306	53	7	2	9
Worden, Salem	.966	54	403	45	16	3	9

PITCHERS

Player and Club	Pct.	G.	PO.	A.	E.	DP.
Ahern, Salem°	.765	12	1	12	4	1
Balderston, Walla Walla	.800	5	1	7	2	0
Bankowski, Salem°	.875	24	3	4	1	1
BOOKER, Walla Walla	1.000	11	4	12	0	1
Burroughs, Salem	.944	12	2	15	1	1
Canavan, Eugene°	.889	19	0	8	1	0
Childress, Bend	.833	25	2	8	2	0
Davisson, Bend	.895	18	5	12	2	0
Dixon, Bellingham°	.929	22	2	11	1	0
Eldridge, Bellingham	.750	14	3	3	2	0
Fenton, Eugene	1.000	19	0	3	0	0
Ferguson, Eugene	.800	14	3	5	2	1
Funk, Eugene	1.000	23	5	1	0	0
Gale, Medford	.750	14	0	3	1	0
Gaynor, Bend	.909	33	1	9	1	1
Giacomazzi, Walla Walla	.903	16	6	22	3	0
Giovacchini, Bend	1.000	9	0	1	0	0
Grame, Walla Walla	.933	13	5	9	1	1

PITCHERS—Continued

Player and Club	Pct.	G.	PO.	A.	E.	DP.	Player and Club	Pct.	G.	PO.	A.	E.	DP.
Guetterman, Bellingham°	.852	13	4	19	4	1	McAnally, Bend°	.667	16	0	4	2	1
Halicki, Salem	.885	13	3	20	3	2	McMahon, Salem	.909	13	3	7	1	0
Hayes, Bellingham°	.909	15	3	7	1	0	Mine, Medford	.667	12	1	1	1	0
HECKMAN, Medford	1.000	13	7	9	0	1	Oberbruner, Walla Walla	.909	26	2	8	1	0
Heidenreich, Eugene	.929	16	7	19	2	3	Ochal, Walla Walla	.929	15	3	10	1	0
Herron, Medford°	.857	25	1	5	1	0	Ochoa, Eugene	1.000	17	6	1	0	0
Holland, Bellingham	.800	13	3	5	2	2	Parent, Bellingham	.889	12	7	9	2	0
Hubbard, Eugene	.920	12	5	18	2	0	Purchatzke, Walla Walla	.867	12	4	9	2	1
Hunter, Bend	.893	13	5	20	3	1	Robins, Salem	1.000	5	2	1	0	0
Hutchinson, Bend	.773	11	2	15	5	1	Rodriguez, Bellingham	.750	8	2	1	1	0
Irions, Bend°	1.000	16	2	2	0	0	Rodriguez, Bend	.800	13	3	9	3	0
Jarrett, Medford	1.000	17	4	10	0	0	Sadd, Salem	.000	7	0	0	1	0
Jones, Salem	1.000	20	0	2	0	0	Salgueiro, Eugene	1.000	17	2	3	0	0
Kain, Walla Walla	1.000	22	3	7	0	0	Schwab, Salem°	1.000	2	0	1	0	0
Kammeyer, Salem	.944	14	5	12	1	3	Seiler, Bend°	.905	14	6	13	2	0
Kincanon, Eugene	1.000	4	1	5	0	0	Skaggs, Salem	1.000	5	1	3	0	0
Knight, Bend	.692	14	2	7	4	1	Smith, Walla Walla	1.000	20	3	2	0	0
Kobernus, Medford°	1.000	17	0	8	0	0	Stalp, Eugene	.960	16	5	19	1	2
Koenig, Bellingham°	.900	22	1	8	1	0	Stearns, Salem	.800	18	0	4	1	0
Kolotka, Medford	.917	9	6	5	1	0	Stein, Walla Walla	1.000	17	1	4	0	0
LaBounty, Bellingham	.944	13	7	10	1	0	Tuchalski, Medford	.500	3	1	0	1	0
Langston, Bellingham°	.906	13	6	23	3	3	Vavrock, Medford	.905	13	5	14	2	0
Layton, Eugene	1.000	18	3	3	0	0	Vela, Medford°	1.000	9	1	4	0	0
Long, Salem	.909	14	3	7	1	1	Weatherman, Medford	1.000	7	3	5	0	1
Macias, Eugene°	.667	13	1	3	2	1	Williams, Walla Walla°	.917	13	3	8	1	0
Martin, Bellingham	1.000	30	1	5	0	0	C. YOUNG, Medford°	1.000	8	6	10	0	1

The following players do not have any recorded accepted chances at the positions indicated; therefore, are not listed in the fielding averages for those particular positions: Ashman, p; Bailey, p; Boni, 2b; Feeley, p; Kinley, p; Morris, 2b; Oppenheimer, of; Quinones, of; Slettvet, p; Talia, p; Towey, p; White, 2b.

CLUB PITCHING

Club	ERA.	G.	CG.	ShO.	Sv.	IP.	H.	R.	ER.	HR.	HB.	BB.	Int. BB.	SO.	WP.	Bk.
Medford	3.85	70	19	4	12	620	602	338	265	55	10	288	15	520	61	7
Eugene	4.21	70	12	5	11	605	542	370	283	42	21	345	3	497	39	6
Bellingham	4.21	70	10	1	15	596	589	353	279	28	12	380	8	508	45	11
Salem	4.40	70	13	4	18	603	557	361	295	21	20	400	3	535	71	10
Bend	4.44	70	6	2	15	606	588	421	299	41	20	387	11	507	60	3
Walla Walla	4.69	70	11	3	13	624	630	438	325	38	32	370	10	500	61	8

PITCHERS' RECORDS
(Leading Qualifiers for Earned-Run Average Leadership — 56 or More Innings)

°Throws lefthanded.

Pitcher—Club	W.	L.	Pct.	ERA.	G.	GS.	CG.	GF.	ShO.	Sv.	IP.	H.	R.	ER.	HR.	HB.	BB.	Int. BB.	SO.	WP.
Heidenreich, Eugene	5	7	.417	2.39	16	14	4	1	2	0	98	74	39	26	3	7	50	0	96	2
Vavrock, Medford	9	3	.750	2.53	13	13	6	0	0	0	96	88	39	27	8	1	27	1	58	5
Heckman, Medford	7	0	1.000	2.53	13	13	3	0	0	0	89	78	30	25	5	0	29	1	72	2
Hunter, Bend	7	4	.636	2.64	13	13	3	0	1	0	92	78	41	27	1	1	34	1	72	6
Guetterman, Bellingham°	6	4	.600	2.68	13	13	3	0	0	0	84	85	36	25	3	2	42	2	55	4
Kain, Walla Walla	2	2	.500	2.75	22	0	0	12	0	2	59	52	31	18	4	2	14	3	63	3
Kammeyer, Salem	8	4	.667	2.81	14	14	4	0	1	0	96	79	38	30	2	3	40	0	108	8
Grame, Walla Walla	5	4	.556	2.93	13	12	1	0	0	0	80	79	40	26	1	5	59	0	61	15
Ferguson, Eugene	6	3	.667	3.00	14	9	2	3	1	0	60	40	30	20	4	4	39	0	50	3
Jarrett, Medford	7	4	.636	3.07	17	9	3	7	1	3	85	80	39	29	10	1	26	1	76	8

Departmental Leaders: G—Gaynor, 33; GS—Giacomazzi, Ochal, 15; CG—Giacomazzi, Vavrock, 6; ShO—Heidenreich, 2; W—Vavrock, 9; L—Giacomazzi, 9; Sv—Gaynor, Jones, L., 10; Pct.—Heckman, 1.000; IP—Giacomazzi, 105; H—Giacomazzi, 117; R—Giacomazzi, 77; ER—Giacomazzi, 58; HR—Ochal, 11; BB—Long, 77; IBB—Childress, Gale, Smith, W., 4; HB—Heidenreich, 7; SO—Kammeyer, 108; WP—Long, 16.

(All Pitchers—Listed Alphabetically)

Pitcher—Club	W.	L.	Pct.	ERA.	G.	GS.	CG.	GF.	ShO.	Sv.	IP.	H.	R.	ER.	HR.	HB.	BB.	Int. BB.	SO.	WP.
Ahern, Salem°	5	6	.455	4.88	12	12	1	0	0	0	72	64	45	39	2	2	65	0	53	10
Ashman, Medford	0	0	.000	0.00	1	0	0	1	0	0	3	1	0	0	0	0	1	0	3	0
Bailey, Medford	0	0	.000	9.00	3	0	0	0	0	0	5	6	5	5	0	0	5	0	6	1
Balderston, Walla Walla	3	2	.600	3.86	5	5	1	0	0	0	35	30	20	15	1	0	15	0	22	2
Bankowski, Salem°	4	1	.800	4.71	24	0	0	15	0	4	42	41	25	22	0	1	21	0	34	5
Booker, Walla Walla	2	3	.400	5.26	11	11	0	0	0	0	53	55	41	31	1	4	35	1	25	6
Burroughs, Bend	2	5	.286	6.20	12	9	1	0	0	0	74	90	62	51	4	3	55	0	48	9
Canavan, Eugene°	1	6	.143	2.72	19	3	1	7	0	1	43	31	16	13	2	0	29	2	35	5
Childress, Bend	4	5	.444	4.50	25	0	0	15	0	4	46	56	36	23	5	0	21	4	38	2
Davisson, Bellingham	4	1	.800	3.60	18	4	1	7	0	0	65	57	35	26	6	2	24	0	60	1
Dixon, Bellingham°	3	0	1.000	3.63	22	1	0	8	0	2	57	42	28	23	6	0	42	1	41	4
Eldridge, Bellingham	3	2	.600	6.55	14	3	0	3	0	1	33	30	29	24	1	2	39	1	31	3
Feeley, Medford	0	0	.000	36.00	7	0	0	2	0	0	4	11	23	16	1	3	16	0	3	8
Fenton, Eugene	0	1	.000	10.96	14	0	0	8	0	0	23	23	30	28	3	0	33	0	28	2
Ferguson, Eugene	6	3	.667	3.00	14	9	2	3	1	0	60	40	30	20	4	4	39	0	50	3
Funk, Eugene	4	1	.800	3.98	23	1	0	18	0	8	43	46	22	19	4	3	8	0	30	4
Gale, Medford	2	0	1.000	5.67	14	0	0	6	0	0	27	24	21	17	2	1	23	4	22	3
Gaynor, Bend	1	1	.500	2.44	33	0	0	25	0	10	48	32	19	13	2	1	35	2	56	11
Giacomazzi, Walla Walla	5	9	.357	4.97	16	15	6	1	1	0	105	117	77	58	6	5	60	0	67	7
Giovacchini, Bend	0	1	.000	18.00	9	0	0	4	0	0	11	21	24	22	3	1	17	1	10	6
Grame, Walla Walla	5	4	.556	2.93	13	12	1	0	0	0	80	79	40	26	1	5	59	0	61	15
Guetterman, Bellingham°	6	4	.600	2.68	13	13	3	0	0	0	84	85	36	25	3	2	42	2	55	4
Halicki, Salem	7	3	.700	3.58	13	13	2	0	0	0	78	73	39	31	2	0	33	0	47	8
Hayes, Bellingham°	1	4	.200	5.20	15	5	0	6	0	1	45	51	31	26	3	0	31	1	49	3
Heckman, Medford	7	0	1.000	2.53	13	13	3	0	0	0	89	78	30	25	5	0	29	1	72	2
Heidenreich, Eugene	5	7	.417	2.39	16	14	4	1	2	0	98	74	39	26	3	7	50	0	96	2
Herron, Medford°	4	4	.500	2.93	25	0	0	20	0	9	40	40	22	13	3	0	23	3	52	8

Pitcher—Club	W.	L.	Pct.	ERA.	G.	GS.	CG.	GF.	ShO.	Sv.	IP.	H.	R.	ER.	HR.	HB.	BB.	Int. BB.	SO.	WP.
Holland, Bellingham	1	5	.167	3.74	13	11	2	1	0	1	65	65	39	27	1	1	43	0	48	4
Hubbard, Eugene	3	4	.429	3.50	12	12	2	0	0	0	72	67	43	28	5	0	27	0	53	0
Hunter, Bend	7	4	.636	2.64	13	13	3	0	1	0	92	78	41	27	1	1	34	1	72	6
Hutchinson, Bend	3	7	.300	4.14	11	11	0	0	0	0	63	58	39	29	2	5	42	0	43	5
Irions, Bend°	1	2	.333	7.68	16	2	0	8	0	0	34	43	40	29	7	1	26	0	26	3
Jarrett, Medford	7	4	.636	3.07	17	9	3	7	1	3	85	80	39	29	10	1	26	1	78	8
Jones, Salem	0	3	.000	5.46	20	0	0	17	0	10	28	28	19	17	2	6	19	1	30	4
Kain, Walla Walla	2	2	.500	2.75	22	0	0	12	0	2	59	52	31	18	4	2	14	3	63	3
Kammeyer, Salem	8	4	.667	2.81	14	14	4	0	1	0	96	79	38	30	2	3	40	0	108	8
Kincanon, Eugene	1	1	.500	3.81	4	4	1	0	0	0	26	25	18	11	0	3	11	0	22	2
Kinley, Bellingham	0	0	.000	18.00	1	0	0	0	0	0	1	2	2	2	0	0	3	0	0	0
Knight, Bend	3	6	.333	4.13	14	14	1	0	0	0	72	63	46	33	5	1	58	0	68	6
Kobernus, Medford°	4	1	.800	3.64	17	3	1	9	0	0	42	43	19	17	4	0	17	1	50	2
Koenig, Bellingham°	4	3	.571	6.43	22	1	0	10	0	1	42	52	37	30	1	3	27	2	52	3
Kolotka, Medford	2	3	.400	3.49	9	6	1	1	0	0	49	51	25	19	2	1	24	3	37	7
LaBounty, Bellingham	5	4	.556	4.30	13	11	0	0	0	0	67	75	39	32	4	1	20	0	55	4
Langston, Bellingham°	7	3	.700	3.39	13	13	5	0	1	0	85	81	37	32	2	0	46	0	97	4
Layton, Eugene	2	2	.500	5.73	18	6	1	4	0	0	44	42	31	28	5	0	40	1	29	2
Long, Salem	3	7	.300	4.73	14	14	4	0	1	0	78	52	51	41	3	2	77	2	107	16
Macias, Eugene°	0	3	.000	7.88	13	1	0	5	0	0	24	27	26	21	4	0	11	0	25	1
Martin, Bellingham	4	2	.667	4.95	30	0	0	26	0	9	40	31	26	22	3	0	29	1	37	3
McAnally, Bend°	1	1	.500	8.44	16	1	0	4	0	1	32	39	36	30	2	3	32	2	45	3
McMahon, Salem	2	3	.400	4.50	13	6	1	2	1	0	58	54	34	29	5	1	46	0	44	0
Mine, Medford	2	5	.286	4.67	12	6	0	2	0	0	54	57	33	28	8	0	20	0	35	0
Oberbruner, Walla Walla	3	3	.500	3.63	26	0	0	20	0	3	52	57	30	21	4	3	27	1	48	5
Ochal, Walla Walla	5	5	.500	5.03	15	15	3	0	1	0	93	84	60	52	11	2	36	0	58	5
Ochoa, Eugene	4	4	.500	6.75	17	5	0	4	0	0	52	61	49	39	7	1	33	0	44	4
Parent, Bellingham	5	4	.556	4.58	12	12	0	0	0	0	55	45	35	28	3	2	43	0	33	12
Purchatzke, Walla Walla	0	8	.000	6.60	12	10	0	1	0	1	45	57	56	33	3	3	41	1	25	7
Robins, Salem	0	0	.000	0.00	5	1	0	4	0	0	7	5	2	0	0	1	3	0	7	0
Rodriguez, Bellingham	0	0	.000	2.57	8	0	0	1	0	0	14	18	5	4	1	0	8	0	5	0
Rodriguez, Bend	4	3	.571	4.17	13	11	1	1	0	0	69	68	39	32	4	1	35	1	40	6
Sadd, Salem	1	0	1.000	5.40	7	0	0	3	0	1	15	12	12	9	0	0	13	0	10	0
Salgueiro, Eugene	2	2	.500	3.66	17	1	1	6	0	1	32	24	19	13	1	2	20	0	24	4
Schwab, Salem°	0	0	.000	15.00	2	0	0	2	0	0	3	7	5	5	0	0	2	0	1	0
Seiler, Bend°	3	8	.273	4.68	14	14	0	0	0	0	73	73	66	38	4	4	63	0	49	11
Skaggs, Salem	1	1	.500	5.73	5	1	0	2	0	0	11	12	10	7	0	0	12	0	8	5
Slettvet, Walla Walla	0	0	.000	9.00	1	0	0	1	0	0	1	2	1	1	0	0	1	0	0	0
Smith, Walla Walla	2	3	.400	2.45	20	0	0	17	0	6	44	23	17	12	0	1	19	4	73	2
Stalp, Eugene	5	3	.625	3.74	16	14	0	2	0	0	89	82	47	37	4	1	44	0	61	10
Stearns, Salem	3	1	.750	3.32	18	0	0	10	0	2	38	34	19	14	1	1	12	0	33	4
Stein, Walla Walla	2	1	.667	7.15	17	0	0	1	0	1	34	38	32	27	1	3	43	0	48	8
Talia, Salem	0	0	.000	0.00	2	0	0	2	0	1	4	6	0	0	0	0	2	0	5	2
Towey, Bellingham	0	0	.000	6.75	5	0	0	5	0	0	8	12	9	6	0	1	7	0	5	1
Tuchalski, Medford	0	1	.000	9.00	3	0	0	0	0	0	4	8	9	4	0	1	3	0	3	1
Vavrock, Medford	9	3	.750	2.53	13	13	6	0	0	0	96	88	39	27	8	1	27	1	58	5
Vela, Medford°	0	2	.000	7.56	9	5	0	3	0	0	25	27	26	21	4	1	23	0	22	6
Weatherman, Medford	3	3	.000	4.09	7	7	2	0	1	0	44	43	20	20	4	0	19	0	30	2
Williams, Walla Walla°	0	1	.000	12.13	13	2	0	6	0	0	23	36	33	31	6	4	20	0	10	1
C. Young, Medford°	2	2	.500	4.25	8	8	3	0	1	0	53	45	27	25	4	1	32	1	49	8

BALKS—Ahern, 4; Parent 3; Dixon, Giacomazzi, Grame, Halicki, Heckman, Hutchinson, Kammeyer, Langston, McMahon, Ochal, Williams, 2 each; Guetterman, Hayes, Herron, Hubbard, Kain, Kinley, Kobernus, Kolotka, Mine, Rodriguez, Seiler, Stalp, Stein, Vavrock, 1 each.

COMBINATION SHUTOUTS—Hunter-Childress, Bend; Heidenreich-Funk, Stalp-Funk, Eugene; Vavrock-Kobernus-Feeley, Medford; Kammeyer-Talia, Salem; Grame-Kain, Walla Walla.

NO-HIT GAME—None.

South Atlantic League

CLASS A

CHAMPIONSHIP WINNERS IN PREVIOUS YEARS

1948—Lincolnton° .627	1964—Rock Hill .672	1973—Spartanburg‡ .646
1949—Newton-Conover .667	Salisbury‡ .631	Gastonia .619
Ruth'ford Co. (2nd)† .627	1965—Salisbury .641	1974—Gastonia .606
1950—Newton-Conover .627	Rock Hill‡ .603	Gastonia .672
Lenoir (2nd)† .626	1966—Spartanburg .682	1975—Spartanburg .543
1951—Morganton .645	Spartanburg .767	Spartanburg .614
Shelby (2nd)† .604	1967—Spartanburg .730	1976—Asheville .544
1952—Lincolnton .649	Spartanburg .567	Greenwood‡ .600
Shelby (2nd)† .645	1968—Greenwood‡ .597	1977—Greenwood .557
1953-59—League inactive.	Greenwood‡ .597	Gastonia‡ .590
1960—Lexington .707	1969—Greenwood‡ .587	1978—Greenwood .614
Salisbury (2nd)† .650	Shelby .565	Greenwood .565
1961—Salisbury .627	1970—Greenville .576	1979—Greenwood‡ .565
Shelby (4th)† .481	Greenville .619	Spartanburg .525
1962—Statesville .563	1971—Greenwood .631	1980—Greensboro‡ .590
Statesville .700	Greenwood .759	Charleston .561
1963—Greenville† .576	1972—Spartanburg‡ .788	
Salisbury .631	Greenville .652	

°Won championship and four-club playoff. †Won four-club playoff. ‡Won split-season playoff. (NOTE—Known as Western Carolina League from 1948 through 1962 and known as Western Carolinas League through 1979.)

STANDING OF CLUBS AT CLOSE OF FIRST HALF, JUNE 19

NORTHERN DIVISION

Club	W.	L.	T.	Pct.	G.B.
Greensboro (Yankees)	47	23	0	.671	....
Gastonia (Cardinals)	37	35	0	.514	11
Spartanburg (Phillies)	34	37	0	.479	13½
Asheville (Rangers)	34	38	0	.472	14
Shelby (Mets)	30	40	0	.429	17

SOUTHERN DIVISION

Club	W.	L.	T.	Pct.	G.B.
Greenwood (Pirates)	42	30	0	.583	....
Charleston (Royals)	41	31	0	.569	1
Macon (Tigers)	33	36	0	.478	7½
Florence (Blue Jays)	31	38	0	.449	9½
Anderson (Braves)	25	46	0	.352	16½

STANDING OF CLUBS AT CLOSE OF SECOND HALF, AUGUST 31

NORTHERN DIVISION

Club	W.	L.	T.	Pct.	G.B.
Greensboro (Yankees)	51	20	0	.718	....
Asheville (Rangers)	40	30	1	.571	10½
Spartanburg (Phillies)	37	33	0	.529	13½
Gastonia (Cardinals)	31	41	0	.431	20½
Shelby (Mets)	29	43	0	.403	22½

SOUTHERN DIVISION

Club	W.	L.	T.	Pct.	G.B.
Greenwood (Pirates)	37	35	0	.514	....
Florence (Blue Jays)	35	34	0	.507	½
Charleston (Royals)	34	36	1	.486	2
Anderson (Braves)	32	40	0	.444	5
Macon (Tigers)	29	43	0	.403	8

COMPOSITE STANDING OF CLUBS AT CLOSE OF SEASON, AUGUST 31

Club	Gbr.	Gwd.	Char.	Ash.	Spar.	Flo.	Gas.	Mac.	Shel.	And.	W.	L.	T.	Pct.	G.B.
Greensboro (Yankees)	..	11	12	8	13	9	11	12	10	12	98	43	0	.695	....
Greenwood (Pirates)	5	..	6	11	8	9	10	10	8	12	79	65	0	.549	20½
Charleston (Royals)	4	10	..	5	10	8	11	11	6	10	75	67	1	.528	23½
Asheville (Rangers)	8	5	9	..	6	9	7	7	12	11	74	68	1	.521	24½
Spartanburg (Phillies)	3	8	6	10	..	9	9	7	12	7	71	70	0	.504	27
Florence (Blue Jays)	5	7	8	7	5	..	10	8	11	5	66	72	0	.478	30½
Gastonia (Cardinals)	5	6	5	9	7	6	..	8	10	12	68	76	0	.472	31½
Macon (Tigers)	4	6	5	9	8	7	8	..	6	9	62	79	0	.440	36
Shelby (Mets)	5	8	10	4	4	5	6	9	..	8	59	83	0	.415	39½
Anderson (Braves)	4	4	6	5	9	10	4	7	8	..	57	86	0	.399	42

Major league affiliations in parentheses.

Playoffs—Greensboro, Northern Division champion, defeated Greenwood, Southern Division champion, three games to two, for League Championship.

Regular-Season Attendance—Anderson, 34,349; Asheville, 70,957; Charleston, 83,934; Florence, 74,645; Gastonia, 80,869; Greensboro, 260,340; Greenwood, 20,740; Macon, 72,557; Shelby, 51,324; Spartanburg, 43,404. Total, 793,119. Playoffs, 5,983. All-star game, 3,441.

Managers: Anderson, Sonny Jackson; Asheville, Tom Robson; Charleston, Rick Mathews; Florence, Dennis Holmberg; Gastonia, Joe Rigoli; Greensboro, Bob Schaefer; Greenwood, Joe Frisina; Macon, Tom Kotchman; Shelby, Dan Monzon; Spartanburg, Tom Harmon.

All-Star Team: 1B—Larry Pittman, Shelby; 2B—Garry Harris, Florence; 3B—Jeffrey Reynolds, Greensboro; SS—(tie) Ralph Wheeler, Florence; Robert Meacham, Gastonia; OF—Joseph Orsulak, Greenwood; Jeffery Stone, Spartanburg; Daniel Murphy, Asheville; C—Joel Skinner, Greenwood; DH—Matthew Winters, Greensboro; P—Glenn Ray, Charleston; Christopher Green, Greenwood. MVP—(tie) Daniel Murphy, Asheville; Jeffrey Reynolds, Greensboro; Pitcher of Year—Glenn Ray, Charleston; Manager of Year—Bob Schaefer, Greensboro.

(Compiled by Howe News Bureau, Boston, Mass.)

CLUB BATTING

Club	Pct.	G.	AB.	R.	OR.	H.	TB.	2B.	3B.	HR.	RBI.	GW.	SH.	SF.	HP.	BB.	Int. BB.	SO.	SB.	CS.	LOB.
Greensboro	.270	141	4537	788	560	1223	1923	197	31	147	713	86	18	53	61	649	17	868	104	64	1030
Greenwood	.269	144	4835	681	705	1301	1748	184	49	55	565	58	38	51	39	395	29	855	151	56	984
Asheville	.266	143	4724	773	666	1256	1896	223	36	115	676	54	52	33	49	600	32	780	112	45	1064
Macon	.252	141	4603	647	670	1158	1642	161	28	89	577	52	48	37	39	547	16	853	112	41	1012
Charleston	.251	143	4818	632	642	1209	1624	184	39	51	523	46	39	36	51	561	18	871	138	52	1116
Florence	.243	138	4505	628	638	1095	1570	193	27	76	518	50	51	28	36	532	16	910	98	42	993
Shelby	.238	142	4522	635	763	1078	1482	147	37	61	511	46	54	30	38	690	15	907	204	59	1057
Anderson	.234	143	4575	614	746	1071	1434	170	35	41	510	47	64	41	50	582	11	762	135	51	1047
Gastonia	.231	144	4658	541	557	1078	1469	182	34	47	454	52	45	37	41	486	24	857	79	20	1015
Spartanburg	.230	141	4450	641	633	1022	1470	189	35	63	506	48	23	33	47	586	16	952	274	78	899

INDIVIDUAL BATTING
(Leading Qualifiers for Batting Championship—389 or More Plate Appearances)

°Bats lefthanded.   †Switch-hitter.

Player and Club	Pct.	G.	AB.	R.	H.	TB.	2B.	3B.	HR.	RBI.	GW.	SH.	SF.	HP.	BB.	Int. BB.	SO.	SB.	CS.
Murphy, Daniel, Asheville°	.369	116	409	93	151	241	28	4	18	88	7	5	6	2	69	9	54	20	3
Orsulak, Joseph, Greenwood°	.315	118	460	80	145	197	18	8	6	70	3	2	7	1	29	3	32	18	7
Tarver, Laschelle, Shelby°	.314	110	427	78	134	158	14	5	0	27	2	2	0	4	48	1	44	57	12
Reynolds, Jeffrey, Greensboro	.306	125	474	83	145	257	28	3	26	103	16	0	7	3	41	3	91	6	9
Ojeda, Luis, Gastonia	.304	109	398	58	121	160	18	6	3	53	7	2	8	3	38	5	28	8	1
Clack, Marvin, Greenwood	.303	122	468	87	142	164	11	4	1	27	1	4	2	5	63	3	89	30	15
Winters, Matthew, Greensboro°	.300	125	404	85	121	196	23	2	16	76	13	1	9	6	94	5	66	7	4
Davis, Trench, Greenwood°	.298	141	530	70	158	212	24	9	4	73	10	2	3	2	41	5	81	31	6
Ubri, Fermin, Shelby	.297	133	468	63	139	173	20	4	2	52	4	8	7	3	32	0	52	11	3
Gagne, Gregory, Greensboro	.297	104	364	71	108	162	21	3	9	48	4	5	5	2	49	0	72	14	9

Departmental Leaders: G—T. Davis, Hansen, 141; AB—T. Davis, Dunbar, 530; R—Stone, 108; H—T. Davis, 158; TB—Reynolds, 257; 2B—Dunbar, 33; 3B—Delarosa, 10; HR—Dodd, 29; RBI—Reynolds, 103; GWRBI—Reynolds, 16; SH—Best, 11; SF—Tiamo, 11; BB—Dowell, 114; HP—Stone, 15; SO—Schroeder, 142; SB—Stone, 123; CS—Clack, 15.

(All Players—Listed Alphabetically)

Player and Club	Pct.	G.	AB.	R.	H.	TB.	2B.	3B.	HR.	RBI.	GW.	SH.	SF.	HP.	BB.	Int. BB.	SO.	SB.	CS.
Aguayo, Carmelo, Asheville	.295	86	308	59	91	141	19	5	7	48	2	0	0	2	48	1	30	2	2
Arias, Juan, Greenwood	.170	36	112	12	19	27	3	1	1	10	2	1	0	0	7	0	50	3	1
Arroyo, Hector, Charleston°	.232	93	353	39	82	94	8	2	0	32	1	3	0	1	40	0	54	12	8
Ayala, Eric, Anderson-Shelby	.231	59	186	35	43	47	2	1	0	16	2	3	1	5	29	0	22	17	5
Bailey, David, Greensboro	.212	66	203	22	43	63	8	0	4	20	3	0	2	0	25	0	33	2	1
Bailey, Welby, Anderson	.203	18	48	7	10	19	3	0	2	13	2	0	0	1	10	0	6	0	0
Baker, Christopher, Macon	.293	89	259	31	76	98	7	0	5	41	5	2	3	4	26	2	31	3	4
Benza, Brett, Asheville	.232	85	280	48	65	81	10	3	0	18	0	8	3	5	32	3	37	15	1
Best, William, Charleston°	.275	123	447	61	123	170	20	3	7	47	3	11	6	3	74	2	51	10	3
Bonner, Mark, Anderson	.223	28	94	16	21	30	6	0	1	14	1	1	2	1	18	0	20	0	0
Brill, Clinton, Anderson	.139	30	72	7	10	14	1	0	1	8	0	5	0	1	8	0	20	0	0
Bryeans, Christopher, Charleston	.248	53	149	20	37	42	5	0	0	15	0	2	2	5	14	1	27	4	2
Bundy, Lorenzo, Asheville°	.290	24	69	10	20	35	4	1	3	17	1	0	2	2	9	1	8	0	0
Burley, Anthony, Greenwood†	.250	16	36	5	9	11	0	1	0	3	1	3	0	0	9	0	8	0	0
Cadahia, C. Benito, Charleston	.220	110	346	47	76	103	16	1	3	32	5	7	1	0	54	0	72	1	0
Campbell, R. Thomas, Macon	.182	11	22	3	4	4	0	0	0	1	0	0	0	0	1	0	2	0	0
Canady, Chuckie, Asheville	.300	35	120	20	36	48	6	0	2	26	2	0	1	2	17	1	18	3	0
Carroll, Preston, Spartanburg	.000	1	2	0	0	0	0	0	0	0	0	0	0	0	2	0	0	0	0
Casasnovas, Roberto, Macon°	.226	113	349	60	79	157	12	3	20	64	6	4	2	7	73	4	107	11	3
Casteneda, Nick, Greenwood°	.301	57	186	25	56	73	11	0	2	26	4	1	1	2	17	1	29	1	0
Cazares, Jose, Gastonia	.254	125	418	49	106	132	18	4	0	31	5	4	2	4	48	0	59	8	3
Chamberlain, William, Shelby	.257	31	109	11	28	39	5	0	2	22	4	0	1	2	13	0	24	1	1
Chavez, Pedro, Macon	.247	99	324	42	80	100	10	2	2	24	4	5	2	1	8	0	47	5	0
Chmil, Steven, Anderson	.245	68	233	25	57	72	8	2	1	22	2	6	2	3	11	0	33	11	1
Cicatiello, Gary, Gastonia°	.235	135	523	59	123	161	17	3	5	56	11	6	1	2	29	5	71	3	2
Clack, Marvin, Greenwood	.303	122	468	87	142	164	11	4	1	27	1	4	2	5	63	3	89	30	15
Clow, Dennis, Anderson	.219	57	187	30	41	63	10	0	4	19	1	1	1	6	33	0	41	0	0
Cooperrider, James, Shelby°	.000	31	1	0	0	0	0	0	0	0	0	0	0	0	0	0	1	0	0
Cordova, Wilfrido, Greenwood	.000	39	2	0	0	0	0	0	0	0	0	0	0	0	0	0	1	0	0
Cormack, Terry, Anderson°	.250	27	68	2	17	22	3	1	0	8	3	1	0	0	9	0	17	0	0
Crafort, Samuel, Asheville†	.143	16	42	9	6	7	1	0	0	3	1	0	0	0	8	0	19	4	1
Currier, William, Spartanburg°	.228	63	197	30	45	72	9	0	6	20	2	1	2	0	27	1	59	9	3
D'Aloia, James, Greensboro	.294	6	17	0	5	5	0	0	0	0	0	1	0	0	1	0	1	1	1
Darkis, William, Spartanburg	.235	70	226	34	53	92	17	2	6	32	5	0	3	0	26	0	78	6	1
Darling, Edward, Greensboro†	.250	11	32	4	8	10	2	0	0	1	0	0	2	7	0	0	13	0	1
Davis, Trench, Greenwood°	.298	141	530	70	158	212	24	9	4	73	10	2	3	2	41	5	81	31	6
Delarosa, Nelson, Greenwood°	.249	131	449	52	112	172	19	10	7	51	4	2	5	1	33	5	80	9	5
DelMonte, John, Gastonia°	.225	88	280	26	63	85	18	2	0	30	1	2	1	3	40	1	56	7	1
Demeter, Todd, Greensboro	.220	124	378	53	83	153	9	2	19	64	4	2	3	4	59	0	113	7	4
Denby, Darryl, Shelby	.150	38	100	16	15	24	2	2	1	6	0	1	0	0	20	0	28	11	0
Dennis, Roberto, Greensboro	.221	17	68	10	15	18	1	1	0	5	0	1	0	2	4	0	8	3	3
Dodd, Thomas, Greensboro	.274	103	351	77	96	208	15	5	29	95	11	0	2	10	50	3	115	5	4
Douglas, Claude, Macon	.308	30	91	17	28	34	3	0	1	7	0	0	1	3	7	0	15	2	2
Dowell, Kenneth, Spartanburg	.226	137	451	70	102	137	19	5	2	51	2	4	3	6	114	0	76	24	12
Dunbar, Thomas, Asheville°	.296	138	530	101	157	249	33	7	15	76	5	1	3	1	74	1	77	26	12
Dykstra, Lenny, Shelby°	.261	48	157	34	41	52	7	2	0	18	0	4	1	0	37	0	31	15	5
Echstenkamper, T. Michael, Gboro	.200	7	20	3	4	4	0	0	0	3	0	0	1	0	2	0	2	0	0
Ellenberg, K. Wayne, Spartanburg	.203	54	133	18	27	33	6	0	0	11	2	2	2	1	17	1	22	4	2
Escobar, Jose, Florence	.238	35	105	12	25	28	3	0	0	4	1	2	0	0	12	0	19	0	4
Filkins, Randy, Greensboro	.296	105	341	70	101	170	24	3	13	62	8	0	6	11	67	2	66	7	3
Ford, Kenneth, Greenwood	.311	21	74	12	23	31	3	1	1	11	2	0	1	5	0	0	12	3	0
Freeney, Delano, Spartanburg°	.199	63	181	23	36	67	11	1	6	24	2	1	2	1	36	0	34	2	0
Fuller, Leonard, Shelby°	.250	18	36	5	9	11	2	0	0	1	0	0	0	0	5	0	4	2	1
Gagne, Gregory, Greensboro	.297	104	364	71	108	162	21	3	9	48	4	5	5	2	49	0	72	14	9
Garcia, Agustin, Shelby	.191	109	304	30	58	80	7	3	3	24	1	8	1	2	20	0	89	7	4
Garnett, Bradley, Greenwood°	.205	52	146	17	30	54	4	1	6	21	2	1	1	0	20	2	58	2	1
Giansanti, Ralph, Anderson	.143	30	77	10	11	14	3	0	0	6	0	1	1	2	8	0	14	0	0
Gibbons, John, Shelby	.189	109	360	33	68	111	11	4	8	57	6	3	3	4	50	1	86	2	3
Gilmore, Lawrence, Macon°	.223	44	148	21	33	49	4	0	4	16	0	0	1	1	22	2	27	0	1
Gither,, Thomas, Macon	.254	51	181	27	46	60	7	2	1	19	2	1	0	1	25	1	20	7	3
Gomez, George, Asheville	.289	106	356	58	103	176	22	3	15	68	5	2	0	3	51	3	63	2	1
Gonzalez, Robinson, Spartanburg	.158	26	57	6	9	10	1	0	0	1	0	2	0	0	3	0	12	0	4
Good, James, Macon	.189	36	106	8	20	26	3	0	1	14	0	0	1	2	7	1	25	0	0
Granek, Lawrence, Charleston°	.197	22	66	6	13	17	2	1	0	7	0	0	0	6	1	1	17	0	0
Guerrero, Inocencio, Anderson	.199	60	146	21	29	44	4	1	3	11	2	2	0	2	28	1	40	0	0
Guzman, Luis, Florence	.244	92	295	38	72	103	12	2	5	32	4	6	4	1	13	0	52	2	0
Hansen, Roger, Charleston	.242	141	516	55	125	183	28	6	6	71	6	1	5	4	62	4	79	9	1
Haro, Samuel, Greenwood	.248	83	303	37	75	78	3	0	0	19	0	2	4	4	20	1	56	11	2
Harris, Garry, Florence	.253	130	495	73	125	194	20	2	15	64	7	3	1	5	48	2	94	22	4
Harris, Michael, Gastonia†	.209	62	220	17	46	60	9	1	1	24	5	8	2	0	3	0	35	3	1

Player and Club	Pct.	G.	AB.	R.	H.	TB.	2B.	3B.	HR.	RBI.	GW.	SH.	SF.	HP.	BB.	Int. BB.	SO.	SB.	CS.
Harry, Whitney, Spartanburg	.163	78	215	18	35	48	4	0	3	25	5	0	0	4	20	0	79	2	5
Hatcher, Harold, Charleston	.274	105	391	39	107	160	18	4	9	59	5	0	6	3	25	1	73	2	1
Hegman, Robert, Charleston	.260	100	311	43	81	91	8	1	0	22	3	2	2	2	41	1	57	7	8
Heiser, Bruce, Anderson	.235	72	260	28	61	74	9	2	0	25	4	9	1	1	24	1	31	5	2
Heller, John, Shelby°	.223	108	341	36	76	90	9	1	1	34	3	4	2	2	27	1	49	9	4
Helsom, Robert, Greensboro°	.289	118	394	79	114	190	17	4	17	68	9	1	2	1	78	1	78	4	5
Hennessy, Michael, Shelby†	.234	125	385	62	90	120	16	4	2	36	3	10	4	3	90	1	76	17	6
Hernandez, Gustavo, Anderson	.152	22	46	7	7	9	2	0	0	2	0	1	0	0	11	0	15	0	1
Hibner, David, Asheville	.237	23	76	15	18	31	4	0	3	6	0	1	0	2	14	0	26	2	2
Hicks, Robert, Gastonia	.191	103	371	38	71	122	16	1	11	45	4	1	2	3	22	1	119	2	1
Hilton, Gary, Shelby	.215	111	363	36	78	115	8	1	9	46	5	0	2	3	44	1	103	7	4
Hool, Gerald, Florence	.261	36	115	12	30	41	5	0	2	16	1	3	2	2	15	1	11	1	0
Howser, Thomas, Greensboro	.219	27	64	9	14	15	1	0	0	6	1	0	1	3	11	0	15	3	3
Hurdle, Michael, Florence	.196	69	204	28	40	57	7	2	2	21	0	3	2	2	30	2	57	8	1
Jackson, John, Shelby	.256	32	82	15	21	24	0	0	1	6	0	0	0	1	7	1	10	4	1
Jacoby, Donald, Gastonia°	.250	93	280	39	70	113	15	2	8	32	2	4	2	3	43	1	50	1	2
Jonson, Greg, Charleston°	.261	130	510	56	133	156	15	1	2	50	7	5	3	6	54	1	56	3	1
Kastelic, Bruce, Shelby°	.208	63	178	17	37	48	8	0	1	14	0	4	1	2	28	1	41	3	1
Kelly, D. Patrick, Florence	.284	90	324	53	92	133	14	0	9	38	5	0	1	1	51	0	59	5	5
Kingery, Michael, Charleston°	.268	69	213	33	57	77	3	4	3	25	4	3	1	2	26	1	45	12	3
Kinnard, Kenneth, Florence	.179	27	78	11	14	22	0	1	2	5	0	0	0	0	4	0	33	1	0
Klaus, Leonard, Anderson	.000	18	1	0	0	0	0	0	0	0	0	0	0	0	0	0	0	0	0
Kneuer, Frank, Greensboro	.252	85	278	38	70	109	16	1	7	43	7	0	5	4	30	2	29	1	2
Kolbe, Brian, Shelby	.000	20	1	0	0	0	0	0	0	0	0	0	0	0	0	0	0	0	0
Kovar, Jerome, Spartanburg	.143	9	21	3	3	3	0	0	0	2	1	1	0	0	4	0	1	2	0
Langham, Thomas, Florence°	.196	95	276	42	54	68	8	3	0	20	2	7	1	3	50	1	50	14	4
Laurie, Robert, Macon	.238	123	445	59	106	136	17	2	3	40	4	7	5	5	49	0	81	18	6
Lavalliere, Michael, Spartanburg°	.268	39	123	15	33	48	9	0	2	23	0	0	1	0	31	3	16	3	2
Lee, John, Anderson	.231	92	290	34	67	79	7	1	1	35	2	4	3	5	28	0	30	2	5
Lewis, Amos, Asheville	.249	78	249	45	62	106	9	1	11	48	6	1	2	0	51	4	87	1	3
Liggins, Danny, Gastonia	.203	46	153	13	31	41	3	2	1	13	2	0	0	7	0	35	3	1
Lowry, Dwight, Macon°	.251	67	231	30	58	70	6	0	2	32	4	0	3	0	25	3	39	6	2
Luzon, Robert, Florence	.232	116	380	52	88	112	13	1	3	48	2	8	4	6	47	0	83	31	7
Maloney, Joseph, Macon	.238	109	323	55	77	125	16	1	10	61	4	8	2	2	68	0	74	4	3
Marcano, Jose, Shelby	.077	6	13	3	1	1	0	0	0	1	0	0	0	0	2	0	6	1	0
Marte, Alexis, Florence°	.314	14	51	9	16	16	0	0	0	0	0	1	0	0	6	0	11	5	3
Martinez, Z. Tomas, Greenwood	.210	44	105	12	22	25	3	0	0	11	1	0	1	2	8	0	16	3	2
Mastro, Steven, Macon†	.262	23	61	9	16	17	1	0	0	2	1	2	1	2	16	0	12	1	0
Mata, Victor, Greensboro	.261	102	353	59	92	117	11	4	2	39	5	2	3	5	26	0	56	8	3
Maxwell, Jamie, Asheville°	.254	110	402	56	102	163	23	1	12	53	5	5	5	2	42	1	88	7	2
McCulla, Henry, Gastonia	.220	135	454	67	100	157	18	3	11	52	3	3	4	6	85	6	133	4	1
McNair, Robert, Florence	.266	137	518	77	138	204	23	2	13	75	11	4	7	2	57	1	90	8	1
Meacham, Robert, Gastonia	.182	74	274	24	50	65	8	2	1	18	1	5	4	3	37	1	47	11	1
Mead, Fred, Florence	.221	30	95	9	21	34	8	1	1	9	0	2	0	1	9	0	24	1	1
Mejia, Oscar, Asheville	.318	57	236	42	75	114	16	1	7	44	3	5	3	3	16	0	13	1	1
Melendez, Francisco, Spartanburg°	.268	85	306	44	82	106	13	1	3	36	1	1	3	0	32	1	57	5	3
Melvin, Robert, Macon	.272	114	412	56	112	175	19	1	14	64	10	3	3	2	35	1	71	5	4
Menzhuber, Charles, Gastonia†	.232	42	168	18	39	52	6	2	1	8	0	0	0	0	8	0	29	4	1
Michalek, James, Florence	.125	20	48	4	6	8	2	0	0	1	0	0	0	0	8	0	14	0	0
Millholland, John, Greensboro°	.261	85	272	42	71	77	3	0	1	19	0	3	0	2	36	0	27	26	8
Milligan, Randy, Shelby	.283	130	406	90	115	164	16	6	7	58	7	2	1	6	98	2	85	49	5
Murphy, Daniel, Asheville°	.369	116	409	93	151	241	28	4	18	88	7	5	6	2	69	9	54	20	3
Neal, Bryan, Anderson	.239	59	188	30	45	66	10	1	3	26	2	0	0	1	28	1	34	0	2
Neal, Willie, Charleston	.240	121	434	64	104	142	13	8	3	44	2	0	1	7	59	3	107	34	10
Neufang, Gerald, Asheville	.252	76	222	34	56	62	6	0	0	23	1	2	1	2	41	1	27	2	0
Norman, Gregory, Macon	.261	44	119	18	31	39	5	0	1	10	1	1	1	1	21	0	17	3	1
O'Leath, Robert, Greensboro°	.266	58	188	23	50	75	8	1	5	27	2	0	1	0	21	2	57	1	2
Ojeda, Luis, Gastonia	.304	109	398	58	121	160	18	6	3	53	7	2	8	3	38	5	28	8	1
Orsulak, Joseph, Greenwood°	.315	118	460	80	145	197	18	8	6	70	3	2	7	1	29	3	32	18	7
Palma, Michael, Anderson	.234	67	244	29	57	75	9	0	3	20	0	2	2	0	10	0	31	2	0
Pastornicky, Clifford, Charleston	.216	80	296	36	64	98	15	2	5	36	2	3	1	2	16	0	23	6	4
Paula, Julio, Florence†	.248	58	222	30	55	74	12	2	1	27	3	1	2	2	21	1	32	6	1
Payano, Vidal, Anderson	.216	72	222	33	48	64	9	2	1	19	0	7	2	2	34	0	52	12	2
Perry, Jerry, Gastonia	1.000	28	1	1	1	1	0	0	0	0	0	0	0	0	1	0	0	0	0
Pierce, Walter, Gastonia	.214	34	14	0	3	4	1	0	0	1	0	0	0	0	2	0	5	0	0
Pittman, Larry, Shelby	.247	89	279	42	69	140	10	2	19	66	9	7	0	3	4	71	5	79	2	1
Plante, Daniel, Greensboro	.261	70	188	24	49	63	6	1	2	20	2	1	3	3	25	0	41	2	3
Powell, H. Lee, Spartanburg	.219	103	329	46	72	122	14	3	10	34	2	2	1	1	47	1	67	3	4
Pustorino, Frederick, Shelby†	.224	27	67	5	15	18	0	0	1	3	0	1	1	1	13	0	14	1	0
Quezada, Rafael, Anderson	.261	40	119	16	31	47	4	3	2	17	0	0	0	0	14	0	33	11	1
Ray, Steven, Shelby°	.143	30	7	0	1	2	1	0	0	0	0	0	0	0	0	0	2	0	0
Reeder, Michael, Macon†	.222	12	27	6	6	6	0	0	0	5	0	0	0	0	11	0	11	0	0
Renteria, Richard, Greenwood	.286	127	510	90	146	187	19	5	4	48	3	6	7	10	26	3	53	8	5
Reynolds, Jeffrey, Greensboro	.306	125	474	83	145	257	28	3	26	103	16	0	7	3	41	3	91	6	9
Reynolds, Larry, Asheville	.345	23	84	20	29	32	3	0	0	9	0	1	0	1	7	1	4	8	3
Reynolds, Leonardo, Spartanburg	.215	90	317	25	68	91	14	0	3	33	2	3	0	0	14	0	66	8	6
Ricciardi, John, Shelby	.178	104	292	31	52	58	4	1	0	21	4	6	1	1	49	0	48	4	5
Rice, Arlanda, Greenwood	.228	43	127	22	29	40	5	0	2	14	1	0	1	1	18	0	42	7	3
Rigby, Kevin, Anderson°	.217	46	115	15	25	29	4	0	0	7	2	1	0	1	14	0	14	1	2
Rivas, Rafael, Florence†	.237	55	173	12	41	48	7	0	0	22	3	2	0	3	12	0	43	2	4
Rizzo, Richard, Charleston	.251	133	518	95	130	190	26	5	8	46	3	2	5	10	56	1	61	31	6
Robertson, Glen, Greensboro	.261	84	276	45	72	94	12	2	2	37	3	1	4	3	32	1	28	1	0
Rollins, Rip, Spartanburg	.160	21	50	2	8	13	2	0	1	5	0	0	0	1	13	0	28	0	1
Samuel, Juan, Spartanburg°	.248	135	512	88	127	198	22	8	11	74	6	1	7	10	36	2	132	53	10
Sanchez, Jose, Gastonia	.261	53	165	17	43	52	7	1	0	18	3	1	2	2	8	2	21	1	2
Santos, Edward, Florence	.249	135	486	73	121	180	31	2	8	67	6	5	3	4	53	2	90	7	1
Sayler, Barry, Gastonia	.182	41	121	15	22	23	1	0	0	9	2	3	1	5	25	1	21	4	0
Schroeder, Jay, Florence	.204	131	417	51	85	134	17	1	10	47	3	4	6	4	81	0	142	4	5
Scott, Richard, Greenwood	.212	14	33	4	7	8	1	0	0	2	0	0	3	0	4	0	12	1	0
Silverio, Virgilio, Macon°	.274	110	409	66	112	146	13	9	1	45	4	9	3	4	37	0	65	22	3
Siriano, Rick, Anderson°	.290	115	383	69	111	154	24	8	1	38	7	4	6	7	51	2	64	19	8
Skinner, Joel, Greenwood	.266	117	428	48	114	176	25	2	11	63	9	4	4	4	27	2	99	2	0

Player and Club	Pct.	G.	AB.	R.	H.	TB.	2B.	3B.	HR.	RBI.	GW.	SH.	SF.	HP.	BB.	Int. BB.	SO.	SB.	CS.
Smith, Daniel, Greenwood	.294	5	17	2	5	5	0	0	0	1	0	0	0	1	0	0	6	0	0
Smith, Keith, Greensboro	.200	33	60	14	12	12	0	0	0	4	0	0	0	0	12	0	14	7	1
Smith, Mark, Macon	.242	125	454	48	110	160	16	5	8	48	3	4	6	1	31	1	64	6	5
Smith, Robert, Shelby	.125	13	32	4	4	5	1	0	0	4	0	0	1	0	4	1	6	0	0
Spears, Kenneth, Gastonia°	.253	135	513	66	130	166	17	5	3	43	3	3	6	3	64	1	82	15	3
Stefanski, James, Anderson	.251	107	359	40	90	122	13	2	5	40	5	2	7	3	47	1	19	3	2
Stephans, Russell, Charleston	.301	47	163	23	49	57	2	0	2	19	2	0	2	5	21	2	19	5	0
Stone, Jeffery, Spartanburg°	.277	134	516	108	143	183	13	9	3	53	9	0	1	15	60	4	90	123	13
Stryffeler, Daniel, Gastonia°	.227	17	44	5	10	11	1	0	0	3	1	0	0	0	7	0	7	1	0
Tabor, Craig, Asheville	.169	39	136	13	23	28	3	1	0	4	0	3	1	1	7	0	23	4	5
Tarver, Laschelle, Shelby°	.314	110	427	78	134	158	4	5	0	27	2	2	0	4	48	1	44	57	12
Thomas, Reginald, Macon°	.278	67	216	35	60	97	11	1	8	34	1	1	1	1	36	0	44	12	1
Tiamo, Jesus, Greenwood	.267	131	449	63	120	171	24	6	5	75	10	4	11	5	41	2	38	13	5
Tiburcio, Fredrick, Anderson°	.259	83	328	43	85	116	13	6	2	39	2	3	3	3	28	3	56	10	10
Tinkler, Jack, Gastonia	.098	22	41	4	4	4	0	0	0	2	0	0	2	2	2	0	13	2	0
Tjader, James, Asheville	.240	26	75	9	18	32	1	2	3	10	1	1	0	0	5	1	24	2	0
Trimble, David, Florence	.188	23	80	5	15	22	4	0	1	3	1	1	0	0	4	1	32	1	1
Tumpane, Robert, Anderson°	.204	57	196	20	40	66	6	1	6	28	3	2	0	2	26	2	32	1	1
Ubri, Fermin, Shelby	.297	133	468	63	139	173	20	4	2	52	4	8	7	3	32	0	52	11	3
Vann, Jesse, Shelby	.250	35	96	23	24	46	6	2	4	11	0	0	1	0	30	0	29	1	2
Vazquez, Francisco, Macon	.232	92	284	39	66	91	6	2	5	32	2	1	1	2	32	0	72	6	2
Venger, Tad, Charleston°	.267	30	105	15	28	44	5	1	3	18	3	0	1	1	13	0	40	2	0
Venner, W. Gary, Asheville°	.201	84	264	24	53	91	6	1	10	38	4	1	1	5	21	1	34	0	1
Villa, Boris, Greenwood	.184	77	212	20	39	42	3	0	0	13	3	6	0	0	6	0	36	8	2
Wallace, Brooks, Asheville	.154	55	169	16	26	29	3	0	0	11	1	3	1	1	14	0	34	1	1
Warner, Harold, Spartanburg°	.231	119	428	48	99	143	22	5	4	49	4	0	3	1	31	2	79	14	6
Weaver, Dale, Anderson°	.252	64	210	31	53	63	6	2	0	38	3	0	4	0	41	0	29	4	2
Weems, Charles, Gastonia	.176	32	102	6	18	23	2	0	1	7	1	1	2	0	7	0	23	0	0
Wheeler, Ralph, Florence	.277	133	523	89	145	204	20	9	7	67	3	7	4	8	58	5	57	11	7
Whistler, Randall, Anderson	.191	47	141	15	27	36	1	1	2	12	1	2	0	0	26	0	26	6	1
Wilkerson, Curt, Asheville	.204	106	333	45	68	81	7	3	0	19	2	9	4	5	26	0	53	12	5
Wilkinson, Rich, Asheville°	.266	111	364	57	97	149	19	3	9	67	8	4	3	7	48	4	61	0	2
Williams, Melvin, Spartanburg	.163	36	86	15	14	16	2	0	0	3	1	3	0	2	16	0	17	2	0
Winters, Matthew, Greensboro°	.300	125	404	85	121	196	23	2	16	76	13	1	9	6	94	5	66	7	4
Wirkus, Paul, Gastonia	.167	7	24	6	4	6	2	0	0	0	0	0	0	2	3	0	3	2	0
Ysambert, Sergio, Spartanburg	.133	15	30	4	4	4	0	0	0	1	0	1	0	1	1	0	4	0	1
Zunino, Gary, Gastonia	.245	31	94	13	23	31	5	0	1	9	1	0	1	0	7	0	20	0	0
Zureich, Jonathon, Macon°	.268	47	142	17	38	52	5	0	3	18	1	0	1	0	17	1	29	1	1

The following pitchers had no plate appearances primarily through use of designated hitters, listed alphabetically by club, games in parentheses:

ANDERSON—Ames, Kenneth (17); Ayers, Lynn (20); Clay, David (6); Coatney, Rick (12); Fisher, Brian (25); Fuller, Timothy (13); Hamer, Michael (19); Hinton, Michael (40); Rymer, Carlos (18); Soderberg, Jon (10); Treadway, Andre (28); Waddell, Thomas (13); Walker, Alan (27); Wex, Gary (25).

ASHEVILLE—Courtney, Matthew (15); Gammage, Mark (18); Hartman, Albert (36); Henke, Thomas (28); Henry, Dwayne (25); Henry, Timothy (18); Hudson, Anthony (16); Leach, Martin (9); Long, Dennis (12); Maki, Timothy (15); Mason, Michael (12); Mengwasser, Bradley (41); Moharten, David (1); Schmid, Michael (10); Smith, Darrl (29); Taylor, William (14); Zwolenski, Mitchell (9).

CHARLESTON—Albright, David (28); Cook, Douglas (17); Cutty, Francis (20); Gladden, Jeffrey (37); Huismann, Mark (28); Johnson, Abner (13); Johnson, Bert (17); Kennedy, Robert (Anderson) (23); Krauss, Ronald (16); McMichael, Charles (37); Meyer, Randy (6); Olsen, Michael (19); Ray, Glenn (29); Shaw, Theodore (6); Strode, Lester (8); Wong, David (52); Wyatt, Reggie (9).

FLORENCE—Blackmon, Thomas (5); Dickerson, Edwin (7); Holton, Mark (23); Langfield, Paul (16); Lovins, Steven (35); McKnight, Jonathan (27); Nawrocki, Matt (29); Pierce, Donald (34); Pursell, Joseph (27); Rahmer, Daniel (6); Schneider, Edwin (5); Shipanoff, David (52); Smith, Steven (38); Tackitt, Robert (12); Welenc, Douglas (24); Williams, Matthew (15).

GASTONIA—Alba, Gibson (5); Brown, Brian (3); Clark, Terry (53); Davis, Russell (16); Dozier, Thomas (11); Epple, Thomas (18); Martin, John (28); Neely, Alex (15); Pittman, Michael (10); Rhodes, Michael (48); Sanford, Edmund (22); Silva, Freddie (11); Warburton, Jeffrey (7).

GREENSBORO—Cartwright, Mark (23); Collins, Joseph (21); Fontenot, Ray (9); Foster, Michael (25); Gilliam, Melvin (Asheville) (24); Hernandez, Carlo (5); Kuhn, Lawrence (27); Mason, Martin (50); Mendez, Mark (18); Olwine, Edward (51); Peltola, William (7); Quirk, Kevin (5); Scott, Kelly (24); Szymczak, David (12); Toliver, Freddie (17); Vanderplas, Jeffrey (14).

GREENWOOD—Acker, Larry (8); Bielicki, Michael (28); Dodd, Lance (9); Edwards, Christopher (14); Fiepke, Scott (8); Gonzalez, Fernando (27); Green, Christopher (27); Horne, Jeffrey (23); Marcheskie, Lee (26); Muench, Timothy (13); Padgett, Glenn (5); Palmer, Bradley (14); Reams, Brian (12); Tingler, Meredith (2); Wheeler, Timothy (27); Williams, Donald (3).

MACON—Berthelson, Laurence (7); Cary, Charles (13); Davis, William (34); Gonzalski, Thomas (8); Hayford, Donald (5); Jacob, Mark (2); Kelly, Bryan (11); Lackey, John (6); Mason, Roger (26); Nail, Charles (13); O'Connor, Donald (13); O'Connor, Nicholas (25); Pankratz, Carl (33); Ross, James (37); Sanchez, Luis (5); Untisz, Michael (17); Valdez, Miguel (33); Vercoe, John (11); Woody, Harley (22).

SHELBY—Begue, Roger (15); Guinn, Wayne (26); Johnston, Jody (23); Magdzvik, Donald (8); Merlack, Scott (14); Pina, Elvin (45); Rech, Edward (20); Replogle, Mickey (6); Shockley, Lee (2); Spicer, Kevin (15); Sunderlage, Jeffrey (34); Teate, Kevin (25); Tibbs, Jay (13); Vaughn, Wayne (12); Webster, Richard (4).

SPARTANBURG—Acevedo, Julio (31); Darnell, Jimmy (24); Dorin, Matthew (33); Ghelfi, Anthony (27); Griffin, Frankie (37); Gross, Kevin (28); Johnson, William (52); Richardson, Ronald (28); Rodriguez, Yonis (11); Schiavo, Edward (20); True, Steven (24); Wojna, Edward (27).

GRAND SLAM HOME RUNS—Dodd, 2; Best, Cadahia, Cassanovas, Chamberlain, Cicatiello, Demeter, Gagne, Gomez, Helsom, Hilton, Lowry, McNair, Rice, Samuel, Skinner, Wheeler, 1 each.

AWARDED FIRST BASE ON INTERFERENCE—Winters 2 (McCulla, Powell); Gilmore (McCulla); Jacoby (Lowry); Johnson (Guerrero).

CLUB FIELDING

Club	Pct.	G.	PO.	A.	E.	DP.	PB.	Club	Pct.	G.	PO.	A.	E.	DP.	PB.
Charleston	.966	143	3774	1625	192	112	33	Gastonia	.954	144	3694	1551	251	105	29
Greensboro	.965	141	3589	1627	187	149	16	Spartanburg	.953	141	3602	1629	260	115	31
Macon	.959	141	3589	1470	218	128	28	Shelby	.947	142	3610	1367	279	93	22
Florence	.958	138	3508	1544	221	105	33	Anderson	.946	143	3615	1405	286	98	60
Asheville	.955	143	3637	1779	258	135	15	Greenwood	.945	144	3707	1416	298	107	22

Triple Plays—Greenwood, Macon, Spartanburg.

INDIVIDUAL FIELDING

°Throws lefthanded.

FIRST BASEMEN

Player and Club	Pct.	G.	PO.	A.	E.	DP.	Player and Club	Pct.	G.	PO.	A.	E.	DP.
Bailey, Greensboro	.995	25	204	8	1	30	Benza, Asheville	1.000	1	8	0	0	1
Bailey, Anderson	.900	6	17	1	2	2	Bundy, Asheville	.982	11	104	5	2	11

FIRST BASEMEN—Continued

Player and Club	Pct.	G.	PO.	A.	E.	DP.	Player and Club	Pct.	G.	PO.	A.	E.	DP.
Castaneda, Greenwood	.989	39	315	28	4	27	Maloney, Macon	1.000	1	8	0	0	0
Cicatiello, Gastonia°	.978	134	1233	82	29	80	Mata, Greensboro	1.000	1	13	0	0	0
Clow, Anderson	.990	37	288	13	3	21	Maxwell, Asheville	.985	20	180	12	3	15
Darling, Greensboro	1.000	5	44	4	0	5	McNair, Florence°	.987	137	1314	107	18	91
Davis, Greenwood°	.971	104	838	28	26	62	Melendez, Spartanburg°	.985	76	749	55	12	60
DEMETER, Greensboro	.988	123	1088	62	14	85	Norman, Macon	.990	35	272	14	3	28
Freeney, Spartanburg°	.976	18	151	14	4	11	O'Leath, Greenwood	.958	7	41	5	2	4
Garnett, Greenwood°	.900	1	8	1	1	0	Pittman, Shelby	.968	52	371	21	13	28
Gilmore, Macon°	.954	40	360	10	18	29	Rollins, Spartanburg	.857	1	6	0	1	0
Good, Macon	.955	2	18	3	1	1	Sayler, Gastonia	.929	2	13	0	1	2
Guerrero, Anderson	1.000	1	4	0	0	0	Smith, Macon	.996	25	218	8	1	21
Hansen, Charleston	.987	135	1180	74	17	93	Spears, Gastonia°	.909	3	7	3	1	0
Harry, Spartanburg	.974	58	472	20	13	35	Stefanski, Anderson	.988	85	724	33	9	50
Hatcher, Charleston	1.000	7	67	5	0	3	Tiamo, Greenwood	.750	1	3	0	1	0
Heller, Shelby	.967	20	136	9	5	8	Tjader, Asheville	1.000	4	48	3	0	3
Hennessy, Shelby	1.000	1	3	0	0	0	Tumpane, Anderson°	.979	22	177	12	4	17
Hilton, Shelby	.987	83	627	47	9	46	Wilkinson, Asheville°	.984	91	908	61	16	74
Jonson, Charleston	1.000	1	5	0	0	0	Winters, Greensboro	1.000	2	8	0	0	1
Kelly, Florence	1.000	1	6	0	0	1	Wirkus, Gastonia	.984	7	58	4	1	12
Laurie, Macon	1.000	7	55	1	0	2	Zunino, Gastonia	1.000	1	10	1	0	0
Lewis, Asheville	.966	25	194	7	7	18	Zureich, Macon°	.988	45	362	32	5	36

Triple Plays—Harry, Zureich.

SECOND BASEMEN

Player and Club	Pct.	G.	PO.	A.	E.	DP.	Player and Club	Pct.	G.	PO.	A.	E.	DP.
Aguayo, Asheville	.962	36	79	121	8	25	Kinnard, Florence	1.000	1	2	1	0	0
Arroyo, Charleston	.952	91	211	243	23	46	Laurie, Macon	.945	108	241	325	33	69
Ayala, Anderson-Shelby	.857	5	5	7	2	2	Maloney, Macon	.943	14	31	35	4	9
Bailey, Greensboro	.947	13	27	45	4	9	Mata, Greensboro	.938	5	7	8	1	2
Bryeans, Charleston	.948	42	93	109	11	20	Mejia, Asheville	.957	7	20	25	2	2
Burley, Greenwood	.983	15	20	38	1	9	Menzhuber, Gastonia	1.000	5	13	11	0	2
Cazares, Gastonia	.955	84	156	245	19	36	Millholland, Greensboro	.956	71	118	189	14	37
Currier, Spartanburg	1.000	2	4	1	0	0	Norman, Macon	.750	1	1	2	1	0
D'Aloia, Greensboro	.955	5	9	12	1	2	Ojeda, Gastonia	1.000	1	0	6	0	2
Dowell, Spartanburg	.918	10	20	36	5	2	Pastornicky, Charleston	1.000	1	0	1	0	0
Gagne, Greensboro	.961	63	100	169	11	37	Payano, Anderson	.904	44	100	125	24	20
Garcia, Shelby	1.000	1	0	1	0	0	Ricciardi, Shelby	.977	47	112	103	5	17
Giansanti, Anderson	.919	27	49	75	11	14	Rigby, Anderson	.951	11	14	25	2	2
Gither, Macon	1.000	1	1	2	0	0	Samuel, Spartanburg	.932	133	280	409	50	82
Gomez, Asheville	.935	30	67	105	12	25	Scott, Greenwood	.927	14	22	29	4	7
Gonzalez, Spartanburg	.500	2	2	2	4	1	Tabor, Asheville	.961	10	31	18	2	10
Guzman, Florence	1.000	19	25	49	0	9	Tinkler, Gastonia	.931	9	11	16	2	3
Haro, Greenwood	.938	76	165	213	25	41	Tjader, Asheville	.978	19	38	50	2	8
HARRIS, Florence	.960	111	194	340	22	50	Ubri, Shelby	.935	108	200	260	32	45
Hegman, Charleston	.950	14	31	45	4	6	Vazquez, Macon	.934	25	44	70	8	12
Heiser, Anderson	.947	72	153	204	20	33	Villa, Greenwood	.935	55	89	111	14	24
Howser, Greensboro	1.000	10	18	24	0	6	Wallace, Asheville	.922	9	12	35	4	4
Jacoby, Gastonia	.956	59	117	165	13	28	Wheeler, Florence	.980	12	12	37	1	4
Jonson, Charleston	1.000	1	0	1	0	0	Wilkerson, Asheville	.943	44	100	163	16	27

Triple Plays—Maloney, Villa.

THIRD BASEMEN

Player and Club	Pct.	G.	PO.	A.	E.	DP.	Player and Club	Pct.	G.	PO.	A.	E.	DP.
Ayala, Anderson-Shelby	.800	12	5	15	5	2	Lavalliere, Spartanburg	.900	18	13	32	5	2
Bailey, Greensboro	1.000	6	3	12	0	0	Lee, Anderson	.873	78	53	147	29	12
Bryeans, Charleston	1.000	1	0	3	0	0	Maloney, Macon	.920	73	62	145	18	15
Casasnovas, Macon	.909	4	4	6	1	1	Martinez, Greenwood	.857	20	13	29	7	4
Cazares, Gastonia	.902	42	36	74	12	8	Mata, Greensboro	.920	12	8	15	2	0
Chamberlain, Shelby	.921	15	8	27	3	0	Maxwell, Asheville	.937	89	71	153	15	15
Clow, Anderson	.842	9	7	9	3	1	Mejia, Asheville	.880	24	26	55	11	3
Dowell, Spartanburg	.932	84	52	179	17	12	Ojeda, Gastonia	.916	102	88	195	26	14
Ellenberg, Spartanburg	.897	49	25	80	12	4	Palma, Anderson	.903	46	29	73	11	5
Escobar, Florence	.833	2	0	5	1	0	Pastornicky, Charleston	1.000	1	1	2	0	0
Filkins, Greensboro	.000	2	0	0	1	0	Paula, Florence	.891	57	37	127	20	7
Gagne, Greensboro	.950	7	7	12	1	2	Reeder, Macon	.840	7	6	15	4	1
Gither, Macon	.920	43	34	70	9	3	Renteria, Greenwood	.887	122	81	225	39	12
Gomez, Asheville	.825	29	24	42	14	7	Reynolds, Greensboro	.936	121	88	277	25	27
Guzman, Florence	.864	10	4	15	3	0	Ricciardi, Shelby	.877	49	52	62	16	10
Hansen, Charleston	.920	5	17	6	2	2	Rigby, Anderson	.795	14	7	24	8	0
Haro, Greenwood	.947	7	5	13	1	1	Schroeder, Florence	.869	69	34	95	21	6
Harris, Gastonia	1.000	2	2	6	0	1	Smith, Greensboro	1.000	2	0	7	0	0
Harry, Spartanburg	.727	4	2	6	3	0	Smith, Shelby	.821	12	6	17	5	2
Hegman, Charleston	.897	15	10	25	4	4	Ubri, Shelby	.938	21	23	37	4	4
Heller, Shelby	.825	19	13	20	7	2	Vann, Shelby	.831	24	22	27	10	2
Jacoby, Gastonia	.800	2	2	2	1	1	Vazquez, Macon	.947	20	19	35	3	3
JONSON, Charleston	.943	124	87	261	21	22	Wallace, Asheville	.733	9	9	13	8	1
Kastelic, Shelby	.907	15	12	27	4	2	Wheeler, Florence	.909	3	4	6	1	0
Laurie, Macon	.909	3	2	8	1	2							

SHORTSTOPS

Player and Club	Pct.	G.	PO.	A.	E.	DP.	Player and Club	Pct.	G.	PO.	A.	E.	DP.
Ayala, Shelby	1.000	1	1	2	0	0	Gagne, Greensboro	.927	44	65	99	13	21
Bailey, Greensboro	1.000	4	4	14	0	2	Garcia, Shelby	.892	105	168	269	53	36
Bryeans, Charleston	.909	4	2	8	1	2	Gonzalez, Spartanburg	.929	19	18	47	5	4
Chavez, Macon	.926	96	147	303	36	44	Guzman, Florence	.800	1	1	3	1	1
Chmil, Anderson	.929	68	93	194	22	33	Harris, Florence	.849	14	17	28	8	6
Clack, Greenwood	.875	121	167	349	74	61	Harris, Gastonia	.875	60	74	149	32	22
Dowell, Spartanburg	.936	44	64	142	14	19	Hegman, Charleston	.932	67	109	191	22	32
Dykstra, Shelby°	1.000	1	1	0	0	0	Heiser, Anderson	.000	1	0	0	1	0
Escobar, Florence	.899	26	31	67	11	13	Hernandez, Anderson	.896	19	29	31	7	8

SHORTSTOPS—Continued

Player and Club	Pct.	G.	PO.	A.	E.	DP.
Jacoby, Gastonia	1.000	3	1	4	0	0
Jonson, Charleston	1.000	3	5	6	0	2
Kastelic, Shelby	.884	38	50	80	17	14
Laurie, Macon	1.000	3	8	7	0	2
Lee, Anderson	.865	6	11	21	5	5
Marcano, Shelby	.850	5	5	12	3	2
Meacham, Gastonia	.932	73	107	235	25	30
Mejia, Asheville	.942	24	54	93	9	16
Millholland, Greensboro	.818	7	2	16	4	1
Milligan, Shelby	1.000	1	2	1	0	0
Ojeda, Gastonia	1.000	2	1	1	0	0
Pastornicky, Charleston	.964	74	144	231	14	34
Paula, Florence	1.000	1	1	2	0	1
Payano, Anderson	.868	21	39	53	14	6
Pierce, Gastonia	1.000	1	1	0	0	0
Reeder, Macon	.750	1	1	2	1	0
Renteria, Greenwood	1.000	4	6	7	0	0
Reynolds, Spartanburg	.936	85	132	308	30	62
Ricciardi, Shelby	.815	13	9	13	5	3
Robertson, Greensboro	.948	82	110	237	19	49
Smith, Greenwood	.923	5	5	19	2	2
Smith, Greensboro	.955	28	25	60	4	12
Tabor, Asheville	.891	30	59	113	21	17
Tinkler, Gastonia	.905	13	14	24	4	5
Ubri, Shelby	.824	3	4	10	3	2
Vazquez, Macon	.918	47	86	104	17	27
Villa, Greenwood	.899	22	27	44	8	11
Wallace, Asheville	.915	40	62	122	17	25
Weaver, Anderson	.878	36	55	89	20	13
WHEELER, Florence	.943	100	167	297	28	52
Wilkerson, Asheville	.961	59	88	209	12	30

Triple Plays—Reynolds, Vazquez.

OUTFIELDERS

Player and Club	Pct.	G.	PO.	A.	E.	DP.
Arias, Greenwood	.917	34	53	2	5	1
Bailey, Greensboro	1.000	1	1	0	0	0
Baker, Macon	.987	52	71	2	1	1
Benza, Asheville	.965	77	127	9	5	1
Best, Charleston	.978	108	170	8	4	2
Bonner, Anderson	1.000	26	36	2	0	0
Canady, Asheville	.956	32	39	4	2	0
Casasnovas, Macon	.949	101	145	5	8	1
Crafort, Asheville	.938	14	15	0	1	0
Currier, Spartanburg	.949	54	73	1	4	0
Darkis, Spartanburg	.990	69	96	2	1	1
Daulton, Spartanburg	1.000	2	7	0	0	0
Davis, Greenwood	.943	38	79	3	5	0
De La Rosa, Greenwood°	.944	130	224	10	14	0
DelMonte, Gastonia°	.969	87	204	13	7	4
Demeter, Greensboro	1.000	1	2	0	0	0
Denby, Shelby	.986	36	64	4	1	2
Dennis, Greensboro	.947	17	34	2	2	0
Dodd, Greensboro	.964	68	105	3	4	0
Douglas, Macon	1.000	24	39	0	0	0
Dowell, Spartanburg	1.000	6	3	0	0	0
Dunbar, Charleston°	.939	134	184	15	13	1
Dykstra, Shelby°	.957	44	85	3	4	3
Echstenkamper, Greensboro	1.000	4	7	0	0	0
Filkins, Greensboro	.977	87	114	11	3	2
Ford, Greenwood	.976	21	37	3	1	0
Fuller, Shelby	1.000	13	16	0	0	0
Garnett, Greenwood°	.778	14	14	0	4	0
Gomez, Asheville	.967	12	27	2	1	0
Grahek, Charleston°	1.000	4	6	1	0	0
Harris, Florence	1.000	1	1	0	0	0
Harry, Spartanburg	.000	1	0	0	1	0
Hegman, Charleston	1.000	1	1	0	0	0
Heller, Shelby	1.000	15	19	0	0	0
Helsom, Greensboro	.966	109	193	7	7	1
Hennessy, Shelby	.972	123	198	9	6	3
Hibner, Asheville	.973	20	32	4	1	1
Hicks, Gastonia	.946	100	178	15	11	4
Hool, Florence	1.000	4	2	0	0	0
Hurdle, Florence	.971	66	130	6	4	0
Jackson, Shelby	.929	19	25	1	2	0
Kelly, Florence	1.000	2	2	0	0	0
Kingery, Charleston°	.956	62	80	7	4	0
Kinnard, Florence	.944	13	17	0	1	0
Langham, Florence°	.940	90	133	8	9	0
Lavalliere, Spartanburg	1.000	1	3	0	0	0
Lewis, Asheville	.920	21	21	2	2	0
Liggins, Gastonia	.971	44	62	5	2	0
Luzon, Anderson	.966	113	215	13	8	1
Marte, Florence°	.900	13	18	0	2	0
Martinez, Greenwood	1.000	2	1	0	0	0
Mastro, Macon	1.000	17	27	0	0	0
Mata, Greensboro	.954	81	137	9	7	4
Mead, Florence	.957	17	20	2	1	0
Melendez, Spartanburg°	.722	9	11	2	5	1
Menzhuber, Gastonia	.982	33	48	6	1	1
Michalek, Florence	1.000	2	3	0	0	0
Milligan, Shelby	.926	104	172	4	14	1
Murphy, Asheville°	.951	111	133	4	7	0
Neal, Anderson°	.969	53	88	6	3	0
Neal, Charleston	.953	121	170	11	9	1
ORSULAK, Greenwood°	.985	113	249	16	4	4
Palma, Anderson	.897	20	32	3	4	0
Quezada, Anderson	.889	31	52	4	7	0
Reynolds, Asheville	.936	19	27	2	2	0
Rice, Greenwood	.922	40	54	5	5	1
Rigby, Anderson	1.000	1	3	0	0	0
Rizzo, Charleston	.979	132	262	18	6	4
Rollins, Spartanburg	.950	16	19	0	1	0
Sanchez, Gastonia	.972	36	67	3	2	1
Santos, Florence	.935	133	178	9	13	1
Schroeder, Florence	.923	61	78	6	7	1
Silverio, Macon°	.952	101	190	8	10	3
Siriano, Anderson°	.964	114	196	15	8	3
Smith, Macon	.980	93	143	3	3	0
Spears, Charleston	.926	130	198	15	17	2
Stone, Spartanburg	.948	134	264	11	15	3
Stryffeler, Gastonia	.880	17	19	3	3	1
Tarver, Shelby°	.985	106	247	9	4	1
Thomas, Macon°	.944	64	80	4	5	0
Tiamo, Greenwood	.990	66	93	6	1	0
Tiburcio, Anderson	.955	83	183	10	9	1
Trimble, Florence	.970	22	30	2	1	0
Venger, Charleston	1.000	18	22	1	0	0
Warner, Spartanburg°	.955	110	170	19	9	1
Weaver, Anderson	1.000	4	3	0	0	0
Wheeler, Florence	.968	12	28	2	1	1
Williams, Spartanburg	.902	30	44	2	5	0
Winters, Greensboro	.957	80	101	10	5	1
Ysambert, Spartanburg	1.000	8	8	1	0	0

CATCHERS

Player and Club	Pct.	G.	PO.	A.	E.	DP.	PB.
Aguayo, Asheville	.965	7	49	6	2	1	6
Bailey, Greensboro	.987	12	67	6	1	1	0
Bailey, Anderson	.944	13	64	4	4	0	3
Brill, Anderson	.974	30	168	20	5	2	9
Cadahia, Charleston	.981	110	772	101	17	11	26
Campbell, Macon	.958	5	19	4	1	0	0
Carroll, Spartanburg	1.000	1	2	1	0	0	0
Cormack, Anderson	1.000	26	140	12	0	0	10
Daulton, Spartanburg	.990	70	371	34	4	2	13
Gibbons, Shelby	.975	103	629	65	18	5	16
Good, Macon	.971	26	146	22	5	0	10
Guerrero, Anderson	.965	39	210	10	8	0	23
Hatcher, Charleston	.969	12	85	8	3	2	5
Heller, Shelby	.969	21	116	7	4	0	3
Hicks, Gastonia	1.000	1	7	0	0	0	0
Hool, Florence	.977	10	37	6	1	2	0
Kelly, Florence	.977	77	501	59	13	2	11
Kneuer, Greensboro	.989	79	481	57	6	15	11
Kovar, Spartanburg	1.000	5	28	3	0	0	1
Lowry, Macon	.980	39	225	22	5	5	6
Martinez, Greenwood	1.000	4	11	0	0	0	3
McCulla, Gastonia	.971	75	461	48	15	5	16
MELVIN, Macon	.996	78	456	67	2	4	12
Michalek, Florence	.962	15	97	4	4	0	4
Neufang, Asheville	.979	75	401	62	10	5	6
Plante, Greensboro	.967	66	334	45	13	12	5
Powell, Spartanburg	.976	73	440	53	12	3	17
Pustorino, Shelby	.983	26	157	20	3	3	3
Rivas, Florence	.973	47	297	31	9	1	18
Sayler, Gastonia	.974	30	197	28	6	2	5
Skinner, Greensboro	.974	112	766	42	22	5	11
Stefanski, Anderson	.950	8	36	2	2	0	2
Stephans, Charleston	.975	25	173	21	5	1	2
Tiamo, Greenwood	.979	36	258	27	6	1	8
Venner, Asheville	.975	72	319	34	9	4	8
Weems, Gastonia	.991	17	107	8	1	1	3
Whistler, Anderson	.963	46	288	25	12	2	13
Zunino, Gastonia	.979	21	130	10	3	0	5

Triple Play—Lowry.

PITCHERS

Player and Club	Pct.	G.	PO.	A.	E.	DP.
Acker, Greenwood°	1.000	8	1	0	0	0
Alba, Gastonia°	.500	5	1	0	1	0
Albright, Charleston°	1.000	28	2	16	0	2
Ames, Anderson	1.000	17	2	5	0	0
Ayers, Anderson	1.000	20	3	3	0	1
Begue, Shelby	1.000	15	1	4	0	0
Berthelson, Macon°	1.000	7	0	2	0	1
Bielicki, Greenwood	.941	28	7	25	2	0
Blackmon, Florence	1.000	5	1	4	0	0
Cartwright, Greensboro	.923	23	7	17	2	3
Cary, Macon°	.923	13	5	19	2	1
Clark, Gastonia°	1.000	53	6	14	0	2
Clay, Anderson	.938	6	2	13	1	0
Coatney, Anderson	.875	11	0	14	2	2
Collins, Greensboro	.895	21	7	10	2	1
Cook, Charleston	.950	17	5	14	1	1
Cooperrider, Shelby°	.882	31	3	12	2	0
Cordova, Greenwood	.900	39	6	12	2	0
Courtney, Asheville°	1.000	15	0	6	0	0
Cutty, Charleston	.880	20	5	17	3	0
Darnell, Spartanburg	.938	24	5	10	1	1
Davis, Gastonia	.947	16	5	13	1	1
Davis, Macon	.867	34	3	10	2	1
Dickerson, Florence	1.000	7	0	2	0	0
Dodd, Greenwood	.833	9	1	4	1	0
Dorin, Spartanburg	.857	33	3	9	2	1
Dozier, Gastonia	1.000	11	2	5	0	0
Edwards, Greenwood	1.000	14	0	5	0	0
Epple, Gastonia°	.933	18	3	11	1	0
Fiepke, Greenwood°	1.000	8	2	1	0	0
Fisher, Anderson	.842	25	4	12	3	0
Fontenot, Greensboro°	1.000	9	3	16	0	1
Foster, Greensboro°	.952	25	5	15	1	1
Fuller, Anderson	1.000	13	5	14	0	0
Gammage, Asheville	.706	18	1	11	5	0
Ghelfi, Spartanburg	.864	27	7	31	6	2
Gilliam, Ashe-Gboro°	.900	24	2	7	1	0
Gladden, Charleston	.902	37	4	33	4	0
Gonzalez, Greenwood	.917	27	12	21	3	0
Gonzalski, Macon	.500	8	1	0	1	0
Green, Greenwood°	.886	27	3	28	4	0
Griffin, Spartanburg°	.917	37	5	6	1	1
Gross, Spartanburg	.923	28	14	22	3	0
Guinn, Shelby	.909	26	3	17	2	1
Hamer, Anderson	.857	19	2	4	1	1
Hartman, Asheville	.973	36	8	28	1	1
Hayford, Macon	1.000	5	0	4	0	0
Henke, Asheville	.889	28	6	18	3	4
D. Henry, Asheville	.968	25	7	23	1	0
T. Henry, Asheville°	1.000	18	2	5	0	1
Hernandez, Greensboro°	.750	5	1	5	2	0
Hinton, Anderson°	1.000	40	2	10	0	1
Holton, Florence	.933	23	11	17	2	1
Horne, Greenwood	.913	23	4	17	2	1
Hudson, Asheville	.889	16	7	9	2	1
Huismann, Charleston	.882	28	4	11	2	1
Johnson, Charleston	.870	13	4	16	3	2
Johnson, Charleston°	.938	17	3	12	1	2
Johnson, Spartanburg	1.000	52	5	13	0	0
Johnston, Shelby	.913	23	4	17	2	1
Kelly, Macon	1.000	11	1	8	0	1
Kelly, Florence	1.000	1	0	1	0	0
Kennedy, Anderson-Charleston	1.000	23	4	10	0	1
Klaus, Anderson	1.000	18	3	6	0	0
Kolbe, Shelby	1.000	20	3	5	0	1
Krauss, Charleston°	1.000	16	4	12	0	0
Kuhn, Greensboro	.947	27	2	16	1	1
Lackey, Macon	1.000	6	3	4	0	0
Langfield, Florence	1.000	16	6	9	0	0
Leach, Asheville	.950	9	6	13	1	2
Long, Asheville	1.000	12	3	5	0	0
Lovins, Florence	.875	35	1	6	1	0
Magdzuik, Shelby	1.000	8	2	8	0	0
Maki, Asheville	1.000	15	3	7	0	0
Marcheskie, Greenwood	.818	26	8	10	4	1
Martin, Gastonia	.974	28	15	22	1	2
Mason, Greensboro	.865	50	8	24	5	1
Mason, Asheville°	.971	12	7	27	1	2

Player and Club	Pct.	G.	PO.	A.	E.	DP.
Mason, Macon	.909	26	8	12	2	1
McKnight, Florence	.938	27	12	33	3	4
McMichael, Charleston°	.963	37	5	21	1	1
Mendez, Greensboro	.950	18	4	15	1	0
Mengwasser, Asheville	.914	41	8	24	3	2
Merlack, Shelby°	.846	14	5	6	2	0
Meyer, Charleston	.833	6	3	2	1	0
Muench, Greenwood	.800	13	2	2	1	0
Nail, Macon	.966	13	8	20	1	0
Nawrocki, Florence	.936	29	10	19	2	1
Neely, Gastonia	1.000	15	0	1	0	0
D. O'Connor, Macon	.813	13	8	5	3	1
N. O'Connor, Macon	.947	25	7	11	1	1
Olson, Charleston	.889	19	5	19	3	5
Olwine, Greensboro°	.813	51	2	11	3	1
Padgett, Greenwood	1.000	5	1	3	0	0
Palmer, Greenwood°	.600	14	0	3	2	0
Pankratz, Macon	1.000	33	5	9	0	1
Peltola, Greensboro	1.000	7	1	6	0	1
Perry, Gastonia	.943	28	10	23	2	1
Pierce, Florence°	.833	34	3	12	3	1
Pierce, Gastonia	.919	27	10	24	3	1
Pina, Shelby	.867	45	3	10	2	0
Pittman, Gastonia°	.667	10	1	3	2	0
Pursell, Florence	.957	27	11	33	2	7
Quirk, Gastonia	.875	5	1	6	1	0
Rahmer, Florence°	.833	6	1	4	1	0
Ray, Charleston	.852	29	8	15	4	0
Ray, Shelby°	.938	26	6	24	2	2
Reams, Greenwood	1.000	12	3	4	0	0
Rech, Shelby°	.880	20	6	16	3	2
Replogle, Shelby	1.000	6	0	2	0	1
Rhodes, Macon	.889	48	2	22	3	0
Richardson, Spartanburg	.917	28	8	25	3	1
Rodriguez, Spartanburg	1.000	11	1	3	0	0
Ross, Macon	1.000	37	4	13	0	0
Rymer, Anderson	.667	18	3	5	4	0
Sanford, Gastonia	.941	22	9	23	2	2
Schiavo, Spartanburg	.800	20	2	2	1	0
Schneider, Florence°	1.000	5	1	3	0	0
Scott, Greensboro	.907	24	13	26	4	0
Shaw, Charleston	1.000	6	2	4	0	0
Shipanoff, Florence	.966	52	8	20	1	0
Shockley, Shelby	1.000	2	0	1	0	0
Silva, Gastonia	1.000	11	8	12	0	2
Smith, Asheville	.962	29	18	32	2	2
Smith, Florence	.939	38	4	27	2	5
Soderberg, Anderson	.600	10	0	3	2	0
Spicer, Shelby°	.914	15	3	29	3	0
Strode, Charleston°	1.000	8	3	12	0	3
Sunderlage, Shelby°	.933	33	2	12	1	1
Szymczak, Greensboro°	.909	12	2	8	1	0
Tackitt, Florence	.750	12	0	3	1	0
Taylor, Asheville	.882	14	3	12	2	0
Teate, Shelby	.909	25	8	12	2	0
Tibbs, Shelby	.800	13	3	9	3	1
Toliver, Greensboro	.955	17	5	16	1	0
Treadway, Anderson	.926	28	10	15	2	0
True, Spartanburg°	.867	24	4	9	2	1
Untisz, Macon	1.000	17	0	3	0	0
Valdez, Macon	.941	33	11	5	1	0
Vanderplas, Greensboro°	1.000	14	4	14	0	4
Vaughn, Shelby	.833	12	1	4	1	0
Vercoe, Macon°	1.000	11	1	3	0	1
Waddell, Anderson	1.000	13	1	7	0	0
Walker, Anderson	.950	27	3	16	1	1
Warburton, Gastonia°	.000	7	0	0	1	0
Webster, Macon	.857	4	1	5	1	0
Welenc, Florence	1.000	24	7	14	0	1
Wex, Anderson	.889	25	2	6	1	0
WHEELER, Greenwood	.976	27	13	27	1	0
Williams, Greenwood°	1.000	3	0	1	0	0
Williams, Florence	.944	15	11	23	2	2
Wojna, Spartanburg	.875	27	14	28	6	2
Wong, Charleston	.931	52	8	19	2	3
Woody, Macon°	.917	22	3	8	1	1
Wyatt, Charleston°	1.000	9	4	5	0	1
Zwolensky, Asheville	1.000	9	0	5	0	1

Triple Play—Green.

The following players do not have any recorded accepted chances at the positions indicated; therefore, are not listed in the fielding averages for those particular positions: Aguayo, of; Ayala, of; Brown, p; Cazares, p; Daulton, 3b; Delarosa, 3b; L. Fuller, p; Garnett, 2b; Guzman, of; Jackson, ss; Jacob, p; Jacoby, of; Kinnard, ss; Langham, ss; Lee, p-3b; Lewis, p-3b; Maloney, of; Mead, 3b; Millholland, 3b; Moharten, p; Neofang, of; Quezada, 2b; Ray, ss; Rigby, c; Rivas, ss, of; Sanchez, p; Schmid, p; Stefanski, 3b-of; Tingler, p; Zunino, of.

CLUB PITCHING

Club	ERA.	G.	CG.	ShO.	Sv.	IP.	H.	R.	ER.	HR.	HB.	BB.	Int. BB.	SO.	WP.	Bk.
Gastonia	3.11	144	37	10	23	1231⅓	1039	557	426	79	41	479	25	817	68	11
Greensboro	3.26	141	36	14	35	1196⅓	1087	560	433	72	24	526	21	851	87	4
Spartanburg	3.58	141	24	9	20	1200⅔	1146	633	477	68	49	512	36	776	80	10
Greenwood	3.71	144	44	5	17	1235⅔	1197	705	509	83	29	540	15	962	75	10

Club	ERA.	G.	CG.	ShO.	Sv.	IP.	H.	R.	ER.	HR.	HB.	BB.	Int. BB.	SO.	WP.	Bk.
Charleston	3.72	143	11	7	29	1258	1222	642	520	57	58	637	8	993	109	11
Florence	3.83	138	25	9	16	1169⅓	1140	638	497	63	48	501	18	893	92	9
Asheville	3.91	143	23	6	21	1212⅓	1143	666	527	89	54	585	14	724	89	4
Anderson	4.08	143	39	6	15	1205	1204	746	546	71	47	605	21	856	111	12
Macon	4.08	141	20	8	18	1196⅓	1187	670	542	68	52	545	17	810	45	8
Shelby	4.20	142	29	2	17	1203⅓	1126	763	561	95	51	698	19	843	85	16

PITCHERS' RECORDS
(Leading Qualifiers for Earned-Run Average Leadership — 115 or More Innings)

*Throws lefthanded.

Pitcher—Club	W.	L.	Pct.	ERA.	G.	GS.	CG.	GF.	ShO.	Sv.	IP.	H.	R.	ER.	HR.	HB.	BB.	Int. BB.	SO.	WP.
Gladden, Charleston	10	9	.526	2.09	37	4	2	21	0	7	116	88	36	27	5	9	26	0	112	3
Martin, Gastonia	11	13	.458	2.12	28	28	10	0	2	0	212	166	71	50	11	8	56	4	148	12
Ray, Charleston	13	7	.650	2.65	29	16	4	9	1	0	146	120	57	43	6	2	70	0	155	11
Sanford, Gastonia	13	7	.650	2.73	22	22	6	0	2	0	142	124	59	43	5	0	58	1	83	6
Mason, Greensboro	11	2	.846	2.73	50	0	0	28	0	10	122	97	61	37	9	2	39	5	86	5
Smith, Asheville	16	5	.762	2.76	29	22	7	4	0	1	160	136	65	49	7	4	57	0	64	9
Scott, Greensboro	16	6	.727	2.98	24	22	10	2	2	1	169	136	69	56	16	3	51	2	130	7
Welenc, Florence	10	3	.769	3.05	24	18	4	4	3	0	118	105	50	40	4	3	34	0	102	5
Ghelfi, Spartanburg	10	11	.476	3.07	27	27	4	0	2	0	164	165	85	56	7	8	55	4	108	4
Green, Greenwood*	15	7	.682	3.08	27	27	9	0	0	0	184	148	87	63	13	0	86	0	128	8

Departmental Leaders: G—Clark, 53; GS—Bielicki, Gross, Martin, Perry, Richardson, 28; CG—Wheeler, 15; ShO—Welenc, 3; W—Scott, D. Smith, 16; L—Pierce, 14; SV—Olwine, 19; Pct.—Mason, .846; IP—Martin, 212; H—Wheeler, 185; R—Treadway, Wojna, 107; ER—Treadway, Wojna, 82; HR—Teate, 24; BB—Ray, 103; IBB—Clark, 8; HB—Guinn, 12; SO—Wheeler, 166; WP—Hinton, 22.

(All Pitchers—Listed Alphabetically)

Pitcher—Club	W.	L.	Pct.	ERA.	G.	GS.	CG.	GF.	ShO.	Sv.	IP.	H.	R.	ER.	HR.	HB.	BB.	Int. BB.	SO.	WP.
Acevedo, Spartanburg	1	6	.143	4.38	31	6	1	17	0	3	72	80	44	35	5	2	23	6	26	6
Acker, Greenwood*	0	0	.000	6.23	8	0	0	8	0	0	13	19	11	9	1	0	5	0	11	3
Alba, Gastonia*	0	0	.000	3.75	5	1	0	2	0	0	12	7	5	5	1	1	8	0	13	1
Albright, Charleston*	1	0	1.000	3.83	28	0	0	11	0	1	80	74	36	34	3	4	35	0	51	8
Ames, Anderson	5	4	.556	3.71	17	0	0	16	0	2	34	31	20	14	4	3	17	4	20	0
Ayers, Anderson	1	2	.333	5.29	20	0	0	13	0	1	34	49	26	20	2	0	4	1	16	2
Begue, Shelby	2	0	1.000	1.29	15	0	0	12	0	4	21	19	7	3	0	1	4	0	18	0
Berthelson, Macon	0	0	.000	6.00	7	1	0	5	0	0	12	13	8	8	2	2	7	0	9	1
Bielicki, Greenwood	12	11	.522	3.42	28	28	10	0	2	0	192	172	95	73	11	3	82	2	163	6
Blackmon, Florence	0	1	.000	11.25	5	2	0	2	0	0	8	10	10	10	1	0	8	0	7	1
Brown, Gastonia	0	0	.000	6.00	3	0	0	0	0	0	6	10	5	4	0	0	6	0	7	1
Cartwright, Greensboro	15	4	.789	3.37	23	22	10	0	2	0	147	124	63	55	6	4	58	1	89	10
Cary, Macon*	5	5	.500	2.59	13	13	4	0	0	0	87	77	32	25	2	3	19	1	55	3
Cazares, Gastonia	0	0	.000	0.00	1	0	0	0	0	0	1	1	0	0	0	0	0	0	0	0
Clark, Gastonia	4	5	.444	2.16	53	0	0	51	0	13	75	56	23	18	4	1	25	8	66	2
Clay, Anderson	1	3	.250	1.88	6	6	4	0	1	0	43	35	10	9	0	1	24	2	17	3
Coatney, Anderson	4	5	.444	4.03	11	11	2	0	0	0	58	57	40	26	2	4	36	0	37	10
Collins, Greensboro	7	1	.875	4.50	21	8	1	7	1	1	68	77	40	34	3	1	26	1	37	6
Cook, Charleston	3	7	.300	5.79	17	17	1	0	0	0	87	98	65	56	9	3	64	0	71	10
Cooperrider, Shelby*	1	6	.143	4.10	31	6	0	9	0	0	90	98	66	41	6	5	50	5	47	6
Cordova, Greenwood	7	6	.538	1.78	39	1	1	36	0	11	81	44	22	16	2	3	51	3	106	3
Courtney, Asheville*	0	3	.000	3.48	15	2	0	7	0	2	31	30	16	12	1	1	19	0	27	5
Cutty, Charleston	2	8	.200	5.38	20	13	1	1	0	0	82	99	56	49	6	3	55	0	49	8
Darnell, Spartanburg	3	2	.600	3.12	24	8	1	8	1	0	78	85	40	27	6	2	18	1	29	7
Davis, Gastonia	6	8	.429	4.30	16	16	4	0	1	0	92	89	51	44	11	4	46	1	55	4
Davis, Macon	1	4	.200	4.03	34	9	0	12	0	2	96	104	62	43	3	8	52	0	63	4
Dickerson, Florence	0	1	.000	7.36	7	0	0	3	0	0	11	18	10	9	2	1	6	0	6	2
Dodd, Greenwood	1	2	.333	6.39	9	5	1	3	1	0	31	38	23	22	1	1	18	0	24	4
Dorin, Spartanburg	6	1	.857	1.61	33	1	1	17	1	1	84	69	20	15	2	2	30	5	54	2
Dozier, Gastonia	1	0	1.000	1.47	11	0	0	5	0	0	43	26	8	7	2	1	10	0	26	1
Edwards, Greenwood	3	0	1.000	3.88	14	3	0	6	0	0	58	68	34	25	4	2	17	1	35	3
Epple, Gastonia*	4	5	.444	4.37	18	8	3	4	2	0	68	53	37	33	8	4	34	1	54	10
Fiepke, Greenwood*	1	3	.250	5.59	8	7	0	0	0	0	29	29	27	18	0	0	30	0	27	6
Fisher, Anderson	6	8	.429	4.26	25	23	6	1	1	0	152	139	96	72	7	7	94	0	152	11
Fontenot, Greensboro*	4	2	.667	2.75	9	9	3	0	0	0	59	53	22	18	7	1	23	0	62	10
Foster, Greensboro*	8	3	.727	3.77	25	11	1	10	0	1	86	87	45	36	4	3	40	1	55	8
Fuller, Shelby	0	0	.000	9.00	1	0	0	1	0	0	1	1	1	1	0	0	2	0	1	0
Fuller, Anderson	7	4	.636	3.58	13	10	4	2	1	1	78	70	46	31	7	2	24	1	54	4
Gammage, Asheville	4	4	.500	4.21	18	15	3	0	0	0	92	91	53	43	12	3	53	1	53	7
Ghelfi, Spartanburg	10	11	.476	3.07	27	27	4	0	2	0	164	165	85	56	7	8	55	4	108	4
Gilliam, Ashe-Gboro*	3	1	.750	4.83	24	5	0	12	0	1	69	68	41	37	8	3	42	0	58	5
Gladden, Charleston	10	9	.526	2.09	37	4	2	21	0	7	116	88	36	27	5	9	26	0	112	3
Gonzalez, Greenwood	10	11	.476	3.52	27	25	6	1	1	0	161	170	92	63	16	5	52	2	128	6
Gonzalski, Macon	0	0	.000	6.00	8	0	0	6	0	1	18	19	22	12	1	1	30	0	10	6
Green, Greenwood*	15	7	.682	3.08	27	27	9	0	0	0	184	148	87	63	13	0	86	0	128	8
Griffin, Spartanburg*	4	4	.500	3.48	37	2	0	13	0	3	62	52	29	24	2	2	46	7	54	6
Gross, Spartanburg	13	12	.520	3.56	28	28	8	0	2	0	192	173	94	76	18	6	62	4	123	7
Guinn, Shelby	0	2	.000	4.91	26	3	0	11	0	0	44	45	41	24	1	12	39	1	22	2
Hamer, Anderson	2	3	.400	2.55	19	1	0	13	0	4	53	46	18	15	2	1	8	3	29	2
Hartman, Asheville	6	6	.500	4.11	36	4	0	17	0	4	105	110	67	48	9	7	52	4	54	7
Hayford, Macon	1	4	.200	6.55	5	5	1	0	0	0	22	26	21	16	0	1	17	0	15	4
Henke, Asheville	8	6	.571	2.93	28	8	0	19	0	3	92	77	36	30	5	3	35	4	67	6
D. Henry, Asheville	8	7	.533	4.43	25	25	1	0	0	0	134	120	81	66	21	4	58	0	86	8
T. Henry, Asheville*	3	2	.600	4.36	18	8	0	5	0	1	64	55	39	31	1	2	42	0	42	9
Hernandez, Greensboro*	1	1	.500	3.18	5	4	0	1	0	0	17	19	11	6	0	1	16	0	13	2
Hinton, Anderson*	3	7	.300	4.44	40	1	1	22	0	4	73	77	54	36	3	3	63	3	52	22
Holton, Florence	7	6	.538	3.50	23	17	2	2	0	0	113	103	55	44	8	4	47	0	92	12
Horne, Greenwood	4	4	.500	3.56	23	9	1	9	0	2	86	104	63	34	4	1	39	4	58	10
Hudson, Asheville	2	5	.286	5.58	16	6	0	8	0	2	50	60	41	31	3	4	36	0	23	4
Huismann, Charleston	3	2	.600	1.64	28	0	0	22	0	10	44	36	16	8	0	1	17	3	42	4
Jacob, Macon	0	1	.000	4.50	2	0	0	0	0	0	2	2	2	1	0	0	3	0	2	0
Johnson, Charleston	8	4	.667	2.54	13	13	3	0	0	0	85	84	37	24	2	0	37	0	49	8

Pitcher—Club	W.	L.	Pct.	ERA.	G.	GS.	CG.	GF.	ShO.	Sv.	IP.	H.	R.	ER.	HR.	HB.	BB.	Int. BB.	SO.	WP.
Johnson, Charleston°	4	4	.500	4.23	17	17	0	0	0	0	83	103	55	39	3	3	38	0	62	5
Johnson, Spartanburg	8	3	.727	2.84	52	0	0	48	0	12	57	45	26	18	2	8	40	2	40	5
Johnston, Shelby	11	8	.579	3.66	23	23	6	0	0	0	160	132	86	65	11	3	81	0	120	8
Kelly, Macon	4	3	.571	4.58	11	10	0	0	0	0	53	50	30	27	3	4	45	0	46	5
Kelly, Florence	0	0	.000	0.00	1	0	0	1	0	0	2	0	0	0	0	0	1	0	2	0
Kennedy, Anderson-Chstn	5	6	.455	5.46	23	13	1	4	0	0	89	86	68	54	8	11	89	1	64	16
Klaus, Anderson	2	3	.400	3.75	18	2	1	11	0	1	48	48	26	20	1	1	28	0	36	5
Kolbe, Shelby	3	2	.600	1.71	20	1	0	15	0	5	42	31	8	8	3	1	24	1	38	0
Krauss, Charleston°	2	3	.400	6.59	16	10	0	3	0	0	56	75	46	41	4	0	51	0	37	10
Kuhn, Greensboro	5	5	.500	3.19	27	11	3	4	1	0	96	89	41	34	5	3	46	1	65	6
Lackey, Macon	1	4	.200	5.91	6	6	1	0	0	0	35	47	27	23	3	0	18	1	19	0
Langfield, Florence	2	5	.286	7.96	16	10	1	1	1	0	52	64	54	46	3	2	34	0	44	11
Leach, Asheville	3	0	1.000	1.88	9	5	2	3	1	0	48	32	13	10	1	1	10	0	25	0
Lee, Anderson	0	0	.000	7.50	4	0	0	2	0	0	6	6	5	5	0	0	5	0	3	0
Lewis, Asheville	0	0	.000	13.50	1	0	0	1	0	0	2	3	4	3	1	1	2	0	1	0
Long, Asheville	1	1	.500	0.72	12	0	0	12	0	1	25	18	5	2	0	1	2	0	18	0
Lovins, Florence	2	2	.500	4.50	35	0	0	22	0	2	44	42	33	22	4	2	38	2	42	4
Magdzuik, Shelby	0	3	.000	7.59	8	5	0	0	0	0	32	40	31	27	1	1	22	0	14	4
Maki, Asheville	3	7	.300	5.23	15	15	2	0	0	0	74	81	49	43	5	6	47	0	40	3
Marcheskie, Greenwood	6	4	.600	5.22	26	5	1	12	0	3	81	93	68	47	2	8	33	0	43	11
Martin, Gastonia	11	13	.458	2.12	28	28	10	0	2	0	212	166	71	50	11	8	56	4	148	12
Mason, Greensboro	11	2	.846	2.73	50	0	0	28	0	10	122	97	61	37	9	2	39	5	86	5
Mason, Asheville°	8	3	.727	2.12	12	12	6	0	1	0	85	58	28	20	4	2	35	0	39	11
Mason, Macon	10	10	.500	3.89	26	26	4	0	1	0	148	153	77	64	10	7	50	0	105	4
McKnight, Florence	9	8	.529	3.24	27	27	7	0	2	0	172	139	73	62	12	9	77	0	119	6
McMichael, Charleston°	7	1	.875	3.43	37	1	0	21	0	3	84	80	37	32	2	5	25	0	62	9
Mendez, Greensboro	7	4	.636	3.00	18	18	3	0	2	0	114	109	49	38	5	2	55	1	67	9
Mengwasser, Asheville	8	5	.615	4.50	41	5	0	22	0	5	94	80	61	47	7	4	48	1	74	5
Merlack, Shelby°	3	3	.500	4.11	14	4	0	3	0	1	46	42	26	21	2	0	28	1	24	2
Meyer, Charleston	0	2	.000	7.67	6	6	0	0	0	0	27	38	29	23	4	2	19	0	24	1
Moharten, Asheville°	0	1	.000	6.75	1	1	0	0	0	0	4	5	4	3	0	1	1	0	2	0
Muench, Greenwood	1	2	.333	5.18	13	1	0	2	0	0	33	38	29	19	2	0	37	1	23	2
Nail, Macon	6	5	.545	2.70	13	13	3	0	1	0	90	68	38	27	3	3	34	1	73	3
Nawrocki, Florence	7	9	.438	4.30	29	16	1	4	0	0	115	122	72	55	3	5	55	2	75	11
Neely, Gastonia	3	2	.600	4.66	15	0	0	9	0	3	29	25	18	15	4	2	12	2	31	2
D. O'Connor, Macon	4	7	.364	4.80	13	13	0	0	0	0	75	74	44	40	7	4	28	1	58	3
N. O'Connor, Macon	7	6	.538	3.95	25	11	1	11	0	1	98	110	51	43	6	5	35	1	52	0
Olson, Charleston	3	6	.333	4.92	19	19	0	0	0	0	106	109	67	58	3	6	62	0	69	8
Olwine, Greensboro°	8	5	.615	3.00	51	0	0	43	0	19	75	67	35	25	0	1	25	5	73	5
Padgett, Greenwood	1	1	.500	4.05	5	4	0	1	0	0	20	18	14	9	1	2	11	0	7	3
Palmer, Greenwood°	2	1	.667	4.34	14	2	0	9	0	0	29	25	19	14	0	1	18	2	20	0
Pankratz, Macon	3	2	.600	4.88	33	3	0	20	0	2	83	85	55	45	6	1	38	4	50	2
Peltola, Greensboro	1	0	1.000	1.20	7	0	0	5	0	2	15	12	3	2	0	0	1	1	5	0
Perry, Gastonia	14	7	.667	3.19	28	28	5	0	2	0	178	143	79	63	15	5	61	0	118	9
Pierce, Florence°	3	5	.375	2.63	34	0	0	18	0	3	48	46	20	14	2	0	22	0	47	5
Pierce, Gastonia	5	14	.263	3.49	27	27	8	0	0	0	188	176	90	73	11	4	65	2	97	3
Pina, Shelby	2	6	.250	5.75	45	1	0	20	0	3	83	81	62	53	7	7	54	2	73	6
Pittman, Gastonia°	0	1	.000	6.19	10	0	0	3	0	0	16	17	21	11	1	3	16	1	7	2
Pursell, Florence	7	11	.389	3.53	27	24	4	1	0	0	148	167	81	58	8	3	34	2	78	9
Quirk, Greensboro	0	0	.000	3.38	5	0	0	1	0	0	16	13	8	6	2	1	15	1	15	0
Rahmer, Florence°	1	3	.250	14.06	6	4	0	0	0	0	16	24	26	25	2	3	19	0	12	4
Ray, Charleston	13	7	.650	2.65	29	16	4	9	1	0	146	120	57	43	6	2	70	0	155	11
Ray, Shelby°	2	12	.143	4.69	26	22	2	3	0	0	119	112	81	62	13	7	103	0	95	20
Reams, Greenwood	2	0	1.000	1.91	12	0	0	9	0	1	33	27	8	7	2	0	8	0	17	1
Rech, Shelby°	9	7	.563	3.82	20	20	7	0	0	0	139	114	79	59	11	3	65	0	113	6
Replogle, Shelby	0	1	.000	7.00	6	0	0	2	0	0	9	15	7	7	0	0	6	1	4	0
Rhodes, Gastonia°	6	8	.429	1.75	48	3	0	28	0	7	103	74	43	20	3	5	46	3	77	4
Richardson, Spartanburg	11	11	.500	3.53	28	28	5	0	1	0	176	155	93	69	6	7	95	3	100	7
Rodriguez, Spartanburg	0	1	.000	7.56	11	1	0	4	0	1	25	34	21	21	4	0	6	0	19	2
Ross, Macon	6	5	.545	3.32	37	0	0	31	0	6	76	67	37	28	4	2	28	4	60	2
Rymer, Anderson	0	7	.000	6.00	18	10	0	3	0	0	60	71	55	40	1	5	55	0	33	16
Sanchez, Macon	0	1	.000	13.0	5	1	0	3	0	0	9	13	16	13	0	0	13	0	5	0
Sanford, Gastonia	13	7	.650	2.73	22	22	6	0	2	0	142	124	59	43	5	0	58	1	83	6
Schiavo, Spartanburg	2	3	.400	5.54	20	0	0	5	0	0	39	38	37	24	5	1	26	0	17	8
Schmid, Asheville°	1	2	.333	5.06	10	0	0	6	0	0	16	21	10	9	1	1	8	1	8	0
Schneider, Florence°	1	0	1.000	4.85	5	1	1	1	1	0	13	10	7	7	1	1	4	0	9	0
Scott, Greensboro	16	6	.727	2.98	24	22	10	2	2	1	169	136	69	56	16	3	51	2	130	7
Shaw, Charleston	1	2	.333	3.90	6	6	0	0	0	0	30	27	15	13	2	1	25	0	24	2
Shipanoff, Florence	7	7	.500	2.67	52	0	0	34	0	8	101	78	40	30	4	2	44	7	101	0
Shockley, Shelby	0	0	.000	1.80	2	0	0	2	0	0	5	2	1	1	0	0	2	0	3	1
Silva, Gastonia	1	6	.143	5.64	11	11	1	0	0	0	59	62	43	37	3	3	31	2	28	10
Smith, Asheville	16	5	.762	2.76	29	22	7	4	0	1	160	136	65	49	7	4	57	0	64	9
Smith, Florence	3	6	.333	3.29	38	4	1	16	0	2	93	102	51	34	5	4	39	3	70	7
Soderberg, Anderson	0	6	.000	6.38	10	10	0	0	0	0	48	57	48	34	3	5	22	0	20	5
Spicer, Shelby°	5	9	.357	3.48	15	15	4	0	0	0	88	77	56	34	5	2	63	1	75	8
Strode, Charleston°	3	2	.600	2.54	8	8	0	0	0	0	46	39	14	13	0	1	32	0	35	4
Sunderlage, Shelby°	7	2	.778	2.80	33	0	0	25	0	3	45	38	19	14	1	1	19	2	27	4
Szymczak, Greensboro°	2	0	1.000	5.25	12	4	0	3	0	1	36	47	28	21	2	1	18	1	23	3
Tackitt, Florence	0	1	.000	7.43	12	0	0	4	0	1	23	29	23	19	2	2	12	1	16	6
Taylor, Asheville	1	7	.125	4.64	14	12	1	0	0	0	64	76	43	33	2	5	35	0	44	11
Teate, Shelby	8	10	.444	5.33	25	25	4	0	0	0	135	138	106	80	24	4	82	3	84	9
Tibbs, Shelby	4	8	.333	3.84	13	11	4	2	0	0	89	87	56	38	6	1	33	0	57	6
Tingler, Greensboro	0	0	.000	10.29	2	0	0	1	0	0	7	11	10	8	3	0	5	0	3	0
Toliver, Greensboro	5	3	.625	3.49	17	14	2	1	1	0	80	67	38	31	7	0	56	0	62	7
Treadway, Anderson	7	13	.350	4.17	28	27	8	1	0	0	177	176	107	82	17	5	73	3	157	9
True, Spartanburg°	2	3	.400	3.65	24	13	0	5	0	0	74	69	37	30	2	4	42	2	76	7
Untisz, Macon	1	5	.167	5.47	17	2	0	6	0	0	51	57	37	31	4	3	29	1	23	2
Valdez, Macon	4	5	.444	3.93	33	3	1	23	1	5	71	61	33	31	2	4	26	1	60	2
Vanderplas, Greensboro°	6	6	.500	3.33	14	14	3	0	0	0	73	70	37	27	3	1	46	1	47	8
Vaughn, Shelby	1	3	.250	3.10	12	2	1	8	0	1	29	27	17	10	3	1	10	1	18	2
Vercoe, Macon°	1	2	.333	4.06	11	3	0	4	0	1	31	34	16	14	4	1	18	0	24	1
Waddell, Anderson	6	3	.667	2.86	13	5	4	6	1	1	63	57	24	20	4	0	12	0	51	0

Pitcher—Club	W.	L.	Pct.	ERA.	G.	GS.	CG.	GF.	ShO.	Sv.	IP.	H.	R.	ER.	HR.	HB.	BB.	Int. BB.	SO.	WP.
Walker, Anderson	8	12	.400	3.61	27	25	8	0	2	0	167	179	98	67	12	1	59	2	96	7
Warburton, Gastonia°	0	0	.000	3.00	7	0	0	5	0	0	9	10	4	3	0	0	5	0	7	1
Webster, Shelby	1	1	.500	4.50	4	4	1	0	0	0	26	27	13	13	1	2	11	1	10	1
Welenc, Florence	10	3	.769	3.05	24	18	4	4	3	0	118	105	50	40	4	3	34	0	102	5
Wex, Anderson	1	3	.250	3.52	25	3	0	13	0	1	64	57	35	25	2	5	37	2	52	3
Wheeler, Greenwood	14	13	.519	3.60	27	27	15	0	0	0	195	185	98	78	21	3	47	0	166	9
Williams, Greenwood°	0	0	.000	9.00	3	0	0	3	0	0	4	8	5	4	0	0	1	0	3	0
Williams, Florence	7	4	.636	2.18	15	15	4	0	0	0	91	81	33	22	2	7	27	1	76	9
Wojna, Spartanburg	11	13	.458	4.15	27	27	4	0	0	0	178	181	107	82	9	5	69	2	130	19
Wong, Charleston	9	6	.600	2.52	52	0	0	41	0	8	82	66	29	23	3	11	22	3	65	5
Woody, Macon°	8	10	.444	3.30	22	22	5	0	2	0	139	127	62	51	8	3	55	2	81	3
Wyatt, Charleston°	5	1	.833	1.86	9	9	0	0	0	0	63	49	17	13	1	0	14	0	53	6
Zwolensky, Asheville	1	4	.200	6.67	9	2	1	4	0	1	27	42	20	20	4	1	14	3	21	0

BALKS—Fisher, Ray, 4 each; Cooperrider, Green, N. O'Connor, Pierce, Purcell, Treadway, Walker, Webster, Wong, 3 each, Acevedo, Epple, Ghelfi, Maki, Nawrocki, Olwine, Rech, Sanford, Shipanoff, Strode, True, Vercoe, 2 each. Bielicki, Clark, Cordova, Cutty, Davis, Dickerson, Dorin, Gammage, Gladden, Gonzalez, Griffin, Hamer, Hartman, Hayford, Horne, W. Johnson, Johnston, McKinght, Meyer, Neely, Olson, Padgett, Pankratz, Pina, Rhodes, Sanchez, Shaw, Soderberg, Sunderlage, Tibbs, Tingler, Toliver, Vanderplas, Wheeler, Wojna, Wyatt, 1 each.

COMBINATION SHUTOUTS—Henke-Coatney-Mengwasser, D. Henry-Hartman, D. Henry-Henke, Mason-Long, Asheville; Cutty-Albright, Johnson-Albright-Huismann, Krauss-Huismann, Ray-Gladden, Ray-McMichael-Wong, Strode-Gladden, Charleston; Holton-Pierce, Holton-Shipanoff, Pierce-Rhodes, Gastonia; Collins-Cartwright-Mason-Olwine, Fontenot-Mason, Hernandez-Scott, Mendez-Scott, Toliver-Mason, Greensboro; Bielicki-Cordova, Greenwood; Cary-Ross-Valdez, Kelly-Valdez, Nail-Valdez, Macon; Johnstone-Colby, Merlach-Pina, Shelby; Richardson-Acevedo, Richardson-Johnson, Spartanburg.

NO-HIT GAMES—Scott, Greensboro, defeated Charleston, 3-0, June 9, first game (seven innings); Walker, Anderson, defeated Florence, 5-0, August 15, second game (seven innings).

Appalachian League

SUMMER CLASS A CLASSIFICATION

CHAMPIONSHIP WINNERS IN PREVIOUS YEARS

1921—Greenville .... .608	1946—New River‡ .... .675	1965—Salem .... .614
Johnson City° .... .627	1947—Pulaski‡ .... .648	1966—Marion .... .623
1922—Bristol .... .557	New River (3rd)† .... .516	1967—Bluefield .... .627
1923—Knoxville .... .635	1948—Pulaski‡ .... .680	1968—Marion .... .583
1924—Knoxville° .... .642	1949—Bluefield‡ .... .721	1969—Pulaski a .... .576
Bristol .... .607	1950—Bluefield .... .600	Johnson City...................... .544
1925—Greenville .... .667	Bluefield z .... .745	1970—Bluefield .... .638
1926-36—Did not operate.	1951—Kingsport‡ .... .659	1971—Bluefield a. .... .609
1937—Elizabethton .... .559	1952—Johnson City .... .595	Kingsport........................... .559
Pennington Gap° .... .580	Welch (3rd)† .... .509	1972—Bristol a .... .588
1938—Elizabethton .... .664	1953—Welch° .... .705	Covington.......................... .586
Greenville (3rd)† .... .571	Johnson City...................... .672	1973—Kingsport .... .757
1939—Elizabethton‡ .... .597	1954—Bluefield‡ .... .619	1974—Bristol a .... .754
1940—Johnson City§ .... .726	1955—Salem°° .... .689	Bluefield .... .536
Elizabethton .... .750	1956—Did not operate.	1975—Marion .... .515
1941—Johnson City .... .614	1957—Bluefield .... .701	Johnson City a .... .603
Elizabethton° .... .661	1958—Johnson City .... .662	1976—Johnson City a .... .714
1942—Bristol .... .667	1959—Morristown .... .603	Bluefield .... .600
Bristol x .... .660	1960—Wytheville .... .614	1977—Kingsport .... .623
1943—Bristol .... .755	1961—Middlesboro .... .591	1978—Elizabethton .... .594
Bristol y .... .617	1962—Bluefield .... .671	1979—Paintsville .... .800
1944—Kingsport‡ .... .575	1963—Bluefield .... .652	1980—Paintsville .... .657
1945—Kingsport‡ .... .670	1964—Johnson City .... .662	

°Won split-season playoff. †Won four-team playoff. ‡Won championship and four-team playoff. §Johnson City, first-half winner, won playoff involving six clubs. xWon both halves and defeated second-place Elizabethton in playoff. yWon both halves, but Erwin won four-team playoff. zWon both halves, but Bristol won two-club playoff. °°Salem and Johnson City declared playoff co-champions when weather forced cancellation of final series. aLeague was divided into Northern, Southern divisions; declared league champion, based on highest won-lost percentage.

STANDING OF CLUBS AT CLOSE OF SEASON, AUGUST 31

Club	Pvl.	Eliz.	J.C.	Blu.	Bri.	Kpt.	W.	L.	T.	Pct.	G.B.
Paintsville (Yankees)	...	7	7	10	11	11	46	24	0	.657	....
Elizabethton (Twins)	7	....	9	5	12	9	42	28	0	.600	4
Johnson City (Cardinals)..................	7	5	....	7	7	10	36	34	0	.514	10
Bluefield (Orioles)	4	9	7	....	7	9	36	34	0	.514	10
Bristol (Tigers)...............................	3	2	7	7	....	10	29	41	0	.414	17
Kingsport (Mets)............................	3	5	4	5	4	....	21	49	0	.300	25

Major league affiliations in parentheses.

Playoffs—None.

Regular-Season Attendance—Bluefield, 21,525; Bristol, 9,486; Elizabethton, 11,932; Johnson City, 32,035; Kingsport, 22,630; Paintsville, 21,520. Total, 119,128. No playoffs or all-star game.

Managers: Bluefield, Lance Nichols; Bristol, Joe Lewis; Elizabethton, Fred Waters; Johnson City, Johnny Lewis; Kingsport, Al Jackson; Paintsville, Mike Easom.

All-Star Team: 1B—Orestes Destrade, Paintsville; 2B—Curtis Ford, Johnson City; 3B—Kevin Mitchell, Kingsport; SS—Steve Lombardozzi, Elizabethton; OF—Michael Reddish, Paintsville; Thomas Jones, Paintsville; David Hoyt, Elizabethton; C—Stanley Haas, Johnson City; Utility INF—Michael Williams, Bristol; Utility OF—David Falcone, Bluefield; LHP—Paul Cherry, Johnson City; RHP—Daniel Cox, Johnson City. Manager of Year—Fred Waters, Elizabethton.

(Compiled by Howe News Bureau, Boston, Mass.)

CLUB BATTING

Club	Pct.	G.	AB.	R.	OR.	H.	TB.	2B.	3B.	HR.	RBI.	GW.	SH.	SF.	HP.	BB.	Int. BB.	SO.	SB.	CS.	LOB.
Paintsville	.294	70	2324	426	325	684	985	104	10	59	377	34	26	15	10	313	18	342	54	26	546
Bluefield	.263	70	2303	384	365	606	828	89	14	35	338	24	23	20	19	339	17	350	74	27	541
Johnson City	.259	70	2267	341	324	588	852	91	16	47	291	24	18	16	27	284	11	392	63	21	516
Kingsport	.250	70	2209	318	452	553	766	89	11	34	270	9	11	15	22	233	3	405	66	15	448
Elizabethton	.245	70	2256	402	335	552	815	98	15	45	344	18	11	28	21	387	12	405	85	15	554
Bristol...................	.244	70	2223	326	396	543	817	94	9	54	283	22	10	12	11	253	9	388	68	22	457

INDIVIDUAL BATTING

(Leading Qualifiers for Batting Championship—189 or More Plate Appearances)

°Bats lefthanded. †Switch-hitter.

Player and Club	Pct.	G.	AB.	R.	H.	TB.	2B.	3B.	HR.	RBI.	GW.	SH.	SF.	HP.	BB.	Int. BB.	SO.	SB.	CS.
Jones, Thomas, Paintsville°	.348	55	204	42	71	84	13	0	0	31	3	1	0	0	22	0	31	22	5
Falcone, David, Bluefield°	.346	62	214	56	74	127	14	0	13	55	4	0	2	1	50	5	33	1	2
Hoyt, David, Elizabethton	.337	66	252	59	85	131	15	2	9	50	2	0	2	0	32	1	31	18	0
Mitchell, Kevin, Kingsport	.335	62	221	39	74	108	9	2	7	45	2	0	3	0	22	0	31	5	5
Lombardozzi, Stephen, Elizabethton..	.321	65	246	48	79	114	13	2	6	38	3	2	1	2	46	2	28	9	1
Williams, Michael, Bristol	.321	60	224	40	72	131	23	0	12	60	8	0	2	0	24	0	34	0	0
Perdomo, Felix, Kingsport................	.310	56	213	40	66	100	17	1	5	29	1	3	1	3	9	0	37	6	0
O'Shea, Shane, Paintsville°	.310	53	187	30	58	70	6	0	2	30	2	1	1	0	25	3	13	1	0
Gallegos, Matthew, Paintsville†	.304	61	194	39	59	67	4	2	0	19	1	6	0	4	33	0	16	19	10
Reddish, Michael, Paintsville............	.298	64	242	42	72	117	8	2	11	48	4	1	2	1	22	1	31	2	3

Departmental Leaders: G—Luther, 70; AB—Simmons, 267; R—Hoyt, 59; H—Hoyt, 85; TB—Hoyt, Williams, 131; 2B—Williams, 23; 3B—Young, 5; HR—Destrade, 14; RBI—Williams, 60; GWRBI—Williams, 8; SH—Johnson, 14; SF—Tirado, 5; BB—Young, 51; IBB—Falcone, Pina, Tirado, 5; HP—McNutt, 10; SO—Burns, 54; SB—Salery, 26; CS—Gallegos, 10.

(All Players—Listed Alphabetically)

Player and Club	Pct.	G.	AB.	R.	H.	TB.	2B.	3B.	HR.	RBI.	GW.	SH.	SF.	HP.	BB.	Int. BB.	SO.	SB.	CS.
Aiello, Talbot, Elizabethton	.250	18	60	8	15	19	4	0	0	16	0	0	0	0	15	0	14	0	1
Alexander, Tommy, Bluefield	.000	25	1	0	0	0	0	0	0	0	0	0	0	0	0	0	1	0	0
Andujar, Jose, Kingsport	.111	10	18	1	2	2	0	0	0	0	0	0	0	0	0	0	14	0	0
Bertucio, Charles, Bluefield	.210	65	210	20	44	55	8	0	1	14	0	1	0	1	23	0	49	2	6
Blaser, Mark, Paintsville	.327	17	52	10	17	21	1	0	1	8	3	1	0	0	9	0	6	0	1
Bone, Patrick, Paintsville†	.257	9	35	5	9	9	0	0	0	0	0	0	0	0	4	0	6	1	0
Borriello, Sebastian, Elizabethton	.252	48	155	24	39	60	5	2	4	17	2	0	3	2	24	0	36	3	0
Brister, Walter, Bristol	.180	39	111	12	20	27	7	0	0	10	1	1	1	1	16	1	27	5	2
Brophy, Martin, Kingsport	.176	7	17	4	3	3	0	0	0	2	0	0	0	1	4	0	4	0	0
Burns, Carl, Bristol†	.000	1	2	0	0	0	0	0	0	0	0	0	0	0	0	0	1	0	0
Burns, James, Johnson City°	.279	66	208	25	58	89	7	0	8	35	3	4	0	2	24	1	54	7	4
Butler, Mark, Bluefield†	.000	13	1	0	0	0	0	0	0	0	0	0	0	0	0	0	0	0	0
Cardieri, Ronald, Bluefield°	.331	47	154	22	51	61	8	1	0	25	4	1	1	1	16	2	18	0	0
Carreon, Mark, Kingsport	.289	64	232	30	67	78	8	0	1	36	0	1	2	1	24	1	13	12	2
Carroll, Carson, Elizabethton	.253	64	221	33	56	78	12	2	2	27	1	3	2	0	39	0	23	10	2
Carter, Herbert, Elizabethton	.229	44	144	16	33	41	3	1	1	22	0	1	3	0	15	0	39	0	0
Cazet, James, Kingsport†	.113	33	71	10	8	12	2	1	0	3	0	0	1	0	15	0	26	1	0
Charley, Tandy, Bluefield°	.000	17	1	0	0	0	0	0	0	0	0	0	0	0	0	0	1	0	0
Cisco, Galen, Johnson City	.265	37	102	8	27	33	6	0	0	8	1	1	0	0	18	0	18	1	0
Costello, Robert, Kingsport	.280	58	186	28	52	67	9	0	2	34	1	0	2	0	21	0	19	1	1
Cusack, David, Bluefield	.273	68	238	53	65	103	12	1	8	44	3	2	3	1	41	1	46	8	1
Czeszewski, Lawrence, Kingsport	.252	38	115	8	29	33	2	1	0	9	1	0	1	1	8	0	20	1	0
D'ercole, Stephen, Kingsport	.000	22	1	0	0	0	0	0	0	0	0	0	0	0	0	0	0	0	0
Destrade, Orestes, Paintsville†	.274	63	208	51	57	113	12	1	14	46	4	1	1	2	48	3	49	2	1
Digioia, John, Johnson City	.219	30	73	5	16	25	3	0	2	5	1	0	0	0	11	1	33	0	1
Duhon, Guy, Bluefield	.300	4	10	1	3	3	0	0	0	1	0	0	0	1	0	0	3	0	1
Dummar, George, Bluefield°	.198	26	81	11	16	25	3	0	2	10	0	0	0	4	14	1	9	0	0
Dye, Charles, Bristol†	.000	2	3	0	0	0	0	0	0	0	0	0	0	0	0	0	0	0	0
Earl, William, Bristol	.260	52	181	38	47	62	6	0	3	18	1	0	1	0	31	0	35	13	0
Englin, Lance, Kingsport	1.000	7	1	0	1	1	0	0	0	0	0	0	0	0	0	0	0	0	0
Falcone, David, Bluefield°	.346	62	214	56	74	127	14	0	13	55	4	0	2	1	50	5	33	1	2
Fink, Bill, Johnson City°	.226	61	199	31	45	70	7	0	6	17	1	0	3	2	22	0	30	12	2
Fleming, Paul, Elizabethton	.184	37	98	27	18	22	1	0	1	5	0	0	0	4	28	0	39	7	2
Ford, Curtis, Johnson City°	.298	63	218	36	65	95	11	2	5	38	5	1	4	8	19	0	16	6	5
Franko, Phillip, Elizabethton°	.210	52	162	26	34	42	8	0	0	26	2	2	2	1	31	2	16	2	0
Franks, Michael, Kingsport	.261	38	115	13	30	33	3	0	0	12	0	1	1	0	14	0	9	2	2
Gallegos, Matthew, Paintsville†	.304	61	194	39	59	67	4	2	0	19	1	6	0	4	33	0	16	19	10
Gambeski, Michael, Johnson City	.240	36	100	17	24	44	3	1	5	14	0	1	0	1	11	1	19	1	0
Garcia, Luis, Kingsport	.056	9	18	2	1	2	1	0	0	1	0	0	0	0	3	0	11	0	0
Gilmore, Lawrence, Bristol°	.202	35	104	13	21	34	4	0	3	13	0	0	0	0	14	0	20	1	2
Gjesdal, Brent, Paintsville	.254	61	193	39	49	71	10	0	4	25	2	1	0	1	25	1	35	2	2
Gonzales, James, 1 J. City-2 King	.375	3	8	0	3	3	0	0	0	2	0	0	0	1	0	1	1	0	0
Goodyear, Christopher, Bristol	.254	37	114	25	29	43	3	1	3	17	0	1	0	2	22	0	12	4	2
Granger, L. Randall, Bluefield†	.320	32	128	34	41	56	3	3	2	23	0	1	1	1	20	0	15	11	1
Gray, Cedric, Elizabethton	.235	6	17	6	4	5	1	0	0	1	0	0	0	0	4	0	2	0	0
Griggs, David, Bluefield†	.227	15	44	2	10	10	0	0	0	2	0	0	0	0	5	1	7	0	0
Grove, Trent, Paintsville°	.280	61	214	19	60	79	13	0	0	36	2	4	0	0	16	0	28	2	1
Guinn, Charles, Bluefield	.000	15	1	0	0	0	0	0	0	0	0	0	0	0	0	0	1	0	0
Haas, Stanley, Johnson City	.293	52	167	28	49	72	12	1	3	25	2	3	3	1	18	0	23	1	0
Hawkins, Johnny, Paintsville†	.351	36	114	24	40	54	5	0	3	18	1	0	1	0	11	2	13	0	0
Haynes, Kennie, Bristol	.195	39	118	13	23	24	1	0	0	4	0	1	0	1	12	0	26	9	1
Heimerl, Robert, Elizabethton°	.188	33	96	16	18	30	3	0	3	13	0	0	1	0	19	1	32	0	1
Henderson, Craig, Elizabethton	1.000	2	1	1	1	1	0	0	0	0	0	0	0	0	0	0	0	0	0
Hoffman, Randall, Kingsport	.138	25	58	9	8	13	2	0	1	5	0	1	0	1	14	0	26	2	0
Hoyt, David, Elizabethton	.337	66	252	59	85	131	15	2	9	50	2	0	2	0	32	1	31	18	0
Hubert, Guy, Bluefield	.146	37	103	7	15	19	4	0	0	4	1	3	0	1	15	0	14	2	0
Hunsinger, Alan, Johnson City	.295	61	207	49	61	102	8	0	11	37	2	0	2	3	38	4	24	8	3
Isherwood, Michael, Paintsville	.256	41	133	23	34	42	5	0	1	12	2	2	1	1	26	0	18	1	0
Javier, Stanley, Johnson City†	.250	53	144	30	36	58	5	4	3	19	1	0	2	1	40	1	34	2	2
Johnson, Duane, Bluefield†	.196	64	230	24	45	59	7	2	1	21	1	7	0	0	23	1	46	7	3
Jones, Michael, Bristol°	.333	2	3	0	1	1	0	0	0	0	0	0	0	0	1	0	1	0	0
Jones, Thomas, Paintsville°	.348	55	204	42	71	84	13	0	0	31	3	1	0	0	22	0	31	22	5
Kappes, Dean, Elizabethton	.000	3	8	1	0	0	0	0	0	1	0	0	0	0	1	0	3	0	0
Kelly, Ronald, Bluefield°	.278	45	144	20	40	57	6	1	3	24	2	2	1	3	23	3	15	1	0
Labastidas, Mario, Bluefield	.171	14	41	4	7	7	0	0	0	3	0	2	0	2	5	0	13	0	0
Lauck, Jeffrey, Johnson City†	.182	41	99	11	18	25	2	1	1	10	1	2	0	0	12	0	25	3	1
Lindsey, William, Paintsville	.296	51	162	28	48	82	8	1	8	28	2	3	1	1	11	2	28	0	1
Lombardozzi, Stephen, Elizabethton	.321	65	246	48	79	114	13	2	6	38	3	2	1	2	46	2	28	9	1
Lucido, John, Paintsville	.289	34	83	9	24	27	3	0	0	14	0	1	2	0	6	0	11	1	0
Luther, Bradley, Johnson City	.241	70	249	36	60	71	11	0	0	20	2	5	0	4	19	0	25	7	1
Martin, Jeffrey, Elizabethton	.135	14	37	6	5	7	2	0	0	2	1	1	0	0	9	0	10	0	1
Martinez, Louis, Kingsport†	.199	47	136	11	27	40	4	0	3	14	0	0	1	0	8	0	20	1	2
Maull, Oliver, Bluefield°	.202	36	94	11	19	22	1	1	0	16	2	1	2	0	9	0	19	1	1
McNutt, Lawrence, Kingsport	.273	57	172	30	47	71	7	1	5	29	2	1	3	10	15	0	29	5	0
Merkle, Thomas, Bristol	.273	5	11	2	3	3	0	0	0	1	0	0	0	0	4	0	4	0	0
Miller, David, Bluefield†	.313	23	80	13	25	35	7	0	1	21	1	0	0	0	16	1	8	0	0
Mitchell, Kevin, Kingsport	.335	62	221	39	74	108	9	2	7	45	2	0	3	0	22	0	31	5	5
Moore, Alan, Johnson City°	.284	48	134	19	38	54	9	2	1	18	1	0	0	2	19	2	16	2	0
Moriarty, James, Bristol	.226	48	159	13	36	40	4	0	0	9	1	0	0	0	5	0	23	5	1
O'Shea, Shane, Paintsville†	.310	53	187	30	58	70	6	0	2	30	2	1	1	0	25	3	13	1	0
Orrick, Russell, Kingsport°	.300	4	10	1	3	3	0	0	0	0	0	0	0	1	1	0	1	0	0
Perdomo, Felix, Kingsport	.310	56	213	40	66	100	17	1	5	29	1	3	1	3	9	0	37	6	0
Perna, Joseph, Paintsville°	.262	57	187	38	49	92	10	3	9	37	4	2	2	0	27	5	43	0	2
Perrett, Kevin, Bristol	.000	1	3	0	0	0	0	0	0	0	0	0	0	0	1	0	3	0	0
Phillip, Daniel, Bristol°	.154	12	26	2	4	4	0	0	0	1	0	0	0	0	3	0	7	1	0
Phillips, Steven, Kingsport°	.281	34	89	15	25	43	6	0	4	10	0	1	0	1	12	1	19	3	0
Piatnik, Michael, Elizabethton	.209	18	67	9	14	16	2	0	0	8	0	0	1	1	6	0	15	2	1
Porter, Eric, Elizabethton	.182	5	11	2	2	2	0	0	0	1	0	0	0	1	1	0	1	0	0
Priessman, Kraig, Bristol	.227	26	75	9	17	24	2	1	1	4	0	2	0	0	4	0	20	0	0
Prosper, Michael, Kingsport°	.000	5	11	0	0	0	0	0	0	0	0	0	0	0	1	0	2	0	0
Reddish, Michael, Paintsville	.298	64	242	42	72	117	8	2	11	48	4	1	2	1	22	1	31	2	3

Player and Club	Pct.	G.	AB.	R.	H.	TB.	2B.	3B.	HR.	RBI.	GW.	SH.	SF.	HP.	BB.	Int. BB.	SO.	SB.	CS.
Rembielak, Richard, Bluefield	.209	59	187	24	39	54	7	1	2	24	1	3	4	2	28	0	26	8	0
Riche, Timothy, Bluefield°	.236	32	106	20	25	32	2	1	1	11	0	0	1	3	21	1	16	11	1
Robertson, Gary, Elizabethton°	.242	12	33	6	8	15	2	1	1	7	0	0	1	0	8	0	4	0	0
Rodriguez, Claudio, Johnson City°	.283	26	60	7	17	24	3	2	0	9	2	0	1	0	8	0	17	2	1
Rodriguez, Jose, Johnson City	.252	63	238	33	60	66	3	0	1	27	0	0	1	1	11	0	35	10	1
Rooney, James, Bluefield°	.000	12	3	0	0	0	0	0	0	0	0	0	0	0	0	0	1	0	0
Sadey, Richard, Bluefield	.444	2	9	2	4	4	0	0	0	1	0	0	0	0	0	0	0	1	0
Salery, John, Elizabethton	.229	49	175	38	40	64	6	0	6	27	1	2	2	3	38	0	42	26	2
Sanchez, Miguel, Kingsport	.172	40	99	7	17	23	3	0	1	6	0	1	0	1	6	0	28	2	0
Schaffer, Jeffrey, Bluefield	.268	62	250	45	67	81	7	2	1	31	4	3	4	0	35	0	26	17	9
Schlemmer, Mark, Bristol	.444	3	9	2	4	4	0	0	0	0	0	0	0	0	0	0	0	0	0
Shirley, Gregory, Kingsport°	.122	18	41	2	5	10	2	0	1	2	0	1	0	1	8	1	17	0	0
Silva, Albert, Bristol	.257	25	74	9	19	27	6	1	0	8	0	1	1	1	7	0	18	1	1
Simmons, Nelson, Bristol†	.296	69	267	36	79	125	14	1	10	45	5	0	4	2	18	2	38	2	4
Skeens, George, Elizabethton	.103	10	39	2	4	6	2	0	0	5	0	0	1	0	3	0	14	0	0
Stuart, Richard, Johnson City	.209	29	67	6	14	24	1	3	1	9	2	1	0	2	13	1	22	1	0
Thornton, Louis, Kingsport°	.209	48	153	23	32	45	7	0	2	17	1	0	0	0	15	0	34	4	1
Tirado, Julio, Elizabethton°	.226	62	217	30	49	85	7	4	7	49	2	0	5	4	29	5	29	5	2
Tutt, Johnny, Bluefield	.408	20	76	22	31	37	4	1	0	12	2	0	1	0	9	1	9	3	2
Vila, Jesus, Bristol	.217	62	235	27	51	84	9	0	8	31	2	0	1	0	10	1	35	0	1
Ward, Willie, Bristol	.071	5	14	0	1	1	0	0	0	0	0	0	0	0	1	0	6	0	0
Whisman, Rhett, Elizabethton	.221	60	217	44	48	77	12	1	5	30	3	0	4	3	39	1	27	3	2
Williams, Leon, Kingsport	.045	8	22	1	1	3	0	1	0	0	0	0	0	0	0	0	14	0	0
Williams, Michael, Bristol	.321	60	224	40	72	131	23	0	12	60	8	0	2	0	24	0	34	0	0
Williamson, Robert, Bristol°	.257	46	152	22	39	72	6	0	9	31	3	0	1	2	16	1	20	3	0
Winningham, Herman, Kingsport°	.255	58	204	44	52	73	7	4	2	14	1	1	0	2	33	0	31	20	2
Young, Kevin, Bristol°	.266	66	233	56	62	92	5	5	5	27	0	1	1	1	51	4	43	22	8
Zayas, Edgar, Bristol	.000	1	2	0	0	0	0	0	0	0	0	0	0	0	0	0	1	0	0
Zunino, Gregory, Paintsville	.319	45	116	27	37	57	6	1	4	25	4	2	4	0	28	1	14	1	0

The following pitchers had no plate appearances primarily through use of designated hitters, listed alphabetically by club, games in parentheses:

BLUEFIELD—Arnold, Tony (5); Cratch, Richard (9); Crumley, Hubert (12); Dixon, Kenneth (3); Gessell, Steven (6); Gray, David (3); Hebert, Michael (1); Lackie, Jeffrey (13); McDonough, Brian (16); Mitcheltree, John (17); Wadley, Anthony (10).

BRISTOL—Barlow, Ricky (11); Berthelson, Laurence (9); Corcoran, Thomas (14); Edwards, David (7); Jacob, Mark (12); Lockenmeyer, Mark (11); Mastro, Steven (17); McFadden, Robert (13); Miguel, George (13); Moya, Ernest (12); O'Connor, Donald (10); Pardo, Gerardo (1); Schultz, Terry (12); Thoel, Ronald (14).

ELIZABETHTON—Anderson, Craig (5); Borgini, Donald (5); Everett, Albert (10); Fregin, Douglas (11); Henkemeyer, Richard (10); Korczyk, Steven (28); Kribell, Michael (15); Larcom, Mark (8); Muhlenburg, Michael (2); Page, Marc (1); Portugal, Mark (14); Valencia, Arthur (9); Weiermueller, Michael (23); Wright, Mark (13).

JOHNSON CITY—Bear, David (15); Brown, Brian (12); Cherry, Paul (14); Cox, Danny (13); Finnegan, William (8); Fish, Timothy (1); Frey, John (12); Hayes, Robert (19); Hoag, George (12); Mitchell, William (14); Parks, James (18); Travers, Steven (13); Warburton, Jeffrey (10).

KINGSPORT—Alba, Fernando (20); Bautista, Jose (13); Fitts, Matthew (14); Hampton, Timothy (12); Oates, Malcolm (16); Thomas, Keith (15); Tirado, Aris (13); Walker, Steven (10); Webster, Richard (6); Williams, David (17).

PAINTSVILLE—Bailey, Boyce (6); Bratton, Reggie (13); Easley, Logan (22); Elston, Guy (27); Fincher, Steven (11); Marks, Jeffrey (4); Niemiec, David (10); Raftice, Robert (9); Repass, Scott (13); Silva, Mark (13); Swope, Andrew (11); Woodworth, David (12).

GRAND SLAM HOME RUNS—M. Williams, 2; Gilmore, Heimerl, Schaffer, Zunino, 1 each.

AWARDED FIRST BASE ON INTERFERENCE—Gilmore 4 (Martin 2, Borriello, Haas); Earl (Borriello).

CLUB FIELDING

Club	Pct.	G.	PO.	A.	E.	DP.	PB.	Club	Pct.	G.	PO.	A.	E.	DP.	PB.
Bluefield	.962	70	1789	786	102	78	9	Elizabethton	.950	70	1769	726	130	57	18
Johnson City	.959	70	1759	715	107	48	8	Bristol	.947	70	1712	765	139	63	18
Paintsville	.956	70	1746	729	115	60	7	Kingsport	.936	70	1677	688	163	56	14

INDIVIDUAL FIELDING

°Throws lefthanded.

FIRST BASEMEN

Player and Club	Pct.	G.	PO.	A.	E.	DP.	Player and Club	Pct.	G.	PO.	A.	E.	DP.
Brophy, Kingsport	1.000	3	26	0	0	2	Kelly, Bluefield°	.990	13	93	5	1	17
Burns, Johnson City°	.983	64	526	46	10	38	Lindsey, Paintsville	.989	25	163	13	2	12
Costello, Kingsport	1.000	2	10	1	0	1	Martinez, Kingsport	.929	3	26	0	2	2
Destrade, Paintsville	.978	52	461	22	11	42	McNutt, Kingsport	.956	25	174	21	9	9
Dummar, Bluefield°	.970	12	88	10	3	14	Robertson, Elizabethton	1.000	2	19	0	0	2
FALCONE, Bluefield	.985	50	434	32	7	42	Rodriguez, Johnson City°	.960	15	91	4	4	5
Ford, Johnson City	1.000	1	5	1	0	0	Silva, Bristol	.972	11	101	3	3	5
Franko, Elizabethton	.983	11	111	3	2	7	Thornton, Kingsport	.960	44	338	43	16	36
Gambeski, Johnson City	1.000	1	0	0	0	0	Tirado, Elizabethton°	.967	58	521	38	19	42
Gilmore, Bristol°	.977	32	279	14	7	25	Ward, Bristol	1.000	3	31	2	0	4
Hunsinger, Johnson City	1.000	2	4	0	0	1	Williams, Bristol	.989	26	250	14	3	22

SECOND BASEMEN

Player and Club	Pct.	G.	PO.	A.	E.	DP.	Player and Club	Pct.	G.	PO.	A.	E.	DP.
Carroll, Elizabethton	.973	64	138	183	9	39	Labastidas, Bluefield	1.000	1	2	3	0	0
Cisco, Johnson City	.968	21	38	53	3	13	Lauck, Johnson City°	1.000	1	0	1	0	0
Cusack, Bluefield	.917	2	8	3	1	1	Lucido, Paintsville	.949	32	56	73	7	13
Earl, Bristol	.952	45	89	169	13	34	Orrick, Kingsport°	.800	1	3	1	1	0
Ford, Johnson City	.935	54	110	148	18	18	Perdomo, Kingsport	.945	37	53	84	8	12
Franks, Kingsport	.968	36	70	114	6	24	Phillips, Paintsville	1.000	1	0	1	0	0
Gallegos, Paintsville	.966	6	10	18	1	3	Piatnik, Elizabethton	.918	8	15	30	4	4
Goodyear, Bristol	.965	27	63	75	5	16	Rembielak, Bluefield	1.000	2	3	1	0	1
Grove, Paintsville	.952	42	84	114	10	24	Rodriguez, Johnson City°	1.000	1	2	2	0	0
Johnson, Bluefield	.903	5	12	16	3	4	SCHAFFER, Bluefield	.984	62	170	189	6	56
Jones, Bristol	1.000	1	2	3	0	0							

THIRD BASEMEN

Player and Club	Pct.	G.	PO.	A.	E.	DP.	Player and Club	Pct.	G.	PO.	A.	E.	DP.
Blaser, Paintsville	.333	2	0	1	2	0	Martinez, Kingsport	.818	12	11	16	6	1
Cusack, Bluefield	.870	65	39	108	22	7	Merkle, Bristol	.857	4	3	3	1	0
Falcone, Bluefield	.556	5	2	3	4	2	Mitchell, Kingsport	.889	58	42	102	18	12
Franko, Elizabethton	.810	8	8	9	4	1	O'Shea, Paintsville	.912	53	47	77	12	6
Gambeski, Johnson City	.870	23	14	26	6	3	Piatnik, Elizabethton	.857	5	1	11	2	0
Gjesdal, Paintsville	.821	20	7	25	7	2	Sadey, Bluefield	1.000	2	0	2	0	0
Hubert, Bristol	.870	7	7	13	3	3	Schlemmer, Bristol	1.000	1	0	3	0	0
HUNSINGER, Johnson City	.915	53	32	86	11	2	Vila, Bristol	.908	62	49	108	16	11
Johnson, Bluefield	1.000	1	0	1	0	0	Whisman, Elizabethton	.865	57	36	98	21	4

SHORTSTOPS

Player and Club	Pct.	G.	PO.	A.	E.	DP.	Player and Club	Pct.	G.	PO.	A.	E.	DP.
Bone, Paintsville	.667	5	3	9	6	2	Hubert, Bristol	.925	30	38	86	10	23
Brister, Bristol	.692	5	1	8	4	2	Johnson, Bluefield	1.000	4	1	1	0	0
Cazet, Kingsport	.920	30	50	53	9	13	Labastidas, Bluefield	.953	12	21	40	3	8
Cisco, Johnson City	1.000	2	4	2	0	0	LOMBARDOZZI, Elizabethton	.953	59	89	192	14	38
Cusack, Bluefield	.833	1	2	3	1	0	Luther, Johnson City	.948	70	120	206	18	38
Franko, Elizabethton	.933	11	20	22	3	8	O'Shea, Paintsville	1.000	6	2	1	0	0
Gallegos, Paintsville	.932	54	86	188	20	31	Perdomo, Kingsport	.862	18	24	51	12	13
Goodyear, Bristol	.833	6	5	15	4	5	Phillips, Kingsport	.864	30	45	57	16	10
Grove, Paintsville	.952	17	21	39	3	5	Piatnik, Elizabethton	1.000	1	3	1	0	0
Haynes, Bristol	.890	33	54	84	17	12	Rembielak, Bluefield	.927	58	86	195	22	46

OUTFIELDERS

Player and Club	Pct.	G.	PO.	A.	E.	DP.	Player and Club	Pct.	G.	PO.	A.	E.	DP.
Aiello, Elizabethton	1.000	14	15	2	0	0	Maull, Bluefield	1.000	1	3	1	0	0
Andujar, Elizabethton	.750	8	6	0	2	0	McNutt, Kingsport	.955	23	41	1	2	0
Bertucio, Bluefield°	.982	63	98	9	2	0	Miller, Bluefield	1.000	17	23	2	0	0
Bone, Paintsville	1.000	7	10	0	0	0	Mitchell, Kingsport	1.000	2	2	0	0	0
Brister, Bristol	.906	31	45	3	5	0	Moriarty, Kingsport	.947	45	67	4	4	0
Carreon, Kingsport°	.963	63	99	6	4	1	Orrick, Kingsport°	1.000	3	2	0	0	0
Carter, Elizabethton	.948	42	50	5	3	1	Perna, Paintsville°	.963	54	73	4	3	1
Duhon, Bluefield	1.000	4	2	0	0	0	Prosper, Kingsport°	.857	3	6	0	1	0
Falcone, Bluefield	.846	6	10	1	2	0	Reddish, Paintsville	.923	46	46	2	4	0
Fink, Johnson City	.962	59	98	2	4	0	Riche, Bluefield°	.976	30	38	2	1	0
Fleming, Elizabethton	.971	26	32	1	1	0	Rodriguez, Johnson City°	1.000	2	1	0	0	0
Gjesdal, Paintsville	.939	45	57	5	4	0	Rodriguez, Johnson City	.957	62	146	11	7	1
Granger, Bluefield	.924	32	56	5	5	0	Salery, Elizabethton	.901	48	88	3	10	0
Gray, Elizabethton	.875	6	7	0	1	0	Sanchez, Kingsport	.909	39	66	4	7	2
Haynes, Bristol	.778	6	13	1	4	0	Shirley, Kingsport	.917	15	10	1	1	0
Heimerl, Elizabethton°	.846	24	22	0	4	0	Simmons, Bristol	.896	69	62	7	8	0
Hoffman, Kingsport	.882	20	28	2	4	0	Stuart, Johnson City°	.936	24	29	0	2	0
Hoyt, Elizabethton	.944	62	126	10	8	3	Tutt, Bluefield	.950	13	19	0	1	0
Javier, Johnson City	.948	51	53	2	3	0	Williams, Bristol	.889	6	8	0	1	0
Johnson, Bluefield	.968	52	110	10	4	1	WINNINGHAM, Kingsport	.985	56	128	3	2	2
Jones, Paintsville	.951	54	95	2	5	0	Young, Bristol	.950	65	161	9	9	1
Lauck, Johnson City°	.938	33	44	1	3	0	Zunino, Paintsville	.946	28	31	4	2	3

CATCHERS

Player and Club	Pct.	G.	PO.	A.	E.	DP.	PB.	Player and Club	Pct.	G.	PO.	A.	E.	DP.	PB.
Borriello, Elizabethton	.968	46	275	23	10	3	8	Martin, Elizabethton	.958	13	62	6	3	0	4
Brophy, Kingsport	1.000	3	12	2	0	0	0	Martinez, Kingsport	1.000	4	7	0	0	0	2
CARDIERI, Bluefield	.993	42	257	25	2	2	5	Maull, Bluefield	.953	17	90	12	5	1	2
Carreon, Kingsport°	1.000	1	2	1	0	0	0	Moore, Johnson City	.993	24	132	11	1	0	2
Costello, Kingsport	.968	36	161	18	6	2	4	Perrett, Bristol	.857	1	3	3	1	0	1
Czeszewski, Kingsport	.961	25	107	15	5	3	3	Phillip, Bristol	.971	8	30	3	1	0	1
Digioia, Johnson City	.966	11	24	4	1	0	0	Porter, Elizabethton	1.000	5	31	2	0	0	2
Garcia, Kingsport	.957	7	20	2	1	0	5	Priessman, Bristol	1.000	20	80	10	0	0	6
Gonzales, JCity-King	.842	3	13	3	3	0	0	Silva, Bristol	.979	8	41	5	1	0	1
Griggs, Bluefield	.987	15	64	10	1	1	2	Skeens, Elizabethton	.934	9	54	3	4	0	4
Haas, Johnson City	.983	40	201	33	4	1	6	Williams, Bristol	.976	16	72	9	2	2	2
Hawkins, Paintsville	.974	34	204	23	6	1	3	Williamson, Bristol	.932	24	115	8	9	0	7
Hunsinger, Johnson City	1.000	1	5	2	0	0	0	Zayas, Bristol	1.000	1	5	2	0	0	0
Isherwood, Paintsville	.989	40	248	23	3	4	4								

PITCHERS

Player and Club	Pct.	G.	PO.	A.	E.	DP.	Player and Club	Pct.	G.	PO.	A.	E.	DP.
Alexander, Bluefield	1.000	25	6	6	0	0	D'Ercole, Kingsport	.952	22	7	13	1	3
Anderson, Elizabethton	1.000	5	1	4	0	0	Dixon, Bluefield	1.000	3	2	0	0	1
Arnold, Bluefield	.600	5	2	1	2	0	Easley, Paintsville	.867	22	3	10	2	1
Bailey, Paintsville	1.000	6	0	1	0	1	Edwards, Bristol	1.000	7	1	1	0	0
Barlow, Bristol	.900	11	4	14	2	0	Elston, Paintsville	1.000	27	2	4	0	0
Bautista, Kingsport	.889	13	13	11	3	0	Englin, Kingsport	.750	7	2	4	2	1
Bear, Johnson City	.933	15	8	6	1	1	Everett, Elizabethton	.833	10	3	7	2	1
Berthelson, Bristol	1.000	9	0	4	0	1	Fincher, Paintsville°	.950	11	3	16	1	0
Borgini, Elizabethton	.800	5	0	4	1	0	Finnegan, Johnson City	.667	8	2	2	2	0
Bratton, Paintsville	1.000	13	5	3	0	1	Fitts, Kingsport	.900	14	11	7	2	2
Brown, Johnson City	1.000	12	8	11	0	0	Fregin, Elizabethton	.947	11	7	11	1	1
Butler, Bluefield°	.960	13	6	18	1	4	Frey, Johnson City°	.667	12	0	2	1	0
Charley, Bluefield°	1.000	16	1	0	0	0	Gessell, Bluefield	1.000	6	2	2	0	0
Cherry, Johnson City°	1.000	14	3	13	0	0	Gray, Bluefield	1.000	3	2	0	0	0
Corcoran, Bristol	1.000	14	2	5	0	0	Guinn, Bluefield	1.000	15	4	11	0	0
Cox, Johnson City	.929	13	26	13	3	1	Hampton, Kingsport	.929	12	11	15	2	1
Cratch, Bluefield	1.000	9	4	7	0	0	Hayes, Johnson City	1.000	19	1	3	0	0
Crumley, Bluefield	1.000	12	1	3	0	1	Hebert, Bluefield°	1.000	1	1	0	0	0

PITCHERS—Continued

Player and Club	Pct.	G.	PO.	A.	E.	DP.
Henderson, Elizabethton°	1.000	2	0	2	0	0
Henkemeyer, Elizabethton°	1.000	10	1	3	0	0
Hoag, Johnson City	.909	12	7	3	1	1
Jacob, Bristol	.962	12	9	16	1	0
Korczyk, Elizabethton	.938	28	7	8	1	1
Kribell, Elizabethton°	1.000	15	2	15	0	0
Lackie, Bluefield°	.895	13	8	9	2	0
Larcom, Elizabethton°	1.000	8	6	2	0	0
Lockenmeyer, Bristol	.929	11	5	8	1	1
Mastro, Bristol	.857	17	2	10	2	1
McDonough, Bluefield	.957	16	12	10	1	0
McFadden, Bristol	.944	13	4	13	1	0
Miguel, Bristol°	1.000	13	0	6	0	1
Mitchell, Johnson City	.867	14	8	5	2	0
Mitcheltree, Bluefield	1.000	17	4	15	0	1
Moya, Bristol	1.000	12	9	9	0	0
Muhlenburg, Elizabethton°	1.000	2	0	1	0	0
Niemiec, Paintsville	1.000	10	3	2	0	1
O'Connor, Bristol	1.000	10	9	9	0	0
Oates, Kingsport°	1.000	16	4	7	0	1
Pardo, Bristol	1.000	1	0	1	0	0
Parks, Johnson City	1.000	18	5	7	0	0
Portugal, Elizabethton	.905	14	9	10	2	0
Raftice, Paintsville°	1.000	9	1	1	0	0
REPASS, Paintsville°	1.000	13	9	17	0	0
Rooney, Bluefield°	1.000	12	3	9	0	3
Shultz, Bristol°	.667	12	1	3	2	0
Silva, Paintsville	.958	13	12	11	1	1
Swope, Paintsville	.875	11	3	11	2	0
Thoel, Bristol°	1.000	14	0	2	0	0
Thomas, Kingsport	1.000	15	5	7	0	0
Tirado, Kingsport	.864	13	9	10	3	2
Travers, Johnson City	.900	13	5	4	1	0
Valencia, Elizabethton	1.000	9	0	2	0	0
Wadley, Bluefield	1.000	10	0	6	0	0
Walker, Kingsport	.700	10	4	3	3	1
Warburton, Johnson City°	1.000	10	3	3	0	0
Webster, Kingsport	.722	6	7	6	5	1
Weiermiller, Elizabethton°	1.000	23	1	5	0	0
Williams, Kingsport	.857	17	5	1	1	0
Woodworth, Paintsville°	.917	12	1	10	1	1
Wright, Elizabethton	.950	13	9	10	1	0

The following players do not have any recorded accepted chances at the positions indicated; therefore, are not listed in the fielding averages for those particular positions: Cazet, 3b; Cisco, of; Fish, p; Gambeski, of; Grove, 3b; Hunsinger, of; Kappes, c; Lindsey, 3b; Marks, p; Martinez, of; Maull, 2b; Page, p; Prosper, p; Schlemmer, 2b.

CLUB PITCHING

Club	ERA.	G.	CG.	ShO.	Sv.	IP.	H.	R.	ER.	HR.	HB.	BB.	Int. BB.	SO.	WP.	Bk.
Johnson City	3.92	70	18	7	3	586⅓	555	324	255	42	11	266	21	379	59	1
Paintsville	3.96	70	21	9	13	582	551	325	256	36	23	293	3	452	45	3
Elizabethton	4.31	70	12	3	8	589⅔	554	335	282	39	21	317	11	398	50	4
Bluefield	4.71	70	9	3	8	596⅓	627	365	312	52	16	316	7	404	37	5
Bristol	5.02	70	20	2	8	570⅔	604	396	318	32	24	317	9	347	39	3
Kingsport	5.57	70	14	3	8	559	635	452	346	73	18	300	19	302	45	11

PITCHERS' RECORDS
(Leading Qualifiers for Earned-Run Average Leadership — 56 or More Innings)

°Throws lefthanded.

Pitcher—Club	W.	L.	Pct.	ERA.	G.	GS.	CG.	GF.	ShO.	Sv.	IP.	H.	R.	ER.	HR.	HB.	BB.	Int. BB.	SO.	WP.
Cox, Johnson City	9	4	.692	2.06	13	13	10	0	4	0	109	80	27	25	3	1	36	1	87	3
Rooney, Bluefield°	6	0	1.000	2.08	12	12	2	0	1	0	78	65	27	18	5	3	32	1	76	2
Cherry, Johnson City°	10	2	.833	2.50	14	14	6	0	1	0	101	87	33	28	8	1	17	1	70	4
Mitcheltree, Bluefield	7	2	.778	2.54	17	6	3	9	1	2	71	57	27	20	1	4	25	0	65	3
Silva, Paintsville	6	4	.600	3.00	13	11	4	1	3	0	81	59	37	27	3	3	38	0	77	2
Fregin, Elizabethton	6	2	.750	3.18	11	11	2	0	1	0	68	67	37	24	2	4	23	2	36	2
McFadden, Bristol	3	6	.333	3.45	13	8	4	4	0	1	60	57	34	23	1	0	35	1	39	6
Lockenmeyer, Bristol	5	5	.500	3.47	11	11	4	0	0	0	70	75	38	27	3	3	24	1	42	3
McDonough, Bluefield	4	3	.571	3.50	16	7	2	4	0	0	72	69	31	28	3	1	19	1	37	5
Swope, Paintsville	5	2	.714	3.51	11	0	0	3	0	1	59	48	29	23	1	5	38	0	42	7

Departmental Leaders: G—Korczyk, 28; GS—Cherry, 14; CG—Cox, 10; ShO—Cox, 4; W—Cherry, 10; L—Tirado, 8; Sv—Elston, 11; Pct.—Elston, Woodworth, 1.000; IP—Cox, 109; H—Butler, 88; R—Tirado, 61; ER—Tirado, 45; HR—Guinn, Portugal, Tirado, 11; BB—Tirado, 48; IBB—Oates, Weiermiller, 5; HB—Everett, Miguel, Moya, Portugal, 5; SO—Cox, 87; WP—Portugal, 12.

(All Pitchers—Listed Alphabetically)

Pitcher—Club	W.	L.	Pct.	ERA.	G.	GS.	CG.	GF.	ShO.	Sv.	IP.	H.	R.	ER.	HR.	HB.	BB.	Int. BB.	SO.	WP.
Alba, Kingsport	3	1	.750	4.11	20	0	0	18	0	5	35	35	19	16	3	0	20	1	23	1
Alexander, Bluefield	4	2	.667	4.14	25	0	0	15	0	1	50	41	28	23	2	2	37	1	38	6
Anderson, Elizabethton	0	2	.000	10.29	5	2	0	1	0	0	14	23	20	16	5	0	9	0	10	2
Arnold, Bluefield	2	1	.667	8.22	5	3	1	1	0	0	23	32	22	21	2	2	11	0	15	0
Bailey, Paintsville	3	3	.500	4.15	6	5	2	0	0	0	39	37	23	18	2	1	15	0	30	1
Barlow, Bristol	6	3	.667	4.34	11	11	2	0	1	0	58	63	38	28	2	1	36	0	24	6
Bautista, Kingsport	3	6	.333	4.64	13	11	3	1	2	0	66	84	54	34	10	2	17	1	34	1
Bear, Johnson City	2	1	.667	3.44	15	2	0	4	0	1	55	63	29	21	1	0	17	2	11	4
Berthelson, Bristol	1	3	.250	6.60	9	2	1	5	0	0	30	32	26	22	3	0	23	1	16	1
Borgini, Elizabethton	1	1	.500	6.00	5	2	1	2	0	1	21	29	17	14	3	0	7	0	19	2
Bratton, Paintsville	1	0	1.000	5.40	13	2	0	7	0	0	30	39	21	18	4	1	17	1	25	3
Brown, Johnson City	2	7	.222	4.35	12	12	1	0	0	0	60	56	41	29	3	0	34	2	43	5
Butler, Bluefield°	2	4	.333	3.89	13	13	0	0	0	0	74	88	41	32	8	1	29	1	35	1
Charley, Bluefield°	1	2	.333	3.43	16	0	0	11	0	2	21	19	8	8	2	0	13	0	19	2
Cherry, Johnson City°	10	2	.833	2.50	14	14	6	0	1	0	101	87	33	28	8	1	17	1	70	4
Corcoran, Bristol	0	1	.000	6.12	14	0	0	4	0	0	25	25	21	17	3	2	28	0	12	2
Cox, Johnson City	9	4	.692	2.06	13	13	10	0	4	0	109	80	27	25	3	1	36	1	87	3
Cratch, Bluefield	2	3	.400	8.70	9	6	0	1	0	0	30	41	32	29	4	1	19	0	21	2
Crumley, Bluefield	0	0	.000	6.00	12	0	0	9	0	1	21	22	14	14	2	0	15	0	11	2
D'Ercole, Kingsport	2	2	.500	5.63	22	0	0	12	0	2	48	57	37	30	8	2	21	1	33	2
Dixon, Bluefield	2	1	.667	6.00	3	3	1	0	0	0	18	23	12	12	1	0	11	0	22	1
Easley, Paintsville	2	2	.500	3.91	22	1	0	8	0	2	53	60	36	23	2	2	24	0	26	4
Edwards, Bristol	2	2	.500	4.26	7	0	0	4	0	1	19	13	10	9	1	2	11	1	13	2
Elston, Paintsville	9	0	1.000	0.60	27	0	0	27	0	11	45	25	4	3	2	1	7	1	67	1
Englin, Kingsport	3	4	.429	6.62	7	7	1	0	0	0	34	45	29	25	1	1	15	1	17	2
Everett, Bristol	3	4	.429	4.19	10	7	0	1	0	0	43	41	27	20	0	5	38	0	19	4
Fincher, Paintsville°	1	5	.167	6.53	11	10	1	0	0	0	51	55	47	37	3	3	44	0	28	0
Finnegan, Johnson City	1	1	.500	7.58	8	4	0	0	0	0	19	16	19	16	2	0	29	0	13	11
Fish, Johnson City°	0	0	.000	6.75	1	0	0	0	0	0	4	4	3	3	2	0	3	0	3	0
Fitts, Kingsport	3	6	.333	4.96	14	12	1	1	0	0	69	74	50	38	10	1	33	2	22	6
Fregin, Elizabethton	6	2	.750	3.18	11	11	2	0	1	0	68	67	37	24	2	4	23	2	36	2

Pitcher—Club	W.	L.	Pct.	ERA.	G.	GS.	CG.	GF.	ShO.	Sv.	IP.	H.	R.	ER.	HR.	HB.	BB.	Int. BB.	SO.	WP.
Frey, Johnson City°	0	0	.000	8.47	12	0	0	7	0	0	17	18	26	16	2	2	13	1	5	2
Gessell, Bluefield	1	1	.500	12.00	6	3	0	0	0	0	12	17	17	16	1	1	17	0	2	4
Gray, Bluefield	0	0	.000	5.40	3	0	0	1	0	0	5	5	3	3	1	0	5	0	1	0
Guinn, Bluefield	3	5	.375	6.65	15	4	0	6	0	1	46	48	35	34	10	0	28	2	30	4
Hampton, Kingsport	4	5	.444	4.50	12	12	4	0	1	0	76	78	48	38	9	2	31	1	28	7
Hayes, Johnson City	0	1	.000	5.04	19	0	0	15	0	1	25	30	17	14	0	0	10	2	10	5
Hebert, Bluefield°	0	1	.000	9.00	1	0	0	1	0	0	2	4	6	2	2	0	1	0	1	1
Henderson, Elizabethton°	2	0	1.000	2.81	2	2	2	0	0	0	16	16	5	5	1	0	4	0	18	0
Henkemeyer, Elizabethton°	2	3	.400	7.69	10	9	0	0	0	0	48	51	41	41	2	2	42	0	36	1
Hoag, Johnson City	2	3	.400	3.66	12	1	0	6	0	0	32	27	16	13	4	2	17	1	17	3
Jacob, Bristol	2	6	.250	4.22	12	11	5	0	0	0	81	72	48	38	3	2	31	1	61	3
Korczyk, Elizabethton	6	4	.600	1.50	28	0	0	26	0	5	48	34	11	8	1	0	9	0	33	2
Kribell, Elizabethton°	4	1	.800	3.54	15	9	0	1	0	0	61	55	31	24	3	3	38	1	42	10
Lackie, Bluefield	2	5	.286	6.46	13	10	0	1	0	0	46	56	41	33	5	1	45	1	24	4
Larcom, Elizabethton°	0	0	.000	5.87	8	1	0	6	0	0	23	20	15	15	5	0	9	0	9	4
Lockenmeyer, Bristol	5	5	.500	3.47	11	11	4	0	0	0	70	75	38	27	3	3	24	1	42	3
Marks, Paintsville°	0	0	.000	18.00	4	0	0	1	0	0	4	5	8	8	0	1	8	0	2	2
Mastro, Bristol	1	2	.333	5.82	17	1	0	10	0	3	34	43	24	22	0	0	23	0	15	2
McDonough, Bluefield	4	3	.571	3.50	16	7	2	4	0	0	72	69	31	28	3	1	19	1	37	5
McFadden, Bristol	3	6	.333	3.45	13	8	4	4	0	1	60	57	34	23	1	0	35	1	39	6
Miguel, Bristol°	0	4	.000	8.00	13	6	0	3	0	1	36	46	36	32	2	5	26	1	26	5
Mitchell, Johnson City	2	7	.222	6.27	14	13	0	0	0	0	56	48	53	39	4	4	45	3	29	8
Mitcheltree, Bluefield	7	2	.778	2.54	17	6	3	9	1	2	71	57	27	20	1	4	25	0	65	3
Moya, Bristol	6	3	.667	3.52	12	10	3	1	0	0	69	68	33	27	4	5	24	0	56	2
Muhlenburg, Elizabethton°	0	0	.000	21.00	2	0	0	1	0	0	3	7	7	7	0	0	7	0	4	1
Niemiec, Paintsville	1	4	.200	5.73	10	4	0	3	0	0	33	47	27	21	1	3	17	0	15	7
O'Connor, Bristol	2	4	.333	5.79	10	7	1	1	0	0	42	51	35	27	4	1	14	0	13	3
Oates, Kingsport°	0	5	.000	7.41	16	2	1	8	0	1	34	39	34	28	6	2	24	5	29	2
Page, Elizabethton	0	1	.000	9.00	1	1	0	0	0	0	4	5	4	4	0	0	5	0	2	0
Pardo, Bristol	0	0	.000	3.00	1	0	0	1	0	0	3	2	1	1	0	0	4	0	1	0
Parks, Johnson City	4	2	.667	3.00	18	0	0	16	0	1	33	37	11	11	1	0	18	4	33	3
Portugal, Elizabethton	7	1	.875	3.71	14	13	2	1	0	1	85	65	41	35	11	5	39	3	65	12
Prosper, Bristol	0	0	.000	27.00	1	0	0	0	0	0	1	0	3	3	0	0	6	0	0	0
Raftice, Paintsville°	4	2	.667	3.98	9	6	2	0	1	0	43	43	26	19	5	3	24	0	36	3
Repass, Paintsville°	5	2	.714	3.57	13	9	2	2	1	0	63	53	30	25	1	2	37	1	45	4
Rooney, Bluefield°	6	0	1.000	2.08	12	12	0	1	0	0	78	65	27	18	5	3	32	1	76	2
Schultz, Bristol°	0	1	1.000	7.33	12	1	0	7	0	1	27	33	27	22	4	0	22	1	17	2
Silva, Paintsville	6	4	.600	3.00	13	11	4	1	3	0	81	59	37	27	3	3	38	0	77	2
Swope, Paintsville	5	2	.714	3.51	11	10	3	0	1	0	59	48	29	23	5	2	38	0	42	7
Thoel, Bristol°	1	1	.500	11.50	14	0	0	10	0	1	18	24	25	23	2	0	16	2	12	2
Thomas, Kingsport	2	2	.500	9.28	15	3	0	5	0	0	32	46	40	33	6	0	30	2	17	5
Tirado, Kingsport	1	8	.111	5.70	13	13	1	0	0	0	71	76	61	45	11	4	48	2	41	9
Travers, Johnson City	3	4	.429	3.90	13	11	1	1	0	0	67	71	35	29	7	1	17	1	52	7
Valencia, Elizabethton	1	0	1.000	7.20	9	0	0	4	0	0	20	20	17	16	1	0	16	0	7	2
Wadley, Bluefield	0	4	.000	6.11	10	3	0	2	0	1	28	40	21	19	2	0	9	0	7	0
Walker, Kingsport	0	4	.000	12.86	10	4	0	2	0	0	21	29	39	30	3	1	27	0	11	9
Warburton, Johnson City°	1	2	.333	9.90	10	0	0	3	0	0	10	18	14	11	1	0	10	3	6	4
Webster, Kingsport	0	4	.000	3.00	6	6	3	0	0	0	33	35	18	11	4	2	10	0	16	0
Weiermiller, Eliz.°	4	4	.500	3.00	23	0	0	15	0	1	51	41	20	17	1	1	38	5	62	4
Williams, Kingsport	0	2	.000	3.46	17	0	0	9	0	0	39	37	20	15	2	1	18	3	31	1
Woodworth, Paintsville°	9	0	1.000	3.73	12	12	7	0	1	0	82	80	37	34	8	1	24	0	59	11
Wright, Elizabethton	6	5	.545	3.90	13	13	5	0	1	0	83	80	42	36	4	1	33	0	36	4

BALKS—Hampton, 4; Alba, Bautista, 3 each; Butler, Weiermiller, 2 each; Borgini, Dixon, Easley, Henkemeyer, Jacob, Lackie, McFadden, Mitchell, Niemiec, O'Conner, Oates, Wadley, Woodworth, 1 each.

COMBINATION SHUTOUTS—Butler-Mitcheltree, Bluefield; Lockenmeyer-Shultz, Bristol; Fregin-Weiermiller, Elizabethton; Cherry-Parks, Brown-Hoag, Johnson City; Woodworth-Easley, Repass-Elston, Paintsville.

NO-HIT GAME—Cox, Johnson City, defeated Bristol, 11-0, August 9.

Gulf Coast League

SUMMER CLASS A CLASSIFICATION

CHAMPIONSHIP WINNERS IN PREVIOUS YEARS

1964—Sarasota Braves	.610	1970—Chicago A.L.	.600	1975—Texas	.774
1965—Bradenton Astros	.632	1971—Kansas City	.755	1976—Texas	.704
1966—New York A.L.	.667	1972—Chicago N.L. a	.651	1977—Chicago-AL	.731
1967—Kansas City	.614	Kansas City a	.651	1978—Texas	.600
1968—Oakland	.650	1973—Texas	.732	1979—Houston	.635
1969—Montreal	.585	1974—Chicago N.L.	.702	1980—Kansas City-Blue	.635

(Note—Known as Sarasota Rookie League in 1964 and Florida Rookie League in 1965.) aDeclared co-champions; no playoff.

STANDING OF CLUBS AT CLOSE OF SEASON, AUGUST 31

Club	K.C. Gold	Chi. AL	K.C. Blue	Hous. Org.	Pitt.	Tex.	N.Y. AL	Atl.	Tor.	Chi. NL	S.D.	Hous. Blue	W.	L.	T.	Pct.	G.B.
Kansas City-Gold	...	4	2	2	4	5	4	3	5	4	5	6	44	20	1	.688	......
Chicago-AL	2	...	3	6	2	3	4	4	6	2	4	5	41	23	0	.641	3
Kansas City-Blue	3	3	...	3	3	5	0	4	2	4	4	4	35	28	1	.556	8½
Houston-Orange	4	0	1	...	3	2	5	4	3	5	3	3	33	28	0	.541	9½
Pittsburgh	2	4	3	2	...	2	2	3	4	4	3	3	32	28	1	.533	10
Texas	1	3	1	4	2	...	4	3	5	3	3	3	32	30	1	.516	11
New York-AL	2	2	6	1	3	1	...	2	4	4	4	1	30	29	0	.508	12½
Atlanta	3	2	2	0	3	3	4	...	1	3	3	4	28	34	0	.452	15
Toronto	1	0	4	3	2	1	1	5	...	2	4	3	26	39	0	.400	18½
Chicago-NL	2	3	2	1	2	3	1	2	4	...	1	4	25	38	1	.397	18½
San Diego	0	1	2	3	3	2	2	3	2	5	...	2	25	38	1	.397	18½
Houston-Blue	0	1	2	3	1	3	2	1	3	2	4	...	22	38	0	.367	20

Kansas City-Gold declared league champion on basis of highest won-lost percentage.

Club names indicate major league connections.

Games played at Bradenton and Sarasota, Fla.

Regular-Season Attendance—At Payne Park, Sarasota, 15,025; no admission charged at other parks. Playoffs, 1,825. No all-star game.

Managers: Atlanta—Pedro Gonzalez; Chicago-AL—John Boles; Chicago-NL—Hugh Yancy; Houston-Blue—Eric Swanson; Houston-Orange—Lyle Olsen; Kansas City-Blue—Joe Jones; Kansas City-Gold—Roy Tanner; New York-AL—Carlos Tosca; Pittsburgh—Woody Hyke; San Diego—Jim Zarilla; Texas—Andy Hancock; Toronto—Richard Hacker.

All-Star Team: 1B—Kyle Sanford, Atlanta; 2B—Philander Smith, Houston-Blue; 3B—Denio Gonzales, Pitttsburgh; SS—Steven McAllister, Houston-Orange; OF—Richard Plautz, Kansas City-Gold; Kevin Buckley, Texas; Rolund Oruna, Kansas City-Blue; C—Mitchell Ashmore, Kansas City-Gold; Starting Pitcher—Ramon Vargas, Atlanta; Relief Pitcher—Guillermo Castro, Houston-Orange.

(Compiled by Howe News Bureau, Boston, Mass.)

CLUB BATTING

Club	Pct.	G.	AB.	R.	OR.	H.	TB.	2B.	3B.	HR.	RBI.	GW.	SH.	SF.	HP.	BB.	Int. BB.	SO.	SB.	CS.	LOB.
Houston-Orange	.272	61	1994	312	289	543	717	75	21	19	263	28	26	20	20	220	8	305	151	64	403
Texas	.253	63	2019	263	227	510	624	62	11	10	215	27	9	5	20	249	4	289	97	32	461
Chicago-AL	.252	64	2040	316	235	515	645	65	16	11	255	33	30	20	13	255	5	338	69	30	436
Kansas City-Gold	.251	65	2013	317	224	506	658	65	30	9	244	35	16	19	25	261	10	295	101	42	428
Toronto	.249	65	2055	247	312	512	643	70	17	9	198	18	18	18	24	166	7	428	141	54	375
Pittsburgh	.249	61	1957	259	260	488	627	81	14	10	209	24	7	20	16	213	4	373	133	42	410
New York-AL	.249	59	1853	260	254	461	594	79	18	6	214	27	33	16	17	215	4	309	55	34	379
Kansas City-Blue	.246	64	2002	313	237	492	664	68	19	22	247	23	33	15	25	297	6	361	85	38	469
Houston-Blue	.238	60	1942	207	278	462	592	65	13	13	175	17	14	18	15	171	3	344	81	44	401
Atlanta	.228	62	1968	227	262	448	591	72	13	15	200	26	21	15	19	249	9	389	49	30	456
Chicago-NL	.217	64	1931	216	302	419	519	52	15	6	154	18	21	13	22	226	6	456	98	41	407
San Diego	.214	64	1994	235	292	427	535	60	9	10	179	15	37	20	15	226	7	404	57	18	415

INDIVIDUAL BATTING

(Leading Qualifiers for Batting Championship—178 or More Plate Appearances)

°Bats lefthanded.   †Switch-hitter.

Player and Club	Pct.	G.	AB.	R.	H.	TB.	2B.	3B.	HR.	RBI.	GW.	SH.	SF.	HP.	BB.	Int. BB.	SO.	SB.	CS.
Henderson, Wendell, Chicago-NL	.356	60	202	31	72	89	13	2	0	28	4	1	3	3	26	1	17	11	6
Gonzales, Denio, Pittsburgh	.346	50	179	32	62	79	5	3	2	24	5	2	1	0	29	0	15	9	5
Thompson, Thomas, KC-G-KC-B	.328	62	186	28	61	101	10	0	10	44	3	1	3	4	41	2	25	7	4
Pecota, William, Kansas City-Blue	.317	61	208	61	66	94	11	4	3	22	0	1	0	1	39	0	18	14	1
Sanford, Kyle, Atlanta°	.317	58	186	34	59	79	12	1	2	34	9	0	5	1	38	1	15	1	2
Koch, Donn, Chicago-AL	.313	55	166	21	52	62	6	2	0	33	3	0	1	2	23	2	15	2	1
Rivera, Ricardo, Houston-Orange†	.309	53	191	25	59	74	5	5	0	26	1	5	1	1	19	0	29	33	17
Ortiz, Miguel, Toronto	.297	63	212	27	63	85	12	2	2	33	1	0	5	4	20	1	37	19	6
Oruna, Roland, Kansas City-Gold	.296	64	199	43	59	76	7	5	0	35	10	0	2	7	48	3	32	14	5
Buckley, Kevin, Texas	.295	50	176	21	52	72	8	3	2	29	4	0	0	0	16	0	25	2	1

Departmental Leaders: G—West, 65; AB—West, 250; R—Pecota, 61; H—Henderson, 72; TB—Plautz, Thompson, 101; 2B—Gomez, Lynch, Medina, 14; 3B—Plautz, 10; HR—Thompson, 10; RBI—Thompson, 44; GWRBI—Oruna, 10; SH—Langhorne, 9; SF—Ashmore, Ortiz, Sanford, Thompson, 5; BB—Oruna, 48; IBB—McHugh, Reyes, 3; SO—Roomes, 79; SB—Marte, 50; CS—Rivera, 17.

(All Players—Listed Alphabetically)

Player and Club	Pct.	G.	AB.	R.	H.	TB.	2B.	3B.	HR.	RBI.	GW.	SH.	SF.	HP.	BB.	Int. BB.	SO.	SB.	CS.
Aaron, Lawrence, Atlanta°	.190	28	63	5	12	13	1	0	0	5	0	6	0	2	2	0	8	1	0
Abraham, Miguel, Pittsburgh	.245	25	53	12	13	15	2	0	0	2	0	2	0	2	3	0	10	6	2
Acosta, Eduardo, Pittsburgh	.250	3	8	1	2	2	0	0	0	1	0	0	0	0	0	0	0	0	0

Player and Club	Pct.	G.	AB.	R.	H.	TB.	2B.	3B.	HR.	RBI.	GW.	SH.	SF.	HP.	BB.	Int. BB.	SO.	SB.	CS.
Adams, Patrick, Chicago-AL	.289	15	45	6	13	19	3	0	1	9	0	0	1	0	4	0	7	0	0
Alcala, Jesus, New York-AL	.306	16	49	10	15	20	1	2	0	8	0	1	1	1	4	0	8	4	0
Amaris, Orlando, Kansas City-Gold	.202	38	114	14	23	28	5	0	0	11	1	1	0	3	7	0	6	4	3
Amoros, Andres, Toronto	.286	5	7	0	2	2	0	0	0	0	0	0	0	0	2	0	0	0	0
Antonelli, John, Kansas City-Gold	.204	20	49	4	10	13	3	0	0	5	0	2	0	0	2	0	4	0	0
Antonetty, Elliot, Houston-Blue	.188	40	133	10	25	43	3	0	5	24	3	1	1	2	5	0	40	1	0
Arias, Juan, Pittsburgh	.261	6	23	6	6	11	1	2	0	3	0	0	0	0	2	0	7	2	0
Arnerich, Kenneth, Chicago-NL	.200	50	145	7	29	34	3	1	0	9	0	0	1	2	22	0	64	4	4
Ashmore, Mitchell, 5 KCB-44 KCG	.292	49	154	19	45	58	7	3	0	25	4	1	5	3	16	1	15	0	2
Bachmeier, Ronald, Chicago-NL	.217	32	106	12	23	27	2	1	0	3	0	0	0	2	13	0	21	8	5
Barton, Shaun, Chicago-AL	.176	26	51	11	9	9	0	0	0	4	0	5	1	0	14	0	4	3	1
Bass, Barry, Texas	.000	15	2	1	0	0	0	0	0	0	0	0	0	0	0	0	0	0	0
Battle, Kevin, Pittsburgh	.176	11	34	2	6	7	1	0	0	3	0	0	0	0	5	0	9	1	1
Beede, Walter, Chicago-NL	.068	27	73	5	5	8	0	0	1	6	0	0	0	5	0	0	29	1	0
Behan, Scott, Kansas City-Blue	.000	13	1	1	0	0	0	0	0	0	0	0	0	0	1	0	0	0	0
Benjamin, Julio, Houston-Blue	.200	50	170	13	34	47	6	2	1	19	2	1	4	1	11	0	18	7	4
Berti, Donald, Houston-Orange	.325	43	126	23	41	50	4	1	1	16	2	0	2	0	19	2	14	3	2
Blaser, Mark, New York-AL	.284	21	67	11	19	26	2	1	1	8	0	1	1	1	5	0	9	3	2
Blaylock, Russell, 43 HouB-8 HouO	.203	51	172	17	35	43	6	1	0	13	1	0	3	2	18	0	40	4	6
Bohi, Robert, Pittsburgh	.200	3	10	0	2	2	0	0	0	0	0	0	0	0	0	0	1	0	0
Bomerito, Robert, New York-AL	.233	30	103	12	24	33	1	1	2	11	2	0	0	1	6	1	17	2	2
Bonilla, Roberto, Pittsburgh	.217	22	69	6	15	20	5	0	0	7	0	0	2	1	7	1	17	2	1
Borges, Edward, Chicago-NL	.173	41	110	6	19	20	1	0	0	8	0	7	1	1	16	0	24	3	1
Boston, Daryl, Chicago-AL°	.291	56	189	30	55	70	6	3	1	30	5	4	1	0	16	0	45	12	3
Braun, Randall, 25 HouO-24 HouB°	.273	49	143	17	39	62	8	3	3	18	3	0	4	1	13	1	15	5	1
Brittman, James, Kansas City-Gold°	.333	13	27	3	9	11	0	1	0	4	0	0	2	0	3	0	5	0	1
Brown, Kenneth, Pittsburgh	.206	19	68	5	14	18	4	0	0	5	2	0	0	3	0	0	28	5	1
Brown, S. Craig, Pittsburgh	.259	50	170	21	44	56	12	0	0	23	1	1	4	0	14	0	27	13	5
Buckley, Kevin, Texas	.295	50	176	21	52	72	8	3	2	29	4	0	0	0	16	0	25	2	1
Buggs, Michael, Chicago-AL	.214	4	14	2	3	3	0	0	0	0	0	0	0	0	2	0	2	0	1
Bullock, Eric, Houston-Orange°	.293	56	184	38	54	71	8	3	1	15	1	2	0	3	34	1	23	24	5
Burger, Randall, Kansas City-Blue	.265	49	151	16	40	50	3	2	1	27	5	1	3	1	22	1	29	7	1
Burke, Curtis, Houston-Blue	.218	51	179	21	39	57	7	4	1	16	0	0	1	3	10	0	41	5	2
Burley, Anthony, Pittsburgh†	.227	25	66	6	15	18	3	0	0	5	0	0	0	0	7	0	6	2	1
Burton, Jeffrey, Pittsburgh	.232	28	99	14	23	31	2	0	2	15	2	0	3	2	15	0	22	5	1
Canady, Chuckie, Texas	.167	8	30	3	5	7	0	1	0	1	0	0	0	1	1	0	2	0	1
Cannon, Timothy, San Diego	.233	15	30	4	7	8	1	0	0	3	1	1	0	0	10	0	8	1	1
Carmona, Williams, Toronto	.267	47	120	14	32	36	4	0	0	13	2	1	2	3	8	1	20	0	2
Carpenter, Glenn, Houston-Orange	.265	53	166	24	44	57	6	2	1	13	1	2	0	1	26	0	25	7	7
Castenada, Nick, Pittsburgh°	.357	11	42	6	15	20	2	0	1	7	0	0	0	0	5	1	4	1	0
Castillo, Carlos, San Diego	.279	33	104	12	29	32	3	0	0	8	0	2	2	1	8	0	21	4	1
Chirrick, Mark, Kansas City-Blue	.000	16	0	1	0	0	0	0	0	0	0	0	0	0	0	0	0	0	0
Chmil, Steven, Atlanta	.200	1	5	0	1	1	0	0	0	0	0	0	0	0	0	0	1	0	0
Church, Daniel, Atlanta	.176	46	131	12	23	31	6	1	0	11	1	0	0	2	14	1	29	3	3
Churchill, James, Pittsburgh	.245	49	151	14	37	39	2	0	0	14	2	1	3	0	21	1	24	2	1
Citari, Joseph, Kansas City-Gold	.233	40	103	19	24	39	6	0	3	10	0	0	0	1	18	0	24	2	0
Clark, Henry, Houston-Orange	.254	52	189	22	48	61	8	1	1	27	4	3	4	2	11	2	24	9	4
Clark, Thomas, Atlanta	.197	41	122	12	24	29	3	1	0	6	1	0	0	1	14	0	26	5	4
Classes, Ramon, Pittsburgh†	.000	1	3	2	0	0	0	0	0	0	0	0	0	0	0	0	0	0	0
Clinton, Mark, Houston-Orange	.155	33	84	8	13	15	2	0	0	4	0	0	2	7	0	35	6	1
Colbert, Anthony, Chicago-NL	.000	15	1	0	0	0	0	0	0	0	0	0	0	0	0	0	1	0	0
Cormack, Terry, Atlanta°	.360	22	75	12	27	43	8	1	2	16	0	1	0	4	0	9	0	1	
Costa, Jason, Chicago-AL	.087	11	23	0	2	2	0	0	0	1	0	1	0	2	0	11	0	1	
Crum, George, Texas	.265	31	102	10	27	28	1	0	0	13	2	0	1	2	12	0	12	10	6
Daugherty, William, San Diego	.220	48	150	17	33	42	3	0	2	21	3	1	2	3	22	0	44	0	0
Davis, Douglas, Texas	.238	37	122	11	29	40	5	0	2	8	1	1	0	0	15	1	17	1	0
Davis, Glenn, Houston-Orange	.261	54	188	27	49	76	7	1	6	35	6	0	1	2	18	3	31	7	3
Davis, Johnny, Houston-Blue	.237	32	97	11	23	31	3	1	1	8	1	0	0	2	8	0	25	7	1
De La Rosa, Emilio, Texas	.238	12	21	2	5	5	0	0	0	3	1	0	0	0	1	0	9	1	1
Delgado, Juan, Hou-Or-Hou-Blue	.287	50	174	30	50	65	6	3	1	20	2	1	0	5	17	0	29	14	7
Delgado, Rumaldo, Pittsburgh°	.279	37	122	16	34	51	8	3	1	13	2	0	2	2	6	0	31	14	2
DePaula, Elvido, Houston-Blue	1.000	18	1	0	1	1	0	0	0	0	0	0	0	0	0	0	0	0	0
DeSena, Sergio, Houston-Orange	.229	45	131	15	30	36	3	0	1	13	0	1	3	0	7	0	22	7	5
DeSoto, Juan, Atlanta	.222	18	45	1	10	11	1	0	0	3	1	0	0	5	0	13	2	0	
Diaz, Angel, Toronto	.221	36	86	8	19	24	3	1	0	4	0	0	4	6	0	31	2	1	
Diaz, Eduardo, Atlanta	.256	17	43	5	11	15	4	0	0	5	0	1	0	1	0	7	0	0	
Diaz, Max, Chicago-AL	.200	12	20	2	4	6	0	1	0	0	0	0	3	0	4	0	0		
Donovan, Dennis, New York-AL	.280	33	82	9	23	27	2	1	0	8	0	6	0	1	9	0	9	3	2
Doolittle, Charles, Kansas City-Blue	.079	32	38	6	3	3	0	0	0	1	0	1	0	0	5	0	19	2	0
Duarte, Carlos, Toronto	.143	18	28	2	4	4	0	0	0	3	0	0	1	4	0	9	0	0	
Emmert, Kenneth, Chicago-NL	.230	54	178	27	41	46	5	0	0	10	1	4	0	5	23	1	36	8	4
Epperson, Charles, Chicago-AL†	.333	9	30	7	10	23	2	1	3	6	0	0	0	1	2	0	4	0	0
Espinal, Nelson, Houston Orange	.170	27	47	5	8	10	0	1	0	2	0	3	0	1	2	0	11	1	1
Espinoza, Ernesto, Houston Orange	.000	10	1	0	0	0	0	0	0	0	0	0	0	0	0	0	0	0	0
Espy, Cecil, Chicago-AL†	.282	43	142	24	40	45	2	3	1	16	2	3	1	1	11	1	13	9	4
Falls, Robert, Houston Blue	.243	55	202	23	49	56	7	0	0	15	3	2	0	1	20	1	48	14	8
Farmer, C. Theodore, New York-AL	.222	4	9	2	2	2	0	0	0	0	0	1	0	0	2	0	2	1	0
Faucette, Charles, Toronto	.167	51	156	16	26	37	5	0	2	8	2	0	0	3	20	1	39	2	6
Ferrante, Joseph, Houston Blue	.000	12	1	0	0	0	0	0	0	0	0	0	0	0	0	0	0	0	0
Flenoir, Keith, Chicago-AL°	.325	18	40	7	13	14	1	0	0	1	0	2	0	0	4	0	5	1	1
Flores, Edison, Chicago-AL	.286	24	56	8	16	20	2	1	0	7	1	0	0	0	2	0	4	1	0
Gaeta, Thomas, San Diego	.218	34	87	8	19	24	3	1	0	5	0	1	2	1	13	1	26	3	2
Garcia, Anthony, Texas	.231	8	26	3	6	6	0	0	0	2	0	0	0	1	1	0	1	0	0
Garcia, Ramone, Houston Blue	.228	39	127	8	29	36	5	1	0	7	0	1	1	0	5	0	18	1	2
Gatlin, Michael, New York-AL°	.283	55	173	28	49	62	6	2	1	22	4	3	4	3	37	1	29	6	5
Gaunce, David, Kansas City Gold	.343	17	35	4	12	17	2	0	1	7	1	0	0	0	4	0	5	0	0
Gayton, William, Chicago-AL°	.239	36	109	7	26	30	4	0	0	11	4	0	0	7	0	15	0	1	
Giansanti, Ralph, Atlanta	.197	40	127	12	25	30	3	1	0	15	1	5	0	2	14	0	10	5	3
Gil, Luis, Pittsburgh	.500	3	6	0	3	3	0	0	0	1	0	0	0	0	0	0	0	0	0
Gil, Thomas, Pittsburgh	.261	40	138	19	36	48	12	0	0	11	0	1	1	1	11	0	23	14	3
Gleissner, James, Kansas City Blue	.250	14	36	4	9	10	1	0	0	3	1	0	0	0	4	0	4	3	0
Gohde, George, New York-AL	.238	31	84	7	20	23	3	0	0	10	0	0	0	6	0	15	3	1	

Player and Club	Pct.	G.	AB.	R.	H.	TB.	2B.	3B.	HR.	RBI.	GW.	SH.	SF.	HP.	BB.	Int. BB.	SO.	SB.	CS.
Gomez, Jose, San Diego°	.290	61	200	34	58	88	14	2	4	35	3	1	2	2	35	0	51	6	2
Gompper, Christopher, K. City Gold	.158	7	19	3	3	3	0	0	0	1	0	0	0	0	2	0	5	1	0
Gonsoulin, Robert, San Diego†	.217	60	184	21	40	53	10	0	1	14	1	3	0	0	24	2	20	5	2
Gonzales, Agustin, Toronto	.156	23	45	4	7	8	1	0	0	3	0	1	0	1	1	0	9	2	0
Gonzales, Denio, Pittsburgh	.346	50	179	32	62	79	5	3	2	24	5	2	1	0	29	0	15	9	5
Gonzalez, Joaquin, New York-AL	.286	7	14	0	4	5	1	0	0	3	0	0	0	0	4	0	0	0	0
Gonzalez, Otto, Texas	.217	33	120	17	26	32	3	0	1	11	2	0	0	0	6	0	16	2	1
Goodin, Craig, Texas	.149	28	67	7	10	14	2	1	0	4	1	2	0	1	16	0	14	2	1
Gordon, Kenneth, Texas	.250	16	48	7	12	17	2	0	1	9	1	1	0	1	6	1	9	2	0
Guillen, Ozzie, San Diego†	.259	55	189	26	49	55	4	1	0	16	2	7	1	1	13	0	24	8	2
Hall, Tracy, Kansas City Gold	.132	28	53	7	7	8	1	0	0	3	0	2	0	1	4	0	21	7	2
Harris, James, Chicago-AL	.183	25	60	8	11	12	1	0	0	6	0	1	0	0	16	0	6	1	0
Harwell, Bryan, Texas	.188	21	64	9	12	13	1	0	0	5	0	1	1	0	14	1	16	2	0
Hawley, Mitchell, Kansas City Blue	.000	21	1	0	0	0	0	0	0	0	0	0	0	0	0	0	1	0	0
Heiser, Bruce, Atlanta	.667	1	3	0	2	2	0	0	0	1	0	0	0	0	1	0	1	0	0
Hempfield, Vaughn, Kansas City Blue	.324	39	102	13	33	41	2	3	0	8	0	2	0	0	8	0	19	3	6
Henderson, Wendell, Chicago-NL	.356	60	202	31	72	89	13	2	0	28	4	1	3	3	26	1	17	11	6
Henley, Michael, Chicago-AL	.240	47	146	16	35	55	10	2	2	30	5	3	4	0	14	0	29	2	4
Hennessey, Brendan, Texas	.278	24	79	8	22	24	2	0	0	7	0	0	0	0	9	0	20	0	0
Hodde, Rodney, Texas°	.291	38	110	16	32	36	2	1	0	14	2	2	0	3	19	0	12	3	0
Hodge, Patrick, Atlanta°	.120	41	92	15	11	17	1	1	1	5	1	0	0	0	28	2	27	1	2
Isaac, Johnny, Houston Orange	.317	45	123	28	39	59	6	1	4	18	1	1	1	1	10	0	32	9	6
Jackson, Darrin, Chicago-NL	.186	62	210	29	39	47	5	0	1	15	3	3	2	1	28	0	53	18	4
Janssen, Henry, Houston Orange	.248	42	117	21	29	37	5	0	1	17	1	0	1	1	22	0	12	10	2
Jeffries, James, Texas	.270	39	141	16	38	51	6	2	1	26	1	0	0	3	14	0	21	0	1
Jewett, Gregory, New York-AL	.189	13	37	5	7	13	3	0	1	4	1	0	2	0	5	0	12	2	0
Johnson, Aubrey, Kansas City Gold	.189	30	90	13	17	18	1	0	0	4	2	1	1	1	2	0	10	5	2
Johnson, Donald, Kansas City Gold	.241	24	58	6	14	14	0	0	0	7	0	0	0	0	10	0	19	2	0
Johnson, Michael, Texas	.284	30	88	13	25	36	5	0	2	16	1	0	1	1	21	0	12	3	1
Jones, Keith, Texas†	.291	54	175	36	51	56	5	0	0	13	3	0	0	0	16	0	21	30	5
Jones, Kevin, Chicago-AL°	.143	33	42	5	6	7	1	0	0	0	0	0	0	0	2	0	17	5	1
Kellam, Steven, Pittsburgh°	.000	4	11	0	0	0	0	0	0	0	0	0	0	0	0	0	3	0	0
Kent, Wesley, Chicago-AL	.188	20	64	3	12	16	1	0	1	12	0	1	0	1	4	0	12	0	0
Kinnard, Kenneth, Toronto	.275	63	233	55	64	83	11	4	0	12	0	0	0	0	29	0	61	38	9
Koch, Donald, Chicago-AL	.313	55	166	21	52	62	6	2	0	33	3	0	1	2	23	2	15	2	1
Lance, Mark, Atlanta	.000	13	1	0	0	0	0	0	0	0	0	0	0	0	0	0	0	0	0
Lane, Ira, Houston Blue	.188	35	80	15	15	16	1	0	0	1	0	3	0	0	14	0	16	7	3
Langhorne, Meade, Kan. City Blue°	.225	55	178	32	40	52	4	1	2	24	1	9	3	3	29	0	27	8	4
Ledna, Michael, Chicago-AL	.254	26	63	13	16	17	1	0	0	7	2	3	0	0	9	0	10	1	0
Llewellyn, Paul, Atlanta	.237	40	118	6	28	37	4	1	1	12	1	0	0	4	40	3	20	3	0
Lombardi, Phillip, New York-AL	.245	20	53	9	13	16	3	0	0	6	4	3	0	0	9	1	7	1	0
Loscalzo, Robert, Pittsburgh°	.111	4	9	0	1	1	0	0	0	0	0	0	0	0	4	0	2	1	0
Lowe, Andre, Atlanta	.161	30	56	7	9	12	0	0	1	4	0	1	1	0	12	0	16	1	0
Lucas, William, Atlanta	.214	41	103	10	22	27	3	1	0	10	0	1	2	0	16	1	21	4	1
Lucido, John, New York-AL	.333	1	3	1	1	1	0	0	0	1	0	0	0	0	1	0	0	0	0
Luzinski, William, Chicago-AL	.189	23	74	7	14	21	2	1	1	11	2	0	1	2	12	0	17	0	0
Lynch, Robyn, Atlanta°	.284	54	169	19	48	77	14	0	5	31	5	0	1	2	16	0	35	1	1
Malave, Omar, Toronto	.253	53	158	17	40	47	1	3	0	16	0	4	1	1	9	0	23	6	5
Mallet, Jeff, Hou-Or-Hous-B°	.203	27	74	7	15	19	1	0	1	9	1	0	1	0	8	0	21	2	0
Marmalejos, Leonida, San Diego	.086	22	58	4	5	5	0	0	0	2	1	1	0	0	5	0	15	1	0
Marte, Alexis, Toronto°	.293	49	157	35	46	54	4	2	0	15	3	3	0	0	23	0	24	50	4
Martin, Darrel, Texas	.308	7	13	1	4	4	0	0	0	1	0	0	0	0	1	0	4	0	1
Martin, Leonardo, Pittsburgh	.000	2	4	0	0	0	0	0	0	0	0	0	0	0	3	0	1	0	0
Masterson, Thomas, Pittsburgh	.273	33	88	14	24	28	2	1	0	8	2	0	2	1	24	0	15	6	1
Matos, Carlos, New York-AL	.208	9	24	5	5	5	0	0	0	1	0	0	0	0	7	0	3	0	0
Maynor, Howard, New York-AL	.218	38	110	17	24	31	3	2	0	8	0	2	0	0	11	0	18	2	2
McAllister, Steven, Houston Orange	.273	58	205	27	56	65	7	1	0	31	5	6	3	2	14	0	19	10	4
McCorkle, Robert, Houston Orange	.171	22	35	6	6	7	1	0	0	6	2	1	1	0	10	0	8	5	1
McGriff, Fredrick, New York-AL°	.148	29	81	6	12	14	2	0	0	9	2	0	1	1	11	0	20	0	0
McHugh, Thomas, Kansas City Gold°	.223	63	179	23	40	49	7	1	0	31	5	1	3	4	47	4	29	2	3
McIvar, Lawrence, Houston Orange	.263	36	114	20	30	42	6	0	2	19	0	2	0	2	11	0	31	9	0
Medina, Pedro, New York-AL	.268	56	209	34	56	74	14	2	0	17	2	4	0	2	14	0	13	7	6
Mejia, Oscar, Texas	.143	3	7	1	1	1	0	0	0	0	0	0	0	0	1	0	0	0	0
Mieses, Rafael, Toronto	.000	2	3	0	0	0	0	0	0	0	0	0	0	0	0	0	2	0	0
Miles, J. Edward, Chicago-AL	.164	30	55	5	9	13	2	1	0	3	0	0	0	0	8	0	16	1	1
Mohr, Thomas, Kansas City Blue°	.186	49	129	20	24	35	4	2	1	16	1	4	0	3	23	0	38	3	1
Moreno, Jamie, San Diego	.192	56	172	23	33	44	6	1	1	16	0	5	3	2	14	0	21	2	0
Morrison, Bruce, New York-AL	.371	20	62	11	23	29	4	1	0	14	1	0	1	1	6	0	10	1	2
Moser, Lawrence, Atlanta†	.279	57	190	26	53	64	6	1	1	13	2	3	3	0	16	1	24	5	4
Mundie, Donald, Houston Orange	.000	9	0	1	0	0	0	0	0	0	0	0	0	0	0	0	0	0	0
Neal, Bryan, Altanta°	.250	1	4	1	1	1	0	0	0	0	0	0	0	0	0	0	1	0	0
Newman, Mark, Kansas City Gold	.273	55	194	27	53	66	5	1	2	23	4	1	1	1	13	0	31	8	5
Nivar, Felix, Atlanta	.286	26	28	6	8	10	1	0	0	0	0	1	0	0	3	0	4	4	1
Nix, David, Chicago-AL°	.265	48	166	46	44	62	8	2	2	19	3	0	1	1	13	0	16	8	2
Nunez, Daniel, San Diego†	.277	38	119	21	33	37	2	1	0	11	1	2	0	0	21	1	20	10	3
O'Shea, Shane, New York-AL†	.275	13	40	8	11	13	2	0	0	4	0	0	0	2	7	0	3	0	2
Ochoa, Warren, Kansas City Blue	.183	57	186	23	34	39	5	0	0	9	0	4	0	3	21	0	52	5	2
Ortiz, Miguel, Toronto	.297	63	212	27	63	85	12	2	2	33	1	0	5	4	20	1	37	19	6
Oruna, Roland, Kansas City Gold	.296	64	199	43	59	76	7	5	0	35	10	0	2	7	48	3	32	14	5
Oterson, David, New York-AL°	.207	8	29	2	6	7	1	0	0	5	1	0	0	0	1	0	7	1	0
Ozoria, T. Ramon, Atlanta	.261	15	46	4	12	18	1	1	1	3	1	2	0	1	2	0	7	0	2
Palmer, Meade, New York-AL°	.000	9	7	1	0	0	0	0	0	1	0	0	0	0	2	0	3	0	0
Palmore, Stanley, Kansas City Gold	.148	22	61	8	9	11	0	1	0	3	0	2	0	0	6	0	19	5	4
Peake, Allen, Kansas City Blue°	.154	35	52	8	8	10	2	0	0	5	0	1	0	0	8	0	17	0	2
Pecota, William, Kansas City Blue	.317	61	208	61	66	94	11	4	3	22	0	1	0	1	39	0	18	14	1
Pena, Jorge, San Diego†	.184	56	179	15	33	36	1	1	0	10	0	3	0	4	24	0	31	9	2
Peraza, Oswald, Toronto	.125	23	40	1	5	5	0	0	0	0	0	0	2	0	1	0	8	2	1
Perez, Edgar, Chicago-AL	.222	10	27	3	6	7	1	0	0	4	2	0	1	0	2	0	6	0	0
Perez, Onesimo, Toronto°	.286	59	185	17	53	75	9	2	3	33	1	1	4	2	15	2	29	4	1
Perry, Scott, Texas	.211	23	76	10	16	20	4	0	0	6	0	0	0	0	12	0	15	2	1
Pettis, Stacey, Pittsburgh°	.224	40	143	20	32	40	5	0	1	9	1	0	1	1	16	1	41	21	6

Player and Club	Pct.	G.	AB.	R.	H.	TB.	2B.	3B.	HR.	RBI.	GW.	SH.	SF.	HP.	BB.	Int. BB.	SO.	SB.	CS.
Plautz, Richard, Kansas City Gold	.291	62	227	42	66	101	9	10	2	33	3	1	2	0	27	1	15	27	4
Polemir, Miguel, Houston Orange	.000	19	1	0	0	0	0	0	0	0	0	0	0	0	0	0	0	0	0
Portale, Joseph, New York-AL	.238	29	84	11	20	27	5	1	0	14	4	0	1	0	8	0	25	1	0
Powers, Mac, Chicago-NL°	.429	2	7	0	3	3	0	0	0	1	0	0	0	0	1	0	1	3	0
Ragsdale, Jerry, Atlanta	.091	21	44	2	4	4	0	0	0	1	0	0	0	2	3	0	8	0	1
Ramirez, Alvaro, New York-AL	.000	1	2	0	0	0	0	0	0	0	0	0	0	0	0	0	0	0	0
Ramirez, Francisco, Houston Blue	.088	21	57	6	5	5	0	0	0	3	0	0	0	2	13	1	18	0	1
Ramos, Luis, Pittsburgh	.273	38	143	20	39	48	5	2	0	19	1	0	1	0	9	0	20	15	6
Reyes, Rafael, Chicago-NL	.217	48	166	16	36	48	6	0	2	15	4	1	0	0	8	4	30	2	1
Rice, Arlanda, Pittsburgh	.000	3	10	0	0	0	0	0	0	0	0	0	0	0	0	0	5	0	0
Rivas, Hector, San Diego	.115	38	113	6	13	13	0	0	0	4	0	1	0	0	8	0	26	1	2
Rivas, Pedro, San Diego	.153	39	124	10	19	26	4	0	1	8	1	4	2	0	8	1	33	1	0
Rivas, Rafael, Toronto†	.304	45	148	13	45	55	7	0	1	22	2	3	4	0	8	2	19	5	3
Rivera, Ricardo, Houston Orange†	.309	53	191	25	59	74	5	5	0	26	1	5	1	1	19	0	29	33	17
Roberts, Darryl, Chicago-AL†	.128	21	47	2	6	6	0	0	0	3	0	0	2	0	6	0	13	0	0
Roberts, R. Jay, Atlanta	.172	42	122	10	21	27	3	0	1	8	2	0	0	6	19	0	42	6	3
Robertson, Charles, Houston Blue	.000	10	1	0	0	0	0	0	0	0	0	0	0	0	0	0	0	0	0
Rodriguez, Efrain, New York-AL	.231	40	121	17	28	37	9	0	0	16	1	2	1	0	7	0	22	2	1
Rodriguez, Miguel, Toronto	.216	49	148	9	32	41	7	1	0	13	4	1	1	0	5	0	29	1	3
Ridriguez, Wilmer, New York-AL	.283	32	113	15	32	36	4	0	0	5	0	4	0	1	4	0	8	4	4
Roomes, Rolando, Chicago-NL	.232	63	207	31	48	76	4	9	2	25	2	2	1	3	21	0	79	18	7
Rosario, Pedro, Atlanta	.333	3	3	0	1	1	0	0	0	0	0	0	0	0	0	0	1	0	0
Rossi, Domingo, Toronto	.229	35	83	9	19	22	1	1	0	9	1	0	1	1	3	0	17	3	3
Rowdon, Wade, Chicago-AL	.500	3	6	2	3	3	0	0	0	1	0	0	0	0	2	0	2	0	0
Sanford, Kyle, Atlanta°	.317	58	186	34	59	79	12	1	2	34	9	0	5	1	38	1	15	1	2
Sarmiento, Ramon, Toronto	.211	48	114	12	24	32	3	1	1	7	1	0	3	6	0	42	3	6
Scott, Richard, D., Pittsburgh†	.244	12	41	4	10	13	3	0	0	3	0	0	0	1	0	5	1	3
Scott, Richard E., New York-AL	.235	48	132	11	31	40	5	2	0	15	2	3	1	0	21	0	33	5	3
Sears, Hubert, Atlanta	.000	13	1	0	0	0	0	0	0	0	0	0	0	0	0	0	0	0	0
Sedar, Edward, Chicago-AL	.333	26	69	20	23	31	6	1	0	18	3	0	1	1	17	0	14	7	2
Seeker, Donald, Kansas City Blue°	.234	59	145	24	34	51	7	2	2	23	2	1	4	0	32	3	18	5	1
Seid, Bruce, Chicago-NL	.211	36	123	18	26	30	4	0	0	9	3	0	3	1	18	0	8	3	2
Serazio, Christopher, Texas°	.200	26	55	2	11	13	2	0	0	2	0	2	0	0	15	0	4	0	2
Sharp, Gary, Texas	.216	33	111	8	24	30	3	0	1	8	2	0	0	2	8	1	12	1	1
Shult, James, Texas	.326	17	46	10	15	19	2	1	0	4	1	0	0	0	10	0	9	2	1
Sierra, Julio, Atlanta	.000	9	1	0	0	0	0	0	0	0	0	0	0	0	0	0	1	0	0
Silverio, Luis, Kansas City Blue	.226	44	137	22	31	52	8	2	3	18	3	5	2	3	18	0	20	13	3
Simcox, Larry, Houston Blue	.268	41	149	18	40	50	10	0	0	19	2	4	3	0	14	0	4	6	4
Simmons, John, Atlanta	.130	13	23	1	3	3	0	0	0	2	0	1	1	0	3	1	4	0	0
Simonetti, David, Houston Blue	.250	14	52	2	13	13	0	0	0	1	1	0	0	0	7	0	8	1	5
Skelton, Warren, Kansas City Blue	.252	58	202	22	51	57	2	2	0	24	3	3	0	2	25	0	39	5	7
Smajstrla, Craig, Chicago-AL	.336	40	110	15	37	38	1	0	0	4	0	3	1	2	3	0	11	4	2
Smith, Daniel, Pittsburgh	.213	54	174	25	37	51	4	2	2	20	5	0	2	1	19	0	34	9	2
Smith, Philander, Houston Blue	.396	38	144	18	57	66	3	3	0	9	0	1	1	0	9	0	10	22	6
Smith, Randy, Kansas City Blue	.167	34	84	10	14	20	3	0	1	9	2	0	0	2	9	0	12	4	3
Smith, Scott, New York AL°	.000	3	1	1	0	0	0	0	0	0	0	0	0	0	0	0	0	0	0
Spalt, David, Kansas City Blue	.247	44	162	23	40	45	5	0	0	16	2	0	0	3	10	0	24	6	1
Speeney, Michael, New York AL	.200	22	20	4	4	4	0	0	0	2	0	0	0	0	0	0	6	2	0
Stabile, Edward, Chicago NL	.250	32	84	7	21	25	2	1	0	5	0	0	1	0	10	0	19	1	3
Stafford, Keith, Pittsburgh	.182	9	11	1	2	2	0	0	0	1	0	0	0	0	0	0	4	0	0
Stevens, Roger, Chicago AL°	.275	35	69	9	19	20	1	0	0	7	1	2	1	0	14	1	6	3	0
Storer, Kevin, Chicago AL	.167	19	48	3	8	9	1	0	0	5	0	1	1	1	7	0	11	1	1
Street, Keith, Atlanta°	.224	46	125	23	28	34	2	2	0	15	1	0	1	0	20	2	27	4	2
Surratt, Lewis, Texas	.169	27	77	7	13	14	1	0	0	3	0	0	1	1	15	0	10	1	0
Sweeder, David, New York AL	.000	14	1	1	0	0	0	0	0	0	0	0	0	0	0	0	1	0	0
Swinney, Steven, New York AL°	.206	31	63	10	13	21	3	1	1	7	0	2	1	1	14	0	17	3	1
Tabor, Craig, Texas	.320	9	25	4	8	9	1	0	0	5	0	0	0	1	3	0	1	4	1
Thompson, Scott, San Diego	.190	47	168	22	32	43	6	1	1	20	2	2	5	1	17	1	51	3	0
Thompson, Thomas, KC G—KC B	.328	62	186	28	61	101	10	0	10	44	3	1	3	4	41	2	25	7	4
Thorpe, Randy, Texas	.270	40	141	27	38	44	4	1	0	12	4	0	0	1	12	0	17	24	6
Tribble, Lawrence, Chicago NL	.204	33	98	11	20	22	2	0	0	5	1	1	0	2	12	0	15	6	2
Triplett, Antonio, Texas	.301	32	93	13	28	33	3	1	0	13	1	0	0	2	5	0	9	5	1
Tumpane, Robert, Atlanta°	.250	1	4	0	1	1	0	0	0	0	0	0	0	0	0	0	1	0	0
Valdez, Angel, San Diego	.205	33	117	12	24	29	3	1	0	6	0	3	1	0	4	1	13	3	1
Veon, Mark, Pittsburgh°	.195	30	82	13	16	24	3	1	1	15	1	0	4	9	0	20	4	1
Vitato, Richard, Kansas City Gold°	.254	55	205	29	52	68	8	4	0	24	3	2	2	3	23	0	30	3	5
Vizcaino, Tomas, Toronto	.235	48	132	8	31	33	2	0	0	7	1	2	0	0	6	0	29	4	4
Wagner, John, Atlanta†	.105	22	38	4	4	4	0	0	0	0	0	0	0	0	14	0	12	2	0
Walsh, John, Chicago AL	.077	9	13	4	1	1	0	0	0	0	0	1	0	0	3	0	4	1	0
Wayne, Gary, Chicago NL	.200	31	85	4	17	21	2	1	0	9	0	0	1	0	12	0	16	3	0
West, Reggie, Kansas City Gold	.268	65	250	52	67	82	5	5	0	16	2	2	1	1	31	1	24	21	8
Wiesler, Mark, Chicago AL†	.259	34	81	28	21	23	2	0	0	6	0	2	0	2	31	1	12	7	4
Williams, Millard, New York AL°	.238	33	80	12	19	28	5	2	0	15	3	1	2	2	14	1	12	2	1
Wilson, Lawrence, Chicago NL	.132	21	53	4	7	8	1	0	0	2	0	2	0	4	0	9	3	1
Wittmayer, Brent, Houston Blue°	.267	46	161	18	43	54	8	0	1	18	2	0	2	0	16	0	16	2	1
Wright, Andrew, Texas	.000	1	4	0	0	0	0	0	0	0	0	0	0	0	0	0	1	0	0

The following pitchers had no plate appearances primarily through use of designated hitters, listed alphabetically by club, games in parentheses:

ATLANTA—Clay, David (8); Edlefson, Bradley (9); Hamer, Michael (2); Hatcher, Richard (12); Klaus, Richard (2); McBride, Kevin (13); Napoleon, Esteban (9); Perdue, Joseph (2); Smith, Mark (8); Sperto, Carmine (12); Thompkins, James (2); Torres, Rudy (9); Vargas, Ramon (12); Waddell, Thomas (2); West, Matthew (9).

CHICAGO-AL—Babcock, William (6); Butler, Gregory (9); Cruz, Gregorio (9); Enrique, Martin (1); Guzman, Pedro (11); Hardy, John (13); Heath, Allan (10); Jones, Alfornia (12); McAnnally, Terry (14); Moses, John (14); Neimann, Arthur (13); Soth, Paul (2); Sutton, James (8); Tanzi, Michael (13); Welch, Dennis (9).

CHICAGO-NL—Buonantony, Richard (13); Carpio, Jorge (13); Clarke, Timothy (11); Cook, Mitchell (12); Gordon, Rocetto (13); Hook, Robert (14); Isgett, Thomas (11); Lovelace, Vance (7); Nowlin, Mark (16); Shuleeta, Michael (17); Trotter, Gregory (12).

HOUSTON-BLUE—Coplon, Mitchell (14); Corniel, Rafael (16); Godwin, Roger (18); Meadows, Geoffrey (9); Perez, Virgilio (7); Ross, Michael (22); Schimpf, Red (12); Snyder, Benjamin (14); Solano, Julio (17); Turner, Mark (12).

HOUSTON-ORANGE—Callahan, Michael (14); Castro, Guillermo (17); Cerefin, Michael (2); Happel, Craig (7); Malloy, David (16); Matos, Alexander (Atlanta) (5); Mize, Gregory (5); Reilly, Edward (13); Riewerth, Thomas (17).

KANSAS CITY-BLUE—Cone, David (14); Cook, Douglas (7); Davis, John (10); Harsh, Nicholas (7); Miner, James (13); Psaltis, Spiro (17); Schiavo, Edward (12); Strode, Lester (4); Swank, Kenneth (12); Villalba, Libardo (9).

KANSAS CITY-GOLD—Ballard, Timothy (22); Barnard, Jeffrey (8); Bloomfield, Mark (17); Bryant, John (12); Cutty, Francis (4); Ferreira, Anthony (12); Gubicza, Mark (11); King, Olice (10); Lewis, Tod (11); Olson, Michael (7); Shaw, Robert (5); Sturm, Randy (13); Swanson, Perry (21); Wyatt, Reggie (4).

NEW YORK-AL—Bailey, Boyce (6); Blasano, Mark (1); Corpa, Amaury (1); Ferrin, Trent (6); Flores, Wilfredo (18); Herrera, Henry (6); Humphrey, Daryl (13); Jones, Jeffrey (9); Marks, Jeffrey (7); Martin, Kenneth (3); Peltola, William (11); Plunk, Eric (11); Raftice, Robert (4); Rijo, Jose (11); Rodriguez, Nelson (7); Williams, Stanley (7).

PITTSBURGH—Adams, Marvin (1); Allman, Michael (1); Andujar, Ramon (2); Azcona, Ramon (1); Cassell, Timothy (12); Colina, Edgar (5); Daiker, Ronald (1) Gonzalez, Jose (7); Krawczyk, Raymond (4); Lamonde, Lawrence (12); Manzanillo, Ravello (9); Mejia, Manuel (14); Mott, Richard (5); Pellien, Kenneth (12); Plasencia, Homero (1); Plasencia, Omar (2); Rondon, Julio (3); Sanchez, Leopoldo (5); Santana, Gervacio (8); Storm Luis (1); Styles, Lawrence (3); Taylor, Ronald (13); Torres, Nelson (5); Tunnell, Byron (1); Tuthill, Robert (1); Winn, James (1).

SAN DIEGO—Blamay, Patrick (14); Christy, Mark (13); Collet, Jose (13); Figueroa, Ismael (8); Huyck, Paul (11); Katsukos, Peter (15); Leopold, James (13); Macias, Robert (10); Majer, Joseph (23); Schefsky, Steven (4); Solomon, William (2); Sullivan, Daniel (1); White, Jeffrey (including Pittsburgh) (13).

TEXAS—Barnes, Jeffrey (9); Benes, Joseph (13); Brosious, Frank (14); Cook, Glen (14); Guzman, Jose (14); Kouba, Curtis (13); Lachowicz, Allen (6); Leach, Martin (6); Mayfield, Montye (13); McLane, Larry (5); Schmid, Michael (9); Schulte, Todd (7); Taylor, William (12); Thomas, Bobby Joe (2); Warren, Raymond (14); Watson, Carl (14); Zwolenski, Mitchell (6).

TORONTO—Buchanan, Jeffrey (12); Cerrud, Roberto (11); Cook, Dale (14); Diaz, Gumercindo (15); Fagnani, Richard (18); Goffena, David (11); Leal, Obdulio (16); Malave, Benito (14); Palencia, Edwin (13); Reish, Stephan (14); Ruetter, Derrick (12); Schneider, Edwin (14).

GRAND SLAM HOME RUNS—Davis, Henley, Kent, Perez, 1 each.

AWARDED FIRST BASE ON INTERFERENCE—Skelton 2 (Gonzalez 2); Buckley (Koch); Emmert (Cormack); Espy (Garcia); Gaeta (Davis); Hodde (Cormack); Nix (Moreno); Rivera (Diaz); Roberts (Burton); Roomes (Moreno); West (Garcia).

CLUB FIELDING

Club	Pct.	G.	PO.	A.	E.	DP.	PB.	Club	Pct.	G.	PO.	A.	E.	DP.	PB.
Chicago-AL	.962	64	1624	791	95	55	13	Pittsburgh	.948	61	1555	741	125	44	22
Kansas City-Gold	.962	65	1627	755	95	54	21	New York-AL	.946	59	1499	652	123	37	9
Texas	.962	63	1583	742	93	66	15	Atlanta	.945	62	1582	708	134	52	28
Kansas City-Blue	.960	64	1605	705	95	51	18	San Diego	.945	64	1627	684	134	42	18
Houston-Blue	.956	60	1526	760	105	57	16	Chicago-NL	.939	64	1576	740	150	41	25
Houston-Orange	.949	61	1572	774	127	53	15	Toronto	.931	65	1633	733	174	36	14

Triple Plays—Atlanta, Chicago-NL, Texas.

INDIVIDUAL FIELDING

*Throws lefthanded.

FIRST BASEMEN

Player and Club	Pct.	G.	PO.	A.	E.	DP.	Player and Club	Pct.	G.	PO.	A.	E.	DP.
Adams, Chicago AL	1.000	13	99	8	0	10	Malave, Toronto	1.000	1	2	0	0	0
Arias, Pittsburgh	.962	2	24	1	1	2	McCorkle, Houston Orange	.900	1	8	1	1	1
Battle, Pittsburgh	1.000	5	34	3	0	2	McGriff, New York AL*	.963	24	176	8	7	10
Beede, Chicago NL	.969	22	174	11	6	12	McHugh, Kansas City Gold	.984	45	418	14	7	33
Benjamin, Houston Blue	.991	41	398	25	4	31	McIvar, Houston Orange	1.000	1	5	2	0	1
Berti, Houston Orange	1.000	1	1	0	0	0	Morrison, New York AL	.987	18	149	4	2	11
Bonilla, Pittsburgh	.974	12	100	13	3	10	Ortiz, Toronto	1.000	1	3	0	0	2
Borges, Chicago NL	1.000	1	10	1	0	2	Peake, Kansas City Blue*	.971	28	131	5	4	15
Brittman, Kansas City Gold*	.980	7	47	3	1	3	Peraza, Toronto	.875	6	20	1	3	0
Burger, Kansas City Blue	1.000	4	37	0	0	3	Perez, Toronto*	.962	36	298	7	12	12
Carpenter, Houston Orange	.990	12	94	4	1	10	Perry, Texas	1.000	1	1	2	0	0
Castaneda, Pittsburgh*	1.000	11	94	11	0	4	Reyes, Chicago NL	1.000	2	9	0	0	0
Churchill, Pittsburgh	.986	36	256	21	4	18	Rivas, San Diego	.971	12	94	8	3	9
Citari, Kansas City Gold	.982	20	155	5	3	13	Roberts, Chicago AL	.986	21	129	7	2	7
Daugherty, San Diego	1.000	1	8	0	0	2	Rodriguez, New York AL	1.000	3	18	1	0	1
Davis, Houston Orange	.973	52	469	37	14	35	Rodriguez, Toronto	.983	34	275	8	5	15
Diaz, Chicago AL	1.000	3	8	1	0	0	Rossi, Toronto	1.000	1	2	0	0	0
Durarte, Toronto	1.000	4	3	1	0	1	SANFORD, Atlanta*	.993	46	402	17	3	32
Garcia, Texas	1.000	3	26	0	0	2	Sarmiento, Toronto	.800	2	4	0	1	0
Gayton, Chicago AL	.996	26	223	12	1	21	Sharp, Texas	.969	4	30	1	1	4
Gomez, San Diego*	.979	54	450	16	10	26	Stabile, Chicago NL	.982	12	100	10	2	6
Henderson, Chicago NL	.989	29	261	15	3	12	Surratt, Texas	1.000	25	214	9	0	23
Hodde, Texas*	.984	37	295	16	5	35	Thompson, KC G-KC B	.988	52	399	27	5	28
Janssen, Houston Orange	1.000	3	24	1	0	1	Tumpane, Atlanta*	1.000	1	8	0	0	0
Kent, Chicago AL	.993	18	125	15	1	10	Wayne, Chicago AL	1.000	6	51	3	0	3
Ledna, Chicago AL	1.000	1	1	0	0	0	Williams, New York AL*	.979	23	173	14	4	12
Lynch, Atlanta*	.985	27	183	10	3	14	Wittmayer, Houston Blue	.981	23	187	20	4	20

Triple Plays—Sanford, Stabile.

SECOND BASEMEN

Player and Club	Pct.	G.	PO.	A.	E.	DP.	Player and Club	Pct.	G.	PO.	A.	E.	DP.
Acosta, Pittsburgh	1.000	2	6	3	0	0	Guillen, San Diego	.989	19	47	45	1	10
Alcala, New York AL	.938	3	8	7	1	0	Harwell, Texas	1.000	21	56	56	0	17
Amaris, Kansas City Gold	.857	2	1	5	1	0	Heiser, Atlanta	1.000	1	1	4	0	0
Bachmeier, Chicago NL	.933	22	40	43	6	6	Hempfield, Kansas City Blue	.965	28	62	75	5	15
Blaylock, Houston Blue	1.000	2	2	8	0	1	Johnson, Texas	.975	25	59	59	3	16
Bohi, Pittsburgh	1.000	1	1	2	0	1	Ledna, Chicago AL	.940	11	19	28	3	5
Burley, Pittsburgh	1.000	5	16	9	0	4	Lowe, Atlanta	.934	13	25	32	4	9
Cannon, San Diego	1.000	1	0	1	0	0	Lucas, Atlanta	.895	13	36	32	8	8
Carmona, Toronto	.977	11	17	26	1	4	Martin, Pittsburgh	.778	1	5	2	2	0
Castillo, San Diego	.714	5	10	5	6	1	Medina, New York AL	.960	55	123	139	11	27
Crum, Texas	.956	19	42	44	4	9	Newman, Kansas City Gold	.931	7	15	12	2	4
Emmert, Chicago NL	.947	4	10	8	1	1	Nix, Chicago AL	.963	38	84	98	7	25
Espinal, Houston Orange	.959	22	30	40	3	12	Ortiz, Toronto	1.000	1	3	2	0	1
Falls, Houston Blue	.981	35	92	110	4	20	Ozoria, Atlanta	.917	5	9	13	2	1
Giansanti, Atlanta	.920	37	81	92	15	16	Pena, San Diego	.978	10	29	16	1	5
Gil, Pittsburgh	.923	16	36	24	5	3	Perry, Texas	.800	1	2	2	1	0
Gompper, Kansas City Gold	.964	7	11	16	1	3	Ramirez, New York AL	1.000	1	0	2	0	1
Gonsoulin, San Diego	.972	8	14	21	1	6	RIVERA, Houston Orange	.978	51	120	143	6	28
Gonzales, Toronto	1.000	1	0	6	0	0	Rossi, Toronto	.913	25	43	41	8	7
Gonzales, Pittsburgh	.960	28	92	74	7	17	Scott, Pittsburgh	.936	12	32	26	4	7
Goodin, Texas	1.000	2	8	5	0	2	Seid, Chicago NL	.963	13	19	33	2	2

SECOND BASEMEN—Continued

Player and Club	Pct.	G.	PO.	A.	E.	DP.
Smith, Pittsburgh	.875	1	3	4	1	0
Smith, Houston Blue	.955	30	68	80	7	20
Spalt, Kansas City Blue	.962	38	94	84	7	16
Speeney, New York AL	1.000	5	1	4	0	0
Tribble, Chicago NL	.877	15	26	45	10	7

Triple Play—Goodin.

Player and Club	Pct.	G.	PO.	A.	E.	DP.
Valdez, San Diego	.945	30	68	70	8	10
Vitato, Kansas City Gold	.972	50	104	178	8	35
Vizcaino, Toronto	.937	43	87	105	13	12
Walsh, Chicago AL	.875	8	15	13	4	3
Wiesler, Chicago AL	.947	16	40	31	4	9
Wilson, Chicago NL	.938	13	20	25	3	1

THIRD BASEMEN

Player and Club	Pct.	G.	PO.	A.	E.	DP.
Battle, Pittsburgh	.867	6	1	12	2	0
Benjamin, Houston Blue	.933	5	4	10	1	1
Blaylock, Hou B-Hou O	.861	48	45	97	23	2
Bohi, Pittsburgh	.769	2	5	5	3	0
Bomerito, New York AL	.932	22	15	54	5	3
Bonilla, Pittsburgh	.900	2	1	8	1	0
Burley, Pittsburgh	.917	18	10	45	5	4
Burton, Pittsburgh	.774	8	6	18	7	2
Cannon, San Diego	.818	14	6	12	4	1
Church, Atlanta	.886	42	28	73	13	5
Clark, Houston Orange	.914	43	40	98	13	9
Delgado, Hou O-Hou B	.896	25	10	59	8	2
Desena, Houston Orange	1.000	2	2	0	0	0
Duarte, Toronto	.842	9	7	9	3	0
Emmert, Chicago NL	.910	43	38	83	12	6
Epperson, Chicago AL	.909	8	8	12	2	0
Espinal, Houston Orange	.667	1	0	2	1	0
Falls, Houston Blue	1.000	4	2	10	0	0
Garcia, Texas	1.000	4	5	8	0	0
Gayton, Chicago AL	1.000	4	1	8	0	0
Gil, Pittsburgh	.833	11	5	15	4	2
Gonsoulin, San Diego	.911	45	43	80	12	5
Gonzales, Toronto	.857	3	4	2	1	0
Gonzales, Pittsburgh	.875	20	10	39	7	3
Gordon, Texas	1.000	4	2	10	0	4
HENLEY, Chicago AL	.922	45	26	104	11	7

Triple Play—Emmert.

Player and Club	Pct.	G.	PO.	A.	E.	DP.
Hennessey, Texas	.857	14	16	26	7	3
Hodge, Atlanta	.898	25	18	35	6	5
Johnson, Kansas City Gold	.890	30	23	58	10	5
Lucas, Atlanta	.875	4	3	11	2	1
Maynor, New York AL	.800	11	10	14	6	1
McHugh, Kansas City Gold	1.000	1	13	1	0	0
Newman, Kansas City Gold	.937	39	33	85	8	7
O'Shea, New York AL	.790	6	6	9	4	1
Ortiz, Toronto	.913	58	59	120	17	5
Ozoria, Atlanta	.765	5	4	9	4	0
Pecota, Kansas City Blue	.907	14	10	29	4	1
Pena, San Diego	.769	4	3	7	3	1
Perez, Chicago AL	1.000	2	0	3	0	0
Perry, Texas	.805	17	8	25	8	4
Rivas, San Diego	.774	9	9	15	7	1
Rodriguez, New York AL	.923	25	21	51	6	2
Rossi, Toronto	.333	5	0	1	2	0
Seid, Chicago NL	.867	6	2	11	2	0
Sharp, Texas	.843	29	16	59	14	3
Skelton, Kansas City Blue	.908	51	31	97	13	11
Stabile, Chicago NL	.818	10	1	17	4	0
Storer, Chicago AL	.872	17	14	27	6	6
Vitato, Kansas City Gold	.714	1	1	4	2	0
Vizcaino, Toronto	1.000	1	1	0	0	0
Wayne, Chicago NL	.885	9	2	21	3	3
Wilson, Chicago NL	.500	1	0	1	1	0

SHORTSTOPS

Player and Club	Pct.	G.	PO.	A.	E.	DP.
Acosta, Pittsburgh	1.000	1	1	2	0	1
Alcala, New York-AL	.851	12	13	27	7	3
Amaris, Kansas City-Gold	.910	36	48	104	15	22
Amoros, Toronto	.778	5	2	5	2	0
Arnerich, Chicago-NL	.870	49	74	146	33	23
Barton, Chicago-AL	.945	25	30	73	6	9
Brown, Pittsburgh	.639	5	10	13	13	1
Burley, Pittsburgh	.846	4	4	7	2	2
Carmona, Toronto	.826	17	22	35	12	6
Castillo, San Diego	1.000	1	1	1	0	0
Chmil, Atlanta	1.000	1	4	1	0	0
Clark, Atlanta	.853	41	31	125	27	21
Delgado, Hou-Or-Hou-Blue	.888	21	25	62	11	9
Emmert, Chicago-NL	.783	9	11	25	10	2
Espinal, Houston-Orange	.500	1	0	1	1	0
Falls, Houston-Blue	.943	9	13	20	2	5
Gonsoulin, San Diego	1.000	3	5	10	0	1
Gonzales, Toronto	.790	17	17	28	12	3
Goodin, Texas	.901	22	31	60	10	5
Gordon, Texas	.893	13	21	29	6	6
Guillen, San Diego	.914	32	58	90	14	16
Johnson, Kansas City-Gold	.900	23	17	55	8	8
Lowe, Atlanta	.902	12	11	26	4	1
Lucas, Atlanta	.922	19	16	43	5	9
Malave, Toronto	.876	38	44	90	19	11
Martin, Pittsburgh	.667	1	1	1	1	0

Player and Club	Pct.	G.	PO.	A.	E.	DP.
McAllister, Houston-Orange	.930	58	84	180	20	33
Medina, New York-AL	1.000	2	5	5	0	2
Mejia, Texas	1.000	3	2	8	0	0
Newman, Kansas City-Gold	.909	12	14	36	5	3
Nix, Chicago-AL	1.000	3	4	13	0	2
Oliver, Kansas City-Blue	.923	57	84	181	22	31
Ozoria, Atlanta	.667	2	3	1	2	1
Pena, San Diego	.905	35	48	86	14	11
Perez, Chicago-AL	.951	8	9	30	2	7
Rivas, San Diego	1.000	1	1	2	0	0
Rivera, Houston-Orange	1.000	2	0	6	0	1
Rodriguez, New York AL	.867	5	7	6	2	1
Rosario, Atlanta	.667	3	0	2	1	0
Rowdon, Chicago-AL	1.000	2	1	3	0	0
Scott, New York-AL	.920	47	66	130	17	18
Simcox, Houston-Blue	.910	40	59	142	20	23
Skelton, Kansas City-Blue	.714	3	3	2	2	1
Smajstrla, Chicago-AL	.922	39	50	103	13	15
SMITH, Pittsburgh	.934	53	105	179	20	24
Spalt, Kansas City-Blue	.900	6	6	21	3	0
Speeney, New York-AL	.667	7	2	6	4	2
Stabile, Chicago-NL	.897	10	8	18	3	2
Tabor, Texas	.936	7	15	29	3	7
Triplett, Texas	.937	28	42	76	8	21
Vitato, Kansas City-Gold	1.000	4	2	9	0	1
Vizcaino, Toronto	1.000	4	3	7	0	0

OUTFIELDERS

Player and Club	Pct.	G.	PO.	A.	E.	DP.
Aaron, Atlanta	1.000	19	21	3	0	0
Abraham, Pittsburgh	1.000	21	19	0	0	0
Alcala, New York-AL	1.000	1	1	0	0	0
Antonetty, Houston-Blue	.951	35	37	2	2	0
Bachmeier, Chicago-NL	.929	5	12	1	1	1
Bass, Texas	1.000	1	1	0	0	0
Blaser, New York-AL	1.000	1	3	0	0	0
Borges, Chicago-NL	.978	39	40	4	1	2
Boston, Chicago-AL°	.969	54	84	9	3	2
Braun, Hou-Or-Hou-Blue	.946	34	50	2	3	0
Brown, Pittsburgh	.875	5	7	0	1	0
Brown, Pittsburgh	.971	44	59	9	2	2
Buckley, Texas	1.000	48	52	9	0	2
Buggs, Chicago-AL°	1.000	3	9	0	0	0
Bullock, Houston-Orange°	.961	52	67	6	3	0
Burke, Houston-Blue	.990	51	89	6	1	0
Canady, Texas	1.000	8	16	1	0	0
Carmona, Toronto	.818	6	9	0	2	0
Carpenter, Houston-Orange°	.961	43	67	6	3	1
Castillo, San Diego	.850	14	17	0	3	1
Church, Atlanta	1.000	1	2	0	0	0
Classes, Pittsburgh	1.000	1	2	0	0	0

Player and Club	Pct.	G.	PO.	A.	E.	DP.
Colbert, Chicago-NL	.933	26	24	4	2	0
Costa, Chicago-AL°	.857	8	6	0	1	0
Daugherty, San Diego	.927	44	48	3	4	0
Davis, Houston-Blue	.875	21	20	1	3	0
Delgado, Pittsburgh°	.988	35	73	6	1	0
DeSena, Houston-Orange	.980	39	47	3	1	1
Donovan, New York-AL	.963	32	77	1	3	0
Doolittle, Kansas City-Blue	.931	29	27	0	2	0
Espy, Chicago-AL°	.932	41	54	1	4	0
Faucette, Toronto	.913	50	72	1	7	0
Flenoir, Chicago-AL	.938	16	15	0	1	0
Gaeta, San Diego	.979	29	45	1	1	0
Gatlin, New York-AL	.952	54	97	3	5	0
Gil, Pittsburgh	1.000	3	2	0	0	0
Gleissner, Kansas City-Blue	1.000	1	0	1	0	0
Gonzales, Toronto	1.000	1	2	0	0	0
Gonzalez, Texas	1.000	1	9	2	0	0
Goodin, Texas	1.000	2	2	0	0	0
Hall, Kansas City-Gold°	.889	17	15	1	2	0
Harris, Chicago-AL	1.000	23	20	4	0	1
Hodge, Atlanta	.960	14	24	0	1	0
Isaac, Houston-Orange	.897	37	33	2	4	0

OUTFIELDERS—Continued

Player and Club	Pct.	G.	PO.	A.	E.	DP.	Player and Club	Pct.	G.	PO.	A.	E.	DP.
Jackson, Chicago-NL	.992	61	121	5	1	1	Pettis, Pittsburgh	.964	37	81	0	3	0
Jeffries, Texas	1.000	35	51	11	0	2	Plautz, Kansas City-Gold	.960	35	47	1	2	1
Jewett, New York-AL	.857	12	10	2	2	1	Powers, Chicago-NL	1.000	2	6	1	0	1
Jones, Texas	.968	47	89	3	3	0	Ramirez, Houston-Blue	1.000	14	18	1	0	0
Jones, Chicago-AL°	.947	23	18	0	1	0	Ramos, Pittsburgh	.907	36	64	4	7	1
Kinnard, Toronto	.960	61	90	6	4	1	Rice, Pittsburgh	.778	3	7	0	2	0
Lane, Houston-Blue	.938	28	42	3	3	0	Rivas, San Diego	.982	36	52	3	1	0
LANGHORNE, K.C.-Blue°	1.000	52	67	4	0	0	Rivas, Toronto	1.000	1	2	0	0	0
Llewellyn, Atlanta	.982	37	53	0	1	0	Rivera, Houston-Orange	.667	2	2	0	1	0
Loscalzo, Pittsburgh°	1.000	4	9	0	0	0	Roberts, Atlanta	.963	38	49	3	2	1
Lucido, New York-AL	1.000	1	2	0	0	0	Rodriguez, New York-AL	.970	37	54	11	2	3
Luzinski, Chicago-AL	1.000	19	17	0	0	0	Roomes, Chicago-NL	.946	63	80	7	5	0
Malave, Toronto	.950	15	18	1	1	0	Rossi, Toronto	1.000	2	1	0	0	0
Mallet, Houston-Blue	1.000	1	1	0	0	0	Sanford, Atlanta°	1.000	1	1	0	0	0
Marmalejos, San Diego	.895	19	17	0	2	0	Sarmiento, Toronto	.958	33	46	0	2	0
Marte, Toronto°	.960	46	92	5	4	1	Seeker, Kansas City-Blue	.963	55	69	10	3	0
Matos, New York-AL	.933	8	14	0	1	0	Seid, Chicago-NL	1.000	1	1	0	0	0
Maynor, New York-AL	1.000	17	25	1	0	1	Serazio, Texas	.944	17	17	0	1	0
McIvar, Houston-Orange	.966	27	27	1	1	0	Shult, Texas	1.000	15	14	2	0	0
Miles, Chicago-AL	1.000	17	19	4	0	2	Silverio, Kansas City-Blue	.977	40	80	3	2	1
Mohr, Kansas City-Blue°	.968	47	86	4	3	0	Simonetti, Houston-Blue	.931	13	23	4	2	1
Morrison, New York-AL	1.000	2	1	0	0	0	Smith, Kansas City-Blue	.900	10	8	1	1	0
Moser, Atlanta°	.981	54	98	3	2	1	Spalt, Kansas City-Blue	1.000	1	1	0	0	0
Neal, Atlanta	1.000	1	1	0	0	0	Stevens, Chicago-AL°	1.000	32	30	5	0	0
Nivar, Atlanta	1.000	14	10	0	0	0	Street, Atlanta	.981	39	49	3	1	0
Nunez, San Diego°	.964	27	50	4	2	0	Swinney, New York-AL	.913	18	18	3	2	0
Oruna, Kansas City-Gold	.976	63	117	5	3	1	Thompson, San Diego	.948	42	86	5	5	1
Oterson, New York-AL°	.867	8	12	1	2	0	Thorpe, Texas	.960	32	45	3	2	1
Palmer, New York-AL	.600	5	3	0	2	0	Veon, Pittsburgh	.938	13	15	0	1	0
Palmore, Kansas City-Gold	1.000	18	24	0	0	0	Wagner, Atlanta	.923	17	12	0	1	0
Peraza, Toronto	.857	2	6	0	1	0	West, Kansas City-Gold	.983	65	105	9	2	1
Perez, Toronto°	1.000	4	3	0	0	0	Wilson, Chicago-NL	1.000	7	4	0	0	0

Triple Play—Street.

CATCHERS

Player and Club	Pct.	G.	PO.	A.	E.	DP.	PB.	Player and Club	Pct.	G.	PO.	A.	E.	DP.	PB.
Antonelli, Kansas City-Gold	.989	18	80	10	1	1	2	Koch, Chicago-AL	.974	53	306	34	9	3	7
ASHMORE, KC-B-KC-G	.985	43	224	32	4	0	14	Lombardi, New York-AL	.965	20	94	17	4	1	1
Berti, Houston-Orange	.975	32	169	24	5	2	5	Mallet, Hou-O-Hou-Blue	.967	23	101	16	4	4	5
Blaser, New York-AL	.976	17	100	20	3	1	7	Martin, Texas	1.000	4	14	1	0	0	0
Bonilla, Pittsburgh	.962	5	23	2	1	0	2	Masterson, Pittsburgh	.979	33	155	35	4	7	8
Burger, Kansas City-Blue	.979	35	213	25	5	2	6	McCorkle, Houston-Orange	.985	18	56	10	1	1	3
Burton, Pittsburgh	.971	9	58	9	2	0	7	McHugh, Kansas City-Gold	.750	2	3	0	1	0	0
Churchill, Pittsburgh	.986	12	56	12	1	1	2	Moreno, San Diego	.949	56	314	56	20	6	11
Cormack, Atlanta	.949	14	67	8	4	0	11	O'Shea, New York-AL	.778	1	5	2	2	0	0
Davis, Texas	.974	34	175	46	6	3	10	Ochoa, Chicago-AL	1.000	8	36	5	0	0	1
DeSoto, Atlanta	.951	18	64	13	4	1	8	Pecota, Kansas City-Blue	.983	18	102	16	2	2	9
Diaz, Toronto	.932	29	96	40	10	2	7	Peraza, Toronto	.905	14	33	5	4	0	4
Diaz, Atlanta	.968	17	83	7	3	0	2	Portale, New York-AL	1.000	3	9	0	0	0	1
Farmer, New York-AL	1.000	2	6	2	0	0	0	Ragsdale, Atlanta	.991	18	92	23	1	1	7
Flores, Chicago-AL	.981	23	94	11	2	2	5	Reyes, Chicago-NL	.951	32	177	37	11	7	12
Garcia, Houston-Blue	.979	37	191	37	5	2	9	Rivas, San Diego	.971	14	89	11	3	0	7
Gaunce, Kansas City-Gold	1.000	16	82	6	0	1	6	Rivas, Toronto	.965	40	227	47	10	3	4
Gleissner, Kansas City-Blue	.986	12	58	11	1	0	0	Simmons, Atlanta	.971	13	63	3	2	0	0
Gohde, New York-AL	.946	28	109	13	7	0	0	Smith, Kansas City-Blue	.923	5	11	1	1	0	2
Gonzalez, New York-AL	.917	7	43	1	4	0	1	Stafford, Pittsburgh	.944	3	14	3	1	0	1
Gonzalez, Texas	.982	30	186	28	4	1	5	Tribble, Chicago-NL	.966	15	70	15	3	1	10
Henderson, Chicago-NL	.960	25	150	18	7	2	3	Veon, Pittsburgh	1.000	7	21	2	0	0	2
Janssen, Houston-Orange	.945	29	157	33	11	4	7	Wittmayer, Houston-Blue	1.000	11	39	6	0	1	2
Kellam, Pittsburgh	1.000	1	1	0	0	0									

Triple Play—Cormack.

PITCHERS

Player and Club	Pct.	G.	PO.	A.	E.	DP.	Player and Club	Pct.	G.	PO.	A.	E.	DP.
Allman, Pittsburgh	1.000	1	1	1	0	0	Collet, San Diego	1.000	13	0	7	0	0
Andujar, Pittsburgh°	1.000	2	0	3	0	0	Cone, Kansas City-Blue	.857	14	1	11	2	0
Babcock, Chicago-AL°	1.000	6	1	8	0	0	Cook, Toronto	.938	14	2	13	1	1
Bailey, New York-AL	.857	6	1	5	1	1	Cook, Kansas City-Blue	1.000	7	1	6	0	0
Ballard, Kansas City-Gold	1.000	22	3	7	0	0	Cook, Texas	1.000	14	1	8	0	1
Barnard, Kansas City-Gold	1.000	8	1	2	0	2	Cook, Chicago-NL	.875	12	2	19	3	1
Barnes, Texas	1.000	9	0	7	0	2	Coplon, Houston-Blue	.933	14	4	10	1	0
Bass, Texas	1.000	13	2	11	0	2	Corniel, Houston-Blue	.889	16	1	7	1	1
Behan, Kansas City-Blue	.870	13	4	16	3	1	Corpa, New York-AL	1.000	1	0	1	0	0
Benes, Texas°	.857	13	0	6	1	0	Cruz, Chicago-AL	1.000	9	1	2	0	0
Blamay, San Diego	.875	10	2	5	1	0	Cutty, Kansas City-Gold	.867	4	2	11	2	0
Bloomfield, Kansas City-Gold°	.667	17	1	3	2	0	Daiker, Pittsburgh	1.000	1	1	0	0	0
Brosious, Texas	1.000	14	2	6	0	1	Davis, Kansas City-Blue	1.000	10	1	7	0	0
Bryant, Kansas City-Gold	.950	12	3	16	1	0	DePaula, Houston-Blue	1.000	18	2	7	0	0
Buonantony, Chicago-NL	.960	13	5	19	1	1	DIAZ, Toronto	1.000	15	3	21	0	1
Buchanan, Toronto	.857	12	0	12	2	1	Edlefson, Atlanta	1.000	9	0	3	0	1
Butler, Chicago-AL	1.000	9	2	1	0	0	Enriquez, Chicago-AL	1.000	1	0	1	0	0
Callahan, Houston-Orange	.667	14	3	5	4	1	Espinoza, Houston-Orange	.790	10	2	13	4	0
Carpio, Chicago-NL	.957	13	3	19	1	1	Fagnani, Toronto°	.857	18	0	6	1	0
Cassell, Pittsburgh	1.000	12	2	9	0	0	Ferrante, Houston-Blue	1.000	12	3	8	0	0
Castro, Houston-Orange°	.667	17	1	5	3	0	Ferreira, Kansas City-Gold°	1.000	12	2	10	0	2
Cerrud, Toronto	1.000	11	0	7	0	0	Ferrin, New York-AL°	.900	6	4	5	1	0
Chirrick, Kansas City-Blue	1.000	15	2	8	0	0	Figueroa, San Diego°	.929	8	0	13	1	0
Christy, San Diego	.941	13	4	12	1	1	Flores, San Diego	1.000	18	2	8	0	1
Clarke, Chicago-NL	.966	11	8	20	1	3	Godwin, Houston-Blue	.941	18	6	10	1	0
Clay, Atlanta	.933	8	3	11	1	0	Goffena, Toronto	.857	11	1	5	1	0
Clinton, Houston-Orange	.923	13	4	8	1	1	Gonzalez, Pittsburgh	.857	7	4	2	1	0

PITCHERS—Continued

Player and Club	Pct.	G.	PO.	A.	E.	DP.
Gordon, Chicago-NL	.727	13	1	7	3	0
Gubicza, Kansas City-Gold	.964	11	5	22	1	1
Guzman, Chicago-AL	1.000	10	2	6	0	0
Guzman, Texas	1.000	14	2	13	0	2
Hamer, Atlanta	.667	2	0	2	1	0
Happel, Houston-Orange	1.000	7	5	2	0	0
Hardy, Chicago-AL	.929	13	6	20	2	1
Harsh, Kansas City-Blue	.857	7	2	4	1	0
Hatcher, Atlanta	1.000	12	1	15	0	0
Hawley, Kansas City-Blue	.800	21	2	6	2	3
Heath, Chicago-AL*	.875	10	2	12	2	1
Herrera, New York-AL	1.000	6	1	3	0	0
Hook, Chicago-NL*	1.000	14	0	8	0	0
Humphrey, New York-AL	1.000	13	4	17	0	0
Huyck, San Diego*	.889	11	1	15	2	1
Isgett, Chicago-NL	1.000	11	2	2	0	0
Jones, Chicago-AL	.966	11	5	23	1	2
Jones, New York-AL*	1.000	9	2	8	0	0
Katsukos, San Diego	1.000	15	4	6	0	1
King, Kansas City-Gold*	.833	10	0	5	1	0
Klaus, Atlanta	1.000	2	1	1	0	0
Kouba, Texas*	1.000	13	0	4	0	0
Krawczyk, Pittsburgh	.800	4	0	8	2	0
Lachowicz, Texas	1.000	6	6	3	0	0
Lamonde, Pittsburgh	.957	12	10	34	2	1
Lance, Atlanta*	.833	13	0	10	2	1
Leach, Texas	1.000	6	0	7	0	0
Leal, Toronto	.667	16	0	4	2	0
Leopold, San Diego	.912	13	2	29	3	0
Lewis, Kansas City-Gold	1.000	11	2	6	0	0
Lovelace, Chicago-NL*	.636	7	2	5	4	0
Macias, San Diego	.938	10	1	14	1	1
Majer, San Diego	1.000	23	1	10	0	1
Malave, Toronto	1.000	14	2	7	0	0
Malloy, Houston Orange*	.900	16	4	5	1	0
Manzanillo, Pittsburgh*	.889	9	2	6	1	1
Marks, New York AL*	1.000	7	1	2	0	0
Martin, New York AL	1.000	3	0	4	0	0
Matos, Atl-Hou-O	1.000	5	0	2	0	0
Mayfield, Texas	.889	13	2	6	1	1
McAnnally, Chicago AL	.900	14	2	7	1	0
McBride, Atlanta	.750	13	2	4	2	0
McLane, Texas*	1.000	5	0	4	0	0
Meadows, Houston Blue	1.000	9	3	5	0	2
Mejia, Pittsburgh	1.000	14	4	14	0	0
Miner, Kansas City Blue	.923	13	5	19	2	2
Mize, Houston Orange	1.000	5	1	4	0	0
Morrison, New York AL	1.000	1	1	0	0	0
Moses, Chicago AL*	.867	14	2	11	2	0
Mott, Pittsburgh	1.000	5	2	1	0	0
Mundie, Houston Orange	.786	8	4	7	3	1
Napoleon, Atlanta	.833	9	1	4	1	0
Neiman, Chicago AL	1.000	13	3	8	0	0
Nowlin, Chicago NL	.889	16	4	12	2	0
Olson, Kansas City Gold	1.000	7	0	8	0	0
Palencia, Toronto	.714	13	1	4	2	0
Pellien, Pittsburgh*	1.000	12	0	15	0	1
Peltola, New York AL	.933	11	3	11	1	0
Perdue, Atlanta	1.000	2	0	1	0	0
Perez, Houston Blue*	.750	7	1	2	1	0
Plunk, New York AL	.818	11	1	8	2	0
Polemir, Houston Orange	1.000	19	5	6	0	1
Psaltis, Kansas City Blue*	1.000	17	3	10	0	1
Raftice, New York AL*	1.000	4	0	1	0	0
Reilly, Houston Orange	.960	13	5	19	1	0
Reish, Toronto	.868	14	4	29	5	1
Riewerth, Houston Orange*	.833	17	1	14	3	0
Rijo, New York AL	1.000	11	0	3	0	0
Robertson, Houston Blue	.778	10	2	5	2	1
Rodriguez, New York AL	.667	7	0	2	1	0
Ross, Houston Blue	.917	22	3	8	1	0
Ruetter, Toronto*	.947	12	3	15	1	0
Sanchez, Pittsburgh*	1.000	5	0	2	0	0
Santana, Pittsburgh	1.000	8	0	1	0	0
Schefsky, San Diego	1.000	4	0	1	0	0
Schiavo, Kansas City Blue	1.000	12	0	2	0	0
Schimpf, Houston Blue	1.000	12	1	7	0	1
Schmid, Texas*	1.000	9	0	2	0	0
Schneider, Toronto*	.833	14	4	11	3	0
Schulte, Texas*	1.000	7	1	2	0	0
Sears, Atlanta	1.000	13	3	8	0	0
Shaw, Kansas City Gold*	1.000	5	1	0	0	0
Shuleeta, Chicago NL	1.000	17	4	11	0	0
Smith, Atlanta	1.000	8	1	6	0	0
Snyder, Houston Blue	.867	14	11	15	4	0
Solano, Houston Orange	.917	17	6	27	3	1
Solomon, San Diego	1.000	2	0	1	0	0
Soth, Chicago AL	1.000	2	1	0	0	0
Sperto, Atlanta	.867	12	2	11	2	0
Stafford, Pittsburgh	.889	6	1	7	1	0
Strode, Kansas City Blue*	1.000	4	1	1	0	0
Sturm, Kansas City Gold	.857	13	2	4	1	0
Styles, Pittsburgh	1.000	3	0	6	0	1
Sutton, Chicago AL	1.000	8	0	5	0	0
Swank, Kansas City Blue*	1.000	12	5	14	0	0
Swanson, Kansas City Gold	.944	21	5	12	1	0
Sweeder, New York AL*	.900	13	0	9	1	0
Tanzi, Chicago AL*	.926	13	1	24	2	1
Taylor, Pittsburgh	1.000	13	2	6	0	0
Taylor, Texas	.778	12	2	12	4	0
Thomas, Texas	1.000	2	1	1	0	0
Thompkins, Atlanta	1.000	2	0	2	0	0
Torres, Pittsburgh	1.000	5	1	4	0	0
Torres, Atlanta	.750	9	2	4	2	0
Trotter, Chicago NL*	.824	12	4	10	3	0
Turner, Houston Blue*	.929	12	0	13	1	1
Vargas, Atlanta	.963	12	7	19	1	0
Villalba, Kansas City Blue	1.000	9	0	1	0	0
Waddell, Atlanta	1.000	2	0	3	0	0
Warren, Texas	1.000	14	0	4	0	0
Watson, Texas	.889	14	1	7	1	0
Welch, Chicago AL	.600	9	2	1	2	0
West, Atlanta	.933	9	4	10	1	0
White, Pitt-SD*	1.000	13	0	4	0	1
Williams, New York AL	.909	7	3	7	1	1
Winn, Pittsburgh	1.000	1	0	2	0	0
Wyatt, Kansas City Gold*	1.000	4	0	3	0	0
Zwolenski, Texas	1.000	6	1	9	0	1

The following players do not have any recorded accepted chances at the positions indicated; therefore, are not listed in the fielding averages for those particular positions: Abraham, 3b; Adams, 2b; Azcona, p; Blasano, p; Caraballo, 2b; Carmona, 1b; Castillo, 3b; Cerefin, p; Clinton, 2b; Colina, p; Crum, 3b; G. Davis, of; De La Rosa, of; Donovan, 1b; Garcia, of; Henderson, of; McCorkle, of; Nivar, 2b; Pecota, 2b; Peraza, p; H. Plasencia, p; O. Plasencia, p; Rodriguez, c; Rondon, p; Scott, of; Sedar, 1b; Sierra, p; P. Smith, of; S. Smith, of; Storm, p; Sullivan, p; Tunnell, p; Tuthill, p.

CLUB PITCHING

Club	ERA.	G.	CG.	ShO.	Sv.	IP.	H.	R.	ER.	HR.	HB.	BB.	Int. BB.	SO.	WP.	Bk.
Kansas City Gold	2.56	65	8	11	19	542⅓	439	224	154	9	23	240	4	366	33	9
Atlanta	2.73	62	4	5	11	527⅓	484	262	160	12	16	226	5	362	46	7
Texas	2.78	63	0	8	13	527⅔	482	227	163	12	26	223	2	359	24	8
Chicago AL	2.84	64	13	9	13	541⅓	465	235	171	13	19	199	3	407	26	5
New York AL	3.08	59	8	1	11	499⅔	480	254	171	15	17	181	5	353	26	12
Kansas City Blue	3.10	64	5	4	12	535	493	237	184	8	16	219	15	371	42	3
Pittsburgh	3.11	61	12	8	11	518⅓	462	260	179	17	23	223	1	298	39	9
Toronto	3.37	65	13	4	3	544⅓	542	312	204	8	20	220	6	338	34	7
San Diego	3.52	64	21	6	5	542⅓	492	292	212	18	12	272	5	376	43	7
Houston Orange	3.52	61	3	3	17	524	472	289	205	8	17	271	8	361	36	6
Chicago NL	3.62	64	13	5	12	525⅓	493	302	211	6	15	238	7	383	42	8
Houston Blue	3.84	60	0	3	11	508⅔	479	278	217	14	27	236	12	317	44	7

PITCHERS' RECORDS

(Leading Qualifiers for Earned-Run Average Leadership — 53 or More Innings)

*Throws lefthanded.

Pitcher—Club	W.	L.	Pct.	ERA.	G.	GS.	CG.	GF.	ShO.	Sv.	IP.	H.	R.	ER.	HR.	HB.	BB.	Int. BB.	SO.	WP.
Reilly, Houston Orange	6	1	.857	1.30	13	11	1	2	0	0	69	48	16	10	0	1	17	0	43	2
Jones, Chicago AL	3	5	.375	1.40	11	9	3	2	2	1	58	50	19	9	0	0	20	0	41	2
Vargas, Atlanta	7	3	.700	1.56	12	12	3	0	2	0	75	61	20	13	1	2	12	0	24	2
Clarke, Chicago NL	6	2	.750	1.80	11	11	3	0	1	0	70	64	25	14	1	2	18	1	53	1

Pitcher—Club	W.	L.	Pct.	ERA.	G.	GS.	CG.	GF.	ShO.	Sv.	IP.	H.	R.	ER.	HR.	HB.	BB.	Int. BB.	SO.	WP.
Macias, San Diego	5	3	.625	1.87	10	9	7	1	3	0	77	57	23	16	2	1	13	1	71	0
Psaltis, Kansas C. Blue°	4	1	.800	1.87	17	3	2	8	1	1	53	27	17	11	1	0	22	2	52	3
Reish, Toronto	6	5	.545	2.17	14	13	6	0	2	0	87	86	40	21	0	2	20	1	63	2
Gubicza, Kansas C. Gold	8	1	.889	2.25	11	11	0	0	0	0	56	39	18	14	0	1	23	0	40	3
Huyck, San Diego°	3	3	.500	2.33	11	6	2	2	1	0	58	44	19	15	0	2	27	0	54	4
Sperto, Atlanta	2	4	.333	2.33	12	10	0	2	0	2	58	56	25	15	1	0	32	0	43	4
Turner, Houston Blue°	2	3	.400	2.33	12	9	0	2	0	0	54	28	18	14	3	2	28	1	24	2

Departmental Leaders: G—Majer, 23; GS—Brosious, 14; CG—Macias, 7; ShO—Macias, 3; W—Gubicza, Hardy, 8; L—Diaz, 9; Sv.—Nowlin, 7; Pct.—Gubicza, .889; IP—Hardy, Leopold, 88; H—Christy, 93; R—Callahan, 52; ER—Christy, 42; HR—Pellien, 5; BB—Blamay, 61; IBB—Chirrick, 4; HB—Snyder, 6; SO—Hardy, 78; WP—McBride, Snyder, 12.

(All Pitchers—Listed Alphabetically)

Pitcher—Club	W.	L.	Pct.	ERA.	G.	GS.	CG.	GF.	ShO.	Sv.	IP.	H.	R.	ER.	HR.	HB.	BB.	Int. BB.	SO.	WP.
Adams, Pittsburgh	0	0	.000	4.50	1	0	0	0	0	0	2	2	1	1	0	0	1	0	1	0
Allman, Pittsburgh	0	0	.000	9.00	1	0	0	0	0	0	2	3	2	2	0	0	2	0	1	1
Andujar, Pittsburgh°	1	0	1.000	0.00	2	1	0	0	0	0	6	2	1	0	0	0	2	0	3	1
Azcona, Pittsburgh	0	0	.000	0.00	1	0	0	0	0	0	1	1	2	0	0	0	2	0	2	0
Babcock, Chicago-AL°	3	2	.600	1.25	6	6	1	0	1	0	36	24	10	5	0	0	10	0	25	1
Bailey, New York-AL°	3	2	.600	2.00	6	6	0	0	0	0	36	28	12	8	0	1	19	0	29	4
Ballard, Kan. City Gold	6	5	.545	3.09	22	3	0	16	0	3	64	69	31	22	3	3	12	3	41	1
Barnard, Kan. City Gold	0	1	.000	3.00	8	1	0	4	0	1	9	9	6	3	0	1	9	0	5	0
Barnes, Texas	2	1	.667	1.80	9	0	0	4	0	0	20	18	7	4	0	3	6	0	10	1
Bass, Texas	3	2	.600	2.00	13	6	0	2	0	1	45	41	16	10	1	4	19	1	30	4
Behan, Kan. City Blue	3	3	.500	3.10	13	12	0	1	0	1	61	63	24	21	1	3	14	0	35	5
Benes, Texas°	3	0	1.000	1.64	13	3	0	5	0	2	33	22	10	6	1	2	11	0	28	1
Blamay, San Diego	0	5	.000	9.32	10	10	0	0	0	2	28	23	37	29	2	3	61	0	11	7
Blasano, New York-AL	0	0	.000	0.00	1	0	0	0	0	0	1	0	0	0	0	0	0	0	0	0
Bloomfield, Kan. City Gold°	2	1	.667	2.54	17	0	0	6	0	4	39	27	17	11	0	1	13	0	22	2
Brosious, Texas	3	6	.333	4.50	14	14	0	0	0	0	64	74	36	32	0	4	29	0	37	5
Bryant, Kan. City Gold	2	2	.500	3.11	12	7	2	2	1	1	55	47	31	19	2	2	32	0	43	8
Buonantony, Chicago-NL	2	6	.250	5.06	13	9	0	2	0	0	64	70	50	36	4	2	38	1	50	5
Buchanan, Toronto	0	4	.000	5.03	12	7	0	5	0	0	34	41	26	19	2	0	22	0	24	2
Butler, Chicago-AL	2	0	1.000	4.91	9	2	0	3	0	0	22	22	15	12	1	1	17	0	9	5
Callahan, Houston Orange	3	6	.333	7.38	14	8	0	5	0	2	50	54	52	41	2	4	44	1	26	8
Carpio, Chicago-NL	3	8	.273	3.84	13	13	4	0	1	0	82	73	47	35	0	2	34	0	57	7
Cassell, Pittsburgh	5	2	.714	2.94	12	6	1	4	0	1	49	41	25	16	1	2	19	0	22	5
Castro, Houston Orange°	4	1	.800	2.60	17	3	0	9	0	3	52	48	22	15	0	0	18	3	43	0
Cerefin, Houston Orange	0	0	.000	13.50	2	0	0	0	0	0	2	3	3	3	0	0	4	0	3	0
Cerrud, Toronto	1	2	.333	5.46	11	2	0	4	0	0	28	33	25	17	0	5	15	0	20	5
Chirrick, Kan. City Blue	1	4	.200	3.43	15	1	0	10	0	2	42	45	23	16	1	2	22	4	24	2
Christy, San Diego	5	4	.556	4.55	13	12	3	0	0	0	83	93	50	42	4	2	39	2	41	9
Clarke, Chicago-NL	6	2	.750	1.80	11	11	3	0	1	0	70	64	25	14	1	2	18	1	53	1
Clay, Atlanta	3	2	.600	1.60	8	7	0	1	0	0	45	42	17	8	0	1	6	0	37	2
Clinton, Houston Orange	3	4	.429	2.89	13	8	0	3	0	1	53	44	25	17	0	1	29	0	54	11
Colina, Pittsburgh	1	1	.500	10.80	5	0	0	5	0	0	5	11	7	6	1	0	4	0	2	3
Collet, San Diego	0	0	.000	5.76	13	2	0	3	0	0	25	18	17	16	1	1	21	0	26	7
Cone, Kan. City Blue	6	4	.600	2.55	14	12	0	0	0	0	67	52	24	19	0	3	33	1	45	8
Cook, Toronto	5	2	.714	2.10	14	1	0	11	0	1	30	15	12	7	1	1	8	0	18	1
Cook, Kan. City Blue	4	2	.667	2.30	7	7	1	0	0	0	43	28	12	11	2	1	24	0	41	6
Cook, Texas	2	2	.500	4.81	14	8	0	4	0	0	43	40	26	23	4	2	20	0	43	3
Cook, Chicago-NL	5	5	.500	2.50	12	7	2	2	0	1	54	35	21	15	0	0	13	0	44	1
Coplon, Houston Blue	0	3	.000	5.67	14	8	0	4	0	1	46	47	34	29	0	4	20	0	25	4
Corniel, Houston Blue	1	1	.500	2.84	16	1	0	4	0	1	38	36	15	12	1	1	13	1	17	3
Corpa, New York-AL	0	0	.000	0.00	1	0	0	1	0	0	3	2	0	0	0	1	0	0	2	0
Cruz, Chicago-AL	1	0	1.000	6.00	9	0	0	7	0	0	12	16	10	8	0	1	7	0	9	2
Cutty, Kan. City Gold	3	1	.750	1.38	4	2	0	1	2	0	26	14	7	4	0	0	12	0	18	3
Daiker, Pittsburgh	0	0	.000	0.00	1	0	0	1	0	0	1	1	0	0	0	0	0	0	2	1
Davis, Kan. City Blue	2	2	.500	5.10	10	4	0	4	0	0	30	28	21	17	0	0	23	1	13	1
Depaula, Houston Blue	3	1	.750	4.09	18	3	0	9	0	2	44	45	22	20	1	3	16	1	23	4
Diaz, Toronto	3	9	.250	4.04	15	10	1	2	0	0	69	77	34	31	2	2	15	0	22	1
Edlefson, Atlanta	0	0	.000	5.06	9	0	0	5	0	1	16	21	13	9	2	2	13	0	10	2
Enriquez, Chicago-AL	0	0	.000	0.00	1	0	0	1	0	0	1	0	0	0	0	0	0	0	0	0
Espinoza, Houston Orange	2	3	.400	5.11	10	5	1	3	0	0	37	29	28	21	1	5	33	0	15	2
Fagnani, Toronto°	2	1	.667	4.06	18	1	0	5	0	0	31	24	16	14	0	3	22	1	13	1
Ferrante, Houston Blue	2	5	.286	4.02	12	8	0	4	0	1	56	59	29	25	3	2	18	1	30	1
Ferreira, Kan. City Gold°	4	0	1.000	2.25	12	11	0	1	0	0	48	40	19	12	1	3	22	0	45	1
Ferrin, New York-AL°	2	3	.400	2.06	6	5	1	0	0	0	35	32	19	8	0	0	8	0	15	2
Figueroa, San Diego°	4	2	.667	2.63	8	8	3	0	2	0	48	45	23	14	0	1	12	0	28	2
Flores, New York-AL°	4	1	.800	2.84	18	1	0	14	0	6	38	37	15	12	2	2	13	1	33	3
Godwin, Houston Blue	3	6	.333	3.41	18	7	0	8	0	1	58	62	29	22	0	3	21	1	36	1
Goffena, Toronto	0	2	.000	1.80	11	1	0	2	0	0	20	21	16	4	0	0	12	1	9	3
Gonzalez, Pittsburgh	1	0	1.000	2.84	7	0	0	2	0	0	19	22	12	6	2	2	10	0	12	0
Gordon, Chicago-NL	2	3	.400	5.56	13	3	0	7	0	0	34	40	28	21	1	1	18	2	41	5
Gubicza, Kan. City Gold	8	1	.889	2.25	11	11	0	0	0	0	56	39	18	14	0	1	23	0	40	3
Guzman, Chicago-AL	0	1	.000	5.09	10	2	0	5	0	2	23	21	20	13	1	5	10	1	12	1
Guzman, Texas	3	3	.500	5.31	14	4	0	3	0	0	39	44	30	23	2	1	14	0	13	1
Hamer, Atlanta	0	1	.000	0.00	2	1	0	0	0	0	5	2	1	0	0	1	0	0	5	1
Happel, Houston Orange	1	0	1.000	4.50	7	0	0	5	0	2	16	11	10	8	0	0	10	0	10	0
Hardy, Chicago-AL	8	2	.800	2.35	13	11	4	1	2	0	88	72	24	23	3	0	7	0	78	2
Harsh, Kan. City Blue	4	0	1.000	0.90	7	3	0	4	0	1	20	12	4	2	0	0	5	0	12	0
Hatcher, Atlanta	4	2	.677	0.79	12	0	0	10	0	3	34	23	6	3	1	1	6	2	26	0
Hawley, Kan. City Blue	3	4	.429	4.50	21	0	0	19	0	3	32	43	19	16	0	1	11	3	31	4
Heath, Chicago-AL	3	3	.500	3.83	10	10	1	0	1	0	47	43	29	20	1	1	36	0	37	4
Herrera, New York-AL	0	1	.000	3.38	6	2	1	2	0	0	24	19	9	9	1	2	14	0	17	2
Hook, Chicago-NL°	0	0	.000	3.55	14	0	0	7	0	2	33	35	15	13	0	1	9	0	12	2
Humphrey, New York-AL	4	3	.571	4.29	13	9	1	4	0	0	63	63	38	30	2	2	24	0	35	2
Huyck, San Diego°	3	3	.500	2.33	11	6	2	2	1	0	58	44	19	15	0	2	27	0	54	4
Isgett, Chicago-NL	0	0	.000	7.36	11	1	0	4	0	0	22	25	21	18	0	1	17	1	12	2
Jones, Chicago-AL	3	5	.375	1.40	11	9	3	2	2	1	58	50	19	9	0	0	20	0	41	5
Jones, New York-AL°	1	4	.200	2.20	9	8	3	0	0	0	49	46	19	12	2	0	10	0	22	1

Pitcher—Club	W.	L.	Pct.	ERA.	G.	GS.	CG.	GF.	ShO.	Sv.	IP.	H.	R.	ER.	HR.	HB.	BB.	Int. BB.	SO.	WP.
Katsukos, San Diego	2	3	.400	3.98	15	0	0	9	0	0	43	45	25	19	3	0	25	0	20	1
King, Kan. City Gold°	4	3	.571	4.40	10	10	0	0	0	0	45	40	23	22	2	2	38	0	24	0
Klaus, Atlanta	0	1	.000	10.80	2	1	0	0	0	0	5	8	6	6	0	0	3	0	5	1
Kouba, Texas°	1	2	.333	0.86	13	0	0	12	0	2	21	16	4	2	1	0	2	0	11	0
Krawczyk, Pittsburgh	0	1	.000	1.50	4	3	1	1	1	1	18	11	5	3	0	1	7	1	14	2
Lachowicz, Texas	2	3	.400	1.88	6	6	0	0	0	0	24	19	9	5	0	0	15	0	14	3
Lamonde, Pittsburgh	3	3	.500	2.65	12	12	5	0	0	0	85	63	39	25	2	5	37	0	53	5
Lance, Atlanta°	1	3	.250	1.32	13	2	0	8	0	2	34	29	19	5	0	1	16	1	22	5
Leach, Texas	0	1	.000	2.00	6	4	0	1	0	0	18	19	5	4	0	2	5	0	11	0
Leal, Toronto	1	1	.500	3.33	16	2	0	9	0	2	27	30	21	10	1	0	8	1	20	2
Leopold, San Diego	3	8	.273	3.07	13	13	4	0	0	0	88	82	51	30	3	0	34	0	48	6
Lewis, Kan. City Gold	2	0	1.000	3.66	11	3	0	5	0	2	32	30	15	13	0	1	15	0	17	3
Lovelace, Chicago-NL°	0	5	.000	3.30	7	7	1	0	0	0	30	27	22	11	0	4	26	0	31	1
Macias, San Diego	5	3	.625	1.87	10	9	7	1	3	0	77	57	23	16	2	1	13	1	71	0
Majer, San Diego	1	3	.250	2.10	23	0	0	21	0	5	30	30	10	7	1	0	7	2	17	2
Malave, Toronto	3	4	.429	3.21	14	11	1	0	1	0	73	61	43	26	2	3	41	0	64	7
Malloy, Houston Orange°	2	2	.500	3.38	16	7	0	6	0	1	48	45	23	18	1	0	25	1	36	4
Manzanillo, Pittsburgh°	3	1	.750	1.13	9	7	0	0	0	0	48	35	11	6	0	2	10	0	34	4
Marks, New York-AL°	3	1	.750	4.33	7	3	0	1	0	0	27	28	15	13	2	1	15	0	18	3
Martin, New York-AL	0	0	.000	10.80	3	1	0	1	0	0	5	4	6	6	0	0	7	0	2	0
Matos, Atl-Hou-Orange	0	1	.000	3.38	5	1	0	2	0	0	8	9	5	3	0	1	5	0	4	0
Mayfield, Texas	0	2	.000	3.19	13	2	0	5	0	2	31	29	15	11	2	0	17	1	16	1
McAnnally, Chicago-AL	2	3	.400	3.75	14	1	0	8	0	1	36	32	25	15	0	0	17	0	32	1
McBride, Atlanta	0	3	.000	5.45	13	2	0	7	0	1	33	40	29	20	1	2	18	0	35	12
McLane, Texas	0	1	.000	1.80	5	0	0	3	0	0	10	12	4	2	0	1	3	0	8	1
Meadows, Houston Blue	0	2	.000	9.50	9	1	0	1	0	0	18	27	29	19	0	1	25	0	11	7
Mejia, Pittsburgh	4	5	.444	4.25	14	4	0	7	0	1	53	60	36	25	1	3	20	0	30	2
Miner, Kan. City Blue	1	2	.333	2.55	13	6	1	3	1	2	53	55	22	15	1	1	15	3	27	3
Mize, Houston Orange	2	1	.667	2.57	5	0	0	2	0	1	7	6	3	2	0	2	1	0	7	1
Morrison, New York-AL	0	0	.000	0.00	1	0	0	1	0	0	2	2	3	0	0	0	1	0	1	0
Moses, Chicago-AL°	6	2	.750	3.10	14	8	2	5	0	0	58	57	25	20	2	0	16	0	32	2
Mott, Pittsburgh	1	1	.500	3.32	5	3	0	2	0	0	19	21	12	7	2	1	6	0	7	1
Mundie, Houston Orange	4	1	.800	2.06	8	5	0	3	0	1	35	33	15	8	0	2	9	0	23	2
Napoleon, Atlanta	1	0	1.000	5.79	9	0	0	4	0	1	14	15	14	9	1	1	13	0	7	1
Neimann, Chicago-AL	3	1	.750	1.70	13	1	0	10	0	6	37	20	10	7	1	2	16	1	35	1
Nowlin, Chicago-NL	3	0	1.000	2.54	16	0	0	16	0	7	39	34	16	11	0	0	17	0	28	2
Olson, Kan. City Gold	3	3	.500	2.25	7	7	2	0	1	0	40	37	16	10	0	3	11	0	28	2
Palencia, Toronto	2	2	.500	4.67	13	2	1	3	1	0	27	38	22	14	1	1	11	0	14	3
Pellien, Pittsburgh°	6	5	.545	3.41	12	11	4	0	2	0	74	80	33	28	5	2	20	0	31	2
Peltola, New York-AL	2	2	.500	3.15	11	3	0	6	0	0	40	44	28	14	1	3	7	1	19	2
Peraza, Toronto	0	0	.000	18.00	2	0	0	1	0	0	1	3	2	2	0	0	0	0	0	0
Perdue, Atlanta	0	1	.000	2.00	2	1	0	0	0	0	9	3	3	2	0	0	11	0	4	0
Perez, Houston Blue°	2	0	1.000	6.00	7	2	0	1	0	0	18	23	15	12	0	0	19	1	15	4
Plasencia, Pittsburgh	0	0	.000	4.50	1	0	0	1	0	0	2	4	2	1	0	0	2	0	4	0
Plasencia, Pittsburgh	0	0	.000	15.00	2	0	0	1	0	0	3	6	5	5	0	0	3	0	2	0
Plunk, New York-AL	3	4	.429	3.83	11	11	1	0	0	0	54	56	29	23	1	2	20	1	47	2
Polemir, Houston Orange	1	3	.250	2.93	19	1	0	10	0	0	43	38	19	14	2	1	25	2	34	3
Psaltis, Kan. City Blue°	4	1	.800	1.87	17	3	2	8	1	1	53	27	17	11	1	0	22	2	52	3
Raftice, New York-AL°	2	1	.667	0.41	4	4	1	0	1	0	22	8	2	1	0	2	6	0	29	1
Reilly, Houston Orange	6	1	.857	1.30	13	11	1	2	0	0	69	48	16	10	0	1	17	0	43	2
Reish, Toronto	6	5	.545	2.17	14	13	6	0	2	0	87	86	40	21	0	2	20	1	63	2
Riewerth, Houston Orange°	1	2	.333	3.75	17	1	0	5	0	0	36	39	25	15	1	0	20	1	21	2
Rijo, New York-AL	3	3	.500	4.50	11	1	0	4	0	1	22	37	16	11	2	0	7	0	22	1
Robertson, Houston Blue	2	2	.500	2.88	10	2	0	5	0	2	25	15	10	8	0	3	9	1	23	1
Rodriguez, New York-AL	0	1	.000	3.91	7	2	0	4	0	1	23	24	14	10	1	0	13	1	14	0
Rondon, Pittsburgh°	0	0	.000	6.00	3	0	0	3	0	0	3	4	2	2	0	0	2	0	1	1
Ross, Houston Blue	2	6	.250	5.57	22	1	0	18	0	2	42	55	28	26	1	1	16	3	27	3
Ruetter, Toronto°	1	3	.250	3.43	12	9	2	0	0	0	63	64	29	24	0	1	16	1	34	1
Sanchez, Pittsburgh°	2	1	.667	2.45	5	0	0	1	0	0	11	4	4	3	0	0	13	0	7	3
Santana, Pittsburgh	0	2	.000	6.75	8	0	0	8	0	2	12	15	11	9	2	2	6	0	11	1
Schefsky, San Diego	1	2	.333	2.33	4	3	2	0	0	0	27	22	10	7	1	0	8	0	24	0
Schiavo, Kan. City Blue	1	2	.333	3.67	12	0	0	6	0	1	27	23	15	11	1	2	9	1	11	5
Schimpf, Houston Blue	5	2	.714	1.29	12	6	0	3	0	1	42	22	12	6	4	1	23	1	42	2
Schmid, Texas°	2	1	.667	2.12	9	0	0	8	0	1	17	14	5	4	0	0	6	0	20	0
Schneider, Toronto°	2	4	.333	2.50	14	6	1	3	0	0	54	49	26	15	0	2	30	1	37	6
Schulte, Texas°	3	0	1.000	1.50	7	1	0	2	0	0	18	18	6	3	0	1	4	0	14	0
Sears, Houston Blue	4	3	.571	3.40	13	4	0	8	0	1	43	46	29	17	1	1	17	0	27	3
Shaw, Kan. City Gold°	3	0	1.000	0.00	5	1	0	0	0	0	14	7	1	0	0	0	6	0	5	1
Shuleeta, Chicago-NL	3	2	.600	3.38	17	3	1	12	0	2	40	41	24	15	0	1	17	2	28	9
Sierra, Atlanta	0	0	.000	5.29	9	0	0	7	0	0	17	25	17	10	1	3	13	0	11	7
Smith, Atlanta	1	1	.500	5.14	8	2	0	4	0	0	21	26	18	12	0	0	12	2	15	0
Snyder, Houston Blue	0	7	.000	3.18	14	12	0	1	0	0	68	60	37	24	1	6	28	1	44	12
Solano, Houston Blue	4	4	.500	3.89	17	12	1	4	0	1	74	71	47	32	1	1	36	0	45	1
Solomon, San Diego	0	1	.000	9.00	2	0	0	2	0	0	1	3	1	1	0	0	0	0	6	0
Soth, Chicago-AL	1	0	1.000	1.29	2	2	0	0	0	0	7	7	3	1	0	0	6	0	6	0
Sperto, Atlanta	2	4	.333	2.33	12	10	0	2	0	2	58	56	25	15	1	0	32	0	43	4
Stafford, Pittsburgh	1	2	.333	3.27	6	4	0	2	0	1	22	13	9	8	0	0	23	0	11	2
Storm, Pittsburgh	0	0	.000	6.00	1	1	0	0	0	0	3	4	2	2	0	1	1	0	1	0
Strode, Kan. City Blue°	0	2	.000	4.24	4	4	0	0	0	0	17	15	9	8	0	0	8	0	17	1
Sturm, Kan. City Gold	3	2	.600	1.88	13	4	2	5	1	4	43	31	18	9	0	4	12	0	19	2
Styles, Pittsburgh	0	0	.000	4.50	3	0	0	1	0	0	8	8	5	4	0	1	7	0	7	1
Sullivan, San Diego	0	0	.000	0.00	1	0	0	1	0	0	2	2	2	0	0	1	1	0	2	0
Sutton, Chicago-AL	1	1	.500	2.00	8	1	0	4	0	1	27	24	7	6	1	3	6	1	23	0
Swank, Kan. City Blue°	5	2	.714	2.74	12	12	1	0	0	0	69	62	30	21	1	4	24	0	56	1
Swanson, Kan. City Gold	2	1	.667	2.12	21	0	0	17	0	4	51	36	19	12	1	2	26	1	39	5
Sweeder, New York-AL°	0	2	.000	3.77	13	1	0	10	0	3	31	32	24	13	1	1	11	1	25	2
Tanzi, Chicago-AL°	5	3	.625	3.09	13	11	2	1	0	0	64	54	27	22	2	3	22	0	54	3
Taylor, Pittsburgh	1	3	.250	1.29	13	3	1	8	0	5	35	28	13	5	0	0	16	0	13	2
Taylor, Texas	4	2	.667	2.72	12	11	0	0	0	0	53	42	23	16	0	3	29	0	35	3
Thomas, Texas	0	0	.000	9.00	2	0	0	1	0	0	3	5	3	3	0	0	4	0	2	0
Thompkins, Atlanta	1	0	1.000	3.38	2	1	0	0	0	0	8	9	3	3	0	0	1	0	8	0
Torres, Pittsburgh	3	0	1.000	2.05	5	2	0	2	0	0	22	13	8	5	1	1	4	0	11	1

Pitcher—Club	W.	L.	Pct.	ERA.	G.	GS.	CG.	GF.	ShO.	Sv.	IP.	H.	R.	ER.	HR.	HB.	BB.	Int. BB.	SO.	WP.
Torres, Atlanta	1	4	.200	2.25	9	9	1	0	0	0	48	35	17	12	1	1	22	0	33	5
Trotter, Chicago-NL°	1	7	.125	3.41	12	10	2	1	0	0	58	49	33	22	0	1	31	0	27	7
Tunnell, Pittsburgh	0	0	.000	0.00	1	1	0	0	0	0	4	0	0	0	0	0	1	0	6	0
Turner, Houston Blue°	2	3	.400	2.33	12	9	0	2	0	0	54	28	18	14	3	2	28	1	24	2
Tuthill, Pittsburgh	0	0-	.000	0.00	1	0	0	0	0	0	1	0	1	0	0	0	0	0	2	0
Vargas, Atlanta	7	3	.700	1.56	12	12	3	0	2	0	75	61	20	13	1	2	12	0	24	2
Villalba, Kan. City Blue	1	0	1.000	6.55	9	0	0	4	0	1	22	40	17	16	0	1	9	0	7	3
Waddell, Atlanta	0	1	.000	0.90	2	1	0	1	0	0	10	5	2	1	1	0	1	0	7	0
Warren, Texas°	1	1	.500	0.88	14	2	0	3	0	0	41	31	12	4	1	2	23	0	40	0
Watson, Texas	1	3	.250	2.67	14	0	0	8	0	2	27	20	11	8	0	1	7	0	11	1
Welch, Chicago-AL	3	0	1.000	3.60	9	0	0	4	0	2	25	23	11	10	1	2	9	0	14	2
West, Atlanta	3	4	.429	2.66	9	8	0	0	0	0	44	32	19	13	1	0	24	0	44	1
White, Pitt-San Diego°	1	5	.167	6.00	13	3	0	4	0	0	39	37	36	26	1	1	29	0	36	6
Williams, New York-AL	3	1	.750	0.38	7	2	0	3	0	0	24	18	5	1	0	1	6	0	23	1
Winn, Pittsburgh	0	0	.000	0.00	1	1	0	0	0	0	4	1	0	0	0	0	0	0	6	0
Wyatt, Kan. City Gold°	2	0	1.000	1.29	4	0	0	0	0	0	21	13	3	3	0	0	9	0	20	2
Zwolenski, Texas	2	0	1.000	1.42	6	2	0	2	0	1	19	18	5	3	0	0	9	0	16	0

BALKS—R. Taylor, 4; Benes, Cone Plunk, 3 each; Ballard, Carpio, Christy, Corniel, Flores, McAnnally, Napoleon, Peltola, Rijo, Schneider, Torres, 2 each; Barnard, Blamay, Bloomfield, Brosious, Buonantony, Buchanan, Callahan, Castro, Clinton, Collet, Coplon, Edlefson, Fagnini, Ferreira, Gordon, J. Guzman, P. Guzman, Hook, Huyck, King, Lamonde, Leopold, Lovelace, Macias, Malave, Manzanillo, Marks, Meadows, Mejia, Morrison, Moses, Nowlin, Olson, Polemir, Raftice, Reilly, Reish, Ross, Ruetter, Sanchez, Schimpf, Schulte, Sears, Snyder, Solano, Sturm, Trotter, Tunnell, Vargas, Warren, Welch, Wyatt, Zwolenski, 1 each.

COMBINATION SHUTOUTS—Clay-Hatcher, Sears-McBride, Vargas-Napoleon, Atlanta; Hardy-Butler-Guzman, Soth-Hardy, Chicago-AL; Clarke-Cook-Nowlin, Cook-Nowlin, Lovelace-Shuleeta, Chicago-NL; Goodwin-Corniel, Schimpf-Meadows-Corniel-Ross, Turner-Schimpf, Houston-Blue; Malloy-Polemir-Castro, Reilly-Mundie, Reilly-Polemir, Houston-Orange; Cook-Davis, Miner-Schiavo, Kansas City Blue; Ferreira-Sturm, Gubicza-Barnard-Ballard, Gubicza-Bloomfield, King-Swanson, Shaw-Ballard, Wyatt-Bryant, Kansas City Gold; Manzanillo-Taylor 2, Pellien-Stafford, Torres-Santana, Winn-Cassell, Pittsburgh; Brosious-Shulte, Cook-Warren-Watson, Cook-Warren-Benes-Guzman-Mayfield-McLane-Watson, Lachowicz-Benes-Kouba, Leach-Benes, Leach-Benes-Watson-Schmid, Guzman-Barnes-Zwolenski, Taylor-Watson, Texas; Schneider-Cook, Toronto.

NO-HIT GAMES—Cook and Nowlin (combination no-hitter), Chicago NL, defeated Atlanta, 3-1, July 13; Tanzi, Chicago AL, defeated Houston-Blue, 4-0, August 12.

Pioneer League

SUMMER CLASS A CLASSIFICATION

CHAMPIONSHIP WINNERS IN PREVIOUS YEARS

1939—Twin Falls° .... .581	1953—Ogden .... .679	1965—Treasure Valley.................... .530
1940—Salt Lake City........................ .608	Salt Lake C. (4th)° .... .527	1966—Ogden .... .591
Ogden (4th)° .... .492	1954—Salt Lake City....................... .595	1967—Ogden .... .621
1941—Boise..................................... .623	Great Falls (4th)° .... .530	1968—Ogden .... .609
Ogden (2nd)° .... .598	1955—Boise..................................... .588	1969—Ogden .... .620
1942—Pocatello†............................. .690	Magic Valley (4th)° .... .489	1970—Idaho Falls........................... .629
Boise..................................... .683	1956—Boise..................................... .561	1971—Great Falls .... .643
1943-44-45—Did not operate.	1957—Salt Lake City....................... .650	1972—Billings................................. .694
1946—Twin Falls‡........................... .585	Billings†................................ .582	1973—Billings................................. .629
Salt Lake City†................ .585	1958—Great Falls .... .582	1974—Idaho Falls........................... .569
1947—Salt Lake City........................ .618	Boise†................................... .615	1975—Great Falls .... .577
Twin Falls†...................... .600	1959—Boise..................................... .633	1976—Great Falls .... .577
1948—Pocatello............................... .611	Billings (2nd)° .... .523	1977—Lethbridge............................ .629
Twin Falls (2nd)° .... .595	1960—Boise†................................... .686	1978—Billings x .... .735
1949—Twin Falls .... .624	Idaho Falls...................... .650	1979—Helena.................................. .623
Pocatello (3rd)° .... .595	1961—Boise..................................... .638	Lethbridge y .... .559
1950—Pocatello............................... .635	Great Falls° .... .571	1980—Lethbridge y .... .743
Billings (3rd)° .... .571	1962—Boise§................................... .565	Billings .... .629
1951—Salt Lake City........................ .618	Billings†................................ .706	
Great Falls (3rd)° .... .559	1963—Idaho Falls............................ .702	
1952—Pocatello............................... .595	Magic Valley†.............. .643	
Idaho Falls (2nd)° .... .573	1964—Treasure Valley.................... .615	

°Won four-club playoff. †Won split-season playoff. ‡Ended first half in tie with Salt Lake City and won one-game playoff. §Ended first half in tie with Billings and Great Falls and won playoff. xBillings (first place) defeated Idaho Falls (second place) in First Place-Second Place playoff. yLeague divided in Northern and Southern divisions; won two-club playoff.

STANDING OF CLUBS AT CLOSE OF SEASON, AUGUST 31
NORTHERN DIVISION

Club	Cal.	Leth.	M.H.	G.F.	But.	Bil.	I.F.	Hel.	W.	L.	T.	Pct.	G.B.
Calgary (Expos)	..	6	7	5	7	7	7	7	46	24	0	.657	....
Lethbridge (Dodgers)	4	..	3	7	7	7	8	7	43	27	0	.614	3
Medicine Hat (Blue Jays)	3	7	..	6	5	5	6	5	37	33	0	.529	9
Great Falls (Giants).........................	5	3	4	..	2	7	5	6	32	38	0	.457	14

SOUTHERN DIVISION

	Cal.	Leth.	M.H.	G.F.	But.	Bil.	I.F.	Hel.	W.	L.	T.	Pct.	G.B.
Butte (Brewers)	3	3	5	8	..	7	6	7	39	31	0	.557	....
Billings (Reds)	3	3	5	3	3	..	5	8	30	40	0	.429	9
Idaho Falls (Angels)	3	2	4	5	4	5	..	4	27	43	0	.386	12
Helena (Phillies)	3	3	5	4	3	2	6	..	26	44	0	.371	13

Major league affiliations in parentheses.

Playoff—Butte defeated Calgary, three games to two.

Regular-Season Attendance—Billings, 79,018; Butte, 30,519; Calgary, 38,748; Great Falls, 58,179; Helena, 25,143; Idaho Falls, 33,283; Lethbridge, 37,361; Medicine Hat, 33,109. Total, 335,440. Playoffs, 7,572. No all-star game.

Managers: Billings—Jim Hoff; Butte—Ken Richardson; Calgary—Junior Miner; Great Falls—Ernie Rodriguez; Helena—Rollie DeArmas; Idaho Falls—Joe Maddon; Lethbridge—Guy LaRocque; Medicine Hat—Wayne Graham.

All-Star Team: 1B—Colclough, Billings; 2B—Carrasco, Idaho Falls; 3B—Fettig, Calgary; SS—Riles, Butte; OF—Peyton, Butte; Stacheit, Calgary; Lewis, Medicine Hat; C—Pinkham, Medicine Hat; P—Fernandez, Lethbridge; Branam, Calgary; Cerutti, Medicine Hat; Manager—La-Rocque, Lethbridge.

(Compiled by William J. Weiss, League Statistician, San Mateo, Calif.)

CLUB BATTING

Club	Pct.	G.	AB.	R.	OR.	H.	TB.	2B.	3B.	HR.	RBI.	GW.	SH.	SF.	HP.	BB.	Int. BB.	SO.	SB.	CS.	LOB.
Butte	.302	70	2491	459	405	752	1067	127	37	38	396	36	20	30	20	265	6	504	109	40	529
Calgary	.286	69	2416	413	354	691	961	93	27	41	335	37	22	33	31	335	11	384	86	29	623
Great Falls	.269	70	2459	379	339	662	903	113	28	24	326	28	15	29	29	317	8	459	98	36	604
Medicine Hat	.269	70	2391	388	402	642	886	111	17	33	320	32	20	23	17	298	11	472	105	19	536
Billings..................	.263	69	2291	377	411	602	877	88	17	31	328	26	31	24	21	329	13	450	46	29	540
Lethbridge	.262	70	2378	403	340	624	815	97	17	20	329	34	17	23	22	309	4	481	73	37	521
Idaho Falls.............	.256	70	2422	378	446	619	834	108	25	19	319	23	23	18	14	335	15	562	113	45	553
Helena	.242	70	2328	363	463	564	802	83	22	37	298	24	10	16	30	293	3	566	94	44	491

INDIVIDUAL BATTING
(Leading Qualifiers for Batting Championship—189 or More Plate Appearances)

°Bats lefthanded.   †Switch-hitter.

Player and Club	Pct.	G.	AB.	R.	H.	TB.	2B.	3B.	HR.	RBI.	GW.	SH.	SF.	HP.	BB.	Int. BB.	SO.	SB.	CS.
Peyton, Eric, Butte°	.403	67	273	64	110	174	24	8	8	65	9	3	6	1	23	4	41	22	4
Carrasco, Norman, Idaho Falls	.374	68	262	44	98	137	22	4	3	57	3	0	5	2	22	3	31	5	8
Baker, Derrell, Calgary	.371	66	272	54	101	119	11	2	1	49	6	2	8	0	35	0	26	7	4
Clayton, Kenneth, Butte..................	.350	55	214	30	75	101	15	1	3	43	2	0	4	0	17	0	24	2	1
Riles, Earnest, Butte†	.348	67	256	63	89	116	11	2	4	43	5	3	5	1	31	0	34	9	4
Bingham, Mark, Idaho Falls°	.333	59	213	41	71	109	15	7	3	48	2	2	2	2	32	2	43	12	2
Jones, Glenn, Great Falls	.327	59	214	45	70	96	10	2	4	24	2	1	1	9	28	0	47	25	7
Olander, John, Helena	.324	61	222	37	72	106	10	3	6	37	4	1	1	2	17	0	59	5	4
O'Neill, Paul, Billings°	.315	66	241	37	76	96	7	2	3	29	1	2	2	0	21	2	35	6	3
Gregory, John, Lethbridge°	.311	67	238	41	74	88	7	2	1	41	7	2	5	2	22	0	36	5	0

Departmental Leaders: G—Aitcheson, Gerber, 70; AB—Gerber, 288; R—Peyton, 64; H—Peyton, 110; TB—Peyton, 174; 2B—Peyton, 24; 3B—Peyton, 8; HR—Fettig, Stacheit, 10; RBI—Peyton, 65; GWRBI—Peyton, 9; SH—Leggitt, Morales, 5; SF—Baker, 8; BB—Schofield, 68; HP—Frishman, Jones, 9; SO—George, 71; SB—Lewis, 51; CS—Ebersberger, Gerber, 9.

(All Players—Listed Alphabetically)

Player and Club	Pct.	G.	AB.	R.	H.	TB.	2B.	3B.	HR.	RBI.	GW.	SH.	SF.	HP.	BB.	Int. BB.	SO.	SB.	CS.
Aitcheson, Kevin, Medicine Hat°	.302	70	265	48	80	95	12	0	1	33	6	3	0	31	1	21	16	4
Baier, Martin, Great Falls°	.301	44	133	22	40	67	6	3	5	33	3	0	2	1	18	2	30	0	1
Baker, Derrell, Calgary	.371	66	272	54	101	119	11	2	1	49	6	2	8	0	35	0	26	7	4
Barling, Glenn, Great Falls	.250	14	8	0	2	2	0	0	0	0	0	0	0	1	0	0	3	1	0
Barros, Eleazar, Idaho Falls	.174	33	69	7	12	14	2	0	0	6	0	1	0	0	11	0	31	0	0
Bass, Frederick, Lethbridge	.000	1	3	0	0	0	0	0	0	0	0	0	0	0	1	0	0	0	0
Bendorf, Jerry, Lethbridge	.269	25	93	16	25	32	5	1	0	17	1	2	0	4	14	0	11	2	2
Berry, Troy, Helena†	.247	22	85	16	21	21	0	0	0	8	0	1	0	0	15	0	15	10	4
Bingham, Mark, Idaho Falls°	.333	59	213	41	71	109	15	7	3	48	2	2	2	2	32	2	43	12	2
Bishop, James, Medicine Hat	.267	68	243	39	65	95	12	3	4	23	2	0	0	0	30	1	63	7	3
Bridges, Cory, Great Falls	.260	56	181	20	47	57	7	0	1	37	3	2	4	4	27	0	25	3	5
Bryant, Ralph, Lethbridge°	.265	50	181	31	48	83	12	4	5	29	5	0	1	1	14	0	53	5	4
Campbell, Chris, Calgary†	.167	18	54	4	9	13	2	1	0	8	1	0	0	2	11	0	9	0	0
Carapezzi, Ronald, Billings	.267	50	120	25	32	42	8	1	0	17	2	2	1	1	31	1	32	0	1
Cardinali, John, Great Falls°	.203	23	59	8	12	15	1	1	0	5	1	2	1	1	7	1	6	4	0
Carrasco, Norman, Idaho Falls	.374	68	262	44	98	137	22	4	3	57	3	0	5	2	22	3	31	5	8
Carter, Don, Calgary°	.277	50	159	31	44	53	3	3	0	11	2	2	1	1	18	1	28	18	3
Cassidy, Michael, Helena	.159	36	113	12	18	26	2	0	2	10	1	0	1	1	15	0	38	1	3
Castillo, Tomas, Medicine Hat	.181	38	83	8	15	23	5	0	1	11	1	2	0	1	9	0	25	0	1
Castillo, Rafael, Idaho Falls	.143	18	49	3	7	10	1	1	0	7	0	2	0	0	4	0	16	2	1
Chavez, Christopher, Lethbridge†	.265	65	223	45	59	76	11	0	2	38	2	3	2	1	61	2	46	8	5
Cipolloni, Joseph, Helena	.217	15	46	5	10	15	2	0	1	4	1	0	0	1	11	0	9	1	0
Clarke, Stanley, Medicine Hat°	.000	17	1	0	0	0	0	0	0	0	0	0	0	0	0	0	1	0	0
Clayton, Kenneth, Butte	.350	55	214	30	75	101	15	1	3	43	2	0	4	0	17	0	24	2	1
Colbert, Ernest, Helena†	.148	12	27	2	4	7	0	0	1	3	0	0	1	0	4	0	15	0	0
Colclough, Charles, Billings°	.256	68	250	45	64	102	9	1	9	45	2	0	4	1	34	3	38	3	1
Coleman, Jerome, Calgary°	.306	58	209	61	64	85	5	5	2	23	1	3	3	4	50	0	22	23	8
Conley, Virgil, Billings°	.100	9	20	2	2	2	0	0	0	0	0	3	0	1	0	0	12	0	0
Contreras, Henry, Butte	.000	1	1	0	0	0	0	0	0	0	0	0	0	0	0	0	1	0	0
Corbett, Craig, Calgary	.267	48	172	22	46	72	7	2	5	17	1	2	2	1	11	0	35	0	1
Crawford, Jack, Idaho Falls	.183	47	153	18	28	37	6	0	1	8	1	4	1	1	10	0	37	10	8
Crump, Adolph, Helena	.218	47	142	23	31	54	4	2	5	33	2	0	3	2	21	0	32	8	1
Culver, Lanell, Billings	.247	32	73	12	18	32	5	0	3	16	1	2	1	3	13	0	34	3	4
Davenport, Gary, Great Falls	.268	18	71	7	19	27	5	0	1	7	0	0	0	2	0	0	11	4	3
Day, Dexter, Billings†	.266	65	237	42	63	104	11	6	6	35	1	1	2	3	27	0	30	7	1
de Jesus, Dionisio, Butte	.295	29	61	11	18	26	4	2	0	2	0	1	0	1	4	0	16	2	0
De Kraai, Bradley, Butte	.286	7	21	5	6	8	0	1	0	2	0	1	0	3	5	0	3	0	1
Delancy, Anthony, Billings	.240	10	25	4	6	6	0	0	0	6	0	0	0	0	0	0	2	0	0
DeSa, Gary, Billings	.261	9	23	4	6	6	0	0	0	3	1	0	0	0	2	0	8	0	0
Des Jarden, Matthew, Lethbridge†	.000	1	0	0	0	0	0	0	0	0	0	0	0	0	0	0	0	0	0
Dodd, Timothy, Billings	.286	13	14	2	4	4	0	0	0	2	0	1	0	0	0	0	2	0	0
Dunn, Michael, Great Falls	.300	6	20	4	6	12	3	0	1	5	1	1	0	0	2	0	2	0	0
Duran, Robert, Helena	.254	40	122	26	31	46	6	3	1	18	1	0	0	2	31	0	34	12	4
Ebersberger, Randolph, Great Falls	.275	61	207	46	57	79	9	5	1	24	3	1	2	3	46	2	50	17	9
Ellis, Thomas, Calgary†	.194	9	31	4	6	6	0	0	0	0	0	0	0	0	5	0	9	3	0
Embser, Richard, Butte	.500	13	2	0	1	1	0	0	0	0	0	0	0	0	0	0	1	0	0
Fettig, Thomas, Calgary	.303	63	244	40	74	126	20	1	10	49	6	1	3	2	42	2	46	3	0
Findeisen, Guy, Billings	.600	13	5	0	3	3	0	0	0	2	0	0	0	0	0	0	2	0	0
Frishman, Mark, Helena	.227	64	229	45	52	83	8	1	7	39	2	0	1	9	26	0	40	9	1
Fryman, Craig, Medicine Hat	.186	35	86	7	16	25	4	1	1	8	1	3	0	1	12	0	18	1	1
George, Thomas, Helena	.214	56	187	34	40	57	8	0	3	18	2	2	2	3	37	0	71	5	2
Gerber, Craig, Idaho Falls°	.267	70	288	52	77	92	13	1	0	15	3	3	0	2	34	2	23	32	9
Gilmore, Myron, Medicine Hat°	.215	37	93	11	20	23	1	1	0	11	0	0	2	0	10	0	23	7	0
Gonzalez, Jose, Lethbridge	.136	34	103	11	14	17	1	1	0	7	0	0	0	0	11	0	44	3	2
Gonzalez, Robinson, Helena	.263	25	95	7	25	28	3	0	0	8	0	0	0	0	5	0	12	1	1
Greene, Jeffrey, Lethbridge°	.172	20	29	10	5	5	0	0	0	1	0	0	0	1	9	0	18	0	0
Gregory, John, Billings°	.311	67	238	41	74	88	7	2	1	41	7	2	5	2	22	0	36	5	0
Grier, David, Billings†	.000	6	6	1	0	0	0	0	0	0	0	0	0	0	0	0	4	0	0
Groninger, Gehret, Billings	.000	2	5	2	0	0	0	0	0	0	0	1	0	0	4	0	2	0	0
Groth, Douglas, Billings	.412	18	17	5	7	8	1	0	0	1	1	0	0	0	5	0	2	0	0
Gutierrez, Felipe, Lethbridge	.238	65	260	40	62	82	12	1	2	35	1	1	6	1	18	0	36	10	5
Hancock, Boris, Medicine Hat	.500	2	2	5	1	1	0	0	0	0	0	0	0	0	2	0	0	1	0
Hartsock, Brian, Idaho Falls°	.312	45	125	17	39	52	3	5	0	21	1	0	0	0	25	1	34	9	3
Hennessy, Michael, Billings	.150	14	20	0	3	3	0	0	0	1	0	0	1	0	3	0	9	0	0
Henry, Mark, Calgary	.149	17	47	6	7	14	2	1	1	7	0	0	0	1	12	0	9	1	2
Higgins, Mark, Butte	.167	4	6	0	1	1	0	0	0	1	0	0	0	0	2	0	0	0	0
Hoff, David, Butte	.169	38	65	10	11	19	1	2	1	5	0	0	0	1	14	0	27	1	1
Hoskins, Daniel, Calgary°	.310	14	29	3	9	9	0	0	0	5	1	0	0	0	3	0	9	0	0
Howell, Toney, Billings	.205	55	161	25	33	44	6	1	1	20	2	1	2	2	18	0	34	2	1
James, Dewey, Butte	.267	60	210	32	56	83	11	2	4	32	2	0	2	5	22	0	56	9	8
Jennings, Charles, Billings	.258	69	244	38	63	79	9	1	1	28	2	3	5	4	53	0	39	10	7
Job, Ryan, Butte	.268	36	82	13	22	33	6	1	1	6	0	1	0	0	4	0	12	1	1
Johns, Richard, Billings	.143	19	7	2	1	1	0	0	0	1	0	2	0	0	1	0	2	0	0
Johnson, Mark, Helena	.500	4	14	2	7	10	3	0	0	5	1	0	0	0	3	0	1	0	0
Jones, Glenn, Great Falls	.327	59	214	45	70	96	10	2	4	24	2	1	1	9	28	0	47	25	7
Jones, Ronnie, Butte†	.286	51	189	38	54	65	9	1	0	14	0	0	0	0	23	1	34	11	7
Kanter, John, Helena†	.222	43	144	20	32	41	2	2	1	15	2	1	1	3	10	0	38	4	1
Kennedy, Jeffrey, Idaho Falls	.138	54	145	26	20	25	2	0	1	13	3	5	1	4	27	0	64	12	3
Kincanon, William, Billings	.231	11	26	5	6	6	0	0	0	7	1	1	0	0	4	0	4	0	0
Kirby, Charles, Butte	.307	64	254	50	78	98	7	2	3	34	3	1	4	1	18	0	62	26	7
Knighten, Kenneth, Great Falls	.239	42	134	15	32	42	4	0	2	12	1	0	2	1	7	0	26	3	1
Knox, Michael, Billings	.308	9	13	3	4	11	1	0	2	2	0	0	1	0	2	0	0	0	0
Kornacker, Dean, Idaho Falls	.290	62	231	33	67	90	12	4	1	33	4	1	5	0	36	1	32	5	1
Larker, Wayne, Idaho Falls°	.262	68	248	39	65	90	15	2	2	44	4	2	6	2	30	4	23	4	1
Le Boeuf, Alan, Helena°	.315	48	168	35	53	82	10	2	5	32	3	1	3	0	13	2	18	1	1
Leclerc, Raymond, Calgary†	.220	18	41	11	9	10	1	0	0	7	2	1	2	1	13	0	10	2	1
Leggitt, Eric, Calgary	.248	45	149	26	37	49	5	2	1	8	2	5	0	0	19	1	30	2	2

Player and Club	Pct.	G.	AB.	R.	H.	TB.	2B.	3B.	HR.	RBI.	GW.	SH.	SF.	HP.	BB.	Int. BB.	SO.	SB.	CS.
Lewis, Herman, Medicine Hat	.298	68	265	60	79	83	4	0	0	14	1	2	1	7	40	1	41	51	3
Liddle, Steven, Idaho Falls	.455	3	11	6	5	8	1	1	0	5	1	0	0	0	3	0	2	0	1
Longa, Ramon, Idaho Falls	.233	24	73	8	17	21	2	1	0	8	0	1	1	0	6	0	15	2	0
Machuca, Freddy, Idaho Falls	.205	13	39	8	8	11	1	1	0	0	0	1	0	0	4	1	15	2	2
Manfre, Michael, Billings	.306	63	222	29	68	92	9	3	3	30	5	1	5	3	20	1	52	6	5
Mathe, Curtis, Idaho Falls°	.311	23	45	11	14	14	0	0	0	5	1	1	0	0	11	1	10	4	2
Matzen, Mark, Billings°	.275	19	51	12	14	17	3	0	0	6	2	0	0	1	11	0	9	0	0
Max, William, Butte	.329	42	152	34	50	88	10	5	6	47	3	1	6	1	26	0	36	7	0
McDaniel, Kevin, Calgary	.340	30	106	17	36	44	3	1	1	9	1	1	1	1	11	0	18	4	1
McFarlen, Randy, Butte†	.240	24	96	13	23	36	5	1	2	16	2	1	1	2	4	1	27	2	0
McGan, Brian, Medicine Hat°	.248	58	161	27	40	70	10	1	6	29	2	0	1	1	25	2	42	0	0
McGriff, Terence, Billings†	.271	42	96	15	26	32	3	0	1	15	2	0	2	1	18	1	11	0	0
Mead, Fred, Medicine Hat	.125	17	40	4	5	9	1	0	1	5	0	0	1	1	7	0	9	0	0
Minyard, John, Billings	.000	17	7	1	0	0	0	0	0	1	0	2	0	0	1	0	4	0	0
Miudes, Wilson, Idaho Falls†	.135	19	37	5	5	7	2	0	0	3	0	0	0	1	5	0	20	0	0
Moore, Michael, Lethbridge	.174	19	46	4	8	8	0	0	0	2	0	2	0	3	5	0	8	0	0
Morales, Joe, Butte†	.296	61	186	37	55	80	6	5	3	35	4	5	1	0	29	0	23	15	2
Morris, Angel, Butte	.282	33	85	15	24	33	6	0	1	8	0	0	0	2	13	0	13	0	1
Murray, William, Lethbridge	.277	33	101	17	28	33	3	1	0	9	1	0	0	1	22	0	15	1	1
Nago, Garrett, Butte°	.261	7	23	1	6	10	2	1	0	6	0	0	0	0	3	0	3	0	1
Nokes, Matthew, Great Falls°	.226	44	146	14	33	43	6	2	0	13	0	0	2	0	11	0	23	0	0
O'Connor, Robert, Great Falls	.307	65	251	35	77	100	15	1	2	37	3	2	4	1	31	2	35	7	4
Olander, John, Helena	.324	61	222	37	72	106	10	3	6	37	4	1	1	2	17	0	59	5	4
O'Neill, Paul, Billings	.315	66	241	37	76	96	7	2	3	29	1	2	2	0	21	2	35	6	3
Ortiz, Rafael, Billings	.167	18	6	0	1	1	0	0	0	1	0	0	0	0	0	0	4	0	0
Ouellette, Philip, Great Falls†	.264	42	129	17	34	45	6	1	1	28	1	3	3	1	16	0	18	4	1
Padia, Steven, Billings°	.231	51	130	19	30	38	5	0	1	22	0	0	0	0	21	2	12	1	3
Parker, Joel, Butte	.195	35	77	7	15	16	1	0	0	7	0	1	1	2	8	0	36	2	2
Parrish, Cletis, Billings†	.286	6	7	2	2	2	0	0	0	0	0	0	0	0	3	1	2	0	1
Penigar, Charles, Helena†	.212	46	165	25	35	50	8	2	1	16	1	0	0	2	25	0	52	12	7
Perez, Paul, Helena	.000	1	1	0	0	0	0	0	0	0	0	0	0	0	0	0	0	0	0
Perkins, Harold, Lethbridge†	.278	66	248	56	69	81	10	1	0	21	4	2	1	2	48	1	48	22	5
Peyton, Byron, Billings	.500	3	4	1	2	2	0	0	0	0	0	0	0	0	0	0	1	0	0
Peyton, Eric, Butte°	.403	67	273	64	110	174	24	8	8	65	9	3	6	1	23	4	41	22	4
Pinkham, William, Medicine Hat	.300	69	283	39	85	133	17	2	9	59	8	1	5	1	12	4	49	2	1
Pitts, Daryl, Great Falls°	.264	60	239	36	63	86	11	3	2	15	4	0	0	0	30	0	24	16	4
Pleis, Scott, Medicine Hat	.310	32	126	15	39	51	7	1	1	17	2	1	0	0	11	0	36	0	0
Poole, Mark, Medicine Hat	.274	56	212	36	58	90	12	1	6	45	3	2	3	3	29	2	40	3	2
Pride, Darrell, Great Falls	.189	29	74	6	14	14	0	0	0	2	0	1	0	1	12	0	29	0	0
Prieto, Omar, Helena	.253	45	158	18	40	47	5	1	0	8	0	2	1	0	9	0	10	6	7
Proctor, John, Helena	.180	36	122	16	22	36	5	3	1	12	1	1	2	1	10	0	45	4	3
Raley, Terry, Medicine Hat†	.287	34	122	24	35	53	11	2	1	17	1	0	1	0	30	0	15	6	1
Reina, Rene, Butte	.129	20	31	4	4	7	1	1	0	2	1	1	0	0	3	0	19	0	0
Reyes, Gilberto, Lethbridge	.258	44	155	28	40	67	9	0	6	24	5	0	1	1	15	0	29	1	1
Rhodes, Jeffrey, Billings	.235	21	34	2	8	11	1	0	0	3	0	0	0	1	0	0	9	0	0
Rhodes, Stephen, Billings	.241	43	54	19	13	17	2	1	0	7	0	0	0	1	19	0	23	4	1
Richmond, Kirk, Medicine Hat	.500	2	2	0	1	1	0	0	0	0	0	0	0	0	1	0	1	0	0
Riles, Earnest, Butte†	.348	67	256	63	89	116	11	2	4	43	5	3	5	1	31	0	34	9	4
Rivera, Hector, Calgary	.283	67	254	34	72	110	8	3	8	47	4	2	4	5	32	1	31	1	1
Robbins, Gary, Idaho Falls	.176	21	51	4	9	11	2	0	0	7	1	1	0	0	6	0	21	0	1
Rosellino, Jose, Idaho Falls	.160	11	25	3	4	7	0	0	1	4	0	0	0	0	0	0	18	0	0
Salazar, Angel, Calgary	.247	63	259	37	64	81	5	3	2	25	3	1	2	5	9	0	23	7	2
Samuel, Michael, Butte	.125	3	8	2	1	1	0	0	0	1	0	1	0	1	2	0	1	0	0
Santiago, Edgar, Idaho Falls	.250	3	8	0	2	2	0	0	0	1	0	0	0	0	1	0	2	0	0
Schofield, Richard, Idaho Falls	.279	66	226	59	63	93	10	1	6	31	2	0	1	0	68	1	60	13	2
Seymour, Robert, Lethbridge	.282	37	142	22	40	58	8	2	2	33	1	1	1	2	15	0	36	2	2
Smith, Kenneth, Helena†	.192	43	146	23	28	35	1	3	0	8	0	1	0	1	22	1	51	15	3
Smith, Michael, Billings	.000	26	11	0	0	0	0	0	0	0	0	0	1	0	1	1	3	0	0
Smith, Todd, Helena	.343	23	70	7	24	34	4	0	2	16	2	0	1	0	7	0	8	0	2
Smoot, Allen, Great Falls	.325	33	114	33	37	55	9	3	1	22	1	1	1	1	26	0	18	2	0
Soto, Domingo, Great Falls	.081	19	37	6	3	5	0	1	0	1	0	0	1	0	2	0	17	2	0
Spinozzi, Michael, Great Falls	.288	24	66	10	19	25	4	1	0	4	0	0	0	0	9	0	18	1	0
Spiroff, George, Great Falls	.222	2	9	2	2	4	0	1	0	0	0	0	0	0	0	0	2	0	0
Stacheit, Glen, Calgary	.302	66	258	42	78	127	15	2	10	53	4	0	3	6	41	4	48	5	3
Stefany, John, Helena	.231	18	39	3	9	10	1	0	0	2	0	0	0	1	4	0	14	0	0
Steinbach, Eugene, Lethbridge	.259	42	143	17	37	48	4	2	1	23	4	1	2	1	19	0	34	0	1
Stout, Timothy, Billings	.100	6	10	1	1	2	1	0	0	2	1	0	0	1	0	0	0	0	0
Strichek, James, Billings	.154	19	13	0	2	2	0	0	0	3	0	1	0	0	2	0	2	1	0
Suggs, Tyris, Calgary	.333	6	9	1	3	3	0	0	0	0	0	1	0	0	3	0	2	2	0
Sylvia, John, Lethbridge	.240	25	75	13	18	22	2	1	0	7	1	0	0	1	11	1	15	0	0
Tackitt, Robert, Medicine Hat	.167	7	18	1	3	3	0	0	0	1	0	0	0	0	0	0	9	0	0
Tanabe, Collin, Butte	.270	54	189	30	51	69	8	2	2	26	5	0	0	1	25	0	32	0	0
Tatis, Bernardo, Medicine Hat†	.194	31	108	17	21	28	2	1	1	14	2	4	0	1	8	0	26	5	0
Thompson, Craig, Lethbridge	.261	45	138	16	36	40	4	0	0	17	0	3	3	1	13	0	23	3	2
Turner, Richard, Idaho Falls	.232	63	228	15	53	67	9	1	1	21	1	0	1	0	21	0	57	2	0
Vaughn, Michael, Calgary°	.278	37	108	16	30	38	6	1	0	17	3	1	4	2	16	1	25	3	1
Ventura, Jose, Lethbridge†	.333	9	9	1	3	4	1	0	0	3	0	0	0	0	0	0	0	0	0
Wahlig, James, Medicine Hat	.299	58	184	38	55	77	11	4	1	22	2	2	3	0	38	0	41	5	2
Weir, James, Great Falls	.206	44	136	20	28	39	5	0	2	24	1	0	3	3	7	0	43	4	0
White, Devon, Idaho Falls	.179	30	106	10	19	21	2	0	0	10	0	0	0	0	12	0	34	4	2
Whitney, Anthony, Calgary°	.133	17	15	4	2	2	0	0	0	0	0	0	0	0	4	1	4	5	0
Williams, Brian, Lethbridge†	.305	54	190	35	58	71	8	1	1	22	2	0	1	0	11	0	26	11	7
Williams, Melvin, Helena	.303	9	33	7	10	14	1	0	1	6	1	0	0	1	8	0	4	0	0
Wilson, David, Billings°	.000	5	4	0	0	0	0	0	0	0	0	0	0	0	0	0	4	0	0
Wood, Johnson, Butte°	.200	32	10	1	2	2	0	0	0	1	0	0	0	0	1	0	1	0	0
Wright, Paul, Idaho Falls	.143	7	21	2	3	6	0	0	1	5	0	0	0	0	3	0	6	0	0
Yari, John-David, Medicine Hat°	.247	42	97	9	24	26	2	0	0	11	1	0	3	0	3	0	12	1	1
Young, Delwyn, Billings†	.326	47	135	22	44	54	7	0	1	23	2	2	1	0	13	1	19	3	1
Young, Steven, Lethbridge	.000	2	1	0	0	0	0	0	0	0	0	0	0	0	0	0	0	0	0

The following pitchers had no plate appearances, primarily through the use of designated hitters, listed alphabetically by club, games in parentheses:

BILLINGS—Barba, Douglas (2).

BUTTE—Clutterbuck, Bryan (6); Dinkins, Charles (6); Evans, Gary (14); Fedor, Christian (27); Herberholz, Craig (4); Myerchin, Michael (25); Orlich, Scott (15); Pena, Hipolito (7); Rice, Richard (18); Roberts, Scott (12); Wegman, William (14); Williams, Bruce (13).

CALGARY—Baldrick, Robert° (16); Branam, Barry (33); Budd, Randy (15); Hinson, Scott (7); Kollman, Ronald (12); Maria, Alan (17); McIntosh, James (14); Mitchell, Frederic (13); Roy, Jacques, (11); Stubberfield, Ian D. (15); Valliant, Robert (20); Waymire, Ronald (18).

GREAT FALLS—Banach, Joseph (6); Bautista, Ramon (8); Biagini, Robert (19); Brecht, Michael (2); Crews, Lawrence (7); Grant, Mark (10; Lambert, Gene (12); Lusted, Charles (5); Malin, Steven (9); Mathiesen, Martin (14); Murtha, Brian (12); Ronan, Kernan (19); Willis, Robert (8); Winters, Mark (12).

HELENA—Abrego, John (12); Bartholow, Foster (23); Campos, Marcos (12); Finch, Timothy (11); Hudson, Charles (14); Mack, Ronald (12); Nye, Scott (13); Oswell, Arby (13); Reilly, James (10); Rubio, Frank (13); Ruiz, Carlos (11); Segura, Jose (25); Sims, Michael (4); Witt, Stephen (13).

IDAHO FALLS—Bryden, Thomas (14); Dowies, Thomas (13); Gast, Robert (5); Gonzalez, Julian (6); Goodin, Richard (17); King, Joseph (27); Lindsey, Douglas (17); Oliver, Scott (14); Price, Kevin (13); Ray, Christopher (19); Robins, Gary (2); Williams, Willie (11); Withrow, Bradley (16).

LETHBRIDGE—Beard, Charles (23); Beuder, Michael (13); Carne, Gregory (8); Fernandez, Sidney (11); Forer, Daniel (18); Guillen, Santiago (8); Lloyd, Richard (12); Montalvo, Rafael (13); Moscaret, Jeffrey (10); Mosher, Peyton (12); O'Malley, Michael (14); Rennicke, Dean (9); Slezak, Robert (4); Whyte, Ronald (8).

MEDICINE HAT—Blackmon, Thomas (19); Campbell, David (16); Cerutti, John (14); Gallagher, Glenn (12); Gorden, Daniel (16); Patterson, Richard (5); Phillips, Christopher (14); Phillips, Jeffery (14); Rodgers, Timothy (2); Stenquist, Steven (23).

GRAND SLAM HOME RUNS—Rivera 2; Baier, Bridges, Fettig, Frishman, James, Rosellino, Tatis, 1 each.

AWARDED FIRST BASE ON INTERFERENCE—Jennings 3 (Morris, Pinkham, Stefany); Vaughn 2 (Johnson, Steinbach); Fryman (Tanabe) Riles (Ouellette), Seymour (Nokes), Stefany (Poole).

CLUB FIELDING

Club	Pct.	G.	PO.	A.	E.	DP.	PB.	Club	Pct.	G.	PO.	A.	E.	DP.	PB.
Lethbridge	.962	70	1845	753	104	56	20	Helena	.946	70	1806	854	151	54	33
Calgary	.955	69	1828	841	126	73	15	Butte	.940	70	1848	806	169	85	29
Idaho Falls	.954	70	1853	859	132	74	16	Billings	.930	69	1773	825	196	53	18
Great Falls	.949	70	1862	765	141	62	32	Medicine Hat	.928	70	1832	708	196	38	21

Triple Plays—Billings, Medicine Hat.

INDIVIDUAL FIELDING

FIRST BASEMEN

Player and Club	Pct.	G.	PO.	A.	E.	DP.	Player and Club	Pct.	G.	PO.	A.	E.	DP.
Bingham, Idaho Falls	.991	15	108	8	1	9	LeBoeuf, Helena	.979	45	455	21	10	25
Campbell, Calgary	.974	17	140	8	4	15	McGan, Medicine Hat°	.960	46	266	23	12	13
Carapezzi, Billings	.944	3	15	2	1	1	McGriff, Billings	.750	1	3	0	1	0
Clayton, Butte	.984	48	410	31	7	48	Mead, Medicine Hat	.975	7	35	4	1	1
Colclough, Billings	.968	68	646	53	23	48	O'Connor, Great Falls	1.000	4	19	2	0	1
Coleman, Calgary°	.985	51	488	26	8	48	Ouellette, Great Falls	.909	1	10	0	1	1
Crump, Helena	.969	7	60	2	2	5	Padia, Billings	1.000	1	1	0	0	0
Dunn, Great Falls	.985	6	60	5	1	6	Parker, Butte	.967	20	114	4	4	17
Ellis, Calgary	1.000	6	52	4	0	2	Proctor, Helena	.965	25	211	7	8	17
Embser, Butte°	1.000	1	2	0	0	0	Reyes, Lethbridge	.969	3	29	2	1	3
Fryman, Medicine Hat	.951	34	227	23	13	11	Richmond, Medicine Hat	.857	2	6	0	1	0
Gregory, Lethbridge°	.985	67	561	39	9	44	Smoot, Medicine Hat	.988	27	228	16	3	18
Hoff, Butte	.951	18	94	4	5	11	Wahlig, Medicine Hat	.980	6	49	1	1	7
Howell, Billings	.800	1	3	1	1	0	Weir, Great Falls	.972	41	285	24	9	28
Kornacker, Great Falls	1.000	1	7	1	0	1	White, Idaho Falls	.800	1	4	0	1	1
LARKER, Idaho Falls°	.986	62	523	52	8	60							

Triple Plays—Colclough, McGan.

SECOND BASEMEN

Player and Club	Pct.	G.	PO.	A.	E.	DP.	Player and Club	Pct.	G.	PO.	A.	E.	DP.
Baker, Calgary	.931	60	147	176	24	47	Leclerc, Calgary	.966	7	11	17	1	3
Bendorf, Lethbridge	.926	25	51	62	9	15	Lewis, Medicine Hat	.900	5	15	3	2	1
Berry, Helena	.935	22	48	67	8	8	Machuca, Idaho Falls	.941	8	19	13	2	3
Carapezzi, Billings	1.000	3	4	4	0	0	McDaniel, Calgary	.944	5	7	10	1	1
Cardinali, Great Falls	.970	14	27	37	2	10	Mead, Medicine Hat	1.000	2	1	3	0	0
CARRASCO, Idaho Falls	.955	65	145	197	16	52	Morales, Butte	.937	40	75	119	13	29
Carter, Calgary	1.000	1	0	2	0	0	Murray, Lethbridge	.971	33	70	65	4	21
Chavez, Lethbridge	1.000	2	2	3	0	1	O'Connor, Great Falls	.926	30	50	75	10	17
Davenport, Great Falls	.943	16	28	55	5	8	Peyton, Billings	1.000	2	0	1	0	0
George, Helena	.957	5	12	10	1	3	Pleis, Medicine Hat	.901	32	48	70	13	8
Gerber, Idaho Falls	1.000	2	4	8	0	0	Poole, Medicine Hat	.964	15	40	40	3	11
Gonzalez, Helena	.930	17	35	45	6	5	Riles, Butte	.500	1	1	1	2	0
Gutierrez, Lethbridge	.966	15	26	31	2	6	Schofield, Idaho Falls	1.000	1	0	1	0	0
Hancock, Medicine Hat	.750	1	2	1	1	0	Spinozzi, Great Falls	.925	15	37	37	6	8
Jennings, Billings	.948	68	144	221	20	41	Stacheit, Calgary	.800	1	2	2	1	0
Job, Butte	.947	31	51	57	6	16	Ventura, Lethbridge	1.000	6	0	2	0	0
Kanter, Helena	.928	31	56	99	12	18	Wahlig, Medicine Hat	.838	20	44	44	17	5
Kirby, Butte	.915	18	33	53	8	14							

Triple Plays—Jennings, Wahlig.

THIRD BASEMEN

Player and Club	Pct.	G.	PO.	A.	E.	DP.	Player and Club	Pct.	G.	PO.	A.	E.	DP.
Baker, Calgary	.895	6	6	11	2	0	Kirby, Butte	.889	9	4	12	2	2
Bishop, Medicine Hat	.812	68	39	108	34	3	KORNACKER, Great Falls	.978	50	36	99	3	13
Bridges, Great Falls	.920	8	9	14	2	4	Manfre, Billings	.868	62	52	113	25	7
Carapezzi, Billings	.842	14	2	14	3	2	Matzen, Billings	.929	5	6	7	1	0
Cardinali, Great Falls	1.000	2	1	1	0	0	Max, Butte	.894	42	44	57	12	11
Castillo, Idaho Falls	1.000	1	0	1	0	0	McDaniel, Calgary	.824	6	3	11	3	1
Chavez, Lethbridge	.940	14	20	27	3	1	McFarlen, Butte	.857	6	5	7	2	2
Clayton, Butte	.000	1	0	0	1	0	Mead, Medicine Hat	.818	9	2	7	2	0
Crump, Helena	1.000	3	4	4	0	1	Morales, Butte	.854	14	14	21	6	5
Day, Billings	1.000	1	2	3	0	0	Nago, Butte	.500	1	1	1	2	0
DeKraai, Butte	.533	7	5	3	7	0	O'Connor, Great Falls	.920	17	17	29	4	3
Fettig, Calgary	.914	59	44	136	17	9	Padia, Billings	.000	2	0	0	1	0
Frishman, Helena	.917	64	51	147	18	12	Rhodes S., Billings	.000	2	0	0	0	0
Gerber, Idaho Falls	.946	64	61	131	11	23	Riles, Butte	1.000	3	0	1	0	0
Gonzalez, Helena	1.000	5	4	11	0	1	Santiago, Idaho Falls	1.000	2	1	4	0	1
Greene, Lethbridge	.950	14	6	13	1	3	Smoot, Great Falls	1.000	1	1	1	0	0
Gutierrez, Lethbridge	.957	52	39	95	6	10	White, Idaho Falls	1.000	5	4	8	0	0
Job, Butte	.947	31	51	57	6	16							

Triple Plays—Bishop, Manfre.

SHORTSTOPS

Player and Club	Pct.	G.	PO.	A.	E.	DP.	Player and Club	Pct.	G.	PO.	A.	E.	DP.
Carapezzi, Billings	.881	32	32	72	14	13	Morales, Butte	.931	9	9	18	2	4
Castillo, Idaho Falls	.880	13	15	29	6	4	Peyton, Billings	1.000	1	2	2	0	1
Chavez, Lethbridge	.945	50	69	171	14	28	Prieto, Helena	.880	13	18	26	6	6
Day, Billings	.868	7	12	21	5	3	Raley, Medicine Hat	.851	34	41	96	24	12
DeSa, Billings	.935	9	4	25	2	1	Riles, Butte	.926	63	96	215	25	45
Ebersberger, Great Falls	.883	58	92	149	32	29	SALAZAR, Calgary	.961	62	89	228	13	45
George, Idaho Falls	.933	51	65	172	17	25	Samuel, Butte	.800	3	6	10	4	1
Gerber, Idaho Falls	1.000	2	8	6	0	1	Schofield, Idaho Falls	.932	60	102	200	22	38
Gonzalez, Helena	.923	3	6	6	1	2	Soto, Great Falls	.796	15	19	24	11	3
Kanter, Helena	.926	9	12	38	4	3	Sylvia, Lethbridge	.867	25	28	63	14	5
Kornacker, Great Falls	.952	7	6	14	1	2	Tatis, Medicine Hat	.874	31	41	81	18	7
Leclerc, Calgary	.810	4	2	15	4	2	Wahlig, Medicine Hat	.757	8	10	18	9	3
McDaniel, Calgary	.737	4	7	7	5	2	Young, Billings	.835	37	43	99	28	18

OUTFIELDERS

Player and Club	Pct.	G.	PO.	A.	E.	DP.	Player and Club	Pct.	G.	PO.	A.	E.	DP.
Aitcheson, Medicine Hat	.960	70	116	4	5	0	Matzen, Billings	1.000	2	2	0	0	0
Baier, Great Falls°	1.000	28	28	3	0	0	McFarlen, Butte	.947	10	17	1	1	0
Barling, Great Falls	1.000	4	4	1	0	1	Miudes, Idaho Falls	.667	10	8	0	4	0
Barros, Idaho Falls	.914	31	29	3	3	0	Morris, Butte	.600	1	3	0	2	0
Bingham, Idaho Falls	.953	35	36	5	2	1	O'Connor, Great Falls	1.000	11	17	1	0	0
Bridges, Great Falls	.962	42	45	5	2	2	Olander, Helena	.944	61	114	5	7	1
Bryant, Lethbridge	.927	39	34	4	3	0	O'Neill, Billings°	.948	65	87	4	5	1
Carter, Calgary	.938	45	54	6	4	2	Parker, Butte	.824	14	14	0	3	0
Cassidy, Helena	.931	23	24	3	2	0	Parrish, Billings	.667	5	2	0	1	0
Castillo, Medicine Hat	.895	30	33	1	4	0	Penigar, Helena	.961	37	45	4	2	1
Coleman, Calgary°	1.000	7	8	1	0	0	Perkins, Lethbridge	.963	42	73	5	3	0
Corbett, Calgary	.946	47	80	7	5	2	Peyton, Butte	.938	67	102	19	8	1
Crawford, Idaho Falls	.929	45	57	8	5	0	Pitts, Great Falls°	.971	56	131	2	4	2
Culver, Billings°	.889	31	31	1	4	0	Pride, Great Falls	.952	17	19	1	1	0
Day, Billings	.908	56	107	11	12	0	Prieto, Helena	.913	30	40	2	4	0
de Jesus, Butte	.897	21	24	2	3	1	Reina, Butte	1.000	16	9	0	0	0
Delancy, Billings	.786	9	9	2	3	1	J. Rhodes, Billings	.667	11	6	0	3	0
Duran, Helena	.860	28	39	4	7	0	S. Rhodes, Billings	.895	17	16	1	2	0
Gilmore, Medicine Hat	1.000	21	31	3	0	1	Robbins, Idaho Falls	.783	15	18	0	5	0
Gonzalez, Lethbridge	.934	30	65	6	5	0	Seymour, Lethbridge	.941	25	46	2	3	0
Henry, Calgary	1.000	9	14	0	0	0	K. Smith, Helena	.833	35	45	5	10	0
Hoskins, Calgary	.889	7	8	0	1	0	Stacheit, Calgary	.970	65	124	7	4	1
HOWELL, Billings	.986	49	66	4	1	1	Stout, Billings	.500	5	1	0	1	0
James, Butte	.917	56	80	8	8	1	Suggs, Calgary	1.000	2	4	0	0	0
Jones, Great Falls	.943	49	58	8	4	0	Tackitt, Medicine Hat	1.000	1	1	0	0	0
Jones, Butte	.942	51	75	6	5	0	Thompson, Lethbridge	.933	40	55	1	4	0
Kennedy, Idaho Falls°	.918	53	74	4	7	0	Wahlig, Medicine Hat	1.000	20	20	4	0	1
Knighten, Great Falls	.975	33	38	1	1	0	White, Idaho Falls	.931	22	25	2	2	0
Larker, Idaho Falls°	.833	5	4	1	1	0	Whitney, Calgary°	.778	9	7	0	2	0
Leggitt, Calgary	.958	42	66	3	3	0	Williams, Lethbridge	.975	47	75	3	2	2
Lewis, Medicine Hat	.949	62	126	5	7	0	Williams, Helena	.900	7	9	0	1	0
Longa, Idaho Falls	.857	19	17	1	3	0	Wright, Idaho Falls	.750	7	6	0	2	0
Machuca, Idaho Falls	1.000	1	1	0	0	0	Yari, Medicine Hat	1.000	32	25	2	0	1
Mathe, Idaho Falls°	.833	15	8	2	2	1	Young, Billings	.909	3	10	0	1	0

CATCHERS

Player and Club	Pct.	G.	PO.	A.	E.	DP.	PB.	Player and Club	Pct.	G.	PO.	A.	E.	DP.	PB.
Cipolloni, Helena	.980	15	85	14	2	0	5	Nokes, Great Falls	.961	41	288	35	13	2	19
Colbert, Helena	1.000	2	4	1	0	0	1	Ouellette, Great Falls	.988	32	224	21	3	0	8
Crump, Helena	.983	28	149	25	3	1	12	Padia, Billings	.974	42	197	29	6	1	6
Fryman, Medicine Hat	1.000	1	1	0	0	0	0	Perez, Helena	1.000	1	2	1	0	0	0
Groninger, Billings	.846	2	9	2	2	0	0	Pinkham, Medicine Hat	.978	46	366	33	9	2	15
Hartsock, Idaho Falls	1.000	6	40	3	0	0	1	Poole, Medicine Hat	.974	25	202	21	6	0	6
Henry, Calgary	1.000	3	25	3	0	0	1	Reyes, Lethbridge	.987	29	211	22	3	3	7
Johnson, Helena	.963	4	26	0	1	0	2	Rivera, Calgary	.961	39	219	29	10	0	7
Knighten, Great Falls	.947	4	33	3	2	0	5	Rosellino, Idaho Falls	1.000	5	23	2	0	0	2
Liddle, Idaho Falls	1.000	3	26	2	0	0	0	T. Smith, Helena	.992	20	104	16	1	1	7
Matzen, Billings	.960	11	44	4	2	0	6	Stefany, Helena	.909	14	49	11	6	1	6
McGriff, Billings	.967	31	163	14	6	0	6	STEINBACH, Lethbridge	.981	35	242	21	5	1	11
Moore, Lethbridge	1.000	19	117	7	0	0	2	Tanabe, Butte	.970	51	343	43	12	5	16
Morris, Butte,	.982	30	141	20	3	3	10	Turner, Idaho Falls	.976	63	435	57	12	3	13
Nago, Butte	.980	6	46	4	1	0	3	Vaughn, Calgary	.995	33	181	19	1	6	7

PITCHERS

Player and Club	Pct.	G.	PO.	A.	E.	DP.	Player and Club	Pct.	G.	PO.	A.	E.	DP.
Abrego, Helena	.889	12	7	17	3	4	Clarke, Medicine Hat°	.850	17	4	13	3	0
Baldrick, Calgary°	.909	16	1	9	1	1	Clutterbuck, Butte	1.000	6	2	4	0	0
Banach, Great Falls°	.667	6	1	1	1	1	Conley, Billings°	.821	9	3	20	5	0
Barling, Great Falls	.882	9	1	14	2	0	Crews, Great Falls	.800	7	3	9	3	0
Bartholow, Helena	1.000	23	2	3	0	0	Dinkins, Butte°	.667	6	1	1	1	0
Bautista, Great Falls	.857	8	3	3	1	0	Dodd, Billings	.833	12	3	2	1	0
Beard, Lethbridge	.800	23	3	9	2	1	Dowies, Idaho Falls	1.000	13	3	15	0	1
Beuder, Lethbridge°	.905	13	1	18	2	0	Embser, Butte°	.700	12	1	6	3	0
Biagini, Great Falls	1.000	19	3	7	0	0	Evans, Butte	.867	14	7	6	2	0
Blackmon, Medicine Hat	1.000	19	2	16	0	0	Fedor, Butte	.933	27	2	12	1	0
Branam, Calgary	1.000	33	6	8	0	1	Fernandez, Lethbridge°	.889	11	4	4	1	0
Brecht, Great Falls°	.800	2	0	4	1	0	Finch, Helena	1.000	11	0	6	0	0
Bryden, Idaho Falls	.889	14	10	14	3	3	Findeisen, Billings	.667	13	1	3	2	0
Budd, Calgary	1.000	15	0	7	0	1	Forer, Lethbridge°	.667	18	0	2	1	0
Campbell, Medicine Hat	1.000	16	5	3	0	0	Gallagher, Medicine Hat	1.000	12	9	14	0	1
Campos, Helena°	.900	12	2	7	1	0	Gonzalez, Idaho Falls	1.000	6	0	2	0	0
Carne, Lethbridge	1.000	8	3	7	0	1	Goodin, Idaho Falls°	.938	17	4	11	1	1
Cerutti, Medicine Hat°	1.000	14	5	14	0	0	Gorden, Medicine Hat	1.000	16	5	3	0	1

PITCHERS—Continued

Player and Club	Pct.	G.	PO.	A.	E.	DP.
Grant, Great Falls	.813	10	8	5	3	0
Groth, Billings	.778	17	5	9	4	1
Guillen, Lethbridge	.800	8	0	4	1	1
Hennessy, Billings	1.000	13	8	4	0	1
Herberholz, Butte	1.000	4	1	6	0	0
Hinson, Calgary	.500	7	0	2	2	0
Hoff, Butte	1.000	3	1	1	0	0
Hudson, Helena	.952	14	5	15	1	0
Johns, Billings	1.000	19	5	8	0	0
Kincanon, Billings	.957	9	6	16	1	0
King, Idaho Falls	.875	27	4	3	1	0
Knox, Billings	.944	6	5	12	1	1
Kollman, Calgary	.889	12	3	5	1	1
Lambert, Great Falls°	.875	12	3	11	2	0
Lindsey, Idaho Falls°	.813	17	2	11	3	0
Lloyd, Lethbridge	.857	12	0	6	1	2
Lusted, Great Falls	1.000	5	3	1	0	0
Mack, Helena°	.875	12	1	6	1	1
Malin, Great Falls	1.000	9	2	4	0	0
Maria, Calgary°	.926	17	5	20	2	2
Mathiesen, Great Falls	.800	14	5	11	4	1
McIntosh, Calgary	.875	14	4	17	3	3
Minyard, Billings	.769	17	3	7	3	0
Mitchell, Calgary	1.000	13	5	3	0	0
Montalvo, Lethbridge	.800	13	1	7	2	0
Moscaret, Lethbridge°	.909	10	2	8	1	1
Mosher, Lethbridge	.500	12	0	1	1	0
Murtha, Great Falls	1.000	12	0	7	0	1
Myerchin, Butte°	.750	25	0	3	1	0
Nye, Helena	.933	13	4	10	1	0
Oliver, Idaho Falls	.935	14	11	18	2	3
O'MALLEY, Lethbridge°	1.000	14	4	22	0	2
Orlich, Butte	.778	15	0	7	2	1
Ortiz, Billings	.909	18	4	6	1	0
Oswell, Helena	.750	13	1	2	1	1
Patterson, Medicine Hat	.500	5	0	1	1	0

Player and Club	Pct.	G.	PO.	A.	E.	DP.
Pena, Butte°	.800	7	0	4	1	0
Phillips C., Medicine Hat	.882	14	6	24	4	3
Phillips J., Medicine Hat	.952	14	5	15	1	1
Price, Idaho Falls	.867	13	10	16	4	0
Ray, Idaho Falls	.889	19	2	6	1	0
Reilly, Helena	.857	10	2	4	1	1
Rennicke, Lethbridge	1.000	9	5	20	0	1
Rhodes S., Billings	.500	5	0	1	1	0
Rice, Butte	.889	18	2	6	1	0
Roberts, Butte	.955	12	6	15	1	0
Robins, Idaho Falls	1.000	2	1	0	0	0
Rodgers, Medicine Hat	.750	2	2	1	1	0
Ronan, Great Falls	.933	19	7	7	1	0
Roy, Calgary	.923	11	11	25	3	3
Rubio, Helena	1.000	13	4	12	0	0
Ruiz, Helena	1.000	11	2	10	0	1
Segura, Helena	.857	25	1	5	1	0
Sims, Helena	1.000	4	2	3	0	0
Slezak, Lethbridge	1.000	4	2	3	0	0
Smith, Billings	1.000	22	4	12	0	0
Stenquist, Medicine Hat	.667	23	2	6	4	1
Strichek, Billings	.846	19	3	8	2	0
Stubberfield, Calgary	.923	15	4	8	1	0
Valliant, Calgary°	1.000	20	0	6	0	0
Waymire, Calgary	1.000	18	1	3	0	0
Wegman, Butte	.882	14	2	13	2	1
Whyte, Lethbridge	.750	8	1	2	1	0
Williams, Butte	1.000	13	3	1	0	0
Williams, Idaho Falls	.900	11	4	5	1	0
Willis, Great Falls°	1.000	8	1	2	0	1
Wilson, Billings	1.000	5	2	7	0	0
Winters, Great Falls	.870	12	5	15	3	1
Withrow, Idaho Falls	.917	16	1	10	1	0
Witt, Helena	.818	13	1	8	2	1
Wood, Butte	.900	26	3	6	1	1

The following players do not have any recorded accepted chances at the positions indicated; therefore, are not listed in the fielding averages for those particular positions: Barba, p; Carapezzi, p; Delancy, 1b; Gast, p; Greene, ss; Grier, of; Hoff, 2b, of; Kirby, of, ss; Leclerc, of; Morales, of; Rhodes, J., p; Soto, of; Spinozzi, 1b, 3b; Tackitt, p; Weir, of; Young, of.

CLUB PITCHING

Club	ERA.	G.	CG.	ShO.	Sv.	IP.	H.	R.	ER.	HR.	HB.	BB.	Int. BB.	SO.	WP.	Bk.
Lethbridge	3.776	70	19	10	9	615	613	340	258	30	15	287	12	552	43	2
Great Falls	3.783	70	19	3	9	620⅔	641	339	261	27	16	272	6	541	40	7
Calgary	4.06	69	7	0	14	609⅓	655	354	275	35	10	234	10	407	51	3
Butte	4.11	70	8	2	17	616	56 9	405	281	27	46	406	14	514	59	5
Medicine Hat	4.27	70	17	6	10	610⅔	601	402	290	35	21	316	4	547	48	11
Billings	4.28	69	11	1	12	591	661	411	281	36	25	250	13	400	40	9
Idaho Falls	5.20	70	7	2	10	617⅔	714	446	357	17	39	370	5	504	54	5
Helena	5.53	70	4	3	11	602	702	463	370	36	12	346	7	413	67	9

PITCHERS' RECORDS
(Leading Qualifiers for Earned-Run Average Leadership — 56 or More Innings)

°Throws lefthanded.

Pitcher—Club	W.	L.	Pct.	ERA.	G.	GS.	CG.	GF.	ShO.	Sv.	IP.	H.	R.	ER.	HR.	HB.	BB.	Int. BB.	SO.	WP.
Fernandez, Lethbridge°	5	1	.833	1.54	11	11	2	0	1	0	76	43	21	13	1	1	31	0	128	3
Beuder, Lethbridge°	7	2	.778	1.82	13	13	3	0	2	0	84	60	21	17	1	2	35	0	72	7
Rennicke, Lethbridge	6	3	.667	1.83	9	9	6	0	4	0	69	62	18	14	2	1	9	0	62	3
Roberts, Butte	6	1	.857	1.85	12	12	2	0	0	0	78	51	23	16	1	12	28	0	74	4
Phillips, C., Med. Hat	6	3	.667	2.27	14	11	4	2	0	1	91	80	45	23	4	3	37	0	71	3
Fedor, Butte	6	3	.667	2.37	27	0	0	17	0	5	57	37	22	15	1	7	35	3	76	7
Branam, Calgary	10	5	.667	2.70	33	0	0	30	0	11	60	38	21	18	2	1	19	2	68	3
Conley, Billings	2	2	.500	3.00	9	8	1	1	0	0	60	62	30	20	3	0	13	1	44	1
Cerutti, Medicine Hat°	8	4	.667	3.03	14	14	5	0	2	0	107	87	45	36	8	1	43	0	120	5
O'Malley, Lethbridge°	6	3	.667	3.43	14	14	4	0	0	0	97	108	46	37	8	0	41	0	68	5

Departmental Leaders: G—Branam, 33; GS—Cerutti, Hudson, Maria, Oliver, O'Malley, 14; CG—Clarke, Rennicke, Winters, 6; ShO—Rennicke, 4; W—Branam, 10; L—Lindsey, 7; Sv—Branam, 11; Pct.—Roberts, .857; IP—Cerutti, 107; H—Oliver, 132; R—Evans, 70; ER—Oliver, 51; HR—Cerutti, O'Malley, Winters, 8; BB—Evans, 63; IBB—Beard, Wood, 5; HB—Roberts, 12; SO—Fernandez, 128; WP—Withrow, 21.

(All Pitchers—Listed Alphabetically)

Pitcher—Club	W.	L.	Pct.	ERA.	G.	GS.	CG.	GF.	ShO.	Sv.	IP.	H.	R.	ER.	HR.	HB.	BB.	Int. BB.	SO.	WP.
Abrego, Helena	3	4	.429	4.70	12	12	1	0	0	0	67	60	40	35	3	5	52	0	52	10
Baldrick, Calgary°	3	0	1.000	3.91	16	6	0	5	0	0	46	45	31	20	5	1	18	0	41	4
Banach, Great Falls°	0	2	.000	3.00	6	4	0	1	0	0	27	32	18	9	2	0	17	0	29	1
Barba, Billings	0	0	.000	12.00	2	0	0	0	0	0	3	3	4	4	0	1	4	0	3	0
Barling, Great Falls	1	3	.250	2.34	9	9	1	0	0	0	50	34	16	13	1	0	35	0	50	3
Bartholow, Helena	0	6	.000	5.81	23	0	0	19	0	6	31	47	27	20	3	0	12	3	30	3
Bautista, Great Falls	1	1	.500	3.52	8	4	0	2	0	0	23	24	18	9	0	1	14	0	19	1
Beard, Lethbridge	5	2	.714	4.67	23	0	0	14	0	0	52	65	41	27	2	3	26	5	43	4
Beuder, Lethbridge°	7	2	.778	1.82	13	13	3	0	2	0	84	60	21	17	1	2	35	0	72	7
Biagini, Great Falls	3	4	.429	3.76	19	2	1	14	0	3	55	46	28	23	1	2	22	1	69	0
Blackmon, Medicine Hat	3	4	.429	5.71	19	3	0	9	0	3	52	70	51	33	3	1	28	0	43	4
Branam, Calgary	10	5	.667	2.70	33	0	0	30	0	11	60	38	21	18	2	1	19	2	68	3
Brecht, Great Falls°	0	1	.000	3.60	2	2	0	0	0	0	10	12	6	4	1	0	3	0	7	0
Bryden, Idaho Falls	2	5	.286	4.91	14	7	0	5	0	1	66	62	42	36	0	5	47	0	51	2

Pitcher—Club	W.	L.	Pct.	ERA	G.	GS.	CG.	GF.	ShO.	Sv.	IP.	H.	R.	ER.	HR.	HB.	BB.	Int. BB.	SO.	WP.
Budd, Calgary	4	1	.800	5.09	15	5	1	2	0	0	46	49	31	26	7	0	29	1	42	3
Campbell, Medicine Hat	2	3	.400	6.70	16	5	0	5	0	0	43	44	38	32	2	2	29	0	36	7
Campos, Helena°	0	5	.000	6.62	12	4	0	2	0	0	34	36	29	25	1	0	32	0	28	5
Carapezzi, Billings	0	0	.000	0.00	1	0	0	1	0	0	4	1	0	0	0	0	1	0	1	0
Carne, Lethbridge°	2	4	.333	3.31	8	8	3	0	0	0	49	48	27	18	3	0	21	1	37	0
Cerutti, Medicine Hat°	8	4	.667	3.03	14	14	5	0	2	0	107	87	45	36	8	1	43	0	120	5
Clarke, Medicine Hat°	8	4	.667	4.02	17	11	6	4	2	0	94	96	54	42	5	7	35	0	112	3
Clutterbuck, Butte	1	1	.500	7.31	6	6	0	0	0	0	16	22	13	13	1	0	7	0	4	1
Conley, Billings°	2	2	.500	3.00	9	8	1	1	0	0	60	62	30	20	3	0	13	1	44	1
Crews, Great Falls	4	1	.800	3.25	7	5	3	2	0	0	36	32	17	13	2	1	15	0	29	4
Dinkins, Butte°	1	2	.333	7.36	6	0	0	1	0	0	11	16	15	9	1	0	7	0	10	1
Dodd, Billings	2	5	.286	5.02	12	7	2	2	1	0	43	58	35	24	4	0	16	0	33	4
Dowies, Idaho Falls	2	6	.250	5.12	13	8	0	2	0	1	51	66	40	29	2	2	32	0	34	1
Embser, Butte°	3	3	.500	5.93	12	6	1	1	0	0	44	45	39	29	5	3	42	0	32	5
Evans, Butte	7	5	.583	5.11	14	13	0	0	0	0	81	83	70	46	4	5	63	1	72	5
Fedor, Butte	6	3	.667	2.37	27	0	0	17	0	5	57	37	22	15	1	7	35	3	76	7
Fernandez, Lethbridge°	5	1	.833	1.54	11	11	2	0	1	0	76	43	21	13	1	1	31	0	128	3
Finch, Helena	0	0	.000	17.44	11	0	0	5	0	0	16	36	34	31	2	1	13	0	14	3
Findeisen, Billings	0	2	.000	5.73	13	2	0	6	0	1	22	36	26	14	5	2	12	0	9	1
Forer, Lethbridge°	1	2	.333	8.63	18	0	0	12	0	3	24	33	28	23	5	3	10	1	18	2
Gallagher, Medicine Hat	4	4	.500	4.58	12	9	1	1	1	0	59	65	38	30	3	1	25	3	41	5
Gast, Idaho Falls	0	0	.000	11.25	5	0	0	4	0	0	8	17	16	10	0	1	10	0	9	5
Gonzalez, Idaho Falls	0	2	.000	11.45	6	1	0	1	0	0	11	17	18	14	0	2	15	0	14	0
Goodin, Idaho Falls°	2	6	.250	4.60	17	4	0	7	0	1	43	46	26	22	1	4	23	1	31	2
Gorden, Medicine Hat	2	4	.333	4.60	16	5	0	10	0	1	47	52	34	24	2	4	30	0	32	7
Grant, Great Falls	2	6	.250	4.36	10	10	4	0	0	0	64	63	36	31	2	5	35	1	50	5
Groth, Billings	4	4	.500	4.14	17	8	0	5	0	2	63	67	42	29	2	7	23	2	35	3
Guillen, Lethbridge	1	3	.250	6.23	8	6	0	1	0	0	26	29	27	18	2	1	27	0	11	5
Hennessy, Billings	2	4	.333	4.77	13	11	2	1	0	0	66	77	46	35	2	3	16	0	36	3
Herberholz, Butte	3	0	.000	5.50	4	4	0	0	0	0	18	19	19	11	1	4	13	0	7	6
Hinson, Calgary	0	0	.000	2.77	7	0	0	2	0	0	13	16	8	4	0	1	9	0	7	4
Hoff, Butte	1	0	1.000	4.50	3	0	0	1	0	0	4	4	2	2	0	1	3	0	4	0
Hudson, Helena	5	5	.500	3.83	14	14	1	0	0	0	87	92	53	37	5	2	27	1	67	6
Johns, Billings	1	2	.333	5.63	19	1	0	3	0	1	40	46	35	25	1	3	26	1	29	2
Kincanon, Billings	5	3	.625	4.43	9	9	4	0	0	0	63	72	36	31	6	3	17	1	31	2
King, Idaho Falls	5	4	.556	3.95	27	0	0	23	0	6	41	32	24	18	1	4	33	4	28	4
Knox, Billings	2	3	.400	3.69	6	6	2	0	0	0	39	44	18	16	4	0	12	2	23	2
Kollman, Calgary	2	2	.500	7.04	12	1	0	3	0	0	23	39	23	18	3	1	8	0	12	1
Lambert, Great Falls°	4	3	.571	4.89	12	7	1	0	1	0	57	67	35	31	2	1	17	0	39	4
Lindsey, Idaho Falls°	1	7	.125	7.98	17	3	0	4	0	0	44	54	46	39	4	7	39	0	37	5
Lloyd, Lethbridge	1	1	.500	5.73	12	0	0	5	0	2	33	45	23	21	3	0	17	1	18	2
Lusted, Great Falls	3	0	1.000	1.80	5	5	2	0	1	0	35	29	9	7	0	2	3	0	33	1
Mack, Helena°	1	5	.167	7.71	12	7	0	2	0	0	42	59	43	36	4	0	40	0	25	5
Malin, Great Falls	1	0	1.000	2.74	9	0	0	5	0	2	23	27	12	7	0	2	10	0	16	2
Maria, Calgary°	6	3	.667	4.34	17	14	3	0	0	0	85	102	55	41	2	0	34	0	54	11
Mathiesen, Great Falls	3	5	.375	4.06	14	4	1	9	0	1	51	55	32	23	2	0	23	0	41	5
McIntosh, Calgary	1	5	.167	7.00	17	8	0	6	0	0	36	47	57	28	5	2	31	0	38	6
Mitchell, Calgary	5	1	.833	2.25	13	4	1	4	0	0	48	38	15	12	2	0	21	1	31	4
Montalvo, Lethbridge	0	0	.000	5.40	13	0	0	4	0	0	20	28	19	12	1	1	13	1	11	1
Moscaret, Lethbridge	5	2	.714	2.03	10	3	1	6	1	1	31	18	8	7	0	2	21	2	32	4
Mosher, Lethbridge	4	1	.800	2.45	12	0	0	6	0	2	22	17	8	6	1	1	6	0	19	1
Murtha, Great Falls°	0	2	.000	4.26	12	3	0	1	0	0	38	48	24	18	2	0	26	1	28	1
Myerchin, Butte°	1	2	.333	2.68	25	0	0	14	0	5	37	29	21	11	2	0	18	2	43	3
Nye, Helena	2	4	.333	4.83	13	13	0	0	0	0	69	74	44	37	4	1	39	0	28	6
Oliver, Idaho Falls	6	4	.600	4.99	14	14	2	0	1	0	92	132	59	51	1	3	27	0	71	3
O'Malley, Lethbridge°	6	3	.667	3.43	14	14	4	0	0	0	97	108	46	37	8	0	41	0	68	5
Orlich, Butte	1	3	.250	4.50	15	5	0	2	0	0	46	54	33	23	2	0	27	1	21	6
Ortiz, Billings	1	0	1.000	4.94	18	1	0	4	0	0	31	33	21	17	1	1	19	0	17	5
Oswell, Helena	1	0	1.000	6.12	13	0	0	5	0	0	25	34	24	17	2	0	16	0	13	3
Patterson, Medicine Hat	0	1	.000	3.75	5	2	0	1	0	0	12	10	9	5	1	0	7	0	7	0
Pena, Butte°	2	1	.667	2.73	7	6	1	0	0	0	33	21	17	10	1	3	33	0	22	3
Phillips, C., Med. Hat	6	3	.667	2.27	14	11	4	2	0	1	91	80	45	23	4	3	37	0	71	3
Phillips, J., Med. Hat	3	4	.429	4.15	14	7	1	3	0	1	52	33	32	24	4	0	45	1	48	11
Price, Idaho Falls	5	4	.556	4.61	13	13	2	0	0	0	82	83	51	42	3	2	55	0	77	3
Ray, Idaho Falls	1	1	.500	5.43	19	3	1	12	0	1	53	68	44	32	3	2	24	0	44	7
Reilly, Helena	0	2	.000	7.83	10	0	0	3	0	0	23	33	26	20	2	0	21	1	12	5
Rennicke, Lethbridge	6	3	.667	1.83	9	9	6	0	4	0	69	62	18	14	2	1	9	0	62	3
Rhodes, J., Billings	0	0	.000	Infin	1	0	0	0	0	0	0	2	5	4	1	0	1	0	0	1
Rhodes, S., Billings	0	0	.000	0.00	1	0	0	0	0	0	2	0	0	0	0	0	2	0	1	1
Rice, Butte	0	0	.000	3.86	18	0	0	6	0	0	28	36	15	12	0	1	12	0	14	2
Roberts, Butte	6	1	.857	1.85	12	12	2	0	0	0	78	51	23	16	1	12	28	0	74	4
Robins, Idaho Falls	0	0	.000	3.60	2	0	0	0	0	0	5	4	2	2	0	3	4	0	4	0
Rodgers, Medicine Hat	1	0	1.000	3.75	2	2	0	0	0	0	12	7	5	5	0	0	8	0	15	0
Ronan, Great Falls	3	6	.333	5.32	19	2	0	15	0	3	44	51	32	26	3	2	16	3	49	10
Roy, Helena	3	2	.600	4.30	11	11	1	0	0	0	67	75	39	32	2	2	19	1	30	5
Rubio, Helena	6	5	.545	3.98	13	13	2	0	1	0	86	89	49	38	4	2	23	1	71	7
Ruiz, Helena	2	0	1.000	5.66	11	1	0	4	0	0	35	46	29	22	1	0	16	0	16	6
Segura, Helena	2	3	.400	4.37	25	0	0	19	0	4	35	42	26	17	1	0	15	0	27	1
Sims, Helena	1	1	.500	1.80	4	0	0	2	0	0	10	8	2	2	0	0	7	0	6	1
Slezak, Lethbridge	0	1	.000	15.30	4	3	0	1	0	0	10	13	18	17	0	0	16	0	10	3
Smith, Billings	5	5	.500	1.37	22	0	0	19	0	8	46	39	21	7	0	1	19	4	52	3
Stenquist, Med. Hat	0	2	.000	8.10	23	1	0	17	0	4	40	57	51	36	3	2	28	0	21	3
Strichek, Billings	4	3	.571	3.98	19	6	0	8	0	0	52	50	30	23	2	1	30	2	32	4
Stubberfield, Calgary	0	4	.000	5.30	15	9	0	1	0	0	56	71	41	33	4	4	20	1	28	5
Tackitt, Medicine Hat	0	0	.000	0.00	1	0	0	1	0	0	1	0	0	0	0	0	0	0	1	0
Valliant, Calgary°	4	1	.800	3.86	20	5	0	6	0	0	42	51	21	18	1	0	26	1	32	7
Waymire, Calgary	2	2	.500	3.00	18	2	0	9	0	3	42	38	16	14	1	0	15	3	33	3
Wegman, Butte	6	5	.545	4.17	14	13	4	0	0	0	82	94	51	38	5	1	44	1	47	3
Whyte, Lethbridge	0	2	.000	10.96	8	3	0	2	0	0	23	44	35	28	1	0	14	1	23	3
Williams, Butte	1	1	.500	12.00	13	5	0	1	0	0	27	30	48	36	2	7	51	1	31	12
Williams, Idaho Falls	0	2	.000	5.44	11	7	0	2	0	0	43	55	35	26	0	3	23	0	27	1
Willis, Great Falls°	0	1	.000	4.50	8	1	0	2	0	0	16	19	11	8	1	0	11	0	11	1

Pitcher—Club	W.	L.	Pct.	ERA.	G.	GS.	CG.	GF.	ShO.	Sv.	IP.	H.	R.	ER.	HR.	HB.	BB.	Int. BB.	SO.	WP.
Wilson, Billings	1	1	.500	1.71	5	2	0	1	0	0	21	24	5	4	0	1	8	0	16	3
Winters, Great Falls°	7	3	.700	3.77	12	12	6	0	1	0	93	102	45	39	8	0	25	0	71	2
Withrow, Idaho Falls	3	2	.600	4.10	16	8	2	3	0	0	79	78	43	36	2	1	38	0	77	21
Witt, Helena	3	4	.429	6.75	13	6	0	5	0	1	44	46	37	33	4	1	33	1	24	6
Wood, Butte	3	1	.750	1.67	26	0	0	20	0	5	54	28	17	10	1	2	23	5	57	1

BALKS—Clarke 6; Cerutti 3; Bautista, Conley, Gonzalez, Hudson, Minyard, Oswell, Pena, Smith, 2 each; Abrego, Baldrick, Banach, Beuder, Brecht, Bryden, Campbell, Campos, Clutterbuck, Gallagher, Gast, Hennessy, Kincanon, Knox, Lambert, Maria, Mathieson, Montalvo, Price, Ronan, Roy, Rubio, Ruiz, Williams, Witt, Wood, 1 each.

COMBINATION SHUTOUTS—Roberts-Fedor, Roberts-Wood, Butte; Rubio-Bartholow, Nye-Bartholow, Helena; Oliver-Roy, Idaho Falls; Fernandez-Mosher-Beard, Lethbridge; Gallagher-Blackmon, Medicine Hat.

NO-HIT GAMES—None.

BILL MADLOCK
• PIRATES •
BATTING CHAMPION (.341)

PETE ROSE
• PHILLIES •
HITS (140)

MIKE SCHMIDT
• PHILLIES •
HOMERS (31)
RUNS BATTED IN (91)
TOTAL BASES (228)
RUNS (78)

1981 NATIONAL LEAGUE LEADERS

NOLAN RYAN
• ASTROS •
EARNED-RUN AVERAGE (1.69)

TOM SEAVER
• REDS •
WINNING PCT. (.875)
WINS (14)

FERNANDO VALENZUELA
• DODGERS •
INNINGS (192)
STRIKEOUTS (180)
SHUTOUTS (8)
COMPLETE GAMES (11)

1982 N.L. EASTERN DIVISION SLATE...

1982	EAST					
	AT CHICAGO	**AT MONTREAL**	**AT NEW YORK**	**AT PHILADELPHIA**	**AT PITTSBURGH**	**AT ST. LOUIS**
CHICAGO		June 11*, 12*, **13** Aug. 9*, 10*, 11* Sept. 17*, 18, **19**	April 20*, 21* Aug. 12*, 13*, 14, **15-15** Sept. 29*, 30*	June 7*, 8*, 9* July 29*, 30*, 31* Aug. **1** Sept. 27*, 28*	April 16*, 17, **18** June 21*, 22*, 23* Sept. 13*, 14*, 15*	May 3*, 4*, 5 July 2*, 3*, **4** Sept. 24*, 25, **26**
MONTREAL	June 17, 18, 19, **20** July 27, 28 Sept. 10, 11, **12**		April 16*, 17, **18** June 21*, 22*, 23*, 24* Sept. 20*, 21	April 9*, 10*, **11** Aug. 2*, 3*, 4*, 5 Sept. 29*, 30*	April 6, 8* July 2 (Tn), 3*, **4** Oct. 1*, 2*, **3**	June 14*, 15*, 16* Aug. 6*, 7*, **8** Sept. 6*, 7*, 8*
NEW YORK	April 9, 10, **11**, 12 Aug. 3, 4, 5 Sept. 22, 23	April 23, 24, **25** June 29*, 30* July 1* Sept. 14*, 15*, 16*		April 6*, 7* June 25*, 26 (Tn), **27** Oct. 1*, 2*, **3**	June 14*, 15*, 16* Aug. 6*, 7*, **8** Sept. 6*, 7*, 8*	June 18 (Tn), 19*, **20** July 27*, 28* Sept. 10*, 11*, **12**
PHILADELPHIA ...	June 14, 15, 16 Aug. 6, 7, **8** Sept. 6, 7, 8	April 19, 20, 21 Aug. 12*, 13*, 14, **15** Sept. 22*, 23*	April 13, 14, 15 July 2*, 3*, **4** Sept. 24*, 25, **26**		June 17*, 18*, 19, **20** July 27*, 28* Sept. 10*, 11*, **12**	April 16*, 17, **18** June 21*, 22*, 23*, 24 Sept. 20*, 21*
PITTSBURGH	April 23, 24, **25** June 28, 29, 30 July 1 Sept. 20, 21	April 13, 15 June 25 (Tn), 26*, **27** Sept. 24*, 25, **26**	June 7*, 8*, 9* July 29*, 30*, 31* Aug. **1** Sept. 27*, 28*	June 11*, 12*, **13** Aug. 9*, 10*, 11* Sept. 17*, 18*, **19**		April 10, **11**, 12 Aug. 2*, 3*, 4*, 5* Sept. 22*, 23*
ST. LOUIS	April 13, 14, 15 June 25, 26-26, **27** Oct. 2, **3**	June 7*, 8*, 9* July 29*, 30*, 31* Aug. **1** Sept. 27*, 28*	June 11*, 12*, **13** Aug. 9*, 10*, 11* Sept. 17*, 18*, **19**	April 23*, 24, **25** June 28*, 29*, 30* Sept. 13*, 14*, 15*	April 20*, 21* Aug. 12*, 13*, 14*, **15-15** Sept. 29*, 30*	
ATLANTA	May 11, 12 July 15, 16, 17, **18**	May 17*, 18*, 19* Sept. 3*, 4*, **5**	May 31 June 1*, 2* Aug. 27*, 28*, **29**	May 28*, 29, **30** Aug. 30*, 31* Sept. 1*	May 3*, 4*, 5* July 23*, 24*, **25**	May 7*, 8*, **9** July 19*, 20*, 21*
CINCINNATI	April 27, 28 July 9, 10-10, **11**	May 28*, 29, **30** Aug. 30*, 31* Sept. 1*	May 17*, 18*, 19* Sept. 3*, 4*, **5**	May 31* June 1*, 2* Aug. 27*, 28*, **29**	May 13*, 14*, 15, **16** July 7*, 8*	May 10*, 11* July 15*, 16*, 17, **18**
HOUSTON	May 7, 8, **9** July 19, 20, 21	May 31* June 1*, 2* Aug. 26*, 28, **29**	May 28*, 29*, **30** Aug. 30*, 31* Sept. 1*	May 17*, 18*, 19* Sept. 3*, 4, **5**	April 29*, 30* May 1*, **2** July 5*, 6*	April 26*, 27*, 28 July 23*, 24, **25**
LOS ANGELES	May 28, 29, **30** Aug. 17, 18, 19	May 6, 7*, 8, **9** July 7*, 8*	May 13*, 14*, 15*, **16** July 5*, 6*	May 10*, 11*, 12* July 9*, 10*, **11**	May 31* June 1*, 2* Aug. 20*, 21*, **22**	June 4*, 5*, **6** Aug. 23*, 24*, 25*
SAN DIEGO	May 31 June 1, 2 Aug. 20, 21, **22**	May 13*, 14*, 15, **16** July 5*, 6*	May 10*, 11*, 12* July 9*, 10*, **11**	May 6*, 7*, 8*, **9** July 7*, 8*	June 4*, 5*, **6** Aug. 23*, 24*, 25*	May 28*, 29*, **30** Aug. 17*, 18*, 19*
SAN FRANCISCO	June 4, 5, **6** Aug. 23, 24, 25	May 10*, 11*, 12* July 9*, 10*, **11**	May 6*, 7*, 8, **9** July 7*, 8*	May 13*, 14*, 15*, **16** July 5*, 6*	May 28*, 29*, **30** Aug. 17*, 18*, 19*	May 31* June 1*, 2* Aug. 20*, 21*, **22**
1982	79 HOME DATES 0 NIGHTS	80 HOME DATES 53 NIGHTS	80 HOME DATES 58 NIGHTS	80 HOME DATES 64 NIGHTS	79 HOME DATES 63 NIGHTS	80 HOME DATES 59 NIGHTS

* NIGHT GAME
NIGHT GAME: Any game starting after 5:00 p.m.
HEAVY BLACK FIGURES DENOTE SUNDAY

AND COMPLETE WESTERN SCHEDULES

1982	WEST					
	AT ATLANTA	AT CINCINNATI	AT HOUSTON	AT LOS ANGELES	AT SAN DIEGO	AT SAN FRANCISCO
CHICAGO	April 29*, 30* May 1*, 2 July 5*, 6*	April 5, 7* July 23*, 24*, 25, 26*	May 13*, 14*, 15*, 16 July 7*, 8*	May 18*, 19*, 20* Aug. 27*, 28*, 29	May 24*, 25*, 26* Sept. 3*, 4*, 5	May 21*, 22, 23-23 Aug. 31* Sept. 1
MONTREAL	June 4*, 5*, 6 Aug. 17*, 18*, 19*	May 21*, 22*, 23 Aug. 23*, 24*, 25*	May 24*, 25*, 26* Aug. 20*, 21, 22*	April 30* May 1, 2 July 19*, 20*, 21*	May 3*, 4* July 15, 16*, 17*, 18	April 27*, 28, 29* July 23*, 24, 25
NEW YORK	May 24*, 25*, 26* Aug. 20*, 21*, 22	June 4*, 5*, 6 Aug. 17*, 18*, 19*	May 21*, 22*, 23* Aug. 23*, 24*, 25	May 3*, 4* July 15*, 16*, 17*, 18	April 27*, 28*, 29 July 23*, 24*, 25	April 30* May 1, 2-2 July 20*, 21
PHILADELPHIA	May 21*, 22, 23 Aug. 23*, 24*, 25*	May 24*, 25*, 26* Aug. 20*, 21*, 22	June 4*, 5*, 6* Aug. 17*, 18*, 19*	April 27*, 28*, 29* July 23*, 24*, 25	April 30* May 1*, 2 July 19*, 20*, 21*	May 3*, 4* July 15*, 16*, 17, 18
PITTSBURGH	April 26*, 27*, 28* July 9*, 10*, 11	May 7*, 8*, 9 July 19*, 20*, 21*	May 10*, 11* July 15*, 16*, 17*, 18	May 24*, 25*, 26* Sept. 3*, 4*, 5	May 21*, 22*, 23 Aug. 30*, 31* Sept. 1*	May 18*, 19, 20 Aug. 27*, 28, 29
ST. LOUIS	May 13*, 14*, 15*, 16 July 7*, 8*	April 30* May 1, 2-2 July 5*, 6*	April 6*, 7*, 8* July 9*, 10*, 11	May 21*, 22*, 23 Aug. 30*, 31* Sept. 1*	May 18*, 19*, 20 Aug. 27*, 29-29 Sept. 1*	May 24*, 25*, 26 Sept. 3*, 4*, 5
ATLANTA		April 12*, 13*, 14 June 25*, 26*, 27 Sept. 17*, 18*, 19	April 16*, 17*, 18 June 14*, 15*, 16* Sept. 20*, 21*, 22*	June 7*, 8*, 9* Aug. 5*, 6*, 7*, 8 Sept. 29*, 30*	April 6*, 7 Aug. 12, 13*, 14*, 15 Oct. 1*, 2*, 3	June 11*, 12, 13-13 Aug. 9*, 10*, 11 Sept. 27*, 28*
CINCINNATI	April 20*, 21*, 22* July 2*, 3*, 4* Sept. 10*, 11*, 12		April 23*, 24*, 25 July 27*, 28*, 29* Oct. 1*, 2*, 3	June 10*, 11*, 12*, 13 Aug. 9*, 10*, 11* Sept. 27*, 28*	June 7*, 8*, 9* Aug. 5*, 6*, 7*, 8 Sept. 29*, 30	April 16*, 17, 18 June 28*, 29*, 30* Sept. 13*, 14*, 15*
HOUSTON	April 9*, 10*, 11 June 28*, 29*, 30* Sept. 13*, 14*, 15*	May 4*, 5 Aug. 13*, 14*, 15, 16* Sept. 24*, 25, 26		April 19*, 20*, 21* July 2*, 3*, 4 Sept. 17*, 18*, 19	June 10, 11*, 12*, 13 Aug. 9*, 10*, 11* Sept. 27*, 28*	June 8*, 9 Aug. 5*, 6*, 7, 8-8 Sept. 29*, 30*
LOS ANGELES	June 22*, 23*, 24* July 30 (Tn), 31 Aug. 1 Sept. 8*, 9*	June 18*, 19, 20, 21* Aug. 2*, 3*, 4 Sept. 6*, 7*	April 12*, 13*, 14* June 25*, 26, 27* Sept. 10*, 11, 12*		April 15*, 16*, 17*, 18 June 14*, 15*, 16* Sept. 21*, 22*	April 23*, 24*, 25 July 26*, 27*, 28* Oct. 1*, 2, 3
SAN DIEGO	April 23*, 24*, 25 July 27*, 28*, 29* Sept. 24*, 25*, 26	June 22*, 23*, 24* July 30*, 31 (Tn) Aug. 1 Sept. 8*, 9*	June 18*, 19*, 20*, 21* Aug. 2*, 3*, 4 Sept. 6*, 7*	April 9*, 10, 11 June 28*, 29*, 30* Sept. 13*, 14*, 15*		April 13, 14* June 25*, 26, 27 Sept. 16*, 17*, 18, 19
SAN FRANCISCO	June 18*, 19*, 20, 21* Aug. 2*, 3*, 4* Sept. 6*, 7*	April 9*, 10, 11 June 15*, 16*, 17 Sept. 21*, 22*, 23	June 22*, 23*, 24* July 30*, 31 (Tn) Aug. 1* Sept. 8*, 9	April 6, 7* Aug. 12, 13*, 14*, 15 Sept. 24*, 25, 26	April 19*, 20*, 21* July 2 (Tn), 3*, 4 Sept. 10*, 11*	
1982	80 HOME DATES 67 NIGHTS	79 HOME DATES 57 NIGHTS	80 HOME DATES 69 NIGHTS	81 HOME DATES 63 NIGHTS	79 HOME DATES 61 NIGHTS	77 HOME DATES 44 NIGHTS

JULY 13—ALL STAR GAME AT MONTREAL

AUGUST 2—HALL OF FAME GAME AT COOPERSTOWN, N.Y. (Chicago White Sox vs. Chicago Cubs)

1982 A.L. EASTERN DIVISION SLATE...

1982	EAST						
	AT MILWAUKEE	**AT DETROIT**	**AT CLEVELAND**	**AT TORONTO**	**AT BALTIMORE**	**AT NEW YORK**	**AT BOSTON**
MILWAUKEE		June 17*, 18*, 19*, **20** Sept. 13*, 14*, 15*	April 13, 14, 15 Aug. 6*, 7*, **8**	April 9, 10, **11** Aug. 2, 3*, 4*	June 14*, 15*, 16* Oct. 1*, 2*, **3**	June 29*, 30* July 1* Sept. 9*, 10*, 11*, **12**	June 25*, 26, **27**, 28* Sept. 28*, 29*, 30*
DETROIT	June 11*, 12*, **13** Sept. 6, 7*, 8*		June 14 (Tn), 15*, 16* Oct. 1*, 2, **3**	April 12, 13*, 14* July 30*, 31 Aug. **1**	June 24*, 25*, 26*, **27** Sept. 20*, 21*, 22*	April 22*, 23*, 24, **25** July 26*, 27*, 28*	June 21*, 22*, 23* Sept. 10*, 11, **12**
CLEVELAND	April 6, 8 July 29*, 30*, 31 Aug. **1-1**	June 8*, 9 (Tn) Sept. 24*, 25, **26**		June 4*, 5, **6-6**, 7* Aug. 16*, 17*	June 29*, 30* July 1* Sept. 17*, 18*, **19**	June 24*, 25*, 26*, **27** Sept. 20*, 21*, 22*	June 11*, 12, **13** Sept. 13*, 14*, 15*
TORONTO	April 20*, 21*, 22* Aug. 12*, 13*, 14*, **15**	April 6, 8 Aug. 5*, 6*, 7, **8-8**	May 18*, 19*, 20* Sept. 3*, 4, **5**		May 28*, 29*, **30** Aug. 24*, 25*, 26*	May 25*, 26* Aug. 20*, 21*, **22**, 23*	April 16, 17, **18**, 19 July 26*, 27*, 28*
BALTIMORE	June 7*, 8*, 9*, 10 Sept. 24*, 25*, **26**	July 2*, 3*, **4** Sept. 28*, 29*, 30*	June 21*, 22*, 23* Sept. 9*, 10*, 11, **12**	May 21*, 22, **23**, 24 Aug. 30, 31 Sept. 1		June 18*, 19*, **20** Sept. 6, 7*, 8*	April 20*, 21* Aug. 13*, 14, **15**, 16*
NEW YORK	June 21*, 22*, 23* Sept. 17*, 18*, **19**	April 16*, 17, **18** Aug. 9*, 10*, 11*	July 2*, 3*, **4** Sept. 28*, 29*, 30*	May 31* June 1*, 2*, 3* Aug. 27*, 28, **29**	June 11*, 12*, **13** Sept. 13*, 14*, 15*, 16*		June 8*, 9*, 10* Sept. 24*, 25, **26**, 27*
BOSTON	July 2*, 3*, **4** Sept. 20*, 21*, 22*	June 29*, 30* July 1* Sept. 16*, 17*, 18, **19**	June 17*, 18*, 19*, **20** Sept. 6*, 7*, 8*	April 23*, 24, **25** Aug. 9*, 10*, 11*	April 9*, 10, **11** Aug. 2*, 3 (Tn), 4*	June 14*, 15*, 16* Oct. 1*, 2, **3**	
SEATTLE	May 21*, 22, **23** Aug. 30*, 31* Sept. 1*	June 4*, 5, **6** Aug. 16*, 17*, 18*	April 27*, 28*, 29* July 23*, 24*, **25**	June 29*, 30* July 1 Oct. 1*, 2, **3**	May 3*, 4* July 15*, 16*, 17*, **18**	April 30* May 1*, **2** July 19*, 20*, 21*	May 18*, 19*, 20* Sept. 3*, 4, **5**
OAKLAND	May 25*, 26* Aug. 26*, 27*, 28*, **29**	May 18*, 19*, 20* Sept. 3*, 4, **5**	April 30* May 1, **2** July 19*, 20*, 21*	June 11*, 12, **13**, 14 Sept. 14*, 15*	April 27*, 28*, 29* July 23*, 24, **25**	May 3*, 4* July 15*, 16*, 17*, **18**	May 21*, 22, **23** Aug. 30*, 31* Sept. 1*
CALIFORNIA	May 18*, 19*, 20 Sept. 3*, 4*, **5**	May 21*, 22, **23** Aug. 31* Sept. 1*, 2*	May 3*, 4* July 15*, 16*, 17, **18**	June 8*, 9* Sept. 16*, 17*, 18, **19**	April 30* May 1*, **2** July 19*, 20*, 21*	April 27*, 28*, 29* July 23*, 24*, **25**	May 24*, 25* Aug. 26*, 27*, 28, **29**
TEXAS	April 16*, 17, **18** Aug. 9*, 10*, 11	May 4*, 5* July 23*, 24, **25-25**	April 10, **11** Aug. 2*, 3 (Tn), 4*	April 27*, 28* July 15*, 16*, 17, **18**	May 31* June 1*, 2* Aug. 27*, 28*, **29**	April 6, 8 Aug. 5*, 6*, 7, **8**	April 30* May 1, **2** July 19*, 20*, 21*
KANSAS CITY ...	May 3*, 4*, 5 July 9*, 10*, **11**	April 19*, 20*, 21 Aug. 13*, 14, **15**	April 16, 17, **18** July 26*, 27*, 28*	May 7*, 8, **9** July 19*, 20*, 21*	April 5, 7* Aug. 5*, 6*, 7*, **8**	June 4*, 5*, **6** Aug. 16*, 17*, 18*	April 27*, 28* July 15*, 16*, 17, **18**
MINNESOTA	May 6*, 7*, 8, **9** July 7*, 8	May 13*, 14*, 15, **16** July 5, 6*	May 31* June 1*, 2* Aug. 20*, 21, **22**	June 25*, 26, **27** Sept. 28*, 29*, 30*	May 18*, 19*, 20* Sept. 3*, 4*, **5**	May 21*, 22*, **23** Aug. 24*, 25*, 26*	May 3*, 4*, 5* July 9*, 10, **11**
CHICAGO	April 27*, 28* July 15*, 16*, 17*, **18**	May 7*, 8, **9** July 19*, 20*, 21*	May 28*, 29, **30** Aug. 23*, 24*, 25*	May 10*, 11*, 12* July 9*, 10*, **11**	April 23*, 24*, **25** July 26*, 27*, 28*	April 9*, 10, **11** Aug. 3 (Tn), 4*	April 12, 14, 15 Aug. 6*, 7, **8**
1982	80 HOME DATES 55 NIGHTS	78 HOME DATES 51 NIGHTS	79 HOME DATES 55 NIGHTS	80 HOME DATES 46 NIGHTS	80 HOME DATES 65 NIGHTS	80 HOME DATES 61 NIGHTS	81 HOME DATES 50 NIGHTS

* NIGHT GAME
NIGHT GAME: Any game starting after 6:00 p.m.
HEAVY BLACK FIGURES DENOTE SUNDAY

AND COMPLETE WESTERN SCHEDULES

1982	WEST						
	AT SEATTLE	AT OAKLAND	AT CALIFORNIA	AT TEXAS	AT KANSAS CITY	AT MINNESOTA	AT CHICAGO
MILWAUKEE	May 31* June 1*, 2* Aug. 20*, 21*, 22*	June 4*, 5, 6 Aug. 17*, 18*, 19	May 27*, 28*, 29, 30 Aug. 23*, 24*	April 23*, 24*, 25 July 26*, 27*, 28*	May 10*, 11*, 12* July 23*, 24*, 25	April 30* May 1, 2 July 19*, 20*, 21*	May 13*, 14*, 15*, 16 July 5*, 6*
DETROIT	May 25*, 26* Aug. 26*, 27*, 28*, 29*	May 28*, 29, 30-30 Aug. 23*, 24	May 31 June 1*, 2* Aug. 20*, 21*, 22	May 10*, 11*, 12* July 9*, 10*, 11*	April 9*, 10*, 11 Aug. 2*, 3*, 4*	April 27*, 28* July 15*, 16*, 17*, 18	April 29*, 30* May 1, 2 July 7*, 8*
CLEVELAND	May 10*, 11*, 12* July 9*, 10*, 11	May 6*, 7*, 8, 9 July 5*, 6	May 13*, 14*, 15*, 16 July 7*, 8*	April 20*, 21*, 22* Aug. 13*, 14*, 15*	April 23*, 24*, 25 Aug. 9*, 10*, 11*	May 24*, 25*, 26* Aug. 27*, 28*, 29	May 21*, 22*, 23 Aug. 30*, 31* Sept. 1*
TORONTO	June 21*, 22*, 23 Sept. 24*, 25*, 26	June 18*, 19, 20 Sept. 6, 7*, 8	June 15*, 16*, 17* Sept. 10*, 11*, 12	May 13*, 14*, 15*, 16 July 5*, 6*	April 29*, 30* May 1*, 2 July 7*, 8*	July 2*, 3*, 4 Sept. 20*, 21*, 22*	May 4*, 5* July 22*, 23*, 24, 25
BALTIMORE	May 13*, 14*, 15*, 16* July 7*, 8*	May 10*, 11*, 12 July 9*, 10, 11	May 6*, 7*, 8*, 9 July 5*, 6*	May 25*, 26*, 27* Aug. 20*, 21*, 22*	April 13*, 14* July 29*, 30*, 31* Aug. 1	June 4*, 5*, 6 Aug. 17*, 18*, 19*	April 16*, 17*, 18 Aug. 9*, 10*, 11*
NEW YORK	May 6*, 7*, 8*, 9* July 5*, 6*	May 13*, 14*, 15, 16 July 7*, 8*	May 10*, 11*, 12* July 9*, 10*, 11	April 12*, 13*, 14* July 30*, 31* Aug. 1*	May 17*, 18*, 19* Sept. 3*, 4, 5	May 28*, 29, 30 Aug. 30*, 31* Sept. 1*	April 20*, 21* Aug. 12*, 13*, 14*, 15
BOSTON	May 27*, 28*, 29*, 30* Aug. 23*, 24*	May 31 June 1*, 2* Aug. 20*, 21, 22	June 4*, 5*, 6 Aug. 17*, 18*, 19*	May 6*, 7*, 8*, 9 July 7*, 8*	May 13*, 14*, 15, 16 July 5*, 6*	May 10*, 11*, 12* July 23*, 24*, 25	April 6, 8 July 29*, 30*, 31* Aug. 1
SEATTLE		April 9*, 10, 11-11 Aug. 2*, 3*, 4	April 13*, 14*, 15* July 29*, 30*, 31* Aug. 1	June 7*, 8*, 9* Sept. 10*, 11*, 12	June 11*, 12*, 13 Sept. 13*, 14*, 15*, 16*	April 6*, 7*, 8 Aug. 13*, 14*, 15	July 2*, 3, 4 Sept. 27*, 28*, 29*
OAKLAND	April 16*, 17*, 18 Aug. 9*, 10*, 11*		April 23*, 24*, 25 July 26*, 27*, 28*	June 24*, 25*, 26*, 27* Sept. 27*, 28*, 29*	June 28*, 29*, 30* Sept. 30* Oct. 1*, 2*, 3	April 13*, 14*, 15 Aug. 6*, 7, 8	June 7*, 8*, 9* Sept. 16*, 17*, 18*, 19
CALIFORNIA	April 19*, 20*, 21* Aug. 6*, 7*, 8*	April 6*, 7*, 8* Aug. 13*, 14, 15*, 16*		June 29*, 30* July 1* Sept. 23*, 24*, 25*, 26	July 2*, 3*, 4 Sept. 27*, 28*, 29*	April 9*, 10, 11 Aug. 9*, 10*, 11*	June 10*, 11*, 12, 13 Sept. 13*, 14*, 15*
TEXAS	June 14*, 15*, 16*, 17* Sept. 17*, 18*, 19	July 2*, 3, 4* Sept. 20*, 21*, 22*	June 21*, 22*, 23* Oct. 1*, 2, 3		May 21*, 22*, 23 Aug. 30*, 31* Sept. 1*	June 18*, 19, 20 Sept. 13*, 14*, 15*, 16	May 17*, 18*, 19* Sept. 2*, 3*, 4*, 5
KANSAS CITY ...	June 18*, 19*, 20* Sept. 6*, 7*, 8*	June 21*, 22*, 23 Sept. 24*, 25, 26	June 24*, 25*, 26*, 27 Sept. 20*, 21*, 22*	May 28*, 29*, 30 Aug. 23*, 24*, 25*, 26*		June 7*, 8*, 9*, 10* Sept. 17*, 18, 19	May 24*, 25*, 26* Aug. 27*, 28*, 29
MINNESOTA	April 22*, 23*, 24*, 25 July 26*, 27*, 28	April 19*, 20*, 21 July 29*, 30*, 31 Aug. 1	April 16*, 17*, 18 Aug. 2*, 3*, 4, 5	June 11*, 12*, 13 Sept. 6*, 7*, 8*	June 14*, 15*, 16* Sept. 10*, 11*, 12		June 21*, 22*, 23* Sept. 24*, 25*, 26
CHICAGO	June 25*, 26*, 27* Sept. 20*, 21*, 22*, 23*	June 15*, 16*, 17 Sept. 10*, 11, 12	June 18*, 19, 20 Sept. 6, 7*, 8*	June 4*, 5*, 6 Aug. 16*, 17*, 18*	May 31* June 1*, 2* Aug. 19*, 20*, 21*, 22	June 28*, 29*, 30* July 1 Oct. 1*, 2*, 3	
1982	81 HOME DATES 74 NIGHTS	79 HOME DATES 43 NIGHTS	81 HOME DATES 62 NIGHTS	81 HOME DATES 73 NIGHTS	81 HOME DATES 66 NIGHTS	81 HOME DATES 58 NIGHTS	81 HOME DATES 62 NIGHTS

JULY 13—ALL STAR GAME AT MONTREAL

AUGUST 2—HALL OF FAME GAME AT COOPERSTOWN, N. Y. (Chicago White Sox vs. Chicago Cubs)

CARNEY LANSFORD
•Angles•
BATTING CHAMPION (.336)

EDDIE MURRAY
•Orioles•
RUNS BATTED IN (78)
HOME RUNS (22—4-way tie)

RICKEY HENDERSON
•A's•
RUNS (89)
HITS (135)

1981 AMERICAN LEAGUE LEADERS

STEVE McCATTY
•A's•
WINS (14—4-way tie)
EARNED-RUN AVERAGE (2.32)

ROLLIE FINGERS
•Brewers•
SAVES (28)

PETE VUCKOVICH
•Brewers•
WINS (14—4-way tie)
WINNING PERCENTAGE (.778)

Index to Contents

All-Star Game 205-212
Championship Series 177-188
Cy Young Award Winners 239
Directory of Organized Ball 260
Division Playoffs 165-176
Draft, Major League 247
Farm Systems for 1982 294
Five-Hit Games 226-227
Hall of Fame 240-242
Most Valuable Player Selections, BBWAA 238
Most Valuable Player and
   Cy Young voting for 1981 27-28

Necrology 253-258
No. 1 Men Selections 291
Perfect and No-Hit Games 215-217
Player Deals 248-252
Players' Association, Major League 292
Presidents of Minor Leagues, 1982 293
Re-Entry Draft 245-246
Review of Year 3
Rookie of Year Selections 239
THE SPORTING NEWS Awards 233-237
Umpires Association, Major League 232
World Series 189-204

AMERICAN LEAGUE

Attendance, 1981 247
Batting Averages, 1981 138-143
Batting Statistics, Miscellaneous, 1981 . 143-145
Designated Hitting, 1981 145-147
Directory for 1982 275
Fielding Averages, 1981 148-153
Home Runs, Grand-Slam 224
Home Runs by Parks 231-232
Home Runs, Three in One Game 225
Low-Hit Games 218-219
1-0 Games 223
Pennant Winners Each Year 136
Pinch-Hitting 228-229
Pitchers vs. Individual Clubs 160-163
Pitching Averages, 1981 154-159
Relief Pitcher Ratings 221-222
Schedule, 1982 452-453
Standings, 1981 136
Strikeout Performances, Top 220
Team Reviews 95-135

NATIONAL LEAGUE

Attendance, 1981 247
Batting Averages, 1981 70-76
Batting Statistics, Miscellaneous, 1981 76-79
Directory for 1982 261
Fielding Averages, 1981 80-84
Home Runs, Grand-Slam 224
Home Runs by Parks 230-231
Home Runs, Three in One Game 225
Low-Hit Games 218-219
1-0 Games 223
Pennant Winners Each Year 68
Pinch-Hitting 228-229
Pitchers vs. Individual Clubs 90-92
Pitching Averages, 1981 85-89
Relief Pitcher Ratings 221-222
Schedule, 1982 450-451
Standings, 1981 68
Strikeout Performances, Top 220
Team Reviews 33-66

1981 Game Scores

Baltimore	102	Milwaukee	98
Boston	108	Minnesota	134
California	128	New York	96
Chicago	126	Oakland	116
Cleveland	110	Seattle	132
Detroit	104	Texas	122
Kansas City	120	Toronto	114

1981 Game Scores

Atlanta	46	New York	64
Chicago	66	Philadelphia	54
Cincinnati	40	Pittsburgh	60
Houston	36	St. Louis	58
Los Angeles	34	San Diego	48
Montreal	52	San Francisco	42

NATIONAL ASSOCIATION (MINOR LEAGUE) AVERAGES

American Association	296	Gulf Coast	430	Pacific Coast	327
Appalachian	424	International	305	Pioneer	441
California	364	Mexican	314	South Atlantic	414
Carolina	372	Midwest	391	Southern	345
Eastern	337	New York-Pennsylvania	400	Texas	355
Florida State	380	Northwest	408		

Index to Minor League Clubs, Cities

Aguascalientes, Mexico 314
Aguila, Mexico 314
Albuquerque, N.M. 328
Alexandria, Va. 372
Amarillo, Tex. 356
Anderson, S.C. 414
Appleton, Wis. 391
Arkansas 356
Asheville, N.C. 414

Batavia, N.Y. 400
Bellingham, Wash. 408
Bend, Ore. 408
Bettendorf, Ia.
  (see Quad Cities) 391
Billings, Mont. 441
Birmingham, Ala. 346
Bluefield, W.Va. 424
Bradenton, Fla. 430
Bristol, Conn. 338
Bristol, Va. 424
Buffalo, N.Y. 338
Burlington, Ia. 391
Butte, Mont. 441

Calgary, Alberta, Can. 441
Campeche, Mexico 314
Cedar Rapids, Ia. 391
Charleston, W.Va. 306
Charleston, S.C. 414
Charlotte, N.C. 346
Chattanooga, Tenn. 346
Chihuahua, Mexico 314
Clinton, Ia. 391
Coatzacoalcos, Mexico 314
Columbus, Ga. 346
Columbus, O. 306

Davenport, Ia.
  (see Quad Cities) 391
Daytona Beach, Fla. 380
Denver, Colo. 297
Des Moines, Ia. (see Iowa) 297
Durham, N.C. 372

Edmonton, Alberta, Can. 328
Elizabethton, Tenn. 424
Elmira, N.Y. 400
El Paso, Tex. 356
Erie, Pa. 400
Eugene, Ore. 408
Evansville, Ind. 297

Florence, S.C. 414
Fort Lauderdale, Fla. 380
Fort Myers, Fla. 380
Fresno, Calif. 364

Gastonia, N.C. 414
Geneva, N.Y. 400
Glens Falls, N.Y. 338
Gomez Palacio, Mexico
  (see Union Laguna) 314
Great Falls, Mont. 441

Greensboro, N.C. 414
Greenwood, S.C. 414

Hagerstown, Md. 372
Hampton, Va.
  (see Peninsula) 372
Hawaii 328
Helena, Mont. 441
Holyoke, Mass. 338
Honolulu, Hawaii
  (see Hawaii) 328

Idaho Falls, Ida. 441
Indianapolis, Ind. 297
Iowa 297

Jackson, Miss. 356
Jacksonville, Fla. 346
Jamestown, N.Y. 400
Johnson City, Tenn. 424
Juarez, Mexico 314

Kingsport, Tenn. 424
Kinston, N.C. 372
Knoxville, Tenn. 346

Lakeland, Fla. 380
Lethbridge, Alberta, Can. 441
Little Falls, N.Y. 400
Little Rock, Ark.
  (see Arkansas) 356
Lodi, Calif. 364
Lynchburg, Va. 372
Lynn, Mass. 338

Macon, Ga. 414
Medicine Hat, Alberta, Can. 441
Medford, Ore. 408
Memphis, Tenn. 346
Mexico City, Mex. Reds 314
Mexico City, Mex. Tigers 314
Miami, Fla. 380
Midland, Tex. 356
Modesto, Calif. 364
Moline, Ill.
  (see Quad Cities) 391
Monterrey, Mexico 314

Nashville, Tenn. 346
Norfolk, Va.
  (see Tidewater) 306
Nuevo Laredo, Mexico 314

Oklahoma City, Okla. 297
Omaha, Neb. 297
Oneonta, N.Y. 400
Orlando, Fla. 346

Paintsville, Ky. 424
Pawtucket, R.I.
  (see Rhode Island) 306
Peninsula 372
Phoenix, Ariz. 328
Portland, Ore. 328

Portsmouth, Va.
  (see Tidewater) 306
Poza Rica, Mexico 314

Quad Cities 391

Reading, Pa. 338
Redwood, Calif. 364
Reno, Nev. 364
Reynosa, Mexico 314
Rhode Island 306
Richmond, Va. 306
Rochester, N.Y. 306
Rock Island, Ill.
  (see Quad Cities) 391

St. Petersburg, Fla. 380
Salem, Ore. 408
Salem, Va. 372
Saltillo, Mexico 314
Salt Lake City, Utah 328
San Antonio, Tex. 356
San Jose, Calif. 364
Sarasota, Fla. 430
Savannah, Ga. 346
Shelby, N.C. 414
Shreveport, La. 356
Spartanburg, S.C. 414
Spokane, Wash. 328
Springfield, Ill. 297
Stockton, Calif. 364
Syracuse, N.Y. 306

Tabasco, Mexico 314
Tacoma, Wash. 328
Tampa, Fla. 380
Tidewater 306
Toledo, O. 306
Torreon, Mexico
  (see Union Laguna) 314
Tucson, Ariz. 328
Tulsa, Okla. 356

Union Laguna, Mexico 314
Utica, N.Y. 400

Vancouver, B.C., Can. 328
Veracruz, Mexico 314
Vero Beach, Fla. 380
Villahermosa, Mexico
  (see Tabasco) 314
Visalia, Calif. 364

Walla Walla, Wash. 408
Waterbury, Conn. 338
Waterloo, Ia. 391
Wausau, Wis. 391
West Haven, Conn. 338
West Palm Beach, Fla. 380
Wichita, Kan. 297
Winston-Salem, N.C. 372
Winter Haven, Fla. 380
Wisconsin Rapids, Wis. 391

Yucatan, Mexico 314

NOTES

NOTES

NOTES

NOTES

NOTES

NOTES